Age	Physical Developments	Neurological Developments	Cognitive Developments	Language Developments	Emotional Developments	Social Developments	Self/Gender/Identity Developments	Moral Developments
18–24 months	Toddler can walk up steps.	Number of synapses increases.	Toddler uses mental representations and symbols. Object permanence is achieved. Toddler can form concepts and categories. Episodic memory emerges.	Naming explosion takes place. First sentences are often telegraphic.	Self-conscious emotions (embarrassment, envy, empathy) have emerged, as well as precursors of shame and guilt. Negativism begins.	Urge for autonomy is developing. Conflicts with older siblings increase.	Child recognizes self in a mirror. Use of first-person pronouns shows consciousness of self. Parental gender-typing peaks.	Child may show prosocial (helping) behavior.
24–30 months	Artwork consists of scribbles.	Number of synapses peaks; unneeded synapses are pruned. Myelination of frontal lobes occurs; this development may underlie self-awareness, self-conscious emotions, and capacity for self-regulation.	Preoperational stage begins.	Child uses many two-word phrases. Child begins to engage in conversations. Child overregularizes language rules.	Self-evaluative emotions (pride, shame, guilt) have emerged. Empathic responses are less egocentric, more appropriate.	Play with others is mostly parallel.	Child can describe and evaluate self. Gender awareness emerges. Preference for gender-appropriate toys and activities emerges.	Guilt, shame, and empathy promote moral development. Aggression occurs primarily in conflicts over toys and space.
30–36 months	Child has full set of primary teeth. Child can jump in place.	Neurons continue to undergo integration and differentiation.	Child can count. Child knows basic color words. Child understands analogies about familiar items. Child can explain familiar causal relations. Child becomes more accurate in gauging others' emotional states.	Child learns new words almost daily. Child combines three or more words. Child understands language well. Child says up to 1,000 words. Child uses past tense.	Child shows growing ability to "read" others' emotions, mental states, and intentions.	Child shows increasing interest in other people, especially children.	Child begins to be aware of a continuous self.	Aggression becomes less physical, more verbal.
3 years	Child draws shapes. Child can pour liquids and eat with silverware. Child can use toilet alone.	Brain is about 90 percent adult weight. Handedness is apparent. Hormonal changes in autonomic nervous system are associated with emergence of evaluative emotions.	Child understands symbolic nature of pictures, maps, and scale models. Autographical memory may begin. Child engages in pretend play. Child can do pictorial calculations involving whole numbers. IQ tests may predict later intelligence.	Vocabulary, grammar, and syntax are improving. Emergent literacy skills are developing.	Negativism peaks; temper tantrums are common.	Initiative is developing. Play with others becomes more coordinated. Child chooses friends and playmates on basis of proximity.	Children play with others of same sex. Peers reinforce gender-typed behavior.	Altruism and other prosocial behavior become more common; motive is to earn praise and avoid disapproval.

Eleventh Edition

A Child's World

Infancy through Adolescence

Diane E. Papalia

Sally Wendkos Olds

Ruth Duskin Feldman

**McGraw-Hill
Higher Education**

Boston   Burr Ridge, IL   Dubuque, IA   New York   San Francisco   St. Louis
Bangkok   Bogotá   Caracas   Kuala Lumpur   Lisbon   London   Madrid   Mexico City
Milan   Montreal   New Delhi   Santiago   Seoul   Singapore   Sydney   Taipei   Toronto

Mc Graw Hill **McGraw-Hill Higher Education**

Published by McGraw-Hill, an imprint of The McGraw-Hill Companies, Inc., 1221 Avenue of the Americas, New York, NY 10020. Copyright © 2008, 2006, 2004, 2002, 1999, 1996, 1993, 1990, 1987, 1982, 1979, 1975. All rights reserved. No part of this publication may be reproduced or distributed in any form or by any means, or stored in a database or retrieval system, without the prior written consent of The McGraw-Hill Companies, Inc., including, but not limited to, in any network or other electronic storage or transmission, or broadcast for distance learning.

This book is printed on acid-free paper.

1 2 3 4 5 6 7 8 9 0 DOW/DOW 0 9 8 7

ISBN: 978-0-07-353197-7
MHID: 0-07-353197-9

Editor in Chief: *Mike Ryan*
Publisher: *Beth Mejia*
Executive Editor: *Mike Sugarman*
Executive Marketing Manager: *James Headley*
Director of Development: *Dawn Groundwater*
Developmental Editor: *Barbara Conover*
Production Editor: *Holly Paulsen*
Manuscript Editor: *Jan Fehler*
Art Director: *Jeanne M. Schreiber*
Senior Design Manager: *Violeta Díaz*
Design Coordinator: *Margarite Reynolds*
Text Designer: *Ellen Pettengell/Glenda King/Jenny El-Shamy*
Cover Designer: *Kiera Pohl*
Art Editor: *Emma Ghiselli*
Illustrators: *Dartmouth Publishing, Joanne Brummett*
Senior Photo Research Coordinator: *Nora Agbayani*
Photo Research: *Toni Michaels/PhotoFind, LLC*
Permissions Editor: *Marty Moga*
Media Project Manager: *Thomas Brierly*
Production Supervisor: *Dennis Fitzgerald*
Composition: *10/12 Times by Aptara, Inc.*
Printing: *45# Pub Matte Plus, R. R. Donnelley & Sons*

Cover: Ellen B. Senisi / The Image Works

Credits: The credits section for this book begins on page C-1 and is considered an extension of the copyright page.

Library of Congress Cataloging-in-Publication Data

Papalia, Diane E.
  A child's world : infancy through adolescence / Diane E. Papalia, Sally Wendkos Olds, Ruth Duskin Feldman. — 11th ed.
    p. cm.
  Includes bibliographical references (p.   ) and indexes.
  ISBN-13: 978-0-07-353197-7 (hardcover : alk. paper)
  ISBN-10: 0-07-353197-9 (hardcover : alk. paper) 1. Child development. 2. Child psychology. 3. Adolescence. I. Olds, Sally Wendkos. II. Feldman, Ruth Duskin. III. Title.
HQ767.9.P36 2008
305.231—dc22   2007034988

The Internet addresses listed in the text were accurate at the time of publication. The inclusion of a Web site does not indicate an endorsement by the authors or McGraw-Hill, and McGraw-Hill does not guarantee the accuracy of the information presented at these sites.

www.mhhe.com

About the Authors

 As a professor, **Diane E. Papalia** taught thousands of undergraduates at the University of Wisconsin–Madison. She received her bachelor's degree, majoring in psychology, from Vassar College and both her master's degree in child development and family relations and her Ph.D. in life-span developmental psychology from West Virginia University. She has published numerous articles in such professional journals as *Human Development, International Journal of Aging and Human Development, Sex Roles, Journal of Experimental Child Psychology,* and *Journal of Gerontology.* Most of these papers have dealt with her major research focus, cognitive development from childhood through old age. She is especially interested in intelligence in old age and factors that contribute to the maintenance of intellectual functioning in late adulthood. She is a Fellow in the Gerontological Society of America. She is the coauthor of *Human Development,* now in its tenth edition, with Sally Wendkos Olds and Ruth Duskin Feldman; of *Adult Development and Aging,* now in its third edition, with Harvey L. Sterns, Ruth Duskin Feldman, and Cameron J. Camp; and of *Child Development: A Topical Approach* with Dana Gross and Ruth Duskin Feldman.

 **Sally Wendkos Olds** is an award-winning professional writer who is the author of more than 200 articles in leading magazines and is the author or coauthor of seven books addressed to general readers, in addition to the three textbooks she has coauthored with Diane E. Papalia. Her newest book, *A Balcony in Nepal: Glimpses of a Himalayan Village,* describes her encounters with the people and way of life in a remote hill village in eastern Nepal. The third edition of her classic book *The Complete Book of Breastfeeding* was published in 1999. She is also the author of *The Working Parents' Survival Guide* and *The Eternal Garden: Seasons of Our Sexuality* and the coauthor of *Raising a Hyperactive Child* (winner of the Family Service Association of America National Media Award) and *Helping Your Child Find Values to Live By.* She has spoken widely on the topics of her books and articles to both professional and lay audiences, in person and on television and radio. She received her bachelor's degree from the University of Pennsylvania, where she majored in English literature and minored in psychology. She was elected to Phi Beta Kappa and was graduated summa cum laude.

 **Ruth Duskin Feldman** is an award-winning writer and educator. With Diane E. Papalia and Sally Wendkos Olds, she coauthored the fourth, seventh, eighth, ninth, and tenth editions of *Human Development* and the eighth, ninth, tenth, and eleventh editions of *A Child's World.* She also is coauthor of *Adult Development and Aging* and of *Child Development: A Topical Approach.* A former teacher, she has developed educational materials for all levels from elementary school through college and has prepared ancillaries to accompany the Papalia-Olds books. She is author or coauthor of four books addressed to general readers, including *Whatever Happened to the Quiz Kids? Perils and Profits of Growing Up Gifted,* republished in 2000 as an Authors Guild Back-in-Print edition of iUniverse. She has written for numerous newspapers and magazines and has lectured extensively and made national and local media appearances throughout the United States on education and gifted children. She received her bachelor's degree from Northwestern University, where she was graduated with highest distinction and was elected to Phi Beta Kappa.

To our parents,
Madeline and Edward Papalia,
Leah and Samuel Wendkos,
and Boris and Rita Duskin,
for their unfailing love, nurturance, and
confidence in us, and for their abiding conviction
that childhood is a wondrous time of life.

And to our children,
Anna Victoria,
Nancy, Jennifer, and Dorri,
Steven, Laurie, and Heidi,
and our grandchildren,
Stefan, Maika, Anna, Lisa, and Nina,
Daniel, Emmett, Rita, Carol, Eve, Isaac, Delilah, and Raphael,
who have helped us revisit childhood
and see its wonders and challenges
through new eyes.

Brief Contents

Contents

Preface

The title *A Child's World* reflects our vision of the study of child development as an exciting journey of exploration into the special world of childhood. Through vibrant illustrations and real-life examples, we seek to make that world come alive. By studying this book, students will gain a perspective, not only on what earlier explorers have discovered about children's development, but also on how the world looks from the standpoint of a child.

Our Aims for This Edition

In recent editions of *A Child's World,* our author team has revamped virtually the entire book—its design, content, and pedagogical features—and substantially streamlined the text. In this eleventh edition our primary aim is to build on these foundations by revising and adding much new material while keeping overall size about the same. As always, we seek to emphasize the continuity of development and its contrasts across cultures, to highlight interrelationships among the physical, cognitive, and psychosocial domains, and to integrate theoretical, research-related, and practical concerns.

Cutting-Edge Research

We have sifted through the plethora of literature published each year to select cutting-edge theory and research that will add significantly to students' understanding.

An important theme of the eleventh edition is a greatly enhanced emphasis on *evolutionary theory* as it affects the study of child development. Beginning with expanded introductory material in Chapter 2, many chapters discuss evolutionary interpretations of topics ranging from maternal nutrition (Chapter 4) and early sensory abilities (Chapter 6) to language (Chapter 7) and gender (Chapters 11 and 14).

With the growing importance of cognitive neuroscience, we now present sections on *brain development* in middle childhood (Chapter 12) and adolescence (Chapter 15), as well as in the fetus and infant (Chapter 6). We include many studies throughout the text that shed light on the role of the brain in cognition and emotions. For example, Chapter 13 has a new section on genetic and neurological influences on intelligence. Also new to this edition are the concept of *epigenesis* (Chapter 3) and extended discussions of Esther Thelen's *dynamic systems theory* of infant development (Chapters 6 and 7).

We have broadened the research base of each chapter and have updated throughout, using the most current statistics available. We have striven to make our coverage as concise and readable as possible while still doing justice to the vast scope and significance of current theoretical and research work.

Cultural and Historical Influences

This edition continues our stress on cultural and historical influences on development. Reviewers have praised our emphasis on culture as a particular strength of this book.

Cross-cultural research is fully integrated throughout the text as well as highlighted in Around the World boxes, reflecting the diversity of the population in the United States and in other societies. For example, in Chapter 1 we present a revised section on influences of culture and race/ethnicity. Chapter 5 includes a new table of regional prevalence of low birth weight worldwide and a revised discussion of parents' roles, including cross-cultural comparisons. Chapter 9 includes an updated discussion of the impact of race/ethnicity and socioeconomic status on health. Chapter 11 has new information on cultural influences on emotional regulation and an expanded in-text discussion of the only child, including effects of China's one-child policy. Our photo illustrations, too, show an ever greater commitment to depicting cultural diversity.

Our emphasis on history begins in Chapter 1 with a summary of the history of the field of child development, a section on historical influences on development (including the concept of historical generations), and a Social World box on Elder's work in studying the life course. Discussions in other parts of the book place such topics as childbirth customs, infant feeding, and the comprehensive high school in a historical context. Many of our chapter-opening Focus vignettes provide historical background as they profile the lives of such figures as Margaret Mead and Charles Darwin's infant son "Doddy."

The Eleventh Edition at a Glance

Organization

This book takes a *chronological* approach, describing all aspects of development at each period of childhood. With this approach students gain a sense of the multifaceted sweep of child development. The 17 chapters fall into six parts:

- Part 1 summarizes the history, basic concepts, theories, and research tools of the field of child development.
- Part 2 describes the beginnings of life, including the influences of heredity and environment, pregnancy and prenatal development, birth, and the newborn baby.
- Parts 3 through 6 are divided into three chapters each, covering physical, cognitive, and psychosocial development during infancy and toddlerhood, early childhood, middle childhood, and adolescence.

In this edition, we have carefully assessed and improved the organization of material within and among chapters. For example, material on child maltreatment, previously presented in Chapter 9, has been moved to Chapter 6 to stress its greater prevalence in infancy.

Pedagogical Features

We are gratified by the overwhelmingly favorable response to the pedagogy we have developed for *A Child's World,* which includes the following features:

Our comprehensive Learning System, a unique, coordinated set of elements that work together to foster active learning. The names of the pedagogical features (Guideposts, Checkpoints), and critical thinking questions (What's Your View?) are designed to reinforce our central theme of exploration and discovery of a child's world. So are the four types of boxed material headed The Research World, The Everyday World, The Social World, and Around the World.

- *Guideposts for Study* This list of questions at the beginning of each chapter highlights the key concepts to learn. Each Guidepost appears again to introduce the related text section.
- *Checkpoints* These questions placed in the margins throughout each chapter serve to help students assess how well they grasp the concepts in the preceding text sections.
- *What's Your View?* These critical thinking questions, placed in the margins throughout each chapter and in the boxed features, encourage students to examine their thoughts about the information presented in the text.
- *Summary and Key Terms* Concluding each chapter, these resources, organized under the Guideposts, help students review the chapter and check their learning.

Each part of the book begins with a distinctive, illustrated two-page spread containing

- a Part Preview table outlining highlights of each chapter
- a Part Overview introducing important themes, and, for Parts 2 through 9,
- a list of Linkups to Look For, examples of interaction among the physical, cognitive, and psychosocial domains of development.

Focus vignettes introduce each chapter by highlighting a famous or remarkable person in the stage of development covered by the chapter. Refocus questions at the end of each chapter refer back to the opening Focus vignettes, encouraging students to apply the chapter's concepts to the life of the person profiled. A Landmark Table in the endpapers helps students find the whole child at each period of development as well as trace various domains of development across childhood and adolescence.

Four types of boxes enhance our text by highlighting topics related to the main text. Each chapter contains at least two of the four types of boxed material. Each box contains a Check It Out section referring the student to relevant Internet links where further information can be found.

- *The Research World* boxes provide an in-depth examination of research topics briefly mentioned in the text. For example, in our eleventh edition you will find new Research World boxes on "The Autism 'Epidemic'" (Chapter 6) and "Does Play Have an Evolutionary Basis?" (Chapter 11).
- *The Everyday World* boxes deal with a variety of practical applications of research. Our eleventh edition offers new Everyday World boxes on "Mourning a Miscarriage or Stillbirth" (Chapter 4) and "Do Barbie Dolls Affect Girls' Body Image?" (Chapter 12).
- *Around the World* boxes explore the way an issue in the chapter is treated or experienced in one or more foreign cultures, or in a United States minority group. Among the new Around the World boxes is "The Globalization of Adolescence" (Chapter 15).
- *The Social World* boxes discuss social issues or problems that have an impact on child development. New Social World boxes in this edition are "Shaken Baby Syndrome" (Chapter 6) and "Should Adolescents Be Exempt From the Death Penalty?" (Chapter 15).

For a detailed preview of the book's pedagogical features, see the Visual Walk-Through following this preface.

Content Changes

Following is a chapter-by-chapter list of the most important new and heavily revised material in our eleventh edition:

Chapter One

- Expanded discussions of race/ethnicity and critical/sensitive periods
- Expanded box on critical period in language development
- Section on "An Emerging Consensus" moved to end of chapter to serve as summary

Chapter Two

- New table on developmental considerations in ethics of research
- Revised figure illustrating Bronfenbrenner's theory
- Revised treatment of Vygotsky, now under cognitive perspective
- Revised introduction to cognitive neuroscience, now under research methods
- Expanded introduction to evolutionary/sociobiological perspective (moved to end of theories section)

Chapter Three

- New box on multiple births
- New table on causes and treatment of infertility
- New figure on increased use of assisted reproductive technology
- Revised discussion of assisted reproductive technology
- New treatment of epigenesis
- Revised discussions of genome imprinting, influences on intelligence, and schizophrenia

Chapter Four

- New table on early signs of pregnancy
- New discussion on evolutionary perspective on maternal nutrition during pregnancy
- New figures on fertilization/implantation and embryonic development
- New figure on miscarriage rates and maternal age
- New box on mourning a miscarriage or stillbirth
- New table on prenatal assessment techniques
- New figure on trends in prenatally acquired AIDS
- Updated sections on prenatal influences, especially maternal nutrition, maternal age, and environmental hazards
- Revised discussion of monitoring prenatal development with emphasis on preconception care

Chapter Five

- Revised discussion of labor and childbirth stages, with new discussion of episiotomy and new section on electronic fetal monitoring
- New discussion of benefits of vaginal birth
- Revised information on neonatal appearance, administration of APGAR scale, and low birth weight
- New table on neonatal skin conditions
- New table of international prevalence of low birth weight by regions
- Revised section on parents' roles, including cross-cultural comparisons (moved from Chapter 8)
- New discussion of evolution and parent-child bonding

Chapter Six

- New discussion of evolutionary perspective on early sensory abilities
- New figures of human nervous system and fetal nervous system development
- New box on autism "epidemic"
- Expanded discussion of Thelen's dynamic systems theory of infant motor development
- Revised figure on trends in infant mortality by race/ethnicity
- New table on recommendations to prevent Sudden Infant Death Syndrome (SIDS)
- Revised information on breastfeeding, brain development (including studies of Romanian orphans), infant mortality, and SIDS
- Child maltreatment section (moved from Chapter 9)
- New box on shaken baby syndrome

Chapter Seven

- New discussion of A, not-B error from perspective of developmental systems theory
- New discussion of plausibility of precocious infant abilities from evolutionary perspective
- New discussion of evolution of language
- Reorganized material on Piagetian tasks and information processing
- Revised language milestones table

Chapter Eight

- New section on gender differences in baby boys and girls
- Revised discussion of parental employment and effects of early child care, including latest NICHD study findings

Chapter Nine

- New information on exposure to pesticides and air pollution
- Revised discussions of obesity (overweight), enuresis, and lead exposure
- Revised discussion of race/ethnicity, socioeconomic status, and health
- Revised box on surviving the first five years of life

Chapter Ten

- Revised discussions of numerical abilities and influences on memory development
- Revised section on literacy and social interaction
- Revised section on the child in kindergarten

Chapter Eleven

- New information on cultural influences on emotional regulation
- New section on evolutionary perspective on gender development
- New box on whether play has an evolutionary basis
- Revised discussions of gender differences and sibling relations
- Expanded discussion of only child

Chapter Twelve

- New section on brain development in middle childhood
- New box on how Barbie dolls affect body image
- Revised discussions of growth hormone therapy, overweight, stuttering, and asthma

Chapter Thirteen

- New discussion of genetic and neurological, and revised discussion of racial/cultural, influences on intelligence
- New discussion of gender and achievement
- New discussion of effects of No Child Left Behind Act
- New section on Julian Stanley's research on the profoundly gifted
- Revised information on executive function
- Revised box on math wars with latest recommendations for teaching math

Chapter Fourteen

- New discussion of gender differences in peer group relations
- New box on talking with children about terrorism and war
- New discussion of evolutionary perspective on gender differences in aggression
- Revised discussion of effects of family structures

Chapter Fifteen

- New box on the globalization of adolescence
- New box, based on brain research, on whether adolescents should be exempt from the death penalty
- Revised discussions of nutrition, eating disorders, and drug use

Chapter Sixteen

- New section on prosocial behavior and volunteer activity
- New section on student motivation and school achievement (an international perspective)

- New box on Fowler's stages of faith
- Revised discussions of gender and school achievement, dropping out of high school, and working outside of school

Chapter Seventeen

- New sections on cliques and crowds
- Revised discussions of ethnic factors in identity formation, sexual orientation, sexual attitudes and behavior, and teen pregnancy and childbearing
- Section on sexually transmitted diseases moved from Chapter 15 for better integration with other material on sexuality
- Revised sections on adolescents and parents and sibling relationships
- Revised discussion of romantic relationships

Supplementary Materials

A Child's World, Eleventh Edition, is accompanied by a complete learning and teaching package keyed into the Learning System. Each component of this package has been thoroughly revised and expanded to include important new course material. Please contact your McGraw-Hill representative for more information.

For the Instructor

The instructor side of the Online Learning Center, located at www.mhhe.com/papaliaacw11, contains the Instructor's Manual, test bank files, PowerPoint slides, and other valuable material to help you design and enhance your course. Ask your local McGraw-Hill representative for your password.

Instructor's Manual

Meghan Fulcher, Washington and Lee University

Designed specifically for the eleventh edition, this manual contains valuable resources for both new and experienced teachers. All content is organized around the same Guideposts for Study used in the text, with each chapter introduced by a Total Teaching Package Outline linking the Guideposts to the lecture topics, discussion topics, and classroom activities that follow. The Classroom Activities include suggestions for independent study assignments, Knowledge-Construction Activities, Applied Activities, a Ten-Minute Test, and the Choosing Sides feature, which provides an overview of contemporary controversial issues for class discussion and debate. Each chapter concludes with a Resources for Instructors section, providing suggestions for publications and videos to enrich your teaching experience.

Test Bank and Computerized Test Bank

Diane Powers, Iowa Central Community College

This comprehensive test bank includes more than 2,000 multiple-choice and approximately 150 essay questions. Organized by chapter, the questions are designed to test factual, applied, and conceptual understanding. All test questions are compatible with EZ Test, McGraw-Hill's computerized test bank program.

PowerPoint Slides

Kim Foreman

These presentations cover the key points of each chapter and include charts and graphs from the text. They can be used as is, or you may modify them to meet your specific needs.

McGraw-Hill's Visual Asset Database
for Lifespan Development (VAD)

McGraw-Hill's Visual Assets Database for Lifespan Development (VAD 2.0; www.mhhe .com/vad) is an online database of videos for use in the developmental psychology classroom, created specifically for instructors. You can customize classroom presentations by downloading the videos to your computer and showing them on their own or by inserting them into your course cartridge or PowerPoint presentations. All videos are available with or without captions. Ask your McGraw-Hill representative for access information.

Multimedia Courseware for Child Development
Charlotte J. Patterson, University of Virginia

This video-based set of two CD-ROMs covers classic and contemporary experiments in child development. Respected researcher Charlotte J. Patterson selected the content and wrote accompanying modules that can be assigned to students. These modules include suggestions for additional projects as well as a testing component. Multimedia Courseware can be packaged with the text at a discount.

For the Student
Online Learning Center
www.mhhe.com/papaliaacw11

The eleventh edition Online Learning Center provides students with access to a variety of learning tools, including a chapter outline, Key Terms glossary, and Guideposts for Study that match those in the text. Resources for content review and practice include multiple-choice quizzes, matching quizzes, and decision-making scenarios, which afford students the opportunity to apply the material learned in the chapter to realistic situations and observe what effects their decisions have.

Acknowledgments

We would like to express our gratitude to the many friends and colleagues who, through their work and their interest, helped us clarify our thinking about child development. We are especially grateful for the valuable help given by those who reviewed the tenth edition of *A Child's World* and the manuscript drafts of this eleventh edition, whose evaluations and suggestions helped greatly in the preparation of this new edition. These reviewers, who are affiliated with both two-year and four-year institutions, are as follows.

Tanisha Billingslea, Cameron University
Lorelei Carvajal, Triton Community College
Mary Beth Miller, Fresno City College
Christina Nigrelli, California State University, Long Beach
Jane Spruill, Pensacola Junior College
Patricia Weaver, Fayetteville Technical Community College

We appreciate the strong support we have had from our publisher. We would like to express our special thanks to Mike Sugarman, executive editor; Dawn Groundwater, director of development; Barbara Conover, freelance developmental editor; Carol Mulligan, who took great care in preparing the bibliography; Holly Paulsen, production editor; Violeta Díaz and Margarite Reynolds, design managers; Toni Michaels, photo researcher; and Emma Ghiselli, art editor.

As always, we welcome and appreciate comments from readers, which help us continue to improve *A Child's World.*

Diane E. Papalia
Sally Wendkos Olds
Ruth Duskin Feldman

Visual Walk-Through

Part Preview

These previews, visually keyed to each chapter of the text, highlight the main features of the chapter. The contents of the part previews for Parts 2 through 6 are coordinated with Table 1-1 in Chapter 1, which summarizes major developments of the life span through adolescence.

Part Four

Early Childhood: A Preview

Chapter 9
Physical Development and Health in Early Childhood
- Growth is steady; appearance becomes more slender and proportions more adultlike.
- Appetite diminishes, and sleep problems are common.
- Handedness appears; fine and gross motor skills and strength improve.

Chapter 10
Cognitive Development in Ear
- Thinking is somewhat egocentric, but und perspectives grows.
- Cognitive immaturity results in some illogi
- Memory and language improve.
- Intelligence becomes more predictable.
- Preschool experience is common, and ki

Chapter 11
Psychosocial Development in
- Self-concept and understanding of emoti is global.
- Independence, initiative, and self-control
- Gender identity develops.
- Play becomes more imaginative, more ela
- Altruism, aggression, and fearfulness are
- Family is still the focus of social life, but o

Infancy and Toddlerhood

Some of the most exciting developmental research during the past quarter-century has been on the period from birth to age 3, known as infancy and toddlerhood. By measuring how long infants look at different patterns or how vigorously they suck on nipples that turn on recordings of women's voices, researchers have discovered that newborns have definite preferences about what they see and hear. By video recording babies' facial expressions, researchers have documented when specific early emotions (such as joy, anger, and fear) first appear. Through imaging techniques, researchers have linked specific functions and emotions with various parts of the brain. All in all, we now know that the world of infants and toddlers is far richer and their abilities far more impressive than was previously suspected.

Infancy begins at birth and ends when a child begins walking and stringing words together—two events that typically take place between age 12 and 18 months. Toddlerhood lasts from about age 18 to 36 months,

Linkups to Look For

- The physical growth of the brain before and after birth makes possible a great burst of cognitive and emotional development. Fetuses whose ears and brains have developed enough to hear sounds from the outside world seem to retain a memory of these sounds after birth.

- An infant's earliest smiles arise from central nervous system activity and may reflect nothing more than a pleasant physiological state, such as drowsiness and a full stomach. As the infant becomes cognitively aware of the warm responses of caregivers and as his or her vision becomes sharp enough to recognize a familiar face, the infant's smiles become more emotionally expressive and more socially directed.

Part Overviews and Linkups to Look For

At the beginning of each part, an overview introduces the period of life discussed in the chapters that follow. The part overviews include Linkups to Look For: bulleted lists that point to examples of the interaction of physical, cognitive, and psychosocial aspects of development.

Chapter-Opening Outlines

At the beginning of each chapter, an outline previews the major topics included in the chapter.

Biographical 'snapshots' from the lives of well-known people introduce and illustrate chapter themes.

Physical Development and Health in Middle Childhood

The healthy human child will keep
Away from home. except to sleep.
Were it not for the common cold.
Our young we never would behold.

—Ogden Nash, *You Can't Get There from Here*

Focus *Ann Bancroft, Polar Explorer*

Ann Bancroft

Ann Bancroft is the first woman in history to reach both the North and South Poles by nonmotorized means. In 1986, she dogsledded 1,000 miles from the Northwest Territories in Canada to the North Pole as the only female member of an international expedition. After surviving 8 months of grueling training and enduring temperatures as low as −70 degrees F for 56 days, Bancroft stood on top of the world. Seven years later she led three other women in a 67-day, 660-mile ski trek to the South Pole, reaching it on January 14, 1993. For these exploits, she was inducted into the National Women's Hall of Fame, was named Woman of the Year by *Ms.* magazine, and won numerous other awards and honors. Bancroft also was the first woman to ski across Greenland. In 2000, she and Liv Arneson of Norway became the first team of women to ski across the landmass of Antarctica; and in 2002 the two women reunited for a kayaking voyage from the north shore of Lake Superior to the St. Lawrence Seaway.

How did this 5-foot-3-inch, 125-pound woman achieve these remarkable feats? The answers go back to her childhood in then-rural Mendota Heights, Minnesota. Born September 29, 1955, into what she calls a family of risk takers, Ann showed her climbing instincts as soon as she could walk. As a toddler, she would climb her grandmother's bookcase to reach things on top. Instead of trying to stop her from climbing, her parents said, "Go ahead and try; you might just get what you want."

Ann was an outdoor girl. She and her two brothers and two sisters spent hours roaming the fields surrounding their farmhouse. Ann would "pretend she was a pirate building rafts to

Focus *Ann Bancroft,*
Polar Explorer

Aspects of
Physical Development

Height and Weight
Tooth Development and Dental Care
Brain Development

Nutrition and Sleep

Nutritional Needs
Sleep Patterns and Problems

Motor Development
and Physical Play

Recess-Time Play
Organized Sports

Health and Safety

Overweight and Body Image
Medical Conditions
Factors in Health and Access
to Health Care
Accidental Injuries

BOXES

12-1 The Everyday World: Do
Barbie Dolls Affect Girls' Body
Image?
12-2 Around the World: How
Cultural Attitudes Affect
Health Care

The story launched a debate about the moral implications of tampering with nature—and, down the road, the possibility of mass baby farms and reproductive engineering, which could alter or custom design the "products" of reproduction. Of more immediate concern were the risks to mother and baby. What if the baby was born grossly deformed? Could *any* baby conceived in a laboratory dish have a normal life?

Lesley was checked and monitored more frequently than most expectant mothers are, and, as a precaution, spent the last 3 months of her pregnancy in the hospital. The birth took place about 2 weeks before the due date, by cesarean delivery, because Lesley had developed toxemia (blood poisoning) and the fetus did not seem to be gaining weight. The delivery went smoothly without further complications.

The blond, blue-eyed, 5-pound 12-ounce baby was, from all accounts, a beautiful, normal infant, who emerged crying lustily. "There's no difference between her and any other little girl," her father maintained. "We just helped nature a bit" ("Louise Brown," 1984, p. 82).

By the time Louise celebrated her fourth birthday, she had a "test-tube" sister, Natalie, born June 14, 1982. Lesley and John used part of the nest egg obtained from interview, book, and film rights to buy a modest house; the rest remained in trust for the children.

Despite her highly publicized start, Louise Brown has led an unassuming life. On her 25th birthday, about 1,000 of the more than 3 million children worldwide now estimated to have been born through in vitro fertilization (Reaney, 2006; ICMART, 2006) gathered to celebrate the occasion. Brown, engaged to a bank security officer whom she has since married, said she had no immediate plans to start a family and just wanted to be treated as a "normal person." Her younger sister Natalie had two children, both conceived normally (Daley, 2003). In January 2007, Louise, at 28, gave birth to a normally conceived son (Associated Press, 2007).

• • •

What made Louise Brown the person she is? Like any other child, she began with a hereditary endowment from her mother and father. For example, she has her father's stocky build, wide forehead, and chubby cheeks and her mother's tilted nose and curved mouth, as well as her mother's sudden temper. Louise also has been affected by a host of environmental influences, from that famous laboratory dish to the tremendous public interest in her story. As a preschooler, she was mentally precocious, mischievous, and (by her parents' admission) spoiled. As a teenager, like many of her classmates, she liked to swim and ride horses, wore two gold studs in each ear, watched MTV, and had a crush on the actor Tom Cruise.

Most children do not become famous, especially at birth; but every child is the product of a unique combination of hereditary and environmental influences set in motion by the parents' decision to form a new life. We begin this chapter by examining how a life is conceived, either through normal reproduction or through alternative technologies, many of them developed since Louise Brown's birth. We consider the mechanisms and patterns of heredity—the inherited factors that affect development—and how genetic counseling can help couples make the decision to become parents. We look at how heredity and environment work together and how their effects on development can be studied.

After you have read and studied this chapter, you should be able to answer each of the Guidepost questions on the following page. Look for them again in the margins throughout the chapter, where they point to important concepts. To check your understanding of these Guideposts, review the end-of-chapter summary. Checkpoints located throughout the chapter will help you verify your understanding of what you have read.

Chapter Overviews

Near the beginning of each chapter, a brief overview of topics to be covered leads the reader smoothly from the opening vignette into the body of the chapter.

A comprehensive, unified **Learning System** helps students focus their reading and review and retain what they learn. It forms the conceptual framework for each chapter, is carried across all text supplements, and contains five parts.

Guideposts for Study

These topical questions, similar to learning objectives, are first posed near the beginning of each chapter to capture students' interest and motivate them to look for answers as they read. The questions are broad enough to form a coherent outline of each chapter's content but specific enough to invite careful study. Each Guidepost is repeated in the margin at the beginning of the section that deals with the topic in question and is repeated in the Chapter Summary to facilitate study.

Guideposts for Study

1. What is child development, and how has its study evolved?

2. What do developmental scientists study?

3. What kinds of influences make one child different from another?

4. What are six fundamental points about child development on which consensus has emerged?

Checkpoints

These detailed marginal questions, placed at the end of major sections of text, enable students to test their understanding of what they have read. Students should be encouraged to pause and review any section for which they cannot answer one or more Checkpoints.

Checkpoint ✔

Can you . . .

✔ Distinguish between quantitative and qualitative development and give an example of each?

✔ Trace highlights in the evolution of the study of child development?

✔ Name some pioneers in that study and summarize their most important contributions?

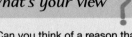

What's your view ❓

• Can you think of a reason that various societies divide the periods of development differently?

What's Your View?

These periodic marginal questions challenge students to interpret, apply, or critically evaluate information presented in the text.

Refocus

This series of interpretive questions near the end of each chapter encourages students to think back over major chapter themes and their application to the notable person featured in the opening vignette.

Refocus

On the basis of the information given about Abel Dorris in the Focus vignette at the beginning of this chapter,

- What light does Abel Dorris's case shed on the role of the prenatal environment in a child's development?
- Why did Michael Dorris's belief that Abel would "catch up," given a positive adoptive home environment, prove unfounded?

- What sorts of information might be helpful in counseling prospective parents on adoption of a child whose prenatal history is unknown?

Good preconception and prenatal care can give every child the best possible chance for entering the world in good condition to meet the challenges of life outside the womb—challenges we discuss in the next three chapters.

Summary and Key Terms

Prenatal Development: Three Stages

Guidepost 1 What are the three stages of prenatal development, and what happens during each stage?

- Prenatal development occurs in three stages of gestation: the germinal, embryonic, and fetal stages.
- Growth and development both before and after birth follow the cephalocaudal principle (head to tail) and the proximodistal principle (center outward).
- As many as 1 in 2 conceptions end in spontaneous abortion, usually in the first trimester of pregnancy.
- As fetuses grow, they move less, but more vigorously. Swallowing amniotic fluid, which contains substances from the mother's body, stimulates taste and smell. Fetuses seem able to hear, exercise sensory discrimination, learn, and remember.

- Important environmental influences involving the mother include nutrition, physical activity, smoking, intake of alcohol or other drugs, maternal illnesses, maternal stress, maternal age, and external environmental hazards, such as chemicals and radiation. External influences and paternal age may affect the father's sperm.

**teratogenic (99) fetal alcohol syndrome (FAS) (101)
acquired immune deficiency syndrome (AIDS) (105)**

Monitoring and Promoting Prenatal Development

Guidepost 3 What techniques can assess a fetus's health and well-being, and what is the importance of prenatal and preconception care?

Summary and Key Terms

The Chapter Summaries are organized by the major topics in the chapter. The Guideposts for Study questions appear under the appropriate major topics. Each Guidepost is followed by a series of brief statements restating the most important points that fall under it, thus creating a self-testing, question-answer format. Students should be encouraged to try to answer each Guidepost question before reading the summary material that follows. In this edition, key terms are listed for review under relevant topics, in the order in which they first appear, and are cross-referenced to pages where they are defined.

Boxed Series in This Edition

This edition includes four types of boxed material. Each box contains a critical-thinking What's Your View? section, as well as Check It Out! Internet links, which direct students to further information located on the World Wide Web.

The Research World Boxes

These boxes report on exciting new developments or current controversies in the field of child development. These include new treatments of such contemporary topics as the increase in the diagnosis of autism and whether there is a critical period for language acquisition.

The Research World

Box 6-1 *The Autism "Epidemic"*

Autism is a severe disorder of brain functioning characterized by lack of normal social interaction, impaired communication, repetitive movements, and a highly restricted range of activities and interests. (See the table for a list of behaviors typical of children with autism.) Autism is usually not diagnosed behaviorally before age 3 (Schieve, Rice, Boyle, Visser, & Blumberg, 2006), but signs of the disorder may be seen as early as age 12 months through brain imaging (Center for Autism Research, n.d.).

Autism is one of a group of *autism spectrum disorders (ASDs)*. One of these, *Asperger syndrome*, is generally milder than autism, so children with Asperger syndrome generally function at a higher level than children with autism. Children with Asperger syndrome have an obsessive interest in a single topic to the exclusion of all others, and they talk about it to anyone who will listen. They have large vocabularies and stilted speech patterns and are often awkward and poorly coordinated. Their odd or eccentric behavior makes social contacts difficult (National Institute of Neurological Disorders and Stroke, 2007).

Perhaps in part because of growing awareness and more accurate diagnosis, the reported prevalence of autism has increased markedly since the mid-1970s in the United States (Newschaffer, Falb, & Gurney, 2005) and other industrialized countries. According to parental reports, at least 300,000 children—approximately 5.6 in 1,000 U.S. children ages 4 through 17—have been diagnosed with autism, 4 out of 5 of them boys (Schieve et al., 2006). A 14-state study in 2002 found that 1 in 150 8-year-olds has autism or one of the related disorders (Autism and Developmental Disabilities Monitoring Network Surveillance Year 2002 Principal Investigators, 2007).

Some parents blame the preservative thimerosal, which contains a form of mercury and was widely used before the development of thimerosal-free vaccines. The prevalence of the disorder did decline after the U.S. Public Health Service recommended that thimerosal be removed from these vaccines as a precaution (Geier & Geier, 2006). However, the Centers for Disease Control and Prevention (2004), on the basis of multiple studies, concludes that no convincing evidence supports a causal connection between vaccines and autism.

Autism seems to involve a lack of coordination between different regions of the brain needed for complex tasks (Just, Cherkassky, Keller, Kana, & Minshew, in press; Williams, Goldstein, & Minshew, 2006). In a brain imaging study, adults with autism used different parts of the brain than did adults without autism in trying to comprehend a sentence. The group with autism showed less activation in the front of the brain, which is involved in higher-level thinking, and more in the rear section, which is involved in perceiving details, suggesting that they focused more on the meanings of individual words than on the sentence as a whole (Just, Cherkassky, Keller, & Minshew, 2004). Postmortem studies have found fewer neurons in the amygdala, a part of the brain involved in emotion and memory, in the brains of people who had autism (Schumann & Amaral, 2006). People with autism also show deficits in executive function and theory of mind (Zelazo & Müller, 2002; see Chapter 10).

Possible Signs of Autism

Children with autism may show the following characteristics in varying combinations and degrees of severity:

Inappropriate laughing or giggling
Lack of fear of danger
Apparent insensitivity to pain
Rejection of cuddling
Sustained unusual or repetitive play
Uneven physical or verbal skills
Avoidance of eye contact
Preferring to be alone
Difficulty expressing needs except through gestures
Inappropriate attachment to objects
Insistence on sameness
Echoing words or phrases
Inappropriate response to sound
Spinning objects or self
Difficulty interacting with others

Source: Autism Society of America, n.d.

Autism and related disorders run in families and have a strong genetic basis (Constantino, 2003; Ramoz et al., 2004; Rodier, 2000). Monozygotic twins are more concordant for autism than dizygotic twins. It is likely that multiple genes are at work. An international team of researchers has identified at least one gene and pinpointed the location of another gene on chromosome 11 that may contribute to autism (Szatmari et al., 2007). An earlier study found strong support for an autism gene on chromosome 7 and also evidence for genes on chromosomes 3, 4 and 11. This study also suggested that different genes may be responsible for the disorder in boys than in girls, and in early-onset as opposed to late-onset autism (Schellenberg et al., 2006).

Environmental factors, such as exposure to certain viruses or chemicals, may trigger an inherited tendency toward autism (Rodier, 2000). Certain complications of pregnancy, such as uterine bleeding and vaginal infection seem to be associated with a higher incidence of autism (Juul-Dam, Townsend, & Courchesne, 2001). So are advanced parental age, first births, threatened fetal loss, epidural anesthesia, induced labor, and cesarean delivery (Glasson et al., 2004; Reichenberg et al., 2006). Major stress during the 24th to 28th week of pregnancy may deform the developing brain (Beversdorf et al., 2001).

Why are children with autism overwhelmingly male? According to one theory, the female brain is predominantly hard-wired for empathy, and the male brain for understanding and building systems: Newborn girls look longer at a face; newborn boys look longer at a mechanical mobile. According to this theory, autism may be an extreme version of the normal male brain. Persons with autism are impaired in empathizing but excellent at systematizing (Baron-Cohen, 2005). In a study of 58 children whose mothers had undergone amniocentesis during pregnancy, high levels of fetal testosterone in amniotic fluid were associated with poorer quality social relationships and more restricted

Box 15-1 *The Globalization of Adolescence*

Young people today live in a global neighborhood, a web of interconnections and interdependencies. Goods, information, electronic images, songs, entertainment, and fads sweep almost instantaneously around the planet. The historical and cultural forces that influence adolescents' lives often arise from events oceans away. Western youth dance to Latin music and watch Japanese films, Western movies undermine the system of arranged marriage in Africa, and Arabic girls draw their images of romance from Indian cinema. Maori youth in New Zealand listen to African American rap music to symbolize their separation from adult society.

Adolescence is no longer solely a Western phenomenon. Globalization and modernization have set in motion societal changes the world over. Among these changes are urbanization, longer and healthier lives, reduced birth rates, and smaller families. Earlier puberty and later marriage are increasingly common. More women and fewer children work outside the home. The rapid spread of advanced technologies has made knowledge a prized resource. Young people need more schooling and skills to enter the labor force. Together these changes result in an extended transitional phase between childhood and adulthood.

Puberty in less-developed countries traditionally was marked by initiation rites such as circumcision. Today adolescents in these countries are increasingly identified by their status as students removed from the working world of adults. In this changing world, new pathways are opening up for them. They are less apt to follow in their parents' footsteps and to be guided by their advice. If they work, they are more likely to work in factories than on the family farm.

This does not mean that adolescence is the same the world over. The strong hand of culture shapes its meaning differently in different societies. Adolescents' choices are influenced by parents, teachers, friends, and broader societal institutions, conditions, and values. In the United States, adolescents tend to spend less time with their parents than before and confide in them less. In India, adolescents may wear Western clothing and use computers, but they maintain strong family ties, and their life decisions often are influenced by traditional Hindu values. In Western countries, teenage girls strive to be as thin as possible. In Niger and other African countries, obesity is considered beautiful, and girls try to fatten themselves with steroids and growth hormones.

Despite the forces of globalization and modernization, preadolescent children in some less-developed societies still follow traditional paths. These 9-year-old schoolgirls in Tehran celebrate the ceremony of Taqlif, which marks their readiness to begin the religious duties of Islam.

on the other hand, gain more freedom and mobility, and their sexual exploits are tolerated by parents and admired by peers.

Puberty also heightens preparation for gender roles, which, for girls in most parts of the world, means preparation for domestic roles. In Laos, a girl may spend 2½ hours a day husking, washing, and steaming rice. In Istanbul, a girl must learn the proper way to serve tea when a suitor comes to call. Whereas boy[...]

Around the World Boxes

This boxed feature offers windows on child development in societies other than our own (in addition to the cultural coverage in the main body of text). A new topic under this heading is the globalization of adolescence.

Box 14-2 *Talking with Children about Terrorism and War*

In today's world, parents are faced with the challenge of explaining violence, terrorism, and war to children. Although difficult, these conversations are extremely important. They give parents an opportunity to help their children feel more secure and understand the world in which they live. The following information can be helpful to parents when discussing these issues.

Listen to Children

1. Create a time and place for children to ask their questions. Don't force children to talk about things until they're ready.
2. Remember that children tend to personalize situations. For example, they may worry about friends or relatives who live in a city or state associated with incidents or events.
3. Help children find ways to express themselves. Some children may not be able to talk about their thoughts, feelings, or fears. They may be more comfortable drawing pictures, playing with toys, or writing stories or poems directly or indirectly related to current events.

Answer Children's Questions

1. Use words and concepts your child can understand. Make your explanation appropriate to your child's age and level of understanding. Don't overload a child with too much information.
2. Give children honest answers and information. Children will usually know if you're not being honest.
3. Be prepared to repeat explanations or have several conversations. Some information may be hard to accept or understand. Asking the same question over and over may be your child's way of asking for reassurance.
4. Acknowledge and support your child's thoughts, feelings, and reactions. Let your child know that you think their questions and concerns are important.
5. Be consistent and reassuring, but don't make unrealistic promises.
6. Avoid stereotyping groups of people by race, nationality, or religion. Use the opportunity to teach tolerance and explain prejudice.
7. Remember that children learn from watching their parents and teachers. They are very interested in how you respond to events. They learn from listening to your conversations with other adults.
8. Let children know how you are feeling. It's OK for them to know if you are anxious or worried about events. However, don't burden them with your concerns.
9. Don't confront your child's way of handling events. If a child feels reassured by saying that things are happening

sports, birthdays, holidays, and group activities take on added importance during stressful times.
3. Coordinate information between home and school. Parents should know about activities and discussions at school. Teachers should know about the child's specific fears or concerns.
4. Children who have experienced trauma or losses may show more intense reactions to tragedies or news of war or terrorist incidents. These children may need extra support and attention.
5. Watch for physical symptoms related to stress. Many children show anxiety and stress through complaints of physical aches and pains.
6. Watch for possible preoccupation with violent movies or war theme video/computer games.
7. Children who seem preoccupied or very stressed about war, fighting, or terrorism should be evaluated by a qualified mental health professional. Other signs that a child may need professional help include ongoing trouble sleeping, persistent upsetting thoughts, fearful images, intense fears about death, and trouble leaving their parents or going to school. The child's physician can assist with appropriate referrals.
8. Help children communicate with others and express themselves at home. Some children may want to write letters to the president, governor, local newspaper, or grieving families.
9. Let children be children. They may not want to think or talk a lot about these events. It is OK if they'd rather play ball, climb trees, or ride their bike, etc.

War and terrorism are not easy for anyone to comprehend or accept. Understandably, many young children feel confused, upset, and anxious. Parents, teachers, and caring adults can help by listening and responding in an honest, consistent, and supportive manner. Most children, even those exposed to trauma, are quite resilient. Like most adults, they can and do get through difficult times and go on with their lives. By creating an open environment where they feel free to ask questions, parents can help them cope and reduce the likelihood of emotional difficulties.

Source: American Academy of Child & Adolescent Psychiatry, 2003.

 What's your view

Which of the suggestions in this box do you think would be most helpful in talking with a child about a war or terrorist attack? Why?

The Everyday World Boxes

These boxes highlight practical applications of research findings. Among the new subjects are how to talk with children about terrorism and war and whether Barbie dolls affect girls' body image.

The Social World Boxes

This box series includes discussions about such topics as Elder's work on growing up in hard times, fetal welfare versus mothers' rights, and the youth violence epidemic.

The Social World

Box 1-1 *Studying the Life Course: Growing up in Hard Times*

Our awareness of the need to look at the life course in its social and historical context is indebted in part to Glen H. Elder, Jr. In 1962, Elder arrived on the campus of the University of California, Berkeley, to work on the Oakland Growth Study, a longitudinal study of social and emotional development in 167 urban young people born around 1920. The study had begun at the outset of the Great Depression of the 1930s, when the participants, about half of whom came from middle-class homes and had spent their childhoods in the boom years of the Roaring '20s, were entering adolescence. Elder (1974) observed how societal disruption can alter family processes and, through them, children's development.

As economic stress changed parents' lives, it changed children's lives, too. Deprived families reassigned economic roles. Fathers, preoccupied with job losses and irritable about loss of status within the family, sometimes drank heavily. Mothers got outside jobs and took on more parental authority. Parents argued more. Adolescents tended to show developmental difficulties.

Still, for boys, particularly, the long-term effects of the ordeal were not entirely negative. Boys who got jobs to help out became more independent and were better able to escape the stressful family atmosphere than were girls, who helped at home. As adults, these men were strongly work oriented but also valued family activities and cultivated dependability in their children.

Effects of a major economic crisis depend on a child's stage of development, Elder noted. The children in the Oakland sample were already teenagers during the 1930s. They could draw on their own emotional, cognitive, and economic resources. A child born in 1929 would have been entirely dependent on the family. On the other hand, the parents of the Oakland children, being older, may have been less resilient in dealing with the loss of a job, and their emotional vulnerability may well have affected the tone of family life and their treatment of their children.

Fifty years after the Great Depression, in the early 1980s, a precipitous drop in the value of midwestern agricultural land pushed many farm families into debt or off the land. This farm crisis gave Elder the opportunity to replicate his earlier research on families suffering from an economic depression, this time in a rural setting. In 1989, he and his colleagues (Conger & Elder, 1994; Conger et al., 1993) interviewed 451 Iowa farm and small-town two-parent families with a seventh grader and a sibling no more than 4 years younger. The researchers also videotaped family interactions. Because virtually no minorities lived in Iowa at the time, all the participating families were white.

As in the Depression-era study, many of these rural parents, under pressure of economic hardship, developed emotional problems. Depressed parents were more likely to fight with each other and to mistreat or withdraw from their children. The children, in turn, tended to lose self-confidence, to be unpopular, and to do poorly in school. But whereas in the 1980s this pattern of parental behavior fit both mothers and fathers, in the 1930s it was less true of mothers, whose economic role before the collapse had been more marginal (Conger & Elder, 1994; Conger et al., 1993; Elder, 1998).

The Iowa study, now called the Family Transitions Project, continues. Family members have been reinterviewed yearly, with a focus on how a family crisis experienced in early adolescence

Glen Elder's studies of children growing up during the Great Depression showed how a major sociohistorical event can affect children's current and future development.

affects the transition to adulthood. The adolescents who were in seventh grade when the study began were followed through high school. Each year they completed a list of stressful events they had experienced and were tested on measures of anxiety and depression and self-reported delinquent activities. For both boys and girls, a self-reinforcing cycle appeared. Such negative family events as economic crisis, illness, and getting in trouble at school tended to intensify sadness, fear, and antisocial conduct, which, in turn, led to future adversities, such as the divorce of parents (Kim, Conger, Elder, & Lorenz, 2003).

Elder's work, like other studies of the life course, gives researchers a window into processes of development and their links with socioeconomic change. Eventually it may enable us to see long-term effects of early hardship on the lives of people who experienced it at different ages and in varying family situations.

Source: Unless otherwise referenced, this discussion is based on Elder, 1998.

What's your view

Can you think of a major cultural event within your lifetime that shaped the lives of families and children? How would you go about studying such effects?

Check it out

For more information on this topic, go to www.michigan.gov/hal/0,1607,7-160-17451_18670_18793-53511--,00.html ["Reminiscences of the Great Depression," originally published in *Michigan History Magazine,* January/February, 1982 (Vol. 66, No. 1).] Read one of the oral histories at this Web site and consider how the Great Depression seems to have affected the person whose story is told.

Other Teaching and Learning Aids

Key Terms

Whenever an important new term is introduced in the text, it is highlighted in **boldface** and defined, both in the text and, sometimes more formally, in the end-of-book glossary. Key terms and their definitions appear in the margins near the place where they are introduced in the text, and all key terms appear in **boldface** in the Chapter Summaries and subject index.

The Information-Processing Approach

The **information-processing approach** attempts to explain cognitive development by analyzing the mental processes involved in perceiving and handling information. The information-processing approach is not a single theory but a framework that underlies a wide range of theories and research.

Some information-processing theorists compare the brain to a computer. Sensory impressions go in; behavior comes out. But what happens in between? How does the brain use sensory perceptions, say, of an unfamiliar face to recognize that face again?

Information-processing researchers *infer* what goes on between a stimulus and a response. For example, they may ask a person to recall a list of words and then observe any difference in performance if the person repeats the list over and over before being asked to recall the words. Through such studies, some researchers have developed computational models or flowcharts that analyze the specific steps children go through in gathering, storing, retrieving, and using information.

zone of proximal development (ZPD) Vygotsky's term for the difference between what a child can do alone and what the child can do with help.

scaffolding Temporary support to help a child master a task.

information-processing approach Approach to the study of cognitive development by observing and analyzing the mental processes involved in perceiving and handling information.

Tables

Frequent tables summarize or illustrate important concepts and developments.

Table 6-4	Physicians' Recommendations to Prevent SIDS

1. Place infant to sleep on the back (not tummy or side).
2. Use a firm sleep surface.
3. Keep soft objects and loose bedding out of the crib.
4. Do not smoke during pregnancy, and avoid exposing infant to second-hand smoke.
5. Let the infant sleep in his or her own bed, near the mother.
6. Consider offering a pacifier at nap time and bedtime during the 1st year of life. For breast-fed infants, delay introducing the pacifier until 1 month, so that breast-feeding is firmly established.
7. Avoid overheating and overbundling. Infant should be clothed lightly, and room temperature should be comfortable for an adult.
8. Avoid commercial devices that claim to reduce the risk of SIDS. These have not been tested for efficacy or safety.
9. Do not use home monitors to reduce the risk of SIDS; there is no evidence for their effectiveness.

Motives for prosocial behavior may change as children grow older and develop more mature moral reasoning (see Chapters 13 and 16). Preschoolers tend to have egocentric motives; they want to earn praise and avoid disapproval. They weigh costs and benefits and consider how they would like others to act toward them. As children grow older, they adopt societal standards of "being good," which eventually become internalized as principles and values (Eisenberg & Fabes, 1998). Individual differences in prosocial behavior may reflect individual differences in moral reasoning (Eisenberg, Guthrie, et al., 1999).

Cultures vary in the degree to which they foster prosocial behavior. Traditional cultures in which people live in extended family groups and share work seem to foster prosocial values more than cultures that stress individual achievement (Eisenberg & Fabes, 1998).

Aggression

When Noah roughly snatches a ball away from Jake, he is interested only in getting the ball, not in hurting or dominating Jake. This is **instrumental aggression,** or aggression used as an instrument to reach a goal—the most common type in early childhood. Between ages 2½ and 5, children commonly struggle over toys and control of space. Instrumental aggression surfaces mostly during social play; children who fight the most also tend to be the most sociable and competent. In fact, the ability to show some instrumental aggression may be a necessary step in psychosocial development.

As children develop more self-control and become better able to express themselves verbally, they typically shift from showing aggression with blows to showing it with words (Coie & Dodge, 1998). However, individual differences remain. Children who more frequently hit or grab toys from other children at age 2 are likely to be more physically aggressive at age 5 (Cummings, Iannotti, & Zahn-Waxler, 1989), and children who, as preschoolers, often engaged in violent fantasy play may, at age 6, be prone to violent displays of anger (Dunn & Hughes, 2001).

Gender Differences in Aggression

Aggression is an exception to the generalization that boys and girls are more similar than different (Hyde, 2005). In all cultures studied, as among most mammals, boys are more physically and verbally aggressive than girls. This gender difference is apparent by age 2 (Archer, 2004; Baillargeon et al., 2007; Pellegrini & Archer, 2005). Research with genetically engineered mice suggests that the Sry gene on the Y chromosome may play a role (Gatewood et al., 2006).

However, girls may be more aggressive than they seem (McNeilly-Choque, Hart, Robinson, Nelson, & Olsen, 1996; Putallaz & Bierman, 2004). Whereas boys engage in more **overt,** or **direct, aggression**—physical or verbal aggression openly directed at its target—girls, especially as they grow older, are more likely to engage in **relational,** or **social, aggression.** This more subtle kind of aggression consists of damaging or interfering with relationships, reputation, or psychological well-being, often through teasing, manipulation, ostracism, or bids for control. It may include spreading rumors, name-calling, putdowns, or excluding someone from a group. It can be either overt or covert (indirect)—for example, making mean faces or ignoring someone. Among preschoolers, it tends to be direct and face-to-face ("You can't come to my party if you don't give me that toy") (Archer, 2004; Brendgen et al., 2005; Crick, Casas, & Nelson, 2002).

From an evolutionary perspective, boys' greater overt aggressiveness, like their greater size and strength, may prepare them to compete for a mate (Archer, 2004). Males produce many sperm; females generally produce only one ovum at a time. Males seek to mate as frequently and widely as possible, and they have less investment in each

Children given responsibilities at home tend to develop prosocial qualities, such as cooperation and helpfulness. This 3-year-old girl, who is learning to care for plants, is likely to have caring relationships with people as well.

instrumental aggression
Aggressive behavior used as a means of achieving a goal.

overt, or direct, aggression
Aggression that is openly directed at its target.

relational, or social, aggression
Aggression aimed at damaging or interfering with another person's relationships, reputation, or psychological well-being; can be overt or covert.

Art Program

Many points in the text are underscored pictorially through carefully selected drawings, graphs, and photographs. The illustration program includes new or revised figures and many full-color photographs.

Index

Separate indexes, by author name and by subject, appear at the end of the book.

End-of-Book Glossary

The extensive glossary at the back of the book gives definitions of key terms.

Glossary

A

A, not-B error Tendency for 8- to 12-month-old infants to search for a hidden object in a place where they previously found it rather than in the place where they most recently saw it being hidden.

feelings without words, us and media.

assimilation Piaget's term f of new information into a cognitive structure.

asthma A chronic respirator characterized by sudden at

Subject Index

Part One

Entering a Child's World:
A Preview

Chapter 1
Studying a Child's World

- The scientific study of child development began during the late 19th century and has evolved to become part of the study of the full life span.
- Developmental scientists study change and stability in the physical, cognitive, and psychosocial domains.
- Development is subject to internal and external influences.
- Important contextual influences on development include family, neighborhood, socio-economic status, race/ethnicity, culture, and history.

Chapter 2
A Child's World: How We Discover It

- Theoretical perspectives on child development differ on two key issues: (1) whether children contribute to their own development, and (2) whether development is continuous or occurs in stages.
- Major theoretical perspectives are psychoanalytic, learning, cognitive, evolutionary/biological, and contextual.
- Research may be quantitative or qualitative and may include case studies, ethnographic studies, correlational studies, and experiments.
- To study development, researchers may follow children over a period of time to see how they change or may compare children of different ages to see how they differ.

Entering a Child's World

If you look at pictures of yourself as a child, it may seem as if you are stepping back onto a terrain that is familiar yet strange. Is that really you in those images frozen in time? When you study a photograph of yourself soon after birth, do you wonder how it felt to come into this world? How about that photo taken on your first day of school—were you nervous about meeting your teacher? Now flip ahead to your high school graduation picture. How did that helpless baby turn into the sturdy schoolchild and then into the cap-and-gowned person about to step into the world of adulthood?

Snapshots tell us little about the processes of change that take place as a child grows up. Even a series of home videos, which can follow children from moment to moment as they get older, will not capture a progression of changes so subtle that we often cannot detect them until after they have occurred. The processes and influences that produce those developmental changes are the subject of this book.

Part I is a map to a child's world. It traces routes that investigators have followed in the quest for information about what makes children develop as they do and points out the main directions students of development follow today. In Chapter 1, we explore how the study of child development has evolved and examine its basic concepts. In Chapter 2, we consider how developmental scientists study children, what theories guide them, what research methods they use, and what ethical standards govern their work.

As you enter a child's world again, remember that real children are not abstractions on the printed page. They are living, laughing, crying, shouting, tantrum-throwing, question-asking human beings. Observe the children about you in grocery stores, parks, movie theaters, and on the street. Listen to them. Look at them. Pause to pay attention as they confront and experience the wonder of life. Look back at the child you once were, and ask yourself what made you the person you are. Jot down questions you hope this course will help you answer. With the insights you gain as you read this book, you will be able to look at yourself and at every child you see with new eyes.

CHAPTER ONE

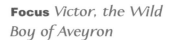

Studying a Child's World

There is nothing permanent except change.

—Heraclitus, fragment (6th century B.C.)

Focus *Victor, the Wild Boy of Aveyron*

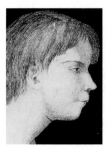

Victor

On January 8, 1800, a naked boy, his face and neck heavily scarred, appeared on the outskirts of the village of Saint-Sernin in the sparsely populated province of Aveyron in south central France. The boy, who was only 4½ feet tall but looked about 12 years old, had been spotted several times during the previous 2½ years, climbing trees, running on all fours, drinking from streams, and foraging for acorns and roots.

When the dark-eyed boy came to Saint-Sernin, he neither spoke nor responded to speech. Like an animal accustomed to living in the wild, he spurned prepared foods and tore off the clothing people tried to put on him. It seemed clear that he had either lost his parents or been abandoned by them, but how long ago this had occurred was impossible to tell.

The boy appeared during a time of intellectual and social ferment, when a new, scientific outlook was beginning to replace metaphysical speculation. Philosophers debated questions about the nature of human beings—questions that would become central to the study of child development. Are the qualities, behavior, and ideas that define what it means to be human inborn or acquired or both? How important is social contact during the formative years? Can its lack be overcome? A study of a child who had grown up in isolation might provide evidence of the relative impacts of *nature* (inborn characteristics) and *nurture* (upbringing, schooling, and other societal influences).

After initial observation, the boy, who came to be called Victor, was sent to a school for deaf-mutes in Paris. There, he was turned over to Jean-Marc-Gaspard Itard, an ambitious 26-year-old practitioner of the emerging science of "mental medicine," or psychiatry. Itard believed that Victor's development had been limited by isolation and that he simply needed to be taught the skills that children in civilized society normally acquire.

Itard took Victor into his home and, during the next 5 years, gradually "tamed" him. Itard first awakened his pupil's ability to discriminate sensory experience through hot baths and dry rubs. He then moved on to painstaking, step-by-step training of emotional responses and instruction in moral and social behavior, language, and thought.

But the education of Victor (which was dramatized in François Truffaut's film *The Wild Child*) was not an unqualified success. The boy did make remarkable progress; he learned the names of many objects and could read and write simple sentences. He could express

Sources of information about the wild boy of Aveyron are Frith (1989) and Lane (1976).

desires, obey commands, and exchange ideas. He showed affection, especially for Itard's housekeeper, Madame Guérin, as well as such emotions as pride, shame, remorse, and the desire to please. However, aside from uttering some vowel and consonant sounds, he never learned to speak. Furthermore, he remained totally focused on his own wants and needs and never seemed to lose his yearning "for the freedom of the open country and his indifference to most of the pleasures of social life" (Lane, 1976, p. 160). When the study ended, Victor—no longer able to fend for himself, as he had done in the wild—went to live with Madame Guérin until his death in his early 40s in 1828.

● ● ●

Why did Victor fail to fulfill Itard's hopes for him? The boy may have been a victim of brain damage, autism (a brain disorder involving lack of social responsiveness), or severe early maltreatment. Itard's instructional methods, advanced as they were for his time, may have been inadequate. Itard himself came to believe that the effects of long isolation could not be fully overcome and that Victor may have been too old, especially for language learning.

Although Victor's story does not yield definitive answers to the questions Itard set out to explore, it is important because it was one of the first systematic attempts to study child development. Since Victor's time, we have learned much about how children develop, but developmental scientists are still investigating such fundamental questions as the relative importance of nature and nurture and how they work together. Victor's story dramatizes the challenges and complexities of the scientific study of child development—the study on which you are about to embark.

In this introductory chapter, we examine how the field of child development has itself developed. We present the goals and basic concepts of the field today. We identify aspects of development and show how they interrelate. We summarize major developments during each period of a child's life. We look at influences on development and the contexts in which each occurs.

After you have read and studied this chapter, you should be able to answer each of the Guidepost questions on the following page. Look for them again in the margins throughout the chapter, where they point to important concepts. To check your understanding of these Guideposts, review the end-of-chapter summary. Checkpoints located throughout the chapter will help you verify your understanding of what you have read.

1. What is child development, and how has its study evolved?
2. What do developmental scientists study?
3. What kinds of influences make one child different from another?
4. What are six fundamental points about child development on which consensus has emerged?

The Study of Child Development: Then and Now

Guidepost 1

What is child development, and how has its study evolved?

The field of **child development** focuses on the scientific study of processes of change and stability in human children. Developmental scientists—people engaged in the professional study of child development—look at ways in which children change from conception through adolescence as well as at characteristics that remain fairly stable.

Developmental scientists study two kinds of change: *quantitative* and *qualitative*. **Quantitative change** is a change in number or amount, such as in height, weight, size of vocabulary, or frequency of communication. Quantitative change is largely *continuous* throughout childhood. **Qualitative change** is a change in kind, structure, or organization. Qualitative change is *discontinuous:* It is marked by the emergence of new phenomena that cannot be anticipated easily on the basis of earlier functioning. One example is the change from a nonverbal child to one who understands words and can use them to communicate.

Along with changes such as these, most people show an underlying *stability,* or constancy, in aspects of personality and behavior. For example, about 10 to 15 percent of children are consistently shy, and another 10 to 15 percent are very bold. Although various influences can modify these traits, they tend to persist to a moderate degree, especially in children at one extreme or the other (see Chapter 3).

Which of a child's characteristics are most likely to endure? Which are likely to change, and why? These are among the questions that developmental scientists seek to answer.

child development Processes of change and stability in children from conception through adolescence.

quantitative change Change in number or amount, such as in height, weight, or size of vocabulary.

qualitative change Change in kind, structure, or organization, such as the change from nonverbal to verbal communication.

Early Approaches

The formal *scientific* study of child development is relatively new. Looking back, we can see dramatic changes in the ways of investigating the world of childhood.

Forerunners of the scientific study of child development were *baby biographies,* journals kept to record the early development of a single child. One journal, published in 1787, contained the German philosopher Dietrich Tiedemann's (1787/1897) observations of his infant son's sensory, motor, language, and cognitive development. Typical of the speculative nature of such observations was Tiedemann's erroneous conclusion, after watching the infant suck more continuously on a cloth tied around something sweet than on a nurse's finger, that sucking appeared to be "not instinctive, but acquired" (Murchison & Langer, 1927, p. 206).

It was Charles Darwin, originator of the theory of evolution, who first emphasized the *developmental* nature of infant behavior. In 1877, in the belief that human beings could better understand themselves by studying their origins—both as a species and as individuals—Darwin published notes on his son Doddy's sensory, cognitive, and emotional development during his first 12 months (Keegan & Gruber, 1985; see the Focus at the beginning of Chapter 7). Darwin's journal gave baby biographies scientific respectability; about 30 more were published during the next three decades (Dennis, 1936).

Developmental Psychology Becomes a Science

By the end of the 19th century, several advances in the western world had paved the way for the scientific study of child development. Scientists had unlocked the mystery of

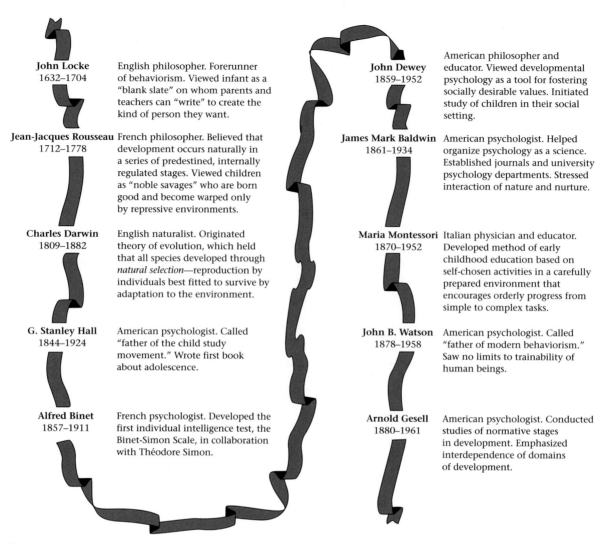

Figure 1-1

A time line of some leading figures and important developments in the study of a child's world. Some major theorists not shown here, such as Sigmund Freud, Erik Erikson, Jean Piaget, and B. F. Skinner, are covered in Chapter 2.

conception and (as in the case of the wild boy of Aveyron) were arguing about the relative importance of nature and nurture (inborn characteristics and external influences). The discovery of germs and immunization made it possible for many more children to survive infancy. Because of an abundance of cheap labor, children were less needed as workers. Laws protecting them from long workdays let them spend more time in school, and parents and teachers became more concerned with identifying and meeting children's developmental needs. The new science of psychology taught that people could understand themselves by learning what had influenced them as children.

Still, this new discipline had far to go. Adolescence was not considered a separate period of development until the early 20th century, when G. Stanley Hall, a pioneer in child study, published a popular (though unscientific) book called *Adolescence* (1904/1916). The establishment of research institutes in the 1930s and 1940s at universities such as Iowa, Minnesota, Columbia, Berkeley, and Yale marked the emergence of child psychology as a true science with professionally trained practitioners. Longitudinal studies, such as Arnold Gesell's (1929) studies of stages in motor development, provided research-based information about developments that normally occur at various ages. Other major studies that began around 1930—the Fels Research Institute Study, the Berkeley Growth and Guidance Studies, and the Oakland (Adolescent) Growth Study— produced much information on long-term development. Figure 1-1 presents summaries, in historical order, of the ideas and contributions of some early pioneers in the study of child development.

Almost from the start, developmental science has been interdisciplinary (Parke, 2004). Today students of child development draw collaboratively from a wide range of disciplines, including psychology, psychiatry, sociology, anthropology, biology, genetics (the study of inherited characteristics), family science (the interdisciplinary study of family relations), education, history, and medicine. This book includes findings from research in all these fields.

Studying the Life Span

Life-span studies in the United States grew out of programs designed to follow children through adulthood. One such study, the Stanford Studies of Gifted Children, which began in 1922 under the direction of Lewis M. Terman, traced through old age the development of a group of people identified as unusually intelligent in childhood.

Today the study of child development is part of the broader study of *human development,* which covers the entire human life span from conception to death. Although growth and development are most obvious in childhood, they occur throughout life. Indeed, such aspects of adult development as the timing of parenthood, maternal employment, and marital satisfaction have an impact on the way children develop.

New Frontiers

Although children have been the focus of scientific study for more than 100 years, this exploration is ever evolving. The questions developmental scientists ask, the methods they use, and the explanations they propose are more sophisticated and more eclectic than they were even 25 years ago. These shifts reflect progress in understanding, as new investigations build on or challenge those that went before. They also reflect the changing cultural and technological context. Sensitive instruments that measure eye movements are revealing intriguing connections between infant visual attentiveness and childhood intelligence. Cameras, videocassette recorders, and computers enable investigators to scan infants' facial expressions for early signs of emotions and to analyze how mothers and babies communicate. Advances in brain imaging make it possible to probe the mysteries of temperament and to pinpoint the sources of logical thought.

The traditional distinction between *basic research,* undertaken purely in a spirit of intellectual inquiry, and *applied research,* which addresses a practical problem, is becoming less meaningful. Increasingly, research findings have direct application to child rearing, education, health, and social policy. For example, research into preschool children's understanding of death can enable adults to help a child deal with bereavement; research on children's memory can help determine the weight to be given children's courtroom testimony; and research on factors that increase the risks of low birth weight, antisocial behavior, and teenage suicide can suggest ways to prevent these ills.

The Study of Child Development:
Basic Concepts

The processes of change and stability that developmental scientists study occur in all three *domains,* or aspects, of the self and throughout all five periods of childhood and adolescence.

Domains of Development

For purposes of study, developmental scientists separate the three domains: *physical development, cognitive development,* and *psychosocial development.* Actually, though, these domains are interrelated (Diamond, 2007).

What's your view

- What reasons do you have for studying child development?

Checkpoint ✔

Can you . . .

✔ Distinguish between quantitative and qualitative development and give an example of each?

✔ Trace highlights in the evolution of the study of child development?

✔ Name some pioneers in that study and summarize their most important contributions?

✔ Give examples of practical applications of research on child development?

Guidepost 2

What do developmental scientists study?

physical development Growth of body and brain, including patterns of change in sensory capacities, motor skills, and health.

cognitive development Pattern of change in mental abilities, such as learning, attention, memory, language, thinking, reasoning, and creativity.

psychosocial development Pattern of change in emotions, personality, and social relationships.

social construction Concept about the nature of reality based on societally shared perceptions or assumptions.

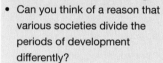
What's your view

- Can you think of a reason that various societies divide the periods of development differently?

Growth of the body and brain, the development of sensory capacities and motor skills, and health are part of **physical development** and influence other aspects of development. For example, a child with frequent ear infections may develop language more slowly than a child without this physical problem. During puberty, dramatic physiological and hormonal changes affect the developing sense of self.

Change and stability in mental abilities, such as learning, memory, language, thinking, moral reasoning, and creativity, constitute **cognitive development.** Cognitive advances are closely related to physical, social, and emotional growth. The ability to speak depends on the physical development of the mouth and brain. A child who has difficulty expressing herself in words may bring out negative reactions in others, affecting her popularity and sense of self-worth.

Change and stability in personality, emotions, and social relationships constitute **psychosocial development,** and this can affect cognitive and physical functioning. Anxiety about taking a test can worsen performance. Social support can help children cope with effects of stress on physical and mental health. Conversely, physical and cognitive capacities affect psychosocial development by contributing to self-esteem and social acceptance.

Although we will look separately at physical, cognitive, and psychosocial development, a child is more than a bundle of isolated parts. Development is a unified process. Throughout the text, we will highlight links among the three domains of development.

Periods of Development

There is no single, objectively definable moment when a child becomes an adolescent, or an adolescent becomes an adult. Thus, the concept of periods of development is an arbitrary one adopted for purposes of social discourse. We call such a concept a **social construction:** an idea about the nature of reality accepted by members of a particular society at a particular time on the basis of shared subjective perceptions or assumptions.

Indeed, the concept of childhood itself can be viewed as a social construction. Some evidence indicates that children in earlier times were regarded and treated much like small adults. However, this suggestion has been disputed (Ariès, 1962; Elkind, 1986; Pollock, 1983). Archaeological finds from ancient Greece show that children played with clay dolls and dice made of bones of sheep and goats. Pottery and tombstones depict children sitting on high chairs and riding goat-pulled carts (Mulrine, 2004).

In industrial societies, as we have mentioned, the concept of adolescence is quite recent. Until the early 20th century, young people in the United States were considered children until they left school (often well before age 13), married or got a job, and entered the adult world. By the 1920s, with the establishment of comprehensive high schools to meet the needs of a growing economy and with more families able to support extended formal education for their children, the teenage years had become a distinct period of development (Keller, 1999). In some preindustrial societies, the concept of adolescence still does not exist. The Chippewa Indians, for example, have only two periods of childhood: from birth until the child walks, and from walking to puberty. What we call *adolescence* is part of adulthood (Broude, 1995), as was true in western societies before industrialization.

In this book, we follow a sequence of five periods generally accepted in Western industrial societies. After examining the crucial changes that occur in the first period, before birth, we will trace physical, cognitive, and psychosocial development through infancy and toddlerhood, early childhood, middle childhood, and adolescence (Table 1-1). Again, these age divisions are approximate and arbitrary.

A Grecian vase painting (from about 460 B.C.) depicts a mother and toddler reaching out to one another. The toddler is seated in a tall stool with a removable potty chamber on top. Such stools, which seem to have been fairly common, are the only type of furniture known to have been made specifically for children.

Table 1-1   Typical Major Developments in Five Periods of Child Development

Age Period	Physical Developments	Cognitive Developments	Psychosocial Developments
Prenatal Period (conception to birth)	Conception occurs by normal fertilization or other means. The genetic endowment interacts with environmental influences from the start. Basic body structures and organs form; brain growth spurt begins. Physical growth is most rapid in the life span. Vulnerability to environmental influences is great.	Abilities to learn and remember and to respond to sensory stimuli are developing.	Fetus responds to mother's voice and develops a preference for it.
Infancy and Toddlerhood (birth to age 3)	All senses and body systems operate at birth to varying degrees. The brain grows in complexity and is highly sensitive to environmental influence. Physical growth and development of motor skills are rapid.	Abilities to learn and remember are present, even in early weeks. Use of symbols and ability to solve problems develop by end of second year. Comprehension and use of language develop rapidly.	Attachments to parents and others form. Self-awareness develops. Shift from dependence to autonomy occurs. Interest in other children increases.
Early Childhood (ages 3 to 6)	Growth is steady; appearance becomes more slender and proportions more adultlike. Appetite diminishes, and sleep problems are common. Handedness appears; fine and gross motor skills and strength improve.	Thinking is somewhat egocentric, but understanding of other people's perspectives grows. Cognitive immaturity results in some illogical ideas about the world. Memory and language improve. Intelligence becomes more predictable. Preschool experience is common, and kindergarten experience is more so.	Self-concept and understanding of emotions become more complex; self-esteem is global. Independence, initiative, and self-control increase. Gender identity develops. Play becomes more imaginative, more elaborate, and usually more social. Altruism, aggression, and fearfulness are common. Family is still the focus of social life, but other children become more important.
Middle Childhood (ages 6 to 11)	Growth slows. Strength and athletic skills improve. Respiratory illnesses are common, but health is generally better than at any other time in the life span.	Egocentrism diminishes. Children begin to think logically but concretely. Memory and language skills increase. Cognitive gains permit children to benefit from formal schooling. Some children show special educational needs and strengths.	Self-concept becomes more complex, affecting self-esteem. Coregulation reflects gradual shift in control from parents to child. Peers assume central importance.
Adolescence (ages 11 to about 20)	Physical growth and other changes are rapid and profound. Reproductive maturity occurs. Major health risks arise from behavioral issues, such as eating disorders and drug abuse.	Ability to think abstractly and use scientific reasoning develops. Immature thinking persists in some attitudes and behaviors. Education focuses on preparation for college or vocation.	Search for identity, including sexual identity, becomes central. Relationships with parents are generally good. Peer group may exert a positive or negative influence.

Checkpoint ✓

Can you . . .

✔ Identify three domains of development and give examples of how they are interrelated?

✔ Name five periods of child development (as defined in this book) and list several key issues or events of each?

Although individual differences exist in the way children deal with the characteristic events and issues of each period, developmental scientists suggest that certain basic needs must be met and certain tasks mastered for normal development to occur. Infants, for example, are dependent on adults for food, clothing, and shelter as well as for human contact and affection. They form attachments to parents and caregivers, who also become attached to them. With the development of speech and self-locomotion, toddlers become more self-reliant; they need to assert their autonomy but also need parents to set limits on their behavior. During early childhood, children develop more self-control and more interest in other children. During middle childhood, control over behavior gradually shifts from parent to child, and the peer group becomes increasingly important. A main task of adolescence is the search for identity—personal, sexual, and occupational. As adolescents become physically mature, they deal with conflicting needs and emotions as they prepare to leave the parental nest.

Influences on Development

Guidepost 3

What kinds of influences make one child different from another?

individual differences Differences among children in characteristics, influences, or developmental outcomes.

Why does one child turn out unlike any other? To find out, students of development must look at the universal processes of development experienced by all children and also at **individual differences,** both in influences on development and in its outcomes. Children differ in gender, height, weight, and body build; in health and energy level; in intelligence; and in temperament, personality, and emotional reactions. The contexts of their lives differ too: the homes, communities, and societies they live in, the relationships they have, the kinds of schools they go to (or whether they go to school at all), and how they spend their free time.

Heredity, Environment, and Maturation

heredity Inborn characteristics inherited from the biological parents.

environment Totality of nonhereditary, or experiential, influences on development.

Some influences on development originate primarily with **heredity,** inborn traits or characteristics inherited from the biological parents. Other influences come largely from the inner and outer **environment,** the world outside the self beginning in the womb, and the learning that comes from experience—including *socialization,* a child's induction into the value system of the culture. Which of these factors—heredity or environment—has more impact on development? This issue (dramatized by our Focus on the wild boy of Aveyron) once aroused intense debate. Theorists differed in the relative importance they gave to *nature* (heredity) and *nurture* (environmental influences both before and after birth).

Today, scientists in the field of behavioral genetics have found ways to measure more precisely the roles of heredity and environment in the development of specific traits within a population. When we look at a particular child, however, research with regard to almost all characteristics points to a blend of inheritance and experience. Thus, even though intelligence is strongly affected by heredity, environmental factors such as parental stimulation, education, and peer influence also affect it. Although there still is considerable dispute about the relative importance of nature and nurture, contemporary theorists and researchers are more interested in finding ways to explain how they work together.

maturation Unfolding of a universal natural sequence of physical and behavioral changes, including readiness to master new abilities.

Many typical changes of infancy and early childhood, such as the emergence of the abilities to walk and talk, are tied to **maturation** of the body and brain—the unfolding of a universal, natural sequence of physical changes and behavior patterns, including readiness to master new abilities such as walking and talking. These maturational processes, which are seen most clearly in the early years, act in concert with the influences of heredity and environment. As children grow into adolescents and then into adults, individual differences in innate characteristics (heredity) and life experience (environment) play an increasing role as children adapt to the internal and external conditions in which they find themselves.

Even in maturational processes that all children undergo, rates and timing of development vary. Throughout this book, we talk about average ages for the occurrence of certain events, such as the first word, the first step, the first menstruation or wet dream, and the development of logical thought. But these ages are *merely* averages. Only when deviation from the average is extreme should we consider development exceptionally advanced or delayed.

In trying to understand child development, then, we need to look at the *inherited* characteristics that are unique to each child. We also need to consider the many *environmental,* or experiential, factors that affect children, especially such major contexts as family, neighborhood, socioeconomic status, ethnicity, and culture. We need to consider how heredity and environment interact; this will be discussed in Chapter 3. We need to understand which developments are primarily maturational and which are more subject to individual differences. We need to look at influences that affect many or most people at a certain age or a certain time in history and also at those that affect only certain individuals. Finally, we need to look at how timing can accentuate the impact of certain influences.

Contexts of Development

Human beings are social beings. Right from the start, they develop within a social and historical context. For an infant, the immediate context normally is the family; and the family in turn is subject to the wider and ever-changing influences of neighborhood, community, and society.

Family

The **nuclear family** is a two-generational kinship, economic, and household unit consisting of one or two parents and their biological children, adopted children, and/or stepchildren. Historically, the two-parent nuclear family has been the dominant family unit in the United States and other Western societies. Parents and children typically worked side by side on the family farm. Today most U.S. families are urban; they have fewer children, and, in many families, both parents work outside the home. Children spend much of their time in school or child care. Children of divorced parents may live with one or the other parent or may move back and forth between them. The household may include a stepparent and stepsiblings or a parent's live-in partner. There are increasing numbers of single and childless adults, unmarried parents, and gay and lesbian households (Hernandez, 1997, 2004; Teachman, Tedrow, & Crowder, 2000).

In many societies in Asia, Africa, and Latin America and among some U.S. families that trace their lineage to those countries, the **extended family**—a multigenerational kinship network of grandparents, aunts, uncles, cousins, and more distant relatives—is the traditional family form. Many or most people live in *extended-family households,* where they have daily contact with kin. Adults often share breadwinning and child raising responsibilities, and children are responsible for younger brothers and sisters. Often these households are headed by women (Aaron, Parker, Ortega, & Calhoun, 1999; Johnson et al., 2003). Today the extended-family household is becoming less typical in developing countries due to industrialization and migration to urban centers (Brown, 1990; Gorman, 1993).

Socioeconomic Status and Neighborhood

Socioeconomic status (SES) includes income, education, and occupation. Throughout this book, we examine many studies that relate SES to developmental processes (such as mothers' verbal interactions with their children) and to developmental outcomes (such as health and cognitive performance; Table 1-2). SES affects these outcomes indirectly, through such associated factors as the kinds of homes and neighborhoods children live in and the quality of nutrition, medical care, supervision, schooling, and other opportunities available to them.

Poverty, especially if it is long-lasting, is harmful to the physical, cognitive, and psychosocial well-being of children and families. Poor children are more likely than other children to have emotional or behavioral problems, and their cognitive potential and school performance suffer even more (Evans, 2004). The harm done by poverty may be indirect, through its impact on parents' emotional state and parenting practices and on the home environment they create (see Chapter 14). Threats to well-being multiply if, as often happens,

nuclear family Two-generational kinship, economic, and household unit consisting of one or two parents and their biological children, adopted children, or stepchildren.

extended family Multigenerational kinship network of parents, children, and other relatives, sometimes living together in an extended-family household.

socioeconomic status (SES) Combination of economic and social factors, including income, education, and occupation, that describe an individual or family.

Table 1-2	Poverty Hurts Children	
Outcomes		**Low-Income Children's Higher Risk**
Health		
Death in infancy		1.6 times more likely
Premature birth (*under 37 weeks*)		1.8 times more likely
Low birth weight		1.9 times more likely
Inadequate prenatal care		2.8 times more likely
No regular source of health care		2.7 times more likely
Having too little food sometime in the past 4 months		8.0 times more likely
Education		
Lower math scores at ages 7 to 8		5 test points lower
Lower reading scores at ages 7 to 8		4 test points lower
Repeating a grade		2.0 times more likely
Being expelled from school		3.4 times more likely
Being a dropout at ages 16 to 24		3.5 times more likely
Finishing a four-year college		50 percent as likely

Source: Children's Defense Fund, 2004.

In Auburn, New York, a family lights the Kinara, a ceremony celebrating the first harvest, part of the African American celebration of Kwanzaa. The family joined others at a local Unitarian Universalist Church to celebrate the winter solstice, Hanukkah, and Kwanzaa. The gathering shared stories and songs from varied cultural traditions.

risk factors Conditions that increase the likelihood of a negative developmental outcome.

several **risk factors**—conditions that increase the likelihood of a negative outcome—coexist. Children in more affluent families also may be at risk. Under pressure to achieve and often left on their own by busy parents, these children have high rates of substance abuse, anxiety, and depression (Luthar & Latendresse, 2005).

The composition of a neighborhood affects the way children turn out. Living in a poor neighborhood with large numbers of people who are unemployed and on welfare makes it less likely that effective social support will be available (Black & Krishnakumar, 1998). Still, the resilience of such people as Oprah Winfrey and former president Bill Clinton, who rose from poverty and deprivation to high achievement, show that positive development can occur despite serious risk factors (Kim-Cohen, Moffitt, Caspi, & Taylor, 2004).

Figure 1-2

KEY

▢ Asian/Pacific Islander, non-Hispanic

▢ American Indian, non-Hispanic

▢ African American, non-Hispanic

▢ Hispanic

▢ White, non-Hispanic

Past and projected percentages
of U.S. children in specified
racial/ethnic groups.

Source: Hernandez, 2004, p. 18, Fig. 1.
Data from Population Projections pro-
gram, Population Division, U.S. Census
Bureau, issued January 13, 2000.

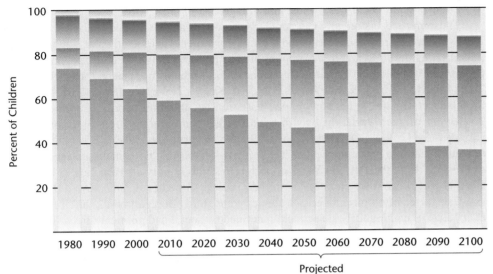

Culture and Race/Ethnicity

Researchers today are paying more attention to cultural and ethnic differences than in the past. However, it is difficult to present a truly comprehensive picture of these differences, in part because minorities still are underrepresented in developmental research and in part because of complications in defining cultural and ethnic identities.

Culture refers to a society's or group's total way of life, including customs, traditions, laws, knowledge, beliefs, values, language, and physical products, from tools to artworks—all of the behavior and attitudes that are learned, shared, and transmitted among members of a social group. Culture is constantly changing, often through contact with other cultures. Today, for example, American music is heard around the world.

An **ethnic group** consists of people united by a distinctive culture, ancestry, religion, language, and/or national origin, all of which contribute to a sense of shared identity and shared attitudes, beliefs, and values. Ethnic and cultural patterns affect child development by their influence on the composition of a household, its economic and social resources, the way its members act toward one another, the foods they eat, the games children play, the way they learn, how well they do in school, the occupations adults engage in, and the way family members think and perceive the world. For example, children of immigrants in the United States are nearly twice as likely as native-born children to live with extended families and are less likely to have mothers who work outside the home (Hernandez, 2004; Shields & Behrman, 2004). In time, however, immigrant or minority groups tend to *acculturate*, or adapt, by learning the language, customs, and attitudes needed to get along in the dominant culture while trying to preserve some of their cultural practices and values (Johnson et al., 2003).

The United States always has been a nation of immigrants and ethnic groups, but the ethnic origins of the immigrant population have shifted from Europe and Canada to Asia and Latin America (Hernandez, 2004). In 2003, 31 percent of the U.S. population belonged to an ethnic minority—African American, Hispanic, American Indian, or Asian and Pacific Islander—representing a threefold increase since the 1930s (U.S. Census Bureau, 1930, 2003). By about 2040 the minority population is projected to rise to 50 percent (Hernandez, 2004; Figure 1-2).

culture A society's or group's total way of life, including customs, traditions, beliefs, values, language, and physical products—all learned behavior passed on from parents to children.

ethnic group A group united by ancestry, race, religion, language, and/or national origins, which contribute to a sense of shared identity.

Furthermore, there is wide diversity *within* ethnic groups. The European-descended "white majority" consists of many distinct ethnicities—German, Belgian, Irish, French, Italian, and so on. Cuban Americans, Puerto Ricans, and Mexican Americans—all Hispanic Americans—have different histories and cultures (Johnson et al., 2003; Sternberg, Grigorenko, & Kidd, 2005). African Americans from the rural South differ from those of Caribbean ancestry. Asian Americans hail from a variety of countries with distinct cultures, from modern, industrial Japan to communist China to the remote mountains of Nepal, where many people still practice their ancient way of life. American Indians consist of hundreds of recognized nations, tribes, bands, and villages.

The term *race,* historically and popularly viewed as an identifiable biological category, is now agreed by most scholars to be a social construct. There is no clear scientific consensus on its definition, and it is impossible to measure reliably (American Academy of Pediatrics Committee on Pediatric Research, 2000; Bonham, Warshauer-Baker, & Collins, 2005; Helms, Jernigan, & Mascher, 2005; Lin & Kelsey, 2000; Smedley & Smedley, 2005; Sternberg et al., 2005). Human genetic variation occurs along a broad continuum, and 90 percent of such variation occurs *within* rather than among socially defined races (Bonham et al., 2005; Ossorio & Duster, 2005). Nevertheless, race as a social category remains a factor in research because it makes a difference in "how individuals are treated, where they live, their employment opportunities, the quality of their health care, and whether [they] can fully participate" in their society (Smedley & Smedley, 2005, p. 23).

Categories of culture, race, and ethnicity are fluid (Bonham et al., 2005; Sternberg et al., 2005), "continuously shaped and redefined by social and political forces" (Fisher et al., 2002, p. 1026). Geographic dispersion and intermarriage together with adaptation to varying local conditions have produced a great heterogeneity of physical and cultural characteristics within populations (Smedley & Smedley, 2005; Sternberg et al., 2005). Thus, a person such as the golf champion Tiger Woods, who has a black father and an Asian-American mother, may fall into more than one racial/ethnic category and may identify more strongly with one or another at different times (Hitlin, Brown, & Elder, 2006; Lin & Kelsey, 2000). A term such as *black* or *Hispanic* can be an **ethnic gloss**: an overgeneralization that obscures or blurs such variations (Parke, 2004; Trimble & Dickson, 2005).

The Historical Context

At one time developmental scientists paid little attention to historical context—the time period in which people live and grow. Then, as the early longitudinal studies of childhood extended into the adult years, investigators began to focus on how certain experiences, tied to time and place, affect the course of children's lives. The Terman sample, for example, reached adulthood in the 1930s, during the Great Depression; the Oakland sample, during World War II (Box 1-1); and the Berkeley sample, around 1950, the postwar boom period. What did it mean to be a child in each of these periods? To be an adolescent? To become an adult? The answers differ in specific and important ways. Today, as we will discuss in the next section, the historical context is an important part of the study of development.

Normative and Nonnormative Influences

To understand similarities and differences in development, we must look at **normative** influences—those that impinge on many or most people—and at those that touch only certain individuals.

Normative age-graded influences are highly similar for people in a particular age group. They include biological events (such as puberty) and social events (such as entry into formal education). The timing of biological events is fixed, within a normal range (children do not experience puberty at age 3). The timing of social events is more flexible and varies in different times and places, within maturational limits. Children in Western industrial societies generally begin formal education around age 5 or 6; but, in some developing countries, schooling begins much later, if at all.

Normative history-graded influences are significant events (such as the Great Depression or World War II) that shape the behavior and attitudes of a **historical generation:** a

What's your view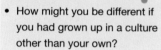

- How might you be different if you had grown up in a culture other than your own?

ethnic gloss Overgeneralization about an ethnic or cultural group that blurs or obscures variations within the group or overlaps with other such groups.

Checkpoint ✔

Can you . . .

✔ Explain why individual differences tend to increase with age?

✔ Give examples of the influences of family and neighborhood composition, socioeconomic status, culture, race/ethnicity, and historical context?

normative Characteristic of an event that occurs in a similar way for most people in a group.

historical generation A group of people strongly influenced by a major historical event during their formative period.

Box 1-1 *Studying the Life Course: Growing up in Hard Times*

Our awareness of the need to look at the life course in its social and historical context is indebted in part to Glen H. Elder, Jr. In 1962, Elder arrived on the campus of the University of California, Berkeley, to work on the Oakland Growth Study, a longitudinal study of social and emotional development in 167 urban young people born around 1920. The study had begun at the outset of the Great Depression of the 1930s, when the participants, about half of whom came from middle-class homes and had spent their childhoods in the boom years of the Roaring '20s, were entering adolescence. Elder (1974) observed how societal disruption can alter family processes and, through them, children's development.

As economic stress changed parents' lives, it changed children's lives, too. Deprived families reassigned economic roles. Fathers, preoccupied with job losses and irritable about loss of status within the family, sometimes drank heavily. Mothers got outside jobs and took on more parental authority. Parents argued more. Adolescents tended to show developmental difficulties.

Still, for boys, particularly, the long-term effects of the ordeal were not entirely negative. Boys who got jobs to help out became more independent and were better able to escape the stressful family atmosphere than were girls, who helped at home. As adults, these men were strongly work oriented but also valued family activities and cultivated dependability in their children.

Effects of a major economic crisis depend on a child's stage of development, Elder noted. The children in the Oakland sample were already teenagers during the 1930s. They could draw on their own emotional, cognitive, and economic resources. A child born in 1929 would have been entirely dependent on the family. On the other hand, the parents of the Oakland children, being older, may have been less resilient in dealing with the loss of a job, and their emotional vulnerability may well have affected the tone of family life and their treatment of their children.

Fifty years after the Great Depression, in the early 1980s, a precipitous drop in the value of midwestern agricultural land pushed many farm families into debt or off the land. This farm crisis gave Elder the opportunity to replicate his earlier research on families suffering from an economic depression, this time in a rural setting. In 1989, he and his colleagues (Conger & Elder, 1994; Conger et al., 1993) interviewed 451 Iowa farm and small-town two-parent families with a seventh grader and a sibling no more than 4 years younger. The researchers also videotaped family interactions. Because virtually no minorities lived in Iowa at the time, all the participating families were white.

As in the Depression-era study, many of these rural parents, under pressure of economic hardship, developed emotional problems. Depressed parents were more likely to fight with each other and to mistreat or withdraw from their children. The children, in turn, tended to lose self-confidence, to be unpopular, and to do poorly in school. But whereas in the 1980s this pattern of parental behavior fit both mothers and fathers, in the 1930s it was less true of mothers, whose economic role before the collapse had been more marginal (Conger & Elder, 1994; Conger et al., 1993; Elder, 1998).

The Iowa study, now called the Family Transitions Project, continues. Family members have been reinterviewed yearly, with a focus on how a family crisis experienced in early adolescence

Glen Elder's studies of children growing up during the Great Depression showed how a major sociohistorical event can affect children's current and future development.

affects the transition to adulthood. The adolescents who were in seventh grade when the study began were followed through high school. Each year they completed a list of stressful events they had experienced and were tested on measures of anxiety and depression and self-reported delinquent activities. For both boys and girls, a self-reinforcing cycle appeared. Such negative family events as economic crisis, illness, and getting in trouble at school tended to intensify sadness, fear, and antisocial conduct, which, in turn, led to future adversities, such as the divorce of parents (Kim, Conger, Elder, & Lorenz, 2003).

Elder's work, like other studies of the life course, gives researchers a window into processes of development and their links with socioecoconomic change. Eventually it may enable us to see long-term effects of early hardship on the lives of people who experienced it at different ages and in varying family situations.

Source: Unless otherwise referenced, this discussion is based on Elder, 1998.

What's your view ?

Can you think of a major cultural event within your lifetime that shaped the lives of families and children? How would you go about studying such effects?

Check it out !

For more information on this topic, go to www.michigan.gov/hal/0,1607,7-160-17451_18670_18793-53511--,00.html ["Reminiscences of the Great Depression," originally published in *Michigan History Magazine,* January/February, 1982 (Vol. 66, No. 1).] Read one of the oral histories at this Web site and consider how the Great Depression seems to have affected the person whose story is told.

group of people who experience the event at a formative time in their lives. For example, the generations that came of age during the Depression and World War II tend to show a strong sense of social interdependence and trust that has declined among more recent generations (Rogler, 2002). Depending on when and where they live, entire generations may feel the impact of famines, nuclear explosions, or terrorist attacks. In Western countries, medical advances as well as improvements in nutrition and sanitation have dramatically reduced infant and child mortality. As children grow up today, they are influenced by computers, digital television, the Internet, and other technological developments. Social changes, such as the increase in employed mothers, have greatly altered family life.

A historical generation is not the same as an age **cohort:** a group of people born at about the same time. A historical generation may contain more than one cohort, but not all cohorts are part of historical generations unless they experience major, shaping historical events at a formative point in their lives (Rogler, 2002).

Nonnormative influences are unusual events that have a major impact on *individual* lives and may cause stress because they are unexpected. They are either typical events that happen at an atypical time of life (such as marriage in the early teens or the death of a parent when a child is young) or atypical events (such as having a birth defect or being in an airplane crash). They can also, of course, be happy events (such as winning the lottery). Young people may help create nonnormative life events—say, by driving after drinking or by applying for a scholarship—and thus participate actively in their own development.

Timing of Influences: Critical or Sensitive Periods

In a well-known study, Konrad Lorenz (1957), an Austrian zoologist, waddled, honked, and flapped his arms—and got newborn ducklings to follow him as they would the mother duck. Lorenz showed that newly hatched ducklings will instinctively follow the first moving object they see, whether or not it is a member of their species. This phenomenon is called **imprinting,** and Lorenz believed that it is automatic and irreversible. Usually, this instinctive bond is with the mother; but if the natural course of events is disturbed, other attachments, like the one to Lorenz—or none at all—can form. Imprinting, said Lorenz, is the result of a *predisposition toward learning:* the readiness of an organism's nervous system to acquire certain information during a brief *critical period* in early life.

A **critical period** is a specific time when a given event, or its absence, has a specific impact on development. If a necessary event does not occur during a critical period of maturation, normal development will not occur; and the resulting abnormal patterns may be irreversible (Knudsen, 1999; Kuhl, Conboy, Padden, Nelson, & Pruitt, 2005). However, the length of a critical period is not absolutely fixed; if ducklings' rearing conditions are varied to slow their growth, the usual critical period for imprinting can be extended, and imprinting itself may even be reversed (Bruer, 2001).

Do human beings experience critical periods? One example occurs during gestation. If a woman receives X-rays, takes certain drugs, or contracts certain diseases at certain times during pregnancy, the fetus may show specific ill effects, depending on the nature of the "shock" and on its timing. Critical periods also occur early in childhood. A child deprived of certain kinds of experience during a critical period is likely to show permanent stunting of physical development. For example, if a muscle problem interfering with the ability to focus both eyes on the same object is not corrected early in life, the brain mechanisms necessary for binocular depth perception probably will not develop (Bushnell & Boudreau, 1993).

The concept of critical periods is controversial. Because many aspects of development, even in the physical domain, have been found to show **plasticity,** or modifiability of performance, it may be more useful to think about **sensitive periods,** when a child's development is especially responsive to certain kinds of experiences, but later experience continues to influence development (Bruer, 2001; Knudson, 1999; Kuhl et al., 2005). Box 1-2 discusses how the concepts of critical and sensitive periods apply to language development.

---

cohort A group of people born at about the same time.

nonnormative Characteristic of an unusual event that happens to a particular person or a typical event that happens at an unusual time of life.

What's your view

- Can you think of a historical event that has molded your life? If so, in what ways?

imprinting Instinctive form of learning in which, during a critical period in early development, a young animal forms an attachment to the first moving object it sees, usually the mother.

critical period Specific time when a given event or its absence has a specific impact on development.

plasticity Modifiability of performance.

sensitive periods Times in development when a person is particularly open to certain kinds of experiences.

Checkpoint

Can you . . .

- Give examples of normative age-graded, normative history-graded, and nonnormative influences? (Include some normative history-graded influences that impacted different generations.)

- Explain the concept of critical periods and give examples?

Box 1-2 *Is There a Critical Period for Language Acquisition?*

In 1970, a 13-year-old girl called Genie (not her real name) was discovered in a suburb of Los Angeles (Curtiss, 1977; Fromkin, Krashen, Curtiss, Rigler, & Rigler, 1974; Pines, 1981; Rymer, 1993). The victim of an abusive father, she had been confined for nearly 12 years to a small room in her parents' home, tied to a potty chair and cut off from normal human contact. She weighed only 59 pounds, could not straighten her arms or legs, could not chew, had no bladder or bowel control, and did not speak. She recognized only her name and the word *sorry*.

Only 3 years before, Eric Lenneberg (1967, 1969) had proposed that there is a critical period for language acquisition, beginning in early infancy and ending around puberty. Lenneberg argued that it would be difficult, if not impossible, for a child who had not yet acquired language to do so after that age.

The discovery of Genie offered the opportunity for a test of Lenneberg's hypothesis. Could Genie be taught to speak, or was it too late? The National Institutes of Mental Health (NIMH) funded a study, and a series of researchers took over Genie's care and gave her intensive testing and language training.

Genie's progress during the next few years (before the NIMH withdrew funding and her mother regained custody and cut her off from contact with the professionals who had been teaching her) both challenges and supports the idea of a critical period for language acquisition. Genie did learn some simple words and could string them together into primitive, but rule-governed, sentences. She also learned the fundamentals of sign language. But she never used language normally, and "her speech remained, for the most part, like a somewhat garbled telegram" (Pines, 1981, p. 29). When her mother, unable to care for her, turned her over to a series of abusive foster homes, she regressed into total silence.

Case studies like those of Genie and Victor, the wild boy of Aveyron, dramatize the *difficulty* of acquiring language after the early years of life, but, because there are so many complicating factors, they do not permit conclusive judgments about whether such acquisition is *possible*. Because of the brain's plasticity, some researchers consider the prepubertal years a sensitive rather than critical period for learning language (Newport, Bavelier, & Neville, 2001; Schumann, 1997). Brain imaging research has found that even if the parts of the brain best suited to language processing are damaged early in childhood, nearly normal language development can continue as other parts of the brain take over (Boatman et al., 1999; Hertz-Pannier et al., 2002; M. H. Johnson, 1998). In fact, shifts in brain organization and utilization occur throughout the course of normal language learning (M. H. Johnson, 1998; Neville & Bavelier, 1998). Neuroscientists also have observed different patterns of brain activity during language

processing between people who learned American Sign Language (ASL) as a native language and those who learned it as a second language, after puberty (Newman, Bavelier, Corina, Jezzard, & Neville, 2002).

Other research has focused on a shorter critical period early in life. Sometime between 6 and 12 months, babies normally begin to "specialize" in perceiving the sounds of their native language and lose the ability to perceive sounds of other languages. In one study (Kuhl, Conboy, Padden, Nelson, & Pruitt, 2005; see Chapter 7), infants who, at 7 months, had already developed this specialized phonetic perception showed more advanced language abilities 2 years later than did 7-month-olds who were better able to discriminate *non*native sounds. This research, these investigators suggest, may point to a critical period for phonetic perception: If infants do not begin to focus exclusively on the sounds of their native language during that period, their language development is slowed. This may explain why learning a second language in adulthood is not as easy as in early childhood (Newport, 1991).

If either a critical or a sensitive period for language learning exists, what explains it? Do the brain's mechanisms for acquiring language decay as the brain matures? That would seem strange, since other cognitive abilities improve. An alternative hypothesis is that this very increase in cognitive sophistication interferes with an adolescent's or adult's ability to learn a language. Young children acquire language in small chunks that can be digested readily. Older learners, when they first begin learning a language, tend to absorb a great deal at once and then may have trouble analyzing and interpreting it (Newport, 1991).

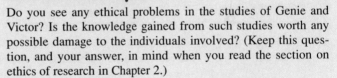

What's your view

Do you see any ethical problems in the studies of Genie and Victor? Is the knowledge gained from such studies worth any possible damage to the individuals involved? (Keep this question, and your answer, in mind when you read the section on ethics of research in Chapter 2.)

Check it out

For more information on this topic, go to www.alphadictionary.com/articles/ling001.html. This page was developed by Professor Robert Beard of the Linguistics Program at Bucknell University. It gives a brief, accurate overview of the nature-nurture question as it concerns language acquisition. Links to other sites of related interest can also be found.

Guidepost 4

What are six fundamental points about child development on which consensus has emerged?

An Emerging Consensus

As the study of children has matured, a broad consensus has emerged on several fundamental points concerning child development, which sum up our introduction to this book:

1. As we have mentioned, *all domains of development are interrelated.* Although developmental scientists often look separately at the three *domains,* or aspects, of development, each affects the others.
2. *Normal development includes a wide range of individual differences within the general processes all children follow as they develop.* Each child, from the start, is unlike anyone else in the world. One is outgoing, another shy. One is agile, another awkward. Some of the influences on individual development are inborn; others come from experience. Most often, both types of influences work together. Family characteristics, gender, social class, race/ethnicity, and the presence or absence of physical, mental, or emotional disability all affect the way a child develops within the universal processes of human maturation.
3. *Children help shape their development and influence others' responses to them.* Right from the start, through the responses they evoke in others, infants mold their environment and then respond to the environment they have helped create. Influence is *bidirectional:* When babies babble and coo, adults tend to talk to them, which then makes babies "talk" more.
4. *Historical and cultural contexts strongly influence development.* Each child develops within a specific environment, bounded by time and place. A child born in the United States today is likely to have very different experiences from a child born in colonial America or from a child born in Greenland or Afghanistan.
5. *Early experience is important, but children can be remarkably resilient.* A traumatic incident or a severely deprived childhood may well have grave emotional consequences, but the life histories of countless people show that the effects of painful experience, such as growing up in poverty or the death of a parent, can often be overcome.
6. *Development in childhood is part of development throughout the life span.* At one time, it was believed that growth and development end, as this book does, with adolescence. Today most developmental scientists agree that development goes on throughout life. As long as people live, they have the potential to change.

Checkpoint ✓

Can you . . .

- Summarize six fundamental points of agreement that have emerged from the study of child development?

Refocus

Thinking back to the Focus vignette about Victor, the wild boy of Aveyron, at the beginning of this chapter, in what way does Victor's story illustrate the following chapter themes?

- How the study of child development has become more scientific
- The interrelationship of domains of development
- The influences of heredity, environment, and maturation

- The importance of contextual and historical influences
- The roles of nonnormative influences and critical or sensitive periods

Now that you have had a brief introduction to the field of child development and its basic concepts, we can look more closely at the issues developmental scientists think about and how they do their work. In Chapter 2, we will discuss some influential theories of how development takes place and the methods investigators commonly use to study it.

Summary and Key Terms

The Study of Child Development: Then and Now

Guidepost 1 What is child development, and how has its study evolved?

- Child development as a field of scientific study focuses on processes of change and stability from conception through adolescence.

- The scientific study of child development began toward the end of the 19th century. Adolescence was not considered a separate phase of development until the early 20th century. The field of child development is now part of the study of the entire life span, or human development.

- Ways of studying child development are still evolving, making use of advanced technologies.

- The distinction between basic and applied research has become less meaningful.

- Developmental scientists study developmental change, both quantitative and qualitative, as well as stability of personality and behavior.

child development (7)   quantitative change (7)
qualitative change (7)

The Study of Child Development: Basic Concepts

Guidepost 2   What do developmental scientists study?

- The three major domains, or aspects, of development that developmental scientists study are physical, cognitive, and psychosocial. Each affects the others.

- The concept of periods of development is a social construction. In this book, child development is divided into five periods: the prenatal period, infancy and toddlerhood, early childhood, middle childhood, and adolescence. In each period, children have characteristic developmental needs and tasks.

physical development (10)   cognitive development (10)
psychosocial development (10)   social construction (10)

Influences on Development

Guidepost 3   What kinds of influences make one child different from another?

- Influences on development come from both heredity and environment. Many typical changes during childhood are related to maturation. Individual differences increase with age.

- In some societies, the nuclear family predominates; in others, the extended family.

- Socioeconomic status (SES) affects developmental processes and outcomes through the quality of home and neighborhood environments and of nutrition, medical care, supervision, and schooling. The most powerful neighborhood influences seem to be neighborhood income and human capital. Multiple risk factors increase the likelihood of poor outcomes.

- Other important environmental influences stem from culture, ethnicity, and historical context. In large, multiethnic societies, immigrant groups often acculturate to the majority culture while preserving aspects of their own.

- Influences may be normative (age graded or history graded) or nonnormative.

- There is strong evidence of critical or sensitive periods for certain types of early development.

individual differences (12)   heredity (12)   environment (12)
maturation (12)   nuclear family (13)   extended family (13)
socioeconomic status (SES) (13)   risk factors (14)   culture (15)
ethnic group (15)   ethnic gloss (16)   normative (16)   historical
generation (16)   cohort (17)   nonnormative (17)
imprinting (17)   critical period (17)   plasticity (17)
sensitive periods (17)

An Emerging Consensus

Guidepost 4   What are six fundamental points about child development on which consensus has emerged?

- Consensus has emerged on several important points. These include (1) the interrelationship of domains of development, (2) the existence of a wide range of individual differences, (3) the bidirectionality of influence, (4) the importance of history and culture, (5) children's potential for resilience, and (6) continuity of development throughout life.

2 CHAPTER TWO

A Child's World:
How We Discover It

There is one thing even more vital to science than intelligent methods; and that is, the sincere desire to find out the truth, whatever it may be.

—Charles Sanders Peirce, *Collected Papers,* vol. 5

Focus *Margaret Mead, Pioneer in Cross-Cultural Research*

Margaret Mead

Margaret Mead (1901–1978) was a world-famous American anthropologist. In the 1920s, at a time when it was rare for a woman to take on the rigors of fieldwork with remote, preliterate peoples, Mead spent 9 months on the South Pacific island of Samoa, studying girls' adjustment to the transition to adulthood. Her best-selling first book, *Coming of Age in Samoa* (1928), challenged accepted views about the inevitability of adolescent rebellion.

An itinerant childhood built around her parents' academic pursuits prepared Mead for a life of roving research. In New Jersey, her mother, who was working on her doctoral thesis in sociology, took Margaret along on interviews with recent Italian immigrants—the child's first exposure to fieldwork. Her father, a professor at the University of Pennsylvania's Wharton business school, taught her respect for facts and "the importance of thinking clearly" (Mead, 1972, p. 40). He stressed the link between theory and application—as Margaret did when, years later, she applied her theories of child rearing to her daughter. Margaret's grandmother, a former schoolteacher, sent her out in the woods to collect and analyze mint specimens. "I was not well drilled in geography or spelling," Mead wrote in her memoir, *Blackberry Winter* (1972, p. 47). "But I learned to observe the world around me and to note what I saw."

Margaret took copious notes on the development of her younger brother and two younger sisters. Her curiosity about why one child in a family behaved so differently from another led to her later interest in temperamental variations within a culture.

How cultures define male and female roles was another research focus. Margaret saw her mother and her grandmother as educated women who had managed to have husbands, children, and professional careers; and she expected to do the same. She was dismayed when, at the outset of her career, the distinguished anthropologist Edward Sapir told her she "would do better to stay at home and have children than to go off to the South Seas to study adolescent girls" (Mead, 1972, p. 11).

Margaret's choice of anthropology as a career was consistent with her homebred respect for the value of all human beings and their cultures. Recalling her father's insistence that the only thing worth doing is to add to the store of knowledge, she saw an urgent need to document once-isolated cultures now "vanishing before the onslaught of modern civilization" (Mead, 1972, p. 137).

"I went to Samoa—as, later, I went to the other societies on which I have worked—to find out more about human beings, human beings like ourselves in everything except their culture," she wrote. "Through the accidents of history, these cultures had developed so differently from ours that knowledge of them could shed a kind of light upon us, upon our potentialities and our limitations" (Mead, 1972, p. 293). The ongoing quest to illuminate those "potentialities and limitations" is the business of theorists and researchers in child development.

● ● ●

Margaret Mead's life was all of a piece. The young girl who filled notebooks with observations about her siblings became the scientist who traveled to distant lands and studied cultures very different from her own.

Mead's story underlines several important points about the study of child development. First, the study of children is not dry, abstract, or esoteric. It deals with the substance of real life.

Second, a cross-cultural perspective can reveal which patterns of behavior, if any, are universal and which are not. Most studies of human development have been done in Western, industrialized societies, using white, middle-class participants. Today developmental scientists are increasingly conscious of the need to expand the research base, as Mead and her colleagues sought to do.

Third, although the goal of science is to obtain verifiable knowledge through open-minded, impartial investigation, observations about human behavior are products of very human individuals whose inquiries and interpretations may be influenced by their backgrounds, values, and experiences. As Mead's daughter, Mary Catherine Bateson (1984), herself an anthropologist, noted in response to methodological criticism of Mead's early work in Samoa, a scientific observer is like a lens, which may introduce some distortion into what is observed. This is why scientists have others check their results. In striving for greater objectivity, investigators must scrutinize how they and their colleagues conduct their work, the assumptions on which it is based, and how they arrive at their conclusions. In studying the results of research, it is important to keep these potential biases in mind.

Fourth, theory and research are two sides of the same coin. As Mead reflected on her experiences and observed the behavior of others, she formed tentative explanations, or theories, to be tested by additional research. Because theory and research are so closely interrelated, we introduce in this chapter an overview both of major theories of child development and of research methods used to study it.

In the first part of this chapter, we present major issues and theoretical perspectives that underlie much research in child development. In the remainder of the chapter, we look at how researchers gather and assess information so that, as you read further in this book, you will be better able to judge whether research findings and conclusions rest on solid ground.

After you have read and studied this chapter, you should be able to answer each of the Guidepost questions on the following page. Look for them again in the margins throughout the chapter, where they point to important concepts. To check your understanding of these Guideposts, review the end-of-chapter summary. Checkpoints located throughout the chapter will help you verify your understanding of what you have read.

Guideposts
for Study

1. What purposes do theories serve, and what are two basic issues on which developmental theorists differ?

2. What are five theoretical perspectives on child development, and what are some theories representative of each?

3. How do developmental scientists study children, and what are the advantages and disadvantages of each research method?

4. What ethical problems may arise in research on children?

Basic Theoretical Issues

Guidepost 1

What purposes do theories serve, and what are two basic issues on which developmental theorists differ?

Developmental scientists have proposed many theories about how children develop. A **theory** is a set of logically related concepts or statements that seeks to describe and explain development and to predict what kinds of behavior might occur under certain conditions. Theories organize and explain data, the information gathered by research. Theories also generate **hypotheses,** tentative explanations or predictions that can be tested by further research.

Theories change to incorporate new findings. Sometimes research supports a hypothesis and the theory on which it was based. At other times, as with Mead's findings challenging the inevitability of adolescent rebellion, scientists must modify their theories to account for unexpected data. Research findings often suggest additional hypotheses to be examined and provide direction for dealing with practical issues.

The way theorists explain development depends in part on the way they view two basic issues: (1) whether children are active or passive in their development; and (2) whether development is continuous or occurs in stages. A third issue, whether development is more influenced by heredity or environment, was introduced in Chapter 1 and will be discussed more fully in Chapter 3.

theory Coherent set of logically related concepts that seeks to organize, explain, and predict data.

hypotheses Possible explanations for phenomena, used to predict the outcome of research.

Issue 1: Are Children Active or Passive in Their Development?

Are children active or passive in their development? This controversy goes back to the 18th century. The English philosopher John Locke held that a young child is a *tabula rasa*—a "blank slate"—on which society "writes." In contrast, the French philosopher Jean-Jacques Rousseau believed that children are born "noble savages" who develop according to their own positive natural tendencies unless corrupted by society. We now know that both views are too simplistic. Children have their own internal drives and needs that influence development; but children also are social animals, who cannot develop optimally in isolation.

The debate over Locke's and Rousseau's philosophies led to two contrasting models, or images, of human development: *mechanistic* and *organismic*. Locke's view was the forerunner of the **mechanistic model** of development. In this model, people are like machines that react to environmental input (Pepper, 1942/1961). If we know enough about how the human "machine" is put together and about the internal and external forces acting on it, we can predict what a person will do. Mechanistic research seeks to identify the factors that make people behave as they do. For example, to explain why some college students drink too much alcohol, a mechanistic theorist might look for environmental influences, such as advertising and whether the students' friends drink to excess.

mechanistic model Model that views human development as a series of passive, predictable responses to stimuli.

Figure 2-1

A major difference among developmental theories is (a) whether development occurs in distinct stages, as Freud, Erikson, and Piaget maintained, or (b) whether it proceeds continuously, as learning theorists and information-processing theorists propose.

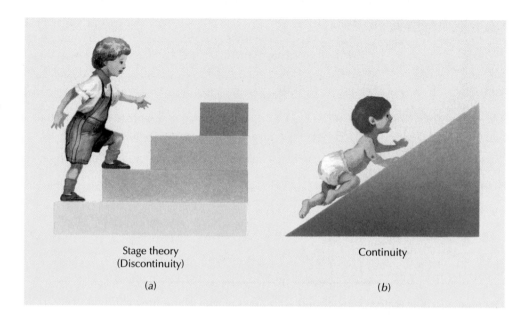

Stage theory
(Discontinuity)

(a)

Continuity

(b)

organismic model Model that views human development as internally initiated by an active organism, and as occurring in a sequence of qualitatively different stages.

Rousseau's ideas were precursors of the **organismic model** of development. This model sees people as active, growing organisms that set their own development in motion (Pepper, 1942/1961). They initiate events; they do not just react. The impetus for change is internal. Environmental influences do not *cause* development, though they can speed or slow it. Because human behavior is an organic whole, it cannot be predicted by breaking it down into simple responses to environmental stimulation. An organismic theorist, in studying why some students drink too much, would be likely to look at what kinds of situations they choose to participate in and with whom. Do they choose friends who like to party or who are more studious?

Issue 2: Is Development Continuous, or Does It Occur in Stages?

The mechanistic and organismic models also differ on the second issue: Is development continuous, or does it occur in stages?

Mechanistic theorists see development as continuous, like walking or crawling up a ramp (Figure 2-1). These theorists describe development as consistently governed by the same underlying processes, enabling prediction of later behaviors from earlier ones. These theorists focus on *quantitative* change: for example, changes in the frequency with which a response is made, rather than changes in the type of response.

Organismic theorists emphasize *qualitative* change. They see development as occurring in a series of distinct stages, like stair steps. At each stage, people cope with different types of problems and develop different abilities. Each stage builds on the previous one and prepares the way for the next.

A Shifting Balance

As the study of child development has evolved, the mechanistic and organismic models have shifted in influence (Parke, Ornstein, Rieser, & Zahn-Waxler, 1994). Most of the early theoretical pioneers, including Sigmund Freud, Erik Erikson, and Jean Piaget, favored organismic or stage approaches. The mechanistic view gained support during the 1960s with the popularity of learning theories derived from the work of John B. Watson. (We discuss all these theorists in the next section.)

Today much theory and research attention is focused on the biological and evolutionary bases of behavior. Instead of looking for broad stages, developmental scientists seek to discover what specific types of behavior show continuity or lack of continuity and what processes are involved in each. Instead of debating active versus passive development, they often find that influences are *bidirectional:* People change their world even as it changes them. A baby girl born with a cheerful disposition is likely to get positive reactions from adults, which strengthen her trust that her smiles will be rewarded and motivate her to smile more. As children grow older, their natural tendencies lead them to choose or initiate activities, such as studying a musical instrument, that further develop those tendencies.

Checkpoint ✓

Can you . . .

✔ State two basic issues regarding the nature of child development?

✔ Contrast the mechanistic and organismic models of development?

Theoretical Perspectives

Guidepost 2

What are five theoretical perspectives on child development, and what are some theories representative of each?

Despite the growing consensus on the basic issues just discussed, many investigators view development from differing theoretical perspectives. Theories generally fall within these broad perspectives, each of which focuses on different aspects of development. These perspectives influence the questions researchers ask, the methods they use, and the ways they interpret data. Therefore, to evaluate and interpret research, it is important to recognize the theoretical perspective on which it is based.

Five major perspectives (summarized in Table 2-1) underlie much influential theory and research on child development: (1) *psychoanalytic,* which focuses on unconscious emotions and drives; (2) *learning,* which studies observable behavior; (3) *cognitive,* which analyzes thought processes; (4) *contextual,* which emphasizes the impact of the historical, social, and cultural context; and (5) *evolutionary/sociobiological,* which considers evolutionary and biological underpinnings of behavior.

Perspective 1: Psychoanalytic

The **psychoanalytic perspective** views development as shaped by unconscious forces that motivate human behavior. Sigmund Freud (1856–1939), a Viennese physician, developed *psychoanalysis,* a therapeutic approach aimed at giving patients insight into unconscious emotional conflicts. Other theorists and practitioners, including Erik H. Erikson, have expanded and modified the psychoanalytic perspective.

psychoanalytic perspective View of human development as being shaped by unconscious forces.

Sigmund Freud: Psychosexual Development

Freud (1953, 1964a, 1964b) believed that people are born with biological drives that must be redirected to make it possible to live in society. By asking his patients questions designed to summon up long-buried memories, Freud concluded that the sources of emotional disturbances lay in repressed traumatic experiences of early childhood.

Freud proposed three hypothetical parts of the personality—the *id,* the *ego,* and the *superego*—that develop early in life. Newborns are governed by the *id,* the seat of unconscious instinctual drives; it seeks immediate gratification under the *pleasure principle.* When gratification is delayed, as when infants have to wait to be fed, they begin to see themselves as separate from the outside world. The *superego,* which develops at about age 5 or 6, contains the conscience; it incorporates socially approved "shoulds" and "should nots" into the child's value system. The superego is highly demanding; if its demands are not met, a child may feel guilty and anxious. The *ego,* the conscious self, develops gradually during the first year or so and operates under the *reality principle.* The ego's aim is to find reasonably realistic ways to gratify the id that are also acceptable to the superego.

Freud proposed that personality forms through unconscious conflicts between the inborn urges of the id and the requirements of civilized life. These conflicts occur in an

The Viennese physician Sigmund Freud developed an influential but controversial theory of childhood emotional development.

Table 2-1   Five Perspectives on Human Development

Perspective	Important Theories	Basic Principles
Psychoanalytic	Freud's psychosexual theory	Behavior is controlled by powerful unconscious urges.
	Erikson's psychosocial theory	Personality is influenced by society and develops through a series of crises.
Learning	Behaviorism, or traditional learning theory (Pavlov, Skinner, Watson)	People are responders; the environment controls behavior.
	Social learning (social cognitive) theory (Bandura)	Children learn in a social context by observing and imitating models. Children are active contributors to learning.
Cognitive	Piaget's cognitive-stage theory	Qualitative changes in thought occur between infancy and adolescence. Children are active initiators of development.
	Vygotsky's sociocultural theory	Social interaction is central to cognitive development.
	Information-processing theory	Human beings are processors of symbols.
Contextual	Bronfenbrenner's bioecological theory	Development occurs through interaction between a developing person and five surrounding, interlocking contextual systems of influences, from microsystem to chronosystem.
Evolutionary/ sociobiological	Bowlby's attachment theory	Human beings have the adaptive mechanisms to survive; critical or sensitive periods are stressed; evolutionary and biological bases for behavior and predisposition toward learning are important.

psychosexual development
In Freudian theory, an unvarying sequence of stages of personality development during infancy, childhood, and adolescence, in which gratification shifts from the mouth to the anus and then to the genitals.

unvarying sequence of five maturationally based stages of **psychosexual development** (Table 2-2), in which pleasure shifts from one body zone to another—from the mouth to the anus and then to the genitals. At each stage, the behavior that is the chief source of gratification (or frustration) changes—from feeding to elimination and eventually to sexual activity.

Freud considered the first three stages—those of the first 5 or 6 years of life—crucial for personality development. He suggested that if children receive too little or too much gratification in any of these stages, they are at risk of *fixation*—an arrest in development that can affect adult personality. Babies whose needs are not met during the *oral stage,* when feeding is the main source of pleasure, may become nail-biters or develop "bitingly" critical personalities. A person who, as a toddler, had too-strict toilet training may be fixated at the *anal stage.* Such a person may be obsessively clean, rigidly tied to schedules and routines, or defiantly messy.

According to Freud, a key event in psychosexual development occurs in the *phallic stage* of early childhood, which focuses on the genitals. Children discover the physical differences between males and females. Boys develop sexual desire for their mothers and have aggressive urges toward their fathers, whom they both fear and regard as rivals. Freud called this development the *Oedipus complex.* Girls, according to Freud, experience *penis envy,* the repressed wish to possess a penis and the power it stands for.

Children eventually resolve their anxiety over these feelings by identifying with the same-sex parent and move into the *latency stage* of middle childhood, a period of relative emotional calm and intellectual and social exploration. They redirect their sexual energies into other pursuits, such as schoolwork, skill-building, relationships, and hobbies.

The *genital stage,* the final one, lasts throughout adulthood. The sexual urges repressed during latency now resurface to flow in socially approved channels, which Freud defined as heterosexual relations with persons outside the family of origin.

Freud's theory made historic contributions and inspired a whole generation of followers, some of whom took psychoanalytic theory in new directions. Some of Freud's ideas, such as his notions of the Oedipus complex and penis envy, now are widely considered obsolete. Others, such as the concepts of the id and superego, cannot be empirically tested. Although Freud opened our eyes to the importance of early sexual urges, many psy-

Technique Used	Stage-Oriented	Causal Emphasis	Active or Passive Individual
Clinical observation	Yes	Innate factors modified by experience	Passive
Clinical observation	Yes	Interaction of innate and experiential factors	Active
Rigorous scientific (experimental) procedures	No	Experience	Passive
Rigorous scientific (experimental) procedures	No	Experience modified by innate factors	Active and passive
Flexible interviews; meticulous observation	Yes	Interaction of innate and experiential factors	Active
Cross-cultural research; observation of child interacting with more competent person	No	Experience	Active
Laboratory research; technological monitoring of physiologic responses	No	Interaction of innate and experiential factors	Active and passive
Naturalistic observation and analysis	No	Interaction of innate and experiential factors	Active
Naturalistic and laboratory observation	No	Interaction of innate and experiential factors	Active and passive (theorists vary)

choanalysts today reject his narrow emphasis on sexual and aggressive drives to the exclusion of other motives. Nevertheless, several of his central themes have stood the test of time (Westen, 1998, p. 334). Freud made us aware of the importance of unconscious thoughts, feelings, and motivations; the role of childhood experiences in forming personality; the ambivalence of emotional responses, especially responses to parents; the role of mental representations of the self and others in the establishment of intimate relationships; and the path of normal development from an immature, dependent state to a mature, interdependent one. In all these ways, Freud left an indelible mark on psychoanalysis and developmental psychology (Westen, 1998).

We need to remember that Freud's theory grew out of his place in history and in society. Freud based his theories about normal development, not on a population of average children, but on a clientele of upper-middle-class adults, mostly women, in therapy. His concentration on the influences of sexual urges and early experience did not take into account other, and later, influences on personality—including the influences of society and culture, which many heirs to the Freudian tradition, such as Erik Erikson, stress.

The psychoanalyst Erik H. Erikson departed from Freudian theory in emphasizing societal, rather than chiefly biological, influences on personality.

Erik Erikson: Psychosocial Development

Erik Erikson (1902–1994), a German-born psychoanalyst who originally was part of Freud's circle in Vienna, modified and extended Freudian theory by emphasizing the influence of society on the developing personality. Erikson was a pioneer in the life-span perspective. Whereas Freud maintained that early childhood experiences permanently shape personality, Erikson contended that ego development is lifelong.

Erikson's (1950, 1982; Erikson, Erikson, & Kivnick, 1986) theory of **psychosocial development** covers eight stages across the life span (refer to Table 2-2), which we will discuss in the appropriate chapters. Each stage involves what Erikson originally called a "crisis" in personality—a major psychosocial theme that is particularly important at that time but will remain an issue to some degree throughout the rest of life.* These issues,

psychosocial development In Erikson's eight-stage theory, the socially and culturally influenced process of development of the ego, or self.

---

*Erikson later dropped the term "crisis" and referred instead to conflicting or competing tendencies.

Table 2-2   Development Stages according to Various Theories

Psychosexual Stages (Freud)	Psychosocial Stages (Erikson)	Cognitive Stages (Piaget)
Oral (birth to 12–18 months). Baby's chief source of pleasure involves mouth-oriented activities (sucking and feeding).	*Basic trust versus mistrust (birth to 12–18 months).* Baby develops sense of whether world is a good and safe place. Virtue: hope.	*Sensorimotor (birth to 2 years).* Infant gradually becomes able to organize activities in relation to the environment through sensory and motor activity.
Anal (12–18 months to 3 years). Child derives sensual gratification from withholding and expelling feces. Zone of gratification is anal region, and toilet training is important activity.	*Autonomy versus shame and doubt (12–18 months to 3 years).* Child develops a balance of independence and self-sufficiency over shame and doubt, Virtue: will.	*Preoperational (2 to 7 years).* Child develops a representational system and uses symbols to represent people, places, and events. Language and imaginative play are important manifestations of this stage. Thinking is still not logical.
Phallic (3 to 6 years). Child becomes attached to parent of the other sex and later identifies with same-sex parent. Supergo develops. Zone of gratification shifts to genital region.	*Initiative versus guilt (3 to 6 years).* Child develops initiative when trying out new activities and is not overwhelmed by guilt. Virtue: purpose.	
Latency (6 years to puberty). Time of relative calm between more turbulent states.	*Industry versus inferiority (6 years to puberty).* Child must learn skills of the culture or face feelings of incompetence. Virtue: skill.	*Concrete operations (7 to 11 years).* Child can solve problems logically if they are focused on the here and now but cannot think abstractly.
Genital (puberty through adulthood). Reemergence of sexual impulses of phallic stage, channeled into mature adult sexuality.	*Identity versus identity confusion (puberty to young adulthood).* Adolescent must determine sense of self ("Who am I?") or experience confusion about roles. Virtue: fidelity.	*Formal operations (11 years through adulthood).* Person can think abstractly, deal with hypothetical situations, and think about possibilities.
	Intimacy versus isolation (young adulthood). Person seeks to make commitments to others; if unsuccessful, may suffer from isolation and self-absorption. Virtue: love.	
	Generativity versus stagnation (middle adulthood). Mature adult is concerned with establishing and guiding the next generation or else feels personal impoverishment. Virtue: care.	
	Integrity versus despair (late adulthood). Elderly person achieves acceptance of own life, allowing acceptance of death, or else despairs over inability to relive life. Virtue: wisdom.	

Note: All ages are approximate.

---

learning perspective View of human development that holds that changes in behavior result from experience or adaptation to the environment.

which emerge according to a maturational timetable, must be satisfactorily resolved for healthy ego development.

Each stage requires the balancing of a positive trait and a corresponding negative one. Although the positive quality should predominate, some degree of the negative is needed as well. The critical theme of infancy, for example, is *basic trust versus basic mistrust.* People need to trust the world and the people in it, but they also need to learn some mistrust to protect themselves from danger. The successful outcome of each stage is the development of a particular "virtue" or strength—in this first stage, the virtue of *hope.*

Erikson's theory is important because of its emphasis on social and cultural influences and on development beyond adolescence. He is perhaps most widely known for his concept of the *identity crisis,* which has entered public parlance and has generated considerable research (see Chapter 17).

Perspective 2: Learning

The **learning perspective** maintains that development results from *learning,* a long-lasting change in behavior based on experience or adaptation to the environment. Learning theorists are concerned with finding out the objective laws that govern changes in observable behavior. They see development as continuous (not in stages) and emphasize quantitative change.

Learning theorists have helped to make the study of human development more scientific. Their terms are defined precisely, and their theories can be tested in the laboratory. Two important learning theories are *behaviorism* and *social learning (social cognitive) theory.*

Learning Theory 1: Behaviorism

Behaviorism is a mechanistic theory, which describes observed behavior as a predictable response to experience. Although biology sets limits on what people do, behaviorists view the environment as much more influential. They hold that human beings at all ages learn about the world the same way other organisms do: by reacting to conditions, or aspects of their environment, that they find pleasing, painful, or threatening. Behavioral research focuses on *associative learning,* in which a mental link is formed between two events. Two kinds of associative learning are *classical conditioning* and *operant conditioning.*

behaviorism Learning theory that emphasizes the predictable role of environment in causing observable behavior.

Classical Conditioning The Russian physiologist Ivan Pavlov (1849–1936) devised experiments in which dogs learned to salivate at the sound of a bell that rang at feeding time. These experiments were the foundation for **classical conditioning**, in which a response (salivation) to a stimulus (the bell) is elicited after repeated association with a stimulus that normally elicits it (food).

The American behaviorist John B. Watson (1878–1958) applied stimulus-response theories to children, claiming that he could mold any infant in any way he chose. His writings influenced a generation of parents to apply principles of learning theory to child raising. In one of the earliest and most famous demonstrations of classical conditioning in human beings (Watson & Rayner, 1920), he taught an 11-month-old baby known as "Little Albert" to fear furry white objects.

In this study, Albert was exposed to a loud noise just as he was about to stroke a furry white rat. The noise frightened him, and he began to cry. After repeated pairings of the rat with the loud noise, Albert whimpered with fear whenever he saw the rat. Although such research would be considered unethical today, the study showed that a baby could be conditioned to fear things he or she had not been afraid of before.

Critics of such methods sometimes associate conditioning with thought control and manipulation. Actually, as we will discuss in Chapter 7, classical conditioning is a natural form of learning that occurs even without intervention.

classical conditioning Learning based on association of a stimulus that does not ordinarily elicit a particular response with another stimulus that does elicit the response.

Operant Conditioning Baby Terrell lies peacefully in his crib. When he happens to smile, his mother goes over to the crib and plays with him. Later his father does the same thing. As this sequence is repeated, Terrell learns that his behavior (smiling) can produce a desirable consequence (loving attention from a parent); and so he smiles again to attract his parents' attention. An originally accidental behavior (smiling) has become a conditioned response.

This type of learning is called **operant conditioning** because the individual learns from the consequences of *operating* on the environment. Unlike classical conditioning, operant conditioning involves voluntary behavior, such as Terrell's smiling (Figure 2-2).

The American psychologist B. F. Skinner (1904–1990), who formulated the principles of operant conditioning, worked primarily with rats and pigeons, but Skinner (1938) maintained that the same principles apply to human beings. He found that an organism will tend to repeat a response that has been reinforced by desirable consequences and will suppress a response that has been punished. Thus, **reinforcement** is the process by which a behavior is strengthened, *increasing* the likelihood that the behavior will be repeated. In Terrell's case, his parents' attention reinforces his smiling. **Punishment** is the process by which a behavior is weakened, *decreasing* the likelihood of repetition. If Terrell's parents frowned when he smiled, he would be less likely to smile again. Whether a consequence is reinforcing or punishing depends on the person. What is reinforcing for one person may be punishing for another. For a child who likes being alone, being sent to his or her room could be reinforcing rather than punishing.

operant conditioning Learning based on association of behavior with its consequences.

reinforcement In operant conditioning, a process that strengthens and encourages repetition of a desired behavior.

punishment In operant conditioning, a process that weakens and discourages repetition of a behavior.

Figure 2-2

Operant conditioning has three steps. An accidental response that is reinforced is likely to be repeated.

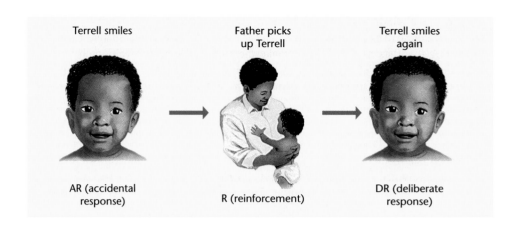

Terrell smiles

Father picks up Terrell

Terrell smiles again

AR (accidental response)

R (reinforcement)

DR (deliberate response)

Reinforcement can be either positive or negative. *Positive reinforcement* consists of *giving* a reward, such as food, gold stars, money, or praise—or playing with a baby. *Negative reinforcement* consists of *removing* something the individual does not like (known as an *aversive event*), such as a wet diaper. Negative reinforcement is sometimes confused with punishment. However, they are different. Punishment *suppresses* a behavior by *bringing on* an aversive event (such as spanking a child) or by *withdrawing* a positive event (such as watching television). Negative reinforcement *encourages* repetition of a behavior by *removing* an aversive event. When an older baby signals a wet diaper, the removal of the diaper may encourage the child to signal again the next time a diaper is wet.

Reinforcement is most effective when it immediately follows a behavior. If a response is no longer reinforced, it will eventually be *extinguished;* that is, it will return to its original (baseline) level. If, after a while, no one plays with Terrell when he smiles, he may not stop smiling but will smile far less than if his smiles continued to bring reinforcement.

Behavior modification, or behavior therapy, is a form of operant conditioning used to eliminate undesirable behavior, such as temper tantrums, or to instill desirable behavior, such as putting away toys after play. For example, every time a child puts toys away, she or he gets a reward, such as praise or a treat or new toy. Behavior modification is particularly effective among children with special needs, such as those with mental or emotional disabilities. However, Skinnerian psychology is limited in application because it does not adequately address individual differences and cultural and social influences.

social learning theory Theory that behaviors are learned by observing and imitating models. Also called *social cognitive theory.*

reciprocal determinism Bandura's concept that behavior is determined bidirectionally, by the child and the environment acting on each other.

observational learning Learning through watching the behavior of others.

The American psychologist B. F. Skinner formulated the principles of operant conditioning.

Figure 2-3

According to social learning theory, children learn by imitating the behavior of adult models—such as Dad mowing the lawn.

Learning Theory 2: Social Learning (Social Cognitive) Theory

The American psychologist Albert Bandura (b. 1925) developed many of the principles of **social learning theory.** Whereas behaviorists see the environment, acting on the child, as the chief impetus for development, Bandura (1977, 1989; Bandura & Walters, 1963) suggests that the impetus for development is bidirectional. Bandura called this concept **reciprocal determinism**—the child acts on the world as the world acts on the child.

Classic social learning theory maintains that people learn appropriate social behavior chiefly by observing and imitating models—that is, by watching other people. This process is called *modeling,* or **observational learning** (Figure 2-3). People initiate or advance their learning by choosing models to imitate—say, a parent or a popular sports hero. According to this theory, imitation of models is the most important element in how children learn a language, deal with aggression, develop a moral sense, and learn gender-appropriate behaviors. However, observational learning can occur even if the child does not imitate the observed behavior.

The specific behavior people imitate depends on what they perceive as valued in their culture. If all the teachers in Carlos's school are women, he probably will not copy their behavior, which he may consider "unmanly." However, if he meets a male teacher he likes, he may change his mind about the value of teachers as models.

Bandura's (1989) newest version of social learning theory is called *social cognitive theory*. The evolution from one name to the next reflects Bandura's increasing emphasis on cognitive processes as central to development. Cognitive processes are at work as people observe models, learn chunks of behavior, and mentally put the chunks together into complex new behavior patterns. Rita, for example, imitates her dance teacher's toes-out walk but models her dance steps after those of Carmen, a slightly more advanced student. Even so, she develops her own style of dancing by putting her observations together into a new pattern.

Through feedback on their behavior, children gradually form standards for judging their actions and become more selective in choosing models who exemplify those standards. They also begin to develop a sense of **self-efficacy,** confidence in their ability to succeed.

self-efficacy Sense of one's capability to master challenges and achieve goals.

cognitive perspective View that thought processes are central to development.

cognitive-stage theory Piaget's theory that children's cognitive development advances in a series of four stages involving qualitatively distinct types of mental operations.

Perspective 3: Cognitive

The **cognitive perspective** focuses on thought processes and the behavior that reflects those processes. This perspective encompasses both organismic and mechanistically influenced theories. It includes Piaget's cognitive-stage theory and Vygotsky's sociocultural theory of cognitive development. It also includes the information-processing approach and neo-Piagetian theories, which combine elements of information-processing and Piagetian theory.

Jean Piaget's Cognitive-Stage Theory

Our understanding of how children think owes a great deal to the work of the Swiss theoretician Jean Piaget (1896–1980). Piaget's **cognitive-stage theory** was the forerunner of today's "cognitive revolution" with its emphasis on mental processes. Piaget, a biologist and philosopher by training, viewed development organismically, as the product of children's efforts to understand and act on their world.

As a young man studying in Paris, Piaget set out to standardize the tests Alfred Binet had developed to assess the intelligence of French schoolchildren. Piaget became intrigued by the children's wrong answers, finding in them clues to their thought processes. Piaget's clinical method combined observation with flexible questioning. To find out how children think, Piaget followed up their answers with more questions, and he designed tasks to test his tentative conclusions. In this way he discovered that a typical 4-year-old believes that pennies or flowers are more numerous when arranged in a line than when heaped or piled up. From his observations of his own and other children, Piaget created a comprehensive theory of cognitive development.

Piaget suggested that cognitive development begins with an inborn ability to adapt to the environment. By rooting for a nipple, feeling a pebble, or exploring the boundaries of a room, young

The Swiss psychologist Jean Piaget studied children's cognitive development by observing and talking with his own youngsters and others.

children develop a more accurate picture of their surroundings and greater competence in dealing with them.

Piaget described cognitive development as occurring in four qualitatively different stages (listed in Table 2-2 and discussed in detail in later chapters), which represent universal patterns of development. At each stage a child's mind develops a new way of operating. From infancy through adolescence, mental operations evolve from learning based on simple sensory and motor activity to logical, abstract thought. This cognitive growth occurs through three interrelated processes: *organization, adaptation,* and *equilibration.*

Organization is the tendency to create increasingly complex cognitive structures: systems of knowledge or ways of thinking that incorporate more and more accurate images of reality. These structures, called **schemes,** are organized patterns of behavior that a person uses to think about and act in a situation. As children acquire more information, their schemes become more and more complex. Take sucking, for example. A newborn infant has a simple scheme for sucking but soon develops varied schemes for how to suck at the breast, a bottle, or a thumb.

Adaptation is how children handle new information in light of what they already know. Adaptation involves two steps: (1) **assimilation,** taking in new information and incorporating it into existing cognitive structures, and (2) **accommodation,** modifying one's cognitive structures to include the new information.

Equilibration—a constant striving for a stable balance, or equilibrium—dictates the shift from assimilation to accommodation. When children cannot handle new experiences within their existing cognitive structures, they experience an uncomfortable state of disequilibrium. By organizing new mental patterns that integrate the new experience, they restore equilibrium. Take sucking, again. A breast- or bottle-fed baby who begins to suck on the spout of a sippy cup is showing assimilation—using an old scheme to deal with a new situation. When the infant discovers that sipping from a cup requires different tongue and mouth movements from those used to suck on a breast or bottle, she accommodates by modifying the old scheme. She has adapted her original sucking scheme to deal with a new experience: the cup. Thus, assimilation and accommodation work together to produce equilibrium. Throughout life, the quest for equilibrium is the driving force behind cognitive growth.

Piaget's observations have yielded much information and some surprising insights. Who, for example, would have thought that most children younger than 7 do not realize that a ball of clay that has been rolled into a worm shape before their eyes still contains the same amount of clay? Or that an infant might think that a person who has moved out of sight no longer exists? Piaget has shown us that children's minds are not miniature adult minds. Knowing how children think makes it easier for parents and teachers to understand them and teach them.

Yet Piaget seems to have seriously underestimated the abilities of infants and young children. Some contemporary psychologists question his distinct stages, pointing instead to evidence that cognitive development is more gradual and continuous. Furthermore, later research has challenged Piaget's idea that thinking develops in a single, universal progression leading to formal thought. Instead, children's cognitive processes seem closely tied to specific content (what they are thinking *about*) as well as to the context of a problem and the kinds of information and thought a culture considers important (Case & Okamoto, 1996).

Lev Vygotsky's Sociocultural Theory

The Russian psychologist Lev Semenovich Vygotsky (1896–1934) focused on the social and cultural processes that guide children's cognitive development. Vygotsky's (1978) **sociocultural theory,** like Piaget's theory, stresses children's active engagement with their environment; but, whereas Piaget described the solo mind taking in and interpreting information about the world, Vygotsky saw cognitive growth as a *collaborative* process. Children, said Vygotsky, learn through social interaction. They acquire cognitive skills as part of their induction into a way of life. Shared activities help children internalize their society's modes of thinking and behaving and make those folkways their own. Vygotsky placed special emphasis on *language*—not merely as an expression

organization Piaget's term for the creation of systems of knowledge.

schemes Piaget's term for organized patterns of behavior used in particular situations.

adaptation Piaget's term for adjustment to new information about the environment.

assimilation Piaget's term for incorporation of new information into an existing cognitive structure.

accommodation Piaget's term for changes in a cognitive structure to include new information.

equilibration Piaget's term for the tendency to seek a stable balance among cognitive elements.

According to the Russian psychologist Lev Semenovich Vygotsky, children learn through social interaction.

sociocultural theory Vygotsky's theory of how contextual factors affect children's development.

Box 2-1 *The Adaptive Value of Immaturity*

In comparison with other animals and even with other primates, human beings take a long time to grow up. Chimpanzees reach reproductive maturity in about 8 years, rhesus monkeys in about four years, and lemurs in only 2 years or so. Human beings, in contrast, do not reach full growth and physical maturity until the early teenage years and, at least in modern industrialized societies, typically reach cognitive and psychosocial maturity even later. During much of that time, they remain largely dependent on their parents or other caregivers.

From the point of view of evolutionary theory, this prolonged period of immaturity may be essential to survival and well-being. Human beings are social animals, and a long, protective childhood may serve as essential preparation for the social problem-solving skills needed in adulthood. Human communities and cultures are highly complex, and there is much to learn in order to know the ropes. Thus, childhood may be an evolved mechanism that allows for the development of social competency.

Human intelligence, too, may be an evolved characteristic. The fossil record indicates that during the past 4 million years, the human brain has tripled in volume. At the same time, its period of development has nearly doubled. The human brain, despite its rapid prenatal growth, is much less fully developed at birth than the brains of other primates; if the human fetus's brain attained full size before birth, its head would be too big to go through the birth canal. Instead, the human brain continues to grow in size and complexity throughout childhood, eventually far surpassing the brains of our simian cousins in the capacities for language and thought. The human brain's slower development gives it greater *plasticity,* or flexibility, as not all connections are hard-wired at an early age. One theorist has called this plasticity "the human species's greatest adaptive advantage" (Bjorklund, 1997, p. 157).

The extended period of immaturity and dependency during infancy and childhood allows children to spend much of their time in play; and, as Piaget maintained, it is largely through play that cognitive development occurs. Play also enables children to develop motor skills and experiment with social roles. It is a ve-

hicle for creative imagination and intellectual curiosity, the hallmarks of the human spirit.

Some aspects of immaturity serve immediate adaptive purposes. For example, some primitive reflexes, such as rooting for the nipple, which are protective for newborns, disappear when no longer needed. Research on animals suggests that the immaturity of early sensory and motor functioning may protect infants from overstimulation. By limiting the amount of information they have to deal with, it may help them focus on experiences essential to survival, such as feeding and attachment to the mother. Later, as mentioned in Box 1-2 in Chapter 1, infants' limited memory capacity may simplify the processing of linguistic sounds and facilitate early language learning.

Limitations on the way young children think also may have adaptive value. For example, young children are unrealistic in assessing their abilities, believing they can do more than they actually can. This immature self-judgment, by reducing fear of failure, may encourage children to try new things.

All in all, evolutionary theory and research suggest that immaturity is not necessarily equivalent to deficiency and that some attributes of infancy and childhood have persisted because they are appropriate to the tasks of a particular time of life.

Source: Bjorklund, 1997; Bjorklund & Pellegrini, 2000, 2002; Flinn & Ward, 2005.

What's your view

Can you think of additional examples of the adaptive value of immaturity? Can you think of ways in which immaturity may *not* be adaptive?

Check it out

For more information on this topic, go to www.brazelton-institute .com. This is the Web site for the Brazelton Institute at Harvard Medical School. Follow the link *The Brazelton Scale: What Is It?* to learn about the scale. The scale shows how much such immature creatures as human newborns can do in responding to the world. This Web site also offers a preview of the discussion of the Brazelton Scale in Chapter 5.

Research Methods

Guidepost 3

How do developmental scientists study children, and what are the advantages and disadvantages of each research method?

Researchers in child development work within two methodological traditions: *quantitative* and *qualitative*. **Quantitative research** deals with objectively measurable data. Quantitative researchers may study, for example, how much fear or anxiety children feel before surgery, as measured by standardized tests, physiological changes, or statistical analysis. **Qualitative research** involves the interpretation of nonnumerical data, such as the nature or quality of participants' subjective experiences, feelings, or beliefs. Qualitative researchers may study how children describe their emotions before surgery (Morse & Field, 1995) or, as in Margaret Mead's research, how girls in the South Sea islands describe their experience of puberty.

Quantitative research is based on the **scientific method,** which characterizes most scientific inquiry. Its usual steps are

1. *identifying a problem* to be studied, often on the basis of a theory or of previous research
2. *formulating hypotheses* to be tested by research
3. *collecting data*

quantitative research Research that deals with objectively measurable data.

qualitative research Research that involves the interpretation of nonnumerical data, such as subjective experiences, feelings, or beliefs.

4. *analyzing the data* to determine whether they support the hypothesis
5. *disseminating findings* so that other observers can check, learn from, analyze, repeat, and build on the results

Qualitative research is more open-ended. Instead of generating hypotheses from previous research, qualitative researchers often gather and examine data to see what hypotheses or theories may emerge. Qualitative research can be a rich source of insights into attitudes and behavior.

Although most developmental scientists have been trained in quantitative methods, the need for qualitative research is increasingly recognized. The selection of quantitative or qualitative methods depends on a number of factors: the topic for study, how much is already known about it, the researcher's theoretical orientation, and the setting. Quantitative research is often done in controlled laboratory settings. Qualitative research is usually conducted in everyday settings. Each of these two distinct methodologies can provide rich information about child development.

Sampling

To be sure that the results of research are true generally, and not just for specific participants, quantitative researchers need to control who gets into the study. Because studying an entire *population* (a group to whom the findings may apply) is usually too costly and time-consuming, investigators select a **sample,** a smaller group within the population. The sample should adequately represent the population under study—that is, it should show relevant characteristics in the same proportions as in the entire population. Otherwise the results cannot properly be *generalized,* or applied to the population as a whole. To judge how generalizable the findings are likely to be, researchers carefully compare the characteristics of the people in the sample with those of the population as a whole.

Often researchers seek to achieve representativeness through **random selection,** in which each person in a population has an equal and independent chance of being chosen. If we wanted to study the effects of an educational program, one way to select a random sample would be to put all the names of participating children into a large bowl, stir it, and then draw out a certain number of names. A random sample, especially a large one, is likely to represent the population well. Unfortunately, a random sample of a large population is often difficult to obtain. Instead, many studies use samples selected for convenience or accessibility (for example, children born in a particular hospital or attending a particular day care center). The findings of such studies may not apply to the population as a whole.

In qualitative research, samples tend to be small and need not be random. Participants in this kind of research may be chosen for their ability to communicate the nature of their experience, such as how it feels to go through a particular type of surgery.

Forms of Data Collection

Common ways of gathering data (Table 2-3) include self-reports (verbal reports by study participants), behavioral or performance measures, and observation of participants in laboratory or natural settings. Depending in part on time and financial constraints, researchers may use one or more of these data collection techniques in any research design. Qualitative research tends to depend heavily on interviews and on observation in natural settings, whereas quantitative research makes use of more structured methods. Currently there is a trend toward increased use of self-reports and observation in combination with more objective measures.

Self-Reports: Diaries, Interviews, Questionnnaires

The simplest form of self-report is a *diary* or log. Adolescents may be asked, for example, to record what they eat each day or the times when they feel depressed. In studying young children, *parental self-reports*—diaries, journals, interviews, or questionnaires—are commonly used, often together with other methods, such as videotaping or recording. Parents may be videotaped playing with their babies and then may be shown the tapes and asked to explain why they acted or reacted as they did.

Table 2-3   Major Methods of Data Collection

Type	Main Characteristics	Advantages	Disadvantages
Self-report: diary, interview, or questionnaire	Participants are asked about some aspect of their lives; questioning may be highly structured or more flexible.	Can provide firsthand information about a person's life, attitudes, or opinions.	Participant may not remember information accurately or may distort responses in a socially desirable way; how question is asked or by whom may affect answer.
Naturalistic observation	People are observed in their normal setting, with no attempt to manipulate behavior.	Provides good description of behavior; does not subject people to unnatural settings that may distort behavior.	Lack of control; observer bias.
Laboratory observation	Participants are observed in the laboratory, with no attempt to manipulate behavior.	Provides good descriptions; offers greater control than naturalistic observation, since all participants are observed under same controlled conditions.	Observer bias; controlled situation can be artificial.
Behavioral measures	Participants are tested on abilities, skills, knowledge, competencies, or physical responses.	Provides objectively measurable information; avoids subjective distortions.	Cannot measure attitudes or other nonbehavioral phenomena; results may be affected by extraneous factors.

In a face-to-face or telephone *interview,* researchers ask questions about attitudes, opinions, or behavior. In a *structured* interview, each participant is asked the same set of questions. An *open-ended* interview is more flexible; the interviewer can vary the topics and order of questions and can ask follow-up questions based on the responses. To reach more people and to protect their privacy, researchers sometimes distribute a printed *questionnaire,* which participants fill out and return.

By questioning a large number of people, investigators can get a broad picture—at least of what the respondents *say* they believe or do or did. However, people willing to participate in interviews or fill out questionnaires tend to be unrepresentative of the population. Furthermore, heavy reliance on self-reports may be unwise because people may not have thought about what they feel and think or honestly may not know. Some people forget when and how events actually took place, and others consciously or unconsciously distort their replies to fit what is considered socially desirable.

How a question is asked, and by whom, can affect the answer. When questioned about risky or socially disapproved behavior, such as sexual habits and drug use, respondents may be more candid in responding to a computerized survey than to a paper-and-pencil one (Turner et al., 1998).

Naturalistic and Laboratory Observation

Observation can take two forms: *naturalistic observation* and *laboratory observation.* In **naturalistic observation,** researchers look at children in real-life settings. The researchers do not try to alter behavior or the environment; they simply record what they see. In **laboratory observation,** researchers observe and record behavior in a controlled situation, such as a laboratory. By observing all participants under the same conditions, investigators can more clearly identify any differences in behavior not attributable to the environment.

Both kinds of observation can provide valuable descriptions of behavior, but they have limitations. For one, they do not explain *why* children behave as they do, though the observers may suggest interpretations. Then, too, an observer's presence can alter behavior. When children know they are being watched, they may act differently. Further, there is a risk of *observer bias:* the researcher's tendency to interpret data to fit expectations or to emphasize some aspects and minimize others. To counteract the effects of observer bias, some studies employ several observers.

naturalistic observation Research method in which behavior is studied in natural settings without intervention or manipulation.

laboratory observation Research method in which all participants are observed under the same controlled conditions.

Figure 2-5

An image of the brain, produced by magnetic resonance imaging (MRI). A large cylindrical magnet creates a magnetic field around the head. Sensors record magnetic signals from various brain structures, such as nerve tissue, blood vessels, fluid, and bone, each of which has different magnetic properties and thus appears differently in the image. MRI can show a three-dimensional image in great anatomical detail. Functional MRI records changes in brain activity by measuring the amount of blood that travels to specific regions of the brain.

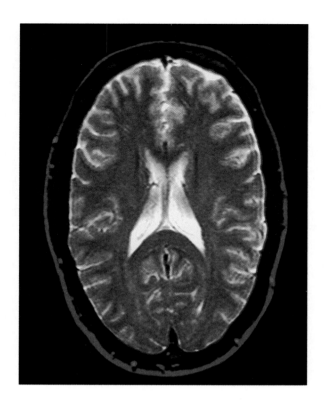

During the 1960s, laboratory observation was used most commonly so as to achieve more rigorous control. Now such technological devices as portable video recorders and computers increase objectivity and enable researchers to analyze moment-by-moment changes in facial expressions or other behavior (Gottman & Notarius, 2000). Such methods can make naturalistic observation more accurate and objective than it otherwise would be.

Behavioral and Performance Measures

For many kinds of research, investigators use more objective measures of behavior or performance instead of, or in addition to, self-reports or observation. Tests and other behavioral and neuropsychological measures, including mechanical and electronic devices, may be used to assess abilities, skills, knowledge, competencies, or physiological responses, such as heart rate and brain activity. Although these measures are less subjective than self-reports or personal observation, such factors as fatigue and self-confidence can affect results.

Some written tests, such as intelligence tests, compare performance with that of other test-takers. Such tests can be meaningful and useful only if they are both *valid* (that is, the tests measure the abilities they claim to measure) and *reliable* (that is, the results are reasonably consistent from one time to another). (The validity of intelligence tests is in question, as we discuss in Chapter 13.) To avoid bias, tests must be *standardized*, that is, given and scored by the same methods and criteria for all test-takers.

When measuring a characteristic such as intelligence, it is important to define exactly what is to be measured in a way that other researchers will understand so that they can comment on the results. For this purpose, researchers use an **operational definition**—a definition stated solely in terms of the operations or procedures used to produce or measure a phenomenon. Intelligence, for example, can be defined as the ability to achieve a certain score on a test covering logical relationships, memory, and vocabulary recognition. Some people may disagree with this definition, but no one can reasonably claim that it is not clear.

For most of the history of psychology, theorists and researchers studied cognitive processes apart from the physical structures of the brain in which these processes occur. Now, sophisticated imaging instruments, such as magnetic resonance imaging (MRI) (Figure 2-5) and positron emission tomography (PET), make it possible to see the brain in action. The field of **cognitive neuroscience** is linking our understanding of cognitive

operational definition Definition stated solely in terms of the operations or procedures used to produce or measure a phenomenon.

cognitive neuroscience Study of links between neural processes and cognitive abilities.

Table 2-4   Basic Research Designs

Type	Main Characteristics	Advantages	Disadvantages
Case study	Study of single individual in depth.	Flexibility; provides detailed picture of one person's behavior and development; can generate hypotheses.	May not generalize to others; conclusions not directly testable; cannot establish cause and effect.
Ethnographic study	In-depth study of a culture or subculture.	Can help overcome culturally based biases in theory and research; can test universality of developmental phenomena.	Subject to observer bias.
Correlational study	Attempt to find positive or negative relationship between variables.	Enables prediction of one variable on basis of another; can suggest hyptheses about causal relationships.	Cannot establish cause and effect.
Experiment	Controlled procedure in which an experimenter controls the independent variable to determine its effect on the dependent variable; may be conducted in the laboratory or field.	Establishes cause-and-effect relationships; is highly controlled and can be repeated by another investigator; degree of control greatest in the laboratory experiment.	Findings, especially when derived from laboratory experiments, may not generalize to situations outside the laboratory.

functioning with what happens in the brain (Gazzaniga, 2000; Humphreys, 2002; Posner & DiGirolamo, 2000). *Developmental cognitive neuroscience* focuses on how cognitive growth occurs as the brain interacts with the environment (Johnson, 1999, 2001) and why some children do not develop normally (Posner & DiGirolamo, 2000). This branch of science may shed light on whether intelligence is general or specialized, what influences readiness for formal learning (Byrnes & Fox, 1998), and why common memory failures occur (Schacter, 1999).

Social cognitive neuroscience is an emerging interdisciplinary field that bridges brain, mind, and behavior, bringing together data from cognitive neuroscience, social psychology, and the information-processing approach. Social cognitive neuroscientists use brain imaging and studies of people with brain injuries to figure out how neural pathways control such behavioral processes as memory and attention, which in turn influence attitudes and emotions, and to identify the brain systems involved in schizophrenia, anxiety, phobias, and learning disorders (Azar, 2002; Ochsner & Lieberman, 2001).

Basic Research Designs

A research design is a plan for conducting a scientific investigation: what questions are to be answered, how participants are to be selected, how data are to be collected and interpreted, and how valid conclusions can be drawn. Four of the basic designs used in developmental research are case studies, ethnographic studies, correlational studies, and experiments. Each design has advantages and drawbacks, and each is appropriate for certain kinds of research problems (Table 2-4).

Case Studies

A **case study** is a study of a single case or individual, such as Genie, the 13-year-old girl who had been confined to her room and never learned to talk (refer back to Box 1-2 in Chapter 1). A number of theories, most notably Freud's, have grown out of clinical case studies, which include careful observation and interpretation of what patients say and do. Case studies also may use behavioral or neuropsychological measures and biographical, autobiographical, or documentary materials.

Case studies offer useful, in-depth information. They can explore sources of behavior and can test treatments. They also can suggest a need for other research. A related advantage is flexibility: The researcher is free to explore avenues of inquiry that arise during the course of the study. However, case studies have shortcomings. From studying Genie, for instance, we learn much about the development of a single child but not how the information applies

Checkpoint ✔

Can you . . .

✔ Compare the advantages and disadvantages of various forms of data collection?

✔ Explain how brain research contributes to the understanding of behaviors?

case study Study of a single subject, such as an individual or family.

Box 2-2 *Purposes of Cross-Cultural Research*

When David, an American child, was asked to identify the missing detail in a picture of a face with no mouth, he said, "The mouth." But Ari, an Asian immigrant child in Israel, said that the *body* was missing. Because art in his culture does not present a head as a complete picture, he thought the absence of a body was more important than the omission of "a mere detail like the mouth" (Anastasi, 1988, p. 360).

By looking at children from different cultural groups, researchers can learn in what ways development is universal (and thus intrinsic to the human condition) and in what ways it is culturally determined. For example, children everywhere learn to speak in the same sequence, advancing from cooing and babbling to single words and then to simple combinations of words. The words vary from culture to culture, but around the world toddlers put them together to form sentences similar in structure. Such findings suggest that the capacity for learning language is universal and inborn.

On the other hand, culture can exert a surprisingly large influence on early motor development. African babies, whose parents often prop them in a sitting position and bounce them on their feet, tend to sit and walk earlier than U.S. babies (Rogoff & Morelli, 1989). The society in which children grow up also influences the skills they learn. In the United States, children learn to read, write, and, increasingly, to operate computers. In rural Nepal, they learn how to drive water buffalo and find their way along mountain paths.

One important reason to conduct research among different cultural groups is to recognize biases in traditional Western theories and research that often go unquestioned until they are shown to be a product of cultural influences. Because much research in child development has focused on Western industrialized societies, there is a tendency to view typical development in these societies as the *norm,* or standard of behavior. Measuring against this norm leads to narrow—and often wrong—ideas about development. Pushed to its extreme, this belief can cause the development of children in other ethnic and cultural groups to be seen as deviant.

Barriers exist to our understanding of cultural differences, particularly those involving minority subcultures. As with David and Ari in our opening example, a question or task may have different conceptual meanings for different cultural groups. Sometimes the

barriers are linguistic. In a study of children's understanding of kinship relations among the Zinacanta people of Chiapas, Mexico (Greenfield & Childs, 1978), instead of asking "How many brothers do you have?" the researchers—knowing that the Zinacantas have separate terms for older and younger siblings—asked, "What is the name of your older brother?" Using the same question across cultures might have obscured, rather than revealed, cultural differences and similarities (Parke, 2004).

Results of observational studies of ethnic or cultural groups may be affected by the ethnicity of the researchers. For example, in one study European American observers noted more conflict and restrictiveness in African American mother-daughter relationships than African American observers did (Gonzales, Cauce, & Mason, 1996).

In this book we discuss several influential theories developed from research in Western societies that do not hold up when tested on people from other cultures—theories about gender roles, abstract thinking, moral reasoning, and a number of other aspects of human development. Throughout this book, we consistently look at children in cultures and subcultures other than the dominant one in the United States to show how closely development is tied to society and culture and to add to our understanding of normal development in many settings. In so doing, however, we need to keep in mind the pitfalls involved in cross-cultural comparisons.

What's your view ?

Can you think of a situation in which you made an incorrect assumption about a person because you were unfamiliar with her or his cultural background?

Check it out !

For more information on this topic, go to http://psych/ucsc.edu. This is the Web site for the Department of Psychology at the University of Santa Cruz. Select the *Faculty* link and read about the work of faculty members who conduct cross-cultural research in human development, including Barbara Rogoff, David Harrington, Per Gjerde, and Margarita Azmitia.

---

to children in general. Furthermore, case studies cannot explain behavior with certainty because there is no way to test their conclusions. Even though it seems reasonable that Genie's severely deprived environment contributed to or even caused her language deficiency, it is impossible to know how she would have developed with a normal upbringing.

Ethnographic Studies

ethnographic study In-depth study of a culture, which uses a combination of methods including participant observation.

participant observation Research method in which the observer lives with the people or participates in the activity being observed.

An **ethnographic study** seeks to describe the pattern of relationships, customs, beliefs, technology, arts, and traditions that make up a society's way of life. Ethnographic research can be qualitative, quantitative, or both. It uses a combination of methods, including informal, unstructured interviewing and **participant observation.** Participant observation is a form of naturalistic observation in which researchers live or participate in the societies or smaller groups they observe, as did Margaret Mead (1928, 1930, 1935)—often for long periods of time.

Because of ethnographers' involvement in the events or societies they are observing, their findings are especially open to observer bias. On the positive side, ethnographic research can help overcome cultural biases in theory and research (Box 2-2). Ethnography

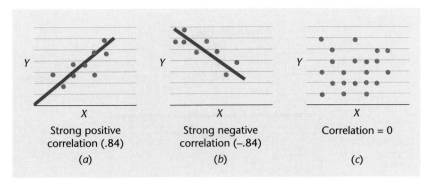

Figure 2-6

Correlational studies may find positive or negative correlations or no correlation. In a positive, or direct, correlation (*a*), data plotted on a graph cluster around a line showing that one variable (*X*) increases as the other variable (*Y*) increases. In a negative, or inverse, correlation (*b*), one variable (*X*) increases as the other variable (*Y*) decreases. No correlation, or a zero correlation (*c*), exists when increases and decreases in two variables show no consistent relationship (that is, data plotted on a graph show no pattern).

demonstrates the error of assuming that principles developed from research in Western cultures are universally applicable.

Correlational Studies

A **correlational study** is an attempt to find a *correlation,* or statistical relationship, between *variables,* phenomena that change or vary among people or can be varied for purposes of research. Correlations are expressed in terms of direction (positive or negative) and magnitude (degree). Two variables that are related *positively* increase or decrease together. As we report in Chapter 14, studies show a positive, or direct, correlation between televised violence and aggressiveness; that is, children who watch more violent television tend to fight more than children who watch less violent television. Two variables have a *negative,* or inverse, correlation if, as one increases, the other decreases. Studies show a negative correlation between amount of schooling and the risk of developing dementia (mental deterioration) due to Alzheimer's disease in old age. In other words, the less education, the more dementia (Katzman, 1993).

Correlations are reported as numbers ranging from −1.0 (a perfect negative relationship) to +1.0 (a perfect positive relationship). Perfect correlations are rare. The closer a correlation comes to +1.0 or −1.0, the stronger the relationship, either positive or negative. A correlation of 0 means that the variables have no relationship (Figure 2-6).

Correlations enable us to predict one variable on the basis of another. On the basis of the positive correlation between watching televised violence and aggression, we can predict that children who watch violent shows are more likely to get into fights than children who do *not* watch such shows. The greater the magnitude of the correlation between two variables, the greater the ability to predict one from the other.

Although strong correlations suggest possible cause-and-effect relationships, these are merely hypotheses and need to be examined and tested very critically. We cannot be sure from a positive correlation between televised violence and aggressiveness that watching televised violence *causes* aggressive play; we can conclude only that the two variables are related. It is possible that the causation goes the other way: Aggressive play may lead children to watch more violent programs. Or a third variable—perhaps an inborn predisposition toward aggressiveness or a violent living environment—may cause a child both to watch violent programs and to act aggressively. Similarly, we cannot be sure that schooling protects against dementia; it may be that another variable, such as socioeconomic status, might explain both lower levels of schooling and higher levels of dementia. The only way to show with certainty that one variable causes another is through experimentation—a method that, when studying human beings, is not always possible for practical or ethical reasons.

correlational study Research design intended to discover whether a statistical relationship between variables exists.

Figure 2-7

Design for an experiment. This experiment takes a random sample from the larger population being studied, randomly assigns participants to either the experimental (*E*) or control (*C*) group, and exposes the experimental group to a treatment that is not given to the control group. By comparing the two groups after the experimental group has received the treatment, the researcher can conclude that any difference between them is due to the experimental treatment.

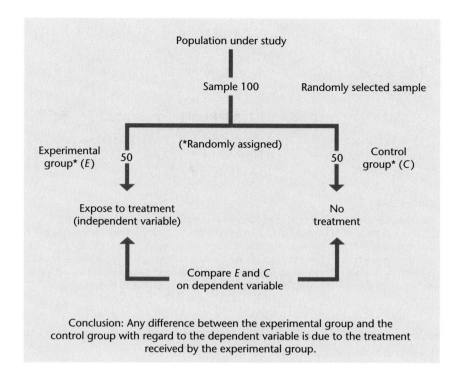

Population under study

Sample 100   Randomly selected sample

(*Randomly assigned)

Experimental group* (*E*)   50   50   Control group* (*C*)

Expose to treatment (independent variable)   No treatment

Compare *E* and *C* on dependent variable

Conclusion: Any difference between the experimental group and the control group with regard to the dependent variable is due to the treatment received by the experimental group.

Experiments

experiment Rigorously controlled, replicable procedure in which the researcher manipulates variables to assess the effect of one on the other.

An **experiment** is a controlled procedure in which the experimenter manipulates variables to learn how one affects another. Scientific experiments must be conducted and reported in such a way that another experimenter can *replicate* them, that is, repeat them in exactly the same way with different participants to verify the results and conclusions. Figure 2-7 shows how an experiment might be designed.

Groups and Variables A common way to conduct an experiment is to divide the participants into two kinds of groups. An **experimental group** consists of people who are to be exposed to the experimental manipulation or *treatment*—the phenomenon the researcher wants to study. Afterward, the effect of the treatment will be measured one or more times to find out what changes, if any, it caused. A **control group** consists of people who are similar to the experimental group but do not receive the treatment or may receive a different treatment. An experiment may include one or more of each type of group. If the experimenter wants to compare the effects of different treatments (say, of two methods of teaching), the overall sample may be divided into *treatment groups,* each of which receives one of the treatments under study. To ensure objectivity, some experiments, particularly in medical research, use *double-blind* procedures, in which neither participants nor experimenters know who is receiving the treatment and who is instead receiving an inert *placebo.*

experimental group In an experiment, the group receiving the treatment under study.

control group In an experiment, a group of people, similar to those in the experimental group, who do not receive the treatment under study.

One team of researchers (Whitehurst et al., 1988) wanted to find out what effect *dialogic reading,* a special method of reading picture books to very young children, might have on their language and vocabulary skills. The researchers compared two groups of middle-class children ages 21 to 35 months. In the *experimental group,* the parents adopted the new read-aloud method (the treatment), which consisted of encouraging children's active participation and giving frequent, age-based feedback. In the *control group,* parents simply read aloud as they usually did. After 1 month, the children in the experimental group were 8½ months ahead of the control group in level of speech and 6 months ahead in vocabulary; after 10 months, the experimental group was still 6 months ahead of the controls. It is fair to conclude, then, that this read-aloud method improves language and vocabulary skills.

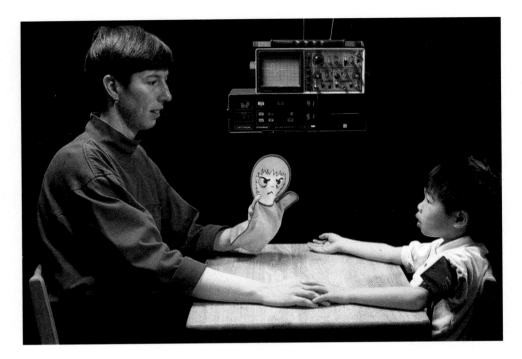

Experiments use strictly controlled procedures that manipulate variables to determine how one affects another. To study emotional resiliency, this research project at the University of California, San Francisco, monitors the heart rate and blood pressure of young children as they explain their feelings in response to a hand puppet's happy or angry face.

In this experiment, the type of reading approach was the *independent variable,* and the children's language skills were the *dependent variable.* An **independent variable** is something over which the experimenter has direct control. A **dependent variable** is something that may or may not change as a result of changes in the independent variable; in other words, it *depends* on the independent variable. In an experiment, a researcher manipulates the independent variable to see how changes in it will affect the dependent variable.

Random Assignment If an experiment finds a significant difference in the performance of the experimental and control groups, how do we know that the cause was the independent variable—in other words, that the conclusion is valid? For example, in the read-aloud study, how can we be sure that the reading method and not some other factor (such as intelligence) caused the difference in language development of the two groups? The best way to control for effects of such extraneous factors is **random assignment:** assigning the participants to groups in such a way that each person has an equal chance of being placed in any group. (Random assignment is different from random selection, which determines who gets into the full sample.)

If assignment is random and the sample is large enough, differences in factors not intended as variables, such as age, sex, race, IQ, and socioeconomic status, will be evenly distributed so that the groups initially are as alike as possible in every respect except for the variable to be tested. Otherwise, unintended differences between the groups might *confound,* or contaminate, the results, and any conclusions drawn from the experiment would have to be viewed with great suspicion. To control for confounds, the experimenter must make sure that everything except the independent variable is held constant during the course of the experiment. For example, in the read-aloud study, parents of the experimental and control groups must spend the same amount of time reading to their children. When participants in an experiment are randomly assigned to treatment groups, and conditions other than the independent variable are carefully controlled, the experimenter can be reasonably confident that a causal relationship has (or has not) been established—that any differences between the reading skills of the two groups are due to the reading method and not some other factor.

Of course, with respect to some variables we might want to study, such as age, gender, and race/ethnicity, random assignment is not possible. We cannot assign Terry to be age 5 and Brett to be 10, or one to be a boy and the other a girl, or one to be African

independent variable In an experiment, the condition over which the experimenter has direct control.

dependent variable In an experiment, the condition that may or may not change as a result of changes in the independent variable.

random assignment Assignment of participants in an experiment to groups in such a way that each person has an equal chance of being placed in any group.

American and the other Asian American. When studying such a variable—for example, whether boys or girls are stronger in certain abilities—researchers can strengthen the validity of their conclusions by randomly selecting participants and by trying to make sure that they are statistically equivalent in other ways that might make a difference in the study.

Because race (as discussed in Chapter 1) has no widely agreed meaning, some researchers argue that racial categories should not be used as independent variables in psychological research, for example, on intergroup variations in intelligence. Instead, researchers can substitute meaningful underlying variables that are often masked by racial categories, such as socioeconomic status and test-taking skills (Helms, Jernigan, & Mascher, 2005).

Laboratory, Field, and Natural Experiments The control necessary for establishing cause and effect is most easily achieved in laboratory experiments. In a *laboratory experiment* the participants are brought to a special place where they experience conditions manipulated by the experimenter. The experimenter records the participants' reactions to these conditions, perhaps comparing them with their own or other participants' behavior under different conditions.

However, not all experiments can be readily done in the laboratory. A *field experiment* is a controlled study conducted in a setting that is part of everyday life, such as a child's home or school. The experiment in which parents tried out a new way of reading aloud was a field experiment.

Laboratory and field experiments differ in two important respects. One is the *degree of control* exerted by the experimenter; the other is the degree to which findings can be generalized beyond the study situation. Laboratory experiments can be more rigidly controlled and are thus easier to replicate; however, the results may be less generalizable to real life. Because of the artificiality of the situation, participants may not act as they normally would. Thus, if children who watch violent television shows in the laboratory become more aggressive in that setting, we cannot be sure that children who watch a lot of violent shows at home hit their younger brothers or sisters more often than children who watch fewer such shows.

When, for practical or ethical reasons, it is impossible to conduct a true experiment, a natural experiment may provide a way of studying certain events. A *natural experiment* compares people who have been accidentally "assigned" to separate groups by circumstances of life—one group of children who were exposed, say, to famine or HIV or superior educational opportunities and another group who were not. A natural experiment, despite its name, is actually a correlational study because controlled manipulation of variables and random assignment to treatment groups are not possible.

One natural experiment dealt with what happened when a casino opened on an Indian reservation in North Carolina, boosting the income of tribal members (Costello, Compton, Keeler, & Angold, 2003). The study found a decline in behavioral disorders among children in tribal families as compared with children in the same area whose families did not receive increased income. However, being correlational, the study could not prove that the increased income *caused* improvements in mental health.

Controlled experiments have important advantages over other research designs: the ability to establish cause-and-effect relationships and to permit replication. However, such experiments can be too artificial and too narrowly focused. In recent decades, therefore, many researchers have concentrated less on laboratory experimentation or have supplemented it with a wider array of methods.

Developmental Research Designs

The two most common research strategies used to study child development are cross-sectional and longitudinal studies (Figure 2-8). *Cross-sectional studies* show similarities and differences among age groups; *longitudinal studies* reveal how children change or stay the same as they grow older. Because each of these designs has drawbacks, researchers also have devised *sequential* designs. To directly observe change, *microgenetic studies* can be used.

Checkpoint ✔

Can you . . .

✔ Compare the uses and drawbacks of case studies, ethnographic studies, correlational studies, and experiments?

✔ Explain why only a controlled experiment can establish causal relationships?

✔ Distinguish among laboratory, field, and natural experiments, and tell what kinds of research seem most suitable to each?

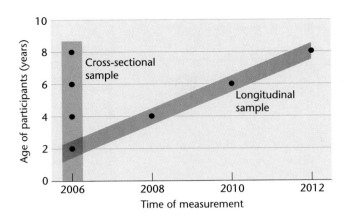

Figure 2-8
Developmental research designs. In the cross-sectional study, groups of 2-, 4-, 6-, and 8-year-olds were tested in 2006 to obtain data about age differences. In the longitudinal study, a group of children were first measured in 2006, when they were 2 years old; follow-up testing is done when the children are 4, 6, and 8, to measure age-related changes in performance.

Cross-Sectional, Longitudinal, and Sequential Studies

In a **cross-sectional study,** children of different ages are assessed at one time. In one cross-sectional study, researchers asked 3-, 4-, 6-, and 7-year-olds such questions as what a pensive-looking woman was doing. These researchers found a striking increase with age in children's awareness of thinking as a mental activity (J. H. Flavell, Green, & Flavell, 1995). These findings strongly suggest that, as children become older, their understanding of mental processes improves. However, we cannot draw such a conclusion with certainty. We don't know whether the 7-year-olds' awareness of mental activity when they were 3 years old was the same as that of the current 3-year-olds in the study. The only way to see whether change occurs with age is to conduct a longitudinal study of a particular person or group.

In a **longitudinal study,** researchers study the same child or children more than once, sometimes years apart. They may measure a single characteristic, such as vocabulary size, height, or aggressiveness, or they may look at several aspects of development to find relationships among them. The Oakland (Adolescent) Growth Study, mentioned in Chapter 1, initially was designed to assess social and emotional development from the preteen through the senior high school years; ultimately, many of the participants were followed into old age. The study found that participants who as teenagers showed self-confidence, intellectual commitment, and dependable effectiveness made good choices in adolescence and also in early adulthood, which often led to promising opportunities (scholarships, good jobs, and competent spouses). Less competent teenagers made poorer early decisions and tended to lead crisis-ridden lives (Clausen, 1993).

Both cross-sectional and longitudinal designs have strengths and weaknesses (Table 2-5). Advantages of cross-sectional research include speed and economy; data can be gathered fairly quickly from large numbers of people. A drawback of cross-sectional studies is that they may overlook individual differences by focusing on group averages. Their major disadvantage, however, is that the results may be affected by cohort differences—the differing experiences of children born at different times, for example, before and after the advent of the Internet. Cross-sectional studies are sometimes interpreted as yielding information about developmental changes, but such information is often misleading. Thus, although cross-sectional studies still dominate the field—no doubt because they are so much easier to do—the proportion of research devoted to longitudinal studies, especially short-term ones, is increasing.

Longitudinal research, in repeatedly studying the same people, can track individual patterns of continuity and change. However, a longitudinal study done on one cohort may not apply to another. (The results of a study of children born in the 1920s, such as the Oakland Growth Study, may not apply to children born in the 1990s.) Furthermore, longitudinal studies generally are more time-consuming and expensive than cross-sectional studies; it is hard to keep track of a large group of participants over the years, to keep records, and to keep the study going despite possible turnover in research personnel. Then there is the problem of attrition; participants may die, move away, or drop out. Also, longitudinal studies tend to be biased; those who stay with the study tend to

cross-sectional study Study designed to assess age-related differences, in which people of different ages are assessed on one occasion.

longitudinal study Study designed to assess changes in a sample over time.

Table 2-5	Longitudinal, Cross-Sectional, and Sequential Research		
Type of Study	**Procedure**	**Advantages**	**Disadvantages**
Longitudinal	Data are collected on same person or persons over a period of time.	Can show age-related change or continuity; avoids confounding age with cohort effects.	Is time-consuming, expensive; presents problems of attrition, bias in sample, and effects of repeated testing; results may be valid only for cohort tested or sample studied.
Cross-sectional	Date are collected on people of different ages at the same time.	Can show similarities and differences among age groups; speedy, economical; presents no problem of attrition or repeated testing.	Cannot establish age effects; masks individual differences; can be confounded by cohort effects.
Sequential	Data are collected on successive cross-sectional or longitudinal samples.	Can avoid drawbacks of both cross-sectional and longitudinal designs.	Requires large amount of time and effort and analysis of very complex data.

Figure 2-9

A sequential design. Two successive cross-sectional groups of 2-, 4-, 6-, and 8-year-olds are tested in 2006 and 2008. Also, a longitudinal study of a group of children first measured in 2006, when they were 2 years old, is followed by a similar longitudinal study of another group of children who were 2 years old in 2008.

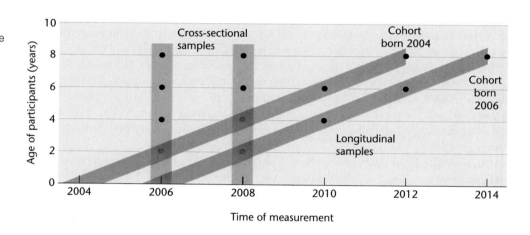

be above average in intelligence and socioeconomic status. Also, results can be affected by repeated testing; participants may do better in later tests because of familiarity with test procedures.

sequential study Study design that combines cross-sectional and longitudinal techniques.

The **sequential study**—a sequence of cross-sectional and/or longitudinal studies—is a complex strategy designed to overcome the drawbacks of longitudinal and cross-sectional research shown in Table 2-5. Researchers may assess a cross-sectional sample on two or more occasions in sequence to find out how members of each age cohort have changed. This procedure permits researchers to separate age-related changes from cohort effects. Another sequential design consists of a sequence of longitudinal studies, running concurrently but starting one after another. This design enables researchers to compare individual differences in the course of developmental change. A combination of cross-sectional and longitudinal sequences (as shown in Figure 2-9) can provide a more complete picture of development than would be possible with longitudinal or cross-sectional research alone. The major drawbacks of sequential studies relate to time, effort, and complexity. Sequential designs require large numbers of participants and the collection and analysis of huge amounts of data over a period of years. Interpreting their findings and conclusions can demand a high degree of sophistication.

Microgenetic Studies

microgenetic study Study design that enables researchers to directly observe change by repeated testing over a short time.

Because change usually happens slowly, developmental scientists rarely can observe it directly in everyday life. But what if the process could be compressed into a very short time frame? A **microgenetic study** does just that. Over a short time span, participants are repeatedly exposed to a stimulus for change or opportunity for learning, enabling researchers to see and analyze the processes by which change occurs. Vygotsky used such "microgenesis experiments" to see how much children's performance could be improved over a brief interval.

In one series of experiments using operant conditioning (Rovee-Collier & Boller, 1995; see Chapter 7), infants as young as 2 months learned to kick to set in motion a brightly colored mobile to which one leg was attached—if the infants were exposed repeatedly to a similar situation within a few days or weeks. Building on this work, Esther Thelen (1994) tied 3-month-olds' left and right legs together with soft elastic fabric. Would they learn to kick with both legs at once to activate the mobile? The infants' movements were videotaped, and the frequency and speed of kicks, using one or both legs, were then analyzed with the help of a computer. The infants gradually switched to kicking with both legs when it proved more effective, and observers were able to chart exactly how and when this change occurred.

Collaborative Research

Throughout much of the history of the field of child development, investigators have worked individually or in small groups at a single laboratory or site. Many important advances have come from such research, but the current trend is to broaden the research base.

Researchers use various means to share and pool data. One is the archiving of data sets for use by other researchers. Another is *meta-analysis,* a statistical analysis of the findings of multiple studies. Another, increasingly common, approach is collaborative research by multiple researchers at multiple sites, sometimes with government or foundation funding. This collaborative model can trace development within a population on a very broad scale. It makes possible larger, more representative, samples; makes it easier to carry out longitudinal studies that might otherwise be hampered by researcher attrition and burnout; and permits a blending of theoretical perspectives (Parke, 2004).

An example of collaborative research is the National Institute of Child Health and Human Development (NICHD) Study of Early Child Care, discussed in Chapter 8. Another example is the planned National Children's Study (2004), a prospective study of influences on children's health. This 21-year, multi-sited study, under the auspices of the U.S. Department of Health and Human Services and other government agencies, will begin with couples of childbearing age who are not yet expecting a child and then follow the children they bear, from conception to adulthood.

A difficulty with the collaborative model is the need for group consensus on all aspects of the research, from the initial design to the writing of the report. Achieving consensus can be cumbersome and may require difficult compromises. The more flexible single-investigator or single-site model may be better suited to experimental work and to the development of novel methods and approaches.

Checkpoint ✔

Can you . . .

✔ List advantages and disadvantages of longitudinal, cross-sectional, and sequential research?

✔ Explain how microgenetic studies are done and what kinds of data they can reveal?

✔ Discuss advantages and disadvantages of collaborative research?

Ethics of Research

Guidepost 4

What ethical problems may arise in research on children?

Should research that might harm its participants ever be undertaken? How can we balance the possible benefits against the risk of mental, emotional, or physical injury to individuals?

Objections to the study of "Little Albert" (described earlier in this chapter), as well as to a number of other early studies, gave rise to today's more stringent ethical standards. Institutional review boards at colleges, universities, and other institutions that receive federal funding must review proposed research from an ethical standpoint. Guidelines of the American Psychological Association (2002) and the Society for Research in Child Development (1996) cover such issues as informed consent, avoidance of deception, protection of participants from harm and loss of dignity, guarantees of privacy and confidentiality, the right to decline or withdraw from an experiment at any time, and the responsibility of investigators to correct any undesirable effects.

Table 2-6	Developmental Considerations in Children's Participation in Research

Younger Children Are Especially Vulnerable to	Older Children Are Especially Vulnerable to
Stressful or unfamiliar situations	Apparent approval or disapproval by the researcher
Absence of parent or caregiver	Sense of failure, threats to self-esteem
Situations arousing inappropriate shame, guilt, or embarrassment	Expressed or implied comparisons with others
Coercion, deception, and unreasonable demands	Implied racial, ethnic, or socioeconomic biases
	Threats to privacy

Source: Based on Thompson, 1990.

In resolving ethical dilemmas, researchers should be guided by three principles: (1) *beneficence*, the obligation to maximize benefits to participants and minimize harm; (2) *respect*, for participants' autonomy and protection of those who are unable to exercise their own judgment; and (3) *justice*, inclusion of diverse groups combined with sensitivity to any special impact the research situation may have on them. In evaluating risks and benefits, researchers should be sensitive to cultural issues and values (Fisher et al., 2002).

Even research that seems to involve minimal risk may be too risky for a particular child at a particular level of development. An important need is to develop standards for age-appropriate treatment of children in research. One ethicist (Thompson, 1990) has suggested research-based guidelines (Table 2-6), which you may wish to review after you have read the relevant chapters in this book. For example, infants' and very young children's ability to cope with the stress of the research situation may hinge on the presence of a parent or trusted caregiver, a familiar setting and procedure, and familiar objects.

Let's look more closely at a few specific ethical considerations that can present problems.

Right to Informed Consent

Informed consent exists when participants voluntarily agree to be in a study, are competent to give consent, are aware of the risks as well as the potential benefits, and are not being exploited. The National Commission for the Protection of Human Subjects of Biomedical and Behavioral Research (1978) recommends that children age 7 or over be asked to give their consent to take part in research and that any children's objections should be overruled only if the research promises direct benefit to the child.

However, some ethicists argue that young children cannot give meaningful, voluntary *consent* because they cannot fully understand what is involved. They can merely *assent*, that is, agree to participate. Young children are less capable than adults of understanding what they are getting into and of making an informed decision on whether to participate. The usual procedure, therefore, when children under age 18 are involved, is to ask the parents or legal guardians and sometimes school personnel to give consent.

Avoidance of Deception

Can informed consent exist if participants are deceived about the nature or purpose of a study or about the procedures to which they will be subjected? Suppose that children are told they are trying out a new game when they are actually being tested on their reactions to success or failure? Experiments like this have added to our knowledge but at the cost of the participants' right to know what they were getting involved in.

Ethical guidelines call for withholding information *only* when it is essential to the study; and then investigators should avoid methods that could cause pain, anxiety, or harm. Participants should be debriefed afterward to let them know the true nature of the study and why deception was necessary and to make sure they have not suffered as a result.

Right to Self-Esteem

Some studies have a built-in *failure factor*. Researchers give harder and harder tasks until the participant is unable to do them. Might this inevitable failure affect a participant's self-worth? Similarly, when researchers publish findings that middle-class children are academically superior to poor children, unintentional harm may be done to some participants' self-esteem. Even if such studies may lead to beneficial interventions for poor children, they also may affect teachers' expectations and students' performance.

Right to Privacy and Confidentiality

Not all ethical issues have clear answers; some hinge on researchers' judgment and scruples. In this gray area are issues having to do with privacy and with protecting the confidentiality of personal information that participants may reveal in interviews or questionnaires.

What if, during the course of research, an investigator suspects that a child may have a learning disability or some other treatable condition? Is the researcher obliged to share such information with the parents or guardians or to recommend services that may help, when sharing the information might contaminate the research findings? Such a decision should not be made lightly; sharing information of uncertain validity might create damaging misconceptions about a child. However, researchers need to know, and inform participants of, their legal responsibility to report abuse or neglect or any other illegal activity of which they become aware.

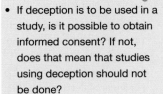

What's your view

- If deception is to be used in a study, is it possible to obtain informed consent? If not, does that mean that studies using deception should not be done?

Checkpoint ✓

Can you . . .

✔ Identify three principles that should govern inclusion of participants in research?

✔ Discuss four rights of research participants?

✔ Give examples of how the developmental needs of children need to be considered in research?

Refocus

On the basis of the information given about Margaret Mead in the Focus vignette at the beginning of this chapter:

- What position do you think Mead might have taken on the issue of the relative influences of heredity, environment, and maturation?

- Does Mead seem to fit within any of the five theoretical perspectives described in this chapter?

- What research methods described in the chapter did she use?

- What advantages and disadvantages existed because her research was done in the field, rather than in a laboratory?

- What ethical issues might be relevant to cross-cultural research such as Mead's?

The final word in these introductory chapters is that this entire book is far from the final word. Although the authors have tried to incorporate the most important and up-to-date information about how children develop, developmental scientists are constantly learning more. As you read this book, you are certain to come up with questions. By thinking about them and perhaps eventually conducting research to find answers, it is possible that you, now embarking on the study of child development, will someday add to our knowledge about the interesting species to which we all belong.

Summary and Key Terms

Basic Theoretical Issues

Guidepost 1 What purposes do theories serve, and what are two basic issues on which developmental theorists differ?

- A theory is used to organize and explain data and generate hypotheses that can be tested by research.

- Developmental theories differ on two basic issues: the active or passive character of development and the existence of stages of development.

- Some theorists subscribe to a mechanistic model of development; others to an organismic model.

theory (25) hypotheses (25) mechanistic model (25) organismic model (26)

Theoretical Perspectives

Guidepost 2 What are five theoretical perspectives on child development, and what are some theories representative of each?

- The psychoanalytic perspective sees development as motivated by unconscious emotional drives and conflicts. Leading examples are Freud's and Erikson's theories.

  psychoanalytic perspective (27) psychosexual development (28) psychosocial development (29)

- The learning perspective views development as a result of learning based on experience. Leading examples are Watson's and Skinner's behaviorism and Bandura's social learning (social cognitive) theory.

  learning perspective (30) behaviorism (31) classical conditioning (31) operant conditioning (31) reinforcement (31) punishment (31) social learning theory (32) reciprocal determinism (32) observational learning (32) self-efficacy (33)

- The cognitive perspective is concerned with thought processes. Leading examples are Piaget's cognitive-stage theory, Vygotsky's sociocultural theory, the information-processing approach, and neo-Piagetian theories.

  cognitive perspective (33) cognitive-stage theory (33) organization (34) schemes (34) adaptation (34) assimilation (34) accommodation (34) equilibration (34) sociocultural theory (34) zone of proximal development (ZPD) (35) scaffolding (35) information-processing approach (35)

- The contextual perspective focuses on interaction between the individual and the social context. A leading example is Bronfenbrenner's bioecological theory.

  contextual perspective (36) bioecological theory (36) microsystem (36) mesosystem (36) exosystem (36) macrosystem (36) chronosystem (37)

- The evolutionary/sociobiological perspective, represented by E. O. Wilson, is based in part on Darwin's theory of evolution and describes adaptive behaviors that promote survival. A leading example is Bowlby's attachment theory.

  evolutionary/sociobiological perspective (37) ethology (38) evolutionary psychology (38)

Research Methods

Guidepost 3 How do developmental scientists study children, and what are the advantages and disadvantages of each research method?

- Research can be quantitative, qualitative, or both.

- To arrive at sound conclusions, quantitative researchers use the scientific method.

- Random selection of a research sample can ensure generalizability.

  quantitative research (39) qualitative research (39) scientific method (40) sample (40) random selection (40)

- Three forms of data collection are self-reports, observation, and behavioral or performance measures.

  naturalistic observation (41) laboratory observation (41) operational definition (42) cognitive neuroscience (42)

- Two basic qualitative designs used in developmental research are the case study and ethnographic study. Cross-cultural research can indicate whether certain aspects of development are universal or culturally influenced.

- Two quantitative designs are the correlational study and experiment. Only experiments can firmly establish causal relationships.

  case study (43) ethnographic study (44) participant observation (44) correlational study (45) experiment (46)

- Experiments must be rigorously controlled so as to be valid and replicable. Random assignment of participants can ensure validity.

- Laboratory experiments are easiest to control and replicate, but findings of field experiments may be more generalizable. Natural experiments may be useful in situations in which true experiments would be impractical or unethical.

  experimental group (46) control group (46) independent variable (47) dependent variable (47) random assignment (47)

- The two most common designs used to study age-related development are longitudinal and cross-sectional. Cross-sectional studies compare age groups; longitudinal studies describe continuity or change in the same participants. The sequential study is intended to overcome the weaknesses of the other two designs. A microgenetic study enables direct observation of change over a short period of time.

  cross-sectional study (49) longitudinal study (49) sequential study (50) microgenetic study (50)

Ethics of Research

Guidepost 4 What ethical problems may arise in research on children?

- Researchers seek to resolve ethical issues on the basis of principles of beneficence, respect, and justice.

- Ethical issues in research on child development involve the rights of participants to informed consent, avoidance of deception, protection from harm and loss of dignity or self-esteem, and guarantees of privacy and confidentiality.

- Children's developmental needs and cultural differences should be considered in designing research.

Part Two

Beginnings: A Preview

Chapter 3
Forming a New Life

- Conception occurs by normal fertilization or other means.
- The genetic endowment interacts with environmental influences from the start.

Chapter 4
Pregnancy and Prenatal Development

- Basic body structures and organs form.
- Brain growth spurt begins.
- Physical growth is most rapid in the life span.
- Abilities to learn and remember and to respond to sensory stimuli are developing.
- Fetus responds to mother's voice and develops a preference for it.
- Vulnerability to environmental influences is great.

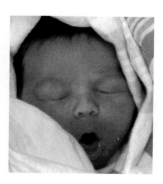

Chapter 5
Birth and the Newborn Baby

- A method and setting for childbirth are chosen, and the progress of the birth is monitored.
- The newborn emerges and is assessed for immediate health, developmental status, and any complications of childbirth.
- All body systems operate at birth to some extent.

Beginnings

Ꮟy the time babies are born, they already have an impressive history, Part of this early history, which began long before conception, is the hereditary endowment. Another part is environmental, for the new organism is affected by many events that occur during its nine months in the womb. As this organism grows from a single cell to a newborn baby, both inheritance and experience affect its development. At birth, babies are already individuals, distinguishable not just by sex, but by size, temperament, appearance, and history.

The changes that occur between conception and the first months after birth are broader and faster paced than any a person will ever experience again. Although these initial changes may seem to be mostly physical, they have repercussions on other aspects of development. For example, the *physical* growth of the brain before and immediately after birth makes possible a great burst of *cognitive* and *emotional* growth.

In Part II, we focus on this earliest period of development. Chapter 3 examines the two great forces—heredity and environment—that work together to make each child a unique person. Chapter 4 considers effects of the prenatal environment. Chapter 5 describes the birth process and the tiny traveler who emerges into a child's world.

Linkups to Look For

- A combination of biological, psychological, social, economic, and cultural factors may shape development beginning at conception.

- A family's socioeconomic status and other aspects of the social and cultural environment may affect the availability and utilization of prenatal care and, thus, the health of a newborn.

- Many prospective mothers are as concerned about emotional and social aspects of the setting in which their infants come into the world as they are about medical arrangements.

- Protective factors that reduce the impact of complications of birth include an affectionate, supportive family and rewarding experiences in school, work, or place of worship.

CHAPTER THREE

Forming a New Life: Conception, Heredity, and Environment

*Of the cell, the wondrous seed
Becoming plant and animal and mind
Unerringly forever after its kind . . .*

—William Ellery Leonard, *Two Lives*, 1925

Focus *Louise Brown, the First "Test-Tube Baby"*

Louise Brown

The writer Aldous Huxley foresaw it in 1932: human life created in the laboratory. As Huxley described it in his novel *Brave New World,* the feat would be accomplished by immersing female *ova* (egg cells), which had been incubated in test tubes, in a dish of free-swimming male sperm. Huxley envisioned his "brave new world" as 600 years off; yet it was only 46 years after Huxley's prediction that a birth through *in vitro fertilization,* or fertilization outside the mother's body, became a reality.

Louise Brown, the world's first documented "test-tube baby," was born July 25, 1978, at a four-story redbrick hospital in the old textile mill town of Oldham in northwest England. She had been conceived, not in a test tube, but by placing a ripe ovum from her 30-year-old mother, Lesley Brown, in a shallow glass dish with fluid containing sperm from her 38-year-old father, John Brown. After 2 days, during which the resulting single-celled organism multiplied to 8 cells, the embryo was implanted in Lesley's womb.

Until this event, Lesley and John, a truck driver for the British Railway Network, were, by their own description, an ordinary couple who lived in a low-rent row house in Bristol. Although they were raising John's 17-year-old daughter from a previous marriage, they desperately wanted to have a baby together. After 7 years of failure to conceive, they turned to the then-experimental in vitro method. The fulfillment of the Browns' wish was the culmination of more than a decade of painstaking preparatory research by Patrick Steptoe, a gynecologist, and Robert Edwards, a physiologist at Cambridge University. The outcome was far more than a single baby. Steptoe's and Edwards's work gave birth to a new branch of medicine: *assisted reproductive technology.*

Questions were in the air as Lesley and John Brown awaited the birth of what was to be called, in banner headlines, the "Miracle Baby" and "Baby of the Century." Despite strenuous efforts to keep the birth secret, the news leaked out. Hordes of newspaper and television reporters from around the world hovered outside the hospital and, later, camped on the Browns' front lawn.

Sources of information about Louise Brown are Barthel, 1982; Daley, 2003; Faltermayer et al., 1996; "The First Test-Tube Baby," 1978; International Committee for Monitoring Assisted Reproductive Technologies (ICMART), 2006; Lawson, 1993; "Louise Brown," 1984; "Louise Brown," 1994; "Test-Tube Baby," 1978; and Van Dyck, 1995.

The story launched a debate about the moral implications of tampering with nature—and, down the road, the possibility of mass baby farms and reproductive engineering, which could alter or custom design the "products" of reproduction. Of more immediate concern were the risks to mother and baby. What if the baby was born grossly deformed? Could *any* baby conceived in a laboratory dish have a normal life?

Lesley was checked and monitored more frequently than most expectant mothers are, and, as a precaution, spent the last 3 months of her pregnancy in the hospital. The birth took place about 2 weeks before the due date, by cesarean delivery, because Lesley had developed toxemia (blood poisoning) and the fetus did not seem to be gaining weight. The delivery went smoothly without further complications.

The blond, blue-eyed, 5-pound 12-ounce baby was, from all accounts, a beautiful, normal infant, who emerged crying lustily. "There's no difference between her and any other little girl," her father maintained. "We just helped nature a bit" ("Louise Brown," 1984, p. 82).

By the time Louise celebrated her fourth birthday, she had a "test-tube" sister, Natalie, born June 14, 1982. Lesley and John used part of the nest egg obtained from interview, book, and film rights to buy a modest house; the rest remained in trust for the children.

Despite her highly publicized start, Louise Brown has led an unassuming life. On her 25th birthday, about 1,000 of the more than 3 million children worldwide now estimated to have been born through in vitro fertilization (Reaney, 2006; ICMART, 2006) gathered to celebrate the occasion. Brown, engaged to a bank security officer whom she has since married, said she had no immediate plans to start a family and just wanted to be treated as a "normal person." Her younger sister Natalie had two children, both conceived normally (Daley, 2003). In January 2007, Louise, at 28, gave birth to a normally conceived son (Associated Press, 2007).

● ● ●

What made Louise Brown the person she is? Like any other child, she began with a hereditary endowment from her mother and father. For example, she has her father's stocky build, wide forehead, and chubby cheeks and her mother's tilted nose and curved mouth, as well as her mother's sudden temper. Louise also has been affected by a host of environmental influences, from that famous laboratory dish to the tremendous public interest in her story. As a preschooler, she was mentally precocious, mischievous, and (by her parents' admission) spoiled. As a teenager, like many of her classmates, she liked to swim and ride horses, wore two gold studs in each ear, watched MTV, and had a crush on the actor Tom Cruise.

Most children do not become famous, especially at birth; but every child is the product of a unique combination of hereditary and environmental influences set in motion by the parents' decision to form a new life. We begin this chapter by examining how a life is conceived, either through normal reproduction or through alternative technologies, many of them developed since Louise Brown's birth. We consider the mechanisms and patterns of heredity—the inherited factors that affect development—and how genetic counseling can help couples make the decision to become parents. We look at how heredity and environment work together and how their effects on development can be studied.

After you have read and studied this chapter, you should be able to answer each of the Guidepost questions on the following page. Look for them again in the margins throughout the chapter, where they point to important concepts. To check your understanding of these Guideposts, review the end-of-chapter summary. Checkpoints located throughout the chapter will help you verify your understanding of what you have read.

Guideposts for Study

1. How does conception normally occur, and how have beliefs about conception changed?

2. What causes infertility, and what are alternative ways of becoming parents?

3. What genetic mechanisms determine sex, physical appearance, and other characteristics?

4. How are birth defects and disorders transmitted?

5. How do scientists study the relative influences of heredity and environment, and how do heredity and environment work together?

6. What roles do heredity and environment play in physical health, intelligence, and personality?

Becoming Parents: How Conception Occurs

Guidepost 1

How does conception normally occur, and how have beliefs about conception changed?

The timing and circumstances of parenthood can have vast consequences for a child. Whether a birth is planned or accidental, whether the pregnancy is welcomed or unwanted, whether it comes about through normal or extraordinary means, whether the parents are married or unmarried, whether they are of the same sex or different sexes, and how old the parents are when a child is conceived or adopted all are factors in the *microsystem* issues, identified by Bronfenbrenner's bioecological approach (discussed in Chapter 2). Whether the culture encourages large or small families, whether it values one sex over the other, and how much it supports families with children are *macrosystem* issues likely to influence the child's development.

We'll explore such contextual issues throughout this book. For now, let's look at the act of conception and then at options for couples unable to conceive normally.

Changing Theories of Conception*

Most adults, and even most children in industrialized countries, have a reasonably accurate idea of where babies come from. Yet only a generation or two ago, many parents told their children that a stork had brought them. The folk belief that children came from wells, springs, or rocks was common in north and central Europe as late as the beginning of the 20th century. Conception was believed to be influenced by cosmic forces. A baby conceived under a new moon would be a boy; during the moon's last quarter, a girl (Gélis, 1991).

Theories about conception go back to ancient times. The Greek physician Hippocrates, known as the father of medicine, held that a fetus results from the joining of male and female seeds. The philosopher Aristotle had a contrary view that "the woman functions only as a receptacle, the child being formed exclusively by means of the sperm" (Fontanel & d'Harcourt, 1997, p. 10). According to Aristotle, the production of male babies was in the natural order of things; a female came about only if development was disturbed.

Between the 17th and 19th centuries, a debate raged between two schools of biological thought. Harking back to Aristotle, the *animalculists* (so named because the male sperm were then called *animalcules*) claimed that fully formed "little people" were contained in the heads of sperm, ready to grow when deposited in the nurturing environment of the womb. The *ovists,* inspired by the work of the English physician William Harvey, held an opposite but equally incorrect view: that a female's ovaries contained tiny, already formed humans whose growth was activated by the male's sperm. Finally, in the late 18th century, the German-born anatomist Kaspar Friedrich Wolff demonstrated that embryos are not preformed in either parent and that both contribute equally to the formation of a new being.

---

*Unless otherwise referenced, this discussion is based on Eccles, 1982, and Fontanel & d'Harcourt, 1997.

How Fertilization Takes Place

fertilization Union of sperm and ovum to produce a zygote; also called *conception*.

zygote One-celled organism resulting from fertilization.

Fertilization, or conception, is the process by which sperm and ovum—the male and female *gametes,* or sex cells—combine to create a single cell called a **zygote,** which then duplicates itself again and again by cell division to become a baby. But conception is not as simple as it sounds. Several independent events need to coincide to conceive a child. And, as we will discuss in the next chapter, not all conceptions end in birth.

At birth, a girl is believed to have about 2 million immature *ova* in her two ovaries, each ovum in its own *folliccle,* or small sac. In a sexually mature woman, *ovulation*—rupture of a mature follicle in either ovary and expulsion of its ovum—occurs about once every 28 days until menopause. The ovum is swept along through the fallopian tube by *cilia,* tiny hair cells, toward the *uterus,* or womb.

Sperm are produced in the *testes* (testicles), or reproductive glands, of a mature male at a rate of several hundred million a day and are ejaculated in the semen at sexual climax. They enter the vagina and try to swim through the *cervix* (the opening of the uterus) and into the fallopian tubes, but only a tiny fraction make it that far.

Fertilization normally occurs while the ovum is passing through the fallopian tube. Contrary to previous guidelines, this 6-day "fertile window" may occur any time between the 6th and 21st days of the menstrual cycle and can be highly unpredictable, even in women whose menstrual periods are regular (Wilcox, Dunson, & Baird, 2000). If fertilization does not occur, the sperm are absorbed by the woman's white blood cells, and the ovum passes through the uterus and exits through the vagina.

Checkpoint

Can you . . .

✔ Compare historic and scientific views of conception?

✔ Explain how and when fertilization normally takes place?

Guidepost 2

What causes infertility, and what are alternative ways of becoming parents?

infertility Inability to conceive after 12 months of trying.

Infertility

An estimated 7 percent of U.S. couples experience **infertility:** inability to conceive a baby after 12 months of trying (Centers for Disease Control and Prevention [CDC], 2005a; Wright, Chang, Jeng, & Macaluso, 2006). Women's fertility begins to decline in the late 20s, with substantial decreases during the 30s. Men's fertility is less affected by age but declines significantly by the late 30s (Dunson, Colombo, & Baird, 2002).

Causes of Infertility

Infertility is far from a new concern. To enhance fertility, ancient doctors advised men to eat fennel, and women to drink the saliva of lambs and wear necklaces of earthworms. It was recommended that, after intercourse, a woman lie flat with her legs crossed and "avoid becoming angry" (Fontanel & d'Harcourt, 1997, p. 10). By the Renaissance, the list of foods recommended to spur conception ranged from squabs and sparrows to cocks' combs and bull's genitals. In the early 17th century, Louise Bourgeois, midwife to Marie de Médicis, the queen of France, advocated bathing the vagina with chamomile, mallow, marjoram, and catmint boiled in white wine.

Today we know that the most common cause of infertility in men is production of too few sperm. Although only one sperm is needed to fertilize an ovum, a sperm count lower than 60 to 200 million per ejaculation makes conception unlikely. In some instances an ejaculatory duct may be blocked, preventing the exit of sperm, or sperm may be unable to swim well enough to reach the cervix. Some cases of male infertility seem to have a genetic basis (King, 1996; Reijo, Alagappan, Patrizio, & Page, 1996; Phillips, 1998).

In a woman, the cause of infertility may be the failure to produce ova or to produce normal ova; mucus in the cervix, which might prevent sperm from penetrating it; or a disease of the uterine lining, which might prevent implantation of the fertilized ovum. A major cause of declining fertility in women after age 30 is deterioration in the quality of ova (van Noord-Zaadstra et al., 1991). However, the most common cause is the problem Lesley Brown had: blockage of the fallopian tubes, preventing ova from reaching the uterus. In about half of these cases, the tubes are blocked by scar tissue from sexually transmitted diseases (King, 1996). Table 3-1 lists major causes and treatments of male and female infertility.

Table 3-1	Common Causes of Infertility in Men and Women	
Condition	**Explanations**	**Treatments**
Male Causes		
Abnormal sperm production or function	Abnormal shape or motility of sperm. Low or no sperm production. Undescended testicles. Varicose veins in the scrotum. Testosterone deficiency. Klinefelter's syndrome. Sexually transmitted diseases.	Fertility drugs Surgery to repair varicose veins or other obstructions. Artificial insemination with donor sperm. Injecting sperm directly into ovum.
Impaired delivery of sperm into vagina	*Sexual problems,* including erectile dysfunction, premature ejaculation, and painful intercourse. *Physical problems,* including failure to produce semen, blockage of ejaculatory ducts, other structural defects, and antibodies that weaken or disable sperm.	*Sexual problems* can be treated with medication or behavioral therapy. *Physical problems* may require surgery. Assisted reproduction techniques may include in vitro fertilization, electrical stimulation of ejaculation, or surgical retrieval of sperm (if blockage is present).
Age	Gradual decline in fertility, commonly in men older than 35.	
General health and lifestyle issues	Emotional stress, malnutrition, obesity, alcohol and drugs, tobacco smoking, cancer treatments, severe injury, surgery, and other medical conditions may impair sperm production.	Correct health and lifestyle problems if possible.
Environmental exposure	Overexposure to heat (in saunas or hot tubs), toxins, and certain chemicals, such as pesticides, lead, and chemical solvents.	Avoid unhealthy exposures.
Female Causes		
Fallopian tube damage or blockage	*Most frequent cause:* inflammation of the fallopian tube due to chlamydia, a sexually transmitted disease; tubal damage with scarring may result in an ectopic pregnancy, in which the fertilized egg is unable to pass through the fallopian tube and implant in the uterus. *Other causes:* benign uterine fibroid tumors and pelvic adhesions (bands of scar tissue) formed after pelvic infections, appendicitis, or pelvic or abdominal surgery.	Laparoscopic surgery to repair or open fallopian tubes; in vitro fertilization.
Endometriosis	Uterine tissue implanted outside the uterus can lead to scarring and inflammation, which may prevent transfer of ovum to fallopian tube and cause pelvic pain. Ovarian cysts.	Ovulation therapy (medication to stimulate ovulation) or in vitro fertilization.
Ovulation disorders	Any condition that prevents the release of a mature ovum from the ovary. Specific causes include hormonal deficiencies, injury to hypothalamus or pituitary gland, pituitary tumors; excessive exercise, and eating disorders.	Fertility drugs.
Polycystic ovary syndrome	Increase in production of the hormone androgen can prevent production of mature ovum. Common symptoms are absent or infrequent menstruation; dark or thick hair on chin, upper lip, or abdomen; acne; and oily skin.	Fertility drugs, particularly clomiphene.
Early menopause	Ovarian failure before age 35 may be associated with autoimmune disease, hypothyroidism (too little thyroid hormone), radiation or chemotherapy for cancer treatment, or tobacco smoking.	In vitro fertilization with donated ova.

Source: Based on Mayo Clinic, 2005.

Infertility can burden a marriage emotionally. Partners may become frustrated and angry with themselves and each other and may feel empty, worthless, and depressed (Abbey, Andrews, & Halman, 1992; Jones & Toner, 1993). However, only when infertility leads to permanent, involuntary childlessness is it associated with long-term psychological distress (McQuillan, Greil, White, & Jacob, 2003).

Treatments for Infertility

Sometimes hormone treatment, drug therapy, or surgery may correct the problem. However, fertility drugs increase the likelihood of multiple, high-risk births (Box 3-1). Also, men undergoing fertility treatment are at increased risk of producing sperm with chromosomal abnormalities (Levron et al., 1998). Daily supplements of coenzyme Q10, an antioxidant, may help increase sperm motility (Balercia et al., 2004).

Couples who have been unable to bear children after 1 year should not necessarily rush into fertility treatments. Unless there is a known cause for failure to conceive, the chances of success after 18 months to 2 years are high (Dunson, 2002). However, pregnancies that occur after a year or more of trying—even without treatment—need to be monitored closely, as there is greater risk of preterm births, low-birth-weight babies, and cesarean deliveries (Basso & Baird, 2003).

Human beings seldom abandon their fondest hopes simply because they run into obstacles, and so it is no surprise that many infertile adults who want children, like Lesley and John Brown, eagerly embrace techniques that bypass ordinary biological processes. Others choose the more traditional route of adoption (discussed in Chapter 14).

Alternative Ways to Parenthood

Since the birth of Louise Brown in 1978, more than 3 million children worldwide have been conceived through *assisted reproduction technology (ART)* (Reaney, 2006; ICMART, 2006). In 2003, 35,785 U.S. women delivered with technological help, giving birth to 48,756 babies, more than 1 percent of babies born in the United States that year (Wright, Chang, Jeng, & Macaluso, 2006; Figure 3-1).

In *in vitro fertilization (IVF),* the most common assisted reproduction procedure and the one Lesley Brown used, fertility drugs are given to increase production of ova. Then one or more mature ova are surgically removed, fertilized in a laboratory dish, and implanted in the woman's uterus. Usually 50,000 to 100,000 sperm are used to increase the chances of fertilization, and several embryos are transferred to the uterus to increase the chances of pregnancy. As we have mentioned, this procedure also increases the likelihood of multiple, usually premature, births—twins, triplets, or higher multiples. In 2003, 16 percent of twins and 44 percent of higher multiples born in the United States were attributable to ART (Wright et al., 2006).

A newer technique, *in vitro maturation (IVM)* is performed earlier in the monthly cycle, when as many as 30 to 50 egg follicles are developing. Normally, only one of these will mature. Harvesting a large number of follicles before ovulation is complete and then allowing them to mature in the laboratory can make hormone injections unnecessary and diminish the likelihood of multiple births (Duenwald, 2003).

IVF also can address severe male infertility. A single sperm can be injected into the ovum—a technique called *intracytoplasmic sperm injection (ICSI).* This procedure is now used in the majority of IVF cycles (Van Voorhis, 2007).

Artificial insemination—injection of sperm into a woman's vagina, cervix, or uterus—can be used to facilitate conception if a man has a low sperm count. Sperm from several ejaculations can be combined for one injection. Thus, with help, a couple can produce their own biological offspring. If the man is infertile, a couple may choose *artificial insemination by a donor (AID).* If the woman has no explain-able cause of infertility, the chances of success can be greatly increased by stimulating her ovaries to produce excess ova and injecting semen directly in the uterus (Guzick et al., 1999).

Box 3-1 *What Causes Multiple Births?*

Laurie and her husband, Steve, had four children, ages 4 to 10. All had been singleton births. So when an ultrasound early in Laurie's fifth pregnancy at age 40 revealed that she was carrying twins, she and Steve were surprised. They learned that Laurie exemplified one of the main risk factors for multiple births: advanced maternal age.

Multiple births occur in two ways. Most commonly, as in Laurie's case, the mother's body releases two ova within a short time (or sometimes a single unfertilized ovum splits) and then both are fertilized. The resulting babies are *dizygotic twins* (*di* means "two"), commonly called *fraternal twins*. Less commonly, a single *fertilized* ovum splits into two. The babies that result from this cell division are *monozygotic twins* (*mono* means "one"), commonly called *identical twins*. Triplets, quadruplets, and other multiple births can result from either of these processes or a combination of both.

Monozygotic twins have the same hereditary makeup and are the same sex, but they can differ in some respects. They may not be identical in temperament. In some physical characteristics, such as hair whorls, dental patterns, and handedness, they may be mirror images of each other; one may be left-handed and the other right-handed. Furthermore, differences between monozygotic twins tend to magnify as twins grow older, especially if they live apart. These differences may result from chemical modifications in a person's genome shortly after conception or may be due to later experiences or environmental factors, such as exposure to smoke or other pollutants (Fraga et al., 2005).

Dizygotic twins, who are created from different sperm cells and usually from different ova, are no more alike in hereditary makeup than any other siblings and may be the same sex or, like Laurie's twins, of different sexes. Dizygotic twins tend to run in families (though not in Laurie's) and so may have a genetic basis, whereas monozygotic twins usually occur purely by chance (Martin & Montgomery, 2002; National Center for Health Statistics [NCHS], 1999). A tendency toward twinning seems to be inherited from a woman's mother; thus, when dizygotic twins skip generations, it is normally because a mother of dizygotic twins has only sons to whom she cannot pass on the tendency (NCHS, 1999). The chance of having twins is also affected by diet; vegan women are only one-fifth as likely to have twins as women who include dairy products in their diet (Steinman, 2006).

The rate of monozygotic twins (about 4 per 1,000 live births) is constant at all times and places, but the rate of dizygotic twins, the more common type, varies (Martin & Montgomery, 2002; NCHS, 1999). For example, West African and African American women are more likely to have dizygotic twins than Caucasian women, who, in turn, are more likely to have them than Chinese or Japanese women (Martin & Montgomery, 2002).

The incidence of dizygotic twins and higher multiple births in the United States has grown rapidly. Between 1980 and 2004, the twin birth rate increased by 70 percent, from 19 to 32.2 twins per 1,000 live births. Twins, triplets, and higher multiples accounted for 3.4 percent of all births in 2004 (Martin, Hamilton, et al., 2006). Two related factors in the rise in multiple births are (1) the trend toward delayed childbearing and (2) the increased use

Pregnancies resulting in triplets or even higher multiples are increasingly common, in part because of the trend toward delayed motherhood and the use of fertility drugs and assisted reproduction techniques.

of fertility drugs, which spur ovulation, and of assisted reproductive techniques such as in vitro fertilization, which tend to be used more by older women (Hoyert et al., 2006; Martin et al., 2005).

The explosion of multiple births, especially triplets and higher multiples, is of concern because such births are associated with increased risks: pregnancy complications, premature delivery, low-birth-weight infants, and disability or death of an infant (Hoyert et al., 2006; Jain, Missmer, & Hornstein, 2004; Martin et al., 2003; Martin, Hamilton, et al., 2005; Wright, Schieve, Reynolds, & Jeng, 2003). Furthermore, triplets may be at higher risk for cognitive delays during the first 2 years. In a comparative study of 23 sets each of triplets, twins, and singleton infants, the triplets scored lowest on tests of mental development at 6, 12, and 24 months. This finding appeared to be related to the difficulty of giving sensitive mothering to three infants at the same time (Feldman & Eidelman, 2005). Perhaps because of such concerns, the proportion of artificial procedures involving three or more embryos declined between 1997 and 2001, and the birth rate for triplets and higher multiples, which had quadrupled since 1980, has since taken a slight downturn (Martin, Hamilton, et al., 2006).

What's your view

- Would you want to have twins or higher multiples?
- If you are a twin or higher multiple, how does that experience affect you?

Check it out

For information about multiple pregnancy and about raising twins, triplets, and higher multiples, go to http://www.parents.com/parents/category.jsp?categoryid=/templatedata/ab/category/data/AB25.xml. Articles cover such issues as breastfeeding, potty training, and sibling rivalry.

Figure 3-1

Increase in use of assisted
reproduction technology (ART),
United States, 1996–2003.

Source: CDC, 2005a.

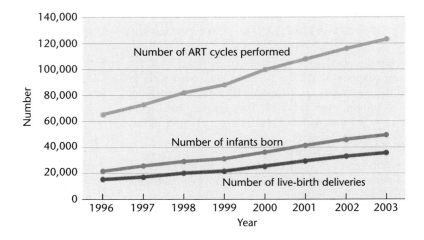

Although success rates have improved since 1978 (Duenwald, 2003), only 84 percent of the 122,872 U.S. women who attempted assisted reproduction in 2003 progressed to the transfer stage, and only 35 percent of these had live births (Wright et al., 2003). For one thing, the likelihood of success with IVF using a woman's own ova drops precipitously with maternal age as the quality of ova declines. A woman who is producing poor-quality ova or who has had her ovaries removed may try *ovum transfer.* In this procedure, a donor egg—provided, usually anonymously, by a fertile young woman—is fertilized in the laboratory and implanted in the prospective mother's uterus. IVF using donor eggs tends to be highly successful (Van Voorhis, 2007). In *blastocyst transfer,* the fertilized ovum is kept in the culture until it grows to the blastocyst stage; but this method has been linked to an increase in identical twin births (Duenwald, 2003). Alternatively, the ovum can be fertilized in the donor's body by artificial insemination. The donor's uterus is flushed out a few days later, and the embryo is retrieved and inserted into the recipient's uterus. Two other techniques with relatively high success rates are *gamete intrafallopian transfer (GIFT)* and *zygote intrafallopian transfer (ZIFT),* in which either the egg and sperm or the fertilized egg are inserted into the fallopian tube (CDC, 2002b; Schieve et al., 2002; Society for Assisted Reproductive Technology, 1993, 2002).

How do children conceived by artificial means turn out? Most of them do fine (Van Voorhis, 2007). A study of Iowa births between 1989 and 2002 did find a slightly increased risk of major birth defects associated with IVF (Van Voorhis et al., 2005). On the other hand, among 36,062 singleton pregnancies studied at Stamford Hospital in Connecticut, 1776 of them conceived through ovulation induction or IVF, use of these technologies was associated with increased risk of adverse outcomes, including fetal loss, but *not* of chromosomal or structural abnormalities (Shevell et al., 2005).

In a longitudinal study of 1,523 British, Belgian, Danish, Swedish, and Greek infants, there were *no* major differences in physical development, health, and other aspects of development at age 5 between those born through IVF or ICSI and those conceived normally. The groups also did not differ in behavioral problems or temperamental difficulties. However, children born through ICSI did have a higher rate of congenital urological and kidney abnormalities (Barnes et al., 2003; Sutcliffe, Loft, Wennerholm, Tarlatzis, & Bonduelle, 2003). Longitudinal studies of children conceived by IVF or by donor insemination found little or no difference in socioemotional development at age 12 between these children and naturally conceived or adopted children (Golombok, MacCallum, & Goodman, 2001; Golombok, MacCallum, Goodman, & Rutter, 2002).

In *surrogate motherhood,* a fertile woman is impregnated by the prospective father, usually by artificial insemination. She agrees to carry the baby to term and give it to the father and his mate. Courts in most states view surrogacy contracts as unenforceable, and some states have either banned the practice or placed strict conditions on it. The American

What's your view ?

- If you or your partner were infertile, would you consider or undertake one of the methods of assisted reproduction described here? Why or why not?

deoxyribonucleic acid (DNA)
Chemical that carries inherited instructions for the development of all cellular forms of life.

genetic code Sequence of bases within the DNA molecule; governs the formation of proteins that determine the structure and functions of living cells.

Academy of Pediatrics (AAP) Committee on Bioethics (1992) recommends that surrogacy be considered a tentative, preconception adoption agreement. The committee also recommends a prebirth agreement on the period of time in which the surrogate may assert parental rights.

Aside from the possibility that a surrogate who decides she wants to keep her baby may be forced to relinquish it, perhaps the most objectionable aspect of surrogacy is the payment of money. The creation of a "breeder class" of disadvantaged women who carry the babies of the well-to-do strikes many people as wrong. Similar concerns have been raised about payment for donor eggs. Exploitation of the would-be parents is an issue, too (Gabriel, 1996). However, a study of 42 families with infants born through surrogacy found that these parents adjusted better to their first year of parenthood than parents in control groups who had conceived children naturally or through egg donation (Golombok, Murray, Jadva, MacCallum, & Lycett, 2004).

Checkpoint

Can you . . .

✔ Identify several causes and treatments of male and female infertility?

✔ Describe four means of assisted reproduction, and mention several issues they raise?

✔ Distinguish between monozygotic and dizygotic twins, and tell how each comes about?

Mechanisms of Heredity

The science of genetics is the study of *heredity*—the inborn factors, inherited from the biological parents, that affect development. When ovum and sperm unite—whether by normal fertilization or by assisted reproduction, as with Louise Brown—they endow the baby-to-be with a genetic makeup that influences a wide range of characteristics from color of eyes and hair to health, intellect, and personality.

Guidepost 3

What genetic mechanisms determine sex, physical appearance, and other characteristics?

The Genetic Code

The basis of heredity is a chemical called **deoxyribonucleic acid (DNA).** The double-helix structure of DNA resembles a long, spiraling ladder whose steps are made of pairs of chemical units called *bases* (Figure 3-2). The bases—adenine (A), thymine (T), cytosine (C), and guanine (G)—are the "letters" of the **genetic code,** which cellular machinery "reads."

Chromosomes are coils of DNA that consist of smaller segments called **genes,** the functional units of heredity. Each gene is located in a definite position on its chromosome and contains thousands of base pairs. The sequence of bases in a gene tells a cell how to make the proteins that enable it to carry out specific functions.

Every cell in the normal human body except the sex cells (sperm and ova) has 23 pairs of chromosomes—46 in all. Through a type of cell division called *meiosis,* which the sex cells undergo when they are developing, each sex cell ends up with only 23 chromosomes—1 from each pair. Thus, when sperm and ovum fuse at conception, they produce a zygote with 46 chromosomes, 23 from the father and 23 from the mother (Figure 3-3).

Three-quarters of the genes every child receives are identical to those received by every other child; they are called *monomorphic genes.* The other one-quarter of a child's genes are *polymorphic genes,* which define each person as an individual. Because many of these come in several variations, and because meiotic division is random, it is virtually impossible for any two children—even siblings, other than monozygotic twins—to receive exactly the same combination of genes.

At conception, then, the single-celled zygote has all the biological information needed to guide its development into a human baby. This happens through *mitosis,* a process by which the cells divide and replicate themselves over and over again. When a cell divides, the DNA spirals duplicate themselves, so that each newly formed cell has the same DNA structure as the others. Thus, each cell division creates a genetic duplicate of the original cell with the same hereditary information. When development is normal, each cell (except the sex cells)

chromosomes Coils of DNA that consist of genes.

genes Small segments of DNA located in definite positions on particular chromosomes; functional units of heredity.

DNA is the genetic material in all living cells. It consists of four chemical units, called bases. These bases are the letters of the DNA alphabet. A (adenine) pairs with T (thymine) and C (cytosine) pairs with G (guanine). There are 3 billion base pairs in human DNA.

Letters of the DNA alphabet

T = Thymine
A = Adenine
G = Guanine
C = Cytosine

Figure 3-2

DNA: The genetic code.

Source: Ritter, 1999.

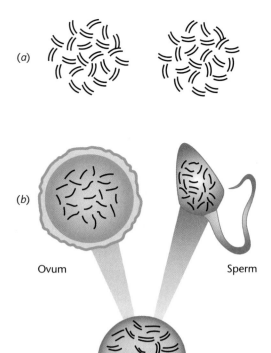

Figure 3-3

Hereditary composition of the zygote. (*a*) Body cells of women and men contain 23 pairs of chromosomes, which carry the genes, the basic units of inheritance. (*b*) Each sex cell (ovum and sperm) has only 23 single chromosomes because of meiosis, a special kind of cell division in which the total number of chromosomes is halved. (*c*) At fertilization, the 23 chromosomes from the sperm join the 23 from the ovum so that the zygote receives 46 chromosomes, or 23 pairs.

(*a*)

(*b*) Ovum   Sperm

(*c*) Zygote

autosomes In humans, the 22 pairs of chromosomes not related to sexual expression.

sex chromosomes Pair of chromosomes that determines sex: XX in the normal human female, XY in the normal human male.

continues to have 46 chromosomes identical to those in the original zygote. As the cells divide and the infant grows and develops, the cells differentiate, specializing in a variety of complex bodily functions.

Genes spring into action when conditions call for the information they can provide. Genetic action that triggers growth of body and brain is often regulated by hormonal levels—both in the mother and in the developing baby—that are affected by such environmental conditions as nutrition and stress. Thus, from the start, heredity and environment are interrelated.

What Determines Sex?

In many villages in Nepal, it is common for a man whose wife has borne no male babies to take a second wife. In some societies, a woman's failure to produce sons is justification for divorce. The irony in these customs is that it is the father's sperm that determines a child's sex.

At the moment of conception, the 23 chromosomes from the sperm and the 23 from the ovum form 23 pairs. Twenty-two pairs are **autosomes,** chromosomes not related to sexual expression. The 23rd pair are **sex chromosomes**— 1 from the father and 1 from the mother—which govern the baby's sex.

Sex chromosomes are either *X chromosomes* or *Y chromosomes*. The sex chromosome of every ovum is an X chromosome, but the sperm may contain either an X or a Y chromosome. The Y chromosome contains a gene for maleness, the *SRY gene*. When an ovum (X) is fertilized by an X-carrying sperm, the zygote formed is XX, a female. When an ovum (X) is fertilized by a Y-carrying sperm, the resulting zygote is XY, a male (Figure 3-4).

Initially, the embryo's rudimentary reproductive system is almost identical in males and in females. About 6 to 8 weeks after conception, male embryos normally start producing the male hormone testosterone. Exposure of a genetically male embryo to steady, high levels of testosterone ordinarily results in the development of a male body with male sexual organs. However, the process is not automatic. Research with mice has found that hormones must first signal the SRY gene, which then triggers cell differentiation and formation of the testes. Without this signaling, a genetically male mouse will develop female genitals instead of male ones (Hughes, 2004; Meeks, Weiss, & Jameson, 2003; Nef et al., 2003). It is likely that a similar mechanism occurs in human males. Conversely, the development of the female reproductive system depends on a signaling molecule called *Wnt-4,* a variant form of which can masculinize a genetically female fetus (Biason-Lauber, Konrad, Navratil, & Schoenle, 2004; Hughes, 2004; Vainio, Heikkiia, Kispert, Chin, & McMahon, 1999). Thus, sexual differentiation appears to be a more complex process than simple genetic determination.

Further complications arise from the fact that women have two X chromosomes, whereas men have only one. For many years researchers believed that the duplicate genes on one of a woman's two X chromosomes are inactivated. Recently, however, researchers sequencing the X chromosome discovered that only 75 percent of the genes on the extra X chromosome are inactive. About 15 percent remain active, and 10 percent are active in some women but not in others (Carrel & Willard, 2005). This variability in gene activity could help explain gender differences both in normal traits and in disorders linked to the X chromosome (discussed later in this chapter). The extra X chromosome also may help explain why women are generally healthier and more long-lived than men: Harmful changes in a gene on one X chromosome may be offset by a backup copy on the other X chromosome (Migeon, 2006).

Patterns of Genetic Transmission

During the 1860s, Gregor Mendel, an Austrian monk, laid the foundation for our understanding of patterns of inheritance. He crossbred pea plants that produced only yellow seeds with pea plants that produced only green seeds. The resulting hybrid plants produced only yellow seeds, meaning, he said, that yellow was *dominant* over green. Yet when he

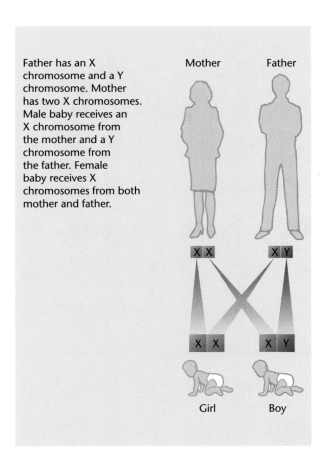

Father has an X chromosome and a Y chromosome. Mother has two X chromosomes. Male baby receives an X chromosome from the mother and a Y chromosome from the father. Female baby receives X chromosomes from both mother and father.

Mother   Father

X X   X Y

X X   X Y

Girl   Boy

Figure 3-4

Determination of sex. Because all babies receive an X chromosome from the mother, sex is determined by whether an X or Y chromosome is received from the father.

bred the yellow-seeded hybrids with each other, only 75 percent of their offspring had yellow seeds, and the other 25 percent had green seeds. This showed, Mendel said, that a hereditary characteristic (in this case, the color green) can be *recessive;* that is, carried by an organism that does not express, or show, it.

Mendel also tried breeding for two traits at once. Crossing pea plants that produced round yellow seeds with plants that produced wrinkled green seeds, he found that color and shape were independent of each other. Mendel thus showed that hereditary traits are transmitted separately.

Today we know that the genetic picture in humans is far more complex than Mendel imagined. Most human traits fall along a continuous spectrum (for example, from light skin to dark). One normal trait that people do inherit through simple dominant transmission is the ability to curl the tongue lengthwise.

Dominant and Recessive Inheritance

Can you curl your tongue? If so, you inherited this ability through *dominant inheritance.* If your parents can curl their tongues but you cannot, *recessive inheritance* occurred. How do these two types of inheritance work?

Genes that can produce alternative expressions of a characteristic (such as ability or inability to curl the tongue) are called **alleles.** Every person receives a pair of alleles for a given characteristic, one from each biological parent. When both alleles are the same, the person is **homozygous** for the characteristic; when they are different, the person is **heterozygous.** In **dominant inheritance,** when a person is heterozygous for a particular trait, the dominant allele governs. In other words, when an offspring receives contradictory alleles for a trait, only one of them, the dominant one, will be expressed. **Recessive inheritance,** the expression of a recessive trait, occurs only when a person receives the recessive allele from both parents.

If you inherited one allele for tongue-curling ability from each parent (Figure 3-5), you are homozygous for tongue curling. If, say, your mother passed on an allele for the ability

alleles Two or more alternative forms of a gene that can occupy the same position on paired chromosomes and affect the same trait.

homozygous Possessing two identical alleles for a trait.

heterozygous Possessing differing alleles for a trait.

dominant inheritance Pattern of inheritance in which, when a child receives different alleles, only the dominant one is expressed.

recessive inheritance Pattern of inheritance in which a child receives identical recessive alleles, resulting in expression of a nondominant trait.

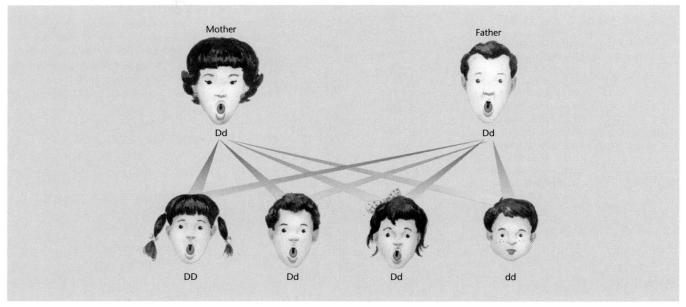

Figure 3-5

Dominant and recessive inheritance. Because of dominant inheritance, the same observable phenotype (in this case, the ability to curl the tongue lengthwise) can result from two different genotypes (DD and Dd). A phenotype expressing a recessive characteristic (such as inability to curl the tongue) must have a homozygous genotype (dd).

polygenic inheritance Pattern of inheritance in which multiple genes at different sites on chromosomes affect a complex trait.

mutations Permanent alterations in genes or chromosomes that may produce harmful characteristics.

multifactorial transmission Combination of genetic and environmental factors to produce certain complex traits.

phenotype Observable characteristics of a person.

genotype Genetic makeup of a person, containing both expressed and unexpressed characteristics.

The ability to curl the tongue lengthwise, as this girl is doing, is unusual in that it is inherited through simple dominant transmission. Most normal traits are influenced by multiple genes, often in combination with environmental factors.

and your father passed on an allele lacking it, you are heterozygous. Either way, since the ability is dominant (D) and its lack is recessive (d), you can curl your tongue. But if you received the recessive allele from both parents, you cannot.

Most traits result from **polygenic inheritance,** the interaction of several genes. Whereas more than 1,000 rare genes individually determine abnormal traits, no known single gene by itself significantly accounts for individual differences in any complex normal behavior. Instead, such behaviors are likely to be influenced by many genes with small but sometimes identifiable effects. Furthermore, there may be an average of twelve versions, or variants, of each gene, each with varying influences (Stephens et al., 2001). Researchers in *molecular genetics* have begun to identify specific genes that contribute to particular behavioral traits (Plomin, 2001). So far, at least 7 genes have been tentatively associated with intelligence and other cognitive abilities (Posthuma & de Gues, 2006).

Traits may be affected by **mutations:** permanent alterations in genetic material. A study comparing genomes of four racial/ethnic groups found that the lighter skin color of Caucasians and Asians resulted from slight mutations—a change of just 1 letter of DNA code out of the 3.1 billion letters in the human genome—tens of thousands of years ago (Lamason et al., 2005). **Multifactorial transmission,** a combination of genetic and environmental factors, plays a role in the expression of most traits.

Genotypes and Phenotypes

If you can curl your tongue, that ability is part of your **phenotype,** the observable characteristics through which your **genotype,** or underlying genetic makeup, is expressed. Except for monozygotic twins, no two people have the same genotype. The phenotype is the product of the genotype and any relevant environmental influences. The difference between genotype and phenotype helps explain why a clone (a genetic copy of an individual) or even an identical twin can never be an exact duplicate of another person.

As Figure 3-5 shows, the same phenotypical characteristic may arise from different genotypes: either a homozygous combination of two dominant alleles or a heterozygous combination of one dominant allele and one recessive allele. If you are heterozygous for tongue curling, and you and a mate who is also heterozygous for the trait have four children, the statistical probability is that one child will be homozygous for the ability, one will be homozygous lacking it, and the other two will be heterozygous. Thus, three of your children will likely have phenotypes that include tongue curling (they will be able to curl their tongues), but this ability will arise from two different genotypical patterns (homozygous and heterozygous).

Tongue curling has a strong genetic base; but, for most traits, experience modifies the expression of the genotype. Imagine that Steven has inherited musical talent. If he takes music lessons and practices regularly, he may delight his family with his performances. If his family likes and encourages classical music, he may play Bach preludes; if the other children on his block influence him to prefer popular music, he may eventually form a rock group. However, if from early childhood he is not encouraged and not motivated to play music, and if he has no access to a musical instrument or to music lessons, his genotype for musical ability may not be expressed (or may be expressed to a lesser extent) in his phenotype. Some physical characteristics (including height and weight) and most psychological characteristics (such as intelligence and personality traits, as well as musical ability) are products of multifactorial transmission.

Checkpoint ✔

Can you . . .

✔ Explain why no two people, other than monozygotic twins, have the same genetic heritage?

✔ Explain why it is the sperm that determines a baby's sex?

✔ Tell how dominant inheritance and recessive inheritance work, and why most normal traits are not the products of simple dominant or recessive transmission?

Genetic and Chromosomal Abnormalities

Guidepost 4

How are birth defects and disorders transmitted?

One of John and Lesley Brown's chief worries before Louise's birth—whether she would be a normal, healthy baby—is shared by every prospective biological parent. Babies born with serious birth defects are at high risk of dying at or shortly after birth or during infancy or childhood. Birth disorders are fairly rare, affecting only about 3 percent of live births (Waknine, 2006); but they are the leading cause of infant death in the United States, accounting for 20 percent of deaths in the first year in 2003 (Hoyert, Heron, Murphy, & Kung, 2006). The most prevalent defects are cleft lip or cleft palate, followed by Down syndrome. Other serious malformations involve the eye or the circulatory, orofacial, gastronomical, or musculoskeletal systems (CDC, 2006b; Table 3-2).

It is in genetic defects and diseases that we see most clearly the operation of dominant and recessive transmission in humans and also of a variation, *sex-linked inheritance.* Some defects are due to abnormalities in genes or chromosomes, which may result from mutations that occur spontaneously or are induced by environmental hazards, such as radiation.

Many disorders arise when an inherited predisposition interacts with an environmental factor, either before or after birth. Attention-deficit/hyperactivity disorder, discussed in Chapter 13, is one of a number of behavioral disorders thought to be transmitted multifactorially. Furthermore, children with attention-deficit/hyperactivity disorder are more likely to show early antisocial behavior if they were of low birth weight and have a variant of a gene called COMT (Thapar et al., 2005).

Not all genetic or chromosomal abnormalities are apparent at birth. Symptoms of Tay-Sachs disease (a fatal degenerative disease of the central nervous system that at one time occurred mostly among Jews of eastern European ancestry) and sickle-cell anemia (a blood disorder most common among African Americans) may not appear until at least age 6 months; cystic fibrosis (a condition, especially common in children of northern European descent, in which excess mucus accumulates in the lungs and digestive tract), not until age 4; and glaucoma (a disease in which fluid pressure builds up in the eye) and Huntington's disease (a progressive degeneration of the nervous system), usually not until middle age.

Table 3-2	Some Birth Defects		
Problem	**Characteristics of Condition**	**Who Is at Risk**	**What Can Be Done**
Alpha₁ antitrypsin deficiency	Enzyme deficiency that can lead to cirrhosis of the liver in early infancy and emphysema and degenerative lung disease in middle age.	1 in 1,000 white births	No treatment.
Alpha thalassemia	Severe anemia that reduces ability of the blood to carry oxygen; nearly all affected infants are stillborn or die soon after birth.	Primarily families of Malaysian, African, and Southeast Asian descent	Frequent blood transfusions.
Beta thalassemia (Cooley's anemia)	Severe anemia resulting in weakness, fatigue, and frequent illness; usually fatal in adolescence or young adulthood.	Primarily families of Mediterranean descent	Frequent blood transfusions.
Cystic fibrosis	Overproduction of mucus, which collects in the lung and digestive tract; children do not grow normally and usually do not live beyond age 30; the most common inherited *lethal* defect among white people.	1 in 2,000 white births	Daily physical therapy to loosen mucus; antibiotics for lung infections; enzymes to improve digestion; gene therapy (in experimental stage).
Duchenne muscular dystrophy	Fatal disease usually found in males, marked by muscle weakness; minor mental retardation is common; respiratory failure and death usually occur in young adulthood.	1 in 3,000 to 5,000 male births	No treatment.
Hemophilia	Excessive bleeding, usually found in males; in its most severe form, can lead to crippling arthritis in adulthood.	1 in 10,000 families with a history of hemophilia	Frequent transfusions of blood with clotting factors.
Neural-tube defects			
Anencephaly	Absence of brain tissues; infants are stillborn or die soon after birth.	1 in 1,000	No treatment.
Spina bifida	Incompletely closed spinal canal, resulting in muscle weakness or paralysis and loss of bladder and bowel control; often accompanied by hydrocephalus, an accumulation of spinal fluid in the brain, which can lead to mental retardation.	1 in 1,000	Surgery to close spinal canal prevents further injury; shunt placed in brain drains excess fluid and prevents mental retardation.
Phenylketonuria (PKU)	Metabolic disorder resulting in mental retardation.	1 in 15,000	Special diet begun in first few weeks of life can prevent mental retardation.
Polycystic kidney disease	*Infantile form:* enlarged kidneys, leading to respiratory problems and congestive heart failure. *Adult form:* kidney pain, kidney stones, and hypertension resulting in chronic kidney failure.	1 in 1,000	Kidney transplants.
Sickle-cell anemia	Deformed, fragile red blood cells that can clog the blood vessels, depriving the body of oxygen; symptoms include severe pain, stunted growth, frequent infections, leg ulcers, gallstones, susceptibility to pneumonia, and stroke.	1 in 500 African Americans	Painkillers, transfusions for anemia and to prevent stroke, antibiotics for infections.
Tay-Sachs disease	Degenerative disease of the brain and nerve cells, resulting in death before age 5.	Historically found mainly in eastern European Jews	No treatment.

Source: Adapted from AAP Committee on Genetics, 1996; NIH Consensus Development Panel, 2001; Tisdale, 1988, pp. 68–69.

Table 3-3 Chances of Genetic Disorders for Various Ethnic Groups

If You Are	The Chance Is About	That
African American	1 in 12	You are a carrier of sickle-cell anemia.
	7 in 10	You will have milk intolerance as an adult.
African American and male	1 in 10	You have a hereditary predisposition to develop hemolytic anemia after taking sulfa or other drugs.
African American and female	1 in 50	You have a hereditary predisposition to develop hemolytic anemia after taking sulfa or other drugs.
White	1 in 25	You are a carrier of cystic fibrosis.
	1 in 80	You are a carrier of phenylketonuria (PKU).
Jewish (Ashkenazic)	1 in 100	You are a carrier of familial dysautonomia.
Italian American or Greek American	1 in 10	You are a carrier of beta thalassemia.
Armenian or Jewish (Sephardic)	1 in 45	You are a carrier of familial Mediterranean fever.
Afrikaner (white South African)	1 in 330	You have porphyria.
Asian	almost 100%	You will have milk intolerance as an adult.

Source: Adapted from Milunsky, 1992, p. 122.

Dominant or Recessive Inheritance of Defects

Most of the time, normal genes are dominant over those carrying abnormal traits, but sometimes the gene for an abnormal trait is dominant. When one parent has one dominant abnormal gene and one recessive normal gene and the other parent has two recessive normal genes, each of their children has a 50/50 chance of inheriting the abnormal gene. Among the 1,800 disorders known to be transmitted by dominant inheritance are achondroplasia (a type of dwarfism) and Huntington's disease.

Recessive defects are expressed only if a child receives the same recessive gene from each biological parent. Some defects transmitted recessively, such as Tay-Sachs disease and sickle-cell anemia, are more common among certain ethnic groups, which, through reproduction within the group, have passed down recessive characteristics (Table 3-3).

Defects transmitted by recessive inheritance are more likely to be lethal at an early age than those transmitted by dominant inheritance. If a dominantly transmitted defect killed before the age of reproduction, it could not be passed on to the next generation and therefore would soon disappear. A recessive defect can be transmitted by carriers who do not have the disorder and thus may live to reproduce.

Some traits are only partly dominant or partly recessive. In **incomplete dominance** a trait is not fully expressed. For example, people with only one sickle-cell allele and one normal allele do not have sickle-cell anemia but do show some manifestations of the condition, such as shortness of breath at high altitudes.

incomplete dominance Pattern of inheritance in which a child receives two different alleles, resulting in partial expression of a trait.

Sex-Linked Inheritance of Defects

In **sex-linked inheritance** (Figure 3-6) certain recessive disorders, linked to genes on the sex chromosomes, affect male and female children differently. Red-green color blindness is one of these sex-linked conditions. Another is hemophilia, a disorder in which blood does not clot when it should.

Sex-linked recessive traits are carried on one of the X chromosomes of an unaffected mother. The mother is a *carrier;* she does not have the disorder but can pass on the gene to

sex-linked inheritance Pattern of inheritance in which certain characteristics carried on the X chromosome inherited from the mother are transmitted differently to her male and female offspring.

Figure 3-6

Sex-linked inheritance.

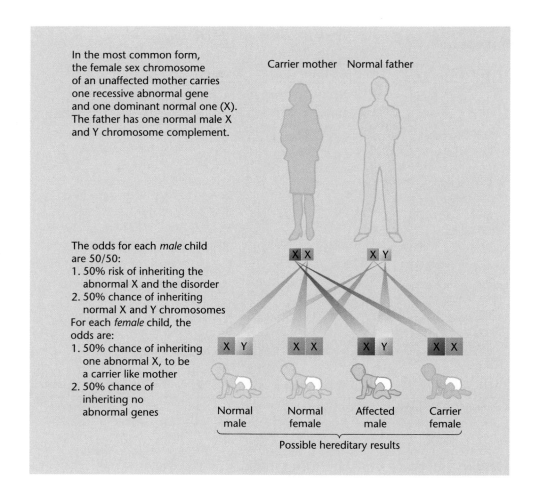

In the most common form, the female sex chromosome of an unaffected mother carries one recessive abnormal gene and one dominant normal one (X). The father has one normal male X and Y chromosome complement.

Carrier mother   Normal father

X X   X Y

The odds for each *male* child are 50/50:
1. 50% risk of inheriting the abnormal X and the disorder
2. 50% chance of inheriting normal X and Y chromosomes

For each *female* child, the odds are:
1. 50% chance of inheriting one abnormal X, to be a carrier like mother
2. 50% chance of inheriting no abnormal genes

X Y   X X   X Y   X X

Normal male   Normal female   Affected male   Carrier female

Possible hereditary results

Checkpoint ✔

Can you . . .

✔ Compare the operation of dominant inheritance, recessive inheritance, and sex-linked inheritance in transmission of birth defects?

her children. Sex-linked disorders almost always appear only in male children; in females, a normal dominant gene on the X chromosome from the father overrides the defective gene on the X chromosome from the mother. Boys are more vulnerable to these disorders because there is no opposite dominant gene on the Y chromosome from the father to override a defect on the X chromosome from the mother.

Occasionally, a female does inherit a sex-linked condition. For example, if her father is a hemophiliac and her mother happens to be a carrier for the disorder, the daughter has a 50 percent chance of receiving the abnormal X chromosome from each parent and having the disease.

Genome Imprinting

Genome, or *genetic, imprinting* is the differential expression of certain genetic traits, depending on whether the trait has been inherited from the mother or the father. In imprinted gene pairs, genetic information inherited from the parent of one sex is activated, but genetic information from the other parent is not. Imprinted genes play an important role in regulating fetal growth and development. When a normal pattern of imprinting is disrupted, abnormal fetal growth or congenital growth disorders may result (Hitchins & Moore, 2002).

Scientists have studied genome imprinting in mice by artificially manipulating their genetic makeup. Mice with two maternal copies of a gene in the region of chromosome 11 and a disabled paternal gene are born 70 percent smaller than their normal littermates, whereas mice with two paternal copies and a disabled maternal gene are about 30 percent larger than normal (Cattanach & Kirk, 1985).

What explains these differences? One widely accepted hypothesis, proposed by the evolutionary biologist David Haig (1993; Haig & Westoby, 1989), is that a pregnant woman unconsciously seeks to ration her nutritive resources between herself and her

Table 3-4   Sex Chromosome Abnormalities

Pattern/Name	Characteristics*	Incidence	Treatment
XYY	Male; tall stature; tendency to low IQ, especially verbal.	1 in 1,000 male births	No special treatment
XXX (triple X)	Female; normal appearance, menstrual irregularities, learning disorders, mental retardation.	1 in 1,000 female births	Special education
XXY (Kleinfelter)	Male; sterility, underdeveloped secondary sex characteristics, small testes, learning disorders.	1 in 1,000 male births	Hormone therapy, special education
XO (Turner)	Female; short stature, webbed neck, impaired spatial abilities, no menstruation, infertility, underdeveloped sex organs, incomplete development of secondary sex characteristics.	1 in 1,500 to 2,500 female births	Hormone therapy, special education
Fragile X	Minor-to-severe mental retardation; symptoms, which are more severe in males, include delayed speech and motor development, speech impairments, and hyperactivity; the most common *inherited* form of mental retardation.	1 in 1,200 male births; 1 in 2,000 female births	Educational and behavioral therapies when needed

*Not every affected person has every characteristic.

fetus, ensuring her ability to survive and have future children. Fathers, on the other hand, are concerned (from an evolutionary point of view) only with their own offspring, not with any other children the mother may have. Thus imprinted genes that limit fetal growth may be a mother's defense against extra demands on her, while imprinted genes from the father may serve as a check so that growth is not abnormally slowed. The fact that imprinting occurs only in mammals and that most imprinted genes are expressed in the mother's placenta, the seat of fetal nourishment, supports this theory (Tilghman, 1999).

Chromosomal Abnormalities

Chromosomal abnormalities typically occur because of errors in cell division, which result in an extra or missing chromosome. Some of these errors happen in the sex cells during meiosis. For example, Klinefelter syndrome is caused by an extra sex chromosome (shown by the pattern XXY). Turner syndrome results from a missing sex chromosome (XO). The likelihoood of errors in meiosis may increase in women age 35 or older (University of Virginia Health System, 2004). Characteristics of the most common sex chromosome disorders are shown in Table 3-4.

Other chromosomal abnormalities occur in the autosomes during cell division. **Down syndrome,** the most common of these, is responsible for about 40 percent of cases of moderate-to-severe mental retardation (Pennington, Moon, Edgin, Stedron, & Nadel, 2003). The condition is also called *trisomy-21,* because it is usually caused by an extra 21st chromosome or the translocation of part of the 21st chromosome onto another chromosome. The most obvious physical characteristic associated with the disorder is a downward-sloping skin fold at the inner corners of the eyes.

Approximately 1 in every 700 babies born alive has Down syndrome (CDC, 2006). The risk is greatest with older parents; when the mother is under age 35, the disorder is more likely to be hereditary. The extra chromosome seems to come from the mother's ovum in 95 percent of cases (Antonarakis & Down Syndrome Collaborative Group, 1991); the other 5 percent of cases seem to be related to the father.

The brains of children with Down syndrome appear normal at birth but shrink in volume by young adulthood, particularly in the hippocampal area, resulting in cognitive

This boy shows the chief identifying characteristic of Down syndrome: a downward sloping skin fold at the inner corner of the eye. Although Down syndrome is a major cause of mental retardation, children with this chromosomal abnormality have a good chance of living productive lives.

Down syndrome Chromosomal disorder characterized by moderate-to-severe mental retardation and by such physical signs as a downward-sloping skin fold at the inner corners of the eyes.

Figure 3-7

A karyotype is a photograph that shows the chromosomes when they are separated and aligned for cell division. We know that this is a karyotype of a person with Down syndrome, because there are three chromosomes instead of the usual two on pair 21. Because pair 23 consists of two Xs, we know that this is the karyotype of a female.

Source: Babu & Hirschhorn, 1992; March of Dimes, 1987.

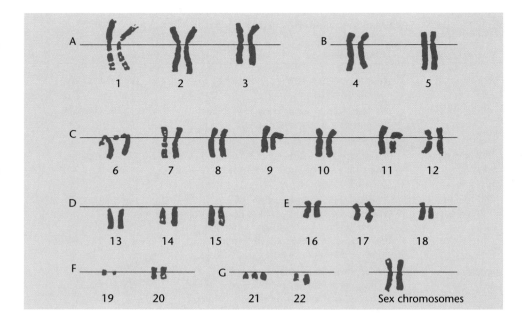

dysfunction (Pennington et al., 2003). The prognosis for these children is brighter than was once thought. As adults, many live in small group homes and support themselves; they tend to do well in structured job situations. More than 70 percent of people with Down syndrome live into their 60s, but they are at elevated risk of dying early from various causes, including leukemia, cancer, Alzheimer's disease, and cardiovascular disease (Hayes & Batshaw, 1993; Hill et al., 2003).

Genetic Counseling and Testing

genetic counseling Clinical service that advises couples of their probable risk of having children with hereditary defects.

Genetic counseling can help prospective parents assess their risk of bearing children with genetic or chromosomal defects. People who have already had a child with a genetic defect, who have a family history of hereditary illness, who suffer from conditions known or suspected to be inherited, or who come from ethnic groups at higher-than-average risk of passing on genes for certain diseases can get information about their likelihood of producing affected children.

Geneticists have made great contributions to avoidance of birth defects. For example, since so many Jewish couples have been tested for Tay-Sachs genes, far fewer Jewish babies have been born with the disease (Kolata, 2003). Similarly, screening and counseling of women of childbearing age from Mediterranean countries, where beta thalassemia (refer back to Table 3-1) is common, have resulted in a decline in births of affected babies and greater knowledge of the risks of being a carrier (Cao, Saba, Galanello, & Rosatelli, 1997).

What's your view

• Should genetic counseling be compulsory before marriage?

A genetic counselor takes a family history and gives the prospective parents and any biological children physical examinations. Laboratory investigations of blood, skin, urine, or fingerprints may be performed. Chromosomes from body tissues may be analyzed and photographed, and the photographs enlarged and arranged according to size and structure on a chart called a *karyotype*. This chart can show chromosomal abnormalities and can indicate whether a person who appears normal might transmit genetic defects to a child (Figure 3-7). The counselor tries to help clients understand the mathematical risk of a particular condition, explains its implications, and presents information about alternate courses of action.

Checkpoint

Can you . . .

✔ Explain how genome imprinting occurs?

✔ Describe three ways in which chromosomal disorders occur?

✔ Explain the purposes of genetic counseling?

Today, researchers are rapidly identifying genes that contribute to many serious diseases and disorders as well as those that influence normal traits. Their work is likely to lead to widespread genetic testing to reveal genetic profiles—a prospect that involves dangers as well as benefits (Box 3-2).

Box 3-2 *Genetic Testing, Genetic Engineering, and Medical Genetics*

The complete sequence of genes in the human body constitutes the *human genome.* Scientists have now finished mapping the human genome, which is estimated to contain between 20,000 and 25,000 genes (International Human Genome Sequencing Consortium, 2004). Among the interesting findings are that all but 300 human genes have counterparts in mice (Wade, 2001), and the genomes of humans and chimpanzees are nearly 99 percent alike (Clark et al., 2003). Indeed, chimps and humans of the same sex are no more different genetically than are men and women (Rozen et al., 2003).

The mapping of the human genome has greatly advanced our ability to identify which genes influence specific traits or behaviors and the developmental unfolding of these traits. A new field of science, *genomics,* the study of the functions and interactions of the various genes, will have untold implications for *medical genetics,* the application of genetic information to therapeutic purposes (McKusick, 2001; Patenaude, Guttmacher, & Collins, 2002). As efforts shift from finding genes to understanding how they affect behavior, scientists will be able to identify genes that cause, trigger, or increase susceptibility to particular disorders so as to screen at-risk population groups.

The genetic information gained from such research could increase our ability to predict, prevent, control, treat, and cure disease—even to pinpoint specific drug treatments to specific individuals. Already, genetic screening of newborns is saving lives and preventing mental retardation by permitting identification and treatment of infants with such disorders as sickle-cell anemia and phenylketonuria (PKU) (Holtzman, Murphy, Watson, & Barr, 1997; Khoury, McCabe, & McCabe, 2003). Genetic screening for breast cancer probably would identify 88 percent of all high-risk persons, significantly more than are currently identified (Pharaoh et al., 2002). Genetic information can help people decide whether to have children and with whom, and it can help people with family histories of a disease to know the worst that is likely to happen.

Gene therapy (repairing genes, or replacing abnormal genes with normal ones), once a bright hope, appears to have dimmed for the time being. In 2000, French researchers reversed severe combined immunodeficiency, a serious immune disease, in ten babies age 1 to 11 months by taking bone marrow cells from the babies, genetically altering the cells, and then injecting them into the babies. One year later, the patients remained healthy (Cavazanna-Calvo et al., 2000). But three of the children have since developed leukemia, and one of the three has died. In 1999 another death occurred in a gene therapy experiment at the University of Pennsylvania (Harris, 2005).

Genetic testing itself involves such ethical and political issues as privacy and fair use of genetic information. Although medical data are supposed to be confidential, it is almost impossible to keep genetic information private. Some courts have ruled that blood relatives have a legitimate claim to information about a patient's genetic health risks that may affect them, even though such disclosures violate confidentiality (Clayton, 2003).

A major concern is *genetic determinism:* the misconception that a person with a gene for a disease is bound to get the disease. All genetic testing can tell us is the *likelihood* that a person will get a disease. Most diseases involve a complex combination of genes or depend in part on lifestyle or other environmental factors. Job and insurance discrimination on the basis of genetic information has occurred—even though tests may be imprecise and unreliable and people deemed at risk of a disease may never develop it (Clayton, 2003; Khoury et al., 2003; Lapham, Kozma, & Weiss, 1996). Federal and state antidiscrimination laws provide some protection, but it is not consistent or comprehensive (Clayton, 2003). Policies protecting confidentiality of research also are needed.

The psychological impact of test results is another concern. Predictions are imperfect; a false positive result may cause needless anxiety, and a false negative result may lull a person into complacency. And what if a genetic condition is incurable? Is there any point in knowing you have the gene for a potentially debilitating condition if you cannot do anything about it? A panel of experts has recommended against genetic testing for diseases for which there is no known cure (Institute of Medicine [IOM], 1993).

Additional concerns involve the testing of children. Should a child be tested to benefit a sibling or someone else? How will a child be affected by learning that he or she is likely to develop a disease 20, 30, or 50 years later? The American Academy of Pediatrics Committee on Bioethics (2001) recommends against genetic testing of children for conditions that cannot be treated in childhood.

Particularly chilling is the prospect that genetic testing could be misused to justify sterilization of people with "undesirable" genes or abortion of a normal fetus with the "wrong" genetic makeup (Harmon, 2005; Plomin & Rutter, 1998). Gene therapy has the potential for similar abuse. Should it be used to make a short child taller or a chubby child thinner? To improve an unborn baby's appearance or intelligence? The path from therapeutic correction of defects to genetic engineering for cosmetic or functional purposes may well be a slippery slope (Anderson, 1998), leading to a society in which some parents could afford to provide the "best" genes for their children and others could not (Rifkin, 1998).

Within the next 15 years, genetic testing "will almost certainly revolutionize the practice of medicine" (Anderson, 1998, p. 30). It is not yet clear whether the benefits will outweigh the risks.

What's your view

Would you want to know that you had a gene predisposing you to lung cancer? To Alzheimer's disease? Would you want your child to be tested for these genes?

Check it out

For more information on this topic, go to http://www.ornl.gov/sci/techresources/Human_Genome/home/shtml. This is the Human Genome Project Web site. Information about disease diagnosis and prediction, disease intervention, genetic counseling, and ethical, legal, and social issues is presented.

Nature and Nurture: Influences of Heredity and Environment

Which is more important, nature or nurture? That question was hotly debated by early psychologists and the general public, as we discussed in Chapter 1. Since then, it has become clear that, although certain rare physical disorders are virtually 100 percent inherited, phenotypes for most complex normal traits, such as those having to do with health, intelligence, and personality, are subject to a complex array of hereditary and environmental forces. Let us explore how scientists study and explain the influences of heredity and environment and how these two forces work together.

Studying the Relative Influences of Heredity and Environment

behavioral genetics Quantitative study of relative hereditary and environmental influences on behavior.

One approach to the study of heredity and environment is quantitative: It seeks to measure how much a certain trait is influenced by heredity and how much by environment. This is the traditional goal of the science of **behavioral genetics.**

Measuring Heritability

heritability Statistical estimate of contribution of heredity to individual differences in a specific trait within a given population.

Heritability is a statistical estimate of how great a contribution heredity makes toward variations in a specific trait at a certain time *within a given population*. Heritability does *not* refer to the relative influence of heredity and environment in a particular individual; those influences may be virtually impossible to separate. Nor does heritability tell us how traits develop. It merely indicates the statistical extent to which genes contribute to a trait.

Heritability is expressed as a percentage ranging from 0.0 to 1.0; the higher the number, the greater the heritability of a trait, with 1.0 meaning that genes are 100 percent responsible for variances in the trait within the population. Because heritability cannot be measured directly, researchers in behavioral genetics rely chiefly on three types of correlational research: family, adoption, and twin studies.

These studies are based on the assumption that immediate family members are more genetically similar than more distant relatives, adopted children are genetically more like their biological families than their adoptive families, and monozygotic twins are more genetically similar than dizygotic twins. Thus, if heredity has a large influence on a particular trait, siblings should be more alike than cousins with regard to that trait, adopted children should be more like their biological parents than their adoptive parents, and monozygotic twins should be more alike than dizygotic twins. By the same token, if a shared environment exerts a large influence on a trait, persons who live together should be more similar with regard to that trait than persons who do not live together.

Family studies go beyond noting similarities in traits among family members, as we did for Louise Brown and her mother and father. Researchers measure the *degree* to which biological relatives share certain traits and whether the closeness of the familial relationship is associated with the degree of similarity. If the correlation is strong, the researchers infer a genetic influence. However, family studies cannot rule out environmental influences. A family study alone cannot tell us whether obese children of obese parents inherited the tendency or whether they are overweight because their diet is like that of their parents. For that reason, researchers do adoption studies, which can separate the effects of heredity from those of a shared environment.

Adoption studies look at similarities between adopted children and their adoptive families and also between adopted children and their biological families. When adopted children are more like their biological parents and siblings in a particular trait (say, obesity), we see the influence of heredity. When they resemble their adoptive families more, we see the influence of environment.

Monozygotic twins separated at birth are sought by researchers who want to study the impact of genes on personality. These twins, adopted by different families and not reunited until age 31, both became firefighters. Was this a coincidence, or did it reflect the influence of heredity?

Twin studies compare pairs of monozygotic twins and same-sex dizygotic twins. (Same-sex twins are used so as to avoid any confounding effects of gender.) Monozygotic twins are twice as genetically similar, on average, as dizygotic twins, who are no more genetically similar than other same-sex siblings. When monozygotic twins are more **concordant** (that is, have a statistically greater tendency to show the same trait) than dizygotic twins, we see the likely effects of heredity. Concordance rates, which may range from 0.0 to 1.0, estimate the probability that a pair of twins in a sample will be concordant for a trait.

concordant Term describing tendency of twins to share the same trait or disorder.

When monozygotic twins show higher concordance for a trait than do dizygotic twins, the likelihood of a genetic factor can be studied further through adoption studies. Studies of monozygotic twins separated in infancy and reared apart have found strong resemblances between the twins. Twin and adoption studies support a moderate to high hereditary basis for many normal and abnormal characteristics (McGuffin et al., 2001).

Critics of behavioral genetics claim that its assumptions and methods tend to maximize the importance of hereditary effects and minimize environmental ones. Furthermore, there are great variations in the findings, depending on the source of the data. For example, twin studies generally come up with higher heritability estimates than adoption studies do. This wide variability, critics say, "means that no firm conclusions can be drawn about the relative strength of these influences on development" (Collins, Maccoby, Steinberg, Hetherington, & Bornstein, 2000, p. 221).

Behavioral geneticists recognize that the effects of genetic influences, especially on behavioral traits, are rarely inevitable. Even in a trait strongly influenced by heredity, the environment can have substantial impact (Rutter, 2002), as much as 50 percent. In fact, environmental interventions sometimes can overcome genetically determined conditions. For example, a special diet begun soon after birth often can prevent mental retardation in children with the genetic disease phenylketonuria (PKU) (Plomin & DeFries, 1999; refer back to Table 3-1).

> ## *Checkpoint* ✔
>
> *Can you . . .*
>
> ✔ State the basic assumption underlying studies of behavioral genetics and explain how it applies to family studies, adoption studies, and twin studies?
>
> ✔ Cite criticisms of the behavioral genetics approach?

How Heredity and Environment Work Together

Today many developmental scientists have come to regard a solely quantitative approach to the study of heredity and environment as simplistic. They see these two forces as fundamentally intertwined. Instead of looking at genes and experience as operating independently on an organism, scientists influenced by contemporary evolutionary and developmental theory see both as part of a complex *developmental system* (Gottlieb, 1991; Lickliter & Honeycutt, 2003).

From conception on, a combination of constitutional (biological and psychological), social, economic, and cultural factors help shape development. The more advantageous these circumstances and the experiences to which they give rise, the greater is the likelihood of optimum development.

Let us consider several ways in which inheritance and experience work together.

Reaction Range and Canalization

Many characteristics vary, within limits, under varying hereditary or environmental conditions. The concepts of *reaction range* and *canalization* can help us visualize how this happens.

Reaction range is the conventional term for a range of potential expressions of a hereditary trait. Body size, for example, depends largely on biological processes, which are genetically regulated. Even so, a range of sizes is possible, depending on environmental opportunities and constraints and a person's own behavior. In societies in which nutrition has dramatically improved, such as the Netherlands, an entire generation has grown up to tower over the generation before. The better-fed children share their parents' genes but also have responded to a healthier world. Once a society's average diet becomes adequate for more than one generation, however, children tend to grow to heights similar to their parents'. Height has genetic limits; we do not see people who are only a foot tall or any who are 10 feet tall.

Heredity can influence whether a reaction range is wide or narrow. For example, a child born with a defect producing mild retardation is more able to respond to a favorable environment than a child born with more severe limitations. Likewise, a child with high native intelligence is likely to benefit more from an enriched home and school environment than a child with less ability (Figure 3-8).

The metaphor of **canalization** illustrates how heredity restricts the range of development for some traits. After a heavy storm, the rainwater that has fallen on a pavement has to go somewhere. If the street has potholes, the water will fill them. If deep canals have been dug along the edges of the street, the water will flow into the canals. Some human characteristics, such as eye color, are so strongly programmed by genes that they are said to be highly *canalized;* there is little opportunity for variance in their expression.

Certain behaviors also develop along genetically dug channels; it takes an extreme change in environment to alter their course. Behaviors that depend largely on maturation seem to appear when a child is ready. Normal babies follow a typical sequence of motor development: crawling, walking, and running, in that order, at certain approximate ages. Still, this development is not completely canalized; experience can affect its pace and timing.

Cognition and personality are more subject to variations in experience: the kinds of families children grow up in, the schools they attend, and the people they encounter. Consider language. Before children can talk, they must reach a certain level of neurological and muscular maturation. No 6-month-old could speak this sentence, no matter how enriched the infant's home life might be. Yet environment does play a large part in language development. If parents encourage babies' first sounds by talking back to them, the babies are likely to start to speak earlier than if their early vocalizing is ignored.

Recently scientists have begun to recognize that a usual or typical *experience,* too, can dig canals, or channels for development (Gottlieb, 1991). For example, infants who hear only the sounds peculiar to their native language soon lose the ability to perceive

reaction range Potential variability, depending on environmental conditions, in the expression of a hereditary trait.

canalization Limitation on variance of expression of certain inherited characteristics.

Pieter Gijselaar, 7 feet tall, poses next to an elevator in Amsterdam. In the past 150 years the Dutch have become the tallest people on earth, and experts say they are still growing. Gijselaar spends much of his life ducking doorways.

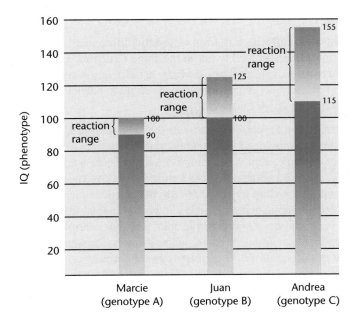

Figure 3-8

Intelligence and reaction range. Children with different genotypes for intelligence will show varying reaction ranges when exposed to a restricted (blue portion of bar) or enriched (entire bar) environment.

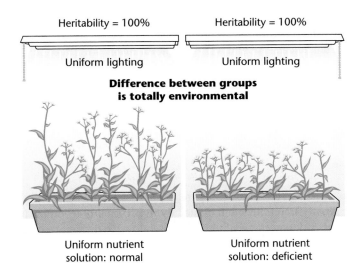

Figure 3-9

Example of gene-environment interaction. The two plants have the same hereditary endowment, but the one grown in a deficient nutrient mix is dwarfed in height.

Source: Gray & Thompson, 2004.

sounds characteristic of other languages. Throughout this book you will find many examples of how socioeconomic status, neighborhood conditions, and educational opportunity can powerfully shape developmental outcomes, from the pace and complexity of language development to the likelihood of early sexual activity and antisocial behavior.

Genotype-Environment Interaction

Genotype-environment interaction usually refers to the effects of similar environmental conditions on genetically different individuals. To take a familiar example, many children are exposed to pollen and dust, but those with a genetic predisposition are more likely to develop allergic reactions. Interactions can work the other way as well: Genetically similar children often develop differently depending on their home environments (Collins et al., 2000; Figure 3-9). As we will discuss in Chapter 8, a child born with a difficult temperament may develop adjustment problems in one family and thrive in another, depending largely on parental handling. Thus, it is the interaction of hereditary and environmental factors, not just one or the other, that produces certain outcomes.

genotype-environment interaction The portion of phenotypic variation that results from the reactions of genetically different individuals to similar environmental conditions.

Genotype-Environment Correlation

genotype-environment correlation Tendency of certain genetic and environmental influences to reinforce each other; may be passive, reactive (evocative), or active. Also called *genotype-environment covariance*.

The environment often reflects or reinforces genetic differences. That is, certain genetic and environmental influences tend to act in the same direction. This is called **genotype-environment correlation,** or *genotype-environment covariance,* and it works in three ways to strengthen the phenotypic expression of a genotypic tendency (Bergeman & Plomin, 1989; Scarr, 1992; Scarr & McCartney, 1983):

- *Passive correlations:* Parents, who provide the genes that predispose a child toward a trait, also tend to provide an environment that encourages the development of that trait. For example, a musical parent is likely to create a home environment in which music is heard regularly, to give a child music lessons, and to take the child to musical events. If the child inherited the parent's musical talent, the child's musicality will reflect a combination of genetic and environmental influences. This type of correlation is called *passive* because the child does not control it. Passive correlations are most applicable to young children, whose parents, the source of their genes, also have a great deal of control over their early experiences.
- *Reactive, or evocative, correlations:* Children with differing genetic makeups evoke different responses from adults. If a child shows interest and ability in music, parents who are not musically inclined may react by making a special effort to provide that child with musical experiences. This response, in turn, strengthens the child's genetic inclination toward music.
- *Active correlations:* As children get older and have more freedom to choose their own activities and environments, they actively select experiences consistent with their genetic tendencies. A child with a talent for music will probably seek out musical friends, take music classes, and go to concerts if such opportunities are available. A shy child is likely to spend more time in solitary pursuits than an outgoing child. This tendency to seek out environments compatible with one's genotype is called *niche-picking;* it helps explain why identical twins reared apart tend to be quite similar.

What Makes Siblings So Different? The Nonshared Environment

Although two children in the same family may bear a striking physical resemblance, siblings can differ greatly in intellect and especially in personality (Plomin, 1989). One reason may be genetic differences, which lead children to need different kinds of stimulation or to respond differently to a similar home environment. For example, one child may be more affected by family discord than another (Rutter, 2002). In addition, studies in behavioral genetics suggest that many of the experiences that strongly affect development differ for different children in a family (McGuffin et al., 2001; Plomin & Daniels, 1987; Plomin & DeFries, 1999).

nonshared environmental effects The unique environment in which each child grows up, consisting of distinctive influences or influences that affect one child differently than another.

These **nonshared environmental effects** result from the unique environment in which each child in a family grows up. Children in a family have a shared environment—the home they live in, the people in it, and the activities a family jointly engages in—but they also, even if they are twins, have experiences that are not shared by their brothers and sisters. Parents and siblings may treat each child differently. Certain events, such as illnesses and accidents, and experiences outside the home (for example, with teachers and peers) affect one child and not another. Indeed, some behavioral geneticists have concluded that although heredity accounts for most of the similarity between siblings, the nonshared environment accounts for most of the difference (McClearn et al., 1997; Plomin, 1996; Plomin & Daniels, 1987; Plomin & DeFries, 1999; Plomin, Owen, & McGuffin, 1994). However, methodological challenges and additional empirical evidence point to the more moderate conclusion that nonshared environmental effects do not greatly outweigh shared ones; rather, there seems to be a balance between the two (Rutter, 2002).

Genotype-environment correlations may play an important role in the nonshared environment. Children's genetic differences may lead parents and siblings to react to them differently and treat them differently, and genes may influence how children perceive and respond to that treatment and what its outcome will be. Children also mold their environments by the choices they make—what they do and with whom—and their genetic makeup influences these choices. A child who has inherited artistic talent may spend a great deal of time creating "masterpieces" in solitude, whereas a sibling who is athletically inclined may spend more time playing ball with friends. Thus, not only will the children's abilities (in, say, painting or soccer) develop differently, but their social lives will be different as well. These differences tend to be accentuated as children grow older and have more experiences outside the family (Bergeman & Plomin, 1989; Bouchard, 1994; Plomin, 1990, 1996; Plomin et al., 1994; Scarr, 1992; Scarr & McCartney, 1983).

The old nature-nurture debate is far from resolved; we know now that the problem is far more complex than previously thought. A variety of research designs can continue to augment and refine our understanding of the forces affecting development.

Epigenesis: Environmental Influence on Gene Expression

At one time, most scientists believed that the genes a child inherits were firmly established during fetal development, though their effects on behavior could be modified by experience. Now, mounting evidence suggests that gene expression itself is controlled by a third component, a mechanism that controls the functioning of genes without affecting their DNA structure. This phenomenon is called *epigenesis*. Furthermore, far from being fixed once and for all, epigenetic activity is affected by a continuing bidirectional interplay with nongenetic influences (Gottlieb, 2007; Rutter, 2007).

Epigenesis (meaning "on the genes"), or the *epigenetic framework,* refers to chemical molecules attached to a gene, which alter the way a cell "reads" the gene's DNA. The epigenetic framework can be visualized as "a code written in pencil in the margins around the DNA" (Gosden & Feinberg, 2007, p. 731). Because every cell in the body inherits the same DNA sequence, the function of these epigenetic markers is to differentiate types of body cells. They do so by switching particular genes on or off during embryonic formation. Sometimes errors arise in the process, which may lead to birth defects or disease (Gosden & Feinberg, 2007).

Epigenetic markers may contribute to such common ailments as cancer, diabetes, and heart disease. Epigenesis also may explain why on monozygotic twin is susceptible to a disease such as schizophrenia whereas the other twin is not and why some twins get the same disease but at different ages (Fraga et al., 2005; Wong, Gottesman, & Petronia, 2005).

Epigenetic changes can occur throughout life in response to environmental factors such as nutrition and stress (Rakyan & Beck, 2006). In one twin study, blood analysis showed epigenetic differences in 35 percent of the sample, and these differences were associated with age and lifestyle (Fraga et al., 2005).

Epigenetic modifications, especially those that occur early in life, may even be heritable. Studies of human sperm cells found age-related epigenetic variations capable of being passed on to future generations (Rakyan & Beck, 2006).

Some Characteristics Influenced by Heredity and Environment

Keeping in mind the complexity of unraveling the influences of heredity and environment, let us look at what is known about their roles in producing certain characteristics.

Physical and Physiological Traits

Not only do monozygotic twins generally look alike, but they also are more concordant than dizygotic twins in their risk for medical disorders such as high blood pressure, heart disease, stroke, rheumatoid arthritis, peptic ulcers, and epilepsy (Brass, Isaacsohn, Merikangas, & Robinette, 1992; Plomin et al., 1994). Life span, too, seems to be influenced by genes (Sorensen, Nielsen, Andersen, & Teasdale, 1988).

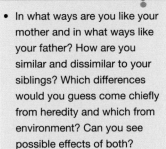

What's your view

- In what ways are you like your mother and in what ways like your father? How are you similar and dissimilar to your siblings? Which differences would you guess come chiefly from heredity and which from environment? Can you see possible effects of both?

epigenesis Mechanism that turns genes on or off and determines functions of body cells.

Checkpoint ✓

Can you . . .

- ✔ Explain and give at least one example of reaction range, canalization, genotype-environment interaction, and genotype-environment correlation?
- ✔ List three types of influences that contribute to nonshared environmental effects?
- ✔ Explain how epigenesis works?

Guidepost 6

What roles do heredity and environment play in physical health, intelligence, and personality?

obesity Extreme overweight in relation to age, sex, height, and body type.

Obesity, sometimes called simply *overweight,* is a multifactorial condition. It is defined in childhood as having a body mass index, or BMI (comparison of weight to height), at or above the 95th percentile for age and sex. Twin studies, adoption studies, and other research suggest that 40 to 70 percent of the risk is genetic. A longitudinal study of risk factors for heart disease, begun in 1973 in the Bogalusa, Louisiana, area, has linked specific genes and their chromosomal locations to body mass measurements taken over several decades (Chen et al., 2004). One key gene, GAD2 on chromosome 10, normally controls appetite; but an abnormal version of this gene can stimulate hunger and overeating (Boutin et al., 2003).

The kind and amount of food eaten in a particular home or in a particular social or ethnic group and the amount of exercise that is encouraged can increase or decrease the likelihood that a person will become overweight. The rapid rise in the prevalence of obesity in Western countries seems to result from the interaction of a genetic predisposition with inadequate exercise (Leibel, 1997). Obesity is discussed further in Chapters 9, 12, and 15.

Intelligence

Heredity exerts a strong influence on general intelligence (as measured by intelligence tests) and, to a lesser extent, on specific abilities such as memory, verbal ability, and spatial ability (McClearn et al., 1997; Petrill et al., 2004; Plomin et al., 1994; Plomin & DeFries, 1999; Plomin & Spinath, 2004). As we mentioned earlier in this chapter, several genes have been tentatively associated with intelligence (Posthuma & de Gues, 2006). Experience counts, too; as Figure 3-8 shows, an enriched or impoverished environment can substantially affect the development and expression of innate ability (Neisser et al., 1996).

Evidence of the role of heredity in intelligence comes from adoption and twin studies. Adopted children's IQs are consistently closer to the IQs of their biological mothers than to those of their adoptive parents and siblings, and monozygotic twins are more alike in intelligence than dizygotic twins. This pattern is also true of performance on elementary school achievement tests and on National Merit Scholarship examinations given to high school students. The studies yield a consistent estimate of heritability of about 50 percent for spatial abilities, meaning that genetic differences explain about half of the observed variation among members of a population. A close correlation between verbal and spatial abilities suggests a genetic link among the components of intelligence (Petrill et al., 2004; Plomin & DeFries, 1999). Indeed, it is likely that the same genes that affect one cognitive ability also affect other cognitive abilities (Plomin & Spinath, 2004).

Furthermore, the genetic influence, which is primarily responsible for stability in cognitive performance, increases with age. The shared family environment seems to have a strong influence on young children but a diminishing influence on adolescents and adults, who are more apt to find their own niche by actively selecting environments compatible with their hereditary abilities and related interests. The nonshared environment, in contrast, is influential throughout life and is primarily responsible for changes in cognitive performance (Bouchard, 2004; Petrill et al., 2004; Plomin & Spinath, 2004).

Personality

Scientists have identified genes directly linked with specific personality traits, such as neuroticism, which may contribute to depression and anxiety (Lesch et al., 1996). Heritability of personality traits appears to be between 40 and 50 percent, and there is little evidence of shared environmental influence (Bouchard, 2004).

temperament Characteristic disposition or style of approaching and reacting to situations.

Temperament, a person's characteristic style of approaching and reacting to situations, appears to be largely inborn and is often consistent over the years, though it may respond to special experiences or parental handling (Thomas & Chess, 1984; Thomas, Chess, & Birch, 1968). Siblings—both twins and nontwins—tend to be similar in temperament (Saudino, Wertz, Gagne, & Chawla, 2004). An observational study of 100 pairs of 7-year-old siblings (half of them adoptive siblings and half siblings by birth) found significant genetic influences on activity, sociability, and emotionality (Schmitz, Saudino, Plomin, Fulker, & DeFries, 1996).

Religiousness is subject to both genetic and environmental influences, according to a study of 169 monozygotic and 104 dizygotic twin pairs from Minnesota. Parenting and family life have the strongest influence in childhood, but genetic influences become more predominant from adolescence on (Koenig, McGue, Krueger, & Bouchard, 2005).

Psychopathology

There is evidence for a strong hereditary influence on such mental disorders as schizophrenia, autism, and depression. All tend to run in families and to show greater concordance between monozygotic twins than between dizygotic twins. However, heredity alone does not produce such disorders; an inherited tendency can be triggered by environmental factors. For example, children with a short form of the serotonin transporter gene 5-HTTLPR are vulnerable to depression if they have cold, unsupportive families but not if they have supportive, nurturing ones (Taylor et al., 2006). (Autism is discussed in Box 6-1 in Chapter 6 and depression in Chapters 14 and 15.)

Schizophrenia is now widely considered a neurological disorder (Gray & Thompson, 2004). Characterized by loss of contact with reality and by such symptoms as hallucinations and delusions, it has multifactorial causes (Berry, Jobanputra, & Pal, 2003; Tuulio-Henriksson et al., 2002; Vaswani & Kapur, 2001). The risk of schizophrenia is ten times greater among siblings and offspring of schizophrenics than among the general population; and twin and adoption studies suggest that this increased risk comes from shared genes, not shared environments. Estimates of heritability are as high as 80 to 85 percent (McGuffin, Owen, & Farmer, 1995; Picker, 2005).

No single gene appears to be responsible (Picker, 2005). Research has identified several gene variants that increase susceptibility to schizophrenia (Xu et al., 2005; Cannon et al., 2005; Egan et al., 2004). A postmortem examination suggests that the disorder may originate in a lack of a chemical called *reelin,* which helps position nerve cells in the developing brain (Impagnatiello et al., 1998).

Because not all monozygotic twins are concordant for the illness, its cause cannot be purely genetic. Schizophrenia may stem from a series of neurological insults in fetal life (Picker, 2005; Rapoport, Addington, & Frangou, 2005), such as exposure to influenza in the first trimester of pregnancy (Brown, Begg, et al., 2004) and to maternal rubella and respiratory infections in the second and third trimesters. Infants born in urban areas or in late winter or early spring appear to be at increased risk, as are those whose mothers experienced obstetric complications or who were poor or severely deprived as a result of war or famine (Picker, 2005). A link between fetal malnutrition and schizophrenia has been demonstrated in studies in the Netherlands (Susser & Lin, 1992), Finland (Wahlbeck, Forsen, Osmond, Barker, & Eriksson, 2001), and China (St. Clair et al., 2005).

Advanced paternal age is a risk factor for schizophrenia. In large population-based studies in Jerusalem and Denmark, the risk of the disorder was greatly increased when the father was age 50 or more (Byrne, Agerbo, Ewald, Eaton, & Mortenson, 2003; Malaspina et al., 2001). A study of 700,000 Swedish births estimated that 15.5 percent of schizophrenia cases involved a father who was over 30 at the time of the birth (Sipos et al., 2004).

What's your view ?

- What practical difference does it make whether a trait such as obesity, intelligence, or shyness is influenced more by heredity or by environment, since heritability can be measured only for a population, not for an individual?

schizophrenia Neurological disorder marked by loss of contact with reality; symptoms include hallucinations and delusions.

Checkpoint ✔

Can you . . .

✔ Assess the evidence for genetic and environmental influences on obesity, intelligence, temperament, and schizophrenia?

Refocus

On the basis of the information given about Louise Brown in the Focus vignette at the beginning of this chapter:

- Since Louise Brown's birth, how have alternate means of conception affected the likelihood of multiple births and the treatment of infertility?

- What hereditary and environmental influences may explain some of Louise Brown's characteristics?

- The Focus vignette gives virtually no information about Louise Brown's test-tube sister, Natalie, but what factors do you imagine might have affected any similarities and differences between them?

In this chapter we have looked at some ways in which heredity and environment act to make children what they are. A child's first environment is the world within the womb, which we discuss in Chapter 4.

Summary and Key Terms

Becoming Parents: How Conception Occurs

Guidepost 1 How does conception normally occur, and how have beliefs about conception changed?

- Early beliefs about conception reflected unscientific approaches to the understanding of nature and of male and female anatomy.

- Fertilization, the union of an ovum and a sperm, results in the formation of a one-celled zygote, which then duplicates itself by cell division.

  fertilization (62) zygote (62)

Infertility

Guidepost 2 What causes infertility, and what are alternative ways of becoming parents?

- The most common cause of infertility in men is a low sperm count; the most common cause in women is blockage of the fallopian tubes.

- Assisted reproduction by in vitro fertilization or other means may involve ethical and practical issues.

- Multiple births can occur either by the fertilization of more than one ovum (or one ovum that has split) or by the splitting of one fertilized ovum.

- Dizygotic (fraternal) twins have different genetic makeups and may be of different sexes; monozygotic (identical) twins have the same genetic makeup but may differ in some respects.

  infertility (62)

Mechanisms of Heredity

Guidepost 3 What genetic mechanisms determine sex, physical appearance, and other characteristics?

- The basic functional units of heredity are the genes, which are made of deoxyribonucleic acid (DNA). DNA carries the biochemical instructions that govern the formation and functions of various body cells. The genetic code, the chemical structure of DNA, determines all inherited characteristics. Each gene seems to be located by function in a definite position on a particular chromosome. The complete sequence of genes in the human body is the human genome.

  deoxyribonucleic acid (DNA) (66) genetic code (66) chromosomes (67) genes (67)

- At conception, each normal human being receives 23 chromosomes from the mother and 23 from the father. These form 23 pairs of chromosomes—22 pairs of autosomes and 1 pair of sex chromosomes. A child who receives an X chromosome from each parent is genetically female. A child who receives a Y chromosome from the father is genetically male.

- The simplest patterns of genetic transmission are dominant and recessive inheritance. When a pair of alleles are the same, a person is homozygous for the trait; when they are different, the person is heterozygous.

  autosomes (68) sex chromosomes (68) alleles (69) homozygous (69) heterozygous (69) dominant inheritance (69) recessive inheritance (69)

- Most normal human characteristics are the result of polygenic inheritance or multifactorial transmission, or sometimes of mutations. Except in the case of monozygotic twins, each child inherits a unique genotype, but the phenotype may not express the underlying genotype.

  polygenic inheritance (70) mutations (70) multifactorial transmission (70) phenotype (70) genotype (70)

Genetic and Chromosomal Abnormalities

Guidepost 4 How are birth defects and disorders transmitted?

- Birth defects and diseases may result from simple dominant, recessive, or sex-linked inheritance; from mutations; from genome imprinting; or from chromosomal abnormalities.

- Genetic counseling can provide information about the mathematical odds of bearing children with certain defects. Genetic testing involves risks as well as benefits.

  incomplete dominance (73) sex-linked inheritance (73) Down syndrome (75) genetic counseling (76)

Nature and Nurture: Influences of Heredity and Environment

Guidepost 5 How do scientists study the relative influences of heredity and environment, and how do heredity and environment work together?

- Research in behavioral genetics is based on the assumption that the relative influences of heredity and environment can be measured statistically. If heredity is an important influence on a trait, genetically closer persons will be more similar in that trait. Family studies, adoption studies, and twin studies enable researchers to measure the heritability of traits.

- Critics claim that traditional behavioral genetics is too simplistic. Instead, they study complex developmental systems, reflecting a confluence of constitutional, economic, social, and biological influences.

- The concepts of reaction range, canalization, genotype-environment interaction, genotype-environment correlation (or covariance), and niche-picking describe ways in which heredity and environment work together.
- Siblings tend to be more different than alike in intelligence and personality. Many experiences that strongly affect development are different for each sibling.

behavioral genetics (78)   **heritability (78)**   **concordant (79)**
reaction range (80)   **canalization (80)**   **genotype-environment interaction (81)**   **genotype-environment correlation (82)**   **nonshared environmental effects (82)**
epigenesis (83)

Some Characteristics Influenced by Heredity and Environment

Guidepost 6   What roles do heredity and environment play in physical health, intelligence, and personality?

- Health, obesity, longevity, intelligence, and temperament are influenced by both heredity and environment, and their relative influences may vary across the life span.
- Schizophrenia is a psychopathological disorder influenced by both heredity and environment.

obesity (84)   **temperament (84)**   **schizophrenia (85)**

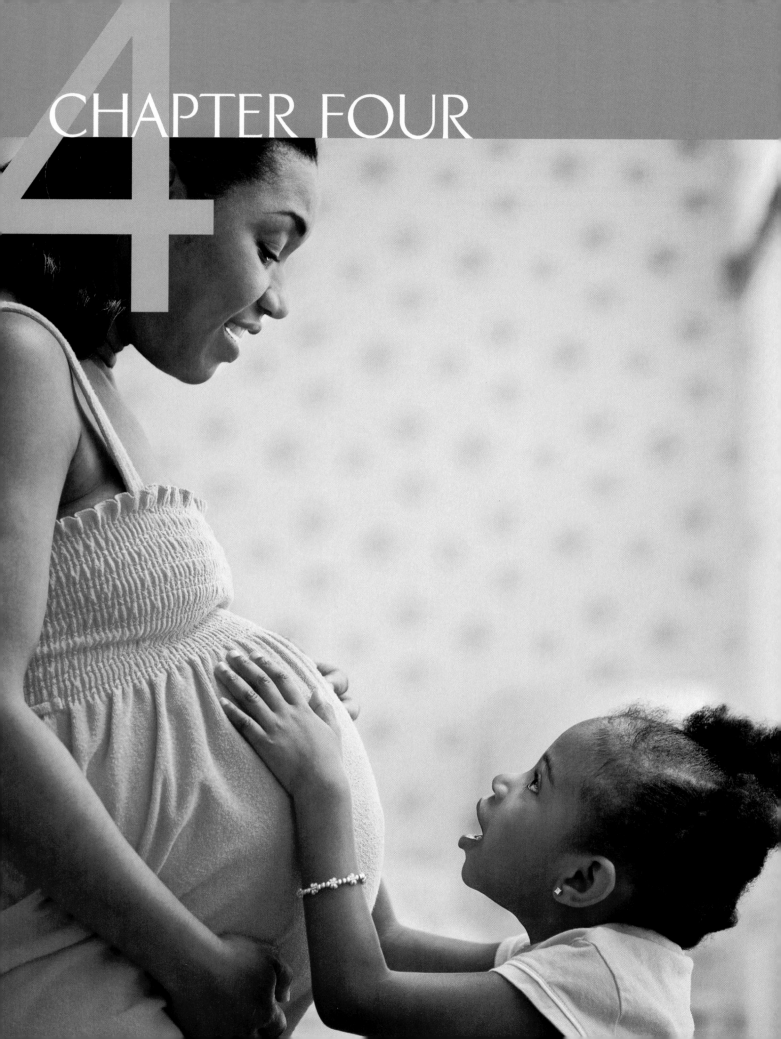

CHAPTER FOUR

Pregnancy and Prenatal Development

If I could have watched you grow
as a magical mother might,
if I could have seen through my magical transparent
belly,
there would have been such ripening within. . . .

—Anne Sexton, 1966

Focus *Abel Dorris and Fetal Alcohol Syndrome*

Abel Dorris

Fetal alcohol syndrome (FAS), a cluster of abnormalities shown by children whose mothers drank during pregnancy, is a leading cause of mental retardation. But in 1971, when the writer Michael Dorris adopted a 3-year-old Sioux boy whose mother had been a heavy drinker, the facts about FAS were not widely publicized or scientifically investigated, though the syndrome had been observed for centuries. Not until 11 years later, as Dorris relates in *The Broken Cord* (1989), did he discover the source of his adopted son's developmental problems.

The boy, named Abel ("Adam" in the book), had been born almost 7 weeks premature, with low birth weight, and had been abused and malnourished before being removed to a foster home. His mother had died at 35 of alcohol poisoning. His birth father had been beaten to death in an alley after a string of arrests. The boy was small for his age, was not toilet-trained, and could speak only about twenty words. Although he had been diagnosed as mildly retarded, Dorris was certain that with a positive environment the boy would catch up.

Abel did not catch up. When he turned 4, he was still in diapers and weighed only 27 pounds. He had trouble remembering names of playmates. His activity level was unusually high, and the circumference of his skull was unusually small. He suffered severe, unexplained seizures.

As the months went by, Abel had trouble learning to count, identify primary colors, and tie his shoes. Before entering school, he was labeled learning disabled. His IQ was, and remained, in the mid-60s. Thanks to the efforts of a devoted first-grade teacher, Abel did learn to read and write, but his comprehension was low. When the boy finished elementary school in 1983, he "still could not add, subtract, count money, or consistently identify the town, state, country, or planet of his residence" (Dorris, 1989, pp. 127–128).

By then, Michael Dorris had solved the puzzle of what was wrong with his son. As an associate professor of Native American studies at Dartmouth College, he was acquainted with the cultural pressures that make drinking prevalent among American Indians. In 1982, the year before Abel's graduation, Michael visited a treatment center for chemically dependent teenagers at a Sioux reservation in South Dakota. There he was astonished to see three boys who "could have been [Abel's] twin brothers" (Dorris, 1989, p. 137). They not only looked like Abel but acted like him.

Fetal alcohol syndrome had been identified during the 1970s, while Abel was growing up. Once alcohol enters a fetus's bloodstream, it remains there in high concentrations for long periods of time, causing brain damage and harming other body organs. There is no cure. As one medical expert wrote, "for the fetus the hangover may last a lifetime" (Enloe, 1980, p. 15).

For the family, too, the effects of FAS can be devastating. The years of constant attempts first to restore Abel to normality and then to come to terms with the damage irrevocably done in the womb may well have been a factor in the later problems in Michael Dorris's marriage to the writer Louise Erdrich, which culminated in divorce proceedings and his suicide in 1997 at age 52. According to Erdrich (personal communication, March 1, 2000), Dorris suffered from extreme depression, possibly exacerbated by the difficulties he faced as a father.

As for Abel Dorris, at age 20 he had entered a vocational training program and had moved into a supervised home, taking along his collections of stuffed animals, paper dolls, newspaper cartoons, family photographs, and old birthday cards. At 23, five years before his father's death, he was hit by a car and killed (Lyman, 1997).

● ● ●

For students of child development, the story of Abel Dorris is a devastating reminder of the responsibility prospective biological parents have for the crucial development that goes on before birth. The womb is the developing child's first environment, and its impact on the child is immense. In addition to what the mother does and what happens to her, there are other environmental influences—from those that affect the father's sperm to the technological, social, and cultural environment—which may affect the kind of prenatal care a woman gets.

In this chapter we begin by looking at the experience of pregnancy and how prospective parents prepare for a birth. We trace how the fertilized ovum becomes an embryo and then a fetus, already with a personality of its own. Then we discuss environmental factors that can affect the developing person-to-be, describe techniques for determining whether development is proceeding normally, and explain the importance of prenatal care.

After you have read and studied this chapter, you should be able to answer each of the Guidepost questions on the following page. Look for them again in the margins throughout the chapter, where they point to important concepts. To check your understanding of these Guideposts, review the end of chapter summary. Checkpoints located throughout the chapter will help you verify your understanding of what you have read.

1. What are the three stages of prenatal development, and what happens during each stage?

2. What environmental influences can affect prenatal development?

3. What techniques can assess a fetus's health and well-being, and what is the importance of prenatal and preconception care?

Prenatal Development: Three Stages

Guidepost 1

What are the three stages of prenatal development, and what happens during each stage?

If you had been born in China, you would probably celebrate your birthday on your estimated date of conception rather than your date of birth. This Chinese custom recognizes the importance of *gestation,* the approximately 38-week period of development between conception and birth. *Gestational age* is usually dated from the first day of an expectant mother's last menstrual cycle. The normal range of gestation is between 38 and 42 weeks.

For many women, the first clear (but not necessarily reliable) sign of pregnancy is a missed menstrual period. But even before that first missed period, a pregnant woman's body undergoes subtle but noticeable changes. Table 4-1 lists early signs and symptoms of pregnancy. Although these signs are not unique to pregnancy, a woman who experiences one or more of them may wish to take a home pregnancy test or to seek medical confirmation that she is pregnant.

Prenatal development takes place in three stages: *germinal, embryonic,* and *fetal.* (Table 4-2 gives a month-by-month description.) During these three stages of gestation, the

Table 4-1	Early Signs and Symptoms of Pregnancy
Physical Change	**Causes and Timing**
Tender, swollen breasts or nipples	Increased production of the female hormones estrogen and progesterone stimulates breast growth to prepare for producing milk (most noticeable in a first pregnancy).
Fatigue; need to take extra naps	Woman's heart is pumping harder and faster to produce extra blood to carry nutrients to the unborn baby. Stepped-up production of hormones takes extra effort. Progesterone depresses central nervous system and may cause sleepiness. Concerns about pregnancy may sap energy.
Slight bleeding or cramping	*Implantation bleeding* may occur about 10 to 14 days after fertilization when fertilized ovum attaches to lining of uterus. Many women also have cramps (similar to menstrual cramps) as the uterus begins to enlarge.
Nausea with or without vomiting	Rising levels of estrogen produced by placenta and fetus cause stomach to empty more slowly. Also, heightened sense of smell may trigger nausea in response to certain odors, such as coffee, meat, dairy products, or spicy foods. *Morning sickness* may begin as early as 2 weeks after conception, but usually around 4 to 8 weeks, and may occur at any time of day.
Food cravings	Hormonal changes may change food preferences, especially during first trimester, when hormones have greatest impact.
Frequent urination	Enlarging uterus during first trimester exerts pressure on the bladder.
Frequent, mild headaches	Increased blood circulation caused by hormonal changes may bring on headaches.
Constipation	Increase in progesterone may slow digestion, so food passes more slowly through intestinal tract.
Mood swings	Flood of hormones early in pregnancy can produce emotional highs and lows.
Faintness and dizziness	Lightheaded feeling may be triggered by blood vessel dilation and low blood pressure; also may be triggered by low blood sugar.
Raised basal body temperature	Basal body temperature (taken first thing in the morning) normally rises soon after ovulation each month and then drops during menstruation. When menstruation ceases, temperature remains elevated.

Source: Mayo Clinic, 2005.

Table 4-2 Prenatal Development

Month	Description

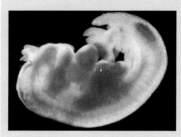

1 month

During the first month, growth is more rapid than at any other time during prenatal or postnatal life: The embryo reaches a size 10,000 times greater than the zygote. By the end of the first month, it measures about ½ inch in length. Blood flows through its veins and arteries, which are very small. It has a minuscule heart, beating 65 times a minute. It already has the beginnings of a brain, kidneys, liver, and digestive tract. The umbilical cord, its lifeline to the mother, is working. By looking very closely through a microscope, it is possible to see the swellings on the head that will eventually become eyes, ears, mouth, and nose. Its sex cannot yet be detected.

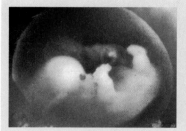

7 weeks

By the end of the second month, the fetus is less than 1 inch long and weighs only ⅓ ounce. Its head is half its total body length. Facial parts are clearly developed, with tongue and teeth buds. The arms have hands, fingers, and thumbs, and the legs have knees, ankles, and toes. The fetus has a thin covering of skin and can make handprints and footprints. Bone cells appear at about 8 weeks. Brain impulses coordinate the function of the organ system. Sex organs are developing; the heartbeat is steady. The stomach produces digestive juices; the liver, blood cells. The kidneys remove uric acid from the blood. The skin is now sensitive enough to react to tactile stimulation. If an aborted 8-week-old fetus is stroked, it reacts by flexing its trunk, extending its head, and moving back its arms.

3 months

By the end of the third month, the fetus weighs about 1 ounce and measures about 3 inches in length. It has fingernails, toenails, eyelids (still closed), vocal cords, lips, and a prominent nose. Its head is still large—about one-third its total length—and its forehead is high. Sex can easily be detected. The organ systems are functioning, and so the fetus may now breathe, swallow amniotic fluid into the lungs and expel it, and occasionally urinate. Its ribs and vertebrae have turned into cartilage. The fetus can now make a variety of specialized responses: It can move its legs, feet, thumbs, and head; its mouth can open and close and swallow. If its eyelids are touched, it squints; if its palm is touched, it makes a partial fist; if its lip is touched, it will suck; and if the sole of the foot is stroked, the toes will fan out. These reflexes will be present at birth but will disappear during the first months of life.

4 months

The body is catching up to the head, which is now only one-fourth the total body length, the same proportion it will be at birth. The fetus now measures 8 to 10 inches and weighs about 6 ounces. The umbilical cord is as long as the fetus and will continue to grow with it. The placenta is now fully developed. The mother may be able to feel the fetus kicking, a movement known as *quickening*, which some societies and religious groups consider the beginning of human life. The reflex activities that appeared in the third month are now brisker because of increased muscular development.

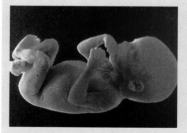

5 months

The fetus, now weighing about 12 ounces to 1 pound and measuring about 1 foot, begins to show signs of an individual personality. It has definite sleep-wake patterns, has a favorite position in the uterus (called its *lie*), and becomes more active—kicking, stretching, squirming, and even hiccuping. By putting an ear to the mother's abdomen, it is possible to hear the fetal heartbeat. The sweat and sebaceous glands are functioning. The respiratory system is not yet adequate to sustain life outside the womb; a baby born at this time does not usually survive. Coarse hair has begun to grow for eyebrows and eyelashes, fine hair is on the head, and a woolly hair called *lanugo* covers the body.

Month	Description

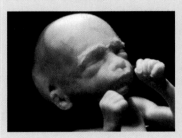

6 months

The rate of fetal growth has slowed down a little—by the end of the sixth month, the fetus is about 14 inches long and weighs 1¼ pounds. It has fat pads under the skin; the eyes are complete, opening, closing, and looking in all directions. It can hear, and it can make a fist with a strong grip. A fetus born during the sixth months still has only a slight chance of survival, because the breathing apparatus has not matured. However, medical advances have made survival increasingly likely.

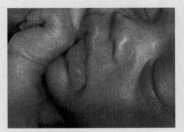

7 months

By the end of the seventh month, the fetus, about 16 inches long and weighing 3 to 5 pounds, has fully developed reflex patterns. It cries, breathes, and swallows, and it may suck its thumb. The lanugo may disappear at about this time, or it may remain until shortly after birth. Head hair may continue to grow. The chances that a fetus weighing at least 3½ pounds will survive are good, provided it receives intensive medical attention. It will probably need to be kept in an isolette until a weight of 5 pounds is attained.

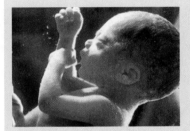

8 months

The 8-month-old fetus is 18 to 20 inches long and weighs between 5 and 7 pounds. It living quarters are becoming cramped, and so its movements are curtailed. During this month and the next, a layer of fat develops over the fetus's entire body, which will enable it to adjust to varying temperatures outside the womb.

9 months—newborn

About a week before birth, the fetus stops growing, having reached an average weight of about 7½ pounds and a length of about 20 inches, with boys tending to be a little longer and heavier than girls. Fat pads continue to form, the organ systems are operating more efficiently, the heart rate increases, and more wastes are expelled through the umbilical cord. The reddish color of the skin is fading. At birth, the fetus will have been in the womb for about 266 days, although gestational age is usually estimated at 280 days because most doctors date the pregnancy from the mother's last menstrual period.

Note: Even in these early stages, individuals differ. The figures and descriptions given here represent averages.

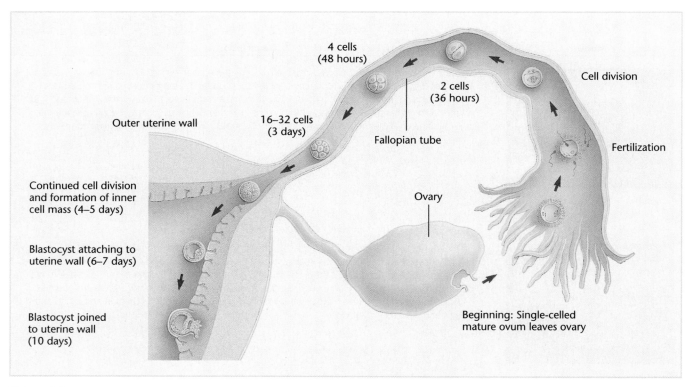

Figure 4-1

Early development of a human embryo. This simplified diagram shows the progress of the ovum as it leaves the ovary, is fertilized in the fallopian tube, and then divides while traveling to the lining of the uterus. Now a blastocyst, it is implanted in the uterus, where it will grow larger and more complex until it is ready to be born.

fertilized ovum, or *zygote,* grows into an *embryo* and then a *fetus.* What turns a single-celled zygote into a creature with a specific shape and pattern? Research suggests that an identifiable group of genes is responsible for this transformation in vertebrates, presumably including human beings. These genes produce molecules called *morphogens,* which are switched on after fertilization and begin sculpting arms, hands, fingers, vertebrae, ribs, a brain, and other body parts (Echeland et al., 1993; Krauss, Concordet, & Ingham, 1993; Riddle, Johnson, Laufer, & Tabin, 1993).

Both before and after birth, development proceeds according to two fundamental principles: Growth and motor development occur from top down and from the center of the body outward.

The **cephalocaudal principle** (from Latin, meaning "head to tail") dictates that development proceeds from the head to the lower part of the trunk. An embryo's head, brain, and eyes develop earliest and are disproportionately large until the other parts catch up. At 2 months of gestation, the embryo's head is half the length of the body. By the time of birth, the head is only one-fourth the length of the body but is still disproportionately large. According to the **proximodistal principle** (from Latin, "near to far"), development proceeds from parts near the center of the body to outer ones. The embryo's head and trunk develop before the limbs, and the arms and legs before the fingers and toes.

The Germinal Stage (Fertilization to 2 Weeks)

During the **germinal stage,** the first 2 weeks after fertilization, the zygote divides, becomes more complex, and is implanted in the wall of the uterus (Figure 4-1).

Within 36 hours after fertilization, the zygote enters a period of rapid cell division and duplication, or *mitosis.* Some 72 hours after fertilization, it has divided into 16 to 32 cells; 24 hours later it has 64 cells. This division continues until the original single cell has developed into the 800 billion or more specialized cells that make up the human body.

While the fertilized ovum is dividing, it is also making its way down the fallopian tube to the uterus, a journey of 3 or 4 days. Its form changes into a *blastocyst,* a fluid-filled

cephalocaudal principle Principle that development proceeds in a head-to-tail direction; that is, that upper parts of the body develop before lower parts of the trunk.

proximodistal principle Principle that development proceeds from within to without; that is, that parts of the body near the center develop before the extremities.

germinal stage First 2 weeks of prenatal development, characterized by rapid cell division, increasing complexity and differentiation, and implantation in the wall of the uterus.

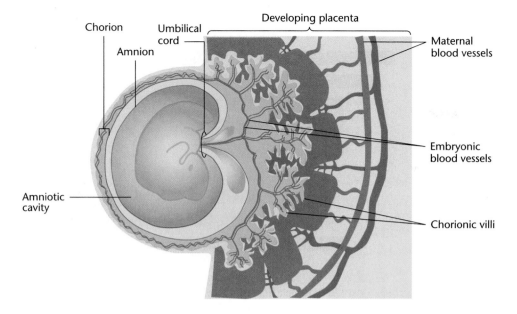

Chorion
Umbilical cord
Amnion
Developing placenta
Maternal blood vessels
Amniotic cavity
Embryonic blood vessels
Chorionic villi

Figure 4-2

The developing embryo. After implantation in the uterine wall, the embryo is enclosed and cushioned by the fluid-filled *amniotic cavity,* or amniotic sac. The surrounding membrane, the *amnion,* gradually expands to enlarge the cavity in which the growing embryo (and later the fetus) floats. Through the *umbilical cord,* the embryo receives nourishment and oxygen from the mother and eliminates wastes. This is accomplished through a complex system of exchange of blood between the maternal and embryonic circulatory systems. This exchange takes place across the *placenta,* without direct contact between the two blood systems. The exchange occurs through the action of tiny hairlike projections from the outer membrane, the *chorion,* which diffuse and exchange the blood.

sphere, which floats freely in the uterus until the 6th day after fertilization, when it begins to implant itself in the uterine wall. The blastocyst actively participates in the implanting process through a complex system of hormonally regulated signaling (Norwitz, Schust, & Fisher, 2001).

Only about 10 to 20 percent of fertilized ova complete the task of implantation and continue to develop. For implantation to be successful, a protein called *L-selectin,* secreted for only a short time during a woman's monthly cycle, must interlock with carbohydrate molecules on the surface of the uterus, stopping the blastocyst's free-floating motion (Genbacev et al., 2003).

Before implantation, as cell differentiation begins, some cells around the edge of the blastocyst cluster on one side to form the *embryonic disk,* a thickened cell mass from which the embryo begins to develop. This mass is already differentiating into two layers. The upper layer, the *ectoderm,* will become the outer layer of skin, the nails, hair, teeth, sensory organs, and the nervous system, including the brain and spinal cord. The lower layer, the *endoderm,* will become the digestive system, liver, pancreas, salivary glands, and respiratory system. Later a middle layer, the *mesoderm,* will develop and differentiate into the inner layer of skin, muscles, skeleton, and excretory and circulatory systems.

Other parts of the blastocyst begin to develop into organs that will nurture and protect the embryo: the *amniotic cavity,* or *amniotic sac,* with its outer layers, the *amnion* and *chorion,* the *placenta,* and the *umbilical cord* (Figure 4-2). The *amniotic sac* is a fluid-filled membrane that encases the developing baby, giving it room to move. The *placenta,* which contains both maternal and embryonic tissue, develops in the uterus to allow oxgen, nourishment, and wastes to pass betweeen mother and baby. It is connected to the embryo by the *umbilical cord.* Nutrients from the mother pass from her blood to the embryonic blood vessels, and are then carried, via the umbilical cord, to the embryo. In turn, embryonic blood vessels in the umbilical cord carry embryonic wastes to the placenta, where they can be eliminated by maternal blood vessels. The mother's and embryo's circulatory systems are not directly linked; instead, this exchange occurs by diffusion across the blood vessel walls. The placenta also helps to combat internal infection and gives the unborn child immunity to various diseases. It produces the hormones that support pregnancy, prepare the mother's breasts for lactation, and eventually stimulate the uterine contractions that will expel the baby from the mother's body.

The Embryonic Stage (2 to 8 Weeks)

During the **embryonic stage,** the second stage of gestation, from about 2 to 8 weeks, the organs and major body systems—respiratory, digestive, and nervous—develop rapidly. This is a critical period, when the embryo is most vulnerable to destructive influences in the prenatal environment (Figure 4-3). An organ system or structure that is still developing at

embryonic stage Second stage of prenatal development (2 to 8 weeks), characterized by rapid growth and development of major body systems and organs.

Figure 4-3

When birth defects occur. Body parts and systems are most vulnerable to damage when they are developing most rapidly (*darkly shaded areas*), generally within the first trimester of pregnancy.

Note: Intervals of time are not all equal.

Source: J. E. Brody, 1995; data from March of Dimes.

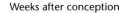

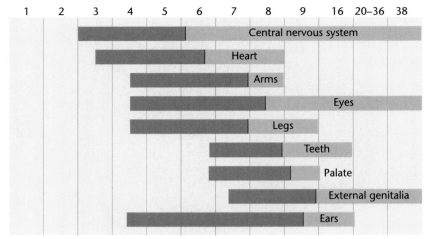

the time of exposure is most likely to be affected. Defects that occur later in pregnancy are likely to be less serious. (In Chapter 6, we discuss brain growth and development, which begins during the embryonic stage and continues after birth and beyond.)

The most severely defective embryos usually do not survive beyond the first *trimester,* or 3-month period, of pregnancy. A **spontaneous abortion,** commonly called a *miscarriage,* is the expulsion from the uterus of an embryo or fetus that is unable to survive outside the womb. As many as 1 in 4 recognized pregnancies end in miscarriage, and the actual figure may be as high as 1 in 2 because many spontaneous abortions take place before the woman realizes she is pregnant. About 3 out of 4 miscarriages occur during the first trimester (Neville n.d.). Most miscarriages result from abnormal pregnancies; about 50 to 70 percent involve chromosomal abnormalities. Losing an unborn baby can be extremely painful, as we discuss in Box 4-1.

Males are more likely than females to be spontaneously aborted or to be *stillborn* (dead at or after the 20th week of gestation; see Chapter 5). Thus, although about 125 males are conceived for every 100 females, only about 105 boys are born for every 100 girls. Males' greater vulnerability continues after birth: More of them die early in life, and at every age they are more susceptible to many disorders. As a result, there are only 96 males for every 100 females in the United States (Martin, Hamilton, et al., 2006; U.S. Department of Health and Human Services [USDHHS] 1996a).

The Fetal Stage (8 Weeks to Birth)

The appearance of the first bone cells at about 8 weeks signals the **fetal stage,** the final stage of gestation. During this period, the fetus grows rapidly to about twenty times its previous length, and organs and body systems become more complex. Right up to birth, "finishing touches" such as fingernails, toenails, and eyelids develop.

Fetuses are not passive passengers in their mothers' wombs. They breathe, kick, turn, flex their bodies, do somersaults, squint, swallow, make fists, hiccup, and suck their thumbs. The flexible membranes of the uterine walls and amniotic sac, which surround the protective buffer of amniotic fluid, permit and stimulate limited movement. Fetuses also can feel pain, but it is unlikely that they do so before the third trimester (Lee, Ralston, Drey, Partridge, & Rosen, 2005).

Scientists can observe fetal movement through **ultrasound,** using high-frequency sound waves to detect the outline of the fetus. Other instruments can monitor heart rate, changes in activity level, states of sleep and wakefulness, and cardiac reactivity. In one study, fetuses monitored from 20 weeks of gestation until term had increasingly slower but more variable heart rates—possibly in response to the increasing stress of the mother's pregnancy—and greater cardiac response to stimulation. They also showed less, but more vigorous, activity—perhaps a result of the increasing difficulty of movement for a growing fetus in a constricted environment, as well as of maturation of the nervous system (DiPietro,

spontaneous abortion Natural expulsion from the uterus of a embryo that cannot survive outside the womb; also called *miscarriage.*

fetal stage Final stage of prenatal development (from 8 weeks to birth), characterized by increased differentiation of body parts and greatly enlarged body size.

ultrasound Prenatal medical procedure using high-frequency sound waves to detect the outline of a fetus and its movements, so as to determine whether a pregnancy is progressing normally.

Box 4-1 *Mourning a Miscarriage or Stillbirth*

At a Buddhist temple in Tokyo, small statues of infants accompanied by toys and gifts are left as offerings to Jizo, an enlightened being who is believed to watch over miscarried and aborted fetuses and eventually, through reincarnation, to guide them into a new life. The ritual of *mizuko kuyo,* a rite of apology and remembrance, is observed as a means of making amends to the lost life (Orenstein, 2002).

The Japanese word *mizuko* means "water child." Japanese Buddhists believe that life flows into an organism gradually, like water, and a mizuko is somewhere on the continuum between life and death (Orenstein, 2002). In English, in contrast, there is no word for a miscarried, aborted, or stillborn fetus, nor any ritual of mourning. Families, friends, and health professionals tend to avoid talking about such losses, which may seem insignificant compared with the loss of a living child (Van, 2001). Or people make unhelpful comments such as, "It was better this way" or "This happens all the time." (See table for advice on what to say to someone who has suffered a pregnancy loss.) Grief can be more wrenching without social support, and "the silence our society casts over the topic makes it hard for women and families to get the information and help they need" (Grady, 2002, p. 1).

How do prospective parents cope with the loss of a child they never knew? Because each person's or couple's experience of loss is unique, it is hard to generalize (Van, 2001). A woman may feel a sense of inadequacy or failure. Often there is anger (at herself or others for not being able to prevent the miscarriage or stillbirth, or at her partner for not being supportive enough), guilt (if the woman had mixed feelings about becoming a mother, or if she thinks the loss of the baby may have resulted from something she did), or anxiety ("Will I be able to have another child?"). Children in the family may blame themselves, especially if they had some negative feelings about the expected birth. The parents may mourn not only for what is now lost but for what the lost child might have become. Feelings of pain and grief may recur, often on the expected due date or on the anniversary of the loss (Neville, n.d.).

Differences in the ways men and women grieve may be a source of tension and divisiveness in a couple's relationship (Caelli, Downie, & Letendre, 2002). The man may have been less focused on the pregnancy, and his body does not give him physical reminders of the loss (Grady, 2002). In one small study, eleven men whose child had died in utero reported being overcome with frustration and helplessness during and after the delivery, but several found relief in supporting their partners (Samuelsson, Radestad, & Segesten, 2001). In another study, grieving parents perceived their spouses and extended families as most helpful and their doctors as least helpful. Some bereaved parents benefited from a support group, and some not (DiMarco,

Talking to Someone Who Has Had a Miscarriage or Stillbirth

When Speaking to a Friend Who Has Experienced Pregnancy Loss

Do . . .	Bring up the subject; Ignoring the loss can be painful.
	Listen with empathy and compassion.
	Express sadness and regret.
	Let your friend grieve, cry, and take the time necessary to heal.
Don't . . .	Minimize or trivialize the loss or pain.
	Ask why it happened—often there is no real answer.
	Expect your friend to move on before she is ready.

Source: Grady, 2002.

Menke, & McNamara, 2001). Couples who have gone through pregnancy loss may need extra-compassionate care during a later pregnancy (Caelli et al., 2002).

Grief counselors suggest that adjustment to a pregnancy loss may be eased if the parents are allowed to see the remains—something that is often not possible. Other suggestions are (Brin, 2004; Grady, 2002; Neville, n.d.)

- Set aside time to talk about the loss.
- Create and hold a memorial ceremony or ritual; online resources may help.
- Name the miscarried or stillborn baby.
- Plant a tree or flowering bush in the lost baby's name.
- Write poetry or keep a journal.
- Put items such as an ultrasound photo in a memory box.
- Create a special certificate.
- Seek private counseling or a support group.

What's your view

- Have you ever had a spontaneous abortion (miscarriage) or stillbirth, or do you know anyone who has? If so, how did you or your acquaintance cope with the loss? How did others react to it?
- Do you think recognition of such losses through ceremonies or rituals would be helpful?

Check it out

Go to www.nationalshareoffice.com for information on pregnancy and infant loss support groups and items for creating appropriate rituals.

Hodgson, Costigan, Hilton, & Johnson, 1996). A significant jump in all these aspects of fetal development seems to occur between 28 and 32 weeks; it may help explain why infants born prematurely at this time are more likely to survive and flourish than those born earlier (DiPietro et al., 1996). This jump occurred among fetuses in two contrasting cultures, Baltimore and Lima, Peru—suggesting that this aspect of fetal neurological development is universal (DiPietro et al., 2004).

The movements and activity level of fetuses show marked individual differences, and their heart rates vary in regularity and speed. There also are differences between males and

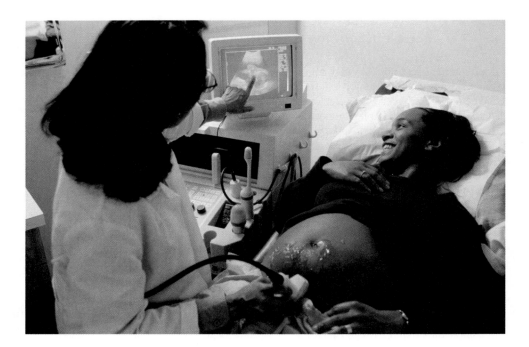

The most effective way to prevent birth complications is early prenatal care, which may include ultrasound checkups, such as this woman is having, to follow the fetus's development. Ultrasound is a diagnostic tool that presents an immediate image of the fetus in the womb.

Checkpoint ✔

Can you . . .

✔ Identify two principles that govern physical development and give examples of their application during the prenatal period?

✔ Describe how a zygote becomes an embryo?

✔ Explain why defects and miscarriages are most likely to occur during the embryonic stage?

✔ Describe findings about fetal activity, sensory development, and memory?

females. Male fetuses, regardless of size, are more active and tend to move more vigorously than female fetuses throughout gestation. Thus infant boys' tendency to be more active than girls may be at least partly inborn (DiPietro et al., 1996).

Beginning at about the 12th week of gestation, the fetus swallows and inhales some of the amniotic fluid in which it floats. The amniotic fluid contains substances that cross the placenta from the mother's bloodstream and enter the fetus's bloodstream. Partaking of these substances may stimulate the budding senses of taste and smell and may contribute to the development of organs needed for breathing and digestion (Mennella & Beauchamp, 1996a; Ronca & Alberts, 1995; Smotherman & Robinson, 1995, 1996). Mature taste cells appear at about 14 weeks of gestation. The olfactory system, which controls the sense of smell, also is well developed before birth (Bartoshuk & Beauchamp, 1994; Mennella & Beauchamp, 1996a).

Fetuses respond to the mother's voice and heartbeat and the vibrations of her body, suggesting that they can hear and feel. Hungry infants, no matter on which side they are held, turn toward the breast in the direction from which they hear the mother's voice (Noirot & Algeria, 1983, cited in Rovee-Collier, 1996). Thus familiarity with the mother's voice may have an evolutionary survival function: to help newborns locate the source of food. Responses to sound and vibration seem to begin at 26 weeks of gestation, rise, and then reach a plateau at about 32 weeks (Kisilevsky, Muir, & Low, 1992).

Fetuses seem to learn and remember. In one experiment, 3-day-old infants sucked more on a nipple that activated a recording of a story their mother had frequently read aloud during the last 6 weeks of pregnancy than they did on nipples that activated recordings of two other stories. Apparently, the infants recognized the pattern of sound they had heard in the womb. A control group, whose mothers had not recited a story before birth, responded equally to all three recordings (DeCasper & Spence, 1986). Similar experiments have found that newborns age 2 to 4 days prefer musical and speech sequences heard before birth. They also prefer their mother's voice to those of other women, female voices to male voices, and their mother's native language to another language (DeCasper & Fifer, 1980; DeCasper & Spence, 1986; Fifer & Moon, 1995; Lecanuet, Granier-Deferre, & Busnel, 1995; Moon, Cooper, & Fifer, 1993).

How do we know that these preferences develop before rather than after birth? When 60 fetuses heard a female voice reading, their heart rate increased if the voice was their mother's and decreased if it belonged to a stranger (Kisilevsky et al., 2003). In another study, newborns were given the choice of sucking to turn on a recording of the mother's voice or a filtered version of her voice as it might sound in the womb. The newborns sucked more often to turn on the filtered version, suggesting that fetuses develop a preference for the kinds of sounds they hear before birth (Fifer & Moon, 1995; Moon & Fifer, 1990).

Prenatal Development: Environmental Influences

Maternal Factors

Because the prenatal environment is the mother's body, virtually everything that affects her well-being, from her diet to her moods, may alter her unborn child's environment and influence its growth. However, not all environmental hazards are equally risky for all fetuses. Some factors that are **teratogenic** (birth defect–producing) in some cases have little or no effect in others. The timing of exposure (refer back to Figure 4-3), the dose, duration, and interaction with other teratogenic factors may make a difference. Sometimes vulnerability may depend on a gene either in the fetus or in the mother. For example, fetuses with a particular variant of a growth gene, called *transforming growth factor alpha,* have six times more risk than other fetuses of developing a cleft palate if the mother smokes while pregnant (Hwang et al., 1995).

teratogenic Capable of causing birth defects.

Technology that permits a woman to view images of her fetus early in her pregnancy may help motivate her to engage in nurturing behaviors, such as eating properly and abstaining from alcohol and drugs (Salisbury, Law, LaGasse, & Lester, 2003).

Nutrition and Maternal Weight

The evolutionary biologist David Haig (1993) suggests that pregnancy creates an unconscious conflict between mother and fetus over the nutrients the mother provides. From an evolutionary perspective, it is adaptive for the fetus to obtain maximum amounts of nutrients from the mother, whereas it is adaptive for the mother to limit the transfer of nutrients to the fetus so as to maintain her health and her ability to bear future children. Yet, because the fetus has direct access to the maternal blood supply through the placenta, the mother does not have much control over the amount of nutrients she "loses" to her fetus. It is important, then, for an expectant mother to take in enough nutrients to adequately feed herself and her fetus.

Pregnant women typically need 300 to 500 additional calories a day, including extra protein. Women of normal weight who gain 25 to 35 pounds are less likely to have birth complications or to bear babies whose weight at birth is dangerously low. However, desirable weight gain depends on individual factors, such as height and weight before pregnancy (Martin, Hamilton, et al., 2006).

Either overweight or underweight can be risky: Among women having their first babies, those who were overweight before pregnancy had the most risk of stillbirth or of losing their babies during the first week of life. On the other hand, underweight women are more likely to have dangerously small babies (Cnattingius et al., 1998). Obese women risk having children with neural-tube defects, as well as heart defects and other birth defects (Shaw, Velie, & Schaffer, 1996; Werler, Louik, Shapiro, & Mitchell, 1996; Watkins, Rasmussen, Honein, Botto, & Moore, 2003). Obesity also increases the risk of other complications of pregnancy, including miscarriage (Cnattingius, Bergstrom, Lipworth, & Kramer, 1998; Goldenberg & Tamura, 1996), difficulty inducing labor, and a greater likelihood of cesarean delivery (Brousseau, 2006).

What an expectant mother eats is important: Fish appears to be brain food for a fetus, too. In one study, the more fish a mother had eaten during the second trimester of pregnancy, the better her 6-month-old infant performed on a test of visual memory. However, eating fish with high mercury levels tended to depress infants' scores (Oken et al., 2005). In other studies, newborns whose mothers' blood contained high levels of docosahexaenoic acid (DHA), an omega-3 fatty acid found in certain fish, such as Atlantic salmon and tuna, showed more mature sleep patterns (a sign of advanced brain development) than infants whose mothers' blood had lower levels of DHA (Cheruku, Montgomery-Downs, Farkas, Thoman, & Lammi-Keefe, 2002) and also were more attentive at 12 and 18 months (Colombo et al., 2004).

Only fairly recently have we learned of the critical importance of folic acid, or folate (a B vitamin), in a pregnant woman's diet. For some time, scientists have known that China has the highest incidence in the world of babies born with anencephaly and spina bifida (refer back to Table 3-1), but it was not until the 1980s that researchers linked that fact with the timing of the babies' conception. Traditionally, Chinese couples marry in January or February and try to conceive as soon as possible. Thus, their pregnancies often begin in the winter, when rural women have little access to fresh fruits and vegetables, important sources of folic acid.

After medical detective work established the lack of folic acid as a cause of anencephaly and spina bifida, China embarked on a massive program to give folic acid supplements to prospective mothers. The result was a large reduction in the prevalence of these defects (Berry et al., 1999). Addition of folic acid to enriched grain products has been mandatory since 1998 in the United States, where the incidence of these defects has also fallen (Honein, Paulozzi, Mathews, Erickson, & Wong, 2001). Women of childbearing age are urged to take folate supplements and to include this vitamin in their diets by eating plenty of fresh fruits and vegetables even before becoming pregnant, since damage from folic acid deficiency can occur during the early weeks of gestation (American Academy of Pediatrics [AAP] Committee on Genetics, 1999; Mills & England, 2001). If all women took 5 milligrams of folic acid each day before pregnancy and during the first trimester, an estimated 85 percent of neural-tube defects could be prevented (Wald, 2004).

Malnutrition

Prenatal malnutrition may have long-range effects. In rural Gambia, in western Africa, people born during the "hungry" season, when foods from the previous harvest are badly depleted, are ten times more likely to die in early adulthood than people born during other parts of the year (Moore et al., 1997). In rural areas of northern England and Wales, rising stroke rates among middle-aged adults were associated with poverty and poor nutrition 50 years earlier, when those adults were born (Barker & Lackland, 2003). Severe prenatal nutritional deficiencies in the first or second trimesters affect the developing brain, increasing the risk of antisocial personality disorders at age 18 (Neugebauer, Hoek, & Susser, 1999). Children whose mothers had low vitamin D levels late in pregnancy had low bone mineral content at age 9, potentially increasing their risk of osteoporosis in later life (Javaid et al., 2006). And, as reported in Chapter 3, a Finnish study found a link between fetal undernutrition and schizophrenia (Wahlbeck et al., 2001).

Malnourished women who take dietary supplements while pregnant tend to have bigger, healthier, more active, and more visually alert infants (J. L. Brown, 1987; Vuori et al., 1979); and women with low zinc levels who take daily zinc supplements are less likely to have babies with low birth weight and small head circumference (Goldenberg et al., 1995). In a large-scale randomized study of low-income households in 347 Mexican communities, women who took nutrient-fortified dietary supplements while pregnant or lactating tended to have infants who grew more rapidly and were less likely to be anemic (Rivera, Sotres-Alvarez, Habicht, Shamah, & Villalpando, 2004).

Physical Activity and Strenuous Work

Moderate exercise does not seem to endanger the fetuses of healthy women (Committee on Obstetric Practice, 2002; Riemann & Kanstrup Hansen, 2000). Regular exercise prevents constipation and improves respiration, circulation, muscle tone, and skin elasticity, all of which contribute to a more comfortable pregnancy and an easier, safer delivery (Committee on Obstetric Practice, 2002). Employment during pregnancy generally entails no special hazards. However, strenuous working conditions, occupational fatigue, and long working hours may be associated with a greater risk of premature birth (Luke et al., 1995).

The American College of Obstetrics and Gynecology (1994) recommends that women in low-risk pregnancies be guided by their own abilities and stamina. The safest course seems to be for pregnant women to exercise moderately, not pushing themselves and not raising their heart rate above 150, and, as with any exercise, to taper off at the end of each session rather than stop abruptly.

Checkpoint ✔

Can you . . .

✔ Summarize recommendations concerning an expectant mother's diet and physical activity?

Drug Intake

Practically everything an expectant mother takes in makes its way to the uterus. Drugs may cross the placenta, just as oxygen, carbon dioxide, and water do. Vulnerability is greatest in the first few months of gestation, when development is most rapid. Some problems resulting from prenatal exposure to drugs can be treated if the presence of a drug can be detected early.

What are the effects of the use of specific drugs during pregnancy? Let's look first at medical drugs; then at alcohol, nicotine, and caffeine; and finally at some illegal drugs: marijuana, cocaine, and methamphetamine.

Medical Drugs It once was thought that the placenta protected the fetus against drugs the mother took during pregnancy—until the early 1960s, when a tranquilizer called *thalidomide* was banned after it was found to have caused stunted or missing limbs, severe facial deformities, and defective organs in some 12,000 babies. The thalidomide disaster sensitized medical professionals and the public to the potential dangers of taking drugs while pregnant.

Moderate, regular exercise is beneficial for pregnant women and does not seem to endanger the fetus.

According to a review of data from six health maintenance organizations, nearly 40 percent of women who were given medications during pregnancy received drugs whose safety for the fetus has not been established, and an additional 10 percent received drugs for which evidence of risk to a fetus has been found (Andrade et al., 2004). Among the medicinal drugs that may be harmful are the antibiotic tetracycline; certain barbiturates, opiates, and other central nervous system depressants; several hormones, including diethylstilbestrol and androgens; certain anticancer drugs, such as methotrexate; and Accutane, a drug often prescribed for severe acne (Koren, Pastuszak, & Ito, 1998). Angiotensin-converting enzyme (ACE) inhibitors and nonsteroidal anti-inflammatory drugs (NSAIDs), such as naproxen and ibuprofen, have been linked to birth defects when taken anytime from the first trimester on (Ofori, Oraichi, Blais, Rey, & Berard, 2006; Cooper et al., 2006).

The effects of taking a drug during pregnancy do not always become apparent immediately. In the late 1940s and early 1950s, the synthetic hormone diethylstilbestrol (DES) was widely prescribed (ineffectually, as it turned out) to prevent miscarriage. Not until years later, when the daughters of women who had taken DES during pregnancy reached puberty, did as many as 1 in 1,000 develop a rare form of vaginal or cervical cancer (Giusti, Iwamoto, & Hatch, 1995; Swan, 2000; Treffers, Hanselaar, Helmerhorst, Koster, & van Leeuwen, 2001). Now in midlife, DES women have nearly twice the risk of breast cancer as women who were not exposed to DES in utero (Palmer et al., 2006). DES sons have had malformations in the genital tract (Treffers et al., 2001; Wilcox, Baird, Weinberg, Hornsby, & Herbst, 1995).

Infants whose mothers took antidepressants such as Prozac during pregnancy tend to show signs of disrupted neurobehavioral activity (Zeskind & Stephens, 2004). These infants also have an increased risk of severe respiratory failure (Chambers et al., 2006). Certain antipsychotic drugs used to manage severe psychiatric disorders may have serious potential effects on the fetus, including withdrawal symptoms at birth (AAP Committee on Drugs, 2000). The AAP Committee on Drugs (1994) recommends that *no* medication be prescribed for a pregnant or breast-feeding woman unless it is essential for her health or her child's. Pregnant women should not take over-the-counter drugs without consulting a doctor (Koren et al., 1998).

Alcohol Like Abel Dorris, as many as 5 infants in 1000 born in the United States suffers from **fetal alcohol syndrome (FAS),** a combination of retarded growth, facial and bodily malformations, and disorders of the central nervous system. FAS and other, less severe, alcohol-related conditions are estimated to occur in nearly 1 in every 100 births (Sokol, Delaney-Black, & Nordstrom, 2003).

Prenatal alcohol exposure is the most common cause of mental retardation and the leading preventable cause of birth defects in the United States (Sokol et al., 2003) and

What's your view

- Thousands of adults now alive suffered gross abnormalities because, during the 1950s, their mothers took the tranquilizer thalidomide during pregnancy. As a result, the use of thalidomide was banned in the United States and some other countries. Now thalidomide has been found to be effective in treating or controlling many illnesses, from mouth ulcers to brain cancer. Should its use for these purposes be permitted even though there is a risk that pregnant women might take it? If so, what safeguards should be required?

fetal alcohol syndrome (FAS)
Combination of mental, motor, and developmental abnormalities affecting the offspring of some women who drink during pregnancy.

A woman who drinks and smokes while pregnant is taking grave risks with her future child's health.

is a risk factor for development of drinking problems and alcohol disorders in young adulthood (Alati et al., 2006; Baer, Sampson, Barr, Connor, & Streissguth, 2003). Yet about 10 percent of pregnant women in the United States report using alcohol, 2 percent heavily or frequently. Furthermore, more than 50 percent of women of childbearing age who do not use birth control (and therefore could become pregnant) report alcohol use (Tsai & Floyd, 2004).

Even small amounts of social drinking may harm a fetus (Sokol et al., 2003), and the more the mother drinks, the greater the effect. Moderate or heavy drinking during pregnancy seems to disturb an infant's neurological and behavioral functioning, and this may affect early social interaction with the mother, which is vital to emotional development (Nugent, Lester, Greene, Wieczorek-Deering, & Mahony, 1996). Heavy drinkers who continue to drink after becoming pregnant are likely to have babies with reduced skull and brain growth as compared with babies of nondrinking women or expectant mothers who stop drinking (Handmaker et al., 2006). Because there is no known safe level of drinking during pregnancy, it is best to avoid alcohol from the time a woman begins *thinking* about becoming pregnant until she stops breast-feeding (AAP Committee on Substance Abuse and Committee on Children with Disabilities, 1993; Sokol et al., 2003).

FAS-related problems can include, in infancy, reduced responsiveness to stimuli, slow reaction time, and reduced visual acuity (sharpness of vision) (Carter et al., 2005; Sokol et al., 2003); and, throughout childhood, short attention span, distractibility, restlessness, hyperactivity, learning disabilities, memory deficits, and mood disorders (Sokol et al., 2003) as well as aggressiveness and problem behavior (Sood et al., 2001).

Some FAS problems recede after birth; but others, such as retardation, behavioral and learning problems, and hyperactivity, tend to persist. As with Abel Dorris, enriching these children's education or general environment does not seem to enhance their cognitive development (Kerns, Don, Mateer, & Streissguth, 1997; Spohr, Willms, & Steinhausen, 1993; Streissguth et al., 1991; Strömland & Hellström, 1996), but they may be less likely to develop behavioral and mental health problems if they are diagnosed early and are reared in stable, nurturing environments (Streissguth et al., 2004).

Nicotine The percentage of U.S. women who smoke during pregnancy has been declining since 1989. Still, 10.2 percent reported doing so in 2004 (Martin, Hamilton, et al., 2006). Women who smoke during pregnancy are more than one and a half times as likely as nonsmokers to bear low-birth-weight babies (weighing less than 5½ pounds at birth). Even light smoking (fewer than five cigarettes a day) is associated with a greater risk of low birth weight (Martin, Hamilton, et al., 2005; Shankaran et al., 2004; Hoyert, Mathews, Menacker, Strobino, & Guyer, 2006). Indeed, maternal smoking has been identified as the single most important factor in low birth weight in developed countries (DiFranza, Aligne, & Weitzman, 2004).

Tobacco use during pregnancy also brings increased risks of miscarriage, growth retardation, stillbirth, small head circumference, sudden infant death, colic in early infancy, hyperkinetic disorder (excessive movement), and long-term respiratory, neurological, cognitive, and behavioral problems (AAP Committee on Substance Abuse, 2001; DiFranza et al., 2004; Hoyert, Mathews, et al., 2006; Linnet et al., 2005; Martin, Hamilton, et al., 2006; Shankaran et al., 2004; Smith et al., 2006; Sondergaard, Henriksen, Obel, & Wisborg, 2001; Shah, Sullivan, & Carter, 2006).

In a controlled study, newborns whose mothers had smoked during pregnancy (but had not used drugs and had taken no more than three alcoholic drinks per month) showed more evidence of neurological toxicity (such as overexcitability and stress) than infants of nonsmoking mothers (Law et al., 2003). The effects of prenatal exposure to secondhand smoke on cognitive development tend to be worse when the child also experiences socioeconomic hardships, such as substandard housing, malnutrition, and inadequate clothing during the first 2 years of life (Rauh et al., 2004).

Women who smoke during pregnancy also tend to smoke after giving birth, and each type of exposure seems to have independent effects (DiFranza et al., 2004). One study separated the effects of prenatal and postnatal exposure by examining 500 newborns about 48 hours after birth, while they were still in the hospital's nonsmoking maternity ward and thus had not been exposed to smoking outside the womb. Newborns whose mothers had smoked during pregnancy were shorter and lighter and had poorer respiratory functioning than babies of nonsmoking mothers (Stick, Burton, Gurrin, Sly, & LeSouëf, 1996).

Smoking during pregnancy seems to have some of the same effects on children when they reach school age as drinking during pregnancy: poor attention span, hyperactivity, anxiety, learning and behavior problems, perceptual-motor and linguistic problems, poor IQ scores, low grade placement, and neurological problems (Milberger, Biederman, Faraone, Chen, & Jones, 1996; Naeye & Peters, 1984; Olds, Henderson, & Tatelbaum, 1994a, 1994b; Thapar et al., 2003; Wakschlag et al., 1997; Weitzman, Gortmaker, & Sobol, 1992; Weissman, Warner, Wickramaratne, & Kandel, 1999).

Caffeine Can the caffeine a pregnant woman ingests in coffee, tea, cola, or chocolate cause trouble for her fetus? For the most part, the answer is no (Leviton & Cowan, 2002). It does seem clear that caffeine is not a teratogen for human babies (Christian & Brent, 2001; Hinds, West, Knight, & Harland, 1996). A controlled study of 1,205 new mothers and their babies showed no effect of reported caffeine use on low birth weight, premature birth, or retarded fetal growth (Santos, Victora, Huttly, & Carvalhal, 1998). However, eight or more cups of coffee a day may dramatically increase the risk of fetal death (Bech, Nohr, Vaeth, Henriksen, & Olsen, 2005), and four or more cups a day, of sudden death in infancy (Ford et al., 1998). Studies of a possible link between caffeine consumption and spontaneous abortion have had mixed results (Cnattingius et al., 2000; Dlugosz et al., 1996; Infante-Rivard, Fernández, Gauthier, David, & Rivard, 1993; Klebanoff, Levine, DerSimonian, Clemens, & Wilkins, 1999; Mills et al., 1993; Signorello et al., 2001).

Marijuana, Cocaine, and Methamphetamine Studies of marijuana use by pregnant women are sparse and their findings mixed (Fried & Smith, 2001). However, some evidence suggests that heavy marijuana use can lead to birth defects, low birth weight, withdrawal-like symptoms (excessive crying and tremors) at birth, and increased risk of attention disorders and learning problems later in life (Fried, Watkinson, & Willan, 1984; March of Dimes Birth Defects Foundation, 2004b). In two longitudinal studies, prenatal use of marijuana was associated with impaired attention, impulsivity, and difficulty in use of visual and perceptual skills after age 3, suggesting that the drug may affect functioning of the brain's frontal lobe (Fried & Smith, 2001). In a study of pregnant mice, marijuana use at the time of conception or early in pregnancy tended to prevent implantation in the uterus (Wang et al., 2006).

Cocaine use during pregnancy has been associated with spontaneous abortion, delayed growth, premature labor, low birth weight, small head size, birth defects, and impaired neurological development (Bunikowski et al., 1998; Chiriboga, Brust, Bateman, & Hauser, 1999; Macmillan et al., 2001; March of Dimes Birth Defects Foundation, 2004a; Scher, Richardson, & Day, 2000; Shankaran et al., 2004). In some studies, cocaine-exposed newborns showed acute withdrawal symptoms and sleep disturbances (O'Brien & Jeffery, 2002; Wagner, Katikaneni, Cox, & Ryan, 1998). In a more recent study, high prenatal cocaine exposure was associated with childhood behavior problems, independent of the effects of alcohol and tobacco exposure (Bada et al., 2007). So great has been the concern about crack babies that some states have taken criminal action against expectant mothers suspected of using cocaine (Box 4-2).

Other studies, however, have found no specific connection between prenatal cocaine exposure and physical, motor, cognitive, emotional, or behavioral deficits that could not also be attributed to other risk factors, such as low birth weight, exposure to tobacco, alcohol, marijuana, or a poor home environment (Frank, Augustyn, Knight, Pell, & Zuckerman, 2001; Messinger et al., 2004; Singer et al., 2004).

Methamphetamine use among pregnant women is an increasing concern in the United States. In a study of 1,618 infants, 84 were found to have been exposed to methamphetamine. The methamphetamine-exposed infants were more likely to have low birth weight and to be small for their gestational age than the remainder of the sample. This finding suggests that prenatal methamphetamine exposure is associated with fetal growth restriction (Smith et al., 2006).

Box 4-2 *Fetal Welfare Versus Mothers' Rights*

A South Carolina hospital routinely tested the urine of pregnant women suspected to be using illegal drugs and reported the evidence to police. Ten women were arrested, some of them in their hospital rooms almost immediately after childbirth. They sued, arguing that the urine tests constituted an unconstitutional search of their persons without their consent (Greenhouse, 2000a). In March 2001 the U.S. Supreme Court invalidated the hospital's drug testing policy (Harris & Paltrow, 2003).

In another South Carolina case, a young woman who had a stillbirth was convicted of homicide after an autopsy revealed evidence of cocaine in the baby's body. The woman was sentenced to 12 years in prison. The South Carolina Supreme Court upheld the conviction, and the U.S. Supreme Court declined to hear an appeal (Drug Policy Alliance, 2004).

In both these cases the issue was the conflict between protection of a fetus and a woman's right to privacy or to make her own decisions about her body. It is tempting to require a pregnant woman to adopt practices that will ensure her baby's health or to stop or punish her if she does not. But what about her personal freedom? Can civil rights be abrogated for the protection of the unborn?

The argument about the right to choose abortion, which rests on similar grounds, is far from settled. But the examples just given deal with a different aspect of the problem. What can or should society do about a woman who does not choose abortion but instead goes on carrying her baby while engaging in behavior destructive to it or refuses tests or treatment that medical providers consider essential to the baby's welfare?

Ingesting Harmful Substances

Does a woman have the right to knowingly ingest a substance, such as alcohol or another drug, which can permanently damage her unborn child? Some advocates for fetal rights think such behavior should be against the law even though it is legal for other adults. Others argue that incarceration for substance abuse is unworkable and self-defeating. They say that expectant mothers who have a drinking or drug problem need education and treatment, not prosecution (Drug Policy Alliance, 2004; Marwick, 1997, 1998).

Since 1985, at least 240 women in 35 states have been prosecuted for using illegal drugs or alcohol during pregnancy, even though no state legislature has specifically criminalized such activity (Harris & Paltrow, 2003; Nelson & Marshall, 1998). Instead, these women have been charged with the broader crimes of child endangerment or abuse, illegal drug delivery to a minor, murder, or manslaughter. In all states except South Carolina, courts have refused to expand these existing laws to cover claims of fetal rights. Only in South Carolina has drug use during pregnancy been held to be a crime (Harris & Paltrow, 2003).

Intrusive Medical Procedures

In January 2004, Melissa Ann Rowland of Salt Lake City was charged with the murder of one of her newborn twins, who was born dead. Until it was too late, Rowland had refused doctors' urgent recommendation that she have a cesarean section. The second child, a girl, was born alive with cocaine and alcohol in her system and was subsequently adopted. Rowland, who had a history of mental health problems, pleaded guilty to a reduced charge of child endangerment, agreed to enter a drug treatment program, and was sentenced to 18 months of probation (Associated Press, 2004b; Johnson, 2004).

Should a woman be forced to submit to intrusive procedures that pose a risk to her, such as a surgical delivery or intrauterine transfusions, when doctors say such procedures are essential to the delivery of a healthy baby? Should a woman from a fundamentalist sect that rejects modern medical care be taken into custody until she gives birth? Such measures have been defended as protecting the rights of the unborn, but women's rights advocates claim that they reflect a view of women as mere vehicles for carrying offspring and not as persons in their own right (Greenhouse, 2000b). Also, forcing intrusive measures on a pregnant woman may jeopardize the doctor-patient relationship. If failure to follow medical advice could bring forced surgery, confinement, or criminal charges, some women might avoid doctors altogether and thus deprive their fetuses of needed prenatal care (Nelson & Marshall, 1998).

Courts have held that "neither fetal rights nor state interests on behalf of the fetus supersede[s] women's rights as ultimate medical decision maker" (Harris & Paltrow, 2003, p. 1698). Yet, the U.S. Congress in March 2004, in response to the notorious murder of a pregnant woman that also took the life of her unborn son, made it a federal crime to harm or kill an unborn child (Reuters, 2004b). That law, if not overturned by the courts, for the first time establishes a fetal right to life separate from the mother's and could have repercussions in cases in which fetal welfare conflicts with women's rights.

What's your view ?

Does society's interest in protecting an unborn child justify coercive measures against pregnant women who ingest harmful substances or refuse medically indicated treatment?

   a. Should pregnant women who refuse to stop drinking or to get treatment be incarcerated until they give birth?

   b. Should mothers who repeatedly give birth to children with FAS be sterilized?

   c. Should liquor companies be held liable if adequate warnings against use during pregnancy are not on their products?

   d. Would your answers be the same regarding smoking or use of cocaine or other potentially harmful substances?

Check it out

For more information on this topic, go to www.nofas.org. You will find information on behaviors of those affected by Fetal Alcohol Syndrome and Fetal Alcohol Effects, including national statistics and contacts. Resources include newsletters, support groups, audiovisual materials, and information packets.

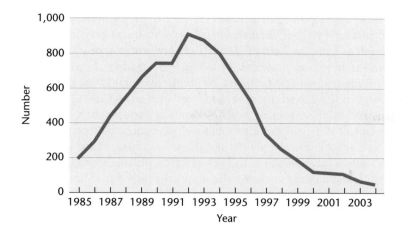

Figure 4-4

Estimated cases of perinatally acquired AIDS—United States, 1985–2004. The number of perinatally acquired AIDS cases has dropped precipitously with widespread screening and retroviral treatment.

Source: CDC, 2006.

HIV/AIDS

Acquired immune deficiency syndrome (AIDS) is a disease caused by the *human immunodeficiency virus* (*HIV*), which undermines functioning of the immune system. If an expectant mother has the virus in her blood, *perinatal transmission* may occur: The virus may cross over to the fetus's bloodstream through the placenta during pregnancy, labor, or delivery or, after birth, through breast milk.

The biggest risk factor for perinatal HIV transmission is a mother who is unaware she has HIV. In the United States, new pediatric AIDS cases have declined steadily since 1992 due to routine testing and treatment of pregnant women and newborn babies and to advances in the prevention, detection, and treatment of HIV infection in infants. This decline accelerated in 1994 with the introduction of continuous pre- and postnatal administration of the drug zidovudine, commonly known as AZT, as well as other antiviral drugs. As a result, the estimated rate of perinatal HIV infection is now less than 2 percent. In 2004, an estimated 48 perinatally acquired cases of HIV/AIDS were reported, down 95 percent from 1992 (Figure 4-4). However, as with adults, HIV/AIDS tends to be underreported in children. The risk of transmission also can be reduced by choosing cesarean delivery, especially when a woman has not received antiretroviral therapy, and by promotion of alternatives to breast-feeding (CDC, 2006a).

acquired immune deficiency syndrome (AIDS) Viral disease that undermines effective functioning of the immune system.

Other Maternal Illnesses

Prospective parents should try to prevent any infections—colds, flu, urinary tract and vaginal infections, as well as sexually transmitted diseases. If the mother does contract an infection, it should be treated promptly. Pregnant women also should be screened for thyroid deficiency, which can affect their children's cognitive performance (Haddow et al., 1999).

Rubella (German measles), if contracted by a woman before her 11th week of pregnancy, is almost certain to cause deafness and heart defects in her baby. Chances of catching rubella during pregnancy have been greatly reduced in Europe and the United States since the late 1960s, when a vaccine was developed that is now routinely administered to infants and children. However, rubella is still a serious problem in developing countries where inoculations are not routine (Plotkin, Katz, & Cordero, 1999).

Offspring of mothers with diabetes are two to five times more likely to develop birth defects, especially of the heart and of the spinal cord (neural tube defects), than offspring of other women. Research on mice suggests why: High blood glucose levels, typical in diabetics, deprive an embryo of oxygen, with resultant cell damage, during the first 8 weeks of pregnancy, when its organs are forming. Women with diabetes need to be sure their blood glucose levels are under control *before* becoming pregnant (Li, Chase, Jung, Smith, & Loeken, 2005). Use of multivitamin supplements during the 3 months before conception and the first 3 months of pregnancy can help reduce the risk of diabetes-associated birth defects (Correa, Botto, Lin, Mulinare, & Erickson, 2003).

An infection called *toxoplasmosis,* caused by a parasite harbored in the bodies of cattle, sheep, and pigs and in the intestinal tracts of cats, typically produces either no symptoms or symptoms like those of the common cold. In a pregnant woman, however, especially in the second and third trimesters of pregnancy, it can cause fetal brain damage, severely impaired eyesight or blindness, seizures, or miscarriage, stillbirth, or death of the baby. Although as many as 9 out of 10 of these babies may appear normal at birth, more than half of them have later problems, including eye infections, hearing loss, and learning disabilities. Treatment with two antiparasitic drugs, pyrimethamine and sulfadiazine, during the 1st year of life can reduce brain and eye damage (McLeod et al., 2006).

To avoid infection, expectant mothers should not eat raw or very rare meat, should wash hands and all work surfaces after touching raw meat, should peel or thoroughly wash raw fruits and vegetables, and should not dig in a garden where cat feces are buried. Women who have a cat should have it checked for the disease, should not feed it raw meat, and, if possible, should have someone else empty the litter box (March of Dimes Foundation, 2002) or should do it often, wearing gloves (Kravetz & Federman, 2002).

Maternal Stress

Some tension and worry during pregnancy are normal and do not necessarily increase risks of birth complications, such as low birth weight, according to an analysis of many studies (Littleton, Breitkopf, & Berenson, 2006). Moderate maternal stress may even spur organization of the developing brain. In a series of studies, 2-year-olds whose mothers had shown moderate anxiety midway through pregnancy scored higher on measures of motor and mental development (DiPietro, 2004; DiPietro, Novak, Costigan, Atella, & Reusing, 2006).

On the other hand, unusual maternal stress during pregnancy may negatively affect the offspring (Dingfelder, 2004; Huizink, Mulder, & Buitelaar, 2004). In one study, women whose partners or children died or were hospitalized for heart attacks or cancer were at elevated risk of giving birth to children with malformations, such as cleft lip, cleft palate, and heart malformations (Hansen, Lou, & Olsen, 2000). As reported in Chapter 6, major stress during the 24th to 28th weeks of pregnancy may influence the development of autism by deforming the developing brain (Beversdorf et al., 2001).

A mother's self-reported anxiety during pregnancy has been associated with 8-month-olds' inattentiveness during a developmental assessment (Huizink, Robles de Medina, Mulder, Visser, & Buitelaar, 2002) and preschoolers' negative emotionality or behavioral disorders in early childhood (Martin, Noyes, Wisenbaker, & Huttunen, 2000; O'Connor, Heron, Golding, Beveridge, & Clover, 2002). Other studies found links between expectant mothers' perceptions of stress and their fetuses' activity levels (DiPietro, Hilton, Hawkins, Costigan, & Pressman, 2002).

Maternal Age

On December 30, 2006, in Barcelona, Spain, a 67-year-old woman became the oldest woman on record to give birth. The woman (whose name was not released) had become pregnant after in vitro fertilization. She gave birth to twins by cesarean section.

Births to U.S. women in their 30s and 40s—and, to a lesser extent, even in their 50s and 60s—have nearly doubled since 1980, from 19 percent to more than 37 percent of all births (Martin, Hamilton, et al., 2006)—an example of a history-graded influence. How does delayed childbearing affect the risks to mother and baby?

Although most risks to the baby's health are not much greater than for babies born to younger mothers, the chance of miscarriage or stillbirth rises with maternal age (Figure 4-5). In fact, the risk of miscarriage reaches 90 percent for women age 45 or older (Heffner, 2004). Women over 30 to 35 are more likely to suffer complications due to diabetes, high blood pressure, or severe bleeding. There is also more likelihood of premature delivery, retarded fetal growth, birth defects, and chromosomal abnormalities, such as Down syndrome. However, due to widespread screening among older expectant mothers, fewer malformed babies are born nowadays (Berkowitz, Skovron, Lapinski, & Berkowitz, 1990; P. Brown, 1993; Cunningham & Leveno, 1995; Heffner, 2004). Women age 40 and over are at increased risk of needing operative deliveries (Gilbert, Nesbitt, & Danielsen, 1999). Women who give birth after age 50 are two to three times more likely than younger women to have babies who are very small, born prematurely, or stillborn (Salihu, Shumpert, Slay, Kirby, & Alexander, 2003).

Not all of these risks apply to women who become pregnant by in vitro fertilization, using ova donated by younger women. In those pregnancies, which are generally screened

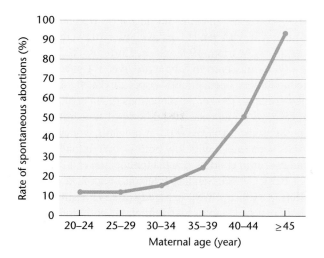

Figure 4-5

Miscarriage rates as a function of maternal age.

Source: Heffner, 2004, p. 1927; adapted from Menken et al., 1986; and Anderson, Wohlfahrt, Christens, Olsen, & Melbye, 2000.

and monitored closely, the risks of both miscarriage and chromosomal abnormalities are consistent with the age of the donor (Heffner, 2004).

Adolescents also tend to have premature or underweight babies—perhaps because a young girl's still-growing body consumes vital nutrients the fetus needs (Fraser, Brockert, & Ward, 1995). These newborns are at heightened risk of death in the 1st month, disabilities, or health problems. Risks of teenage pregnancy are discussed further in Chapter 17.

Outside Environmental Hazards

Air pollution, chemicals, radiation, extremes of heat and humidity, and other hazards of modern life can affect prenatal development. Pregnant women who regularly breathe air that contains high levels of fine combustion-related particles are more likely to bear infants who are premature or undersized (Parker, Woodruff, Basu, & Schoendorf, 2005) or have chromosomal abnormalities (Bocskay et al., 2005). Exposure to high concentrations of disinfection by-products is associated with low birth weight and slowed fetal growth (Hinckley, Bachand, & Reif, 2005). Women who work with chemicals used in manufacturing semiconductor chips have about twice the rate of miscarriage as other female workers (Markoff, 1992), and women exposed to DDT tend to have more preterm births (Longnecker, Klebanoff, Zhou, & Brock, 2001). Two common insecticides, chlorpyrifos and diazinon, apparently have caused stunting of prenatal growth (Whyatt et al., 2004). Research in the United Kingdom found a 33 percent increase in risk of nongenetic birth defects among families living within 2 miles of hazardous waste sites (Vrijheld et al., 2002).

Fetal exposure to low levels of environmental toxins, such as lead, mercury, and dioxin, as well as nicotine and ethanol, may help explain the sharp rise in asthma, allergies, and autoimmune disorders such as lupus (Dietert, 2005). Childhood cancers, including leukemia, have been linked to pregnant mothers' drinking chemically contaminated groundwater (Boyles, 2002) and use of home pesticides (Menegaux et al., 2006). Infants exposed prenatally even to low levels of lead, especially during the third trimester, tend to show IQ deficits at ages 6 to 10 (Schnaas et al., 2006).

Women who have routine dental X-rays during pregnancy triple their risk of having full-term, low-birth-weight babies (Hujoel, Bollen, Noonan, & del Aguila, 2004). In utero exposure to radiation 8 through 15 weeks after fertilization has been linked to mental retardation, small head size, chromosomal malformations, Down syndrome, seizures, and poor performance on IQ tests and in school (Yamazaki & Schull, 1990).

Paternal Factors

A man's exposure to lead, marijuana or tobacco smoke, large amounts of alcohol or radiation, DES, pesticides, or high ozone levels may result in abnormal or poor quality sperm (Sokol et al., 2006; Swan et al., 2003) Offspring of male workers at a British nuclear processing plant were at elevated risk of being born dead (Parker, Pearce, Dickinson, Aitkin, &

Checkpoint ✔

Can you . . .

✔ Describe the short-term and long-term effects on the developing fetus of a mother's use of medical and recreational drugs during pregnancy?

✔ Summarize the risks of maternal illnesses and stress, delayed childbearing, and exposure to chemicals and radiation?

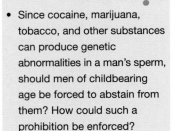
Checkpoint

Can you . . .

✔ Identify at least three ways in which environmentally caused defects can be influenced by the father?

Guidepost 3

What techniques can assess a fetus's health and well-being, and what is the importance of prenatal and preconception care?

Craft, 1999). Babies whose fathers had diagnostic X-rays within the year prior to conception or had high lead exposure at work tended to have low birth weight and slowed fetal growth (Lin, Hwang, Marshall, & Marion, 1998; Shea, Little, & ALSPAC Study Team, 1997). Among nearly 238,000 infants born in Singapore over a 4-year period, birth defects were more strongly linked to fathers' occupations—especially such jobs as plant and machine operation and assembly—than to mother's occupations (Chia et al., 2004).

Men who smoke have an increased likelihood of transmitting genetic abnormalities (AAP Committee on Substance Abuse, 2001). A pregnant woman's exposure to the father's secondhand smoke has been linked with low birth weight, infant respiratory infections, sudden infant death, and cancer in childhood and adulthood (Ji et al., 1997; Rubin, Krasilnikoff, Leventhal, Weile, & Berget, 1986; Sandler, Everson, Wilcox, & Browder, 1985; Wakefield, Reid, Roberts, Mullins, & Gillies, 1998). In a study of 214 nonsmoking mothers in New York City, exposure to *both* paternal smoking and urban air pollution resulted in a 7 percent reduction in birth weight and a 3 percent reduction in head circumference (Perera et al., 2004).

Older fathers may be a significant source of birth defects due to damaged or deteriorated sperm. In 2004 about 10 percent of fathers of new babies were ages 35 to 55 and over (Martin, Hamilton, et al., 2006). Advancing paternal age is associated with increases in the risk of several rare conditions, including dwarfism (Wyrobek et al., 2006). Advanced age of the father also may be a factor in a disproportionate number of cases of schizophrenia (Byrne et al., 2003; Malaspina et al., 2001) and of autism and related disorders (Reichenberg et al., 2006).

Monitoring and Promoting Prenatal Development

Not long ago, almost the only decision parents had to make about their babies before birth was the decision to conceive; most of what happened in the intervening months was beyond their control. Now scientists have developed an array of tools to assess an unborn baby's progress and well-being (Table 4-3).

Progress is being made in the use of noninvasive procedures, such as ultrasound and blood tests, to detect chromosomal abnormalities. Contrary to earlier findings, amniocentesis and chorionic villus sampling, which can be used earlier in pregnancy, carry only a slightly higher miscarriage risk (Caughey, Norton, 2006; Eddleman et al., 2006). Screening is most effective when begun during the first trimester (Simpson, 2005). In one study, a combination of three noninvasive tests conducted at 11 weeks of gestation predicted the presence of Down syndrome with 87 percent accuracy. When the 11-week tests were followed by further noninvasive testing early in the second trimester, accuracy reached 96 percent (Malone et al., 2005).

Screening for defects and diseases is only one reason for the importance of early prenatal care. Early, high-quality prenatal care, which includes educational, social, and nutritional services, can help prevent maternal or infant death and other birth complications. It can provide first-time mothers with information about pregnancy, childbirth, and infant care. Poor women who get prenatal care benefit by being put in touch with other needed services, and they are more likely to get medical care for their infants after birth (Shiono & Behrman, 1995).

Disparities in Prenatal Care

In the United States prenatal care is widespread, but not universal as in many European countries; and it lacks uniform national standards and guaranteed financial coverage. Use of early prenatal care (during the first 3 months of pregnancy) has risen modestly since 1990 from 75.6 percent to 83.9 percent of pregnant women. Still, in 2004, 3.6 percent of expectant mothers received no care until the last trimester or no care at all (Hoyert et al., 2006; Martin, Hamilton, et al., 2006). (Utilization rates are poorer in seven states in which revised definitions of prenatal care were put into effect in 2004.) Furthermore, rates of low birth weight and premature birth continue to rise (see Chapter 5). Why?

One answer is the increasing number of multiple births, which require especially close prenatal attention. These pregnancies often end, for precautionary reasons, in early births,

Table 4-3 Prenatal Assessment Techniques

Technique	Description	Uses and Advantages	Risks and Notes
Ultrasound (sonogram), sonoembryology	High-frequency sound waves directed at the mother's abdomen produce a picture of fetus in uterus. Sonoembryology uses high-frequency transvaginal probes and digital image processing to produce a picture of embryo in uterus.	Monitor fetal growth, movement, position, and form; assess amniotic fluid volume; judge gestational age; detect multiple pregancies. Detect major structural abnormalities or death of a fetus. Guide amniocentesis and chorionic villus sampling. Help diagnose sex-linked disorders. Sonoembryology can detect unusual defects during embryonic stage.	No known risks; done routinely in many places. Can be used for sex-screening of unborn babies.
Embryoscopy, fetoscopy	Tiny viewing scope is inserted in woman's abdomen to view embryo or fetus.	Can guide fetal blood transfusions and bone marrow transplants. Can assist in diagnosis of nonchromosomal genetic disorders.	Embryoscopy is still in research stage. Riskier than other prenatal diagnostic procedures.
Amniocentesis	Sample of amniotic fluid is withdrawn and analyzed under guidance of ultrasound. Most commonly used procedure to obtain fetal cells for testing.	Can detect chromosomal disorders and certain genetic or multifactorial defects; more than 99 percent accuracy rate. Usually performed in women age 35 and over; recommended if prospective parents are known carriers of Tay-Sachs disease or sickle-cell anemia or have family history of Down syndrome, spina bifida, or muscular dystrophy. Can help diagnose sex-linked disorders.	Normally not performed before 15 weeks' gestation. Results usually take 1 to 2 weeks. Small (0.5 percent to 1 percent) added risk of fetal loss or injury; early amniocentesis (at 11 to 13 weeks' gestation) is more risky and not recommended. Can be used for sex-screening of unborn babies.
Chorionic villus sampling (CVS)	Tissues from hairlike chorionic villi (projections of membrane surrounding fetus) are removed from placenta and analyzed.	Early diagnosis of birth defects and disorders. Can be performed between 10 and 12 weeks' gestation; yields highly accurate results within a week.	Should not be performed before 10 weeks' gestation. Some studies suggest 1 to 4 percent more risk of fetal loss than with amniocentesis.
Preimplantation genetic diagnosis	After in vitro fertilization, a sample cell is removed from the blastocyst and analyzed.	Can avoid transmission of genetic defects or predispositions known to run in the family; a defective blastocyst is not implanted in uterus. Can test for more than 100 disorders. Can screen for defective embryo that might be miscarried. Often used with in vitro fertilization.	No known risks.
Umbilical cord sampling (cordocentesis, or fetal blood sampling)	Needle guided by ultrasound is inserted into blood vessels of umbilical cord.	Allows direct access to fetal DNA for diagnostic measures, including assessment of blood disorders and infections, and therapeutic measures such as blood transfusions.	Fetal loss or miscarriage is reported in 1 percent to 2 percent of cases; increases risk of bleeding from umbilical cord and fetal distress.
Maternal blood test	A sample of the prospective mother's blood is tested for alpha fetoprotein (AFP).	May indicate defects in formation of brain or spinal cord (anencephaly or spina bifida); also can predict Down syndrome and other abnormalities. Permits monitoring of pregnancies at risk for low birth weight or stillbirth.	No known risks, but false negatives are possible. Ultrasound and/or amniocentesis needed to confirm suspected conditions.

Sources: Chodirker et al., 2001; Cicero, Curcio, Papageorghiou, Sonek, & Nicolaides, 2001; Cunniff & Committee on Genetics, 2004; Kurjak, Kupesic, Matijevic, Kos, & Marton, 1999; Tarkan, 2005; and Verlinsky et al., 2002.

either induced or by cesarean delivery (Hamilton, Martin, & Sutton, 2004; Hoyert et al., 2006; Martin, Hamilton, et al., 2006).

Another answer is that the benefits of prenatal care are not evenly distributed. Although usage of prenatal care has grown, especially among ethnic groups that have tended not to receive early care, the women most at risk of bearing low-birth-weight babies—teenage and unmarried women, those with little education, and some minority women—are still least likely to receive it (Martin, Hamilton, et al., 2006; National Center for Health

Figure 4-6

Proportion of U.S. mothers with late or no prenatal care, according to race or ethnicity, 2004. Late prenatal care begins in the last 3 months of pregnancy.

Source: NCHS, 2006.

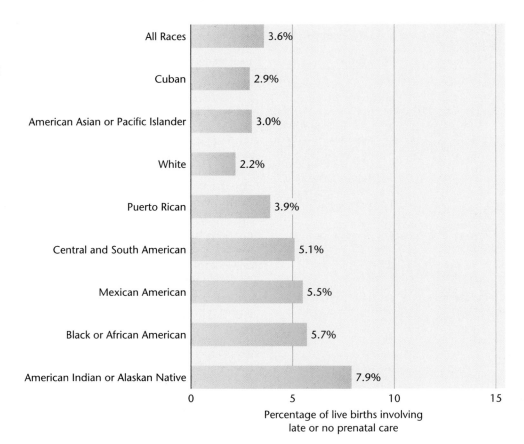

Percentage of live births involving late or no prenatal care

Statistics [NCHS], 2005; USDHHS, 1996a). In 2004, 89 percent of non-Hispanic white expectant mothers, but only 77.5 percent of Hispanic American and 76.5 percent of non-Hispanic black expectant mothers, began prenatal care in the first trimester (Martin, Hamilton, et al., 2006). Figure 4-6 shows percentages of various ethnic groups that receive late or no prenatal care.

A related concern is an ethnic disparity in fetal and postbirth mortality. After adjusting for such risk factors as SES, overweight, smoking, hypertension, and diabetes, the chances of perinatal death (death between 20 weeks gestation and 1 week after birth) remain 3.4 times higher for blacks, 1.5 times higher for Hispanics, and 1.9 times higher for other minorities than for whites (Healy et al., 2006).

The Need for Preconception Care

A more fundamental answer is that even early prenatal care is insufficient; care should begin *before* pregnancy to identify preventable risks. The Centers for Disease Control and Prevention (CDC) (2006c) has issued comprehensive, research-based guidelines for *preconception care* for all women of childbearing age. Such care should include

- *Physical examinations* and the taking of medical and family histories.
- *Vaccinations* for rubella and hepatitis B.
- *Risk screening* for genetic disorders and infectious diseases such as STDs.
- *Counseling* women to avoid smoking and alcohol, maintain a healthy body weight, and take folic acid supplements.

Interventions should be provided where risks are indicated and also between pregnancies for women who have had poor pregnancy outcomes in the past.

The CDC (2006c) urges all adults to create a reproductive life plan so as to focus attention on reproductive health, avoid unintended pregnancies, and improve pregnancy outcomes. The CDC also calls for increased health insurance for low-income women to make sure they have access to preventive care.

What's your view

- Can you suggest ways to induce more pregnant women to seek early prenatal or preconception care?

Checkpoint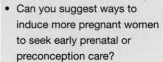

Can you . . .

✔ Describe seven techniques for identifying defects or disorders prenatally?

✔ Discuss possible reasons for disparities in utilization of prenatal care?

✔ Tell why early, high-quality prenatal care is important and why preconception care is needed?

Refocus

On the basis of the information given about Abel Dorris in the Focus vignette at the beginning of this chapter,

- What light does Abel Dorris's case shed on the role of the prenatal environment in a child's development?
- Why did Michael Dorris's belief that Abel would "catch up," given a positive adoptive home environment, prove unfounded?

- What sorts of information might be helpful in counseling prospective parents on adoption of a child whose prenatal history is unknown?

Good preconception and prenatal care can give every child the best possible chance for entering the world in good condition to meet the challenges of life outside the womb—challenges we discuss in the next three chapters.

Summary and Key Terms

Prenatal Development: Three Stages

Guidepost 1 What are the three stages of prenatal development, and what happens during each stage?

- Prenatal development occurs in three stages of gestation: the germinal, embryonic, and fetal stages.
- Growth and development both before and after birth follow the cephalocaudal principle (head to tail) and the proximodistal principle (center outward).
- As many as 1 in 2 conceptions end in spontaneous abortion, usually in the first trimester of pregnancy.
- As fetuses grow, they move less, but more vigorously. Swallowing amniotic fluid, which contains substances from the mother's body, stimulates taste and smell. Fetuses seem able to hear, exercise sensory discrimination, learn, and remember.

cephalocaudal principle (94)   proximodistal principle (94) germinal stage (94)   embryonic stage (95)   spontaneous abortion (96)   fetal stage (96)   ultrasound (96)

Prenatal Development: Environmental Influences

Guidepost 2 What environmental influences can affect prenatal development?

- The developing organism can be greatly affected by its prenatal environment. The likelihood of a birth defect may depend on the timing and intensity of an environmental event and its interaction with genetic factors.

- Important environmental influences involving the mother include nutrition, physical activity, smoking, intake of alcohol or other drugs, maternal illnesses, maternal stress, maternal age, and external environmental hazards, such as chemicals and radiation. External influences and paternal age may affect the father's sperm.

teratogenic (99)   fetal alcohol syndrome (FAS) (101) acquired immune deficiency syndrome (AIDS) (105)

Monitoring and Promoting Prenatal Development

Guidepost 3 What techniques can assess a fetus's health and well-being, and what is the importance of prenatal and preconception care?

- Ultrasound, amniocentesis, chorionic villus sampling, embryoscopy, preimplantation genetic diagnosis, umbilical cord sampling, and maternal blood tests can be used to determine whether an unborn baby is developing normally.
- High-quality prenatal care, begun early, is essential for healthy development. It can lead to detection of defects and disorders and may help reduce low birth weight and other birth complications.
- Racial/ethnic disparities in prenatal care may be a factor in disparities in low birth weight and perinatal death.
- Preconception care for every woman of childbearing age would reduce unintended pregnancies and increase the chances of good pregnancy outcomes.

Birth and the Newborn Baby

A newborn baby is an extraordinary event; and I have never seen two babies who looked exactly alike. Here is the breathing miracle who could not live an instant without you, with a skull more fragile than an egg, a miracle of eyes, legs, toenails, and lungs.

—James Baldwin, *No Name in the Street*, 1972

Focus *The Birth of Elvis Presley*

Elvis Presley

Elvis Presley (1935–1977) was born in a 30- by 15-foot cottage in East Tupelo, Mississippi. Today, the modest birthplace of the now-legendary king of rock music is painted sparkling white, the walls are papered with primroses, and dainty curtains hang at the windows—among the many homey touches added for the benefit of tourists. But, like many of the popular myths about Elvis's early life, this "cute little doll house" (Goldman, 1981, p. 60) bears only slight resemblance to the reality: a bare board shack with no indoor plumbing or electricity, set in a dirt-poor hamlet that wasn't much more than "a wide spot in the road" (Clayton & Heard, 1994, p. 8).

During the Great Depression, Elvis's near-illiterate father, Vernon Presley, sometimes did odd jobs for a farmer named Orville Bean, who owned much of the town. Elvis's mother, Gladys, was vivacious and high-spirited, as talkative as Vernon was taciturn. She, like Vernon, came from a family of sharecroppers and migrant workers. She had moved to East Tupelo to be close to the garment factory where she worked.

Gladys first noticed handsome Vernon on the street and then, soon after, met him in church. They eloped on June 17, 1933. Vernon was 17 and Gladys, 21. They borrowed $3 for the marriage license.

At first the young couple lived with friends and family. When Gladys became pregnant, Vernon borrowed $180 from his employer, Bean, to buy lumber and nails and, with the help of his father and older brother, built a two-room cabin next to his parents' house on Old Saltillo Road. Bean, who owned the land, was to hold title to the house until the loan was paid off.

Vernon and Gladys moved into their new home in December 1934, about a month before Gladys gave birth. Her pregnancy was a difficult one; her legs swelled, and she finally quit her job at the garment factory, where she had to stand on her feet all day pushing a heavy steam iron.

When Vernon got up for work in the wee hours of January 8, a bitterly cold morning, Gladys was hemorrhaging. The midwife told Vernon to get the doctor, Will Hunt. (His $15 fee was paid by welfare.) At about 4 o'clock in the morning, Dr. Hunt delivered a stillborn baby

Sources of information about Elvis Presley's birth were Clayton & Heard (1994); Dundy (1985); Goldman (1981); Guralnick (1994); and Marling (1996).

boy, Jesse Garon. The second twin, Elvis Aron, was born about 35 minutes later. Gladys—extremely weak and losing blood—was taken to the hospital charity ward with baby Elvis. They stayed there for more than 3 weeks.

Baby Jesse remained an important part of the family's life. Gladys frequently talked to Elvis about his brother. "When one twin died, the one that lived got the strength of both," she would say (Guralnick, 1994, p. 13). Elvis took his mother's words to heart. Throughout his life, his twin's imagined voice and presence were constantly with him.

Elvis lived in his birthplace only until age 3, when his father went to prison for altering a $4 check. When the payment on the house loan came due, Bean evicted Gladys and her son, who had to move in with family members. In later years, Elvis would drive back to East Tupelo (now Tupelo's suburban Presley Heights). He would sit in his car in the dark, looking at the cottage on what is now called Elvis Presley Drive and "thinking about the course his life had taken" (Marling, 1996, p. 20).

● ● ●

Elvis Presley is just one of many well-known people—including almost all the presidents of the United States—who were born at home. At one time, medical care during pregnancy was rare even in the United States. Many infants, like Jesse Presley, were born dead, and many women died in childbirth. Today, medical advances and a rising standard of living in industrialized countries have reduced the risks of giving birth. Today, the overwhelming majority of births in the United States (but a smaller proportion in some European countries) now occur in hospitals. However, as we will see, there is a small but growing movement back to home birth—still the norm in many developing countries.

In this chapter, we examine how babies come into the world. We describe how newborn infants look and how their body systems work. We discuss ways to assess their health and how birth complications can affect development. We also consider how the birth of a baby affects the people most vital to the infant's well-being: the parents.

After you have read and studied this chapter, you should be able to answer each of the Guidepost questions on the following page. Look for them again in the margins throughout the chapter, where they point to important concepts. To check your understanding of these Guideposts, review the end-of-chapter summary. Checkpoints located throughout the chapter will help you verify your understanding of what you have read.

Guideposts for Study

1. How do customs surrounding birth reflect culture, and how has childbirth changed in developed countries?

2. How does labor begin, what happens during each of the three stages of childbirth, and what alternative methods of delivery are available?

3. How do newborn infants adjust to life outside the womb, and how can we tell whether a new baby is healthy and is developing normally?

4. What complications of childbirth can endanger newborn babies, and what are the long-term prospects for infants with complicated births?

5. How do parents bond with and care for their baby?

Childbirth and Culture:
How Birthing Has Changed*

Guidepost 1

How do customs surrounding birth reflect culture, and how has childbirth changed in developed countries?

Customs surrounding childbirth reflect the beliefs, values, and resources of a culture. A Mayan woman in Yucatan gives birth in the hammock in which she sleeps every night; the father-to-be is expected to be present, along with the midwife. To evade evil spirits, mother and child remain at home for a week (Jordan, 1993). In contrast, among the Ngoni in East Africa, men are excluded from the birth. In rural Thailand, a new mother generally resumes normal activity within a few hours of giving birth (Broude, 1995; Gardiner & Kosmitzki, 2005).

Before the 20th century, childbirth in Europe and in the United States followed somewhat similar patterns. Birth was a female social ritual. The woman, surrounded by female relatives and neighbors, sat up in her bed or perhaps in the stable, modestly draped in a sheet; if she wished, she might stand, walk around, or squat over a birth stool. Chinks in the walls, doors, and windows were stuffed with cloth to keep out chills and evil spirits. The prospective father was nowhere to be seen. Not until the 15th century was a doctor present, and then only for wealthy women if complications arose.

The midwife who presided over the event had no formal training; she offered "advice, massages, potions, irrigations, and talismans." Salves made of fat of viper, gall of eel, powdered hoof of donkey, tongue of chameleon, or skin of snake or hare might be rubbed on the prospective mother's abdomen to ease her pain or hasten her labor; but "the cries of the mother during labor were considered to be as natural as those of the baby at birth" (Fontanel & d'Harcourt, 1997, p. 28).

Given the lack of accurate knowledge about female anatomy and the birth process, the midwives' ministrations sometimes did more harm than good. A 16th-century textbook instructed midwives to stretch and dilate the membranes of the genital parts and cut or break them with their fingernails, to urge the patient to go up and down stairs screaming at the top of her lungs, to help her bear down by pressing on her belly, and to pull out the placenta immediately after the birth (Fontanel & d'Harcourt, 1997).

After the baby emerged, the midwife cut and tied the umbilical cord and cleaned and examined the newborn, testing the reflexes and joints. The other women helped the new mother wash and dress, made her bed with clean sheets, and served her food to rebuild her strength. Within a few hours or days, a peasant mother would be back at work in the fields; a more affluent or noble woman could "lie in" and rest for several weeks.

---

*This discussion is based largely on Eccles, 1982; Fontanel & d'Harcourt, 1997; Gélis, 1991; and Scholten, 1985.

Reducing the Risks of Childbirth

Childbirth in those times was "a struggle with death" (Fontanel & d'Harcourt, 1997, p. 34) for both mother and baby. In 17th- and 18th-century France, a woman had a 1 in 10 chance of dying while or shortly after giving birth. Thousands of babies were stillborn, and 1 out of 4 who were born alive died during their first year. At the end of the 19th century in England and Wales, an expectant mother was almost fifty times more likely to die in childbirth than is a woman giving birth today (Saunders, 1997).

The development of the science of obstetrics early in the 19th century professionalized childbirth, especially in urban settings. Most deliveries still occurred at home and women were on hand to help and offer emotional support, but a (male) physician was usually in charge, with surgical instruments ready in case of trouble. Midwives were now trained, and obstetrics manuals were widely disseminated.

After the turn of the 20th century, maternity hospitals, where conditions were antiseptic and medical management was easier, became the birth setting of choice for those who could afford them (though not for many country women, such as Gladys Presley). In 1900, only 5 percent of U.S. deliveries occurred in hospitals; by 1920, rates in various cities ranged from 30 to 65 percent (Scholten, 1985). A similar trend took place in Europe. In the United States in 2004, 99 percent of babies were born in hospitals, and 91.5 percent of births were attended by physicians. Nearly 8 percent were attended by midwives, usually certified nurse-midwives (Martin, Hamilton, et al., 2006).

The dramatic reductions in risks surrounding pregnancy and childbirth in the industrialized world, particularly during the past 50 years, are largely due to the availability of antibiotics, blood transfusions, safe anesthesia, improved hygiene, and drugs for inducing labor when necessary. In addition, improvements in prenatal assessment and care make it far more likely that a baby will be born healthy.

Still, childbirth is not risk-free for women or babies. Among the nearly 4 million U.S. women giving birth each year between 1993 and 1997, 31 percent experienced medical problems (Daniel, Berg, Johnson, & Atrash, 2003). Black women, obese women, those with difficult medical histories, those who have had previous cesarean deliveries, and those who have had several children are at elevated risk of hemorrhage and other dangerous complications; and the risk of dying in childbirth is at least four times higher for black women than for white women (Chazotte, quoted in Bernstein, 2003).

Contemporary Settings for Childbirth

The medicalization of childbirth has had social and emotional costs. To many modern women, "a hospital birth has become a surgical act in which the woman is hooked up to a monitor and stretched out on a table under glaring lights and the stares of two or three strangers, her feet in stirrups" (Fontanel & d'Harcourt, 1997, p. 57). Today a small but growing percentage of women in economically developed countries are reviving the intimate, personal experience of home birth, which can involve the whole family. Home births usually are attended by a trained nurse-midwife, with the resources of medical science close at hand in case of need. Freestanding, homelike birth centers are another option. Studies suggest that both of these settings can be as safe and much less expensive than hospital births in low-risk deliveries attended by skilled practitioners (Anderson & Anderson, 1999; Durand, 1992; Guyer, Strobino, Ventura, & Singh, 1995; Korte & Scaer, 1984).

Hospitals, too, are finding ways to "humanize" childbirth. Labor and delivery may take place in a quiet, homelike birthing room, under soft lights, with the father present as a coach and older siblings invited to visit after the birth. The woman is given local anesthesia if she wants and needs it, but she can see and consciously participate in the birth process and can hold her newborn on her belly immediately afterward. Rooming-in policies allow a baby to stay in the mother's room much or all of the time. By "demedicalizing the experience, some hospitals and birthing centers are seeking to establish—or reestablish—around childbirth an environment in which tenderness, security, and emotion carry as much weight as medical techniques" (Fontanel & d'Harcourt, 1997, p. 57).

Checkpoint ✔

Can you . . .

✔ Identify three ways in which childbirth has changed in developed countries?

✔ Give reasons for the reduction in risks of pregnancy and childbirth?

✔ Weigh the comparative advantages of various settings and attendants for childbirth?

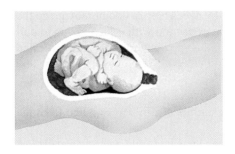

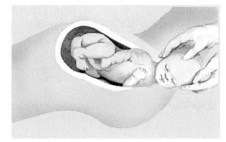

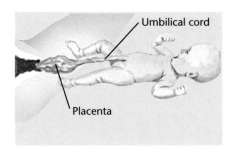

(a) First stage

(b) Second stage

(c) Third stage

Figure 5-1

The first three stages of childbirth. (a) During the first stage of labor, a series of stronger and stronger contractions dilates the cervix, the opening to the mother's womb. (b) During the second stage, the baby's head moves down the birth canal and emerges from the vagina. (c) During the brief third stage, the placenta and umbilical cord are expelled from the womb. Then the cord is cut.

Source: Adapted from Lagercrantz & Slotkin, 1986.

The Birth Process

Guidepost 2

How does labor begin, what happens during each of the three stages of childbirth, and what alternative methods of delivery are available?

Labor is an apt term for the process of giving birth. Chiefly because of the size of the fetal head, birth is hard work for both mother and baby. From an evolutionary perspective, the advantage of an enlarged head that can contain a brain capable of advanced thought outweighs the difficulty of passing through the birth canal (Bjorklund & Pellegrini, 2000).

What brings on labor, or normal vaginal childbirth, is a series of uterine, cervical, and other changes called **parturition.** Parturition typically begins about two weeks before delivery, when sharply rising estrogen levels stimulate the uterus to contract and the cervix to become more flexible. The timing of parturition seems to be determined by a dramatic increase in the rate at which the placenta produces a protein called *corticotropin-releasing hormone (CRH)*. This protein also promotes maturation of the fetal lungs to ready them for life outside the womb. The rate of CRH production as early as the fifth month of pregnancy may help predict whether a baby will be born early, on time, or late (Smith, 1999, 2007).

The uterine contractions that expel the fetus begin—typically, at 40 weeks of gestation—as tightenings of the uterus. A woman may have felt false contractions (known as *Braxton-Hicks contractions*) at times during the final months of pregnancy, or even as early as the second trimester, when the muscles of the uterus would tighten for 30 to 60 seconds or as long as 2 minutes. These contractions may help tone the uterine muscles and promote the flow of blood to the placenta. In comparison with Braxton-Hicks contractions, which are relatively mild and irregular and then subside, real labor contractions are more frequent, rhythmic, and painful, and they increase in frequency and intensity.

parturition Process of uterine, cervical, and other changes, usually lasting about 2 weeks preceding childbirth.

Stages of Childbirth

Labor takes place in three overlapping stages (Figure 5-1). The *first stage, dilation of the cervix,* is the longest, typically lasting 12 to 14 hours for a woman having her first child. In subsequent births the first stage tends to be shorter. During this stage, regular and increasingly frequent uterine contractions—15 to 20 minutes apart at first—cause the cervix to shorten and dilate, or widen, in preparation for delivery. Toward the end of the first stage, contractions occur every 2 to 5 minutes. This stage lasts until the cervix is fully open (10 centimeters, or about 4 inches) so the baby can descend into the birth canal.

The *second stage, descent and emergence of the baby,* typically lasts up to an hour or two. It begins when the baby's head begins to move through the cervix into the vaginal canal, and it ends when the baby emerges completely from the mother's body. If this stage lasts longer than 2 hours, signaling that the baby needs help, a doctor may grasp the baby's head with forceps or, more often, use vacuum extraction with a suction cup to pull it out of the mother's body. At the end of this stage, the baby is born but is still attached to the placenta in the mother's body by the umbilical cord, which must be cut and clamped.

The *third stage, expulsion of the placenta,* lasts between 10 minutes and 1 hour. During this stage the placenta and the remainder of the umbilical cord are expelled from the mother.

At one time, an *episiotomy,* a surgical cut between the vagina and anus, was made just before delivery to enlarge the vaginal opening, speed delivery, and prevent the vagina from tearing. The assumption was that a "clean" incision would heal better than a spontaneous tear. However, many studies have disproved this theory, and experts now agree that episiotomy should not be done routinely. It is recommended only under special circumstances, such as a very large baby, a forceps birth, or indications of trouble with the baby's heart rate.

Electronic Fetal Monitoring

Electronic fetal monitoring can be used to track the fetus's heartbeat during labor and delivery and to indicate how the fetal heart is responding to the stress of uterine contractions. Monitoring can detect any serious problems and alert the attending physician or midwife that a fetus needs help. Sometimes electronic fetal monitoring is used late in pregnancy if there are signs that the fetus may be at risk. The procedure was used in 85.4 percent of live births in the United States in 2003 (Martin, Hamilton, et al., 2005).

Electronic fetal monitoring can be done *externally,* by placing a monitor on the mother's abdomen and securing it with elastic belts, or *internally,* by inserting a wire into the cervix and resting it on the baby's head. The internal method is more accurate but can be used only when the cervix is already open, and it carries a risk of infection. Monitoring can be done remotely by *telemetry,* sending information about the fetal heart rate and the woman's contractions to a monitor at another location, such as the nurses' station.

Electronic fetal monitoring can provide valuable information in high-risk deliveries, including those in which the fetus is very small, is premature, is in a breech position (feet or buttocks down), or seems to be in distress, or in which labor is induced through administration of drugs. The rate of inductions in the United States has more than doubled since 1990; more than 21 percent of live births were induced in 2004, in part reflecting an increase in elective inductions (Martin, Hamilton, et al., 2006).

Monitoring can have drawbacks if used routinely in low-risk pregnancies. It is costly; it restricts the mother's movements during labor; and, most important, it has an extremely high false-positive rate, suggesting that fetuses are in trouble when they are not. Such warnings may prompt doctors to deliver by the riskier cesarean method rather than the vaginal one (Nelson, Dambrosia, Ting, & Grether, 1996).

Vaginal versus Cesarean Delivery

The usual method of childbirth, previously described, is *vaginal delivery.* Alternatively, **cesarean delivery** can be used to surgically remove the baby from the uterus through an incision in the mother's abdomen. In 2004, 29.1 percent of U.S. births occurred this way, a 41 percent increase since 1996 and a record high (Hoyert, Mathews, et al., 2006). Use of this procedure also increased in European countries during the 1990s, but cesarean birthrates in the United States are among the highest in the world (International Cesarean Awareness Network, 2003; Notzon, 1990; Sachs et al., 1999).

The operation is commonly performed when labor progresses too slowly, when the fetus seems to be in trouble, or when the mother is bleeding vaginally. Often a cesarean is needed when the fetus is in the breech position or in the transverse position (lying crosswise in the uterus) or when the head is too big to pass through the mother's pelvis.

Surgical deliveries are more likely when the birth involves a first baby, a large baby, an older mother, or a mother who has had a previous cesarean. Thus, the increase in cesarean rates since 1970 is in part a reflection of a proportional increase in first births, a rise in average birth weight, and a trend toward later childbirth (Guyer et al., 1999; Martin et al., 2003; Martin, Hamilton, et al., 2005). Other suggested explanations include the increased use of electronic fetal monitoring; physicians' fear of malpractice litigation; and women's desire to avoid a difficult labor (Martin et al., 2003; Martin, Hamilton, et al., 2005, 2006; Sachs, Kobelin, Castro, & Frigoletto, 1999).

Cesarean deliveries carry risks of serious maternal complications, such as bleeding, infections, and bowel injury (Nelson, Dambrosia, Ting, & Grether, 1996; Silver et al., 2006). They also (as we will discuss in a subsequent section) deprive the baby of important benefits of normal birth. However, despite these disadvantages of cesarean birth, a vaginal delivery for a woman who has had an earlier cesarean delivery should be attempted only with caution. A comparison of 17,898 U.S. women who attempted vaginal births after a previous cesarean (VBAC) with 15,801 U.S. women who elected a repeat cesarean found greater (though still low) risks of uterine rupture and brain damage associated with VBAC (Landon et al., 2004). And, among 313,238 Scottish women giving birth after previous cesareans, the risk of the infant's dying during delivery was about 11 times higher in vaginal deliveries than in planned repeat cesareans (Smith, Pell, Cameron, & Dobbie, 2002). As risks of such deliveries have become widely known, the rate of vaginal births after a previous cesarean has fallen by 67 percent in U.S. women since 1996 (Hoyert, Mathews, et al., 2006), Today, if a woman has had a cesarean delivery, chances are more than 90 percent that any subsequent deliveries will be cesarean (Martin, Hamilton, et al., 2006).

Medicated versus Nonmedicated Delivery

For centuries, pain was considered an unavoidable part of giving birth. Then, in the mid-19th century, England's Queen Victoria became the first woman in history to be sedated during delivery, that of her eighth child. Sedation with ether or chloroform became common practice as more births took place in hospitals (Fontanel & d'Harcourt, 1997).

During the 20th century, several alternative methods of **natural, or prepared, childbirth** were developed. These methods minimize or eliminate the use of drugs that may pose risks for babies and enable both parents to participate fully in a natural, empowering experience. In 1914 Dr. Grantly Dick-Read, an English gynecologist, suggested that pain in childbirth was caused mostly by fear of the unknown and the resulting muscular tension. His "Childbirth without Fear" method educates expectant mothers about the physiology of reproduction and trains them in physical fitness and in breathing and relaxation during labor and delivery.

The Lamaze method, introduced by the French obstetrician Fernand Lamaze in the late 1950s, teaches expectant mothers to work actively with their bodies through controlled breathing. The woman is trained to pant or breathe rapidly in sync with the increasing intensity of her contractions and to concentrate on other sensations to ease the perception of pain. She learns to relax her muscles as a conditioned response to the voice of her coach (usually the prospective father or a friend), who attends classes with her, takes part in the delivery, and helps with the exercises. Other methods use mental imagery, massage, gentle pushing, and deep breathing. One technique, introduced by the French physician Michael Odent, is submersion of the laboring mother in a soothing pool of water. Perhaps most extreme is the Bradley Method, which disavows all obstetrical procedures and other medical interventions.

Today, improvements in medicated delivery have led many mothers to choose pain relief, sometimes along with natural methods. *General anesthesia,* which renders the woman completely unconscious and greatly increases the risks to mother and baby, is rarely used, even in cesarean births (Eltzschig et al., 2003). A woman may be given *local (vaginal) anesthesia,* also called a *pedunal block,* if she wants and needs it, usually during the second stage of labor or when forceps are used. Or she can receive an *analgesic* (painkiller), which reduces the perception of pain by depressing the activity of the central nervous system.

natural, or prepared, childbirth Methods of childbirth that seek to reduce or eliminate use of drugs, enable both parents to participate fully, and control perceptions of pain.

What's your view

- If you or your partner were expecting a baby, and the pregnancy seemed to be going smoothly, would you prefer (a) hospital, birth center, or home birth, (b) attendance by a physician or midwife, and (c) medicated or nonmedicated delivery? Give reasons.

- If you are a man, would you choose to be present at the birth?

- If you are a woman, would you want your partner present?

However, analgesics may slow labor, cause maternal complications, and make the baby less alert after birth. Approximately 60 percent of women in labor have *regional (epidural or spinal) anesthesia* (Eltzschig et al., 2003). Regional anesthesia, which is injected into a space in the spinal cord between the vertebrae in the lumbar (lower) region, blocks the nerve pathways that would carry the sensation of pain to the brain. Epidurals given early can shorten labor with no added risk of needing cesarean delivery (Wong et al., 2005).

With any of these newer forms of anesthesia, the woman can see and participate in the birth process and can hold her newborn immediately afterward. However, these drugs pass through the placenta to the fetal blood supply and tissues and thus may pose some danger to the baby.

Pain relief should not be the only consideration in a decision about whether a woman should have anesthesia. More important to her satisfaction with the childbirth experience may be her involvement in decision making, her relationship with the professionals caring for her, and her expectations about labor. Social and cultural attitudes and customs also may play a part (Eltzschig et al., 2003). A woman and her doctor should discuss the various options early in pregnancy, but her choices may change once labor is under way.

In many traditional cultures, childbearing women are attended by a *doula,* an experienced mentor, coach, and helper who can furnish emotional support and information and can stay at a woman's bedside throughout labor. Unlike a midwife, a doula does not participate in the delivery but supports the mother throughout the process (Box 5-1). In eleven randomized, controlled studies, women attended by doulas had shorter labor, less anesthesia, and fewer forceps and cesarean deliveries than mothers who had not had doulas (Klaus & Kennell, 1997). Approximately 5,000 U.S. women were registered as professional doulas in 2004 (Wilgoren, 2005).

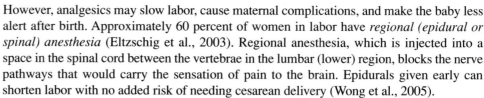

The Newborn Baby

Birth is stressful for babies. The struggle to be born apparently stimulates the infant's body to produce huge amounts of two stress hormones, adrenaline and noradrenaline. The surge of these hormones at birth clears the lungs of excess fluid to permit breathing, mobilizes stored fuel to nourish cells, and sends blood to the heart and brain. Also, by making the baby more alert and ready to interact with another person, these hormones may promote bonding with the mother. These, as we have mentioned, are important advantages of vaginal birth. Cesarean deliveries bypass the experience of labor, which may help a baby adjust to life outside the womb (Lagercrantz & Slotkin, 1986).

The first 4 weeks of life, the **neonatal period,** is a time of transition from the uterus, where a fetus is supported entirely by the mother, to an independent existence. What are the physical characteristics of newborn babies, and how are they equipped for this crucial transition?

Size and Appearance

An average newborn, or **neonate,** in the United States is about 20 inches long and weighs about 7½ pounds. At birth, the vast majority of full-term babies weigh between 5½ and 10 pounds and are between 18 and 22 inches long. Boys tend to be slightly longer and heavier than girls, and a firstborn child is likely to weigh less at birth than laterborns. In their first few days, neonates lose as much as 10 percent of their body weight, primarily because of a loss of fluids. They begin to gain weight again by about the fifth day and are generally back to birth weight by the 10th to the 14th day.

New babies have distinctive features, including a large head (one-fourth the body length), red skin (which soon fades), various skin conditions (which are temporary—Table 5-1), birthmarks (which are permanent), and a receding chin (which makes it easier to nurse). For about a week after birth, a neonate's head may be long and misshapen because of the molding that eased its passage through the mother's pelvis, but it assumes

Checkpoint

Can you . . .

✔ Describe the three stages of vaginal childbirth?

✔ Explain the purpose of electronic fetal monitoring and the dangers of its routine use?

✔ Discuss the uses and disadvantages of cesarean births?

✔ Compare medicated delivery with natural or prepared childbirth?

✔ Compare the functions of a midwife and a doula?

Guidepost 3

How do newborn infants adjust to life outside the womb, and how can we tell whether a new baby is healthy and is developing normally?

neonatal period First 4 weeks of life, a time of transition from intrauterine dependency to independent existence.

neonate Newborn baby, up to 4 weeks old.

Box 5-1 *Having a Baby in the Himalayas*

Between 1993 and 1995, Sally Olds, one of the authors of this book, made four visits to Badel, a remote hill village in the small Asian country of Nepal, where she stayed with local families. The following account (Olds, 2002) describes a visit that she, the friend she traveled with, and their guide, Buddi, made to the village midwife.

Sabut Maya Mathani Rai has been helping childbearing mothers for almost 50 of her 75 years. Only 3 days ago she attended the birth of a baby girl.

When Sabut Maya attends a woman about to give birth, she says, "First I feel on the outside of the woman's belly. I look to see where is the head and the other organs. I help the mother push down when her time comes."

She does not use forceps. "I don't have any instruments," she says. "I just use my hands. If the baby is upside down, I turn it from the outside."

Nepali hill women usually give birth right after, or in the middle of, working in house or fields. The delivery may occur inside or outside of the house, depending on when the woman goes into labor. Women usually give birth on their knees. This kneeling position allows the mother to use her strong thigh and abdominal muscles to push the baby out. If the mother has other children, they usually watch, no matter how small they are. But the husbands don't want to watch, and the women don't want them there.

Most women are not attended by a midwife; they handle the delivery and dispose of the placenta and umbilical cord themselves. Buddi's mother once gave birth on the path as she was walking back from working in the fields and then asked for her husband's knife to cut the cord.

"If the baby is not coming fast, I use special medicine," the midwife says. "I put grasses on the mother's body and I massage her with oil from a special plant. I don't give the mother any herbs or anything like that to eat or drink, only hot water or tea."

In a complicated birth—if, say, the baby is not emerging or the mother gets sick—the midwife calls the *shaman* (spiritual healer). Inevitably, some babies and some mothers die. In most cases, however, all goes well, and most deliveries are easy and quick.

How is the newborn cared for? "After the baby is born I wash the baby," says the midwife. "I leave this much of the cord on the baby [indicating about half an inch] and I tie it up with very good cotton. Then I wrap a piece of cotton cloth around the baby's tummy. This stays on for a few days until the cord falls off." Sometimes a small piece of the umbilical cord is saved and inserted into a metal bead that will be given to the child to wear on a string around the neck, to ward off evil spirits. A family member flings the placenta high up on a tree near the house to dry out; eventually it is thrown away.

No one but the mother—not even the father—is allowed to hold the baby at first. This custom may help to protect both

A midwife in Kathmandu, Nepal, oils a newborn baby.

mother and baby from infection and disease when they are most vulnerable. Then, at age 4 days for a girl or 7 days for a boy (girls are thought to mature earlier), a purification rite and naming ceremony take place.

My friend and I tell how in our culture women lie on their backs, a position unknown in most traditional societies, and how the doctor sometimes breaks the woman's water. We also describe how a doctor sometimes puts on surgical gloves and reaches inside the woman to turn a baby in a breech or other position. "We don't have gloves and we don't have instruments," the midwife repeats. "We don't do any of those things. I'm just a helper." What Sabut Maya really is is a combination of midwife and doula [described in this chapter]—a kind of helper now seen with growing frequency in Western delivery rooms. It seems ironic that it has taken the Western world so long to rediscover some of the wisdom that "primitive" societies have known for centuries.

What's your view

- What aspects of traditional ways of delivering babies might enhance Western childbearing practices without giving up medical techniques that save lives?
- Could advanced medical techniques be introduced into traditional societies without invalidating practices that seem to serve women in those societies well?

Check it out

For more information on this topic, go to www.dona.org. This is the Web site for Doulas of North America (DONA), an international association of doulas, founded in 1992 by Marshall Klaus, John Kennell, and others.

Table 5-1	Neonatal Skin Conditions		
Condition	**Description**	**Cause**	**Duration**
Blue coloring	Bluish color on hands and feet*	Immature blood circulation	Normal color should appear within several days
Milia	Tiny, white, hard, pimplelike spots on nose, chin, or forehead	Immature oil glands	Disappear on their own
Stork bites (or salmon patches)	Small pink or red patches on eyelids, between the eyes, on upper lip, or back of neck, most visible during crying	Concentration of immature blood vessels	Most soon fade and disappear
Mongolian spots	Blue or purple splotches on lower back and buttocks	Concentration of pigmented cells; tends to occur in dark-skinned babies	Usually disappears within first 4 years
Erythema toxicum	Red rash similar to flea bites, usually on chest and back	Cause unknown; appears in half of all babies, but most commonly in premature babies	Usually disappears in a few days
Acne neonatorum (baby acne)	Pimples on cheeks and forehead	Maternal hormones; about one-fifth of neonates develop this condition in 1st month	Disappears in a few months
Strawberry hemangioma (strawberry mark)	Bright or dark red, raised or swollen, bumpy area, usually on head	Concentration of tiny, immature blood vessels; often develop within first 2 months; most common in premature babies and in girls	Often grow in size for several months and then fade gradually, disappearing by age 9
Port wine stain	Flat pink, red, or purple birthmark, usually on head or neck but may cover large areas of body	Concentration of dilated capillaries (tiny, immature blood vessels)	Do not disappear; may become darker and bleed as child grows older; may be treated by laser surgery

*Bluish coloring on other parts of body is abnormal.

a normal shape by the end of the first week. This temporary molding is possible because an infant's skull bones are not yet fused; they will not be completely joined for 18 months. The places on the head where the bones have not yet grown together—the soft spots, or *fontanels*—are covered by a tough membrane.

Many newborns have a pinkish cast; their skin is so thin that it barely covers the capillaries through which blood flows. However, a baby's skin color can vary greatly, depending on the baby's age, racial or ethnic origin, health status, temperature, the environment, and whether the baby is crying. During the first few days, some neonates are very hairy because some of the *lanugo,* a fuzzy prenatal hair on the shoulders, back, forehead, and cheeks, has not yet fallen off. It appears most often in premature babies. Almost all new babies (except those born postterm, after 41 weeks of gestation), are covered with *vernix caseosa* ("cheesy varnish"), a white, oily, cheeselike substance that is formed in the womb by secretions from the fetal oil glands and protects against infection. This coating is absorbed into the skin after birth.

Table 5-2

Characteristic	Prenatal Life	Postnatal Life
Environment	Amniotic fluid	Air
Temperature	Relatively constant	Fluctuates with atmosphere
Stimulation	Minimal	All senses stimulated by various stimuli
Nutrition	Dependent on mother's blood	Dependent on external food and functioning of digestive system
Oxygen supply	Passed from maternal bloodstream via placenta	Passed from neonate's lungs to pulmonary blood vessels
Metabolic elimination	Passed into maternal bloodstream via placenta	Discharged by skin, kidneys, lungs, and gastrointestinal tract

"Witch's milk," a secretion that sometimes leaks from the swollen breasts of newborn boys and girls around the 3rd day of life, was believed during the Middle Ages to have special healing powers. Like the whitish or blood-tinged vaginal discharge of some newborn girls, this fluid emission results from high levels of the hormone estrogen, which is secreted by the placenta just before birth, and goes away within a few days or weeks. A newborn, especially if premature, also may have swollen genitals.

Body Systems

Before birth, blood circulation, respiration, nourishment, elimination of waste, and temperature regulation are accomplished through the mother's body. After birth, all of the baby's systems and functions must operate on their own (Table 5-2). Most of this transition occurs during the first 4 to 6 hours after delivery (Ferber & Makhoul, 2004).

As we discussed in Chapter 4, the fetus and mother have separate circulatory systems and separate heartbeats; the fetus's blood is cleansed through the umbilical cord, which carries old blood to the placenta and returns a fresh supply (refer back to Figure 4-2). A neonate's blood circulates wholly within the baby's body; the heartbeat at first is fast and irregular, and blood pressure does not stabilize until about the 10th day of life.

The fetus gets oxygen through the umbilical cord, which also carries away carbon dioxide. A newborn needs much more oxygen than before and must now get it alone. Most babies start to breathe as soon as they are exposed to air. If breathing has not begun within about 5 minutes, the baby may suffer permanent brain injury from **anoxia,** lack of oxygen, or *hypoxia,* a reduced oxygen supply. Because infants' lungs have only one-tenth as many air sacs as adults' do, infants (especially those born prematurely) are susceptible to respiratory problems. Anoxia or hypoxia may occur during delivery (though rarely so) as a result of repeated compression of the placenta and umbilical cord with each contraction. This form of *birth trauma* can leave permanent brain damage, causing mental retardation, behavior problems, or even death.

In the uterus, the fetus relies on the umbilical cord to bring food from the mother and to carry fetal body wastes away. At birth, babies have a strong sucking reflex to take in milk and gastrointestinal secretions to digest it. During the first few days infants secrete *meconium,* a stringy, greenish-black waste matter formed in the fetal intestinal tract. When the bowels and bladder are full, the sphincter muscles open automatically; a baby will not be able to control these muscles for many months.

About 3 or 4 days after birth, about half of all babies (and a larger proportion of babies born prematurely) develop **neonatal jaundice:** their skin and eyeballs look yellow. This kind of jaundice is caused by the immaturity of the liver. Usually it is not serious, does not need treatment, and has no long-term effects. However, because healthy U.S. newborns usually go home from the hospital within 48 hours or less, jaundice may go unnoticed and may lead to complications (American Academy of Pediatrics [AAP] Committee on Quality Improvement, 2002). Severe jaundice that is not monitored and treated promptly may result in brain damage.

The layers of fat that develop during the last two months of fetal life enable healthy full-term infants to keep their body temperature constant after birth despite changes in air

anoxia Lack of oxygen, which may cause brain damage.

neonatal jaundice Condition, in many newborn babies, caused by immaturity of the liver and evidenced by yellowish appearance; can cause brain damage if not treated promptly.

Checkpoint ✔

Can you . . .

✔ Describe the normal size and appearance of a newborn, and name several temporary skin conditions and other changes that occur within the first few days?

✔ Compare four fetal and neonatal body systems?

✔ Identify two dangerous conditions that can appear soon after birth?

Table 5-3	Apgar Scale			
Sign*	**0**	**1**	**2**
Appearance (color)	Blue, pale	Body pink, extremities blue	Entirely pink
Pulse (heart rate)	Absent	Slow (below 100 beats per minute)	Rapid (over 100 beats per minute)
Grimace (reflex irritability)	No response	Grimace	Coughing, sneezing, crying
Activity (muscle tone)	Limp	Weak, inactive; some flexing of arms and legs	Strong, active
Respiration (breathing)	Absent	Irregular, slow	Good, crying

*Each sign is rated in terms of absence or presence from 0 to 2; highest overall score is 10.

temperature. Newborn babies also maintain body temperature by increasing their activity when air temperature drops.

Medical and Behavioral Assessment

Although the great majority of births result in normal, healthy babies, some do not. The first few minutes, days, and weeks after birth are crucial for development. It is important to know as soon as possible whether a baby has any problem that needs special care.

The Apgar Scale

At 1 minute after delivery and then again at 5 minutes after birth (measured by a timer), babies are assessed using the **Apgar scale** (Table 5-3). Its name, after its developer, Dr. Virginia Apgar (1953), helps us remember its five subtests: *a*ppearance (color), *p*ulse (heart rate), *g*rimace (reflex irritability), *a*ctivity (muscle tone), and *r*espiration (breathing). The newborn is rated 0, 1, or 2 on each measure, for a maximum score of 10. A 5-minute score of 7 to 10—achieved by 98.5 percent of babies born in the United States in 2004—indicates that the baby is in good to excellent condition (Martin, Hamilton, et al., 2006). A score of 5 to 7 at 1 minute may mean the baby needs help to establish breathing; nurses may dry him vigorously with a towel while oxygen is held under his nose, and the test should be repeated every 5 minutes up to 20 minutes (AAP Committee on Fetus and Newborn & American College of Obstetricians and Gynecologists (ACOG) Committee on Obstetric Practice, 2006).

A score below 5 (unlikely except in a small percentage of premature newborns or those delivered by emergency cesarean) may reflect problems with the heart or respiratory system. A mask may be placed over the newborn's face to pump oxygen directly into the lungs; or, if breathing still does not start, a tube can be placed in the windpipe, and medications and fluids may be administered through the blood vessels in the umbilical cord to strengthen the heartbeat. If resuscitation is successful, bringing the baby's score to 5 or more, no long-term damage is likely to result. Scores of 0 to 3 at 10, 15, and 20 minutes after birth are increasingly associated with cerebral palsy (muscular impairment due to brain damage before or during birth) or other neurological problems (AAP Committee on Fetus and Newborn and ACOG Committee on Obstetric Practice, 1996, 2006).

In general, Apgar scores at 5 minutes reliably predict survival during the 1st month of life (Casey, McIntire, & Leveno, 2001). However, a low Apgar score alone does not necessarily indicate anoxia or predict neonatal death. Prematurity, low birth weight, trauma, infection, birth defects, medication given to the mother, and other conditions may affect

Apgar scale Standard measurement of a newborn's condition; it assesses appearance, pulse, grimace, activity, and respiration.

the scores (AAP Committee on Fetus and Newborn and ACOG Committee on Obstetric Practice, 1996, 2006).

Assessing Neurological Status: The Brazelton Scale

The **Brazelton Neonatal Behavioral Assessment Scale (NBAS)** is used in high-risk situations to help parents, health care providers, and researchers assess neonates' responsiveness to their physical and social environment, to identify strengths and possible vulnerabilities in neurological functioning, and to predict future development. The test, suitable for infants up to 2 months old, is named for its developer, Dr. T. Berry Brazelton (1973, 1984; Brazelton & Nugent, 1995). It assesses *motor organization* as shown by such behaviors as activity level and the ability to bring a hand to the mouth; *reflexes; state changes,* such as irritability, excitability, and ability to quiet down after being upset; *attention and interactive capacities,* as shown by general alertness and response to visual and auditory stimuli; and indications of *central nervous system instability,* such as tremors and changes in skin color. The NBAS takes about 30 minutes, and scores are based on a baby's best performance. A newer version, the Newborn Behavioral Observations (NBO) system (Nugent, Keefer, O'Brien, Johnson, & Blanchard, 2005) was developed specifically for clinicians caring for newborns in hospital, clinic, or home settings.

Brazelton Neonatal Behavioral Assessment Scale (NBAS) Neurological and behavioral test to measure a neonate's responses to the environment.

Neonatal Screening for Medical Conditions

Children who inherit the enzyme disorder phenylketonuria, or PKU (refer back to Table 3-1), will become mentally retarded unless they are fed a special diet beginning in the first 3 to 6 weeks of life (National Institutes of Health [NIH] Consensus Development Panel, 2001). Screening tests administered soon after birth often can discover such correctable defects. In one study, newborns identified by screening were less likely to be retarded or to need hospitalization than those identified by clinical diagnosis. One drawback is that the tests can generate false-positive results, which suggest that a problem exists when it does not and may trigger anxiety and costly, unnecessary treatment (Waisbren et al., 2003).

Until recently, routine screening of all newborn babies for such rare genetic conditions as PKU (1 case in 15,000 births), congenital hypothyroidism (1 in 3,600 to 5,000), galactosemia (1 in 60,000 to 80,000), and other, even rarer, biochemical disorders could be extremely expensive because of the need for separate tests for each disorder. So, although all states require screening for PKU and hypothyroidism, requirements for other screening tests vary (AAP Newborn Screening Task Force, 2000; NIH Consensus Development Panel, 2001).

Now, the advent of tandem mass spectrometry, in which a single blood specimen can be screened for 20 or more disorders, has prompted about half of the states as well as many developed countries to expand their mandatory screening programs (Howell, 2006). The American College of Medical Genetics (ACMG) recommends that screening nationwide be extended to 29 treatable conditions as well as 25 related but secondary conditions (USDHHS, Maternal and Child Health Bureau, 2005), and further expansion may follow (Howell, 2006). Critics warn against expanding screening too rapidly without adequate research support, including cost-benefit data (Botkin et al., 2006). Advocates argue that, although problems remain to be worked out in the operation of these programs, it is wrong to let children who might have been helped by screening suffer or even die in the meantime.

Checkpoint ✔

Can you . . .

✔ Discuss the uses of the Apgar test, the Brazelton Scale, and routine postbirth screening for rare disorders?

States of Arousal and Activity Levels

Babies have an internal clock that regulates their daily cycles of eating, sleeping, and elimination and perhaps even their moods. These periodic cycles of wakefulness, sleep, and

Table 5-4	States of Arousal in Infancy			
State	**Eyes**	**Breathing**	**Movements**	**Responsiveness**
Regular sleep	Closed; no eye movement	Regular and slow	None, except for sudden, generalized startles	Cannot be aroused by mild stimuli.
Irregular sleep	Closed; occasional rapid eye movements	Irregular	Muscles twitch, but no major movements	Sounds or light bring smiles or grimaces in sleep.
Drowsiness	Open or closed	Irregular	Somewhat active	May smile, startle, suck, or have erections in response to stimuli.
Alert inactivity	Open	Even	Quiet; may move head, limbs, and trunk while looking around	An interesting environment (with people or things to watch) may initiate or maintain this state.
Waking activity and crying	Open	Irregular	Much activity	External stimuli (such as hunger, cold, pain, being restrained, or being laid down) bring about more activity, perhaps starting with soft whimpering and gentle movements and turning into a rhythmic crescendo of crying or kicking, or perhaps beginning and enduring as uncoordinated thrashing and spasmodic screeching.

Source: Adapted from Prechtl & Beintema, 1964; P. H. Wolff, 1966.

state of arousal Infant's physiological and behavioral status at a given moment in the periodic daily cycle of wakefulness, sleep, and activity.

activity, which govern an infant's **state of arousal,** or degree of alertness (Table 5-4), seem to be inborn and highly individual. Changes in state are coordinated by multiple areas of the brain and are accompanied by changes in the functioning of virtually all body systems (Ingersoll & Thoman, 1999).

Most new babies spend about 75 percent of their time—up to 18 hours a day—asleep but awaken every 3 to 4 hours, day and night, for feeding (Ferber & Makhoul, 2004; Hoban, 2004). Newborns' sleep alternates between quiet (regular) and active (irregular) sleep. Active sleep appears rhythmically in cycles of about 1 hour and accounts for up to 50 percent of a newborn's sleep time. It is probably the equivalent of rapid eye movement (REM) sleep, which in adults is associated with dreaming. The amount of active sleep declines to less than 30 percent of daily sleep time by age 3 and continues to decrease steadily throughout life (Hoban, 2004).

Beginning in the 1st month, nighttime sleep periods gradually lengthen and total sleep time diminishes as babies grow more wakeful in the daytime. Some infants begin to sleep through the night as early as age 3 months. By 6 months, an infant typically sleeps for 6 hours straight at night, but brief nighttime waking is normal even during late infancy and toddlerhood. A 2-year-old typically sleeps about 13 hours a day, including a single nap, usually in the afternoon (Hoban, 2004).

Babies' sleep rhythms and schedules vary across cultures. Among the Micronesian Truk and the Canadian Hare peoples, babies and children have no regular sleep schedules; they fall asleep whenever they feel tired. Some U.S. parents try to time the evening feeding to encourage nighttime sleep. Mothers in rural Kenya allow their babies to nurse as they please, and their 4-month-olds continue to sleep only 4 hours at a stretch (Broude, 1995).

Some parents and caregivers spend a great deal of time and energy trying to change babies' states—mostly by soothing a fussy infant to sleep. Although crying is usually more distressing than serious, it is particularly important to quiet low-birth-weight babies, because quiet babies maintain their weight better. Steady stimulation is the time-proven way to soothe crying babies: by rocking or walking them, wrapping them snugly, or letting them hear rhythmic sounds (Box 5-2).

Checkpoint ✔

Can you . . .

✔ Discuss patterns of sleep, arousal, and activity and variations in newborns' states?

✔ Tell how sleep patterns change, and how cultural practices can affect these patterns?

Box 5-2 *Comforting a Crying Baby*

All babies cry. It is their only way to let us know they are hungry, uncomfortable, lonely, or unhappy. And because few sounds are as distressing as a baby's cry, parents or other caregivers usually rush to feed or pick up a crying infant. As babies quiet down and fall asleep or gaze about in alert contentment, they may show that their problem has been solved. At other times, the caregiver cannot figure out what the baby wants. The baby keeps crying. It is worth trying to find ways to help. Babies whose cries bring relief seem to become more self-confident, feeling that they can affect their own lives.

In Chapter 8 we will discuss several kinds of crying and what the crying may mean. Unusual, persistent crying patterns may be early signs of trouble. For healthy babies who just seem unhappy, the following may help (Eiger & Olds, 1999):

- Hold the baby, perhaps laying the baby on his or her stomach on your chest, to feel your heartbeat and breathing. Or sit with the baby in a comfortable rocking chair.
- Put the baby in a carrier next to your chest and walk around.
- If you are upset, ask someone else to hold the baby; infants sometimes sense and respond to their caregivers' moods.
- Pat or rub the baby's back, in case a bubble of air is causing discomfort.
- Wrap the baby snugly in a small blanket; some infants feel more secure when firmly swaddled from neck to toes, with arms held close to the sides.
- Make the baby warmer or cooler; put on or take off clothing or change the room temperature.
- Give the baby a massage or a warm bath.
- Sing or talk to the baby. Or provide a continuous or rhythmic sound, such as music from the radio, a simulated heartbeat, or background noise from a whirring fan, vacuum cleaner, or other appliance.
- Take the baby out for a ride in a stroller or car seat—at any hour of the day or night. In bad weather, some parents walk around in an enclosed mall; the distraction helps them as well as the baby.
- If someone other than a parent is taking care of the baby, it sometimes helps if the caregiver puts on a robe or a sweater that the mother or father has recently worn so the baby can sense the familiar smell.
- Pick up on the baby's signals.

What's your view ?

Have you ever tried to soothe a crying baby? What techniques seemed to work best?

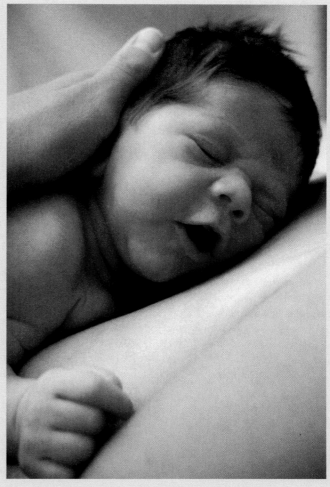

This crying baby may quiet when held stomach down on his mother's chest.

Check it out !

For more information on this topic, go to www.pantley.com/elizabeth/advice/0071398856.php?nid=435. This article by parenting educator Elizabeth Pantley discusses various types of cries and offers advice about whether and how parents should respond.

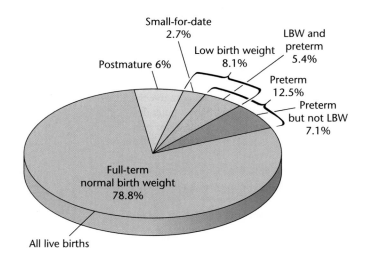

preterm (premature) infants
Infants born before completing the 37th week of gestation.

small-for-date (small-for-gestational-age) infants Infants whose birth weight is less than that of 90 percent of babies of the same gestational age, as a result of slow fetal growth.

Complications of Childbirth— and Their Aftermath

"It must be a boy," say some mothers whose labor and delivery prove long and difficult. This old adage seems to bear some truth: boys' deliveries are somewhat more likely to involve complications than girls', in part because boy babies tend to be larger. In two large Irish and Dutch studies, male babies took longer to emerge and were more likely to suffer fetal distress, to require forceps or caesarean delivery, and to have low Apgar scores than female babies (Bekedam, Engelsbel, Mol, Buitendijk, & van der Pal-de Bruin, 2002; Eogan, Geary, O'Connell, & Keane, 2003).

Most babies are born healthy, but some remain in the womb too briefly or too long or are born too small—complications that can impair their chances of survival and well-being. Others are born dead or die soon after birth. Let's look at some of these potential complications of birth and at ways to increase the chances of favorable outcomes.

Low Birth Weight

Low-birth-weight babies may be either *preterm* or *small-for-date,* or both (Figure 5-2). About 2 out of 3 babies with low birth weight are **preterm (premature) infants,** born before completing the 37th week of gestation (Martin, Hamilton, Sutton, et al., 2005). (Preterm babies born close to term may be of normal birth weight and may have few or mild health problems.) **Small-for-date (small-for-gestational age) infants,** who may or may not be preterm, weigh less than 90 percent of all babies of the same gestational age. Their small size is generally a result of inadequate prenatal nutrition, which slows fetal growth.

Prematurity and low birth weight together constitute the second leading cause of death in infancy in the United States after birth defects (Hoyert, Heron, et al., 2006) and the leading cause during the neonatal period (Anderson & Smith, 2005). Preventing or treating these conditions can greatly increase the number of babies who survive the first year of life.

How Many Babies Are Preterm, and Why?

In 2004, 12.5 percent of U.S. infants were born preterm, 18 percent more than in 1990 and 33 percent more than in 1981. The causes of preterm birth are not fully understood, but this trend may in part reflect the rise in multiple births and induced and cesearean deliveries (Martin, Hamilton, et al., 2006).

Preterm birth accounts for nearly half of all neurological birth defects, such as cerebral palsy, and more than two-thirds of infant deaths. More than 70 percent of preterm births are late preterm, delivered between 34 and 36 weeks' gestation; these babies tend to weigh more and to be at lower risk than those born earlier in gestation (Martin, Hamilton, et al., 2006).

Such measures as enhanced prenatal care, nutritional interventions, home monitoring of uterine activity, and administration of drugs, bed rest, and hydration for women who go into labor early have failed to stem the tide of premature births (Goldenberg & Rouse, 1998; Lockwood, 2002). One promising treatment is a form of the hormone progesterone called *hydroxyprogesterone caproate,* or *17P.* In a 2½-year trial at 13 major medical research centers, giving 17P to women who had borne premature babies reduced repeat preterm births by as much as one-third (Meis et al., 2003).

How Many Babies Are Low Birth Weight, and Why?

In 2004, 8.1 percent of babies born in the United States had **low birth weight,** weighing less than 2,500 grams (5½ pounds) at birth—the highest rate of low birth weight since 1969. *Very-low-birth-weight* babies, who weigh less than 1,500 grams (3½ pounds), accounted for nearly 1.5 percent of births. Very-low-birth-weight babies are nearly 100 times more likely to die during their 1st year of life than babies of normal birth weight, and moderately low-birth-weight babies (between 1,500 and 2,499 grams at birth) are more than 5 times more likely to die. Much of the increase in low birth weight since the mid-1980s, like the rise in premature births, is likely due to increased use of induced and cesarean deliveries, delayed childbearing, fertility drugs, and multiple births; but low birth weight also is increasing among single births (Martin, Hamilton, et al., 2006).

The United States is more successful than any other country in the world in saving low-birth-weight babies, but the rate of such births to U.S. women remains higher than in many European and Asian nations. Overall, 15.5 percent of all births, or more than 20 million infants worldwide—more than 95 percent of them in developing countries—have low birth weight (Table 5-5). (The true extent of low birth weight may be much higher because as many as 3 out of 4 newborns in the developing world are not weighed.) Low birth weight in developing regions stems primarily from the mother's poor health and nutrition; in the industrialized world smoking during pregnancy is the leading factor (United Nations Children's Fund and World Health Organization, 2004).

low birth weight Weight of less than 5½ pounds (2,500 grams) at birth because of prematurity or being small-for-date.

Who Is Likely to Have a Low-Birth-Weight Baby?

Factors increasing the likelihood that a woman will have an underweight baby include (1) *demographic and socioeconomic factors,* such as being African American, under age 17 or over 40, poor, unmarried, or undereducated, and being born in certain regions, such as the southern and plains states (Thompson, Goodman, Chang, & Stukel, 2005); (2) *medical factors predating the pregnancy,* such as having no children or more than four, being short or thin, having had previous low-birth-weight infants or multiple miscarriages, having had low birth weight oneself, or having genital or urinary abnormalities or chronic hypertension; (3) *prenatal behavioral and environmental factors,* such as poor nutrition, inadequate prenatal care, smoking, use of alcohol or other drugs, or exposure to stress, high altitude, or toxic substances; and (4) *medical conditions associated with the pregnancy,* such as vaginal bleeding, infections, high or low blood pressure, anemia, too little weight gain (Arias, MacDorman, Strobino, & Guyer, 2003; S. S. Brown, 1985; Chomitz, Cheung, & Lieberman, 1995; Nathanielsz, 1995; Shiono & Behrman, 1995; Wegman, 1992; Zhu, Rolfs, Nangle, & Horan, 1999), and having last given birth less than 6 months or more than 5 years before (Conde-Agudelo, Rosas-Bermúdez, Kafury-Goeta, 2006). Depression during pregnancy is another risk factor; screening for depression is a critical part of prenatal care (Yonkers, quoted in Bernstein, 2003).

The high proportion (13.7 percent) of low-birth-weight babies in the African American population—about twice as high as in white and Hispanic babies—is the major factor in the high mortality rates of black babies (Hoyert, Mathews, et al., 2006; Martin, Hamilton, et al., 2006; see Table 6-3 in Chapter 6). Researchers have identified a genetic variant that

Table 5-5 — Percentage and Number of Low-Birth-Weight Infants by United Nations Regions, 2000*

	% Low-Birth-Weight Infants
WORLD	**15.5**
More developed countries	7.0
Less developed countries	16.5
Least developed countries	18.6
AFRICA	**14.3**
Eastern Africa	13.5
Middle Africa	12.3
Northern Africa	15.3
Southern Africa	14.6
Western Africa	15.4
ASIA**	**18.3**
Eastern Asia**	5.9
South-central Asia	27.1
South-eastern Asia	11.6
Western Asia	15.4
EUROPE	**6.4**
Eastern Europe	6.4
Northern Europe	6.5
Southern Europe	5.9
Western Europe	6.7
LATIN AMERICA AND CARIBBEAN	**10.0**
Caribbean	13.7
Central America	10.1
South America	9.6
NORTHERN AMERICA	**7.7**
OCEANIA**	**10.5**
Australia/New Zealand	6.5
Melanesia	10.8
Micronesia	12.7
Polynesia	3.8

*The latest available estimates by country and territory, on which these global and regional estimates are calculated, may refer to an earlier or a more recent year than 2000. However, considering that low-birth-weight rates are changing only slowly, the latest rates available have been taken to also refer to the year 2000 for the calculation of these global and regional estimates.

**Australia, Japan, and New Zealand have been excluded from the regional estimates, but are included in the total for developed countries.

Source: United Nations Children's Fund & World Health Organization (2004).

may account for the high rates of premature delivery among African American women (Wang et al., 2006). Other suggested reasons for the greater prevalence of low birth weight, preterm births, and infant mortality among African American babies include (1) health behaviors and SES; (2) higher levels of stress in African American women; (3) greater susceptibility to stress; (4) the impact of racism, which may contribute to or exacerbate stress; and (5) ethnic differences in stress-related body processes, such as blood pressure and immune reactions (Giscombé & Lobel, 2005).

Data from a national longitudinal study of three generations of family members suggest that SES is a more important factor for white mothers than for black mothers. For white women who had been poor in childhood, upward socioeconomic mobility was associated with a 48 percent lower likelihood of having a low-birth-weight baby; for black women, this relationship was not statistically significant. Maternal health behaviors, such as smoking and inadequate weight gain, failed to account for the disparity. On the other hand, the presence of a grandmother in the household reduced the risk of low birth weight by 56 percent among black women but not among white women. As SES increases, black women are less likely to have their mothers in the household and may be less able to rely on them for support during pregnancy (Colen, Geronimus, Bound, & James, 2006).

Immediate Treatment and Outcomes

The most pressing fear regarding very small babies is that they will die in infancy. Because their immune systems are not fully developed, they are especially vulnerable to infection, which has been linked to slowed growth and developmental delays (Stoll et al., 2004). Also, these infants' nervous systems may be too immature for them to perform functions basic to survival, such as sucking, so they may need to be fed intravenously (through the veins). Feeding them mothers' milk can help prevent infection (AAP Section on Breastfeeding, 2005; Furman, Taylor, Minich, & Hack, 2003). Because they do not have enough fat to insulate them and to generate heat, it is hard for them to stay warm. Low Apgar scores in a preterm newborn are a strong indication of the need for intensive care (Weinberger et al., 2000).

A low-birth-weight or at-risk preterm baby is placed in an *isolette* (an antiseptic, temperature-controlled crib) and fed through tubes. To counteract the sensory impoverishment of life in an isolette, hospital workers and parents are encouraged to give these small babies special handling. Gentle massage seems to foster growth, weight gain, motor activity, alertness, and behavioral organization, as assessed by the Brazelton NBAS (T. Field, 1998b; T. Field, Diego, Hernandez-Reif, 2007), and can shorten the hospital stay (T. Field, Hernandez-Reif, & Freedman, 2004; Standley, 1998).

The antiseptic, temperature-controlled crib, or isolette, in which this premature baby lies has holes through which the infant can be examined, touched, and massaged. Frequent human contact helps low-birth-weight infants thrive.

Premature infants tend to show uneven state development. Compared with full-term infants the same age, they are more alert and wakeful and have longer stretches of quiet sleep and more REMs in active sleep. On the other hand, their sleep can be more fragmented, with more transitions between sleeping and waking (Ingersoll & Thoman, 1999). Kangaroo care, a method of skin-to-skin contact in which a newborn is laid face down between the mother's breasts for an hour or so after birth, can help preterm—and full-term—infants make the adjustment from fetal life to the jumble of sensory stimuli in the outside world. This soothing maternal contact seems to reduce stress on the central nervous system and help with self-regulation of sleep and activity (Ferber & Makhoul, 2004).

Respiratory distress syndrome, also called *hyaline membrane disease,* is common in preterm babies who lack an adequate amount of *surfactant,* an essential lung-coating substance that keeps air sacs from collapsing. These babies may breathe irregularly or stop breathing altogether. Since 1994, administering surfactant to high-risk preterm newborns has dramatically increased survival rates (Corbet et al., 1995; Goldenberg & Rouse, 1998; Horbar et al., 1993; Martin, Hamilton, et al., 2005; Msall, 2004; Stoelhorst et al., 2005) as well as neurological and developmental status at 18 to 22 months (Vohr, Wright, Poole, & McDonald for the NICHD Neonatal Research Network Follow-up Study, 2005). Since 2000 the percentage of extremely low-birth-weight infants who survived unimpaired has increased further (Wilson-Costello et al., 2007).

Long-Term Outcomes

Even if low-birth-weight babies survive the dangerous early days, there is concern for their future. For example, both preterm and small-for-gestational-age infants may be at increased risk of adult-onset diabetes (Hofman et al., 2004; Sperling, 2004). Small-for-gestational-age infants appear to be at increased risk of cardiovascular disease (Sperling, 2004).

In longitudinal studies of extremely low-birth-weight infants (about 1 to 2 pounds at birth) and infants born before 26 weeks of gestation, the survivors tend to be smaller than full-term children and more likely to have neurological, sensory, cognitive, educational, and behavioral problems (Anderson, Doyle, and the Victorian Infant Collaborative Study Group, 2003; Marlow, Wolke, Bracewell, & Samara for the EPICure Study Group, 2005; Mikkola et al., 2005; Saigal, Stoskopf, Streiner, & Burrows, 2001). Among a cohort of extremely low-birth-weight infants born in Finland in 1996–1997, only 26 percent showed normal development at age 5 (Mikkola et al., 2005).

The less low-birth-weight children weigh at birth, the lower their IQs and achievement test scores tend to be and the more likely they are to require special education or to repeat a grade (Saigal, Hoult, Streiner, Stoskopf, & Rosenbaum, 2000). Cognitive deficits, especially in memory and processing speed, have been noted among very-low-birth-weight babies (about 2 to 3½ pounds at birth) by age 5 or 6 months, continuing through childhood (Rose & Feldman, 2000; Rose, Feldman, & Jankowski, 2002), and tend to persist into adulthood (Fearon et al., 2004; Greene, 2002; Hack et al., 2002; Hardy, Kuh, Langenberg, & Wadsworth, 2003). Very-low-birth-weight children and adolescents also tend to have more behavioral and mental health problems than those born at normal weight (Hack et al., 2004).

On the other hand, in a longitudinal study of 296 infants who weighed, on average, just over 2 pounds at birth and were considered borderline retarded, most showed cognitive improvement in early childhood and intelligence in the normal range by age 8. Children in two-parent families, those whose mothers were highly educated, those who had not suffered significant brain damage, and those who did not need special help did best (Ment et al., 2003). And, in a prospective longitudinal study of 166 extremely low-birth-weight babies born in 1977 to 1982 in Ontario, Canada, where health care is universal, a significant majority overcame earlier difficulties to become functioning young adults, finishing high school, working, and living independently and many of them pursuing postsecondary education. The children were predominantly white and from two-parent families, about half of them of high SES. Children with disabilities had been integrated into regular schools and provided with classroom assistants (Saigal et al., 2006). Birth weight alone, then, does not necessarily determine the outcome. Environmental factors make a difference, as we discuss in a subsequent section.

Postmaturity

postmature A fetus not yet born as of 42 weeks' gestation.

About 6 percent of pregnant women in the United States have not gone into labor after 42 or more weeks' gestation (Martin, Hamilton, et al., 2006). At that point, a baby is considered **postmature.** Postmature babies tend to be long and thin, because they have kept growing in the womb but have had an insufficient blood supply toward the end of gestation. Possibly because the placenta has aged and become less efficient, it may provide less oxygen. The baby's greater size also complicates labor; the mother has to deliver a baby the size of a normal 1-month-old.

Because postmature fetuses are at risk of brain damage or even death, doctors sometimes induce labor or perform cesarean deliveries. The increasing use of these techniques probably explains a decline in postterm births in recent years (Martin, Hamilton, et al., 2006).

Stillbirth

stillbirth Death of a fetus at or after the 20th week of gestation.

A stillbirth is a tragic union of opposites—birth and death. Sometimes fetal death is diagnosed prenatally; in other cases, as with Elvis Presley's twin brother, the baby's death is discovered during labor or delivery.

Stillbirth, the death of a fetus at or after the 20th week of gestation, accounts for more than half of *perinatal deaths* (deaths that occur during or within 24 hours after childbirth) in developing countries. Some 4 babies per 1,000 are born dead in the United States (Surkan, Stephansson, Dickman, & Cnattingius, 2004). Boys are more likely to be stillborn than girls (Bekedam, Engelsbel, Mol, Buitendijk, & van der Pal-de Bruin, 2002; Eogan,

Geary, O'Connell, & Keane, 2003). Although the cause of stillbirth is not clearly understood, many stillborn infants are small for their gestational age, indicating malnourishment in the womb (Surkan et al., 2004).

The incidence of third-trimester stillbirths in the United States has dropped substantially during the past two decades, by 33 percent among African American women and 46 percent among white women. However, for unknown reasons, rates of stillbirth are still twice as high among black women (6.6 per 1,000 live births) as among white women (3.2 per 1,000 live births). Women over age 35 are more likely than other women to experience stillbirth, and stillbirth rates for this age group have increased, as have rates among women under age 20 (Ananth, Liu, Kinzler, & Kramer, 2005; Heffner, 2004). The overall reduction in stillbirths may be due to electronic fetal monitoring, ultrasound, and other measures to identify fetuses at risk for preeclampsia (a toxic condition) or restricted growth. Fetuses believed to have these problems can then be delivered prematurely (Goldenberg & Rouse, 1998).

Can a Supportive Environment Overcome Effects of Birth Complications?

From an evolutionary standpoint, people—like other organisms—thrive, reproduce, and survive in environments suitable to their needs and expectations. Thus, appropriate environmental characteristics can help an infant develop optimally. Furthermore, human beings are adaptable, especially during the early years; if early disadvantages are remedied, the outcome may be surprisingly positive (MacDonald, 1988). Two major studies, the Infant Health and Development Program and the Kauai Study, suggest that, given a supportive or improved environment, resilience can occur even in the face of a difficult start in life.

The Infant Health and Development Program

The Infant Health and Development Program (IHDP) (1990) followed the cognitive development of 985 preterm, low-birth-weight babies—most of them from poor and disadvantaged families in which the mother had no more than a high school education—in eight parts of the United States from birth to age 3 (Brooks-Gunn, 2003). One-third of the heavier (but still low-birth-weight) babies and one-third of the lighter babies were randomly assigned to intervention groups. Their parents received home visits, counseling, information about children's health and development, and instruction in children's games and activities; at 1 year, these babies entered an educational day care/preschool program.

When the program stopped, the 3-year-olds in both intervention groups were doing better on cognitive and social measures, were much less likely to show mental retardation, and had fewer behavioral problems than control groups of similar birth weight who had received only pediatric follow-up (Brooks-Gunn, Klebanov, Liaw, & Spiker, 1993). By age 5, however, the lighter intervention group had lost its cognitive edge over the weight-matched controls (Brooks-Gunn et al., 1994), and by age 8, the heavier intervention group averaged only 4 IQ points higher than its control group. All groups had substantially below-average IQs and vocabulary scores (McCarton et al., 1997; McCormick, McCarton, Brooks-Gunn, Belt, & Gross, 1998).

Still, the intervention did seem to yield some long-term benefits. At age 18, among the 636 youths who remained in the study, those in the heavier intervention group scored modestly higher in math achievement, and those in the lighter intervention group in reading, than their respective control groups—if they had experienced the preschool program. Still, both groups performed well below age norms (McCormick et al., 2006). Perhaps for such an intervention to have more lasting effects, it needs to continue beyond age 3 (Blair, 2002).

Closer studies of the full IHDP sample underline the importance of what goes on in the home. Children whose mothers reported having experienced stressful events—illnesses,

Thanks to positive environments and their own resilience, fully a third of the at-risk children studied by Emmy Werner and her colleagues developed into self-confident, successful adults.

deaths of friends or family members, moves, or changes in schooling or work—during the last six months of the child's first year showed less cognitive benefit from the intervention at age 3 (Klebanov, Brooks-Gunn, & McCormick, 2001). Children who got little parental attention and care were more likely to be undersized and to do poorly on cognitive tests than children from more favorable home environments (Kelleher et al., 1993; McCormick et al., 1998). Those whose cognitive performance stayed high had mothers who themselves scored well on cognitive tests and were responsive and stimulating. Babies with more than one risk factor (such as poor neonatal health plus a less educated or less responsive mother) fared worst (Liaw & Brooks-Gunn, 1993).

The Kauai Study

The Kauai Study had even more encouraging results. For more than 5 decades, Emmy E. Werner (1987, 1995; Werner & Smith, 2001) and a team of pediatricians, psychologists, public health workers, and social workers have followed 698 children born in 1955 on the Hawaiian island of Kauai, from gestation to middle adulthood. The researchers interviewed the mothers-to-be, monitored their pregnancies, and interviewed them again when the children were 1, 2, and 10 years old. They observed the children at home; gave them aptitude, achievement, and personality tests in elementary and high school; obtained progress reports from their teachers; and interviewed the young people themselves periodically as adults.

The physical and psychological development of children who had low birth weight or other complications of birth were seriously impaired *only* when the children grew up in persistently poor environmental circumstances. Unless the early damage was so serious as to require institutionalization, those children who had a stable and enriching environment did well (E. E. Werner, 1985, 1987). They had fewer language, perceptual, emotional, and school problems than children who had not experienced unusual stress at birth but who had received little intellectual stimulation or emotional support at home (E. E. Werner, 1989; E. E. Werner et al., 1968). The children who had been exposed to birth-related problems and later stressful experiences had the worst health and the most retarded development (E. E. Werner, 1987).

Most remarkable is the resilience of children who escaped damage despite multiple sources of stress. Even when birth complications were combined with chronic poverty, family discord, divorce, or parents who were mentally ill, many children came through relatively unscathed. Of the 276 children who at age 2 had been identified as having four or more risk factors, two-thirds developed serious learning or behavior problems by age 10 or, by age 18, had become pregnant, gotten in trouble with the law, or become emotionally disturbed. Yet by age 30, one-third of these highly at-risk children had managed to become "competent, confident, and caring adults" (E. E. Werner, 1995, p. 82). Of the full sample, about half of those on whom the researchers were able to obtain follow-up data successfully weathered the age-30 and age-40 transitions (E. Werner & Smith, 2001).

Protective factors, which tended to reduce the impact of early stress, fell into three categories: (1) individual attributes that may be largely genetic, such as energy, sociability, and intelligence; (2) affectionate ties with at least one supportive family member; and (3) rewards at school, work, or place of worship that provide a sense of meaning and control over one's life (E. E. Werner, 1987). Although the home environment seemed to have the most marked effect in childhood, in adulthood the individuals' own qualities made a greater difference (E. E. Werner, 1995).

These studies underline the need to look at child development in context. They show how biological and environmental influences interact, making resiliency possible even in babies born with serious complications. Although most births are uneventful and most children turn out well, risk factors, protective factors, and resiliency are concerns that will come up again and again throughout this book (especially in Chapter 14) as we report on what developmental scientists have learned about ways to promote the most desirable outcomes for children.

protective factors Factors that reduce the impact of potentially negative influences and tend to predict positive outcomes.

Checkpoint ✔

Can you . . .

✔ Discuss the effectiveness of the home environment and of intervention programs in overcoming effects of low-birth-weight and other birth complications?

✔ Name three protective factors identified by the Kauai study?

Newborns and Parents

Guidepost 5

How do parents bond with and care for their baby?

Childbirth is a major transition, not only for the baby, but for the parents as well. Suddenly almost all their time and energy (it seems) is focused on this newcomer in their lives. Especially with a first birth, a newborn brings insistent demands that challenge the parents' ability to cope. At the same time, parents (and, perhaps, siblings) are getting acquainted with this newcomer and developing emotional bonds.

Childbirth and Bonding

How and when does the **mother-infant bond**—the close, caring connection between mother and newborn—develop? Some researchers studying this topic have followed the ethological approach (introduced in Chapter 2), which considers behavior in human beings, as in animals, to be biologically determined and emphasizes critical or sensitive periods for development of certain behaviors.

As we mentioned in Chapter 1, Konrad Lorenz (1957) demonstrated that newly hatched ducklings will follow the first moving object they see, usually the mother—a phenomenon called **imprinting.** However, research has concluded that, unlike the animals Lorenz studied, a critical period for bonding does *not* exist in human beings (Chess & Thomas, 1982; Klaus & Kennell, 1982; Lamb, 1983). This finding can relieve the worry and guilt sometimes felt by adoptive parents and those who have to be separated from their infants after birth.

Fathers, like mothers, form close bonds with their babies. The babies contribute simply by doing the things normal babies do: opening their eyes, grasping their fathers' fingers, or moving in their fathers' arms. Fathers who are present at the birth of a child often see the event as a "peak emotional experience" (May & Perrin, 1985), but a man can become emotionally committed to his newborn whether or not he attended the birth (Palkovitz, 1985).

From an evolutionary perspective, parental bonding may be a mechanism to ensure that the parents invest the tremendous energy and resources needed to enable a helpless infant to survive and reproduce. Evolutionary developmental psychologists point out that child rearing involves a balancing act between the needs of the parents and those of the offspring (Bjorklund & Pellegrini, 2000). Bonding helps ensure that the benefits to the parents are worth the cost.

In a series of classic experiments, Harry Harlow and Margaret Harlow showed that food is not the most important way to a baby's heart. When infant rhesus monkeys could choose whether to go to a wire surrogate mother or a warm, soft terry-cloth mother, they spent more time clinging to the cloth mother, even if they were being fed by bottles connected to the wire mother.

mother-infant bond Mother's feeling of close, caring connection with her newborn.

imprinting Instinctive form of learning in which, during a critical period in early development, a young animal forms an attachment to the first moving object it sees, usually the mother.

What Do Newborns Need from Their Mothers?

A series of pioneering experiments with monkeys by Harry Harlow and his colleagues established that more than feeding is involved in the mother-infant bond. In these experiments, rhesus monkeys were separated from their mothers 6 to 12 hours after birth and raised in a laboratory. The infant monkeys were put into cages with one of two kinds of surrogate mothers: a plain cylindrical wire-mesh form or a form covered with terry cloth. Some monkeys were fed from bottles connected to the wire mothers; others were fed by the warm, cuddly cloth mothers. When the monkeys were allowed to spend time with either kind of mother, they all spent more time clinging to the cloth surrogates, even if they were being fed only by the wire ones. In an unfamiliar room, the babies "raised" by cloth surrogates showed more natural interest in exploring than those "raised" by wire surrogates, even when the appropriate mothers were there.

Apparently, the monkeys also remembered the cloth surrogates better. After a year's separation, the "cloth-raised" monkeys eagerly ran to embrace the terry-cloth forms, whereas the "wire-raised" monkeys showed no interest in the wire forms (Harlow & Zimmerman, 1959). None of the monkeys in either group grew up normally, however (Harlow & Harlow, 1962), and none were able to nurture their own offspring (Suomi & Harlow, 1972).

In another study, baby rats whose mothers licked them frequently turned out to be less anxious and fearful and produced lower levels of stress hormones than rats who had been licked less. The researchers found that maternal licking activated a gene that relieves stress (Caldji, Diorio, & Meaney, 2003).

It is hardly surprising that a dummy mother would not provide the same kinds of stimulation and opportunities for positive development as a live mother and that a mother's physical demonstrativeness would soothe her baby's stress. These experiments show that feeding is not the most important thing babies get from their mothers. Mothering includes the comfort of close bodily contact and, at least in monkeys, the satisfaction of an innate need to cling.

Human infants also have needs that must be satisfied if they are to grow up normally. It is the task of parents to try to meet those needs.

The Father's Role

The fathering role is a social construction, having different meanings in different cultures. The role may be taken or shared by someone other than the biological father: the mother's brother, as in Botswana (where young mothers remain with their childhood family until their partners are in their 40s), or a grandfather, as in Vietnam (Engle & Breaux, 1998; Richardson, 1995; Townsend, 1997). In some societies, fathers are more involved in their young children's lives—economically, emotionally, and in time spent—than in other cultures. In many parts of the world, what it means to be a father has changed—and is changing (Engle & Breaux, 1998).

Concepts of fathering have changed in recent decades. This father comforting his son will play an important part in the child's development.

Among the Huhot of Inner Mongolia, a province of China, fathers traditionally are responsible for economic support and discipline and mothers for nurturing (Jankowiak, 1992). Fathers are stern and aloof, and their children respect and fear them. Men almost never hold infants. Fathers interact more with toddlers but perform child care duties only if the mother is absent. However, urbanization and maternal employment are changing these attitudes. Fathers—especially college-educated fathers—now seek more intimate relationships with children, especially sons. China's official one-child policy has accentuated this change, leading both parents to be more deeply involved with their only child (Engle & Breaux, 1998; see Box 11-2).

Among the Aka of central Africa, in contrast with the Huhot, fathers are as nurturant and emotionally supportive as mothers. In fact, "Aka fathers provide more direct infant care than fathers in any other known society" (Hewlett, 1992, p. 169).

In the United States and some other countries, fathers' involvement in caregiving and play has greatly increased since 1970 as more mothers have begun to work outside the home and concepts of fathering have changed (Cabrera et al., 2000; Casper, 1997; Pleck, 1997). A father's frequent and positive involvement with his child, from infancy on, is directly related to the child's well-being and physical, cognitive, and social development (Cabrera et al., 2000; Kelley, Smith, Green, Berndt, & Rogers, 1998; Shannon, Tamis-LeMonda, London, & Cabrera, 2002).

Infant Care: A Cross-Cultural View

Infant care practices and patterns of interaction with infants vary greatly around the world, depending on environmental conditions and the culture's view of infants' nature and needs. In Bali, infants are believed to be ancestors or gods brought to life in human form and thus must be treated with utmost dignity and respect. The Beng of West Africa think that young babies can understand all languages, whereas people in the Micronesian atoll of Ifaluk believe that babies cannot understand language at all, and therefore adults do not speak to them (DeLoache & Gottlieb, 2000).

In some societies, as Margaret Mead found in the South Seas, infants have multiple caregivers. Among the Efe people of central Africa, for example, infants typically receive care from five or more people in a given hour and are routinely breast-fed by other women besides the mother (Tronick, Morelli, & Ivey, 1992). Among the Gusii in western Kenya, where infant mortality is high, parents are more likely than those in industrial societies to keep their infants close to them, respond quickly when they cry, and feed them on demand (LeVine, 1974, 1989, 1994). The same is true of Aka foragers in central Africa, who move around frequently in small, tightly knit groups marked by extensive sharing, cooperation, and concern about danger. However, Ngandu farmers in the same region, who tend to live farther apart and to stay in one place for long periods of time, are more likely to leave their infants alone and to let them fuss or cry, smile, vocalize, or play (Hewlett, Lamb, Shannon, Leyendecker, & Schölmerich, 1998).

We need to remember, then, that patterns of parent-infant interaction we take for granted may be culture-based.

Checkpoint

Can you . . .

✔ Summarize findings on bonding between parents and newborns?

✔ Compare the roles of mothers and fathers in meeting newborns' needs?

✔ Give examples of cultural differences in care and treatment of newborns?

Refocus

On the basis of the information given about Elvis Presley's birth in the Focus vignette at the beginning of this chapter,

- What changes in the customs and risks surrounding childbirth have occurred since Presley's birth?

- How might resources widely available today have changed the course of Gladys Presley's pregnancy and delivery?

The birth of a baby, as momentous an achievement as it is, marks the launching of a challenging but rewarding journey—the journey through a child's world. In Part 3, we will examine our rapidly growing understanding of the physical, cognitive, and psychosocial developments of infancy and toddlerhood.

Summary and Key Terms

Childbirth and Culture:
How Birthing Has Changed

Guidepost 1 How do customs surrounding birth reflect culture, and how has childbirth changed in developed countries?

- In Europe and the United States, childbirth before the 20th century was similar to childbirth in some developing countries today. Birth was a female ritual that occurred at home and was attended by a midwife. Pain relief was minimal, and risks for mother and baby were high.

- The development of the science of obstetrics professionalized childbirth. Births took place in hospitals, attended by physicians. Medical advances dramatically improved safety.

- Today delivery at home or in birth centers attended by midwives can be a relatively safe alternative to physician-attended hospital delivery for women with normal, low-risk pregnancies.

The Birth Process

Guidepost 2 How does labor begin, what happens during each of the three stages of childbirth, and what alternative methods of delivery are available?

- Labor normally begins after a preparatory period of parturition.

- The vaginal birth process consists of three stages: (1) dilation of the cervix; (2) descent and emergence of the baby; (3) expulsion of the umbilical cord and the placenta.

- Electronic fetal monitoring is widely used during labor and delivery. It is intended to detect signs of fetal distress, especially in high-risk births.

- The rate of cesarean births in the United States is at a record high.

- Natural or prepared childbirth can minimize the need for pain-killing drugs and maximize parents' active involvement. Modern epidurals can give effective pain relief with smaller doses of medication than in the past.

- The presence of a doula can provide physical benefits as well as emotional support.

parturition (117)   electronic fetal monitoring (118)   cesarean delivery (118)   natural, or prepared, childbirth (119)

The Newborn Baby

Guidepost 3 How do newborn infants adjust to life outside the womb, and how can we tell whether a new baby is healthy and is developing normally?

- The neonatal period is a time of transition from intrauterine to extrauterine life. During the first few days, the neonate loses weight and then regains it; the lanugo (prenatal hair) falls off, and the protective coating of vernix caseosa dries up. The fontanels (soft spots) in the skull close within the first 18 months.

- At birth, the circulatory, respiratory, gastrointestinal, and temperature regulation systems become independent of the mother's. If a newborn cannot start breathing within about 5 minutes, brain injury may occur.

- Newborns have a strong sucking reflex and secrete meconium from the intestinal tract. They are commonly subject to neonatal jaundice, due to immaturity of the liver.

- At 1 minute and 5 minutes after birth, a neonate's Apgar score can indicate how well he or she is adjusting to extrauterine life. The Brazelton Neonatal Behavioral Assessment Scale can assess an infant's responses to the environment and predict future development.

- Neonatal screening is done for certain rare conditions, such as PKU and congenital hypothyroidism. It is being expanded to include more conditions.

- A newborn's state of arousal is governed by periodic cycles of wakefulness, sleep, and activity, which seem to be inborn.

- Sleep takes up the major but a diminishing amount of a neonate's time.

- Individual differences in newborns' activity levels show stability and may be early indicators of temperament.

- Parents' responsiveness to babies' states and self-initiated activity levels is an important bidirectional influence on development.

  neonatal period (120) neonate (120) anoxia (123) neonatal jaundice (123) Apgar scale (124) Brazelton Neonatal Behavioral Assessment Scale (NBAS) (125) state of arousal (126)

Complications of Childbirth— and Their Aftermath

Guidepost 4 What complications of childbirth can endanger newborn babies, and what are the long-term prospects for infants with complicated births?

- Complications of childbirth include prematurity, low birth weight, postmature birth, and stillbirth.

- Low-birth-weight babies may be either preterm (premature) or small-for-date (small-for-gestational-age). Low birth weight is a major factor in infant mortality and can cause long-term physical and cognitive problems. Very-low-birth-weight babies have an even less promising prognosis.

- A supportive postnatal environment and other protective factors often can improve the outcome for babies who experienced birth complications.

- Postmature births have decreased with the increase in induced and cesarean deliveries.

- Stillbirth has been substantially reduced in the United States but still accounts for half of perinatal deaths in the developing world.

  preterm (premature) infants (128) small-for-date (small-for-gestational-age) infants (128) low birth weight (129) postmature (132) stillbirth (132) protective factors (134)

Newborns and Parents

Guidepost 5 How do parents bond with and care for their baby?

- Researchers following the ethological approach have suggested that there is a critical period for the formation of the mother-infant bond, much like imprinting in some animals. However, research has not confirmed this hypothesis. Fathers can bond with their babies whether or not they are present at the birth.

- Infants have strong needs for maternal closeness and warmth as well as physical care.

- Fatherhood is a social construction. Fathering roles differ in various cultures.

- Child raising practices and caregiving roles vary around the world.

  mother-infant bond (135) imprinting (135)

Part Three

Infancy and Toddlerhood: A Preview

Chapter 6
Physical Development and Health during the First Three Years

- All senses and body systems operate at birth to varying degrees.
- The brain grows in complexity and is highly sensitive to environmental influence.
- Physical growth and development of motor skills are rapid.

Chapter 7
Cognitive Development during the First Three Years

- Abilities to learn and remember are present even in early weeks.
- Use of symbols and ability to solve problems develop by end of second year.
- Comprehension and use of language develop rapidly.

Chapter 8
Psychosocial Development during the First Three Years

- Attachments to parents and others form.
- Self-awareness develops.
- Shift from dependence to autonomy occurs.
- Interest in other children increases.

Infancy and Toddlerhood

Some of the most exciting developmental research during the past quarter-century has been on the period from birth to age 3, known as infancy and toddlerhood. By measuring how long infants look at different patterns or how vigorously they suck on nipples that turn on recordings of women's voices, researchers have discovered that newborns have definite preferences about what they see and hear. By video recording babies' facial expressions, researchers have documented when specific early emotions (such as joy, anger, and fear) first appear. Through imaging techniques, researchers have linked specific functions and emotions with various parts of the brain. All in all, we now know that the world of infants and toddlers is far richer and their abilities far more impressive than was previously suspected.

Infancy begins at birth and ends when a child begins walking and stringing words together—two events that typically take place between age 12 and 18 months. Toddlerhood lasts from about age 18 to 36 months, a period when children become more verbal, independent, and able to move about. As we study how newborns become infants and toddlers (and, later, grow into children and adolescents), we see how each of the three aspects of development is bound up with the others. Thus, although we focus on the *physical* development of infants and toddlers in Chapter 6, on their *cognitive* development in Chapter 7, and on their *psychosocial* development in Chapter 8, we will see many examples of how these aspects of development intertwine.

CHAPTER SIX

Physical Development and Health during the First Three Years

There he lay upon his back
The yearling creature, warm and moist with life
To the bottom of his dimples,——to the ends
Of the lovely tumbled curls about his face.

—Elizabeth Barrett Browning, *Aurora Leigh*, 1857

Focus *Helen Keller and the World of the Senses*

Helen Keller

"What we have once enjoyed we can never lose," the author Helen Keller (1880–1968) once wrote. "A sunset, a mountain bathed in moonlight, the ocean in calm and in storm—we see these, love their beauty, hold the vision to our hearts. All that we love deeply becomes a part of us" (Keller, 1929, p. 2).

This quotation is especially remarkable—and especially poignant—in view of the fact that Helen Keller never saw a sunset, or a mountain, or moonlight, or an ocean, or anything else after age 19 months. It was then that she contracted a mysterious fever, which left her deaf and with inexorably ebbing sight.

Before her illness, Helen had been a normal, healthy baby—lively, affectionate, and precocious, with excellent vision. After her illness, she became expressionless and unresponsive. At 1 year, she had begun to walk; after her illness, she clung to her mother's skirts or sat in her lap, endlessly rubbing her face. She had also begun to talk; one of her first words was *water*. After her illness, she continued to say, "wah-wah," but not much else.

Her distraught parents first took her to a mineral spa and then to medical specialists, but there was no hope for a cure. At a time when physical and cognitive development normally enter a major growth spurt, the sensory gateways to the exploration of Helen's world had slammed shut—but not entirely. Deprived of two senses, she leaned more heavily on the other three, especially smell and touch. She later explained that she could tell a doctor from a carpenter by the odors of ether or wood that came from them. She used her ever-active fingertips to trace the "delicate tremble of a butterfly's wings . . . , the soft petals of violets . . . , the clear, firm outline of face and limb, the smooth arch of a horse's neck and the velvety touch of his nose" (Keller, 1920, pp. 6–7). Memories of the daylight world she had once inhabited helped her make sense of the unrelieved night in which she now found herself.

Sources of information about Helen Keller include Keller (1903/1905, 1920, 1929, 2003), Herrmann (1999), Lash (1980), and Ozick (2003).

Helen realized that she was not like other people, but at first she had no clear sense of who or what she was. She later wrote, "I lived in a world that was a no-world. . . . I did not know that I knew [anything], or that I lived or acted or desired" (1920, p. 113). Sometimes, when family members were talking to each other, she would stand between them and touch their lips and then frantically move her own—but nothing happened. Her frustration found its outlet in violent, inconsolable tantrums; she would kick and scream until she was exhausted.

Out of pity, her parents indulged her whims. Finally, more in desperation than in hope, they engaged a teacher for her: a young woman named Anne Sullivan, who herself had limited vision and who had been trained in a school for the blind. Arriving at the Keller home, Sullivan found 6-year-old Helen to be "wild, wilful, and destructive" (Lash, 1980, p. 348). On meeting her new teacher, the child knocked out one of Sullivan's front teeth. Once, after figuring out how to use a key, she locked her mother in the pantry. Another time, she overturned her baby sister's cradle. Frustrated by her teacher's attempts to spell the word *doll* into her palm, Helen hurled her new doll to the floor, smashing it to bits.

Yet, that same day, the little girl made her first linguistic breakthrough. As she and her teacher walked in the garden, they stopped to get a drink at the pump. Sullivan placed Helen's hand under the spout, at the same time spelling "w-a-t-e-r" over and over into her other hand. "I stood still," Keller later wrote, "my whole attention fixed upon the motions of her fingers. Suddenly I felt a misty consciousness as of something forgotten—a thrill of returning thought; and somehow the mystery of language was revealed to me. I knew then that 'w-a-t-e-r' meant the wonderful cool something that was flowing over my hand. That living word awakened my soul, gave it light, hope, joy, set it free!" (Keller, 1905, p. 35).

● ● ●

The story of how Anne Sullivan tamed this unruly child and brought her into the light of language and thought is a familiar and inspiring one. One lesson we can draw from the story of Helen Keller's early development is the central importance of the senses—the windows to a baby's world—and their connection with all other aspects of development. Had Helen Keller not lost her vision and hearing, or had she been born without one or the other or both, her physical, cognitive, and psychosocial development undoubtedly would have been quite different.

In this chapter, we explore how sensory perception goes hand in hand with an infant's growing motor skills and shapes the astoundingly rapid development of the brain. We examine typical growth patterns of body and brain, and we see how a nourishing environment can stimulate both. We study how infants, who spend most of their time sleeping and eating, become busy, active toddlers and how parents and other caregivers can foster healthy growth and development. We discuss threats to infants' life and health, including abuse and neglect, and ways to ward them off.

After you have read and studied this chapter, you should be able to answer each of the Guidepost questions on the following page. Look for them again in the margins throughout the chapter, where they point to important concepts. To check your understanding of these Guideposts, review the end-of-chapter summary. Checkpoints located throughout the chapter will help you verify your understanding of what you have read.

1. How do babies grow, and how and what should they be fed?

2. How does the brain develop, and how do environmental factors affect its early growth?

3. How do the senses develop during infancy?

4. What are the early milestones in motor development, and what are some influences on it?

5. How can we enhance babies' chances of survival and health?

6. What are the causes and consequences of child abuse and neglect, and what can be done about them?

Growth and Nutrition

Guidepost 1

How do babies grow, and how and what should they be fed?

The genes an infant inherits have a strong influence on whether the child will be tall or short, thin or stocky, or somewhere in between. This genetic influence interacts with such environmental influences as nutrition and living conditions, which also affect general health and well-being. Well-nourished, well-nurtured children grow taller and heavier than less well-nourished and -nurtured children. Thus, Japanese American children are taller and weigh more than children the same age in Japan, probably because of dietary differences (Broude, 1995).

Patterns of Growth

Children grow faster during the first 3 years, especially during the first few months, than they ever will again (Figure 6-1). By 5 months, the average baby boy's birth weight has doubled to 16 pounds and, by 1 year, has nearly tripled to 23 pounds. This rapid growth rate tapers off during the 2nd and 3rd years. A boy typically gains about 5 pounds by his second birthday and 3½ pounds by his third, when he tips the scales at 31½ pounds. A boy's height typically increases by 10 inches during the 1st year (making the average 1-year-old boy nearly 30 inches tall), by almost 5 inches during the 2nd year (so that the average 2-year-old boy is approaching 3 feet tall), and by a little more than 3 inches during the 3rd year to top 37 inches. Girls follow a similar pattern but are slightly smaller. At 3, the average girl weighs a pound less and is half an inch shorter than the average boy (Kuczmarski et al., 2000).

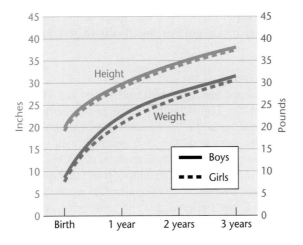

Figure 6-1

Growth in height and weight during infancy and toddlerhood. Babies grow most rapidly in both height and weight during the first few months of life and then taper off somewhat by age 3. Baby boys are slightly larger, on average, than baby girls.

Note: Curves shown are for the 50th percentiles for each sex.

Source: Kuczmarski et al., 2000.

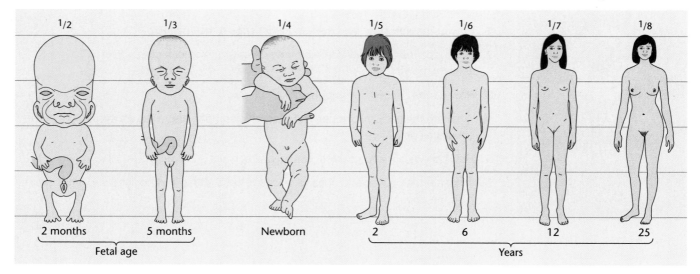

Figure 6-2

Changes in proportions of the human body during growth. The most striking change is that the head becomes smaller relative to the rest of the body. The fractions indicate head size as a proportion of total body length at several ages. More subtle is the stability of the trunk proportion (from neck to crotch). The increasing leg proportion is almost exactly the reverse of the decreasing head proportion.

Checkpoint ✔

Can you . . .

✔ Summarize typical patterns of growth during the first 3 years?

✔ Discuss two principles that affect growth?

Teething usually begins around 3 or 4 months, when infants begin grabbing almost everything in sight to put into their mouths; but the first tooth may not actually arrive until sometime between 5 and 9 months, or even later. By the first birthday, babies generally have six to eight teeth. By age 2½, they have a mouthful of 20.

As a baby grows, body shape and proportions change too; a 3-year-old typically is slender compared with a chubby, potbellied 1-year-old. Physical growth and development follow the maturational principles introduced in Chapter 3: the *cephalocaudal principle* and *proximodistal principle.* According to the *cephalocaudal principle,* growth occurs from top down. Because the brain grows so rapidly before birth, a newborn baby's head is disproportionately large. By 1 year, the brain is 70 percent of its adult weight, but the rest of the body is only about 10 to 20 percent of adult weight. The head becomes proportionately smaller as the child grows in height and the lower parts of the body develop (Figure 6-2). As we'll see later in this chapter, sensory and motor development proceed according to the same principle; infants learn to use the upper parts of the body before the lower parts. They see objects before they can control their trunk, and they learn to do many things with their hands long before they can crawl or walk. According to the *proximodistal principle* (inner to outer), growth and motor development proceed from the center of the body outward. In the womb, the head and trunk develop before the arms and legs, then the hands and feet, and then the fingers and toes. During infancy and early childhood, the limbs continue to grow faster than the hands and feet. Similarly, babies first develop the ability to use their upper arms and upper legs (which are closest to the center of the body), then the forearms and forelegs, then hands and feet, and finally fingers and toes.

Nourishment

From the beginnings of human history, babies were breast-fed. Babies fed nonhuman milk were likely to fall ill and die. Following the discovery of germs in 1878, mothers were warned to avoid the "poisonous bottle" at all costs (Fontanel & d'Harcourt, 1997, p. 121).

Beginning in the first decade of the 20th century, with the advent of dependable refrigeration, pasteurization, and sterilization, manufacturers began to develop formulas to modify and enrich cow's milk for infant consumption and to improve the design of bottles. Bottle-feeding became safe, nutritious, and popular. During the next half-century, formula feeding became the norm in the United States and some other industrialized countries. By 1971, only 25 percent of U.S. mothers even tried to nurse (Ryan, 1997).

Since then, recognition of the benefits of breast milk has brought a dramatic reversal of this trend. In 2002, more than two-thirds (71.4 percent) of children in the United States (the highest proportion ever recorded) had been breast-fed. However, only about 35 percent were still breast-fed at 6 months, only about 13 percent exclusively so. At 1 year, only 16 percent of infants received some breast milk (Li, Darling, Maurice, Barker, & Grummer-Strawn, 2005). Worldwide, only about one-half of infants are ever breast-fed (UNICEF, 2002).

Breast-Feeding: Benefits and Cautions

Feeding a baby is an emotional as well as physical act. Warm contact with the mother's body fosters the emotional connection between mother and baby. Such bonding can take place through either breast- or bottle-feeding and through many other caregiving activities, most of which can be performed by fathers as well as mothers.

Nutritionally speaking, however, breast milk is almost always the best food for infants. The only acceptable alternative is an iron-fortified formula that is based on either cow's milk or soy protein and contains supplemental vitamins and minerals. The American Academy of Pediatrics (AAP) Section on Breastfeeding (2005) recommends that babies be exclusively breast-fed for 6 months. If direct breast-feeding is not possible, as with premature infants, the baby should receive expressed human milk—milk squeezed from the mother's, or another mother's, breast. Breast-feeding should begin immediately after birth and should continue for *at least* the 1st year. Infants weaned during the 1st year should receive iron-fortified formula. At 1 year, babies can switch to cow's milk.

The health advantages of breast-feeding are striking. Among the illnesses prevented or minimized by breast-feeding are diarrhea, respiratory infections, otitis media (an infection of the middle ear), and staphylococcal, bacterial, and urinary tract infections (AAP Section on Breastfeeding, 2005; Black, Morris, & Bryce, 2003). Breast-feeding may reduce the risk of postneonatal death (death that occurs between 28 days and 1 year) (Chen & Rogan, 2004).

Breast-feeding seems to have benefits for visual acuity (Makrides, Neumann, Simmer, Pater, & Gibson, 1995), neurological development (Lanting, Fidler, Huisman, Touwen, & Boersma, 1994), and long-term cardiovascular health (Owen, Whincup, Odoki, Gilg, & Cook, 2002), including cholesterol levels (Singhal, Cole, Fewtrell, & Lucas, 2004). It may help prevent obesity, diabetes, lymphoma, leukemia, and Hodgkin disease (AAP Section on Breastfeeding, 2005; Owen, Martin, Whincup, Smith, & Cook, 2005; Stuebe, Rich-Edwards, Willett, Manson, & Michels, 2005). Babies who breast-feed are less likely to be overfed, as they actively regulate their intake (American Heart Association et al., 2006). Studies also have shown slight benefits for cognitive development (AAP Section on Breastfeeding, 2005), even into young adulthood (Mortensen, Michaelson, Sanders, & Reinisch, 2002).

Breast-feeding also benefits the mother. Nursing mothers typically have less postpartum bleeding, quicker physical recovery, and an earlier return to their previous weight. After menopause, they have less risk of breast cancer and ovarian cancer and possibly less risk of osteoporosis and hip fractures (AAP Section on Breastfeeding, 2005).

Nursing mothers need to be as careful as pregnant women about what they take into their bodies. They should avoid the use of alcohol. Breast-feeding is inadvisable if a mother is infected with HIV/AIDS or any other infectious illness, if she has untreated active tuberculosis, if she has been exposed to radiation, or if she is taking any drug that would not be safe for the baby (AAP Section on Breastfeeding, 2005). The risk of transmitting HIV infection to an infant continues as long as an infected mother breast-feeds (The Breastfeeding and HIV International Transmission Study Group, 2004).

Encouraging Breast-Feeding

Since 1991, 16,000 hospitals and birthing centers worldwide and at least 32 U.S. hospitals have been designated as "Baby-Friendly" under a United Nations initiative for encouraging institutional support of breast-feeding. These institutions offer new mothers rooming-in, tell them of

Breast milk can be called the "ultimate health food" because it offers so many benefits to babies—physical, cognitive, and emotional.

the benefits of breast-feeding, help them start nursing within 1 hour of birth, show them how to maintain lactation, encourage on-demand feeding, give infants nothing but breast milk unless medically necessary, and establish ongoing breast-feeding support groups. Breast-feeding in the U.S. hospitals greatly increased after the program went into effect, and mothers were more likely to continue nursing (Merewood, Mehta, Chamberlain, Philipp, & Bauchner, 2005). In studies in France and Belarus (in the former Soviet Union), mothers trained to support breast-feeding were more likely to breast-feed exclusively, were less likely to report difficulties with breast-feeding, and tended to continue longer (Kramer et al., 2001; Labarere et al., 2005).

Increases in breast-feeding in the United States are most notable in socioeconomic groups that historically have been less likely to breast-feed—black women, teenage women, poor women, working women, and those with no more than high school education—but many of these women do not continue breast-feeding. Flexible scheduling and privacy for nursing mothers at work and at school as well as education about the benefits of breast-feeding and availability of breast pumping facilities might increase its prevalence in these groups (Ryan et al., 2002; Taveras et al., 2003).

Nutritional Concerns

Pediatric experts recommend that iron-enriched solid foods—usually beginning with cereal—be introduced gradually between ages 6 and 12 months. At this time, too, fruit juice may be introduced (AAP Section on Breastfeeding, 2005). Unfortunately, many parents do not follow these guidelines. According to random telephone interviews with parents and caregivers of more than 3,000 U.S. infants and toddlers, 29 percent of infants are given solid food before 4 months, 17 percent drink juice before 6 months, and 20 percent drink cow's milk before 12 months. Furthermore, like older children and adults, many infants and toddlers eat too much, and the wrong kinds, of food. From 7 to 24 months, the median food intake is 20 to 30 percent above normal daily requirements (Fox, Pac, Devaney, & Jankowski, 2004). By 19 to 24 months, French fries become the most commonly consumed vegetable. About 30 percent of children this age eat no fruit, but 60 percent eat baked desserts, 20 percent candy, and 44 percent sweetened beverages each day (American Heart Association et al., 2006).

In many low-income communities around the world, malnutrition in early life is widespread—and often fatal. Malnutrition is implicated in more than half of deaths of children globally, and many children are irreversibly damaged by age 2 (World Bank, 2006). Undernourished children who survive their first 5 years are at high risk for stunted growth and poor health and functioning throughout life. However, a longitudinal study of a large-scale government-sponsored nutritional program in 347 poor rural communities of Mexico offers encouraging results. Infants who received fortified nutrition supplements—along with nutrition education, health care, and financial assistance for the family—showed better growth and lower rates of anemia than a control group of infants not yet assigned to the program (Rivera, Sotres-Alvarez, Habicht, Shamah, & Villalpando, 2004). (Malnutrition is further discussed in Chapter 9.)

Overweight has increased in infancy as in all age groups in the United States. In 2000–2001, 5.9 percent of U.S. infants up to 6 months old were classified as overweight, meaning that their weight for height was in the 95th percentile for age and gender, up from 3.4 percent in 1980. An additional 11.1 percent were at risk for overweight, in the 85th percentile, compared with 7 percent in 1980 (Kim et al., 2006).

Two factors seem to influence most strongly the chances that an overweight child will become an obese adult: whether the child has an obese parent and the age of the child. Before age 3, parental obesity is a stronger predictor of a child's obesity as an adult than is the child's own weight. Having one obese parent increases the odds of obesity in adulthood to 3 to 1, and if both parents are obese, the odds increase to more than 10 to 1 (AAP Committee on Nutrition, 2003). Among 70 children followed from age 3 months to 6 years, little difference in weight and body composition appeared by age 2 between children with overweight mothers and children with lean mothers. However, by age 4, those with overweight mothers tended to weigh more and, by age 6, also had more body fat than those with lean mothers (Berkowitz, Stallings, Maislin, & Stunkard, 2005). Thus, a 1- or 2-year-old who has an obese parent—or especially two obese parents—may be a candidate for preventive efforts.

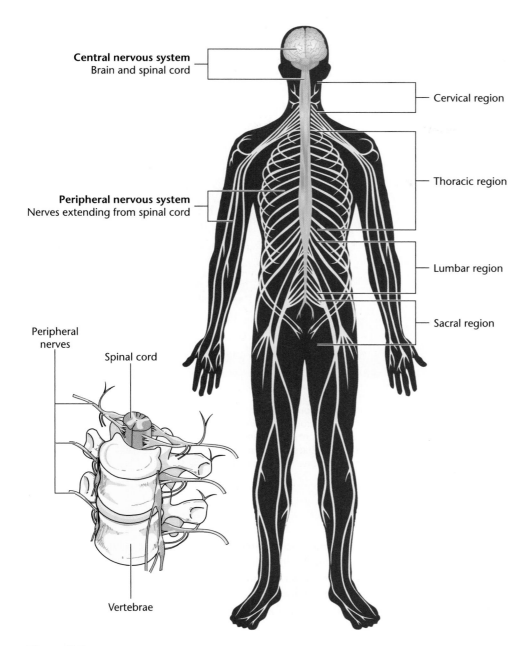

Central nervous system
Brain and spinal cord

Cervical region

Thoracic region

Peripheral nervous system
Nerves extending from spinal cord

Lumbar region

Sacral region

Peripheral nerves

Spinal cord

Vertebrae

Figure 6-3

The human nervous system. The central nervous system consists of the brain and spinal cord. The brain sends nerve signals to specific parts of the body through peripheral nerves; these are known as the peripheral nervous system. Peripheral nerves connect skeletal muscles with cells specialized to respond to sensations such as touch and pain. Peripheral nerves in the cervical region serve the neck and arms; those in the thoracic region serve the trunk, or main part of the body; those in the lumbar region serve the legs; and those in the sacral region serve the bowels and bladder.

Source: Adapted from Society for Neuroscience, 2005.

The Brain and Reflex Behavior

What makes newborns respond to a nipple? What tells them to start the sucking movements that allow them to control their intake of fluids? These are functions of the **central nervous system**—the brain and *spinal cord* (a bundle of nerves running through the backbone)— and of a growing peripheral network of nerves extending to every part of the body (Figure 6-3). Through this network, sensory messages travel to the brain, and motor commands travel back.

Guidepost 2

How does the brain develop, and how do environmental factors affect its early growth?

central nervous system Brain and spinal cord.

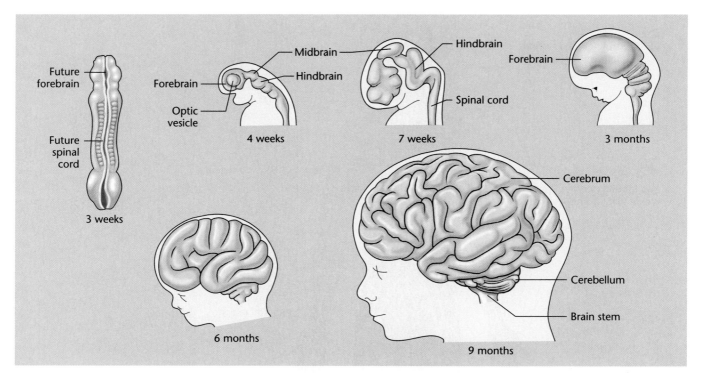

Figure 6-4

Brain development during gestation. Fetal nervous system development begins at about 3 weeks with the closing of the neural tube (left), from which will develop the brain and spinal cord. By 4 weeks, major regions of the brain appear in primitive form: the forebrain, midbrain, hindbrain, and optic vesicle, from which the eye develops. As the brain grows, the front part expands greatly to form the cerebrum, the large, convoluted upper mass which will be the seat of conscious brain activity. The brain stem, an extension of the spinal cord, is almost fully developed at birth, but the cerebellum (above the brain stem) grows most rapidly during the 1st year of life.

Source: Society for Neuroscience, 2005.

Building the Brain

The growth of the brain is a lifelong process fundamental to physical, cognitive, and emotional development. Through various brain-imaging tools, researchers are gaining a clearer picture of how brain growth occurs (Toga, Thompson, & Sowell, 2006).

The brain at birth is only about one-fourth to one-third of its eventual adult volume (Toga et al., 2006); It reaches nearly 90 percent of adult weight (3½ pounds) by age 3. By age 6, it is almost adult weight; but specific parts of the brain continue to grow and develop functionally into adulthood (Gabbard, 1996*). The brain's growth occurs in fits and starts called **brain growth spurts.** Different parts of the brain grow more rapidly at different times.

brain growth spurts Periods of rapid brain growth and development.

Major Parts of the Brain

Beginning about 3 weeks after conception, the brain gradually develops from a long hollow tube into a spherical mass of cells (Society for Neuroscience, 2005; Figure 6-4). By birth, the growth spurt of the spinal cord and *brain stem* (the part of the brain responsible for such basic bodily functions as breathing, heart rate, body temperature, and the sleep-wake cycle) has nearly run its course. The *cerebellum* (the part of the brain that maintains balance and motor coordination) grows fastest during the 1st year of life (Casaer, 1993).

The *cerebrum,* the largest part of the brain, is divided into right and left halves, or hemispheres, each with specialized functions. This specialization of the hemispheres is called **lateralization.** The left hemisphere is mainly concerned with language and logical thinking, the right hemisphere with visual and spatial functions such as map reading and

lateralization Tendency of each of the brain's hemispheres to have specialized functions.

*Unless otherwise referenced, the discussion in this section is largely based on Gabbard (1996), Society for Neuroscience (2005), and Toga et al. (2006).

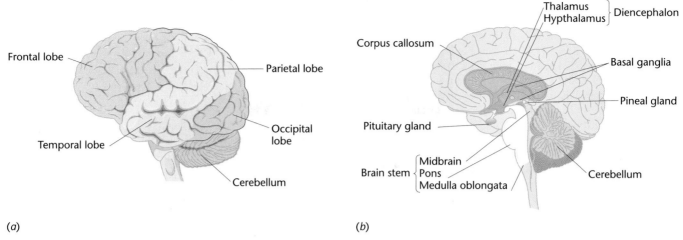

(a)   (b)

Figure 6-5

Parts of the brain, side view. The brain consists of three main parts: the brain stem, the cerebellum, and, above those, the large cerebrum. The brain stem controls such basic bodily functions as breathing, sleep, circulation, and reflexes. The cerebellum, at birth, begins to control balance and muscle tone; later it coordinates sensory and motor activity. The cerebrum constitutes almost 70 percent of the weight of the nervous system and handles thought, memory, language, and emotion, as well as sensory input and conscious motor control. (a) *Exterior view of left side of brain:* The cerebrum is divided into two halves, or hemispheres, each of which has four sections, or lobes: The *occipital lobe,* which processes visual information; the *temporal lobe,* which helps with hearing and language; the *parietal lobe,* which receives touch sensations and spatial information and facilitates eye-hand coordination; and the *frontal lobe,* which develops gradually during the 1st year and permits such higher-level functions as speech and reasoning. The cerebral cortex, the outer surface of the cerebrum, consists of gray matter, made up of closely packed neurons; it is the seat of thought processes and mental activity. (b) *Interior view of right hemisphere (left hemisphere removed):* Several important structures deep within the cerebrum—the thalamus, hippocampus (not shown), and basal ganglia, all of which control basic movements and functions, are largely developed at birth.

drawing. Joining the two hemispheres is a tough band of tissue called the *corpus callosum,* which allows them to share information and coordinate commands. The corpus callosum grows dramatically during childhood, reaching adult size by about age 10.

Each cerebral hemisphere has four lobes, or sections: the *occipital, parietal, temporal,* and *frontal lobes,* which control different functions (Figure 6-5) and develop at different rates. The regions of the *cerebral cortex* (the outer surface of the cerebrum) that govern vision, hearing, and other sensory information grow rapidly in the first few months after birth and are mature by age 6 months, but the areas of the frontal cortex responsible for abstract thought, mental associations, remembering, and deliberate motor responses grow little during this period and remain immature for several years (Gilmore et al., 2007).

The brain growth spurt that begins at about the third trimester of gestation and continues until at least age 4 is important to the development of neurological functioning. Smiling, babbling, crawling, walking, and talking—all the major sensory, motor, and cognitive milestones of infancy and toddlerhood—reflect the rapid development of the brain, particularly the cerebral cortex. (Box 6-1 discusses autism, a disorder related to abnormal brain growth.)

Brain Cells

The brain is composed of *neurons* and *glia.* **Neurons,** or nerve cells, send and receive information. *Glia,* or glial cells, nourish and protect the neurons.

neurons Nerve cells.

Beginning in the 2nd month of gestation, an estimated 250,000 immature neurons are produced every minute through mitosis (cell division). At birth, most of the more than 100 billion neurons in a mature brain are already formed but are not yet fully developed. The number of neurons increases most rapidly between the 25th week of gestation and the first few months after birth. This cell proliferation is accompanied by a dramatic growth in cell size.

Originally the neurons are simply cell bodies with a nucleus, or center, composed of deoxyribonucleic acid (DNA), which contains the cell's genetic programming. As the brain

Box 6-1 *The Autism "Epidemic"*

Autism is a severe disorder of brain functioning characterized by lack of normal social interaction, impaired communication, repetitive movements, and a highly restricted range of activities and interests. (See the table for a list of behaviors typical of children with autism.) Autism is usually not diagnosed behaviorally before age 3 (Schieve, Rice, Boyle, Visser, & Blumberg, 2006), but signs of the disorder may be seen as early as age 12 months through brain imaging (Center for Autism Research, n.d.).

Autism is one of a group of *autism spectrum disorders (ASDs)*. One of these, *Asperger syndrome,* is generally milder than autism, so children with Asperger syndrome generally function at a higher level than children with autism. Children with Asperger syndrome have an obsessive interest in a single topic to the exclusion of all others, and they talk about it to anyone who will listen. They have large vocabularies and stilted speech patterns and are often awkward and poorly coordinated. Their odd or eccentric behavior makes social contacts difficult (National Institute of Neurological Disorders and Stroke, 2007).

Perhaps in part because of growing awareness and more accurate diagnosis, the reported prevalence of autism has increased markedly since the mid-1970s in the United States (Newschaffer, Falb, & Gurney, 2005) and other industrialized countries. According to parental reports, at least 300,000 children—approximately 5.6 in 1,000 U.S. children ages 4 through 17—have been diagnosed with autism, 4 out of 5 of them boys (Schieve et al., 2006). A 14-state study in 2002 found that 1 in 150 8-year-olds has autism or one of the related disorders (Autism and Developmental Disabilities Monitoring Network Surveillance Year 2002 Principal Investigators, 2007).

Some parents blame the preservative thimerosal, which contains a form of mercury and was widely used before the development of thimerosal-free vaccines. The prevalence of the disorder did decline after the U.S. Public Health Service recommended that thimerosal be removed from these vaccines as a precaution (Geier & Geier, 2006). However, the Centers for Disease Control and Prevention (2004), on the basis of multiple studies, concludes that no convincing evidence supports a causal connection between vaccines and autism.

Autism seems to involve a lack of coordination between different regions of the brain needed for complex tasks (Just, Cherkassky, Keller, Kana, & Minshew, 2007; Williams, Goldstein, & Minshew, 2006). In a brain imaging study, adults with autism used different parts of the brain than did adults without autism in trying to comprehend a sentence. The group with autism showed less activation in the front of the brain, which is involved in higher-level thinking, and more in the rear section, which is involved in perceiving details, suggesting that they focused more on the meanings of individual words than on the sentence as a whole (Just, Cherkassky, Keller, & Minshew, 2004). Postmortem studies have found fewer neurons in the amygdala, a part of the brain involved in emotion and memory, in the brains of people who had autism (Schumann & Amaral, 2006). People with autism also show deficits in executive function and theory of mind (Zelazo & Müller, 2002; see Chapter 10).

Possible Signs of Autism

Children with autism may show the following characteristics in varying combinations and degrees of severity:

Inappropriate laughing or giggling

Lack of fear of danger

Apparent insensitivity to pain

Rejection of cuddling

Sustained unusual or repetitive play

Uneven physical or verbal skills

Avoidance of eye contact

Preferring to be alone

Difficulty expressing needs except through gestures

Inappropriate attachment to objects

Insistence on sameness

Echoing words or phrases

Inappropriate response to sound

Spinning objects or self

Difficulty interacting with others

Source: Autism Society of America, n.d.

Autism and related disorders run in families and have a strong genetic basis (Constantino, 2003; Ramoz et al., 2004; Rodier, 2000). Monozygotic twins are more concordant for autism than dizygotic twins. It is likely that multiple genes are at work. An international team of researchers has identified at least one gene and pinpointed the location of another gene on chromosome 11 that may contribute to autism (Szatmari et al., 2007). An earlier study found strong support for an autism gene on chromosome 7 and also evidence for genes on chromosomes 3, 4 and 11. This study also suggested that different genes may be responsible for the disorder in boys than in girls, and in early-onset as opposed to late-onset autism (Schellenberg et al., 2006).

Environmental factors, such as exposure to certain viruses or chemicals, may trigger an inherited tendency toward autism (Rodier, 2000). Certain complications of pregnancy, such as uterine bleeding and vaginal infection seem to be associated with a higher incidence of autism (Juul-Dam, Townsend, & Courchesne, 2001). So are advanced parental age, first births, threatened fetal loss, epidural anesthesia, induced labor, and cesarean delivery (Glasson et al., 2004; Reichenberg et al., 2006). Major stress during the 24th to 28th week of pregnancy may deform the developing brain (Beversdorf et al., 2001).

Why are children with autism overwhelmingly male? According to one theory, the female brain is predominantly hard-wired for empathy, and the male brain for understanding and building systems: Newborn girls look longer at a face; newborn boys look longer at a mechanical mobile. According to this theory, autism may be an extreme version of the normal male brain. Persons with autism are impaired in emphathizing but excellent at systematizing (Baron-Cohen, 2005). In a study of 58 children whose mothers had undergone amniocentesis during pregnancy, high levels of fetal testosterone in amniotic fluid were associated with poorer quality social relationships and more restricted interests at age 4. This finding suggests that high levels of fetal testosterone may be involved in the male vulnerability to autism (Knickmeyer, Baron-Cohen, Raggatt, & Taylor, 2005).

Autism has no known cure, but improvement—sometimes substantial—can occur, especially with early intervention. Some children with autism can be taught to speak, read, and write. Behavior therapy can help them learn such basic social skills as paying attention, sustaining eye contact, and feeding and dressing themselves (AAP Committee on Children with Disabilities, 2001). However, only about 2 percent of these children grow up to live independently; most need some degree of care throughout life. Children with Asperger's syndrome generally fare better ("Autism—Part II," 2001).

grows, these rudimentary cells migrate to various parts of it (Bystron, Rakic, Molnar, & Blakemore, 2006). Most of the neurons in the cortex are in place by 20 weeks of gestation, and its structure becomes fairly well-defined during the next 12 weeks.

Once in place, the neurons sprout *axons* and *dendrites*—narrow, branching, fiberlike extensions. Axons send signals to other neurons, and dendrites receive incoming messages from them, through *synapses,* the nervous system's communication links. The synapses are tiny gaps, which are bridged with the help of chemicals called *neurotransmitters,* which are released by the neurons. Eventually a particular neuron may have anywhere from 5,000 to 100,000 synaptic connections to and from the body's sensory receptors, its muscles, and other neurons within the central nervous system.

The multiplication of dendrites and synaptic connections, especially during the last 2½ months of gestation and the first 6 months to 2 years of life (Figure 6-6), accounts for much of the brain's growth and permits the emergence of new perceptual, cognitive, and motor abilities. As the neurons multiply, migrate to their assigned locations, and develop connections, they undergo the complementary processes of *integration* and *differentiation.* Through **integration,** the neurons that control various groups of muscles coordinate their activities. Through **differentiation,** each neuron takes on a specific, specialized structure and function.

At first the brain produces more neurons and synapses than it needs. Those that are not used or do not function well die out. This process of **cell death,** or pruning of excess cells, begins during the prenatal period and continues after birth (Figure 6-7), helping create an efficient nervous system.

Only about half the neurons originally produced survive and function in adulthood (Society for Neuroscience, 2005). Yet, even as unneeded neurons die out, others continue to form during adult life (Eriksson et al., 1998; Gould, Reeves, Graziano, & Gross, 1999). Meanwhile, connections among cortical cells continue to strengthen and to become more reliable and precise, enabling more flexible and more advanced motor and cognitive functioning (Society for Neuroscience, 2005).

integration Process by which neurons coordinate the activities of muscle groups.

differentiation Process by which cells acquire specialized structure and function.

cell death In brain development, normal elimination of excess cells to achieve more efficient functioning.

Myelination

Much of the credit for improvement in efficiency of communication goes to the glia, which coat the neural pathways with a fatty substance called *myelin.* This process of **myelination** enables signals to travel faster and more smoothly, permitting the achievement of mature functioning. Myelination begins about halfway through gestation in some parts of the brain and continues into adulthood in others. The pathways related to the sense of touch—the first sense to develop—are myelinated by birth. Myelination of visual pathways, which are slower to mature, begins at birth and continues during the first 5 months. Pathways related to hearing may begin to be myelinated as early as the 5th month of gestation, but the process is not complete until about age 4.

myelination Process of coating neurons with myelin, a fatty substance that enables faster communication between cells.

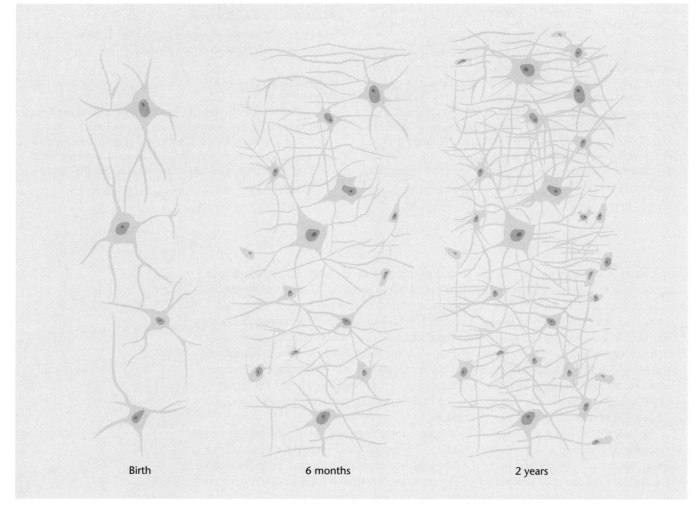

Birth	6 months	2 years

Figure 6-6

Growth of neural connections during the first 2 years of life. The rapid increase in the brain's density and weight is due largely to the formation of dendrites, extensions of nerve cell bodies, and the synapses that link them. This mushrooming communications network sprouts in response to environmental stimulation and makes possible impressive growth in every domain of development.

Source: Reprinted by permission of the publisher from *The Postnatal Development of the Human Cerebral Cortex, Vols. I–VIII* by Jesse LeRoy Conel, Cambridge, Mass.: Harvard University Press. Copyright © 1939, 1975 by the President and Fellows of Harvard College.

Myelination of sensory and motor pathways, first in the fetus's spinal cord and later, after birth, in the cerebral cortex, may account for the appearance and disappearance of early reflexes.

Early Reflexes

reflex behavior Automatic, involuntary, innate response to stimulation.

When you blink at a bright light, your eyelids are acting involuntarily. Such an automatic, innate response to stimulation is called a **reflex behavior.** Reflex behaviors are controlled by the lower brain centers that govern other involuntary processes, such as breathing and heart rate.

Human infants have an estimated 27 major reflexes, many of which are present at birth or soon after (Gabbard, 1996; see Table 6-1 for examples). *Primitive reflexes,* such as sucking, rooting for the nipple, and the Moro reflex (a response to being startled or beginning to fall), are related to instinctive needs for survival and protection. Some primitive reflexes may be part of humankind's evolutionary legacy. One example is the grasping reflex, by which infant monkeys hold on to the hair of their mothers' bodies. As the higher brain centers become active during the first 2 to 4 months, infants begin to show *postural reflexes:* reactions to changes in position or balance. For example, infants who are tilted downward extend their arms in the parachute reflex, an instinctive attempt to break a fall. *Locomotor*

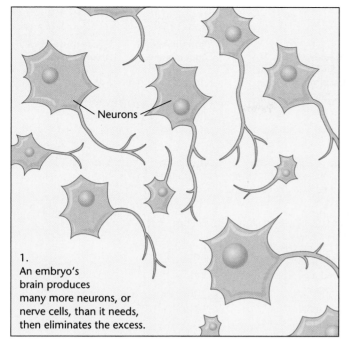

1.
An embryo's brain produces many more neurons, or nerve cells, than it needs, then eliminates the excess.

Neurons

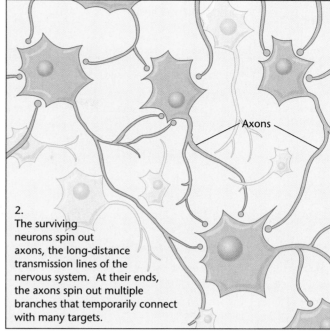

2.
The surviving neurons spin out axons, the long-distance transmission lines of the nervous system. At their ends, the axons spin out multiple branches that temporarily connect with many targets.

Axons

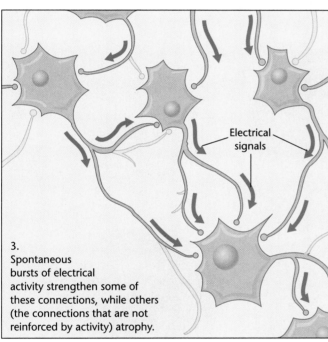

3.
Spontaneous bursts of electrical activity strengthen some of these connections, while others (the connections that are not reinforced by activity) atrophy.

Electrical signals

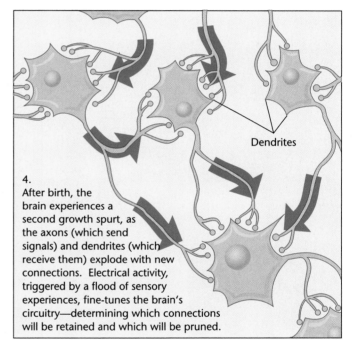

4.
After birth, the brain experiences a second growth spurt, as the axons (which send signals) and dendrites (which receive them) explode with new connections. Electrical activity, triggered by a flood of sensory experiences, fine-tunes the brain's circuitry—determining which connections will be retained and which will be pruned.

Dendrites

Figure 6-7

Wiring the brain: development of neural connections before and after birth.

Source: Nash, 1997, p. 51.

reflexes, such as the walking and swimming reflexes, resemble voluntary movements that do not appear until months after these reflexes have disappeared.

Most of the early reflexes disappear during the first 6 months to 1 year. Reflexes that continue to serve protective functions, such as blinking, yawning, coughing, gagging, sneezing, shivering, and the pupillary reflex (dilation of the pupils in the dark), remain. Disappearance of unneeded reflexes on schedule is a sign that motor pathways in the cortex have been partially myelinated, enabling a shift to voluntary behavior. Thus, a physician can evaluate a baby's neurological development by seeing whether certain reflexes are present or absent.

Reflex	Stimulation	Baby's Behavior	Typical Age of Appearance	Typical Age of Disappearance
Moro	Baby is dropped or hears loud noise.	Extends legs, arms, and fingers; arches back, draws back head.	7th month of gestation	3 months
Darwinian (grasping)	Palm of baby's hand is stroked.	Makes strong fist, can be raised to standing position if both fists are closed around a stick.	7th month of gestation	4 months
Tonic neck	Baby is laid down on back.	Turns head to one side, assumes "fencer" position, extends arms and legs on preferred side, flexes opposite limbs.	7th month of gestation	5 months
Babkin	Both of baby's palms are stroked at once.	Mouth opens, eyes close, neck flexes, head tilts forward.	Birth	3 months
Babinski	Sole of baby's foot is stroked.	Toes fan out, foot twists in.	Birth	4 months
Rooting	Baby's cheek or lower lip is stroked with finger or nipple.	Head turns, mouth opens, sucking movements begin.	Birth	9 months
Walking	Baby is held under arms, with bare feet touching flat surface.	Makes steplike motions that look like well-coordinated walking.	1 month	4 months
Swimming	Baby is put into water face down.	Makes well-coordinated swimming movements.	1 month	4 months

Table 6-1 Early Human Reflexes

Moro reflex

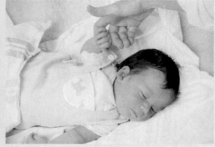

Darwinian reflex

Tonic neck reflex

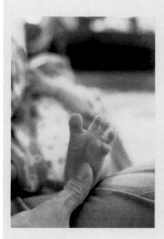

Baoinski reflex

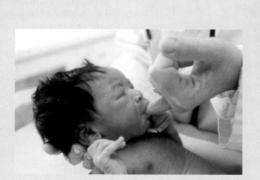

Rooting reflex

Walking reflex

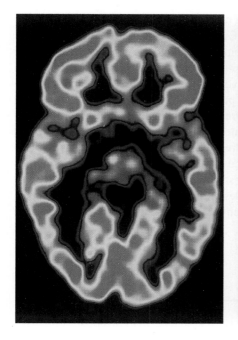
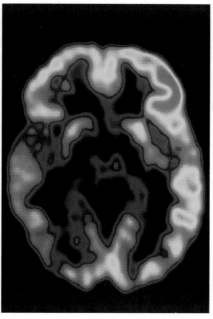

Extreme environmental deprivation in infancy can affect the structure of the brain, resulting in cognitive and emotional problems. A PET scan of a normal child's brain (*left*) shows regions of high (*red*) and low (*blue* and *black*) activity. A PET scan of the brain of a Romanian orphan institutionalized after birth (*right*) shows little activity.

Molding the Brain: The Role of Experience

Although the brain's early development is genetically directed, it can be modified both positively and negatively by environmental experience (Toga et al., 2006). The technical term for this modifiability of the brain is **plasticity.** Early experience can have lasting effects on the capacity of the central nervous system to learn and store information (Society for Neuroscience, 2005). Individual differences in intelligence may reflect differences in the brain's ability to develop neural connections in response to experience (Garlick, 2003).

During this formative period, the brain is especially vulnerable. Exposure to hazardous drugs, environmental toxins, or maternal stress before or after birth can threaten the developing brain, and malnutrition can interfere with normal cognitive growth (Rose, 1994; Thompson, 2001). So, too, early abuse or sensory impoverishment may leave an imprint on the brain (J. E. Black, 1998). In one study, a monkey raised until age 6 months with one eyelid closed became permanently blind in that eye, apparently through loss of working connections between that eye and the visual cortex (Society for Neuroscience, 2005). Thus, if certain cortical connections are not made early in life, these circuits may shut down forever.

By the same token, enriched experience can spur brain development (Society for Neuroscience, 2005) and even make up for past deprivation (J. E. Black, 1998). Animals raised in toy-filled cages sprout more axons, dendrites, and synapses than animals raised in bare cages (Society for Neuroscience, 2005). Plasticity continues throughout life as neurons change in size and shape in response to environmental experience (Rutter, 2002). Such findings have sparked successful efforts to stimulate the brain development of premature infants (Als et al., 2004) and children with Down syndrome and to help victims of brain damage recover function. These findings also explain why the sensory and cognitive stimulation Anne Sullivan provided was so important in Helen Keller's development.

Ethical constraints prevent controlled experiments on the effects of environmental deprivation on human infants. However, the discovery of thousands of infants and young children who had spent virtually their entire lives in overcrowded Romanian orphanages offered a natural experiment (Ames, 1997). Found after the fall of the dictator Nicolae Ceausescu in December 1989, these abandoned children appeared to be starving, passive, and emotionless. They had spent much of their time lying quietly in their cribs or beds with nothing to look at. They had had little contact with one another or with their caregivers and

plasticity Modifiability of the brain through experience.

What's your view

- In view of what is known about the plasticity of the infant brain, should every baby have access to an appropriately stimulating environment? If so, how can this goal be accomplished?

Checkpoint ✔

Can you . . .

✔ Describe important features of early brain development?

✔ Explain the functions of reflex behaviors and why some drop out during the early months?

✔ Discuss how early experience affects brain growth and development?

had heard little conversation or even noise. Most of the 2- and 3-year-olds did not walk or talk, and the older children played aimlessly. PET scans of their brains showed extreme inactivity in the temporal lobes, which regulate emotion and receive sensory input.

Many of these orphans were placed in adoptive homes in the United Kingdom or in foster care in Romania. In both cases, age of adoption and length of previous institutionalization were key factors in the children's prospects for cognitive improvement. In an English study, for example, Romanian children who had been removed from institutions before age 6 months showed no associated cognitive impairment by age 11 as compared with a control group of English children adopted within the United Kingdom, but the average IQs of Romanian children adopted into English families after age 6 months were 15 points lower. At ages 6 and 11, the latest-placed adoptees were the most cognitively impaired, though this group did show modest progress (Beckett et al., 2006). Apparently, then, it may take very early environmental stimulation to fully overcome the effects of extreme deprivation.

Guidepost 3

How do the senses develop during infancy?

Early Sensory Capacities

The developing brain enables newborn infants to make fairly good sense of what they touch, see, smell, taste, and hear; and their senses develop rapidly in the early months of life as infants adapt to the world around them.

Touch and Pain

Touch seems to be the first sense to develop, and for the first several months it is the most mature sensory system. When a newborn's cheek is stroked near the mouth, the baby responds by trying to find a nipple, probably an evolved survival mechanism (Rakison, 2005). By 32 weeks of gestation, all body parts are sensitive to touch, and this sensitivity increases during the first 5 days of life (Haith, 1986).

In the past, physicians performing surgery (such as circumcision) on newborn babies often used no anesthesia because of a mistaken belief that neonates cannot feel pain or feel it only briefly. Actually, as we reported in Chapter 4, there is evidence that the capacity for pain perception may emerge by the third trimester of pregnancy (Lee et al., 2005). Newborns can and do feel pain; and they become more sensitive to it during their first few days. The AAP and the Canadian Paediatric Society (2000) now maintain that prolonged or severe pain can do long-term harm to newborns and that pain relief is essential.

Smell and Taste

The senses of smell and taste also begin to develop in the womb. The flavors and odors of foods an expectant mother consumes may be transmitted to the fetus through the amniotic fluid. After birth, a similar transmission occurs through breast milk (Mennella & Beauchamp, 1996b).

A preference for pleasant odors seems to be learned in utero and during the first few days after birth, and the odors transmitted through the mother's breast milk may further contribute to this learning (Bartoshuk & Beauchamp, 1994). This attraction to the fragrance of the mother's milk may be another evolutionary survival mechanism (Rakison, 2005). In a study of French 3- and 4-day-olds, both those who were being breast-fed and those who were being formula-fed showed a preference for the odor of human milk (Marlier & Schaal, 2005).

Certain taste preferences seem to be largely innate (Bartoshuk & Beauchamp, 1994). Newborns prefer sweet tastes to sour, bitter, or salty ones (Haith, 1986). Sweetened water calms crying newborns, whether full term or 2 to 3 weeks premature—evidence that, not only the taste buds themselves (which seem to be fairly well developed by 20 weeks of gestation), but also the mechanisms that produce this calming effect are functional before normal term (Smith & Blass, 1996). An inborn sweet tooth may help a baby adapt to life outside the womb, since breast milk is quite sweet (Harris, 1997). Newborns' rejection of bitter tastes is probably another survival mechanism, since many bitter substances are toxic (Bartoshuk & Beauchamp, 1994).

Most infants begin to eat solid foods after 6 months. Even at this age, infants show definite taste preferences. An infant exposed to the flavors of healthy foods through breast-feeding is more likely to accept healthy foods, such as cereal and vegetables.

Taste preferences developed in infancy may last into early childhood. In one study, 4- and 5-year-olds who, as infants, had been fed different types of formula had differing food preferences (Mennella & Beauchamp, 2002). Exposure to the flavors of healthy foods through breastfeeding may improve acceptance of healthy foods after weaning and later in life (American Heart Association et al., 2006).

Hearing

Hearing, too, is functional before birth; fetuses respond to sounds and seem to learn to recognize them. From an evolutionary perspective, early recognition of voices and language heard in the womb may lay the foundation for the relationship with the mother, which is critical to early survival (Rakison, 2005).

Auditory discrimination develops rapidly after birth. Even 3-day-old infants can tell new speech sounds from those they have heard before (L. R. Brody, Zelazo, & Chaika, 1984). At 1 month, babies can distinguish sounds as close as *ba* and *pa* (Eimas, Siqueland, Jusczyk, & Vigorito, 1971).

Because hearing is a key to language development, hearing impairments should be identified as early as possible. Hearing loss occurs in 1 to 3 of 1,000 live births and, if left undetected, can lead to developmental delays (Gaffney et al., 2003). Early hearing detection and intervention programs have been established in all 50 states and are mandated in 39 of them, as well as in several European countries.

Sight

Vision is the least developed sense at birth, perhaps because there is so little to see in the womb. From an evolutionary developmental perspective, the other senses are more directly related to a newborn's survival. Visual perception and the ability to use visual information—identifying caregivers, finding food, and avoiding dangers—become more important as infants become more alert and active (Rakison, 2005).

The eyes of newborns are smaller than those of adults, the retinal structures are incomplete, and the optic nerve is underdeveloped. A neonate's eyes focus best from about 1 foot away—just about the typical distance from the face of a person holding a newborn. This focusing distance may have evolved to promote mother-infant bonding. There is some evidence that the ability to recognize faces—specifically, a caregiver's face—may be an innate survival mechanism (Rakison, 2005).

Newborns blink at bright lights. Their peripheral vision is very narrow; it more than doubles between ages 2 and 10 weeks (Tronick, 1972). The ability to follow a moving target also develops rapidly in the first months, as does color perception (Haith, 1986).

Visual acuity at birth is approximately 20/400 but improves rapidly, reaching the 20/20 level by about 8 months (Kellman & Arterberry, 1998; Kellman & Banks, 1998). (This measure of vision means that a person can read letters on a specified line on a standard eye chart from 20 feet away.) *Binocular vision*—the use of both eyes to focus, enabling perception of depth and distance—usually does not develop until 4 or 5 months (Bushnell & Boudreau, 1993).

Early screening is essential to detect any problems that interfere with vision, such as retinal abnormalities, congenital cataracts, muscle imbalances, and amblyopia (failure of coordination between the images produced by the two eyes). Infants should be examined by 6 months for visual fixation preference, ocular alignment, and any signs of eye disease. Formal vision screening should begin by 3 years (AAP Committee on Practice and Ambulatory Medicine and Section on Ophthalmology, 1996, 2002).

Motor Development

Babies do not have to be taught such basic motor skills as rolling over, crawling, and walking. They just need room to move and freedom to see what they can do. When the central nervous system, muscles, and bones are ready and the environment offers the right opportunities for exploration and practice, babies keep surprising the adults around them with their new abilities.

Checkpoint ✔

Can you . . .

✔ Give evidence for early development of the senses?

✔ Tell how breast-feeding plays a part in the development of smell and taste?

✔ Tell how auditory discrimination in newborns is related to fetal hearing?

✔ List three ways in which newborns' vision is underdeveloped?

Guidepost 4

What are the early milestones in motor development, and what are some influences on it?

Table 6-2	Milestones of Motor Development	
Skill	**50 percent**	**90 percent**
Rolling over	3.2 months	5.4 months
Grasping rattle	3.3 months	3.9 months
Sitting without support	5.9 months	6.8 months
Standing while holding on	7.2 months	8.5 months
Grasping with thumb and finger	8.2 months	10.2 months
Standing alone well	11.5 months	13.7 months
Walking well	12.3 months	14.9 months
Building tower of two cubes	14.8 months	20.6 months
Walking up steps	16.6 months	21.6 months
Jumping in place	23.8 months	2.4 years
Copying circle	3.4 years	4.0 years

Note: This table shows the approximate ages when 50 percent and 90 percent of children can perform each skill, according to the Denver Training Manual II.

Source: Adapted from Frankenburg et al., 1992.

Milestones of Motor Development

Motor development is marked by a series of milestones: achievements that develop systematically, each newly mastered ability preparing a baby to tackle the next. Babies first learn simple skills and then combine them into increasingly complex **systems of action,** which permit a wider or more precise range of movement and more effective control of the environment. In developing the precision grip, for example, an infant first tries to pick things up with the whole hand, fingers closing against the palm. Later the baby masters the *pincer grasp,* in which thumb and index finger meet at the tips to form a circle, making it possible to pick up tiny objects. In learning to walk, an infant first gains control of separate movements of the arms, legs, and feet before putting these movements together to take that momentous first step.

The **Denver Developmental Screening Test** (Frankenburg, Dodds, Fandal, Kazuk, & Cohrs, 1975) is used to chart normal progress between ages 1 month and 6 years and to identify children who are not developing normally. The test measures **gross motor skills** (those using large muscles), such as rolling over and catching a ball, and **fine motor skills** (using small muscles), such as grasping a rattle and copying a circle. It also assesses language development (such as knowing the definitions of words) and personality and social development (such as smiling spontaneously and dressing without help). The newest edition, the Denver II Scale (Frankenburg et al., 1992), includes revised norms (Table 6-2 gives examples).

When we talk about what the "average" baby can do, we refer to the 50 percent Denver norms. Actually, normality covers a wide range; about half of all babies master these skills before the ages given, and about half do so afterward. The Denver norms were developed with reference to a Western population and are not necessarily valid in assessing children from other cultures. For example, Southeast Asian children who were given the Denver test did not play pat-a-cake, did not pick up raisins, and did not dress themselves at the expected ages (V. Miller, Onotera, & Deinard, 1984). Yet that did not indicate slow development. In their culture, children do not play pat-a-cake; raisins look like a medicine they are taught to avoid; and their parents continue to help them dress much longer than western parents do.

As we trace typical progress in head control, hand control, and locomotion, notice how these developments follow the cephalocaudal (head to tail) and proximodistal (inner to outer) principles outlined earlier. Note, too, that although boy babies tend to be a little bigger and more active than girl babies, there are no gender differences in infants' motor development (Mondschein, Adolph, & Tamis-LeMonda, 2000).

systems of action Increasingly complex combinations of motor skills that permit a wider or more precise range of movement and more control of the environment.

Denver Developmental Screening Test Screening test given to children age 1 month to 6 years to determine whether they are developing normally.

gross motor skills Physical skills that involve the large muscles.

fine motor skills Physical skills that involve the small muscles and eye-hand coordination.

Head Control

At birth, most infants can turn their heads from side to side while lying on their backs. While lying chest down, many can lift their heads enough to turn them. Within the first 2 to 3 months, they lift their heads higher and higher—sometimes to a point at which they lose their balance and roll over on their backs. By age 4 months, almost all infants can keep their heads erect while being held or supported in a sitting position.

Hand Control

At about 3½ months, most infants can grasp an object of moderate size, such as a rattle, but have trouble holding a small object. Next they begin to grasp objects with one hand and transfer them to the other and then to hold (but not pick up) small objects. Some time between 7 and 11 months, their hands become coordinated enough to pick up a tiny object, such as a pea, using the pincer grasp. After that, hand control becomes increasingly precise. By 15 months, the average baby can build a tower of two cubes. A few months after the third birthday, the average toddler can copy a circle fairly well.

At 4 months, Delilah can raise her head high from a prone position. She was a little later in doing so than some babies, but such variations in timing are normal.

Locomotion

After 3 months, the average baby begins to roll over deliberately (rather than accidentally, as before)—first from front to back and then from back to front. The average baby can sit without support by 6 months and can assume a sitting position without help by about 8½ months.

Between 6 and 10 months, most babies begin to get around under their own power by creeping or crawling. This achievement of *self-locomotion* has striking cognitive and psychosocial benefits (Bertenthal & Campos, 1987; Bertenthal, Campos, & Barrett, 1984; Bertenthal, Campos, & Kermoian, 1994; J. Campos, Bertenthal, & Benson, 1980). Crawling infants become more sensitive to where objects are, how big they are, whether they can be moved, and how they look. Crawling helps babies learn to better judge distances and perceive depth. They learn to look to others for clues as to whether a situation is safe or frightening—a skill known as *social referencing* (Hertenstein & Campos, 2004), which we discuss in Chapter 8.

By holding on to a helping hand or a piece of furniture, the average baby can stand at a little past age 7 months. The average baby can let go and stand well alone at about 11½ months.

All these developments are milestones along the way to the major motor achievement of infancy: walking. Humans begin to walk later than other species, possibly because babies' heavy heads, short legs, and relatively weak muscles make balance difficult. Again, practice is the most important factor in overcoming these difficulties (Adolph, Vereijken, & Shrout, 2003). For some months before they can stand without support, babies practice walking while holding on to furniture. Soon after they can stand alone well and take their first unaided steps. At this stage a baby typically practices standing and walking more than 6 hours a day, on and off, and may take enough steps (9,000) to cover the length of 29 football fields! Within a few weeks, soon after the 1st birthday, the baby is walking fairly well and thus achieves the status of toddler.

Many U.S. parents put their babies in mobile walkers in the belief that the babies will learn to walk earlier. Actually, by restricting babies' motor exploration, and sometimes their view of their movements, walkers may *delay* motor skill development (Siegel & Burton, 1999). Furthermore, walkers can be dangerous. An estimated 197,200 walker-related injuries to children younger than 15 months were treated in U.S. hospital emergency departments between 1990 and 2001, but the number of such injuries decreased markedly after 1994, when stationary activity centers for babies came on the market (Shields & Smith, 2006). The American Academy of Pediatrics has called for a ban on the manufacture

What's your view

- Is it advisable to try to teach babies skills such as walking before they develop them on their own?

and sale of infant walkers (AAP Committee on Injury and Poison Prevention, 2001b). In 2004, Canada became the first country to ban their sale, advertising, and importation (Reuters, 2004a).

During the 2nd year, children begin to climb stairs one at a time, putting one foot after another on each step; later, they will alternate feet. Walking down stairs comes later. In their 2nd year, toddlers also begin to run and jump. By age 3½, most children can balance briefly on one foot and begin to hop.

Motor Development and Perception

Sensory perception enables infants to learn about themselves and their environment so they can make better judgments about how to navigate in it. Motor experience, together with awareness of their changing bodies, sharpens and modifies their perceptual understanding of what is likely to happen if they move in a certain way. This bidirectional connection between perception and action, mediated by the developing brain, gives infants much useful information about themselves and their world (Adolph & Eppler, 2002).

Sensory and motor activity seem to be fairly well coordinated from birth (Bertenthal & Clifton, 1998). Infants as young as 2 months realize that an object's size and shape are constant, even though it looks smaller if it is farther away (Bower, 1966).

Infants begin reaching for objects at about 4 to 5 months; by 5½ months, they can adapt their reach to moving or spinning objects (Wentworth, Benson, & Haith, 2000). Piaget and other researchers long believed that reaching depended on **visual guidance:** the use of the eyes to guide the movement of the hands (or other parts of the body). Now, research has found that infants in that age group can use other sensory cues to reach for an object. They can locate an unseen rattle by its sound, and they can reach for a glowing object in the dark, even though they cannot see their hands (Clifton, Muir, Ashmead, & Clarkson, 1993). They even can reach for an object based only on their memory of its location (McCarty, Clifton, Ashmead, Lee, & Goubet, 2001). Slightly older infants, at 5 to 7½ months, can grasp a moving, fluorescent object in the dark—a feat that requires awareness, not only of how their hands move, but also of the object's path and speed, so as to anticipate the likely point of contact (Robin, Berthier, & Clifton, 1996).

Depth perception, the ability to perceive objects and surfaces in three dimensions, depends on several kinds of cues that affect the image of an object on the retina of the eye. These cues involve not only binocular coordination, but also motor control (Bushnell & Boudreau, 1993). *Kinetic cues* are produced by movement of the object or the observer, or both. To find out whether an object is moving, a baby might hold his or her head still for a moment, an ability that is well established by about 3 months.

Sometime between 5 and 7 months, babies respond to such cues as relative size and differences in texture and shading. These cues depend on **haptic perception,** the ability to acquire information by handling objects rather than just looking at them. Haptic perception comes only after babies develop enough eye-hand coordination to reach for objects and grasp them (Bushnell & Boudreau, 1993).

Eleanor and James Gibson's Ecological Theory of Perception

In a classic experiment by Richard Walk and Eleanor Gibson (1961), 6-month-old babies were placed on a Plexiglas tabletop laid over a checkerboard pattern that created the illusion of a vertical drop in the center of the table—a **visual cliff.** Would the infants perceive this illusion of depth? The babies did see a difference between the "ledge" and the "drop": They crawled freely on the ledge but avoided the drop, even when they saw their mothers beckoning from the far side of the table.

How do babies decide whether to move across a ledge or down a hill? According to Eleanor Gibson's and James J. Gibson's **ecological theory of perception** (E. J. Gibson, 1969; J. J. Gibson, 1979; Gibson & Pick, 2000), infants size up the **affordance,** or the fit, between their changing physical attributes (such as arm and leg length, endurance, balance, and strength) and the changing characteristics of their environment. Knowledge of this fit enables babies to make decisions about what they can do in a given situation (Is the ground

visual guidance Use of the eyes to guide movements of the hands or other parts of the body.

depth perception Ability to perceive objects and surfaces in three dimensions.

haptic perception Ability to acquire information about properties of objects, such as size, weight, and texture, by handling them.

visual cliff Apparatus designed to give an illusion of depth and used to assess depth perception in infants.

ecological theory of perception Theory developed by Eleanor and James Gibson, which describes developing motor and perceptual abilities as interdependent parts of a functional system that guides behavior in varying contexts.

affordance In the Gibsons' ecological theory of perception, the fit between a person's physical attributes and capabilities and characteristics of the environment.

too rough to walk on? Can I keep my balance if I try?) (Adolph, 2000; Adolph & Eppler, 2002). According to the Gibsons, perceptual learning occurs through a growing ability to differentiate the many features of a rich sensory environment. It is this ability, which may be inborn (Gibson & Walk, 1960), that permits infants and toddlers to recognize affordances and thus to successfully negotiate a terrain.

Locomotor development depends on increasing sensitivity to affordances and is an outcome of both perception and action (Adolph & Eppler, 2002). With experience, babies become better able to gauge the environment in which they move and to act accordingly (Adolph, 2000; Adolph et al., 2003; Adolph & Eppler, 2002). In visual cliff experiments, infants who have been crawling for some time are more likely than novices to avoid the cliff. Similarly, when faced with actual downward slopes of increasing steepness, infants' judgments become more accurate and their explorations more efficient as they gain practice in crawling. They apparently learn from experience how far they can push their limits without losing their balance (Adolph & Eppler, 2002).

This learning is flexible but posture-specific. Babies who learn how far they can reach for a toy across a gap while in a sitting position must acquire this knowledge anew when they begin to crawl (Adolph, 2000; Adolph & Eppler, 2002). Likewise, when crawling babies who have mastered slopes begin to walk, they have to learn to cope with slopes all over again (Adolph, 1997; Adolph & Eppler, 2002).

No matter how enticing a mother's arms are, this baby is staying away from them. As young as he is, he can perceive depth and wants to avoid falling off what looks like a cliff.

How Motor Development Occurs: Thelen's Dynamic Systems Theory

The typical sequence of motor development was traditionally thought to be genetically programmed—a largely automatic, preordained series of steps directed by the maturing brain. Today, many developmental scientists consider this view too simplistic. Instead, according to Esther Thelen (1995; Smith & Thelen, 2003), motor development is a continuous process of interaction between baby and environment.

Thelen pointed to the *walking reflex:* stepping movements a neonate makes when held upright with the feet touching a surface. This behavior usually disappears by the 4th month. Not until the latter part of the 1st year, when a baby is getting ready to walk, do such movements appear again. The usual explanation is a shift to cortical control: Thus, an older baby's deliberate walking is a new skill masterminded by the developing brain. But, Thelen observed, a newborn's stepping involves the same kinds of movements the neonate makes while lying down and kicking. Why would stepping stop, only to reappear months later, whereas kicking continues? The answer, she suggested, might be that babies' legs become thicker and heavier during the early months but not yet strong enough to carry the increased weight (Thelen & Fisher, 1982, 1983). In fact, when infants who had stopped stepping were held in warm water, which helps support their legs, stepping reappeared. Their ability to produce the movement had not changed—only the physical and environmental conditions that inhibited or promoted it.

Maturation alone cannot explain such an observation, said Thelen. Development does not have a single, simple cause. Infant and environment form an interconnected, dynamic system, which includes the infant's motivation as well as his muscular strength and position in the environment at a particular moment in time (for example, lying in a crib or being held in a pool). Similarly, when an infant tries to reach for a rattle or mobile, opportunities and constraints presented by the infant's physical characteristics, the intensity of her desire, her energy level, the speed and direction of her arm, and the changing positions of her arm and hand at each point in the process affect whether and how she can achieve the goal. Ultimately, a solution emerges as the baby explores various combinations of movements and selects and assembles those that most efficiently contribute to that end. Furthermore, the solution must be flexible, subject to modification in changing circumstances. Rather than being solely in charge of this process, the maturing brain is only one part of it.

These initial insights grew into Thelen's **dynamic systems theory (DST)**. According to dynamic systems theory, "behavior emerges in the moment from the self-organization of multiple components" (Spencer et al., 2006, p. 1523). According to Thelen, normal babies develop the same skills in the same order because they are built approximately the same way and have similar physical challenges and needs. Thus, they eventually discover that walking is more efficient than crawling in most situations. However, this discovery arises from each particular baby's physical characteristics and experience in a particular context. That this is so may explain why some babies learn to walk earlier and differently than others.

Thelen believed that the principles of DST apply in all realms of development. Like a jazz musician, infants improvise their personal solutions to problems by selecting and integrating multiple patterns or strands of behavior (Spencer et al., 2006).

Cultural Influences on Motor Development

Dynamic systems theory includes an emphasis on the context in which development occurs. Thus, although motor development follows a virtually universal sequence, its pace does respond to certain cultural factors. When children are well fed and well cared for and have physical freedom and the chance to explore their surroundings, their motor development is likely to be normal. However, what is normal in one culture may not be in another.

African babies tend to be more advanced than U.S. and European infants in sitting, walking, and running. In Uganda, for example, babies typically walk at 10 months, as compared with 12 months in the United States and 15 months in France (Gardiner & Komitzki, 2005). Asian babies tend to develop these skills more slowly. Such differences may be related in part to ethnic differences in temperament (H. Kaplan & Dove, 1987; see Chapter 8) or may reflect a culture's child-rearing practices (Gardiner & Komitzki, 2005).

Some cultures actively encourage early development of motor skills. In many African and West Indian cultures with advanced infant motor development, adults use special *handling routines,* such as bouncing and stepping exercises, to strengthen babies' muscles (Hopkins & Westra, 1988). In one study, Jamaican infants, whose mothers used such handling routines daily, sat, crawled, and walked earlier than English infants, whose mothers gave them no such special handling (Hopkins & Westra, 1990).

Other cultures discourage early motor development. Children of the Ache in eastern Paraguay do not begin to walk until age 18 to 20 months (H. Kaplan & Dove, 1987). Ache mothers pull their babies back to their laps when the infants begin to crawl away. The Ache mothers closely supervise their babies to protect them from the hazards of nomadic life and also because the women's primary responsibility is child raising rather than subsistence labor. Yet, as 8- to 10-year-olds, Ache children climb tall trees, chop branches, and play in ways that enhance their motor skills (H. Kaplan & Dove, 1987). Normal development, then, need not follow the same timetable to reach the same destination.

Checkpoint ✔

Can you . . .

✔ Trace a typical infant's progress in head control, hand control, and locomotion, according to the Denver norms?

✔ Discuss how maturation, perception, and cultural influences relate to early motor development?

Guidepost 5

How can we enhance babies' chances of survival and health?

Health

Infancy and toddlerhood are risky times of life, though far less so than they were when Helen Keller contracted her mysterious illness. How many babies die during the 1st year, and why? What can be done to prevent injuries and dangerous or debilitating childhood diseases? How can we ensure that infants and toddlers live, grow, and develop as they should?

Infant Mortality

Great strides have been made in protecting the lives of new babies, but these advances are not evenly distributed. Worldwide, in 2000, about 8 million infants—more than 1 in 20 born alive—died before their 1st birthday (Population Reference Bureau, 2005; UNICEF, 2002). Of these deaths, nearly half—about 4 million—occurred during the neonatal period, 3 out

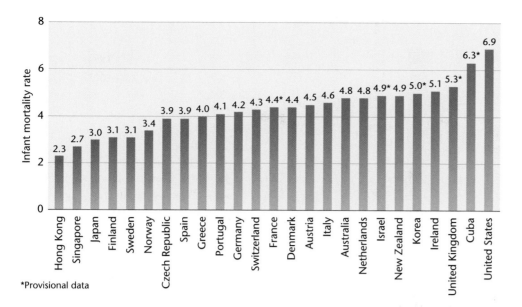

Figure 6-8

Infant mortality rates in industrialized countries, 2003. Despite dramatic improvement, the United States has a higher infant mortality rate than 25 other industrialized nations, largely because of its diverse population, health disparities for disadvantaged groups, and its high percentage of low-birth-weight infants, especially among African American babies.

Source: Hamilton et al., 2007; from United Nations Demographic Yearbook, 2003.

of 4 of them in the 1st week of life, and 2 out of 3 in Africa and Southeast Asia (Lawn, Cousens, & Zupan for the Lancet Neonatal Survival Steering Team, 2005). The primary causes of neonatal death worldwide are preterm delivery (28 percent), sepsis or pneumonia (26 percent), and asphyxiation at birth (23 percent) (Bryce, Boschi-Pinto, Shibuya, and the WHO Child Health Epidemiology Reference Group, 2005). Many of these deaths are preventable, resulting from a combination of poverty, poor maternal health and nutrition, infection, and poor medical care (Lawn et al., 2005; UNICEF, 2003).

In the United States, the **infant mortality rate**—the proportion of babies who die within the 1st year—has fallen almost every year since 1950 (Hamilton et al., 2007; NCHS, 2005). In 2004, 6.79 infants died for every 1,000 live births (Hamilton et al., 2007). Mortality rates for twins and triplets have diminished along with rates for single births (Luke & Brown, 2006). More than half of all infant deaths occur during the 1st week of life, and two-thirds occur during the neonatal weeks (Hoyert, Heron, Murphy, & Kung, 2006; Kochanek & Smith, 2004; Kochanek, Murphy, Anderson, & Scott, 2004).

infant mortality rate Proportion of babies born alive who die within the 1st year.

Birth defects (congenital malformations) are the leading cause of infant deaths in the United States, followed by disorders related to prematurity or low birth weight (refer back to Chapter 5), sudden infant death syndrome (SIDS), maternal complications of pregnancy, and unintentional injuries. These five causes together account for more than half of all infant deaths (Hamilton et al., 2007).

The improvement in U.S. infant mortality rates since 1990, even at a time when more babies were born perilously small, is attributable largely to prevention of sudden infant death syndrome (discussed on pages 167–168) as well as to effective treatment for respiratory distress and medical advances in keeping very small babies alive (Arias et al., 2003). Still, mainly because of the prevalence of low birth weight, U.S. babies have a poorer chance of reaching their first birthday than do babies in many other developed countries (Arias et al., 2003; Hamilton et al., 2007; Figure 6-8). Indeed, nearly half (49 percent) of all infant deaths in the United States in 2003 were among the 0.8 percent of infants whose birth weight was less than 1,000 grams (about 2 pounds) (Mathews & MacDorman, 2006).

Racial/Ethnic Disparities in Infant Mortality

Although infant mortality has declined for all races and ethnic groups in the United States, large disparities remain (Hesso & Fuentes, 2005; Figure 6-9). Black babies are nearly two and a half times as likely to die in their 1st year as white and Hispanic babies (Hoyert, Heron, et al., 2006; Table 6-3). This disparity largely reflects the greater prevalence of low birth weight and SIDS among African Americans (Kochanek & Smith, 2004; Kochanek et al., 2004). Infant mortality among American Indians and Alaska Natives is about one and a

Figure 6-9

Infant mortality rates by race/ ethnicity of mother, 1995 and 2003. Despite some decline, non-Hispanic blacks continue to have the highest infant mortality rates.

Source: Centers for Disease Control & Prevention, 2006d.

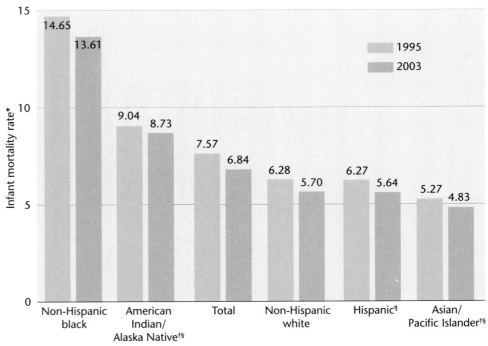

* Deaths of infants age <1 year per 1,000 live births.
† Includes persons of Hispanic and non-Hispanic origin.
§ Difference not significant at *p* < 0.05 (*z* test).
¶ Persons of Hispanic origin might be of any race.

Table 6-3	Birth Weight, Mortality, and Race, 2003				
	Low Birth Weight (less than 5.5 pounds, or 2,500 grams), % of births	**Very Low Birth Weight (less than 3.3 pounds, or 1,500 grams), % of births**	**Infant Mortality Rate* per 1,000**	**Neonatal Mortality Rate** per 1,000**	**Postneonatal Mortality Rate*** per 1,000**
Black infants	11.6	2.6	13.9	9.3	4.9
White (non-Hispanic) infants	5.1	0.8	5.8	3.9	1.9
Hispanic infants	5.6	0.9	5.6	3.8	1.8

Note: Black infants are more likely than white or Hispanic infants to die in the 1st year from birth defects or disorders, sudden infant death syndrome, respiratory distress syndrome, and disorders related to short gestation and low birth weight and as a result of maternal complications of pregnancy.

  * Deaths during the 1st year of life
 ** Deaths during first 4 weeks
***Deaths between 4 weeks and 11 months

Source: Martin, Hamilton, et al., 2005; Martin, Kochanek, et al., 2005.

half times that among white babies (NCHS, 2005), mainly due to SIDS and fetal alcohol syndrome (American Public Health Association, 2004).

Intragroup variations are often overlooked. Within the Hispanic population, Puerto Rican infants are more than twice as likely to die as Cuban infants (Hoyert, Heron, et al., 2006). Asian Americans, overall, are least likely to die in infancy, but Hawaiian infants are more than three times as likely to die as Chinese American infants (NCHS, 2005).

Racial or ethnic disparities in access to and quality of health care for minority children (Flores, Olson, & Tomany-Korman, 2005) may help account for differences in mortality, but behavioral factors also may play a part. Obesity, smoking, and alcohol consumption contribute to poor outcomes of pregnancy. African Americans have the highest obesity rates, and American Indians and Alaska Natives tend to be heavy smokers and drinkers. Rates of prenatal care vary from 85 percent of white expectant mothers down to 69 percent of American Indians and Alaska Natives (American Public Health Association, 2004). Because causes and risk factors for infant mortality vary among ethnic groups, efforts to further reduce infant deaths need to focus on factors specific to each ethnic group (Hesso & Fuentes, 2005).

Sudden Infant Death Syndrome (SIDS)

Sudden infant death syndrome (SIDS), sometimes called *crib death,* is the sudden death of an infant under age 1 year in which the cause of death remains unexplained after a thorough investigation that includes an autopsy. SIDS is the leading cause of postneonatal infant death in the United States (Anderson & Smith, 2005). It peaks between 2 and 3 months and is most common among African American and American Indian/Alaska Native babies; boy babies; those born preterm; and those whose mothers are young and received late or no prenatal care (AAP Task Force on Sudden Infant Death Syndrome, 2005).

sudden infant death syndrome (SIDS) Sudden and unexplained death of an apparently healthy infant.

About 20 percent of SIDS deaths occur while the infant is in the care of someone other than the parents (AAP Task Force on Sudden Infant Death Syndrome, 2005), 16.5 percent among infants in child care (Moon, Sprague, & Patel, 2005). Because families who experience one SIDS death often experience another after a later pregnancy, foul play is sometimes suspected. However, the vast majority of these deaths have natural causes (AAP Task Force on Sudden Infant Death Syndrome, 2005). One likely explanation is that women who have experienced a SIDS death tend to have low-birth-weight babies, who are especially susceptible to SIDS (Smith, Wood, Pell, & Dobbie, 2005).

SIDS most likely results from a combination of factors. An underlying biological defect may make some infants vulnerable during a critical period to certain contributing or triggering experiences, such as prenatal exposure to smoke—an identified risk factor (AAP Task Force on Sudden Infant Death Syndrome, 2005). The underlying defect may be a delay in maturation of the neural network that is responsible for arousal from sleep in the presence of life-threatening conditions (AAP Task Force on Sudden Infant Death Syndrome, 2005), a disturbance in the brain mechanism that regulates breathing (Tryba, Peña, & Ramirez, 2006), or a genetic factor (Opdal & Rognum, 2004).

At least six gene mutations affecting the heart have been linked to SIDS cases (Ackerman et al., 2001; Cronk et al., 2006; Tester et al., 2006). Nearly 10 percent of victims have mutations or variations in genes associated with arrhythmias (irregular heart rhythms), according to a survey of 201 SIDS deaths in a single cohort in Norway (Arnestad et al., 2007; Wang et al., 2007). A gene variant that appears in 1 out of 9 African Americans may help explain the greater incidence of SIDS among black babies (Plant et al., 2006; Weese-Mayer et al., 2004).

An important clue has emerged from the discovery of defects in the brain stem, which regulates breathing, heartbeat, body temperature, and arousal. Autopsies of 31 SIDS babies and 10 babies who had died of other causes found that all 31 SIDS babies (but not the other babies) had defects in the brain's ability to use serotonin (Paterson et al., 2006). These defects may prevent SIDS babies who are sleeping face down or on their sides from waking or turning their heads when they breathe stale air containing carbon dioxide trapped under their blankets (AAP Task Force, 2000; Kinney et al., 1995; Panigrahy et al., 2000; Waters, Gonzalez, Jean, Morielli, & Brouillette, 1996). Even in normal infants, *tummy sleeping* inhibits the swallowing reflex, a natural protection against choking (Jeffery, Megevand, & Page, 1999).

Research strongly supports a relationship between SIDS and sleeping on the stomach. SIDS rates declined in the United States by 53 percent between 1992 and 2001 (AAP Task Force on Sudden Infant Death Syndrome, 2005) and in some other countries by as much as 70 percent following recommendations that healthy babies be laid on their backs to sleep (Dwyer, Ponsonby, Blizzard, Newman, & Cochrane, 1995; Hunt, 1996; Skadberg et al., 1998; Willinger, Hoffman, & Hartford, 1994).

Table 6-4	Physicians' Recommendations to Prevent SIDS

1. Place infant to sleep on the back (not tummy or side).

2. Use a firm sleep surface.

3. Keep soft objects and loose bedding out of the crib.

4. Do not smoke during pregnancy, and avoid exposing infant to second-hand smoke.

5. Let the infant sleep in his or her own bed, near the mother.

6. Consider offering a pacifier at nap time and bedtime during the 1st year of life. For breast-fed infants, delay introducing the pacifier until 1 month, so that breast-feeding is firmly established.

7. Avoid overheating and overbundling. Infant should be clothed lightly, and room temperature should be comfortable for an adult.

8. Avoid commercial devices that claim to reduce the risk of SIDS. These have not been tested for efficacy or safety.

9. Do not use home monitors to reduce the risk of SIDS; there is no evidence for their effectiveness.

10. Encourage tummy time when the infant is awake and someone is watching.

Source: AAP Task Force on Sudden Infant Death Syndrome, 2005.

Doctors recommend that infants not sleep on soft surfaces, such as pillows, quilts, or sheepskin, or under loose covers, which, especially when the infant is face down, may increase the risk of overheating or rebreathing (breathing exhaled waste products) (AAP Task Force on Sudden Infant Death Syndrome, 2005; see Table 6-4 for a list of the Task Force's recommendations). The risk of SIDS is increased twentyfold when infants sleep in adult beds, sofas, or chairs, or on other surfaces not designed for infants (Scheers, Rutherford, & Kemp, 2003). Studies associate use of pacifiers with lower risk of SIDS (AAP Task Force on Sudden Infant Death Syndrome, 2005; Hauck et al., 2003, 2005; Mitchell, Blair, & L'Hoir, 2006). Contrary to popular reports, studies show no connection between immunizations and SIDS (AAP Task Force on Sudden Infant Death Syndrome, 2005).

Sharing a bed with the mother is a common practice in some cultures; its possible role in preventing or promoting SIDS has been controversial (Box 6-2).

Injuries

Unintentional injuries are the fifth leading cause of death in infancy in the United States (Hoyert, Heron, et al., 2006) and the third leading cause of death after the first 4 weeks of life, following SIDS and birth defects (Anderson & Smith, 2005). Black infants are two and a half times as likely to die of injuries as white infants and more than three times as likely to be victims of homicide (Tomashek, Hsia, & Iyasu, 2003).

Many accidental injuries occur at home. In a study of 990 infants brought to emergency rooms in Kingston, Ontario, by far the most injuries were caused by falls (61.1 percent), by ingesting harmful substances (6.6 percent), and by burns (5.7 percent) (Pickett, Streight, Simpson, & Brison, 2003).

Immunization for Better Health

Such once-familiar and sometimes fatal childhood illnesses as measles, pertussis (whooping cough), and polio are now largely preventable, thanks to the development of vaccines that mobilize the body's natural defenses. Unfortunately, many children still are not adequately protected.

Worldwide, an estimated 2 million child deaths were prevented by vaccinations in 2003. An estimated 70 to 78 percent of children age 12 to 23 months worldwide had full routine vaccination coverage between 1990 and 2004. At least 90 percent of European,

Thanks to widespread immunization of infants and toddlers, rates of infectious diseases have plummeted in the United States. However, many children, especially in low-income urban areas, do not get all required shots or receive them late. Nearly 1 out of 5 deaths of young children in the developing world are from vaccine-preventable diseases.

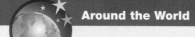
Box 6-2 *Sleep Customs*

In many cultures, infants do not have special places to sleep. Gusii infants in Kenya fall asleep in someone's arms or on a caregiver's back. In many societies, infants sleep in the same room with their mothers for the first few years of life and frequently in the same bed, making it easier to nurse at night (Broude, 1995). In the United States, it is customary to have a separate bed or a separate room for the infant, but bed sharing is common in low-income, inner-city families (Brenner et al., 2003). This practice has become controversial.

In interviews, middle-class U.S. parents and Mayan mothers in rural Guatemala revealed their societies' child-rearing values and goals in their explanations about sleeping arrangements (Morelli, Rogoff, Oppenheim, & Goldsmith, 1992). The U.S. parents, many of whom kept their infants in the same room but not in the same bed for the first 3 to 6 months, said they moved the babies to separate rooms because they wanted to make them self-reliant and independent. The Mayan mothers kept infants and toddlers in the maternal bed until the birth of a new baby, when the older child would sleep with another family member or in a bed in the mother's room. The Mayan mothers valued close parent-child relationships and expressed shock at the idea that anyone would let a baby sleep in a room all alone.

Some investigators find benefits in the shared sleeping pattern, sometimes called bed sharing or cosleeping. Observational studies have found that the physical closeness of mother and baby tends to facilitate breast-feeding, touching, and maternal responsiveness (AAP Task Force on Sudden Infant Death Syndrome, 2005; Baddock, Gallan, Bolton, Williams, & Taylor, 2006; McKenna & Mosko, 1993; McKenna, Mosko, & Richard, 1997). By snuggling up together, mother and baby stay oriented toward each other's subtle body signals, and mothers can respond more quickly and easily to an infant's first whimpers of hunger.

However, under certain conditions, bed sharing can increase the risk of sudden infant death syndrome, as a parent may roll over onto the baby while asleep. The risk seems to be particularly high when the infant is under 8 to 11 weeks, when more than one person cosleeps with the baby, or when a bed sharer has been smoking, drinking alcohol, or is overtired (AAP Task Force on Sudden Infant Death Syndrome, 2005). Both the United Kingdom Department of Health and the American Academy of Pediatrics advise that the safest place for an infant to sleep is in a crib in the parents' room for the first 6 months (AAP Task Force on Sudden Infant Death Syndrome, 2005).

Why is it, then, that Japan, where mothers and infants commonly sleep in the same bed, has one of the lowest SIDS rates in the world (Hoffman & Hillman, 1992)? This may be because Japanese families—as in many developing countries where bed sharing is practiced—generally sleep on thin mats on the floor. Societal values influence parents' attitudes and behaviors. Throughout this book we will see many ways in which such culturally determined attitudes and behaviors affect children.

What's your view ?

In view of medical evidence that bed sharing between mother and infant may contribute to SIDS, should mothers from cultures in which sharing a bed is customary be discouraged from doing so?

Check it out !

For more information on this topic, go to www.askdrsears.com/html/10/t102200.asp (a discussion on "Sleeping Safely with Pour Baby" from AskDrSears.com).

Western Pacific, and U.S. children were fully covered, as compared with only 69 percent of southeast Asian children and 66 percent of African children. Still, during 2002, there were 2.5 million vaccine-preventable deaths among children less than 5 years old; nearly 2 million of these were in Africa and southeast Asia. A Global Immunization Vision Strategy for 2006–2015 seeks to extend routine vaccinations to every eligible person (Department of Immunization, Vaccines, and Biologicals, WHO; United Nations Children's Fund; Global Immunization Division, National Center for Immunization and Respiratory Diseases; & McMorrow, 2006).

In the United States, thanks to a nationwide immunization initiative, vaccine-preventable infectious diseases have dropped more than 95 percent since 1993 (AAP Committee on Infectious Diseases, 2000). In 2005, 76.1 percent of 19- to 35-month-olds completed a recommended series of childhood vaccinations. Still, many children lack one or more of the required shots, and there is substantial regional variation in coverage (CDC, 2006c).

Some parents hesitate to immunize their children because of speculation that certain vaccines—particularly the diphtheria-pertussis-tetanus (DPT) and measles-mumps-rubella (MMR) vaccines—may cause autism or other neurodevelopmental disorders, but the preponderance of evidence suggests no reason for this concern (refer to Box 6-1). Another parental worry is that infants receive too many vaccines for their immune system to handle safely. (Today's children routinely receive 11 vaccines and as many as 20 shots by age 2.) Actually, the opposite is true. Multiple vaccines fortify the immune system against a variety of bacteria and viruses and reduce related infections (Offit et al., 2002).

Checkpoint ✓

Can you . . .

✔ Summarize trends in infant mortality, and explain why black infants are less likely to survive than white infants?

✔ Discuss risk factors for, causes of, and prevention of sudden infant death syndrome?

✔ Explain why full immunization of all infants and preschoolers is important?

Figure 6-10

Deaths from maltreatment by age, 2004. More than three-quarters (81 percent) of fatalities are of children younger than 4, and 45 percent are of infants younger than 1 year.

Source: USDHHS Administration on Children, Youth, and Families, 2006.

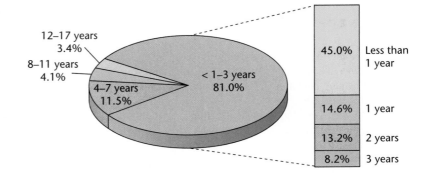

Guidepost 6

What are the causes and consequences of child abuse and neglect, and what can be done about it?

Maltreatment: Abuse and Neglect

Although most parents are loving and nurturing, some cannot or will not take proper care of their children, and some deliberately harm them. *Maltreatment,* whether perpetrated by parents or others, is deliberate or avoidable endangerment of a child.

Children are abused and neglected at all ages, but the highest rates of victimization and of death from maltreatment are for age 3 and younger (USDHHS, Administration on Children, Youth, & Families, 2006; Figure 6-10). Many of the infants are victims of shaken baby syndrome (Box 6-3). Others die of *failure to thrive,* often due to neglect. Failure to thrive can result from a combination of inadequate nutrition, disturbed interactions with parents, and other factors, such as disease, difficulties in breast-feeding, and improper formula preparation or feeding techniques. Poverty is the greatest single risk factor for failure to thrive worldwide (Block, Krebs, and the Committee on Child Abuse and Neglect, and the Committee on Nutrition, 2005).

Maltreatment: Facts and Figures

Maltreatment takes several specific forms, and the same child can be a victim of more than one type (USDHHS, Administration on Children, Youth, & Families, 2006). These types include

physical abuse Action taken deliberately to endanger another person, involving potential bodily injury.

neglect Failure to meet a dependent's basic needs.

sexual abuse Physical or psychologically harmful sexual activity, or any sexual activity involving a child and an older person.

emotional maltreatment Action or inaction that may cause behavioral, cognitive, emotional, or mental disorders.

- **Physical abuse,** injury to the body through punching, beating, kicking, or burning
- **Neglect,** failure to meet a child's basic needs, such as food, clothing, medical care, protection, and supervision
- **Sexual abuse,** any sexual activity involving a child and an older person
- **Emotional maltreatment,** including rejection, terrorization, isolation, exploitation, degradation, ridicule, or failure to provide emotional support, love, and affection

The rate of child abuse and neglect in the U.S. population has dropped from 13.4 children per 1,000 in 1990 to 11.9 in 2004. Still, state and local child protective services agencies investigated and confirmed some 872,000 cases in 2004 (USDHHS, Administration on Children, Youth, & Families, 2006), and the actual number may have been considerably higher (Theodore et al., 2005).

More than 60 percent of children identified as maltreated are neglected. About 18 percent are physically abused, 10 percent are sexually abused, and 7 percent are emotionally maltreated. An estimated 1,490 U.S. children died of abuse or neglect in 2004, and infant boys were the most frequent victims. More than one-third of child fatalities were attributed to neglect (USDHHS, Administration on Children, Youth, & Families, 2006).

Contributing Factors: An Ecological View

As in Bronfenbrenner's bioecological theory, abuse and neglect reflect the interplay of multiple layers of contributing factors involving the family, the community, and the larger society.

Box 6-3 *Shaken Baby Syndrome*

The scenario is all too common. A baby, usually 6 weeks to 4 months old, is brought to the emergency room by a parent or caregiver. The infant may show symptoms ranging from lethargy, irritability, breathing problems, tremors, or vomiting and pale or bluish skin to seizures, convulsions, stupor, or coma and may be unable to suck or swallow, make sounds, or follow an object with his or her eyes. However, there is no visible sign of injury, and the parent or caregiver denies knowledge of what caused the condition or claims that the child fell. Closer examination may or may not reveal bruises indicative of abuse, but radiological studies (a CT scan, possibly followed by an MRI) find hemorrhaging of the brain or retina—a result of the infant's having been violently shaken, dropped, or thrown (AAP Committee on Child Abuse and Neglect, 2001; Dowshen, Crowley, & Palusci, 2004; National Center on Shaken Baby Syndrome, 2000; National Institute of Neurological Disorders and Stroke [NINDS], 2006).

Shaken baby syndrome (SBS) is a form of maltreatment, found mainly in children under 2 years and especially in infants. Because a baby has weak neck muscles and a large, heavy head, shaking makes the fragile brain bounce back and forth inside the skull. This causes bruising, bleeding, and swelling and can lead to permanent, severe brain damage, paralysis, or death (AAP, 2000; NINDS, 2006). The damage is even worse when the baby is thrown against a wall or into bed. Head trauma is the leading cause of death in child abuse cases in the United States (Dowshen et al., 2004). The vast majority of these deaths are of babies cared for at home (Wrigley & Dreby, 2005). About 60 percent of the victims are boys, and an estimated 65 to 90 percent of the perpetrators are males—usually either the father or the mother's boyfriend (Dowshen et al., 2004).

Because the milder symptoms of SBS may be mistaken for those of infant colic, feeding problems, or fussiness, the condition is frequently misdiagnosed and underreported (AAP Committee on Child Abuse and Neglect, 2001; King, MacKay, Sirnick, & Canadian Shaken Baby Study Group, 2003). Incidence estimates range from 600 to 1,400 cases each year in the United States alone. Often these children have suffered previous abuse. About 20 percent die within a few days of being shaken.

Survivors may be left with a range of disabilities, from learning and behavioral disorders to neurological injuries, retardation, paralysis, or blindness, or in a permanent vegetative state (King et al., 2003; National Center on Shaken Baby Syndrome, 2000; NINDS, 2006).

Why would an adult inflict such harm on a helpless baby? A caregiver who is frustrated or angered by an infant's crying, and who is unable to handle stress or has unrealistic expectations for infant behavior, may lose control and shake a crying baby in a desperate attempt to quiet the child. If the injured infant becomes drowsy or loses consciousness, the caregiver may think the shaking worked and may do it again when the crying resumes. Or the caregiver may put an unconscious baby to bed, hoping the infant will recover, thus missing the opportunity for immediate treatment (AAP Committee on Child Abuse and Neglect, 2001; National Center on Shaken Baby Syndrome, 2000), which could save the child's life (AAP, 2000).

Adults need to know that a baby's crying is normal and is not a reflection on their caregiving skills, that shaking is *never* okay, and that help is available. (One resource is the National Center on Shaken Baby Syndrome, 888-273-0071.) Parents also need to know what age-appropriate physical play with a baby is not injurious (Dowshen et al., 2004; National Center on Shaken Baby Syndrome, 2000).

What's your view

Have you ever cared for a baby that seemingly would not stop crying? If so, what did you do?

Check it out

For more information on Shaken Baby Syndrome, go to www.kidshealth.org/parent/medical/brain/shaken.html. This is the Web site of Kids Health, an educational site sponsored by the Nemours Foundation. Here you will find a detailed, physician-reviewed article on causes, effects, symptoms, diagnosis, and prognosis of Shaken Baby Syndrome, as well as recommendations for parents and caregivers on how to deal with a baby who won't stop crying.

Characteristics of Abusive and Neglectful Parents and Families

In nearly 80 percent of cases of maltreatment the perpetrators are the child's parents, usually the mother; and 63 percent of maltreatment cases involve neglect. Some 7 percent of perpetrators are other relatives, 4 percent are unmarried partners of parents, and 75 percent of perpetrators are family friends and neighbors (USDHHS, Administration on Children, Youth, & Families, 2006).

Maltreatment by parents is a symptom of extreme disturbance in child rearing, usually aggravated by other family problems, such as poverty, lack of education, alcoholism, depression, or antisocial behavior. A disproportionate number of abused and neglected children are in large, poor, or single-parent families, which tend to be under stress and to have trouble meeting children's needs (Sedlak & Broadhurst, 1996; USDHHS, 2004). Yet what pushes one parent over the edge, another may take in stride. Although most neglect cases occur in very poor families, most low-income parents do not neglect their children.

The likelihood that a child will be physically abused has little to do with the child's characteristics and more to do with the household environment, according to a nationally representative longitudinal study of twins (Jaffee et al., 2004). Abuse may begin when a parent who is already anxious, depressed, or hostile tries to control a child physically but loses self-control and ends up shaking or beating the child. Parents who abuse children tend to have marital problems and to fight physically. Their households are often disorganized, and they experience more stressful events than other families.

Parents who are neglectful distance themselves from their children. They may be critical or uncommunicative. Many of the mothers were neglected themselves as children and are depressed or feel hopeless. Many of the fathers have deserted or do not give enough financial or emotional support (Dubowitz, 1999).

Abuse and neglect sometimes occur in the same families (USDHHS, Administration on Children, Youth, & Families, 2006). Such families tend to have no one to turn to in times of stress and no one to see what is happening (Dubowitz, 1999). Substance abuse is a factor in at least one-third of cases of abuse and neglect (USDHHS, 1999a). Sexual abuse often occurs along with other family disturbances such as physical abuse, emotional maltreatment, substance abuse, and family violence (Kellogg and the Committee on Child Abuse and Neglect, 2005).

Community Characteristics and Cultural Values

What makes one low-income neighborhood a place where children are highly likely to be maltreated and another, matched for ethnic population and income levels, safer? In one inner-city Chicago neighborhood, the proportion of children who died from maltreatment (1 death for every 2,541 children) was about twice the proportion in another inner-city neighborhood. In the high-abuse neighborhood, criminal activity was rampant, and facilities for community programs were dreary. People in the low-abuse neighborhood described it as a poor but decent place to live. They painted a picture of a neighborhood with robust social support networks, well-known community services, and strong political leadership. In a community like this, maltreatment is less likely to occur (Garbarino & Kostelny, 1993).

Two cultural factors associated with child abuse are societal violence and physical punishment of children. In countries where violent crime is infrequent and children are rarely spanked, such as Japan, China, and Tahiti, child abuse is rare (Celis, 1990). In the United States, homicide, domestic violence, and rape are common, and many states still permit corporal punishment in schools. According to a representative sampling, more than 90 percent of parents of preschoolers and about 50 percent of parents of school-age children report using physical punishment at home (Straus & Stewart, 1999; see Box 11-2 in Chapter 11 for a discussion of effects of corporal punishment).

Helping Families in Trouble

State and local child protective services agencies investigate reports of maltreatment. After making a determination of maltreatment, they determine what steps, if any, need to be taken and marshal community resources to help. Agency staff may try to help the family resolve their problems or arrange for alternative care for children who cannot safely remain at home. In 2004, approximately 60 percent of victims received such services (USDHHS, Administration on Children, Youth, & Families, 2006).

Services for children who have been abused and for their parents include shelters, education in parenting skills, and therapy. Parents Anonymous and other organizations offer free, confidential support groups. Children may receive play or art therapy and day care in a therapeutic environment. However, availability of services is often limited. In a nationally representative survey, about 48 percent of 2- to 14-year-olds investigated by child welfare agencies after reported maltreatment had clinically significant emotional or behavioral problems, but only one-fourth of those with such problems received mental health care (Burns et al., 2004).

When authorities remove children from their homes, the usual alternative is foster care. In 2004, about 19 percent of victims of maltreatment were placed in foster homes

(USDHHS, Administration on Children, Youth, & Families, 2006). Foster care removes a child from immediate danger, but it is often unstable, further alienates the child from the family, and may turn out to be another abusive situation. Often a child's basic health and educational needs are not met (David and Lucile Packard Foundation, 2004; NRC, 1993b).

In part because of a scarcity of traditional foster homes and an increasing caseload, a growing proportion of placements (31 percent), especially of African American children, are in kinship foster care—under the care of grandparents or other family members (Berrick, 1998; Geen, 2004). Although most foster children who leave the system are reunited with their families, about 28 percent reenter foster care within the next 10 years (Wulczyn, 2004). Children who have been in foster care are more likely than other children to become homeless, to become involved in criminal activity, and to become teenage mothers (David and Lucile Packard Foundation, 2004).

Long-Term Effects of Maltreatment

Consequences of abuse or neglect may depend on the child's age and developmental status; the type, frequency, duration, and severity of the maltreatment; the relationship between the victim and perpetrator; and the child's personal characteristics. Without help, maltreated children often grow up with serious problems, at great cost to themselves and to society, and may continue the cycle of maltreatment when they have children of their own. An estimated one-third of adults who were abused and neglected in childhood victimize their own children (NCCANI, 2004).

Consequences of maltreatment may be physical, emotional, cognitive, and social, and these types of consequences are often interrelated. A physical blow to a child's head can cause brain damage resulting in cognitive delays and emotional and social problems. Similarly, severe neglect or unloving parents can have traumatic effects on the developing brain (Fries et al., 2005).

Long-term consequences of maltreatment may include poor physical, mental, and emotional health; impaired brain development (Glaser, 2000); cognitive, language, and academic difficulties; problems in attachment and social relationships (NCCANI, 2004); memory problems (Brunson et al., 2005); and, in adolescence, heightened risks of poor academic achievement, delinquency, teenage pregnancy, alcohol and drug use, and suicide (Dube et al., 2003; Dube et al., 2001; Lansford et al., 2002; NCCANI, 2004).

In a study that followed 68 sexually abused children for 5 years, these children showed more disturbed behavior, had lower self-esteem, and were more depressed, anxious, or unhappy than a control group (Swanston, Tebbutt, O'Toole, & Oates, 1997). Sexually abused children may become sexually active at an early age (Fiscella, Kitzman, Cole, Sidora, & Olds, 1998). Adults who were sexually abused as children tend to be anxious, depressed, angry, or hostile; to mistrust people; to feel isolated and stigmatized; to be sexually maladjusted (Browne & Finkelhor, 1986); and to abuse alcohol or drugs (NRC, 1993b; USDHHS, 1999a).

Why do some abused children grow up to become antisocial or abusive, while others do not? One possible difference is genetic; some genotypes may be more resistant to trauma than others (Caspi et al., 2002; Jaffee et al., 2005). Research with rhesus monkeys suggests another answer. When baby monkeys endured high rates of maternal rejection and abuse in the 1st month of life, their brains produced less serotonin, a neurotransmitter. Low levels of serotonin are associated with anxiety, depression, and impulsive aggression in humans as well as in monkeys. Abused female monkeys who became abusive mothers had less serotonin in their brains than abused females who did not become abusive mothers. This finding suggests that treatment with drugs that increase serotonin levels early in life may prevent an abused child from growing up to abuse her children (Maestripieri et al., 2006).

Many maltreated children show remarkable resilience. Optimism, self-esteem, intelligence, creativity, humor, and independence are protective factors, as is the social support of a caring adult (NCCANI, 2004). In Chapter 14 we further discuss factors that affect resilience.

Checkpoint ✔

Can you . . .

✔ Define four types of child abuse and neglect?

✔ Discuss the incidence of maltreatment and explain why it is hard to measure?

✔ Identify contributing factors having to do with the family, the neighborhood, and the wider society?

✔ Describe ways to prevent or stop maltreatment and help its victims?

✔ Give examples of long-term effects of child abuse and neglect?

Refocus

Thinking back to the information about Helen Keller in the Focus vignette at the beginning of this chapter,

- What connections does Keller's story show among physical health, sensory capabilities, cognition, and pyschosocial development?

- How would a cognitive neuroscientist explain why Keller's senses of smell and touch became unusually sharp when she lost her hearing and sight?

- What hypotheses might explain why Keller's language development regressed and how she regained it? How might such hypotheses be tested?

- Would the mysterious fever that Helen contracted likely be as damaging today? Why or why not?

Fortunately, most babies survive and grow up healthy and well cared for. Their physical development forms the underpinning for cognitive and psychosocial developments that enable infants and toddlers to become more at home in their world, as we will see in Chapters 7 and 8.

Summary and Key Terms

Growth and Nutrition

Guidepost 1   How do babies grow, and how and what should they be fed?

- Normal physical growth and sensory and motor development proceed according to the cephalocaudal and proximodistal principles.

- A child's body grows most dramatically during the 1st year of life; growth proceeds at a rapid but diminishing rate throughout the first 3 years.

- Historic shifts in feeding practices reflected efforts to improve infant survival and health.

- Breast-feeding offers many health advantages and sensory and cognitive benefits. However, the quality of the relationship between parents and infant may be more important than the feeding method.

- Babies should not start solid foods and fruit juices until age 6 months and should not get cow's milk until 1 year.

- Obese babies are not at special risk of becoming obese adults, unless they have obese parents.

The Brain and Reflex Behavior

Guidepost 2   How does the brain develop, and how do environmental factors affect its early growth?

- The central nervous system controls sensorimotor functioning. Lateralization enables each hemisphere of the brain to specialize in different functions.

- The brain grows most rapidly during the months before and immediately after birth as neurons migrate to their assigned locations, form synaptic connections, and undergo integration and differentiation. Cell death and myelination improve the efficiency of the nervous system.

- Reflex behaviors—primitive, locomotor, and postural—are indicators of neurological status. Most early reflexes drop out during the 1st year as voluntary, cortical control develops.

- Especially during the early period of rapid growth, environmental experience can influence brain development positively or negatively.

central nervous system (149)   brain growth spurts (150) lateralization (150)   neurons (151)   integration (153) differentiation (153)   cell death (153)   myelination (153) reflex behavior (154)   plasticity (157)

Early Sensory Capacities

Guidepost 3   How do the senses develop during infancy?

- Sensory capacities, present from birth and even in the womb, develop rapidly in the first months of life. Very young infants can discriminate among stimuli.

- Touch seems to be the first sense to develop and mature. Newborns are sensitive to pain. Smell, taste, and hearing also begin to develop in the womb.

- Vision is the least well-developed sense at birth but sharpens within the first 6 months.

Motor Development

Guidepost 4   What are the early milestones in motor development, and what are some influences on it?

- Motor skills develop in a certain sequence, which may depend largely on maturation but also on context, experience, and motivation. Simple skills combine into increasingly complex systems. The Denver Developmental Screening Test assesses gross and fine motor skills as well as linguistic, personality, and social development.

- Depth perception is present at a very early age and is related to motor development.

- According to Gibson's ecological theory, sensory perception and motor activity are coordinated from birth, helping infants figure out how to navigate in their environment.

- Thelen's dynamic systems theory holds that infants develop motor skills, not by maturation alone, but by active coordination of multiple systems of action within a changing environment.

- Environmental factors, including cultural practices, may affect the pace of early motor development.

systems of action (160)   Denver Developmental Screening Test (160)   gross motor skills (160)   fine motor skills (160)   visual guidance (162)   depth perception (162)   haptic perception (162) visual cliff (162)   ecological theory of perception (162) affordance (162)   dynamic systems theory (DST) (164)

Health

Guidepost 5 How can we enhance babies' chances of survival and health?

- Although infant mortality in the United States has diminished, it is still disturbingly high for African American babies. Birth defects are the leading cause of death in the 1st year; for black infants, low birth weight is the leading cause.

- Sudden infant death syndrome (SIDS) is the third leading cause of death in infants in the United States. Major risk factors include exposure to smoke and sleeping in the prone position. SIDS rates have dropped dramatically since doctors have advised parents to lay infants on their backs to sleep.

- Injuries are the third leading cause of death of U.S. infants after the 1st month.

- Vaccine-preventable diseases have declined as rates of immunization have improved, but many toddlers are not fully protected.

infant mortality rate (165)   sudden infant death syndrome (SIDS) (167)

Maltreatment: Abuse and Neglect

Guidepost 6 What are the causes and consequences of child abuse and neglect, and what can be done about it?

- The incidence of confirmed maltreatment of children has declined since the 1990s, but many more cases may go unreported.

- Forms of maltreatment are physical abuse, neglect, sexual abuse, and emotional maltreatment.

- Characteristics of the abuser or neglecter, the victim, the family, the community, and the larger culture all contribute to child abuse and neglect.

- Maltreatment can interfere with physical, cognitive, emotional, and social development, and its effects can continue into adulthood. Still, many maltreated children show remarkable resilience.

- Preventing or stopping maltreatment may require multifaceted, coordinated community efforts.

physical abuse (170)   neglect (170)   sexual abuse (170)   emotional maltreatment (170)

CHAPTER SEVEN

Cognitive Development during the First Three Years

So runs my dream; but what am I?
An infant crying in the night;
An infant crying for the light,
And with no language but a cry.

—Alfred, Lord Tennyson, *In Memoriam,* Canto 54

Focus *William Erasmus Darwin, Naturalist's Son*

Charles and "Doddy" Darwin

On December 27, 1839, when the naturalist Charles Darwin was 30 years old, his first baby, William Erasmus Darwin, affectionately known as Doddy, was born. That day—20 years before his publication of *Origin of Species,* which outlined his theory of evolution based on natural selection—the proud father began keeping a diary of observations of his newborn son. It was these notes, published in 1877, that first called scientific attention to the developmental nature of infant behavior.

What abilities are babies born with? How do they learn about their world? How do they communicate, first nonverbally and then through language? These were among the questions Darwin sought to answer—questions still central to the study of cognitive development.

Darwin's keen eye illuminates how coordination of physical and mental activity helps an infant adapt to the world—as in this entry written when Doddy was 4 months old:

> Took my finger to his mouth & as usual could not get it in, on account of his own hand being in the way; then he slipped his own back & so got my finger in.—This was not chance & therefore a kind of reasoning. (diary, p. 12; quoted in Keegan & Gruber, 1985, p. 135)

In Darwin's notes, we can see Doddy developing new cognitive skills through interaction, not only with his father's finger, but with other objects as well. The diary depicts a series of encounters with reflected images. In these episodes Doddy gains knowledge, not in sudden bursts or jumps, but through gradual integration of new experience with existing patterns of behavior. In Darwin's view—as, later, in Piaget's—this was not merely a matter of piling new knowledge on old; it involved an actual transformation of the way the mind is organized.

The source for analysis of Darwin's diary is Keegan and Gruber (1985).

When Doddy, at 4½ months, saw his likeness and his father's in a mirror, Darwin noted that the baby "seemed surprised at my voice coming from behind him, my image being in front" (diary, p. 18; quoted in Keegan & Gruber, 1985, p. 135). Two months later, Doddy apparently had solved the mystery: Now, when his father, standing behind him, made a funny face in the mirror, the infant "was aware that the image . . . was not real & therefore . . . turned round to look" (diary, pp. 21–22; quoted in Keegan & Gruber, 1985, pp. 135–136).

At first, this newfound understanding did not generalize to other reflective materials. Two weeks later, Doddy seemed puzzled to see his father's reflection in a window. By 9 months, however, the boy realized that "the shadow of a hand, made by a candle, was to be looked for behind, in [the] same manner as in [a] looking glass" (diary, p. 23; quoted in Keegan & Gruber, 1985, p. 136). His recognition that reflections could emanate from objects behind him now extended to shadows, another kind of two-dimensional image.

Darwin was particularly interested in documenting his son's progress in communication. He believed that language acquisition is a natural process, akin to earlier physical expressions of feelings. Through smiling, crying, laughing, facial expressions, and sounds of pleasure or pain, Doddy managed to communicate quite well with his parents even before uttering his first word. One of his first meaningful verbal expressions was "Ah!"—uttered when he recognized an image in a glass.

● ● ●

Darwin made these observations more than 160 years ago, at a time when infants' cognitive abilities were widely underestimated. We now know—as Darwin inferred from his observations of Doddy—that normal, healthy infants are born with the ability to learn and remember and with a capacity for acquiring and using speech. They use their growing sensory and cognitive capacities to exert control over their behavior and their world.

In this chapter we look at infants' and toddlers' cognitive abilities from three classic perspectives—behaviorist, psychometric, and Piagetian—and then from three newer perspectives: information processing, cognitive neuroscientific, and social-contextual. We trace the early development of language and discuss how it comes about.

After you have read and studied this chapter, you should be able to answer each of the Guidepost questions on the following page. Look for them again in the margins throughout the chapter, where they point to important concepts. To check your understanding of these Guideposts, review the end-of-chapter summary. Checkpoints located throughout the chapter will help you verify your understanding of what you have read.

Guideposts
for Study

1. What are six approaches to the study of cognitive development?

2. How do infants learn, and how long can they remember?

3. Can infants' and toddlers' intelligence be measured, and how can it be improved?

4. How did Piaget describe infants' and toddlers' cognitive development, and how have his claims stood up?

5. How can we measure infants' ability to process information, and when do babies begin to think about characteristics of the physical world?

6. What can brain research reveal about the development of cognitive skills?

7. How does social interaction with adults advance cognitive competence?

8. How do babies develop language, and what influences linguistic progress?

Studying Cognitive Development: Six Approaches

Guidepost 1

What are six approaches to the study of cognitive development?

How and when do babies learn to solve problems? How and when does memory develop? What accounts for individual differences in cognitive abilities? Can we measure a baby's intelligence? Can we predict how smart that baby will be in the future? These questions have long intrigued developmental scientists, many of whom have taken one of three classic approaches to their study:

- The **behaviorist approach** studies the basic *mechanics* of learning, which fall in the domain of cognitive development. Behaviorists are concerned with how behavior changes in response to experience.
- The **psychometric approach** seeks to *measure quantitative differences* in cognitive abilities by using tests that indicate or predict these abilities.
- The **Piagetian approach** looks at changes, or stages, in the *quality* of cognitive functioning. It is concerned with how the mind structures its activities and adapts to the environment.

During the past few decades, researchers have turned to three newer approaches to add to our knowledge about cognitive development:

- The **information-processing approach** focuses on the processes involved in perception, learning, memory, and problem solving. It seeks to discover what children do with information from the time they encounter it until they use it.
- The **cognitive neuroscience approach** examines the "hardware" of the central nervous system. It seeks to identify what brain structures are involved in specific aspects of cognition.
- The **social-contextual approach** examines the influence of environmental aspects of the learning process, particularly the role of parents and other caregivers.

All six of these approaches help us understand how cognition develops.

behaviorist approach Approach to the study of cognitive development that is concerned with the basic mechanics of learning.

psychometric approach Approach to the study of cognitive development that seeks to measure the quantity of intelligence a person possesses.

Piagetian approach Approach to the study of cognitive development that describes qualitative stages in cognitive functioning.

Checkpoint ✔

Can you . . .

✔ Compare six approaches to the study of cognitive development and identify their goals?

Behaviorist Approach: Basic Mechanics of Learning

Guidepost 2

How do infants learn, and how long can they remember?

Babies are born with the ability to learn from what they see, hear, smell, taste, and touch, and they have at least some ability to remember what they learn. Of course, maturation is essential to this process, as learning theorists recognize; but the main interest of these

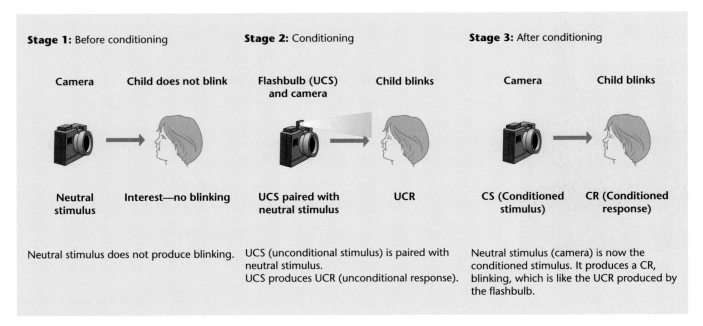

Stage 1: Before conditioning

Camera → Child does not blink

Neutral stimulus → Interest—no blinking

Neutral stimulus does not produce blinking.

Stage 2: Conditioning

Flashbulb (UCS) and camera → Child blinks

UCS paired with neutral stimulus → UCR

UCS (unconditional stimulus) is paired with neutral stimulus.
UCS produces UCR (unconditional response).

Stage 3: After conditioning

Camera → Child blinks

CS (Conditioned stimulus) → CR (Conditioned response)

Neutral stimulus (camera) is now the conditioned stimulus. It produces a CR, blinking, which is like the UCR produced by the flashbulb.

Figure 7-1

Three steps in classical conditioning.

information-processing approach Approach to the study of cognitive development by observing and analyzing processes involved in perceiving and handling information.

cognitive neuroscience approach Approach to the study of cognitive development that links brain processes with cognitive ones.

social-contextual approach Approach to the study of cognitive development that focuses on environmental influences, particularly parents and other caregivers.

classical conditioning Learning based on associating a stimulus that does not ordinarily elicit a particular response with another stimulus that does elicit the response.

operant conditioning Learning based on reinforcement or punishment.

theorists is in mechanisms of learning. Because behaviorists do not focus on developmental change, we will discuss this theory here but not in subsequent chapters.

Let's look first at two simple learning processes (introduced in Chapter 2) that behaviorists study: *classical conditioning* and *operant conditioning.* Later we will consider *habituation,* a form of learning that information-processing researchers study.

Classical and Operant Conditioning

Eager to capture Anna's memorable moments on film, her father took pictures of the infant smiling, crawling, and showing off her other achievements. Whenever the flash went off, Anna blinked. One evening when Anna was 11 months old, she saw her father hold the camera up to his eye—and she blinked *before* the flash. She had learned to associate the camera with the bright light, so that the sight of the camera alone activated her blinking reflex.

Anna's blinking (Figure 7-1) is an example of **classical conditioning,** in which a person learns to make a reflex or involuntary response (in this case, blinking) to a stimulus (the camera) that originally did not provoke the response. Classical conditioning enables infants to anticipate an event before it happens by forming associations between stimuli (such as the camera and the flash) that regularly occur together. Classically conditioned learning become *extinct,* or will fade, if it is not reinforced. Thus, if Anna frequently saw the camera without the flash, she eventually would stop blinking.

In classical conditioning, the learner is passive, absorbing and automatically reacting to stimuli. In contrast, in **operant conditioning**—as when a baby learns that smiling brings loving attention—the learner operates, or acts, on the environment. The infant learns to make a certain response to an environmental stimulus (smiling at the sight of her or his parents) in order to produce a particular effect (parental attention). Researchers often use operant conditioning to study other phenomena, such as memory.

Infant Memory

Can you remember anything that happened to you before you were about 2 years old? Chances are you can't. This inability to remember early events is called *infantile amnesia.* Developmental scientists have proposed various explanations for this common phenomenon. One explanation, held by Piaget (1969) and others, is that early events are not retained in memory because the brain is not yet developed enough to store them. Freud, in contrast,

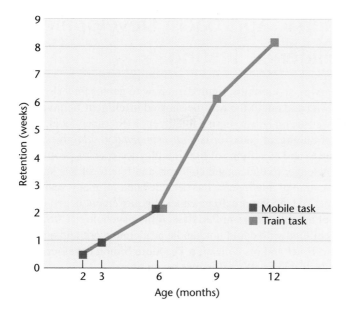

Figure 7-2

Maximum number of weeks that infants of varying ages show retention of how to operate either a mobile or a miniature train. Regardless of the task, retention improves with age.

Source: Rovee-Collier, 1999, Fig. 4, p. 83.

believed that early memories are stored but are repressed because they are emotionally troubling. Other researchers suggest that children cannot store events in memory until they can talk about them (Nelson, 1992).

More recent research using operant conditioning with nonverbal, age-appropriate tasks suggests that infants' memory processes may not differ fundamentally from those of older children and adults except that infants' retention time is shorter. These studies have found that babies will repeat a learned action days or weeks later—if they are periodically reminded of the situation in which they originally learned it (Rovee-Collier, 1999).

In a series of experiments by Carolyn Rovee-Collier and her associates, infants were operantly conditioned to kick in order to activate a mobile attached to one ankle by a ribbon. Babies 2 to 6 months old, when shown the same mobiles days or weeks later, repeated the kicking, even though their ankles were no longer attached to the mobiles. When the infants saw these mobiles, they kicked more than before the conditioning, showing that recognition of the mobiles triggered a memory of their initial experience with them (Rovee-Collier, 1996, 1999). In a similar task designed for older infants and toddlers, a child was conditioned to press a lever to make a miniature train go around a track. The length of time a conditioned response could be retained increased with age, from 2 days for 2-month-olds to 13 weeks for 18-month-olds (Hartshorn et al., 1998; Rovee-Collier, 1996, 1999; Figure 7-2).

Young infants' memory of a behavior seems to be linked specifically to the original cue. Two- to 6-month-olds repeated the learned behavior *only* when they saw the original mobile or train. However, 9- to 12-month-olds would try out the behavior on a different train if no more than 2 weeks had gone by since the training (Rovee-Collier, 1999).

A familiar context can improve recollection when a memory has weakened. Thus, 3-, 9-, and 12-month-olds initially could recognize the mobile or train in a different setting from the one in which they were trained, but not after long delays. Periodic nonverbal reminders through brief exposure to the original stimulus can sustain a memory from early infancy through age 1½ to 2 years (Rovee-Collier, 1999).

At least one prominent memory researcher disputes the claim that such conditioned memories are qualitatively the same as the memories of older children and adults. From an evolutionary developmental perspective, abilities develop as they can fulfill useful functions in adapting to the environment. The early procedural and perceptual knowledge demonstrated by infants kicking a mobile is not the same as an older child's or adult's explicit memory of specific events. Infancy is a time of great change, and retention of specific experiences is unlikely to be useful for long. This may be one reason that adults do not remember events that occurred when they were infants (Nelson, 2005). Later in this chapter we will discuss brain research that sheds more light on the development of memory in infancy.

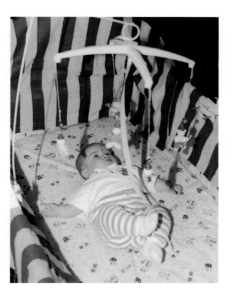

Babies 2 to 6 months old can remember, after a hiatus of 2 days to 2 weeks, that they were able to activate a mobile by kicking; they show this by kicking as soon as they see the mobile.

Checkpoint

Can you . . .

✔ Give examples of classical and operant conditioning in infants?

✔ Summarize what studies of operant conditioning have shown about infant memory?

intelligent behavior Behavior that is goal oriented and adaptive to circumstances and conditions of life.

IQ (intelligence quotient) tests Psychometric tests that seek to measure intelligence by comparing a test-taker's performance with standardized norms.

Bayley Scales of Infant and Toddler Development Standardized test of infants' and toddlers' mental and motor development.

Checkpoint ✓

Can you . . .

✔ Tell why developmental tests are sometimes given to infants and toddlers, and describe one such widely used test?

Home Observation for Measurement of the Environment (HOME) Instrument to measure the influence of the home environment on children's cognitive growth.

Psychometric Approach: Developmental and Intelligence Testing

When Doddy Darwin, at 4 months, figured out how to get his father's finger into his mouth by moving his own hand out of the way, he showed **intelligent behavior.** Although there is no scientific consensus on how to define intelligence (Sternberg et al., 2005), most professionals agree that intelligent behavior is *goal-oriented* and *adaptive:* directed at adjusting to the circumstances and conditions of life. Intelligence enables people to acquire, remember, and use knowledge; to understand concepts and relationships; and to solve problems.

The precise nature of intelligence has been debated for many years, and so has the best way to measure it. The modern intelligence testing movement began in the early 20th century, when school administrators in Paris asked the psychologist Alfred Binet to devise a way to identify children who could not handle academic work and needed special instruction. The test that Binet and his colleague Theodore Simon developed was the forerunner of psychometric tests that score intelligence by numbers.

The goals of psychometric testing are to measure quantitatively the factors that are thought to make up intelligence (such as comprehension and reasoning), and, from the results of that measurement, to predict future performance (such as school achievement). **IQ (intelligence quotient) tests** consist of questions or tasks that are supposed to show how much of the measured abilities a person has, by comparing that person's performance with that of other test-takers. For school-age children, as we discuss in Chapter 13, intelligence test scores can predict academic performance fairly accurately and reliably.

However, testing infants and toddlers is another matter. Since babies cannot tell us what they know and how they think, the most obvious way to gauge their intelligence is by assessing what they can do. But if they do not grasp a rattle, it is hard to tell whether they do not know how, do not feel like doing it, do not realize what is expected of them, or have simply lost interest.

Testing Infants and Toddlers

Although it is virtually impossible to measure infants' intelligence, it is possible to test their cognitive development. Developmental tests compare a baby's performance on a series of tasks with norms established on the basis of what large numbers of infants and toddlers can do at particular ages.

The **Bayley Scales of Infant and Toddler Development** (Bayley, 1969, 1993, 2005) is a widely used developmental test designed to assess children from 1 month to 3½ years. Scores on the Bayley-III (2005) indicate a child's strengths and weaknesses in each of five developmental areas: *cognitive, language, motor, social-emotional,* and *adaptive behavior.* An optional *behavior rating scale* can be completed by the examiner, in part on the basis of information from the child's caregiver. Separate scores, called *developmental quotients (DQs),* are calculated for each scale. DQs are most useful for early detection of emotional disturbances and sensory, neurological, and environmental deficits and in helping parents and professionals plan for a child's needs.

Assessing the Impact of the Home Environment

Intelligence was once thought to be fixed at birth, but we now know that it is influenced by both inheritance and experience. As discussed in Chapter 6, early brain stimulation is a key to future cognitive development. What characteristics of the early home environment may influence measured intelligence and other measures of cognitive development?

Using the **Home Observation for Measurement of the Environment (HOME)** (R. H. Bradley, 1989; Caldwell & Bradley, 1984), trained observers interview the primary caregiver and rate on a yes-or-no checklist the intellectual stimulation and support observed in a child's home. The version for infants and toddlers (Table 7-1) lasts about 1 hour. HOME scores after age 2 are significantly correlated with measures of cognitive development (Totsika & Sylva, 2004).

Table 7-1   The Infant-Toddler HOME Inventory (age 0 to 3)

Name of Subscale	Description	Example Item
Emotional and verbal responsivity of the primary caregiver (*items* 1–11)	The communicative and affective interactions between the caregiver and the child	Mother spontaneously vocalizes to the child at least twice during visit Mother caresses or kisses child at least once during visit
Avoidance of restriction and punishment (*items* 12–19)	How the adult disciplines the child	Primary caregiver (PC) does not shout at child during visit PC does not express overt annoyance with or hostility toward the child
Organization of the physical and temporal environment (*items* 20–25)	How the child's time is organized outside the family house. What the child's personal space looks like	When PC is away, care is provided by one of three regular substitutes The child's play environment appears safe and free of hazards
Provision of appropriate play materials (*items* 26–34)	Presence of several types of toys available to the child and appropriate for his/her age	Child has one or more large muscle activity toys or pieces of equipment Provides equipment appropriate to age, such as infant seat, infant rocker, playpen
Parental involvement with the child (*items* 35–40)	How the adult interacts physically with the child	PC tends to keep child within visual range and look at him/her often PC talks to child while doing her work
Opportunities for variety in daily stimulation (*items* 40–45)	The way the child's daily routine is designed to incorporate social meetings with people other than the mother	Father provides some care-giving every day. Family visits or receives visits from relatives approximately once a month

Source: Totsika & Sylva (2004).

One important factor that HOME assesses is parental responsiveness. HOME gives credit to the parent of an infant or toddler for caressing or kissing the child during an examiner's visit, to the parent of a preschooler for spontaneously praising the child, and to the parent of an older child for answering the child's questions. A longitudinal study found positive correlations between parents' responsiveness to their 6-month-olds and the children's IQs, achievement test scores, and teacher-rated classroom behavior through age 13 (Bradley, Corwyn, Burchinal, McAdoo, & Coll, 2001).

HOME also assesses the number of books in the home, the presence of playthings that encourage the development of concepts, and parents' involvement in children's play. In an analysis of HOME assessments of 29,264 European American, African American, and Hispanic American children, learning stimulation was consistently associated with kindergarten achievement scores, as well as with language competence and motor and social development (Bradley, Corwyn, Burchinal, et al., 2001).

Of course, some HOME items may be less culturally relevant in non-Western than in Western families (Bradley, Corwyn, McAdoo, & Coll, 2001). Also, we cannot be sure on the basis of HOME and correlational findings that parental responsiveness or an enriched home environment actually increases a child's intelligence. All we can say is that these factors are associated with high intelligence and achievement. Intelligent, well-educated parents may be more likely to provide a positive, stimulating home environment; and, because they also pass their genes on to their children, there may be a genetic influence as well. This is an example of a *passive genotype-environment correlation,* described in Chapter 3.

Other research has identified seven aspects of the early home environment that enable cognitive and psychosocial development and help prepare children for school. These aspects are (1) encouraging exploration of the environment; (2) mentoring in basic cognitive and social skills; (3) celebrating developmental advances; (4) guidance in practicing and extending skills; (5) protection from inappropriate disapproval, teasing, and punishment; (6) communicating richly and responsively; and (7) guiding and limiting behavior. The consistent presence of all seven aspects early in life is "causally linked to many areas of brain functioning and cog-

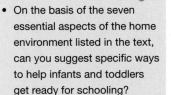

What's your view

- On the basis of the seven essential aspects of the home environment listed in the text, can you suggest specific ways to help infants and toddlers get ready for schooling?

Table 7-2	Fostering Competence

Findings from studies using the HOME scales, and from neurological studies and other research suggest the following guidelines for fostering infants' and toddlers' cognitive development:

- In the early months, *provide sensory stimulation* but avoid overstimulation and distracting noises.
- As babies grow older, *create an environment that fosters learning*—one that includes books, interesting objects (which do not have to be expensive toys), and a place to play.
- *Respond to babies' signals.* This establishes a sense of trust that the world is a friendly place and gives babies a sense of control over their lives.
- *Give babies the power to effect changes,* through toys that can be shaken, molded, or moved. Help a baby discover that turning a doorknob opens a door, flicking a light switch turns on a light, and opening a faucet produces running water for a bath.
- *Give babies freedom to explore.* Do not confine them regularly during the day in a crib, jump seat, or small room and only for short periods in a playpen. Baby-proof the environment and let them go!
- *Talk to babies.* They will not pick up language from listening to the radio or television; they need interaction with adults.
- In talking to or playing with babies, *enter into whatever they are interested in* at the moment instead of trying to redirect their attention to something else.
- *Arrange opportunities to learn basic skills,* such as labeling, comparing, and sorting objects (say, by size or color), putting items in sequence, and observing the consequences of actions.
- *Applaud new skills and help babies practice and expand them.* Stay nearby but do not hover.
- *Read to babies in a warm, caring atmosphere from an early age.* Reading aloud and talking about the stories develop preliteracy skills.
- *Use punishment sparingly.* Do not punish or ridicule results of normal trial-and-error exploration.

Sources: R. R. Bradley & Caldwell, 1982; R. R. Bradley, Caldwell, & Rock, 1988; R. H. Bradley et al., 1989; C. T. Ramey & Ramey, 1998a, 1998b, 2003; S. L. Ramey & Ramey, 1992; Staso, quoted in Blakeslee, 1997; J. H. Stevens & Bakeman, 1985; B. L. White, 1971; B. L. White, Kaban, & Attanucci, 1979.

early intervention Systematic process of providing services to help families meet young children's developmental needs.

nitive development" (C. T. Ramey & S. L. Ramey, 2003, p. 4). (Table 7-2 lists specific suggestions for helping babies develop cognitive competence.)

Early Intervention

Children who have had limited learning opportunities early in life are likely to start kindergarten at least 2 years behind their peers and are unlikely to catch up without special help. **Early intervention** is an effort to prevent or reduce that gap (C. T. Ramey & S. L. Ramey, 2003). The Individuals with Disabilities Education Act defines early intervention as a process of planning and providing therapeutic and educational services for families that need help in meeting children's developmental needs. Two randomly assigned, controlled studies have demonstrated the effectiveness of early intervention.

Project CARE (Wasik, Ramey, Bryant, & Sparling, 1990) and the Abecedarian (ABC) Project (C. T. Ramey & Campbell, 1991) involved a total of 174 babies from at-risk homes in North Carolina. In each project, from age 6 weeks through age 5, an experimental group was enrolled in Partners for Learning, a full-day, year-round early childhood education program at a university child development center. The program had a low child-teacher ratio and used learning games to foster specific cognitive, linguistic, perceptual-motor, and social skills. While the children in the experimental group were in Partners for Learning, their teenage mothers were able to pursue their own education. Control groups received pediatric and social work services, formula, and home visits, as the experimental groups did, but were not enrolled in Partners for Learning (C. T. Ramey & S. L. Ramey, 2003).

In both projects, the children who received the early intervention showed a widening advantage over the control groups in developmental test scores between 12 and 18 months. By age 3, the average IQ of the Abecedarian experimental group was 101 and of the CARE experimental group, 105—equal to or better than average for the general population—as compared with only 84 and 93 for the control groups (C. T. Ramey & S. L. Ramey, 1998b).

As often happens with early intervention, these early gains were not fully maintained. Still, scores remained higher and more stable among children who had been in Partners for

Learning than in the control groups (Burchinal et al., 1997). Both the experimental and control groups' IQs and math scores increasingly fell below national norms while reading scores held steady but below average. However, the children in the Abecedarian Project who had been enrolled in Partners for Learning continued to outdo the control group on all measures and were less likely to repeat a grade or to be placed in special education (Campbell, Pungello, Miller-Johnson, Burchinal, & Ramey, 2001; C. T. Ramey et al., 2000; C. T. Ramey & S. L. Ramey, 2003). At 21, 70 percent of the Abecedarian experimental group were in skilled jobs or higher education, in contrast with only 40 percent of the control group. Those in the experimental group were three times more likely to attend a 4-year college and were less likely to experience teen pregnancy, to smoke, or to use drugs (C. T. Ramey & S. L. Ramey, 2003).

These findings, and others like them, show that early educational intervention can help offset environmental risks (Brooks-Gunn, 2003). The most effective early interventions are those that (1) start early and continue throughout the preschool years; (2) are highly time-intensive (i.e., occupy more hours in a day or more days in a week, month, or year); (3) are center-based, providing direct educational experiences, not just parental training; (4) take a comprehensive approach, including health, family counseling, and social services; and (5) are tailored to individual differences and needs. As occurred in the two North Carolina projects, initial gains tend to diminish without sufficient ongoing environmental support (Brooks-Gunn, 2003; C. T. Ramey & S. L. Ramey, 1996, 1998a).

Early Head Start, a federally funded intervention for low-income families, is discussed in Chapter 10.

Checkpoint

Can you . . .

✔ Summarize findings about the value of early intervention?

Piagetian Approach: The Sensorimotor Stage

Guidepost 4

How did Piaget describe infants' and toddlers' cognitive development, and how have his claims stood up?

The first of Piaget's four stages of cognitive development is the **sensorimotor stage.** During this stage, from birth to approximately age 2, infants learn about themselves and their world through their developing sensory and motor activity. Babies change from creatures who respond primarily through reflexes and random behavior into goal-oriented toddlers. In Darwin's diary, for example, we saw Doddy progress from simple exploration of his father's finger to purposeful attempts to solve the mysteries of mirrors and shadows.

Substages of the Sensorimotor Stage

The sensorimotor stage consists of six substages (Table 7-3) that flow from one to another as a baby's **schemes,** organized patterns of thought and behavior, become more elaborate. During the first five substages, babies learn to coordinate input from their senses and organize their activities in relation to their environment. They do this by the processes of *organization, adaptation,* and *equilibration,* which we discussed in Chapter 2. During the sixth substage, they progress from trial-and-error learning to the use of symbols and concepts to solve simple problems.

Much of this early cognitive growth comes about through **circular reactions,** in which an infant learns to reproduce pleasurable or interesting events originally discovered by chance. Initially, an activity produces a sensation so enjoyable that the baby wants to repeat it. The repetition then feeds on itself in a continuous cycle in which cause and effect keep reversing (Figure 7-3). The original chance behavior has been consolidated into a new scheme.

In the *first substage* (birth to about 1 month), neonates begin to exercise some control over their inborn reflexes, engaging in a behavior even when its normal stimulus is not present. For example, newborns suck reflexively when their lips are touched. But they soon learn to find the nipple even when they are not touched, and they suck at times when they are not hungry. These newer behaviors illustrate how infants modify and extend the scheme for sucking.

In the *second substage* (about 1 to 4 months), babies learn to repeat a pleasant bodily sensation first achieved by chance (say, sucking their thumbs, as shown in Figure 7-3a). Piaget called this a *primary circular reaction.* Also, babies begin to turn toward sounds, showing the ability to coordinate different kinds of sensory information (vision and hearing).

sensorimotor stage In Piaget's theory, first stage in cognitive development, during which infants learn through senses and motor activity.

schemes Piaget's term for organized patterns of thought and behavior used in particular situations.

circular reactions Piaget's term for processes by which an infant learns to reproduce desired occurrences originally discovered by chance.

Table 7-3		Six Substages of Piaget's Sensorimotor Stage of Cognitive Development*	
Substages	**Ages**	**Description**	**Behavior**
1. Use of reflexes	Birth to 1 month	Infants exercise their inborn reflexes and gain some control over them. They do not coordinate information from their senses. They do not grasp an object they are looking at.	Dorri begins sucking when her mother's breast is in her mouth.
2. Primary circular reactions	1 to 4 months	Infants repeat pleasurable behaviors that first occur by chance (such as thumb sucking). Activities focus on the infant's body rather than the effects of the behavior on the environment. Infants make first acquired adaptations; that is, they suck different objects differently. They begin to coordinate sensory information and grasp objects.	When given a bottle, Dylan, who is usually breast-fed, is able to adjust his sucking to the rubber nipple.
3. Secondary circular reactions	4 to 8 months	Infants become more interested in the environment; they repeat actions that bring interesting results (such as shaking a rattle) and prolong interesting experiences. Actions are intentional but not initially goal directed.	Alejandro pushes pieces of dry cereal over the edge of his high chair tray one at a time and watches each piece as it falls to the floor.
4. Coordination of secondary schemes	8 to 12 months	Behavior is more deliberate and purposeful (intentional) as infants coordinate previously learned schemes (such as looking at and grasping a rattle) and use previously learned behaviors to attain their goals (such as crawling across the room to get a desired toy). They can anticipate events.	Anica pushes the button on her musical nursery rhyme book, and "Twinkle, Twinkle, Little Star" plays. She pushes this button over and over again, choosing it instead of the buttons for the other songs.
5. Tertiary circular reactions	12 to 18 months	Toddlers show curiosity and experimentation; they purposefully vary their actions to see results (for example, by shaking different rattles to hear their sounds). They actively explore their world to determine what is novel about an object, event, or situation. They try out new activities and use trial and error in solving problems.	When Bjorn's big sister holds his favorite board book up to his crib bars, he reaches for it. His first efforts to bring the book into his crib fail because the book is too wide. Soon, Bjorn turns the book sideways and hugs it, delighted with his success.
6. Mental combinations	18 to 24 months	Because toddlers can mentally represent events, they are no longer confined to trial and error to solve problems. Symbolic thought enables toddlers to begin to think about events and anticipate their consequences without always resorting to action. Toddlers begin to demonstrate insight. They can use symbols, such as gestures and words, and can pretend.	Jenny plays with her shape box, searching carefully for the right hole for each shape before trying—and succeeding.

*Note: Infants show enormous cognitive growth during Piaget's sensorimotor stage, as they learn about the world through their senses and their motor activities. Note their progress in problem solving and the coordination of sensory information. All ages are approximate.

The *third substage* (about 4 to 8 months) coincides with a new interest in manipulating objects and learning about their properties. Babies engage in *secondary circular reactions:* intentional actions repeated not merely for their own sake, as in the second substage, but to get results *beyond the infant's own body.* For example, a baby this age will repeatedly shake a rattle to hear its noise or (as shown in Figure 7-3b) coo when a friendly face appears, so as to make the face stay longer.

By the time infants reach the *fourth substage, coordination of secondary schemes* (about 8 to 12 months), they have built on the few schemes they were born with. They have learned to generalize from past experience to solve new problems, and they can distinguish means from ends. They will crawl to get something they want, grab it, or push away a barrier to it (such as someone else's hand). They try out, modify, and coordinate previous schemes to find one that works. This substage marks the development of complex, goal-directed behavior.

In the *fifth substage* (about 12 to 18 months), babies begin to experiment with new behavior to see what will happen. Once they begin to walk, they can more easily explore their

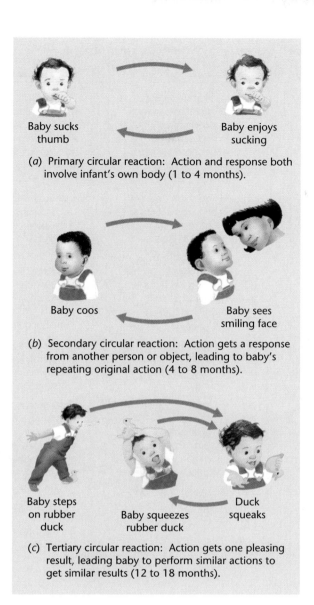

Figure 7-3

Primary, secondary, and tertiary circular reactions.

(a) Primary circular reaction: Action and response both involve infant's own body (1 to 4 months).

(b) Secondary circular reaction: Action gets a response from another person or object, leading to baby's repeating original action (4 to 8 months).

(c) Tertiary circular reaction: Action gets one pleasing result, leading baby to perform similar actions to get similar results (12 to 18 months).

environment. They now engage in *tertiary circular reactions,* varying an action to get a similar result, rather than merely repeating pleasing behavior they have accidentally discovered. For example, a toddler may squeeze a rubber duck that squeaked when stepped on, to see whether it will squeak again (as shown in Figure 7-3c). For the first time, children show originality in problem solving. By trial and error, they try out behaviors until they find the best way to attain a goal.

The *sixth substage, mental combinations* (about 18 months to 2 years) is a transition into the preoperational stage of early childhood. Toddlers develop **representational ability,** the ability to mentally represent objects and events in memory, largely through *symbols* such as words, numbers, and mental pictures. The ability to manipulate symbols frees children from immediate experience. They can pretend, and their representational ability affects the sophistication of their pretending. They can think about actions before taking them. They no longer have to go through laborious trial and error to solve problems. Piaget's daughter Lucienne seemed to show representational ability when, in figuring out how to pry open a partially closed box, she opened her mouth wider to represent her idea of widening the opening of the box (Piaget, 1936/1952).

During the sensorimotor stage, infants develop certain specific abilities—such as imitation—and knowledge about certain aspects of the physical world—notably, about objects and spatial relationships. Researchers following in Piaget's footsteps have found that some of these developments conform fairly closely to his observations, but others,

representational ability Piaget's term for capacity to store mental images or symbols of objects and events.

Table 7-4	Key Developments of the Sensorimotor Stage	
Concept or Skill	**Piaget's View**	**More Recent Findings**
Imitation	Invisible imitation develops around 9 months; deferred imitation begins after development of mental representations in the sixth substage (18–24 months).	Controversial studies have found invisible imitation of facial expressions in newborns and deferred imitation as early as 6 weeks. Deferred imitation of complex activities seems to exist as early as 6 months.
Object permanence	Develops gradually between the third and sixth substage. Infants in the fourth substage (8–12 months) make the A, not-B error.	Infants as young as 3½ months (second substage) seem to show object knowledge, though interpretation of findings is in dispute.
Symbolic development	Depends on representational thinking, which develops in the sixth substage (18 to 24 months).	Understanding that pictures stand for something else occurs at about 19 months. Children under 3 tend to have difficulty interpreting scale models.
Categorization	Depends on representational thinking, which develops during the sixth substage (18–24 months).	Infants as young as 3 months seem to recognize perceptual categories, and 7-month-olds categorize by function.
Causality	Develops slowly between 4–6 months and 1 year, based on an infant's discovery, first of effects of own actions and then of effects of outside forces.	Some evidence suggests early awareness of specific causal events in the physical world, but general understanding of causality may be slower to develop.
Number	Depends on use of symbols, which begins in the sixth substage (18–24 months).	Infants as young as 5 months may recognize and mentally manipulate small numbers, but interpretation of findings is in dispute.

Checkpoint ✔

Can you . . .

✔ Summarize major developments during the six substages of the sensorimotor stage?

✔ Explain how primary, secondary, and tertiary circular reactions work?

✔ Tell why the development of representational ability is important?

invisible imitation Imitation with parts of one's body that one cannot see.

visible imitation Imitation with parts of one's body that one can see.

including representational ability, may occur earlier than Piaget believed possible. (Table 7-4 compares Piaget's views on these and other topics with more recent findings; refer back to this table as you read on.)

Do Imitative Abilities Develop Earlier than Piaget Thought?

Imitation is an important way of learning; it becomes especially valuable toward the end of the first year, as babies try out new skills (Nelson, 2005). Piaget maintained that **invisible imitation**—imitation using parts of their body that babies cannot see, such as the mouth—develops at about 9 months, after **visible imitation,** using parts that babies can see, such as the hands or feet. Yet in a series of studies by Andrew Meltzoff and M. Keith Moore (1983, 1989), babies less than 72 hours old appeared to imitate adults by opening their mouths and sticking out their tongues—a response that other research has found to disappear by about age 2 months (Bjorklund & Pellegrini, 2000). According to Meltzoff and Gopnik (1993), this early imitative behavior reflects an evolved "like me" mechanism; the infant seeks to imitate faces that have the same properties (tongues that can stick out) as his or her own. Meltzoff and Moore (1994) further suggest that infants have an inborn predisposition to imitate human faces—a tendency that may serve the evolutionary purpose of communication with a caregiver (Rakison, 2005). Other researchers have suggested that the tongue thrust may be an early attempt to interact with the mother or simply exploratory behavior aroused by the sight of an adult tongue (Bjorklund, 1997; S. S. Jones, 1996). In any event, as with some other early capacities, imitation appears to serve a different adaptive purpose for the young infant than for an older infant (Bjorklund & Pellegrini, 2000).

Piaget also held that children under 18 months cannot engage in **deferred imitation** of an act they saw some time before because they have not yet developed the ability to retain mental representations. However, Piaget may have underestimated infants' and toddlers' representational ability because of their limited ability to talk about what they remember. Babies as young as 6 weeks have imitated an adult's facial movements after a 24-hour delay, in the presence of the same adult, who this time was expressionless. This suggests that very young babies can retain a mental representation of an event (Meltzoff & Moore, 1994, 1998). Deferred imitation of novel or complex events seems to begin by 6 to 9 months (Meltzoff & Moore, 1998; Bauer, 2002). Thus, the findings on deferred imitation agree with those on operant conditioning (Rovee-Collier, 1999); infants do seem capable of remembering after a delay.

In **elicited imitation,** researchers induce infants and toddlers to imitate a specific series of actions they have seen but not necessarily done before. The initial demonstration may be accompanied by a simple verbal explanation (Bauer, 1996, 2002; Bauer, Wenner, Dropik, & Wewerka, 2000; Bauer, Wiebe, Carver, Waters, & Nelson, 2003). After a 1-month delay, with no further demonstration or explanation, more than 40 percent of 9-month-olds can reproduce a simple two-step procedure, such as dropping a toy car down a vertical chute and then pushing the car with a rod to make it roll to the end of a track and turn on a light (Bauer, 2002; Bauer et al., 2003). One study reliably predicted individual differences in performance of this task from scans of the infants' brains as they looked at photos of the same procedure a week after first seeing it. The memory traces of infants who could not repeat the procedure in the right order were less robust, indicating that they had failed to consolidate the memory for long-term storage (Bauer et al., 2003).

Elicited imitation is much more reliable during the 2nd year of life; nearly 8 out of 10 toddlers 13 to 20 months old can repeat an unfamiliar, multistep sequence (such as putting together a metal gong and causing it to ring) as much as a year later (Bauer, 1996; Bauer et al., 2000). Prior practice helps to reactivate children's memories, especially if some new items have been substituted for the original ones (Hayne, Barr, & Herbert, 2003). Four factors seem to determine young children's long-term recall: (1) the number of times a sequence of events has been experienced, (2) whether the child actively participates or merely observes, (3) whether the child is given verbal reminders of the experience, and (4) whether the sequence of events occurs in a logical, causal order (Bauer et al., 2000).

Development of Knowledge about Objects and Space

The ability to perceive the size and shape of objects and to discern their movements may be an early evolved mechanism for avoidance of predators (Rakison, 2005). The *object concept*—the idea that objects have independent existence, characteristics, and locations in space—is a later *cognitive* development fundamental to an orderly view of physical reality. The object concept is the basis for children's awareness that they themselves exist apart from objects and other people. It is essential to understanding a world full of objects and events. Doddy Darwin's struggle to understand the existence and location of reflective images was part of his development of an object concept.

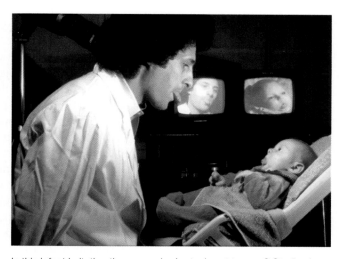

Is this infant imitating the researcher's stuck-out tongue? Studies by Andrew N. Meltzoff suggest that infants as young as 2 weeks are capable of invisible imitation. But other researchers found that only the youngest babies make this response, suggesting that the tongue movement may merely be exploratory behavior.

deferred imitation Piaget's term for reproduction of an observed behavior after the passage of time by calling up a stored symbol of it.

elicited imitation Research method in which infants or toddlers are induced to imitate a specific series of actions they have seen but not necessarily done before.

This 8-month-old baby crawling after a ball is in the fourth substage of Piaget's sensorimotor stage, coordination of secondary schemes.

When Does Object Permanence Develop?

object permanence Piaget's term for the understanding that a person or object still exists when out of sight.

A, not-B error Tendency for 8- to 12-month-old infants to search for a hidden object in a place where they previously found it rather than in the place where they most recently saw it being hidden.

One aspect of the object concept is **object permanence,** the realization that an object or person continues to exist when out of sight. The development of this concept in many cultures can be seen in the game of peekaboo (Box 7-1).

Object permanence develops gradually during the sensorimotor stage. At first, infants have no such concept. By the third substage, from about 4 to 8 months, they will look for something they have dropped, but if they cannot see it, they act as if it no longer exists. In the fourth substage, about 8 to 12 months, they will look for an object in a place where they first found it after seeing it hidden, even if they later saw it being moved to another place. Piaget called this the **A, not-B error.** In the fifth substage, 12 to 18 months, they no longer make this error; they will search for an object in the last place they saw it hidden. However, they will not search for it in a place where they did not see it hidden. By the sixth substage, 18 to 24 months, object permanence is fully achieved; toddlers will look for an object even if they did not see it hidden.

A study of 48 14-month-olds seems to support the existence of Piaget's fifth substage in the development of object permanence. Even after a 24-hour delay, the babies successfully searched for and found a silver bell in the same place they had seen it hidden. However, when brought to a different or rearranged room, their search was unsuccessful, even if the container in which they had seen the object hidden was still there, and even if the bell itself had been placed on the floor in full view (Moore & Meltzoff, 2004).

A new interpretation of the A, not-B error comes from Esther Thelen's dynamic systems theory (introduced in Chapter 6). The decision where to search for a hidden object, Thelen and her colleagues observed, is not about what babies *know,* but about what they *do,* and why. Infants' reaching behavior is influenced by multiple processes, including vision, perception, attention, movement, and memory. One factor is how much time has elapsed between the infant's seeing the object hidden in a new place (B) and the infant's reaching for it. If the elapsed time is brief, the infant is more likely to reach for the object in the new location. When the time interval is longer, however, the perceptual and motor memory of having previously found the object in the old place (A) inclines the infant to search there again, and that inclination grows stronger the more times the object has been found in the same place (Smith & Thelen, 2003; Spencer, Smith, & Thelen, 2001; Spencer et al., 2006).

Other research suggests that Piaget may have underestimated younger infants' grasp of object permanence because of his testing methods. Babies may fail to search for hidden objects because they cannot yet carry out a two-step or two-handed sequence of actions, such as moving a cushion or lifting the cover of a box before grasping the object. When given repeated opportunities, over a period of 1 to 3 months, to explore, manipulate, and learn about such a task, infants in the last half of their 1st year can succeed (Bojczyk & Corbetta, 2004).

When object permanence is tested with a more age-appropriate procedure, in which the object is hidden only by darkness and thus can be retrieved in one motion, infants in the third substage (4 to 8 months) perform surprisingly well. In one study, 6½-month-olds saw a ball drop down a chute and land in one of two spots, each identifiable by a distinctive sound. When the light was turned off and the procedure was repeated, the babies reached for the ball in the appropriate location, guided only by the sound (Goubet & Clifton, 1998). This showed that they knew the ball continued to exist and could tell where it had gone.

Methods based only on infants' looking behavior eliminate the need for any motor activity and thus can be used at very early ages. As we will discuss later in this chapter, recent, controversial research using information-processing methodology suggests that infants as young as 3 or 4 months old seem not only to have a sense of object permanence but also to understand causality and categorization, to have a rudimentary concept of number, and to know other principles governing the physical world.

Symbolic Development, Pictorial Competence, and Understanding of Scale

Much of the knowledge people acquire about their world is gained, not through direct observation or experience, but through *symbols,* intentional representations of reality. Learning to interpret symbols is, then, an essential task of childhood. First, however,

Box 7-1 *Playing Peekaboo*

In rural South Africa, a Bantu mother smiles at her 9-month-old son, covers her eyes with her hands, and asks, "Uphi?" (Where?). After 3 seconds, the mother says, "Na-a-a-a-n *ku!*" (Here!) and uncovers her eyes to the baby's delight. In Tokyo, a Japanese mother plays the same game with her 12-month-old daughter, who shows the same joyous response. In suburban Connecticut, a 15-month-old boy who sees his grandfather for the first time in 2 months raises his shirt to cover his eyes—as Grandpa did on his previous visit.

Peekaboo is played across diverse cultures, using similar routines (Fernald & O'Neill, 1993). In all cultures in which the game is played,* the moment when the mother or other caregiver reappears is exhilarating. It is marked by exaggerated gestures and voice tones. Infants' pleasure from the immediate sensory stimulation of the game is heightened by their fascination with faces and voices, especially the high-pitched tones an adult usually uses.

The game serves several important purposes. Psychoanalysts say that it helps babies master anxiety when their mother disappears. Cognitive psychologists see it as a way babies play with developing ideas about object permanence. It may also be a social routine that helps babies learn rules that govern conversation, such as taking turns. It may provide practice in paying attention, a prerequisite for learning.

As babies develop the cognitive competency to predict future events, the game takes on new dimensions. Between 3 and 5 months, the baby's smiles and laughter as the adult's face moves in and out of view signal the infant's developing expectation of what will happen next. At 5 to 8 months, the baby shows anticipation by looking and smiling as the adult's voice alerts the infant to the adult's imminent reappearance. By 1 year, babies are no longer merely observers but usually initiate the game, actively engaging adults in play. Now it is the adult who generally responds to the baby's physical or vocal cues, which can become quite insistent if the adult doesn't feel like playing.

To help infants who are in the process of learning peekaboo or other games, parents often use *scaffolding* (see Chapter 2). In an 18-month longitudinal study at the University of Montreal, 25 mothers were videotaped playing peekaboo with their babies, using a doll as a prop (Rome-Flanders, Cronk, & Gourde, 1995). The amount and type of scaffolding varied with the infant's age and skill. Mothers frequently tried to attract a 6-month-old's attention to begin the game; this became less and less necessary as time went on. Modeling (performing the peekaboo sequence to encourage a baby to imitate it) also was most frequent at 6 months and decreased significantly by 12 months, when there was an increase in direct verbal instruction ("Cover the doll") as babies became more able to understand spoken language. Indirect

"Peekaboo!" This game, played the world over, helps babies to overcome anxiety about a parent's disappearance and to develop cognitive concepts, such as anticipation of future events.

verbal instruction ("Where is the doll?"), used to focus attention on the next step in the game, remained constant throughout the entire age range. Reinforcement (showing satisfaction with the infant's performance, for example, by saying, "Peekaboo!" when the infant uncovered the doll) was fairly constant from 9 months on. The overall amount of scaffolding dropped substantially at 24 months, by which time most babies have fully mastered the game.

*The cultures included in this report are found in Malaysia, Greece, India, Iran, Russia, Brazil, Indonesia, Korea, and South Africa.

What's your view ?

Have you ever played peekaboo periodically with the same infant? If so, did you notice changes with age in the child's participation, as described in this box?

Check it out

For more information on this topic, go to http://wik.ed.uiuc.edu/index.php/Attachment. On this page you can find an article by Steve Harvey, Ph.D., from *Zero to Three,* titled "Dynamic Play Therapy: An Integrated Expressive Arts Approach to the Family Treatment of Infants and Toddlers."

children must become *symbol-minded:* attentive to symbols and their relationships to the things they represent (DeLoache, 2004). One aspect of symbolic development, studied by Judy DeLoache and her colleagues, is the growth of *pictorial competence,* the ability to understand the nature of pictures (De Loache, Pierroutsakos, & Uttal, 2003).

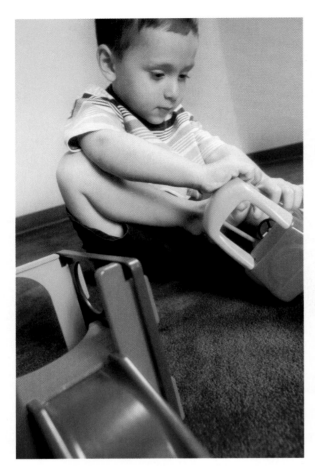

In one experiment (DeLoache, Uttal, & Rosengren, 2004), toddlers were observed trying to fit into toy cars or slide down miniature slides. Such scale errors may result from lack of impulse control and from lack of coordination between brain systems.

dual representation hypothesis
Proposal that children under age 3 have difficulty grasping spatial relationships because of the need to keep more than one mental representation in mind at the same time.

What's your view

- On the basis of Piaget's observations and the research they inspired, what factors would you consider in buying a toy for an infant or toddler?

In studies carried out in both the United States and Africa's Ivory Coast, infants were observed using their hands to explore pictures as if they were objects—feeling, rubbing, patting, or grasping them or attempting to lift a depicted object off the page. This manual exploration of pictures diminishes by 15 months, but not until about 19 months—according to Piaget, the dawn of representational thought—do children show, by pointing at a picture of a bear or telephone while saying its name ("beh" or "teltone"), an understanding that a picture is meant to be a representation, or symbol, of something else (DeLoache et al., 2003; DeLoache, Pierroutsakos, Uttal, Rosengren, & Gottlieb, 1998; Pierroutsakos & DeLoache, 2003).

Although toddlers may spend a good deal of time watching television, they at first seem unaware that what they are seeing is a representation of reality (Troseth, Saylor, & Archer, 2006). In one series of experiments, 2- and 2½-year-olds watched on a video monitor as an adult hid an object in an adjoining room. When taken to the room, the 2½-year-olds found the hidden object easily, but 2-year-olds could not. Yet the younger children did find the object if they had watched through a window as it was being hidden (Troseth & DeLoache, 1998). Apparently, what the 2-year-olds lacked was representational understanding of screen images. In a follow-up experiment, 2-year-olds who were told face to face where to find a hidden toy were able to do so, whereas 2-year-olds who received the same information from a person on video did not (Troseth, Saylor, & Archer, 2006).

Toddlers often make *scale errors*—momentary misperceptions of the relative sizes of symbolic and real objects. In one study, 18- to 36-month-olds were videotaped trying to slide down tiny slides, sit in dollhouse chairs, and squeeze into miniature cars after similar, but child-sized, objects were removed from their playroom. Such scale errors are clearly distinguishable from pretend play (DeLoache, Uttal, & Rosengren, 2004) and may in part result from lack of impulse control. In addition, the researchers suggested that two different brain systems normally work together during interactions with familiar objects. One system enables the child to recognize and categorize an object ("That's a buggy") and plan what to do with it ("I'm going to lie in it"). A separate system may be involved in perceiving the size of the object and using this information to control actions pertaining to it. Faulty communication between these immature brain systems is a possible reason for young children's frequent scale errors (DeLoache, 2006).

According to the **dual representation hypothesis,** it is difficult for toddlers to mentally represent both a symbol and the object it represents at the same time, and so they may confuse the two (DeLoache, 2006; DeLoache et al., 2003). This may be why 2-year-olds tend to have problems interpreting scale models. They can use representational thinking to guide them to the actual location of something shown in a photograph (Suddendorf, 2003), but apparently they think of the model as an object in itself, rather than a representation of something else (DeLoache, 2000).

In one experiment, 2½-year-olds who were told that a "shrinking machine" had shrunk a room to the size of a miniature model were more successful in finding a toy hidden in the room on the basis of its position in the model than were children the same age who were told that the "little room" was just like the "big room." What seems to make the second task harder is that it requires a child to mentally represent both the symbol (the "little room") and its relationship to the thing it stands for (the "big room") at the same time. With the "shrinking machine," children do not have to perform this dual operation, because they are told that the room and the model are one and the same. Three-year-olds do not seem to have this problem with models (DeLoache, Miller, & Rosengren, 1997).

Evaluating Piaget's Sensorimotor Stage

According to Piaget, the journey from reflex behavior to the beginnings of thought is a long, slow one. For a year and a half or so, babies learn only from their senses and movements; not until the last half of the 2nd year do they make the breakthrough to conceptual thought. Now, as we have seen, research using simplified tasks and modern tools suggests that certain limitations Piaget saw in infants' early cognitive abilities, such as object permanence, may instead have reflected immature linguistic and motor skills.

In some ways, then, infants and toddlers seem to be more cognitively competent than Piaget imagined. This does not mean that infants come into the world with minds fully formed. As Piaget observed, immature forms of cognition precede more mature forms. We can see this, for example, in the errors young infants make in searching for hidden objects. However, Piaget may have been mistaken in his emphasis on motor experience as the primary engine of cognitive growth. Infants' perceptions are far ahead of their motor abilities, and today's methods enable researchers to make observations and inferences about those perceptions. The relationship between perception and cognition is a major area of investigation, as we will discuss in the next section.

Checkpoint ✔

Can you . . .

✔ Summarize Piaget's views on imitation, object permanence, pictorial competence, and understanding of scale?

✔ Explain why Piaget may have underestimated some of infants' cognitive abilities, and discuss the implications of more recent research?

Information-Processing Approach: Perceptions and Representations

Guidepost 5

How can we measure infants' ability to process information, and when do babies begin to think about characteristics of the physical world?

Information-processing research uses new methods to test ideas about cognitive development that sprang from the psychometric and Piagetian approaches. For example, information-processing researchers analyze the separate parts of a complex task, such as Piaget's object search tasks, to figure out what abilities are necessary for each part of the task and at what age these abilities develop. Information-processing researchers also measure and draw inferences from what infants pay attention to and for how long.

Habituation

At about 6 weeks, Stefan lies peacefully in his crib near a window, sucking a pacifier. It is a cloudy day, but suddenly the sun breaks through, and an angular shaft of light appears on the end of the crib. Stefan stops sucking for a few moments, staring at the pattern of light and shade. Then he looks away and starts sucking again.

We don't know what was going on in Stefan's mind when he saw the shaft of light, but we can tell by his sucking and looking behavior at what point he began paying attention and when he stopped.

Much information-processing research with infants is based on **habituation,** a type of learning in which repeated or continuous exposure to a stimulus, such as the shaft of light, reduces attention to that stimulus. In other words, familiarity breeds loss of interest.

Researchers study habituation in newborns by repeatedly presenting a stimulus (usually a sound or visual pattern) and then monitoring such responses as heart rate, sucking, eye movements, and brain activity. A baby who has been sucking typically stops when the stimulus is first presented and pays attention to the new stimulus, as Stefan did. After the same sound or sight has been presented again and again, it loses its novelty and no longer causes the baby to stop sucking. Resumption of sucking shows that the infant has *habituated* to the stimulus. A new sight or sound, however, will capture the baby's attention and the baby will again stop sucking. This response to a new stimulus is called **dishabituation.**

Researchers gauge the efficiency of infants' information processing by measuring how quickly babies habituate to familiar stimuli, how fast their attention recovers when they are exposed to new stimuli, and how much time they spend looking at the new and the old. Efficiency of habituation correlates with later signs of cognitive development, such as a preference for complexity, rapid exploration of the environment,

habituation Type of learning in which familiarity with a stimulus reduces, slows, or stops a response.

dishabituation Increase in responsiveness after presentation of a new stimulus.

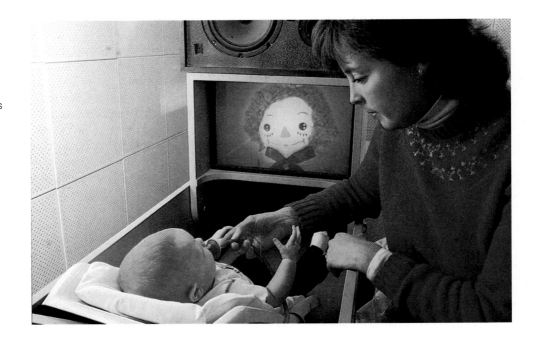

Can this baby tell the difference between Raggedy Ann and Raggedy Andy? This researcher may find out by seeing whether the baby has habituated—gotten used—to one face (as shown by sucking on a nipple) and then stops sucking on the nipple when a new face appears, showing recognition of the difference.

sophisticated play, quick problem solving, and the ability to match pictures. In fact, as we will see, speed of habituation and other information-processing abilities show promise as predictors of intelligence (Bornstein & Sigman, 1986; Colombo, 1993; McCall & Carriger, 1993).

Visual and Auditory Processing Abilities

visual preference Tendency of infants to spend more time looking at one sight than another.

The amount of time a baby spends looking at different kinds of sights is a measure of **visual preference,** which is based on the ability to make visual distinctions. Babies less than 2 days old prefer curved lines to straight lines, complex patterns to simple patterns, three-dimensional objects to two-dimensional objects, and moving objects to stationary objects—again, possibly an evolved mechanism to enable awareness of predators. Newborns also prefer pictures of faces or facelike configurations to pictures of other things and new sights to familiar ones (Fantz, 1963, 1964, 1965; Fantz, Fagen, & Miranda, 1975; Fantz & Nevis, 1967; Rakison, 2005; Turati, Simion, Milani, & Umilta, 2002). The latter tendency is called *novelty preference.*

visual recognition memory
Ability to distinguish a familiar visual stimulus from an unfamiliar stimulus when shown both at the same time.

Visual recognition memory can be measured by showing an infant two stimuli side by side, one familiar and one novel. A longer gaze at the novel stimulus indicates that the infant recognizes the other stimulus as familiar, as something the infant has seen before. Visual recognition memory depends on comparing incoming information with information the infant already has—in other words, on the ability to form and refer to mental representations (P. R. Zelazo, Kearsley, & Stack, 1995).

Contrary to Piaget's view, habituation and novelty preference studies suggest that at least a rudimentary representational ability exists at birth or soon after and quickly becomes more efficient. Individual differences in efficiency of information processing reflect the speed with which infants form and refer to such mental images. When shown two sights at the same time, infants who quickly shift attention from one to another tend to have better recognition memory and stronger novelty preference than infants who take longer looks at each sight (Jankowski, Rose, & Feldman, 2001; Rose, Feldman, & Jankowski, 2001; Stoecker, Colombo, Frick, & Allen, 1998). Speed of processing increases rapidly during the 1st year of life. It continues to increase during the 2nd and 3rd years, as toddlers become better able to separate new information from information they have already processed (P. R. Zelazo et al., 1995).

Auditory discrimination studies also are based on attentional preference. Such studies have found that newborns can tell sounds they have already heard from those they have not. In one study, infants who heard a certain speech sound 1 day after birth appeared to remember that sound 24 hours later, as shown by a reduced tendency to turn their heads toward the familiar sound and even a tendency to turn away (Swain, Zelazo, & Clifton, 1993).

Piaget believed that the senses are unconnected at birth and are only gradually integrated through experience. If so, this integration begins almost immediately. The fact that neonates will look at a source of sound shows that they associate hearing and sight. A more sophisticated ability is **cross-modal transfer,** the ability to use information gained from one sense to guide another—as when a person negotiates a dark room by feeling for the location of familiar objects or identifies objects by sight after feeling them with eyes closed. In one study, 1-month-olds showed that they could transfer information gained from sucking (touch) to vision. When the infants saw a rigid object (a hard plastic cylinder) and a flexible one (a wet sponge) being manipulated by a pair of hands, the infants looked longer at the object they had just sucked (Gibson & Walker, 1984).

cross-modal transfer Ability to use information gained by one sense to guide another.

Researchers also study how attention itself develops (Colombo, 2001). From birth to about 2 months, the amount of time infants typically gaze at a new sight increases. Between about 2 and 9 months, looking time decreases as infants learn to scan objects more efficiently and shift attention. Later in the 1st year and into the 2nd, when sustaining attention becomes more voluntary and task oriented, looking time plateaus or increases (Colombo, 2002; Colombo et al., 2004).

The capacity for *joint attention*—which may contribute to social interaction, language acquisition, and the understanding of others' mental states—develops between 10 and 12 months, when babies follow an adults' gaze by looking or pointing in the same direction (Brooks & Meltzoff, 2002, 2005). Joint attention develops slowly during the months of dependence on adult caregivers (Nelson, 2005). In one study, 10- and 11-month-olds' ability to follow an adult's gaze predicted higher language scores 8 months later. (Brooks & Meltzoff, 2005). *Gaze-following* also may be an important step toward understanding the intentions of others (Brooks & Meltzoff, 2005).

Watching television (Box 7-2) may impede attentional development. In a nationally representative longitudinal study, the more hours children spent viewing television at ages 1 and 3, the more likely they were to have attentional problems by age 7 (Christakis, Zimmerman, DiGiuseppe, & McCarty, 2004). Children who watched at least 3 hours a day scored lower on cognitive measures at age 6 (Zimmerman & Christakis, 2005).

Information Processing as a Predictor of Intelligence

Because of a weak correlation between infants' scores on developmental tests (such as the Bayley Scales) and their later IQ, many psychologists believed that the cognitive functioning of infants had little in common with that of older children and adults—in other words, that there was a discontinuity in cognitive development. Piaget believed this too. However, when researchers assess how infants and toddlers process information, some aspects of mental development seem to be fairly continuous from birth (McCall & Carriger, 1993). Children who, from the start, are efficient at taking in and interpreting sensory information later score well on intelligence tests.

In many longitudinal studies, habituation and attention-recovery abilities during the first 6 months to 1 year of life were moderately useful in predicting childhood IQ. So was visual recognition memory (Bornstein & Sigman, 1986; Colombo, 1993; McCall & Carriger, 1993). In one study, a combination of visual recognition memory at 7 months and cross-modal transfer at 1 year predicted IQ at age 11 and also showed a modest (but nonetheless remarkable after 10 years) relationship to processing speed and memory at that age (Rose & Feldman, 1995, 1997).

A young child who watches television several hours a day may develop attentional problems and be late in learning to read.

Box 7-2 *Do Infants and Toddlers Watch Too Much Television?*

Six-month-old Jenny reclines in her bouncy seat, watching a Baby Einstein DVD. She bounces up and down, claps, and laughs out loud as bright images flash across the screen. Jenny has been watching Baby Einstein videos since she was 5 weeks old.

Jenny is neither precocious nor unusual, according to a nationally representative random-dialed survey of 1,000 parents of preschoolers, sponsored by the Henry J. Kaiser Family Foundation. On a typical day, 59 percent of children under 2 watch television, 42 percent watch a video or DVD, 5 percent use a computer, and 3 percent play video games. These children spend an average of about 2 hours a day in front of a screen, more than twice as much time as they spend being read to (see figure).

An avalanche of media geared to infants and toddlers has occurred since the late 1990s: the first television show targeting children as young as 12 months, computer games with special keyboard toppers for infants as young as 9 months, and educational videotapes and DVDs (with accompanying books, flashcards, and puppets) aimed at infants from 1 to 18 months. In 2006, creators of the widely respected TV program *Sesame Street* released a series of DVDs for babies as young as 6 months to watch with their parents, and HBO featured a series called "Classical Baby," featuring works of music, art, and dance. A BabyFirstTV channel now offers round-the-clock programming for infants and toddlers.

According to the Kaiser survey, 74 percent of children under 2 watch television, and 26 percent have TV sets in their bedrooms. Some 66 percent of children 3 and younger turn on the TV by themselves, 52 percent change channels with a remote device, and 30 percent put in a video or DVD by themselves.

Babies in whose households television is frequently on are more likely to start watching before their first birthday than babies not exposed to such heavy doses of TV. The "heavy watchers" are more likely to watch every day, watch for a longer time, and spend less time being read to. They also are less likely to learn to read by age 6.

All of this flies in the face of recommendations by the American Academy of Pediatrics Committee on Public Education (2001) that children under 2 be discouraged from watching television and instead be engaged in interactive activities that promote brain development, such as talking, playing, singing, and reading with parents. Most parents in the Kaiser survey expressed faith in the educational value of the media and said their children were more likely to imitate positive behaviors, such as sharing and helping, than aggressive behaviors. Parents who value and exhibit positive behavior tend to steer children toward stories, films, and television programs that depict such behavior (Singer & Singer, 1998).

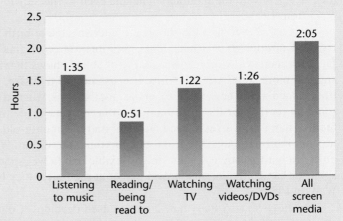

Average amount of time children under 2 spend on media and other activities in a typical day, according to mothers' reports.

Note: These data include only children who participate in these activities.

Source: Rideout et al., 2003.

Further study is needed to find out how heavy exposure to television affects infants and toddlers. Researchers need to investigate such questions as whether the constant presence of background media interferes with the development of physical coordination and language; whether time spent with media takes away time from playing outdoors, reading, or interacting with parents; whether it contributes to a sedentary lifestyle; whether video and computer games help visual and spatial skills or risk eyestrain and ergonomic problems; how various types of media impact cognitive development and attention span; and what is the extent and effect of young children's exposure to noneducational content.

Source: Unless otherwise referenced, this box is based on Rideout, Vandewater, & Wartella, 2003.

What's your view

At what age would you let a baby watch television or a videotape or play a computer game, and what restrictions, if any, would you place on such activities?

Check it out

For more information on this topic, go to http://www.kff.org/entmedia/3378.cfm (the Kaiser Family Foundation report discussed in this box).

Visual reaction time and *visual anticipation* can be measured by the *visual expectation paradigm.* In this research design, a series of computer-generated pictures briefly appears, some on the right and some on the left side of an infant's peripheral visual field. The same sequence of pictures is repeated several times. The infant's eye movements are measured to see how quickly his or her gaze shifts to a picture that has just appeared (reaction time) or to the place where the infant expects the next picture to appear (anticipation). These measurements are thought to indicate attentiveness and processing speed, as well as the tendency to form expectations on the basis of experience. In a longitudinal study, visual reaction time and visual anticipation at 3½ months correlated with IQ at age 4 (Dougherty & Haith, 1997).

All in all, there is much evidence that the abilities infants use to process sensory information are related to the cognitive abilities intelligence tests measure. Still, we need to be cautious in interpreting these findings. Most of the studies used small samples. Also, the predictability of childhood IQ from measures of habituation and recognition memory is only modest. Furthermore, predictions based on information-processing measures alone do not take into account the influence of environmental factors (Colombo & Janowsky, 1998; Laucht, Esser, & Schmidt, 1994; McCall & Carriger, 1993). For example, maternal responsiveness in early infancy seems to play a part in the link between early attentional abilities and cognitive abilities later in childhood (Bornstein & Tamis-LeMonda, 1994) and even at age 18 (Sigman, Cohen, & Beckwith, 1997).

Information Processing and the Development of Piagetian Abilities

As we mentioned in a previous section, new evidence suggests that several of the cognitive abilities Piaget identified as developing toward the end of the sensorimotor stage actually seem to arise much earlier. Research based on infants' visual processing—independent of motor abilities—has given developmental scientists a new window into the timing of such cognitive developments as categorization, causality, object permanence, and number, all of which depend on formation of mental representations (refer back to Table 7-4).

Categorization

Dividing the world into meaningful categories is vital to thinking about objects or concepts and their relationships. It is the foundation of language, reasoning, problem solving, and memory; without it, the world would seem chaotic and meaningless (Rakison, 2005).

According to Piaget, the ability to classify, or group things into categories, does not appear until the sixth sensorimotor substage, around 18 months. Yet, by looking longer at items in a new category, even 3-month-olds seem to know, for example, that a dog is not a cat (Quinn, Eimas, & Rosenkrantz, 1993). Indeed, brain imaging has found that basic components of the neural structures needed to support categorization are functional within the first 6 months of life (Quinn, Westerlund, & Nelson, 2006). From an evolutionary perspective, infants may be born with a rudimentary ability to discern certain limited categories (such as snakes and spiders) that are dangerous to humans (Rakison, 2005).

For the most part, infants at first seem to categorize on the basis of *perceptual* features, such as shape, color, and pattern. Toward the end of the 1st year their categories become *conceptual,* based on real-world knowledge (Oakes, Coppage, & Dingel, 1997), particularly of function (Mandler, 1998a; Mandler & McDonough, 1993, 1996, 1998). In one series of experiments, 10- and 11-month-olds recognized that chairs with zebra-striped upholstery belong in the category of furniture, not animals (Pauen, 2002). In the 2nd year, language becomes a factor in learning to categorize. Hearing an experimenter name an object and/or point out its function can help 14- to 18-month-olds with category formation (Booth & Waxman, 2002).

Causality

An understanding of *causality,* the principle that one event causes another, is important because it "allows people to predict and control their world" (L. B. Cohen, Rundell, Spellman, & Cashon, 1999). Piaget believed that this understanding develops slowly during the 1st year of life. At about 4 to 6 months, as infants become able to grasp objects, they begin to recognize that they can act on their environment. Thus, said Piaget, the concept of causality is rooted in a dawning awareness of the power of one's own intentions. However, according to Piaget, infants do not yet know that causes must come before effects; and not until close to 1 year do they realize that forces outside of themselves can make things happen.

Some information-processing research suggests that a mechanism for recognizing causality may exist much earlier (Mandler, 1998a), possibly even at birth. Infants 6½ months old have shown by habituation and dishabituation that they seem to see a difference between events that are the immediate cause of other events (such as a brick striking a second brick,

Checkpoint ✔

Can you . . .

✔ Explain how habituation measures the efficiency of infants' information processing?

✔ Identify several early perceptual and processing abilities that serve as predictors of intelligence?

Figure 7-4

How early do infants show object permanence? In this violation-of-expectations experiment, 3½-month-olds watched a short carrot and then a tall carrot slide along a track, disappear behind a screen, and then reappear. After they became accustomed to seeing these events, the opaque screen was replaced by a screen with a large notch at the top. The short carrot did not appear in the notch when passing behind the screen; the tall carrot, which should have appeared in the notch, also did not. The babies looked longer at the tall, than at the short, carrot event, suggesting that they were surprised that the tall carrot did not reappear in the notch.

Source: Baillargeon & DeVos, 1991.

Habituation Events

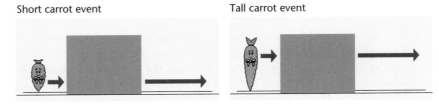

Test Events

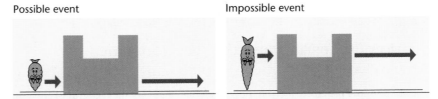

violation-of-expectations
Research method in which dishabituation to a stimulus that conflicts with experience is taken as evidence that an infant recognizes the new stimulus as surprising.

which is then pushed out of position) and events that occur with no apparent cause (such as a brick moving away from another brick without having been struck by it) (Leslie, 1982, 1984).

Other researchers have replicated these findings with 6½-month-olds but not with younger infants (L. B. Cohen & Amsel, 1998). These investigators attribute the growth of causal understanding to a gradual improvement in information-processing skills. As infants accumulate more information about how objects behave, they are better able to see causality as a general principle operating in a variety of situations (L. B. Cohen & Amsel, 1998; L. B. Cohen & Oakes, 1993; L. B. Cohen et al., 1999; Oakes, 1994).

Research also has explored infants' expectations about hidden causes. In one experiment, 10- to 12-month-olds looked longer when a human hand emerged from the opposite side of a lighted stage onto which a beanbag had been thrown than when the hand emerged from the same side as the beanbag, suggesting that the infants understood that the hand probably had thrown the beanbag. The infants did not have the same reaction when a toy train rather than a hand appeared or when the thrown object was a self-propelled puppet. Thus, infants that age apparently can figure out that (1) an object incapable of self-motion must have a causal agent to set it in motion, and (2) a hand is a more likely causal agent than a toy train (Saxe, Tenenbaum, & Carey, 2005).

Object Permanence

Violation-of-expectations research begins with a familiarization phase, in which infants see an event or series of events happen normally. After the infant is habituated to this procedure, the event is changed in a way that violates (conflicts with) normal expectations. An infant's tendency to look longer at the changed event is interpreted as evidence that the infant recognizes it as surprising.

Using the violation-of-expectations method, Renée Baillargeon and her colleagues claim to have found evidence of object permanence in infants as young as 3½ months. The babies appeared surprised by the failure of a tall carrot that slid behind a screen of the same height to show up in a large notch in the upper part of the screen before appearing again on the other side (Baillargeon & DeVos, 1991; Figure 7-4).

In other research, the ability to visually follow the path of a ball that briefly passed behind a box was present at 4 months and more firmly established at 6 months (Johnson et al., 2003). Of course, the perception that an object that disappears on one side of a visual barrier looks the same as the object that reappears on the other side does not necessarily imply cognitive knowledge that the object continues to exist behind the barrier (Meltzoff & Moore, 1998).

Number

Some violation-of-expectations research suggests that an understanding of number may begin long before Piaget's sixth substage, when he claimed children first begin to use symbols. Karen Wynn (1992) tested whether 5-month-old babies can add and subtract small numbers of objects. The infants watched as Mickey Mouse dolls were placed behind a screen, and a doll was either added or taken away. The screen then was lifted to reveal either the expected number or a different number of dolls. Babies looked longer at surprising "wrong" answers than at expected "right" ones, suggesting (according to Wynn) that they had mentally computed the right answers.

According to Wynn, this research suggests that numerical concepts are inborn—that when parents teach their babies numbers, they may merely be teaching them the names ("one, two, three") for *concepts* the babies already know. However, skeptics point out that the idea that these concepts is inborn is mere speculation, since the infants in these studies were already 5 and 6 months old. Furthermore, the infants might simply have been responding *perceptually* to the puzzling presence of a doll they saw removed from behind the screen or the absence of a doll they saw placed there (Haith, 1998; Haith & Benson, 1998). Other researchers suggest that, although infants do seem to discriminate visually between sets of, say, two and three objects, they may merely notice differences in the overall contours, area, or collective mass of sets of objects rather than compare the number of objects in the sets (Clearfield & Mix, 1999; Mix, Huttenlocher, & Levine, 2002).

In response to that criticism, McCrink and Wynn (2004) designed an experiment to show that 9-month-olds can add and subtract numbers too large for mere perceptual discrimination. The infants saw five abstract objects go behind an opaque square. Five more objects then appeared and went behind the square. The infants looked longer when the screen dropped to reveal five objects than when it revealed ten. Similarly, when ten objects went behind the square and five emerged and went away, the infants looked longer when the screen dropped to reveal ten objects than when it revealed five. The authors concluded that "humans possess an early system that supports numerical combination and manipulation" (p. 780). This experiment does not, however, shed light on whether that system is inborn.

Evaluating Information-Processing Research on Infants

Violation-of-expectations studies and other recent information-processing research with infants raises the possibility that at least rudimentary forms of categorization, causal reasoning, object permanence, and numerical understanding may be present in the early months of life.

One proposal is that infants are born with reasoning abilities—*innate learning mechanisms* that help them make sense of the information they encounter—or that they acquire these abilities very early (Baillargeon, 1994a). Some investigators go further, suggesting that infants at birth may already have intuitive *core knowledge* of basic physical principles in the form of specialized brain modules that help infants organize their perceptions and experience (Spelke, 1994, 1998).

However, these interpretations are controversial. In violation-of-expectations studies, does an infant's visual interest in an "impossible event" reveal a *conceptual* understanding of the way things work or merely a *perceptual* awareness that something unusual has happened? The fact that an infant looks longer at one scene than at another may show only that the infant can see a difference between the two. It does not show what the infant knows about the difference or that the infant is actually surprised. The mental representation the infant refers to may be no more than a brief sensory memory of something just seen. It's also possible that an infant, in becoming accustomed to the habituation event, develops the expectations that are then violated by the impossible event and did not have such knowledge or expectations before (Goubet & Clifton, 1998; Haith, 1998; Haith & Benson, 1998; Mandler, 1998a; Munakata, 2001; Munakata, McClelland, Johnson, & Siegler, 1997).

Defenders of this research insist that a conceptual interpretation best accounts for the findings (Baillargeon, 1999; Spelke, 1998), but a recent variation on one of Baillargeon's experiments suggests otherwise. In her original research, Baillargeon (1994a) showed infants of various ages a "drawbridge" rotating 180 degrees. When the infants became habituated to the rotation, a barrier was introduced in the form of a box. At 4½ months, infants seemed to show (by longer looking) that they understood that the drawbridge could not move through the entire box (Figure 7-5). Later investigators replicated the experiment but eliminated the box. Five-month-olds still looked longer at the 180-degree rotation than at

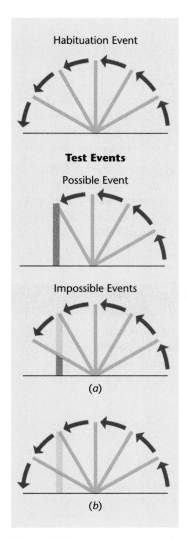

Figure 7-5

Test for infants' understanding of how a barrier works. Infants first become accustomed to seeing a "drawbridge" rotate 180 degrees on one edge. Then a box is placed beside the drawbridge. In the possible event, the drawbridge stops when it reaches the edge of the box. In the impossible events, the drawbridge rotates through part or all of the space occupied by the box. On the basis of how long they stare at each event, at 4½ months, infants seem to know that the drawbridge cannot pass through the entire box (b); but not until 6½ months do infants recognize that the drawbridge cannot pass through part of the box (a).

Source: Adapted from Baillargeon, 1994a.

Can you . . .

✔ Describe the violation-of-expectations research method, tell how and why it is used, and list some criticisms of it?

✔ Discuss four areas in which information-processing research seems to contradict Piaget's account of development?

a lesser degree of rotation, even though no barrier was present—suggesting that they simply were demonstrating a preference for greater movement (Rivera, Wakeley, & Langer, 1999). Thus, until further research clarifies these issues, we must be cautious about inferring the existence of adultlike cognitive abilities from data that may have simpler explanations or may represent only partial achievement of mature abilities (Haith, 1998).

Is it plausible that mechanisms to acquire knowledge of physical principles would become functional long before babies can put that knowledge to practical use? According to some evolutionary theorists (Nelson, 2005; Rakison, 2005), the answer is no. Evolutionary principles suggest that people develop various capacities at times of life when they are adaptive, or useful. Thus, infants are endowed at birth with basic attentional, perceptive, and learning abilities that adequately meet their needs for that period of life. It is likely, then, that the ability to find meaning in what they perceive develops later, as do specialized learning abilities for specific domains such as language (Rakison, 2005).

Cognitive Neuroscience Approach: The Brain's Cognitive Structures

Guidepost 6

What can brain research reveal about the development of cognitive skills?

Piaget's belief that neurological maturation is a major factor in cognitive development is borne out by current brain research. Brain growth spurts (periods of rapid growth and development) coincide with changes in cognitive behavior similar to those Piaget described (Fischer & Rose, 1994, 1995).

Some researchers have used brain scans to determine which brain structures affect which cognitive functions and to chart developmental changes. Brain scans provide physical evidence of the location of two separate long-term memory systems—*implicit* and *explicit*—that acquire and store different kinds of information (Squire, 1992; Vargha-Khadem et al., 1997). **Implicit memory,** which develops early in infancy, refers to remembering that occurs without effort or even conscious awareness; it pertains to habits and skills, such as knowing how to throw a ball—or an infant's kicking on seeing a familiar mobile (Nelson, 2005). **Explicit memory,** also called *declarative memory,* is conscious or intentional recollection, usually of facts, names, events, or other things that can be stated or declared. Delayed imitation of complex behaviors is evidence that declarative memory is developing in late infancy and toddlerhood.

implicit memory Unconscious recall, generally of habits and skills; sometimes called *procedural memory.*

explicit memory Intentional and conscious memory, generally of facts, names, and events; sometimes called *declarative memory.*

In early infancy, when the structures responsible for memory storage are not fully formed, memories are relatively fleeting (Serres, 2001). The maturing of the *hippocampus,* a structure deep in the temporal lobes, along with the development of cortical structures coordinated by the hippocampal formation make longer-lasting memories possible (Bauer, 2002; Bauer et al., 2000, 2003). The hippocampal system continues to develop at least through the 5th year (Serres, 2001).

The *prefrontal cortex* (the large portion of the frontal lobe directly behind the forehead) is believed to control many aspects of cognition. This part of the brain develops more slowly than any other (M. H. Johnson, 1998). During the second half of the 1st year, the prefrontal cortex and associated circuitry develop the capacity for **working memory**—short-term storage of information the brain is actively processing, or working on. It is in working memory that mental representations are prepared for, or recalled from, storage.

working memory Short-term storage of information being actively processed.

The relatively late appearance of working memory may be largely responsible for the slow development of object permanence, which seems to be seated in a rearward area of the prefrontal cortex (Nelson, 1995). By 12 months, this region may be developed enough to permit an infant to avoid the A, not-B error by controlling the impulse to search in a place where the object previously was found (Bell & Fox, 1992; Diamond, 1991).

Although memory systems continue to develop beyond infancy, the early emergence of the brain's memory structures underlines the importance of environmental stimulation from the first months of life. Social-contextual theorists and researchers pay particular attention to the impact of environmental influences.

Social-Contextual Approach: Learning from Interactions with Caregivers

Researchers influenced by Vygotsky's sociocultural theory study how the cultural context affects early social interactions that may promote cognitive competence. **Guided participation** refers to mutual interactions with adults that help structure children's activities and bridge the gap between a child's understanding and an adult's. This concept was inspired by Vygotsky's view of learning as a collaborative process. Guided participation often occurs in shared play and in ordinary, everyday activities in which children learn informally the skills, knowledge, and values important in their culture.

In one cross-cultural study (Rogoff, Mistry, Göncü, & Mosier, 1993), researchers visited the homes of fourteen 1- to 2-year-olds in each of four places: a Mayan town in Guatemala, a tribal village in India, and middle-class urban neighborhoods in Salt Lake City and Turkey. The investigators interviewed caregivers about their child-rearing practices and watched them help the toddlers learn to dress themselves and to play with unfamiliar toys.

Cultural differences affected the types of guided participation the researchers observed. In the Guatemalan town, where toddlers normally saw their mothers sewing and weaving at home to help support the family, and in the Indian village, where they accompanied their mothers at work in the fields, the children customarily played alone or with older siblings while the mother worked nearby. After initial demonstration and instruction, mostly nonverbal, in, for example, how to tie shoes, the children took over, while the parent or other caregiver remained available to help. The U.S. toddlers, who had full-time homemaker mothers or were in day care, interacted with their parents in the context of child's play rather than in the parents' work or social worlds. Caregivers spoke with the children as peers and managed and motivated their learning with praise and excitement. Turkish families, who were in transition from a rural to an urban way of life, showed a pattern somewhere between the other two.

The cultural context, then, influences the way caregivers contribute to cognitive development. Direct adult involvement in children's play and learning may be better adapted to a middle-class urban community, in which parents or caregivers have more time, greater verbal skills, and possibly more interest in children's play and learning, than in a rural community in a developing country, in which children frequently observe and participate in adults' work activities (Rogoff et al., 1993).

guided participation Participation of an adult in a child's activity in a manner that helps to structure the activity and to bring the child's understanding of it closer to that of the adult.

Checkpoint ✔

Can you . . .

✔ Identify the brain structures apparently involved in explicit, implicit, and working memory, and mention a task made possible by each?

✔ Tell how brain research helps explain Piagetian developments and memory operations?

✔ Explain how cultural patterns affect guided participation in toddlers' learning?

Language Development

Guidepost 8

How do babies develop language, and what influences linguistic progress?

Doddy Darwin's exclamation "Ah!" to express his recognition of an image in a glass is a striking example of the connection between **language,** a communication system based on words and grammar, and cognitive development. Once children know words, they can use them to represent objects and actions. They can reflect on people, places, and things; and they can communicate their needs, feelings, and ideas in order to exert control over their lives. How did language evolve, and how do infants "crack the code" of language?

language Communication system based on words and grammar.

The Evolution of Language*

The evolution of language in the human species and its development in each individual illustrate the interaction of all domains of development.

The emergence of human language was made possible by several important physiological adaptations. First, between 10 million and 7 million years ago, the shift from four legs to two was accompanied by an expansion of social groupings. As the brain brought the vocal system under cortical control, it became possible for these groups to adopt distinguishing patterns of utterance and gesture. Imitation of vocalizations and gestures facilitated group cohesion and the linguistic initiation of the young.

*This section is indebted to MacWhinney (2005).

Table 7-5	Language Milestones from Birth to 3 Years

Age in Months	Development
Birth	Can perceive speech, cry, make some response to sound.
1½ to 3	Coos and laughs.
3	Plays with speech sounds.
5 to 6	Recognizes frequently heard sound patterns.
6 to 7	Recognizes all phonemes of native language.
6 to 10	Babbles in strings of consonants and vowels.
9	Uses gestures to communicate and plays gesture games.
9 to 10	Intentionally imitates sounds.
9 to 12	Uses a few social gestures.
10 to 12	No longer can discriminate sounds not in own language.
10 to 14	Says first word (usually a label for something).
10 to 18	Says single words.
12 to 13	Understands symbolic function of naming; passive vocabulary grows.
13	Uses more elaborate gestures.
14	Uses symbolic gesturing.
16 to 24	Learns many new words, expanding expressive vocabulary rapidly, going from about 50 words to as many as 400; uses verbs and adjectives.
18 to 24	Says first sentence (2 words).
20	Uses fewer gestures; names more things.
20 to 22	Has comprehension spurt.
24	Uses many two-word phrases; no longer babbles; wants to talk.
30	Learns new words almost every day; speaks in combinations of three or more words; understands very well; makes grammatical mistakes.
36	Says up to 1,000 words, 80 percent intelligible; makes some mistakes in syntax.

Source: Bates, O'Connell, & Shore, 1987; Capute, Shapiro, & Palmer, 1987; Kuhl, 2004; Lalonde & Werker, 1995; Lenneberg, 1969; Newman, 2005.

The next step was the development of enough brain storage to commit visual and auditory images and their significance to memory. Beginning about 2 million years ago, the size of the brain gradually tripled. Between 300,000 and 50,000 years ago, with the emergence of *Homo sapiens,* or human beings, the brain underwent changes that enabled the systematization of language. People were able to learn, store, and retrieve almost limitless names for things, to combine them into sentences, and to develop principles for grammatical constructions. Four other physiological adaptations—loss of canine teeth, changes in the muscles of the larynx, bending of the vocal tract, and shaping of the tongue muscles—played an important part in the production of speech.

Similarly, each infant acquires language through a combination of physical, cognitive, and social developments. As the physical structures needed to produce sounds mature and the neuronal connections necessary to associate sound and meaning become activated, social interaction motivates and facilitates the communicative nature of speech. Let's look at the typical sequence of language development (Table 7-5).

Sequence of Early Language Development

prelinguistic speech Forerunner of linguistic speech; utterance of sounds that are not words. Includes crying, cooing, babbling, and accidental and deliberate imitation of sounds without understanding their meaning.

Before babies can use words, they make their needs and feelings known—as Doddy Darwin did—through sounds that progress from crying to cooing and babbling, then to accidental imitation, and then to deliberate imitation. These sounds are known as **prelinguistic speech.** Infants also grow in the ability to recognize and understand speech sounds and to use meaningful gestures. Babies typically say their first word around the end of their 1st year, and toddlers begin speaking in sentences about 8 months to 1 year later.

Early Vocalization

Crying is a newborn's only means of communication. Different pitches, patterns, and intensities signal hunger, sleepiness, or anger (Lester & Boukydis, 1985).

Between 6 weeks and 3 months, babies start *cooing* when they are happy—squealing, gurgling, and making vowel sounds like "ahhh." At about 3 to 6 months, babies begin to play with speech sounds, matching the sounds they hear from people around them.

Babbling—repeating consonant-vowel strings, such as "ma-ma-ma-ma"—occurs between ages 6 and 10 months and is often mistaken for a baby's first word. Babbling is not real language, since it does not hold meaning for the baby, but it becomes more wordlike.

As we have seen, *imitation* was a key to the evolution of human language, and so it is with language development in infants. Babies accidentally imitate language sounds and then imitate themselves making these sounds. At about 9 to 10 months, infants deliberately imitate sounds without understanding them. Once they have a repertoire of sounds, they string them together in patterns that sound like language but seem to have no meaning. Once infants become familiar with the sounds of words and phrases, they begin to attach meanings to them (Fernald, Perfors, & Marchman, 2006; Jusczyk & Hohne, 1997).

Perceiving Language Sounds and Structure

Imitation of language sounds requires the ability to perceive subtle differences between sounds, and infants can do this from or even before birth. Their brains seem to be preset to discriminate basic linguistic units, perceive linguistic patterns, and categorize them as similar or different. This complex set of abilities seems to be unique to human infants (Kuhl, 2004).

At first, infants can discriminate the sounds of any language. In time, however, the ongoing process of pattern perception and categorization seems to commit the brain's neural networks to further learning of similar patterns—typically, the patterns of the infant's native language. This *neural commitment* also seems to constrain future learning of non-native-language patterns. Babies who lack early exposure to this patterning feature of language—whether spoken or signed—during a critical or sensitive period are unlikely to acquire language normally (Kuhl, 2004; Kuhl, Conboy, Padden, Nelson, & Pruitt, 2005; refer back to Box 1-2 in Chapter 1).

The process apparently begins in the womb. In one experiment, the heart rates of fetuses in the 35th week of gestation slowed when a tape recording of a rhyme the mother had spoken frequently was played near her abdomen. The fetal heart rate did not slow for a different rhyme another pregnant woman had spoken. Since the voice on the tape was not that of the mother, the fetuses apparently were responding to the linguistic sounds they had heard the mother use. This suggests that hearing the "mother tongue" before birth may "pretune" an infant's ears to pick up its sounds (DeCasper, Lecanuet, Busnel, Granier-Deferre, & Maugeais, 1994).

By age 6 to 7 months, hearing babies have learned to recognize the approximately 40 *phonemes*, or basic sounds, of their native language and to adjust to slight differences in the way different speakers form those sounds (Kuhl, Williams, Lacerda, Stevens, & Lindblom, 1992). The ability to discriminate native-language sounds at this age predicts individual differences in language abilities during the 2nd year (Tsao, Liu, & Kuhl, 2004), whereas non-native sound discrimination does not (Kuhl et al., 2005).

By 10 to 12 months, babies lose their sensitivity to sounds that are not part of the language or languages they usually hear spoken. For example, Japanese infants no longer make a distinction between "ra" and "la," a distinction that does not exist in the Japanese language. Although the ability to perceive non-native sounds is not entirely lost, the brain no longer routinely discriminates them (Bates, O'Connell, & Shore, 1987; Lalonde & Werker, 1995; Werker, 1989). How does this change occur? One hypothesis, for which there is evidence from behavioral studies and brain imaging, is that infants mentally compute the relative frequency of particular phonetic sequences in their language and learn to ignore sequences they infrequently hear (Kuhl, 2004).

Between 6 and 12 months, babies begin to become aware of the phonological rules of their language—how sounds are arranged in speech. In one series of experiments, 7-month-olds

This toddler is communicating with his father by pointing at something that catches his eye. Gesturing seems to come naturally to young children and may be an important part of language learning.

listened longer to "sentences" containing a different order of nonsense sounds (such as "wo fe wo," or ABA) from the order to which the infants had been habituated (such as "ga ti ti," or ABB). The sounds used in the test were different from those used in the habituation phase, so the infants' discrimination must have been based on the patterns of repetition alone. This finding suggests that infants may have a mechanism for discerning abstract rules of sentence structure (Marcus, Vijayan, Rao, & Vishton, 1999). In another series of experiments based on listening time, 9-month-olds appeared to discern patterns of syllabification and pronunciation of initial and final consonants and to apply those patterns to new words that fit or violated them (Saffran & Thiessen, 2003).

Gestures

At 9 months, Maika *pointed* to an object, sometimes making a noise to show that she wanted it. Between 9 and 12 months, she learned some *conventional social gestures:* waving bye-bye, nodding her head to mean "yes," and shaking her head to signify "no." By about 13 months, she used more elaborate *representational gestures:* holding an empty cup to her mouth to show that she wanted a drink, or holding up her arms to show that she wanted to be picked up.

Symbolic gestures, such as blowing to mean "hot" or sniffing to mean "flower," often emerge around the same time as babies say their first words, and they function much like words. By using them, children show an understanding that symbols can refer to specific objects, events, desires, and conditions. Gestures usually appear before children have a vocabulary of 25 words and drop out when children learn the word for the idea they were gesturing and can say it instead (Lock, Young, Service, & Chandler, 1990).

Gesturing seems to come naturally. In an observational study, blind children and adolescents used gestures while speaking as much as sighted children did and even while speaking to a blind listener. Thus, the use of gestures does not depend on having either a model or an observer, but seems to be an inherent part of the speaking process (Iverson & Goldin-Meadow, 1998).

Learning gestures seems to help babies learn to talk. Early gestures often correspond with the words and word combinations children later say (Iverson & Goldin-Meadow, 2005). In one experiment (Goodwyn & Acredolo, 1998), 11-month-olds learned gestures by watching their parents perform them and say the corresponding words. Between 15 and 36 months, when tested on vocal language development, these children outperformed two other groups—one whose parents had only said words and another who had received neither vocal nor gestural training. Gestures, then, can be a valuable alternative or supplement to words, especially during the period of early vocabulary formation.

First Words

linguistic speech Verbal expression designed to convey meaning.

Doddy Darwin, at 11 months, said his first word—"ouchy"—which he attached to a number of objects. Doddy's development was typical in this respect. The average baby says a first word sometime between 10 and 14 months, initiating **linguistic speech**—verbal expression that conveys meaning. At first an infant's total verbal repertoire is likely to be "mama" or "dada." Or it may be a simple syllable that has more than one meaning depending on the context in which the child utters it. "Da" may mean "I want that," "I want to go out," or "Where's Daddy?" A word like this, which expresses a complete thought, is called a **holophrase.**

holophrase Single word that conveys a complete thought.

Babies understand many words before they can use them. Long before infants can connect sounds to meanings, they learn to recognize sound patterns they hear frequently, such as their name. Infants 5 months old listen longer to their name than to other names (Newman, 2005). Six-month-olds look longer at a video of their mothers when they hear the word "mommy" and of their fathers when they hear "daddy," suggesting that they are beginning to associate sound with meaning—at least with regard to special people (Tincoff

& Jusczyk, 1999). Ten-month-olds attach labels to objects they find interesting, whether those labels are correct or not; 12-month-olds pay attention to cues from adults in learning what an object is called (Pruden, Hirsh-Pasek, Golinkoff, & Hennon, 2006).

By 13 months, most children understand that a word stands for a specific thing or event, and they can quickly learn the meaning of a new word (Woodward, Markman, & Fitzsimmons, 1994). *Passive* (receptive, or understood) vocabulary continues to grow as verbal comprehension gradually becomes faster and more accurate and efficient (Fernald, Perfors, & Marchman, 2006). By 18 months. about 3 out of 4 children can understand 150 words and can say 50 of them (Kuhl, 2004). Children with larger vocabularies and quicker reaction times can recognize spoken words from just the first part of the word. For example, when hearing "daw" or "ki," they will point to a picture of a dog or kitten (Fernald, Swingley, & Pinto, 2001).

Addition of new words to the *expressive* (spoken) vocabulary is slower at first. Then, sometime between 16 and 24 months, a "naming explosion" may occur, though this phenomenon does not appear to be universal (Ganger & Brent, 2004). Within a few weeks, a toddler may go from saying about 50 words to saying about 400 (Bates, Bretherton, & Snyder, 1988). Rapid gains in spoken vocabulary reflect increases in speed and accuracy of word recognition during the 2nd year (Fernald, Pinto, Swingley, Weinberg, & McRoberts, 1998; Fernald et al., 2006).

Nouns seem to be the easiest type of word to learn. In a cross-cultural study, it did not matter whether a family's native language was Spanish, Dutch, French, Hebrew, Italian, Korean, or American English; in all these languages, parents reported that their 20-month-old children knew more nouns than any other class of words (Bornstein & Cote et al., 2004). At 24 months, children quickly recognize names of familiar objects in the absence of visual cues (Swingley & Fernald, 2002). At 24 to 36 months, children can figure out the meaning of unfamiliar adjectives from context or from the nouns they modify (Mintz, 2005).

First Sentences

The next linguistic breakthrough comes when a toddler puts two words together to express one idea ("Dolly fall"). Generally, children do this between 18 and 24 months, about 8 to 12 months after they say their first word. However, this age range varies greatly. Although prelinguistic speech is fairly closely tied to chronological age, linguistic speech is not. Most children who begin talking fairly late catch up eventually—and many make up for lost time by talking nonstop to anyone who will listen! (True delayed language development is discussed in Chapter 10.)

A child's first sentences typically deal with everyday events, things, people, or activities (Braine, 1976; Rice, 1989; Slobin, 1973). Darwin noted that Doddy expressed his developing moral sense in words. At 27 months the boy gave his sister the last bit of his gingerbread, exclaiming, "Oh, kind Doddy, kind Doddy!"

At first children typically use **telegraphic speech,** consisting of only a few essential words. When Rita says, "Damma deep," she seems to mean "Grandma is sweeping the floor." Children's use of telegraphic speech and the form it takes vary, depending on the language being learned (Braine, 1976; Slobin, 1983). Word order generally conforms to what a child hears; Rita does not say, "Deep Damma," when she sees her grandmother pushing a broom.

telegraphic speech Early form of sentence use consisting of only a few essential words.

Does the omission of functional words such as *is* and *the* mean that a child does not know these words? Not necessarily; the child may merely find them hard to reproduce. Even during the 1st year, infants are sensitive to the presence of functional words; at 10½ months, they can tell a normal passage from one in which the functional words have been replaced by similar-sounding nonsense words (Jusczyk, 2003).

Sometime between 20 and 30 months, children show increasing competence in **syntax,** the rules for putting sentences together in their language. They become more comfortable with articles (*a, the*), prepositions (*in, on*), conjunctions (*and, but*), plurals, verb endings, past tense, and forms of the verb *to be* (*am, are, is*). They also become increasingly aware of the communicative purpose of speech and of whether their words are being understood (Shwe & Markman, 1997)—a sign of growing sensitivity to the mental lives of others. By age 3, speech is fluent, longer, and more complex; although children often omit parts of speech, they usually get their meaning across well.

syntax Rules for forming sentences in a particular language.

Characteristics of Early Speech

Early speech has a character all its own—no matter what language a child is speaking (Slobin, 1971).

As we have seen, children *simplify.* They use telegraphic speech to say just enough to get their meaning across ("No drink milk!").

Children *understand grammatical relationships they cannot yet express.* At first, Nina may understand that a dog is chasing a cat, but she cannot string together enough words to express the complete action. Her sentence comes out as "Puppy chase" rather than "Puppy chase kitty."

Children *underextend word meanings.* Lisa's uncle gave her a toy car, which the 13-month-old called her "koo-ka." Then her father came home with a gift, saying, "Look, Lisa, here's a little car for you." Lisa shook her head. "Koo-ka," she said and ran and got the one from her uncle. To her, *that* car—and *only* that car—was a little car, and it took some time before she called any other toy cars by the same name. Lisa was underextending the word *car* by restricting it to a single object.

Children also *overextend word meanings.* At 14 months, Eddie jumped in excitement at the sight of a gray-haired man on the television screen and shouted, "Gampa!" Eddie was *overextending,* or overgeneralizing, a word; he thought that because his grandfather had gray hair, all gray-haired men could be called "Grandpa." As children develop a larger vocabulary and get feedback from adults on the appropriateness of what they say, they overextend less. ("No, honey, that man looks a little like Grandpa, but he's somebody else's grandpa, not yours.")

Children *overregularize rules.* They apply them rigidly, without exception—as when 21-month-old Delilah, looking out the window with her father on a gloomy day, repeated after him, "Windy . . . cloudy . . . rainy . . .," and then added, "coldy." When children first learn the rules for, in this instance, forming adjectives from nouns, they apply them universally. The next step is to learn the exceptions to the rules, which they generally do by early school age.

Classic Theories of Language Acquisition: The Nature-Nurture Debate

Is linguistic ability learned or inborn? In the 1950s, a debate raged between two schools of thought: one led by B. F. Skinner, the foremost proponent of learning theory, and the other by the linguist Noam Chomsky.

Skinner (1957) maintained that language learning, like other learning, is based on experience. According to classic learning theory, children learn language through operant conditioning. At first, babies utter sounds at random. Caregivers reinforce the sounds that happen to resemble adult speech with smiles, attention, and praise. Infants then repeat these reinforced sounds. According to social-learning theory, babies imitate the sounds they hear adults make and, again, are reinforced for doing so. Word learning depends on selective reinforcement; the word "kitty" is reinforced only when the family cat appears. As this process continues, children are reinforced for speech that is more and more adultlike.

Observation, imitation, and reinforcement probably do contribute to language development, but, as Chomsky (1957) persuasively argued, they cannot fully explain it. For one thing, word combinations and nuances are so many and so complex that they cannot all be acquired by specific imitation and reinforcement. Then, caregivers often reinforce utterances that are not strictly grammatical, as long as they make sense ("Gampa go bye-bye"). Adult speech itself is an unreliable model to imitate, as it is often ungrammatical, containing false starts, unfinished sentences, and slips of the tongue. Also, learning theory does not account for children's imaginative ways of saying things they have never heard—as when 2-year-old Anna described a sprained ankle as a "sprangle" and said she didn't want to go to sleep yet because she wasn't "yawny."

Chomsky's view is called **nativism.** Unlike Skinner's learning theory, nativism emphasizes the active role of the learner. Chomsky (1957, 1972) proposed that the human brain has an innate capacity for acquiring language; babies learn to talk as naturally as they learn to walk. He suggested that an inborn **language acquisition device (LAD)** programs

> *Checkpoint* ✔
>
> Can you . . .
>
> ✔ Trace the typical sequence of milestones in early language development, pointing out the influence of the language babies hear around them?
>
> ✔ Describe five ways in which early speech differs from adult speech?

nativism Theory that human beings have an inborn capacity for language acquisition.

language acquisition device (LAD) In Chomsky's terminology, an inborn mechanism that enables children to infer linguistic rules from the language they hear.

children's brains to analyze the language they hear and to figure out its rules. More recently, Chomsky (1995) has sought to identify a simple set of universal principles that underlie all languages and a single multipurpose mechanism for connecting sound to meaning.

Support for the nativist position comes from newborns' ability to differentiate similar sounds, suggesting that they are "born with perceptual mechanisms that are tuned to the properties of speech" (Eimas, 1985, p. 49). Nativists point out that almost all children master their native language in the same age-related sequence without formal teaching. Furthermore, the brains of human beings, the only animals with fully developed language, contain a structure that is larger on one side than on the other, suggesting that an inborn mechanism for sound and language processing may be localized in the larger hemisphere—the left for most people (Gannon, Holloway, Broadfield, & Braun, 1998). Language lateralization of the brain increases with age, enabling growth in language skills (Szaflarski, Holland, Schmithorst, & Weber-Byars, 2004).

Still, the nativist approach does not explain precisely how such a mechanism operates. It does not tell us why some children acquire language more rapidly and efficiently than others, why children differ in linguistic skill and fluency, or why (as we'll see) speech development appears to depend on having someone to talk with, not merely on hearing spoken language.

Aspects of both learning theory and nativism have been used to explain how deaf babies learn sign language, which is structured much like spoken language and is acquired in the same sequence. Just as hearing babies of hearing parents imitate vocal utterances, deaf babies of deaf parents seem to imitate the sign language they see their parents using, first stringing together meaningless motions and then repeating them over and over in what has been called *hand-babbling*. As parents reinforce these gestures, the babies attach meaning to them (Petitto & Marentette, 1991; Petitto, Holowka, Sergio, & Ostry, 2001).

However, some deaf children make up their own sign language when they do not have models to follow—evidence that imitation and reinforcement alone cannot explain the emergence of linguistic expression (Goldin-Meadow & Mylander, 1998). Since the 1970s, successive waves of Nicaraguan deaf schoolchildren who were being taught only lip-reading in Spanish have developed a true sign language, which has gradually evolved from simple gestures into words and sentences that follow linguistic rules (Senghas & Coppola, 2001; Senghas, Kita, & Ozyürek, 2004). Likewise, Al-Sayyid Bedouin Sign Language, which evolved spontaneously in an isolated village in Israel's Negev desert, has a distinct, systematic grammatical structure unlike that of Israeli Sign Language or of the Arabic dialect spoken by hearing members of the community (Sandler, Meir, Padden, & Aronoff, 2005).

Furthermore, learning theory does not explain the correspondence between the ages at which linguistic advances in both hearing and nonhearing babies typically occur (Padden, 1996; Petitto, Katerelos, et al., 2001; Petitto & Kovelman, 2003). Deaf babies begin hand-babbling between ages 7 and 10 months, about the age when hearing infants begin voice-babbling (Petitto, Holowka, et al., 2001; Petitto & Marentette, 1991). Deaf babies also begin to use sentences in sign language at about the same time that hearing babies begin to speak in sentences (Meier, 1991; Newport & Meier, 1985). This suggests that an inborn language capacity may underlie the acquisition of both spoken and signed language and that advances in both kinds of language are tied to brain maturation.

Most developmental scientists today believe that language acquisition, like most other aspects of development, depends on an intertwining of nature and nurture. Children, whether hearing or deaf, probably have an inborn capacity to acquire language, which may be activated or constrained by experience.

Influences on Language Development

What determines how quickly and how well children learn to understand and use language? Research has focused on influences both within and outside the child.

Brain Development

The tremendous brain growth during the early months and years is closely linked with language development. A newborn's cries are controlled by the *brain stem* and *pons,* the most primitive parts of the brain and the earliest to develop (refer back to Figure 6-4). Repetitive

Checkpoint

Can you . . .

✔ Summarize how learning theory and nativism seek to explain language acquisition, and point out strengths and weaknesses of each theory?

babbling may emerge with the maturation of parts of the *motor cortex,* which control movements of the face and larynx. Not until early in the 2nd year, when most children begin to talk, do the pathways that link auditory and motor activity mature (Owens, 1996). As we have discussed, there is evidence that the development of language actively affects brain networks, committing them to the recognition of native-language sounds only (Kuhl, 2004; Kuhl et al., 2005). Cortical regions associated with language continue to develop until at least the late preschool years or beyond—some regions, not even until adulthood.

In about 98 percent of people, the left hemisphere is dominant for language, though the right hemisphere participates as well (Nobre & Plunkett, 1997; Owens, 1996). Videotapes of babbling babies show that, as in adult speech, the mouth opens more on the right side than on the left. Since the left hemisphere of the brain controls activity on the right side of the body, lateralization of linguistic functions apparently takes place very early in life (Holowka & Petitto, 2002; refer back to Chapter 6). Language lateralization increases into young adulthood, enabling continued growth in language skills (Szaflarski, Holland, Schmithorst, & Weber-Byars, 2004).

Social Interaction: The Role of Parents and Caregivers

Language is a social act. At each stage of language development, interaction with parents or other caregivers plays an essential role (Kuhl, 2004).

Prelinguistic Period At the babbling stage, adults help an infant advance toward true speech by repeating the sounds the baby makes. The baby soon joins in the game and repeats the sounds back. Parents' imitation of babies' sounds affects the amount of infant vocalization (Goldstein, King, & West, 2003) and the pace of language learning (Hardy-Brown & Plomin, 1985; Hardy-Brown, Plomin, & DeFries, 1981). It also helps babies experience the social aspect of speech, the sense that a conversation consists of alternating or taking turns (Kuhl, 2004), an idea most babies seem to grasp at about age 7½ to 8 months. Even as early as 4 months, babies in a game of peekaboo show sensitivity to the structure of social exchange with an adult (Rochat, Querido, & Striano, 1999; refer back to Box 7-1).

Caregivers may help babies understand spoken words by, for example, pointing to a doll and saying, "Please give me Kermit," encouraging the infant to follow the caregiver's gaze (Kuhl, 2004). If the baby doesn't respond, the adult may pick up the doll and say, "Kermit." In one longitudinal study, mothers' responsiveness to 9-month-olds' and, even more so, to 13-month-olds' vocalization and play predicted the timing of language milestones, such as first spoken words and sentences (Tamis-LeMonda, Bornstein, & Baumwell, 2001).

Vocabulary Development As we have noted, babies learn by listening to what adults say. When babies begin to talk, parents or caregivers can boost vocabulary development by repeating their first words and pronouncing them correctly.

A strong relationship has appeared between the frequency of specific words in mothers' speech and the order in which children learn these words (Huttenlocher, Haight, Bryk, Seltzer, & Lyons, 1991) as well as between mothers' talkativeness and the size of toddlers' vocabularies (Huttenlocher, 1998). Mothers with higher socioeconomic status tend to use richer vocabularies and longer utterances, and their 2-year-olds have larger spoken vocabularies (Hoff, 2003)—as much as eight times as large (C. T. Ramey & Ramey, 2003). By age 3, vocabularies of low-income children vary greatly, depending in large part on the diversity of word types they have heard their mothers use, especially around the child's second birthday (Pan, Rowe, Singer, & Snow, 2005).

However, sensitivity and responsiveness to a child's level of development may count more than the number of words a mother uses. In a year-long study of 290 low-income families with 2-year-olds, both parents' sensitivity, positive regard for the child, and the cognitive stimulation they provided during play predicted the child's receptive vocabulary and cognitive development at ages 2 and 3 (Tamis-LeMonda et al., 2004).

In households where more than one language is spoken, babies achieve similar milestones in each language on the same schedule as children who hear only one language (Petitto, Katerelos, et al., 2001; Petitto & Kovelman, 2003). Bilingual children often use elements

Checkpoint ✓

Can you . . .

✔ Name areas of the brain involved in early language development, and tell the function of each?

✔ Give evidence for plasticity in the brain's linguistic areas?

Despite controversy over the value of child-directed speech, or parentese, this simplified way of speaking does appeal to babies.

of both languages, sometimes in the same utterance—a phenomenon called **code mixing.** However, code mixing does not cause them to confuse the two languages (Petitto, Katerelos, et al., 2001; Petitto & Kovelman, 2003). A naturalistic observation in Montreal (Genesee, Nicoladis, & Paradis, 1995) suggests that children as young as 2 in dual-language households differentiate between the two languages, using French, for example, with a predominantly French-speaking father and English with a predominantly English-speaking mother. This ability to shift from one language to another is called **code switching.** (Chapter 13 discusses second-language learning.)

Child-Directed Speech

You do not have to be a parent to speak like a parent. If, when you talk to an infant or toddler, you speak slowly in a high-pitched voice with exaggerated ups and downs, simplify your speech, exaggerate vowel sounds, and use short words and sentences and much repetition, you are using **child-directed speech (CDS;** sometimes called *parentese* or *motherese*). Most adults and even children do it naturally. Such "baby talk" has been documented in many languages and cultures (Kuhl et al., 1997).

Many researchers believe that CDS helps infants learn their native language or at least pick it up faster by exaggerating and directing attention to the distinguishing features of speech sounds (Kuhl et al., 2005). In one cross-cultural observational study, mothers in the United States, Russia, and Sweden were audiotaped speaking to their 2- to 5-month-old infants. Whether the mothers were speaking English, Russian, or Swedish, they produced more exaggerated vowel sounds when talking to the infants than when talking to other adults. At 20 weeks, the babies' babbling contained distinct vowels that reflected the phonetic differences to which their mothers' speech had alerted them (Kuhl et al., 1997).

Other investigators challenge the value of CDS. They contend that babies speak sooner and better if they hear and can respond to more complex adult speech. In fact, some researchers say, children discover the rules of language faster when they hear complex sentences that use these rules more often and in more ways (Gleitman, Newport, & Gleitman, 1984; Oshima-Takane, Goodz, & Derevensky, 1996). Nonetheless, infants themselves prefer to hear simplified speech. This preference is clear before age 1 month, and it does not seem to depend on any specific experience (Cooper & Aslin, 1990; Kuhl et al., 1997; Werker, Pegg, & McLeod, 1994).

code mixing Use of elements of two languages, sometimes in the same utterance, by young children in households where both languages are spoken.

code switching Changing one's speech to match the situation, as in people who are bilingual.

child-directed speech (CDS) Form of speech often used in talking to babies or toddlers; includes slow, simplified speech, a high-pitched tone, exaggerated vowel sounds, short words and sentences, and much repetition; also called *parentese.*

Preparing for Literacy: The Benefits of Reading Aloud

Most babies love to be read to, and the frequency with which parents or caregivers read to them, as well as the way they do it, can influence how well children speak and eventually how well and how soon they develop **literacy**—the ability to read and write.

Adults tend to have one of three styles of reading to children: the *describer style, comprehender style,* and or *performance-oriented style.* A *describer* focuses on describing what is going on in the pictures and inviting the child to do so ("What are the Mom and Dad having for breakfast?"). A *comprehender* encourages the child to look more deeply at the meaning of a story and to make inferences and predictions ("What do you think the lion will do now?"). A *performance-oriented* reader reads the story straight through, introducing the main themes beforehand and asking questions afterward.

An adult's read-aloud style is best tailored to the needs and skills of the child. In an experimental study of 50 4-year-olds in Dunedin, New Zealand, the describer style resulted in the greatest overall benefits for vocabulary and print skills, but the performance-oriented style was more beneficial for children who started out with large vocabularies (Reese & Cox, 1999).

A promising technique, similar to the describer style, is *dialogic,* or *shared, reading.* In this method (Whitehurst & Lonigan, 1998, p. 859) parents ask challenging, open-ended questions rather than those calling for a simple yes or no ("What is the cat doing?" instead of "Is the cat asleep?"). They follow up the child's answers with more questions, repeat and expand on what the child says, correct wrong answers and give alternative possibilities, help the child as needed, and give praise and encouragement. They encourage the child to relate a story to the child's experiences ("Have you ever seen a duck swimming? What did it look like?").

Children who are read to often, especially in this way, when they are ages 1 to 3 show better language skills at ages 2 to 5 and better reading comprehension at age 7 (Crain-Thoreson & Dale, 1992; Wells, 1985). However, dialogic reading does not come naturally to most parents, according to a study of 120 rural families with 2- and 3-year-olds. Small-group instruction with video increased parents' use of the method more than fourfold and had significant positive effects on children's vocabulary and language use (Huebner & Meltzoff, 2005).

literacy Ability to read and write.

Checkpoint ✓

Can you . . .

✔ Explain the importance of social interaction, and give at least three examples of how parents or caregivers help babies learn to talk?

✔ Assess the arguments for and against the value of child-directed speech (CDS)?

✔ Tell why reading aloud to children at an early age is beneficial, and describe an effective way of doing so?

Refocus

Thinking back to the information about "Doddy" Darwin in the Focus vignette at the beginning of this chapter,

- Which approach to cognitive development seems closest to the one Darwin took in observing and describing his son's development? Why?

- How might a behaviorist, a Piagetian, a psychometrician, an information-processing researcher, a cognitive neuroscientist,

and a social-contextual theorist attempt to study and explain the developments Darwin described?

- Did Doddy's early linguistic development seem more consistent with Skinner's theory of language development or Chomsky's? How does it illustrate the role of social interaction?

Social interaction in reading aloud, play, and other daily activities is a key to much of childhood development. Children call forth responses from the people around them and, in turn, react to those responses. In Chapter 8, we will look more closely at these bidirectional influences as we explore early psychosocial development.

Summary and Key Terms

Studying Cognitive Development: Six Approaches

Guidepost 1 What are six approaches to the study of cognitive development?

- Three classic approaches to the study of cognitive development are the behaviorist, psychometric, and Piagetian approaches.

- Three newer approaches are information processing, cognitive neuroscience, and social-contextual.

- All of these approaches can shed light on how early cognition develops.

  behaviorist approach (179)   psychometric approach (179) Piagetian approach (179)   information-processing approach (180) cognitive neuroscience approach (180)   social-contextual approach (180)

Behaviorist Approach: Basic Mechanics of Learning

Guidepost 2   How do infants learn, and how long can they remember?

- Two simple types of learning that behaviorists study are classical conditioning and operant conditioning.

  classical conditioning (180)   operant conditioning (180)

- Rovee-Collier's research suggests that infants' memory processes are much like those of adults, though this conclusion has been questioned. Infants' memories can be jogged by periodic reminders.

Psychometric Approach: Developmental and Intelligence Testing

Guidepost 3   Can infants' and toddlers' intelligence be measured, and how can it be improved?

- Psychometric tests measure factors presumed to make up intelligence.
- Developmental tests, such as the Bayley Scales of Infant and Toddler Development, can indicate current functioning but are generally poor predictors of later intelligence.
- Socioeconomic status, parenting practices, and the home environment may affect measured intelligence.
- If the home environment does not provide the necessary conditions that pave the way for cognitive competence, early intervention may be needed.

  intelligent behavior (182)   IQ (intelligence quotient) tests (182) Bayley Scales of Infant and Toddler Development (182)   Home Observation for Measurement of the Environment (HOME) (182) early intervention (184)

Piagetian Approach: The Sensorimotor Stage

Guidepost 4   How did Piaget describe infants' and toddlers' cognitive development, and how have his claims stood up?

- During Piaget's sensorimotor stage, infants' schemes become more elaborate. They progress from primary to secondary to tertiary circular reactions and finally to the development of representational ability, which makes possible deferred imitation, pretending, and problem solving.
- Object permanence develops gradually, according to Piaget.
- Research suggests that a number of abilities, including imitation and object permanence, develop earlier than Piaget described. He may have underestimated young infants' grasp of object permanence and their imitative abilities.

  sensorimotor stage (185)   schemes (185)   circular reactions (185) representational ability (187)   invisible imitation (188)   visible imitation (188)   deferred imitation (189)   elicited imitation (189)

object permanence (190)   A, not-B, error (190)   dual representation hypothesis (192)

Information-Processing Approach; Perceptions and Representations

Guidepost 5   How can we measure infants' ability to process information, and when do babies begin to think about characteristics of the physical world?

- Information-processing researchers measure mental processes through habituation and other signs of visual and perceptual abilities. Contrary to Piaget's ideas, such research suggests that representational ability is present virtually from birth.
- Indicators of the efficiency of infants' information processing, such as speed of habituation, tend to predict later intelligence.
- Such information-processing research techniques as habituation, novelty preference, and the violation-of-expectations method have yielded evidence that infants as young as 3½ to 5 months may have a rudimentary grasp of such Piagetian abilities as categorization, causality, object permanence, a sense of number, and an ability to reason about characteristics of the physical world. Some researchers suggest that infants may have innate learning mechanisms for acquiring such knowledge. However, the meaning of these findings is in dispute.

  habituation (192)   dishabituation (192)   visual preference (194) visual recognition memory (194)   cross-modal transfer (195) violation-of-expectations (198)

Cognitive Neuroscience Approach: The Brain's Cognitive Structures

Guidepost 6   What can brain research reveal about the development of cognitive skills?

- Explicit memory and implicit memory are located in different brain structures.
- Working memory emerges between ages 6 and 12 months.
- Neurological developments help explain the emergence of Piagetian skills and memory abilities.

  implicit memory (200)   explicit memory (200)   working memory (200)

Social-Contextual Approach: Learning From Interactions with Caregivers

Guidepost 7   How does social interaction with adults advance cognitive competence?

- Social interactions with adults contribute to cognitive competence through shared activities that help children learn skills, knowledge, and values important in their culture.

  guided participation (201)

Language Development

Guidepost 8   How do babies develop language, and what influences linguistic progress?

- The acquisition of language is an important aspect of cognitive development.

- Prelinguistic speech includes crying, cooing, babbling, and imitating language sounds. By 6 months, babies have learned the basic sounds of their language and have begun to link sound with meaning. Perception of categories of sounds in the native language may commit the neural circuitry to further learning in that language only.

- Before they say their first word, babies use gestures.

- The first word typically comes sometime between 10 and 14 months, initiating linguistic speech. A "naming explosion" typically occurs sometime between ages 16 and 24 months.

- The first brief sentences generally come between 18 and 24 months. By age 3, syntax and communicative abilities are fairly well developed.

- Early speech is characterized by simplification, underextending and overextending word meanings, and overregularizing rules.

- Two classic theoretical views about how children acquire language are learning theory and nativism. Today, most developmentalists hold that an inborn capacity to learn language may be activated or constrained by experience.

- Influences on language development include neural maturation and social interaction.

- Family characteristics, such as socioeconomic status, adult language use, and maternal responsiveness, affect a child's vocabulary development.

- Children who hear two languages at home generally learn both at the same rate as children who hear only one language, and they can use each language in appropriate circumstances.

- Child-directed speech (CDS) seems to have cognitive, emotional, and social benefits, and infants show a preference for it. However, some researchers dispute its value.

- Reading aloud to a child from an early age helps pave the way for literacy.

language (201)   **prelinguistic speech (202)**   **linguistic speech (204)**
holophrase (204)   **telegraphic speech (205)**   **syntax (205)**
nativism (206)   **language acquisition device (LAD) (206)**
code mixing (209)   **code switching (209)**
child-directed speech (CDS) (209)   **literacy (210)**

CHAPTER EIGHT

Psychosocial Development during the First Three Years

I'm like a child
trying to do everything
say everything
and be everything
all at once

—John Hartford, "Life Prayer," 1971

Focus *Mary Catherine Bateson, Anthropologist*

Mary Catherine
Bateson

Mary Catherine Bateson (b. 1939) is an anthropologist, the daughter of two famous anthropologists: Margaret Mead (refer back to Chapter 2 Focus) and Gregory Bateson, Mead's third husband and research partner. Hers was probably one of the most documented infancies on record—her mother taking notes, her father behind the camera. Margaret Mead's memoir, *Blackberry Winter* (1972), and Mary Catherine Bateson's *With a Daughter's Eye* (1984) together provide a rare and fascinating dual perspective on a child's first 3 years of life.

Cathy—Mead's only child—was born when her mother was 38 years old. Her parents divorced when Cathy was 11. Their work during World War II often necessitated long absences and separations. But during her infancy and toddlerhood, when they were still together, Cathy was the focus of their love and wholehearted attention. Her early recollections include sitting with her parents on a blanket outdoors, being read to on her mother's lap, and watching the two of them hold up their breakfast spoons to reflect the morning light, making a pair of "birds" flash across the walls for her amusement.

To avoid subjecting her to frustration, her parents tried to respond quickly to her needs. Mead arranged her professional commitments around breast-feeding and nursed "on demand," like the mothers in the island cultures she had studied.

Like their friend Erik Erikson, Mead and Bateson placed great importance on the development of trust. They never left Cathy in a strange place with a strange person; she always met a new caregiver in a familiar place. "Her warm responsiveness, her trustingness, and her outgoing interest in people and things . . . set the stage for her expectation that the world was

Sources of biographical information about Mary Catherine Bateson are Bateson (1984) and Mead (1972).

215

a friendly place" (Mead, 1972, p. 266). As an adult, Catherine observed that, during difficult periods in her life, she often found "resources of faith and strength, a foundation that must have been built in those [first] two years" (Bateson, 1984, p. 35). Yet, as Mead wrote, "How much was temperament? How much was felicitous accident? How much could be attributed to up-bringing? We may never know" (1972, p. 268).

Mead tried to avoid overprotectiveness and to let Cathy be herself. Catherine remembers her father pushing her swing so high that he could run under it. Later he taught her to climb tall pine trees, testing every branch for firmness and making sure that she could find her way back down, while her mother, watching, tried not to show her fear.

When Cathy was 2 and her parents' wartime travel increased, they merged their household with that of a friend and colleague, Lawrence Frank. The decision fit in with Mead's belief, gleaned from her studies, that children benefit from having multiple caregivers and learning to adapt to different situations.

The ménage in Frank's brownstone in Greenwich Village included his infant son and five older children. "Thus," Catherine writes, "I did not grow up in a nuclear family or as an only child, but as a member of a flexible and welcoming extended family . . . , in which five or six pairs of hands could be mobilized to shell peas or dry dishes." Her summertime memories are of a lakeside retreat in New Hampshire, where "each child was cared for by enough adults so that there need be no jealousy, where the garden bloomed and the evenings ended in song. . . . I was rich beyond other children . . . and yet there were all those partings. There were all those beloved people, yet often the people I wanted most were absent" (Bateson, 1984, pp. 38–39).

● ● ●

In Margaret Mead's and Mary Catherine Bateson's complementary memoirs, we can see how Mead put into practice the beliefs she had developed about child rearing, in part from memories of her own childhood and in part from observations of distant cultures. We see her seeking solutions to a problem that has become increasingly common: child care for children of working parents. And we see a bidirectionality of influence: how early experiences with parents help shape a child's development and how a child's needs can shape parents' lives.

This chapter is about the shift from the dependence of infancy to the independence of childhood. We first examine foundations of psychosocial development: emotions, temperament, and early experiences with parents. We consider Erikson's views about the development of trust and autonomy. We look at relationships with caregivers, at the emerging sense of self, and at the foundations of conscience. We explore relationships with siblings and other children and with grandparents. Finally, we consider the increasingly widespread impact of early day care.

After you have read and studied this chapter, you should be able to answer each of the Guidepost questions on the following page. Look for them again in the margins throughout the chapter, where they point to important concepts. To check your understanding of these Guideposts, review the end-of-chapter summary. Checkpoints located throughout the chapter will help you verify your understanding of what you have read.

Guideposts
for Study

1. When and how do emotions develop, and how do babies show them?

2. How do infants show temperamental differences, and how enduring are those differences?

3. How do infants gain trust in their world and form attachments, and how do infants and caregivers read each other's nonverbal signals?

4. When and how does the sense of self arise, and how do toddlers exercise autonomy and develop standards for socially acceptable behavior?

5. When and how do gender differences appear?

6. How do infants and toddlers interact with siblings and other children?

7. How do parental employment and early child care affect infants' and toddlers' development?

Foundations of Psychosocial Development

Guidepost 1

When and how do emotions develop, and how do babies show them?

Although babies share common patterns of development, they also—from the start—show distinct personalities, which reflect both inborn and environmental influences. From infancy on, personality development is intertwined with social relationships (Table 8-1).

Emotions

Emotions, such as sadness, joy, and fear, are subjective reactions to experience that are associated with physiological and behavioral changes (Sroufe, 1997). Fear, for example, is accompanied by a faster heartbeat and, often, by self-protective action. A person's characteristic pattern of emotional reactions begins to develop during infancy and is a basic element of personality. People differ in how often they feel a particular emotion, in the

emotions Subjective reactions to experience that are associated with physiological and behavioral changes.

Table 8-1	Highlights of Infants' and Toddlers' Psychosocial Development, Birth to 36 Months
Approximate Age, Months	**Characteristics**
0–3	Infants are open to stimulation. They begin to show interest and curiosity, and they smile readily at people.
3–6	Infants can anticipate what is about to happen and experience disappointment when it does not. They show this by becoming angry or acting warily. They smile, coo, and laugh often. This is a time of social awakening and early reciprocal exchanges between the baby and the caregiver.
6–9	Infants play "social games" and try to get responses from people. They "talk" to, touch, and cajole other babies to get them to respond. They express more differentiated emotions, showing joy, fear, anger, and surprise.
9–12	Infants are intensely preoccupied with their principal caregiver, may become afraid of strangers, and act subdued in new situations. By 1 year, they communicate emotions more clearly, showing moods, ambivalence, and gradations of feeling.
12–18	Toddlers explore their environment, using the people they are most attached to as a secure base. As they master the environment, they become more confident and more eager to assert themselves.
18–36	Toddlers sometimes become anxious because they now realize how much they are separating from their caregiver. They work out their awareness of their limitations in fantasy and in play and by identifying with adults.

Source: Adapted from Sroufe, 1979.

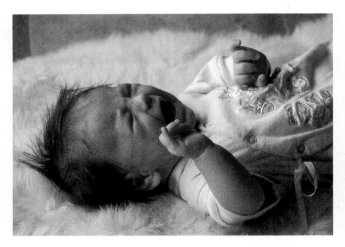

Crying enables this 7-week-old baby to communicate his needs. Parents generally learn to recognize whether their baby is crying because of hunger, anger, frustration, or pain.

An infant's earliest smiles are involuntary, but beginning at 1 month, smiles generally become more frequent and more social. This baby may be smiling at the sight of a parent or caregiver.

kinds of events that may produce it, in the physical manifestations they show, and in how they act as a result. Culture influences the way people feel about a situation and the way they show their emotions. For example, some Asian cultures, which stress social harmony, discourage expression of anger but place much importance on shame. The opposite is often true in American culture, which stresses self-expression, self-assertion, and self-esteem (Cole, Bruschi, & Tamang, 2002).

First Signs of Emotion

Newborns plainly show when they are unhappy. They let out piercing cries, flail their arms and legs, and stiffen their bodies. It is harder to tell when they are happy. During the 1st month, they become quiet at the sound of a human voice or when they are picked up, and they may smile when their hands are moved together to play pat-a-cake. As time goes by, infants respond more to people—smiling, cooing, reaching out, and eventually going to them.

These early signals or clues to babies' feelings are important indicators of development. When babies want or need something, they cry; when they feel sociable, they smile or laugh. When their messages bring a response, their sense of connection with other people grows. Their sense of control over their world grows, too, as they see that their cries bring help and comfort and that their smiles and laughter elicit smiles and laughter in return. They become more able to participate actively in regulating their states of arousal and their emotional life.

Crying Crying is the most powerful way—and sometimes the only way—infants can communicate their needs. Some research has distinguished four patterns of crying (Wolff, 1969): the basic *hunger cry* (a rhythmic cry, which is not always associated with hunger); the *angry cry* (a variation of the rhythmic cry, in which excess air is forced through the vocal cords); the *pain cry* (a sudden onset of loud crying without preliminary moaning, sometimes followed by holding the breath); and the *frustration cry* (two or three drawn-out cries, with no prolonged breath-holding) (Wood & Gustafson, 2001).

Some parents worry that picking up a crying baby will spoil the infant. In one study, delays in responding to fussing did seem to reduce fussing during the first 6 months, perhaps because the babies learned to deal with minor irritations on their own (Hubbard & van IJzendoorn, 1991). However, if parents wait until cries of distress escalate to shrieks of rage, it may become more difficult to soothe the baby; and such a pattern, if experienced repeatedly, may interfere with an infant's developing ability to regulate, or manage, his or her emotional state (R. A. Thompson, 1991). Ideally, the most developmentally sound approach may be the one Cathy Bateson's parents followed: to *prevent* distress, making soothing unnecessary.

Smiling and Laughing The earliest faint smiles occur spontaneously soon after birth, apparently as a result of subcortical nervous system activity. These involuntary smiles frequently appear during periods of REM sleep (refer back to Chapter 5). They become less frequent during the first 3 months as the cortex matures (Sroufe, 1997).

The earliest *waking* smiles may be elicited by mild sensations, such as gentle jiggling or blowing on the infant's skin. In the 2nd week, a baby may smile drowsily after a feeding. By the 3rd week, most infants begin to smile when they are alert and paying attention to a caregiver's nodding head and voice. At about 1 month, smiles generally become more frequent and more social. During the 2nd month, as visual recognition develops, babies smile more at visual stimuli, such as faces they know (Sroufe, 1997; Wolff, 1963).

At about the 4th month, infants laugh out loud when kissed on the stomach or tickled. As babies grow older, they become more actively engaged in mirthful exchanges. A 6-month-old may giggle in response to the mother making unusual sounds or appearing with a towel over her face; a 10-month-old may laughingly try to put the towel back on her face when it falls off. This change reflects cognitive development: By laughing at the unexpected, babies show that they know what to expect. By turning the tables, they show awareness that they can make things happen. Laughter also helps babies discharge tension, such as fear of a threatening object (Sroufe, 1997).

When Do Emotions Appear?

Identifying infants' emotions is a challenge because babies cannot tell us what they feel. Researchers disagree about how many emotions there are, when they arise, and how they should be defined and measured.

Carroll Izard and his colleagues have videotaped infants' facial expressions and have interpreted them as showing joy, sadness, interest, and fear, and to a lesser degree anger, surprise, and disgust (Izard, Huebner, Resser, McGinness, & Dougherty, 1980). Of course, we do not know that these babies actually had the feelings they were credited with, but their facial expressions were remarkably similar to adults' expressions when experiencing these emotions.

Facial expressions are not the only, or necessarily the best, index of infants' emotions; motor activity, body language, and physiological changes also are important indicators. An infant can be fearful without showing a "fear face"; the baby may show fear by turning away or averting the gaze, or by a faster heartbeat. Different indicators may point to different conclusions about the timing of emergence of specific emotions. In addition, this timetable shows a good deal of individual variation (Sroufe, 1997).

Basic Emotions Emotional development is an orderly process; complex emotions unfold from simpler ones. According to one model of emotional development (Lewis, 1997; Figure 8-1), babies soon after birth show signs of contentment, interest, and distress. These are diffuse, reflexive, mostly physiological responses to sensory stimulation or internal processes. During the next 6 months or so, these early emotional states differentiate into true emotions: joy, surprise, sadness, disgust, and last, anger and fear—reactions to events that have meaning for the infant. As we'll discuss in a subsequent section, the emergence of these basic, or primary, emotions is related to the biological clock of neurological maturation.

Emotions Involving the Self Two types of emotions involving the self are *self-conscious emotions* and *self-evaluating emotions*.

Self-conscious emotions, such as embarrassment, empathy, and envy, arise only after children have developed **self-awareness:** the cognitive understanding that they have a recognizable identity, separate and different from the rest of their world. This consciousness of self seems to emerge between 15 and 24 months. Self-awareness is necessary before children can be aware of being the focus of attention, identify with what other "selves" are feeling, or wish they had what someone else has.

By about age 3, having acquired self-awareness plus a good deal of knowledge about their society's accepted standards, rules, and goals, children become better able to evaluate their thoughts, plans, desires, and behavior against what is considered socially

self-conscious emotions
Emotions, such as embarrassment, empathy, and envy, that depend on self-awareness.

self-awareness Realization that one's existence and functioning are separate from those of other people and things.

Figure 8-1

Differentiation of emotions during the first 3 years. The primary, or basic, emotions emerge during the first 6 months or so; the self-conscious emotions develop around 18 to 24 months, as a result of the emergence of self-awareness (consciousness of self) together with accumulation of knowledge about societal standards and rules.

Note: There are two kinds of embarrassment. The earlier kind does not involve evaluation of behavior and may simply be a response to being singled out as the object of attention. The second kind, evaluative embarrassment, which emerges during the 3rd year, is a mild form of shame.

Source: Adapted from Lewis, 1997, Fig. 1, p. 120.

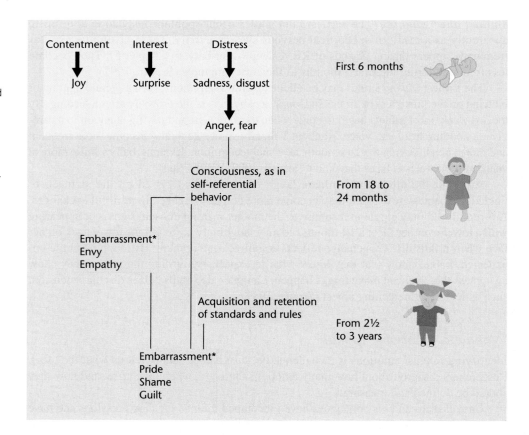

self-evaluative emotions
Emotions, such as pride, shame, and guilt, that depend on both self-awareness and knowledge of socially accepted standards of behavior.

empathy Ability to put oneself in another person's place and feel what the other person feels.

social cognition Ability to understand that other people have mental states and to gauge their feelings and intentions.

egocentrism Piaget's term for inability to consider another person's point of view; a characteristic of young children's thought.

appropriate. Only then can they demonstrate the **self-evaluative emotions** of pride, guilt, and shame (Lewis, 1995, 1997, 1998).

Guilt and shame are distinct emotions, even though both may be responses to wrongdoing. Children who fail to live up to behavioral standards may feel guilty (that is, regret their behavior), but they do not necessarily feel a lack of self-worth, as when they feel ashamed. Their focus is on a bad *act*, not a bad *self* (Eisenberg, 2000).

Empathy: Feeling What Others Feel **Empathy**—the ability to "put oneself in another person's place" and feel what that person feels, or would be expected to feel, in a particular situation—is thought to arise during the 2nd year. Like guilt, empathy increases with age (Eisenberg, 2000; Eisenberg & Fabes, 1998).

Empathy depends on **social cognition,** the cognitive ability to understand that others have mental states and to gauge their feelings and intentions. Piaget believed that **egocentrism** (inability to see another person's point of view) delays the development of this ability until the concrete operational stage of middle childhood. Other research suggests that social cognition begins much earlier. In one study, 9-month-olds (but not 6-month-olds) reacted differently to a person who was unwilling to give them a toy than to a person who tried to give them a toy but accidentally dropped it. This finding suggests that the older infants had gained some understanding of another person's intentions (Behne, Carpenter, Call, & Tomasello, 2005).

Brain Growth and Emotional Development

The development of the brain after birth is related to changes in emotional life. This is a bidirectional process: Emotional experiences are affected by brain development and also can have long-lasting effects on the structure of the brain (Mlot, 1998; Sroufe, 1997).

Four apparent shifts in brain organization roughly correspond to changes in emotional processing (Schore, 1994; Sroufe, 1997; refer back to Figure 4-6). During the first 3 months, differentiation of basic emotions begins as the *cerebral cortex* becomes functional, bringing cognitive perceptions into play. REM sleep and reflexive behavior, including the spontaneous neonatal smile, diminish.

The second shift occurs around 9 or 10 months, when the *frontal lobes* begin to interact with the *limbic system,* a seat of emotional reactions. At the same time, limbic structures such as the *hippocampus* become larger and more adultlike. Connections between the frontal cortex and the *hypothalamus* and limbic system, which process sensory information, may facilitate the relationship between the cognitive and emotional spheres. As these connections become denser and more elaborate, an infant can experience and interpret emotions at the same time.

The third shift takes place during the 2nd year, when infants develop self-awareness, self-conscious emotions, and a greater capacity for regulating their emotions and activities. These changes, which may be related to myelination of the frontal lobes, are accompanied by greater physical mobility and exploratory behavior.

The fourth shift occurs around age 3, when hormonal changes in the autonomic (involuntary) nervous system coincide with the emergence of evaluative emotions. Underlying the development of such emotions as shame may be a shift away from dominance by the *sympathetic system,* the part of the autonomic system that prepares the body for action, and the maturation of the *parasympathetic system,* the part of the autonomic system that is involved in excretion and sexual excitation.

Neurological factors also may play a part in temperamental differences (Mlot, 1998), the topic to which we turn next.

Temperament

Temperament is sometimes defined as a person's characteristic, biologically based way of approaching and reacting to people and situations. Temperament has been described as the *how* of behavior: not *what* people do, but *how* they go about doing it (Thomas & Chess, 1977). Two toddlers, for example, may be equally able to dress themselves and may be equally motivated, but one may do it more quickly than the other, be more willing to put on a new outfit, and be less distracted if the cat jumps on the bed. Some researchers look at temperament more broadly. A child may not act the same way in all situations. Also, temperament may affect, not only the way children approach and react to the outside world, but the way they regulate their mental, emotional, and behavioral functioning (Rothbart, Ahadi, & Evans, 2000).

Temperament has an emotional dimension; but unlike emotions such as fear, excitement, and boredom, which come and go, temperament is relatively consistent and enduring. Individual differences in temperament, which are thought to derive from a person's basic biological makeup, form the core of the developing personality.

Studying Temperamental Patterns: The New York Longitudinal Study

In the New York Longitudinal Study (NYLS), a pioneering study on temperament, researchers followed 133 infants into adulthood. The researchers looked at how active the children were; how regular they were in hunger, sleep, and bowel habits; how readily they accepted new people and situations; how they adapted to changes in routine; how sensitive they were to noise, bright lights, and other sensory stimuli; how intensely they responded; whether their mood tended to be pleasant, joyful, and friendly or unpleasant, unhappy, and unfriendly; and whether they persisted at tasks or were easily distracted (A. Thomas, Chess, & Birch, 1968).

Almost two-thirds of the children fell into one of three categories (Table 8-2). Forty percent were **easy children:** generally happy, rhythmic in biological functioning, and accepting of new experiences. This is how Margaret Mead described the infant Cathy. Ten percent were what the researchers called **difficult children:** more irritable and harder to please, irregular in biological rhythms, and more intense in expressing emotion. Fifteen percent were **slow-to-warm-up children:** mild but slow to adapt to new people and situations (A. Thomas & Chess, 1977, 1984).

Many children (including 35 percent of the NYLS sample) do not fit neatly into any of these three groups. A baby may eat and sleep regularly but be afraid of strangers. A child may be easy most of the time, but not always. Another child may warm up slowly to new

Checkpoint ✔

Can you . . .

✔ Explain why infants' emotions are difficult to study?

✔ Explain the significance of patterns of crying, smiling, and laughing?

✔ Trace a proposed sequence of emergence of the basic, self-conscious, and evaluative emotions, and explain its connection with cognitive and neurological development?

Guidepost 2

How do infants show temperamental differences, and how enduring are those differences?

temperament Characteristic disposition, or style of approaching and reacting to situations.

easy children Children with a generally happy temperament, regular biological rhythms, and a readiness to accept new experiences.

difficult children Children with irritable temperament, irregular biological rhythms, and intense emotional responses.

slow-to-warm-up children Children whose temperament is generally mild but who are hesitant about accepting new experiences.

Table 8-2	Three Temperamental Patterns (according to the New York Longitudinal Study)	
Easy Child	**Difficult Child**	**Slow-to-Warm-Up Child**
Has moods of mild to moderate intensity, usually positive.	Displays intense and frequently negative moods; cries often and loudly; also laughs loudly.	Has mildly intense reactions, both positive and negative.
Responds well to novelty and change.	Responds poorly to novelty and change.	Responds slowly to novelty and change.
Quickly develops regular sleep and feeding schedules.	Sleeps and eats irregularly.	Sleeps and eats more regularly than the difficult child, less regularly than the easy child.
Takes to new foods easily.	Accepts new foods slowly.	Shows mildly negative initial response to new stimuli (a first encounter with a new person, place, or situation).
Smiles at strangers.	Is suspicious of strangers.	
Adapts easily to new situations.	Adapts slowly to new situations.	
Accepts most frustrations with little fuss.	Reacts to frustration with tantrums.	
Adapts quickly to new routines and rules of new games.	Adjusts slowly to new routines.	Gradually develops liking for new stimuli after repeated, unpressured exposures.

Source: Adapted from A. Thomas & Chess, "Genesis and evolution of behavioral disorders: From infancy to early adult life." *American Journal of Psychiatry,* 141 (1) 1984, pp. 1–9. Copyright © 1984 by the American Psychiatric Association. Reproduced with permission.

Seven-month-old Daniel's ready smile and willingness to try a new food are signs of an easy temperament.

foods but adapt quickly to new babysitters (A. Thomas & Chess, 1984). A child may laugh intensely but not show intense frustration, and a child with rhythmic toilet habits may show irregular sleeping patterns (Rothbart et al., 2000). All these variations are normal.

How Is Temperament Measured?

Because the complex interviewing and scoring procedures used in the NYLS are cumbersome, many researchers use short-form questionnaires. A parental self-report instrument, the Rothbart Infant Behavior Questionnaire (IBQ) (Gartstein & Rothbart, 2003; Rothbart et al., 2000) focuses on several dimensions of infant temperament similar to those in the NYLS: activity level, positive emotion (smiling and laughing), fear, frustration, soothability, and duration of orienting (a combination of distractibility and attention span) as well as such additional factors as intensity of pleasure, perceptual sensitivity, and attentional shifting. Parents rate their infants with regard to recent concrete events and behaviors ("How often during the past week did the baby smile or laugh when given a toy?" rather than "Does the baby respond positively to new events?").

Although parental ratings are the most commonly used measures of children's temperament, their validity is in question. Studies of twins have found that parents tend to rate a child's temperament by comparison with other children in the family—for example, labeling one child inactive in contrast to a more active sibling (Saudino, 2003a). Still, observations by researchers may reflect biases as well (Seifer, 2003). Parents see their children in a variety of day-to-day situations, whereas a laboratory observer sees only how the child reacts to particular standardized situations. Thus, a combination of methods may provide a more accurate picture of how temperament affects child development (Rothbart & Hwang, 2002; Saudino, 2003a, 2003b).

How Stable Is Temperament?

Temperament appears to be largely inborn, probably hereditary (Braungart, Plomin, DeFries, & Fulker, 1992; Emde et al., 1992; Schmitz et al., 1996; A. Thomas & Chess, 1977, 1984), and fairly stable. Newborn babies show different patterns of sleeping, fussing, and activity, and these differences tend to persist to some degree (Korner, 1996; Korner et al., 1985). Studies using the IBQ have found strong links between infant temperament and childhood personality at age 7 (Rothbart et al., 2000, 2001). Other researchers, using temperamental types similar to those of the NYLS, have found that temperament at age 3 closely predicts personality at ages 18 and 21 (Caspi, 2000; Caspi & Silva, 1995; Newman, Caspi, Moffitt, & Silva, 1997).

That does not mean temperament is fully formed at birth. Temperament develops as various emotions and self-regulatory capacities appear (Rothbart et al., 2000) and can change in response to parental treatment and other life experiences (Belsky, Fish, & Isabella, 1991; Kagan & Snidman, 2004). As Margaret Mead observed, temperament may be affected by culturally influenced child-raising practices. Infants in Malaysia, an island group in Southeast Asia, tend to be less adaptable, more wary of new experiences, and more readily responsive to stimuli than U.S. babies. This may be because Malay parents do not often expose young children to situations that require adaptability, and they encourage infants to be acutely aware of sensations, such as the need for a diaper change (Banks, 1989).

Temperament and Adjustment: Goodness of Fit

According to the NYLS, the key to healthy adjustment is **goodness of fit**—the match between a child's temperament and the environmental demands and constraints the child must deal with. If a very active child is expected to sit still for long periods, if a slow-to-warm-up child is constantly pushed into new situations, or if a persistent child is constantly taken away from absorbing projects, tensions may occur.

goodness of fit Appropriateness of environmental demands and constraints to a child's temperament.

Caregivers' responses to their children may reflect the amount of control the caregivers think they have over a child's behavior. In a home observation, parents who saw themselves as having little control over their 12-month-olds were more likely than other parents to play directively with their babies—urging, reminding, restraining, questioning, and correcting them; and mothers who felt and acted this way were more likely to consider their infants "difficult" (Guzell & Vernon-Feagans, 2004).

When caregivers recognize that a child acts in a certain way, not out of willfulness, laziness, stupidity, or spite, but largely because of inborn temperament, they may be less likely to feel guilty, anxious, or hostile, to feel a loss of control, or to be rigid or impatient. They can anticipate the child's reactions and help the child adapt—for example, by giving early warnings of the need to stop an activity or, as Mead and Bateson did, by gradually introducing a child to new situations.

Shyness and Boldness: Influences of Biology and Culture

As we have mentioned, temperament seems to have a biological basis. In longitudinal research with about 500 children starting in infancy, Jerome Kagan and his colleagues have studied an aspect of temperament called *inhibition to the unfamiliar,* or shyness, which has to do with how boldly or cautiously the child approaches unfamiliar objects and situations and which is associated with certain biological characteristics.

When presented at 4 months with a series of new stimuli, about 20 percent of the infants cried, pumped their arms and legs, and sometimes arched their backs; this group were called "high-reactive." About 40 percent showed little distress or motor activity and were more likely to smile spontaneously; they were called "low-reactive." The rest either showed little motor activity but became very irritable or showed vigorous motor activity but rarely cried. The researchers hypothesized that these differences might be related to the amygdala, a brain organ that detects and reacts to unfamiliar events and is involved in emotional reactions. High-reactive children may be born with a usually excitable amygdala (Kagan & Snidman, 2004).

At 4½ years, in a play session with two unfamiliar children of the same age and sex, children who had been identified as high-reactive in infancy were more likely to be shy, quiet, and timid, whereas low-reactive children were more likely to be sociable and talkative (Kagan & Snidman, 2004). In addition, the shyer children showed higher and less variable heart rates than bolder children, and the pupils of their eyes dilated more. The boldest children (about 10 to 15 percent) tended to be energetic and spontaneous and to have low heart rates (Arcus & Kagan, 1995).

Children who had been identified as inhibited or uninhibited seemed to maintain these patterns to some degree during childhood (Kagan, 1997; Kagan & Snidman, 1991a, 1991b), along with specific differences in physiological characteristics. High-reactive (inhibited)

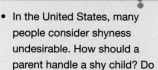

What's your view

- In the United States, many people consider shyness undesirable. How should a parent handle a shy child? Do you think it is best to accept the child's temperament or try to change it?

children were more likely to have a thin body build, narrow face, and blue eyes, whereas low-reactive (uninhibited) children were taller, heavier, and more often brown-eyed. It may be that the genes that contribute to reactivity and timid or bold behavior also influence body size and eye color (Kagan & Snidman, 2004).

Behavioral differences between these two types of children tended to smoothe out by early adolescence, even though the physiological distinctions remained (Woodward et al., 2001). At their last assessment, at about age 11, about 33 percent of both high- and low-reactives behaved consistent with their infant temperament, but 16 percent of each group did not. However, less than 5 percent of each group developed the behavioral features of the other type. For example, some high-reactive children no longer seemed extremely shy, but they still did not show the relaxed spontaneity characteristic of low-reactives (Kagan & Snidman, 2004).

These findings suggest, again, that experience can moderate or accentuate early tendencies. Male toddlers who were inclined to be fearful and shy were more likely to remain so at age 3 if their parents were highly accepting of the child's reactions. If parents encouraged their sons to venture into new situations, the boys tended to become less inhibited (Park, Belsky, Putnam, & Crnic, 1997). Other environmental influences, such as birth order, race/ethnicity, culture, relationships with teachers and peers, and unpredictable events also can reinforce or soften a child's original temperamental bias (Kagan & Snidman, 2004).

Developmental Issues in Infancy

How does a dependent newborn, with a limited emotional repertoire and pressing physical needs, become a child with complex feelings and the abilities to understand and control them? Much of this development revolves around issues regarding relationships with caregivers.

Developing Trust

For a far longer period than the young of other mammals, human babies are dependent on other people for food, for protection, and for their very lives. How do they come to trust that their needs will be met? According to Erikson (1950), early experiences are the key.

The first stage in psychosocial development that Erikson identified (refer back to Table 2-2 in Chapter 2) is **basic trust versus basic mistrust.** This stage begins in infancy and continues until about 18 months. In these early months, babies develop a sense of the reliability of the people and objects in their world. They need to develop a balance between trust (which lets them form intimate relationships) and mistrust (which enables them to protect themselves). If trust predominates, as it should, children develop the virtue, or strength, of *hope:* the belief that they can fulfill their needs and obtain their desires (Erikson, 1982). If mistrust predominates, children will view the world as unfriendly and unpredictable and will have trouble forming relationships.

The critical element in developing trust is sensitive, responsive, consistent caregiving. Erikson saw the feeding situation as the setting for establishing the right mix of trust and mistrust. Can the baby count on being fed when hungry, and can the baby therefore trust the mother as a representative of the world? Trust enables an infant to let the mother out of sight "because she has become an inner certainty as well as an outer predictability" (Erikson, 1950, p. 247). This inner trust, in Cathy Bateson, may have formed a solid foundation for more difficult periods ahead.

Developing Attachments

Attachment is a reciprocal, enduring emotional tie between an infant and a caregiver, each of whom contributes to the quality of the relationship. From an evolutionary point of view, attachments have adaptive value for babies, ensuring that their psychosocial as well as physical needs will be met (MacDonald, 1998). According to ethological theory (see

---

Checkpoint ✔

Can you . . .

✔ List and describe nine aspects and three patterns of temperament identified by the New York Longitudinal Study?

✔ Assess evidence for the stability of temperament?

✔ Discuss how temperament can affect adjustment, and explain the importance of goodness of fit?

✔ Give evidence of biological influences on temperament and of the role of parental handling?

Guidepost 3

How do infants gain trust in their world and form attachments, and how do infants and caregivers read each other's nonverbal signals?

---

basic trust versus basic mistrust Erikson's first stage in psychosocial development, in which infants develop a sense of the reliability of people and objects.

Checkpoint ✔

Can you . . .

✔ Explain the importance of basic trust, and identify the critical element in its development?

---

attachment Reciprocal, enduring tie between two people—especially between infant and caregiver—each of whom contributes to the quality of the relationship.

Chapter 2), infants and parents are biologically predisposed to become attached to each other, and attachment promotes a baby's survival.

Studying Patterns of Attachment

The study of attachment owes much to the ethologist John Bowlby (1951), a pioneer in the study of bonding in animals. From his animal studies and from observations of disturbed children in a London psychoanalytic clinic, Bowlby became convinced of the importance of the mother-baby bond and warned against separating mother and baby without providing good substitute care. Mary Ainsworth (1967), a student of Bowlby's in the early 1950s, went on to study attachment in African babies in Uganda through naturalistic observation in their homes. Ainsworth later devised the **Strange Situation,** a now-classic laboratory-based technique designed to assess attachment patterns between an infant and an adult. Typically, the adult is the mother (though other adults have taken part as well), and the infant is 10 to 24 months old.

The Strange Situation consists of a sequence of eight episodes, which takes less than half an hour. During that time, the mother twice leaves the baby in an unfamiliar room, the first time with a stranger. The second time she leaves the baby alone, and the stranger comes back before the mother does. The mother then encourages the baby to explore and play again and gives comfort if the baby seems to need it (Ainsworth, Blehar, Waters, & Wall, 1978). Of particular concern is the baby's response each time the mother returns.

When Ainsworth and her colleagues observed 1-year-olds in the Strange Situation and at home, they found three main patterns of attachment. These are *secure* (the most common category, into which about 60 to 75 percent of low-risk North American babies fall) and two forms of anxious, or insecure, attachment: *avoidant* (15 to 25 percent) and *ambivalent, or resistant* (10 to 15 percent) (Vondra & Barnett, 1999).

Babies with **secure attachment** cry or protest when the mother leaves and greet her happily when she returns. They use her as secure base, leaving her to go off and explore but returning occasionally for reassurance. They are usually cooperative and relatively free of anger. Babies with **avoidant attachment** rarely cry when the mother leaves, and they avoid her on her return. They tend to be angry and do not reach out in time of need. They dislike being held but dislike being put down even more. Babies with **ambivalent (resistant) attachment** become anxious even before the mother leaves and are very upset when she goes out. When she returns, they show their ambivalence by seeking contact with her while at the same time resisting it by kicking or squirming. Resistant babies do little exploration and are hard to comfort.

These three attachment *patterns* are universal in all cultures in which they have been studied—cultures as different as those in Africa, China, and Israel—though the percentage of infants in each category varies (van IJzendoorn & Kroonenberg, 1988; van IJzendoorn & Sagi, 1999). Attachment *behaviors,* however, vary across cultures. Among the Gusii of East Africa, on the western edge of Kenya, infants are greeted with handshakes, and Gusii infants reach out for a parent's hand much as Western infants cuddle up for a hug (van IJzendoorn & Sagi, 1999).

Other research (Main & Solomon, 1986) identified a fourth pattern, **disorganized-disoriented attachment,** which may be the least secure. Babies with the disorganized pattern seem to lack a cohesive strategy to deal with the stress of the Strange Situation. Instead, they show contradictory, repetitive, or misdirected behaviors (seeking closeness to the stranger instead of the mother). They may greet the mother brightly when she returns but then turn away or approach without looking at her. They seem confused and afraid. It is most likely to occur in babies whose mothers are insensitive, intrusive, or abusive or have suffered unresolved loss. The child's temperament does not seem to be a factor (Carlson, 1998; van IJzendoorn et al., 1999).

Disorganized attachment is thought to occur in at least 10 percent of low-risk infants but in much higher proportions in certain at-risk populations, such as premature children, those with autism or Down syndrome, and those whose mothers abuse alcohol or drugs (Vondra & Barnett, 1999). This attachment pattern seems to be a risk factor for later behavioral problems, especially aggressive conduct (van IJzendoorn et al., 1999).

Table 8-3	Atatchment Behaviors in the Strange Situation
Attachment Classification	**Behavior**
Secure	Gloria plays and explores freely when her mother is nearby. She responds enthusiastically when her mother returns.
Avoidant	When Sam's mother returns, Sam does not make eye contact or greet her. It is almost as if he has not noticed her return.
Ambivalent (Resistant)	James hovers close to his mother during much of the Strange Situation, but he does not greet her positively or enthusiastically during the reunion episode. Instead, he is angry and upset.
Disorganized-Disoriented	Erica responds to the Strange Situation with inconsistent, contradictory behavior. She seems to fall apart, overwhelmed by the stress.

Source: Based on Thompson, 1998, pp. 37–39.

Contrary to Ainsworth's original findings, babies seem to develop attachments to both parents at about the same time, and security of attachment to father and mother is usually quite similar, as it seems to have been with Cathy Bateson (Fox, Kimmerly, & Schafer, 1991). Table 8-3 describes how babies with each of the four patterns of attachment react to the Strange Situation.

How Attachment Is Established

On the basis of a baby's interactions with the mother, proposed Ainsworth and Bowlby, the baby builds a working model of what can be expected from her. As long as the mother continues to act the same way, the model holds up. If her behavior changes—not just once or twice but repeatedly—the baby may revise the model, and security of attachment may change.

A baby's working model of attachment is related to Erikson's concept of basic trust. (Margaret Mead and Gregory Bateson's success as new parents reflected their grasp of this concept.) Secure attachment reflects trust; insecure attachment, mistrust. Securely attached babies have learned to trust not only their caregivers but their own ability to get what they need. Thus, babies who cry a lot and whose mothers respond by soothing them tend to be securely attached (Del Carmen, Pedersen, Huffman, & Bryan, 1993). Mothers of securely attached infants and toddlers tend to be sensitive and responsive (Ainsworth et al., 1978; Braungart-Rieker et al., 2001; De Wolff & van IJzendoorn, 1997; Isabella, 1993; NICHD Early Child Care Research Network, 1997a). Equally important are mutual interaction, stimulation, a positive attitude, warmth and acceptance, and emotional support (De Wolff & van IJzendoorn, 1997; Lundy, 2003).

In a prospective longitudinal study of South African infants at 2 and 18 months, both early and later aspects of the mother-infant relationship influenced security of attachment. Mothers whose infants were insecurely attached at 18 months tended to have been remote (detached) and intrusive or coercive when the infants were 2 months old and to be insensitive and intrusive or coercive when the infants were 18 months. Despite the extreme poverty in which these families lived and the legacy of the apartheid system, an official policy of racial segregation that lasted until the early 1990s, nearly 62 percent of the infants were judged secure, while almost 26 percent were rated as disorganized (Tomlinson, Cooper, & Murray, 2005). In contrast, among institutionalized infants and toddlers in Bucharest, Romania, more than 65 percent were classified as disorganized and only about 19 percent as secure (Zeanah, Smyke, Koga, & Carlson, 2005).

Alternative Methods to Study Attachment

Although much research on attachment has been based on the Strange Situation, some investigators have questioned its validity. The Strange Situation *is* strange; it is also artificial. It asks mothers not to initiate interaction, exposes babies to repeated comings and goings

Diane's sensitivity to Anna's needs contributes to the development of Anna's sense of basic trust— her ability to rely on the people and things in her world. Trust is necessary, according to Erikson, for children to form intimate relationships.

of adults, and expects the infants to pay attention to them. Also, the Strange Situation may be less valid in some non-Western cultures. Research on Japanese infants, who are less commonly separated from their mothers than U.S. babies, showed high rates of resistant attachment, which may reflect the extreme stressfulness of the Strange Situation for these babies (Miyake, Chen, & Campos, 1985).

Because attachment influences a wider range of behaviors than are seen in the Strange Situation, some researchers have begun to supplement it with methods that enable them to study children in natural settings. The Waters and Deane (1985) Attachment Q-set (AQS) has mothers or other home observers sort a set of descriptive words or phrases ("cries a lot"; "tends to cling") into categories ranging from most to least characteristic of the child and then compare these descriptions with expert descriptions of the prototypical secure child. An analysis of 139 studies found the observer version (but not the maternal report version) a valid measure of attachment security, correlating well with results from the Strange Situation and with measures of maternal sensitivity. The AQS also seems to have cross-cultural validity (van IJzendoorn, Vereijken, Bakermans-Kranenburg, & Riksen-Walraven, 2004). In a study using the AQS, mothers in China, Colombia, Germany, Israel, Japan, Norway, and the United States decribed their children as behaving more like than unlike the "most secure child." Furthermore, the mothers' descriptions of "secure-base" be-havior were about as similar across cultures as within a culture. These findings suggest that the tendency to use the mother as a secure base is universal, though it may take somewhat varied forms (Posada et al., 1995).

The Role of Temperament

How much influence does temperament exert on attachment and in what ways? Findings vary (Susman-Stillman, Kalkoske, Egeland, & Waldman, 1996; Vaughn et al., 1992). In a study of 6- to 12-month-olds and their families, both a mother's sensitivity and her baby's temperament influenced attachment patterns (Seifer, Schiller, Sameroff, Resnick, & Riordan, 1996). Neurological or physiological conditions may underlie temperamental differences in attachment. For example, variability in heart rate is associated with irritability, and heart rate seems to vary more in insecurely attached infants (Izard, Porges, et al., 1991).

A baby's temperament may have not only a direct impact on attachment but also an in-direct impact through its effect on the parents. In a series of studies in the Netherlands (van den Boom, 1989, 1994), 15-day-old infants classified as irritable were much more likely than nonirritable infants to be insecurely (usually avoidantly) attached at 1 year. However,

This baby is showing separation anxiety about her parents' leaving her with a baby-sitter. Separation anxiety is common from 6 to 12 months.

stranger anxiety Wariness of strange people and places, shown by some infants from age 6 to 12 months.

separation anxiety Distress shown by someone, typically an infant, when a familiar caregiver leaves.

irritable infants whose mothers received home visits, with instruction on how to soothe their babies, were as likely to be rated as securely attached as the nonirritable infants. Thus, irritability on an infant's part may prevent the development of secure attachment but not if the mother has the skills to cope with the baby's temperament (Rothbart et al., 2000). Goodness of fit between parent and child may well be a key to understanding security of attachment.

Stranger Anxiety and Separation Anxiety

Sophie used to be a friendly baby, smiling at strangers and going to them, continuing to coo happily as long as someone—anyone—was around. Now, at 8 months, she turns away when a new person approaches and howls when her parents try to leave her with a babysitter. Sophie is experiencing both **stranger anxiety,** wariness of a person she does not know, and **separation anxiety,** distress when a familiar caregiver leaves her.

Stranger anxiety and separation anxiety used to be considered emotional and cognitive milestones of the second half of infancy, reflecting attachment to the mother. However, newer research suggests that although stranger anxiety and separation anxiety are fairly typical, they are not universal. Whether a baby cries when a parent leaves or when someone new approaches may say more about the baby's temperament or life circumstances than about security of attachment (R. J. Davidson & Fox, 1989).

Babies rarely react negatively to strangers before age 6 months, commonly do so by 8 or 9 months, and do so more and more throughout the rest of the first year (Sroufe, 1997). This change may reflect cognitive development. Sophie's stranger anxiety involves memory for faces, the ability to compare the stranger's appearance with her mother's, and perhaps the recollection of situations in which she has been left with a stranger. If Sophie is allowed to get used to the stranger gradually in a familiar setting, she may react more positively (Lewis, 1997; Sroufe, 1997). (Remember, Margaret Mead and Gregory Bateson made sure that Cathy always met a new caregiver in a familiar place.)

Separation anxiety may be due not so much to the separation itself as to the quality of substitute care. When substitute caregivers are warm and responsive and play with 9-month-olds *before* they cry, the babies cry less than when they are with less responsive caregivers (Gunnar, Larson, Hertsgaard, Harris, & Brodersen, 1992).

Stability of care is also important. Pioneering work by René Spitz (1945, 1946) on institutionalized children emphasizes the need for substitute care to be as close as possible to good mothering. Research has underlined the value of continuity and consistency in caregiving, so children can form early emotional bonds with their caregivers. As Mead observed in southeast island cultures, bonds can be formed with multiple caregivers, as long as the caregiving situation is stable.

Today, neither intense fear of strangers nor intense protest when the mother leaves is considered to be a sign of secure attachment. Researchers measure attachment more by what happens when the mother returns than by how many tears the baby sheds when she leaves.

Long-Term Effects of Attachment

As attachment theory proposes, security of attachment seems to affect emotional, social, and cognitive competence (van IJzendoorn & Sagi, 1997). The more secure a child's attachment to a nurturing adult, the easier it seems to be for the child to develop good relationships with others.

If children, as infants, had a secure base and could count on parents' or caregivers' responsiveness, they are likely to feel confident enough to be actively engaged in their world (Jacobsen & Hofmann, 1997). In a study of seventy 15-month-olds, those who were securely attached to their mothers, as measured by the Strange Situation, showed less stress in adapting to child care than did insecurely attached toddlers (Ahnert, Gunnar, Lamb, & Barthel, 2004).

Securely attached toddlers tend to have larger, more varied, vocabularies than those who are insecurely attached (Meins, 1998). They have more positive interactions with peers, and their friendly overtures are more likely to be accepted (Fagot, 1997). Insecurely attached toddlers tend to show more fear, distress, and anger, whereas securely attached children are more joyful (Kochanska, 2001).

Between ages 3 and 5, securely attached children are likely to be more curious, competent, empathic, resilient, and self-confident, to get along better with other children; and to form closer friendships than children who were insecurely attached as infants (Arend, Gove, & Sroufe, 1979; Elicker et al., 1992; J. L. Jacobson & Wille, 1986; Waters, Wippman, & Sroufe, 1979; Youngblade & Belsky, 1992). They interact more positively with parents, preschool teachers, and peers and are better able to resolve conflicts (Elicker et al., 1992). They tend to have a more positive self-image (Elicker et al., 1992; Verschueren, Marcoen, & Schoefs, 1996).

Their advantages continue. In a French-Canadian laboratory observation, attachment patterns and the emotional quality of 6-year-olds' interactions with their mothers predicted the strength of the children's communicative skills, cognitive engagement, and mastery motivation at age 8 (Moss & St-Laurent, 2001).

Secure attachment seems to prepare children for the intimacy of friendship (Carlson, Sroufe, & Egeland, 2004). In middle childhood and adolescence, securely attached children (at least in Western cultures, where most studies have been done) tend to have the closest, most stable friendships (Schneider, Atkinson, & Tardif, 2001; Sroufe, Carlson, & Shulman, 1993).

Insecurely attached children, in contrast, often have inhibitions and negative emotions in toddlerhood, hostility toward other children at age 5, and dependency during the school years (Calkins & Fox, 1992; Kochanska, 2001; Lyons-Ruth, Alpern, & Repacholi, 1993; Sroufe, Carlson, et al., 1993). Those with disorganized attachment tend to have behavior problems at all levels of schooling and psychiatric disorders at age 17 (Carlson, 1998).

In a longitudinal study of 1,364 families with 1-month-old infants, children who were avoidantly attached at 15 months tended to be rated by their mothers as less socially competent than secure children and by their teachers as more aggressive or anxious during the preschool and school-age years. However, effects of parenting on the children's behavior during these years were more important than early attachment. Insecure or disorganized children whose parenting had improved were less aggressive in school than those whose parenting did not improve or got worse. Secure children, however, were relatively immune to parenting that became less sensitive, perhaps because their early working models buoyed them up even under changed conditions. This study suggests that the continuity generally found between attachment and later behavior can be explained by continuity in the home environment (NICHD Early Child Care Research Network, 2006b).

Intergenerational Transmission of Attachment Patterns

The *Adult Attachment Interview (AAI)* (George, Kaplan, & Main, 1985; Main, 1995; Main, Kaplan, & Cassidy, 1985) is a semistructured interview that asks adults to recall and interpret feelings and experiences related to their childhood attachments. Studies using the AAI have found that the clarity, coherence, and consistency of the responses reliably predict the security with which the respondent's child will be attached (van IJzendoorn, 1995).

The way adults recall early experiences with parents or caregivers affects their emotional well-being and may influence the way they respond to their children (Adam, Gunnar, & Tanaka, 2004; Dozier, Stovall, Albus, & Bates, 2001; Pesonen, Raïkkönen, Keltikangas-Järvinen, Strandberg, & Järvenpää, 2003; Slade, Belsky, Aber, & Phelps, 1999). A mother who was securely attached to *her* mother, or who understands why she was insecurely attached, can accurately recognize the baby's attachment behaviors, respond encouragingly, and help the baby form a secure attachment to her (Bretherton, 1990). Mothers who are preoccupied with their past attachment relationships tend to show anger and intrusiveness in interactions with their children. Depressed mothers who dismiss memories of their past attachments tend to be cold and unresponsive to their children (Adam et al., 2004). Parents' attachment history also influences their perceptions of their baby's temperament, and those perceptions may affect the parent-child relationship (Pesonen et al., 2003).

Checkpoint ✔

Can you . . .

✔ Describe four patterns of attachment?

✔ Discuss how attachment is established, including the role of temperament?

✔ Discuss factors affecting stranger anxiety and separation anxiety?

✔ Describe how long-term behavioral differences are influenced by attachment patterns?

Emotional Communication with Caregivers: Mutual Regulation

mutual regulation Process
by which infant and caregiver
communicate emotional states
to each other and respond
appropriately.

Infants are communicating beings; they have a strong drive to interact with others (Striano, 2004). A 1-month-old gazes attentively at the mother's face. At 2 months, in response to the mother's emotional feedback, the infant engages more actively in a mutual exchange of positive emotion. By 3 months, the infant becomes more approaching and more playful (Lavelli & Fogel, 2005).

The synchrony of interactions with a caregiver—the ability of both infant and caregiver to respond appropriately and sensitively to each other's mental and emotional states—is known as **mutual regulation.** Infants take an active part in mutual regulation by sending behavioral signals that influence the way caregivers behave toward them (Lundy, 2003). Healthy interaction occurs when a caregiver reads a baby's signals accurately and responds appropriately. When a baby's goals are met, the baby is joyful or at least interested (E. Z. Tronick, 1989). If a caregiver ignores an invitation to play or insists on playing when the baby has signaled, "I don't feel like it," the baby may feel frustrated or sad. When babies do not achieve desired results, they keep on sending signals to repair the interaction. Normally, interaction moves back and forth between well-regulated and poorly regulated states, and babies learn from these shifts how to send signals and what to do when their initial signals are not effective. Mutual regulation helps babies learn to read others' behavior and to develop expectations about it. Even very young infants can perceive emotions expressed by others and can adjust their own behavior accordingly (Legerstee & Varghese, 2001; Montague & Walker-Andrews, 2001; Termine & Izard, 1988), but they are disturbed when someone—whether the mother or a stranger, and regardless of the reason—breaks off interpersonal contact (Striano, 2004). (Box 8-1 discusses how postpartum depression can affect mutual regulation.)

Measuring Mutual Regulation: The "Still-Face" Paradigm

"still-face" paradigm Research
procedure used to measure
mutual regulation in infants
2 to 9 months old.

The **"still-face" paradigm** (Tronick, Als, Adamson, Wise, & Brazelton, 1978) is a research procedure normally used to measure mutual regulation in 2- to 9-month-old infants, though infants as young as 1½ months have been shown to demonstrate the still-face response (Bertin & Striano, 2006). In the *still-face* episode, which follows a normal face-to-face interaction, the mother suddenly becomes stony-faced, silent, and unresponsive. Then, a few minutes later, she resumes normal interaction, the *reunion* episode. During the still-face episode, infants tend to stop smiling and looking at the mother. They may make faces, sounds, or gestures or may touch themselves, their clothing, or a chair, apparently to comfort themselves or to relieve the emotional stress created by the mother's unexpected behavior (Cohn & Tronick, 1983; E. Z. Tronick, 1980, 1989; Weinberg & Tronick, 1996).

How do infants react during the reunion episode? In one study, 6-month-olds showed even more positive behavior during that episode—joyous expressions and utterances and gazes and gestures directed toward the mother—than before the still-face episode. Nonetheless, the persistence of sad or angry facial expressions, "pick-me-up" gestures, distancing, and indications of stress, as well as an increased tendency to fuss and cry, suggested that the negative feelings stirred by a breakdown in mutual regulation were not readily eased (Weinberg & Tronick, 1996).

The still-face reaction seems to be similar in Eastern and Western cultures and in interactions with both fathers and mothers (Braungart-Rieker, Garwood, Powers, & Notaro, 1998; Kisilevsky et al., 1998). Infants whose parents are normally sensitive and responsive to their emotional needs seem better able to comfort themselves and show less negative emotion during the still-face episode and recover more readily during the reunion episode (Braungart-Rieker et al., 2001; Tarabulsy et al., 2003).

Social Referencing

Toward the end of the 1st year, as infants begin to get around on their own and initiate complex behaviors, they experience an important developmental shift: the ability to participate in person-to-person communication about an external event. They can now engage in *affective sharing,* letting a caregiver know how they feel about a situation or object and

What's your view **?**

• Do you see any ethical
problems with the still-face
paradigm or the Strange
Situation? If so, do you think
the benefits of these kinds
of research are worth any
potential risks?

Reading emotional signals lets mothers assess and meet babies' needs; and it lets babies influence or respond to the mother's behavior toward them. What happens, then, if that communication system seriously breaks down, and what can be done about it?

Postpartum depression—major or minor depression occurring within 4 weeks of giving birth—affects about 14.5 percent of new mothers (Wisner, Chambers, & Sit, 2006)—including the actress Brooke Shields, who has written a book about it. First-time mothers are especially at risk, according to a Danish population-based study (Munk-Olsen, Laursen, Pedersen, Mors, & Mortensen, 2006).

Unless treated promptly, postpartum depression may have a negative impact on the way a mother interacts with her baby and on the child's future cognitive and emotional development (Gjerdingen, 2003). Depressed mothers are less sensitive to their infants than nondepressed mothers, and their interactions with their babies are generally less positive (NICHD Early Child Care Research Network, 1999b). Depressed mothers are less likely to interpret and respond to an infant's cries (Donovan, Leavitt, & Walsh, 1998).

Babies of depressed mothers may give up on sending emotional signals and try to comfort themselves by sucking or rocking. If this reaction becomes habitual, babies learn that they have no power to draw responses from other people, that their mothers are unreliable, and that the world is untrustworthy. They also may become depressed themselves (Ashman & Dawson, 2002; Gelfand & Teti, 1995; Teti et al., 1995). We cannot be sure, however, that such infants become depressed through a failure of mutual regulation. They may inherit a predisposition to depression or acquire it prenatally through exposure to hormonal or other biochemical influences.

Infants of depressed mothers tend to show unusual patterns of brain activity, similar to the mothers' own patterns. Within 24 hours of birth, they show relatively less activity in the left frontal region of the brain, which seems to be specialized for *approach emotions* such as joy and anger, and more activity in the right frontal region, which controls *withdrawal emotions* such as distress and disgust (G. Dawson et al., 1992, 1999; T. Field, 1998a, 1998c; T. Field, Fox, Pickens, Nawrocki, & Soutollo, 1995; N. A. Jones, Field, Fox, Lundy, & Davalos, 1997). Newborns of depressed mothers also tend to have higher levels of stress hormones (Lundy et al., 1999), lower scores on the Brazelton Neonatal Behavior Assessment Scale, and lower vagal tone, which is associated with attention and learning (T. Field, 1998a, 1998c; N. A. Jones et al., 1998). These findings suggest that a woman's depression during pregnancy may contribute to her newborn's neurological and behavioral functioning.

It may be that a combination of genetic, prenatal, and environmental factors puts infants of depressed mothers at risk. A bidirectional influence may be at work; an infant who does not respond normally may further depress the mother, and her unresponsiveness may in turn increase the infant's depression (T. Field, 1995, 1998a, 1998c; Lundy et al., 1999). Some depressed mothers do maintain good interactions with their infants, and these infants tend to have better emotional regulation than other infants of depressed mothers (Field, Diego, Hernandez-Reif, Schanberg, & Kuhn, 2003). Interactions with a nondepressed adult can help infants compensate for the effects of depressed mothering (T. Field, 1995, 1998a, 1998c).

Children with depressed mothers tend to be insecurely attached (Gelfand & Teti, 1995; Teti et al., 1995). They are likely to grow poorly, to perform poorly on cognitive and linguistic measures, and to have behavior problems (T. Field, 1998a, 1998c; T. M. Field et al., 1985; Gelfand & Teti, 1995; NICHD Early Child Care Research Network, 1999b; B. S. Zuckerman & Beardslee, 1987). As toddlers these children tend to have trouble suppressing frustration and tension (Cole, Barrett, & Zahn-Waxler, 1992; Seiner & Gelfand, 1995), and in early adolescence they are at risk for violent behavior (Hay, 2003).

Antidepressant drugs such as Zoloft (a selective serotonin reuptake inhibitor) and nortriptyline (a tricyclic) appear to be safe and effective for treating postpartum depression (Wisner et al., 2006). Other techniques that may help improve a depressed mother's mood include listening to music, visual imagery, aerobics, yoga, relaxation, and massage therapy (T. Field, 1995, 1998a, 1998c). Massage also can help depressed babies (T. Field, 1998a, 1998b; T. Field et al., 1996), possibly through effects on neurological activity (N. A. Jones et al., 1997). In one study, such mood-brightening measures—plus social, educational, and vocational rehabilitation for the mother and day care for the infant—improved their interaction behavior. The infants showed faster growth and had fewer pediatric problems, more normal biochemical values, and better developmental test scores than a control group (T. Field, 1998a, 1998b).

What's your view

Can you suggest ways to help depressed mothers and babies, other than those mentioned here?

Check it out

For further information on this topic, go to http://www.nimh.nih.gov/publicat/depwomenknows.cfm, a National Institute of Mental Health Web resource called "Depression: What Every Woman Should Know," or http://www.nimh.nih.gov/publicat/depression.cfm, a general fact sheet about depression, also on the Web site of the National Institute of Mental Health.

reacting to the emotions they discern in the caregiver. These developments are the necessary underpinnings of **social referencing,** the ability to seek out emotional information to guide behavior (Hertenstein & Campos, 2004). In social referencing, one person forms an understanding of how to act in an ambiguous, confusing, or unfamiliar situation by seeking out and interpreting another person's perception of it. Babies seem to use social referencing when they look at their caregivers on encountering a new person or toy.

social referencing Understanding an ambiguous situation by seeking out another person's perception of it.

Research provides experimental evidence of social referencing at 1 year (Moses, Baldwin, Rosicky, & Tidball, 2001). When exposed to jiggling or vibrating toys fastened to the floor or ceiling, both 12- and 18-month-olds moved closer to or farther from the toys depending on the experimenters' expressed emotional reactions ("Yecch!" or "Nice!"). In one pair of studies (Mumme & Fernald, 2003), 12-month-olds (but not 10-month-olds) adjusted their behavior toward certain unfamiliar objects according to nonvocal emotional signals given by an actress on a television screen. In another pair of studies (Hertenstein & Campos, 2004), whether 14-month-olds touched plastic creatures that dropped within their reach was related to the positive or negative emotions they had seen an adult express about the same objects an hour before; 11-month-olds responded to such emotional cues if the delay was very brief (3 minutes).

Social referencing—and the ability to retain information gained from it—may play a role in such key developments of toddlerhood as the rise of self-conscious emotions (embarrassment and pride), the development of a sense of self, and the processes of *socialization* and *internalization,* to which we turn in the remainder of this chapter.

Developmental Issues in Toddlerhood

About halfway between their first and second birthdays, babies become toddlers. This transformation can be seen, not only in such physical and cognitive skills as walking and talking, but in the ways children express their personalities and interact with others. A toddler becomes a more active, intentional partner in interactions and sometimes initiates them. Caregivers can now more clearly read the child's signals. Such in-sync interactions help toddlers gain communicative skills and social competence and motivate compliance with a parent's wishes (Harrist & Waugh, 2002).

Let's look at three psychological issues that toddlers—and their caregivers—have to deal with: the emerging *sense of self;* the growth of *autonomy,* or self-determination; and *socialization,* or *internalization of behavioral standards.*

The Emerging Sense of Self

The **self-concept** is our image of ourselves—our total picture of our abilities and traits. It describes what we know and feel about ourselves and guides our actions (Harter, 1996, 1998). Children incorporate into their self-image the picture that others reflect back to them.

When and how does the self-concept develop? From a jumble of seemingly isolated experiences (say, from one breast-feeding session to another), infants begin to extract consistent patterns that form rudimentary concepts of self and other. Depending on what kind of care the infant receives and how she or he responds, pleasant or unpleasant emotions become connected with experiences such as sucking that play an important part in the growing concept of the self (Harter, 1998).

Between 4 and 10 months, when infants learn to reach, grasp, and make things happen, they experience a sense of personal *agency,* the realization that they can control external events. At about this time infants develop *self-coherence,* the sense of being a physical whole with boundaries separate from the rest of their world (Harter, 1998). These developments occur in interaction with caregivers in games such as peekaboo (refer back to Box 7-1 in Chapter 7), in which the infant becomes increasingly aware of the difference between self and other ("I see you!").

The emergence of *self-awareness*—conscious knowledge of the self as a distinct, identifiable being—builds on this dawning of perceptual discrimination between self and others (Harter, 1998). In an experiment with ninety-six 4- and 9-month-olds, the infants showed more interest in images of others than of themselves (Rochat & Striano, 2002). This early *perceptual* discrimination may be the foundation of the *conceptual* self-awareness that develops between 15 and 18 months.

Self-awareness can be tested by studying whether an infant recognizes himself or herself in a mirror. In a classic line of research, investigators dabbed rouge on the noses of 6- to 24-month-olds and sat them in front of a mirror. Three-fourths of 18-month-olds and

Checkpoint

Can you . . .

✔ Describe how mutual regulation works and explain its importance?

✔ Give examples of how infants seem to use social referencing?

Guidepost 4

When and how does the sense of self arise, and how do toddlers exercise autonomy and develop standards for socially acceptable behavior?

self-concept Sense of self; descriptive and evaluative mental picture of one's abilities and traits.

all 24-month-olds touched their red noses more often than before, whereas babies younger than 15 months never did. This behavior suggests that these toddlers knew they did not normally have red noses and recognized the image in the mirror as their own (Lewis, 1997; Lewis & Brooks, 1974). In a later study, 18- and 24-month-olds were about as likely to touch a sticker on their legs, which was visible only in a mirror, as on their faces (Nielsen, Suddendorf, & Slaughter, 2006). Once children can recognize themselves, they show a preference for looking at their own video image over an image of another child the same age (Nielsen, Dissanayake, & Kashima, 2003).

By 20 to 24 months, toddlers begin to use first-person pronouns, another sign of self-awareness (Lewis, 1997). Between 19 and 30 months, they begin to apply descriptive terms ("big" or "little," "straight hair" or "curly hair") and evaluative ones ("good," "pretty," or "strong") to themselves. The rapid development of language enables children to think and talk about the self and to incorporate parents' verbal descriptions ("You're so smart!" "What a big boy!") into their emerging self-image (Stipek, Gralinski, & Kopp, 1990).

This toddler is showing autonomy—the drive to exert her own power over her environment.

Developing Autonomy

Erikson (1950) identified the period from about 18 months to 3 years as the second stage in psychosocial development, **autonomy versus shame and doubt,** which is marked by a shift from external control to self-control. Having come through infancy with a sense of basic trust in the world and an awakening self-awareness, toddlers begin to substitute their own judgment for their caregivers'. The virtue, or strength, that emerges during this stage is *will.* Toilet training, which in most children is completed most rapidly if begun after 27 months (Blum, Taubman, & Nemeth, 2003), is an important step toward autonomy and self-control. So is language; as children are better able to make their wishes understood, they become more powerful and independent. Since unlimited freedom is neither safe nor healthy, said Erikson, shame and doubt have a necessary place. Toddlers need adults to set appropriate limits, and shame and doubt help them recognize the need for those limits.

In the United States, the "terrible twos" are a normal manifestation of the drive for autonomy. Toddlers have to test the notions that they are individuals, that they have some control over their world, and that they have new, exciting, powers. They are driven to try out their own ideas, exercise their own preferences, and make their own decisions. This drive typically shows itself in the form of *negativism,* the tendency to shout, "No!" just for the sake of resisting authority. Almost all U.S. children show negativism to some degree; it usually begins before age 2, tends to peak at about 3½ to 4, and declines by age 6. Caregivers who view children's expressions of self-will as a normal, healthy striving for independence, not as stubbornness, can help them learn self-control, contribute to their sense of competence, and avoid excessive conflict. (Table 8-4 gives specific, research-based, suggestions for dealing with the terrible twos.)

Many U.S. parents might be surprised to hear that the terrible twos are not universal. In some developing countries, the transition from infancy to early childhood is relatively smooth and harmonious (Mosier & Rogoff, 2003; Box 8-2 on page 235).

autonomy versus shame and doubt Erikson's second stage in psychosocial development, in which children achieve a balance between self-determination and control by others.

Checkpoint ✔

Can you . . .

✔ Trace the early development of the sense of self?

✔ Describe the conflict of autonomy versus shame and doubt?

✔ Explain why the terrible twos is considered a normal phenomenon, and suggest reasons this transition may not exist in some cultures?

Moral Development: Socialization and Internalization

Socialization is the process by which children develop habits, skills, values, and motives that make them responsible, productive members of society. Compliance with parental expectations can be seen as a first step toward compliance with societal standards. Socialization rests on **internalization** of these standards. Children who are successfully socialized no longer merely obey rules or commands to get rewards or avoid punishment; they have made society's standards their own (Grusec & Goodnow, 1994; Kochanska & Aksan, 1995; Kochanska, Tjebkes, & Forman, 1998).

socialization Development of habits, skills, values, and motives shared by responsible, productive members of a society.

internalization During socialization, process by which children accept societal standards of conduct as their own.

Table 8-4	Dealing with the Terrible Twos

The following research-based guidelines can help parents of toddlers discourage negativism and encourage socially acceptable behavior.

- *Be flexible.* Learn the child's natural rhythms and special likes and dislikes.
- *Think of yourself as a safe harbor,* with safe limits, from which a child can set out and discover the world and to which the child can keep coming back for support.
- *Make your home child-safe.* Make unbreakable objects that are safe to explore available.
- *Avoid physical punishment.* It is often ineffective and may even lead a toddler to do more damage.
- *Offer a choice*—even a limited one—to give the child some control. ("Would you like to have your bath now or after we read a book?")
- *Be consistent* in enforcing necessary requests.
- *Don't interrupt an activity unless absolutely necessary.* Try to wait until the child's attention has shifted.
- *If you must interrupt, give warning.* ("We have to leave the playground soon.")
- *Suggest alternative activities* when behavior becomes objectionable. (When Ashley is throwing sand in Keiko's face, say, "Oh, look! Nobody's on the swings now. Let's go over and I'll give you a good push!")
- *Suggest; don't command.* Accompany requests with smiles or hugs, not criticism, threats, or physical restraint.
- *Link requests with pleasurable activities.* ("It's time to stop playing so that you can go to the store with me.")
- *Remind the child of what you expect:* "When we go to this playground, we *never* go outside the gate."
- *Wait a few moments before repeating a request* when a child doesn't comply immediately.
- *Use time-outs to end conflicts.* In a nonpunitive way, remove either yourself or the child from a situation.
- *Expect less self-control during times of stress* (illness, divorce, the birth of a sibling, or a move to a new home).
- *Expect it to be harder for toddlers to comply with "dos" than with "don'ts".* "Clean up your room" takes more effort than "Don't write on the furniture."
- *Keep the atmosphere as positive* as possible. Make your child *want* to cooperate.

Sources: Haswell, Hock, & Wenar, 1981: Kochanska & Aksan, 1995; Kopp, 1982; Kuczynski & Kochanska 1995; Power & Chapieski, 1986.

Developing Self-Regulation

Katy, age 2, is about to poke her finger into an electric outlet. In her child-proofed apartment, the sockets are covered, but not here in her grandmother's home. When Katy hears her father shout, "No!" the toddler pulls her arm back. The next time she goes near an outlet, she starts to point her finger, hesitates, and then says, "No." She has stopped herself from doing something she remembers she is not supposed to do. She is beginning to show **self-regulation:** control of her behavior to conform to a caregiver's demands or expectations, even when the caregiver is not present.

Self-regulation is the foundation of socialization, and it links all domains of development—physical, cognitive, social, and emotional. Until Katy was physically able to get around on her own, electric outlets posed no hazard. To stop herself from poking her finger into an outlet requires that she consciously understand and remember what her father told her. Cognitive awareness, however, is not enough; restraining herself also requires emotional control. By reading their parents' emotional responses to their behavior, children continually absorb information about what conduct their parents approve of. As children process, store, and act on this information, their strong desire to please their parents leads them to do as they know their parents want them to, whether or not the parents are there to see.

Before they can control their behavior, children may need to be able to regulate, or control, their *attentional processes* and to modulate negative emotions (Eisenberg, 2000).

self-regulation A person's independent control of behavior to conform to understood social expectations.

Box 8-2 *Are Struggles with Toddlers Necessary?*

Are the terrible twos a normal phase in child development? Many Western parents and psychologists think so. Actually, though, this transition does not appear to be universal.

In Zinacantan, Mexico, toddlers do not typically become demanding and resistant to parental control. Instead of asserting independence from their mothers, toddlerhood in Zinacantan is a time when children move from being mama's babies to being mother's helpers, responsible children who may tend a new baby and who help with household tasks (Edwards, 1994). A similar developmental pattern seems to occur in Mazahua families in Mexico and among Maya families in San Pedro, Guatemala. San Pedro parents "do not report a particular age when they expect children to become especially contrary or negative" (Mosier & Rogoff, 2003, p. 1058).

One arena in which issues of autonomy and control appear in western cultures is in sibling conflicts over toys and the way children respond to parental handling of these conflicts. To explore these issues, a cross-cultural study compared 16 San Pedro families with 16 middle-class European-American families in Salt Lake City. All of the families had toddlers 14 to 20 months old and older siblings 3 to 5 years old. The researchers interviewed each mother about her child-raising practices. They then handed the mother a series of attractive objects (such as nesting dolls and a jumping-jack puppet) and, in the presence of the older sibling, asked the mother to help the toddler operate them, with no instructions about the older child. Researchers who observed the ensuing interactions found striking differences in the way siblings interacted in the two cultures and in the way mothers viewed and handled sibling conflict.

The older siblings in Salt Lake City often tried to take and play with the objects, but this generally did not happen in San Pedro. Instead, the older San Pedro children would offer to help their younger siblings work the objects, or the two children would play with them together. When there was a conflict over possession of the objects, mothers in both communities were more likely to endorse the toddler's right to have it first, but this tendency was far more characteristic of San Pedro mothers than of Salt Lake City mothers. San Pedro mothers favored the toddlers 94 percent of the time, even taking an object away from the older child if the younger child wanted it; and the older siblings tended to go along, willingly handing the objects to the toddlers or letting them have the objects from the start. In contrast, in more than one-third of the interactions in Salt Lake City, the mothers tried to treat both children equally, negotiating with them or suggesting that they take turns or share. These observations

were consistent with reports of mothers in both cultures of how they handled such issues at home. San Pedro children are given a privileged position until age 3; then they are expected to willingly cooperate with social expectations.

What explains these cultural contrasts? A possible clue emerged when the mothers were asked at what age children can be held responsible for their actions. Most of the Salt Lake mothers maintained that their toddlers already understood the consequences of touching prohibited objects; several said this understanding arises as early as 7 months. Yet all but one of the San Pedro mothers placed the age of understanding social consequences of actions much later—between 2 and 3 years. Whereas the Salt Lake mothers regarded their toddlers as capable of intentionally misbehaving, most San Pedro mothers did not. More than half of the Salt Lake mothers reporting punishing toddlers for such infractions; none of the San Pedro mothers did. All of the Salt Lake preschoolers were under direct caregiver supervision, much like their toddler siblings, while 11 of the 16 San Pedro preschoolers were already on their own much of the time. The San Pedro preschoolers also had greater household responsibilities.

The researchers suggest that the terrible twos may be a phase specific to societies that place individual freedom before the needs of the group. Ethnographic research suggests that, in societies that place higher value on group needs, freedom of choice does exist, but it goes hand in hand with interdependence, responsibility, and expectations of cooperation. Salt Lake parents seem to believe that responsible behavior develops gradually from engaging in fair competition and negotiations. San Pedro parents seem to believe that responsible behavior develops rapidly when children are old enough to understand the need to respect others' desires as well as their own.

What's your view ?

From your experience or observation of toddlers, which of the two ways of handling sibling conflict would you expect to be more effective?

Check it out !

For more information on this topic, go to www.zerotothree.org. Here you will find links to a survey of 3,000 parents and other adults about commonly asked questions regarding the handling of young children and resources covering a variety of key topics.

Attentional regulation enables children to develop willpower and cope with frustration (Sethi, Mischel, Aber, Shoda, & Rodriguez, 2000).

The growth of self-regulation parallels the development of the self-conscious and evaluative emotions, such as empathy, shame, and guilt (Lewis, 1995, 1997, 1998). It requires the ability to wait for gratification. It is correlated with measures of conscience development, such as resisting temptation and making amends for wrongdoing (Eisenberg, 2000). In most children, the full development of self-regulation takes at least 3 years (Kopp, 1982).

Origins of Conscience: Committed Compliance

conscience Internal standards of behavior, which usually control one's conduct and produce emotional discomfort when violated.

Conscience includes both emotional discomfort about doing something wrong and the ability to refrain from doing it. Before children can develop a conscience, they need to have internalized moral standards. Conscience depends on willingness to do the right thing because a child believes it is right, not (as in self-regulation) just because someone else said so. *Inhibitory control*—conscious, or effortful, holding back of impulses, a mechanism of self-regulation that emerges during toddlerhood—may contribute to the development of conscience by first enabling the child to comply voluntarily with parental dos and don'ts (Kochanska, Murray, & Coy, 1997).

Grazyna Kochanska and her colleagues have looked for the origins of conscience in a longitudinal study of a group of toddlers and mothers in Iowa. Researchers videotaped 103 children ages 26 to 41 months and their mothers playing together with toys for 2 to 3 hours, both at home and in a homelike laboratory setting (Kochanska & Aksan, 1995). After a free-play period, a mother would give her child 15 minutes to put the toys away. The laboratory had a special shelf with other, unusually attractive, toys, such as a bubble gum machine, a walkie-talkie, and a music box. The child was told not to touch anything on the shelf. After about 1 hour, the experimenter asked the mother to go into an adjoining room, leaving the child alone with the toys. A few minutes later, a woman entered, played with several of the forbidden toys, and then left the child alone again for 8 minutes.

committed compliance Kochanska's term for wholehearted obedience of a parent's orders without reminders or lapses.

situational compliance Kochanska's term for obedience of a parent's orders only in the presence of signs of ongoing parental control.

Children were judged to show **committed compliance** if they willingly followed the orders to clean up and not touch the special toys, without reminders or lapses. Children showed **situational compliance** if they needed prompting; that is, their compliance depended on ongoing parental control. Committed compliance is related to internalization of parental values and rules (Kochanska, Coy, & Murray, 2001). Children whose mothers rated them as having internalized household rules showed committed compliance: They refrained from touching the forbidden toys even when left alone with them. In contrast, children who showed situational compliance tended to yield to temptation when their mothers were out of sight (Kochanska & Aksan, 1995).

Committed compliance and situational compliance can be distinguished in children as young as 13 months, but their roots go back earlier in infancy. Committed compliers, who are more likely to be girls than boys, tend to be those who, at 8 to 10 months, could refrain from touching when told, "No!" Committed compliance tends to increase with age, while situational compliance decreases (Kochanska, Tjebkes, & Forman, 1998).

What's your view

- In view of Kochanska's research on the roots of conscience, what questions would you ask about the early socialization of antisocial adolescents and adults?

Factors in the Success of Socialization

The way parents go about the job of socializing a child, together with a child's temperament and the quality of the parent-child relationship, may help predict how hard or easy socialization will be (Kochanska, 1993, 1995, 1997a, 1997b, 2002). Factors in the success of socialization may include security of attachment, observational learning from parents' behavior, and the mutual responsiveness of parent and child (Kochanska, Aksan, Knaack, & Rhines, 2004; Maccoby, 1992). All these as well as socioeconomic and cultural factors (Harwood, Schoelmerich, Ventura-Cook, Schulze, & Wilson, 1996) may play a part in motivation to comply. However, not all children respond to socialization in the same way. For example, a temperamentally fearful toddler may respond better to gentle reminders than to strong admonitions (Kochanska, Aksan, & Joy, 2007).

Secure attachment and a warm, mutually responsive parent-child relationship seem to foster committed compliance and conscience development. Starting in the child's 2nd year and extending until early school age, researchers observed more than 200 mothers and children in lengthy, naturalistic interactions: caregiving routines, preparing and eating meals, playing, relaxing, and doing household chores. Children who, based on these interactions, were judged to have mutually responsive relationships with their mothers tended to show *moral emotions* such as guilt and empathy; *moral conduct* in the face of strong temptation to break rules or violate standards of behavior; and *moral cognition,* as judged by their response to hypothetical, age-appropriate moral dilemmas (Kochanska, 2002).

Constructive conflict over a child's misbehavior—conflict that involves negotiation, reasoning, and resolution—can help children develop moral understanding by enabling them to see another point of view. In one observational study, 2½-year-olds whose mothers gave clear explanations for their requests, compromised, or bargained with the child were better able to resist temptation at age 3 than children whose mothers had threatened, teased, insisted, or given in. Discussion of emotions in conflict situations ("How would you feel if . . .") also led to conscience development, probably by fostering the development of moral emotions (Laible & Thompson, 2002).

Receptive cooperation goes beyond committed compliance. It is a child's eager willingness to cooperate harmoniously with a parent, not only in disciplinary situations, but in a variety of daily interactions, including routines, chores, hygiene, and play. Receptive cooperation enables a child to be an active partner in socialization. In a longitudinal study of 101 7-month-olds, those who were prone to anger, who received unresponsive parenting, or who were insecurely attached at 15 months tended to be low in receptive cooperation at 7 months. Children who were securely attached and whose mothers had been responsive to the child during infancy tended to be high in receptive cooperation (Kochanska, Aksan, & Carlson, 2005).

Checkpoint ✔

Can you . . .

✔ Tell when and how self-regulation develops and how it contributes to socialization?

✔ Distinguish among situational compliance, committed compliance, and receptive cooperation?

✔ Discuss factors that affect socialization?

How Different Are Baby Boys and Girls?

Guidepost 5

When and how do gender differences appear?

Being male or female affects how people look, how they move their bodies, and how they work, play, and dress. It influences what they think about themselves and what others think of them. All these characteristics—and more—are included in the word **gender:** what it means to be *male* or *female*.

Gender Differences in Infants and Toddlers

receptive cooperation Kochanska's term for eager willingness to cooperate harmoniously with a parent in daily interactions, including routines, chores, hygiene, and play.

gender Significance of being male or female.

Measurable differences between baby boys and baby girls are few, at least in U.S. samples. Boys are a bit longer and heavier and may be slightly stronger, but, as we mentioned in Chapter 4, they are physically more vulnerable from conception on. Girls are less reactive to stress and more likely to survive infancy (Davis & Emory, 1995; Keenan & Shaw, 1997). Boys' brains at birth are about 10 percent larger than girls' brains, a difference that continues into adulthood (Gilmore et al., 2007). On the other hand, the two sexes are equally sensitive to touch and tend to teethe, sit up, and walk at about the same ages (Maccoby, 1980). They also achieve the other motor milestones of infancy at about the same times.

One of the earliest *behavioral* differences between boys and girls, appearing between ages 1 and 2, is in preferences for toys and play activities and for playmates of the same sex (Campbell, Shirley, Heywood, & Crook, 2000; Serbin et al., 2001; Turner & Gervai, 1995). Boys as young as 17 months tend to play more aggressively than girls (Baillargeon et al., 2007). Between ages 2 and 3, boys and girls tend to say more words pertaining to their own gender (such as "necklace" versus "tractor") than to the other gender (Stennes, Burch, Sen, & Bauer, 2005).

By using age-appropriate tasks, cognitive psychologists have found evidence that infants begin to perceive differences between males and females long before their behavior is gender-differentiated and even before they can talk. Habituation studies have found that 6-month-olds respond differently to male and female voices. By 9 to 12 months, infants can tell the difference between male and female faces, apparently on the basis of hair and clothing. From about 24 to 36 months, infants begin to associate gender-typical toys, such as dolls, with a face of the correct gender. Boys are slower to develop this knowledge than girls (Martin, Ruble, & Szkrybalo, 2002). In elicited imitation studies (refer back to Chapter 7), 25-month-old boys spend more time imitating "boy" tasks, such as shaving a teddy bear, whereas girls spend about the same amount of time imitating activities associated with each gender (Bauer, 1993).

How Parents Shape Gender Differences

Parents in the United States tend to *think* baby boys and girls are more different than they actually are. In a study of 11-month-old infants who had recently begun crawling,

gender-typing Socialization process by which children, at an early age, learn appropriate gender roles.

What's your view **?**

- Should parents try to treat male and female infants and toddlers alike?

Checkpoint ✔

Can you . . .

✔ Compare the roles of mothers and fathers in gender-typing?

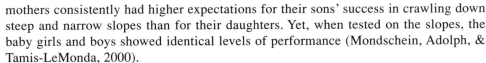

Guidepost 6

How do infants and toddlers interact with siblings and other children?

mothers consistently had higher expectations for their sons' success in crawling down steep and narrow slopes than for their daughters. Yet, when tested on the slopes, the baby girls and boys showed identical levels of performance (Mondschein, Adolph, & Tamis-LeMonda, 2000).

U.S. parents also begin to influence boys' and girls' personalities very early. Fathers, especially, promote **gender-typing,** the process by which children learn behavior that their culture considers appropriate for each sex (Bronstein, 1988). Fathers treat boys and girls more differently than mothers do, even during the 1st year (M. E. Snow, Jacklin, & Maccoby, 1983). During the 2nd year, fathers talk more and spend more time with sons than with daughters (Lamb, 1981). Mothers talk more, and more supportively, to daughters than to sons (Leaper, Anderson, & Sanders, 1998), and girls at this age tend to be more talkative than boys (Leaper & Smith, 2004). Fathers of toddlers play more roughly with sons and show more sensitivity to daughters (Kelley et al., 1998).

However, a highly physical style of play, characteristic of many fathers in the United States, is not typical of fathers in all cultures. Swedish and German fathers usually do not play with their babies this way (Lamb, Frodi, Frodi, & Hwang, 1982; Parke, Grossman, & Tinsley, 1981). African Aka fathers (Hewlett, 1987) and those in New Delhi, India, also tend to play gently with small children (Roopnarine, Hooper, Ahmeduzzaman, & Pollack, 1993; Roopnarine, Talokder, Jain, Josh, & Srivastav, 1992). Such cross-cultural variations suggest that rough play is not a function of male biology, but instead is culturally influenced.

We will discuss gender-typing and gender differences in more depth in Chapter 11.

Contact with Other Children

Although parents exert a major influence on children's lives, relationships with other children—both in the home and out of it—are important too, from infancy on.

Siblings

If you have brothers or sisters, your relationships with them are likely to be the longest lasting you will ever have. They share your roots; they knew you when, they accepted or rejected the same parental values, and they probably deal with you more candidly than almost anyone else you know.

Sibling relationships begin with the birth of a new baby in a household and continue to develop, both positively and negatively, throughout childhood.

Affection and cooperation are common in sibling relationships as the younger sibling learns from the older.

The Arrival of a New Baby

Children react in various ways to the arrival of a sibling. To bid for the mother's attention, some suck their thumbs, wet their pants, or use baby talk. Others withdraw. Some suggest taking the baby back to the hospital or flushing it down the toilet. Some take pride in being the "big ones," who can dress themselves, use the potty, and help care for the baby.

Much of the variation in children's adjustment to a new baby may have to do with such factors as the older child's age, the quality of his or her relationship with the mother, and the family atmosphere. Not surprisingly, attachment to the mother often becomes temporarily less secure (Teti, Sakin, Kucera, Corns, & Eiden, 1996).

The birth of a younger sibling may change the way a mother acts toward an older child, at least until the newcomer settles in. The mother is likely to play less with the older child, to be less sensitive to her or his interests, to give more orders, to have more confrontations, to use physical punishment, and to initiate fewer conversations and games that help develop skills. An older boy, especially, may show temporary behavior problems (Baydar, Greek, & Brooks-Gunn, 1997; Baydar, Hyle, & Brooks-Gunn, 1997; Dunn, 1985; Dunn & Kendrick, 1982). On the positive side, the arrival of a baby tends to enhance the older child's language development, perhaps because the child talks more than before with the father and other family members (Baydar, Greek, & Brooks-Gunn, 1997; Baydar, Hyle, & Brooks-Gunn, 1997).

How Siblings Interact

Sibling relationships play a distinct role in socialization, different from the role of relationships with parents or peers (Vandell, 2000). Sibling conflicts can become a vehicle for understanding social relationships (Dunn & Munn, 1985; Ram & Ross, 2001). Lessons and skills learned from interactions with siblings carry over to relationships outside the home (Brody, 1998).

Young children usually become attached to their older brothers and sisters. Although rivalry may be present, so is affection. The more securely attached siblings are to their parents, the better they get along with each other (Teti & Ablard, 1989).

Nevertheless, as babies begin to move around and become more assertive, they inevitably come into conflict with siblings—at least in U.S. culture (refer back to Box 8-2). Sibling conflict increases dramatically after the younger child reaches age 18 months (Vandell & Bailey, 1992). During the next few months, younger siblings begin to participate more fully in family interactions and become more involved in family disputes. As they do, they become more aware of others' intentions and feelings. They begin to recognize what kind of behavior will upset or annoy an older brother or sister and what behavior is considered naughty or good (Dunn & Munn, 1985).

As this cognitive and social understanding grows, sibling conflict tends to become more constructive, and the younger sibling participates in attempts to reconcile. Constructive conflict helps children recognize each other's needs, wishes, and point of view; and it helps them learn how to fight, disagree, and compromise within the context of a safe, stable relationship (Vandell & Bailey, 1992).

Sociability with Nonsiblings

Infants and—even more so—toddlers show interest in people outside the home, particularly people their size. During the first few months, they show interest in other babies by looking, smiling, and cooing (T. M. Field, 1978). During 6 to 12 months, they increasingly smile at, touch, and babble to another baby (Hay, Pedersen, & Nash, 1982). At about 1 year, when the biggest items on their agenda are learning to walk and to manipulate objects, babies pay more attention to toys and less to other people (T. M. Field & Roopnarine, 1982). This stage does not last long, though; from about 1½ years to almost 3, children show more interest in what other children do and increasing understanding of how to deal with them (Eckerman, Davis, & Didow, 1989; Eckerman & Stein, 1982).

Toddlers learn by imitating one another. Games such as follow-the-leader help toddlers connect with other children and pave the way for more complex games during the preschool years (Eckerman et al., 1989). Imitation of each other's actions leads to more frequent verbal communication ("You go in playhouse," "Don't do it!" or "Look at me"), which helps peers coordinate joint activity (Eckerman & Didow, 1996). Cooperative activity develops during the 2nd and 3rd years as social understanding grows (Brownell, Ramani, & Zerwas, 2006). As with siblings, conflict too can have a purpose: helping children learn how to negotiate and resolve disputes (Caplan, Vespo, Pedersen, & Hay, 1991).

Some children, of course, are more sociable than others, reflecting such temperamental traits as their usual mood, readiness to accept new people, and ability to adapt to change. Sociability is also influenced by experience; babies who spend time with other babies, as in child care, become sociable earlier than those who spend all their time at home alone.

Checkpoint ✔

Can you . . .

✔ Discuss factors affecting a child's adjustment to a new baby sister or brother?

✔ Describe changes in sibling interaction and sibling conflict during toddlerhood?

✔ Trace changes in sociability during the first 3 years, and state two influences on it?

Guidepost 7

How do parental employment and early child care affect infants' and toddlers' development?

Children of Working Parents

Parents' work determines more than the family's financial resources. Much of adults' time, effort, and emotional involvement go into their occupations. How do their working and their child care arrangements affect young children? Most research on this subject pertains to mothers' work. (We'll discuss the impact of parents' work on older children in later chapters.)

Effects of Maternal Employment

More than half, 52.9 percent, of mothers of infants under 1 year and 57.5 percent of women with children under 3 were in the labor force in 2004 (Bureau of Labor Statistics, 2005). How does early maternal employment affect children? The answer varies.

Longitudinal data on 900 European American children from the National Institute of Child Health and Human Development (NICHD) Study of Early Child Care, discussed in the next section, showed negative effects on cognitive development at 15 months to 3 years when mothers worked 30 or more hours a week by a child's 9th month. Maternal sensitivity, a high-quality home environment, and high-quality child care lessened but did not eliminate these negative effects (Brooks-Gunn, Han, & Waldfogel, 2002).

On the other hand, boys and girls in low-income families tend to benefit academically from the more favorable environment a working mother's income can provide (Chase-Lansdale et al., 2003; Goldberg, Greenberger, & Nagel, 1996; Vandell & Ramanan, 1992). A longitudinal study of an ethnically, socioeconomically, and geographically diverse sample of 1,364 children during their first 3 years suggests that the economic and social benefits of maternal employment may outweigh any disadvantages resulting from reduced time with a child. Mothers who worked outside the home compensated for some of their work time by reducing time spent on non–child care activities. Differences in time spent with infants were modestly related to maternal sensitivity but did not seem to affect social or cognitive outcomes. Infants whose mothers spent more time with them did have more stimulating home environments, but so did infants whose mothers spent more time at work. It seems, then, that mothers who are temperamentally prone to be sensitive and to provide stimulating, warm home environments may find ways to do so whether or not they are employed (Huston & Aronson, 2005).

A study of 6,114 children from the National Longitudinal Survey of Youth (NLSY) found that children whose mothers worked full-time in their 1st year after giving birth were more likely to show negative cognitive and behavioral outcomes at ages 3 to 8 than children whose mothers worked part-time or not at all during their 1st year. However, as has been found in other studies, children in disadvantaged families showed less negative cognitive effects than children from more advantaged families (Hill, Waldfogel, Brooks-Gunn, & Han, 2005).

Early Child Care

One factor in the impact of a mother's working outside the home is the type of substitute care a child receives. By age 9 months, about 50 percent of U.S. infants are in some kind of regular nonparental child care arrangement, and 86 percent of these infants enter child care before they are 6 months old. More than half of these babies are in child care more than 30 hours a week (NCES, 2005a).

In 2005, about 60 percent of U.S. children not yet in kindergarten were in some type of regular child care. Some 60 percent of these children were in organized day care centers, 35 percent in a relative's care (usually, a grandparent's), and 22 percent in other care arrangements, including preschools (Iruka & Carver, 2006). Nearly 23 percent of

Caregivers' responsiveness to infants' needs is the most important factor in high-quality child care.

Table 8-5	Checklist for Choosing a Good Child Care Facility

- Is the facility licensed? Does it meet minimum state standards for health, fire, and safety? (Many centers and home care facilities are not licensed or regulated.)
- Is the facility clean and safe? Does it have adequate indoor and outdoor space?
- Does the facility have small groups, a high adult-to-child ratio, and a stable, competent, highly involved staff?
- Are caregivers trained in child development?
- Are caregivers warm, affectionate, accepting, responsive, and sensitive? Are they authoritative but not too restrictive and neither too controlling nor merely custodial?
- Does the program promote good health habits?
- Does it provide a balance between structured activities and free play? Are activities age appropriate?
- Do the children have access to educational toys and materials, which stimulate mastery of cognitive and communicative skills at a child's own pace?
- Does the program nurture self-confidence, curiosity, creativity, and self-discipline?
- Does it encourage children to ask questions, solve problems, express feelings and opinions, and make decisions?
- Does it foster self-esteem, respect for others, and social skills?
- Does it help parents improve their child-rearing skills?
- Does it promote cooperation with public and private schools and the community?

Sources: American Academy of Pediatrics [AAP], 1986; Belsky, 1984; K. A. Clarke-Stewart, 1987; NICHD Early Child Care Research Network, 1996; S. W. Olds, 1989: Scarr, 1998.

preschoolers are in grandparents' care at least part of the time (Johnson, 2005). A similar trend exists in some other developed countries (Kinsella & Velkoff, 2001).

With full-time nonrelative care averaging about $116 a week (Iruka & Carver, 2006), affordability and quality of care are pressing issues, especially for low-income families (Marshall, 2004) and parents of children with disabilities (Shonkoff & Phillips, 2000). Unfortunately, most child care facilities do not meet all recommended guidelines for quality care (Bergen, Reid, & Torelli, 2000; NICHD Early Child Care Research Network, 1998c, 1999a; Table 8-5).

The most important element in quality of care is the caregiver; stimulating interactions with responsive adults are crucial to early cognitive, linguistic, and psychosocial development. Low staff turnover is important; infants need consistent caregiving in order to develop trust and secure attachments (Burchinal, Roberts, Nabors, & Bryant, 1996; Shonkoff & Phillips, 2000).

The NICHD Study: Isolating Child Care Effects

Bronfenbrenner's bioecological theory (refer back to Chapter 2) affords a broad perspective on how early child care can affect children's development. Both the family and the child care setting are microsystems directly affecting the child, but their influences are not fully independent; they are linked through the mesosystem. Parents affect children's child care experience through their selection of particular child care arrangements, which is largely dependent on their means. Child care also may affect family life, for example, when a child learns a new song or game in child care and wants to sing or play it at home. The family–child care mesosystem operates within the exosystem of government policies, subsidies, and regulations that affect the quality and affordability of child care. Above and beyond those specific influences are "the macrosystem of societal beliefs about the desirability of maternal employment and the desired outcomes for children" (Marshall, 2004, p. 167).

Because child care is an integral part of a child's bioecological system, it is difficult to measure its influence alone. It should not be surprising that what look like effects of child care often may be related to family characteristics. After all, stable families with favorable home environments are more able and therefore more likely to place their children in high-quality care. Indeed, parental characteristics are the single best predictor of child care quality (NICHD Early Child Care Research Network, 2006a). The child's temperament also can alter the impact of child care. Shy children experience greater stress in child care than sociable children (Watamura, Donzella, Alwin, & Gunnar, 2003), and insecurely attached children undergo greater stress than securely attached children when placed in full-time care (Ahnert et al., 2004). Boys are more vulnerable to stress, in child care and elsewhere, than are girls (Crockenberg, 2003).

The most comprehensive attempt to separate child care effects from such other factors as family characteristics, the child's characteristics, and the care the child receives at home is an ongoing study sponsored by the NICHD. This longitudinal study of 1,364 children and their families began in 1991 in 10 university centers across the United States, shortly after the children's birth. The sample is diverse socioeconomically, educationally, and ethnically; nearly 35 percent of the families are poor or near poor. Most infants entered nonmaternal care before age 4 months and received, on average, 33 hours of care each week. Child care arrangements varied widely in type and quality. Through observation, interviews, questionnaires, and tests, researchers measured the children's social, emotional, cognitive, and physical development at frequent intervals starting at age 1 month. What do the findings show?

The type, amount, and quality of care children received influenced specific aspects of development. Children in center care tended to have stronger cognitive and language skills at ages 2 and 3 but, according to their caregivers, poorer social skills and more behavior problems than children who had spent little or no time in center care (NICHD Early Child Care Research Network, 2006a).

The more time a child spent in any type of child care up to age 4½, the more likely that child was to be seen by adults as having prosocial skills at age 2 but as having problem behaviors at 3 and 4½. Long days in child care have been associated with stress for 3- and 4-year-olds; and some children that age in the NICHD sample spent up to 92 hours a week in center care (NICHD Early Child Care Research Network, 2003, 2006a). By third grade, children who had spent long hours in child care continued to score higher in math and reading, and their tendency toward aggressive behavior had subsided. However, they still showed poorer work habits and social skills (NICHD Early Child Care Research Network, 2005b).

High-quality child care had a positive influence on both cognitive and social development (NICHD Early Child Care Research Network, 2006a). Children in child care centers with low child-staff ratios, small group sizes, and trained, sensitive, responsive caregivers who provided positive interactions and language stimulation scored higher on tests of language comprehension, cognition, and readiness for school than children in lower quality care. At some ages the mothers of children in high-quality child care centers reported more prosocial skills and fewer behavior problems, and the children showed less negative behavior in interacting with child care peers (NICHD Early Child Care Research Network, 1999a, 2000, 2002, 2006a).

At least some of these findings held up through preadolescence. In fifth grade, children who had been in high-quality care as preschoolers did somewhat better on vocabulary tests than children who had had low-quality care, and in sixth grade those who had spent more time in center care showed somewhat more problem behaviors than those who had had little or no center-care experience (Belsky et al., 2007).

Factors related to child care had varying amounts of influence when compared with family characteristics, such as income, the home environment, the amount of mental stimulation the mother provides, and the mother's sensitivity to her child (NICHD Early Child Care Research Network, 2006a). These characteristics strongly predict developmental outcomes, regardless of how much time children spend in outside care (Marshall, 2004; NICHD Early Child Care Research Network, 1998b, 2000, 2003, 2005b).

Parenting quality was a stronger and more consistent predictor of child outcomes through sixth grade (Belsky et al., 2007). Although a caregiver's sensitivity and responsiveness influence socialization, the mother's sensitivity has a greater influence, according to the NICHD research (NICHD Early Child Care Research Network, 1998a). Maternal sensitivity also is the strongest predictor of attachment. Child care had no direct effect on attachment to the mother, no matter how early infants entered care or how many hours they spent in it. Neither did the stability and quality of care affect attachment in and of themselves. However, when unstable, poor quality, or more-than-minimal time of child care

(10 or more hours a week) were combined with insensitive, unresponsive mothering, insecure attachment was more likely. On the other hand, high-quality care seemed to help offset insensitive mothering (NICHD Early Child Care Research Network, 1997, 2001b).

Children also become attached to their child care providers. An analysis of 40 studies involving 2,867 children found that secure attachments are more likely to develop in home-based than in center-based care and are related to the sensitivity of the provider (Ahnert, Pinquart, & Lamb, 2006).

One area in which the NICHD study found independent effects of child care was in interactions with peers. Between ages 2 and 3, children whose caregivers were sensitive and responsive tended to become more positive and competent in play with other children (NICHD Early Child Care Research Network, 2001a).

To sum up, the NICHD findings so far give high-quality child care good marks overall, especially for its impact on cognitive development and interaction with peers. Some observers say that the areas of concern the study pinpointed—stress levels in infants and toddlers and possible behavior problems related to amounts of care—might be counteracted by activities that enhance children's attachment to caregivers and peers, emphasize child-initiated learning and internalized motivation, and focus on group social development (Maccoby & Lewis, 2003). The study findings support policies that would improve quality of care while enabling parents to reduce the amount of time their children spend in outside care—through welfare benefits, flexible workplace hours, and paid parental leave that could be used anytime within the child's first 5 years (NICHD Early Child Care Research Network, 2006a).

Impact on Disadvantaged Children

Children from low-income families or stressful homes especially benefit from high-quality care that supplies cognitive stimulation and emotional support (Scarr, 1997; Spieker, Nelson, Petras, Jolley, & Barnard, 2003). In a 5-year longitudinal study of 451 poor single mothers who were moving from welfare to work, children demonstrated stronger cognitive growth in center care than in home-based care (Loeb, Fuller, Kagan, & Carrol, 2004). In another study, among more than 14,000 kindergartners, children from poor families gained twice as much from center-based care in language and mathematics learning as did children from middle-class families (Loeb, Bridges, Bassock, Fuller, & Rumberger, 2007).

As we have mentioned, the NICHD study found that the more time a young child spends in nonmaternal care, the greater the risk of problem behavior (NICHD Early Childhood Research Network, 2003). However, data from a study of 2,400 randomly selected low-income children in Boston, Chicago, and San Antonio suggest that extensive child care does not harm poor children's development unless it is of low quality (Votruba-Drzal, Coley, & Chase-Lansdale, 2004). Unfortunately, children from low-income families tend to be placed in lower-cost and lower-quality care than children from more affluent families (Marshall, 2004). Also, the vast majority of children eligible for federal child care subsidies do not receive them (USDHHS, 2000).

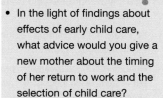

What's your view

- In the light of findings about effects of early child care, what advice would you give a new mother about the timing of her return to work and the selection of child care?

Checkpoint ✔

Can you . . .

✔ Evaluate the impact of a mother's employment on her baby's well-being?

✔ List at least five criteria for good child care?

✔ Discuss the impact of child care and of family characteristics on emotional, social, and cognitive development?

✔ Point out special considerations regarding child care for low-income children?

Refocus

Thinking back to the information about Cathy Bateson in the Focus vignette at the beginning of this chapter,

- Which of the four types of temperament did Cathy Bateson show? Was there goodness of fit in her relationship with her parents?

- Did Cathy appear to be securely or insecurely attached?

- How did the child-raising practices Cathy's parents followed seem to contribute to her psychosocial development?

- Did Cathy's tree-climbing technique suggest that she had internalized her parents' safety rules?

- How did her mother's professional life affect Cathy as an infant? As a toddler? On balance, as an only child, did she seem to benefit from her family's unusual child care arrangement with the Frank family?

The experiences of the first 3 years lay the foundation for future development. In Part 4, we'll see how young children build on that foundation.

Summary and Key Terms

Foundations of Psychosocial Development

Guidepost 1 When and how do emotions develop, and how do babies show them?

- Emotions serve protective functions.

- Crying, smiling, and laughing are early signs of emotion. Other indices are facial expressions, motor activity, body language, and physiological changes.

- The repertoire of basic emotions seems to be universal, but there are cultural variations in their expression.

- Complex emotions seem to develop from earlier, simpler ones. Self-conscious and evaluative emotions arise after the development of self-awareness.

- Separate but interacting regions of the brain may be responsible for various emotional states.

  emotions (217) self-conscious emotions (219) self-awareness (219) self-evaluative emotions (220) empathy (220) social cognition (220) egocentrism (220)

Guidepost 2 How do infants show temperamental differences, and how enduring are those differences?

- Many children seem to fall into one of three categories of temperament: easy, difficult, and slow-to-warm-up. Temperamental patterns appear to be largely inborn and to have a biological basis. They are generally stable but can be modified by experience.

- Goodness of fit between a child's temperament and environmental demands aids adjustment.

- Cross-cultural differences in temperament may reflect child-raising practices.

  temperament (221) easy children (221) difficult children (221) slow-to-warm-up children (221) goodness of fit (223)

Developmental Issues in Infancy

Guidepost 3 How do infants gain trust in their world and form attachments, and how do infants and caregivers read each other's nonverbal signals?

- According to Erikson, infants in the first 18 months are in the first stage of personality development, basic trust versus basic mistrust. Sensitive, responsive, consistent caregiving is the key to successful resolution of this conflict.

- Research based on the Strange Situation has found four patterns of attachment: secure, avoidant, ambivalent (resistant), and disorganized-disoriented.

- Newer instruments measure attachment in natural settings and in cross-cultural research.

- Attachment patterns may depend on a baby's temperament as well as on the quality of parenting and may have long-term implications for development. A parent's memories of childhood attachment can influence his or her own child's attachment.

- Separation anxiety and stranger anxiety may arise during age 6 to 12 months and appear to be related to temperament and circumstances.

basic trust versus basic mistrust (224) attachment (224) Strange Situation (225) secure attachment (225) avoidant attachment (225) ambivalent (resistant) attachment (225) disorganized-disoriented attachment (225) stranger anxiety (228) separation anxiety (228)

- Mutual regulation enables babies to play an active part in regulating their emotional states.

- A mother's depression, especially if severe or chronic, may have serious consequences for her infant's development.

- Social referencing has been observed by 12 months.

  mutual regulation (230) "still-face" paradigm (230) social referencing (231)

Developmental Issues in Toddlerhood

Guidepost 4 When and how does the sense of self arise, and how do toddlers exercise autonomy and develop standards for socially acceptable behavior?

- The self-concept develops between 15 and 18 months and depends on self-awareness.

  self-concept (232)

- Erikson's second stage concerns autonomy versus shame and doubt. Negativism is a normal manifestation of the shift from external control to self-control.

- Socialization, which rests on internalization of societally approved standards, begins with the development of self-regulation.

- A precursor of conscience is committed compliance to a caregiver's demands; toddlers who show committed compliance tend to internalize adult rules more readily than those who show situational compliance.

- Parenting practices, a child's temperament, the quality of the parent-child relationship, and cultural and socioeconomic factors may affect the ease and success of socialization.

  autonomy versus shame and doubt (233) socialization (233) internalization (233) self-regulation (234) conscience (236) committed compliance (236) situational compliance (236) receptive cooperation (237)

How Different Are Baby Boys and Girls?

Guidepost 5 When and how do gender differences appear?

- Although significant gender differences typically do not appear until after infancy, U.S. parents begin gender-typing boys and girls almost from birth.

  gender (237) gender-typing (238)

Contact with Other Children

Guidepost 6 How do infants and toddlers interact with siblings and other children?

- A child's adjustment to a new baby may depend on the child's age, the quality of her or his relationship with the mother, and the family atmosphere.

- Sibling relationships play a distinct role in socialization; what children learn from relations with siblings carries over to relationships outside the home.
- Between ages 1½ and 3 years, children tend to show more interest in other children and increasing understanding of how to deal with them.

Children of Working Parents

Guidepost 7 How do parental employment and early child care affect infants' and toddlers' development?

- In general, mothers' workforce participation during a child's first 3 years seems to have little impact on development, but cognitive development may suffer when a mother works 30 or more hours a week by her child's 9th month.
- Substitute child care varies widely in type and quality. The most important element in quality of care is the caregiver.
- Although quality, quantity, stability, and type of care have some influence on psychosocial and cognitive development, the influence of family characteristics seems greater overall.
- Low-income children, especially, benefit from good child care.

4 Part Four

Early Childhood: A Preview

Chapter 9
Physical Development and Health in Early Childhood

- Growth is steady; appearance becomes more slender and proportions more adultlike.
- Appetite diminishes, and sleep problems are common.
- Handedness appears; fine and gross motor skills and strength improve.

Chapter 10
Cognitive Development in Early Childhood

- Thinking is somewhat egocentric, but understanding of other people's perspectives grows.
- Cognitive immaturity results in some illogical ideas about the world.
- Memory and language improve.
- Intelligence becomes more predictable.
- Preschool experience is common, and kindergarten experience is more so.

Chapter 11
Psychosocial Development in Early Childhood

- Self-concept and understanding of emotions become more complex; self-esteem is global.
- Independence, initiative, and self-control increase.
- Gender identity develops.
- Play becomes more imaginative, more elaborate, and usually more social.
- Altruism, aggression, and fearfulness are common.
- Family is still the focus of social life, but other children become more important.

Early Childhood

During the years from 3 to 6, often called the preschool years, children make the transition from toddlerhood to childhood. Their bodies become slimmer, their motor and mental abilities sharper, and their personalities and relationships more complex.

The 3-year-old is no longer a baby but a sturdy adventurer, at home in the world and eager to explore its possibilities as well as the developing capabilities of his or her own body and mind. A child of this age has come through a relatively dangerous time of life—the years of infancy and toddlerhood—to enter a healthier, less threatening phase.

Growth and change are less rapid in early childhood than in infancy and toddlerhood, but, as we will see in Chapters 9, 10, and 11, all domains of development—physical, cognitive, emotional, and social—continue to intertwine.

Linkups to Look For

- As muscles come under more conscious control, children can tend to more of their personal needs, such as dressing and toileting, and thus gain a greater sense of competence and independence.

- Eating and sleep patterns are influenced by cultural attitudes.

- Even the common cold can have emotional and cognitive implications. Occasional minor illnesses not only build immunity; they also help children learn to cope with physical distress and understand its causes.

- Social interaction plays a major role in the development of preliteracy skills, memory, and measured intelligence.

- Cognitive awareness of gender has far-reaching psychosocial implications, affecting children's sense of self and their attitudes toward the roles males and females play in their society.

CHAPTER NINE

Physical Development and Health in Early Childhood

Children's playings are not sports and should be deemed as their most serious actions.

—Montaigne, *Essays*

Focus *Wang Yani, Self-Taught Artist*

Wang Yani

Wang Yani (b. 1975) is a gifted young Chinese artist. She had her first exhibit in Shanghai at age 4 and had produced 4,000 paintings by age 6. Since she turned 10, her work has been shown throughout Asia and in Europe and the United States.

Yani (her given name)* began painting at 2½. Her father, Wang Shiqiang, was a professional artist and educator. He gave her big brushes and large sheets of paper to permit bold strokes. Rather than teach her, he let her learn in her own way and always praised her work. In contrast with traditional Chinese art education, which emphasizes conformity and imitation, he allowed his daughter's imagination free rein.

Yani went through the usual stages in preschoolers' drawing but far more quickly than usual. Her early paintings were made up of dots, circles, and lines, which represented people, birds, or fruit. By age 3, she could paint recognizable but highly original forms.

Yani's father encouraged her to paint what she saw outdoors near their home in the scenic riverside town of Gongcheng. Like traditional Chinese artists, she did not paint from life but constructed her brightly colored compositions from mental images of what she had seen. Her visual memory has been called astounding. When she was only 4, her father taught her Chinese characters (letters) of as many as 25 strokes by writing them in the air with his finger. Without hesitation, Yani would put them down on paper from memory.

Her father helped her develop powers of observation and imagery by carrying her on his shoulders as he hiked in the fields and mountains or lying with her in the grass and telling stories about the passing clouds. The pebbles along the riverbank reminded her of the monkeys at the zoo, which she painted over and over between ages 3 and 6. Yani made up stories about the monkeys she portrayed. They often represented Yani herself—eating a snack, refereeing an argument among friends, or trying to conquer her fear of her first shot at the

*In Chinese custom, the given name follows the family name.

Sources of biographical information about Wang Yani are Bond (1989), Costello (1990), Ho (1989), Stuart (1991), and Zhensun & Low (1991).

doctor's office. Painting, to Yani, was not an objective representation of reality; it was a mirror of her mind, a way to transform her sensory impressions into simple but powerful semiabstract images onto which she projected her thoughts, feelings, and dreams.

Because of her short arms, Yani's brushstrokes at first were short. Her father trained her to hold her brush tightly by trying to grab it from behind when she was not looking. She learned to paint with her whole arm, twisting her wrist to produce the effect she wanted. As her physical dexterity and experience grew, her strokes became more forceful, varied, and precise: broad, wet strokes to define an animal's shape; fuzzy, nearly dry ones to suggest feathers, fur, or tree bark. The materials she used—bamboo brushes, ink sticks, and rice paper—were traditional, but her style, popularly called *xieyi,* "idea writing," was not. It was and remains playful, free, and spontaneous.

With quick reflexes, a fertile imagination, remarkable visual abilities, strong motivation, and her father's sensitive guidance, Yani's artistic progress has been swift. As a young adult, she is considered an artist of great promise. Yet she herself finds painting very simple: "You just paint what you think about. You don't have to follow any instruction. Everybody can paint" (Zhensun & Low, 1991, p. 9).

● ● ●

Although Wang Yani's artistic growth has been unusual, it rests on typical developments of early childhood: rapid improvements in muscular control and eye-hand coordination. Children in this age group grow more slowly than before but still at a fast pace, and they make so much progress in muscle development and coordination that they can do much more than before. As is true for other children, Yani's gain in fine motor skills was accompanied by a growing cognitive understanding of the world around her—an understanding guided by her powers of observation and memory and her interactions with her father. Together these physical, cognitive, and social influences helped her express her thoughts and emotions through art.

In this chapter, as we look at physical development during the years from 3 to 6, we will see other examples of its interconnection with cognitive and psychosocial development. Nutrition and handedness are influenced by cultural attitudes, and sleep patterns by emotional experiences. Environmental influences, including the parents' life circumstances, affect health and safety.

After you have read and studied this chapter, you should be able to answer each of the Guidepost questions on the following page. Look for them again in the margins throughout the chapter, where they point to important concepts. To check your understanding of these Guideposts, review the end-of-chapter summary. Checkpoints located throughout the chapter will help you verify your understanding of what you have read.

Guideposts for Study

1. How do children's bodies change between ages 3 and 6, and what are their nutritional and dental needs?

2. What sleep patterns and problems tend to develop during early childhood?

3. What are the main motor achievements of early childhood, and how does children's artwork show their physical and cognitive maturation?

4. What are the major health and safety risks for young children?

Aspects of Physiological Development

Guidepost 1

How do children's bodies change between ages 3 and 6, and what are their nutritional and dental needs?

In early childhood, children slim down and shoot up. They need less sleep than before and are more likely to develop sleep problems. They improve in running, hopping, skipping, jumping, and throwing balls. They also become better at tying shoelaces (in bows instead of knots), drawing with crayons (on paper rather than on walls), and pouring cereal (into the bowl, not onto the floor); and they begin to show a preference for using either the right or left hand.

Bodily Growth and Change

Children grow rapidly between ages 3 and 6 but less quickly than in infancy and toddlerhood. At about age 3, children begin to take on the slender, athletic appearance of childhood. As abdominal muscles develop, the toddler potbelly tightens. The trunk, arms, and legs grow longer. The head is still relatively large, but the other parts of the body continue to catch up as proportions steadily become more adultlike.

The pencil mark on the wall that shows Eve's height at 3 years is 37 inches from the floor, and she weighs about 30 pounds. Her twin brother Isaac, like most boys this age, is a little taller and heavier and has more muscle per pound of body weight, whereas Eve, like most girls, has more fatty tissue. Both boys and girls typically grow 2 to 3 inches a year during early childhood and gain 4 to 6 pounds annually (Table 9-1). Boys' slight edge in height and weight continues until the growth spurt of puberty.

Muscular and skeletal growth progresses, making children stronger. Cartilage turns to bone at a faster rate than before, and bones become harder, giving the child a firmer shape and protecting the internal organs. These changes, coordinated by the still-maturing brain and nervous system, promote the development of a wide range of motor skills. The increased

At age 4½, this boy's 43-inch height is 1½ inches above average but within normal range.

Table 9-1	Physical Growth, Ages 3 to 6 (50th percentile)*			
	Height, Inches		**Weight, Pounds**	
Age	**Boys**	**Girls**	**Boys**	**Girls**
3	37½	37	32	30
3½	39	38½	34	32½
4	40½	39½	36	35
4½	41½	41	38	37
5	43	42½	40	40
5½	44½	44	43	42
6	45½	45½	46	45

*Fifty percent of children in each category are above this height or weight level, and 50 percent are below it.

Source: Kuczmarski et al., 2000.

Box 9-1 *Helping Children Eat and Sleep Well*

One child refuses to eat anything but peanut butter and jelly sandwiches. Another seems to live on bananas. Mealtimes seem more like art class, as preschoolers make snowmen out of mashed potatoes or lakes out of applesauce, and food remains uneaten on the plate.

Although a diminished appetite in early childhood is normal, many parents make the mistake of insisting that children eat more than they want, setting in motion a contest of wills. Bedtime, too, often becomes an issue ("Daddy, leave the light on! . . . I want a drink of water. . . . What's that noise by the window? . . . I'm cold"). When a child delays or has trouble going to sleep or wakes often during the night, parents tend to become irritated, and the entire family feels the strain.

The following research-based suggestions can help make mealtimes and bedtimes pleasanter and children healthier (American Academy of Child and Adolescent Psychiatry [AACAP], 1997; American Academy of Pediatrics [AAP], 1992; American Heart Association et al., 2006; L. A. Adams & Rickert, 1989; Graziano & Mooney, 1982; Rolls, Engell, & Birch, 2000; Williams & Caliendo, 1984):

Encouraging Healthy Eating Habits

- Parents, not children, should choose mealtimes.
- If the child is not overweight, allow him or her to decide how much to eat. Don't pressure the child to clean the plate.
- Serve portions appropriate to the child's size and age.
- Serve simple, easily identifiable foods. Preschoolers often balk at mixed dishes such as casseroles.
- Serve finger foods as often as possible.
- Introduce only one new food at a time, along with a familiar one the child likes. Offer small servings of new or disliked foods; give second helpings if wanted.
- After a reasonable time, remove the food and do not serve more until the next meal. A healthy child will not suffer from missing a meal, and children need to learn that certain times are appropriate for eating.
- Give the child a choice of foods containing similar nutrients: rye or whole wheat bread, a peach or an apple, yogurt or milk.
- Serve nonfat or lowfat dairy products as sources of calcium and protein.
- Encourage a child to help prepare food; a child can help make sandwiches or mix and spoon out cookie dough.
- Limit snacking while watching television or videos. Discourage nutrient-poor foods such as salty snacks, fried foods, ice cream, cookies, and sweetened beverages, and instead suggest nutritious snack foods, such as fruits and raw vegetables.
- Turn childish delights to advantage. Serve food in appealing dishes; dress it up with garnishes or little toys; make a party out of a meal.

- Don't fight rituals, in which a child eats foods one at a time, in a certain order.
- Have regular family meals. Make mealtimes pleasant with conversation on interesting topics, keeping talk about eating itself to a minimum.

Helping Children Go to Sleep

- Establish a regular, unrushed bedtime routine—about 20 minutes of quiet activities, such as reading a story, singing lullabies, or having quiet conversation.
- Allow no scary or loud television shows.
- Avoid highly stimulating, active play before bedtime.
- Keep a small night-light on if it makes the child feel more comfortable.
- Don't feed or rock a child at bedtime.
- Stay calm but don't yield to requests for just one more story, one more drink of water, or one more bathroom trip.
- If you're trying to break a child's habit, offer rewards for good bedtime behavior, such as stickers on a chart or simple praise.
- Try making bedtime a little later. Sending a child to bed too early is a common reason for sleep problems.

Helping Children Go Back to Sleep

- If a child gets up during the night, take him or her back to bed. Speak calmly and pat the child gently on the back, but be pleasantly firm and consistent.
- After a nightmare, reassure a frightened child and occasionally check in on the child. If frightening dreams persist for more than 6 weeks, consult your doctor.
- After night terrors, do not wake the child. If the child wakes, don't ask any questions. Just let the child go back to sleep.
- Help your child get enough sleep on a regular schedule; overtired or stressed children are more prone to night terrors.
- Walk or carry a sleepwalking child back to bed. Childproof your home with gates at the top of stairs and at windows and with bells on the child's bedroom door, so you'll know when she or he is out of bed.

What's your view ?

Have you ever tried to get a child to eat properly or go to sleep on time? If so, did you find any of the tactics suggested helpful?

Check it out !

For more information, go to www.kidsnutrition.org/consumer/nyc/vol1_03/energy_calculator.htm for a Children's Energy Needs Calculator that translates exercise patterns into daily caloric needs. You can also visit the National Sleep Foundation at www.sleepfoundation.org and click on "Topics: A to Zzzzs" for a list of articles on sleep-related topics, including many under "Children."

capacities of the respiratory and circulatory systems build physical stamina and, along with the developing immune system, keep children healthier.

Nutrition: Preventing Overweight

As in infancy and toddlerhood, proper growth and health depend on good nutrition and adequate sleep (Box 9-1). However, preschoolers' dietary requirements and sleep needs (discussed later in this chapter) are quite different from those of infants or toddlers. Beginning at age 2, a healthy diet is the same as for adults: primarily fruits and vegetables, whole grains, low-fat and nonfat dairy products, beans, fish, and lean meats (American Heart Association et al., 2006).

Obesity (sometimes called *overweight*) has become a problem among U.S. preschoolers. In 2003–2004, nearly 14 percent of 2- to 5-year-olds were overweight, and about 12 percent more were considered at risk for overweight. Boys are more affected than girls, and Mexican American boys are especially prone to overweight (Ogden et al., 2004). However, the greatest increase in prevalence of overweight is among children in low-income families (Ritchie et al., 2001), cutting across all ethnic groups (AAP Committee on Nutrition, 2003; Center for Weight and Health, 2001). Even at age 5, overweight is associated with behavioral problems (Datar & Sturm, 2004a) and low reading and math scores (Datar, Sturm, & Magnabosco, 2004).

Worldwide, an estimated 22 million children under age 5 are obese (Belizzi, 2002). As junk food spreads through the developing world, as many as 20 to 25 percent of 4-year-olds in some countries, such as Egypt, Morocco, and Zambia, are overweight or obese—a larger proportion than are malnourished.

A tendency toward obesity can be hereditary, but the main factors driving the obesity epidemic are environmental (AAP, 2004). Excessive weight gain hinges on caloric intake and lack of exercise (AAP Committee on Nutrition, 2003). As growth slows, preschoolers need fewer calories in proportion to their weight than they did before. According to a representative sampling in Glasgow, Scotland, many 3- to 5-year-olds have mostly sedentary lifestyles (Reilly et al., 2004).

An obese child is likely to find it hard to keep up with slimmer peers, both physically and socially. Obesity among preschool and school-age children is more common than in the past.

As children move through the preschool period, their eating patterns become more environmentally influenced. Whereas 3-year-olds will eat only until they are full, 5-year-olds tend to eat more when a larger portion is put in front of them. Thus, a key to preventing obesity may be to make sure older preschoolers are served appropriate portions—and not to admonish them to clean their plates (Rolls et al., 2000). Preschoolers who are allowed to eat when they are hungry and are not pressured to eat everything given to them are more likely to regulate their caloric intake than are children fed on a schedule (S. L. Johnson & Birch, 1994). However, children vary in their ability to recognize their internal cues of hunger and fullness and may be influenced by what their parents eat. In a study of 40 families in two child care facilities, a 6-week program designed to teach children to recognize their own cues improved their ability to self-regulate, independent of what they saw their mothers do (Johnson, 2000).

What children eat is as important as how much they eat. To avoid overweight and prevent cardiac problems, young children should get only about 30 percent of their total calories from fat, and no more than one-third of fat calories should come from saturated fat. Lean meat and dairy foods should remain in the diet to provide protein, iron, and calcium. Milk and other dairy products should be skim or low fat (AAP Committee on Nutrition, 1992). Studies have found no negative effects on height, weight, body mass, or neurological development from a moderately low-fat diet (Rask-Nissilä et al., 2000; Shea et al., 1993).

Prevention of overweight in the early years, when excessive weight gain usually begins, is critical; the long-term success of treatment, especially when it is delayed, is limited (AAP Committee on Nutrition, 2003; Quattrin, Liu, Shaw, Shine, & Chiang, 2005). Overweight children, especially those who have overweight parents, tend to become obese adults (AAP Committee on Nutrition, 2003; Whitaker et al., 1997), and excess body mass is a threat to health. Early childhood is a good time to treat overweight, when a child's diet is still subject to parental influence or control (Quattrin et al., 2005; Whitaker et al., 1997).

Too little exercise and too much sedentary activity are important factors in overweight. Studies have found that each hour of television preschool children watch increases the risk of overweight, and having a TV set in a child's bedroom further increases the risk (Dennison, Erb, & Jenkins, 2002). In a longitudinal study of 8,158 U.S. children born in 1970 (Viner & Cole, 2005) approximately 40 percent watched 3 or more hours of television daily at age 5;

What's your view

• Much television advertising aimed at young children fosters poor nutrition by promoting fats and sugars rather than proteins and vitamins. How might parents counteract these pressures?

each additional hour of TV watching above 2 hours increased the likelihood of obesity at age 30 by 7 percent. (Overweight is discussed further in Chapters 12 and 15.)

Malnutrition

Nearly half, 46 percent, of young children in south Asia, 30 percent in sub-Saharan Africa, 8 percent in Latin America and the Caribbean, and 27 percent worldwide are moderately or severely underweight (UNICEF, 2002). Undernutrition is an underlying cause in more than half of all deaths before age 5 (Bryce, Boschi-Pinto, Shibuya, Black, and the WHO Child Health Epidemiology Reference Group, 2005). Even in the United States, 19 percent of children under 18 lived in food-insecure households in 2004 (Federal Interagency Forum on Child and Family Statistics, 2006).

Because undernourished children usually live in extremely deprived circumstances, the specific effects of malnutrition may be hard to determine. However, taken together, these deprivations may negatively affect not only growth and physical well-being but cognitive and psychosocial development as well. In an analysis of data on a nationally representative sample of 3,286 6- to 11-year-olds, those whose families had insufficient food were more likely to do poorly on arithmetic tests, to have repeated a grade, to have seen a psychologist, and to have had difficulty getting along with other children (Alaimo, Olson, & Frongillo, 2001). Moreover, cognitive effects of malnutrition may be long lasting. Among 1,559 children born on the island of Mauritius in a single year, those who were undernourished at age 3 had poorer verbal and spatial abilities, reading skills, scholastic ability, and neuropsychological performance than their peers at age 11 (Liu, Raine, Venables, Dalais, & Mednick, 2003).

Effects of malnutrition on growth can be largely reversed with improved diet (Lewit & Kerrebrock, 1997), but the most effective treatments go beyond physical care. A longitudinal study (Grantham-McGregor, Powell, Walker, Chang, & Fletcher, 1994) followed two groups of Jamaican children with low developmental levels who had been hospitalized for severe undernourishment in infancy or toddlerhood and who came from extremely poor, often unstable homes. Health care paraprofessionals played with an experimental group in the hospital and, after discharge, visited them at home every week for 3 years, showing the mothers how to make toys and encouraging them to interact with their children. Three years after the program stopped, the experimental group's IQs were well above those of a control group who had received only standard medical care (though not as high as those of a third, well-nourished group). Furthermore, the IQs of the experimental group remained higher than those of the control group as much as 14 years after leaving the hospital.

Early education may help counter the effects of undernourishment. In the Jamaican study, the mothers in the experimental group enrolled their children in preschools at earlier ages than did the mothers in the control group. In another Mauritian study, 100 3- to 5-year-olds received nutritional supplements and medical examinations and were placed in special preschools with small classes. At age 17, these children had lower rates of antisocial behavior and mental health problems than a control group. The effects were greatest among those who had been undernourished to begin with (Raine et al., 2003).

Oral Health

By age 3, all the primary, or deciduous, teeth are in place, and the permanent teeth, which will begin to appear at about age 6, are developing. Thus, parents usually can safely ignore the common habit of thumb sucking in children under 4. If children stop sucking thumbs or fingers by that age, their permanent teeth are not likely to be affected (Herrmann & Roberts, 1987; Umberger & Van Reenen, 1995).

Use of fluoride and improved dental care have dramatically reduced the incidence of tooth decay since the 1970s, but disadvantaged children still have more untreated cavities than other children (Bloom, Cohen, Vickerie, & Wondimu, 2003; Brown, Wall, & Lazar, 2000). Tooth decay in early childhood often stems from overconsumption of sweetened milk and juices in infancy together with a lack of regular dental care. In a longitudinal study of 642 Iowa children followed from age 1 through 5, consumption of regular (nondiet) soda pop, powdered beverages, and, to a lesser extent, 100 percent juice increased the risk of tooth decay (Marshall et al., 2003).

Checkpoint ✔

Can you . . .

✔ Describe typical physiological changes between ages 3 and 6?

✔ Summarize preschoolers' dietary needs and explain why overweight and tooth decay can become concerns at this age?

✔ Identify effects of malnutrition and factors that may influence its long-term outcome?

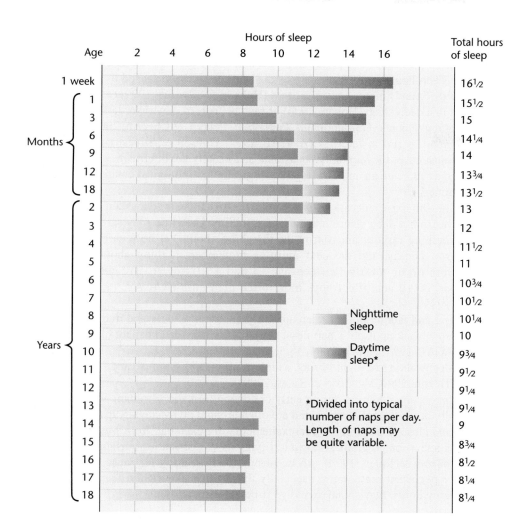

Figure 9-1

Typical sleep requirements in childhood. Unlike infants, who sleep about as long day and night, preschoolers get all or almost all their sleep in one long nighttime period. The number of hours of sleep steadily decreases throughout childhood, but individual children may need more or fewer hours than shown here.

Source: Ferber, 1985; similar data in Iglowstein et al., 2003.

Sleep Patterns and Problems

Guidepost 2

What sleep patterns and problems tend to develop during early childhood?

Sleep patterns change throughout the growing-up years (Iglowstein, Jenni, Molinari, & Largo, 2003; Figure 9-1), and early childhood has its own distinct rhythms. Young children usually sleep more deeply at night than they will later in life. Most U.S. children average about 11 hours of sleep at night by age 5 and give up daytime naps (Hoban, 2004). In some other cultures the timing of sleep may vary. Among the Gusii of Kenya, the Javanese in Indonesia, and the Zuni in New Mexico, young children have no regular bedtime and are allowed to stay up watching adult activities until they are sleepy. Among the Canadian Hare people, 3-year-olds take no naps but go to bed right after dinner and sleep as long as they wish in the morning (Broude, 1995).

Bedtime may bring on a form of separation anxiety, and the child may do all she or he can to avoid it. Young children may develop elaborate routines to put off retiring, and it may take them longer than before to fall asleep. More than half of U.S. parents or caregivers report that their preschool child stalls at bedtime and that it takes 15 minutes or more for the child to fall asleep. About one-third of preschoolers actively resist going to bed, and more than one-third awake at least once each night (National Sleep Foundation, 2004). Regular, consistent sleep routines can help minimize these problems. Young children who have become accustomed to going to sleep while feeding or rocking may find it hard to fall asleep on their own (Hoban, 2004). Children are likely to want a light left on and to sleep with a favorite toy or blanket. Such *transitional objects,* used repeatedly as bedtime companions, help a child shift from the dependence of infancy to the independence of later childhood.

Sleep Disturbances and Disorders

About 1 in 10 parents or caregivers of preschoolers say their child has a sleep problem (National Sleep Foundation, 2004). Sleep disturbances may be caused by accidental activation of the brain's motor control system (Hobson & Silvestri, 1999) or by incomplete arousal from a deep sleep (Hoban, 2004) or may be triggered by disordered breathing or restless leg movements (Guilleminault, Palombini, Pelayo, & Chervin, 2003). These disturbances tend to run in families (AACAP, 1997; Hobson & Silvestri, 1999; Hoban, 2004). In most cases they are only occasional and usually are outgrown. Persistent sleep problems may indicate an emotional, physiological, or neurological condition that needs to be examined.

A child who experiences a *sleep (or night) terror* appears to awaken abruptly early in the night from a deep sleep in a state of agitation. The child may scream and sit up in bed, breathing rapidly and staring or thrashing about. Yet he is not really awake, quiets down quickly, and the next morning remembers nothing about the episode. Night terrors occur mostly between ages 3 and 13 (Laberge, Tremblay, Vitaro, & Montplaisir, 2000) and affect boys more often than girls (AACAP, 1997; Hobson & Silvestri, 1999).

Walking and talking during sleep are fairly common in early and middle childhood. Although sleepwalking itself is harmless, sleepwalkers may be in danger of hurting themselves (AACAP, 1997; Hoban, 2004; Vgontzas & Kales, 1999). However, it is best not to interrupt sleepwalking or night terrors, as interruptions may confuse and further frighten the child (Hoban, 2004; Vgontzas & Kales, 1999).

Nightmares are common during early childhood (Smedje, Broman, & Hetta, 1999). They usually occur toward morning and are often brought on by staying up too late, eating a heavy meal close to bedtime, or overexcitement—for example, from watching an overstimulating television program, seeing a terrifying movie, or hearing a frightening bedtime story (Vgontzas & Kales, 1999). An occasional bad dream is no cause for alarm, but frequent or persistent nightmares, especially those that make a child fearful or anxious during waking hours, may signal excessive stress (Hoban, 2004).

Bed-Wetting

enuresis Repeated urination in clothing or in bed.

Most children stay dry, day and night, by age 3 to 5 years; but **enuresis,** repeated, involuntary urination at night by children old enough to be expected to have bladder control, is not unusual. About 10 to 15 percent of 5-year-olds, more commonly boys, wet the bed regularly, perhaps while sleeping deeply. More than half outgrow bed-wetting by age 8 without special help (Community Paediatrics Committee, 2005).

Children of preschool age normally recognize the sensation of a full bladder while asleep and awaken to empty it in the toilet. Children who wet the bed do not yet have this awareness. Fewer than 1 percent of bed wetters have a physical disorder, though they may have a small bladder capacity. Nor is persistent enuresis primarily an emotional, mental, or behavioral problem—though such problems can develop because of the way bed wetters are treated by playmates and family (Community Paediatrics Committee, 2005; National Enuresis Society, 1995; Schmitt, 1997).

Enuresis runs in families. About 75 percent of bed wetters have a close relative who also wets the bed, and identical twins are more concordant for the condition than fraternal twins (APA, 1994; Fergusson, Horwood, & Shannon, 1986). The discovery of the approximate site of a gene linked to enuresis (Eiberg, 1995; Eiberg, Berendt, & Mohr, 1995) points to heredity as a major factor, possibly in combination with slow motor maturation, allergies, or poor behavioral control (Goleman, 1995). The gene does not appear to account for occasional bed-wetting. Many children who wet the bed are lacking in an antidiuretic hormone, which concentrates urine during sleep. As a result, they produce more urine than their bladders can hold (National Enuresis Society, 1995).

Children and their parents need to be reassured that enuresis is common and not serious. The child is not to blame and should not be punished. Generally parents need not do anything unless children themselves are distressed by bed-wetting. Enuresis that persists beyond age 8 to 10 may be a sign of poor self-concept or other psychological problems (Community Paediatrics Committee, 2005).

The most effective treatment is a device to wake the child when he or she begins to urinate by setting off a bell or buzzer. However, the success rate is less than 50 percent, and the devices are most effective with children older than 7 or 8 who are highly motivated to overcome the problem. Drug therapy with desmopressin acetate can be used in special situations, such as camping and sleepovers. Imipramine hydrochloride may be used as short-term treatment in distressed older children, if other treatments have been unsuccessful or are contraindicated, but care must be taken to avoid overdose. There is insufficient evidence for routine use of behavioral therapy (Community Paediatrics Committee, 2005).

Motor Development

Children ages 3 to 6 make great advances in motor skills—both **gross motor skills,** which involve the large muscles, such as running and jumping (Table 9-2), and **fine motor skills,** manipulative skills involving eye-hand and small-muscle coordination, such as buttoning and drawing. They also begin to show a preference for using either the right or left hand.

Gross and Fine Motor Skills

At 3, David could walk a straight line and jump a short distance. At 4, he could hop a few steps on one foot. At 5, he could jump nearly 3 feet and hop for 16 feet and was learning to roller-skate.

Motor skills do not develop in isolation. The skills that emerge in early childhood build on the achievements of infancy and toddlerhood. Development of the sensory and motor areas of the cerebral cortex permits better coordination between what children want to do and what they can do. Their bones and muscles are stronger, and their lung capacity is greater, making it possible to run, jump, and climb farther, faster, and better. As children's bodies change, permitting them to do more, they integrate their new and previously acquired skills into **systems of action,** producing ever more complex capabilities.

At about 2½, children begin to jump with both feet, a skill they have not been able to master before this time, probably because their leg muscles were not yet strong enough to propel their body weight upward. Hopping is hard to master until about 4. Going upstairs is easier than going down; by 3½, most children comfortably alternate feet going up, but not until about 5 do they easily descend that way. Children begin to gallop at about 4, do fairly well by 5, and are quite skillful by 6½. Skipping is harder; although some 4-year-olds can skip, most children cannot do it until age 6 (Corbin, 1973). Of course, children vary in adeptness, depending on their genetic endowment and their opportunities to learn and practice motor skills.

Checkpoint ✓

Can you . . .

✔ Discuss age differences and cultural variations in sleep patterns?

✔ Identify four common sleep problems and give recommendations for handling them?

Guidepost 3

What are the main motor achievements of early childhood, and how does children's artwork show their physical and cognitive maturation?

gross motor skills Physical skills that involve the large muscles.

fine motor skills Physical skills that involve the small muscles and eye-hand coordination.

systems of action Increasingly complex combinations of skills that permit a wider or more precise range of movement and more control of the environment.

Table 9-2	Gross Motor Skills in Early Childhood	
3-Year-Olds	**4-Year-Olds**	**5-Year-Olds**
Cannot turn or stop suddenly or quickly	Have more effective control of stopping, starting, and turning	Can start, turn, and stop effectively in games
Can jump a distance of 15 to 24 inches	Can jump a distance of 24 to 33 inches	Can make a running jump of 28 to 36 inches
Can ascend a stairway alternating feet, unaided	Can descend a long stairway alternating feet, if supported	Can descend a long stairway alternating feet, unaided
Can hop, using largely an irregular series of jumps with some variations added	Can hop four to six steps on one foot	Can easily hop a distance of 16 feet

Source: Corbin, 1973.

Figure 9-2

Artistic development in early childhood. There is a great difference between the simple shapes shown in (a) and the detailed pictorial drawings in (e).

Source: Kellogg, 1970.

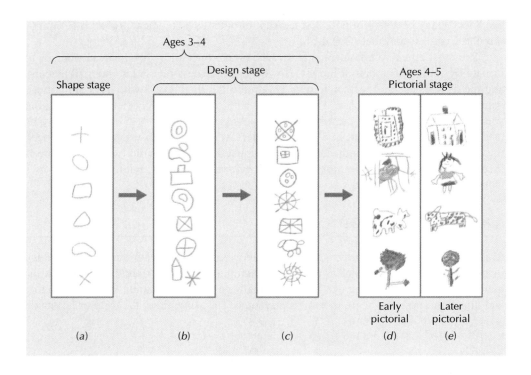

Ages 3–4

Shape stage

Design stage

Ages 4–5
Pictorial stage

Early pictorial

Later pictorial

(a)   (b)   (c)   (d)   (e)

The ability to tie her shoelaces enables this 5-year-old girl to be more self-reliant.

The gross motor skills developed during early childhood are the basis for sports, dancing, and other activities that begin during middle childhood and may continue for a lifetime. However, children under 6 are rarely ready to take part in any organized sport. Only 20 percent of 4-year-olds can throw a ball well, and only 30 percent can catch well (AAP Committee on Sports Medicine and Fitness, 1992).

Young children develop best physically when they can be active at an appropriate maturational level in unstructured free-play. Parents and teachers can help by offering young children the opportunity to climb and jump on safe, properly sized equipment, by providing balls and other toys small enough to be grasped easily and soft enough not to be harmful, and by offering gentle coaching when a child seems to need help.

Gains in *fine motor skills,* such as tying shoelaces and cutting with scissors, allow young children to take more responsibility for their personal care. At 3, Madison can pour milk into her cereal bowl, eat with silverware, and use the toilet alone. She can also draw a circle and a rudimentary person—without arms. At 4, Jordan can dress himself with help. He can cut along a line, draw a fairly complete person, make designs and crude letters, and fold paper into a double triangle. At 5, Juan can dress himself without much help, copy a square or triangle, and draw a more elaborate person than before.

Artistic Development

Most 3- to 5-year-olds may not be as accomplished artists as Wang Yani, but with progress in fine motor coordination, they too can use their growing cognitive powers and express themselves emotionally through art. In pioneering research, Rhoda Kellogg (1970) examined more than one million drawings by children, half of them under age 6. Since she found drawings by young children similar in different cultures, she concluded that stages in early drawing (Figure 9-2) reflect maturation of the brain as well as of the muscles.

Two-year-olds *scribble,* and their scribbles are not random. Kellogg identified 20 basic scribbles, such as vertical and zigzag lines, and 17 patterns of placement of scribbles on paper that appear by age 2. By age 3, the *shape* stage appears. Now a child draws in six basic shapes: circles, squares or rectangles, triangles, crosses, Xs, and odd forms. Children quickly move on to the *design* stage, in which they combine two basic shapes into a more complex abstract pattern. Most children enter the *pictorial* stage between ages 4 and 5, though Yani reached it at 3.

Kellogg views the switch from abstraction to representation during the late pictorial stage as a fundamental change in the purpose of children's drawing. Often, under the "guidance" of adults, children begin to aim for realistic portrayal and lose their concern with form and design, the primary elements of art (Kellogg, 1970).

Kellogg quotes artist Pablo Picasso: "Adults should not teach children to draw but should learn from them" (1970, p. 36). Like Wang Yani's father, adults can sustain children's early creativity by letting them draw what they like without imposing suggestions or standards.

Handedness

Handedness, the preference for using one hand over the other, is usually evident by age 3. Because the left hemisphere of the brain, which controls the right side of the body, is usually dominant, most people favor their right side. In people whose brains are less asymmetrical, the right hemisphere tends to dominate, making them left-handed. Handedness is not always clear-cut; not everybody prefers one hand for every task. Boys are more likely to be left-handed than girls.

Is handedness genetic or learned? That question has been controversial. One theory proposes the existence of a single gene for right-handedness. According to this theory, people who inherit this gene from either or both parents—about 82 percent of the population—are right-handed. Those who do not inherit the gene still have a 50-50 chance of being right-handed; otherwise they will be left-handed or ambidextrous. Random determination of handedness among those who do not receive the gene could explain why some monozygotic twins have differing hand preferences as well as why 8 percent of the offspring of two right-handed parents are left-handed (Klar, 1996).

Health and Safety

Because of widespread immunization, many of what once were the major diseases of childhood are much less common in Western industrialized countries. In the developing world, however, such preventable diseases as pneumonia, diarrhea, and malaria still take a large toll. Measles, once a major scourge of childhood, now causes only 4 percent of deaths in children younger than 5 worldwide (Bryce et al., 2005, Box 9-2).

In the United States, deaths in childhood are relatively few compared with deaths in adulthood, and most are caused by injury rather than illness (Hoyert et al., 2005). Still, environmental influences make this a less healthy time for some children than for others.

Accidental Injuries and Deaths

Because young children are naturally venturesome and often unaware of danger, it is hard for caregivers to protect them from harm without *over*protecting them. Although most cuts, bumps, and scrapes are "kissed away" and quickly forgotten, some accidental injuries result in lasting damage or death. Indeed, accidents are the leading cause of death after infancy throughout childhood and adolescence in the United States (Hamilton et al., 2007).

Many kindergartners and first graders walk alone to school, often crossing busy streets without traffic lights, although they do not know how to do this safely (Zeedyk, Wallace, & Spry, 2002). Some children are risk-prone. In one study, 5- and 6-year-olds who tended to take risks in a gambling game were more likely than their peers to say it was safe to cross a busy street between cars without a traffic light or crosswalk (Hoffrage, Weber, Hertwig, & Chase, 2003).

All 50 states and the District of Columbia require young children in cars to ride in specially designed seats or to wear standard seat belts. Four-year-olds who graduate from car

What's your view

- Drawings from children's early pictorial stage show energy and freedom; those from the later pictorial stage show care and accuracy. Why do you think these changes occur?

handedness Preference for using a particular hand.

Checkpoint ✔

Can you . . .

✔ List at least three gross motor skills and three fine motor skills, and tell when they typically develop?

✔ Identify four stages in young children's drawing?

✔ Tell how brain functioning is related to handedness?

Guidepost 4

What are the major health and safety risks for young children?

Box 9-2 *Surviving the First Five Years of Life*

The chances of a child's living to his or her 5th birthday are substantially better than 38 years ago, but the prospects for survival depend to a great extent on where the child lives. Worldwide, more than 17 million children under 5 died in 1970. Today the number of deaths in this age group has dropped to 10.6 million each year—still far too many (Bryce et al., 2005; WHO, 2003). And, although child mortality has lessened in most parts of the world, these gains have not benefited all children equally.

International efforts to improve child health focus on the first 5 years because nearly 90 percent of deaths of children under age 15 occur during those years. Fully 98 percent of child deaths occur in poor, rural regions of developing countries, where nutrition is inadequate, water is unsafe, and sanitary facilities are lacking; 42 percent of these deaths occur in sub-Saharan Africa and 29 percent in Southeast Asia (Bryce et al., 2005; WHO, 2003; Figure 9-3). A baby born in Sierra Leone is three and a half times more likely to die before age 5 than a child born in India and more than 100 times more likely to die than a child born in Iceland, which has the world's lowest child mortality rate (WHO, 2003).

Worldwide, four major causes of death, accounting for 54 percent of deaths in children younger than 5, are communicable diseases: pneumonia, diarrhea, malaria, and neonatal sepsis or pneumonia (Figure 9-4). In more than half of these deaths, undernutrition is an underlying cause. Ninety-four percent of deaths from malaria occur in Africa (Bryce et al., 2005).

More advanced developing countries of the Eastern Mediterranean region, Latin America, and Asia are experiencing a shift toward the pattern in more developed countries, where child deaths are most likely to be caused by complications of birth (refer back to Chapter 6). At least 169 countries have shown declines in child mortality in the past 3 decades. The most striking reduction was in Oman, on the southern end of the Arabian peninsula, from 242 child deaths per 1,000 live births in 1970 to only 15 per 1,000 in 2002. India and China also have achieved impressive declines. In general, however, the strongest improvement has occurred in rich industrialized nations and in those developing countries where child mortality was already relatively low. Thus, although the mortality gap between the developed and the developing worlds has narrowed, disparities among developing regions have widened (WHO, 2003).

In some African countries, HIV/AIDS is responsible for as many as 60 percent of child deaths, often children who lost their mothers to the disease. Fourteen African countries, after achieving significant reductions in child mortality during the 1970s and 1980s, saw *more* young children die in 2002 than in 1990. On the other hand, eight countries in the region, among them Gabon, Gambia, and Ghana, have reduced child mortality by more than 50 percent since 1970 (WHO, 2003).

In Latin America, the most dramatic reductions in child mortality have taken place in Chile, Costa Rica, and Cuba, where child deaths have dropped more than 80 percent since 1970. In contrast, Haitian children still die at a rate of 133 per 1,000, almost double the rate in Bolivia, which has the next worst mortality record in the Americas (WHO, 2003).

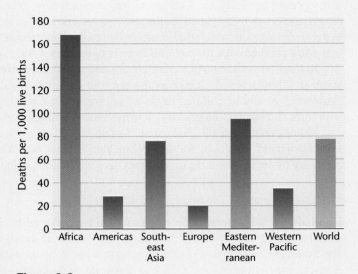

Figure 9-3

Comparative child mortality in six regions of the world, 2002.
Source: WHO, 2003.

In most countries, with the exception of China, India, Pakistan, and Nepal, boys are more likely to die than girls. In China, where families traditionally prefer boys, young girls have a 33 percent greater risk of dying—often, it has been reported, through abandonment or infanticide (Carmichael, 2004; Hudson & den Boer, 2004; Lee, 2004; Rosenthal, 2003). Children in poor countries and children of the poor in rich countries are most likely to die young. Survival gains have been slower in rural than in urban areas and, in some countries, such as the United States, have disproportionately benefited those with higher incomes. But even poor U.S. children are less likely to die young than better-off children in Africa (WHO, 2003).

What's your view ?

What might be done to produce more rapid and more evenly distributed improvements in child mortality throughout the world?

Check it out !

For more information on this topic, go to http://www.who.int/whr/2003/chapter1/en/index2.html. This is the Web site for the WHO report discussed in this box.

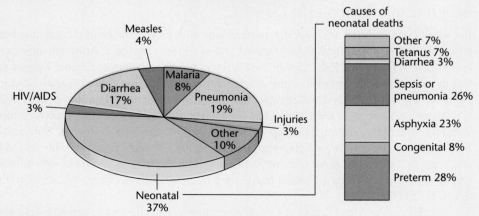

Figure 9-4

Major causes of death in children younger than 5 and in neonates (yearly average, 2000–2003).
Source: Bryce et al., 2005.

Table 9-3	Reducing Accident Risks for Children
Activity	**Precautions**
Bicycling	Helmets reduce risk of head injury by 85 percent and brain injury by 88 percent.
Skateboarding and rollerblading	Children should wear helmets and protective padding on knees, elbows, and wrists.
Using fireworks	Families should not purchase fireworks for home use.
Lawn mowing	Children under 12 should not operate walk-behind mowers; those under 14 should not operate ride-on mowers; small children should not be close to a moving mower.
Swimming	Swimming pools should not be installed in backyards of homes with children under 5; pools already in place need a high fence all around, with gates having high, out-of-reach, self-closing latches. Adults need to watch children very closely near pools, lakes, and other bodies of water.
Playing on a playground	A safe surface under swings, slides, and other equipment can be 10-inch-deep sand, 12-inch-deep wood chips, or rubber outdoor mats; separate areas should be maintained for active play and quiet play, for older and younger children.
Using firearms	Guns should be kept unloaded and locked up, with bullets locked in a separate place; children should not have access to keys; adults should talk with children about the risks of gun injury.
Eating	To prevent choking, young children should not eat hard candies, nuts, grapes, and hot dogs (unless sliced lengthwise, then across); food should be cut into small pieces; children should not eat while talking, running, jumping, or lying down.
Ingesting toxic substances	Only drugs and toxic household products with safety caps should be used; toxic products should be stored out of children's reach. Suspected poisoning should be reported immediately to the nearest poison control center.
Riding in motor vehicles	Young children should sit in approved car seats, in the backseat. Adults should observe traffic laws and avoid aggressive drivers.

Source: Adapted in part from American Academy of Pediatrics (AAP) Committee on Injury and Poison Prevention, 1995; AAP and Center to Prevent Handgun Violence, 1994; Rivara, 1999; Shannon, 2000.

seats to lap and shoulder belts may need booster seats until they grow bigger. Airbags designed to inflate rapidly so as to protect adults riding in the front seat of a car in high-impact collisions *increase* the risk of fatal injury to children under age 13 who are riding in the front seat. The number of child deaths in motor vehicle crashes fell by 200 a year between 1996 and 2003 as a result of a campaign to keep children in the backseats of cars (Glassbrenner, Carra, & Nichols, 2005).

Most deaths from injuries, especially among preschoolers, occur in the home—most of them from fires, drowning in bathtubs, suffocation, poisoning, or falls (Nagaraja et al., 2005). Everyday medications, such as aspirin, acetaminophen, cold and cough preparations, and even vitamins and minerals can be dangerous to inquisitive young children unless they are stored out of reach. During 2001–2003, an estimated 53,517 children age 4 and under were treated each year in U.S. hospital emergency departments for unintentional exposure to prescription and over-the-counter medicines. In 2002, 35 children in this age group died from unintentional drug poisoning. In 2003, pharmaceuticals accounted for 568,939 reports of chemical or substance poisoning of children under 6, according to U.S. poison control centers (Burt, Annest, Ballesteros, & Budnitz, 2006).

U.S. laws requiring childproof caps on medicine bottles and other dangerous household products, regulation of product safety, car seats for young children, mandatory helmets for bicycle riders, and safe storage of firearms and of medicines have improved child safety. Making playgrounds safer would be another valuable measure. (Table 9-3 summarizes suggestions for reducing accident risks in various settings.)

Checkpoint

Can you . . .

✔ Compare the health status of young children in developed and developing countries?

✔ Tell where and how young children are most likely to be injured, and list ways in which injuries can be avoided?

Figure 9-5

Families with children as a percentage of the homeless population in U.S. cities.

Source: Children's Defense Fund, 2004, p. 19. Data taken from U.S. Conference of Mayors, 2003.

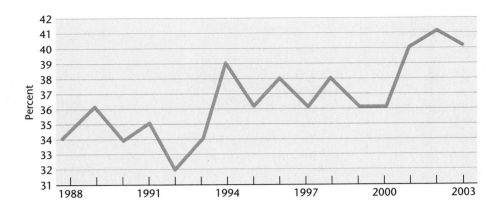

Health in Context: Environmental Influences

Why do some children have more illnesses or injuries than others? The genetic heritage contributes: some children seem predisposed toward some medical conditions. In addition, environmental factors play major roles.

Socioeconomic Status and Race/Ethnicity

The lower a family's SES, the greater a child's risks of illness, injury, and death (Chen, Matthews, & Boyce, 2002). Poor children—who represent 1 in 5 U.S. children under 6 (Federal Interagency Forum on Child and Family Statistics, 2005) and are disproportionately minority children (NCHS, 2005)—are more likely than other children to have chronic conditions and activity limitations, to lack health insurance, and to have unmet medical and dental needs. However, the general health of poor children has been improving; between 1984 and 2003, the percentage of poor children in very good or excellent health rose from 62 percent to 71 percent, as compared with 86 to 89 percent for nonpoor children (Federal Interagency Forum on Child and Family Statistics, 2005).

Medicaid, a government program that provides medical assistance to eligible low-income persons and families, has been a safety net for many poor children since 1965. However, it has not reached millions of children whose families earn too much to qualify but too little to afford private insurance. The federal government in 1997 authorized the State Children's Health Insurance Program (SCHIP) to help states extend health care coverage to uninsured children in poor and near-poor families. At the end of 2004, 3.9 million children were enrolled (Smith & Rousseau, 2005). Still, 11 percent of all children had no health coverage in 2003. Children without insurance are more than 4 times as likely as children with insurance to lack a usual source of health care (Federal Interagency Forum on Child and Family Statistics, 2005).

Access to quality health care is a particular problem among black and Latino children, especially those who are poor or near poor (Flores et al., 2005). In 2003, 21 percent of Hispanic American children lacked health insurance (Federal Interagency Forum on Child and Family Statistics, 2005). In that year, more than 8 percent of Hispanic children under age 6 and more than 14 percent of those ages 6 to 17 had no usual source of health care (NCHS, 2005). Language and cultural barriers and the need for more Latino care providers may help explain these disparities (Flores et al., 2002). Even Asian American children, who tend to be in better health than non-Hispanic white children, are less likely to access and use health care, perhaps because of similar barriers (NCHS, 2005; Yu, Huang, & Singh, 2004).

Homelessness

Since the 1980s, as affordable rental housing has become scarce and poverty has spread, homelessness has increased dramatically in the United States. An estimated 1.35 million children experience homelessness each year (National Coalition for the Homeless, 2004).

Families now make up 40 percent of the homeless population, and the proportion is probably higher in rural areas (National Coalition for the Homeless, 2004; U.S. Conference of Mayors, 2003; Figure 9-5). Many homeless families are headed by single mothers in

Families with children are the fastest-growing part of the homeless population. Homeless children tend to have more health problems than children with homes.

their 20s (Buckner, Bassuk, Weinreb, & Brooks, 1999). Often these families are fleeing domestic violence (National Coalition for the Homeless, 2004).

Many homeless children spend their crucial early years in unstable, insecure, and often unsanitary environments. They and their parents may be cut off from a supportive community, family ties, and institutional resources and from ready access to medical care and schooling; and they often are unable to find stable housing again. These children suffer more health problems than poor children who have homes, and they are more likely to die in infancy. They are three times more likely than other children to lack immunizations and two to three times more likely to have iron deficiency anemia. They experience high rates of diarrhea; severe hunger, and malnourishment; obesity (from eating excessive carbohydrates and fats); tooth decay; asthma and other chronic diseases; respiratory, skin, and eye and ear infections; scabies and lice; trauma-related injuries; and elevated levels of lead. Homeless children also tend to suffer severe depression and anxiety and to have neurological and visual deficits, developmental delays, behavior problems, and learning difficulties. Uprooted from their neighborhoods, as many as half do not go to school; if they do, they tend to have problems, partly because they miss a lot of it and have no place to do homework. They tend to do poorly on standardized reading and math tests, even when their cognitive functioning is normal, and they are more likely to repeat a grade or be placed in special classes than are children with homes (AAP Committee on Community Health Services, 1996; Bassuk, 1991; Children's Defense Fund, 2004; Rafferty & Shinn, 1991; Rubin et al., 1996; Weinreb et al., 2002). In large cities that have provided safe housing for poor and homeless families in stable, lower-poverty neighborhoods, the children's behavior and school performance improved greatly (CDF, 2004).

Exposure to Smoking, Air Pollution, Pesticides, and Lead

Parental smoking, both at home and in the family car, is a preventable cause of childhood illness and death. The potential damage caused by exposure to tobacco is greatest during the early years of life (DiFranza, Aligne, & Weitzman, 2004), when bodies are still developing. Almost 60 percent of U.S. children age 3 to 11 are exposed to secondhand smoke. Children exposed to parental smoke are at increased risk of respiratory infections such as bronchitis and pneumonia, ear problems, worsened asthma, and slowed lung growth. Secondhand smoke contains hundreds of carcinogens, or cancer-causing chemicals, and can lead to premature death (Office on Smoking and Health, 2006).

Air pollution, particularly from chemical particles and ozone, is associated with increased risks of death and of chronic respiratory disease. Environmental contaminants may play a role in certain childhood cancers, neurological disorders, attention-deficit/hyperactivity disorder,

Young children who live in old, dilapidated buildings with peeling lead paint are at risk for lead poisoning, which can adversely affect the developing brain.

and mental retardation (Goldman et al., 2004; Woodruff et al., 2004). In 2003, 62 percent of children up to age 17 lived in counties that failed to meet one or more national air quality standards, the worst offender being ozone levels (Federal Interagency Forum for Child and Family Statistics, 2005). Poverty and minority status are associated with higher exposure to polluted air (Dilworth-Bart & Moore, 2006).

A total of 4.5 billion pounds of chemical pesticides are used annually in the United States. Pesticide residues are found in food, water, homes, schools, workplaces, lawns, and gardens. More than half of all reported pesticide poisonings—almost 50,000 per year—occur in children younger than 6 (Weiss, Amler, & Amler, 2004).

Children are more vulnerable than adults to chronic pesticide damage (Goldman et al., 2004). In a national survey of human exposure to environmental chemicals, urine levels of dimethylthiophosphate, a chemical produced by metabolism of many organic pesticides, were twice as high in 6- through 11-year-olds as in adults (Centers for Disease Control and Prevention, 2003). There is some, though not definitive, evidence that low-dose pesticide exposure may affect the developing brain (Weiss et al., 2004). Pesticide exposure is greater in children in agricultural and inner-city families (Dilworth-Bart & Moore, 2006).

Parents can take precautions against pesticide damage by applying pesticides prudently, storing them in their original containers where children cannot reach them, and washing fresh produce before it is eaten. Insect repellants should be applied only to exposed skin and washed off with soap and water when a child comes indoors (Weiss et al., 2004).

Children can get elevated concentrations of lead from lead-contaminated food or water, from airborne industrial wastes, from putting contaminated fingers in their mouths, or from inhaling dust or playing with paint chips in homes or schools where there is lead-based paint.

Lead poisoning can seriously interfere with cognitive development and can lead to neurological and behavioral problems (AAP Committee on Environmental Health, 2005; Federal Interagency Forum for Child and Family Statistics, 2005). The effects on developing brains may be irreversible (Bellinger, 2004). Very high levels of blood lead concentration may cause headaches, abdominal pain, loss of appetite, agitation, or lethargy and eventually vomiting, stupor, and convulsions (AAP Committee on Environmental Health, 2005). Yet all these effects are completely preventable.

Children's median blood lead levels have dropped by 89 percent in the United States since 1976–1980 due to laws mandating removal of lead from gasoline and paints and reducing smokestack emissions (Federal Interagency Forum for Child and Family Statistics, 2005). Still, about 25 percent of U.S. children, most of them black and poor, live in households with deteriorating lead paint (AAP Committee on Environmental Health, 2005).

There is no safe level of exposure to lead (AAP Committee on Environmental Health, 2005). Even low levels of exposure may have detrimental effects in young preschoolers, particularly those who have other risk factors, such as poverty and maternal depression (Canfield et al., 2003).

In a 5-year longitudinal study, treatment of lead-exposed children decreased blood lead concentrations but proved ineffective in improving psychological, behavioral, and cognitive functioning. Thus, prevention is critical (Rogan et al., 2001). Paint removal can raise lead dust, but professional cleaning and paint stabilization can stop unhealthy exposure. Soil around houses with exterior lead paint and near smokestacks or heavy traffic can be tested, following EPA guidelines (AAP Committee on Environmental Health, 2005).

Checkpoint ✔

Can you . . .

✔ Discuss several environmental influences that endanger children's health and development?

Refocus

Thinking back to the information about Wang Yani in the Focus vignette at the beginning of this chapter,

- What aspects of Wang Yani's physical development in early childhood seem to have been fairly typical? In what ways was her development advanced?

- Can you give examples of how Yani's physical, cognitive, and psychosocial development interacted?

- What more would you like to know about Yani's early development if you had the chance to interview her or her parents?

Fortunately, most children are healthy. Preschool children who are in good health and whose basic physical needs are met are able to make major advances in cognitive development, as we'll see in Chapter 10.

Summary and Key Terms

Aspects of Physiological Development

Guidepost 1 How do children's bodies change between ages 3 and 6, and what are their nutritional and dental needs?

- Physical growth increases during the years from 3 to 6 but more slowly than during infancy and toddlerhood. Boys are on average slightly taller, heavier, and more muscular than girls. Internal body systems are maturing, and all primary teeth are present.

- Preschool children generally eat less for their weight than before—and need less—but the prevalence of obesity has increased.

- Tooth decay has decreased since the 1970s but remains a problem among disadvantaged children.

- Thumb sucking can safely be ignored unless it continues beyond age 4, when permanent teeth begin to develop.

Sleep Patterns and Problems

Guidepost 2 What sleep patterns and problems tend to develop during early childhood?

- Sleep patterns change during early childhood, as throughout life, and are affected by cultural expectations.

- It is normal for preschool children to develop bedtime rituals that delay going to sleep. Prolonged bedtime struggles or persistent sleep terrors or nightmares may indicate emotional disturbances that need attention.

- Bed-wetting is common and is usually outgrown without special help.

    enuresis (256)

Motor Development

Guidepost 3 What are the main motor achievements of early childhood, and how does children's artwork show their physical and cognitive maturation?

- Children progress rapidly in gross and fine motor skills and eye-hand coordination, developing more complex systems of action.

- Stages of art production, which appear to reflect brain development and fine motor coordination, are the scribbling stage, shape stage, design stage, and pictorial stage.

- Handedness is usually evident by age 3, reflecting dominance by one hemisphere of the brain.

    gross motor skills (257)   fine motor skills (257)   systems of action (257)   handedness (259)

Health and Safety

Guidepost 4 What are the major health and safety risks for young children?

- Although major contagious illnesses are rare today in industrialized countries due to widespread immunization, preventable disease continues to be a major problem in the developing world.

- Minor illnesses, such as colds and other respiratory illnesses, are common during early childhood and help build immunity to disease.

- Accidents, most commonly motor vehicle injuries, are the leading cause of death in childhood in the United States. Most fatal nonvehicular accidents occur at home.

- Environmental factors such as exposure to disease, smoking, poverty, and homelessness increase the risks of illness or injury. Lead poisoning can have serious physical, cognitive, and behavioral effects.

Cognitive Development in Early Childhood

Childhood is a world of miracle and wonder: as if creation rose, bathed in light, out of darkness, utterly new and fresh and astonishing. The end of childhood is when things cease to astonish us. When the world seems familiar, when one has got used to existence, one has become an adult.

—Eugene Ionesco, *Fragments of a Journal*, 1976

Focus *Albert Einstein, Nuclear Physicist*

Albert Einstein

In the public mind, the name Albert Einstein (1879–1955) is synonymous with *genius*. His general theory of relativity ("the greatest revolution in thought since Newton"), his discovery of the fundamental principle of quantum physics, and his other contributions to the reshaping of our knowledge of the universe cause him to be considered "one of the greatest physicists of all time" (Whitrow, 1967, p. 1).

Yet the young Einstein, who was born in the German town of Ulm, hardly seemed destined for intellectual stardom. He was slow in learning to walk and did not begin talking until at least his 3rd year. His parents feared he might be mentally retarded. Einstein himself always insisted that he did not *try* to speak until after the age of 3, skipping babbling and going directly to sentences. Actually, his sentences may have come a bit earlier. When his sister, Maja, was born 4 months before Albert's 3rd birthday, Albert (who had been promised a new baby to play with and apparently thought it would be a toy) reportedly asked in disappointment, "Where are the wheels?"

Regardless of the exact timing, "Albert was certainly a late and reluctant talker" (Brian, 1996, p. 1). The reasons may have had more to do with personality than with cognitive development; he was a shy, taciturn child, whom adults thought backward and other children considered dull. He would not play marbles or soldiers or other games with his peers, but he would crouch for hours, observing an ant colony.

When he started school, he did poorly in most subjects; the headmaster predicted he would never amount to anything. Albert hated the regimentation and rote learning stressed in German schools; he did not have a retentive memory and could not give clear answers to his teachers' questions. He was a daydreamer, his questioning mind occupied with its own speculations. He would not even try to learn anything unless he was interested in it—and then his concentration was intense.

Sources of biographical information about Albert Einstein are Bernstein (1973); Brian (1996); French (1979); Goldsmith, Mackay, & Woudhuysen (1980); Michelmore (1962); Quasha (1980); Schilpp (1970); and Whitrow (1967).

His wonder about the workings of the universe was awakened at age 4 or 5, when he was sick in bed and his father gave him a magnetic pocket compass to keep him amused. The boy was astonished: No matter which way he turned the compass, the needle pointed to N (for "north"). What controlled its motion? He pestered his Uncle Jacob, who had studied engineering, with questions. His uncle told him about the earth's north and south poles and about magnetic fields, but Albert still was not satisfied. He believed there must be some mysterious force in what appeared to be the empty space around the needle. He carried the compass around for weeks, trying to figure out its secret. Years later, at the age of 67, he wrote, ". . . this experience made a deep and lasting impression upon me. Something deeply hidden had to be behind things" (Schilpp, 1970, p. 9).

That sense of wonder was reawakened several years later, when Uncle Jacob, noticing that Albert showed an interest in arithmetic, introduced him to algebra and geometry. Albert solved every problem in the books his uncle brought him and then went searching for more. It was that same insatiable curiosity and persistence—what Einstein himself called "a furious impulse to understand" (Michelmore, 1962, p. 24)—that underlay his lifetime quest for scientific knowledge.

● ● ●

Albert Einstein's story touches on several themes of cognitive development in early childhood. One is the variation in normal language development. Another is that although Einstein's reaction to the compass may have been unusually intense, it was characteristic of young children's understanding of the physical world: their growing recognition that natural phenomena have causes, though those causes are not always apparent. Einstein's lifelong memory of that engrossing incident may shed light on why some kinds of early memories last while others do not. Also, his parents' and teachers' underestimation of his cognitive abilities raises issues about how intelligence can be accurately assessed.

In this chapter, we examine these and other aspects of cognitive development in early childhood, as revealed by recent research as well as by such theorists as Piaget and Vygotsky. We see how children's thinking advances after toddlerhood and in what ways it remains immature. We look at children's increasing fluency with language and what impact this has on other aspects of development. We examine the beginnings of autobiographical memory, such as Einstein's memory of the compass; and we compare psychometric intelligence tests with assessments based on Vygotsky's theories. Finally, we look at the widening world of preschool and kindergarten.

After you have read and studied this chapter, you should be able to answer each of the Guidepost questions on the following page. Look for them again in the margins throughout the chapter, where they point to important concepts. To check your understanding of these Guideposts, review the end-of-chapter summary. Checkpoints located throughout the chapter will help you verify your understanding of what you have read.

Guideposts for Study

1. What are typical cognitive advances and immature aspects of preschool children's thinking?

2. What memory abilities expand in early childhood?

3. How is preschoolers' intelligence measured, and what factors influence it?

4. How does language improve, and what happens when its development is delayed?

5. What purposes does early childhood education serve, and how do children make the transition to kindergarten?

Piagetian Approach: The Preoperational Child

Guidepost 1

What are typical cognitive advances and immature aspects of preschool children's thinking?

Jean Piaget called early childhood the **preoperational stage** of cognitive development because children this age are not yet ready to engage in logical mental operations, as they will be in the concrete operational stage in middle childhood (discussed in Chapter 13). However, the preoperational stage, which lasts from approximately ages 2 to 7, is characterized by a great expansion in the use of symbolic thought, or representational ability, which first emerges near the end of the sensorimotor stage. Let's look at some advances and some immature aspects of preoperational thought (Tables 10-1 and 10-2) and at recent research, some of which challenges Piaget's conclusions.

preoperational stage In Piaget's theory, the second major stage of cognitive development, in which children become more sophisticated in their use of symbolic thought but are not yet able to use logic.

Advances of Preoperational Thought

Advances in symbolic thought are accompanied by a growing understanding of causality, identities, categorization, and number. Some of these understandings have roots in infancy and toddlerhood; others begin to develop in early childhood but are not fully achieved until middle childhood.

The Symbolic Function

"I want ice cream!" announces Kerstin, age 4, trudging indoors from the hot, dusty backyard. She has not seen anything that triggered this desire—no open freezer door, no television commercial. She no longer needs this kind of sensory cue to think about something. She remembers ice cream and its coldness and taste, and she purposefully seeks it out. This absence of sensory or motor cues characterizes the **symbolic function:** the ability to use symbols, or mental representations—words, numbers, or images to which a person has attached meaning. Without symbols, people could not communicate verbally, make change, read maps, or treasure photos of distant loved ones. Having symbols for things helps children remember and think about them without having them physically present.

symbolic function Piaget's term for ability to use mental representations (words, numbers, or images) to which a child has attached meaning.

Preschool children show the symbolic function through deferred imitation, pretend play, and language. *Deferred imitation* (refer back to Chapter 7), which becomes more robust after 18 months, is based on having kept a mental representation of an observed action—as when 3-year-old Bart scolds his little sister, using the same words he heard his father say to the delivery boy who was late in bringing the pizza. In **pretend play,** also called *fantasy play, dramatic play,* or *imaginary play,* children may make an object, such as a doll, represent, or symbolize, something else, such as a person. *Language* uses a system of symbols to communicate.

pretend play Play involving imaginary people or situations; also called *fantasy play, dramatic play,* or *imaginary play.*

Understanding of Objects in Space

As reported in Chapter 7, until at least age 3 most children do not reliably grasp the relationships between pictures, maps, or scale models and the larger or smaller objects or spaces they represent. Older preschoolers can use simple maps, and they can transfer the spatial understanding gained from working with models to maps and vice versa (DeLoache,

Table 10-1   Cognitive Advances during Early Childhood

Advance	Significance	Example
Use of symbols	Children do not need to be in sensorimotor contact with an object, person, or event in order to think about it.	Josh asks his mother about the elephants they saw on their trip to the circus several months earlier.
	Children can imagine that objects or people have properties other than those they actually have.	Aidan pretends that a slice of apple is a vacuum cleaner "vrooming" across the kitchen table.
Understanding of identities	Children are aware that superficial alterations do not change the nature of things.	Antonio knows that his teacher is dressed up as a pirate but is still his teacher underneath the costume.
Understanding of cause and effect	Children realize that events have causes.	Seeing a ball roll from behind a wall, Aneko looks behind the wall for the person who kicked the ball.
Ability to classify	Children organize objects, people, and events into meaningful categories.	Rosa sorts the pinecones she collected on a nature walk into two piles according to their size: "big" and "little."
Understanding of number	Children can count and deal with quantities.	Lindsay shares some candy with her friends, counting to make sure that each girl gets the same amount.
Theory of mind	Children become more aware of mental activity and the functioning of the mind.	Bianca wants to save some cookies for herself, so she hides them from her brother in a pasta box. She knows her cookies will be safe there because her brother will not look in a place where he doesn't expect to find cookies.

Table 10-2   Immature Aspects of Preoperational Thought (according to Piaget)

Limitation	Description	Example
Centration: Inability to decenter	Children focus on one aspect of a situation and neglect others.	Justin teases his younger sister that he has more juice than she does because his juice box has been poured into a tall, skinny glass, but hers has been poured into a short, wide glass.
Irreversibility	Children fail to understand that some operations or actions can be reversed, restoring the original situation.	Justin does not realize that the juice in each glass can be poured back into the juice box from which it came, contradicting his claim that he has more than his sister.
Focus on states rather than on transformations	Children fail to understand the significance of the transformation between states.	In the conservation task, Justin does not understand that transforming the shape of a liquid (pouring it from one container into another) does not change the amount.
Transductive reasoning	Children do not use deductive or inductive reasoning; instead they jump from one particular to another and see cause where none exists.	Sarah was mean to her brother. Then her brother got sick. Sarah concludes that she made her brother sick.
Egocentrism	Children assume everyone else thinks, perceives, and feels as they do.	Kara doesn't realize that she needs to turn a book around so that her father can see the picture she is asking him to explain to her. Instead, she holds the book directly in front of her, so only she can see it.
Animism	Children attribute life to inanimate objects.	Amanda says that spring is trying to come but winter is saying, "I won't go! I won't go!"
Inability to distinguish appearance from reality	Children confuse what is real with outward appearance.	Courtney is confused by a sponge made to look like a rock. She states that it looks like a rock and it really is a rock.

Miller, & Pierroutsakos, 1998). In a series of experiments, preschoolers were asked to use a simple map to find or place an object at the corresponding location in a similarly shaped but much larger space, such as a rug. Some 90 percent of 5-year-olds but only 60 percent of 4-year-olds could do this (Vasilyeva & Huttenlocher, 2004).

Understanding of Causality

Piaget maintained that preoperational children cannot yet reason logically about cause and effect. Instead, he said, they reason by **transduction.** They mentally link two events, especially events close in time, whether or not there is logically a causal relationship. For example, Luis may think that his "bad" thoughts or behavior caused his own or his sister's illness or his parents' divorce.

Yet, when tested on situations they can understand, young children do grasp cause and effect. One research team set up a series of experiments using a device called a "blicket detector," rigged to light up and play music only when certain objects (called "blickets") were placed on it. Even 2-year-olds were able to decide, by observing the device in operation, which objects were blickets (because they activated the blicket detector) and which were not (Gopnik, Sobel, Schulz, & Glymour, 2001).

In naturalistic observations of 2½- to 5-year-olds' everyday conversations with their parents, children showed flexible causal reasoning, appropriate to the subject. Types of explanations ranged from physical ("The scissors have to be clean so I can cut better") to social-conventional ("I have to stop now because you said to"). Causal statements were more frequent among older children (Hickling & Wellman, 2001). However, preschoolers seem to view all causal relationships as equally and absolutely predictable. In one series of experiments, 3- to 5-year-olds, unlike adults, were just as sure that a person who does not wash his or her hands before eating will get sick as they were that a person who jumps up will come down (Kalish, 1998).

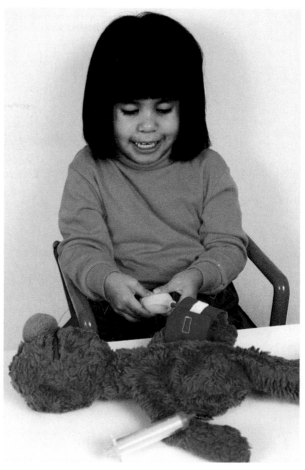

As Anna pretends to take Grover's blood pressure, she is showing a major cognitive achievement: deferred imitation, the ability to repeat an action she observed some time before.

Understanding of Identities and Categorization

The world becomes more orderly and predictable as preschool children develop a better understanding of *identities:* the concept that people and many things are basically the same even if they change in form, size, or appearance. This understanding underlies the emerging self-concept (see Chapter 11).

Categorization, or classification, requires a child to identify similarities and differences. By age 4, many children can classify by two criteria, such as color and shape. Children use this ability to order many aspects of their lives, categorizing people as "good" or "bad," "nice" "mean," and so forth. Thus, categorization is a cognitive ability with psychosocial implications.

One type of categorization is the ability to distinguish living from nonliving things. When Piaget asked young children whether the wind and the clouds were alive, their answers led him to think they were confused about what is alive and what is not. The tendency to attribute life to objects that are not alive is called **animism.** However, when later researchers questioned 3- and 4-year-olds about something more familiar to them—differences between a rock, a person, and a doll—the children showed they understood that people are alive and rocks and dolls are not. They did not attribute thoughts or emotions to rocks, and they cited the fact that dolls cannot move on their own as evidence that dolls are not alive (Gelman, Spelke, & Meck, 1983).

Of course, plants do not move on their own either, nor do they utter sounds, as most animals do. Yet preschoolers know that both plants and animals can grow and decay and, when injured, can heal (Rosengren, Gelman, Kalish, & McCormick, 1991; Wellman & Gelman, 1998). Culture can affect such beliefs. In one study, 5- to 9-year-old Israeli children, whose tradition views plants primarily in terms of their usefulness as food, were

transduction In Piaget's terminology, preoperational child's tendency to mentally link particular experiences, whether or not there is logically a causal relationship.

animism Tendency to attribute life to objects that are not alive.

Table 10-3	Key Elements of Number Sense in Young Children

Area	Components
Counting	Grasping one-to-one correspondence
	Knowing stable order and cardinality principles
	Knowing the count sequence
Number knowledge	Discriminating and coordinating quantities
	Making numerical magnitude comparisons
Number transformation	Simple addition and subtraction
	Calculating in story problems and nonverbal contexts
	Calculating "in the head"
Estimation	Approximating or estimating set sizes
	Using reference points
Number patterns	Copying number patterns
	Extending number patterns
	Discerning numerical relationships

Source: Adapted from Jordan et al., 2006.

less likely than U.S. and Japanese children to attribute to plants the qualities of living things, such as respiration, growth, and death. Japanese children were more likely to attribute such qualities to inanimate objects, such as a stone and a chair, which, in their culture, are sometimes viewed as if they were alive and had feelings (Hatano et al., 1993).

Number

As we discussed in Chapter 7, research by Karen Wynn suggests that infants as young as 4½ months have a rudimentary concept of number. They seem to know that if one doll is added to another doll, there should be two dolls, not just one. Other research has found that *ordinality*—the concept of comparing quantities (*more* or *less, bigger* or *smaller*)—seems to begin at around 12 to 18 months and at first is limited to comparisons of very few objects (Siegler, 1998). By age 4, most children have words for comparing quantities. They can say that one tree is *bigger* than another or one cup holds *more* juice than another. They know that if they have one cookie and then get another cookie, they have more cookies than they had before and that if they give one cookie to another child, they have fewer cookies. They also can solve numerical ordinality problems ("Megan picked six apples, and Joshua picked four apples; which child picked more?") with up to nine objects (Byrnes & Fox, 1998).

Not until age 3½ or older do most children consistently apply the *cardinality* principle in counting (Wynn, 1990). That is, when asked to count six items, children younger than 3½ tend to recite the number-names (one through six) but not to say how many items there are altogether (six). However, there is some evidence that children as young as 2½ use cardinality in practical situations, such as checking to make sure which plate has more cookies on it (Gelman, unpublished ms.). By age 5, most children can count to 20 or more and know the relative sizes of the numbers 1 through 10 (Siegler, 1998). Children intuitively devise strategies for adding by counting on their fingers or by using other objects (Naito & Miura, 2001).

By the time they enter school, most children have developed basic "number sense" (Jordan, Kaplan, Oláh, & Locuniak, 2006). This basic level of number skills (Table 10-3) includes *counting, number knowledge* (ordinality), *number transformations* (simple addition and subtraction), *estimation* ("Is this group of dots more or less than 5?"), and recognition of *number patterns* (2 plus 2 equals 4, and so does 3 plus 1).

SES and preschool experience affect how rapidly children advance in math. By age 4, children from middle-income families have markedly better number skills than low-SES children, and their initial advantage tends to continue. Children whose preschool teachers do a lot of "math talk" (such as asking children to help count days on a calendar) tend to make greater gains (Klibanoff, Levine, Huttenlocher, Vasilyeva, & Hedges, 2006).

Checkpoint

Can you . . .

✔ Summarize findings about preschool children's understanding of symbols, causality, identities, categories, and number?

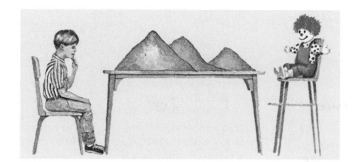

Immature Aspects of Preoperational Thought

According to Piaget, one of the main characteristics of preoperational thought is **centration:** the tendency to focus on one aspect of a situation and neglect others. He said preschoolers come to illogical conclusions because they cannot **decenter**—think about several aspects of a situation at one time. Centration can limit young children's thinking about both physical and social relationships.

Egocentrism

Egocentrism is a form of centration. According to Piaget, young children center so much on their own point of view that they cannot take in another's. Three-year-olds are not as egocentric as newborn babies; but, said Piaget, they still think the universe centers on them. Egocentrism may help explain why young children sometimes have trouble separating reality from what goes on inside their heads and why they may show confusion about what causes what. When Emily believes that her "bad thoughts" have made her brother sick or that she caused her parents' marital troubles, she is thinking egocentrically.

To study egocentrism, Piaget designed the *three-mountain task* (Figure 10-1). A child sits facing a table that holds three large mounds. A doll is placed on a chair at the opposite side of the table. The investigator asks the child how the mountains would look to the doll. Piaget found that young children usually could not answer the question correctly; instead, they described the mountains from their own perspective. Piaget saw this as evidence that preoperational children cannot imagine a point of view different from their own (Piaget & Inhelder, 1967).

However, another experimenter who posed a similar problem in a different way got different results (Hughes, 1975). A child sat in front of a square board divided by "walls" into four sections. A toy police officer stood at the edge of the board; a doll was moved from one section to another. After each move the child was asked, "Can the police officer see the doll?" Then another toy police officer was brought into the action, and the child was told to hide the doll from both officers. Thirty children between ages 3½ and 5 were correct 9 out of 10 times.

Why were these children able to take another person's point of view (the police officer's) when those doing the mountain task were not? It may be because the "police officer" task calls for thinking in more familiar, less abstract ways. Most children do not look at mountains and do not think about what other people might see when looking at one, but most preschoolers know something about dolls and police officers and hiding. Thus young children may show egocentrism primarily in situations beyond their immediate experience.

Conservation

Another classic example of centration is the failure to understand **conservation,** the fact that two things that are equal remain so if their appearance is altered, so long as nothing is added or taken away. Piaget found that children do not fully grasp this principle until the

centration In Piaget's theory, tendency of preoperational children to focus on one aspect of a situation and neglect others.

decenter In Piaget's terminology, to think simultaneously about several aspects of a situation.

egocentrism Piaget's term for inability to consider another person's point of view; a characteristic of young children's thought.

conservation Piaget's term for awareness that two objects that are equal according to a certain measure remain equal in the face of perceptual alteration so long as nothing has been added to or taken away from either object.

Table 10-4   Tests of Various Kinds of Conservation

Conservation Task	What Child Is Shown*	Transformation	Question for Child	Preoperational Child's Usual Answers
Number	Two equal, parallel rows of candies	Space the candies in one row farther apart.	"Are there the same number of candies in each row or does one row have more?"	"The longer one has more."
Length	Two parallel sticks of the same length	Move one stick to the right.	"Are both sticks the same size or is one longer?"	"The one on the right (or left) is longer."
Liquid	Two identical glasses holding equal amounts of liquid	Pour liquid from one glass into a taller, narrower glass.	"Do both glasses have the same amount of liquid or does one have more?"	"The taller one has more."
Matter (mass)	Two balls of clay of the same size	Roll one ball into a sausage shape.	"Do both pieces have the same amount of clay or does one have more?"	"The sausage has more."
Weight	Two balls of clay of the same weight	Roll one ball into a sausage shape.	"Do both weigh the same or does one weigh more?"	"The sausage weighs more."
Area	Two toy rabbits, two pieces of cardboard (representing grassy fields), with blocks or toys (representing barns on the fields); same number of "barns" on each board	Rearrange the blocks on one piece of cardboard.	"Does each rabbit have the same amount of grass to eat or does one have more?"	"The one with the blocks close together has more to eat."
Volume	Two glasses of water with two equal-sized balls of clay in them	Roll one ball into a sausage shape.	"If we put the sausage back in the glass, will the water be the same height in each glass, or will one be higher?"	"The water in the glass with the sausage will be higher."

*Child then acknowledges that both items are equal.

irreversibility Piaget's term for a preoperational child's failure to understand that an operation can go in two or more directions.

Checkpoint ✓

Can you . . .

✔ Tell how centration limits preoperational thought?

✔ Discuss research that challenges Piaget's views on egocentrism in early childhood?

✔ Give several reasons preoperational children have difficulty with conservation?

theory of mind Awareness and understanding of mental processes.

stage of concrete operations. (Table 10-4 shows how various dimensions of conservation have been tested.)

In one type of conservation task, conservation of liquid, 5-year-old Justin is shown two identical clear glasses, each short and wide and each holding the same amount of water. Justin is asked, "Is the amount of water in the two glasses equal?" When he agrees, the researcher pours the water in one glass into a third glass, a tall, thin one. Justin is now asked, "Do both glasses contain the same amount of water? Or does one contain more? Why?" In early childhood—even after watching the water being poured out of one of the short, fat glasses into a tall, thin glass or even after pouring it himself—Justin will say that either the taller glass or the wider one contains more water. When asked why, he says, "This one is bigger this way," stretching his arms to show the height or width. Preoperational children cannot consider height *and* width at the same time. Since they center on one aspect, they cannot think logically, said Piaget.

The ability to conserve is also limited by **irreversibility:** failure to understand that an operation or action can go in two or more directions. Once Justin can imagine restoring the original state of the water by pouring it back into the other glass, he will realize that the amount of water in both glasses must be the same.

Preoperational children commonly think as if they were watching a slide show with a series of static frames: they *focus on successive states,* said Piaget, and do not recognize the transformation from one state to another. In the conservation experiment, they focus on the water as it stands in each glass rather than on the water being poured from one glass to another, and so they fail to realize that the amount of water is the same.

Do Young Children Have Theories of Mind?

Piaget (1929) was the first scholar to investigate children's **theory of mind,** their awareness of their own mental processes and those of other people. He asked children such questions as "Where do dreams come from?" and "What do you think with?" On the basis of their answers, he concluded that children younger than 6 cannot distinguish between thoughts or dreams and real physical entities and therefore have no theory of mind. However, more recent research indicates that between ages 2 and 5 and especially around age 4, children's knowledge about mental processes grows dramatically.

Again, methodology seems to have made the difference. Piaget's questions were abstract, and he expected children to be able to put their understanding into words. Contemporary researchers observe children in everyday activities or give them concrete examples. In this way, we have learned, for example, that 3-year-olds can tell the difference between a boy who has a cookie and a boy who is thinking about a cookie; they know which boy can touch, share, and eat it (Astington, 1993). Let's look at several aspects of theory of mind.

The young girl on the right is old enough to know that her cousin needs consoling. Empathy, the ability to understand another person's feelings, begins at an early age.

Knowledge about Thinking and Mental States

Between ages 3 and 5, children come to understand that thinking goes on inside the mind; that it can deal with either real or imaginary things; that someone can be thinking of one thing while doing or looking at something else; that a person whose eyes and ears are covered can think about objects; that someone who looks pensive is probably thinking; and that thinking is different from seeing, talking, touching, and knowing (Flavell et al., 1995).

However, preschoolers generally believe that mental activity starts and stops. Not until middle childhood do children know that the mind is continuously active (Flavell, 1993; Flavell et al., 1995). Preschoolers also have little or no awareness that they or other people think in words, or "talk to themselves in their heads," or that they think while they are looking, listening, reading, or talking (Flavell, Green, Flavell, & Grossman, 1997).

Preschoolers tend to believe they can dream about anything they wish. Five-year-olds show a more adultlike understanding, recognizing that physical experiences, emotions, knowledge, and thoughts can affect the content of dreams. Not until age 11, however, do children fully realize that they cannot control their dreams (Woolley & Boerger, 2002).

Social cognition, the recognition that others have mental states accompanies the decline of egocentrism and the development of empathy. By age 3, children realize that if someone gets what he wants he will be happy, and, if not, he will be sad (Wellman & Woolley, 1990). By age 4, children begin to understand that people have differing beliefs about the world—true or mistaken—and that these beliefs affect their actions.

False Beliefs and Deception

A researcher shows 3-year-old Madeline a candy box and asks what is in it. "Candy," she says. But when Madeline opens the box, she finds crayons, not candy. "What will a child who hasn't opened the box think is in it?" the researcher asks. "Crayons," says Madeline, not understanding that another child would be fooled by the box as she was. And then she says that she originally thought crayons would be in the box (Flavell, 1993; Flavell et al., 1995).

The understanding that people can hold false beliefs flows from the realization that people hold mental representations of reality, which can sometimes be wrong. Three-year-olds, like Madeline, appear to lack such an understanding (Flavell et al., 1995). An analysis of 178 studies in various countries, using a number of variations on false-belief tasks, found this consistent developmental pattern (Wellman & Cross, 2001; Wellman, Cross, & Watson, 2001).

However, some researchers claim that 3-year-olds do have a rudimentary understanding of false beliefs but may not show it when presented with complicated situations (Hala & Chandler, 1996). When preschoolers were taught to respond to a false-belief task with gestures rather than with words, children near their fourth birthday—but not younger children—did better than on the traditional verbal-response tasks. Thus, gestures may help children on the verge of grasping the idea of false beliefs to make that conceptual leap (Carlson, Wong, Lemke, & Cosser, 2005).

Three-year-olds' failure to recognize false beliefs may stem from egocentric thinking. At that age, children tend to believe that everyone else knows what they know and believes what they do, and, like Madeline, they have trouble understanding that their beliefs can be false (Lillard & Curenton, 1999). Four-year-olds understand that people who see or hear different versions of the same event may come away with different beliefs. Not until about age 6, however, do children realize that two people who see or hear the same thing may interpret it differently (Pillow & Henrichon, 1996).

Deception is a deliberate effort to plant a false belief in someone else's mind, and it requires a child to suppress the impulse to be truthful. Some studies have found that children become capable of deception as early as age 2 or 3, and others, at 4 or 5. The difference may have to do with the means of deception children are expected to use. In a series of experiments, 3-year-olds were asked whether they would like to play a trick on an experimenter by giving a false clue about which of two boxes a ball was hidden in. The children were better able to carry out the deception when asked to put a picture of the ball on the wrong box or to point to that box with an arrow than when they pointed with their fingers, which children this age are accustomed to doing truthfully (Carlson, Moses, & Hix, 1998).

Piaget maintained that young children regard all falsehoods—intentional or not—as lies. However, when 3- to 6-year-olds were told a story about a subject close to their experience—the danger of eating contaminated food—and were asked whether a character's incorrect statement about the food was a lie or a mistake, about three-fourths of the children of all ages characterized it accurately (Siegal & Peterson, 1998). Apparently, then, even 3-year-olds have some understanding of the role of intent in deception.

Distinguishing between Appearance and Reality

According to Piaget, not until about age 5 or 6 do children understand the distinction between what *seems* to be and what *is*. Much research bears him out, though some studies have found this ability beginning to emerge before age 4 (Friend & Davis, 1993; Rice, Koinis, Sullivan, Tager-Flusberg, & Winner, 1997).

In one classic series of experiments (Flavell, Green, & Flavell, 1986), 3-year-olds apparently confused appearance and reality in a variety of tests. For example, when the children put on special sunglasses that made milk look green, they said the milk *was* green, even though they had just seen white milk. However, when 3-year-olds were shown a sponge that looked like a rock and were asked to help trick someone else into thinking it was a rock, the children were able to make the distinction between the way the sponge looked (like a rock) and what it actually was (a sponge). Apparently, putting the task in the context of a deception helped the children realize that an object can be perceived as other than what it actually is (Rice et al., 1997).

Three-year-olds' difficulty distinguishing appearance from reality may itself be more apparent than real. When children were asked questions about the uses of such objects as a candle wrapped like a crayon, only 3 out of 10 answered correctly. But when asked to respond with actions rather than words ("I want a candle to put on a birthday cake"), 9 out of 10 handed the experimenter the crayonlike candle (Sapp, Lee, & Muir, 2000).

Distinguishing between Fantasy and Reality

Sometime between 18 months and 3 years, children learn to distinguish between real and imagined events. Three-year-olds know the difference between a real dog and a dog in a dream, and between something invisible (such as air) and something imaginary. They can pretend and can tell when someone else is pretending (Flavell et al., 1995). By age 3, and, in some cases, by age 2, they know that pretense is intentional; they can tell the difference between trying to do something and pretending to do the same thing (Rakoczy, Tomasello, & Striano, 2004).

Still, the line between fantasy and reality may seem to blur at times. In one study (Harris, Brown, Marriott, Whittall, & Harmer, 1991), 4- to 6-year-olds, left alone in a room, preferred to touch a box holding an imaginary bunny rather than a box holding an imaginary monster, even though most of the children claimed they were just pretending. However, in a partial replication of the study, in which the experimenter stayed in the room and clearly ended the pretense, only about 10 percent of the children touched or looked in either of the boxes, and almost all showed a clear understanding that the creatures were imaginary

Box 10-1 *Imaginary Companions*

At 3½, Anna had 23 "sisters" with such names as Och, Elmo, Zeni, Aggie, and Ankie. She often talked to them on the telephone, since they lived about 100 miles away, in the town where her family used to live. During the next year, most of the sisters disappeared, but Och continued to visit, especially for birthday parties. Och had a cat and a dog (which Anna had begged for in vain), and whenever Anna was denied something she saw advertised on television, she announced that she already had one at her sister's house. But when a live friend came over and Anna's mother happened to mention one of her imaginary companions, Anna quickly changed the subject.

All 23 sisters—and some "boys" and "girls" who have followed them—lived only in Anna's imagination, as she well knew. Like an estimated 25 to 65 percent of children between ages 3 and 10 (Woolley, 1997), she created imaginary companions, with whom she talked and played. This normal phenomenon of childhood is seen most often in firstborn and only children, who lack the close company of siblings. Like Anna, most children who create imaginary companions have many of them (Gleason, Sebanc, & Hartup, 2000). Girls are more likely than boys to have imaginary friends, or at least to acknowledge them; boys are more likely to impersonate imaginary characters (Carlson & Taylor, 2005).

Children who have imaginary companions can distinguish fantasy from reality, but in free-play sessions they are more likely to engage in pretend play than are children without imaginary companions (M. Taylor, Cartwright, & Carlson, 1993). They play more happily and more imaginatively than other children and are more cooperative with other children and adults (D. G. Singer & Singer, 1990; J. L. Singer & Singer, 1981); and they do not lack for friends at preschool (Gleason et al., 2000). They are more fluent with language, watch less television, and show more curiosity, excitement, and persistence

during play. In one study of 152 preschoolers, 4-year-olds who reported having imaginary companions did better on theory-of-mind tasks (such as differentiating appearance and reality and recognizing false beliefs) than children who did not create such companions (M. Taylor & Carlson, 1997), and these children showed greater emotional understanding 3 years later. Having imaginary companions remains common in the early school years; almost one-third of the children who reported having had imaginary companions (65 percent of the sample in all) were still playing with them at age 7 (Taylor, Carlson, Maring, Gerow, & Charley, 2004).

Children's relationships with imaginary companions are like peer relationships; they are usually sociable and friendly, in contrast with the way children "take care of" personified objects, such as stuffed animals and dolls (Gleason et al., 2000). Imaginary playmates are good company for an only child like Anna. They provide wish-fulfillment mechanisms ("There was a monster in my room, but Elmo scared it off with magic dust"), scapegoats ("I didn't eat those cookies—Och must have done it!"), a safe way to express the child's own fears ("Aggie is afraid she's going to be washed down the drain"), and support in difficult situations (When Anna went to a scary movie, she "took" her imaginary companion with her).

What's your view ?

How should parents respond to children's talk about imaginary companions?

Check it out

For more information, go to www.imaginarycompanions.com. This is a Web site about children's imaginary companions by Marjorie Taylor.

(Golomb & Galasso, 1995). Thus it is difficult to know, when questioning children about pretend objects, whether children are giving serious answers or are keeping up the pretense (M. Taylor, 1997).

Magical thinking in children age 3 and older does not seem to stem from confusion between fantasy and reality. Often, magical thinking is a way to explain events that do not seem to have obvious realistic explanations (usually because children lack knowledge about them) or simply to indulge in the pleasures of pretending—as with the belief in imaginary companions (Box 10-1). Children, like adults, generally are aware of the magical nature of such fantasy figures but are more willing to entertain the possibility that they may be real (Woolley, 1997). Magical thinking tends to decline near the end of the preschool period (Woolley, Phelps, Davis, & Mandell, 1999).

All in all, then, the research on various theory-of-mind topics suggests that young children may have a clearer picture of reality than Piaget believed.

Influences on Individual Differences in Theory-of-Mind Development

Some children develop theory-of-mind abilities earlier than others. In part this development reflects brain maturation and general improvements in cognition. What other influences explain individual differences?

Social competence and language development contribute to an understanding of thoughts and emotions (Cassidy, Werner, Rourke, Zubernis, & Balaraman, 2003). Children whose teachers and peers rate them high on social skills are better able to recognize false beliefs, to distinguish between real and feigned emotion, and to take another person's point of view. These children also tend to have strong language skills (Cassidy et al., 2003; Watson, Nixon, Wilson, & Capage, 1999). The *kind* of talk a young child hears at home may affect the child's understanding of mental states. Three-year-olds whose mothers talk with them about others' mental states tend to show better theory-of-mind skills (Ruffman, Slade, & Crowe, 2002).

Families that encourage pretend play stimulate the development of theory-of-mind skills. As children play roles, they try to assume others' perspectives. Talking with children about how the characters in a story feel helps them develop social understanding (Lillard & Curenton, 1999). Empathy usually arises earlier in children whose families talk a lot about feelings and causality (Dunn, Brown, Slomkowski, Tesla, & Youngblade, 1991; Dunn, 1991).

Bilingual children, who speak and hear more than one language at home, do somewhat better than children with only one language on certain theory-of-mind tasks (Bialystok & Senman, 2004; Goetz, 2003). Bilingual children know that an object or idea can be represented linguistically in more than one way, and this knowledge may help them see that different people may have different perspectives. Bilingual children also recognize the need to match their language to that of their partner, and this may make them more aware of others' mental states. Finally, bilingual children tend to have better attentional control, and this may enable them to focus on what is true or real rather than on what only seems to be so (Bialystok & Senman, 2004; Goetz, 2003).

Guidepost 2

What memory abilities expand in early childhood?

Information-Processing Approach: Memory Development

During early childhood, children improve in attention and in the speed and efficiency with which they process information; and they begin to form long-lasting memories. Still, young children do not remember as well as older ones. For one thing, young children tend to focus on exact details of an event, which are easily forgotten, whereas older children and adults generally concentrate on the gist of what happened. Also, young children, because of their lesser knowledge of the world, may fail to notice important aspects of a situation, such as when and where it occurred, which could help jog their memory.

Basic Processes and Capacities

Information-processing theorists think of memory as a filing system that has three steps, or processes: *encoding, storage,* and *retrieval*. **Encoding** is like putting information in a folder to be filed in memory; it attaches a "code" or "label" to the information so that it will be easier to find when needed. Events are encoded along with information about the context in which they are encountered. **Storage** is putting the folder away in the filing cabinet. **Retrieval** occurs when the information is needed; the child then searches for the file and takes it out. Difficulties in any of these processes can interfere with efficiency.

The way the brain stores information is believed to be universal, though the efficiency of the system varies from one person to another (Siegler, 1998). Information-processing models depict the brain as containing three "storehouses": *sensory memory, working memory,* and *long-term memory.*

Sensory memory is a temporary "storehouse" for incoming sensory information. Sensory memory shows little change from infancy on (Siegler, 1998). However, without processing (encoding), sensory memories fade quickly.

Information being encoded or retrieved is kept in **working memory,** a short-term storehouse for information a person is actively working on: trying to understand, remember, or think about. Brain imaging studies have found that working memory is located partly in the *prefrontal cortex,* the large portion of the frontal lobe directly behind the forehead (Nelson et al., 2000).

encoding Process by which information is prepared for long-term storage and later retrieval.

storage Retention of information in memory for future use.

retrieval Process by which information is accessed or recalled from memory storage.

sensory memory Initial, brief, temporary storage of sensory information.

working memory Short-term storage of information being actively processed.

The efficiency of working memory is limited by its capacity. Researchers may assess the capacity of working memory by asking children to recall a series of scrambled digits (for example, 2-8-3-7-5-1 if they heard 1-5-7-3-8-2). The capacity of working memory—the number of digits a child can recall—increases rapidly (Cowan, Nugent, Elliott, Ponomarev, & Saults, 1999). At age 4, children typically remember only two digits; at 12 they typically remember six (Zelazo, Müller, Frye, & Marcovitch, 2003).

The growth of working memory may permit the development of **executive function,** the conscious control of thoughts, emotions, and actions to accomplish goals or solve problems. Executive function enables children to plan and carry out goal-directed mental activity. It probably emerges around the end of an infant's 1st year and develops in spurts with age. Changes in executive function between ages 2 and 5 enable children to make up and use complex rules for solving problems (Zelazo et al., 2003; Zelazo & Müller, 2002).

According to a widely used model, a **central executive** controls processing operations in working memory (Baddeley, 1981, 1986, 1992, 1996, 1998). The central executive orders information encoded for transfer to **long-term memory,** a storehouse of virtually unlimited capacity that holds information for long periods of time. The central executive also retrieves information from long-term memory for further processing. The central executive can temporarily expand the capacity of working memory by moving information into two separate subsidiary systems while the central executive is occupied with other tasks. One of these subsidiary systems holds verbal information (as in the digit task) and the other, visual/spatial images.

Recognition and Recall

Recognition and *recall* are types of retrieval. **Recognition** is the ability to identify something encountered before (for example, to pick out a missing mitten from a lost-and-found box). **Recall** is the ability to reproduce knowledge from memory (for example, to describe the mitten to someone). Preschool children, like all age groups, do better on recognition than on recall, but both abilities improve with age. The more familiar children are with an item, the better they can recall it. Recall also depends on motivation and on the strategies a child uses to enhance it (Lange, MacKinnon, & Nida, 1989).

Young children often fail to use strategies for remembering—even strategies they already know—unless reminded (Flavell, 1970). This tendency to not generate efficient strategies may reflect lack of awareness of how a strategy would be useful (Sophian, Wood, & Vong, 1995). Older children tend to become more efficient in the spontaneous use of memory strategies, as we discuss in Chapter 13.

Forming and Retaining Childhood Memories

Memory of experiences in early childhood is rarely deliberate: young children simply remember events that made a strong impression, and most of these early conscious memories seem to be short-lived.

Early Memories: Three Types

One investigator has distinguished three types of childhood memory that serve different functions: *generic, episodic,* and *autobiographical* (Nelson, 1993b).

Generic memory, which begins at about age 2, produces a **script,** or general outline of a familiar, repeated event without details of time or place. The script contains routines for situations that come up again and again; it helps a child know what to expect and how to act. For example, a child may have scripts for riding the bus to preschool or having lunch at Grandma's house.

Episodic memory refers to awareness of having experienced a particular event or episode that occurred at a specific time and place. Early episodic memories enable young children to build a mental picture of their world by organizing their experience around events (Nelson, 2005). Young children remember more clearly events that are new to them. Given a young child's limited memory capacity, episodic memories are temporary. Unless they recur several times (in which case they are transferred to generic memory), they last

executive function Conscious control of thoughts, emotions, and actions to accomplish goals or solve problems.

central executive In Baddeley's model, element of working memory that controls the processing of information.

long-term memory Storage of virtually unlimited capacity that holds information for long periods.

recognition Ability to identify a previously encountered stimulus.

Checkpoint ✔

Can you . . .

✔ Identify the three basic processes and three storehouses of memory and discuss their development?

✔ Compare preschoolers' recognition and recall ability?

recall Ability to reproduce material from memory.

generic memory Memory that produces scripts of familiar routines to guide behavior.

script General remembered outline of a familiar, repeated event, used to guide behavior.

episodic memory Long-term memory of specific experiences or events, linked to time and place.

for a few weeks or months and then fade. As children grow, older memories become obsolete and are replaced by newer, more up-to-date accounts of the child's changing world (Nelson, 2005).

autobiographical memory
Memory of specific events in one's own life; a type of episodic memory.

Autobiographical memory is a type of episodic memory; it refers to specific and long-lasting memories that form a person's life history. Not everything in episodic memory becomes part of autobiographical memory—only those memories that have a special, personal meaning to the child (Fivush & Nelson, 2004).

Autobiographical memory generally emerges between ages 3 and 4 and becomes continuous around age 4½, though some people can recall isolated events, such as the birth of a sibling, from age 2 (Howe, 2003; Fivush & Nelson, 2004; Nelson, 2005). One suggested explanation for the relatively late arrival of autobiographical memory is that children cannot store in memory events pertaining to their own lives until they develop a concept of self around which to organize those memories (Howe, 2003; Howe & Courage, 1993, 1997).

Influences on Memory Retention

Why do some early memories last longer than others? One factor is the uniqueness of the event. Another is children's active participation, either in the event itself or in its retelling or reenactment. Preschoolers tend to remember things they *did* better than things they merely *saw* (Murachver, Pipe, Gordon, Owens, & Fivush, 1996).

Another reinforcing factor is talking about past events. The emergence of autobiographical memory seems to be linked with the development of language (Fivush & Nelson, 2004; Nelson, 2005). The ability to talk about an event, as Albert Einstein and his uncle Jacob did about the workings of the compass, may affect whether and how the memory is carried into later life (Fivush & Schwarzmueller, 1998). In one study, 2½- to 3-year-olds engaged in pretend play with their mothers about a camping trip, a bird-watching adventure, and the opening of an ice cream shop. Children who jointly handled *and* jointly discussed with their mothers various items connected with these events recalled them better 1 to 3 days later than children who had only handled or only discussed the items (Haden, Ornstein, Eckerman, & Didow, 2001).

The way adults talk with a child about a shared experience can influence how well the child will remember it (Cleveland & Reese, 2005; Haden & Fivush, 1996; McGuigan & Salmon, 2004; Reese & Fivush, 1993). When a child gets stuck, adults with a *repetitive* conversational style tend to repeat their own previous statements or questions. A repetitive-style parent might ask, "Do you remember how we traveled to Florida?" and, then, receiving no answer, ask, "How did we get there? We went in the _____." Adults with an *elaborative* style would move on to a different aspect of the event or ask a question that includes more information: "Did we go by car or by plane?" Elaborative parents seem focused on having a mutually rewarding conversation and affirming the child's responses, whereas repetitive parents seem focused on checking the child's memory performance. Children of elaborative-style parents take part in longer, more detailed conversations about events at age 3 and tend to remember the events better at 5 and 6 (Reese, Haden, & Fivush, 1993).

In a study of 3- and 5-year-olds who participated in a staged event (a visit to a "zoo"), elaborative talk a few days *after* the event had greater influence on correct recall 2 weeks later than did such talk before or during the event. In fact, for 3-year-olds, elaborative talk before or during an event had no more effect on later recall than *empty talk*—talk that conveyed no specific information (McGuigan & Salmon, 2004).

How does elaborative talk enhance recall? Such talk may help a child encode recently experienced information by providing verbal labels for aspects of the event and by giving it an orderly, comprehensible structure. Elaborative talk also may create boundaries around children's mental representations of the event, preventing intrusion by irrelevant or distorted information (McGuigan & Salmon, 2004). In one study, at ages 2½ and 3½ children whose mothers had been trained in elaborative techniques recalled richer memories than children of untrained mothers. In addition, at 3½, children who had begun the experiment with higher levels of self-awareness retold their memories more accurately (Reese & Newcombe, 2007).

Children also remember better when a parent supports their autonomy and is not controlling. Autonomy-supportive parents follow the child's lead, encouraging the child to continue or expand on what he or she is trying to say. Controlling parents may push the child to talk when she or he doesn't want to, contradict the child, or comment negatively on the child's statements or behavior. In a longitudinal study of 50 New Zealand mothers and children, the children at age 3 were able to give more information about shared memories when their mothers were both elaborative and autonomy-supporting, not controlling. By age 5, the mothers' elaborative questions remained important in eliciting a child's memories, but autonomy support no longer made a difference—perhaps because children that age are more sure of what they remember (Cleveland & Reese, 2005).

Constructing Shared Memories: The Role of Culture

Conversation not only helps children remember; it may be crucial to memory formation. Some investigators influenced by Vygotsky's sociocultural theory support a **social interaction model,** which holds that children collaboratively construct autobiographical memories with parents or other adults as they talk about shared events (Nelson, 1993a). In reminiscing together, the adult provides a linguistic scaffold to help the child focus and organize a memory and compare that memory with what the adult remembers (Fivush & Nelson, 2004). As adults initiate and guide these conversations, children learn how memories are organized in narrative form in their culture (Welch-Ross, 1997). When parents prompt 2- and 3-year-olds with frequent questions about context ("When did you find the pinecone?" "Where did you find it?" "Who was with you?"), children soon learn to include this information (Peterson & McCabe, 1994). When parents of 3-year-olds comment on subjective reactions ("You *wanted* to go on the slide," "It was a *huge* bowl," "Mommy was *wrong*"), the children at 5½ are more likely to weave such comments into their reminiscences (Haden, Haine, & Fivush, 1997).

Culture affects what children remember about an experience and the way parents talk with them about it. In one study (Wang, 2004), 180 European American and Chinese preschoolers, kindergartners, and second graders were asked such questions as "How did you spend your last birthday?" and "Tell me about a time when your mom or dad scolded you about something." The U.S. children told about particular events; their narratives were longer and more detailed and contained more opinion and emotion than those of the Chinese children. The Chinese children's accounts were shorter and more succinct and centered more on daily routines, group activities, and social interactions and roles. The U.S. children were the chief characters of their stories, whereas the Chinese children shared the stage with others. In discussions of shared memories with 3-year-olds, U.S. mothers used elaboration to encourage the child's active participation ("Do you remember when you went swimming at Nana's? What did you do that was really neat?"). Chinese mothers asked leading questions containing most of the content of the memory, and the child added little ("What did you play at the place of skiing? Sat on the ice ship, right?").

social interaction model Model, based on Vygotsky's sociocultural theory, which proposes that children construct autobiographical memories through conversation with adults about shared events.

Checkpoint ✔

Can you . . .

✔ Identify three types of memories in early childhood?

✔ Identify three factors that affect how well a preschool child will remember an event?

✔ Explain how language development may contribute to the onset of autobiographical memory?

✔ Discuss how conversations with adults influence memory construction and retention?

✔ Give an example of how culture influences memories

Intelligence: Psychometric and Vygotskian Approaches

Guidepost 3

How is preschoolers' intelligence measured, and what factors influence it?

One factor that may affect the strength of early cognitive skills is intelligence. Let's look at two ways intelligence is measured—through traditional psychometric tests and through newer tests of cognitive potential—and at influences on children's performance.

Traditional Psychometric Measures

Although preschool children are easier to test than infants and toddlers, they still need to be tested individually. Because 3- to 5-year-olds are more proficient with language than younger children, intelligence tests for this age group can include more verbal items; and

Giving suggestions and strategies for solving a puzzle or problem—without showing approval or disapproval—can foster cognitive growth. Parental influence on cognitive development may be strongest in early childhood.

Stanford-Binet Intelligence Scales Individual intelligence test for ages 2 and up, used to measure knowledge, quantitative reasoning, visual-spatial processing, and working memory.

Wechsler Preschool and Primary Scale of Intelligence, Revised (WPPSI-III) Individual intelligence test for children ages 2½ to 7 that yields verbal and performance scores as well as a combined score.

these tests produce more reliable results than the largely nonverbal tests used in infancy. The two most commonly used individual tests for preschoolers are the Stanford-Binet Intelligence Scale and the Wechsler Preschool and Primary Scale of Intelligence.

The **Stanford-Binet Intelligence Scales,** used for ages 2 and up, is an American version of the traditional Binet-Simon tests. The test takes 45 to 60 minutes. The child is asked to define words, string beads, build with blocks, identify the missing parts of a picture, trace mazes, and show an understanding of numbers. The child's score is supposed to measure fluid reasoning (the ability to solve abstract or novel problems), knowledge, quantitative reasoning, visual-spatial processing, and working memory. The fifth edition, revised in 2003, includes nonverbal methods of testing all five of these dimensions of cognition and permits comparisons of verbal and nonverbal performance. In addition to providing a full-scale IQ, the Stanford-Binet yields separate measures of verbal and nonverbal IQ plus composite scores spanning the five cognitive dimensions.

The **Wechsler Preschool and Primary Scale of Intelligence, Revised (WPPSI-III),** an individual test taking 30 to 60 minutes, has different levels for ages 2½ to 4 and 4 to 7. It yields separate verbal and performance scores as well as a combined score. The 2002 revision includes new subtests designed to measure both verbal and nonverbal fluid reasoning, receptive versus expressive vocabulary, and processing speed. Both the Stanford-Binet and the WPPSI-III have been restandardized on samples of children representing the population of preschool-age children in the United States. The WPPSI-III also has been validated for special populations, such as children with intellectual disabilities, developmental delays, language disorders, and autistic disorders.

Intelligence tests, beginning at age 5, tend to be fairly reliable in predicting measured intelligence and school success later in childhood (Bornstein & Sigman, 1986; Neisser et al., 1996). However, despite the widespread use of these tests, fierce controversies remain over what intelligence is and how it can be measured—or whether it can be fairly measured at all (see Chapter 13).

Influences on Measured Intelligence

A common misconception is that IQ scores represent a fixed quantity of inborn intelligence. In reality, an IQ score is simply a measure of how well a child can do certain tasks at a certain time in comparison with others of the same age. Indeed, test scores of children in most industrialized countries have risen steadily since testing began, forcing test developers to raise standardized norms (Flynn, 1984, 1987). This trend may in part reflect exposure to educational television, preschools, better-educated parents, and a wider variety of experiences, as well as changes in the tests themselves.

How well a particular child does on IQ tests may be influenced by several factors: temperament, social and emotional maturity, ease in the testing situation, preliteracy or literacy skills, socioeconomic status, ethnicity or culture, and the match between the child's cognitive style and the tasks posed. (We will examine several of these factors in Chapter 13.)

The degree to which family environment influences a child's intelligence is in question. We do not know how much of parents' influence on intelligence comes from their genetic contribution and how much comes from their provision of a child's earliest environment for learning. Twin and adoption studies suggest that family life has its strongest influence in early childhood, and this influence diminishes greatly by adolescence (McGue, 1997; Neisser et al., 1996). However, these studies have been done largely with white, middle-class samples; their results may not apply to low-income and nonwhite families (Neisser et al., 1996). In a longitudinal study of low-income African American children, the influence of the home environment remained substantial—at least as strong as the influence of the mother's IQ (Burchinal et al., 1997).

The correlation between socioeconomic status and IQ is well documented (Neisser et al., 1996). Family income is associated with cognitive development and achievement in the preschool years and beyond. Family economic circumstances can exert a powerful influence, not so much in themselves as in the way they affect other factors such as health, stress, parenting practices, and the atmosphere in the home (Brooks-Gunn, 2003; Evans, 2004; McLoyd, 1990, 1998; NICHD Early Child Care Research Network, 2005a; Rouse, Brooks-Gunn, & McLanahan, 2005; see Chapter 10).

Why do some economically deprived children do better on IQ tests than others? Both genetic and environmental factors are involved. In a study of 1,116 twin pairs born in England and Wales in 1994 and 1995 and assessed at age 5 (Kim-Cohen, Moffitt, Caspi, & Taylor, 2004), children in deprived families tended, as in other studies, to have lower IQs. However, children with outgoing temperament, warm mothering, and stimulating activities in the home (which, again, may be influenced by parental IQ) tended to do better than other economically deprived children.

Testing and Teaching Based on Vygotsky's Theory

According to Vygotsky, children learn by internalizing the results of interactions with adults. This interactive learning is most effective in the **zone of proximal development (ZPD);** that is, with regard to tasks children are almost ready to accomplish on their own. The ZPD can be assessed by *dynamic tests* (see Chapter 13), which, according to Vygotskyan theory, provide a better measure of children's intellectual potential than do traditional psychometric tests that measure what children have already mastered.

The ZPD, in combination with the related concept of **scaffolding,** also can help parents and teachers efficiently guide children's cognitive progress. The less able a child is to do a task, the more scaffolding, or support, an adult must give. As the child can do more and more, the adult helps less and less. When the child can do the task alone, the adult takes away the scaffolding that is no longer needed.

By enabling children to become aware of and monitor their cognitive processes and to recognize when they need help, parents can help children take responsibility for learning. Prekindergarten children who receive this kind of scaffolding are better able to regulate their learning when they get to kindergarten (Neitzel & Stright, 2003). In a longitudinal study of 289 families with infants, the skills children developed during interactions with their mothers at 2 and 3½ enabled them, at 4½, to regulate goal-directed problem solving and to initiate social interactions. Also, 2-year-olds whose mothers helped maintain the child's interest in an activity—for example, by asking questions, making suggestions or comments, or offering choices—tended, at 3½ and 4½, to show independence in cognitive and social skills, such as solving a problem and initating social interaction (Landry, Smith, Swank, & Miller-Loncar, 2000).

Language Development

Preschoolers are full of questions: "How many sleeps until tomorrow?" "Who filled the river with water?" "Do babies have muscles?" "Do smells come from inside my nose?" Young children's growing facility with language helps them express their unique view of the world. Between ages 3 and 6, children make rapid advances in vocabulary, grammar, and syntax. The child who, at 3, describes how Daddy "hatches" wood (chops with a hatchet) or asks Mommy to "piece" her food (cut it into little pieces) may, by age 5, tell her mother, "Don't be ridiculous!" or proudly point to her toys and say, "See how I organized everything?"

Vocabulary

At 3 the average child knows and can use 900 to 1,000 words. By age 6, a child typically has an *expressive* (speaking) vocabulary of 2,600 words and understands more than 20,000 (Owens, 1996). With the help of formal schooling, a child's *passive,* or *receptive,* vocabulary (words she can understand) will quadruple to 80,000 words by the time the child enters high school (Owens, 1996).

What's your view

- If you were a preschool or kindergarten teacher, would you find it more helpful to know a child's IQ or ZPD?

zone of proximal development (ZPD) Vygotsky's term for the difference between what a child can do alone and what the child can do with help.

scaffolding Temporary support to help a child master a task.

Checkpoint

Can you . . .

✔ Describe two commonly used individual intelligence tests for preschoolers?

✔ List and discuss several influences on measured intelligence?

✔ Explain why an intelligence test score using the ZPD might be significantly different from a traditional psychometric test score?

Guidepost 4

How does language improve, and what happens when its development is delayed?

This preschool boy can use his growing vocabulary and knowledge of grammar and syntax to communicate more effectively. He has learned how to ask his father for things, to carry on a conversation, and to tell a story, perhaps about what happened at preschool.

fast mapping Process by which a child absorbs the meaning of a new word after hearing it once or twice in conversation.

This rapid expansion of vocabulary may occur through **fast mapping,** which allows a child to pick up the approximate meaning of a new word after hearing it only once or twice in conversation. From the context, children seem to form a quick hypothesis about the meaning of the word, which then is refined with further exposure and usage. Linguists are not sure how fast mapping works, but it seems likely that children draw on what they know about the rules for forming words, about similar words, about the immediate context, and about the subject under discussion. Names of objects (nouns) seem to be easier to fast map than names of actions (verbs), which are less concrete. Yet one experiment showed that children just under age 3 can fast map a new verb and apply it to another situation in which the same action is being performed (Golinkoff, Jacquet, Hirsh-Pasek, & Nandakumar, 1996).

Many 3- and 4-year-olds seem able to tell when two words refer to the same object or action (Savage & Au, 1996). They know that a single object cannot have two proper names (a dog cannot be both Spot and Fido). They also know that more than one adjective can apply to the same noun ("Fido is spotted and furry") and that an adjective can be combined with a proper name ("smart Fido!") (Hall & Graham, 1999).

Grammar and Syntax

The ways children combine syllables into words, and words into sentences, grow increasingly sophisticated during early childhood. At 3, children typically begin to use plurals, possessives, and past tense and know the difference between *I, you,* and *we.* However, they still overregularize because they have not yet learned or absorbed exceptions to rules (refer back to Chapter 7). Their sentences are generally short and simple, often omitting articles, such as *a* and *the,* but including some pronouns, adjectives, and prepositions. Although they most often use declarative sentences ("Kitty wants milk"), they can ask—and answer—*what* and *where* questions. (*Why* and *how* are harder to grasp.)

Between ages 4 and 5, sentences average four to five words and may be declarative, negative ("I'm not hungry"), interrogative ("Why can't I go outside?"), or imperative ("Catch the ball!"). Four-year-olds use complex, multiclause sentences ("I'm eating because I'm hungry") more frequently if their parents often use such sentences (Huttenlocher, Vasilyeva, Cymerman, & Levine, 2002). Children this age tend to string sentences together in long run-on stories (". . . And then . . . And then . . ."). In some respects, comprehension may be immature. For example, 4-year-old Noah can carry out a command that includes more than one step ("Pick up your toys and put them in the cupboard"). However, if his mother tells him, "You may watch TV after you pick up your toys," he may process the words in the order in which he hears them and think he can first watch television and then pick up his toys.

By ages 5 to 7, children's speech has become quite adultlike. They speak in longer and more complicated sentences. They use more conjunctions, prepositions, and articles. They use compound and complex sentences and can handle all parts of speech.

Still, although children this age speak fluently, comprehensibly, and fairly grammatically, they have yet to master many fine points of language. They rarely use the passive voice ("I was dressed by Grandpa"), conditional sentences ("If I were big, I could drive the bus"), or the auxiliary verb *have* ("I have seen that lady before") (C. S. Chomsky, 1969). They often make errors because they have not yet learned exceptions to rules. Saying "holded" instead of "held" or "eated" instead of "ate" is a normal sign of linguistic progress. When young children discover a rule, such as adding *-ed* to a verb for past tense, they tend to overgeneralize—to use it even with words that do not conform to the rule. Eventually, they notice that *-ed* is not always used to form the past tense of a verb.

Training can help children master such syntactical forms. Every school day for 2 weeks, 72 preschoolers were told narrative stories containing either predominantly active or predominantly passive constructions. When tested the following week, the children who

Box 10-2 *Private Speech: Piaget versus Vygotsky*

Anna, age 4, was alone in her room painting. When she finished, she was overheard saying aloud, "Now I have to put the pictures somewhere to dry. I'll put them by the window. They need to get dry now. I'll paint some more dinosaurs."

Private speech—speaking to oneself—is normal and common in childhood, accounting for 20 to 50 percent of what 4- to 10-year-old children say (Berk, 1986a). Two- to 3-year-olds engage in "crib talk," playing with sounds and words. Four- and 5-year-olds use private speech as a way to express fantasies and emotions (Berk, 1992; Small, 1990). Older children "think out loud" or mutter in barely audible tones (Table 10-5).

Piaget (1962/1923) saw private speech as a sign of cognitive immaturity. Because young children are egocentric, he suggested, they are unable to recognize others' viewpoints and therefore are unable to communicate meaningfully. Instead, they simply vocalize whatever is on their minds. Another reason young children talk while they do things, said Piaget, is that they do not yet distinguish between words and the actions the words stand for, or symbolize. By the end of the preoperational stage, with cognitive maturation and social experience, children become less egocentric and more capable of symbolic thought and so discard private speech.

Like Piaget, Vygotsky (1962/1934) believed that private speech helps young children integrate language with thought. However, Vygotsky did not look on private speech as egocentric. He saw it as a special form of communication: conversation with the self. As such, he said, it serves an important function in the transition between early social speech (often experienced in the form of adult commands) and inner speech (thinking in words)—a transition toward the internalization of socially derived control of behavior ("Now I have to put the pictures somewhere to dry").

Research generally supports Vygotsky as to the functions of private speech. In an observational study of 3- to 5-year-olds, 86 percent of the children's remarks were *not* egocentric (Berk, 1986a). The most sociable children and those who engage in the most social speech tend to use the most private speech as well,

apparently supporting Vygotsky's view that private speech is stimulated by social experience (Berk, 1986a, 1986b, 1992; Berk & Garvin, 1984; Kohlberg, Yaeger, & Hjertholm, 1968). There also is evidence for the role of private speech in self-regulation, as Anna was doing (Berk & Garvin, 1984; Furrow, 1984). Private speech tends to increase when children are trying to perform difficult tasks, especially without adult supervision (Berk, 1992; Berk & Garvin, 1984).

Vygotsky proposed that private speech increases during the preschool years and then fades away during the early part of middle childhood as children become more able to guide and master their actions. However, the pattern now appears to be more complex than Vygotsky suggested. Some studies have reported no age changes in overall use of private speech; others have found variations in the timing of its decline. The brightest children tend to use it earliest. Whereas Vygotsky considered the need for private speech a universal stage of cognitive development, studies have found a wide range of individual differences, with some children using it very little or not at all (Berk, 1992).

Understanding the significance of private speech has practical implications, especially in school (Berk, 1986a). Talking to oneself or muttering should not be considered misbehavior; a child may be struggling with a problem, and thinking out loud may help in solving it.

What's your view?

Have you ever seen a child talking to himself or herself? What purpose did the speech seem to serve?

Check it out!

For more information on this topic, go to www.iuj.ac.jp/faculty/mkahmed/privatespeech.html. This article by Mohammed K. Ahmed of the English Language Program at the International University of Japan applies the concept of private speech to the way adults learn a second language.

---

had heard the passive voice stories correctly comprehended and accurately produced more passive sentences than the children who had heard stories with active sentences (Vasilyeva, Huttenlocher, & Waterfall, 2006).

Pragmatics and Social Speech

As children learn vocabulary, grammar, and syntax, they become more competent in **pragmatics**—the practical knowledge of how to use language to communicate. This includes knowing how to ask for things, how to tell a story or joke, how to begin and continue a conversation, and how to adjust comments to the listener's perspective (M. L. Rice, 1982). These are all aspects of **social speech:** speech intended to be understood by a listener. (Box 10-2 discusses **private speech,** talking aloud to oneself with no intent to communicate with others.)

pragmatics Practical knowledge needed to use language for communicative purposes.

social speech Speech intended to be understood by a listener.

private speech Talking aloud to oneself with no intent to communicate with others.

Table 10-5	Types of Private Speech	

Type	Child's Activity	Examples
Wordplay, repetition	Repeating words and sounds, often in playful, rhythmic recitation	José wanders around the room, repeating in a singsong manner, "Put the mushroom on your head, put the mushroom in your pocket, put the mushroom on your nose."
Solitary fantasy play and speech addressed to nonhuman objects	Talking to objects; playing roles; producing sound effects for objects	Ethan says, "Ka-powee ka-powee," aiming his finger like a gun. Ashley says in a high-pitched voice while playing in the doll corner, "I'll be better after the doctor gives me a shot." As she pokes herself with her finger (a pretend needle), she says, "Ow!"
Emotional release and expression	Expressing emotions or feelings directed inward rather than to a listener	Keiko is given a new box of crayons and says to no one in particular, "Wow! Neat!" Rachel is sitting at her desk with an anxious expression on her face, repeating to herself, "My mom's sick, my mom's sick."
Egocentric communication	Communicating with another person but expressing the information so incompletely or peculiarly that it can't be understood.	David and Mark are seated next to one another on the rug. David says to Mark, "It broke," without explaining what or when. Susan says to Ann at the art table, "Where are the paste-ons?" Ann says, "What paste-ons?" Susan shrugs and walks off.
Describing or guiding one's own activity	Narrating one's actions; thinking out loud	Omar sits down at the art table and says to himself, "I want to draw something. Let's see, I need a big piece of paper. I want to draw my cat." Working in her arithmetic workbook, Cathy says to no one in particular, "Six." Then, counting on her fingers, she continues, "Seven, eight, nine, ten. It's ten, it's ten. The answer's ten."
Reading aloud, sounding out words	Reading aloud or sounding out words while reading	While reading a book, Tyler begins to sound out a difficult word. "Sher-lock Holm-lock, he says slowly and quietly. Then he tries again. "Sher-lock-Holm-lock, Sherlock Holme," he says leaving off the final s in his most successful attempt.
Inaudible muttering	Speaking so quietly that the words cannot be understood by an observer	Tony's lips move as he works a math problem.

Source: Berk, L. and R. Garvin. Adapted from "Development of private speech among low income Appalachian children," *Developmental Psychology,* 202(2) 1984, 271–284. Copyright © 1984 by the American Psychological Association. Adapted with permission.

Checkpoint

Can you . . .

✔ Trace normal progress in 3- to 6-year-olds' vocabulary, grammar, syntax, and conversational abilities?

✔ Give reasons why children of various ages use private speech?

With improved pronunciation and grammar, it becomes easier for others to understand what children say. Most 3-year-olds are quite talkative, and they pay attention to the effect of their speech on others. If people cannot understand them, they try to explain themselves more clearly. Most 4-year-olds, especially girls, use parentese when speaking to 2-year-olds (Owens, 1996; Shatz & Gelman, 1973; refer back to Chapter 7).

Most 5-year-olds can adapt what they say to what the listener knows. They can use words to resolve disputes, and they use more polite language and fewer direct commands in talking to adults than to other children. Almost half of 5-year-olds can stick to a conversational topic for about a dozen turns—if they are comfortable with their partner and if the topic is one they know and care about (Owens, 1996).

Delayed Language Development

The fact that Albert Einstein did not start to speak until he was close to 3 years old may encourage parents of other children whose speech develops later than usual. About 5 to 8 percent of preschool children show speech and language delays (U.S. Preventive Services Task Force, 2006).

It is unclear why some children speak late. They do not necessarily lack linguistic input at home. Hearing problems and head and facial abnormalities may be associated with speech and language delays, as are premature birth, family history, socioeconomic factors, and some developmental delays (Dale et al., 1998; U.S. Preventive Services Task Force, 2006). Heredity seems to play a major role (Lyytinen, Poikkeys, Laakso, Eklund, & Lyytinen, 2001; Spinath, Price, Dale, & Plomin, 2004). Boys are more likely than girls to be late talkers (Dale et al., 1998; U.S. Preventive Services Task Force, 2006). Children with language delays may have problems in fast mapping; they may need to hear a new word more often than other children do before they can incorporate it into their vocabularies (Rice, Oetting, Marquis, Bode, & Pae, 1994).

Like Albert Einstein, many children who speak late—especially those whose comprehension is normal—eventually catch up (Dale, Price, Bishop, & Plomin, 2003; Thal, Tobias, & Morrison, 1991). However, some 40 to 60 percent of children with early language delays, if left untreated, may experience far-reaching cognitive, social, and emotional consequences (U.S. Preventive Services Task Force, 2006).

It is not always easy to predict whether a late talker will need help. In longitudinal, community-based studies of 8,386 2-year-old twins born in England and Wales in 1994 and 1995, only about 40 percent of those reported to have early language delays continued to show language problems at ages 3 and 4 (Dale et al., 2003). Speech and language therapy sometimes can be effective, but samples studied are generally small and findings vary (U.S. Preventive Services Task Force, 2006).

Preparation for Literacy

To understand what is on the printed page, children first need to master certain prereading skills (Lonigan, Burgess, & Anthony, 2000; Muter, Hulme, Snowling, & Stevenson, 2004). **Emergent literacy** refers to the development of these skills.

Prereading skills can be divided into two types: (1) oral language skills, such as vocabulary, syntax, narrative structure, and the understanding that language is used to communicate; and (2) specific skills that help in decoding the printed word. Among this latter group are the phonological skills of *phonemic awareness,* the realization that words are composed of distinct *phonemes,* or sounds, and *phoneme-grapheme correspondence,* the ability to link sounds with the corresponding letters or combinations of letters. Each of these factors seems to have an independent effect (NICHD Early Child Care Research Network, 2005c; Lonigan et al., 2000; Whitehurst & Lonigan, 1998). In a 2-year longitudinal study of 90 British schoolchildren, the development of word recognition appeared critically dependent on phonological skills, whereas oral language skills such as vocabulary and grammatical skills were more important predictors of reading comprehension (Muter et al., 2004).

Does heredity influence literacy development? Apparently so. In a longitudinal study of 3,052 same-sex twin pairs—about half of them monozygotic and the other half dizygotic—both early preliteracy experience with books or recordings of nursery rhymes or stories and preliteracy knowledge at age 4 (saying the alphabet, knowing letter sounds, sounding out words, knowing word meanings, and recognizing rhymes) showed separate genetic influences that played a role in the children's ability to read and write at age 7 (Oliver, Dale, & Plomin, 2005).

Social interaction can promote emergent literacy. Children are more likely to become good readers and writers if, during the preschool years, parents provide conversational challenges the children are ready for—if they use a rich vocabulary and center dinner-table talk on the day's activities, on mutually remembered past events, or on questions about why people do things and how things work (Reese, 1995; Snow, 1990, 1993).

As children learn the skills they will need to translate the written word into speech, they also learn that writing can express ideas, thoughts, and feelings. Preschool children in the United States pretend to write by scribbling, lining up their marks from left to right (Brenneman, Massey, Machado, & Gelman, 1996). Later they begin using letters, numbers, and letterlike shapes to represent words, syllables, or phonemes.

emergent literacy Preschoolers' development of skills, knowledge, and attitudes that underlie reading and writing.

What's your view

• Suppose you wanted to set up a program to encourage preliteracy development in high-risk children. What elements would you include in your program, and how would you judge its success?

Checkpoint ✓

Can you . . .

✔ Discuss possible causes, consequences, and treatment of delayed language development?

✔ Identify two types of prereading skills and explain how social interaction can promote preparation for literacy?

Guidepost 5

What purposes does early childhood education serve, and how do children make the transition to kindergarten?

Often their spelling is so inventive that they cannot read it themselves (Whitehurst & Lonigan, 1998)!

Reading to children is one of the most effective paths to literacy. According to a U.S. government report, 86 percent of girls and 82 percent of boys are read to at home at least three times a week (Freeman, 2004). Children who are read to from an early age learn that reading and writing in English move from left to right and from top to bottom and that words are separated by spaces. They also are motivated to learn to read (Siegler, 1998; Whitehurst & Lonigan, 1998).

Moderate exposure to educational television can help prepare children for literacy, especially if parents talk with children about what they see. In one study, the more time 3- to 5-year-olds spent watching *Sesame Street,* the more their vocabulary improved (M. L. Rice, Huston, Truglio, & Wright, 1990). In a longitudinal study, the content of television programs viewed at ages 2 and 4 predicted academic skills 3 years later (Wright et al., 2001).

Early Childhood Education

Going to preschool is an important step that widens a child's physical, cognitive, and social environment. The transition to kindergarten, the beginning of "real school," is another momentous step. In 2001, 64 percent of U.S. 3- to 5-year-olds were enrolled in preprimary or primary education,* and the rates were higher in many industrial countries (Sen, Partelow, & Miller, 2005).

Goals and Types of Preschools

In some countries, such as China, preschools are expected to provide academic preparation for schooling. In contrast, most preschools in the United States and many other Western countries have followed a child-centered philosophy stressing social and emotional growth in line with young children's developmental needs—though some, such as those based on the theories of Piaget or the Italian educator Maria Montessori (refer back to Figure 1-1 in Chapter 1), have a stronger cognitive emphasis.

Montessori preschools are part of a worldwide movement. The Montessori method enables children to learn independently and undisturbed, at their own pace, as they work with developmentally appropriate materials and self-chosen tasks. Teachers serve merely as guides, and older children help younger ones. An evaluation of Montessori education in Milwaukee, where urban minority children who apply are randomly selected for enrollment, found that 5-year-old Montessori students were better prepared for elementary school in reading and math than children who attended other schools (Lillard & Else-Quest, 2006).

As part of a debate over how to improve education, pressures have built to offer instruction in basic academic skills in U.S. preschools. Defenders of the traditional developmental approach maintain that academically oriented programs neglect young children's need for exploration and free play and that too much teacher-centered instruction may stifle young children's interest and interfere with self-initiated learning (Elkind, 1986; Zigler, 1987).

What type of preschool is best for children? Studies in the United States support a child-centered, developmental approach. One field study (Marcon, 1999) compared 721 randomly selected, predominantly low-income and African American 4- and 5-year-olds from three types of preschool classrooms in Washington, D.C.: *child-initiated, academically directed,* and *middle-of-the-road* (a blend of the other two approaches). Children from child-initiated programs, in which they actively directed their own learning experiences, excelled in basic academic skills in all subject areas. They also had more advanced motor skills than the other two groups and scored higher than the middle-of-the-road group in behavioral and communicative skills. These findings suggest that a single,

*Seven percent of U.S. 5-year-olds were enrolled in primary schooling.

These children in a Head Start program are getting a "head start" toward readiness for school. The most successful compensatory education programs start early and have well-trained staff, parental participation, and low staff-to-child ratios.

coherent philosophy of education may work better than an attempt to blend diverse approaches and that a child-initiated approach seems more effective than an academically directed approach.

Compensatory Preschool Programs

The higher the family's socioeconomic status, the more likely a child is to be ready for school (Rouse et al., 2005). According to one estimate, more than two-thirds of children in poor urban areas enter school unprepared to learn (Zigler, 1998). Since the 1960s, large-scale programs have been developed to help such children compensate for what they have missed and to prepare them for school.

The best-known compensatory preschool program for children of low-income families in the United States is Project Head Start, a federally funded program launched in 1965. Consistent with its whole child approach, its goals are not only to enhance cognitive skills but also to improve physical health and to foster self-confidence, relationships with others, social responsibility, and a sense of dignity and self-worth for the child and the family. The program provides medical, dental, and mental health care, social services, and at least one hot meal a day.

Has Head Start lived up to its name? Data support its effectiveness in improving school readiness (USDHHS, 2003b). Similarly, children who attend newer state-sponsored programs tend to show better cognitive and language skills and do better in school than children who do not attend (USDHHS, 2003a). Yet, even though Head Start children make gains in vocabulary, letter recognition, early writing, and early mathematics, their readiness skills remain far below average (USDHHS, 2003b). And, although they do better on intelligence tests than other children from comparable backgrounds, this advantage disappears after they start school (Ripple et al., 1999; Zigler & Styfco, 1993, 1994). Still, children from Head Start and other compensatory programs are less likely to be placed in special education or to repeat a grade and are more likely to finish high school than low-income children who did not attend such programs (Neisser et al., 1996).

Outcomes are best with earlier and longer-lasting intervention through high quality, center-based programs (Brooks-Gunn, 2003; Reynolds & Temple, 1998; Zigler & Styfco, 1993, 1994, 2001). The most successful Head Start programs are those with the most parental participation, the best-trained teachers, the lowest staff-to-child ratios, the longest school days and weeks, and the most extensive services (Ramey, 1999).

In 1995, an Early Head Start program began offering child and family development services to low-income families with infants and toddlers. By 2004, the program was operating in more than 700 communities and serving about 62,000 families (Love et al., 2005). At ages 2 and 3, according to randomized studies, participants scored higher on standardized developmental and vocabulary tests and were at less risk of slow development than children not in the program. At age 3, they were less aggressive, more attentive to playthings, and more positively engaged with their parents. Early Head Start parents were more emotionally supportive, provided more learning and language stimulation, read to their children more, and spanked less. Programs that offered a mix of center-based services and home visits showed better results than those that concentrated on one setting or the other (Commissioner's Office of Research and Evaluation and Head Start Bureau, 2001; Love et al., 2002, 2005).

A growing consensus among early childhood educators is that the most effective way to ensure that gains achieved in early intervention and compensatory education programs are maintained is through a *PK–3* approach—a systematic program extending from prekindergarten through third grade. Such a program would (1) offer prekindergarten to all 3- and 4-year olds; (2) require full-day kindergarten; and (3) coordinate and align educational experiences and expectations from prekindergarten through grade 3 through a sequenced curriculum based on children's developmental needs and abilities and taught by skilled professionals (Bogard & Takanishi, 2005).

State-funded prekindergarten is becoming a national trend. Most of these programs are for disadvantaged children, but a few states have universal prekindergarten programs. (In practice, "universal" usually means that the program is available to all on a voluntary basis.) Programs vary greatly in length of school day, teacher qualifications, and other characteristics. Almost two-thirds of Oklahoma's 4-year-olds are enrolled in that state's universal prekindergarten program. A comparison of Tulsa children who had just completed the program and children who were just starting the program showed significant effects of prekindergarten education on reading, writing, and numerical skills (Gormley, Gayer, Phillips, & Dawson, 2005).

The Child in Kindergarten

Originally a year of transition between the relative freedom of home or preschool and the structure of grade school, kindergarten in the United States has become more like first grade. Children spend less time on self-chosen activities and more time on worksheets and preparing to read. A successful transition to kindergarten lays the foundation for future academic achievement (Schultin, Malone, & Dodge, 2005).

Although some states do not require kindergarten, most 5-year-olds attend either a public or private kindergarten; and an increasing number (60 percent in 2001) spend a full day in school instead of the traditional half day (National Center for Education Statistics, 2004a). Do children learn more in full-day kindergarten? Initially, they do. According to ongoing longitudinal research on a nationally representative sample of children who started kindergarten in the fall of 1998, children in full-day public kindergarten are more likely than children in half-day kindergarten to receive daily instruction in prereading skills, math skills, social studies, and science (Walston & West, 2004) and tend to do better through the primary grades (Vecchiotti, 2003; Walston & West, 2004). However, by the end of third grade, amount of time spent in kindergarten makes no substantial difference in reading, math, and science achievement (Rathbun, West, & Germino-Hausken, 2004).

Findings highlight the importance of the preparation a child receives *before* kindergarten. The resources with which children come to kindergarten—preliteracy skills and the richness of a home literacy environment—predict reading achievement in first grade, and these individual differences tend to persist or increase throughout the first 4 years of school (Denton, West, & Walston, 2003; Rathbun et al., 2004). Also, children with extensive preschool experience tend to adjust to kindergarten more easily than those who spent little or no time in preschool (Ladd, 1996).

Emotional and social adjustment affect readiness for kindergarten and strongly predict school success. More important than knowing the alphabet or being able to count to 20, kindergarten teachers say, are the abilities to sit still, follow directions, wait one's turn, and regulate one's own learning (Blair, 2002; Brooks-Gunn, 2003; Raver, 2002). Adjustment to kindergarten can be eased by enabling preschoolers and parents to visit before the start of kindergarten, shortening school days early in the school year, having teachers make home visits, holding parent orientation sessions, and keeping parents informed about what is going on in school (Schulting, Malone, & Dodge, 2005).

About 5 percent of children repeat kindergarten, according to a national longitudinal study of children who first entered kindergarten in 1998–1999. Low-SES children, those who did not attend preschool, and those with developmental delays were most likely to repeat kindergarten—typically, in the belief that a 2nd year of kindergarten would help them gain the skills they need to keep up. However, these children still tended to have lower reading and mathematics skills at the end of first grade than those who had spent only 1 year in kindergarten (Malone, West, Flanagan, & Park, 2006).

Proposals have been made to lengthen the school year. When an elementary school in a midsized southeastern city added 30 days to its school year, children who completed kindergarten outperformed their counterparts in a traditional 180-day program on tests of math, reading, general knowledge, and cognitive competence (Frazier & Morrison, 1998).

Checkpoint ✓

Can you . . .

✔ Compare goals of varying types of preschool programs?

✔ Summarize findings on the short-term and long-term effects of academic and child-centered preschool programs?

✔ Assess the benefits of compensatory preschool education?

✔ Discuss factors that affect adjustment to kindergarten?

Refocus

Thinking back to the information about Albert Einstein in the Focus vignette at the beginning of this chapter,

- What aspects of preoperational thought are illustrated by Einstein's ideas about the compass?

- What does Einstein's story suggest about the relationship between delayed language development and intelligence? Between memory and intelligence?

- What information in this chapter would explain why Einstein's memory of the gift of a compass stayed with him throughout his life?

- Which do you think would have been more useful in testing Einstein's cognitive abilities: a traditional IQ test or a test based on Vygotsky's concept of the ZPD?

- Which type of preschool described in this chapter do you think would have been best for young Einstein?

The burgeoning physical and cognitive skills of early childhood have psychosocial implications, as we'll see in Chapter 11.

Summary and Key Terms

Piagetian Approach: The Preoperational Child

Guidepost 1 What are typical cognitive advances and immature aspects of preschool children's thinking?

- Children in the preoperational stage show several important advances, as well as some immature aspects of thought.

- The symbolic function enables children to reflect on people, objects, and events that are not physically present. It is shown in deferred imitation, pretend play, and language.

- Early symbolic development helps preoperational children make more accurate judgments of spatial relationships. They can understand the concept of identity, link cause and effect, categorize living and nonliving things, and understand principles of counting.

- Centration keeps preoperational children from understanding principles of conservation, which develop gradually in middle childhood. Preoperational logic is limited also by irreversibility and a focus on states rather than transformations.

- Preoperational children appear to be less egocentric than Piaget thought; they (and even younger children) are capable of empathy.

- The theory of mind, which develops markedly between ages 3 and 5, includes awareness of one's own thought processes, social cognition, understanding that people can hold false beliefs, ability to deceive, ability to distinguish appearance from reality, and ability to distinguish fantasy from reality. Hereditary and environmental influences affect individual differences in theory-of-mind development.

preoperational stage (269) symbolic function (269) pretend play (269) transduction (271) animism (271) centration (273) decenter (273) egocentrism (273) conservation (273) irreversibility (274) theory of mind (274)

Information-Processing Approach: Memory Development

Guidepost 2 What memory abilities expand in early childhood?

- Information-processing models describe three steps in memory: encoding, storage, and retrieval.

- Although sensory memory shows little change with age, the capacity of working memory increases greatly. The central executive controls the flow of information to and from long-term memory.

- At all ages, recognition is better than recall, but both increase during early childhood.

- Early episodic memory is only temporary; it fades or is transferred to generic memory. Autobiographical memory begins at about age 3 or 4 and may be related to early self-recognition ability and language development. According to the social interaction model, children and adults co-construct autobiographical memories by talking about shared experiences.

- Children are more likely to remember unusual activities that they actively participate in. The way adults talk with children about events influences memory formation.

encoding (278) storage (278) retrieval (278) sensory memory (278) working memory (278) executive function (279) central executive (279) long-term memory (279) recognition (279) recall (279) generic memory (279) script (279) episodic memory (279) autobiographical memory (280) social interaction model (281)

Intelligence: Psychometric and Vygotskian Approaches

Guidepost 3 How is preschoolers' intelligence measured, and what factors influence it?

- The two most commonly used psychometric intelligence tests for young children are the Stanford-Binet Intelligence Scale and the Wechsler Preschool and Primary Scale of Intelligence, Revised (WPPSI-III).

- Intelligence test scores may be influenced by social and emotional functioning as well as by parent-child interaction and socioeconomic factors.

- Newer tests based on Vygotsky's concept of the zone of proximal development (ZPD) indicate immediate potential for achievement. Such tests, when combined with scaffolding, can help parents and teachers guide children's progress.

Stanford-Binet Intelligence Scales (282) Wechsler Preschool and Primary Scale of Intelligence, Revised (WPPSI-III) (282) zone of proximal development (ZPD) (283) scaffolding (283)

Language Development

Guidepost 4 How does language improve, and what happens when its development is delayed?

- During early childhood, vocabulary increases greatly, and grammar and syntax become fairly sophisticated. Children become more competent in pragmatics.

- Private speech is normal and common; it may aid in the shift to self-regulation and usually disappears by age 10.

- Causes of delayed language development are unclear. If untreated, language delays may have serious cognitive, social, and emotional consequences.

- Interaction with adults can promote emergent literacy.

fast mapping (284) pragmatics (285) social speech (285) private speech (285) emergent literacy (287)

Early Childhood Education

Guidepost 5 What purposes does early childhood education serve, and how do children make the transition to kindergarten?

- Goals of preschool education vary across cultures. Since the 1970s, the academic content of early childhood education programs in the United States has increased.

- Compensatory preschool programs have had positive outcomes, but participants generally have not equaled the performance of middle-class children. Compensatory programs that start early and extend into the primary grades have better long-term results.

- Many children today attend full-day kindergarten. Success in kindergarten depends in part on emotional and social adjustment and prekindergarten preparation.

Psychosocial Development in Early Childhood

"I love you,"
said a great mother.
"I love you for what you are
knowing so well what you are.
And I love you more yet, child,
deeper yet than ever, child,
for what you are going to be,
knowing so well you are going far,
knowing your great works are ahead,
ahead and beyond,
yonder and far over yet."

—Carl Sandburg, *The People, Yes,* 1936

Focus *Isabel Allende, Militant Writer*

Isabel Allende

Isabel Allende has been called Latin America's foremost woman writer. Her best-selling novels and short stories, which evoke her imaginative inner world, have been translated into 30 languages and have sold an estimated 11 million copies worldwide. Perhaps her most moving work is *Paula* (1995), the memoir she began scribbling on yellow pads as she sat at the bedside of her 27-year-old daughter, Paula Frías, in a Madrid hospital, waiting for her to awaken from a coma that never ended. The words Allende poured out were as much a reminiscence of her own tempestuous life as a tribute to her dying daughter.

Isabel Allende was born August 2, 1942, in Lima, Peru. Her father was a Chilean diplomat, a cousin of the Chilean revolutionary hero Salvador Allende, who was assassinated in a military coup in 1973. Her emotional connection with the cause of her oppressed people became the backdrop for much of her later writing. Her major theme is the role of women in a highly patriarchal society.

When Isabel was about 3, her father abandoned her mother, Doña Panchita, in childbirth; Isabel never saw him alive again. Left with no means of support and humiliated by the failure of her marriage, Doña Panchita returned in disgrace with her three young children to her parents' household in Santiago. She found a low-paying job in a bank and supplemented

Sources of information on Isabel Allende are Agosin (1999), Allende (1995), Ojito (2003), Perera (1995), Piña (1999), Rodden (1999), and Allende's Web site, http://www.isabelallende.com.

her salary by making hats. There was no divorce in Chile, so the marriage was annulled. "Those were difficult years for my mother," Allende (1995, p. 32) wrote; "she had to contend with poverty, gossip, and the snubs of people who had been her friends." For Isabel, the middle child and only daughter of "an attractive, abandoned woman who had many suitors and no money" (Ojito, 2003, p. E1), her mother's status was an embarrassment; because of it, Isabel once was expelled from a Roman Catholic school.

Another blow to young Isabel was the death of her beloved grandmother. Suddenly her home became dim and cheerless. A small, fearful, isolated child, often left in the care of a harsh, threatening maid, Isabel found refuge in silent games and in the fanciful stories her mother told at night in the dark. She felt "different," "like an outcast" (Allende, 1995, p. 50), and she had a rebellious streak. Although she loved her mother deeply and wanted to protect her, she did not want to be like her. She wanted to be strong and independent like her grandfather. "I think Tata was always sorry I wasn't a boy," she wrote in *Paula* (1995, p. 37); "had I been, he could have taught me to play jai alai, and use his tools, and hunt." He tacitly condoned the "character-building" tactics of the two bachelor uncles who lived in the household and played rough "games" with the children that today would be considered physically or emotionally abusive. It was during these pivotal early years that Allende's fervent feminism was born. "When I was a little girl," she says, "I felt anger towards my grandfather, my stepfather, and all the men in the family, who had all the advantages while my mother was the victim. . . . She had to please everyone and everyone told her what to do" (Piña, 1999, pp. 174–175).

When Isabel was about 5, Ramón Huidobro, the Chilean consul who had helped the family return to Chile, moved in with Doña Panchita, displacing Isabel and her brothers from their mother's bedroom. It took Isabel years to accept her stepfather. "He raised us with a firm hand and unfailing good humor; he set limits and sent clear messages, without sentimental demonstrations, and without compromise. . . . he put up with my contrariness without trying to buy my esteem or ceding an inch of his authority, until he won me over totally," she writes (Allende, 1995, pp. 48–49).

Through her books, Allende has come to a greater understanding and acceptance of herself and her gender. Many of her characters are extraordinary women who break with tradition despite their place in society. Being a woman, she says, "was like being handicapped in many ways. In that macho culture where I was brought up . . . I would have liked to be a man." Not until she was 40 did she "finally accept that I was always going to . . . be the person I am" (Foster, 1999, p. 107).

● ● ●

The years from age 3 to 6 are pivotal ones in children's psychosocial development, as they were for Isabel Allende. A child's emotional development and sense of self are rooted in the experiences of those years. Yet the story of the self is not completed in early childhood; like Allende, we continue to write it even as adults. Allende's story also highlights the importance of the cultural context. As a girl growing up in a male-dominated culture, she faced attitudes very different from what she might have experienced in a less tightly gender-based society.

In this chapter we discuss preschool children's understanding of themselves and their feelings. We see how their sense of male or female identity arises and how it affects their behavior. We discuss the activity on which children, at least in industrialized cultures, typically spend most of their time: play. We consider the influence, for good or ill, of what parents do. Finally, we discuss relationships with siblings and other children.

After you have read and studied this chapter, you should be able to answer each of the Guidepost questions on the following page. Look for them again in the margins throughout the chapter, where they point to important concepts. To check your understanding of these Guideposts, review the end-of-chapter summary. Checkpoints located throughout the chapter will help you verify your understanding of what you have read.

Guideposts for Study

1. How does the self-concept develop during early childhood, and how do children show self-esteem, emotional growth, and initiative?

2. How do boys and girls become aware of the meaning of gender, and what explains differences in behavior between the sexes?

3. How do preschoolers play, and how does play contribute to and reflect development?

4. How do parenting practices influence development?

5. Why do young children help or hurt others, and why do they develop fears?

6. How do young children get along with—or without—siblings, playmates, and friends?

The Developing Self

"Who in the world am I? Ah, *that's* the great puzzle," said Alice in Wonderland, after her size had abruptly changed—again. Solving Alice's "puzzle" is a lifelong process of getting to know one's self.

Guidepost 1

How does the self-concept develop during early childhood, and how do children show self-esteem, emotional growth, and initiative?

The Self-Concept and Cognitive Development

The **self-concept** is our total picture of our abilities and traits. It is "a *cognitive construction,* . . . a system of descriptive and evaluative representations about the self," that determines how we feel about ourselves and guides our actions (Harter, 1996, p. 207). The sense of self also has a social aspect: Children incorporate into their self-image their growing understanding of how others see them.

The self-concept begins to come into focus in toddlerhood, as children develop self-awareness. It becomes clearer as a person gains in cognitive abilities and deals with the developmental tasks of childhood, of adolescence, and then of adulthood.

self-concept Sense of self; descriptive and evaluative mental picture of one's abilities and traits.

Changes in Self-Definition: The 5 to 7 Shift

Changes in *self-definition,* or self-description, reflect self-concept development. Between about ages 5 and 7, as evidenced by changes in **self-definition,** the way children describe themselves typically changes. At age 4, Jason says,

self-definition Cluster of characteristics used to describe oneself.

> My name is Jason and I live in a big house with my mother and father and sister, Lisa. I have a kitty that's orange and a television set in my own room. . . . I like pizza and I have a nice teacher. I can count up to 100, want to hear me? I love my dog, Skipper. I can climb to the top of the jungle gym, I'm not scared! Just happy. You can't be happy *and* scared, no way! I have brown hair, and I go to preschool. I'm really strong. I can lift this chair, watch me! (Harter, 1996, p. 208)

The way Jason describes himself is typical of U.S. children his age. He talks mostly about concrete, observable behaviors; external characteristics, such as physical features; preferences; possessions; and members of his household. He mentions a particular skill (climbing) rather than general abilities (being athletic). His self-descriptions are unrealistically positive. Not until around age 7 will he describe himself in terms of generalized traits, such as *popular, smart,* or *dumb;* recognize that he can have conflicting emotions; and be self-critical while holding a positive overall self-concept.

What specific changes make up this age 5 to 7 shift? A neo-Piagetian analysis (Case, 1985, 1992; Fischer, 1980) describes the 5 to 7 shift as occurring in three steps.* At 4, Jason

---

*This discussion of children's developing understanding of themselves from age 4 on, including their understanding of their emotions, is indebted to Susan Harter (1990, 1993, 1996, 1998).

single representations In neo-Piagetian terminology, first stage in development of self-definition, in which children describe themselves in terms of individual, unconnected characteristics and in all-or-nothing terms.

real self Self one actually is.

ideal self Self one would like to be.

representational mappings In neo-Piagetian terminology, second stage in development of self-definition, in which a child makes logical connections between aspects of the self but still sees these characteristics in all-or-nothing terms.

is at the first step, **single representations.** His statements about himself are one-dimensional ("I like pizza . . . I'm really strong"). His thinking jumps from particular to particular, without logical connections. At this stage he cannot imagine having two emotions at once ("You can't be happy *and* scared"). Because he cannot decenter, he cannot consider different aspects of himself at the same time. His thinking about himself is all-or-nothing. He cannot acknowledge that his **real self,** the person he actually is, is not the same as his **ideal self,** the person he would like to be. So he describes himself as a paragon of virtue and ability.

At about age 5 or 6, Jason moves up to the second step, **representational mappings.** He begins to make logical connections between one aspect of himself and another: "I can run fast, and I can climb high. I'm also strong. I can throw a ball real far, I'm going to be on a team some day!" (Harter, 1996, p. 215). However, his image of himself is still expressed in completely positive, all-or-nothing terms. He cannot see how he might be good at some things and not at others.

The third step, *representational systems,* takes place in middle childhood (see Chapter 14), when children begin to integrate specific features of the self into a general, multidimensional concept. As all-or-nothing thinking declines, Jason's self-descriptions will become more balanced and realistic ("I'm good at hockey but bad at arithmetic").

Cultural Differences in Self-Definition

Parents transmit, often through everyday conversations, cultural ideas and beliefs about how to define the self. For example, Chinese parents tend to encourage *interdependent* aspects of the self: compliance with authority, appropriate conduct, humility, and a sense of belonging to the community. European American parents encourage *independent* aspects of the self: individuality, self-expression, and self-esteem.

A comparative study of 180 European American and Chinese preschoolers, kindergartners, and second graders (Wang, 2004) found that children absorb differing cultural styles of self-definition as early as age 3 or 4, and these differences increase with age. European American children tend to describe themselves in terms of personal attributes and beliefs ("I am big"), whereas Chinese children talk more about social categories and relationships ("I have a sister"). European American children more often describe themselves in terms of personality traits and tendencies ("I'm good at sports"), whereas Chinese children describe specific, overt behaviors ("I play Snowmoon with my neighbor"). European American children tend to put themselves in an unqualifiedly positive light ("I am smart"), whereas Chinese children and adults describe themselves more neutrally ("I sometimes forget my manners"). Thus, differing cultural values influence the way children in each culture perceive and define themselves.

Self-Esteem

self-esteem Judgment a person makes about his or her self-worth.

Self-esteem is the evaluative part of the self-concept, the judgment children make about their overall self-worth. Self-esteem is based on children's growing cognitive ability to describe and define themselves.

Developmental Changes in Self-Esteem

Children do not generally articulate a concept of self-worth until about age 8, but younger children often show by their behavior that they have one. In a study in Belgium (Verschueren, Buyck, & Marcoen, 2001), researchers measured various aspects of 5-year-olds' self-perceptions, such as physical appearance, scholastic and athletic competence, social acceptance, and behavioral conduct. The researchers also used puppets to reveal children's perceptions of what other people think of them. Children's positive or negative self-perceptions at age 5 tended to predict their self-perceptions and socioemotional functioning at age 8.

Still, before the 5 to 7 shift, young children's self-esteem is not necessarily based on reality. They tend to accept the judgments of adults, who often give positive, uncritical feedback, and thus children may overrate their abilities (Harter, 1990, 1993, 1996, 1998). Like the overall self-concept, self-esteem in early childhood tends to be all-or-none: "I am good" or "I am bad" (Harter, 1996, 1998). Not until middle childhood does it become more realistic, as personal evaluations of competence based on internalization of parental and societal standards begin to shape and maintain self-worth (Harter, 1990, 1996, 1998).

What's your view **?**

• Can you think of ways in which your parents or other adults helped you develop self-esteem?

Contingent Self-Esteem: The "Helpless" Pattern

When self-esteem is high, a child is motivated to achieve. However, if self-esteem is *contingent* on success, children may view failure or criticism as an indictment of their worth and may feel helpless to do better. About one-third to one-half of preschoolers, kindergartners, and first-graders show elements of this "helpless" pattern (Burhans & Dweck, 1995; Ruble & Dweck, 1995). Instead of trying a different way to complete a puzzle, as a child with unconditional self-esteem might do, "helpless" children feel ashamed and give up. They do not expect to succeed, and so they do not try. Whereas older children who fail may conclude that they are "dumb," preschoolers interpret poor performance as a sign of being "bad." Furthermore, this sense of being a bad person may persist into adulthood.

Children whose self-esteem is contingent on success tend to become demoralized when they fail. Often these children attribute poor performance or social rejection to their personality deficiencies, which they believe they are helpless to change. Rather than trying new strategies, they repeat unsuccessful ones or just give up. Children with noncontingent self-esteem, in contrast, tend to attribute failure or disappointment to factors outside themselves or to the need to try harder. If initially unsuccessful or rejected they persevere, trying new strategies until they find one that works (Erdley, Cain, Loomis, Dumas-Hines, & Dweck, 1997; Harter, 1998; Pomerantz & Saxon, 2001). Children with high self-esteem tend to have parents and teachers who give specific, focused feedback rather than criticize the child as a person ("Look, the tag on your shirt is showing in front," not, "Can't you see your shirt is on backwards?" or "When are you going to learn to dress yourself?").

Being able to control and talk about their emotions is an important step in young children's psychosocial development.

Understanding and Regulating Emotions

"I hate you!" Maya, age 5, shouts to her mother. "You're a mean mommy!" Angry because her mother sent her to her room for pinching her baby brother, Maya cannot imagine ever loving her mother again. "Aren't you ashamed of yourself for making the baby cry?" her father asks Maya a little later. Maya nods, but only because she knows what response he wants. In truth, she feels a jumble of emotions—not the least of which is feeling sorry for herself.

The ability to understand and regulate, or control, one's feelings is one of the key advances of early childhood (Dennis, 2006). Children who can understand their emotions are better able to control the way they show them and to be sensitive to how others feel (Garner & Power, 1996). Emotional self-regulation helps children guide their behavior (Laible & Thompson, 1998) and contributes to their ability to get along with others (Denham et al., 2003).

Preschoolers can talk about their feelings and often can discern the feelings of others, and they understand that emotions are connected with experiences and desires (Saarni, Mumme, & Campos, 1998). They understand that someone who gets what he wants will be happy, and someone who does not get what she wants will be sad (Lagattuta, 2005).

Emotional understanding becomes more complex with age. In one study, 32 largely middle-class 4- through 8-year-olds and 32 adults were asked to tell, for example, how a young boy would feel if his ball rolled into the street and he either retrieved or refrained from retrieving it. The results revealed a "5 to 7 shift" in emotional understanding much like that found for self-concept development. The 4- and 5-year-olds tended to believe that the boy would be happy if he got the ball—even though he would be breaking a rule—and unhappy if he didn't. The older children, like the adults, were more inclined to believe that obedience to a rule would make the boy feel good and disobedience would make him feel bad (Lagattuta, 2005).

Understanding Conflicting Emotions

One reason for younger children's confusion about their feelings is that they do not understand that they can experience contrary emotional reactions at the same time, as Isabel Allende did toward her grandfather. Individual differences in understanding conflicting emotions are evident by age 3. In one study, 3-year-olds who could identify whether a face looked happy or sad and who could tell how a puppet felt when enacting a situation involving happiness, sadness, anger, or fear were better able at the end of kindergarten to explain a story character's conflicting emotions. These children tended to come from families that often discussed why people behave as they do (Brown & Dunn, 1996). Most children acquire a more sophisticated understanding of conflicting emotions during middle childhood (Harter, 1996; see Chapter 14).

Understanding Emotions Directed toward the Self

Emotions directed toward the self, such as guilt, shame, and pride, typically develop by the end of the 3rd year, after children gain self-awareness and accept the standards of behavior their parents have set. However, even children a few years older often lack the cognitive sophistication to recognize these emotions and what brings them on (Kestenbaum & Gelman, 1995).

In one study (Harter, 1993), 4- to 8-year-olds were told two stories. In the first story, a child takes a few coins from a jar after being told not to do so; in the second story, a child performs a difficult gymnastic feat—a flip on the bars. Each story was presented in two versions: one in which a parent sees the child doing the act and another in which no one sees the child. The children were asked how they and the parent would feel in each circumstance.

Again, the answers revealed a gradual progression in understanding of feelings about the self, reflecting the 5 to 7 shift (Harter, 1996). At age 4 to 5, children did not say that either they or their parents would feel pride or shame. Instead they used such terms as "worried" or "scared" (for the money jar incident) and "excited" or "happy" (about the gymnastic accomplishment). At 5 to 6, children said their parents would be ashamed or proud of them but did not acknowledge feeling these emotions themselves. At 6 to 7, children said they would feel ashamed or proud, but only if they were observed. Not until age 7 to 8 did children say that they would feel ashamed or proud of themselves even if no one saw them.

Cultural Influences on Emotional Regulation

Culture influences the socialization of emotional expression through interaction with caregivers. In four rural villages in Nepal—two populated almost entirely by Brahmans, high-caste Hindus, and two by Tamang, a Buddhist minority—researchers compared the way caregivers respond to 3- to 5-year-olds who express shame or anger. In both cultures, social harmony is an important value, but it is achieved in different ways. Brahman caregivers ignore a child's expression of shame, which is considered inappropriate among this high-status group, but deal openly and sympathetically with anger, coaxing the child to control it. The Tamang, on the other hand, rebuke displays of anger but use nurturance and reason to deal with shame (Cole, Tamang, & Shrestha, 2006). Thus, when presented with the same hypothetical upsetting situation (such as someone spilling a drink on their homework), Brahman schoolchildren say they would feel—but control—anger, whereas Tamang children say they would be ashamed of having left their homework near the drink (Cole et al., 2002).

Erikson: Initiative versus Guilt

The need to deal with conflicting feelings about the self is at the heart of Erikson's (1950) third stage of psychosocial development: **initiative versus guilt.** The conflict arises from the growing sense of purpose, which spurs a child to plan and carry out activities, and the growing pangs of conscience the child may have about such plans.

Preschool children can do—and want to do—more and more. At the same time, they are learning that some of the things they want to do meet social approval and others do not. How do they reconcile their desire to *do* with their desire for approval? Children who learn how to regulate these opposing drives develop the virtue of *purpose,* the courage to envision and pursue goals without being unduly inhibited by guilt or fear of punishment (Erikson, 1982).

If this conflict is not resolved adequately, said Erikson, a child may grow into an adult who is constantly striving for success or showing off; is inhibited and unspontaneous or self-righteous and intolerant; or suffers from impotence or psychosomatic illness. With ample opportunities to do things on their own—but under guidance and consistent limits—children can attain a healthy balance and avoid the tendency to overdo competition and achievement and the tendency to be repressed and guilt ridden.

initiative versus guilt Erikson's third stage in psychosocial development, in which children balance the urge to pursue goals with moral reservations that may prevent carrying them out.

Checkpoint ✔

Can you . . .

✔ Trace self-concept development between ages 3 and 6 and discuss cultural influences on self-definition?

✔ Tell how young children's self-esteem differs from that of school-age children?

✔ Describe how the "helpless" pattern arises and how it can affect children's reactions to failure?

✔ Describe the typical progression in understanding of conflicting emotions and emotions directed toward the self?

✔ Discuss the conflict involved in Erikson's third stage of psychosocial development?

Gender

Gender identity, awareness of one's femaleness or maleness and all it implies, is an important aspect of the developing self-concept. Isabel Allende's awareness of what it meant to be a female in a "man's world" went back to her early years.

How different are young boys and girls? What causes those differences? How do children develop gender identity, and how does it affect their attitudes and behavior?

Gender Differences

Gender differences are psychological or behavioral differences between males and females. As we discussed in Chapter 8, measurable differences between baby boys and girls are few. Although some gender differences become more pronounced after age 3, boys and girls on average remain more alike than different. Extensive evidence from many studies supports this *gender similarities hypothesis.* Fully 78 percent of gender differences are small to negligible, and some differences, such as in self-esteem, change with age.

Among the larger differences are boys' superior motor performance, especially after puberty, and their moderately greater propensity for physical aggression (Hyde, 2005) beginning by age 2 (Archer, 2004; Baillargeon et al., 2007; Pellegrini & Archer, 2005). (Aggression is discussed later in this chapter.) Temperamentally, from infancy on, girls are better able to pay attention and to inhibit inappropriate behavior. Boys are more active and take more intense pleasure in physical activity (Else-Quest, Hyde, Goldsmith, & Van Hulle, 2006).

Cognitive gender differences are few and small (Spelke, 2005). Overall, intelligence test scores show no gender differences (Keenan & Shaw, 1997), perhaps because the most widely used tests are designed to eliminate gender bias (Neisser et al., 1996). Boys and girls do equally well on tasks involving basic mathematical skills and are equally capable of learning math. However, there are small differences in specific abilities. Girls tend to excel on tests of verbal fluency, mathematical computation, and memory for locations of objects. Boys tend to excel in verbal analogies, mathematical word problems, and memory for spatial configurations. In most studies, these differences do not emerge until elementary school or later (Spelke, 2005). In early childhood and again during preadolescence and adolescence, girls tend to use more responsive language, such as praise, agreement, acknowledgment, and elaborating on what someone else has said (Leaper & Smith, 2004).

We need to remember, of course, that gender differences are valid for large groups of boys and girls but not necessarily for individuals. By knowing a child's sex, we cannot predict whether that *particular* boy or girl will be faster, stronger, smarter, more obedient, or more assertive than another child.

Perspectives on Gender Development

What accounts for gender differences, and why do some of them emerge as children grow older? Some explanations center on the differing experiences and social expectations that boys and girls meet almost from birth. These experiences and expectations concern three related aspects of gender identity: *gender roles, gender-typing,* and *gender stereotypes.*

Gender roles are the behaviors, interests, attitudes, skills, and personality traits that a culture considers appropriate for males or females. All societies have gender roles. Historically, in most cultures, as in Isabel Allende's Chile, women have been expected to devote most of their time to caring for the household and children, and men have been providers and protectors. Women have been expected to be compliant and nurturant; men, to be active, aggressive, and competitive. It is these culturally defined roles that Allende rebelled against. Today, gender roles in Western cultures have become more diverse and more flexible.

Gender-typing (refer back to Chapter 8), the acquisition of a gender role, takes place early in childhood; but children vary greatly in the degree to which they become gender-typed (Iervolino, Hines, Golombok, Rust, & Plomin, 2005). **Gender stereotypes** are overgeneralizations about male or female behavior ("All females are passive and dependent; all males are aggressive and independent"). Gender stereotypes pervade many cultures. They

gender identity Awareness, developed in early childhood, that one is male or female.

Checkpoint

Can you . . .

✔ Summarize the main behavioral and cognitive differences between boys and girls?

gender roles Behaviors, interests, attitudes, skills, and traits that a culture considers appropriate for each sex; differs for males and females.

gender-typing Socialization process whereby children, at an early age, learn appropriate gender roles.

gender stereotypes Preconceived generalizations about male or female role behavior.

Table 11-1	Five Perspectives on Gender Development		
Theories	**Major Theorists**	**Key Processes**	**Basic Beliefs**
Biological Approach		Genetic, neurological, and hormonal activity	Many or most behavioral differences between the sexes can be traced to biological differences.
Evolutionary Developmental Approach	Charles Darwin	Natural sexual selection	Children develop gender roles in preparation for adult mating and reproductive behavior.
Psychoanalytic Approach			
Psychosexual theory	Sigmund Freud	Resolution of unconscious emotional conflict	Gender identity occurs when child identifies with same-sex parent.
Social Learning Approach			
Social cognitive theory	Albert Bandura	Observation of models, reinforcement	Child mentally combines observations of multiple models and creates own behavioral variations.
Cognitive Approach			
Cognitive-developmental theory	Lawrence Kohlberg	Self-categorization	Once a child learns she is a girl or he is a boy, child sorts information about behavior by gender and acts accordingly.
Gender-schema theory	Sandra Bem, Carol Lynn Martin & Charles F. Halverson	Self-categorization based on processing of cultural information	Child organizes information about what is considered appropriate for a boy or a girl on the basis of. what a particular culture dictates and behaves accordingly. Child sorts by gender because the culture dictates that gender is an important schema.

appear to some degree in children as young as 2 or 3, increase during the preschool years, and reach a peak at age 5 (Campbell, Shirley, & Candy, 2004; Ruble & Martin, 1998).

How do children acquire gender roles, and why do they adopt gender stereotypes? Are these purely social constructs, or do they reflect innate differences between males and females? The answers are not either-or. Let's look at five theoretical perspectives on gender development (summarized in Table 11-1): *biological, evolutionary developmental, psychoanalytic, social learning,* and *cognitive.* Each of these perspectives can contribute to our understanding; though, none fully explains why boys and girls differ in some respects but not in others.

Biological Approach

The existence of similar gender roles in many cultures suggests that some gender differences may be biologically based. Investigators are uncovering evidence of genetic, hormonal, and neurological explanations for gender differences.

Scientists have identified more than 50 genes that may explain differences in anatomy and function between the brains of male and female mice. If similar genetic differences exist in humans, then sexual identity may be hardwired into the brain even before sexual organs form and hormonal activity begins (Dewing, Shi, Horvath, & Vilain, 2003).

By age 5, when the brain reaches approximate adult size, boys' brains are about 10 percent larger than girls' brains, mostly because boys have more gray matter in the cerebral cortex, whereas girls have greater neuronal density (Reiss, Abrams, Singer, Ross, & Denckla, 1996). Size differences in the *corpus callosum,* the band of tissue joining the right and left hemispheres, are correlated with verbal fluency (Hines, Chiu, McAdams, Bentler, & Lipcamon, 1992). Because girls have a larger corpus callosum, better coordination between the two hemispheres may help explain girls' superior verbal abilities (Halpern, 1997).

Hormones in the bloodstream before or about the time of birth may affect the developing brain. The male hormone testosterone is related to aggressiveness in adult animals, but the relationship in humans is less clear (Simpson, 2001). For one thing, hormonal influences are hard to disentangle from genetic or later environmental influences (Iervolino et al., 2005). In any event, testosterone levels do not appear to be related to aggressiveness in children (Constantino et al., 1993).

Some research focuses on children with unusual prenatal hormonal histories. Girls with a disorder called *congenital adrenal hyperplasia (CAH)* have high prenatal levels of *androgens* (male sex hormones). Although raised as girls, they tend to develop into tomboys, showing preferences for "boys' toys," rough play, and male playmates, as well as strong spatial skills. *Estrogens* (female hormones), seem to have less influence on boys' gender-typed behavior. However, these studies are natural experiments and cannot establish cause and effect. Other factors besides hormonal differences may play a role (Ruble & Martin, 1998).

Perhaps the most dramatic examples of biologically based research have to do with infants born with ambiguous sexual structures that appear to be part male and part female. John Money and his colleagues (Money, Hampson, & Hampson, 1955) developed guidelines for infants born with such disorders. He recommended that the child be assigned as early as possible to the gender that holds the potential for the most nearly normal functioning and for stable gender identity.

In the case of a 7-month-old boy whose penis was accidentally cut off during circumcision, the decision was not made until 17 months to rear the child as a girl, and four months later doctors performed surgical reconstruction (Money & Ehrhardt, 1972). Although initially described as developing into a normal female, the child later rejected female identity and, at puberty, switched to living as a male. After a second surgical reconstruction, he married a woman and adopted her children. This case seems to suggest that gender identity may be rooted in chromosomal structure or prenatal development and cannot easily be changed (Diamond & Sigmundson, 1997)—at least not by waiting until the child is 17 months old.

The only other documented case of this kind had a different outcome. This time, the accident occurred at 2 months, and penile removal and sexual reassignment took place by 7 months. When interviewed at ages 16 and 26, the patient identified as a female, was living as a woman, and had had sexual relationships with both men and women (Bradley, Oliver, Chernick, & Zucker, 1998). Thus assignment of gender—at least during early infancy—may have some flexibility after all.

According to the report of an international conference on intersex disorders, psychosexual development is influenced by a number of factors, including sex-chromosome genes, brain structure, family dynamics, social circumstances, and prenatal androgen exposure. The conferees recommended that decisions about gender assignment of babies with disordered sex development be made carefully but as quickly as thorough diagnostic evaluation and sensitive consultation with parents permits (Houk, Hughes, Ahmed, Lee, and Writing Committee for the International Intersex Consensus Conference Participants, 2006).

Evolutionary Developmental Approach

The evolutionary developmental approach sees gendered behavior as biologically based—with a purpose. From this controversial perspective, children's gender roles underlie the evolved mating and child-rearing strategies of adult males and females.

According to Darwin's (1871) **theory of sexual selection,** the selection of sexual partners is a response to the differing reproductive pressures that early men and women confronted in the struggle for survival of the species (Wood & Eagly, 2002). The more widely a man can "spread his seed," the greater his chances to pass on his genetic inheritance. Thus, men tend to seek as many partners as possible. They value physical prowess because it enables them to compete for mates and for control of resources and social status, which women value. Because a woman invests more time and energy in pregnancy and can bear only a limited number of children, each child's survival is of utmost importance to her. Thus, she looks for a mate who will remain with her and support their

theory of sexual selection
Darwinian theory, which holds that selection of sexual partners is influenced by the differing reproductive pressures that early men and women confronted in the struggle for survival of the species.

offspring. The need to raise each child to reproductive maturity also explains why women tend to be more caring and nurturant than men (Bjorklund & Pellegrini, 2000; Wood & Eagly, 2002).

According to evolutionary theory, male competitiveness and aggressiveness and female nurturance develop during childhood as preparation for these adult roles. Boys play at fighting; girls play at parenting. In caring for children, women often must put a child's needs and feelings ahead of their own. Thus young girls tend to be better able than young boys to control and inhibit their emotions and to refrain from impulsive behavior (Bjorklund & Pellegrini, 2000).

If this theory is correct, gender roles should be universal and resistant to change. Evidence in support of the theory is that in all cultures, women tend to be children's primary caregivers, though in some societies this responsibility is shared with the father or others (Wood & Eagly, 2002). Evidence against the theory is men's greater involvement in child raising today than in the past in the United States and other Western societies.

Critics of evolutionary theory suggest that society and culture are as important as biology in determining gender roles. Evolutionary theory claims that men's primary role is to provide for subsistence while women's primary role is child care, but in some nonindustrial societies women are the main or equal providers. In an analysis of mating preferences in 37 cultures, women in traditional societies did tend to prefer older men with financial resources, and men to prefer younger women with homemaking skills; but these preferences were less pronounced in more egalitarian societies where women had reproductive freedom and educational opportunities (Wood & Eagly, 2002).

Some evolutionary theorists, therefore, see the evolution of gender roles as a dynamic process. They acknowledge that gender roles (such as men's involvement in child rearing) may change in an environment different from that in which these roles initially evolved (Crawford, 1998).

Psychoanalytic Approach

"Dad, where will you live when I grow up and marry Mommy?" asks Juan, age 4. From the psychoanalytic perspective, Juan's question is part of his acquisition of gender identity. That process, according to Freud, is one of **identification,** the adoption of characteristics, beliefs, attitudes, values, and behaviors of the parent of the same sex. Freud considered identification an important personality development of early childhood; some social learning theorists also have used the term.

According to Freud, identification will occur for Juan when he represses or gives up the wish to possess the parent of the other sex (his mother) and identifies with the parent of the same sex (his father). But although this explanation for gender development has been influential, it has been difficult to test and has little research support (Maccoby, 1992). Despite some evidence that preschoolers tend to act more affectionately toward the other-sex parent and more aggressively toward the same-sex parent (Westen, 1998), most developmental psychologists today favor other explanations.

Social Learning Approach

According to Walter Mischel (1966), a traditional social learning theorist, children acquire gender roles by imitating models and being rewarded for gender-appropriate behavior—in other words, by responding to environmental stimuli. Children generally choose models they see as powerful or nurturing. Typically, one model is a parent, often of the same sex, but children also pattern their behavior after other adults or after peers. (Isabel Allende, uncomfortable with the subordinate roles of the women she saw, sought to model herself after her grandfather.) Behavioral feedback, together with direct teaching by parents and other adults, reinforces gender-typing. A boy who models his behavior after his father is commended for acting "like a boy." A girl gets compliments on a pretty dress or hairstyle. In this model, *gendered behavior precedes gender knowledge* ("I am rewarded for doing boy things, so I must be a boy").

Since the 1970s, however, studies have cast doubt on the power of same-sex modeling alone to account for gender differences. As cognitive explanations (discussed in the next

identification In Freudian theory, process by which a young child adopts characteristics, beliefs, attitudes, values, and behaviors of the parent of the same sex.

section) have come to the fore, traditional social learning theory has lost favor (Martin, Ruble, & Szkrybalo, 2002). Albert Bandura's (1986; Bussey & Bandura, 1999) newer **social cognitive theory,** an expansion of social learning theory, incorporates some cognitive elements.

According to social cognitive theory, observation enables children to learn much about gender-typed behaviors before performing them. They can mentally combine observations of multiple models and generate their own behavioral variations. Instead of viewing the environment as a given, social cognitive theory recognizes that children select or even create their environments through their choice of playmates and activities. However, critics say that social cognitive theory does not explain how children differentiate between boys and girls before they have a concept of gender, or what initially motivates children to acquire gender knowledge, or how gender norms become internalized—questions that other cognitive theories attempt to answer (Martin et al., 2002).

social cognitive theory Albert Bandura's expansion of social learning theory; holds that children learn gender roles through socialization.

Cognitive Approaches

Sarah figures out she is a girl because people call her a girl. As she continues to observe and think about her world, she concludes that she will always be female. She comes to understand gender by actively thinking about and constructing her own gender-typing. This is the heart of Lawrence Kohlberg's (1966) cognitive-developmental theory.

Kohlberg's Cognitive-Developmental Theory In Kohlberg's theory, *gender knowledge precedes gendered behavior* ("I am a boy, so I like to do boy things"). Children *actively* search for cues about gender in their social world. As children come to realize which gender they belong to, they adopt behaviors they perceive as consistent with being male or female. Thus, 3-year-old Sarah prefers dolls to trucks because she sees girls playing with dolls and therefore views playing with dolls as consistent with her being a girl. And she plays mostly with other girls, whom she assumes will share her interests (Ruble & Martin, 1998; Martin & Ruble, 2004).

The acquisition of gender roles, said Kohlberg, hinges on **gender constancy,** more recently called *sex-category constancy*—a child's realization that his or her sex will always be the same. Once children achieve this realization, they are motivated to adopt behaviors appropriate to their sex. Gender constancy seems to develop in three stages: *gender identity, gender stability,* and *gender consistency* (Martin et al., 2002; Ruble & Martin, 1998; Szkrybalo & Ruble, 1999). *Gender identity* (awareness of one's own gender and that of others) typically occurs between ages 2 and 3. *Gender stability* comes when a girl realizes that she will grow up to be a woman, and a boy that he will grow up to be a man—in other words, that gender does not change. However, children at this stage may base judgments about gender on superficial appearances (clothing or hairstyle) and stereotyped behaviors. Sometime between ages 3 and 7, or even later—comes *gender consistency:* the realization that a girl remains a girl even if she has a short haircut and wears pants, and a boy remains a boy even if he has long hair and wears earrings. Once children realize that their behavior or dress will not affect their sex, they may become less rigid in their adherence to gender norms (Martin et al., 2002).

gender constancy Awareness that one will always be male or female. Also called *sex-category constancy.*

Much research challenges Kohlberg's view that gender-typing depends on gender constancy. Long before children attain the final stage of gender constancy, they show gender-typed preferences (Bussey & Bandura, 1992; Martin & Ruble, 2004; Ruble & Martin, 1998). For example, gender preferences in toys and playmates appear as early as 12 to 24 months. However, these findings do not challenge Kohlberg's basic insight: that gender concepts influence behavior (Martin et al., 2002).

Today, cognitive-developmental theorists no longer claim that gender constancy must precede gender-typing (Martin et al., 2002). Instead, they suggest, gender-typing may be heightened by the more sophisticated understanding that gender constancy brings (Martin & Ruble, 2004). Each stage of gender constancy increases children's receptivity to gender-relevant information. The achievement of gender identity may motivate children to learn more about gender; gender stability and gender consistency may motivate them to be sure they are acting "like a boy" or "like a girl." Studies have found significant linkage between levels of gender constancy and various aspects of gender development (Martin et al., 2002).

gender-schema theory Theory, proposed by Bem, that children socialize themselves in their gender roles by developing a mentally organized network of information about what it means to be male or female in a particular culture.

Anna's enjoyment of her truck shows that she is not restricted in her play by gender stereotypes. According to Bem's gender-schema theory, parents can help their children avoid such stereotypes by encouraging them to pursue their own interests, even when these interests are unconventional for their sex.

Gender-Schema Theory Another cognitive approach is **gender-schema theory.** Like cognitive-developmental theory, it views children as actively extracting knowledge about gender from their environment *before* engaging in gender-typed behavior. However, gender-schema theory places more emphasis on the influence of culture. Once children know what sex they are, they develop a concept of what it means to be male or female *in their culture*. Children then match their behavior to their culture's view of what boys and girls are "supposed" to be and do. Among the theory's leading proponents are Sandra Bem (1983, 1985, 1993), Carol Lynn Martin, and Charles F. Halverson (Martin & Halverson, 1981; Martin et al., 2002),).

One of the key contributions of gender-schema theory is the concept of the gender schema. A *gender schema* (much like Piaget's *schemes*) is a mentally organized network of information about gender that influences behavior. Gender schemas develop with age in response to experience. Even before they can talk, children organize their observations around the schema of gender because they see that their society classifies people that way: males and females wear different clothes, play with different toys, and use separate bathrooms. Children then generalize this information to other members of the same category. As children's knowledge about gender increases, it influences not only what they do but also what they pay attention to and remember (Martin et al., 2002).

It has been suggested that gender schemas promote gender stereotypes by leading children to overgeneralize. When a new boy his age moves in next door, 4-year-old Brandon knocks on his door, carrying a toy truck—apparently assuming that the new boy will like the same toys he likes. However, there is little evidence that gender schemas are at the root of stereotyped behavior (Yunger, Carver, & Perry, 2004). Furthermore, gender-stereotyping does not always become stronger with increased gender knowledge; in fact, the opposite is often true (Bussey & Bandura, 1999).

A current view, which has research support, is that gender-stereotyping rises and then falls in a developmental pattern (Ruble & Martin, 1998; Welch-Ross & Schmidt, 1996). Around ages 4 to 6, when children are constructing and then consolidating their gender schemas, they notice and remember information consistent with these schemas and even exaggerate it. In fact, they tend to *mis*remember information that challenges gender stereotypes, such as photos of a girl sawing wood or a boy cooking, and to insist that the genders in the photos were the other way around (Martin, Eisenbud, & Rose, 1995; Martin & Ruble, 2004; Ruble & Martin, 1998).

Between ages 5 and 7, children have developed a repertoire of rigid stereotypes about gender that they apply to themselves and others. A boy will pay more attention to what he considers "boys' toys" and a girl to "girls' toys." A boy will expect to do better at "boy things" and a girl, at "girl things." Then, around age 7 or 8, schemas become more complex as children begin to take in and integrate contradictory information, such as the fact that some girls like to play football. As children develop more complex beliefs about gender, they become more flexible in their views about gender roles (Martin & Ruble, 2004; Martin et al., 2002; Ruble & Martin, 1998; M. G. Taylor, 1996; Trautner et al., 2005).

Cognitive approaches to gender development (including social cognitive theory) have made an important contribution by exploring how children think about gender and what they know about it at various ages. However, the various theories differ as to what prompts children to enact gender roles and why some children become more strongly gender-typed than others (Bussey & Bandura, 1992, 1999; Martin et al., 2002; Martin & Ruble, 2004; Ruble & Martin, 1998). One important factor, according to both cognitive and social cognitive theorists, may be socialization.

The Role of Socialization

Socialization begins in infancy, long before a conscious understanding of gender begins to form. Gradually, as children begin to regulate their activities, standards of behavior become internalized. Children feel good about themselves when they live up to their internal standards and feel bad when they do not. A substantial part of this shift from socially guided control to self-regulation of gender-related behavior may take place between ages 3 and 4 (Bussey & Bandura, 1992). How do parents, peers, and the media influence this development?

Family Influences When Louisiana governor Kathleen Blanco's 4-year-old grandson, David, was asked what he wanted to be when he grew up, he wasn't sure. He shrugged off all his mother's suggestions: firefighter, soldier, policeman, airplane pilot. Finally, she asked whether he'd like to be governor. "Mom," he replied, "I'm a boy!" (Associated Press, 2004a).

David's response illustrates how strong family influences may be, even fostering counterstereotypical preferences. Usually, though, experience in the family seems to reinforce gender-typical preferences and attitudes. We say "seems" because it is difficult to separate parents' genetic influence from the influence of the environment they create. Also, parents may be responding to, rather than encouraging, children's gender-typed behavior (Iervolino et al., 2005).

Boys tend to be more strongly gender-socialized concerning play preferences than girls. Parents, especially fathers, generally show more discomfort if a boy plays with a doll than if a girl plays with a truck (Lytton & Romney, 1991; Ruble & Martin, 1998; Sandnabba & Ahlberg, 1999). Girls have more freedom than boys in their clothes, games, and choice of playmates (Miedzian, 1991).

In egalitarian households, the father's role in gender socialization seems especially important (Fagot & Leinbach, 1995). In an observational study of 4-year-olds in British and Hungarian cities, boys and girls whose fathers did more housework and child care were less aware of gender stereotypes and engaged in less gender-typed play (Turner & Gervai, 1995).

Siblings also influence gender development, according to a 3-year longitudinal study of 198 first- and secondborn siblings (median ages 10 and 8) and their parents. Secondborns tend to become more like their older siblings in attitudes, personality, and leisure activities, whereas firstborns are more influenced by their parents and less by their younger siblings (McHale, Updegraff, Helms-Erikson, & Crouter, 2001). Young children with an older sibling of the same sex tend to be more gender-typed than those whose older sibling is of the other sex (Iervolino et al., 2005).

Peer Influences Anna, at age 5, insisted on dressing in a new way. She wanted to wear leggings, with a skirt over them, and boots—indoors and out. When her mother asked her why, Anna replied, "Because Katie dresses like this—and Katie's the king of the girls!"

Even in early childhood, the peer group is a major influence on gender-typing. By age 3, preschoolers generally play in sex-segregated groups, which reinforce gender-typed behavior, and the influence of the peer group increases with age (Martin et al., 2002; Ruble & Martin, 1998). Children who play in same-sex groups tend to be more gender-typed than children who do not (Maccoby, 2002; Martin & Fabes, 2001). Peer groups show more disapproval of boys who act "like girls" than of girls who are tomboys (Ruble & Martin, 1998). Indeed, play choices at this age may be more strongly influenced by peers and the media than by the models children see at home (Turner & Gervai, 1995). Generally, however, peer and parental attitudes reinforce each other (Bussey & Bandura, 1999).

Cultural Influences At age 5, Isabel Allende was admonished to sit with her legs together and knit while her brothers were out climbing trees. In this way she learned that as a female she was restricted from acts her brothers were allowed to perform (D. Skinner, 1989).

In the United States, television is a major channel for the transmission of cultural attitudes toward gender. Social cognitive theory predicts that children who watch a lot of television will become more gender-typed by imitating the models they see on the screen. Dramatic supporting evidence emerged from a natural experiment in several Canadian towns that obtained access to television transmission for the first time. Children who had had relatively unstereotyped attitudes before television programming became available showed marked increases in traditional views 2 years afterward (Kimball, 1986).

Children's books have long been a source of gender stereotypes. Today, the proportion of women as main characters has greatly increased, and children are more frequently shown in nontraditional activities (girls dressing up as pilots or boys helping with laundry).

What's your view

- Where would you place your views on the continuum between the following extremes? Explain.

1. Family A thinks girls should wear only ruffly dresses and boys should never wash dishes or cry.

2. Family Z treats sons and daughters exactly alike, without making any references to the children's sex.

Checkpoint

Can you . . .

✔ Distinguish among five basic approaches to the study of gender development?

✔ Assess evidence for biological explanations of gender differences?

✔ Compare how various theories explain the acquisition of gender roles, and assess the support for each theory?

✔ Discuss the role of socialization in gender acquisition?

Guidepost 3

How do preschoolers play, and how does play contribute to and reflect development?

However, women are still shown mostly in domestic roles, whereas men are seldom seen doing housework or caring for children (Gooden, 2001). Fathers, in fact, are largely absent and, when they do appear, are often shown as withdrawn and ineffectual (Anderson & Hamilton, 2005).

Studies of the role of socialization leave unanswered questions. What aspects of the home environment promote gender-typing? Do parents and peers treat boys and girls differently because they *are* different or because the culture says they *should be* different? Does differential treatment *produce* or *reflect* gender differences, or is there a bidirectional relationship? Further research may help show how socializing agents mesh with children's own biological tendencies and cognitive understandings in respect to gender-related attitudes and behavior.

It seems likely that none of the theories we have discussed has the full answer to how gender identity and gender-typing develop. Today "it is widely acknowledged that . . . cognitive, environmental, and biological factors are all important" (Martin et al., 2002, p. 904). A recent *biosocial theory,* for example, holds that psychological aspects of gender arise from interaction between the physical characteristics of the sexes (such as men's greater physical strength and women's reproductive capacity), their developmental experiences, and the character of the societies in which they live (Wood & Eagly, 2002).

Play: The Business of Early Childhood

Carmen, age 3, pretends that the pieces of cereal floating in her bowl are "fishies" swimming in the milk, and she "fishes," spoonful by spoonful. After breakfast, she puts on her mother's hat, picks up a briefcase, and is a "mommy" going to work. She rides her tricycle through the puddles, comes in for an imaginary telephone conversation, turns a wooden block into a truck and says, "Vroom, vroom!" Carmen's day is one round of play after another.

It would be a mistake to dismiss Carmen's activities as just fun. Although play may not seem to serve any obvious purpose, it has important current and long-term evolutionary functions (Bjorklund & Pellegrini, 2002; Smith, 2005b; Box 11-1). Play is important to healthy development of body and brain. It enables children to engage with the world around them, to use their imagination, to discover flexible ways to use objects and solve problems, and to prepare for adult roles.

Play contributes to all domains of development. Through play, children stimulate the senses, exercise their muscles, coordinate sight with movement, gain mastery over their bodies, make decisions, and acquire new skills. As they sort blocks of different shapes, count how many they can pile on each other, or announce that "my tower is bigger than yours," they lay the foundation for mathematical concepts. As they cooperate to build sandcastles or tunnels on the beach, they learn skills of negotiation and conflict resolution (Ginsburg and the Committee on Communications and the Committee on Psychosocial Aspects of Child and Family Health, 2007). Indeed, play is so important to children's development that the United Nations High Commissioner for Human Rights (1989) has recognized it as a right of every child.

Children need plenty of time for free exploratory play. Today, many parents expose young children to enrichment videos and academically oriented playthings. These activities may be valuable in themselves, but not if they interfere with child-directed play. The trend to full-day kindergarten also has markedly reduced time for free play (Ginsburg et al., 2007).

Children of differing ages have differing styles of play, play with different things, and spend different amounts of time in various types of play (Bjorklund & Pellegrini, 2002). Physical play, for example, begins in infancy with apparently aimless rhythmic movements. As gross motor skills improve, preschoolers exercise their muscles by running, jumping, skipping, hopping, and throwing. Toward the end of this period and into middle childhood, *rough-and-tumble play* involving wrestling, kicking, and chasing becomes more common, especially among boys (see Chapter 12).

Box 11-1 *Does Play Have an Evolutionary Basis?*

Children appear to engage in play for the pure pleasure it brings. Yet, from an evolutionary standpoint, an activity that (1) takes up considerable time and energy, (2) shows a characteristic age progression, peaking in childhood and declining with sexual maturity, (3) is encouraged by parents, and (4) occurs in all cultures would seem to have been naturally selected as having significant benefits for children (Bjorklund & Pellegrini, 2000; Smith, 2005b).

Investigators differ on the value and function of play. One early psychologist, Herbert Spencer (1878/1898), dismissed play as a "useless exercise" of excess energy. The German philosopher Karl Groos (1898, 1901), whose view more closely foreshadows current thinking, argued that play has the essential function of skill practice—indeed, that the main purpose of childhood is for play to occur. G. Stanley Hall (1904/1916) claimed that play serves a cathartic function, allowing children to "play out" primitive human instincts that characterized our evolutionary past.

Today, many psychologists and educators see play as an adaptive activity characteristic of the long period of immaturity and dependence, during which children gain the physical attributes and cognitive and social learning necessary for adult life. Play aids bone and muscle development and gives children a chance to try out and master activities and develop a sense of their own capabilities (Bjorklund & Pellegrini, 2000). Through play, children practice, in a risk-free environment, behaviors and skills they will need in adult life (Hawes, 1996). Animal studies suggest that the evolution of play may be linked to the evolution of intelligence. The most intelligent animals—birds and mammals—play, whereas less intelligent species—fish, reptiles, and amphibians—do not, as far as we can tell (Hawes, 1996).

Parents, according to evolutionary theory, encourage play because the future benefits of children's skill acquisition outweigh any benefits of current productive activity in which children, at their relatively low skill levels, might engage (Smith, 2005b). Gender differences in children's play enable boys and girls to practice adult behaviors important for reproduction and survival (Bjorklund & Pellegrini, 2002; Geary, 1999).

Different types of play serve different adaptive functions. Early locomotor play is common among all mammals and may support brain development. Later, exercise play may help develop muscle strength, endurance, physical skills, and efficiency of movement (Smith, 2005b). Play with objects is found mainly among primates: humans, monkeys, and apes. Object play may have served an evolutionary purpose in the development of tools, by enabling people to learn the properties of objects and what can

be done with them (Bjorklund & Pellegrini, 2002). In premodern societies, the objects used in play can be any materials picked up from the surrounding environment. Object play in such societies tends to focus on developing useful skills, such as making baskets and pounding grain (Smith, 2005b). Young mammals, like human children, engage in social play, such as wrestling and chasing each other. Social play may strengthen social bonds, facilitate cooperation, and lessen aggression (Hawes, 1996).

Unlike other types of play, dramatic play seems to be an almost exclusively human activity. Apes, gorillas, and chimpanzees in captivity have been observed to engage only in simple make-believe play with objects, such as sipping from an empty cup. This rudimentary ability may have been the basis for the evolution of true symbolic play in humans, independent of the presence of physical objects (Bjorklund & Pellegrini, 2002; Smith, 2005b).

Dramatic play seems to be universal in humans but is less frequent in societies in which children are expected to participate in adult work (Smith, 2005a). In traditional hunter-gatherer societies, children's pretense focuses on imitating adult subsistence activities such as hunting, fishing, and preparing food. These highly repetitive routines seem to serve primarily as practice for adult activities (Smith, 2005b). As humans began to settle in permanent communities, dramatic play may have evolved so as to practice the changing skills needed for new ways of life. In modern urban industrial societies, themes of dramatic play are highly influenced by the mass media. At least in higher-SES families, dramatic play is encouraged by an abundance of toys, the absence of demands on children to help in subsistence activities, heavy parental involvement in play, and play-based preschool curricula (Smith, 2005a).

Investigators still have much to learn about the functions and benefits of play, but one thing seems clear: The time children spend playing is time well spent.

What's your view ❓

From your observations of children's play, what immediate and long-range purposes does it appear to serve?

Check it out ❗

For more information on this topic, go to http://nationalzoo.si.edu/Publications/ZooGoer/1996/1/junglegyms.cfm. This is the Web site for *Zoogoer*, a newsletter of the Smithsonian National Zoological Park. It features an article on the evolution of play in animals and humans.

Researchers categorize children's play in varying ways. One common classification system is by *cognitive complexity.* Another classification is based on the *social dimension* of play.

Cognitive Levels of Play

Courtney, at 3, talked for a doll, using a deeper voice than her own. Miguel, at 4, wore a kitchen towel as a cape and "flew" around as Batman. These children were engaged in pretend play involving make-believe people or situations.

functional play In Smilansky's terminology, lowest cognitive level of play, involving repetitive muscular movements; also called *locomotor play.*

constructive play In Smilansky's terminology, second cognitive level of play, involving use of objects or materials to make something; also called *object play.*

dramatic play Play involving imaginary people or situations; also called *fantasy play, pretend play,* or *imaginative play.*

formal games with rules organized games with known procedures and penalties.

Pretend play is one of four levels of play identified by Smilansky (1968) as showing increasing cognitive complexity: *functional play, constructive play, dramatic play,* and *games with rules.*

The simplest level, which begins during infancy, is **functional play** (sometimes called *locomotor play*). It consists of repeated practice in large muscular movements, such as rolling a ball (Bjorklund & Pellegrini, 2002).

The second level, **constructive play** (also called *object play*), is the use of objects or materials to make something, such as a house of blocks or a crayon drawing. Children spend an estimated 10 to 15 percent of their time playing with objects, such as blocks (Bjorklund & Pellegrini, 2002).

The third level, which Smilansky called **dramatic Play** (also called *pretend play, fantasy play,* or *imaginative play*), involves make-believe objects, actions, or roles; it rests on the symbolic function, which emerges during the last part of the 2nd year (Piaget, 1962). Although functional play and constructive play precede dramatic play in Smilanksy's hierarchy, these three types of play often occur at the same ages (Bjorklund & Pellegrini, 2002; Smith, 2005a).

Dramatic play peaks during the preschool years, increasing in frequency and complexity (Bjorklund & Pellegrini, 2002; Smith, 2005a), and then declines as school-age children become more involved in **formal games with rules**—organized games with known procedures and penalties, such as hopscotch and marbles. However, many children continue to engage in pretending well beyond the elementary school years. An estimated 12 to 15 percent of preschoolers' time is spent in pretend play (Bjorklund & Pellegrini, 2002), but the trend toward academically oriented kindergarten programs may limit the amount of time children can spend in such play (Bergen, 2002; Ginsburg et al., 2007).

Dramatic play at age 2 is largely imitative, often initiated by an adult caregiver and following familiar scripts such as feeding a baby doll or taking a stuffed animal's temperature. By age 3 or 4, pretense becomes more imaginative and self-initiated. Children may use a block to represent a cup or just imagine the cup (Smith, 2005a).

Dramatic play involves a combination of cognition, emotion, language, and sensorimotor behavior. It may strengthen the development of dense connections in the brain and strengthen the later capacity for abstract thought. Children who watch a great deal of television tend to play less imaginatively, perhaps because they are accustomed to passively absorbing images and plots rather than generating their own (Howes & Matheson, 1992). Studies have found the quality of dramatic play to be associated with social and linguistic competence (Bergen, 2002). By making "tickets" for an imaginary train trip or "reading eye charts" in a "doctor's office," children build emergent literacy skills (Christie, 1991, 1998). Pretend play also may further the development of theory-of-mind skills (refer back to Chapter 10). The peak period for pretend play, early childhood, is also the peak period for acquisition of such skills as recognizing false beliefs (Smith, 2005b).

The Social Dimension of Play

In a classic study done in the 1920s, Mildred B. Parten (1932) identified six types of play ranging from the least to the most social (Table 11-2). She found that as children get older, their play tends to become more social—that is, more interactive and more cooperative. At first children play alone, then alongside other children, and finally together. Today, however, many researchers view Parten's characterization of children's play development as too simplistic, as children of all ages engage in all of Parten's categories of play (K. H. Rubin et al., 1998).

Parten apparently regarded nonsocial play as less mature than social play. She suggested that young children who continue to play alone may develop social, psychological, or educational problems. However, certain types of nonsocial play, particularly parallel play and solitary independent play, may consist of activities that *foster* cognitive, physical, and social development. In one study of 4-year-olds, *parallel constructive play* (for example, working on puzzles near another child who is also doing so) was most common among children who were good problem solvers, were popular with other children, and were seen by teachers as socially skilled (K. Rubin, 1982).

Table 11-2	Parten's Categories of Social and Nonsocial Play

Category	Description
Unoccupied behavior	The child does not seem to be playing but watches anything of momentary interest.
Onlooker behavior	The child spends most of the time watching other children play. The onlooker talks to them, asking questions or making suggestions, but does not enter into the play. The onlooker is definitely observing particular groups of children rather than anything that happens to be exciting.
Solitary independent play	The child plays alone with toys that are different from those used by nearby children and makes no effort to get close to them.
Parallel play	The child plays independently but among the other children, playing with toys like those used by the other children but not necessarily playing with them in the same way. Playing *beside* rather than *with* the others, the parallel player does not try to influence the other children's play.
Associative play	The child plays with other children. They talk about their play, borrow and lend toys, follow one another, and try to control who may play in the group. All the children play similarly if not identically; there is no division of labor and no organization around any goal. Each child acts as she or he wishes and is interested more in being with the other children than in the activity itself.
Cooperative or organized supplementary play	The child plays in a group organized for some goal—to make something, play a formal game, or dramatize a situation. One or two children control who belongs to the group and direct activities. By a division of labor, children take on different roles and supplement each other's efforts.

Source: Adapted from Parten, 1932, pp. 249–251.

Researchers now look not only at *whether* a child plays alone but at *why*. Among 567 kindergartners, teachers, observers, and classmates rated almost 2 out of 3 children who played alone as socially and cognitively competent; they simply preferred to play that way (Harrist, Zain, Bates, Dodge, & Pettit, 1997).

On the other hand, solitary play can be a sign of shyness, anxiety, fearfulness, or social rejection (Coplan et al., 2004; Henderson, Marshall, Fox, & Rubin, 2004; Spinrad et al., 2004). In two Canadian studies of preschoolers and kindergartners, boys who engaged in solitary *passive* play, drawing pictures or building with blocks while peers played nearby, tended to be shy or maladjusted (Coplan, Gavinski-Molina, Lagacé-Séguin, & Wichman, 2001; Coplan, Prakash, O'Neil, & Armer, 2004).

Reticent play, a combination of Parten's onlooker and unoccupied categories, is often a manifestation of shyness (Coplan et al., 2004). However, such reticent behaviors as playing near other children, watching what they do, or wandering aimlessly may sometimes be a prelude to joining in others' play (K. H. Rubin, Bukowski, & Parker, 1998; Spinrad et al., 2004). In a short-term longitudinal study, preschool children were observed in daily free play. Reticent children, though hesitant to join in other children's play, were well liked and showed few problem behaviors (Spinrad et al., 2004). Nonsocial play, then, seems to be far more complex than Parten imagined.

One kind of play that becomes more social during the preschool years is dramatic play (K. H. Rubin et al., 1998; Singer & Singer, 1990). Children typically engage in more dramatic play when playing with someone else than when playing alone (Bjorklund & Pellegrini, 2002). As dramatic play becomes more collaborative, story lines become more complex and innovative, offering rich opportunities to practice interpersonal and language skills and to explore social conventions and roles. In pretending together, children develop joint problem-solving, planning, and goal-seeking skills; gain understanding of other people's perspectives; and construct an image of the social world (Bergen, 2002; Bodrova & Leong, 1998; Bjorklund & Pellegrini, 2002; J. I. F. Davidson, 1998; J. E. Johnson, 1998; Nourot, 1998; Smith, 2005a).

What's your view

- How do you think the growing use of computers for both games and educational activities might affect preschool children's social and cognitive development?

Checkpoint

Can you . . .

✔ Describe four cognitive levels of play, according to Smilansky and others, and six categories of social and nonsocial play, according to Parten?

✔ Explain the connection between the cognitive and social dimensions of play?

✔ Discuss the functions of dramatic play?

Preschool boys and girls prefer different types of play. Boys engage in rough-and-tumble play; girls play more quietly and cooperatively.

How Gender Influences Play

Boys of all ages engage in more physical play than girls (Bjorklund & Pellegrini, 2002; Smith, 2005b). Boys and girls are equally likely to play with objects, but boys do so more vigorously (Smith, 2005b). Girls tend to use objects for making things, such as puzzles and art projects, whereas boys are more likely to use objects as weapons (Pellegrini & Gustafson, 2005).

As we have mentioned, sex segregation is common among preschoolers and becomes more prevalent in middle childhood. This tendency seems to be universal across cultures (Smith, 2005a). Although biology (sex hormones), gender identification, and adult reinforcement all seem to influence gender differences in play, the influence of the peer group may be more powerful (Smith, 2005a). Boys tend to like active, outdoor physical play in large mixed-age groups; girls prefer quiet, harmonious play with one playmate. Boys play spontaneously on sidewalks, streets, or empty lots; girls tend to choose more structured, adult-supervised activities (Benenson, 1993; Bjorklund & Pellegrini, 2002; Fabes, Martin, & Hanish, 2003; Serbin, Moller, Gulko, Powlishta, & Colburne, 1994; Smith, 2005a).

Girls engage in more dramatic play than boys. Boys' pretend play often involves danger or discord and competitive, dominant roles, as in mock battles. Girls' pretend stories generally focus on social relationships and nurturing, domestic roles, as in playing house (Bjorklund & Pellegrini, 2002; Pellegrini & Archer, 2005; Smith, 2005a). However, boys' play is more strongly gender-stereotyped than girls' (Bjorklund & Pellegrini, 2002). Thus, in mixed-sex groups, play tends to revolve around traditionally masculine activities (Fabes et al., 2003).

How Culture Influences Play

Cultural values affect the play environments adults set up for children, and these environments in turn affect the frequency of specific forms of play across cultures (Bodrova & Leong, 1998). One observational study compared 48 middle-class Korean American and 48 middle-class Anglo American children in separate preschools (Farver, Kim, & Lee, 1995). The three Anglo American preschools, in keeping with normative U.S. values, encouraged independent thinking and active involvement in learning by letting children select from a wide range of activities. The Korean American preschool, in keeping with traditional Korean values, emphasized developing academic skills and completing tasks. The Anglo American preschools encouraged social interchange among children and collaborative activities with teachers. In the Korean American preschool, children were allowed to talk and play only during outdoor recess.

Not surprisingly, the Anglo American children engaged in more social play, whereas the Korean Americans engaged in more unoccupied or parallel play. At the same time, Korean American children played more cooperatively, often offering toys to other children—very likely a reflection of their culture's emphasis on group harmony. Anglo American children were more aggressive and often responded negatively to other children's suggestions, reflecting the competitiveness of American culture.

Checkpoint

Can you . . .

✔ Tell how gender and culture influence the way children play, and give examples?

Parenting

Guidepost 5

How do parenting practices influence development?

As children increasingly become their own persons, their upbringing can be a complex challenge. Parents must deal with small people who have minds and wills of their own but who still have a lot to learn about what kinds of behavior work well in society. How do parents handle discipline? Are some ways of parenting more effective than others?

Forms of Discipline

The word *discipline* means "instruction" or "training." In the field of child development, **discipline** refers to methods of molding character and of teaching self-control and acceptable behavior. It can be a powerful tool for socialization with the goal of developing self-discipline. What forms of discipline work best? Researchers have looked at a wide range of techniques.

discipline Methods of molding children's character and of teaching them to exercise self-control and engage in acceptable behavior.

Reinforcement and Punishment

"What are we going to do with that child?" Noel's mother says. "The more we punish him, the more he misbehaves!"

Parents sometimes punish children to stop undesirable behavior, but children usually learn more from being reinforced for good behavior. *External* reinforcements may be tangible (candy, money, toys, or gold stars) or intangible (a smile, a word of praise, a hug, extra attention, or a special privilege). Whatever the reinforcement, the child must see it as rewarding and must receive it fairly consistently after showing the desired behavior. Eventually, the behavior should provide its own *internal* reward: a sense of pleasure or accomplishment. In Noel's case, his parents often ignore him when he behaves well but scold or spank him when he acts up. In other words, they unwittingly reinforce his *mis*behavior by rewarding him with attention when he does what they do *not* want him to do.

Still, at times punishment, such as isolation or denial of privileges, is necessary. Children cannot be permitted to run out into traffic or hit another child. Sometimes a child is willfully defiant. In such situations, punishment, if consistent, immediate, and clearly tied to the offense, may be effective. It should be administered calmly, in private, and aimed at eliciting compliance, not guilt. It is most effective when accompanied by a short, simple explanation (AAP Committee on Psychosocial Aspects of Child and Family Health, 1998; Baumrind, 1996a, 1996b).

Harsh punishment can be counterproductive. Children who are punished harshly and frequently may have trouble interpreting other people's actions and words; they may attribute hostile intentions where none exist (B. Weiss, Dodge, Bates, & Pettit, 1992). Young children who have been punished harshly may later act aggressively, even though the punishment is intended to stop what a parent sees as purposely aggressive behavior (Nix et al., 1999). Or such children may become passive because they feel helpless. Children may become frightened if parents lose control and may eventually try to avoid a punitive parent, undermining the parent's ability to influence behavior (Grusec & Goodnow, 1994).

Corporal punishment has been defined as "the use of physical force with the intention of causing a child to experience pain, but not injury, for the purpose of correction or control of the child's behavior" (Straus, 1994a, p. 4). It can include spanking, hitting, slapping, pinching, shaking (which can be fatal to infants—refer back to Box 6-3 in Chapter 6), and other physical acts. Corporal punishment is popularly believed to be more effective than other remedies and to be harmless if done in moderation by loving parents (McLoyd & Smith, 2002); but a growing body of evidence points to serious negative consequences (Straus, 1999; Straus & Stewart, 1999; Box 11-2).

corporal punishment Use of physical force with the intention of causing pain but not injury so as to correct or control behavior.

Unlike child abuse, which bears little or no relationship to the child's personality or behavior, corporal punishment is more frequently used with children who are aggressive and hard to manage, characteristics that may be genetically based (Jaffee et al., 2004).

Box 11-2 *The Case against Corporal Punishment*

"Spare the rod and spoil the child" may sound old-fashioned, but corporal punishment has become a hot issue. Many people still believe that spanking instills respect for authority, motivates good behavior, and is a necessary part of responsible parenting (Kazdin & Benjet, 2003). Alternatively, some child development professionals view any corporal punishment as verging on child abuse (Straus, 1994b); they consider it wrong to inflict pain on children and warn that "violence begets violence" (Kazdin & Benjet, 2003). Other professionals find no harm in corporal punishment in moderation when prudently administered by loving parents (Baumrind, 1996a, 1996b; Baumrind et al., 2002).

Corporal punishment is banned in many countries, including Austria, Bulgaria, Croatia, Cyprus, Denmark, Finland, Germany, Hungary, Iceland, Israel, Latvia, Norway, Romania, Sweden, and Ukraine. In the United States, corporal punishment in schools has been outlawed in at least 28 states (Randall, 2005). All states except Minnesota allow parents to administer it, though some insist that it be reasonable, appropriate, moderate, or necessary, and some recognize that excessive corporal punishment can be abusive (Gershoff, 2002). The Supreme Court of Canada in January 2004 ruled out corporal punishment in schools and also forbade it for infants or teenagers in any setting (Center for Effective Discipline, 2005). The United Nations Convention on the Rights of Children opposes all forms of physical violence against children.

Nevertheless, some form of corporal punishment is widely used on U.S. infants and is near-universal among parents of toddlers. In interviews with a nationally representative sample of 991 parents in 1995, 35 percent reported using corporal punishment—usually hand slapping—on infants and fully 94 percent on 3- and 4-year-olds. About 50 percent of the parents used corporal punishment on 12-year-olds, 30 percent on 14-year-olds, and 13 percent on 17-year-olds (Straus & Stewart, 1999).

Why do parents hit children? No doubt, because hitting gets children to comply (Gershoff, 2002). However, a large body of research has found negative short- and long-term associations with its use. Apart from the risk of injury or abuse, these outcomes may include, in childhood, lack of moral internalization; poor parent-child relationships; increased physical aggressiveness, antisocial behavior, and delinquency; and diminished mental health. Outcomes in adulthood can include aggression, criminal or antisocial behavior, anxiety disorders, depression, alcohol problems, and partner or child abuse (Gershoff, 2002; MacMillan et al., 1999; Strassberg, Dodge, Pettit, & Bates, 1994).

Most of this research was cross-sectional or retrospective or did not consider that the spanked children may have been aggressive in the first place and that their aggressive behavior or some other factor might have led their parents to spank them (Gershoff, 2002). Since 1997, several large, nationally representative landmark studies of children from age 3 through adolescence (Brezina, 1999; Gunnoe & Mariner, 1997; Simons, Lin, & Gordon, 1998; Strauss & Paschall, 1999; Straus, Sugarman, & Giles-Sims, 1997) have controlled for the child's behavior at the time of first measurement. These studies found that the more physical punishment a child receives, the more aggressive the child becomes and the more likely the child is to be antisocial or aggressive as an adult (Straus & Stewart, 1999).

Why the link between corporal punishment and aggressive behavior? As social learning theory would predict, children may imitate the punisher and may come to consider infliction of pain an acceptable response to problems. Corporal punishment also may arouse anger and resentment, causing children to focus on their own hurts instead of on the wrong they have done to others. Furthermore, as with any punishment, the effectiveness of spanking diminishes with repeated use; children may feel free to misbehave if they are willing to take the consequences. Also, reliance on physical punishment may

A child who is spanked is likely to imitate that behavior. Studies show that children who are spanked tend to become aggressive.

weaken parents' authority when children become teenagers, too big and strong to spank even if spanking were appropriate (AAP Committee on Psychosocial Aspects of Child and Family Health, 1998; Gershoff, 2002; McCord, 1996). Frequent spanking may even inhibit cognitive development (Straus & Paschall, 1999).

Critics of this research point out that corporal punishment does not occur in isolation; we cannot be sure that the observed outcomes were attributable to it and not to other parental behaviors or family circumstances, such as stressful events, marital discord, lack of parental warmth, or substance abuse (Kazdin & Benjet, 2003). A 6-year study of 1,990 European American, African American, and Hispanic children found that spanking does not predict an increase in problem behavior, if it is done in the context of a mother's strong emotional support (McLoyd & Smith, 2002). Also, physical discipline is less likely to cause aggression or anxiety in cultures where it is seen as normal, such as in Kenya (Lansford et al., 2005).

Still, the research strongly suggests that frequent or severe corporal punishment is potentially harmful to children. Furthermore, there is no clear line between mild and harsh spanking, and one often leads to the other (Kazdin & Benjet, 2003). Thus, even though no harm from very mild spanking has been established (Larzalere, 2000), it seems prudent to choose other, less risky, means of discipline that have no potentially adverse effects (Kazdin & Benjet, 2003).

The American Academy of Pediatrics Committee on Psychosocial Aspects of Child and Family Health (1998) urges parents to avoid spanking. Instead, the committee suggests teaching children to use words to express feelings, giving them choices and helping them evaluate the consequences, and modeling orderly behavior and cooperative conflict resolution. The committee recommends positive reinforcement to encourage desired behaviors and verbal reprimands, time-outs (brief isolation to give the child a chance to cool down), or removal of privileges to discourage undesired behaviors—all within a positive, supportive, loving parent-child relationship.

What's your view ?

Did your parents ever spank you? If so, how often and in what kinds of situations? Would you spank, or have you ever spanked, your own child? Why or why not?

Check it out !

For more information on this topic, go to the World Wide Web: http://www.aap.org/policy/re9740.html. This is a policy statement from the American Academy of Pediatrics, "Guidance for Effective Discipline" (RE9740). Or go to www.stophitting.com, the Web site of the Center for Effective Discipline. This site offers research-based information about corporal punishment in the home and in schools as well as up-to-date information on related legislation and court decisions.

The line between some forms of punishment and physical or emotional abuse is not always easy to draw, but discipline clearly becomes abusive when it results in injury to a child.

Psychological aggression refers to verbal attacks that may result in psychological harm, such as yelling or screaming, threatening to spank or hit the child, swearing or cursing at the child, threatening to send the child away or kick the child out of the house, and calling the child dumb or lazy. Some psychologists equate the last three categories with emotional abuse. Psychological aggression, like physical aggression (spanking), is almost universal among U.S. parents. In a nationally representative sampling of 991 parents, 98 percent reported using some form of psychological aggression by the time a child was 5, and about 90 percent thereafter (Straus & Field, 2003).

psychological aggression Verbal attack by a parent that may result in psychological harm to a child.

Power Assertion, Induction, and Withdrawal of Love

Focusing on reinforcement and punishment alone may be an oversimplification of how parents influence behavior. Contemporary research looks at three broader categories of discipline: *power assertion, induction,* and *temporary withdrawal of love.*

Power assertion is intended to stop or discourage undesirable behavior through physical or verbal enforcement of parental control; it includes demands, threats, withdrawal of privileges, spanking, and other types of punishment. Some of these techniques, when used by the feared maid who took care of the Allende children, left psychological scars on Isabel. **Inductive techniques** are designed to encourage desirable behavior (or discourage undesirable behavior) by reasoning with a child; they include setting limits, demonstrating logical consequences of an action, explaining, discussing, negotiating, and getting ideas from the child about what is fair. **Withdrawal of love** may include ignoring, isolating, or showing dislike for a child.

When Sara took candy from a store, her father did not lecture her on honesty, spank her, or tell her what a bad girl she had been. Instead, he explained how the owner of the store would be harmed by her failure to pay for the candy, asked her how she thought the store owner might feel, and then took her back to the store to return the candy. Inductive techniques, such as those Sara's father used, are usually the most effective and power assertion the least effective methods of getting children to accept parental standards (M. L. Hoffman, 1970a, 1970b; Jagers, Bingham, & Hans, 1996; McCord, 1996). Inductive reasoning tends to arouse empathy for the victim of wrongdoing as well as guilt on the part of the wrongdoer (Krevans & Gibbs, 1996). Kindergartners whose mothers report using reasoning are more likely to see the moral wrongness of behavior that hurts other people (as opposed to merely breaking rules) than children whose mothers took away privileges (Jagers et al., 1996).

However, the choice and effectiveness of a disciplinary strategy may depend on the parent's personality, the child's personality and age, and the quality of the parent-child relationship, as well as on culturally based customs and expectations (Grusec & Goodnow, 1994). Most parents call on more than one strategy, depending on the situation. Parents tend to use reasoning to get a child to show concern for others. They use power assertion to

power assertion Disciplinary strategy designed to discourage undesirable behavior through physical or verbal enforcement of parental control.

inductive techniques Disciplinary techniques designed to induce desirable behavior by appealing to a child's sense of reason and fairness.

withdrawal of love Disciplinary strategy that involves ignoring, isolating, or showing dislike for a child.

What's your view ?

- As a parent, what form of discipline would you favor if your 3-year-old snuck a cookie from the cookie jar? Refused to take a nap? Hit his little sister? Tell why.

stop play that gets too rough, and they use both power assertion and reasoning to deal with lying and stealing (Grusec & Goodnow, 1994). The strategy parents choose may depend, not only on their belief in its effectiveness, but also on their confidence that they can carry it out (Perozynski & Kramer, 1999).

Above all, the effectiveness of parental discipline may hinge on how well the child understands and accepts the parent's message, both cognitively and emotionally (Grusec & Goodnow, 1994). For the child to accept the message, the child has to recognize it as appropriate; so parents need to be fair and accurate as well as clear and consistent about their expectations. They need to fit the discipline to the misdeed and to the child's temperament and cognitive and emotional level. A child may be more motivated to accept the message if the parents are normally warm and responsive and if they arouse the child's empathy for someone the child has harmed (Grusec & Goodnow, 1994). How well children accept a disciplinary method also may depend on whether the type of discipline used is normative, that is, accepted in the family's culture (Lansford et al., 2005).

One point on which many experts agree is that a child interprets and responds to discipline in the context of an ongoing relationship with a parent. Some researchers therefore look beyond specific parental practices to overall styles, or patterns, of parenting.

Parenting Styles

Why does Stacy hit and bite the nearest person when she cannot finish a jigsaw puzzle? What makes David sit and sulk when he cannot finish the puzzle, even though his teacher offers to help him? Why does Consuelo work on the puzzle for 20 minutes and then shrug and try another? Why are children so different in their responses to the same situation? Temperament is a major factor, of course; but some research suggests that styles of parenting may affect children's competence in dealing with their world.

Diana Baumrind and the Effectiveness of Authoritative Parenting

In pioneering research, Diana Baumrind (1971, 1996b; Baumrind & Black, 1967) studied 103 preschool children from 95 families. Through interviews, testing, and home studies, she measured how children were functioning, identified three parenting styles, and described typical behavior patterns of children raised according to each. Baumrind's work and the large body of research it inspired have established strong associations between each parenting style and a particular set of child behaviors (Baumrind, 1989; Darling & Steinberg, 1993; Pettit, Bates, & Dodge, 1997).

Authoritarian parents, according to Baumrind, value control and unquestioning obedience. They try to make children conform rigidly to a set standard of conduct and punish them for violating it, often using power-assertive techniques. They are more detached and less warm than other parents. Their children tend to be more discontented, withdrawn, and distrustful.

Permissive parents value self-expression and self-regulation. They make few demands and allow children to monitor their own activities as much as possible. They consult with children about policy decisions and rarely punish. They are warm, noncontrolling, and undemanding or even indulgent. Their preschool children tend to be immature—the least self-controlled and the least exploratory.

Authoritative parents value a child's individuality but also stress social constraints. They have confidence in their ability to guide children, but they also respect children's independent decisions, interests, opinions, and personalities. They are loving and accepting but also demand good behavior and are firm in maintaining standards. They impose limited, judicious punishment when necessary, within the context of a warm, supportive relationship. They favor inductive discipline, explaining the reasoning behind their stands and encouraging verbal negotiation and give-and-take. Their children apparently feel secure in knowing both that they are loved and what is expected of them. These preschoolers tend to be the most self-reliant, self-controlled, self-assertive,

Checkpoint ✔

Can you . . .

✔ Compare various forms of discipline, and identify factors that influence their effectiveness?

authoritarian In Baumrind's terminology, parenting style emphasizing control and obedience.

permissive In Baumrind's terminology, parenting style emphasizing self-expression and self-regulation.

authoritative In Baumrind's terminology, parenting style blending respect for a child's individuality with an effort to instill social values.

exploratory, and content. (Isabel Allende's description of how her stepfather, Tió Ramón, took charge and raised her and her brothers fits this description of authoritative parenting, and his parenting style was more effective than those of their authoritarian grandfather and permissive mother.)

Eleanor Maccoby and John Martin (1983) added a fourth parenting style—*neglectful, or uninvolved*—to describe parents who, sometimes because of stress or depression, focus on their own needs rather than on those of the child. Neglectful parenting has been linked with a variety of behavioral disorders in childhood and adolescence (Baumrind, 1991; Parke & Buriel, 1998; R. A. Thompson, 1998).

Why does authoritative parenting tend to enhance children's social competence? It may be because authoritative parents set sensible expectations and realistic standards. By making clear, consistent rules, they let children know what is expected of them. In authoritarian homes, children are so strictly controlled that often they cannot make independent choices about their behavior; in permissive homes, children receive so little guidance that they may be uncertain and anxious about whether they are doing the right thing. In authoritative homes, children know when they are meeting expectations and can decide whether it is worth risking parental displeasure to pursue a goal. These children are expected to perform well, fulfill commitments, and participate actively in family duties as well as in family fun. They know the satisfaction of accepting responsibilities and achieving success. Parents who make reasonable demands show that they believe their children can meet them—and that they care enough to insist that their children do so.

When conflict arises, an authoritative parent can teach children positive ways to communicate their point of view and negotiate acceptable alternatives ("If you don't want to throw away those rocks you found, where do you think we should keep them?"). Internalization of this broader set of skills, not just of specific behavioral demands, may well be a key to the success of authoritative parenting (Grusec & Goodnow, 1994).

What's your view

- To what extent would you like your children to adopt your values and behavioral standards? Give examples.

Support and Criticisms of Baumrind's Model

In research based on Baumrind's work, the superiority of authoritative parenting (or similar conceptions of parenting style) has repeatedly been supported. For example, in a longitudinal study of 585 ethnically and socioeconomically diverse families in Tennessee and Indiana with children from prekindergarten through grade 6, four aspects of early supportive parenting—warmth, use of inductive discipline, interest and involvement in children's contacts with peers, and proactive teaching of social skills—predicted positive behavioral, social, and academic outcomes (Pettit, Bates, & Dodge, 1997).

Still, Baumrind's model has provoked controversy because it seems to suggest that there is one "right" way to raise children. Also, because Baumrind's findings are correlational, they merely establish associations between each parenting style and a particular set of child behaviors. They do not show that different styles of child rearing *cause* children to be more or less competent. It is also impossible to know whether the children Baumrind studied were, in fact, raised in a particular style. It may be that some of the better-adjusted children were raised inconsistently, but by the time of the study their parents had adopted the authoritative pattern (Holden & Miller, 1999). In addition, Baumrind did not consider innate factors, such as temperament, that might have affected children's competence and exerted an influence on the parents.

Cultural Differences in Parenting Styles

Another concern is that Baumrind's categories reflect the dominant North American view of child development and may not apply to some other cultures or socioeconomic groups. Among Asian Americans, obedience and strictness are not associated with harshness and domination but instead with caring, concern, involvement, and maintenance of family harmony. Traditional Chinese culture, with its emphasis on respect for elders, stresses adults' responsibility to maintain the social order by teaching children socially proper behavior. This obligation is carried out through firm and just control and

Checkpoint ✔

Can you . . .

✔ Describe and evaluate Baumrind's model of parenting styles?

✔ Discuss how parents' way of resolving conflicts with young children can contribute to the success of authoritative child rearing?

✔ Discuss criticisms of Baumrind's model and cultural variations in parenting styles?

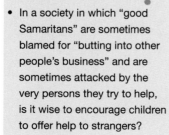

Guidepost 6

Why do young children help or hurt others, and why do they develop fears?

altruism Motivation to help others without expectation of reward; may involve self-denial or self-sacrifice.

prosocial behavior Any voluntary behavior intended to help others.

What's your view ?

• In a society in which "good Samaritans" are sometimes blamed for "butting into other people's business" and are sometimes attacked by the very persons they try to help, is it wise to encourage children to offer help to strangers?

governance of the child and even by physical punishment if necessary (Zhao, 2002). Although Asian American parenting is frequently described as authoritarian, the warmth and supportiveness that characterize Chinese American family relationships may more closely resemble Baumrind's authoritative parenting but without the emphasis on the American values of individuality, choice, and freedom (Chao, 1994) and with stricter parental control (Chao, 2001).

Still, a dichotomy between the individualistic values of Western parenting and the collectivist values of Asian parenting may be overly simplistic. In interviews with 64 Japanese mothers of 3- to 6-year-olds (Yamada, 2004), the mothers' descriptions of their parenting practices reflected the search for a balance between granting appropriate autonomy and exercising disciplinary control. The mothers let children make their own decisions within what they saw as the child's personal domain, such as play activities, playmates, and clothing, and this domain enlarged with the child's age. When health, safety, moral issues, or conventional social rules were involved, the mothers set limits or exercised control. When conflicts arose, the mothers used reason rather than power-assertive methods or sometimes gave in to the child, apparently on the theory that the issue wasn't worth struggling over—or that the child might be right after all.

Special Behavioral Concerns

Three specific issues of special concern to parents, caregivers, and teachers of preschool children are how to promote altruism, curb aggression, and deal with fears that often arise at this age.

Prosocial Behavior

Alex, at 3½, responded to two preschool classmates' complaints that they did not have enough modeling clay, his favorite plaything, by giving them half of his. Alex was showing **altruism:** motivation to help another person with no expectation of reward. Altruistic acts like Alex's often entail cost, self-sacrifice, or risk. Altruism is at the heart of **prosocial behavior,** voluntary activity intended to benefit another.

Even before the second birthday, children often help others, share belongings and food, and offer comfort. Such behaviors may reflect a growing ability to imagine how another person might feel (Zahn-Waxler, Radke-Yarrow, Wagner, & Chapman, 1992). Girls tend to be more prosocial than boys, but the differences are small (Eisenberg & Fabes, 1998).

Is there a prosocial personality or disposition? A longitudinal study that followed 32 4- and 5-year-olds into early adulthood suggests that there is and that it emerges early and remains somewhat consistent throughout life. Preschoolers who were sympathetic and spontaneously shared with classmates tended to show prosocial understanding and empathic behavior as much as 17 years later. Preschoolers who are shy or withdrawn tend to be less prosocial, perhaps because they hesitate to reach out to others (Coplan et al., 2004).

Genes and environment each contribute to individual differences in prosocial behavior, an example of gene-environment correlation. This finding comes from a study of 9,319 twin pairs whose prosocial behavior was rated by parents and teachers at ages 3, 4, and 7. Parents who showed affection and followed positive (inductive) disciplinary strategies tended to encourage their children's natural tendency to prosocial behavior (Knafo & Plomin, 2006). Parents of prosocial children typically are prosocial themselves. They point out models of prosocial behavior and steer children toward stories, films, and television programs that depict cooperation, sharing, and empathy and encourage sympathy, generosity, and helpfulness (Singer & Singer, 1998). Relationships with siblings provide an important laboratory for trying out caring behavior and learning to see another person's point of view. Peers and teachers also can model and reinforce prosocial behavior (Eisenberg, 1992; Eisenberg & Fabes, 1998).

Motives for prosocial behavior may change as children grow older and develop more mature moral reasoning (see Chapters 13 and 16). Preschoolers tend to have egocentric motives; they want to earn praise and avoid disapproval. They weigh costs and benefits and consider how they would like others to act toward them. As children grow older, they adopt societal standards of "being good," which eventually become internalized as principles and values (Eisenberg & Fabes, 1998). Individual differences in prosocial behavior may reflect individual differences in moral reasoning (Eisenberg, Guthrie, et al., 1999).

Cultures vary in the degree to which they foster prosocial behavior. Traditional cultures in which people live in extended family groups and share work seem to foster prosocial values more than cultures that stress individual achievement (Eisenberg & Fabes, 1998).

Aggression

When Noah roughly snatches a ball away from Jake, he is interested only in getting the ball, not in hurting or dominating Jake. This is **instrumental aggression,** or aggression used as an instrument to reach a goal—the most common type in

Children given responsibilities at home tend to develop prosocial qualities, such as cooperation and helpfulness. This 3-year-old girl, who is learning to care for plants, is likely to have caring relationships with people as well.

early childhood. Between ages 2½ and 5, children commonly struggle over toys and control of space. Instrumental aggression surfaces mostly during social play; children who fight the most also tend to be the most sociable and competent. In fact, the ability to show some instrumental aggression may be a necessary step in psychosocial development.

As children develop more self-control and become better able to express themselves verbally, they typically shift from showing aggression with blows to showing it with words (Coie & Dodge, 1998). However, individual differences remain. Children who more frequently hit or grab toys from other children at age 2 are likely to be more physically aggressive at age 5 (Cummings, Iannotti, & Zahn-Waxler, 1989), and children who, as preschoolers, often engaged in violent fantasy play may, at age 6, be prone to violent displays of anger (Dunn & Hughes, 2001).

Gender Differences in Aggression

Aggression is an exception to the generalization that boys and girls are more similar than different (Hyde, 2005). In all cultures studied, as among most mammals, boys are more physically and verbally aggressive than girls. This gender difference is apparent by age 2 (Archer, 2004; Baillargeon et al., 2007; Pellegrini & Archer, 2005). Research with genetically engineered mice suggests that the Sry gene on the Y chromosome may play a role (Gatewood et al., 2006).

However, girls may be more aggressive than they seem (McNeilly-Choque, Hart, Robinson, Nelson, & Olsen, 1996; Putallaz & Bierman, 2004). Whereas boys engage in more **overt,** or **direct, aggression**—physical or verbal aggression openly directed at its target—girls, especially as they grow older, are more likely to engage in **relational,** or **social, aggression.** This more subtle kind of aggression consists of damaging or interfering with relationships, reputation, or psychological well-being, often through teasing, manipulation, ostracism, or bids for control. It may include spreading rumors, name-calling, putdowns, or excluding someone from a group. It can be either overt or covert (indirect)—for example, making mean faces or ignoring someone. Among preschoolers, it tends to be direct and face-to-face ("You can't come to my party if you don't give me that toy") (Archer, 2004; Brendgen et al., 2005; Crick, Casas, & Nelson, 2002).

From an evolutionary perspective, boys' greater overt aggressiveness, like their greater size and strength, may prepare them to compete for a mate (Archer, 2004). Males produce many sperm; females generally produce only one ovum at a time. Males seek to mate as frequently and widely as possible, and they have less investment in each

instrumental aggression
Aggressive behavior used as a means of achieving a goal.

overt, or direct, aggression
Aggression that is openly directed at its target.

relational, or social, aggression
Aggression aimed at damaging or interfering with another person's relationships, reputation, or psychological well-being; can be overt or covert.

In a classic experiment by Albert Bandura, children who had seen a film of an adult hitting and kicking an inflated clown were more likely to imitate the aggressive behavior if they had seen the adult being rewarded or experiencing no consequences than if they had seen the adult being punished.

individual offspring; thus they can afford to take the risks of physical aggression. Females are strongly motivated to protect and nurture the few offspring they have; thus they shy away from direct confrontations that could put them at physical risk (Pellegrini & Archer, 2005).

Influences on Aggression

Why are some children more aggressive than others? Temperament may play a part. Children who are intensely emotional and low in self-control tend to express anger aggressively (Eisenberg, Fabes, Nyman, Bernzweig, & Pinuelas, 1994).

Both physical and social aggression have genetic and environmental sources, but their relative influence differs. Among 234 6-year-old twins, physical aggression was 50 to 60 percent heritable; the remainder of the variance was attributable to nonshared environmental influences (unique experiences). Social aggression was much more environmentally influenced; the variance was only 20 percent genetic, 20 percent explained by shared environmental influences, and 60 percent by unshared experiences (Brendgen et al., 2005).

Parental behaviors strongly influence aggressiveness. In longitudinal studies, insecure attachment and lack of maternal warmth and affection in infancy predict aggressiveness in early childhood (Coie & Dodge, 1998; MacKinnon-Lewis, Starnes, Volling, & Johnson, 1997). Manipulative behaviors such as withdrawal of love and making a child feel guilty or ashamed may foster social aggression (Brendgen et al., 2005). Negative parent-child relationships may set the stage for prolonged, destructive sibling conflicts, in which children imitate their parents' hostile behavior. These coercive family processes may foster aggressive tendencies that carry over to peer relations (MacKinnon-Lewis et al., 1997) and are reinforced by prolonged interaction with aggressive peers (Brendgen et al., 2005). Aggression may be bred from early childhood by a combination of a stressful and unstimulating home atmosphere, harsh discipline, lack of maternal warmth and social support, exposure to aggressive adults and neighborhood violence, and transient peer groups, which prevent stable friendships (Dodge, Pettit, & Bates, 1994; Grusec & Goodnow, 1994). In a study of 431 Head Start participants in an inner-city neighborhood, parents reported that more than half had witnessed gang activity, drug trafficking, police pursuits and arrests, or people carrying weapons, and some of the children and families had been victimized themselves. These children showed symptoms of distress at home and aggression at school (Farver, Xu, Eppe, Fernandez, & Schwartz, 2005).

Why does witnessing violence lead to aggression? In a classic social learning experiment (Bandura, Ross, & Ross, 1961), 3- to 6-year-olds individually watched films of adult models playing with toys. Children in one experimental group saw the adult model play quietly. The model for a second experimental group spent most of the 10-minute session punching, throwing, and kicking a life-size inflated doll. A control group did not see any model. After the sessions, the children, who were mildly frustrated by seeing toys they were not allowed to play with, went into another playroom. The children who had seen the aggressive model acted much more aggressively than those in the other groups, imitating many of the same things they had seen the model say and do. The children who had seen the quiet model were less aggressive than the control group. This finding suggests that parents may be able to moderate the effects of frustration by modeling nonaggressive behavior.

Television has enormous power for modeling either prosocial behavior or aggression. In Chapter 14 we discuss the influence of televised violence on aggressive behavior.

Culture and Aggression

How much influence does culture have on aggressive behavior? One research team asked closely matched samples of 30 Japanese and 30 U.S. middle- to upper-middle-class preschoolers to choose pictured solutions to hypothetical conflicts or stressful situations (such as having one's block tower knocked down, having to stop playing and go to bed,

Table 11-3	Childhood Fears
Age	**Fears**
0–6 months	Loss of support; loud noises
7–12 months	Strangers; heights; sudden, unexpected, and looming objects
1 year	Separation from parent; toilet; injury; strangers
2 years	Many stimuli, including loud noises (vacuum cleaners, sirens and alarms, trucks, and thunder), animals, dark rooms, separation from parent, large objects or machines, changes in personal environment, unfamiliar peers
3 years	Masks; dark; animals; separation from parent
4 years	Separation from parent; animals; dark; noises (including noises at night)
5 years	Animals; "bad" people; dark; separation from parent; bodily harm
6 years	Supernatural beings (e.g., ghosts, witches); bodily injury; thunder and lightning; dark; sleeping or staying alone; separation from parent
7–8 years	Supernatural beings; dark; media events (e.g., news reports on the threat of nuclear war or child kidnapping); staying alone; bodily injury
9–12 years	Tests and examinations in school; school performances; bodily injury; physical appearance; thunder and lightning; death; dark

Source: From Morris, R. J. & Kratochwill, T. R. *Treating Children's Fears and Phobias: A Behavioral Approach,* Allyn and Bacon, Boston, MA. Copyright © 1983 by Pearson Education. Reprinted by permission of the publisher.

being hit, hearing parents argue, or fighting on a jungle gym). The children also were asked to act out such situations using dolls and props. The U.S. children showed more anger, more aggressive behavior and language, and less emotional control than the Japanese children (Zahn-Waxler, Friedman, Cole, Mizuta, & Hiruma, 1996).

These results are consistent with child-rearing values in the two cultures. In Japan, anger and aggression contradict the cultural emphasis on harmony. Japanese mothers are more likely than U.S. mothers to use inductive discipline, pointing out how aggressive behavior hurts others. Japanese mothers show strong disappointment when children fail to meet behavioral standards. However, the cross-cultural difference in children's anger and aggressiveness was significant even apart from mothers' behavior, suggesting that temperamental differences also may have been at work (Zahn-Waxler et al., 1996).

What's your view

- Are there situations in which a child should be encouraged to be aggressive?

Fearfulness

"My childhood was a time of unvoiced fears," writes Isabel Allende (1995, p. 50): fear of her family's tyrannical maid; fear that her mother would die and her father would come back to claim her; fear of the devil; fear of her sadistic uncles; fear of gypsies; and fear of what "bad men can do to little girls."

Passing fears are common in early childhood. Many 2- to 4-year-olds are afraid of animals, especially dogs. By age 6, children are more likely to be afraid of the dark. Other common fears are of thunderstorms, doctors, and imaginary creatures (DuPont, 1983; Stevenson-Hinde & Shouldice, 1996). Most of these disappear as children grow older and lose their sense of powerlessness.

Young children's fears stem largely from their intense fantasy life and their tendency to confuse appearance with reality. Sometimes their imaginations get carried away, and they worry about being attacked by a lion or being abandoned. Also, they are more likely to be frightened by something that looks scary, such as a cartoon monster, than by something capable of doing great harm, such as a nuclear explosion (Cantor, 1994). For the most part, older children's fears are more realistic and self-evaluative (for example, fear of failing a test) (Stevenson-Hinde & Shouldice, 1996; Table 11-3).

Fears may stem from personal experience or from hearing about other people's experiences (Muris, Merckelbach, & Collaris, 1997). A preschooler whose mother is sick in bed may become upset by a story about a mother's death, even the death of an animal mother. Often fears result from appraisals of danger, such as the likelihood of being bitten by a dog, or are triggered by events, such as when a child who was hit by a car becomes afraid to cross the street. Children who have lived through an earthquake, a kidnapping, or some other frightening event may fear that it will happen again (Kolbert, 1994).

Parents can allay children's fears by instilling a sense of trust and normal caution without being too protective—and also by overcoming their own unrealistic fears. They can reassure a fearful child and encourage open expression of feelings. Ridicule ("Don't be such a baby!"), coercion ("Pat the nice doggie—it won't hurt you"), and logical persuasion ("The closest bear is 20 miles away, locked in a zoo!") are not helpful. Not until elementary school can children tell themselves that what they fear is not real (Cantor, 1994).

Systematic desensitization is a therapeutic technique in which a child is exposed in gradually increasing amounts to a feared object or situation. This technique has been used successfully to help children overcome fears ranging from snakes to elevators (Murphy & Bootzin, 1973; Sturges & Sturges, 1998).

Checkpoint ✔

Can you . . .

✔ Discuss influences that contribute to altruism, aggression, and fearfulness?

Guidepost 7

How do young children get along with—or without—siblings, playmates, and friends?

self-efficacy Sense of capability to master challenges and achieve goals.

Relationships with Other Children

Although the most important people in young children's world are the adults who take care of them, relationships with siblings and playmates become more important in early childhood. Virtually every characteristic activity and personality issue of this age, from gender development to prosocial or aggressive behavior, involves other children. Sibling and peer relationships in early childhood strengthen social cognition, or "mind reading"—the ability to understand others' intentions, desires, and feelings (Dunn, 1999). These relationships also provide a measuring stick for **self-efficacy,** children's growing sense of their ability to master challenges and achieve goals. By competing with and comparing themselves with other children, they can gauge their physical, social, cognitive, and linguistic competencies and gain a more realistic sense of self (Bandura, 1994).

Siblings—or Their Absence

Ties between brothers and sisters often set the stage for later relationships. Let's look at sibling relationships and then at children who grow up with no siblings.

Brothers and Sisters

"It's mine!"
"No, it's mine!"
"Well, I was playing with it first!"

The earliest, most frequent, and most intense disputes among siblings are over property rights—who owns a toy or who is entitled to play with it. Although exasperated adults may not always see it that way, sibling disputes and their settlement can be viewed as socialization opportunities, in which children learn to stand up for principles and negotiate disagreements (Ross, 1996). Joint dramatic play is another arena for socialization. Siblings who frequently play "let's pretend" develop a history of shared understandings that allow them to more easily resolve issues and build on each other's ideas (Howe et al., 2005).

Despite the frequency of conflict, sibling rivalry is not the main pattern between brothers and sisters early in life. Although some rivalry exists, so do affection, interest, companionship, and influence. Observations spanning 3½ years that began when younger siblings were about age 1½ and older siblings ranged from 3 to 4½ found prosocial and play-oriented behaviors to be more common than rivalry, hostility, and competition (Abramovitch, Corter, & Lando, 1979; Abramovitch, Corter, Pepler, & Stanhope, 1986; Abramovitch, Pepler, & Corter, 1982). Older siblings initiated more behavior, both friendly and unfriendly; younger siblings tended to imitate the older siblings. As the younger children reached age 5, the siblings became less physical and more verbal, both in showing aggression and in showing care and affection. At least one finding of this research has been replicated in many studies: Same-sex siblings, particularly girls, are closer and play together more peaceably than boy-girl siblings (Kier & Lewis, 1998). Because older siblings tend to dominate younger siblings, the quality of the relationship is more affected by the emotional and social adjustment of the older child (Pike et al., 2005).

The quality of sibling relationships tends to carry over to relationships with other children. A child who is aggressive with siblings is likely to be aggressive with friends as well (Abramovitch et al., 1986), whereas siblings who frequently play amicably together tend to develop prosocial behaviors (Pike, Coldwell, & Dunn, 2005).

By the same token, friendships can influence sibling relationships. Older siblings who have experienced a good relationship with a friend before the birth of a new baby are likely to treat their younger siblings better and are less likely to develop antisocial behavior in adolescence (Kramer & Kowal, 2005). For a young child at risk for behavioral problems, a positive relationship with *either* a sibling or a friend can buffer the effect of a negative relationship with the other (McElwain & Volling, 2005).

The Only Child

In the United States, 21 percent of children under 18 have no siblings in the home (Kreider & Fields, 2005). Are only children spoiled, selfish, lonely, or maladjusted? That stereotype goes back to some of the early pioneers in psychology. Sigmund Freud claimed that only children were at risk for problems of sexual identity, and G. Stanley Hall maintained that being an only child is damaging (Falbo, 2006). Yet, such apparently well-adjusted public figures as the musician Van Cliburn, the football Hall-of-Famer Roger Staubach, and the movie actress Natalie Portman all were only children.

An analysis of 115 studies found that "onlies" do comparatively well. In occupational and educational achievement and verbal intelligence, they perform slightly better than children with siblings. Only children tend to be more motivated to achieve and to have slightly higher self-esteem; and they do not differ in emotional adjustment, sociability, or popularity. Perhaps these children do better because, consistent with evolutionary theory, parents, who have limited time and resources to spend, focus more attention on only children, talk to them more, do more with them, and expect more of them than do parents with more than one child (Falbo, 2006; Falbo & Polit, 1986; Polit & Falbo, 1987). And, because most children today spend considerable time in play groups, child care, and preschool, only children do not lack opportunities for social interaction with peers. Such factors as genetic predispositions and parents' educational level, SES, emotional health, values, and parenting styles play a much bigger part in a child's development than family size (Falbo, 2006).

Research in China also has produced largely encouraging findings about only children. In 1979, to control an exploding population, the People's Republic of China established an official policy of limiting families to one child, enforced by a system of rewards and punishments. Although the policy has since been relaxed somewhat, most urban families now have only one child, and most rural families no more than two (Hesketh, Lu, & Xing, 2005). Thus, in many Chinese cities, schoolrooms are almost completely filled with children who have no brothers or sisters. This situation offered researchers a natural experiment: an opportunity to study the adjustment of large numbers of only children.

A review of the literature found no significant differences in behavioral problems (Tao, 1998). Indeed, only children seemed to be at a distinct psychological advantage in a society that favors and rewards such a child. Among 731 urban children and adolescents, those

Checkpoint ✓

Can you . . .

✔ Explain how the resolution of sibling disputes contributes to socialization?

✔ Tell how birth order and gender affect typical patterns of sibling interaction?

with siblings reported higher levels of fear, anxiety, and depression than only children, regardless of sex or age (Yang et al., 1995).

Among 4,000 third and sixth graders, personality differences between only children and those with siblings—as rated by parents, teachers, peers, and the children themselves—were few. Only children's academic achievement and physical growth were about the same as, or better than, those with siblings (Falbo & Poston, 1993). In a randomized study in Beijing first-grade classrooms (Jiao, Ji, & Jing, 1996), only children outperformed classmates with siblings in memory, language, and mathematics skills. This finding may reflect the greater attention, stimulation, hopes, and expectations that parents shower on a child they know will be their first and last.

Most of the studies used urban samples. Further research may reveal whether the findings hold up in rural areas and small towns, where children with siblings are more numerous, and whether only children maintain their cognitive superiority as they move through school.

Checkpoint ✓

Can you . . .

✔ Compare development of only children with that of children with siblings?

Playmates and Friends

Friendships develop as people develop. Toddlers play alongside or near each other, but not until about age 3 do children begin to have friends. Through friendships and interactions with casual playmates, young children learn how to get along with others. They learn that being a friend is the way to have a friend. They learn how to solve problems in relationships, they learn how to put themselves in another person's place, and they see models of various kinds of behavior. They learn moral values and gender-role norms, and they practice adult roles.

Choosing Playmates and Friends

Preschoolers usually like to play with children of their own age and sex. Children who have frequent positive experiences with each other are most likely to become friends (Rubin et al., 1998; Snyder et al., 1996). About 3 out of 4 preschoolers have such mutual friendships (Hartup & Stevens, 1999).

The traits that young children look for in a playmate are similar to the traits they look for in a friend (C. H. Hart, DeWolf, Wozniak, & Burts, 1992). In one study, 4- to 7-year-olds rated the most important features of friendships as doing things together, liking and caring for each other, sharing and helping one another, and, to a lesser degree, living nearby or going to the same school. Younger children rated physical traits, such as appearance and size, higher than did older children and they rated affection and support lower (Furman & Bierman, 1983).

Preschool children prefer prosocial playmates (C. H. Hart et al., 1992). They reject disruptive, demanding, intrusive, or aggressive children and tend to ignore those who are withdrawn, or tentative (Ramsey & Lasquade, 1996; Roopnarine & Honig, 1985).

Well-liked preschoolers and kindergartners and those who are rated by parents and teachers as socially competent generally cope well with anger. They respond directly, in ways that minimize further conflict and keep relationships going. They avoid insults and threats. Unpopular children tend to hit, hit back, or tattle (Fabes & Eisenberg, 1992).

Characteristics and Effects of Friendships

Preschoolers act differently with their friends than with other children. They have more positive, prosocial interactions but also more quarrels and fights (Rubin et al., 1998). Children may get just as angry with a friend as with someone else, but they are more likely to control their anger and express it constructively with a friend (Fabes, Eisenberg, Smith, & Murphy, 1996). Friendships are more satisfying—and more likely to last—when children see them as relatively harmonious and as validating their self-worth. Being able to confide in friends and get help from them is less important at this age than when children get older (Ladd, Kochenderfer, & Coleman, 1996).

Children with friends enjoy school more. Among 125 kindergartners, those who had friends in their class when they entered in August liked school better 2 months later, and those who kept up these friendships continued to like school better the following May (Ladd et al., 1996).

Parenting and Popularity

Parenting styles and practices can influence peer relationships. Popular children generally have warm, positive relationships with both mother and father. The parents are likely to be authoritative and the children to be both assertive and cooperative (Coplan et al., 2004; Isley, O'Neil, & Parke, 1996; Kochanska, 1992; Roopnarine & Honig, 1985). Children whose parents are authoritarian may become shy or withdrawn (Coplan et al., 2004). Children who are insecurely attached or whose parents are harsh, neglectful, or depressed or have troubled marriages are at risk of being rejected by peers (Rubin et al., 1998). Children, especially boys, with overprotective parents tend to be wary of associating with peers. Parents who place importance on their child's peer relationships tend to have more sociable children than parents who do not show such concern (Coplan et al., 2004).

Children whose parents rely on power-assertive discipline tend to use coercive tactics in peer relations; children whose parents engage in give-and-take reasoning are more likely to resolve conflicts with peers that way (Crockenberg & Lourie, 1996). Children whose parents clearly communicate disapproval rather than anger—as well as strong positive feelings—are more prosocial, less aggressive, and better liked (Boyum & Parke, 1995).

Young children learn the importance of *being* a friend in order to *have* a friend. One way of being a friend is for a sighted child to help a blind playmate enjoy the feel of the sand and the sound of the surf.

Checkpoint ✔

Can you . . .

✔ Explain how preschoolers choose playmates and friends, how they behave with friends, and how they benefit from friendships?

✔ Discuss how relationships at home can influence relationships with peers?

Refocus

Thinking back to the information about Isabel Allende in the Focus vignette at the beginning of this chapter,

- From what you have read, would you guess that Isabel Allende had high or low self-esteem as a young child? Why?

- Which of the theories of gender formation seems to best describe Allende's development? Which do you think she would agree with most?

- Isabel Allende describes herself as a solitary child, living largely in the world of her imagination. Would Parten have considered her immature? Would you?

- Allende and her mother shared an unconditional love, yet she seemed to have greater respect for her stepfather. Why?

- Allende says little about relationships with other children besides her younger brothers. Thinking about her personality, would you expect her to have been popular or unpopular with peers?

Peer relationships become even more important during middle childhood, which we will examine in Chapters 12, 13, and 14.

Summary and Key Terms

The Developing Self

Guidepost 1 How does the self-concept develop during early chldhood, and how do children show self-esteem, emotional growth, and initiative?

- The self-concept undergoes major change in early childhood. According to neo-Piagetians, self-definition shifts from single

representations to representational mappings. Young children do not see the difference between the real self and the ideal self.

- Culture affects self-definition.

- Self-esteem in early childhood tends to be global and unrealistic, reflecting adult approval.

- Understanding of emotions directed toward the self and of simultaneous emotions develops gradually.
- According to Erikson, the developmental conflict of early childhood is initiative versus guilt. Successful resolution of this conflict results in the virtue of *purpose*.

self-concept (page 297) self-definition (297) single representations (298) real self (298) ideal self (298) representational mappings (298) self-esteem (298) initiative versus guilt (300)

Gender

Guidepost 2   How do boys and girls become aware of the meaning of gender, and what explains differences in behavior between the sexes?

- Gender identity is an aspect of the developing self-concept.
- The main gender difference in early childhood is boys' greater aggressiveness. Girls tend to be more empathic and prosocial and less prone to problem behavior. Some cognitive differences appear early and others not until preadolescence or later.
- Children learn gender roles at an early age through gender-typing. Gender stereotypes peak during the preschool years.
- Five major perspectives on gender development are biological, evolutionary, psychoanalytic, social learning, and cognitive approaches.
- Evidence suggests that some gender differences may be biologically based.
- Evolutionary theory sees children's gender roles as preparation for adult mating behavior.
- In Freudian theory, a child identifies with the same-sex parent after giving up the wish to possess the other parent.
- Traditional social-learning theory attributed the learning of gender roles to imitation of models and reinforcement. The expanded social cognitive theory credits cognitive elements as well.
- Cognitive-developmental theory maintains that gender identity develops from thinking about one's gender. Gender constancy enhances the acquisition of gender roles. Gender-schema theory holds that children categorize gender-related information by observing what males and females do in their culture.
- Children also learn gender roles through socialization. Parents, peers, the media, and culture influence gender-typing.

gender identity (301) gender roles (301) gender-typing (301) gender stereotypes (301) theory of sexual selection (303) identification (304) social cognitive theory (305) gender constancy (305) gender-schema theory (306)

Play: The Business of Early Childhood

Guidepost 3   How do preschoolers play, and how does play contribute to and reflect development?

- Play has physical, cognitive, and psychosocial benefits and may have had evolutionary functions.
- Changes in the types of play children engage in reflect cognitive and social development.
- According to Smilansky, children progress cognitively from functional play to constructive play, dramatic play, and then formal games with rules. Dramatic play becomes increasingly common during early childhood and helps children develop social and cognitive skills. Rough-and-tumble play also begins during early childhood.
- According to Parten, play becomes more social during early childhood. However, later research has found that nonsocial play is not necessarily immature.
- Children prefer to play with (and play more socially with) others of their sex.
- Cognitive and social aspects of play are influenced by the culturally approved environments adults create for children.

functional play (310) constructive play (310) dramatic play (310) formal games with rules (310)

Parenting

Guidepost 4   How do parenting practices influence development?

- Discipline can be a powerful tool for socialization.
- Both positive reinforcement and prudently administered punishment can be appropriate tools of discipline within the context of a positive parent-child relationship.
- Power assertion, inductive techniques, and withdrawal of love each can be effective in certain situations. Reasoning is generally the most effective and power assertion the least effective in promoting internalization of parental standards. Spanking and other forms of corporal punishment can have negative consequences.
- Baumrind identified three child-rearing styles: authoritarian, permissive, and authoritative. A fourth style, neglectful or uninvolved, was identified later by Maccoby and Martin. Authoritative parents tend to raise more competent children. However, Baumrind's findings may not apply to some cultures or socioeconomic groups.

discipline (313) corporal punishment (313) psychological aggression (315) power assertion (315) inductive techniques (315) withdrawal of love (315) authoritarian (316) permissive (316) authoritative (316)

Special Behavioral Concerns

Guidepost 5   Why do young children help or hurt others, and why do they develop fears?

- The roots of altruism and prosocial behavior appear early. This may be an inborn disposition that can be cultivated by parental modeling and encouragement.
- Instrumental aggression—first physical, then verbal—is most common in early childhood.
- Most children become less aggressive after age 6 or 7, but the proportion of hostile aggression increases. Boys tend to practice overt aggression, whereas girls engage in relational or social aggression.
- Preschool children show temporary fears of real and imaginary objects and events; older children's fears tend to be more realistic.

altruism (318) prosocial behavior (318) instrumental aggression (319) overt, or direct, aggression (319) relational, or social, aggression (319)

Relationships with Other Children

Guidepost 6 How do young children get along with—or without— siblings, playmates, and friends?

- Sibling and peer relationships contribute to self-efficacy.
- Siblings learn to resolve disputes and negotiate differences.
- Most sibling interactions are positive. Older siblings tend to initiate activities, and younger ones to imitate. Same-sex siblings, especially girls, get along best.
- The kind of relationship children have with siblings often carries over into other peer relationships.
- Only children seem to develop at least as well as children with siblings in most respects.
- Preschoolers choose playmates and friends who are like them and with whom they have positive experiences. Aggressive children are less popular than prosocial children.
- Friends have more positive and negative interactions than other playmates.
- Parenting can affect children's social competence with peers.

self-efficacy (322)

Part Five

Middle Childhood:
A Preview

Chapter 12
Physical Development and Health in Middle Childhood

- Growth slows.
- Strength and athletic skills improve.
- Respiratory illnesses are common, but health is generally better than at any other time in the life span.

Chapter 13
Cognitive Development in Middle Childhood

- Egocentrism diminishes. Children begin to think logically but concretely.
- Memory and language skills increase.
- Cognitive gains permit children to benefit from formal schooling.
- Some children show special educational needs and strengths.

Chapter 14
Psychosocial Development in Middle Childhood

- Self-concept becomes more complex, affecting self-esteem.
- Coregulation reflects gradual shift in control from parents to child.
- Peers assume central importance.

Middle Childhood

The middle years of childhood, from about age 6 to 11, are also called the *school years*. School is the central experience during this time—a focal point for physical, cognitive, and psychosocial development. As we will see in Chapter 12, children grow taller, heavier, and stronger and acquire the motor skills needed to participate in organized games and sports. As we will see in Chapter 13, they make major advances in thinking, in moral judgment, in memory, and in literacy. Individual differences become more evident and special needs more important as competencies affect success in school.

Competencies also affect self-esteem and popularity, as we will discuss in Chapter 14. Although parents continue to be important, the peer group is more influential than before. Children develop physically, cognitively, and emotionally as well as socially through contacts with other children.

Linkups to Look For

- Undernourishment can have cognitive and psychosocial as well as physical effects.

- Obese children often suffer social rejection.

- Moral development may be linked to cognitive growth.

- IQ can be affected by nutrition, socioeconomic status, culture, rapport with the examiner, and familiarity with the surroundings.

- Parenting styles can affect school achievement.

- Physical appearance plays a large part in self-esteem.

- A decline in egocentric thinking permits deeper, more intimate friendships.

- Children who are good learners and problem solvers tend to be resilient in coping with stress.

Physical Development and Health in Middle Childhood

The healthy human child will keep
Away from home, except to sleep.
Were it not for the common cold,
Our young we never would behold.

—Ogden Nash, *You Can't Get There from Here*

Focus *Ann Bancroft, Polar Explorer*

Ann Bancroft

Ann Bancroft is the first woman in history to reach both the North and South Poles by nonmotorized means. In 1986, she dogsledded 1,000 miles from the Northwest Territories in Canada to the North Pole as the only female member of an international expedition. After surviving 8 months of grueling training and enduring temperatures as low as –70 degrees F for 56 days, Bancroft stood on top of the world. Seven years later she led three other women in a 67-day, 660-mile ski trek to the South Pole, reaching it on January 14, 1993. For these exploits, she was inducted into the National Women's Hall of Fame, was named Woman of the Year by *Ms.* magazine, and won numerous other awards and honors. Bancroft also was the first woman to ski across Greenland. In 2000, she and Liv Arneson of Norway became the first team of women to ski across the landmass of Antarctica; and in 2002 the two women reunited for a kayaking voyage from the north shore of Lake Superior to the St. Lawrence Seaway.

How did this 5-foot-3-inch, 125-pound woman achieve these remarkable feats? The answers go back to her childhood in then-rural Mendota Heights, Minnesota. Born September 29, 1955, into what she calls a family of risk takers, Ann showed her climbing instincts as soon as she could walk. As a toddler, she would climb her grandmother's bookcase to reach things on top. Instead of trying to stop her from climbing, her parents said, "Go ahead and try; you might just get what you want."

Ann was an outdoor girl. She and her two brothers and two sisters spent hours roaming the fields surrounding their farmhouse. Ann would "pretend she was a pirate building rafts to float down the creek, or an adventurer canoeing in the far north. During the winter she would build snow forts, sleeping shacks, and tunnels" (Wenzel, 1990, p. 15).

Biographical information about Ann Bancroft came primarily from Noone (2000), Wenzel (1990), and Bancroft's Web site, http://www.yourexpedition.com. Other sources were "Ann Bancroft, 1955–" (1998), "Ann Bancroft, 1955–" (1999), "Ann Bancroft, Explorer" (undated), "First Woman to Both Poles" (1997), and "Minnesota Explorer Ann Bancroft" (2002).

Her father often took the family on camping and canoe trips in the wilds of northern Minnesota. When she was 8, Ann started camping out in her backyard in winter with her cousins and the family dog. When she was 10, her parents went to Africa as missionaries. Ann's 2 years in Kenya kindled her thirst to see other parts of the world.

In school Ann was a poor student. A natural athlete, she liked gym the best. Not until seventh grade did she learn that she had dyslexia, a reading disability. Around that time Ann came across a book about Sir Ernest Shackleton's unsuccessful effort to reach the South Pole in 1914. She was drawn to the photographs. "I was so fascinated by the images that I no longer was intimidated by the words and thickness of the book," Ann recalls. "I wanted to know about this adventure at the bottom of the world. This began my curiosity with Antarctica and the dream of one day crossing it."

Ann became a physical education teacher and athletic director in St. Paul. In 1983, she and a friend climbed Alaska's Mount McKinley, the highest peak in North America—an expedition that could have ended in disaster for her partner, who developed hypothermia, had it not been for Ann's training in first aid and emergency medicine. Two years later, Ann was invited to join the Steger International Polar Expedition to the North Pole as a medic and trip photographer.

"The goal was not so much reaching the pole itself," Bancroft recalls. "It was . . . more universal. Why do we all take on struggles? Why run a marathon? I think we're all striving to push ourselves. And in the process of overcoming struggle and challenges, we get to know ourselves better."

Today Bancroft is an instructor for Wilderness Inquiry, a program for both able-bodied people and those with disabilities. During her first South Pole expedition, she lugged a 30-pound radio set across the ice so she could send progress reports to students around the world. On her last expedition to Antarctica with Arneson, children in more than 40 countries followed the journey by e-mail, with the help of an interactive Web site and curriculum. Bancroft has coauthored a book about her adventures (Loewen & Bancroft, 2001). Her goal is to "inspire children around the globe to pursue their dreams" as she has (Noone, 2000, p. 1). "It is totally energizing," she says, "to step out each day living a dream."

● ● ●

As a schoolgirl, Ann Bancroft may not have seemed extraordinary except that her dyslexia marked her as a child with special needs. Yet her achievements, based on her indomitable energy and will, are impressive. Her story illustrates how a dream formed in childhood can inspire later accomplishments. She is a living example of the power of attitudes and desires to shape development.

Although motor abilities improve less dramatically in middle childhood than before, these years are important for development of the strength, stamina, endurance, and motor proficiency needed for sports and outdoor activities. In this chapter we look at these and other physical developments, beginning with normal growth and brain development, which depend on proper nutrition, adequate sleep, and good health. As we explore health concerns, we examine children's understanding of health and illness, which links physical, cognitive, and emotional issues. As children do more, their risk of accidents increases; we examine some ways to lower the risks.

After you have read and studied this chapter, you should be able to answer each of the Guidepost questions on the following page. Look for them again in the margins throughout the chapter, where they point to important concepts. To check your understanding of these Guideposts, review the end-of-chapter summary. Checkpoints located throughout the chapter will help you verify your understanding of what you have read.

Guideposts for Study

1. How do school-age children's bodies and brains grow and develop?

2. What are the nutritional and sleep needs of middle childhood?

3. What gains in motor skills typically occur at this age, and what kinds of physical play do boys and girls engage in?

4. What are the principal health and safety concerns in middle childhood?

Aspects of Physical Development

Guidepost 1

How do school-age children's bodies and brains grow and develop?

If we were to walk by a typical elementary school just after the three o'clock bell, we would see a virtual explosion of children of all shapes and sizes. Tall ones, short ones, husky ones, and skinny ones would be bursting out of the school doors into the open air. We would see that school-age children look very different from children a few years younger.

Height and Weight

Growth during middle childhood slows considerably. Still, although day-by-day changes may not be obvious, they add up to a startling difference between 6-year-olds, who are still small children, and 11-year-olds, many of whom are now beginning to resemble adults.

Children grow about 2 to 3 inches each year between ages 6 and 11 and approximately double their weight during that period (Ogden, Fryar, Carroll, & Flegal, 2004). Girls retain somewhat more fatty tissue than boys, a characteristic that will persist through adulthood. The average 10-year-old weighs about 11 pounds more than 40 years ago—nearly 85 pounds for a boy and 88 pounds for a girl (Ogden et al., 2004). African American boys and girls tend to grow faster than white children. By about age 6, African American girls have more muscle and bone mass than European American (white) or Mexican American girls, and Mexican American girls have a higher percentage of body fat than white girls the same size (Ellis, Abrams, & Wong, 1997).

Although most children grow normally, some do not. One type of growth disorder arises from the body's failure to produce enough growth hormone. Administration of synthetic growth hormone in such cases can produce rapid growth in height, especially during the first 2 years (Albanese & Stanhope, 1993; Vance & Mauras, 1999).

Synthetic (recombinant) growth hormone therapy is sometimes used for children who are much shorter than other children their age but whose bodies are producing normal quantities of the hormone. Although its use for this purpose has been controversial, it was approved by the Food and Drug Administration in 2003 for healthy children whose projected growth rate is too slow to reach a normal adult height (63 inches for men and 59 inches for women). Hormone therapy typically increases adult height only 1 to 2½ inches, and the therapy must be continued daily for 4 to 7 years. However, some children show no response at all. Because the treatment is fairly new, long-term effects are unknown. If unsuccessful, the therapy may do psychological harm by creating unfulfilled expectations or by giving short children the feeling that something is wrong with them (Lee, 2006).

These girls proudly show off a childhood milestone—the normal loss of baby teeth, which will be replaced by permanent ones. U.S. children today have fewer dental cavities than in the early 1970s, probably owing to better nutrition, widespread use of fluoride, and better dental care.

Tooth Development and Dental Care

Most of the adult teeth arrive early in middle childhood. The primary teeth begin to fall out at about age 6 and are replaced by permanent teeth at a rate of about four teeth per year for the next 5 years.

Between 1971–1974 and 1988–1994, the number of U.S. children ages 6 to 18 with untreated cavities dropped nearly 80 percent. Improvements cut across ethnic and socio-economic lines (Brown, Wall, & Lazar, 1999). Much of the improvement in children's dental health is attributed to use of adhesive sealants on the rough, chewing surfaces (Brown, Kaste, Selwitz, & Furman, 1996).

Brain Development

Brain development during childhood is less dramatic than during infancy, but important changes occur. Brain scans of children studied longitudinally are enabling neuroscientists to map these developmental changes (Blakemore & Choudhury, 2006; Kuhn, 2006).

One such change is a *loss in the density of gray matter* (closely packed neuronal bodies) in certain regions of the cerebral cortex (Figure 12-1). This process, which reflects pruning of unused dendrites, is balanced by a steady *increase in white matter,* axons or nerve fibers that transmit information between neurons to distant regions of the brain. These connections thicken and myelinate (become insulated), beginning with the frontal lobes and moving toward the rear of the brain. Between ages 6 and 13, striking growth takes place in connections between the temporal and parietal lobes, which deal with sensory functions, language, and spatial understanding. White matter growth in these regions then drops off around the end of the critical period for language learning (Giedd et al., 1999; Kuhn, 2006; NIMH, 2001b; Paus et al., 1999). Together these changes increase the speed and efficiency of brain processes.

Whereas the myelination of white matter proceeds from front to back, the loss of gray matter seems to move roughly in the opposite direction. In a longitudinal study of 13 children from age 4 to 21, the decline in gray matter began between ages 4 and 8 in the regions that support basic sensory and motor activity; then, around ages 11 to 13, moved in a back-to-front direction to the areas of the parietal lobes involved in attention, language, and spatial orientation; and finally, in late adolescence, to the areas of the prefrontal cortex that control reasoning and other higher-order functions. This sequence corresponds roughly to the order in which these parts of the brain developed in human evolution (Gogtay et al., 2004).

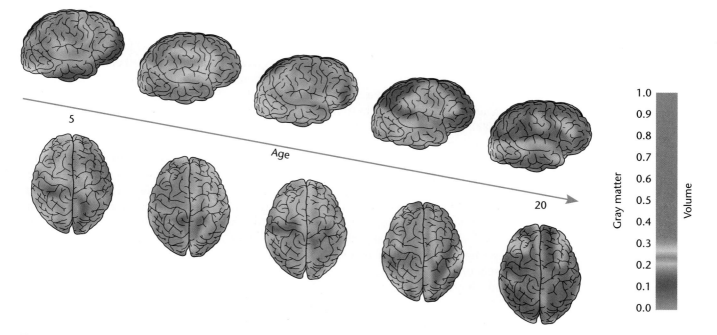

Figure 12-1

Reductions in gray matter density in the cerebral cortex, right side and top views, ages 5 to 20. Losses in gray matter density reflect maturation of various regions of the cortex, permitting more efficient functioning.

Source: Gogtay et al., 2004.

Another way neuroscientists measure brain development is by changes in the *thickness* of the cortex. Researchers have observed cortical thickening between ages 5 and 11 in the regions of the temporal and frontal lobes that handle language. At the same time, thinning occurs in the rear portion of the frontal and parietal cortex in the brain's left hemisphere. This change correlates with improved performance on the vocabulary portion of an intelligence test (Toga et al., 2006).

Developmental changes also have been mapped in the corpus callosum, which links the left and right hemispheres. Progressive myelination of fibers in the corpus callosum leads to more rapid transmission of information between the two hemispheres (Toga et al., 2006). Longitudinal mapping of the corpus callosum from age 3 to 15 revealed a front-to-back growth pattern (Thompson et al., 2000). Between ages 3 and 6, the most rapid growth occurred in the frontal areas that regulate the planning and organizing of actions. Between ages 6 and 11, the most rapid growth was in an area that primarily supports associative thinking, language, and spatial relations; this growth slowed between ages 11 and 15, which may coincide with the end of the critical period that has been proposed for learning a new language.

Sex differences have been found in these patterns of brain development. In a cross-sectional study of 61 boys and 57 girls ages 6 to 17, boys showed markedly greater loss in gray matter and growth in white matter and corpus callosum fibers. Girls showed these changes as well, but at a slower rate (De Bellis et al., 2001).

Nutrition and Sleep

To support their steady growth, brain development, and constant exertion, school-age children need to eat properly and get enough sleep. Unfortunately, too many children do neither.

Nutritional Needs

Schoolchildren need, on average, 2,400 calories every day—more for older children and less for younger ones. Nutritionists recommend a varied diet including plenty of grains,

---

Checkpoint ✔

Can you . . .

✔ Summarize typical growth patterns of boys and girls in middle childhood and give reasons for variations?

✔ Explain why health of permanent teeth has improved?

✔ Summarize changes in the brain during childhood and discuss their possible effects?

Guidepost 2

What are the nutritional and sleep needs of middle childhood?

---

fruits, and vegetables and high levels of complex carbohydrates, found in potatoes, pasta, bread, and cereals.

To avoid overweight and prevent cardiac problems, children (like adults) should get only about 30 percent of their total calories from fat and less than 10 percent of the total from saturated fat (AAP Committee on Nutrition, 1992; U.S. Department of Agriculture & USDHHS, 2000). Studies have found no negative effects on height, weight, body mass, or neurological development from a moderately low-fat diet at this age (Rask-Nissilä et al., 2000; Shea et al., 1993). Fruit juice and sweetened beverages should be limited to 8 to 12 ounces a day.

As children grow older, pressures and opportunities for unhealthy eating increase. Many children do not eat breakfast, or eat it hurriedly, and get at least one-third of their calories from snacks, including sweetened beverages (American Heart Association et al., 2006). School cafeterias and vending machines often offer unhealthy foods (National Center for Education Statistics, 2006). Children frequently eat out, often at fast-food restaurants. Many children prepare their own meals and snacks. The media strongly influence children's food choices, and not for the better. Nutrition education in schools can be helpful when combined with parental education and changes in school lunch menus. Changes in food labeling, taxes on unhealthy foods, restrictions on foods provided by government-supported school lunch programs, regulation of food advertising directed toward children, and requiring restaurants to list nutrition information on their menus are among proposed legislative recommendations (American Heart Association et al., 2006).

Sleep Patterns and Problems

Sleep needs decline from about 11 hours a day at age 5 to little more than 10 hours at age 9 and about 9 hours at age 13. Even so, many U.S. children get less sleep than they need. First through fifth graders average 9½ hours a day, short of the recommended 10 to 11 hours. And, as children get older, about 1 in 4 get less sleep on weekends (National Sleep Foundation, 2004). Sleep problems, such as resistance to going to bed, insomnia, and daytime sleepiness are common during these years, in part because many children, as they grow older, are allowed to set their own bedtimes (Hoban, 2004).

More than 40 percent of school-age children have a television set in their bedrooms, and these children get less sleep than other children (National Sleep Foundation, 2004). The more time children spent watching TV, especially at bedtime, the more likely they are to resist going to bed, to be slow in falling asleep, to be anxious around bedtime, and to wake up early (Owens et al., 1999).

A study of sleep patterns of 140 7- to 12-year-olds in Israel found significant age and gender differences. The older children went to sleep later and slept less (an hour less for 12-year-olds than for 7-year-olds). Older children also reported more morning drowsiness and were more likely to fall asleep during the day. At all ages, children woke up an average of almost twice each night. Girls slept longer and more soundly than boys. Family stress was associated with lower sleep quality (Sadeh, Raviv, & Gruber, 2000).

Although 1 in 5 children in this study experienced significant sleep difficulties, most of them—and their parents—were unaware of them (Sadeh et al., 2000). Similarly, in the United States, according to a National Sleep Foundation (2004) poll, only 11 percent of parents or caregivers of school-age children think their child has a sleep problem. Yet much higher proportions report that children regularly stall about going to bed (42 percent), have difficulty getting up in the morning (29 percent), snore (18 percent), or awaken at night in need of help or attention (14 percent). In one study, teachers noted that at least 10 percent of kindergarten through fourth-grade students struggled to stay awake in class (Owens, Spirito, McGuinn, & Nobile, 2000).

The prevalence of sleep problems declines between preschool and school age, but earlier sleep problems tend to predict later ones. Children with sleep problems often have allergies, ear infections, or hearing problems. Sleep problems also are highly correlated with psychological and behavioral problems (Stein et al., 2001).

Table 12-1	Motor Development in Middle Childhood
Age	**Selected Behaviors**
6	Girls are superior in movement accuracy; boys are superior in forceful, less complex acts. Skipping is possible. Children can throw with proper weight shift and step.
7	One-footed balancing without looking becomes possible. Children can walk 2-inch-wide balance beams. Children can hop and jump accurately into small squares. Children can execute accurate jumping-jack exercise.
8	Children have 12-pound pressure on grip strength. The number of games participated in by both sexes is greatest at this age. Children can engage in alternate rhythmic hopping in a 2-2, 2-3, or 3-3 pattern. Girls can throw a small ball 40 feet.
9	Boys can run 16½ feet per second. Boys can throw a small ball 70 feet.
10	Children can judge and intercept pathways of small balls thrown from a distance. Girls can run 17 feet per second.
11	A standing broad jump of 5 feet is possible for boys and of 4½ feet for girls.

Source: From Bryant J. Cratty, *Perceptual and Motor Development in Infants and Children,* 3rd ed. Copyright © 1986 by Allyn & Bacon. Adapted by permission of the publisher.

Motor Development and Physical Play

Guidepost 3

What gains in motor skills typically occur at this age, and what kinds of physical play do boys and girls engage in?

Motor skills continue to improve in middle childhood (Table 12-1). By this age, however, children in most nonliterate and transitional societies go to work, and this plus more household labor, especially for girls, leaves them little time and freedom for physical play (Larson & Verma, 1999). In the United States, children's lives today are more sedentary than they were when Ann Bancroft was camping out in her backyard. A nationally representative survey based on time-use diaries found that school-age children spend less time each week on sports and other outdoor activities than in the early 1980s and more hours on schooling and homework, in addition to time spent on television—an average of 12 to 14 hours a week—and on computer activities, which barely existed 20 years ago (Juster, Ono, & Stafford, 2004).

Recess-Time Play

The games schoolchildren play at recess tend to be informal and spontaneously organized. One child may play alone while nearby a group of classmates are chasing each other around the schoolyard. Boys play more physically active games, whereas girls favor games that include verbal expression or counting aloud, such as hopscotch and jumprope. Such recess-time activities promote growth in agility and social competence and foster adjustment to school (Pellegrini, Kato, Blatchford, & Baines, 2002).

About 10 percent of schoolchildren's free play in the early grades consists of **rough-and-tumble play,** vigorous play that involves wrestling, kicking, tumbling, grappling, and chasing, often accompanied by laughing and screaming (Bjorklund & Pellegrini, 2002). This kind of play may look like fighting but is done playfully among friends (Smith, 2005a).

Rough-and-tumble play peaks in middle childhood; the proportion typically drops to about 5 percent at age 11, about the same as in early childhood (Bjorklund & Pellegrini, 2002). Seemingly universal, rough-and-tumble play has been reported in such diverse

rough-and-tumble play Vigorous play involving wrestling, hitting, and chasing, often accompanied by laughing and screaming.

According to a nationally representative survey, 38.5 percent of 9- to 13-year-olds participate in organized afterschool sports, such as soccer. To help children improve motor skills, such programs should emphasize skill-building rather than competition and should include as many children as possible regardless of ability.

places as India, Mexico, Okinawa, the Kalahari in Africa, the Philippines, Great Britain, and the United States as well as among most mammals (Bjorklund & Pellegrini, 2002; Humphreys & Smith, 1984). Boys around the world participate in rough-and-tumble play more than girls do, perhaps because of hormonal differences and socialization, and this may be one reason for sex segregation during play (Bjorklund & Pellegrini, 2002; Pellegrini et al., 2002; Smith, 2005a). From an evolutionary standpoint, rough-and-tumble play has important adaptive benefits: It hones skeletal and muscle development, offers safe practice for hunting and fighting skills, and channels aggression and competition. By age 11, it often becomes a way to establish dominance within the peer group (Bjorklund & Pellegrini, 2000, 2002; Smith, 2005b).

Organized Sports

After children outgrow rough-and-tumble play and begin playing games with rules, some join organized, adult-led sports. In a nationally representative survey of U.S. 9- to 13-year-olds and their parents, 38.5 percent reported participation in organized athletics outside of school hours—most of them in baseball, softball, soccer, or basketball. About twice as many children (77.4 percent) participated in unorganized physical activity, such as bicycling and shooting baskets (Duke, Huhman, & Heitzler, 2003). Girls tend to spend less time than boys on sports and more time on housework, studying, and personal care (Juster et al., 2004).

Besides improving motor skills, regular physical activity has immediate and long-term health benefits: weight control, lower blood pressure, improved cardiorespiratory functioning, and enhanced self-esteem and well-being. Active children tend to become active adults. Thus, organized athletic programs should include as many children as possible rather than concentrating on a few natural athletes like Ann Bancroft and should focus on building skills rather than winning games. Programs should include a variety of sports that can be part of a lifetime fitness regimen, such as tennis, bowling, running, swimming, golf, and skating (AAP Committee on Sports Medicine & Fitness, 1997; Council on Sports Medicine and Fitness and Council on School Health, 2006). Six- to 9-year-olds need more flexible rules, shorter instruction time, and more free time for practice than older children. At this age girls and boys are about equal in weight, height, endurance and motor skill development. Older children are better able to process instruction and learn team strategies, so they are better equipped to engage in team sports (Council on Sports Medicine and Fitness and Council on School Health, 2006).

Checkpoint ✔

Can you . . .

✔ Tell how boys' and girls' recess-time activities differ?

✔ Explain the evolutionary significance of rough-and-tumble play?

✔ Tell what proportion of children remain physically active as they get older and what types of physical play they engage in?

Guidepost 4

What are the principal health and safety concerns in middle childhood?

Health and Safety

The development of vaccines for major childhood illnesses has made middle childhood a relatively safe time of life. The death rate in these years is the lowest in the life span. Still, too many children are overweight, and some suffer from chronic medical conditions or accidental injuries or from lack of access to health care.

Overweight and Body Image

Overweight in children is becoming a major health issue worldwide. Since 1980, the prevalence of childhood obesity has increased in almost all countries for which data are

Box 12-1 *Do Barbie Dolls Affect Girls' Body Image?*

"I looked at a Barbie doll when I was 6 and said, 'This is what I want to look like,'" the model Cindy Jackson said on CBS News (2004). "I think a lot of little 6-year-old girls or younger even now are looking at that doll and thinking, 'I want to be her.'"

Barbie is the best-selling fashion doll around the world and the favorite toy of many young girls. In the United States, 99 percent of 3- to 10-year-olds own at least one Barbie doll, and the average girl owns eight. Yet Barbie's body proportions are "unrealistic, unattainable, and unhealthy" (Dittmar, Halliwell, & Ive, 2006, p. 284). Fewer than 1 in 100,000 women actually have Barbie's body proportions; her waist, as compared to her bust size, is 39 percent smaller than that of a woman with the eating disorder anorexia (see Chapter 15).

By age 6, studies show, many girls wish to be thinner than they are. According to Bandura's social cognitive theory, Barbie dolls are role models for young girls, transmitting a cultural ideal of beauty. The media reinforce this ideal. Girls who do not measure up may experience *body dissatisfaction*—negative thoughts about their bodies, leading to low self-esteem.

To test Barbie's effect on young girls' body image, researchers read aloud picture books to 162 English girls, ages 5½ to 8½. One group saw picture stories about Barbie; control groups saw stories about a full-figured fashion doll called Emme or about no doll (Dittmar et al., 2006). Afterward, the girls completed questionnaires in which they were asked to agree or disagree with such statements as "I'm pretty happy about the way I look" and "I really like what I weigh." The girls also were given an assortment of line drawings of female figures. Each girl was asked to color in the figure whose body looked most like her own, as well as the figures that showed the way she wanted to look, now and when she grew up.

The findings were striking. Among the youngest girls, ages 5½ to 6½, a single exposure to the Barbie picture book significantly lowered body esteem and increased the discrepancy between actual and ideal body size. This did not happen with the girls who saw the Emme book or no doll. The effect of Barbie on body image was even stronger on girls ages 6½ to 7½. However, the findings for the oldest girls, ages 7½ to 8½, were completely different: Pictures of Barbie had no direct effect on body image at this age. What accounts for this difference? Girls up to age 7

may be in a sensitive period in which they acquire idealized images of beauty. As girls grow older, they may internalize the ideal of thinness as part of their emerging identity. Once the ideal is internalized, its power no longer depends on direct exposure to the original role model (Dittmar et al., 2006).

Or, it may be that girls simply outgrow Barbie. In another study (Kuther & McDonald, 2004), sixth- through eighth-grade girls were asked about their childhood experiences with Barbie. All the girls had owned at least two Barbie dolls but said they no longer played with them. Looking back, some of the girls saw Barbie as a positive influence: "She is like the perfect person . . . that everyone wants to be like." But most of the young people, girls and boys alike, saw Barbie as an unrealistic role model for girls:

- "Barbie dolls provide a false stereotype . . . as it is physically impossible to attain the same body size. . . . There wouldn't be enough room for organs and other necessary things."
- "Barbie has this perfect body and now every girl is trying to have her body because they are so unhappy with themselves."

Barbie now has a major competitor: Bratz, an ultra-thin doll with a large round face, sassy mouth, and heavy makeup. Longitudinal research will help determine whether fashion dolls such as Barbie and Bratz have a lasting impact on body image.

What's your view ❓

If you had (or have) a young daughter, would you allow her to play with Barbie dolls? Why or why not?

Check it out ✏️

For more information on this topic, go to http://www.bam.gov/ teachers/body_image_dolls.html. This Web page describes a classroom activity in which students take measurements of toy action figures and fashion dolls and figure out how they would look if they were the height of a normal adult man or woman. They then discuss how playing with these toys might shape perceptions of what is normal and might affect mental and physical health.

---

available. By 2010, if current trends continue, nearly 50 percent of the children in North and South America, 39 percent in Europe, and 20 percent in China will be overweight (Wang & Lobstein, 2006).

In the United States, almost 19 percent of school-age children—about three times as many as in 1980—were overweight in 2003–2004. Boys are more likely to be overweight than girls (Ogden et al., 2006). Although overweight has increased in all ethnic groups (Center for Weight and Health, 2001), it is most prevalent among Mexican American boys (more than 25 percent) and non-Hispanic black girls (26.5 percent) (Ogden et al., 2006).

Unfortunately, children who try to lose weight are not always the ones who need to do so. Concern with **body image**—how one believes one looks—begins to be important early in middle childhood, especially for girls, and may develop into eating disorders that become more common in adolescence (see Chapter 15). Playing with Barbie dolls may be an influence in that direction (Box 12-1).

body image Descriptive and evaluative beliefs about one's appearance.

Children who spend many hours watching television tend to be overweight. They are likely to get too little exercise and eat too many fattening snacks.

What's your view

- Since overweight tends to run in families, either because of heredity or lifestyle, how can parents who have not been able to control their weight help their children?

Causes of Overweight

As we reported in Chapters 3 and 9, overweight (or obesity) often results from an inherited tendency aggravated by too little exercise and too much or the wrong kinds of food (AAP Committee on Nutrition, 2003; Chen et al., 2004). Children are more likely to be overweight if they have overweight parents or other relatives. From earlier in this chapter, we know that poor nutrition, encouraged by media advertising and wide availability of snack foods and beverages, also contributes (Council on Sports Medicine and Fitness and Council on School Health, 2006). On a typical day, more than 30 percent of a nationally representative sample of 6,212 children and adolescents reported eating fast foods high in fat, carbohydrates, and sugar additives (Bowman, Gortmaker, Ebbeling, Pereira, & Ludwig, 2004). Eating out is one culprit; children who eat outside the home consume an estimated 200 more calories a day than when the same foods are eaten at home (French, Story, & Jeffery, 2001).

Inactivity is a major factor in the sharp rise in overweight. As we have mentioned, school-age children today spend less time than the children of 20 years ago in outdoor play and sports (Juster et al., 2004). Although the National Association of State Boards of Education (2000) recommends 150 minutes of physical education each week for elementary students, the average school offers it only two to three times a week for a total of 85 to 98 minutes (National Center for Education Statistics, 2006). Yet, 1 additional hour of physical education per week in kindergarten and first grade could reduce by half the number of overweight girls that age (Datar & Sturm, 2004b).

Outside school, many children are not as active as they should be. According to one national survey, 22.6 percent of 9- to 13-year-olds engage in *no* free-time physical activity (Duke et al., 2003). Preadolescent girls in ethnic minorities, children with disabilities, children who live in public housing, and children in unsafe neighborhoods where facilities for outdoor exercise are lacking are most likely to be sedentary (Council on Sports Medicine and Fitness and Council on School Health, 2006).

Excessive television viewing contributes to overweight. Children who watch TV 5 hours a day are 4.6 times as likely to be overweight as those who watch no more than 2 hours daily (Institute of Medicine, 2005).

Why Is Childhood Overweight a Serious Concern?

Being overweight is a decided disadvantage for school-age children. In a longitudinal study of 1,456 primary students in Victoria, Australia, children classified as overweight or obese fell behind their classmates in physical and social functioning by age 10 (Williams, Wake, Hesketh, Maher, & Waters, 2005). When 106 severely obese children and adolescents were asked to rate their health-related quality of life (for example, their ability to walk more than one block, to sleep well, to get along with others, and to keep up in school), they reported significant impairment as compared with healthy peers (Schwimmer, Burwinkle, & Varni, 2003).

Overweight children often suffer emotionally and may compensate by indulging themselves with treats, making their physical and social problems even worse. These children are at risk for behavior problems, depression, and low self-esteem (AAP Committee on Nutrition, 2003; Datar & Sturm, 2004a; Mustillo et al., 2003). They commonly have medical problems, including high blood pressure (discussed in the next section), high cholesterol, and high insulin levels (AAP Committee on Nutrition, 2003; NCHS, 2004).

Overweight children tend to become obese adults, at risk for high blood pressure, heart disease, orthopedic problems, and diabetes. Indeed, childhood overweight may be a stronger predictor of some diseases than adult overweight (AAP Committee on Nutrition, 2003; AAP, 2004; Li et al., 2004; Center for Weight and Health, 2001; Must, Jacques, Dallal, Bajema, & Dietz, 1992). Even children in the upper half of the normal weight range are more likely than their peers to become overweight or obese in adulthood (Field, Cook, & Gillman, 2005). In one longitudinal study, girls who were overweight before puberty were 7.7 times as likely as their peers to be overweight as adults (Must et al., 2005).

Table 12-2	A Coordinated Strategy to Stop the "Overweight Epidemic"

What parents can do:
- Make sure children are offered healthy foods and get plenty of outdoor play time
- Limit food choices
- Limit television time and video games to 2 hours a day, and monitor what children watch
- Provide healthy role models

What schools can do:
- Develop school wellness policies in partnership with the local school board, parents, students, physical education teachers, and health care professionals
- Provide healthier foods in the cafeteria, vending machines, and school stores.
- Make sure that all children spend at least 30 minutes a day in moderate to vigorous physical activity
- Eliminate advertising of low-nutrient foods on school buses and scoreboards and at school functions

What private industry can do:
- Offer employee medical benefits that include preventive coverage
- Develop healthy products that are attractive to children
- Offer incentives for healthy eating
- Use television advertising aimed at children to promote healthy products

What health care professionals can do:
- Identify and track children and adolescents at risk for obesity due to genetic and environmental factors
- Calculate body mass index annually for children and adolescents and refer to a weight control specialist those who are overweight or at risk of overweight
- Encourage parents and caregivers to promote healthy eating by offering nutritious snacks, letting children eat what they want within appropriate limits, and modeling healthy food choices.
- Promote physical activity, including unstructured play time
- Recommend limiting screen time to a maximum of 2 hours a day
- Give parents information on appropriate nutrition and advise families on adopting healthier lifestyles

What communities can do:
- Offer after-school recreational programs emphasizing physical activity and classes in cooking, nutrition, health, and fitness
- Develop pedestrian-friendly neighborhoods with shops and grocery stores within walking distance

What federal, state, or local governments can do:
- Give the Secretary of Agriculture authority over all foods available in schools—in vending machines and after-school programs as well as in the cafeteria
- Publish nutritional guidelines for all foods and beverages sold in schools
- Give the Federal Trade Commission authority to establish guidelines for advertising of junk foods aimed at children
- Sponsor media campaigns to promote healthy nutrition and physical activity
- Support community programs that foster an active environment, for example, road projects that accommodate bicycles and pedestrians
- Tax soft drinks and snack foods and partially subsidize the cost of fresh fruits and vegetables

Source: Krishnamoorthy, Hart, & Jelalian, 2006.

Prevention and Treatment of Overweight

Prevention of weight gain is easier, less costly, and more effective than treating overweight (Center for Weight and Health, 2001; Council on Sports Medicine and Fitness and Council on School Health, 2006). Effective weight-management programs should include efforts of parents, schools, physicians, communities, and the larger culture (Krishnamoorthy, Hart, & Jelalian, 2006; Table 12-2). Less time in front of television and computers, changes in food labeling and advertising, healthier school meals, education to help children make better food choices, and more time spent in physical education would help (AAP, 2004).

Parents can make exercise a family activity by hiking or playing ball together, building strength on playground equipment, walking whenever possible, using stairs instead of elevators, and limiting television. Parents should watch children's eating and activity patterns and address excessive weight gain before a child becomes severely overweight (AAP Committee on Nutrition, 2003). A 2004 federal law (Public Law 108-265) requires that every school receiving federal funding for school lunches or breakfasts must set goals for healthy nutrition, physical activity, and wellness promotion with emphasis on prevention of childhood obesity.

Treatment of overweight should begin early, involve the family, and promote permanent changes in lifestyle, not weight loss alone (Barlow & Dietz, 1998; Miller-Kovach, 2003). During a 12-week experiment with 10 obese 8- to 12-year-olds, those whose television viewing was limited to the amount of time they spent pedaling an exercise bicycle watched much less television and showed significantly greater reductions in body fat than a control group (Faith et al., 2001).

Overweight and Childhood Hypertension

hypertension High blood pressure.

Hypertension (high blood pressure) once was relatively rare in childhood, but it has been termed an "evolving epidemic" of cardiovascular risk, especially among ethnic minorities (Sorof, Lai, Turner, Poffenbarger, & Portman, 2004, p. 481). In nationally representative samples of U.S. children and adolescents ages 8 to 17, average blood pressure rose between 1988 and 2000, in part due to increases in overweight (Muntner, He, Cutler, Wildman, & Whelton, 2004). A series of screenings of 5,102 children ages 10 to 19 in eight Houston public schools found an estimated 4.5 percent prevalence of hypertension, with overweight the major contributing factor (Sorof et al., 2004).

Weight reduction through dietary modification and regular physical activity is the primary treatment for overweight-related hypertension. If blood pressure does not come down, drug treatment can be considered. However, care must be taken in prescribing such drugs, as their long-term effects on children are unknown—as are the long-term consequences of untreated hypertension in children (National High Blood Pressure Education Program Working Group on High Blood Pressure in Children and Adolescents, 2004).

Medical Conditions

acute medical conditions
Occasional illnesses that last a short time.

Illness in middle childhood tends to be brief. **Acute medical conditions**—occasional, short-term conditions, such as infections and warts—are common. Six or seven bouts a year with colds, flu, or viruses are typical as germs pass among children at school or at play (Behrman, 1992).

As children's experience with illness increases, so does their understanding of the causes of health and illness and of how people can promote their own health (Crisp, Underer, & Goodnow, 1996). From a Piagetian perspective, children's understanding of health and illness is tied to cognitive development. As they mature, their explanations for disease change. Before middle childhood, children are egocentric; they believe that illness is magically produced by human actions, often their own ("I was a bad boy, so now I feel bad"). Later they explain all diseases—only a little less magically—as the doing of all-powerful germs. As children approach adolescence, they see that there can be multiple causes of disease, that contact with germs does not automatically lead to illness, and that people can do much to keep healthy.

chronic medical conditions
Physical, developmental, behavioral, and/or emotional conditions that require special health services.

According to a nationally representative survey of more than 200,000 households, an estimated 12.8 percent of U.S. children have or are at risk for **chronic medical conditions:** physical, developmental, behavioral, or emotional conditions requiring special health services (Kogan, Newacheck, Honberg, & Strickland, 2005). Let's look at some chronic conditions that affect everyday living.

Vision and Hearing Problems

Most children have keener vision in middle childhood than when they were younger. Children under 6 years old tend to be farsighted. By age 6, vision typically is more acute; and because the two eyes are better coordinated, they can focus better.

Checkpoint ✔

Can you . . .

✔ Discuss why childhood overweight has increased, how it can affect health, and how it can be treated?

Almost 13 percent of children under 18 are estimated to be blind or to have impaired vision. Vision problems are reported more often for white and Latino children than for African Americans (Newacheck, Stoddard, & McManus, 1993).

About 15 percent of 6- to 19-year-olds, preponderantly boys, have some hearing loss. Current screening guidelines may miss many children with very high frequency impairments. This is of concern, since even slight hearing loss can affect communication, behavior, and social relationships (Niskar et al., 1998).

Stuttering

Stuttering is involuntary audible or silent repetition or prolongation of sounds or syllables. It usually begins between ages 2 and 5 (Büchel & Sommer, 2004). By fifth grade, it is four times more common in boys than in girls. Five percent of children stutter for a period of 6 months or more, but three-quarters of these recover by late childhood, leaving about 1 percent with a long-term problem (Stuttering Foundation, 2006).

Stuttering is now widely regarded as a neurological condition. It sometimes results from brain damage (for example, head trauma or a stroke). The more common type, *persistent developmental stuttering (PDS),* is especially noticeable at the beginning of a word or phrase or in long, complex sentences. The concordance rate is about 70 percent for monozygotic twins, 30 percent for dizygotic twins, and 18 percent for same-sex siblings, suggesting a genetic component. It seems likely that two factors are at work in PDS. The basic cause may be a structural or functional disorder of the central nervous system. This may then be reinforced by parental reactions to the stuttering, which may make the child nervous or anxious about speaking (Büchel & Sommer, 2004).

There is no known cure for stuttering, but speech therapy can help a child talk more easily and fluently (Stuttering Foundation, 2006). If stutterers become frustrated or anxious about their speech, they may learn to avoid speaking as much as possible. On the other hand, the actor Bruce Willis treated himself by joining a drama club, which forced him to speak before an audience (Büchel & Sommer, 2004). Many other famous people, including the actress Julia Roberts and the actor James Earl Jones, have succeeded despite having PDS.

Asthma

Asthma is a chronic respiratory disease, apparently allergy-based and characterized by sudden attacks of coughing, wheezing, and difficulty in breathing. These symptoms reflect an extreme narrowing of the airways when a sufferer inhales certain substances, such as smoke (Eder, Ege, & von Mutius, 2006).

Asthma is increasing worldwide (Asher et al., 2006) but may have plateaued in parts of the Western world (Eder, Ege, & von Mutius, 2006). In 2005, 12.7 percent of U.S. children and adolescents up to age 17 had been diagnosed with asthma at some time, and 8.9 percent currently had it. It is 30 percent more common in boys than in girls. Its prevalence in the United States more than doubled between 1980 and 1995 and has since remained at this historically high level (Akinbami, 2006). Asthma is the third-leading cause of hospitalization of children under 18 in the United States, following pneumonia and injuries (NCHS, 2005).

In a nationally representative survey of parents of 14,487 non-Hispanic black children and 49,042 non-Hispanic white children, even when such factors as SES and access to health care were controlled, black children were 20 percent more likely to be diagnosed with asthma and twice as likely to have visited a hospital emergency department due to an asthma attack during the previous year (McDaniel, Paxson, & Waldfogel, 2006).

The causes of the asthma explosion are uncertain, but a genetic predisposition is likely to be involved (Eder et al., 2006). Some researchers point to environmental factors: tightly insulated houses that intensify exposure to indoor air pollutants and allergens (Nugent, 1999; Sly, 2000; Stapleton, 1998), such as tobacco smoke, molds, and cockroach droppings. Allergies to household pets also have been suggested as risk factors (Bollinger, 2003;

stuttering Involuntary, frequent repetition or prolongation of sounds or syllables.

asthma A chronic respiratory disease characterized by sudden attacks of coughing, wheezing, and difficulty in breathing.

Etzel, 2003; Lanphear, Aligne, Auinger, Weitzman, & Byrd, 2001). Findings regarding these proposed causes, except for smoke exposure, are inconclusive. However, indoor exposure to allergens may contribute to the *persistence* of symptoms in children who already have asthma (Eder et al., 2006). In one study of 174 asthmatic schoolchildren, exposure to higher levels of dust mites and nitrogen dioxide, a product of unflued gas appliances, was linked to worsened asthma symptoms (Nitschke et al., 2006). A 1-year program to reduce indoor allergens and tobacco smoke in the homes of children with asthma significantly reduced asthma symptoms and asthma-related illnesses (Morgan et al., 2004). Increasing evidence points to an association between obesity and asthma, perhaps because of an underlying lifestyle factor related to both conditions. Asthma also has been linked to the use of antibiotics (Eder et al., 2006).

Children with asthma miss an average of 10 days of school each year and experience 20 days of limited activity (Newacheck & Halfon, 2000). Attacks tend to follow severely stressful events, such as illness, parental separation or divorce, the death of a grandparent, a close friend moving away, or becoming a victim of bullying (Sandberg, Järvenpää, Penttinen, Paton, & McCann, 2004). Children with asthma may be at risk for social and psychological problems (Berz, Murdock, & Mitchell, 2005).

Many children get inadequate treatment (Halterman, Aligne, Auinger, McBride, & Szilagyi, 2000; Shields, Comstock, & Weiss, 2004). In a randomized, controlled study of 134 asthmatic inner-city children ages 8 to 16, use of the Internet to educate patients and their families in symptom monitoring and medication led to improved compliance and reduced symptoms (Dorsey & Schneider, 2003).

HIV and AIDS

Worldwide, an estimated 2.2 million children under age 15 are living with the human immunodeficiency virus (HIV) (UNAIDS/WHO, 2004). These children are at high risk of developing AIDS (acquired immune deficiency syndrome), if they have not done so already. In 2004, 510,000 children under 15 died of AIDS (UNAIDS/WHO, 2004).

Prospects for survival and health of children born with HIV infection have improved greatly due to antiretroviral therapy (AAP Committee on Pediatric AIDS, 2000; Gortmaker et al., 2001; Lee et al., 2006). Although some of these children develop AIDS by age 1 or 2, others live for years without apparent effects (European Collaborative Study, 1994; Grubman et al., 1995; Nielsen et al., 1997; Nozyce et al., 1994). Genetic factors may affect the immune system's response to the virus, causing symptoms to develop more slowly in some children than in others (Singh et al., 2003).

Most children infected with HIV who reach school age function normally, though their quality of life may be affected, especially if they are not getting antiretroviral treatment (Lee et al., 2006). Because there is virtually no risk of infecting classmates, children who carry the AIDS virus do not need to be isolated. They should be encouraged to participate in all school activities, including athletics, to the extent they are able (AAP Committee on Sports Medicine and Fitness, 1999; AAP Committee on Pediatric AIDS, 2000).

Because symptoms may not appear until a disease has progressed to the point of causing serious long-term complications, early detection is important. Regular, school-based screening and treatment, together with programs that promote abstention from or postponement of sexual activity, responsible decision making, and ready availability of condoms for those who are sexually active may have some effect in controlling the spread of STDs (AAP Committee on Adolescence, 1994; AGI, 1994; Cohen, Nsuami, Martin, & Farley, 1999; Rotheram-Borus & Futterman, 2000).

Factors in Health and Access to Health Care

Social disadvantage plays an important part in children's health. Poor children—who are disproportionately minority children—and those living with a single parent or parents with low educational status are more likely than other children to be in fair or poor health, to have chronic conditions or health-related limitations on activities, to miss

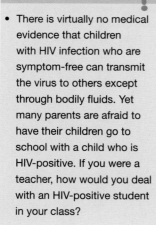

What's your view

• There is virtually no medical evidence that children with HIV infection who are symptom-free can transmit the virus to others except through bodily fluids. Yet many parents are afraid to have their children go to school with a child who is HIV-positive. If you were a teacher, how would you deal with an HIV-positive student in your class?

school due to illness or injury, to be hospitalized, to have unmet medical and dental needs, and to experience delayed medical care (Bauman, Silver, & Stein, 2006; Bloom et al., 2003; Collins & LeClere, 1997; Flores et al., 2002; Newacheck et al., 1998), and the chances of health problems compound when more than one of these risk factors is present. Ethnic minority status is not a risk factor in itself but is associated with low income (Bauman et al., 2006).

Why is this so? Parents with higher socioeconomic and educational status tend to know more about good health habits and have better access to insurance and health care. Two-parent families tend to have higher incomes and more wholesome diets than single-parent families (Collins & LeClere, 1997), and their children are more likely to have health insurance (Fields, 2003). Children in low-income and minority families are more likely than other children to be uninsured, to have no usual place of health care, or to go to clinics or hospital emergency rooms rather than doctors' offices (Bloom et al., 2003).

As many as 33 percent of children with chronic health problems are underinsured (Kogan et al., 2005), and 60 percent of all children experience coverage gaps of at least 4 months (Satchell & Pati, 2005). Many of these children have unmet health care needs. Access to health care is a particularly severe problem among Latino children, especially those who are poor or near poor and who have foreign-born parents with less than a high school education (Scott & Ni, 2004).

However, lack of access to insurance and health care accounts for only part of the disparity in disadvantaged children's health (Bauman et al., 2006). Asian American children, who tend to be in better health than non-Hispanic white children, are less likely to access and use health care, perhaps because of cultural and linguistic barriers (Yu, Huang, & Singh, 2004). Indeed, one factor in variations in health care is differing beliefs and attitudes about health and healing among cultural and ethnic groups (Box 12-2).

Safety-approved helmets protect children of all ages from disabling or fatal head injuries.

Accidental Injuries

As in early childhood, accidental injuries are the leading cause of death among school-age U.S. children (Anderson & Smith, 2003; Kochanek et al., 2004). In a 9-year study of 96,359 children born in Alberta, Canada, 21 percent suffered at least one injury each year, and 73 percent had repeat injuries during the study period. Boys were more likely to be injured than girls and to have repeat injuries (Spady, Saunders, Schopflocher, & Svenson, 2004).

An estimated 23,000 children each year suffer serious brain injuries from bicycle accidents; as many as 88 percent of these injuries could be prevented by using helmets (AAP Committee on Injury and Poison Prevention, 2001a). Protective headgear also is vital for baseball and softball, football, roller skating, rollerblading, skateboarding, scooter riding, horseback riding, hockey, speed sledding, snowmobiling, and tobogganing. For soccer, protective goggles and mouth guards may help reduce head and facial injuries. "Heading" the ball should be minimized because of the danger of brain injury (AAP Committee on Sports Medicine and Fitness, 2000, 2001). The AAP Committee on Accident and Poison Prevention (1988) recommends that children under 16 not use snowmobiles, and that older riders be required by law to be licensed. Because of the need for stringent safety precautions and constant supervision for trampoline use, the AAP Committee on Injury and Poison Prevention and Committee on Sports Medicine and Fitness (1999) recommend that parents not buy trampolines and that children not use them on playgrounds or at school.

Checkpoint ✔

Can you . . .

✔ Distinguish between acute and chronic medical conditions, and tell how specific chronic conditions can affect everyday life?

✔ Explain why socially disadvantaged children tend to have more health problems than their peers?

✔ Identify factors that increase the risks of accidental injury?

Box 12-2 *How Cultural Attitudes Affect Health Care*

One morning Buddi Kumar Rai, a university-educated resident of Badel, a remote hill village in Nepal, carried his 2½-year-old daughter, Kusum, to the shaman, the local medicine man. Kusum's little face was sober, her usually golden complexion pale, and her almond-shaped eyes droopy from the upper-respiratory infection she had been suffering with the past week, complete with fever and a hacking cough.

Two days before, Kusum had been in her father's arms when he had slipped and fallen backward off a veranda to the ground about 3 feet below, still tightly holding his little daughter. Neither was hurt, but little Kusum had screamed in fright.

Now the shaman told Buddi that Kusum's illness was due to that fright. He prescribed incantations and put a mark, a charcoal smudge the size of a silver dollar, on the child's forehead to drive away the evil spirit that had entered her body when she had her scare.

Adherence to ancient beliefs about illness is common in parts of the industrialized world where peoples still cling to beliefs that are at odds with mainstream scientific and medical thinking. To provide better medical care to members of ethnic minorities, policymakers need to understand the cultural beliefs and attitudes that influence what people do and the decisions they make and how they interact with the broader society.

Many cultures see illness and disability as a form of punishment inflicted on someone who has transgressed in this or a previous life or is paying for an ancestor's sin. Another belief, common in Latin America and Southeast Asia, is that an imbalance of elements in the body causes illness, and the patient has to reestablish equilibrium. Arab Americans tend to attribute disease to such causes as the evil eye, grief and loss, exposure to drafts, and eating the wrong combinations of foods.

In many societies people believe that a severely disabled child will not survive. Since there is no hope, they do not expend time, effort, or money on the child—which often creates a self-fulfilling prophecy. In some religious households, parents hold out hope for a miracle and refuse surgery or other treatment.

Of course, standard medical practice in the United States is also governed by a cultural belief system. Often parents must make decisions about their child quickly, without consulting members of the extended family as would be done in many cultures. To foster independence and self-sufficiency, parents are discouraged from babying a disabled child. People from other cultures may not agree with these American values; parents may feel a need to consult their own parents about medical decisions and may not consider it important for a child with a disability to become self-sufficient.

Professionals need to explain clearly, in the family's language whenever possible, what course of treatment they recommend,

This Peruvian healer treats a child with traditional methods, such as herbs and incantations. In many Latin American cultures, such practices are believed to cure illness by restoring the natural balance of elements in the body.

why they favor it, and what they expect to happen. Such concern can help prevent incidents like one that occurred when an Asian mother became hysterical as an American nurse took her baby to get a urine sample. The mother had had three children taken from her in Cambodia. None had returned.

Sources: Al-Oballi Kridli, 2002; S. W. Olds, 2002; Groce & Zola, 1993.

What's your view ?

- How would Piaget interpret the belief in some cultures that illness and disabilities are punishments for human actions?
- Does such a belief suggest that Piaget's theory is limited in its applicability to non-Western cultures?

Check it out !

For more information on this topic, go to http://www.who.int/whr/2000/en/index.html. This is the "World Health Report 2000, Health Systems: Improving Performance," published by the World Health Organization.

Refocus

Thinking back to the information about Ann Bancroft in the Focus vignette at the beginning of this chapter,

- How much impact do you think psychosocial factors such as motivation, determination, and self-confidence had in Ann Bancroft's physical development?

- How did Bancroft's childhood experiences with her parents and siblings influence her later achievements?

- What can we learn from Bancroft's experience about the kinds of activities that can lead to lifetime fitness?

One reason for some accidents is children's immaturity, both cognitive (preventing them from being aware of some dangers) and emotional (leading them to take dangerous risks). We will discuss cognitive development in middle childhood in Chapter 13 and emotional and social development in Chapter 14.

Summary and Key Terms

Aspects of Physical Development

Guidepost 1 How do school-age children's bodies and brains grow and develop?

- Physical development is less rapid in middle childhood than in earlier years. Wide differences in height and weight exist.

- Children with retarded growth due to growth hormone deficiency may be given synthetic growth hormone. The hormone is sometimes prescribed for short children who do not have hormone deficiency; extreme caution is advised in such cases.

- The permanent teeth arrive in middle childhood. Dental health has improved, in part because of the use of sealants on chewing surfaces.

- Brain growth continues during childhood with a gradual increase in white matter and decrease in gray matter. The corpus callosum connecting the two hemispheres becomes progressively myelinated.

Nutrition and Sleep

Guidepost 2 What are the nutritional and sleep needs of middle childhood?

- Proper nutrition and adequate sleep are essential for normal growth and health.

- Most children do not get enough sleep, and many have sleep problems.

Motor Development and Physical Play

Guidepost 3 What gains in motor skills typically occur at this age, and what kinds of physical play do boys and girls engage in?

- Because of improved motor development, boys and girls in middle childhood can engage in a wide range of motor activities.

- About 10 percent of schoolchildren's recess-time play, especially among boys, is rough-and-tumble play.

- Informal, spontaneous play helps develop physical and social skills. Boys' games are more physical and girls' games more verbal.

- Many children, mostly boys, engage in organized, competitive sports.

- A sound physical education program should aim at skill development for all children and should emphasize enjoyment and lifelong fitness rather than competition.

rough-and-tumble play (337)

Health and Safety

Guidepost 4 What are the principal health and safety concerns in middle childhood?

- Middle childhood is a relatively healthy period; the death rate is the lowest in the life span. However, respiratory infections and other acute medical conditions are common.

- Concern with body image, especially among girls, may lead to eating disorders.

- Overweight, which is increasingly common among children, is influenced by genetic and environmental factors and can be prevented more easily than it can be treated.

- Vision becomes keener during middle childhood, but a minority of children have defective vision or hearing.

- Stuttering is fairly common but usually not permanent.

- Most children who are HIV-positive function normally in school and should not be excluded from any activities of which they are physically capable.

- Chronic conditions such as asthma are most prevalent among poor and minority children, who are least likely to be insured and to have regular health care.

- Children's understanding of health and illness is related to their cognitive level. Cultural beliefs affect expectations regarding health care.

- Accidents are the leading cause of death in middle childhood. Use of helmets and other protective devices and avoidance of trampolines, snowmobiling, and other dangerous sports can greatly reduce injuries.

body image (339)   hypertension (342)   acute medical conditions (342)   chronic medical conditions (342)   stuttering (343)   asthma (343)

Cognitive Development in Middle Childhood

What we must remember above all in the education of our children is that their love of life should never weaken.

—Natalia Ginzburg, *The Little Virtues*, 1985

Focus *Akira Kurosawa, Master Filmmaker*

Akira Kurosawa

The Japanese filmmaker Akira Kurosawa (1910–1998), who wrote and directed such classics as the Academy Award–winning *Rashomon* (1951) and *Seven Samurai* (1954), has been called a cinematographic genius. Kurosawa used the screen as if it were a canvas. Artistic intelligence—an unerring sense of composition, form, color, and texture—pervades his scenes.

In his mid-20s, as an apprentice to the great film director Kajiro Yamamoto, he was a quick study. Assigned to write scenarios, the talented novice came up with idea after idea. "He is completely creative," Yamamoto said of him (Richie, 1984, p. 12).

Yet, as a child, during his first 2 years at a Westernized school in Tokyo, Kurosawa was a slow learner. Because he had trouble following the lessons, he just sat quietly, trying to amuse himself. His teacher eventually moved Akira's desk and chair away from the other students and frequently aroused snickers with such comments as "Akira probably won't understand this, but . . ." (Kurosawa, 1983, p. 8).

That initial school experience left an indelible mark on Kirosawa. He felt isolated and miserable. Then, toward the end of his 2nd year of school, his family moved to another part of the city, and he was transferred to a traditional Japanese school. His new classmates, with their close-shaved heads, duck-cloth trousers, and wooden clogs, made fun of Akira's long hair and European-style clothing. The youngest of seven children, Akira had been a crybaby; now he became a laughingstock.

It was in third grade that he came out of his intellectual and emotional fog. The strongest catalyst for this change was his teacher, Mr. Tachikawa. In art class, instead of having all the students copy a picture and giving the top grade to the closest imitation, as was the custom, he let the children draw whatever they liked. Akira became so carried away that he pressed on his colored pencils until they broke, and then he licked his fingertips and smeared the colors all over the paper. When Mr. Tachikawa held up Akira's drawing, the class laughed boisterously. But the teacher lavished it with praise and gave it the highest grade.

"From that time on," Kurosawa later wrote, ". . . I somehow found myself hurrying to school in anticipation on the days when we had art classes. . . . I became really good at

Sources of biographical information about Akira Kurosawa are Goodwin (1994), Kurosawa (1983), and Richie (1984).

Educating Children
with Special Needs

Second-Language Education
Children with, Learning Problems
Gifted Children

BOXES

drawing. At the same time my marks in other subjects suddenly began to improve. By the time Mr. Tachikawa left . . . , I was the president of my class, wearing a little gold badge with a purple ribbon on my chest" (1983, p. 13).

Academically, his performance was uneven: The best in his class in the subjects he liked, he did barely passable work in science and math. Still, he graduated as valedictorian. According to former classmate Uekusa Keinosuke, who became a scriptwriting colleague, "He certainly was not the little-genius type who merely gets good grades" but a "commanding" figure who became popular seemingly without effort (Richie, 1984, p. 10).

It was Mr. Tachikawa who introduced Akira to the fine arts and to film. Akira's father and his older brother Heigo discussed great literature with him and took him to Japanese vaudeville and Western movies.

Even after Mr. Tachikawa left the school, Akira and his friend Uekusa would go to the teacher's home and sit around talking for hours. So strong was Akira's spirit by this time that when Mr. Tachikawa's conservative successor lambasted one of his paintings, the boy simply made up his mind to "work so hard that this teacher would never be able to criticize me again" (Kurosawa, 1983, p. 25).

● ● ●

We can learn several lessons from Akira Kurosawa's school experience. First, children—even highly gifted ones—develop at different rates. Second, Kurosawa's story illustrates the strong impact a teacher can have and how the influences of home and school interact. Third, we see once again the tie-in between cognitive and psychosocial development. The flowering of Kurosawa's cognitive and social competence followed closely after Mr. Tachikawa's move to boost his self-esteem. As Kurosawa later wrote, "When someone is told over and over again that he's no good at something, he loses more and more confidence and eventually does become poor at it. Conversely, if he's told he's good at something, his confidence builds and he actually becomes better at it" (1983, p. 40).

School is a major formative experience in middle childhood, impinging on every aspect of development. Children typically gain in self-confidence as they read, think, talk, play, and imagine in ways that were well beyond them only a few years before.

In this chapter we examine cognitive advances during the first 5 or 6 years of formal schooling, from about age 6 to 11. Entry into Piaget's stage of concrete operations enables children to think logically and to make more mature moral judgments. As children improve in memory and problem solving, intelligence tests become more accurate in predicting school performance. The abilities to read and write open the door to a wider world. We discuss all these changes, and we look at controversies over IQ testing, bilingual education, homework, and mathematics instruction. Finally, we examine influences on school achievement and how schools try to meet special educational needs.

After you have read and studied this chapter, you should be able to answer each of the Guidepost questions on the following page. Look for them again in the margins throughout the chapter, where they point to important concepts. To check your understanding of these Guideposts, review the end-of-chapter summary. Checkpoints located throughout the chapter will help you verify your understanding of what you have read.

Guideposts for Study

1. How do school-age children's thinking and moral reasoning differ from those of younger children?

2. What advances in information-processing skills occur during middle childhood?

3. How accurately can schoolchildren's intelligence be measured?

4. How do communicative abilities expand during middle childhood?

5. What factors influence school achievement?

6. How do schools meet special needs?

Piagetian Approach: The Concrete Operational Child

At about age 7, according to Piaget, children enter the stage of **concrete operations** when they can use mental operations to solve concrete (actual) problems. Children now can think logically because they can take multiple aspects of a situation into account. However, their thinking is still limited to real situations in the here and now.

Cognitive Advances

Children in the stage of concrete operations can perform many tasks at a much higher level than they could in the preoperational stage (Table 13-1). They have a better understanding

Guidepost 1

How do school-age children's thinking and moral reasoning differ from those of younger children?

concrete operations Third stage of Piagetian cognitive development (approximately from age 7 to 12), during which children develop logical but not abstract thinking.

Table 13-1	Advances in Selected Cognitive Abilities during Middle Childhood
Ability	**Example**
Spatial thinking	Danielle can use a map or model to help her search for a hidden object and can give someone else directions for finding the object. She can find her way to and from school, can estimate distances, and can judge how long it will take her to go from one place to another.
Cause and effect	Douglas knows which physical attributes of objects on each side of a balance scale will affect the result (i.e., number of objects matters but color does not). He does not yet know which spatial factors, such as position and placement of the objects, make a difference.
Categorization	Elena can sort objects into categories, such as shape, color, or both. She knows that a subclass (roses) has fewer members than the class of which it is a part (flowers).
Seriation and transitive inference	Catherine can arrange a group of sticks in order, from the shortest to the longest, and can insert an intermediate-size stick into the proper place. She knows that if one stick is longer than a second stick, and the second stick is longer than a third, then the first stick is longer than the third.
Inductive and deductive reasoning	Dominic can solve both inductive and deductive problems and knows that inductive conclusions (based on particular premises) are less certain than deductive ones (based on general premises).
Conservation	Felipe, at age 7, knows that if a clay ball is rolled into a sausage, it still contains the same amount of clay (conservation of substance). At age 9, he knows that the ball and the sausage weigh the same. Not until early adolescence will he understand that they displace the same amount of liquid if dropped in a glass of water.
Number and mathematics	Kevin can count in his head, can add by counting up from the smaller number, and can do simple story problems.

of spatial concepts, causality, categorization, inductive and deductive reasoning, conservation, and number.

Space and Causality

Why can many 6- or 7-year-olds find their way to and from school, whereas most younger children cannot? One reason is that children in the stage of concrete operations can better understand spatial relationships. They have a clearer idea of how far it is from one place to another and how long it will take to get there, and they can more easily remember the route and the landmarks along the way. Experience plays a role in this development: A child who walks to school becomes more familiar with the neighborhood.

Both the ability to understand maps and models and the ability to communicate spatial information improve with age (Gauvain, 1993). So do judgments about cause and effect. When 5- to 12-year-olds were asked to predict how levers and balance scales would perform under varying conditions, the older children gave more correct answers. Children understood the influence of physical attributes (the number of objects on each side of a scale) earlier than they recognized the influence of spatial factors (the distance of objects from the center of the scale) (Amsel, Goodman, Savoie, & Clark, 1996).

Categorization

The ability to categorize helps children think logically. Categorization includes such relatively sophisticated abilities as *seriation, transitive inference,* and *class inclusion,* which improve gradually between early and middle childhood. Children show that they understand **seriation** when they can arrange objects in a series according to one or more dimensions, such as length (shortest to longest) or color (lightest to darkest). By 7 or 8, children can grasp the relationships among a group of sticks on sight and arrange them in order of size (Piaget, 1952).

Transitive inference is the ability to infer a relationship between two objects from the relationship between each of them and a third object. Catherine is shown three sticks: a yellow one, a green one, and a blue one. She is shown that the yellow stick is longer than the green one, and the green one is longer than the blue. Without physically comparing the yellow and blue sticks, she immediately says that the yellow one is longer than the blue one (Chapman & Lindenberger, 1988; Piaget & Inhelder, 1967).

Class inclusion is the ability to see the relationship between a whole and its parts. Piaget (1964) showed preoperational children a bunch of 10 flowers—7 roses and 3 carnations—and asked whether there were more roses or more flowers. The children tended to say there were more roses because they were comparing the roses with the carnations rather than with the whole bunch. Not until age 7 or 8, and sometimes not even then, do children consistently reason that roses are a subclass of flowers and that, therefore, there cannot be more roses than flowers (Flavell, 1963; Flavell et al., 2002). However, even 3-year-olds show a rudimentary awareness of class inclusion, depending on the type of task, the practical cues they receive, and their familiarity with the categories of objects they are tested on (Johnson, Scott, & Mervis, 1997).

Inductive and Deductive Reasoning

According to Piaget, children in the stage of concrete operations use only **inductive reasoning.** Starting with observations about particular members of a class of people, animals, objects, or events, they draw general conclusions about the class as a whole. ("My dog barks. So does Terry's dog and Melissa's dog. So it looks as if all dogs bark.") Inductive conclusions must be tentative because it is always possible to come across new information (a dog that does not bark) that does not support the conclusion.

Deductive reasoning, which Piaget believed does not develop until adolescence, starts with a general statement (premise) about a class and applies it to particular members of the

seriation Ability to order items along a dimension.

transitive inference Understanding of the relationship between two objects by knowing the relationship of each to a third object.

class inclusion Understanding of the relationship between a whole and its parts.

inductive reasoning Type of logical reasoning that moves from particular observations about members of a class to a general conclusion about that class.

deductive reasoning Type of logical reasoning that moves from a general premise about a class to a conclusion about a particular member or members of the class.

class. If the premise is true of the whole class and the reasoning is sound, then the conclusion must be true: "All dogs bark. Spot is a dog. Spot barks."

Researchers gave 16 inductive and deductive problems to 16 kindergartners, 17 second graders, 16 fourth graders, and 17 sixth graders. The problems were designed so as to not call on knowledge of the real world. For example, one deductive problem was "All poggops wear blue boots. Tombor is a poggop. Does Tombor wear blue boots?" The corresponding inductive problem was "Tombor is a poggop. Tombor wears blue boots. Do all poggops wear blue boots?" Contrary to Piagetian theory, second graders (but not kindergartners) were able to answer both kinds of problems correctly (Galotti, Komatsu, & Voelz, 1997).

Conservation

In solving various types of conservation problems (refer back to Chapter 10), children in the stage of concrete operations can work out the answers in their heads; they do not have to measure or weigh objects.

If one of two identical clay balls is rolled or kneaded into a different shape—say, a long, thin sausage—Felipe, who is in the stage of concrete operations, will say that the ball and the sausage still contain the same amount of clay. Stacy, who is in the preoperational stage, is deceived by appearances. She says the long, thin roll contains more clay because it is longer.

Felipe, unlike Stacy, understands the principle of *identity:* he knows the clay is still the same clay even though it has a different shape. He also understands the principle of *reversibility:* he knows he can change the sausage back into a ball. And he can *decenter:* he can focus on both length and width. He recognizes that although the ball is shorter than the sausage, it is also thicker. Stacy centers on one dimension (length) while excluding the other (thickness).

Typically, children can solve problems involving conservation of substance, like this one, by about age 7 or 8. However, in tasks involving conservation of weight—in which they are asked, for example, whether the ball and the sausage weigh the same—children typically do not give correct answers until about age 9 or 10. In tasks involving conservation of volume—in which children must judge whether the sausage and the ball displace an equal amount of liquid when placed in a glass of water—correct answers are rare before age 12. Piaget's term for this inconsistency in the development of different types of conservation is **horizontal décalage.** Children's thinking at this stage is so concrete, so closely tied to a particular situation, that they cannot readily transfer what they have learned about one type of conservation to another type, even though the underlying principles are the same.

Number and Mathematics

By age 6 or 7, many children can count in their heads. They also learn to *count on:* to add 5 and 3, they start counting at 5 and then go on to 6, 7, and 8 to add the 3. It may take 2 or 3 more years for them to perform a comparable operation for subtraction, but by age 9 most children can either count up from the smaller number or down from the larger number to get the answer (Resnick, 1989).

Children also become more adept at solving simple story problems, such as "Pedro went to the store with $5 and spent $2 on candy. How much did he have left?" When the original amount is unknown ("Pedro went to the store, spent $2 and had $3 left. How much did he start out with?"), the problem is harder because the operation needed to solve it (addition) is not as clearly indicated. Few children can solve this kind of problem before age 8 or 9 (Resnick, 1989).

Research with minimally schooled people in developing countries suggests that children learn to add and subtract through concrete experience in a cultural context (Guberman, 1996; Resnick, 1989). These intuitive procedures are different from those taught in school. In a study of Brazilian street vendors ages 9 to 15, a researcher acting as a customer said, "I'll take two coconuts." Each one cost 40 cruzeiros; she paid with a 500-cruzeiros bill and

What's your view

- How can parents and teachers help children improve their reasoning ability?

horizontal décalage Piaget's term for inability to transfer learning about one type of conservation to other types, which causes a child to master different types of conservation tasks at different ages.

According to Piaget, children develop concepts of fairness through interaction with peers, often in games with rules, such as this three-legged race. As children grow older, they realize that rules need not be externally imposed but can be changed by mutual agreement.

asked, "What do I get back?" The child counted up from 80: "Eighty, 90, 100, . . . " and gave the customer 420 cruzeiros. However, when this same child was given a similar problem in the classroom ("What is 500 minus 80?"), he arrived at the wrong answer by incorrectly using a series of steps learned in school (Carraher, Schliemann, & Carraher, 1988). This observation suggests that teaching math through concrete applications may be more effective than teaching abstract rules,.

Some intuitive understanding of fractions seems to exist by age 4, as children show when they distribute portions of pizza (Mix, Levine, & Huttenlocher, 1999; Sophian, Garyantes, & Chang, 1997). Young children tend not to think about the quantity a fraction represents; instead, they focus on the numerals that make it up. Thus, they may say that ½ plus ⅓ equals ⅖. Also difficult for many children to grasp at first is the fact that ½ is bigger than ¼ —that the smaller fraction (¼) has the larger denominator (Siegler, 1998; Sophian & Wood, 1997).

The ability to estimate progresses with age. When asked to place 24 numbers along a line from 0 to 100, almost all kindergartners exaggerate the distances between low numbers and minimize the distances between high numbers. Most second graders produce number lines that are more evenly spaced (Siegler & Booth, 2004). Second, fourth, and sixth graders show a similar progression in producing number lines from 0 to 1,000 (Siegler & Opfer, 2003), most likely reflecting the experience older children gain in dealing with larger numbers. Besides improving in *number line estimation,* school-age children also improve in three other types of estimation: *computational estimation,* such as estimating the sum in an addition problem; *numerosity estimation,* such as estimating the number of candies in a jar; and *measurement estimation,* such as estimating the length of a line (Booth & Siegler, 2006).

Checkpoint ✔

Can you . . .

✔ Identify six types of cognitive abilities that emerge or strengthen during middle childhood, and explain how?

✔ Name three principles that help school-aged children understand conservation, and explain why children master different kinds of conservation at different ages?

✔ Give examples of how neurological development and schooling can affect ability to perform Piagetian tasks?

Influences of Neurological Development and Schooling

Piaget maintained that the shift from the rigid, illogical thinking of younger children to the flexible, logical thinking of older children depends on both neurological development and experience in adapting to the environment. Support for a neurological influence comes from scalp measurements of brain activity during a conservation task. Children who had achieved conservation of volume had different brain wave patterns from those who had not yet achieved it, suggesting that they may have been using different brain regions for the task (Stauder, Molenaar, & Van der Molen, 1993).

Today's schoolchildren may not be advancing through Piaget's stages as rapidly as their parents did. When 10,000 British 11- and 12-year-olds were tested on conservation of volume and weight, their performance was 2 to 3 years behind that of their counterparts 30 years earlier (Shayer, Ginsburg, & Coe, 2007). These results suggest that today's schoolchildren may be getting too much drilling on the three Rs and not enough hands-on experience with the way materials behave.

Moral Reasoning

To draw out children's moral thinking, Piaget (1932) would tell them a story about two little boys: "One day Augustus noticed that his father's inkpot was empty and decided to help his father by filling it. While he was opening the bottle, he spilled a lot of ink on the tablecloth. The other boy, Julian, played with his father's inkpot and spilled a little ink on the cloth." Then Piaget would ask, "Which boy was naughtier, and why?" Children younger than 7 usually considered Augustus naughtier, since he made the bigger stain. Older children recognized that Augustus meant well and made the large stain by accident, whereas Julian made a small stain while doing something he should not have been doing. Immature moral judgments, Piaget concluded, center only on the degree of offense; more mature judgments consider intent.

Piaget (1932; Piaget & Inhelder, 1969) proposed that moral reasoning develops in three stages. Children move gradually from one stage to another, at varying ages.

The first stage (around ages 2 to 7, corresponding with the preoperational stage) is based on *rigid obedience to authority*. Because young children are egocentric, they cannot imagine more than one way of looking at a moral issue. They believe that rules cannot be bent or changed, that behavior is either right or wrong, and that any offense (like Augustus's) deserves punishment, regardless of intent.

The second stage (around ages 7 to 11, corresponding with the stage of concrete operations) is characterized by *increasing flexibility*. As children interact with more people and come into contact with a wider range of viewpoints, they begin to discard the idea that there is a single, absolute standard of right and wrong and to develop their own sense of justice based on fairness or equal treatment for all. Because they can consider more than one aspect of a situation, they can make more subtle moral judgments, such as taking into consideration the intent behind Augustus's and Julian's behavior.

Around age 11 or 12, when children may become capable of formal reasoning, the third stage of moral development arrives. The belief that everyone should be treated alike gives way to the ideal of *equity*, of taking specific circumstances into account. Thus, a child of this age might say that a 2-year-old who spilled ink on the tablecloth should be held to a less demanding moral standard than a 10-year-old who did the same thing.

We discuss Lawrence Kohlberg's theory of moral reasoning, which builds on Piaget's, in Chapter 16.

What's your view

- Do you agree that intent is an important factor in morality?
- How does the criminal justice system reflect this view?

Checkpoint ✔

Can you . . .

✔ Describe Piaget's three stages of moral development and explain their links to cognitive maturation?

Information-Processing Approach: Attention, Memory, and Planning

Guidepost 2

What advances in information-processing skills occur during middle childhood?

As children move through the school years, they make steady progress in the abilities to regulate and sustain attention, process and retain information, and plan and monitor their own behavior. All of these interrelated developments are central to **executive function,** the conscious control of thoughts, emotions, and actions to accomplish goals or solve problems (Luna et al., 2004; NICHD Early Child Care Research Network, 2005d; Zelazo & Müller, 2002). As their knowledge expands, children become more aware of what kinds of information are important to pay attention to and remember. School-age children also understand more about how memory works, and this knowledge enables them to plan and use strategies, or deliberate techniques, to help them remember.

executive function Conscious control of thoughts, emotions, and actions to accomplish goals or solve problems.

How Do Executive Skills Develop?

The gradual development of executive function from infancy through adolescence accompanies the development of the brain, in particular, the *prefrontal cortex,* the region that enables planning, judgment, and decision making (Lamm, Zelazo, & Lewis, 2006). As unneeded synapses are pruned away and pathways become myelinated, *processing speed*—usually measured by reaction time—improves dramatically, especially in girls (Camarata & Woodcock, 2006; Luna, Garver, Urban, Lazar, & Sweeney, 2004). Faster, more efficient processing increases the amount of information children can keep in working memory, enabling complex thinking and goal-directed planning (Flavell et al., 2002; Luna et al., 2004).

The home environment, too, contributes to the development of executive skills. In a longitudinal study of 700 children from infancy on, the quality of the family environment, especially between ages 4½ and 6—including such factors as available resources, cognitive stimulation, and maternal sensitivity—predicted attentional and memory performance in first grade (NICHD Early Child Care Research Network, 2005d).

School-age children develop planning skills by making decisions about their everyday activities. Parenting practices and culture affect the pace at which children are allowed to do this. In a 3-year longitudinal study of 79 European American and 61 Latino children in a southwestern U.S. city, the responsibility for planning children's informal activities gradually shifted between second and fourth grades from parent to child, and this change was reflected in improved ability to plan classroom work. This shift occurred at an earlier age for European American children than for Latino children. More acculturated Latino parents let boys (but not girls) plan their own activities earlier than did nonacculturated Latino parents (Gauvain & Perez, 2005).

Selective Attention

School-age children can concentrate longer than younger children and can focus on the information they need and want while screening out irrelevant information. For example, they can summon up from memory the appropriate meaning of a word and suppress other meanings that do not fit the context. Fifth graders are better able than first graders to keep unwanted information from reentering working memory and vying with other material for attention (Harnishfeger & Pope, 1996). This growth in *selective attention*—the ability to deliberately direct one's attention and shut out distractions—may hinge on the executive skill of *inhibitory control,* the voluntary suppression of unwanted responses (Luna et al., 2004).

The increasing capacity for selective attention is believed to be due to neurological maturation and is one of the reasons memory improves during middle childhood (Bjorklund & Harnishfeger, 1990; Harnishfeger & Bjorklund, 1993). Older children may make fewer mistakes in recall than younger children because they are better able to select what they want to remember and what they can forget (Lorsbach & Reimer, 1997).

Working Memory Span

The efficiency of working memory increases greatly in middle childhood, laying the foundation for a wide range of cognitive skills. What changes produce that vast improvement? In one study, 120 British 6- to 10-year-olds were asked to perform complex memory span tasks involving computerized visual and verbal images. Improvements both in processing speed and in storage capacity were found to underlie the development of working memory in this age group (Bayliss, Jarrod, Baddeley, Gunn, & Leigh, 2005).

Metamemory: Understanding Memory

metamemory Understanding of processes of memory.

Between ages 5 and 7, the brain's frontal lobes undergo significant development and reorganization. These changes may make possible improved **metamemory,** knowledge about the processes of memory (Janowsky & Carper, 1996).

From kindergarten through fifth grade, children advance steadily in understanding memory (Flavell et al., 2002; Kreutzer, Leonard, & Flavell, 1975). Kindergartners and first graders know that people remember better if they study longer, that people forget things with time, and that relearning something is easier than learning it for the first time. By third grade, children know that some people remember better than others and that some things are easier to remember than others.

Mnemonics: Strategies for Remembering

mnemonic strategies Techniques to aid memory.

Devices to aid memory are called **mnemonic strategies.** The most common mnemonic strategy among both children and adults is use of *external memory aids.* Other common mnemonic strategies are *rehearsal, organization,* and *elaboration.*

Contestants in a spelling bee can make good use of mnemonic strategies—devices to aid memory—such as rehearsal (repetition), organization, and elaboration.

Writing down a telephone number, making a list, setting a timer, and putting a library book by the front door are examples of **external memory aids:** prompts by something outside the person. Saying a telephone number over and over after looking it up, so as not to forget it before dialing, is a form of **rehearsal,** or conscious repetition. **Organization** is mentally placing information into categories (such as animals, furniture, vehicles, and clothing) to make it easier to recall. In **elaboration,** children associate items with something else, such as an imagined scene or story. To remember to buy lemons, ketchup, and napkins, for example, a child might imagine a ketchup bottle balanced on a lemon, with a pile of napkins handy to wipe up spilled ketchup.

As children grow older, they develop better strategies, use them more effectively, and tailor them to meet specific needs (Bjorklund, 1997; Table 13-2). When taught to use a strategy, older children are more likely to apply it spontaneously to other situations (Flavell et al., 2002). Children often use more than one strategy for a task and choose different kinds of strategies for different problems (Coyle & Bjorklund, 1997).

Information Processing and Piagetian Tasks

Improvements in information processing may help explain the advances Piaget described. For example, 9-year-olds may be better able than 5-year-olds to find their way to and from school because they can scan a scene, take in its important features, and remember objects in context in the order in which they were encountered (Allen & Ondracek, 1995).

Improvements in memory may contribute to the mastery of conservation tasks. Young children's working memory is so limited that they may not be able to remember all the relevant information (Siegler & Richards, 1982). They may forget, for example, that two differently shaped pieces of clay were originally identical. Gains in working memory may enable older children to solve such problems.

Robbie Case (1985, 1992), a neo-Piagetian theorist, suggested that as a child's application of a concept or scheme becomes more automatic, it frees space in working memory to deal with new information. This may help explain horizontal décalage: Children may need to be able to use one type of conservation without conscious thought before they can extend that scheme to other types of conservation.

external memory aids Mnemonic strategies using something outside the person.

rehearsal Mnemonic strategy to keep an item in working memory through conscious repetition.

organization Mnemonic strategy of categorizing material to be remembered.

elaboration Mnemonic strategy of making mental associations involving items to be remembered.

Checkpoint ✔

Can you . . .

✔ Identify at least three specific ways in which information processing improves during middle childhood?

✔ Name four common mnemonic aids?

✔ Tell of how improved information processing helps explain advances Piaget described?

Table 13-2	Four Common Memory Strategies		
Strategy	**Definition**	**Development in Middle Childhood**	**Example**
External memory aids	Prompting by something outside the person	5- and 6-year-olds can do this, but 8-year-olds are more likely to think of it.	Dana makes a list of the things she has to do today.
Rehearsal	Conscious repetition	6-year-olds can be taught to do this; 7-year-olds do it spontaneously.	Ian says the letters in his spelling words over and over until he knows them.
Organization	Grouping by categories	Most children do not do this until at least age 10, but younger children can be taught to do it.	Luis recalls the animals he saw in the zoo by thinking first of the mammals, then the reptiles, then the amphibians, then the fish, and then the birds.
Elaboration	Associating items to be remembered with something else, such as a phrase, scene, or story	Older children are more likely to do this spontaneously and remember better if they make up their own elaboration; younger children remember better if someone else makes it up.	Yolanda remembers the lines of the musical staff (E, G, B, D, F) by associating them with the phrase "*Every good boy does fine.*"

Guidepost 3

How accurately can schoolchildren's intelligence be measured?

Wechsler Intelligence Scale for Children (WISC-III) Individual intelligence test for schoolchildren that yields verbal and performance scores as well as a combined score.

Otis-Lennon School Ability Test (OLSAT8) Group intelligence test for kindergarten through twelfth grade.

Psychometric Approach: Assessment of Intelligence

Schoolchildren's intelligence may be measured by either individual or group tests. The most widely used individual test is the **Wechsler Intelligence Scale for Children (WISC-III).** This test for ages 6 through 16 measures verbal and performance abilities, yielding separate scores for each as well as a total score. The separate subtest scores pinpoint a child's strengths and help diagnose specific problems. For example, if a child does well on verbal tests (such as general information and basic arithmetic operations) but poorly on performance tests (such as doing a puzzle or drawing the missing part of a picture), the child may be slow in perceptual or motor development. A child who does well on performance tests but poorly on verbal tests may have a language problem. Another commonly used individual test is the Stanford-Binet Intelligence Scale, described in Chapter 10.

A popular group test, the **Otis-Lennon School Ability Test (OLSAT8),** has levels for kindergarten through twelfth grade. Children are asked to classify items, show an understanding of verbal and numerical concepts, display general information, and follow directions. Separate scores for verbal comprehension, verbal reasoning, pictorial reasoning, figural reasoning, and quantitative reasoning can identify strengths and weaknesses.

The IQ Controversy

The use of psychometric intelligence tests is controversial. On the positive side, because IQ tests have been standardized and widely used, there is extensive information about their norms, validity, and reliability (refer back to Chapter 2). IQ scores taken during middle childhood are fairly good predictors of school achievement, especially for highly verbal children, and scores are more reliable than during the preschool years. IQ at age 11 even has been found to predict length of life, functional independence late in life, and the presence or absence of dementia (Starr, Deary, Lemmon, & Whalley, 2000; Whalley & Deary, 2001; Whalley et al., 2000).

On the other hand, critics claim that the tests underestimate the intelligence of children who are in ill health or, for one reason or another, do not do well on tests (Anastasi, 1988; Ceci, 1991; Sternberg, 2004). Because the tests are timed, they equate intelligence with speed and penalize a child who works slowly and deliberately. Their appropriateness for diagnosing learning disabilities has been questioned (Benson, 2003).

A more fundamental criticism is that IQ tests do not directly measure native ability; instead, they *infer* intelligence from what children already know. As we'll see, it is virtually impossible to design a test that requires no prior knowledge. Further, the tests are validated against measures of achievement, such as school performance, which are affected by such factors as schooling and culture (Sternberg, 2004, 2005). As we will discuss in a subsequent section, there is also controversy over whether intelligence is a single, general ability or whether there are types of intelligence not captured by IQ tests. For these and other reasons, there is strong disagreement over how accurately these tests assess children's intelligence.

Influences on Intelligence

As we discussed in Chapter 3, both heredity and environment influence intelligence. Keeping in mind the controversy over whether IQ tests actually measure intelligence, let's look more closely at these influences.

Genes and Brain Development

Brain imaging research shows a moderate correlation between brain size or amount of gray matter and general intelligence, especially reasoning and problem solving abilities (Gray & Thompson, 2004). One study found that the amount of gray matter in the frontal cortex is largely inherited, varies widely among individuals, and is linked with differences in IQ (Thompson, Cannon, et al., 2001). A later study suggests that the key is not the *amount* of gray matter a child has at a certain age, but rather the *pattern of development* of the prefrontal cortex, the seat of executive function and higher-level thinking. In children of average IQ, the prefrontal cortex is relatively thick at age 7, peaks in thickness by age 8, and then gradually thins as unneeded connections are pruned. In the most intelligent 7-year-olds, by the cortex does not peak in thickness until age 11 or 12. The prolonged thickening of the prefrontal cortex may represent an extended critical period for developing high-level thinking circuits (Shaw et al., 2006).

Although reasoning, problem solving, and executive function are linked to the prefrontal cortex, other brain regions under strong genetic influence contribute to intelligent behavior. So does the speed and reliability of transmission of messages in the brain. Environmental factors, such as the family, schooling, and culture, also play a part; but heritability of intelligence (the degree to which individual differences in intelligence are genetically caused) increases with age as children select or create environments that fit their genetic tendencies (Gray & Thompson, 2004).

Influence of Schooling on IQ

Schooling seems to increase tested intelligence (Ceci & Williams, 1997; Neisser et al., 1996). Children whose school entrance was significantly delayed—as happened, for example, in South Africa due to a teacher shortage and in the Netherlands during the Nazi occupation—lost as many as 5 IQ points each year, and some of these losses were never recovered (Ceci & Williams, 1997).

IQ scores also drop during summer vacation (Ceci & Williams, 1997). Among a national sample of 1,500 children, language, spatial, and conceptual scores improved much more between October and April, the bulk of the school year, than between April and

October, which includes summer vacation and the beginning and end of the school year (Huttenlocher, Levine, & Vevea, 1998).

Influences of Race/Ethnicity on IQ

Average test scores vary among racial/ethnic groups, inspiring claims that the tests are unfair to minorities. Although some blacks score higher than most whites, black children, on average, historically scored about 15 points lower than white children and showed a comparable lag on school achievement tests (Neisser et al., 1996). However, those gaps have narrowed in recent years—as much as 4 to 7 IQ points (Dickens & Flynn, 2006). Average IQ scores of Hispanic children fall between those of black and white children, and their scores, too, tend to predict school achievement (Neisser et al., 1996).

What accounts for these racial/ethnic differences in IQ? Some writers have argued for a substantial genetic factor (Herrnstein & Murray, 1994; Jensen, 1969; Rushton & Jensen, 2005). But although there is strong evidence of a genetic influence on *individual* differences in intelligence, there is no direct evidence that differences among ethnic, cultural, or racial groups are hereditary (Gray & Thompson, 2004; Neisser et al., 1996; Sternberg et al., 2005). Instead, many studies attribute ethnic differences in IQ largely or entirely to inequalities in environment (Nisbett, 1998, 2005)—in income, nutrition, living conditions, health, parenting practices, early child care, intellectual stimulation, schooling, culture, or other circumstances such as the effects of oppression and discrimination that can affect self-esteem, motivation, and academic performance. Environmental differences also affect readiness for school (Rouse et al., 2005), which, in turn, affects measured intelligence as well as achievement.

The recent narrowing of the gap between white and black children's test scores parallels an improvement in the life circumstances and educational opportunities of many black children (Nisbett, 2005). In addition, as we discussed in Chapter 7, some early intervention programs have had significant success in raising disadvantaged children's IQs (Nisbett, 2005).

The strength of genetic influence itself appears to vary with socioeconomic status. In a longitudinal study of 319 pairs of twins followed from birth, the genetic influence on IQ scores at age 7 among children from impoverished families was close to zero and the influence of environment was strong, whereas among children in affluent families the opposite was true. In other words, high SES strengthens genetic influence, whereas low SES tends to override it (Turkheimer, Haley, Waldron, D'Onofrio, & Gottesman, 2003). Still, although socioeconomic status and IQ are strongly related, SES does not seem to explain the entire intergroup variance in IQ (Neisser et al., 1996; Suzuki & Valencia, 1997).

What about Asian Americans, whose scholastic achievements consistently outstrip those of other ethnic groups? Although there is some controversy about their relative performance on intelligence tests, most researchers find that they do *not* seem to have a significant edge in IQ (Neisser et al., 1996). Instead, Asian American children's strong scholastic achievement seems to be best explained by their culture's emphasis on obedience and respect for elders, the supreme importance Asian American parents place on education as a route to upward mobility, and the devotion of Asian American students to homework and study (Chao, 1994, 1996; Fuligni & Stevenson, 1995; Huntsinger & Jose, 1995; Stevenson, 1995; Stevenson, Chen, & Lee, 1993; Stevenson, Lee, Chen, & Lummis, 1990; Stevenson, Lee, Chen, Stigler, et al., 1990; Sue & Okazaki, 1990).

Influence of Culture on IQ

cultural bias Tendency of intelligence tests to include items calling for knowledge or skills more familiar or meaningful to some cultural groups than to others.

Some critics of IQ tests attribute ethnic differences in IQ to **cultural bias:** a tendency to include questions that use vocabulary or call for information or skills more familiar to some cultural groups than to others (Sternberg, 1985, 1987). These critics argue that intelligence tests are built around the dominant thinking style and language of white people of European ancestry, putting minority children at a disadvantage (Heath, 1989; Helms, 1992). However, controlled studies have failed to show that cultural bias contributes substantially to overall group differences in IQ (Neisser et al., 1996).

Test developers have tried to design **culture-free** tests—tests with no culture-linked content—by posing tasks that do not require language, such as tracing mazes, putting the right shapes in the right holes, and completing pictures; but they have been unable to eliminate all cultural influences. Test designers also have found it virtually impossible to produce **culture-fair** tests consisting only of experiences common to people in various cultures.

Robert Sternberg (2004) maintains that intelligence and culture are inextricably linked. Behavior seen as intelligent in one culture may be viewed as foolish in another. For example, when given a sorting task, North Americans would be likely to place a robin under the category of birds, whereas the Kpelle people in North Africa would consider it more intelligent to place the robin in the functional category of flying things (Cole, 1998). Thus a test of intelligence developed in one culture may not be equally valid in another. Furthermore, the schooling offered in a culture may prepare a child to do well in certain tasks and not in others, and the competencies taught and tested in school are not necessarily the same as the practical skills needed to succeed in everyday life (Sternberg, 2004, 2005).

Sternberg (2004) defines *successful intelligence* as the skills and knowledge needed for success within a particular social and cultural context. The mental processes that underlie intelligence may be the same across cultures, says Sternberg, but their products may be different—and so should the means of assessing performance. Sternberg proposes **culture-relevant** tests that take into account the adaptive tasks that confront children in particular cultures.

According to Howard Gardner, musical ability—which includes the ability to perceive and create patterns of pitch and rhythm—is one of eight separate kinds of intelligence.

Is There More Than One Intelligence?

As we have mentioned, a serious criticism of IQ tests is that they focus almost entirely on abilities used in school. They do not cover other important aspects of intelligent behavior, such as common sense, social skills, creative insight, and self-knowledge. Yet these abilities, in which some children with modest academic skills excel, may become equally or more important in later life and may even be considered separate forms of intelligence. Two of the chief advocates of this position are Howard Gardner and Robert Sternberg.

Gardner's Theory of Multiple Intelligences

Is a child who is good at analyzing paragraphs and making analogies more intelligent than one who can play a challenging violin solo or organize a closet or pitch a curve ball at the right time? The answer is no, according to Gardner's (1993) **theory of multiple intelligences.**

Gardner, a neuropsychologist and educational researcher at Harvard University, originally identified seven distinct kinds of intelligence. According to Gardner, conventional intelligence tests tap only three "intelligences": linguistic, logical-mathematical, and, to some extent, spatial. The other four, which are not reflected in IQ scores, are musical, bodily-kinesthetic, interpersonal, and intrapersonal. Gardner (1998) recently added an eighth intelligence, naturalist, to his original list. (Table 13-3 gives definitions of each intelligence and examples of fields in which it is most useful.)

High intelligence in one area does not necessarily accompany high intelligence in any of the others. A person may be extremely gifted in art (a spatial ability), precision of movement (bodily-kinesthetic), social relations (interpersonal), or self-understanding (intrapersonal), but not have a high IQ. Thus Akiru Kurosawa, the painter Mary Cassatt, and the cellist Pablo Casals may have been equally intelligent, each in a different area.

Checkpoint ✔

Can you . . .

✔ Name and describe two traditional intelligence tests for schoolchildren?

✔ Discuss influences on measured intelligence and explanations that have been advanced for differences in the performance of children of various racial/ethnic and cultural groups?

culture-free Describing an intelligence test that, if it were possible to design, would have no culturally linked content.

culture-fair Describing an intelligence test that deals with experiences common to various cultures, in an attempt to avoid cultural bias.

culture-relevant Describing an intelligence test that takes into account the adaptive tasks children face in their culture.

theory of multiple intelligences Gardner's theory that each person has several distinct forms of intelligence.

Table 13-3	Eight Intelligences, according to Gardner	
Intelligence	Definition	Fields or Occupations Where Used
Linguistic	Ability to use and understand words and nuances of meaning	Writing, editing, translating
Logical-mathematical	Ability to manipulate numbers and solve logical problems	Science, business, medicine
Spatial	Ability to find one's way around in an environment and judge relationships between objects in space	Architecture, carpentry, city planning
Musical	Ability to perceive and create patterns of pitch and rhythm	Musical composition, conducting
Bodily-kinesthetic	Ability to move with precision	Dancing, athletics, surgery
Interpersonal	Ability to understand and communicate with others	Teaching, acting, politics
Intrapersonal	Ability to understand the self	Counseling, psychiatry, spiritual leadership
Naturalist	Ability to distinguish species and their characteristics	Hunting, fishing, farming, gardening, cooking

Source: Based on Gardner, 1993, 1998.

What's your view

- Which of Gardner's types of intelligence are you strongest in?
- Did your education include a focus on any of these aspects?

Gardner (1995) would assess each intelligence directly by observing its products—how well a child can tell a story, remember a melody, or get around in a strange area—and not by standardized tests. To monitor spatial ability, for example, the examiner might hide an object from a 1-year-old, ask a 6-year-old to do a jigsaw puzzle, and give a Rubik's cube to a preadolescent. The purpose would be, not to compare individuals, but to reveal strengths and weaknesses so as to help children realize their potential. Of course, such assessments would be far more time-consuming and more open to observer bias than paper-and-pencil tests.

Sternberg's Triarchic Theory of Intelligence

Sternberg's (1985, 2004) **triarchic theory of intelligence** identifies three elements, or aspects, of intelligence: *componential, experiential,* and *contextual.*

- The **componential element** is the *analytic* aspect of intelligence; it determines how efficiently people process information. It tells people how to solve problems, how to monitor solutions, and how to evaluate the results.
- The **experiential element** is *insightful* or *creative;* it determines how people approach novel or familiar tasks. It allows people to compare new information with what they already know and to come up with new ways of putting facts together— in other words, to think originally.
- The **contextual element** is *practical;* it determines how people deal with their environment. It is the ability to size up a situation and decide what to do: adapt to it, change it, or get out of it.

According to Sternberg, everyone has these three kinds of abilities to a greater or lesser extent. A person may be strong in one, two, or all three.

Conventional IQ tests measure mainly componential ability; and because this ability is the kind most school tasks require in Western societies, it's not surprising that the tests are fairly good predictors of school performance. Their failure to measure experiential (insightful or creative) and contextual (practical) intelligence, says Sternberg, may explain why they are less useful in predicting success in the outside world. In studies in Usenge, Kenya and among Yup'ik Eskimo children in southwestern Alaska, children's **tacit knowledge** of such practical matters as medicinal herbs, hunting, fishing, and preserving plants—information

triarchic theory of intelligence Sternberg's theory describing three types of intelligence: componential (analytical ability), experiential (insight and originality), and contextual (practical thinking).

componential element Sternberg's term for the analytic aspect of intelligence.

experiential element Sternberg's term for the insightful aspect of intelligence.

contextual element Sternberg's term for the practical aspect of intelligence.

tacit knowledge Sternberg's term for information that is not formally taught or openly expressed but is necessary to get ahead.

gleaned informally, not explicitly taught—showed no correlation with conventional measures of intelligence (Grigorenko et al., 2004; Sternberg, 2004; Sternberg et al., 2001).

The *Sternberg Triarchic Abilities Test (STAT)* (Sternberg, 1993) seeks to measure each of the three aspects of intelligence—analytic, creative, and practical—through multiple-choice and essay questions in three domains: *verbal, quantitative,* and *figural* (or spatial). For example, a test of practical-quantitative intelligence might be to solve an everyday math problem having to do with buying tickets to a ball game or following a recipe for making cookies. A creative-verbal item might ask children to solve deductive reasoning problems that start with factually false premises (such as, "Money falls off trees"). An analytical-figural item might ask children to identify the missing piece of a figure.

Validation studies have found correlations between the STAT and several other tests of critical thinking, creativity, and practical problem solving. As predicted, the three kinds of abilities are only weakly correlated with each other (Sternberg, 1997; Sternberg & Clinkenbeard, 1995).

New Directions in Intelligence Testing

The STAT is only one of several new directions in intelligence testing. Other new diagnostic and predictive tools are based on neurological research and information-processing theory. The second edition of the *Kaufman Assessment Battery for Children (K-ABC-II)* (Kaufman & Kaufman, 1983, 2003), an individual test for ages 3 to 18, is designed to evaluate diverse cognitive needs and abilities in children with autism, hearing impairments, and language disorders and from varying cultural and linguistic backgrounds. It has subtests that minimize verbal instructions and responses. It also has items with limited cultural content.

Dynamic tests based on Vygotsky's theories emphasize potential rather than present achievement. These tests, which seek to capture the dynamic nature of intelligence, offer an alternative to traditional static tests that measure a child's current abilities. Dynamic tests contain items up to 2 years above a child's current level of competence. Examiners help the child when necessary by asking leading questions, giving examples or demonstrations, and offering feedback; thus, the test itself is a learning situation. The difference between the items a child can answer alone and the items the child can answer with help is the child's zone of proximal development (ZPD) (refer back to Chapter 2).

By pointing to what a child is ready to learn, dynamic testing may give teachers more useful information than does a psychometric test and can aid in designing interventions to help children progress. It can be particularly effective with disadvantaged children and with children in non-Western cultures (Grigorenko & Sternberg, 1998; Rutland & Campbell, 1996; Sternberg, 2005). However, the ZPD has had little experimental validation (Grigorenko & Sternberg, 1998) and may be inherently difficult to measure precisely.

Despite such innovations, it seems likely that conventional psychometric intelligence tests will remain dominant for some time to come (Daniel, 1997). They are widely entrenched, heavily researched, and readily available; and their developers continue to respond to criticisms with each new revision, seeking to better reflect the abilities of children from various cultural and linguistic backgrounds. Rather than rely on a single score, competent practitioners assess *patterns* of performance along with clinical observations to provide a better picture of the whole child. The results can guide the development of appropriate teaching strategies for a particular child (Benson, 2003).

Checkpoint ✔

Can you . . .

✔ Compare Gardner's and Sternberg's theories, and name the specific abilities each proposed?

✔ Describe several new types of intelligence tests?

Language and Literacy

Guidepost 4

How do communicative abilities expand during middle childhood?

Language abilities continue to grow during middle childhood. Children become better able to understand and interpret oral and written communication and to make themselves understood.

Vocabulary, Grammar, and Syntax

As vocabulary grows during the school years, children use increasingly precise verbs (*hitting, slapping, striking, pounding*). They learn that a word like *run* can have more than

School-age children's use of language is more sophisticated than before. They are better able to tell stories and secrets and to make themselves understood.

one meaning, and they can tell from the context which meaning is intended. *Simile* and *metaphor,* figures of speech in which a word or phrase that usually designates one thing is compared or applied to another, become increasingly common (Owens, 1996; Vosniadou, 1987). Although grammar is quite complex by age 6, children during the early school years rarely use the passive voice (as in "The sidewalk is being shoveled"), verb tenses that include the auxiliary *have* ("I have already shoveled the sidewalk"), and conditional sentences ("If Barbara were home, she would help shovel the sidewalk") (Chomsky, 1969).

Children's understanding of rules of *syntax* (how words are organized into phrases and sentences) becomes more sophisticated with age (Chomsky, 1969). For example, most children under 5 or 6 years old think the sentences "John promised Bill to go shopping" and "John told Bill to go shopping" both mean that Bill is the one to go to the store. Many 6-year-olds have not yet learned how to interpret constructions such as the one in the first sentence, even though they know what a promise is and can use and understand the word correctly in other sentences. By age 8, most children can interpret the first sentence correctly, and by age 9 virtually all children can. They now look at the meaning of a sentence as a whole instead of focusing on word order alone.

Sentence structure continues to become more elaborate. Older children use more subordinate clauses ("The boy *who delivers the newspapers* rang the doorbell"). Still, some constructions, such as clauses beginning with *however* and *although,* do not become common until early adolescence (Owens, 1996).

Pragmatics: Knowledge about Communication*

pragmatics Practical knowledge needed to use language for communicative purposes.

The major area of linguistic growth during the school years is in **pragmatics:** the practical use of language to communicate. Pragmatics includes both conversational and narrative skills.

Good conversationalists probe by asking questions before introducing a topic with which the other person may not be familiar. They quickly recognize a breakdown in communication and do something to repair it. There are wide individual differences in such skills; some 7-year-olds are better conversationalists than some adults (Anderson, Clark, & Mullin, 1994). There also are gender differences. In one study, 120 middle-class London fourth graders worked in pairs to solve a mathematical problem. When boys and girls worked together, boys tended to use more controlling statements and to make more negative interruptions, whereas girls phrased their remarks in a more tentative, conciliatory way. Children's communication was more collaborative when working with a partner of their own sex (Leman, Ahmed, & Ozarow, 2005).

When first graders tell stories, they usually do not make them up; they are more likely to relate a personal experience. Most 6-year-olds can retell the plot of a short book, movie, or television show. They are beginning to describe motives and causal links. By second grade, children's stories become longer and more complex. Fictional tales often have conventional beginnings and endings ("Once upon a time . . . " and "They lived happily ever after," or simply "The end"). Word use is more varied than before, but characters do not show growth or change, and plots are not fully developed.

Older children usually begin the story with introductory information about the setting and characters, and they clearly indicate changes of time and place during the story. They

*This section is largely indebted to Owens (1996).

construct more complex episodes than younger children do, but with less unnecessary detail. They focus more on the characters' motives and thoughts, and they think through how to resolve problems in the plot.

Literacy

Learning to read and write frees children from the constraints of face-to-face communication. Now they have access to the ideas and imagination of people in faraway lands and long-ago times. Once children can translate the marks on a page into patterns of sound and meaning, they can develop increasingly sophisticated strategies to understand what they read. They also learn that they can use written words to express ideas, thoughts, and feelings.

Reading

Children can identify a printed word in two contrasting ways. One is called **decoding:** the child sounds out the word, translating it from print to speech before retrieving it from long-term memory. To do this, the child must master the phonetic code that matches the printed alphabet to spoken sounds. The second method is **visually based retrieval:** the child simply looks at the word and then retrieves it. The traditional approach, which emphasizes decoding, is called the **phonetic, or code emphasis, approach.** The more recent **whole-language approach** emphasizes visual retrieval and the use of contextual cues.

The whole-language approach is based on the belief that children can learn to read and write naturally, much as they learn to understand and use speech. Whole-language proponents assert that children learn to read with better comprehension and more enjoyment if they experience written language from the outset as a way to gain information and express ideas and feelings, not as a system of isolated sounds and syllables to be learned by memorization and drill. In contrast with the rigorous, teacher-directed tasks involved in phonics instruction, whole-language programs feature real literature and open-ended, student-initiated activities.

Despite the popularity of the whole-language approach, research has found little support for its claims. Critics say that whole-language teaching encourages children to skim through a text, guessing at words and their meanings without trying to correct reading or spelling errors. A long line of research supports the view that phonemic awareness and early phonics training are keys to reading proficiency for most children (Booth, Perfetti, & MacWhinney, 1999; Hatcher, Hulme, & Ellis, 1994; Jeynes & Littell, 2000; Liberman & Liberman, 1990; National Reading Panel, 2000; Stahl, McKenna, & Pagnucco, 1994).

Many experts now recommend a blend of the best of both approaches (National Reading Panel, 2000). Children can learn phonetic skills along with strategies to help them understand what they read. Because reading skills are the joint product of many functions in different parts of the brain, instruction solely in specific subskills—phonetics or comprehension—is less likely to succeed (Byrnes & Fox, 1998). Children who can summon both visually based and phonetic strategies, using visual retrieval for familiar words and phonetic decoding for unfamiliar words, become better, more versatile, readers (Siegler, 1998).

The developmental processes that improve comprehension are similar to those that improve word memory. As word identification becomes more automatic and the capacity of working memory increases, children can focus on the meaning of what they read and can adjust their speed and attentiveness to the importance and difficulty of the material. And, as children's store of knowledge increases, they can more readily check new information against what they already know (Siegler, 1998).

Metacognition, awareness of one's own thinking processes, helps children monitor their understanding of what they read and enables them to develop strategies to clear up any problems—such strategies as reading slowly, rereading difficult passages, trying to visualize information, and thinking of examples. Having students recall, summarize, and ask questions about what they read can enhance comprehension (National Reading Panel, 2000).

decoding Process of phonetic analysis by which a printed word is converted to spoken form before retrieval from long-term memory.

visually based retrieval Process of retrieving the sound of a printed word on seeing the word as a whole.

phonetic, or code-emphasis, approach Approach to teaching reading that emphasizes decoding of unfamiliar words.

whole-language approach Approach to teaching reading that emphasizes visual retrieval and use of contextual clues.

metacognition Awareness of one's own mental processes.

What's your view

- Why might social interaction improve children's writing?

Checkpoint ✓

Can you . . .

✔ Compare the phonetic and whole-language methods of teaching reading, and discuss how comprehension improves?

✔ Discuss factors that affect reading improvement in low-income beginning readers?

✔ Explain why writing is harder for younger children than for older children?

✔ Summarize trends in reading and writing achievement?

Guidepost 5

What factors influence school achievement?

Children who have early reading difficulties are not necessarily condemned to reading failure. One longitudinal study followed the progress of 146 low-income children whose first-grade reading scores fell below the 30th percentile. Thirty percent of the children showed steady movement toward average reading skills from second through fourth grade. The children who improved the most were those who, as kindergartners, had shown relatively strong emergent literacy skills (refer back to Chapter 10) and better classroom behavior, which permitted them to pay attention and benefit from instruction (Spira, Bracken, & Fischel, 2005). Another longitudinal study of low-income 4- to 6-year-olds found consistent associations between social skills and literacy achievement in first, third, and fifth grades (Miles & Stipek, 2006).

Writing

The acquisition of writing skills goes hand in hand with the development of reading. Older preschoolers begin using letters, numbers, and letterlike shapes as symbols to represent words or parts of words—syllables or phonemes. Often their spelling is quite inventive—so much so that they may not be able to read it themselves (Whitehurst & Lonigan, 1998).

Writing is difficult for young children. Unlike conversation, which offers constant feedback, writing requires the child to judge independently whether the communicative goal has been met. The child also must keep in mind a variety of other constraints: spelling, punctuation, grammar, and capitalization, as well as the basic physical task of forming letters (Siegler, 1998).

In many classrooms, children are discouraged from discussing their work with other children in the belief that they will distract one another. Research based on Vygotsky's social interaction model of language development suggests that such policies are misguided. In one study, fourth graders working in pairs wrote stories with more solutions to problems, more explanations and goals, and fewer errors in syntax and word use than did children working alone (Daiute, Hartup, Sholl, & Zajac, 1993).

Efforts to improve the teaching of reading and writing seem to be paying off. U.S. fourth graders scored higher than their counterparts in any of eight other industrialized countries except England on an international literacy test (Sen, Partelow, & Miller, 2005). The National Assessment of Educational Progress in 2002, 2003, and 2005 found significant improvements in the proportions of fourth and eighth graders who read and write proficiently. Still, fewer than one-third of students in both grades read and write at that level (NCES, 2004c, 2005b).

The Child in School

School is a major formative experience, as it was for Akira Kurosawa, affecting every aspect of development. In school, children gain knowledge, skills, and social competence, stretch their bodies and minds, and prepare for adult life. Worldwide, more children are going to school than ever before. In highly developed countries such as the United States, Canada, France, Germany, Italy, Japan, and the United Kingdom, participation in elementary education is almost universal (Sen, Partelow, & Miller, 2005). Worldwide, however, 103.5 million primary-age children—57 percent of them girls—are not in school, and, in nearly one-third of 91 countries reporting, less than 75 percent of students reach fifth grade (UNESCO, 2004).

Early school experiences are critical in setting the stage for future success or failure in school and in adult life (Feinstein & Bynner, 2004). Let's look at the first-grade experience and at influences on school achievement. In the next major section we'll consider how schools educate children with special needs.

Entering First Grade

"What will the teacher be like?" 6-year-old Julia wonders as she walks up the steps to her new school, wearing her new backpack. "Will the work be too hard? Will the kids like me? What games will we play at recess?"

Even today, when nearly 3 out of 4 U.S. children go to kindergarten (National Center for Education Statistics, 2004a), children often approach the start of first grade with a mixture of eagerness and anxiety. The first day of "regular" school is a milestone—a sign of the developmental advances that make this new status possible.

To make the most academic progress, a child needs to be involved in what is going on in class (Valeski & Stipek, 2001). Interest, attention, and active participation are positively associated with achievement test scores and, even more so, with teachers' marks from first grade through at least fourth (Alexander, Entwisle, & Dauber, 1993).

In a national longitudinal study, first graders at risk of school failure—either because of low SES or academic, attentional, or behavioral problems—progressed as much as their low-risk peers when teachers offered strong instructional and emotional support. Such support took the form of frequent literacy instruction, evaluative feedback, engaging students in discussions, responding to their emotional needs, encouraging responsibility, and creating a positive classroom atmosphere (Hamre & Pianta, 2005).

Checkpoint ✓

Can you . . .

✔ Explain the impact of the first-grade experience on a child's school career, and identify factors that affect success in first grade?

Influences on School Achievement: An Ecological Analysis

As Bronfenbrenner's bioecological theory would predict, in addition to children's own characteristics, each level of the context of their lives influences how well they do in school—from the immediate family to what goes on in the classroom to the messages children receive from peers and from the larger culture (such as "It's not cool to be smart"). Let's look at this web of influences. (We discuss the influence of culture on student motivation in Chapter 16.)

Self-Efficacy Beliefs

Students who are high in *self-efficacy*—who believe that they can master schoolwork and regulate their own learning—are more likely to succeed than students who do not believe in their own abilities (Bandura, Barbaranelli, Caprara, & Pastorelli, 1996; Zimmerman, Bandura, & Martinez-Pons, 1992). Self-regulated learners set challenging goals and use appropriate strategies to achieve them. They try hard, persist despite difficulties, and seek help when necessary. Students who do not believe in their ability to succeed tend to become frustrated and depressed—feelings that make success more elusive. When Akira Kurosawa's self-efficacy increased, he began to shine in school.

Gender

Girls tend to do better in school than boys; they are less likely to repeat grades, have fewer school problems, and outperform boys in national reading and writing assessments (Freeman, 2004). In one study, fifth- and seventh-grade girls got better math grades than boys but did no better on math achievement tests. The explanation for the girls' better grades may lie in the way they approached schoolwork. Girls tended to aim for mastery of the subject matter, whereas boys were more interested in how smart they looked in class. Girls had better classroom behavior and adopted more effective strategies for learning. However, girls had less confidence in their abilities, an important factor in performance on achievement tests (Kenney-Benson, Pomerantz, Ryan, & Patrick, 2006). Interestingly, in a study of more than 8,000 males and females ranging from 2 to 90 years old, girls and women tended to do better than boys and men on timed tests (Camarata & Woodcock, 2006).

Boys' advantage in spatial skills has been widely noted, but a study of 547 urban second and third graders found that socioeconomic status makes a difference. Although middle- and high-SES boys did better than high-SES girls on spatial tasks, low-SES boys did not do better than low-SES girls, perhaps because higher-SES boys are more likely to engage in spatially-oriented activities such as building with Legos and playing video games (Levine, Vasilyeva, Lourenco, Newcombe, & Huttenlocher, 2005).

This father's attention to his daughter's school progress makes it more likely that she will succeed. As children grow older, they take on more responsibility for getting schoolwork done on their own.

Parenting Practices

Parents of achieving children create an environment for learning. They provide a place to study and to keep books and supplies; they set times for meals, sleep, and homework; they monitor how much television their children watch and what their children do after school; and they show interest in their children's lives by talking with them about school and being involved in school activities. Children whose parents are involved in their schools do better in school (Hill & Taylor, 2004).

Parents' perceived self-efficacy—their belief in their ability to promote their children's academic growth—affects their success in doing so. Parents who are economically secure and who have high aspirations for their children and a strong sense of parental efficacy tend to have children with high academic goals and achievement (Bandura et al., 1996).

How do parents motivate children to achieve? Some use *extrinsic* (external) means—giving money or treats for good grades or punishment for bad ones. Others encourage *intrinsic* (internal) motivation by praising ability and hard work. Intrinsic motivation seems more effective. In a study of 77 third and fourth graders, those who were interested in the work itself did better in school than those who mainly sought grades or parents' approval (Miserandino, 1996).

Parenting styles may affect motivation. In one study, the highest achieving fifth graders had *authoritative* parents. These children were curious and interested in learning; they liked challenging tasks and enjoyed solving problems. *Authoritarian* parents, who kept after children to do homework, supervised closely, and relied on extrinsic motivation, tended to have lower-achieving children. So did *permissive* parents, who did not seem to care how the children did in school (G. S. Ginsburg & Bronstein, 1993).

Socioeconomic Status

Socioeconomic status can be a powerful factor in educational achievement—not in and of itself, but through its influence on such factors as family atmosphere, choice of neighborhood, and parenting practices (Evans, 2004; National Research Council [NRC], 1993a; Rouse et al., 2005). Children of poor parents are more likely to experience negative home and school atmospheres, stressful events, and unstable, chaotic households (Evans, 2004; Felner et al., 1995). SES can affect parents' ability to provide an environment that enhances learning (Brody, Flor, & Gibson, 1999; Brody, Stoneman, & Flor, 1995; Rouse et al., 2005). In a nationally representative study of children who entered kindergarten in 1998, achievement gaps between advantaged and disadvantaged students widened during the first 4 years of schooling (Rathbun, West, & Germino-Hausken, 2004); and in a longitudinal study of 11,200 British children born in 1970, low SES increased the likelihood that early progress would not be maintained (Feinstein & Bynner, 2004).

However, SES is not the only factor in school achievement. In a longitudinal study, 8-year-olds whose home environment was cognitively stimulating showed higher intrinsic motivation for academic learning at ages 9, 10, and 13 than children who lived in less stimulating homes. This was true over and above effects of SES (Gottfried, Fleming, & Gottfried, 1998).

How can some young people from disadvantaged homes and neighborhoods do well in school and improve their condition in life? One factor is **social capital:** the networks of community resources children and families can draw on (Coleman, 1988). In a 3-year experimental antipoverty intervention in which working poor parents received wage supplements and subsidies for child care and health insurance, their school-age children's academic achievement and behavior improved in comparison with a control group who did not participate (Huston et al., 2001). Two years after the families had left the program, the impact on school achievement and motivation held steady, especially for older boys, though the effect on social and problem behavior declined (Huston et al., 2005).

social capital Family and community resources on which a person or family can draw.

Peer Acceptance

As we discuss in Chapter 14, children who are liked and accepted by peers tend to do better in school. Among 248 fourth graders, those whose teachers reported that they were not liked by peers had poorer academic self-concepts and more symptoms of anxiety or depression in fifth grade and lower reading and math grades in sixth grade. Early teacher identification of children who exhibit social problems could lead to interventions that would improve such children's academic as well as emotional and social outcomes (Flook, Repetti, & Ullman, 2005).

The Educational System

How can school best enhance children's development? Throughout the 20th century, conflicting educational philosophies, along with historical events, brought great swings in educational theory and practice—from the "three R's" (reading, 'riting, and 'rithmetic) to "child-centered" methods that focused on children's interests and then—when competition from Russia and, later, from Japan loomed and standardized test scores plummeted— "back to the basics." In the 1980s, a series of governmental and educational commissions proposed plans for improvement, ranging from more homework (Box 13-1) to a longer school day and school year to a total reorganization of schools and curricula.

The federal No Child Left Behind (NCLB) Act of 2001 is a sweeping educational reform emphasizing accountability, parental options, and expanded local control and flexibility. The intent is to funnel federal funding to research-based programs and practices, with special emphasis on reading and mathematics. Students in grades 3 through 8 are tested annually to see if they are meeting statewide progress objectives. Children in schools that fail to meet state standards can transfer to another school.

More than 50 national education, civil rights, children's, and citizens groups have called for substantial changes in NCLB. Critics such as the National Education Association, a national teachers' organization, claim that NCLB emphasizes punishment rather than assistance for failing schools; rigid, largely unfunded mandates rather than support for proven practices; and standardized testing rather than teacher-led, classroom-focused learning. Research on Sternberg's triarchic theory, for example, suggests that students learn better when taught in a variety of ways, emphasizing creative and practical skills as well as memorization and critical thinking (Sternberg, Torff, & Grigorenko, 1998). (Box 13-2 discusses the controversy over the best way to teach math.)

What's your view

- Which approach to education do you favor for children in the primary grades: instruction in the basics, a more flexible, child-centered curriculum, or a combination of the two?

The School Environment Children learn better and teachers teach better in a comfortable, healthful school environment. Most educators consider small class size a key factor, especially in the early grades, but findings on this point are mixed (Schneider, 2002). A longitudinal study of 11,600 kindergarten and primary students in Tennessee public elementary schools found lasting academic benefits for students randomly assigned to classes of about 15 students in kindergarten through third grade, and—especially for low-SES students— greater likelihood of finishing high school (Finn, Gerber, & Boyd-Zaharias, 2005; Krueger, 2003; Krueger & Whitmore, 2000).

Box 13-1 *The Homework Debate*

The homework debate is far from new. In the United States, historical swings in homework use have reflected shifts in educational philosophy (Cooper, 1989; Gill & Schlossman, 1996). During the 19th century, the mind was considered a muscle and homework a means of exercising it. Antihomework crusaders argued that assignments lasting far into the evening endangered children's physical and emotional health and interfered with family life. By the 1940s, "progressive," child-centered education had become popular and homework had lost favor. Many states and school districts banned it (Gill & Schlossman, 1996). In the 1950s, when the Soviet Union's Sputnik launch brought calls for more rigorous science and math education, and again in the early 1980s, amid worries about the United States' competitive position toward Japan, "More homework!" became a battle cry in campaigns to upgrade U.S. educational standards (Cooper, 1989).

Homework advocates claim that it disciplines the mind, develops good work habits, improves retention, and enables students to cover more ground than they could in the classroom alone. Homework also is a bridge between home and school, increasing parental involvement. Opponents claim that too much homework leads to boredom, anxiety, or frustration; puts unnecessary pressure on children; discourages intrinsic motivation; and usurps time from other worthwhile activities. They say that parental help can be counterproductive if parents become overly intrusive or use teaching methods that conflict with those used at school (Cooper, 1989). Once again, some critics want to ban homework, at least for young children (Kralovec & Buell, 2000).

Research supports a balanced view (Larson & Verma, 1999). A comprehensive review of nearly 120 studies found that the value of homework depends on many factors, including the age, ability, and motivation of the child; the amount and purpose of homework; the home situation; and classroom follow-up. Although homework has strong benefits for high school students, it has only moderate benefits for junior high school students (and then only if limited to 2 hours a night), and virtually no benefits for elementary school students as compared with in-class study

(Cooper, 1989). Research-based recommendations range from one to three 15-minute assignments a week in the primary grades to four or five assignments a week, each lasting 75 to 120 minutes, in grades 10 to 12. Instead of grading homework, researchers suggest, teachers should use it to diagnose learning problems (Cooper, 1989).

Homework, then, has value—but only in moderation and when geared to students' developmental levels. For grade school children, it can develop good study habits and an understanding that learning can take place at home as well as in school. In junior high, a mix of mandatory and voluntary homework can promote academic goals and motivate children to pursue studies that interest them. In high school, homework can provide opportunities for practice, review, and integration of what is being learned at school (Cooper, 1989).

Should parents help with homework? In an 18-month study of 166 fourth through sixth graders, mothers tended to give "intrusive support"—helping with or checking homework without being asked—when their children were uncertain about their performance or when the mothers were worried about it. Intrusive support tended to help low achievers improve but sometimes fostered failure, perhaps because the learning was not internalized (Pomerantz & Eaton, 2001). In a study of 109 8- to 12-year-olds, mothers who helped with homework tended to see their children as helpless and to become irritated and annoyed. However, this did not affect the mothers' positive feelings for their children or undermine the children's motivation and emotional functioning (Pomerantz, Wang, & Ng, 2005).

What's your view ?

How much homework do you think is appropriate for children of various ages, and how much help should parents give?

Check it out !

For more information on this topic, go to www.nces.ed.gov. This is the site of the National Center for Education Statistics.

However, in most schools small classes are larger than that. In classroom observations of 890 first graders, classes with 25 students or less tended to be more social and interactive (with a bit more disruptive behavior) and to enable higher quality instruction and emotional support. Students in these classes tended to score higher on standardized achievements tests and beginning reading skills (NICHD Early Childhood Research Network, 2004b).

social promotion Policy of automatically promoting children even if they do not meet academic standards.

Current Educational Developments When the Chicago public schools in 1996 ended **social promotion,** the practice of promoting children to keep them with their age-mates even when they do not meet academic standards, many observers hailed the change. Others warned that, although grade retention in some cases can be a "wake-up call," more often it is the first step on a remedial track that leads to lowered expectations, poor performance, and dropping out of school (Fields & Smith, 1998; Lugaila, 2003; McCoy & Reynolds, 1999; McLeskey, Lancaster, & Grizzle, 1995; Temple, Reynolds, & Miedel, 2000). Indeed, studies by University of Chicago researchers found that Chicago's retention policy did not improve third graders' test scores, hurt sixth graders' scores, and greatly increased eighth-grade

Should children learn math by rules and formulas or by manipulating colored blocks or pie-shaped segments to illustrate mathematical concepts? By memorizing and drilling with the multiplication tables or by using computer simulations and relating math problems to real life?

Such questions have spurred heated argument between proponents of *traditional "skill-and-drill" math* teaching and advocates of *constructivist math* (or *whole math*), in which children actively build their own mathematical concepts. The latter approach came into nationwide use after 1989, when the National Council of Teachers of Mathematics (NCTM) issued new standards of instruction based on constructivist principles.

The new standards deemphasized basic skills. Instead, they stressed understanding how mathematics works. Rather than passively absorb rules from a teacher or textbook, children were to discover mathematical concepts for themselves, often on the basis of intuitive learning gleaned from telling time, playing board games, dealing with money, and other everyday experiences. Instead of arriving at precise answers by multiplying, say, 19 × 6, children were encouraged to make estimates from more obvious relationships, such as 20 × 5.

Much like older arguments about reading instruction, the math wars split educators into opposing camps. Many parents complained that their children could not add, subtract, multiply, divide, or do simple algebra (Jackson, 1997a, 1997b). But although the reforms were widely pronounced a failure, the first scientific studies on their effectiveness were generally favorable. Among 2,369 big-city middle-school students, the NCTM guidelines actually improved algebra performance (Mayer, 1998). Contrary to claims that the constructivist approach was inappropriate for diverse populations, a randomized study of 104 low-achieving, mostly poor and minority third and fourth graders' performance on computation and word problems found otherwise. Students taught by problem solving and/or peer collaboration outperformed students taught by more traditional methods (Ginsburg-Block & Fantuzzo, 1998).

Nevertheless, in the 1998 Third International Mathematics and Science Study (TIMSS), U.S. twelfth graders scored lower than all but 2 of 21 competing nations on math literacy. Even students of advanced math lagged behind their counterparts in most nations (Smith, 1998). Furthermore, whereas in 1995 U.S. fourth graders had scored above average in math, by eighth grade their scores dipped below average (Holden, 2000).

The TIMSS intensified the math wars. Some educators blamed constructivist teaching, while others insisted the real problem was the persistence of traditional methods in many schools (Murray, 1998). Some argued that the reforms did not go far enough in rooting out the worst features of old curricula (Jackson, 1997a, 1997b). Superficial teaching and textbooks were among the reformers' complaints.

As in the reading wars, the best approach may be a combination of old and new methods. That is what the NCTM now advocates. Its revised standards and principles, issued in 2000, strive for a balance between conceptual understanding and computational skills. In 2003, math scores on the National Assessment of Educational Progress rose sharply to their highest levels since the test began in 1990 (NCES, 2004b). In 2005 they inched higher. The percentage of fourth graders scoring at or above the basic level of achievement increased by 30 points since 1990, from 50 to 80 percent; and the percentage of eighth graders at that level increased 17 points, from 52 to 69 percent. However, only 36 percent of fourth graders and 30 percent of eighth graders were judged "proficient" in 2005 (NCES, 2005a).

Meanwhile, in 2003, U.S. fourth and eighth graders scored well above average in the TIMSS but not as well as Asian students. The eighth graders scored higher than their counterparts in the 1990s, but fourth graders showed no improvement. Achievement gaps between white and black students at both grade levels narrowed (Gonzales et al., 2004).

A further step back to the basics is the NCTM's (2006) issuance of "curriculum focal points." To help teachers and students wade through the dozens of topics set forth in state curriculum standards, the focal points specify the most important skills students need to learn in each grade.

What's your view

Based on your own experience, which method of teaching math do you think would be more effective, or would you advocate a combination of both?

Check it out

For more information on this topic, go to www.nctm.org. This is the site of the National Council of Teachers of Mathematics. Also visit http://www.ams.org, the site of the American Mathematical Society. At www.nces.ed.gov/timss you will find data from the TIMSS.

and high school dropout rates for retained students (Nagaoka & Roderick, 2004; Roderick et al., 2003).

Many educators say the only real solution to a high failure rate is to identify at-risk students early and intervene before they fail (Bronner, 1999). In 2000–2001, 39 percent of U.S. public school districts provided alternative schools or programs for at-risk students, offering smaller classes, remedial instruction, counseling, and crisis intervention (NCES, 2003). Summer school may be effective as an early intervention. In one study, first graders who attended summer instruction in reading and writing at least 75 percent of the time outscored 64 percent of their peers who did not participate (Borman, Boulay, Kaplan, Rachuba, & Hewes, 1999).

Figure 13-1

Percentage of children ages 3 to 17 who use computers at home for various purposes, 2003.

Source: Day, Janus, & Davis, 2005; Data from U.S. Census Bureau, Current Population Survey, October 2003.

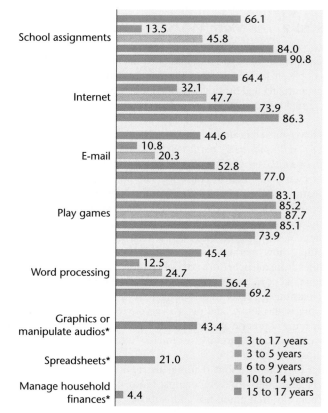

*Asked only of children ages 15 to 17.

Checkpoint ✔

Can you . . .

✔ Tell how self-efficacy beliefs and parenting practices can influence school success?

✔ Discuss the impact of socioeconomic status and peer acceptance on school achievement?

✔ Describe changes and innovations in educational philosophy and practice, and discuss views about social promotion, homework, and the teaching of math?

Some parents, unhappy with their public schools or seeking a particular style of education, are choosing charter schools or homeschooling. More than 1 million U.S. children now attend charter schools, some privately operated and others under charter from public school boards (Center for Education Reform, 2005). Charter schools tend to be smaller than regular public schools and have a unique philosophy, curriculum, structure, or organizational style. Although parents are generally satisfied with their charter schools, studies of their effects on student outcomes have had mixed results (Braun, Jenkins, & Grigg, 2006; Bulkley & Fisler, 2002; Center for Education Reform, 2004; Detrich, Phillips, & Durett, 2002; Hoxby, 2004; National Assessment of Educational Progress, 2004; Schemo, 2004).

Homeschooling is legal in all 50 states. In 2003 some 1.1 million U.S. students representing 2.2 percent of the school-age population were homeschooled, 4 out of 5 of them full-time—a 29 percent increase from 1999. In a nationally representative government survey, the main reasons parents gave for choosing to homeschool their children were concern about a poor or unsafe learning environment in the schools and the desire to provide religious or moral instruction (Princiotta, Bielick, & Chapman, 2004).

Computer and Internet Use In 2003, about 91 percent of children and adolescents used computers at home or at school, and about 59 percent used the Internet. However, fewer black, Hispanic, and American Indian children than white and Asian children, and fewer poor children than nonpoor children, use these technologies. Girls and boys spend about the same amount of time on computer and Internet use (Day, Janus, & Davis, 2005; DeBell & Chapman, 2006). Figure 13-1 shows the percentages of children who use computers at home.

Computer literacy and the ability to navigate the World Wide Web are opening new possibilities for individualized instruction, global communication, and early training in independent research skills. However, this tool poses dangers. Foremost is the risk of exposure to harmful or inappropriate material. Also, students need to learn to critically evaluate information they find in cyberspace and to separate facts from opinion and advertising. Finally, a focus on "visual literacy" could divert financial resources from other areas of the curriculum.

Educating Children with Special Needs

Public schools have a tremendous job educating children of varying abilities from all sorts of families and cultural backgrounds. They also must educate children who have special needs: children for whom English is a second language, those who have learning problems, and those who are gifted, talented, or creative.

Second-Language Education

In 2004, more than 19 percent of the U.S. population spoke a language other than English at home. The primary language most of these children speak is Spanish, and 5 percent have difficulty speaking English (Federal Interagency Forum on Child and Family Statistics, 2006). About 7 percent of the public school population are defined as English Language Learners (ELLs) (National Center for Education Statistics, 2004a).

Some schools use an **English-immersion** approach (sometimes called ESL, or English as a Second Language), in which language-minority children are immersed in English from the beginning, in special classes. Other schools have adopted programs of **bilingual education,** in which children are taught in two languages, first learning in their native language with others who also speak it and then switching to regular classes in English when they become more proficient in it. These programs can encourage children to become **bilingual** (fluent in two languages) and to feel pride in their cultural identity.

Advocates of early English immersion claim that the sooner children are exposed to English and the more time they spend speaking it, the better they learn it. Proponents of bilingual programs claim that children progress faster academically in their native language and later make a smoother transition to all-English classrooms (Padilla et al., 1991). Some educators maintain that the English-only approach stunts children's cognitive growth; because foreign-speaking children can understand only simple English at first, the curriculum must be watered down, and children are less prepared to handle complex material later (Collier, 1995).

Statistical analyses of multiple studies conclude that children in bilingual programs typically outperform those in all-English programs on tests of English proficiency (Crawford, 2007; Krashen & McField, 2005). Even more successful, according to some research, is a third, less common, approach: **two-way,** or **dual-language, learning,** in which English-speaking and foreign-speaking children learn together in their own and each other's languages. This approach avoids any need to place minority children in separate classes. By valuing both languages equally, it reinforces self-esteem and improves school performance. An added advantage is that English speakers learn a foreign language at an early age, when they can acquire it most easily (Collier, 1995;. Thomas & Collier, 1997, 1998). However, less than 2 percent of ELLs nationwide are enrolled in two-way programs (Crawford, 2007).

Regardless of the scientific findings, public opinion has turned against bilingual education. Enrollment in bilingual programs declined from 37 percent to 17 percent between 1992 and 2002 (Crawford, 2007). California, Arizona, and Massachusetts, which together account for one-half of students who speak languages other than English at home, have outlawed bilingual education by referendum and required English immersion. In 2002 the federal Bilingual Education Act was eliminated as part of No Child Left Behind. The new law includes tough accountability provisions; schools are to be assessed each year by the percentage of ELLs who have become fluent in English. This change is expected to discourage bilingual instruction (Crawford, 2002).

English-immersion Approach to teaching English as a second language in which instruction is presented only in English.

bilingual education System of teaching non-English-speaking children in their native language while they learn English and later switching to all-English instruction.

bilingual Fluent in two languages.

two-way, or dual-language, learning Approach to second-language education in which English speakers and non-English speakers learn together in their own and each other's languages.

Checkpoint ✓

Can you . . .

✔ Describe and evaluate various types of second-language education?

Children with Learning Problems

Some children, like Akira Kurosawa, are late bloomers when it comes to schoolwork. An unfortunate minority have more serious learning problems.

Mental Retardation

Mental retardation is significantly subnormal cognitive functioning. It is indicated by an IQ of about 70 or less, coupled with a deficiency in age-appropriate adaptive behavior (such as communication, social skills, and self-care), appearing before age 18 (Kanaya, Scullin, & Ceci, 2003). Fewer than 1 percent of U.S. children are mentally retarded (NCHS, 2004; Woodruff et al., 2004).

In 30 to 50 percent of cases the cause of mental retardation is unknown. Known causes include genetic disorders, traumatic accidents, prenatal exposure to infection or alcohol, and environmental exposure to lead or high levels of mercury (Woodruff et al., 2004). Many cases of retardation may be preventable through genetic counseling, prenatal care, amniocentesis, routine screening and health care for newborns, and nutritional services for pregnant women and infants.

Most retarded children can benefit from schooling. Intervention programs have helped many mildly or moderately retarded adults and those considered borderline (with IQs ranging from 70 up to about 85) to hold jobs, live in the community, and function in society. The profoundly retarded need constant care and supervision, usually in institutions. For some, day care centers, hostels for retarded adults, and homemaking services for caregivers can be less costly and more humane alternatives.

Learning Disabilities

Nelson Rockefeller, former vice president of the United States, had so much trouble reading that he ad-libbed speeches instead of using a script. Rockefeller is one of many eminent persons who have **dyslexia,** a language-processing disorder in which reading is substantially below the level predicted by IQ or age. Other famous persons reportedly having dyslexia include actors Tom Cruise, Whoopi Goldberg, and Cher; baseball Hall-of-Famer Nolan Ryan; television host Jay Leno; and Albert Einstein, father of nuclear energy.

Dyslexia is the most commonly diagnosed of a large number of **learning disabilities (LDs).** These disorders interfere with specific aspects of school achievement, such as listening, speaking, reading, writing, or mathematics, resulting in performance substantially lower than would be expected given a child's age, intelligence, and amount of schooling (APA, 1994). Mathematical disabilities, as an example, include difficulty in counting, comparing numbers, calculating, and remembering basic arithmetic facts. Each of these may involve distinct disabilities. A growing number of children—almost 2.9 million, or 5 percent of the U.S. school population—are served by federally supported programs for students with LDs (National Center for Learning Disabilities, 2004b).

Children with LDs often have near-average to higher-than-average intelligence and normal vision and hearing, but they seem to have trouble processing sensory information. Although causes are uncertain, one factor is genetic. A review of quantitative genetic research concluded that the genes most responsible for the high heritability of the most common LDs—language impairment, reading disability, and mathematical disability—are also responsible for normal variations in learning abilities and that genes that affect one type of disability are also likely to affect other types. However, some genes are specific to particular learning disabilities (Plomin & Kovas, 2005). Environmental factors may include complications of pregnancy or birth, injuries after birth, nutritional deprivation, and exposure to lead (National Center for Learning Disabilities, 2004b).

Children with LDs tend to be less task oriented and more easily distracted than other children; they are less well organized as learners and less likely to use memory strategies. Of course, not all children who have trouble with reading, arithmetic, or other specific school subjects have LDs. Some haven't been taught properly, are anxious, have trouble reading or hearing directions, lack motivation or interest in the subject, or have a developmental delay, which may eventually disappear (Geary, 1993; Ginsburg, 1997; Roush, 1995).

About 4 out of 5 children with LDs have been identified as dyslexic. Dyslexia is generally considered to be a chronic, persistent medical condition that tends to run in families (Shaywitz, 1998, 2003). It hinders the development of oral as well as written language skills and may cause problems with reading, writing, spelling, grammar, and understanding speech (National Center for Learning Disabilities, 2004a). Reading disability is more frequent in boys than in girls (Rutter et al., 2004).

Dyslexia in English-speaking children is believed to result from a neurological defect in processing speech sounds: an inability to recognize that words consist of smaller units of sound, which are represented by printed letters. This defect in *phonological processing* makes it harder to decode words (Morris et al., 1998; Shaywitz, 1998, 2003). Brain imaging has revealed differences or underactivity in the regions of the brain activated during the processing of spoken and written language in dyslexic as compared with normal readers (Breier et al., 2003; Casanova et al., 2005; Eden et al., 2004; Shaywitz, 2003) and significantly reduced volumes of gray matter in persons with familial dyslexia (Brambati et al., 2004). Several identified genes contribute to these abnormalities (Meng et al., 2005; Kere et al., 2005).

The biology of dyslexia may vary by culture. In brain-imaging studies, Chinese children used different parts of the brain in reading than English speakers do, and different parts were affected by dyslexia. This finding is not surprising, as the Chinese language is not phonological but instead relies on memory of visual symbols. About 2 to 7 percent of Chinese children are dyslexic (Sick, Perfetti, Jin, & Tan, 2004).

Many children—and even adults—with dyslexia can be taught to read through systematic phonological training. However, the process does not become automatic, as it does with most readers (Eden et al., 2004; Shaywitz, 1998, 2003).

Hyperactivity and Attention Deficits

Attention-deficit/hyperactivity disorder (ADHD) has been called the most common mental disorder in childhood (Wolraich et al., 2005). It is a chronic condition usually marked by persistent inattention, distractibility, impulsivity, low tolerance for frustration, and a great deal of activity at the wrong time and in the wrong place, such as the classroom (APA, 1994; Woodruff et al., 2004). Among well-known people who reportedly have had ADHD are the singer and composer John Lennon, Senator Robert Kennedy, and the actors Robin Williams and Sylvester Stallone.

ADHD may affect an estimated 2 to 11 percent of school-age children worldwide (Zametkin & Ernst, 1999) and 3 to 7 percent in the United States (Dey et al., 2004; NCHS, 2004; Schneider & Eisenberg, 2006; Zelazo & Müller, 2002). However, its prevalence is in dispute: Some research suggests that it may be underdiagnosed (Rowland et al., 2002). However, some physicians warn that the it may be overdiagnosed, resulting in unnecessary overmedication of children whose parents or teachers do not know how to control them (Elliott, 2000). ADHD diagnosis rates vary greatly by gender, ethnicity, geographic area, and other contextual factors and may in part be related to pressures on children to succeed in school (Schneider & Eisenberg, 2006).

ADHD has two different but sometimes overlapping sets of symptoms, making diagnosis imprecise. Some children are inattentive but not hyperactive; others show the reverse pattern (USDHHS, 1999b). However, in 85 percent of cases, the two types of symptoms go together (Barkley, 1998a). Because these characteristics appear to some degree in many normal children, some practitioners question whether ADHD is actually a distinct neurological or psychological disorder (Bjorklund & Pellegrini, 2002; Furman, 2005). However, most experts agree that there is cause for concern when the symptoms are unusually frequent and so severe as to interfere with the child's functioning in school and in daily life (AAP Committee on Children with Disabilities and Committee on Drugs, 1996; Barkley, 1998b; USDHHS, 1999b).

Many studies have linked ADHD to abnormalities in the prefrontal cortex and impairment of executive function (Zelazo & Müller, 2002). Children with ADHD have unusually small brain structures in the cortical regions that regulate attention and impulse

attention-deficit/hyperactivity disorder (ADHD) Syndrome characterized by persistent inattention and distractibility, impulsivity, low tolerance for frustration, and inappropriate overactivity.

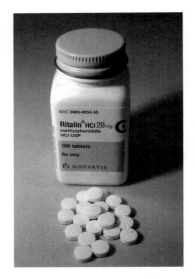

Ritalin can be effective in treating attention-deficit/hyperactivity disorder (ADHD), but its long-term effects are unknown. Some physicians warn that Ritalin may be overprescribed, resulting in overmedication of children.

What's your view ❓

• Long-term effects of drug treatment for ADHD are unknown, and leaving the condition untreated also carries risks. If you had a child with ADHD, what would you do?

Checkpoint ✔

Can you . . .

✔ Describe the causes and prognoses for three common types of conditions that interfere with learning?

✔ Discuss the impact of federal requirements for the education of children with disabilities?

control (Sowell et al., 2003). They tend to forget responsibilities, to speak aloud rather than give themselves silent directions, to be frustrated or angered easily, and to give up when they don't see how to solve a problem. Parents and teachers may be able to help these children by breaking down tasks into small "chunks," providing frequent prompts about rules and time, and giving frequent, immediate rewards for small accomplishments (Barkley, 1998b).

ADHD seems to have a substantial genetic basis with heritability approaching 80 percent (Acosta, Arcos-Burgos, & Muenke, 2004; APA, 1994; Barkley, 1998b; Elia, Ambrosini, & Rapoport, 1999; USDHHS, 1999b; Zametkin, 1995; Zametkin & Ernst, 1999). Symptoms of ADHD may be products of gene-environment interaction. In one study, exposure to high levels of lead impaired executive function, but only in children with certain variations of a gene that helps regulate brain levels of dopamine, a brain chemical essential for attention and cognition (Froehlich, Lamphear, Dietrich, Cory-Slechta, & Kahn, 2006). Birth complications that may play a part in ADHD include prematurity, a prospective mother's alcohol or tobacco use, and oxygen deprivation (Barkley, 1998b; Thapar et al., 2003; USDHHS, 1999b; Woodruff et al., 2004).

Most children diagnosed with ADHD continue to show symptoms as adolescents. Problems with impulse control and hyperactivity often decline, but inattention persists. Academic problems, cumulative family stress, and troubled peer relationships become more apparent (Whalen, Jamner, Henker, Delfino, & Lozano, 2002; Wolraich et al., 2005). Adolescents with ADHD often show learning disorders, excessive injuries, antisocial behavior, risky driving, substance abuse or dependence, anxiety or depression, and other personality disorders (Barkley, 1998b; Barkley, Murphy, & Kwasnik, 1996; Elia et al., 1999; McGee, Partridge, Williams, & Silva, 1991; Molina & Pelham, 2003; USDHHS, 1999b; Wender, 1995; Whalen et al., 2002; Wolraich et al., 2005; Zametkin, 1995). ADHD sometimes continues into adulthood; it affects an estimated 4 percent of adults worldwide (Wilens, Faraone, & Biederman, 2004).

ADHD is often managed with drugs, sometimes combined with behavioral therapy, counseling, training in social skills, and special classroom placement. Contrary to the popular impression that drug treatment is dramatically increasing among children, 2.2 million U.S. children—2.9 percent of the child population—were treated with stimulant drugs such as Ritalin in 2002, as compared with 2.7 percent in 1997 (Zuvekas, Vitello, & Norquist, 2006). In a 14-month randomized study of 579 children with ADHD, a carefully monitored program of Ritalin treatment, alone or in combination with behavior modification, was more effective than the behavioral therapy alone or standard community care (MTA Cooperative Group, 1999). However, the superior benefits of the program diminished during the following 10 months (MTA Cooperative Group, 2004a). A side effect of the combined treatment was slower growth in height and weight (MTA Cooperative Group, 2004b). Furthermore, long-term effects of Ritalin are unknown (Wolraich et al., 2005). Because of known cardiovascular risks of stimulant drugs, in 2006 the Drug Safety and Risk Management Advisory Committee of the Food and Drug Administration recommended that a warning accompany these drugs (Nissen, 2006).

Educating Children with Disabilities

In 2000–2001, 13.3 percent of public school students in the United States were receiving special educational services under the Individuals with Disabilities Education Act, which ensures a free, individualized public education for all children with disabilities. About 45 percent of these children had learning disabilities, 17 percent had speech or language impairments, and 9.5 percent had mental retardation (Snyder & Hoffman, 2003). Children must be educated in the "least restrictive environment" appropriate to their needs, which means, whenever possible, the regular classroom.

Many of these students can be served by "inclusion" programs, in which they are integrated with nondisabled children for all or part of the day. In 2003–2004, about half of U.S. students with disabilities spent 80 percent or more of their school day in regular classrooms (NCES, 2005b).

This deaf girl learns in a class with hearing children through the aid of a special teacher who communicates with her in sign language.

Gifted Children

Akira Kurosawa was not the only gifted person who was considered backward as a child. Sir Isaac Newton, who discovered gravity, did poorly in grade school. Thomas Edison, inventor of the lightbulb, was told as a boy that he was too stupid to learn. The British prime minister Winston Churchill failed sixth grade. The great operatic tenor Enrico Caruso was told as a child that he could not sing.

Giftedness is hard to define and identify. Educators disagree on who qualifies as gifted, on what basis, and on what kinds of educational programs these children need. Another source of confusion is that creativity and artistic talent are sometimes viewed as aspects or types of giftedness and sometimes as independent of it.

Identifying Gifted Children

The traditional criterion of giftedness is high general intelligence as shown by an IQ score of 130 or higher. This definition tends to exclude highly creative children (whose unusual answers often lower their test scores), children from minority groups (whose abilities may not be well developed, though the potential is there), and children with specific aptitudes (who may be only average or even show learning problems in other areas). Most states and school districts have therefore adopted the broader definition in the U.S. Elementary and Secondary Education Act, which encompasses children who show high intellectual, creative, artistic, or leadership capacity or ability in specific academic fields, and who need special educational services and activities in order to fully develop those capabilities. Many school districts now use multiple criteria for admission to programs for the gifted, including achievement test scores, grades, classroom performance, creative production, parent and teacher nominations, and student interviews; but IQ remains an important and sometimes the determining factor. An estimated 6 percent of the student population are considered gifted (NAGC, n.d.).

Some children are "globally gifted." Others excel, say, in math but not in reading, or may be talented in art but have a below-normal IQ or be uninterested in academics. As Gardner suggested, they may have intelligences in some areas but not in others. Thus, programs that rely on IQ to identify gifted children may miss those who are unevenly gifted. Instead, some experts say, it makes more sense to place children in special programs tailored to their particular gifts, including the arts as well as academics (Winner, 2000).

What Causes Giftedness?

Psychologists who study the lives of extraordinary achievers find that high levels of performance require strong intrinsic motivation and years of rigorous training (Bloom, 1985; Czikszentmihalyi, 1996; Gardner, 1993; Gruber, 1981; Keegan, 1996). However, motivation

$$ACG = 2n + 66$$
$$HGF = m\angle ACG$$
$$5n = 2n + 66$$
$$-2n = -2n$$
$$3n = 66$$
$$\frac{3n}{3} = \frac{66}{3}$$
$$n = 22$$

$$(x-3)(x+1) = 0$$
$$x - 3 = 0 \text{ or } x + 1 = 0$$
$$3 = 3 \quad -1 = -1$$
$$x = 3 \quad x = -1$$

Pythagore Theorem

$$x^2 + 12^2$$
$$x^2 + 144$$
$$x^2 = 22$$
$$= 8$$
$$x =$$
$$x > 0$$

Mahito Takahashi of New Jersey made a perfect score in a worldwide mathematics Olympiad and won close to 200 other awards. A well-rounded youth, he sang in a chamber choir and acted in a school production of Shakespeare's *Romeo and Juliet*. The key to helping such children achieve lies in recognizing and nurturing their natural gifts.

and training will not produce giftedness unless a child is endowed with unusual ability (Winner, 2000). Conversely, children with innate gifts are unlikely to show exceptional achievement without motivation and hard work (Achter & Lubinski, 2003).

Gifted children tend to grow up in enriched family environments with much intellectual or artistic stimulation. Their parents recognize and often devote themselves to nurturing the children's gifts but also give their children an unusual degree of independence. Parents of gifted children typically have high expectations and are hard workers and high achievers themselves. But although parenting can enhance the development of gifts, it cannot create them (Winner, 2000).

Brain research suggests that gifted children "are born with unusual brains that enable rapid learning in a particular domain" (Winner, 2000, p. 161). For example, children with mathematical, musical, and artistic gifts tend to have unusual activity in the right hemisphere while doing tasks normally done by the left. They are also more likely to be left-handed (Winner, 2000).

Lewis M. Terman and the Lives of Gifted Children

A classic longitudinal study of gifted children began in 1921, when Lewis M. Terman (who brought the Binet intelligence test to the United States) identified more than 1,500 California children with IQs of 135 or higher, approximately the top 1 percent of intellectual ability. The study demolished the widespread stereotype of the bright child as a puny, pasty-faced bookworm. Terman's children were taller, healthier, better coordinated, better adjusted, and more popular than the average child, and, as a group, their cognitive, scholastic, and vocational superiority have held up in adulthood and old age (Shurkin, 1992; Terman & Oden, 1959).

However, none of Terman's sample grew up to be Einsteins or Kurosawas, and those with the highest IQs became no more illustrious than those who were only moderately gifted. This lack of a close correlation between high IQ and adult eminence has been supported by later research (Winner, 1997).

Terman's findings about the physical and psychological health of gifted children have been confirmed by later, more controlled, studies (Achter & Lubinski, 2003). However, *profoundly* gifted children (often defined as having an IQ of 180 or higher) are more likely to have social and emotional difficulties than the less highly gifted. Feeling different and socially isolated, they may try to hide their gifts. This is a strong argument for placing these children in classes or groups with others like themselves (Winner, 2000).

Defining and Measuring Creativity

In Kurosawa's directorial debut in *Sanshiro Saguto* in 1943, he surprised audiences and critics by combining traditional Japanese samurai themes with tension-building techniques from Western action movies. Throughout his career, innovation was his hallmark.

One definition of *creativity* is the ability to see things in a new light—to produce something never seen before or to discern problems others fail to recognize and find new and unusual solutions. High creativity and high academic intelligence (IQ) do not necessarily go hand in hand. Classic research found only modest correlations (Anastasi & Schaefer, 1971; Getzels, 1964, 1984; Getzels & Jackson, 1962, 1963).

J. P. Guilford (1956, 1959, 1960, 1967, 1986) distinguished two kinds of thinking: *convergent* and *divergent*. **Convergent thinking**—the kind IQ tests measure—seeks a single correct answer; **divergent thinking** comes up with a wide array of fresh possibilities. Tests of creativity call for divergent thinking. The Torrance Tests of Creative Thinking (Torrance, 1966, 1974; Torrance & Ball, 1984), among the most widely known tests of

convergent thinking Thinking aimed at finding the one right answer to a problem.

divergent thinking Thinking that produces a variety of fresh, diverse possibilities.

creativity, include such tasks as listing unusual uses for a paper clip, completing a figure, and writing down what a sound brings to mind.

A problem with these tests is that the score often depends partly on speed, which is not a hallmark of creativity. Moreover, although the tests yield fairly reliable results, there is dispute over whether they are valid—whether they identify children who are creative in everyday life (Simonton, 1990).

Educating Gifted Children

In 2002, about 68 percent of public elementary and secondary schools had special programs for gifted children (Snyder & Hoffman, 2003). Children in these programs not only make academic gains but also tend to improve in self-concept and social adjustment (Ford & Harris, 1996). However, the federal No Child Left Behind Act, with its focus on basic skills, has resulted in reductions of services to the gifted (NAGC, n.d.).

Enrichment versus Acceleration Programs for gifted children generally stress either *enrichment* or *acceleration*. **Enrichment** deepens knowledge and skills through extra classroom activities, research projects, field trips, or expert coaching. **Acceleration,** sometimes recommended for highly gifted children, speeds up their education through early school entrance, grade skipping, placement in fast-paced classes, or advanced courses. Other options include ability grouping within the classroom (which has been found to help children academically and not harm them socially—Winner, 2000), dual enrollment (for example, an eighth grader taking algebra at a nearby high school), magnet schools, and specialized schools for the gifted.

Moderate acceleration does not seem to harm social adjustment, at least in the long run (Winner, 1997). A 30-year study of 3,937 young people who took advanced placement (AP) courses in high school found that they were more satisfied with their school experience and ultimately achieved more than equally gifted young people who did not take AP courses (Bleske-Rechek, Lubinski, & Benbow, 2004).

Julian Stanley: Seeking and Nurturing the Profoundly Gifted In 1971 Julian Stanley founded the Study of Mathematically Precocious Youth (SMPY) at Johns Hopkins University. Highly intelligent and highly motivated 12- and 13-year-olds who qualify can take advanced summer courses at participating universities and can apply for very early college entrance.

Whereas Terman selected children in the top 1 percent of intellectual ability, Stanley looked for profoundly gifted young people in the top 0.001 percent—1 in 10,000. Rather than take IQ as a criterion, Stanley used college entrance examinations, primarily the SAT, to identify children capable of exceptional reasoning in math. Later the program was extended to children profoundly gifted in verbal intelligence (Achter & Lubinski, 2003; Lubinski, Webb, Morelock, & Benbow, 2001).

How did Stanley's finds turn out? By early adulthood, among 320 SMPY participants, several already had won significant awards and had noteworthy literary, scientific, or technical accomplishments. The vast majority said that accelerating their education had promoted their academic progress and social-emotional development (Lubinski et al., 2001).

By their mid-30s, more than half of 380 SMPY participants had earned doctor's degrees, twice the rate found in studies of persons in the top 1 percent of cognitive ability (Lubinski, Benbow, Webb, & Bleske-Rechek, 2006). More SMPY men than women had gone into math and science careers, but the women who had not done so obtained similar proportions of advanced degrees and high level careers in other fields, such as law and medicine, where they could use their advanced reasoning skills (Lubinski & Benbow, 2006). As compared with a control group of graduate students from top universities, the SMPY group achieved exceptional career success, higher incomes, and similar life satisfaction (Lubinski et al., 2006). However, even in this group, not everyone was a top achiever—again underlining the importance of motivation and effort (Achter & Lubinski, 2003).

enrichment Approach to educating the gifted that broadens and deepens knowledge and skills through extra activities, projects, field trips, or mentoring.

acceleration Approach to educating the gifted that moves them through the curriculum at an unusually rapid pace.

What's your view

- Would you favor strengthening, cutting back, or eliminating special educational programs for gifted students?

Checkpoint

Can you . . .

✔ Tell why identification of gifted children is an issue?

✔ Discuss the relationships between giftedness and life achievements, and between IQ and creativity?

✔ Describe two approaches to the education of gifted children?

Refocus

Thinking back to the information about Akira Kurosawa in the Focus vignette at the beginning of this chapter,

- How might a Piagetian or information-processing theorist explain Akira Kurosawa's cognitive advances in third grade?
- What kind of intelligence test would have been most likely to show accurately Kurosawa's abilities?
- What influences on school achievement mentioned in this chapter seemed most applicable to Kurosawa?

- What evidence of creativity did Kurosawa show as a child, and how does this tie in with his adult achievements?
- What does Kurosawa's story suggest about the difficulty of identifying gifted children, especially in the early years?

There is no firm dividing line between being gifted and not being gifted, creative and not creative. All children benefit from being encouraged in their areas of interest and ability. What we learn about fostering intelligence, creativity, and talent in the most able children may help all children make the most of their potential. The degree to which they do this will affect their self-concept and other aspects of personality, discussed in Chapter 14.

Summary and Key Terms

Piagetian Approach: The Concrete Operational Child

Guidepost 1 How do school-age children's thinking and moral reasoning differ from those of younger children?

- A child from about age 7 to age 12 is in the stage of concrete operations. Children are less egocentric than before and are more proficient at tasks requiring logical reasoning, such as spatial thinking, understanding of causality, categorization, inductive and deductive reasoning, conservation, and working with numbers. However, their reasoning is largely limited to the here and now.
- Cultural experience, as well as neurological development, seems to contribute to the rate of development of conservation and other Piagetian skills.
- According to Piaget, moral development is linked with cognitive maturation and occurs in three stages in which children move from strict obedience to authority toward more autonomous judgments based first on fairness and later on equity.

**concrete operations (351) seriation (352)
transitive inference (352) class inclusion (352)
inductive reasoning (352) deductive reasoning (352)
horizontal décalage (353)**

Information-Processing Approach: Attention, Memory, and Planning

Guidepost 2 What advances in information-processing skills occur during middle childhood?

- Executive function—including attentional, memory, and planning skills—improves during middle childhood as a result of pruning of neurons in the prefrontal cortex.
- Processing speed, inhibitory control, selective attention, working memory capacity, metamemory, metacognition, and use of mnemonic strategies are specific skills that improve during the school years.

- Gains in information processing may help explain the advances Piaget described.

executive function (355) metamemory (356) mnemonic strategies (356) external memory aids (357) rehearsal (357) organization (357) elaboration (357)

Psychometric Approach: Assessment of Intelligence

Guidepost 3 How accurately can schoolchildren's intelligence be measured?

- The intelligence of school-age children is assessed by group or individual tests. Although intended as aptitude tests, they are validated against measures of achievement.
- IQ tests are fairly good predictors of school success but may be unfair to some children.
- Differences in IQ among ethnic groups appear to result to a considerable degree from socioeconomic and other environmental differences. Schooling seems to increase measured intelligence.
- Attempts to devise culture-free or culture-fair tests have been unsuccessful.
- IQ tests tap only three of the intelligences in Howard Gardner's theory of multiple intelligences. According to Robert Sternberg's triarchic theory, IQ tests measure mainly the componential element of intelligence, not the experiential and contextual elements.
- New directions in intelligence testing include the Sternberg Triarchic Abilities Test (STAT), Kaufman Assessment Battery for Children (K-ABC-II), and dynamic tests based on Vygotskyan theory.

**Wechsler Intelligence Scale for Children (WISC-III) (358)
Otis-Lennon School Ability Test (OLSAT8) (358)
cultural bias (360) culture-free (361) culture-fair (361)
culture-relevant (361) theory of multiple intelligences (361)
triarchic theory of intelligence (362) componential element (362)
experiential element (362) contextual element (362)
tacit knowledge (362)**

Language and Literacy

Guidepost 4 How do communicative abilities expand during middle childhood?

- Use of vocabulary, grammar, and syntax become increasingly sophisticated, but the major area of linguistic growth is in pragmatics.
- Metacognition contributes to progress in reading.
- Despite the popularity of whole-language programs, early phonics training is a key to reading proficiency.
- Interaction with peers fosters development of writing skills.

    pragmatics (364)   decoding (365)   visually based retrieval (365)   phonetic, or code-emphasis, approach (365) whole-language approach (365)   metacognition (365)

The Child in School

Guidepost 5 What factors influence school achievement?

- Because schooling is cumulative, the foundation laid in first grade is very important.
- Children's self-efficacy beliefs affect school achievement.
- Parents influence children's learning by becoming involved in their schooling, motivating them to achieve, and transmitting attitudes about learning.
- Socioeconomic status can influence parental beliefs and practices that, in turn, influence achievement. Poor families whose children do well in school tend to have more social capital than poor families whose children do not do well.
- The school environment and class size affect learning.
- Current educational issues and innovations include the amount of homework assigned, methods of teaching math, social promotion, charter schools, homeschooling, and computer literacy.

    social capital (369)   social promotion (370)

Educating Children with Special Needs

Guidepost 6 How do schools meet special needs?

- Methods of second-language education are controversial. Issues include speed and facility with English, long-term achievement in academic subjects, and pride in cultural identity.
- Three frequent sources of learning problems are mental retardation, learning disabilities (LDs), and attention-deficit/hyperactivity disorder (ADHD). Dyslexia is the most common learning disability.
- In the United States, all children with disabilities are entitled to a free, appropriate education. Children must be educated in the least restrictive environment possible, often in the regular classroom.
- An IQ of 130 or higher is a common standard for identifying gifted children. Broader definitions include creativity, artistic talent, and other attributes and rely on multiple criteria for identification. Minorities are underrepresented in programs for the gifted.
- In Terman's classic longitudinal study of gifted children, most turned out to be well adjusted and successful but not outstandingly so.
- Creativity and IQ are not closely linked. Tests of creativity seek to measure divergent thinking, but their validity has been questioned.
- Special educational programs for gifted, creative, and talented children usually stress enrichment or acceleration.

    English-immersion (373)   bilingual education (373) bilingual (373)   two-way (dual-language) learning (373) mental retardation (374)   dyslexia (374)   learning disabilities (LDs) (374)   attention-deficit/hyperactivity disorder (ADHD) (375)   convergent thinking (378)   divergent thinking (378) enrichment (379)   acceleration (379)

CHAPTER FOURTEEN

14

Psychosocial Development in Middle Childhood

Have you ever felt like nobody?
Just a tiny speck of air.
When everyone's around you,
And you are just not there.

—Karen Crawford, age 9

Focus *Marian Anderson, Operatic Trailblazer*

Marian Anderson

The African American contralto Marian Anderson (1897–1993) had—in the words of the great Italian conductor Arturo Toscanini— a voice heard "once in a hundred years." She was also a pioneer in breaking racial barriers. Turned away by a music school in her hometown of Philadelphia, she studied voice privately and in 1925 won a national competition to sing with the New York Philharmonic. When she was refused the use of a concert hall in Washington, D.C., First Lady Eleanor Roosevelt arranged for her to sing on the steps of the Lincoln Memorial. The unprecedented performance on Easter Sunday, 1939, drew 75,000 people and was broadcast to millions. Several weeks later, Marian Anderson became the first black singer to perform at the White House. But not until 1955 did Anderson, at age 57, become the first person of her race to sing with New York's Metropolitan Opera.

A remarkable story lies behind this woman's "journey from a single rented room in South Philadelphia" (McKay, 1992, p. xxx). It is a story of nurturing family ties—bonds of mutual support, care, and concern that extended from generation to generation.

Marian Anderson was the eldest of three children of John and Annie Anderson. Two years after her birth, the family left their one-room apartment to move in with her father's parents and then into a small rented house nearby.

At age 6, Marian joined the junior choir at church. There she made a friend, Viola Johnson, who lived across the street from the Andersons. Within a year or two, they sang a duet together—Marian's first public performance.

The chief source of biographical material about Marian Anderson and her family is Anderson (1992). Some details come from Freedman (2004), Heilbut (1993), Jones (2004), Kernan (1993), "Marian Anderson plans move to Portland," 1992; Women in History (2004), and from obituaries published in *Time* (April 19, 1993), *People Weekly,* and *Jet* (April 26, 1993). Although Anderson always gave her birthdate as 1902, her birth certificate, released after her death, showed it as 1897.

When Marian was in eighth grade, her beloved father died, and the family again moved in with his parents, his sister, and her two daughters. Marian's grandfather had a steady job. Her grandmother took care of all the children, her aunt ran the house, and her mother contributed by cooking dinners, working as a cleaning woman, and taking in laundry, which Marian and her sister Alyce delivered.

The most important influence in Marian Anderson's life was the counsel, example, and spiritual guidance of her hardworking, unfailingly supportive mother. Annie Anderson placed great importance on her children's schooling and saw to it that they didn't skimp on homework. Even when she was working full-time, she cooked their dinner every night, and she taught Marian to sew her own clothes. "Not once can I recall . . . hearing Mother lift her voice to us in anger . . . ," Marian wrote. "She could be firm, and we learned to respect her wishes" (Anderson, 1992, p. 92).

When Marian Anderson became a world-renowned concert artist, she often returned to her old neighborhood in Philadelphia. Her mother and sister Alyce shared a modest house, and her other sister, Ethel, lived next door with her son, James.

"It is the pleasantest thing in the world to go into that home and feel its happiness . . . ," the singer wrote. "They are all comfortable, and they cherish and protect one another. . . . I know that it warms [Mother] to have her grandson near her as he grows up, just as I think that when he gets to be a man, making his own life, he will have pleasant memories of his home and family" (1992, p. 93). Anderson married but had no children. In 1992, widowed and frail at age 95, she went to live with her nephew, James DePriest, then music director of the Oregon Symphony. She died of a stroke at his home the following year.

● ● ●

Marian Anderson "lived through momentous changes in America and the world" and in African American life (McKay, 1992, p. xxiv), but one thing that never changed in her life was the strong, supportive network of relationships that sustained her and her family. The kind of household a child lives in and the relationships within the household can have profound effects on psychosocial development in middle childhood, when children are developing a stronger sense of what it means to be responsible, contributing members, first of a family and then of society. The family is part of a web of contextual influences, including the peer group, the school, and the neighborhood in which the family lives. Marian Anderson's first friend, her church choir, and the neighbors for whom she did odd jobs to earn the price of a violin all played parts in her development. Above and beyond these influences were the overarching cultural patterns of time and place, which presented special challenges to African American families and communities and called forth mutually supportive responses.

In this chapter, we trace the rich and varied emotional and social lives of school-age children. We see how children develop a more realistic concept of themselves and achieve more competence, self-reliance, and emotional control. Through being with peers they make discoveries about their own attitudes, values, and skills. Still, as Anderson's story shows, the family remains a vital influence. Children's lives are affected, not only by the way parents approach child rearing, but also by whether and how they are employed, by the family's economic circumstances, and by its structure or composition—whether the child lives with one parent or two; whether the child has siblings and if so, how many; and whether the household includes other relatives, such as grandparents, aunt, and cousins. Although most children are emotionally healthy, some have mental health problems. We examine several of these. We also consider resilient children, who emerge from the stresses of childhood healthier and stronger.

After you have read and studied this chapter, you should be able to answer each of the Guidepost questions on the following page. Look for them again in the margins throughout the chapter, where they point to important concepts. To check your understanding of these Guideposts, review the end-of-chapter summary. Checkpoints located throughout the chapter will help you verify your understanding of what you have read.

1. How do the self-concept and self-esteem change in middle childhood, and how do school-age children show emotional growth?

2. What are the effects of family atmosphere and family structure, and what part do siblings play in children's development?

3. How do relationships with peers change in middle childhood, and what factors influence popularity and aggressive behavior?

4. What are some common mental health problems of childhood, and how do children respond to the stresses of modern life?

Guideposts for Study

The Developing Self

The cognitive growth that takes place during middle childhood enables children to develop more complex concepts of themselves and to grow in emotional understanding and control.

Self-Concept Development

Around age 7 or 8, children reach the third of the neo-Piagetian stages of self-concept development. Judgments about the self become more realistic and balanced as children form **representational systems:** broad, inclusive self-concepts that integrate various aspects of the self (Harter, 1993, 1996, 1998). "At school I'm feeling pretty smart in certain subjects, Language Arts and Social Studies," says 8-year-old Lisa. "I got As in these subjects on my last report card and was really proud of myself. But I'm feeling really dumb in Arithmetic and Science, particularly when I see how well the other kids are doing. . . . I still like myself as a person, because Arithmetic and Science just aren't that important to me. How I look and how popular I am are more important" (Harter, 1996, p. 208).

Lisa's self-description shows that she can focus on more than one dimension of herself. She has outgrown an all-or-nothing, black-or-white self-definition; she recognizes that she can be "smart" in certain subjects and "dumb" in others. She can verbalize her self-concept better, and she can weigh different aspects of it. She can compare her *real self* with her *ideal self* and can judge how well she measures up to social standards in comparison with others. All of these changes contribute to the development of self-esteem, her assessment of her *global self-worth* ("I still like myself as a person").

Self-Esteem

A major determinant of self-esteem, according to Erikson (1982), is children's view of their capacity for productive work. The central issue of middle childhood is **industry versus inferiority.** Children need to learn skills valued in their society. Arapesh boys in New Guinea learn to make bows and arrows; Arapesh girls learn to plant, weed, and harvest. Inuit children of Alaska learn to hunt and fish. Children in industrialized countries learn to read, write, count, and use computers. Like Marian Anderson, many children learn household skills and help out with odd jobs.

The virtue, or strength, that develops with successful resolution of this stage is *competence,* a view of the self as able to master skills and complete tasks. If children feel inadequate in comparison with their peers, they may retreat to the protective embrace of the family. If, on the other hand, they become too industrious, they may neglect social relationships and turn into workaholics.

Parents strongly influence beliefs about competence. In a longitudinal study of 514 U.S. middle-class children, parents' beliefs about their children's competence in math and sports were strongly associated with the children's beliefs (Fredricks & Eccles, 2002).

Guidepost 1

How do the self-concept and self-esteem change in middle childhood, and how do school-age children show emotional growth?

representational systems In neo-Piagetian terminology, the third stage in development of self-definition, characterized by breadth, balance, and the integration and assessment of various aspects of the self.

industry versus inferiority Erikson's fourth crisis of psychosocial development, in which children must learn the productive skills their culture requires or else face feelings of inferiority.

Checkpoint ✔

Can you . . .

✔ From a neo-Piagetian perspective, tell how the self-concept develops in middle childhood?

✔ Compare Erikson's and Harter's views about sources of self-esteem?

Middle childhood, according to Erikson, is a time for learning the skills one's culture considers important. In driving geese to market, this Vietnamese girl is developing a sense of competence and gaining self-esteem.

Emotional Growth

As children grow older, they are more aware of their own and other people's feelings. They can better regulate their emotions and can respond to others' emotional distress (Saarni et al., 1998).

By age 7 or 8, children typically are aware of feeling shame and pride, and they have a clearer idea of the difference between guilt and shame (Harris, Olthof, Meerum Terwogt, & Hardman, 1987; Olthof, Schouten, Kuiper, Stegge, & Jennekens-Schinkel, 2000). These emotions affect their opinion of themselves (Harter, 1993, 1996). Children also understand their conflicting emotions. As Lisa says, "Most of the boys at school are pretty yukky. I don't feel that way about my little brother Jason, although he does get on my nerves. I love him but at the same time, he also does things that make me mad. But I control my temper; I'd be ashamed of myself if I didn't" (Harter, 1996, p. 208).

By middle childhood, children are aware of their culture's rules for emotional expression (Cole, Bruschi, & Tamang, 2002). They know what makes them angry, fearful, or sad and how other people react to a display of these emotions, and they learn to adapt their behavior accordingly. Kindergartners believe that a parent can make a child less sad by telling the child to stop crying or can make a child less afraid of a dog by telling the child there is nothing to be afraid of. Sixth graders know that an emotion may be suppressed, but it still exists (Rotenberg & Eisenberg, 1997).

Emotional self-regulation involves effortful (voluntary) control of emotions, attention, and behavior (Eisenberg et al., 2004). Children low in effortful control tend to become visibly angry or frustrated when interrupted or prevented from doing something they want to do. Children with high effortful control can stifle the impulse to show negative emotion at inappropriate times. Effortful control may be temperamentally based but generally increases with age. Low effortful control may predict later behavior problems (Eisenberg et al., 2004).

Prosocial Behavior

School-age children generally become more empathic and more inclined to prosocial behavior. Prosocial children tend to act appropriately in social situations, to be relatively free from negative emotion, and to cope with problems constructively (Eisenberg, Fabes, & Murphy, 1996). Parents who acknowledge children's feelings of distress and help them deal with the source of their distress foster empathy, prosocial development, and social skills (Bryant, 1987; Eisenberg et al., 1996). When parents respond with disapproval or punishment, emotions such as anger and fear may become more intense and may impair social adjustment (Fabes, Leonard, Kupanoff, & Martin, 2001), or the child may become secretive and anxious about these negative feelings. As children approach early adolescence, parental intolerance of negative emotion may heighten parent-child conflict (Eisenberg, Fabes, et al., 1999).

Checkpoint ✔

Can you . . .

✔ Identify some aspects of emotional growth in middle childhood, and tell how parental treatment may affect children's handling of negative emotions?

✔ Tell ways in which prosocial behavior increases in middle childhood?

Although school-age children spend less time at home than before, parents continue to be very important in children's lives. Parents who enjoy being with their children tend to raise children who feel good about themselves—and about their parents.

The Child in the Family

School-age children spend more of their free time away from home than when they were younger, visiting and socializing with peers. They also spend more time at school and on studies and less time at family meals than 20 years ago (Juster et al., 2004). Still, home and the people who live there remain an important part of most children's lives. According to a national survey of 10,445 U.S. parents, 65 percent of children ages 6 to 17 have dinner each night with at least one parent, and about 75 percent talk to or play with a parent at least once a day (Lugaila, 2003).

To understand the child in the family we need to look at the family environment—its atmosphere and structure. These in turn are affected by what goes on beyond the walls of the home. As Bronfenbrenner's theory predicts, wider layers of influence—including parents' work and socioeconomic status and societal trends such as urbanization, changes in family size, divorce, and remarriage—help shape the family environment and, thus, children's development. Culture, too, defines rhythms of family life and roles of family members. African American families like Marian Anderson's, for example, carry on traditions that include living near or with kin, a strong sense of family obligation, ethnic pride, and mutual aid (Parke & Buriel, 1998). As we look at the child in the family, then, we need to be aware of outside forces that affect the family.

Family Atmosphere

The most important influences of the family environment on children's development come from the atmosphere within the home. Is it supportive and loving or conflict ridden? One contributing factor is how well parents handle school-age children's growing need—and ability—to make their own decisions. Another factor is the family's economic situation. How does parents' work affect children's well-being? Does the family have enough financial resources to provide for basic needs?

Parenting Issues: Coregulation and Discipline

During the course of childhood, control of behavior gradually shifts from parents to child. Middle childhood brings a transitional stage of **coregulation,** in which parent and child share power. Parents oversee a child's behavior, but children enjoy moment-to-moment

Guidepost 2

What are the effects of family atmosphere and family structure, and what part do siblings play in children's development?

coregulation Transitional stage in the control of behavior in which parents exercise general supervision and children exercise moment-to-moment self-regulation.

Latch-key children, who care for themselves after school while parents work, like this brother and sister, need to be mature, responsible, and resourceful and should know how to get help in an emergency.

self-regulation (Maccoby, 1984). With regard to problems among peers, for example, parents now rely less on direct management and more on discussion with their child (Parke & Buriel, 1998). Children are more apt to follow their parents' wishes when they recognize that the parents are fair and are concerned about the child's welfare and that they may "know better" because of experience. It also helps if parents try to defer to children's maturing judgment and take strong stands only on important issues (Maccoby, 1984).

The shift to coregulation affects the way parents handle discipline (Maccoby, 1984; Roberts, Block, & Block, 1984). Parents of school-age children are more likely to use inductive techniques. For example, 8-year-old Jared's father points out how his actions affect others: "Hitting Jermaine hurts him and makes him feel bad." In other situations, Jared's parents may appeal to his self-esteem ("What happened to the helpful boy who was here yesterday?") or moral values ("A big, strong boy like you shouldn't sit on the train and let an old person stand"). Above all, Jared's parents let him know that he must bear the *consequences* of his behavior ("No wonder you missed the school bus today—you stayed up too late last night! Now you'll have to walk to school").

In one longitudinal study in Finland, 196 kindergartners were followed until second grade. Children whose mothers used guilt-producing disciplinary methods ("I'm so-o-o disappointed in you!") but also were highly affectionate tended to develop behavior problems—perhaps because the mothers communicated inconsistent messages or kept the children too emotionally dependent on maternal approval (Aunola & Nurmi, 2005).

The way parents and children resolve conflicts may be more important than the specific outcomes. If family conflict is constructive, it can help children see the need for rules and standards. They also learn what kinds of issues are worth arguing about and what strategies can be effective (Eisenberg, 1996). However, as children become preadolescents and their striving for autonomy becomes more insistent, the quality of family problem solving often deteriorates (Vuchinich, Angelelli, & Gatherum, 1996).

Effects of Parents' Work

Most studies of the impact of parents' work on children's well-being have focused on employed mothers. In 2005, 70.5 percent of U.S. mothers with children under 18 were in the workforce, and 53.8 percent of mothers with infants went to work within 1 year of giving birth (Bureau of Labor Statistics, 2006). Thus, many children have never known a time when their mothers were not working for pay.

In general, the more satisfied a mother is with her employment status, the more effective she is likely to be as a parent (Parke & Buriel, 1998). However, the impact of a mother's work depends on many other factors, including the child's age, sex, temperament, and personality; whether the mother works full- or part-time; why she is working; whether she has a supportive or unsupportive partner, or none; the family's socioeconomic status; and the kind of care the child receives before and/or after school (Parke & Buriel, 1998). Often a single mother like Marian Anderson's must work to stave off economic disaster. How her working affects her children may hinge on how much time and energy she has left over to spend with them and what sort of role model she is (Barber & Eccles, 1992)—clearly, a positive one in Annie Anderson's case.

How well parents keep track of their children may be more important than whether the mother works for pay (Crouter, MacDermid, McHale, & Perry-Jenkins, 1990). In 2005, 57 percent of students in kindergarten through eighth grade whose mothers worked full-time and 32 percent of those whose mothers worked part-time or were looking for work were in at least one regular nonparental after-school care arrangement, most often a school- or center-based program. Some children of employed mothers, especially younger

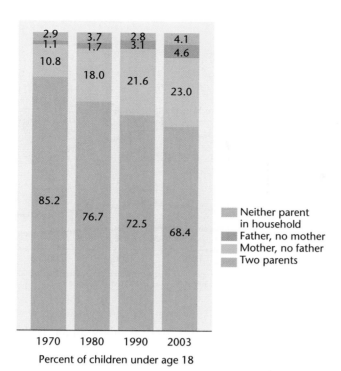

Figure 14-1

Living arrangements of children younger than 18, 1970 to 2003. Most children under 18 in the United States live with two parents, but the prevalence of that household type has been diminishing.

Source: U.S. Census Bureau, 2006.

Neither parent in household
Father, no mother
Mother, no father
Two parents

1970   1980   1990   2003
Percent of children under age 18

children, are supervised by relatives. Many children receive several types of out-of-school care (Carver & Iruka, 2006). Like good child care for preschoolers, good after-school programs have relatively low enrollment, low child-staff ratios, and well-educated staff. Children, especially boys, in organized after-school programs with flexible programming and a positive emotional climate tend to adjust better and do better in school (Pierce, Hamm, & Vandell, 1999; Posner & Vandell, 1999).

About 9 percent of school-age children and 23 percent of early adolescents are reported to be in *self-care,* regularly caring for themselves at home without adult supervision (Hofferth & Jankuniene, 2000; NICHD Early Childhood Research Network, 2004a). This arrangement is advisable only for older children who are mature, responsible, and resourceful and know how to get help in an emergency—and, even then, only if a parent stays in touch by telephone.

Poverty and Parenting

Some 17 percent of U.S. children up to age 17—including 33 percent of black children and 29 percent of Hispanic children—lived in poverty in 2004. Children living with single mothers were nearly 5 times more likely to be poor than children living with married couples—42 percent as compared with 9 percent (Federal Interagency Forum on Child and Family Statistics, 2006; Figure 14-1). Poverty can inspire people like Marian Anderson's mother to work hard and make a better life for their children—or it can crush their spirits.

Poor children are more likely than other children to have emotional or behavioral problems, and their cognitive potential and school performance suffer even more (Brooks-Gunn, Britto, & Brady, 1998; Brooks-Gunn & Duncan, 1997; Duncan & Brooks-Gunn, 1997; McLoyd, 1998). Poverty can harm children's development through its impact on parents' emotional state and parenting practices and on the home environment they create (Evans, 2004; NICHD Early Child Care Research Network, 2005a).

Vonnie McLoyd's (1990, 1998; Mistry, Vandewater, Huston, & McLoyd, 2002) ecological analysis of the effects of poverty traces a route that leads to adult psychological distress, to effects on child rearing, and then to emotional, behavioral, and academic problems in children. Parents who live in poverty are likely to become anxious, depressed, and irritable. They may become less affectionate with and less responsive to their children. They may discipline inconsistently, harshly, and arbitrarily. The children, in turn, tend to become depressed, to have trouble getting along with peers, to lack self-confidence, to develop behavioral and academic problems, and to engage in antisocial acts (Brooks-Gunn

What's your view

• If finances permit, should one parent stay home to take care of the children?

Figure 14-2

Percentage of children ages 0–17 living in poverty. Children living with single mothers (female householder families) are by far the most likely to be poor.

Source: Federal Interagency Forum on Child and Family Statistics, Fig. 3, 2006.

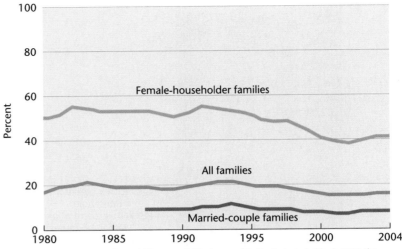

NOTE: Estimates refer to children ages 0–17 who are related to the householder. In 2004, the average poverty threshold for a family of four was $19,307 in annual income.

et al., 1998; Evans, 2004; Evans & English, 2002; Fields & Smith, 1998; McLoyd, 1990, 1998; Mistry et al., 2002).

However, this pattern is not inevitable. In a 4-year longitudinal study of 152 single mother–headed African American families, mothers who, despite economic stress, were emotionally healthy and had relatively high self-esteem tended to have academically and socially competent children who reinforced the mothers' positive parenting. This, in turn, supported the children's continued academic success and socially desirable behavior (Brody, Kim, Murry, & Brown, 2004).

The effects of *persistent* poverty can be complex. In a longitudinal study of 1,364 families of mixed SES, transitory poverty during the first 4 years of a child's life was less damaging to long-term cognitive and social development than later or chronic poverty (NICHD Early Child Care Research Network, 2005a). However, what seemed to be most damaging to children were family characteristics that may accompany poverty—an unstimulating home environment, lack of maternal sensitivity, unstable adult relationships, psychiatric problems, and violent or criminal behavior.

Family Structure

Family structure in the United States has changed dramatically. In earlier generations, the vast majority of children grew up in families with two married parents. Today, about 2 out of 3 children under 18 live with two married biological, adoptive, or stepparents, a proportion that represents a dramatic decline—from 87 percent in 1970 to 67 percent in 2004 (Fields, 2003, 2004; Federal Interagency Forum on Family and Child Statistics, 2006; Figure 14-2). About 10 percent of two-parent families are stepfamilies resulting from divorce and remarriage, and nearly 4 percent are cohabiting families (Kreider & Fields, 2005). Other increasingly common family types are gay or lesbian families and grandparent-headed families.

Other things being equal, children tend to do better in families with two continuously married parents than in cohabiting, divorced, single-parent, or stepfamilies, or when the child is born outside of marriage. The distinction is even stronger for children growing up with two happily married parents. These children tend to experience a higher standard of living, more effective parenting, more cooperative co-parenting, closer relationships with both parents (especially fathers), and fewer stressful events (Amato, 2005). However, the parents' relationship, the quality of their parenting, and their ability to create a favorable family atmosphere may affect children's adjustment more than their marital status (Amato, 2005; Bray & Hetherington, 1993; Bronstein et al., 1993; Dawson, 1991). Adoptive children in two-parent families are equally advantaged as biological children in two-parent families (Hamilton, Cheng, & Powell, 2007).

A father's frequent and positive involvement with his child, from infancy on, is directly related to the child's well-being and physical, cognitive, and social development (Cabrera et al.,

Checkpoint

Can you . . .

✔ Identify ways in which parents' work can affect children?

✔ Discuss effects of poverty on child raising?

2000; Kelley, Smith, Green, Berndt, & Rogers, 1998; Shannon, Tamis-LeMonda, London, & Cabrera, 2002). Unfortunately, among a nationally representative sample of 10,221 children born in the United States in 2001, 20 percent lived in households with no father, and 13 percent had never seen their fathers. Poor children and black and Hispanic children were most likely to have no father in the home (NCES, 2005a).

When Parents Divorce

The United States has one of the highest divorce rates in the world. The annual number of divorces has tripled since 1960 (Harvey & Pauwels, 1999), but the divorce rate has remained stable or declined slightly since 2001 (Munson & Sutton, 2004). More than 1 million children are involved in divorces each year (Harvey & Pauwels, 1999).

Although paternal custody is still relatively rare, it is a growing trend. Whether or not a father has custody, as this man does, his son is likely to adjust better if his father remains involved in his life.

Adjusting to Divorce Divorce is stressful for children. First there is the stress of marital conflict and then of parental separation and the departure of one parent, usually the father. Children may not fully understand what is happening. Divorce is, of course, stressful for the parents as well and may negatively affect their parenting. The family's standard of living is likely to drop; and, if a parent moves away, a child's relationship with the noncustodial parent may suffer (Kelly & Emery, 2003). A divorced parent's remarriage can increase the stress on children, renewing feelings of loss (Ahrons & Tanner, 2003; Amato, 2003).

Children's emotional or behavioral problems may reflect the level of parental conflict *before* the divorce (Amato, 2005). In a longitudinal study of almost 11,000 Canadian children, those whose parents later divorced showed more anxiety, depression, or antisocial behavior than those whose parents stayed married (Strohschein, 2005). If predivorce parental discord is chronic, overt, or destructive, children may be as well or better off, after a divorce (Amato, 2003, 2005; Amato & Booth, 1997).

A child's adjustment to divorce may depend in part on the child's age or maturity, gender, temperament, and psychosocial adjustment before the divorce. Younger children tend to be more anxious about divorce, have less realistic perceptions of what caused it, and are more likely to blame themselves. However, they may adapt more quickly than older children, who better understand what is going on. School-age children are sensitive to parental pressures and loyalty conflicts and, like younger children, may fear abandonment and rejection. Boys find it harder to adjust than girls do and are more susceptible to social and conduct problems (Amato, 2005; Hetherington et al., 1998; Hines, 1997; Parke & Buriel, 1998).

Custody, Visitation, and Co-parenting Children do better after divorce if the custodial parent is warm, supportive, and authoritative, monitors the child's activities, and holds age-appropriate expectations; if parental conflict subsides; and if the nonresident parent maintains close contact and involvement (Ahrons & Tanner, 2003; Kelly & Emery, 2003).

In most divorce cases, the mother gets custody, though paternal custody is a growing trend. Children living with divorced mothers adjust better when the father pays child support, which may be a barometer of the tie between father and child and also of cooperation between the ex-spouses (Amato & Gilbreth, 1999; Kelly & Emery, 2003). Many children of divorce say that losing contact with a father is one of the most painful results of divorce (Fabricius, 2003). However, frequency of contact with the father is not as important as the quality of the father-child relationship and the level of parental conflict. Children who are close to their nonresident fathers and whose fathers are authoritative parents tend to do better in school and are less likely to have behavior problems (Amato & Gilbreth, 1999; Kelly & Emery, 2003).

In a national sample of 354 divorced families, *cooperative parenting*—active consultation between a mother and a nonresident father on parenting decisions—led to more frequent contact between father and child, and this, in turn, led to better father-child relationships and more responsive fathering (Sobolewski & King, 2005). Unfortunately, cooperative parenting is not the norm (Amato, 2005). Parent education programs that teach separated or divorced couples how to prevent or deal with conflict, keep lines of communication open, develop an effective co-parenting relationship, and help children adjust to divorce have been introduced in many courts with measurable success (Wolchik et al., 2002).

Joint custody, custody shared by both parents, can be advantageous if the parents can cooperate, as both parents can continue to be closely involved with the child. When parents have joint *legal* custody, they share the right and responsibility to make decisions regarding the child's welfare. When parents have joint *physical* custody (which is less common), the child lives part-time with each of them. An analysis of 33 studies found that children in either legal or physical joint custody were better adjusted and had higher self-esteem and better family relationships than children in sole custody. In fact, the joint custody children were as well-adjusted as children in nondivorced families (Bauserman, 2002). It is likely, though, that couples who choose joint custody are those that have less conflict.

Long-Term Effects Most children of divorce adjust reasonably well. Still, children with divorced parents tend to have modestly lower levels of cognitive, social, and emotional well-being than children whose parents stay together (Amato, 2005). In adolescence, divorce increases the risk of antisocial behavior, difficulties with authority figures (Amato, 2003, 2005; Kelly & Emery, 2003), and dropping out of school (McLanahan & Sandefur, 1994). According to some research, 25 percent of children of divorce reach adulthood with serious social, emotional, or psychological problems, as compared with 10 percent of children whose parents stay together (Hetherington & Kelly, 2002). As adults, they tend to have lower SES, lower psychological well-being, and a greater chance of having a birth outside marriage. Their marriages tend to be of poorer quality and are more likely to end in divorce (Amato, 2005).

The anxiety connected with parental divorce may surface as children enter adulthood and try to form intimate relationships of their own (Amato, 2003; Wallerstein, Lewis, & Blakeslee, 2000). Having experienced their parents' divorce, some young adults are afraid of making commitments that might end in disappointment and are intent on protecting their independence (Glenn & Marquardt, 2001; Wallerstein & Corbin, 1999). However, much depends on how young people resolve and interpret the experience of parental divorce. Some, who saw a high degree of conflict between their parents, are able to learn from that negative example and to form highly intimate relationships (Shulman, Scharf, Lumer, & Maurer, 2001).

Divorce may have consequences for later generations. In a 20-year longitudinal study of a random sample of 2,033 married persons in the United States, the children of those who divorced tended to have lower educational levels, more instability in their marriages, and increased tension with their children than those whose parents had remained married. The children of these "children of divorce" (the grandchildren of the original respondents) also tended to have lower educational levels and more marital discord, as well as weaker bonds with their parents (Amato & Cheadle, 2005).

Living in a One-Parent Family

One-parent families result from divorce or separation, unwed parenthood, or death. The number of single-parent families in the United States has more than tripled since 1970 (Fields, 2004) with rising rates of divorce and of parenthood outside of marriage. Today 25 percent of U.S. children live with one parent, but more than 11 percent of these households are cohabiting households that include the mother's or father's unwed partner. More than half of all black children live with a single parent, as compared with

19 percent of non-Hispanic white children and 26 percent of Hispanic children (Kreider & Fields, 2005).

Children are far more likely to live with a single mother than with a single father. Still, more than 9 percent of single-parent U.S. families are headed by the father (Kreider & Fields, 2005; refer back to Figure 14-1). The number of father-only families has more than quadrupled since 1970, apparently due largely to the increase in paternal custody after divorce (Fields, 2004).

Although children in single-parent families do fairly well overall, they tend to lag socially and educationally behind peers in two-parent families. This is true of both children born out of wedlock and those whose parents are divorced. Studies on children who experience a parent's death have mixed results, but, overall, they suggest that these children are at risk for more problems than children who grow up with two married parents but less problems than those who are born to unwed mothers or whose parents divorce (Amato, 2005).

What explains these findings? It is possible that people who become single parents out of wedlock or through divorce have personality traits or adjustment problems that "select" them into single parenthood and also make them less effective parents. However, the weight of the evidence is otherwise. Children living with a single parent are exposed to many stressful experiences. For one thing, they tend to be economically disadvantaged; 37 percent of children living with an unmarried mother and 16 percent of children living with an unmarried father live in poverty (Kreider & Fields, 2005). Because their parents are struggling to maintain the household, these children often receive poorer parenting. Losing contact with a parent or observing conflict and hostility between parents can produce emotional insecurity. In many cases, moving to a new neighborhood and changing schools can be upsetting (Amato, 2005). Children living with married parents tend to have more daily interaction with their parents, are read to more often, progress more steadily in school, and participate more in extracurricular activities than children living with a single parent (Lugaila, 2003).

However, negative outcomes for children in one-parent families are far from inevitable. The child's age and level of development, the family's financial circumstances, whether there are frequent moves, and a nonresident father's involvement make a difference (Amato, 2005; Seltzer, 2000). In a longitudinal study of 1,500 white, black, and Hispanic families with 6- and 7-year-old children, the mother's educational and ability level and, to a lesser extent, family income and the quality of the home environment accounted for any negative effects of single parenting on academic performance and behavior (Ricciuti, 1999, 2004).

Because single parents often lack the resources needed for good parenting, potential risks to children in these families might be reduced or eliminated through increased access to economic, social, educational, and parenting support. In international math and science tests, the achievement gap between third and fourth graders living in single-parent households and those living with two biological parents was greater for U.S. children than for any other country except New Zealand. Children of single parents did better in countries with supportive family policies such as child and family allowances, tax benefits to single parents, maternity leave, and released time from work (Pong et al., 2003).

Living in a Cohabiting Family

Cohabiting families are similar in many ways to married families, but the parents tend to be more disadvantaged. They have less income and education, report poorer relationships, and have more mental health problems. Thus, it is not surprising that data from a national survey of 35,938 U.S. families showed worse emotional, behavioral, and academic outcomes for 6- to 11-year-old children living with cohabiting biological parents than for those living with married biological parents. The difference in outcomes was due largely to differences in economic resources, parental well-being, and parenting effectiveness (Brown, 2004).

Furthermore, cohabiting families are more likely to break up than married families. Although about 40 percent of unwed mothers are living with the child's father at the time

This girl has two fathers—and both obviously dote on the child. Contrary to popular stereotypes, children living with homosexual parents are no more likely than other children to have social or psychological problems or to turn out to be homosexual themselves.

of birth, 25 percent of cohabiting parents are no longer together 1 year later, and 31 percent break up after 5 years (Amato, 2005).

Living in a Stepfamily

Most divorced parents eventually remarry, and many unwed mothers marry men who were not the father of their children (Amato, 2005), thus forming step-, or blended, families. Some 15 percent of U.S. children live in blended families (Kreider & Fields, 2005).

Adjusting to a new stepparent may be stressful. A child's loyalties to an absent or dead parent may interfere with forming ties to a stepparent (Amato, 2005). Many stepchildren maintain ties with their noncustodial parents. Noncustodial mothers tend to keep in touch more than do non-custodial fathers and offer more social support (Gunnoe & Hetherington, 2004).

Some studies have found that boys—who often have more trouble than girls in adjusting to divorce and living with a single mother—benefit from a stepfather. A girl, though, may find the new man in the house a threat to her independence and to her close relationship with her mother (Bray & Hetherington, 1993; Hetherington, 1987; Hetherington et al., 1989; Hetherington et al., 1998; Hines, 1997). In a longitudinal study of a nationally representative sample of U.S. adults, mothers who remarried or formed new cohabiting relationships tended to use gentler discipline than mothers who remained single, and their children reported better relationships with them. However, supervision was greater in stable single-mother families (Thomson, Mosley, Hanson, & McLanahan, 2001).

Among 173 college students of mixed ethnicity in a large midwestern U.S. city, those raised in stepfamilies tended to report lower well-being than those raised in intact families, and they also were less likely to recall having been securely attached. Thus, attachment quality may help explain why people from stepfamilies tend not to fare as well emotionally, socially, and psychologically as those from intact families (Love & Murdock, 2004).

Living with Gay or Lesbian Parents

As many as an estimated 9 million U.S. children and adolescents have at least one gay or lesbian parent. Some gays and lesbians are raising children born of previous heterosexual relationships. Others conceive by artificial means, use surrogate mothers, or adopt children (Pawelski et al., 2006; Perrin and AAP Committee on Psychosocial Aspects of Child and Family Health, 2002).

A considerable body of research has examined the development of children of gays and lesbians, including physical and emotional health, intelligence, adjustment, sense of self, moral judgment, and social and sexual functioning, and has indicated no special concerns (APA, 2004). There is no consistent difference between homosexual and heterosexual parents in emotional health or parenting skills and attitudes; and where there are differences, they tend to favor gay and lesbian parents (Brewaeys, Ponjaert, Van Hall, & Golombok, 1997; Meezan & Rauch, 2005; Pawelski et al., 2006; Perrin and AAP Committee on Psychosocial Aspects of Child and Family Health, 2002; Wainright, Russell, & Patterson, 2004). Openly gay or lesbian parents usually have positive relationships with their children, and the children are no more likely than children raised by heterosexual parents to have emotional, social, academic, or psychological problems (APA, 2004; Chan, Raboy, & Patterson, 1998; Gartrell, Deck, Rodas, Peyser, & Banks, 2005; Meezan

& Rauch, 2005; Mooney-Somers & Golombok, 2000; Golombok et al., 2003; Wainright et al., 2004). Furthermore, children of gays and lesbians are no more likely to be homosexual or to be confused about their gender than are children of heterosexuals (Anderssen, Amlie, & Ytteroy, 2002; Golombok et al., 2003; Meezan & Rauch, 2005; Pawelski et al., 2006; Wainright et al., 2004). However, many children of gays and lesbians are teased, and they often seek to hide information about their parents to avoid ridicule (Meezan and Rauch, 2005).

Such findings have social policy implications for legal decisions on custody and visitation disputes, foster care, and adoptions. In the face of controversy over gay and lesbian marriage or civil unions, with its implications for the security of children, several states have considered or adopted legislation sanctioning second-parent adoption by same-sex partners. To promote the economic and emotional well-being of children of these partnerships, the American Academy of Pediatrics supports a right to civil marriage for gays and lesbians (Pawelski et al., 2006) and legislative and legal efforts to permit a partner in a same-sex couple to adopt the other partner's child (AAP Committee on Psychosocial Aspects of Child and Family Health, 2002).

Adoptive Families

Adoption is found in all cultures throughout history. It is not only for infertile people; single people, older people, gay and lesbian couples, and people who already have biological children have become adoptive parents. Famous adoptees include the actress Halle Berry, the writer Maya Angelou, and former presidents Bill Clinton, Gerald Ford, and Herbert Hoover.

In 2001, 1.4 million U.S. children under 18—about 2.5 percent—lived with at least one adoptive parent (Kreider & Fields, 2005). An estimated 60 percent of legal adoptions are by stepparents or relatives, usually grandparents (Kreider, 2003).

Adoptions usually take place through public or private agencies. Agency adoptions are supposed to be confidential, with no contact between the birth mother and the adoptive parents, and the identity of the birth mother is kept secret. However, in recent years independent adoptions, made by agreement between birth parents and adoptive parents, have become more common than in the past. Often these are *open adoptions,* in which the parties share information or have direct contact. Studies suggest that the presumed risks of open adoption, such as fear that a birth mother who knows her child's whereabouts will try to reclaim the child, are overstated (Grotevant, McRoy, Elde, & Fravel, 1994). In a survey of 1,059 California adoptive families, whether an adoption was open bore no relation to the children's adjustment or to the parents' satisfaction with the adoption, both of which were very high (Berry, Dylla, Barth, & Needell, 1998).

Adopting a child carries special challenges: integrating the adopted child into the family, explaining the adoption to the child, helping the child develop a healthy sense of self, and perhaps eventually helping the child find and contact the biological parents. Data from a national longitudinal study show that adoptive parents invest just as much energy and resources in their children as biological parents do (Hamilton, Cheng, & Powell, 2007). A review of the literature found few significant differences in adjustment between adopted and nonadopted children (Haugaard, 1998). Children adopted in infancy are least likely to have adjustment problems (Sharma, McGue, & Benson, 1996b). Any problems that do occur may surface in middle childhood, when children become more aware of differences in the way families are formed, or in adolescence, particularly for boys (Freeark et al., 2005).

Cognitively, adoption is usually beneficial. An analysis of 62 studies of a total of 17,767 adopted children found that they scored higher on IQ tests and performed better in school than siblings or peers who remained in the birth family or in institutional care. Their IQ scores also equaled those of their adoptive siblings and nonadopted peers, but their school performance and language abilities tended to lag, and they were more likely to develop learning problems and to be referred for special education (van IJzendoorn & Juffer, 2005; van IJzendoorn, Juffer, & Poelhuis, 2005).

Adoptions of foreign-born children by U.S. families have nearly quadrupled since 1978 from 5,315 to 20,679 despite a decline in 2006 (Bosch et al., 2003; Crary, 2007). About 17 percent of adoptions are transracial, most often involving white parents adopting

Checkpoint

Can you . . .

✔ Discuss the impact of parental divorce on children and how living in a single-parent household can affect children's well-being?

✔ Identify some special issues and challenges of a stepfamily?

✔ Summarize findings on outcomes of child raising by gay and lesbian parents?

What's your view

• If you were to adopt a child, would you want the adoption to be open? Why or why not?

• If you were giving up your child for adoption, would you want the adoption to be open? Why or why not?

an Asian or Latin American child (Kreider, 2003). Rules governing interracial adoption vary from state to state; some states give priority to same-race adoption, whereas others require that race not be a factor in approval of an adoption.

Does foreign adoption entail special problems? Aside from the possibility of malnourishment or other serious medical conditions in children from developing countries (Bosch et al., 2003), a number of studies find no significant problems with children's psychological adjustment, school adjustment and performance, or observed behavior at home or in the way they cope with being adopted (Levy-Shiff, Zoran, & Shulman, 1997; Sharma, McGue, & Benson, 1996a). However, not all international adoptions proceed so smoothly, especially when the children have experienced substandard care or are older at the time of adoption (refer back to the discussion of children adopted from Romanian orphanages in Chapter 6).

Living with Grandparents

In many developing societies, such as those in Latin America and Asia, extended-family households predominate, and resident grandparents play an integral role in the family. In Thailand and Taiwan, about 40 percent of the population age 50 and over live in the same household with a minor grandchild, and half of those with grandchildren age 10 or younger—usually grandmothers—provide care for the child (Kinsella & Velkoff, 2001). Most children in technologically advanced countries, in contrast, grow up in nuclear families without grandparents or other relatives present in the household.

Yet, in both types of societies, a growing number of grandparents are their grandchildren's sole or primary caregivers. One reason, in developing countries, is rural parents' migration to urban areas to find work. In sub-Saharan Africa, the AIDS epidemic has left many orphans whose grandparents step into the parents' place. Such "skip-generation" families exist in all regions of the world, particularly in Afro-Caribbean countries (Kinsella & Velkoff, 2001).

In the United States, an increasing number of grandparents are serving as "parents by default" for children whose parents are unable to care for them—often as a result of teenage pregnancy, substance abuse, illness, divorce, or early death (Allen et al., 2000). In 2003, about 5 percent of children under 18 lived in grandparent-headed households, and about 40 percent of these children had no parent present. Black children were more likely than children in other ethnic groups to live in a grandparent's household (U.S. Census Bureau, 2006). Many grandparent-headed families are on fixed incomes (Hudnall, 2001), and some are in dire financial straits (Casper & Bryson, 1998; Minkler & Fuller-Thomson, 2005). Many of the grandparent-caregivers (mostly grandmothers) are widowed or divorced (Hudnall, 2001).

Most grandparents who take on the responsibility to raise their grandchildren do it because they love the children and do not want them placed in a stranger's foster home. However, the age difference can become a barrier, and both generations may feel cheated out of their traditional roles (Crowley, 1993; Larsen, 1990–1991). Also, aging grandparents may lack the stamina to keep up with an active child.

Grandparents who do not become foster parents or gain custody have no legal status. They may face many practical problems, from enrolling the child in school and gaining access to academic records to obtaining medical insurance for the child. Grandchildren are usually not eligible for coverage under employer-provided health insurance even if the grandparent has custody. Like working parents, working grandparents need good, affordable child care and family-friendly workplace policies, such as time off to care for a sick child. The federal Family and Medical Leave Act of 1993 does cover grandparents who are raising grandchildren, but many do not realize it.

Sibling Relationships

In remote rural villages of Asia, Africa, Oceania, and Central and South America, it is common to see older girls caring for three or four younger siblings. In such a community, older siblings have an important, culturally defined role. Parents train children early to teach younger sisters and brothers how to gather firewood, carry water, tend animals, and grow

Checkpoint ✔

Can you . . .

✔ Discuss trends in adoption and the adjustment of adopted children?

✔ Discuss the challenges involved in grandparents raising grandchildren?

food. Younger siblings absorb intangible values, such as respecting elders and placing the welfare of the group above that of the individual (Cicirelli, 1994). In industrialized countries such as the United States, parents generally try not to "burden" older children with the regular care of siblings (Weisner, 1993). When older siblings do teach younger ones, this usually happens informally and not as an established part of the social system (Cicirelli, 1994).

The number of siblings in a family and their spacing, birth order, and gender often determine roles and relationships. The larger number of siblings in nonindustrialized societies helps the family carry on its work and provide for aging members. In industrialized societies, siblings tend to be fewer and farther apart in age, enabling parents to focus more resources and attention on each child (Cicirelli, 1994).

Two longitudinal studies in England and in Pennsylvania found that changes in sibling relationships were most likely to occur when one sibling was between ages 7 and 9. Both mothers and children often attributed these changes to outside friendships, which led to jealousy and competitiveness or loss of interest in and intimacy with the sibling (Dunn, 1996).

These Inuit boys in a northern Canadian fishing camp enjoy caring for a baby brother. Children in nonindustrialized societies tend to have regular responsibility for siblings.

Sibling relations can be a laboratory for conflict resolution. Siblings are motivated to make up after quarrels, since they know they will see each other every day. They learn that expressing anger does not end a relationship. Children are more apt to squabble with same-sex siblings; two brothers quarrel more than any other combination (Cicirelli, 1976, 1995).

Siblings influence each other's gender development. In a 3-year longitudinal study of 198 siblings (median ages 8 and 10), secondborns tended to become more like their older siblings in gender-related attitudes, personality, and leisure activities. Firstborns were more influenced by parents and less by younger siblings (McHale, Updegraff, Helms-Erikson, & Crouter, 2001).

Siblings influence each other, not only *directly,* through their own interactions, but also *indirectly* through their impact on each other's relationship with the parents. Parents' experience with an older sibling influences their expectations and treatment of a younger one (Brody, 2004). Conversely, behavior patterns a child establishes with parents tend to "spill over" into the child's behavior with siblings. In a study of 101 English families, when the parent-child relationship was warm and affectionate, siblings tended to have positive relationships as well. When the parent-child relationship was conflictual, sibling conflict was more likely (Pike et al., 2005).

Checkpoint

Can you . . .

✔ Compare the roles and responsibilities of siblings in industrialized and nonindustrialized countries?

✔ Discuss how siblings affect each other's development?

The Child in the Peer Group

In middle childhood the peer group comes into its own. Groups form naturally among children who live near one another or go to school together and often consist of children of the same racial or ethnic origin and similar socioeconomic status. Children who play together are usually close in age and of the same sex (Hartup, 1992; Pellegrini et al., 2002).

How does the peer group influence children? What determines their acceptance by peers and their ability to make friends?

Guidepost 3

How do relationships with peers change in middle childhood, and what factors influence popularity and aggressive behavior?

Positive and Negative Effects of Peer Relations

Children benefit from doing things with peers. They develop skills needed for sociability and intimacy, and they gain a sense of belonging. They are motivated to achieve, and they attain a sense of identity. They learn leadership and communication skills, roles, and rules.

As children begin to move away from parental influence, the peer group opens new perspectives and frees them to make independent judgments. In comparing themselves with others their age, children can gauge their abilities more realistically and gain a clearer sense of self-efficacy. The peer group helps children learn how to get along in society—how to adjust their needs and desires to those of others, when to yield, and when to stand firm. The peer group offers emotional security. It is reassuring for children to find out that they are not alone in harboring thoughts that might offend an adult.

On the negative side, peer groups may reinforce **prejudice:** unfavorable attitudes toward "outsiders," especially members of certain racial or ethnic groups. Children tend to show biases toward children like themselves, but these biases, except for a preference for children of the same sex, diminish with age and cognitive development (Powlishta, Serbin, Doyle, & White, 1994). Prejudice and discrimination can do real damage. In a 5-year longitudinal study of 714 African American 10- to 12-year-olds, those who saw themselves as targets of discrimination tended to show depressive symptoms or conduct problems during the next 5 years (Brody et al., 2006).

The peer group also can foster antisocial tendencies. Preadolescent children are especially susceptible to pressure to conform. It is usually in the company of peers that some children shoplift and begin to use drugs (Hartup, 1992). Of course, some degree of conformity to group standards is healthy. It is unhealthy when it becomes destructive or prompts young people to act against their better judgment.

Gender Differences in Peer-Group Relationships

Boys' and girls' peer groups engage in different types of activities. Groups of boys more consistently pursue gender-typed activities. They play in large groups with well-defined leadership hierarchies and engage in more competitive and rough-and-tumble play. Girls have more intimate conversations characterized by prosocial interactions and shared confidences (Rose & Rudolph, 2006). Also, girls are more likely than boys to engage in cross-gender activities, such as team sports (McHale, Kim, Whiteman, & Crouter, 2004).

Boys are apt to receive less emotional support from their friends than girls do. Girls tend to seek social connections and are more sensitive to others' distress. They are more likely than boys to worry about their relationships, to express emotions, and to seek emotional support (Rose & Rudolph, 2006).

Why do children segregate themselves by sex and engage in such different activities? One obvious reason is that males and females differ in body size, strength, and energy. Boys need more space and more physical exercise to build physical fitness. Another explanation is that same-sex peer groups help socialize children for their future roles as competitors or nurturers (Pellegrini & Archer, 2005). Same-sex peer groups help children learn gender-appropriate behaviors and incorporate gender roles into their self-concept. In a 2-year study of 106 ethnically diverse third through seventh graders, a sense of being typical of one's gender and being content with that gender contributed to self-esteem and well-being, whereas feeling pressure—from parents, peers, or oneself—to conform to gender stereotypes lessened well-being (Yunger, Carver, & Perry, 2004).

Popularity

Popularity becomes more important in middle childhood. Schoolchildren whose peers like them are likely to be well adjusted as adolescents. Those who have trouble getting along with peers are more likely to develop psychological problems, drop out of school, or become delinquent (Hartup, 1992; Kupersmidt & Coie, 1990; Morison & Masten, 1991; Newcomb, Bukowski, & Pattee, 1993).

Popularity can be measured in two ways, and the results may differ. Researchers measure *sociometric popularity* by asking children which peers they like most and least; *perceived popularity* is measured by asking children which children are best liked by their peers.

Sociometric studies have identified five *peer status groups: popular* (youngsters who receive many positive nominations), *rejected* (those who receive many negative nominations), *neglected* (those who receive few nominations of either kind), *controversial* (those who receive many positive and many negative nominations), and *average* (those who do not receive an unusual number of nominations of either kind).

Sociometrically popular children typically have good cognitive abilities, are high achievers, are good at solving social problems, help other children, and are assertive without being disruptive or aggressive. They are kind, trustworthy, cooperative, loyal, and self-disclosing and provide emotional support. Their superior social skills make others enjoy being with them (Cillessen & Mayeux, 2004; LaFontana & Cillessen, 2002; Masten & Coatsworth, 1998). On the other hand, as we will discuss in a subsequent section, some school-age children with *perceived popularity,* that is, high status, may be dominant, arrogant, and aggressive. Children with perceived popularity tend to be physically attractive and to have athletic and, to a lesser extent, academic ability (Cillessen & Mayeux, 2004; LaFontana & Cillessen, 2002).

Children can be *un*popular (either rejected or neglected) for many reasons. Some unpopular children are aggressive; others are hyperactive, inattentive, or withdrawn (Dodge, Coie, Pettit, & Price, 1990; Masten & Coatsworth, 1998; Newcomb et al., 1993; Pope, Bierman, & Mumma, 1991). Still others act silly and immature or anxious and uncertain. Unpopular children are often insensitive to other children's feelings and do not adapt well to new situations (Bierman, Smoot, & Aumiller, 1993). Some show undue interest in being with groups of the other sex (Sroufe, Bennett, Englund, Urban, & Shulman, 1993). Some unpopular children expect not to be liked, and this becomes a self-fulfilling prophecy (Rabiner & Coie, 1989).

It is often in the family that children acquire behaviors that affect popularity (Masten & Coatsworth, 1998). Authoritative parents tend to have more popular children than authoritarian parents (Dekovic & Janssens, 1992). Children of authoritarian parents who punish and threaten are likely to threaten or act mean with other children. They are less popular than children whose authoritative parents reason with them and try to help them understand how another person might feel (Hart, Ladd, & Burleson, 1990).

In both Western and Chinese cultures, sociability and cooperativeness are associated with social and school adjustment, whereas aggression is generally associated with peer rejection and adjustment problems. In both cultures boys tend to be more aggressive and to have more problems in school than girls (Chen, Cen, Li, & He, 2005). One cultural difference is in the social acceptance of shy, sensitive children (Box 14-1).

Friendship

Children may spend much of their free time in groups, but only as individuals do they form friendships. Popularity is the peer group's opinion of a child, but friendship is a two-way street.

Children look for friends who are like them in age, sex, ethnicity, and interests. The strongest friendships involve equal commitment and mutual give-and-take. Even unpopular children can make friends; but they have fewer friends than popular children and tend to find friends among younger children, other unpopular children, or children in a different class or a different school (George & Hartmann, 1996; Hartup, 1992, 1996a, 1996b; Newcomb & Bagwell, 1995).

With their friends, children learn to communicate and cooperate. They help each other weather stressful transitions. The inevitable quarrels help children learn to resolve conflicts (Hartup, 1992, 1996a, 1996b; Hartup & Stevens, 1999; Newcomb & Bagwell, 1995). Friendship seems to help children feel good about themselves, though it's also likely that children who feel good about themselves have an easier time making friends. Peer rejection and friendlessness in middle childhood have long-term effects. In one longitudinal study, fifth graders who had no friends were more likely than their classmates to have low self-esteem in young adulthood and to show symptoms of depression (Bagwell, Newcomb, & Bukowski, 1998).

Box 14-1 *Popularity: A Cross-Cultural View*

How does culture affect popularity? Would a child who is popular in one culture be equally popular in another? Researchers compared 480 second and fourth graders in Shanghai, China, with 296 children the same ages in Ontario, Canada (Chen, Rubin, & Sun, 1992). Although the two samples were quite different—for example, none of the Canadian children came from peasant families, but many of the Chinese children did—both samples were representative of school-age children in the two countries.

The researchers assessed the children's popularity by two kinds of peer perceptions. The children filled out a sociometric rating telling which three classmates they most and least liked to be with and which three classmates were their best friends. The results showed that certain traits were valued similarly in both cultures. A sociable, cooperative child was likely to be popular in both China and Canada, and an aggressive child was likely to be rejected in both countries. However, one important difference emerged: Shy, sensitive children were well liked in China, but not in Canada. This was not surprising. Chinese children traditionally were encouraged to be cautious, to restrain themselves, and to inhibit their urges; thus a quiet, shy youngster was considered well behaved. In a Western culture, in contrast, such a child is likely to be seen as socially immature, fearful, and lacking in self-confidence.

A follow-up study at ages 8 and 10 (Chen, Rubin, & Li, 1995) again found that shy, sensitive Chinese children were popular with peers. They also were rated by teachers as socially competent, as leaders, and as academic achievers. However, by age 12, an interesting twist had occurred: shy, sensitive Chinese children were no longer popular. They tended to be rejected by their peers, just as in Western cultures.

The researchers suggested that shyness and sensitivity might take on different social meanings in China as children enter adolescence, when peer relationships become more important and adult approval becomes less so, and that even in China, with its strong tradition of obedience to authority, the influence of adult social standards may wane as children's urge to make independent judgments of their peers asserts itself.

A more recently published study concerning younger children points to effects of social change resulting from the radical restructuring of China's economic system, particularly since the late 1990s. During that time China has shifted from a completely collectivist system toward a more competitive, technologically advanced market economy with its associated individualistic values.

In the study (Chen, Cen, Li, & He, 2005), researchers administered sociometric measures and peer assessments of social functioning to three cohorts of third and fourth graders in Shanghai schools in 1990, 1998, and 2002. They examined the children's school records and teacher ratings. As in the

During middle childhood, shy, sensitive children are better liked in China than in Western cultures because they are considered well behaved. Children this age tend to accept adult standards of behavior.

earlier studies, prosocial behavior was associated with social status and school achievement, whereas aggression was generally associated with peer rejection and adjustment problems.

However, a striking change emerged with regard to shyness/sensitivity. In the 1990 cohort, shy children were accepted by peers and were high in academic achievement, leadership, and teacher-rated competence. By 2002, the results were just the reverse: shy children tended to be rejected by peers, to be depressed, and to be rated by teachers as low in competence. The results for the 1998 cohort were mixed, likely reflecting the attitudes of a society in transition. These findings suggest that the social acceptability of shy children is closely related to cultural norms. In the quasi-capitalistic society that China has become, social assertiveness and initiative may be more highly appreciated and encouraged than in the past, and shyness and sensitivity may lead to social and psychological difficulties for children.

What's your view ?

How would you advise parents of a shy, sensitive child who complains of being rejected by other children?

Check it out !

For more information on this topic, go to www.pbs.org/kcts/preciouschildren/resources/index.html. Here you will find links about China from the PBS documentary "Precious Children." Or go to http://www.pbs.org/inthemix/. This is the Web site for the PBS program *In the Mix,* which offers transcripts. Search for the show called "Cliques: Behind the Labels."

Table 14-1 | Selman's Stages of Friendship

Stage	Description	Example
Stage 0: Momentary playmateship (ages 3 to 7)	On this *undifferentiated* level of friendship, children are egocentric and have trouble considering another person's point of view; they tend to think only about what they want from a relationship. Most very young children define their friends in terms of physical closeness and value them for material or physical attributes.	"She lives on my street" or "He has the Power Rangers."
Stage 1: One-way assistance (ages 4 to 9)	On this *unilateral* level, a "good friend" does what the child wants the friend to do.	"She's not my friend anymore, because she wouldn't go with me when I wanted her to" or "He's my friend because he always says yes when I want to borrow his eraser."
Stage 2: Two-way fair-weather cooperation (ages 6 to 12)	This *reciprocal* level overlaps stage 1. It involves give-and-take but still serves many separate self-interests, rather than the common interests of the two friends.	"We are friends; we do things for each other" or "A friend is someone who plays with you when you don't have anybody else to play with."
Stage 3: Intimate, mutually shared relationships (ages 9 to 15)	On this *mutual* level, children view a friendship as having a life of its own. It is an ongoing, systematic, committed relationship that incorporates more than doing things for each other. Friends often become possessive and demand exclusivity.	"It takes a long time to make a close friend, so you really feel bad if you find out that your friend is trying to make other friends too."
Stage 4: Autonomous interdependence (beginning at age 12)	In this *interdependent* stage, children respect friends' needs for both dependency and autonomy.	"A good friendship is a real commitment, a risk you have to take; you have to support and trust and give, but you have to be able to let go too."

Source: Selman, 1980; Selman & Selman, 1979.

Children's concepts of friendship and the ways they act with their friends change with age, reflecting cognitive and emotional growth. Preschool friends play together, but friendship among school-age children is deeper and more stable. Children cannot be or have true friends until they achieve the cognitive maturity to consider other people's views and needs as well as their own (Hartup, 1992; Hartup & Stevens, 1999; Newcomb & Bagwell, 1995).

On the basis of interviews with more than 250 people between ages 3 and 45, Robert Selman (1980; Selman & Selman, 1979) traced changing conceptions of friendship through five overlapping stages (Table 14-1). He found that most school-age children are in stage 2 (reciprocal friendship based on self-interest), but some older children, ages 9 and up, may be in stage 3 (intimate, mutually shared relationships).

School-age children distinguish among "best friends," "good friends," and "casual friends" on the basis of intimacy and time spent together (Hartup & Stevens, 1999). Children this age typically have three to five "best" friends but usually play with only one or two at a time (Hartup, 1992; Hartup & Stevens, 1999). School-age girls care less about having many friends than about having a few close friends they can rely on. Boys have more friendships, but they tend to be less intimate and affectionate (Furman, 1982; Furman & Buhrmester, 1985; Hartup & Stevens, 1999).

Aggression and Bullying

Aggression declines and changes in form during the early school years. After age 6 or 7, most children become less aggressive as they grow less egocentric, more empathic, more cooperative, and better able to communicate. They can now put themselves in someone else's place, can understand another person's motives, and can find positive ways of asserting themselves. **Instrumental aggression** (aggression aimed at achieving an objective),

Checkpoint ✔

Can you . . .

✔ Distinguish between popularity and friendship?

✔ List characteristics children look for in friends?

✔ Tell how age and gender affect friendship?

instrumental aggression
Aggressive behavior used as a means of achieving a goal.

hostile aggression Aggressive behavior intended to hurt another person.

the hallmark of the preschool period, becomes much less common (Coie & Dodge, 1998). However, as aggression declines overall, **hostile aggression**—action intended to hurt another person—proportionately increases (Coie & Dodge, 1998), often taking verbal rather than physical form (Pellegrini & Archer, 2005). A high level of physical aggression may lead to a high level of social aggression, which is less likely to be punished (Brendgen et al., 2005).

A small minority of children do not learn to control physical aggression (Coie & Dodge, 1998). These children tend to have social and psychological problems, but it is not clear whether aggression causes these problems or is a response to them, or both (Crick & Grotpeter, 1995). Highly aggressive children often egg each other on to antisocial acts. Thus, school-age boys who are physically aggressive may become juvenile delinquents in adolescence (Broidy et al., 2003).

Gender Differences in Aggressiveness

As we discussed in Chapter 11, from an early age boys are more physically aggressive, whereas relational, or social, aggression seems to be more typical of girls. As children grow older, gender differences in the amount of physical aggression remain. However, gender differences in relational, aggression seem to increase from ages 6 to 17, peaking between ages 11 and 17 (Archer, 2004). Some researchers suggest that relational aggression may be no more frequent in girls than in boys, but its consequences may be more serious for girls, who tend to be more preoccupied with relationships than boys are (Cillessen & Mayeux, 2004; Crick et al., 2002).

Sex-segregated peer groups are the context within which these gender differences develop. Boys tend to be especially aggressive when a group is forming, as they compete for dominance. Later, once their status is achieved, they seek to reconcile with their former adversaries. Girls seek status through more manipulative means involving indirect or relational aggression (Pellegrini & Archer, 2005).

As we have already mentioned, aggressors tend to be personally disliked, but physically aggressive boys and some relationally aggressive girls are perceived as among the most popular in the classroom (Cillessen & Mayeux, 2004; Rodkin, Farmer, Pearl, & Van Acker, 2000). In a study of peer-rejected fourth graders, aggressive boys tended to gain in social status by the end of fifth grade, suggesting that behavior shunned by younger children may be seen as cool or glamorous by preadolescents (Sandstrom & Coie, 1999). In a longitudinal study of a multiethnic group of 905 urban fifth through ninth graders, physical aggression became less disapproved as children moved into adolescence, and relational aggression was increasingly reinforced by high status among peers (Cillessen & Mayeux, 2004).

Types of Aggression and Social Information Processing

What makes children act aggressively? One answer may lie in the way they process social information: what features of the social environment they pay attention to and how they interpret what they perceive (Crick & Dodge, 1994, 1996).

Instrumental, or *proactive,* aggressors view force and coercion as effective ways to get what they want. They act deliberately, not out of anger. In social learning terms, they are aggressive because they expect to be rewarded; and when they are rewarded, their belief in the effectiveness of aggression is reinforced (Crick & Dodge, 1996). In contrast, a child who is accidentally bumped in line may push back angrily, assuming that the other child bumped her on purpose. This is an example of *hostile,* or *reactive,* aggression. Such children often have a **hostile attribution bias;** they see other children as trying to hurt them, and they strike out in retaliation or self-defense (Crick & Dodge, 1996; de Castro, Veerman, Koops, Bosch, & Monshouwer, 2002; Waldman, 1996).

hostile attribution bias Tendency for someone to perceive others as trying to hurt him or her and to strike out in retaliation or self-defense.

Children who seek dominance and control may react aggressively to threats to their status, which they may attribute to hostility (de Castro et al., 2002; Erdley et al., 1997). Rejected children and those exposed to harsh parenting also tend to have a hostile attribution bias (Coie & Dodge, 1998; Masten & Coatsworth, 1998; Weiss, Dodge, Bates, &

Pettit, 1992). Since people often do become hostile toward someone who acts aggressively toward them, a hostile bias may set in motion a cycle of aggression (de Castro et al., 2002). Hostile attribution bias becomes more common between ages 6 and 12 (Aber, Brown, & Jones, 2003).

Both instrumental and hostile aggressors need help in altering the way they process social information so that they do not interpret aggression as either useful or justified. *Instrumental* aggression tends to stop if it is not rewarded (Crick & Dodge, 1996). *Hostile* aggression can be stopped by teaching children how to recognize when they are getting angry and how to control their anger. In a New York City school study, children exposed to a conflict resolution curriculum that involved discussion and group role playing showed less hostile attribution bias, less aggression, fewer behavior problems, and more effective responses to social situations than children who had not participated in the program (Aber et al., 2003).

Does Media Violence Stimulate Aggression?

Children spend more time on entertainment media than on any other activity besides school and sleeping. On average, children spend about 4 hours a day in front of a television or computer screen—some much more than that. Virtually all U.S. families with children have at least one television set, most have VCR or DVD players, 3 out of 4 subscribe to cable or satellite TV, and more than half have access to the Internet (Anderson et al., 2003; DeBell & Chapman, 2006).

About 6 out of 10 U.S. television programs portray violence, usually glamorized, glorified, or trivialized (Yokota & Thompson, 2000), in addition to the constant, repetitive news coverage of natural disasters and violent acts (American Academy of Child & Adolescent Psychiatry, 2002). Among 50 major televised sporting events, such as the Superbowl, 49 percent of commercial breaks contained at least one commercial showing unsafe behavior or violence (Tamburro, Gordon, D'Apolito, & Howard, 2004). Music videos disproportionately feature violence against women and blacks. The motion picture, music, and video game industries aggressively market violent, adult-rated products to children (AAP Committee on Public Education, 2001).

Because of the high proportion of their time that children spend with media, the images they see can become primary role models and sources of information about how people behave in the real world. The vast preponderance of experimental, longitudinal, epidemiological, and cross-cultural studies supports a causal relationship between media violence and aggressive behavior in childhood, adolescence, and adulthood. In fact, the strongest single correlate of violent behavior is previous exposure to violence (AAP Committee on Public Education, 2001; Anderson, Berkowitz, et al., 2003; Anderson, Huston, Schmitt, Linebarger, & Wright, 2001; Huesmann, Moise-Titus, Podolski, & Eron, 2003).

How does media violence lead to long-term aggressiveness? It provides visceral thrills without showing the human cost and leads children to view aggression as acceptable. Children who see both heroes and villains achieving their aims through violence are likely to conclude that force is an effective way to resolve conflicts. They may learn to take violence for granted and may be less likely to intervene when they see it. The more realistically violence is portrayed, the more likely it is to be accepted (AAP Committee on Public Education, 2001; Anderson, Berkowitz, et al., 2003). Furthermore, each hour that children spend watching violent television reduces time spent with friends. Thus, violent TV fare may set off a cycle in which frequent viewers become more aggressive, and their behavior leads to social isolation and, in turn, to viewing more violent television (Bickham & Rich, 2006).

Children are more vulnerable than adults to the influence of televised violence (AAP Committee on Public Education, 2001; Coie & Dodge, 1998). Classic social learning research suggests that children imitate filmed models even more than live ones (Bandura, Ross, & Ross, 1963). The influence is stronger if the child believes the violence on the screen is real, identifies with the violent character, finds that character attractive, and watches without parental supervision or intervention (Anderson,

What's your view

- What can and should be done to reduce children's exposure to violent television programs?

Bullying tends to peak in the middle grades. Boys are more likely to use overt aggression; girls, relational aggression.

Berkowitz, et al., 2003; Coie & Dodge, 1998). Highly aggressive children are more strongly affected by media violence than are less aggressive children (Anderson, Berkowitz, et al., 2003).

The long-term influence of televised violence is greater among school-age children than at earlier ages (Eron & Huesmann, 1986). Among 427 children whose viewing habits were studied at age 8, the best predictor of aggressiveness at age 19 was the degree of violence in the shows they had watched as children (Eron, 1980, 1982). In a follow-up study, the amount of television viewed at age 8 and the preference among boys for violent shows predicted the severity of criminal offenses at age 30 (Huesmann, 1986; Huesmann & Eron, 1984).

Less research has been done on effects of newer, interactive media, such as video games and the Internet, but initial studies suggest that "effects of child-initiated virtual violence may be more profound than those of passive media, such as television." Rather than merely let a child observe rewards for violent behavior, violent video games "place the child in the role of the aggressor and reward him or her for successful violent behavior" (AAP Committee on Public Education, 2001, pp. 1223–1224). In experimental studies, young people, after playing video games, have shown decreases in prosocial behavior and increases in aggressive thoughts and violent retaliation to provocation (Anderson, 2000).

Media-induced aggressiveness can be minimized by cutting down on television use and by parental monitoring and guidance of the shows children watch (Anderson, Berkowitz, et al., 2003). The AAP Committee on Public Education (2001) recommends that parents limit children's media exposure to 1 to 2 hours a day. Third and fourth graders who participated in a 6-month curriculum aimed at motivating them to monitor and reduce the time they spent on television, videotapes, and video games showed significant decreases in peer-rated aggression, as compared with a control group (Robinson, Wilde, Navracruz, Haydel, & Varady, 2001).

Bullies and Victims

bullying Aggression deliberately and persistently directed against a particular target, or victim, typically one who is weak, vulnerable, and defenseless.

Aggression becomes **bullying** when it is deliberately, persistently directed against a particular target: a victim who typically is weak, vulnerable, and defenseless. Bullying can be physical (hitting, punching, kicking, or taking of personal belongings), verbal (name calling or threatening), or psychological (isolating and gossiping) (Veenstra et al., 2005). Some 24 percent of primary schools, 42 percent of middle schools, and 21 percent of high schools report student bullying at school at least once a week (Guerino, Hurwitz, Noonan, & Kaffenberger, 2006). Bullying also is a problem in other industrialized countries, such as England and Japan (Hara, 2002; Kanetsuna & Smith, 2002; Ruiz & Tanaka, 2001). In Japan and Korea, school bullying has been associated with a growing wave of student suicide and suicidal thoughts and behavior (Kim, Koh, & Leventhal, 2005; Rios-Ellis, Bellamy, & Shoji, 2000).

Most bullies are boys (Veenstra et al., 2005) who tend to victimize other boys; girls tend to bully other girls (Pellegrini & Long, 2002). Male bullies tend to use overt, physical aggression; female bullies may use relational aggression (Boulton, 1995; Nansel et al., 2001). Patterns of bullying and victimization may become established as early as kindergarten; as tentative peer groups form, aggressors soon get to know which children make the easiest marks. Bullying and aggression peak during the transition to middle school. During this transition, boys use bullying as a way to establish dominance in the peer group. Unlike the pattern for being a bully, the likelihood of being bullied decreases steadily. As children get older, most of them may learn how to discourage bullying, leaving a smaller pool of available victims (Pellegrini & Long, 2002; Smith & Levan, 1995).

Both bullies and victims exhibit psychological problems, and both tend to be disliked. In fact, about half of bullies say they are victims as well, and they function more poorly than either bullies or victims. Bullies are aggressive, impulsive, hostile, domineering, antisocial, and uncooperative, though they describe themselves as making friends easily. In keeping with the theory of hostile attribution bias, they may claim to pick on their victims because they were provoked (Veenstra et al., 2005).

Risk factors for victimization seem to be similar across cultures (Schwartz, Chang, & Farver, 2001). Victims do not fit in: They tend to be anxious, depressed, cautious, quiet, and submissive and to cry easily, or to be argumentative and provocative (Hodges, Boivin, Vitaro, & Bukowski, 1999; Olweus, 1995; Veenstra et al., 2005). They have few friends and may live in harsh, punitive family environments (Nansel et al., 2001; Schwartz, Dodge, Pettit, & Bates and the Conduct Problems Prevention Research Group, 2000). Victims are apt to have low self-esteem, though it is not clear whether low self-esteem leads to or follows from victimization. Male victims tend to be physically weak (Boulton & Smith, 1994; Olweus, 1995). Among 5,749 Canadian children, those who were overweight were most likely to become either victims or bullies (Janssen, Craig, Boyce, & Pickett, 2004).

Victims of bullying may develop behavior problems, such as hyperactivity. They may become more aggressive themselves or may become depressed (Schwartz, McFadyen-Ketchum, Dodge, Pettit, & Bates, 1998; Veenstra et al., 2005). In the wave of school shootings since 1994, the perpetrators often had been victims of bullying (Anderson, Kaufman, et al., 2001). Bullies are at increased risk of delinquency, crime, or alcohol abuse.

In 2004 the U.S. Department of Health and Human Services announced a campaign to prevent bullying and youth violence. Steps to Respect, a program for grades 3 to 6, aims to (1) increase staff awareness and responsiveness to bullying, (2) teach students social and emotional skills, and (3) foster socially responsible beliefs. A randomized controlled study of 1,023 third to sixth graders found a reduction in playground bullying and argumentative behavior and an increase in harmonious interactions among children who received the program, as well as less bystander incitement to bullying (Frey et al., 2005).

Checkpoint ✔

Can you . . .

✔ Tell how aggression changes during middle childhood and how social information processing and televised violence can contribute to it?

✔ Discuss gender differences in aggression in school-age children?

✔ Tell how patterns of bullying and victimization become established and change?

✔ List risk factors for bullying and victimization?

Mental Health

Guidepost 4

What are some common mental health problems of childhood, and how do children respond to the stresses of modern life?

The term *mental health* may be a misnomer because it usually refers to emotional health. Although most children are fairly well adjusted, at least 1 in 10 children and adolescents has a diagnosed mental illness severe enough to cause some impairment, according to recent estimates (Leslie, Newman, Chesney, & Perrin, 2005). Diagnosis of mental disorders in children is important because they can lead to psychiatric disorders in adulthood (Kim-Cohen et al., 2003). In fact, half of all cases of mental disorders begin by age 14 (Kessler et al., 2005). Let's look at several common emotional disturbances and then at types of treatment.

Common Emotional Disturbances

Children with emotional, behavioral, and developmental problems tend to be an underserved group. Compared with other children who have special health care needs, they are more likely to have conditions that affect their daily activities and cause them to miss school. They often have chronic physical conditions. Many of them lack adequate health insurance and have unmet health care needs (Bethell, Read, & Blumberg, 2005).

A reported 55.7 percent of children diagnosed with emotional, behavioral, and developmental problems have *disruptive conduct disorders:* aggression, defiance, or antisocial behavior. Almost all the rest, 43.5 percent, have *anxiety* or *mood disorders:* feeling sad, depressed, unloved, nervous, fearful, or lonely (Bethell, 2005).

Disruptive Conduct Disorders

Temper tantrums and defiant, argumentative, hostile, or deliberately annoying behavior— common among 4- and 5-year-olds—typically are outgrown by middle childhood. When

oppositional defiant disorder (ODD) Pattern of behavior, persisting into middle childhood, marked by negativity, hostility, and defiance.

conduct disorder (CD) Persistent, repetitive pattern of aggressive, antisocial behavior violating societal norms or the rights of others.

such a pattern of behavior persists until age 8, children (usually boys) may be diagnosed with **oppositional defiant disorder (ODD),** a pattern of defiance, disobedience, and hostility toward adult authority figures lasting at least 6 months and going beyond the bounds of normal childhood behavior. Children with ODD constantly fight, argue, lose their temper, snatch things, blame others, are angry and resentful, have few friends, are in constant trouble in school, and test the limits of adults' patience (APA, 2000; National Library of Medicine, 2004).

Some children with ODD also have **conduct disorder (CD),** a persistent, repetitive pattern, beginning at an early age, of aggressive, antisocial acts, such as truancy, setting fires, habitual lying, fighting, bullying, theft, vandalism, assaults, and drug and alcohol use (APA, 2000; National Library of Medicine, 2003). About 1 to 4 percent of noninstitutionalized 9- to 17-year-olds in the United States have CD (USDHHS, 1999b). Some 11- to 13-year-olds progress from conduct disorder to criminal violence—mugging, rape, and break-ins—and by age 17 may be frequent, serious offenders (Coie & Dodge, 1998). Between 25 and 50 percent of these highly antisocial children become antisocial adults (USDHHS, 1999b).

What determines whether a particular child with antisocial tendencies will become severely and chronically antisocial? Neurobiological deficits, such as weak stress-regulating mechanisms, may fail to warn children to restrain themselves from dangerous or risky behavior. Such deficits may be genetically influenced or may be brought on by adverse environments such as hostile parenting or family conflict, or both (van Goozen, Fairchild, Snoek, & Harold, 2007). (In Chapter 17 we further discuss roots of antisocial behavior and juvenile delinquency.)

School Phobia and Other Anxiety Disorders

school phobia Unrealistic fear of going to school; may be a form of *separation anxiety disorder* or *social phobia.*

separation anxiety disorder Condition involving excessive, prolonged anxiety concerning separation from home or from people to whom a child is attached.

Children with **school phobia** have an unrealistic fear of going to school. Some children have realistic reasons to fear going to school: a sarcastic teacher, overly demanding work, or a bully in the school yard. In such cases, the environment may need changing, not the child (Kochenderfer & Ladd, 1996). True school phobia may be a type of **separation anxiety disorder,** a condition involving excessive anxiety for at least 4 weeks concerning separation from home or from people to whom the child is attached.

Although separation anxiety is normal in infancy, when it persists in older children it is cause for concern. Separation anxiety disorder affects some 4 percent of children and young adolescents and may persist through the college years. These children often come from close-knit, caring families. They may develop the disorder spontaneously or after a stressful event, such as the death of a pet, an illness, or a move to a new school (APA, 2000; Harvard Medical School, 2004). Many children with separation anxiety also show symptoms of depression (USDHHS, 1999b).

social phobia Extreme fear and/or avoidance of social situations.

Sometimes school phobia may be a form of **social phobia,** or *social anxiety:* extreme fear and/or avoidance of social situations, such as speaking in class or meeting an acquaintance on the street. Social phobia affects about 5 percent of children. It runs in families, so there is likely a genetic component. Often these phobias are triggered by traumatic experiences, such as a child's mind going blank after being called on in class (Beidel & Turner, 1998). Social anxiety tends to increase with age, whereas separation anxiety decreases (Costello et al., 2003).

generalized anxiety disorder Anxiety not focused on any single aspect of life.

Some children have a **generalized anxiety disorder,** not focused on any specific aspect of their lives. These children worry about just about everything: school grades, storms, earthquakes, hurting themselves on the playground, or the amount of gas in the tank. They tend to be self-conscious, self-doubting, and excessively concerned with meeting the expectations of others. They seek approval and need constant reassurance, but their worry seems independent of performance or of how they are regarded by others (APA, 1994; Harvard Medical School, 2004; USDHHS, 1999b).

obsessive-compulsive disorder Anxiety aroused by repetitive, intrusive thoughts, images, or impulses, often leading to compulsive ritual behaviors.

Far less common is **obsessive-compulsive disorder (OCD).** Those with this disorder may be obsessed by repetitive, intrusive thoughts, images, or impulses (often involving irrational fears) or may show compulsive behaviors, such as constant hand-washing, or both (APA, 2000; Harvard Medical School, 2004; USDHHS, 1999b).

Anxiety disorders tend to run in families (Harvard Medical School, 2004) and are twice as common among girls as among boys. The heightened female vulnerability to anxiety begins as early as age 6. Females also are more susceptible to depression, which is similar to anxiety and often goes hand in hand with it (Lewinsohn, Gotlib, Lewinsohn, Seeley, & Allen, 1998). Both anxiety and depression may be neurologically based or may stem from insecure attachment, exposure to an anxious or depressed parent, or other early experiences that make children feel a lack of control over what happens around them. Parents who reward an anxious child with attention to the anxiety may unwittingly perpetuate it through operant conditioning (Chorpita & Barlow, 1998; Harvard Medical School, 2004).

Childhood Depression

Childhood depression is a disorder of mood that goes beyond normal, temporary sadness. Depression is estimated to occur in 2 percent of elementary school children (NCHS, 2004). Symptoms include inability to have fun or concentrate, fatigue, extreme activity or apathy, crying, sleep problems, weight change, physical complaints, feelings of worthlessness, a prolonged sense of friendlessness, or frequent thoughts about death or suicide. Childhood depression may signal the beginning of a recurrent problem that is likely to persist into adulthood (Birmaher, 1998; Birmaher et al., 1996; Cicchetti & Toth, 1998; Kye & Ryan, 1995; USDHHS, 1999b; Weissman et al., 1999).

The specific causes of childhood depression are unknown, but depressed children tend to come from families with high levels of parental depression, anxiety, substance abuse, or antisocial behavior. The atmosphere in such families may increase children's risk of depression (Cicchetti & Toth, 1998; USDHHS, 1999b).

Researchers have found two specific genes related to depression. The gene 5-HTT helps to control the brain chemical serotonin and affects mood. In a longitudinal study of 847 people born in the same year in Dunedin, New Zealand, those who had two short versions of this gene were more likely to become depressed than those who had two long versions (Caspi et al., 2003). A short form of another gene, SERT-s, which also controls serotonin, is associated with enlargement of the pulvinar, a brain region involved in negative emotions (Young et al., 2007).

Children as young as 5 or 6 can accurately report depressed moods and feelings that forecast later trouble, from academic problems to major depression and ideas of suicide (Ialongo, Edelsohn, & Kellam, 2001). Depression often emerges during the transition to middle school and may be related to stiffer academic pressures (Cicchetti & Toth, 1998), weak self-efficacy beliefs, and lack of personal investment in academic success (Rudolph, Lambert, Clark, & Kurlakowsky, 2001). Depression becomes more prevalent during adolescence (Costello et al., 2003), as discussed in Chapter 15.

Any child may be sad or lonely at times, but sadness that lasts 2 weeks or more and is accompanied by such symptoms as fatigue, apathy, sleep problems, and inability to concentrate may be a sign of depression.

childhood depression Mood disorder characterized by such symptoms as a prolonged sense of friendlessness, inability to have fun or concentrate, fatigue, extreme activity or apathy, feelings of worthlessness, weight change, physical complaints, and thoughts of death or suicide.

Treatment Techniques

Psychological treatment for emotional disturbances can take several forms. In **individual psychotherapy,** a therapist sees a child one-on-one, to help the child gain insights into his or her personality and relationships and to interpret feelings and behavior. Such treatment may be helpful at a time of stress, such as the death of a parent or parental divorce, even when a child has not shown signs of disturbance. Child psychotherapy is usually more effective when combined with counseling for the parents.

In **family therapy,** the therapist sees the family together, observes how members interact, and points out both growth-producing and growth-inhibiting, or destructive, patterns of family functioning. Therapy can help parents confront their own conflicts and begin to resolve them. This is often the first step toward resolving the child's problems as well.

individual psychotherapy Psychological treatment in which a therapist sees a troubled person one-on-one.

family therapy Psychological treatment in which a therapist sees the whole family together to analyze patterns of family functioning.

behavior therapy Therapeutic approach using principles of learning theory to encourage desired behaviors or eliminate undesired ones; also called *behavior modification.*

art therapy Therapeutic approach that allows a child to express troubled feelings without words, using art materials and media.

play therapy Therapeutic approach in which a child plays freely while a therapist observes and occasionally comments, asks questions, or makes suggestions.

drug therapy Administration of drugs to treat emotional disorders.

Checkpoint ✓

Can you . . .

✔ Identify causes and symptoms of disruptive behavior disorders, anxiety disorders, and childhood depression?

✔ Describe and evaluate five common types of therapy for emotional disorders?

Behavior therapy, or *behavior modification* (refer back to Chapter 2), is a form of psychotherapy that uses principles of learning theory to eliminate undesirable behaviors or to develop desirable ones. A statistical analysis of many studies found that psychotherapy is generally effective with children and adolescents, but behavior therapy is more effective than nonbehavioral methods. Results are best when treatment is targeted to specific problems and desired outcomes (Weisz, Weiss, Han, Granger, & Morton, 1995). *Cognitive behavioral therapy,* which seeks to change negative thoughts through gradual exposure, modeling, rewards, or positive self-talk has proven the most effective treatment for anxiety disorders in children and adolescents (Harvard Medical School, 2004).

When children have limited verbal and conceptual skills or have suffered emotional trauma, **art therapy** can help them describe what is troubling them without the need to put their feelings into words. The child may express deep emotions through choice of colors and subjects (Kozlowska & Hanney, 1999). Observing how a family plans, carries out, and discusses an art project can reveal patterns of family interactions (Kozlowska & Hanney, 1999).

In **play therapy,** a child plays freely while a therapist occasionally comments, asks questions, or makes suggestions. Play therapy has proven effective with a variety of emotional, cognitive, and social problems, especially when consultation with parents or other close family members is part of the process (Athansiou, 2001; Bratton & Ray, 2002; Leblanc & Ritchie, 2001; Ryan & Needham, 2001; Wilson & Ryan, 2001).

The use of **drug therapy**—antidepressants, stimulants, tranquilizers, and antipsychotic medications—to treat childhood emotional disorders is controversial. In 2002, antipsychotic medications were prescribed for 1,438 in every 100,000 children and adolescents, as compared with only 275 per 100,000 during the mid-1990s (Olfson, Blanco, Liu, Moreno, & Laje, 2006). Sufficient research on the effectiveness and safety of many of these drugs, especially for children, is lacking (Murray, de Vries, & Wong, 2004; USDHHS, 1999b; Wong, Murray, Camilleri-Novak, & Stephens, 2004; Zito et al., 2003).

The use of *selective serotonin reuptake inhibitors (SSRIs)* to treat obsessive-compulsive, depressive, and anxiety disorders increased rapidly in the 1990s (Leslie et al., 2005) but has since decreased about 20 percent (Daly, 2005). Some studies show moderate risks of suicidal thought and behavior for children and adolescents under antidepressant treatment, whereas others show no significant added risk (Hammad, Laughren, & Racoosin, 2006; Simon, Savarino, Operskalski, & Wang, 2006) or lessened risk (Simon, 2006). The U.S. Food and Drug Administration in 2004 concluded that antidepressant use can lead to suicidal behavior in children and adolescents, especially in the early months of treatment (Leslie, Newman, Chesney, & Perrin, 2005). (Use of antidepressant drugs for adolescent depression is discussed in Chapter 15.)

Stress and Resilience

Stressful events are part of childhood, and most children learn to cope with them. Stress that becomes overwhelming, however, can lead to psychological problems. Severe stressors, such as war or child abuse, may have long-term effects on physical and psychological well-being. Yet some children show remarkable resilience in surmounting such ordeals.

Stresses of Modern Life

The child psychologist David Elkind (1981, 1986, 1997, 1998) has called today's child the "hurried child." He warns that the pressures of modern life are forcing children to grow up too soon and are making their childhood too stressful. Today's children are expected to succeed in school, to compete in sports, and to meet parents' emotional needs. Children are exposed to many adult problems on television and in real life before they have mastered the problems of childhood. They know about sex and violence, and they often must shoulder adult responsibilities. Many children move frequently and have to change schools and leave old friends. The tightly scheduled pace of life also can be stressful. Yet children are not small adults. They feel and think as children, and they need the years of childhood for healthy development.

Table 14-2	Children's Age-Related Reactions to Trauma
Age	**Typical Reactions**
Age 5 or less	Fear of separation from parent
	Crying, whimpering, screaming, trembling
	Immobility or aimless motion
	Frightened facial expressions
	Excessive clinging
	Regressive behaviors (thumb sucking, bed-wetting, fear of dark)
Ages 6 to 11	Extreme withdrawal
	Disruptive behavior
	Inability to pay attention
	Stomachaches or other symptoms with no physical basis
	Declining school performance, refusal to go to school
	Depression, anxiety, guilt, irritability, or emotional numbing
	Regressive behavior (nightmares, sleep problems, irrational fears, outbursts of anger or fighting)
Ages 12 to 17	Flashbacks, nightmares
	Emotional numbing, confusion
	Avoidance of reminders of the traumatic event
	Revenge fantasies
	Withdrawal, isolation
	Substance abuse
	Problems with peers, antisocial behavior
	Physical complaints
	School avoidance, academic decline
	Sleep disturbances
	Depression, suicidal thoughts

Source: NIMH, 2001a.

Given how much stress children are exposed to, it should not be surprising that anxiety in childhood has increased greatly (Twenge, 2000). Fears of danger and death are the most consistent fears of children at all ages (Gullone, 2000; Silverman, La Greca, & Wasserstein, 1995). This intense anxiety about safety may reflect the high rates of crime and violence in the larger society—including the presence of street gangs and violence in schools (DeVoe, Peter, Noonan, Snyder, & Baum, 2005). In 2003–2004, 94 percent of middle schools and 74 percent of primary schools reported incidents of violent crime, such as rape, robbery, and physical attacks with or without weapons (Guerino et al., 2006).

Findings about children's fears have been corroborated in a wide range of developed and developing societies, including Australia, China, the United Kingdom, Israel, Italy, Nigeria, and Northern Ireland, in addition to the United States. Poor children—who may see their environment as threatening—tend to be more fearful than children of higher socioeconomic status (Gullone, 2000; Ollendick, Yang, King, Dong, & Akande, 1996). Children who grow up constantly surrounded by violence often have trouble concentrating and sleeping. Some become aggressive, and some come to take brutality for granted. Many do not allow themselves to become attached to other people for fear of more hurt and loss (Garbarino et al., 1992).

Children are more susceptible than adults to psychological harm from a traumatic event such as war or terrorism, and their reactions vary with age (Wexler, Branski, & Kerem, 2006; Table 14-2). Younger children, who do not understand why the event occurred, tend to focus on the consequences. Older children are more aware of, and worried about, the underlying forces that caused the event (Hagan et al., 2005).

Table 14-3	Characteristics of Resilient Children and Adolescents
Source	**Characteristic**
Individual	Good Intellectual functioning
	Appealing, sociable, easygoing disposition
	Self-efficacy, self-confidence, high self-esteem
	Talents
	Faith
Family	Close relationship to caring parent figure
	Authoritative parenting: warmth, structure, high expectations
	Socioeconomic advantages
	Connections to extended supportive family networks
Extrafamilial context	Bonds to prosocial adults outside the family
	Connections to prosocial organizations
	Attending effective schools

Source: Masten & Coatsworth, 1998, p. 212.

The impact of a traumatic event is also influenced by the type of event, how much exposure children have to it, and how much they and their families and friends are personally affected. Human-caused disasters, such as terrorism and war, are much harder on children psychologically than natural disasters, such as earthquakes and floods. Exposure to graphic news coverage can worsen the effects (Wexler et al., 2006). Most children who watched news coverage of the September 11, 2001, terrorist attacks on New York and Washington, D.C., experienced profound stress, even if they were not directly affected (Walma van der Molen, 2004).

Children's responses to a traumatic event typically occur in two stages: *first,* fright, disbelief, denial, grief, and relief if their loved ones are unharmed; *second,* several days or weeks later, developmental regression and signs of emotional distress—anxiety, fear, withdrawal, sleep disturbances, pessimism about the future, or play related to themes of the event. If symptoms last for more than 1 month, the child should receive counseling (Hagan et al., 2005).

For some children, the effects of a traumatic event may remain for years. Children who have been exposed to war or terrorism have high rates of depression, disruptive behaviors, and unexplained, recurring physical symptoms. If they and their household have been personally affected, physical pain and loss of home and family may compound the psychological effects (Wexler et al., 2006). Parents' responses to a violent event or disaster and the way they talk with a child about it strongly influence the child's ability to recover (NIMH, 2001a). Box 14-2 gives suggestions for talking with children about terrorism and war.

Coping with Stress: The Resilient Child

resilient children Children who weather adverse circumstances, function well despite challenges or threats, or bounce back from traumatic events.

protective factors Influences that reduce the impact of early stress and tend to predict positive outcomes.

Resilient children, like Marian Anderson, are those who weather circumstances that might blight others, who maintain their composure and competence under challenge or threat, or who bounce back from traumatic events. These children do not possess extraordinary qualities. They simply manage, despite adverse circumstances, to hold on to the basic systems and resources that promote positive development in normal children (Masten, 2001; Table 14-3). The two most important **protective factors** that help children and adolescents overcome stress and contribute to resilience are good *family relationships* and *cognitive functioning* (Masten & Coatsworth, 1998).

Resilient children are likely to have good relationships and strong bonds with at least one supportive parent (Pettit et al., 1997) or caregiver or other caring, competent adult (Masten & Coatsworth, 1998). Resilient children tend to have high IQs and to be good problem solvers. Their superior information-processing skills may help them cope with adversity, protect themselves, regulate their behavior, and learn from experience. They may attract the interest of teachers, who can act as guides, confidants, or mentors (Masten &

Box 14-2 *Talking with Children about Terrorism and War*

In today's world, parents are faced with the challenge of explaining violence, terrorism, and war to children. Although difficult, these conversations are extremely important. They give parents an opportunity to help their children feel more secure and understand the world in which they live. The following information can be helpful to parents when discussing these issues.

Listen to Children

1. Create a time and place for children to ask their questions. Don't force children to talk about things until they're ready.
2. Remember that children tend to personalize situations. For example, they may worry about friends or relatives who live in a city or state associated with incidents or events.
3. Help children find ways to express themselves. Some children may not be able to talk about their thoughts, feelings, or fears. They may be more comfortable drawing pictures, playing with toys, or writing stories or poems directly or indirectly related to current events.

Answer Children's Questions

1. Use words and concepts your child can understand. Make your explanation appropriate to your child's age and level of understanding. Don't overload a child with too much information.
2. Give children honest answers and information. Children will usually know if you're not being honest.
3. Be prepared to repeat explanations or have several conversations. Some information may be hard to accept or understand. Asking the same question over and over may be your child's way of asking for reassurance.
4. Acknowledge and support your child's thoughts, feelings, and reactions. Let your child know that you think their questions and concerns are important.
5. Be consistent and reassuring, but don't make unrealistic promises.
6. Avoid stereotyping groups of people by race, nationality, or religion. Use the opportunity to teach tolerance and explain prejudice.
7. Remember that children learn from watching their parents and teachers. They are very interested in how you respond to events. They learn from listening to your conversations with other adults.
8. Let children know how you are feeling. It's OK for them to know if you are anxious or worried about events. However, don't burden them with your concerns.
9. Don't confront your child's way of handling events. If a child feels reassured by saying that things are happening "very far away," it's usually best not to disagree. The child may need to think about events this way to feel safe.

Provide Support

1. Don't let children watch lots of violent or upsetting images on TV. Repetitive, frightening images or scenes can be very disturbing, especially to young children.
2. Help children establish a predictable routine and schedule. Children are reassured by structure and familiarity. School,

sports, birthdays, holidays, and group activities take on added importance during stressful times.
3. Coordinate information between home and school. Parents should know about activities and discussions at school. Teachers should know about the child's specific fears or concerns.
4. Children who have experienced trauma or losses may show more intense reactions to tragedies or news of war or terrorist incidents. These children may need extra support and attention.
5. Watch for physical symptoms related to stress. Many children show anxiety and stress through complaints of physical aches and pains.
6. Watch for possible preoccupation with violent movies or war theme video/computer games.
7. Children who seem preoccupied or very stressed about war, fighting, or terrorism should be evaluated by a qualified mental health professional. Other signs that a child may need professional help include ongoing trouble sleeping, persistent upsetting thoughts, fearful images, intense fears about death, and trouble leaving their parents or going to school. The child's physician can assist with appropriate referrals.
8. Help children communicate with others and express themselves at home. Some children may want to write letters to the president, governor, local newspaper, or grieving families.
9. Let children be children. They may not want to think or talk a lot about these events. It is OK if they'd rather play ball, climb trees, or ride their bike, etc.

War and terrorism are not easy for anyone to comprehend or accept. Understandably, many young children feel confused, upset, and anxious. Parents, teachers, and caring adults can help by listening and responding in an honest, consistent, and supportive manner. Most children, even those exposed to trauma, are quite resilient. Like most adults, they can and do get through difficult times and go on with their lives. By creating an open environment where they feel free to ask questions, parents can help them cope and reduce the likelihood of emotional difficulties.

Source: American Academy of Child & Adolescent Psychiatry, 2003.

What's your view ?

Which of the suggestions in this box do you think would be most helpful in talking with a child about a war or terrorist attack? Why?

Check it out

For more information on this topic, go to www.nccev.org/violence/events.html. This is a page on the Web site of the National Center for Children Exposed to Violence, which deals specifically with catastrophic events. It has summaries of research and statistics, recommended reading, and links to relevant Web sites.

Coatsworth, 1998). They may even have protective genes, which may buffer the effects of an unfavorable environment (Caspi et al., 2002; Kim-Cohen, Moffitt, Caspi, & Taylor, 2004).

Other frequently cited protective factors (Ackerman, Kogos, Youngstrom, Schoff, & Izard, 1999; Eisenberg et al., 2004; Eisenberg et al., 1997; Masten et al., 1990; Masten & Coatsworth, 1998; Werner, 1993) include the following:

What's your view ?

- How can adults contribute to children's resilience? Give examples.

Checkpoint ✔

Can you . . .

✔ Explain Elkind's concept of the "hurried child"?

✔ Name the most common sources of stress, fear, and anxiety in children?

✔ Identify protective factors that contribute to resilience?

- *The child's temperament or personality:* Resilient children are adaptable, friendly, well liked, independent, and sensitive to others. They are competent and have high self-esteem. They are creative, resourceful, independent, and pleasant to be with. When under stress, they can regulate their emotions by shifting attention to something else.
- *Compensating experiences:* A supportive school environment or successful experiences in studies, sports, or music or with other children or adults can help make up for a destructive home life.
- *Reduced risk:* Children who have been exposed to only one of a number of risk factors for psychiatric disorder (such as parental discord, low social status, a disturbed mother, a criminal father, and experience in foster care or an institution) are often better able to overcome stress than children who have been exposed to more than one risk factor.

All this does not mean that bad things that happen in a child's life do not matter. In general, children with unfavorable backgrounds have more adjustment problems than children with more favorable backgrounds. Even some outwardly resilient children may suffer internal distress that may have long-term consequences (Masten & Coatsworth, 1998). Still, what is heartening about these findings is that negative childhood experiences do not necessarily determine the outcome of a person's life and that many children have the strength to rise above the most difficult circumstances.

Refocus

Thinking back to the information about Marian Anderson in the Focus vignette at the beginning of this chapter,

- What do you think were major sources of self-esteem for Marian Anderson as a child? Would you estimate her self-esteem as high or low?
- How would you describe the family atmosphere in Anderson's home? Was her upbringing primarily authoritarian, authoritative, or permissive?
- How did poverty and the need for her mother to work outside the home affect Anderson?

- How did Anderson's experience living in an extended-family household affect her?
- Was Anderson's choice of her first friend consistent with what you have learned in this chapter about children's choice of friends?
- Can you point to examples of resilience in Marian Anderson's childhood and adult life? What do you think accounted for her resilience?

Adolescence, too, is a stressful, risk-filled time—more so than middle childhood. Yet most adolescents develop the skills and competence to deal with the challenges they face, as we'll see in Part 6.

Summary and Key Terms

The Developing Self

Guidepost 1 How do the self-concept and self-esteem change in middle childhood, and how do school-age children show emotional growth?

- The self-concept becomes more realistic during middle childhood, when, according to neo-Piagetian theory, children form representational systems.
- According to Erikson, the chief source of self-esteem is children's view of their productive competence. This virtue

develops through resolution of the crisis of industry versus inferiority.

- School-age children have internalized shame and pride and can better understand and control negative emotions.
- Empathy and prosocial behavior increase.
- Emotional growth is affected by parents' reactions to displays of negative emotions.

representational systems (385)   industry versus inferiority (385)

The Child in the Family

Guidepost 2 What are the effects of family atmosphere and family structure, and what part do siblings play in children's development?

- School-age children spend less time with parents and are less close to them than before; but relationships with parents continue to be important. Culture influences family relationships and roles.

- The family environment has two major components: family structure and family atmosphere. Family atmosphere includes both emotional tone and economic well-being.

- Development of coregulation may affect the way a family handles conflicts and discipline.

- The impact of mothers' employment depends on many factors concerning the child, the mother's work and her feelings about it; whether she has a supportive partner; the family's socioeconomic status; and the kind of care the child receives.

- Parents living in persistent poverty may have trouble providing effective discipline and monitoring and emotional support.

- Many children today grow up in nontraditional family structures. Children tend to do better in traditional two-parent families than in divorced families, single-parent families, and stepfamilies. The structure of the family, however, is less important than its effects on family atmosphere.

- The amount of conflict in a marriage and the likelihood of its continuing after divorce may influence whether children are better off if the parents stay together.

- Children living with only one parent are at heightened risk of behavioral and academic problems, in part related to socioeconomic status.

- Remarriages are more likely to fail than first marriages. Boys tend to have more trouble than girls in adjusting to divorce and single-parent living but tend to adjust better to the mother's remarriage.

- Studies have found positive outcomes in children living with gay or lesbian parents.

- Adopted children are generally well adjusted, though they face special challenges.

- The roles and responsibilities of siblings in nonindustrialized societies are more structured than in industrialized societies.

- Siblings learn about conflict resolution from their relationships with each other. Relationships with parents affect sibling relationships.

coregulation (387)

The Child in the Peer Group

Guidepost 3 How do relationships with peers change in middle childhood, and what factors influence popularity and aggressive behavior?

- The peer group becomes more important in middle childhood. Peer groups generally consist of children who are similar in age, sex, ethnicity, and socioeconomic status and who live near one another or go to school together.

- The peer group helps children develop social skills, allows them to test and adopt values independent of parents, gives

them a sense of belonging, and helps develop the self-concept. It also may encourage conformity and prejudice.

- Popularity influences self-esteem and future adjustment. Popular children tend to have good cognitive abilities and social skills. Behaviors that affect popularity may be derived from family relationships and cultural values.

- Intimacy and stability of friendships increase during middle childhood. Boys tend to have more friends, whereas girls tend to have closer friends.

- During middle childhood, aggression typically declines. Relational aggression becomes more common than overt aggression. Also, instrumental aggression generally gives way to hostile aggression, often with a hostile bias. Highly aggressive children tend to be unpopular, but this may change as children move into adolescence.

- Aggressiveness promoted by exposure to televised violence can extend into adult life.

- Middle childhood is a prime time for bullying; patterns may be established in kindergarten. Victims tend to be weak and submissive or argumentative and provocative and to have low self-esteem.

prejudice (398)   instrumental aggression (401)
hostile aggression (402)   hostile attribution bias (402)
bullying (404)

Mental Health

Guidepost 4 What are some common mental health problems of childhood, and how do children respond to the stresses of modern life?

- Common emotional and behavioral disorders among school-age children include disruptive behavioral disorders, anxiety disorders, and childhood depression.

- Treatment techniques include individual psychotherapy or family therapy, behavior therapy, art therapy, play therapy, and drug therapy. Often therapies are used in combination.

oppositional defiant disorder (ODD) (406)   conduct
disorder (CD) (406)   school phobia (406)   separation anxiety
disorder (406)   social phobia (406)   generalized anxiety
disorder (406)   obsessive-compulsive disorder (406)
childhood depression (407)   individual psychotherapy (407)
family therapy (407)   behavior therapy (408)   art therapy (408)
play therapy (408)   drug therapy(408)

- As a result of the pressures of modern life, many children experience stress. Children tend to worry about school, health, and personal safety.

- Resilient children are better able than others to withstand stress. Protective factors involve cognitive ability, family relationships, personality, degree of risk, and compensating experiences.

resilient children (410)   protective factors (410)

6

Part Six

Adolescence: A Preview

Chapter 15
Physical Development and Health in Adolescence

- Physical growth and other changes are rapid and profound.
- Reproductive maturity occurs.
- Major health risks arise from behavioral issues, such as eating disorders and drug abuse.

Chapter 16
Cognitive Development in Adolescence

- Ability to think abstractly and use scientific reasoning develops.
- Immature thinking persists in some attitudes and behaviors.
- Education focuses on preparation for college or vocations.

Chapter 17
Psychosocial Development in Adolescence

- Search for identity, including sexual identity, becomes central.
- Relationships with parents are generally good.
- Peer group may exert a positive or negative influence.

Adolescence

In adolescence, young people's appearance changes; as a result of the hormonal events of puberty, they take on the bodies of adults. Their thinking changes, too; they are better able to think abstractly and hypothetically. And their feelings change about almost everything. All areas of development converge as adolescents confront their major task: establishing an identity, including a sexual identity, that will carry over to adulthood.

In Chapters 15, 16, and 17, we see how adolescents incorporate their drastically changed appearance, their puzzling physical yearnings, and their new cognitive abilities into their sense of self. We look at risks and problems that arise during the teenage years, as well as at characteristic strengths of adolescents.

Linkups to Look For

- Early or late physical maturation can affect emotional and social adjustment.

- Conflict between adolescents and their parents may sometimes stem from immature aspects of adolescent thinking.

- Parental involvement and parenting styles influence academic achievement.

- The ability of low-income adolescents to do well in school may depend on the availability of family and community resources.

- Physical characteristics play an important part in molding adolescents' self-concept.

- Girls who are knowledgeable about sex are most likely to postpone sexual activity.

- The intensity and intimacy of adolescent friendships is related to cognitive development.

Physical Development and Health in Adolescence

What I like in my adolescents is that they have not yet hardened. We all confuse hardening and strength. Strength we must achieve, but not callousness.

—Anaïs Nin, *The Diaries of Anaïs Nin,* Vol. IV

Focus *Anne Frank, Diarist of the Holocaust*

Anne Frank

For her thirteenth birthday on June 12, 1942, Anne Frank's parents gave her a diary. This small, cloth-covered volume was the first of several notebooks in which Anne recorded her experiences and reflections during the next 2 years. Little did she dream that her jottings would become one of the most famous published accounts by victims of the Holocaust.

Anne Frank (1929–1945), her parents, Otto and Edith Frank, and her older sister, Margot, were German Jews who fled to Amsterdam after Hitler came to power in 1933, only to see the Netherlands fall to Nazi conquest 7 years later. In the summer of 1942, when the Nazis began rounding up Dutch Jews for deportation to concentration camps, the family went into hiding on the upper floors of the building occupied by Otto Frank's pharmaceutical firm. Behind a door concealed by a movable cupboard, a steep stairway led to the four rooms Anne called the "Secret Annexe." For 2 years, the Franks stayed in those confined quarters with the Van Daans, their 15-year-old son, Peter, and a middle-aged dentist, Albert Dussel,* who shared Anne's room. Then, on August 4, 1944, German and Dutch security police raided the Secret Annexe and sent its occupants to concentration camps, where all but Anne's father died.

Anne's writings, published by Otto Frank after the war, describe the life the fugitives led. During the day they had to be completely quiet so as not to alert people in the offices below. They saw no one except a few trusted Christian helpers who risked their lives to bring food, books, newspapers, and essential supplies. To venture outside—which would have been necessary to replace Anne's quickly outgrown clothes or to correct her worsening nearsightedness—was unthinkable.

The diary reveals the thoughts, feelings, daydreams, and mood swings of a high-spirited, introspective adolescent coming to maturity under traumatic conditions. Anne wrote

---

*Fictional names Anne invented for use in her diary.

Sources of biographical information about Anne Frank are Bloom (1999), Frank (1958, 1995), Lindwer (1991), Müller (1998), and Netherlands State Institute for War Documentation (1989). Page references are to the 1958 paperback version of the diary.

of her concern about her "ugly" appearance, of her wish for "a real mother who understands me," and of her adoration for her father (Frank, 1958, pp. 36, 110). She expressed despair at the adults' constant criticism of her failings and at her parents' apparent favoritism toward her sister. She wrote about her fears, her urge for independence, her hopes for a return to her old life, and her aspirations for a writing career.

As tensions rose in the Secret Annexe, Anne lost her appetite and began taking antidepressant medication. But, as time went on, she became less self-pitying and more serious-minded. When she thought back to her previous carefree existence, she felt like a different person from the Anne who had "grown wise within these walls" (p. 149).

She was deeply conscious of her sexual awakening: "I think what is happening to me is so wonderful, and not only what can be seen on my body, but all that is taking place inside. . . . Each time I have a period . . . I have the feeling that . . . I have a sweet secret, and . . . I always long for the time that I shall feel that secret within me again" (pp. 115–116).

Anne originally had regarded Peter as shy and gawky—not a very promising companion; but eventually she began visiting his attic room for long, intimate talks and, finally, her first kiss. Her diary records the conflict between her stirring sexual passion and her strict moral upbringing.

One of the last diary entries is dated July 15, 1944, less than 3 weeks before the raid and 8 months before Anne's death in the concentration camp at Bergen-Belsen: ". . . in spite of everything, I still believe that people are really good at heart. . . . I hear the ever approaching thunder, which will destroy us too, I can feel the suffering of millions and yet, if I look up into the heavens, I think that it will all come right, that this cruelty too will end, and that peace and tranquility will return again" (p. 233).

● ● ●

The moving story of Anne Frank's tragically abbreviated adolescence points to the insistent role of biology and its interrelationships with inner and outer experience. Anne's "coming of age" occurred under highly unusual conditions. Yet her normal physical maturation went on, along with cognitive and psychosocial changes heightened by her stressful circumstances.

In this chapter, we examine the physical transformations of adolescence and how they affect young people's feelings. We consider the impact of early or late maturation. We discuss health issues associated with this time of life, and we examine two serious problems: depression and teenage suicide.

After you have read and studied this chapter, you should be able to answer each of the Guidepost questions on the following page. Look for them again in the margins throughout the chapter, where they point to important concepts. To check your understanding of these Guideposts, review the end-of-chapter summary. Checkpoints located throughout the chapter will help you verify your understanding of what you have read.

Guideposts
for Study

1. What is adolescence, and what opportunities and risks does it entail?
2. What physical changes do adolescents experience, and how do these changes affect them psychologically?
3. What brain developments occur during adolescence, and how do they affect adolescent behavior?
4. What are some common health problems and health risks of adolescence, and how can they be prevented?

Adolescence: A Developmental Transition

Guidepost 1

What is adolescence, and what opportunities and risks does it entail?

Rituals to mark a child's coming of age are common in many societies. For example, Apache tribes celebrate a girl's first menstruation with a 4-day ritual of sunrise-to-sunset chanting. In most modern societies, the passage from childhood to adulthood is marked, not by a single event, but by a long period known as **adolescence**—a developmental transition that involves physical, cognitive, emotional, and social changes and takes varying forms in different social, cultural, and economic settings (Larson & Wilson, 2004).

An important physical change is the onset of **puberty,** the process that leads to sexual maturity, or fertility—the ability to reproduce.* Traditionally, adolescence and puberty were thought to begin at the same time, around age 13, but, as we will discuss, physicians in some Western societies now see pubertal changes before age 10. In this book, we define adolescence as encompassing the years between 11 and 19 or 20.

adolescence Developmental transition between childhood and adulthood entailing major physical, cognitive, and psychosocial changes.

puberty Process by which a person attains sexual maturity and the ability to reproduce.

Adolescence as a Social Construction

Adolescence is a social construction. In preindustrial societies, children entered the adult world when they matured physically or when they began a vocational apprenticeship. Not until the 20th century was adolescence defined as a separate stage of life in the Western world. Today, adolescence is global (Box 15-1). In most parts of the world, entry into adulthood takes longer and is less clear-cut than in the past. Puberty begins earlier than it used to; and entrance into a vocation occurs later, often requiring longer periods of education or vocational training to prepare for adult responsibilities. Marriage with its attendant responsibilities typically comes later as well. Adolescents spend much of their time in their own world, largely separate from that of adults (Larson & Wilson, 2004).

Adolescence: A Time of Risks and Opportunities

Early adolescence (approximately ages 11 to 14) offers opportunities for growth, not only in physical dimensions, but also in cognitive and social competence, autonomy, self-esteem, and intimacy. This period also carries risks. Some young people have trouble handling so many changes at once and may need help in overcoming dangers along the way. Adolescence is a time of increasing divergence between the majority of young people, who are headed for a fulfilling and productive adulthood, and a sizable minority who will be dealing with major problems (Offer, Kaiz, Ostrov, & Albert, 2002; Offer, Offer, & Ostrov, 2004; Offer & Schonert-Reichl, 1992).

*Some people use the term *puberty* to mean the end point of sexual maturation and refer to the process as *pubescence,* but our usage conforms to that of most psychologists today.

Box 15-1 *The Globalization of Adolescence*

Young people today live in a global neighborhood, a web of interconnections and interdependencies. Goods, information, electronic images, songs, entertainment, and fads sweep almost instantaneously around the planet. The historical and cultural forces that influence adolescents' lives often arise from events oceans away. Western youth dance to Latin music and watch Japanese films, Western movies undermine the system of arranged marriage in Africa, and Arabic girls draw their images of romance from Indian cinema. Maori youth in New Zealand listen to African American rap music to symbolize their separation from adult society.

Adolescence is no longer solely a Western phenomenon. Globalization and modernization have set in motion societal changes the world over. Among these changes are urbanization, longer and healthier lives, reduced birth rates, and smaller families. Earlier puberty and later marriage are increasingly common. More women and fewer children work outside the home. The rapid spread of advanced technologies has made knowledge a prized resource. Young people need more schooling and skills to enter the labor force. Together these changes result in an extended transitional phase between childhood and adulthood.

Puberty in less-developed countries traditionally was marked by initiation rites such as circumcision. Today adolescents in these countries are increasingly identified by their status as students removed from the working world of adults. In this changing world, new pathways are opening up for them. They are less apt to follow in their parents' footsteps and to be guided by their advice. If they work, they are more likely to work in factories than on the family farm.

This does not mean that adolescence is the same the world over. The strong hand of culture shapes its meaning differently in different societies. Adolescents' choices are influenced by parents, teachers, friends, and broader societal institutions, conditions, and values. In the United States, adolescents tend to spend less time with their parents than before and confide in them less. In India, adolescents may wear Western clothing and use computers, but they maintain strong family ties, and their life decisions often are influenced by traditional Hindu values. In Western countries, teenage girls strive to be as thin as possible. In Niger and other African countries, obesity is considered beautiful, and girls try to fatten themselves with steroids and growth hormones. Furthermore, the progress of modernization and globalization is uneven. For adolescents in poor, developing countries—and for the rural and urban poor everywhere—opportunities and choices are more limited than in advanced technological societies.

In many non-Western countries, adolescent boys and girls seem to live in two separate worlds. In parts of the Middle East, Latin America, Africa, and Asia, puberty brings more restrictions on girls, whose virginity must be protected to uphold family status and ensure girls' marriageability. They are closely watched and are not allowed to go out in public alone. Girls who are suspected of sexual activity or even of flirting with boys may be ostracized, whipped, or killed by their fathers and brothers. Boys,

Despite the forces of globalization and modernization, preadolescent children in some less-developed societies still follow traditional paths. These 9-year-old schoolgirls in Tehran celebrate the ceremony of Taqlif, which marks their readiness to begin the religious duties of Islam.

on the other hand, gain more freedom and mobility, and their sexual exploits are tolerated by parents and admired by peers.

Puberty also heightens preparation for gender roles, which, for girls in most parts of the world, means preparation for domestic roles. In Laos, a girl may spend 2½ hours a day husking, washing, and steaming rice. In Istanbul, a girl must learn the proper way to serve tea when a suitor comes to call. Whereas boys are expected to prepare for adult work and to maintain family honor, adolescent girls in many less-developed countries, such as rural regions of China, do not even go to school because the skills they would learn would be of no use after they married. Instead they are expected to spend most of their time helping at home. As a result, they have less opportunity to develop independent thinking and decision making. Boys, on the other hand, face greater risks of harm or death due to violence, accidents, and suicide.

This traditional pattern is changing in some parts of the developing world, as women's employment and self-reliance become financial necessities. During the past quarter-century, the advent of public education has enabled more girls to go to school. In East and Southwest Asia, as many girls as boys now enroll in high school (but not in college). Being able to go to school has broken down some of the taboos and restrictions on girls' activities, has given them wider exposure to contexts and role models outside the family, and has increased their options for the future. Better-educated girls tend to marry later and have fewer children, which enables them to seek skilled employment in the new technological society.

In many other developing countries, however, girls' education still lag behind or differs from that of boys. In Saudi Arabia, girls go to separate schools, where they spend less time on academic studies and more on cooking, sewing, and child care. In many places schoolgirls still carry a heavy burden of domestic work at home. Even after completing their schooling, girls' employment opportunities are more limited than boys'.

Cultural change is complex; it can be both liberating and challenging. Today's adolescents are charting a new course, not always certain where it will lead. We will further discuss how globalization affects adolescents in Chapters 16 and 17.

Source: Larson & Wilson, 2004.

What's your view ❓

Can you think of examples from your own experience of how globalization affects adolescents?

Check it out ❗

For more information on the globalization of adolescence, go to www.unfpa.org/adolescents/about.htm. This Web page, part of the Web site of the United Nations Population Fund, contains an article on "Adolescent Realities in a Changing World."

U.S. adolescents face hazards to their physical and mental well-being, including high death rates from accidents, homicide, and suicide (National Center for Health Statistics [NCHS], 2005). As we will see, such risky behaviors may reflect immaturity of the adolescent brain. However, young people who have supportive connections with parents, school, and community tend to develop in a positive, healthful way (Young-blade et al., 2007).

A national survey of some 14,000 high school students reveals encouraging trends. Since the 1990s, students have become less likely to use alcohol, tobacco, or marijuana; to ride in a car without wearing a seat belt or to ride with a driver who has been drinking; to carry weapons; to have sexual intercourse or to have it without condoms; or to attempt suicide (CDC, 2006f). Avoidance of such risky behaviors increases the chances that young people will come through the adolescent years in good physical and mental health.

Checkpoint ✔

Can you . . .

✔ Explain why adolescence is a social construction?

✔ Point out similarities and differences among adolescents in various parts of the world?

✔ Identify risky behavior patterns common during adolescence?

Puberty: The End of Childhood

Guidepost 2

What physical changes do adolescents experience, and how do these changes affect them psychologically?

Puberty involves dramatic biological changes. These changes are part of a long, complex process of maturation that begins even before birth, and their psychological ramifications may continue into adulthood.

How Puberty Begins: Hormonal Changes

Puberty results from heightened production of sex-related hormones, which occurs in two stages: **adrenarche,** the maturing of the adrenal glands, followed a few years later by **gonadarche,** the maturing of the sex organs.

In the first stage, adrenarche, beginning around age 7 or 8, the adrenal glands located above the kidneys secrete gradually increasing levels of androgens, principally *dehydroepiandrosterone* (DHEA) (Susman & Rogol, 2004). DHEA plays a part in the growth of pubic, axillary (underarm), and facial hair, as well as in faster body growth, oilier skin, and the development of body odor. By age 10, levels of DHEA are 10 times what they were between ages 1 and 4. In several studies, adolescent boys and girls— whether homosexual or heterosexual—recalled their earliest sexual attraction as having taken place at age 9 or 10 (McClintock & Herdt, 1996).

The maturing of the sex organs triggers a second burst of DHEA production, which then rises to adult levels (McClintock & Herdt, 1996). In this second stage, gonadarche, a girl's ovaries step up their output of estrogen, which stimulates growth of female genitals and development of breasts and pubic and underarm hair. In boys, the testes increase the manufacture of androgens, particularly testosterone, which stimulate growth of male genitals, muscle mass, and body hair. Boys and girls have both types of hormones, but

adrenarche Maturation of adrenal glands.

gonadarche Maturation of testes or ovaries.

girls have higher levels of estrogen, and boys have higher levels of androgens. In girls, testosterone influences growth of the clitoris as well as of the bones and of pubic and axillary hair.

The precise time when this rush of hormonal activity begins seems to depend on reaching a critical amount of body fat necessary for successful reproduction. Thus, girls with a higher percentage of body fat in early childhood and those who experience unusual weight gain between ages 5 and 9 tend to show earlier pubertal development (Davison, Susman, & Birch, 2003). Studies suggest that leptin, a hormone identified as having a role in overweight, may trigger the onset of puberty by signaling the brain that sufficient fat has accumulated. An accumulation of leptin in the bloodstream may stimulate the hypothalamus to signal the pituitary gland, which in turn may signal the sex glands to increase their secretion of hormones (Chehab, Mounzih, Lu, & Lim, 1997; Clément et al., 1998; O'Rahilly, 1998; Strobel, Camoin, Ozata, & Strosberg, 1998; Susman & Rogol, 2004). Scientists have identified a gene, *GPR54*, on chromosome 19 that is essential for this development to occur (Seminara et al., 2003).

Some research attributes the heightened emotionality and moodiness of early adolescence, so apparent in Anne Frank's diary, to these hormonal developments. Indeed, negative emotions such as distress and hostility, as well as symptoms of depression in girls, do tend to rise as puberty progresses (Susman & Rogol, 2004). However, other influences, such as sex, age, temperament, and the timing of puberty, may moderate or even override hormonal influences (Buchanan, Eccles, & Becker, 1992).

Timing, Signs, and Sequence of Puberty and Sexual Maturity

Changes that herald puberty now typically begin at age 8 in girls and age 9 in boys (Susman & Rogol, 2004), but a wide range of ages exists for various changes (Table 15-1). Recently, pediatricians have seen a significant number of girls with breast budding before age 8 (Slyper, 2006). The pubertal process typically takes about 3 to 4 years for both sexes. African American and Mexican American girls generally enter puberty earlier than white girls (Wu, Mendola, & Buck, 2002). Some African American girls experience pubertal changes as early as age 6 (Kaplowitz et al., 1999).

Primary and Secondary Sex Characteristics

primary sex characteristics
Organs directly related to reproduction, which enlarge and mature during adolescence.

secondary sex characteristics
Physiological signs of sexual maturation (such as breast development and growth of body hair) that do not involve the sex organs.

The **primary sex characteristics** are the organs necessary for reproduction. In the female, the sex organs include the ovaries, fallopian tubes, uterus, clitoris, and vagina. In the male, they include the testes, penis, scrotum, seminal vesicles, and prostate gland. During puberty, these organs enlarge and mature.

The **secondary sex characteristics** (Table 15-2) are physiological signs of sexual maturation that do not directly involve the sex organs, for example, the breasts of females and the broad shoulders of males. Other secondary sex characteristics are changes in the voice and skin texture, muscular development, and the growth of pubic, facial, axillary, and body hair.

These changes unfold in a sequence that is much more consistent than their timing, though it does vary somewhat. One girl may develop breasts and body hair at about the same rate; in another girl, body hair may reach adultlike growth a year or so before breasts develop. Similar variations in pubertal status (degree of pubertal development) and timing occur among boys. Let's look more closely at these changes.

Signs of Puberty

The first external signs of puberty typically are breast tissue and pubic hair in girls and enlargement of the testes in boys (Susman & Rogol, 2004). A girl's nipples enlarge and protrude, the *areolae* (the pigmented areas surrounding the nipples) enlarge, and the breasts assume first a conical and then a rounded shape. Some adolescent boys experience temporary breast enlargement, much to their distress; however, this is normal and may last up to 18 months.

Table 15-1 — Usual Sequence of Physiological Changes in Adolescence

Female Characteristics	Age of First Appearance
Growth of breasts	6–13
Growth of pubic hair	6–14
Body growth spurt	9.5–14.5
Menarche	10–16.5
Appearance of underarm hair	About 2 years after appearance of pubic hair
Increased output of oil- and sweat-producing glands (which may lead to acne)	About the same time as appearance of underarm hair

Male Characteristics	Age of First Appearance
Growth of testes, scrotal sac	9–13.5
Growth of pubic hair	12–16
Body growth spurt	10.5–16
Growth of penis, prostate gland, seminal vesicles	11–14.5
Change in voice	About the same time as growth of penis
Sperrmarche	About 1 year after beginning of growth of penis
Appearance of facial and underarm hair	About 2 years after appearance of pubic hair
Increased output of oil- and sweat-producing glands (which may lead to acne)	About the same time as appearance of underarm hair

Table 15-2 — Secondary Sex Characteristics

Girls	Boys
Breasts	Pubic hair
Pubic hair	Axillary (underarm) hair
Axillary (underarm) hair	Muscular development
Changes in voice	Facial hair
Changes in skin	Changes in voice
Increased width and depth of pelvis	Changes in skin
Muscular development	Broadening of shoulders

Pubic hair, at first straight and silky, eventually becomes coarse, dark, and curly. It appears in different patterns in males and females. Adolescent boys are usually happy to see hair on the face and chest; but girls are usually dismayed at the appearance of even a slight amount of hair on the face or around the nipples, though this is normal.

The voice deepens, especially in boys, partly in response to the growth of the larynx and partly in response to the production of male hormones. The skin becomes coarser and oilier. Increased activity of the sebaceous glands may give rise to pimples and blackheads. Acne is more common in boys and seems related to increased amounts of testosterone.

The Adolescent Growth Spurt

In Anne Frank's diary, she made rueful references to her physical growth—to shoes she could no longer get into and vests "so small that they don't even reach my tummy" (1958, p. 71). Anne obviously was in the **adolescent growth spurt**—a rapid increase in height, weight, and muscle and bone growth that occurs during puberty.

adolescent growth spurt Sharp increase in height and weight that precedes sexual maturity.

During the years from ages 11 to 13, girls are, on average, taller, heavier, and stronger than boys, who reach their adolescent growth spurt later than girls do.

The adolescent growth spurt generally begins in girls between ages 9½ and 14½ (usually at about 10) and in boys, between 10½ and 16 (usually at 12 or 13). It typically lasts about 2 years; soon after it ends, the young person reaches sexual maturity. Both growth hormone and the sex hormones (androgens and estrogen) contribute to this normal pubertal growth (Susman & Rogol, 2004).

Because girls' growth spurt usually occurs 2 years earlier than that of boys, girls between ages 11 and 13 tend to be taller, heavier, and stronger than boys the same age. After their growth spurt, boys are again larger, as before. Girls usually reach full height at age 15 and boys by age 17. The rate of muscular growth peaks at age 12½ for girls and 14½ for boys (Gans, 1990).

Boys and girls grow differently, not only in rate of growth, but also in form and shape. A boy becomes larger overall: his shoulders wider, his legs longer relative to his trunk, and his forearms longer relative to his upper arms and his height. A girl's pelvis widens to make childbearing easier, and layers of fat accumulate under her skin, giving her a more rounded appearance. Fat accumulates twice as rapidly in girls as in boys (Susman & Rogol, 2004).

Because each of these changes follows its own timetable, parts of the body may be out of proportion for a while. The result is the familiar teenage gawkiness Anne noticed in Peter Van Daan, which accompanies unbalanced, accelerated growth.

These striking physical changes have psychological ramifications. Most young teenagers are more concerned about their appearance than about any other aspect of themselves, and some do not like what they see in the mirror. As we will discuss in a subsequent section, these attitudes can lead to eating problems.

Signs of Sexual Maturity: Sperm Production and Menstruation

spermarche Boy's first ejaculation.

The maturation of the reproductive organs brings the beginning of menstruation in girls and the production of sperm in boys. The principal sign of sexual maturity in boys is the production of sperm. The first ejaculation, or **spermarche,** occurs at an average age of 13. A boy may wake up to find a wet spot or a dried, hardened spot on the sheets—the result of a *nocturnal emission,* an involuntary ejaculation of semen (commonly referred to as a *wet dream*). Most adolescent boys have these emissions, sometimes in connection with an erotic dream.

menarche Girl's first menstruation.

The principal sign of sexual maturity in girls is *menstruation,* a monthly shedding of tissue from the lining of the womb—what Anne Frank called her "sweet secret." The first menstruation, called **menarche,** occurs fairly late in the sequence of female development; its normal timing can vary from ages 10 to 16½ (refer back to Table 15-1). The average age of menarche in U.S. girls has fallen from older than age 14 before 1900 to age 12½ in the

1990s. On average, a black girl first menstruates shortly after her 12th birthday and a white girl about 6 months later (S. E. Anderson et al., 2003).

Influences on Timing of Puberty

Puberty is an evolved mechanism to maximize the chances of successful reproduction, and it is still evolving in response to environmental circumstances and demands (Susman & Rogol, 2004). On the basis of historical sources, developmental scientists have found a **secular trend**—a trend that spans several generations—in the onset of puberty: a drop in the ages when puberty begins and when young people reach adult height and sexual maturity. The trend, which also involves increases in adult height and weight, began about 100 years ago. It has occurred in the United States, western Europe, and Japan and continues in the United States (Anderson, Dallal, & Must, 2003).

One proposed explanation for the secular trend is a higher standard of living. Children who are healthier, better nourished, and better cared for might be expected to mature earlier and grow bigger. Thus, the average age of sexual maturity is earlier in developed countries than in developing ones. A contributing factor in the United States during the last part of the 20th century may be the increase in overweight among young girls (S. E. Anderson et al., 2003), but the evidence for this hypothesis is inconclusive. Another proposed factor is changes in lifestyle and nutrition that produce insulin resistance, increasing the risk of diabetes and heart disease (Slyper, 2006).

A combination of genetic, physical, emotional, and contextual influences may affect the timing of menarche (Graber, Brooks-Gunn, & Warren, 1995). Twin studies have documented the heritability of age of menarche (Mendle et al., 2006). Other research has found that the age of a girl's first menstruation tends to be similar to that of her mother *if* nutrition and standard of living remain stable from one generation to the next (Susman & Rogol, 2004). Bigger girls and those whose breasts are more developed tend to menstruate earlier (Moffitt, Caspi, Belsky, & Silva, 1992); so do girls who have low SES (Mendle et al., 2006). In several studies, family conflict was associated with early menarche, whereas parental warmth, harmonious family relationships, and paternal involvement in child rearing were related to later menarche (Mendle et al., 2006).

The relationship with the father seems particularly important. In one longitudinal study, girls who, as preschoolers, had had close, supportive relationships with their parents—especially with an affectionate, involved father—entered puberty later than girls whose parental relationships had been cold or distant or girls who were raised by single mothers (Ellis, McFadyen-Ketchum, Dodge, Pettit, & Bates, 1999). In another study, the presence of a stepfather was more closely associated with early menarche than the absence of a father (Ellis & Garber, 2000).

How might family relationships affect pubertal development? One possibility is that human males, like some animals, may give off *pheromones*, odorous chemicals that attract mates. As a natural incest-prevention mechanism, sexual development may be inhibited in girls who are heavily exposed to their fathers' pheromones, as would happen in a close father-daughter relationship. Contrarily, frequent exposure to the pheromones of unrelated adult males, such as a stepfather or a single mother's boyfriend, may speed up pubertal development (Ellis & Garber, 2000). Because both a father's absence and early pubertal timing have been identified as risk factors for sexual promiscuity and teenage pregnancy, the father's early presence and active involvement may be important to girls' healthy sexual development (Ellis et al., 1999).

Another possibility is that both a father's tendency toward family abandonment and his daughter's tendency toward early puberty and precocious sexual activity may stem from a shared gene: a sex-linked variant of the androgen receptor (AR) gene, which is carried on the X chromosome of affected fathers and can be transmitted to daughters but not to sons. Among 121 men and 164 unrelated women, men with this allele tended to be aggressive, impulsive, and sexually promiscuous. Women with the same allele tended to have had early menarche and to have experienced parental divorce and father absence before age 7 (Comings, Muhleman, Johnson, & MacMurray, 2002). This hypothesis needs to be tested more directly by genetic analysis of absent fathers and their biological daughters.

secular trend Trend that can be seen only by observing several generations, such as the trend toward earlier attainment of adult height and sexual maturity, which began a century ago.

Psychological Effects of Early and Late Maturation

The effects of early and late maturation vary in boys and girls, and the timing of maturation tends to predict adolescent mental health and health-related behaviors in adulthood (Susman & Rogol, 2004). Research on early maturing boys has had mixed results. Some studies found that most boys like to mature early, and those who do so seem to gain in self-esteem (Alsaker, 1992). They tend to be more poised, relaxed, good-natured, and popular and less impulsive than late maturers, and also more cognitively advanced. In contrast, other studies have found early maturing boys to be more anxious or aggressive, more worried about being liked, more cautious, more reliant on others, and more bound by rules and routines (Ge, Conger, & Elder, 2001b; Graber, Lewinsohn, Seeley, & Brooks-Gunn, 1997; Gross & Duke, 1980). Some early maturers may have trouble living up to expectations that they will act as mature as they look. Late maturing boys, however, have been found to feel more inadequate, self-conscious, rejected, and dominated; to be more dependent, aggressive, insecure, or depressed; to have more conflict with parents and more trouble in school; and to have poorer social and coping skills (Graber et al., 1997; Mussen & Jones, 1957).

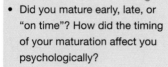

Girls are generally happier if their timing is about the same as that of their peers. Early maturing girls tend to be less sociable, less expressive, and less poised; more introverted and shy; and more negative about menarche than later maturing girls (Livson & Peskin, 1980; Ruble & Brooks-Gunn, 1982; Stubbs, Rierdan, & Koff, 1989). Perhaps because they feel rushed into confronting the pressures of adolescence before they are ready (Susman & Rogol, 2004), they are more vulnerable to psychological distress. They are more likely to associate with antisocial peers (Ge, Conger, & Elder, 1996). They may have a poor body image and lower self-esteem than later maturing girls (Alsaker, 1992; Graber et al., 1997; Simmons, Blyth, Van Cleave, & Bush, 1979). Early maturing girls are at increased risk of anxiety and depression, disruptive behavior, eating disorders, early smoking, drinking, and substance abuse, precocious sexual activity, early pregnancy, and attempted suicide (Deardorff, Gonzalez, Christopher, Roosa, & Millsap, 2005; Dick, Rose, Kaprio, & Viken, 2000; Graber et al., 1997; Susman & Rogol, 2004). However, this is less true of girls with no history of behavior problems (Susman & Rogol, 2004). Among both boys and girls, early maturers tend to be vulnerable to risky behavior and the influence of deviant peers (D. P. Orr & Ingersoll, 1995; Susman & Rogol, 2004).

It is hard to generalize about the psychological effects of pubertal timing because they depend on how the adolescent and other people in his or her world interpret the accompanying changes. Effects of early or late maturation are most likely to be negative when adolescents are much more or less developed than their peers; when they do not see the changes as advantageous; and when several stressful events, such as the advent of puberty and the transition to junior high school, occur at about the same time (Petersen, 1993; Simmons, Blyth, & McKinney, 1983). Contextual factors such as ethnicity, school, and neighborhood can make a difference. For example, African American and Hispanic late maturers report less satisfaction with their bodies, but timing of puberty for Asian American and European American youth does not seem to affect body image (Susman & Rogol, 2004). Also, early maturing girls are more likely to show problem behavior in mixed-gender schools than in all-girl schools and in disadvantaged urban communities than in rural or middle-class urban communities (Caspi et al., 1993; Dick et al., 2000; Ge et al., 2002).

What's your view ?

- Did you mature early, late, or "on time"? How did the timing of your maturation affect you psychologically?

Checkpoint ✔

Can you . . .

✔ Tell how puberty begins and how its timing and length vary?

✔ Identify typical pubertal changes in boys and girls and factors that affect psychological reactions to these changes?

Guidepost 3

What brain developments occur during adolescence, and how do they affect adolescent behavior?

The Adolescent Brain

Not long ago, most scientists believed that the brain is fully mature by puberty. Now brain imaging studies reveal that the adolescent brain is still a work in progress. Dramatic changes in brain structures involved in emotions, judgment, organization of behavior, and self-control take place between puberty and young adulthood. These findings may help explain teenagers' tendency toward emotional outbursts and risky behavior (ACT for Youth, 2002) and raise questions about the extent to which adolescents should be held legally responsible for their actions; Box 15-2).

Box 15-2 *Should Adolescents Be Exempt from the Death Penalty?*

On March 1, 2005, the U.S. Supreme Court, in a controversial 5–4 decision, ruled the death penalty unconstitutional for a convicted murderer who was 17 years old when he committed the crime (Mears, 2005). The Court had previously permitted the death penalty for 16- and 17-year-olds but not for younger minors.

The new decision invalidates laws of 19 states that permitted execution of offenders who were 16 or 17 years old at the time of their crimes and brings U.S. juvenile criminal policy in line with that of almost all other countries in the world. Execution of juveniles is expressly forbidden in the International Covenant on Civil and Political Rights, the American Convention on Human Rights, the Geneva Convention relating to protection of civilians in times of war, and the United Nations Convention on the Rights of the Child (Montaldo, 2005).

Opponents of exempting adolescent offenders from the death penalty argue that the decision should be made on a case-by-case basis, depending on the nature of the crime and the maturity of the offender. However, the Supreme Court majority gave weight to published research which suggested that adolescents *as a group* should not be held to the same criminal standard as adults because they are developmentally less mature.

Laurence Steinberg, a Temple University psychologist specializing in adolescent behavior, and Elizabeth S. Scott, a professor at the University of Virginia School of Law, offer three reasons that adolescence should be a mitigating factor, whether in a capital case or a trial for a lesser offense: (1) Adolescents are deficient in decision-making capacity; (2) they are especially vulnerable to coercive circumstances, such as peer pressure; and (3) their character, or personality, is not yet fully formed (Steinberg & Scott, 2003).

Deficiencies in Decision-Making Capacity

Even if adolescents are capable of logical reasoning (and many are not), they do not always use it in decision making. This is especially true in highly emotional situations. Adolescents are prone to risky behavior; whether because of cognitive limitations or limited life experience, they think less about hypothetical future consequences and more about immediate rewards. Also, adolescents are more impulsive than adults and have more difficulty regulating their moods and behavior.

Some of these well-known differences between adolescent and adult decision making seem to have a neurological basis. The regions of the brain involved in long-term planning, regulation of emotion, impulse control, and evaluation of risk and reward are still developing during adolescence. Changes in the limbic system around puberty may lead adolescents to seek novelty and take risks and may contribute to heightened emotionality and vulnerability to stress. The prefrontal cortex, which is involved in long-term planning, judgment, and decision making, may be immature until late adolescence or adulthood. Steinberg and Scott argue that adolescents, because of their immature judgment, should no more be held fully responsible for their actions than should adults who are mentally retarded.

Vulnerability to Peer Influence

Because of their immaturity, adolescents may give in to pressures that adults would be able to resist. Peer influence increases in adolescence as young people seek independence from parental control. Young people's desire for peer approval and fear of social rejection affect their decisions, even in the absence of overt coercion. Popular peers serve as models for an adolescent's behavior.

Unformed Character

Courts typically allow mitigation of the penalty based on evidence, provided by character witnesses, of a defendant's good character or citizenship. Steinberg and Scott argue that adolescents' character, identity, and values are not yet fully formed. Juvenile crime often represents a temporary phase of experimentation and risk taking, not a deep-seated, lasting moral deficiency. As we point out in Chapter 17, most adolescent offenders grow up to be law-abiding citizens.

Steinberg and Scott call for more research that would (a) link developmental changes in decision making to changes in brain structure and (b) examine age differences in decision making in real-life circumstances. Until more definitive knowledge is available, they urge that courts err, if anything, on the side of life for juvenile offenders, as the Supreme Court has now done.

Source: Steinberg and Scott, 2003.

What's your view

Are there circumstances under which you think an adolescent should be eligible for the death penalty? If so, at what age? What other factors, if any, should enter into such a decision?

Check it out

For more information on Laurence Steinberg's work, go to http://astro.temple.edu/~lds/. This site contains links to several of Steinberg's books on adolescent psychology and parenting.

Adolescents process information about emotions differently than adults do. In one line of research, researchers scanned adolescents' brain activity while they identified emotions on pictures of faces on a computer screen. Early adolescents (ages 11 to 13) tended to use the amygdala, a small, almond-shaped structure deep in the temporal lobe that is heavily involved in emotional and instinctual reactions (refer back to Figure 6-4 in Chapter 6). Older adolescents, like adults, were more likely to use the frontal lobes, which handle planning, reasoning, judgment, emotional regulation, and impulse control and thus permit more accurate, reasoned judgments. This suggests a possible reason for some early adolescents' unwise choices, such as substance abuse and sexual risk taking: Immature brain development may permit feelings to override reason and may keep some adolescents from heeding warnings that seem logical and persuasive to adults (Baird et al., 1999; Yurgelon-Todd, 2002). Underdevelopment of frontal cortical systems associated with motivation, impulsivity, and addiction may help explain adolescents' thrill and novelty seeking and also may explain why many adolescents find it hard to focus on long-term goals (Bjork et al., 2004; Chambers, Taylor, & Potenza, 2003).

To understand the immaturity of the adolescent brain, we need to look at changes in the structure and composition of the frontal cortex. In Chapter 12, we summarized two important childhood brain developments. First, a steady increase in white matter (nerve fibers that connect distant portions of the brain) permits faster transmission of information. In adolescence, this process continues in the frontal lobes (ACT for Youth, 2002; Blakemore & Choudhury, 2006; Kuhn, 2006; NIMH, 2001b). Second, the pruning of unused dendritic connections during childhood results in a reduction in density of gray matter (nerve cells), increasing the brain's efficiency. This process begins in the rear portions of the brain and moves forward. For the most part, however, it has not yet reached the frontal lobes.

A major spurt in production of gray matter in the frontal lobes begins around puberty. After the growth spurt, the density of gray matter declines greatly, particularly in the prefrontal cortex, as unused synapses (connections between neurons) are pruned and those that remain are strengthened (ACT for Youth, 2002; Blakemore & Choudhury, 2006; Kuhn, 2006; NIMH, 2001b). Thus, by mid- to late adolescence young people have fewer but stronger, smoother, and more effective neuronal connections, making cognitive processing more efficient (Kuhn, 2006).

Cognitive stimulation in adolescence makes a critical difference in the brain's development. The process is bidirectional: A young person's activities and experiences determine which neuronal connections will be retained and strengthened, and this in turn supports further cognitive growth in those areas (Kuhn, 2006). Adolescents who "'exercise' their brains by learning to order their thoughts, understand abstract concepts, and control their impulses are laying the neural foundations that will serve them for the rest of their lives" (ACT for Youth, 2002, p. 1).

Checkpoint

Can you . . .

✔ Describe two major changes in the adolescent brain?

✔ Identify immature features of the adolescent brain, and explain how this immaturity can affect behavior?

Guidepost 4

What are some common health problems and health risks of adolescence, and how can they be prevented?

Physical and Mental Health

Some 9 out of 10 early and midadolescents consider themselves healthy. That finding comes from a school-based survey of more than 120,000 11-, 13-, and 15-year-olds in the United States and 27 other Western industrialized countries under auspices of the World Health Organization (WHO) (Scheidt, Overpeck, Wyatt, & Aszmann, 2000). However, many adolescents, especially girls, report frequent health problems, such as headache, stomachache, backache, nervousness, and feeling tired, lonely, or low. Such reports are especially common in the United States and Israel, where life tends to be fast paced and stressful (Scheidt et al., 2000).

Health Problems and Health-Related Behaviors

Many health problems are preventable, stemming from lifestyle or poverty. In industrialized countries, according to the WHO survey, adolescents from less affluent families tend to report poorer health and more frequent symptoms. More affluent adolescents tend to have healthier diets and to be more physically active (Mullan & Currie, 2000).

Let's look at several specific health concerns: physical fitness, sleep needs, eating disorders, drug abuse, depression, and causes of death in adolescence.

Physical Activity

Exercise—or lack of it—affects both physical and mental health. Frequent participation in sports improves strength and endurance, helps build healthy bones and muscles, helps control weight, reduces anxiety and stress, and increases self-esteem, school grades, and well-being. It also decreases the likelihood that an adolescent will participate in risky behavior.

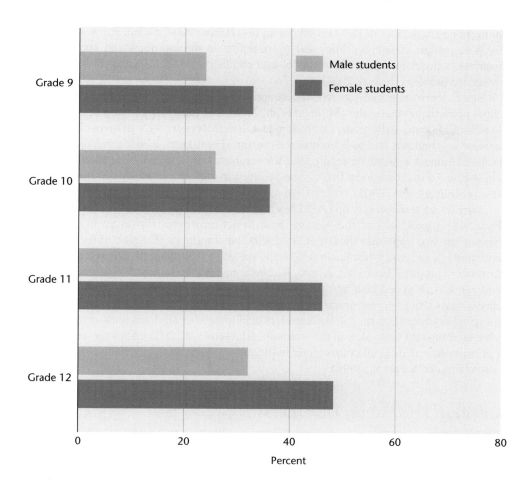

Figure 15-1

High school students who do not engage in recommended amounts of physical activity (moderate or vigorous) by grade and sex, United States, 2003.

Source: NCHS, 2004, Fig. 14, p. 34.

Even moderate physical activity has health benefits if done regularly for at least 30 minutes almost every day. A sedentary lifestyle that carries over into adulthood may result in increased risk of overweight, heart disease, cancer, and type 2 diabetes—a growing problem among children and adolescents (Carnethon, Gulati, & Greenland, 2005; CDC, 2000a; Hickman, Roberts, & de Matos, 2000; NCHS, 2004; Nelson & Gordon-Larsen, 2006; Troiano, 2002).

Unfortunately, one-third of U.S. high school students do not engage in the recommended amounts of physical activity, and the proportion of young people who are inactive increases throughout the high school years (NCHS, 2005; Figure 15-1). U.S. adolescents exercise less often than in past years and less often than adolescents in most other industrialized countries (CDC, 2000a; Hickman et al., 2000). About 75 percent of sixth through eighth graders participate in extracurricular team sports (Kleiner, Nolin, & Chapman, 2004), but just 55 percent of high school senior boys and 30 percent of senior girls do (Snyder & Hoffman, 2002).

Sleep Needs

Sleep deprivation among adolescents has been called an epidemic (Hansen et al., 2005). In the WHO study, an average of 40 percent of adolescents (mostly boys) in 28 industrialized countries reported morning sleepiness at least once a week, and 22 percent said they are sleepy most days (Scheidt et al., 2000).

Children generally go to sleep later and sleep less on school days the older they get. The average adolescent who slept more than 10 hours at night at age 9 gets less than 8 hours' sleep at age 16 (Hoban, 2004). Students who work 20 or more hours a week also tend to get insufficient sleep. As a result, many adolescents doze or sleep in class (Millman et al., 2005).

Actually, adolescents need as much or more sleep than when they were younger (Hoban, 2004; Iglowstein, Jenni, Molinari, & Largo, 2003). Sleeping in on weekends does not make up for the loss of sleep on school nights (Hoban, 2004; Sadeh, Raviv, & Gruber, 2000). A pattern of late bedtimes and oversleeping in the mornings can contribute to insomnia, a problem that often begins in late childhood or adolescence. Daytime naps worsen the problem (Hoban, 2004).

Sleep deprivation can sap motivation and cause irritability, and concentration and school performance can suffer (Millman et al., 2005). In a longitudinal study of 2,259 middle school students, sixth-graders who slept less than their peers were more likely to show depressive symptoms and to have low self-esteem (Fredriksen, Rhodes, Reddy, & Way, 2004). Sleepiness also can be deadly for adolescent drivers. Studies have found that young people ages 16 to 29 are most likely to be involved in crashes caused by the driver falling asleep (Millman et al., 2005).

Why do adolescents stay up late? They may need to do homework, want to talk on the phone with friends or surf the Web, or wish to act grown up. However, physiological changes are also important (Sadeh et al., 2000). The timing of secretion of the hormone *melatonin* is a gauge of when the brain is ready for sleep. After puberty, this secretion takes place later at night (Carskadon, Acebo, Richardson, Tate, & Seifer, 1997). Thus, adolescents *need* to go to bed later and get up later than younger children. Yet most secondary schools start earlier than elementary schools. Their schedules are out of sync with students' biological rhythms (Hoban, 2004). Teenagers tend to be least alert and most stressed early in the morning and more alert in the afternoon (Hansen et al., 2005). Starting school later, or at least offering difficult courses later in the day, would help improve students' concentration (Crouter & Larson, 1998).

Nutrition and Eating Disorders

Good nutrition is important to support the rapid growth of adolescents. Unfortunately, U.S. adolescents tend to have unhealthier diets than those in most other Western industrialized countries. They eat fewer fruits and vegetables and more sweets, chocolate, soft drinks, and other junk foods such as pizza and French fries, which are high in cholesterol, fat, and calories and low in nutrients (American Heart Association et al., 2006; Vereecken & Maes, 2000). Deficiencies of calcium, zinc, and iron are common at this age (Lloyd et al., 1993; Bruner, Joffe, Duggan, Casella, & Brandt, 1996).

Worldwide, poor nutrition is most common in economically depressed or isolated populations. However, it also may result from concern with body image and weight control (Vereecken & Maes, 2000). Eating disorders, including obesity or overweight, are most prevalent in industrialized societies, where food is abundant and attractiveness is equated with slimness; but eating disorders appear to be increasing in non-Western countries as well (Makino, Tsuboi, & Dennerstein, 2004).

Obesity/Overweight

The average teenage girl needs about 2,200 calories per day; the average teenage boy needs about 2,800. Many adolescents eat more calories than they expend and thus accumulate excess body fat.

The percentage of U.S. adolescents who are overweight more than tripled between 1980 and 2004, from 5 percent to 17 percent (Ogden et al., 2006). Among older adolescents, overweight is 50 percent more prevalent in those from poor families (Miech et al., 2006). Mexican American and non-Hispanic black adolescents, who tend to be poorer than their peers, are 1½ times more likely to be overweight than non-Hispanic white adolescents (NCHS, 2005).

U.S. teens are about twice as likely to be overweight as their age-mates in 14 other industrialized countries, according to self-reports of height and weight from 29,242 boys and girls ages 13 and 15. About 26 to 31 percent of U.S. teens had a body mass index (BMI) at or above the 85th or 95th percentiles for age and sex, as compared with an average of 15 percent for all 15 countries (Lissau et al., 2004).

Overweight teenagers tend to be in poorer health than their peers and are more likely to have functional limitations, such as difficulty attending school, performing household

Checkpoint ✓

Can you . . .

✔ Summarize the status of adolescents' health and list prevalent health problems?

✔ Explain why physical activity is important in adolescence?

✔ Explain why adolescents often get too little sleep and how sleep deprivation can affect them?

chores, or engaging in strenuous activity or personal care (Swallen, Reither, Haas, & Meier, 2005). They are at heightened risk of high cholesterol, hypertension, and diabetes (NCHS, 2005). They tend to become obese adults, subject to a variety of physical, social, and psychological risks (Gortmaker, Must, Perrin, Sobol, & Dietz, 1993).

Genetic and other factors having nothing to do with willpower or lifestyle choices seem to put some young people at risk for overweight (refer back to Chapters 3 and 9). Among these factors are faulty regulation of metabolism (Morrison et al., 2005) and, at least in girls, depressive symptoms and having obese parents (Stice, Presnell, Shaw, & Rohde, 2005). In such cases, targeted, early prevention efforts are advisable (Morrison et al., 2005; Stice et al., 2005). In a study of 878 California 11- to 15-year-olds, lack of exercise was the main risk factor for overweight in boys and girls (Patrick et al., 2004).

Weight-loss programs that use behavioral modification techniques to help adolescents make changes in diet and exercise have had some success. For many preadolescents and adolescents, however, dieting may be counterproductive. In a prospective 3-year study of 8,203 girls and 6,769 boys ages 9 to 14, those who dieted gained more weight than those who did not diet (Field et al., 2003). Use of sibutramine, a weight-loss medication usually used with adults, in conjunction with behavioral modification may improve results, but more study is needed on the drug's safety and efficacy with this age group (Berkowitz, Wadden, Tershakovec, & Cronquist, 2003).

Body Image and Eating Disorders

Sometimes a determination not to become overweight can result in graver problems than overweight itself. Concern with body image may lead to obsessive efforts at weight control (Davison & Birch, 2001; Vereecken & Maes, 2000). This pattern is more common among girls than among boys and is less likely to be related to actual weight problems.

Because of girls' normal increase in body fat during puberty, many girls, especially if they are advanced in pubertal development, become unhappy about their appearance, reflecting the cultural emphasis on women's physical attributes (Susman & Rogol, 2004). Girls' dissatisfaction with their bodies increases over the course of early to midadolescence, while boys, who are becoming more muscular, become more satisfied with their bodies (Feingold & Mazella, 1998; Rosenblum & Lewis, 1999; Swarr & Richards, 1996). By age 15, more than half the girls sampled in 16 countries were dieting or thought they should be. The United States was at the top of the list, with 47 percent of 11-year-old girls and 62 percent of 15-year-olds concerned about overweight (Vereecken & Maes, 2000). Black girls are generally more satisfied with their bodies and less concerned about weight and dieting than white girls (Kelly, Wall, Eisenberg, Story, & Neumark-Sztainer, 2004; Wardle et al., 2004).

According to a large prospective cohort study, parental attitudes and media images play a greater part than peer influences in encouraging weight concerns. Girls who try to look like the unrealistically thin models they see in the media tend to develop excessive concern about weight and may develop eating disorders (Striegel-Moore & Bulik, 2007). In addition, both girls and boys who believe that thinness is important to their parents, especially to their fathers, tend to become constant dieters (Field et al., 2001).

Body image problems are often overlooked by medical practitioners. Among 208 adolescent inpatients at a psychiatric hospital who were not being specifically treated for such problems, one-third were found to have severe weight and body image concerns, and they tended to be more anxious, depressed, and suicidal than the other mentally ill adolescents (Dyl, Kittler, Phillips, & Hunt, 2006).

Excessive concern with weight and body image may be signs of *anorexia nervosa* or *bulimia nervosa*. Both disorders involve abnormal patterns of food intake (Harvard Medical School, 2002), such as erratic eating, self-starvation, or binge eating followed by either self-induced vomiting or use of laxatives to purge the system. Ironically, such radical weight control efforts can result in weight gain rather than loss because such practices alter normal appetite and metabolic patterns (Stice et al., 2005).

These chronic disorders affect mostly adolescent girls (Striegel-Moore & Bulik, 2007). They are especially common among girls driven to excel in ballet, competitive swimming,

Anorexics have an unrealistic body image. Despite the evidence of their mirrors, they think they are too fat.

anorexia nervosa Eating disorder characterized by self-starvation and extreme weight loss.

long-distance running, figure skating, and gymnastics; girls with single or divorced parents; and girls who frequently eat alone ("Eating Disorders—Part II," 1997; Martínez-González et al., 2003; Skolnick, 1993). Twin studies have found high heritability from about 50 percent up (Striegel-Moore & Bulik, 2007).

Anorexia Nervosa

Anorexia nervosa is a disorder typically beginning in adolescence and characterized by an obsessive preoccupation with being thin. There are two types of anorexia. One is characterized by self-starvation, often accompanied by compulsive, excessive exercise. The other type is characterized by binge eating, purging, or both (Yager & Andersen, 2005). Anorexics have a distorted body image; though they are at least 15 percent below natural body weight (McGilley & Pryor, 1998), they think they are too fat. An estimated 0.5 percent of adolescent girls and young women and a smaller but growing percentage of boys and men in Western countries have anorexia (AAP Committee on Adolescence, 2003; Martínez-González et al., 2003).

Anorexia has the highest death rate and the highest suicide rate of any mental disorder (Bulik et al., 2006; Crow, 2006). Medical complications affect almost every organ in the body (Yager & Andersen, 2005). Among the early warning signs are determined, secret dieting; dissatisfaction after losing weight; setting new, lower, weight goals after reaching an initial desired weight; excessive exercising; interruption of regular menstruation; hair loss; low body temperature; and growth of soft, fuzzy body hair.

The causes of anorexia probably are multifactorial (Yager & Andersen, 2005). It is estimated to be 56 percent heritable (Bulik et al., 2006). A variant of a gene that may lead to decreased feeding signals has been found in anorexic patients (Vink et al., 2001). In addition, certain complications of birth increase the risk of developing anorexia. These include maternal anemia, diabetes, and death of a portion of the placenta. Risk factors during the neonatal period include heart problems, low body temperature, tremors, and low reactivity (Favaro, Tenconi, & Santonastaso, 2006). People with anorexia tend to have reduced blood flow to certain parts of the brain, including an area thought to control visual self-perception and appetite (Gordon, Lask, Bryantwaugh, Christie, & Timini, 1997).

Personality also may play a role. Young people with anorexia often are good students, described by their parents as model children. They may be withdrawn or depressed and may engage in repetitive, perfectionist behavior. Other suggested causes are anxiety disorders, a family history of depression and obesity, and familial, peer, and cultural pressures to be slender (Yager & Andersen, 2005).

Because anorexia is potentially life threatening, the immediate goal of treatment is to get patients to eat and gain weight. Therapy should focus on educating the patient and the family about the disorder, its risks, and the benefits of treatment and on reducing unhealthful attitudes (Yager & Andersen, 2005). Patients may be given drugs to inhibit vomiting and to treat associated medical problems. Psychotherapy—either behavioral or cognitive—has had some success in getting patients to put on weight (Yager & Andersen, 2005). Family therapy in which parents take control of their child's eating patterns until progress is achieved has had the most effective results (Wilson, Grilo, & Vitousek, 2007).

Patients who show signs of severe malnutrition, are resistant to treatment, show medical danger signs or poor motivation, or do not make progress on an outpatient basis may be admitted to a hospital, where they can be given 24-hour nursing. Once their weight is stabilized, patients may enter less intensive day care that includes ongoing psychotherapy; but if they fail to sustain their weight, they should be rehospitalized (McCallum & Bruton, 2003; Yager & Andersen, 2005). About 50 to 70 percent of anorexia patients make a full recovery; the process may take 5 to 7 years (Yager & Andersen, 2005).

Bulimia Nervosa

In **bulimia nervosa,** a person regularly goes on huge eating binges within a short time, usually 2 hours or less, and then may try to undo the high caloric intake with self-induced vomiting, strict dieting or fasting, excessively vigorous exercise, or laxatives, enemas, or diuretics to purge the body (APA, 1994).

Bulimia differs from the binging-and-purging form of anorexia in that people with bulimia are not abnormally underweight. Some people move back and forth between anorexia and bulimia as their eating and weight patterns change (McGilley & Pryor, 1998). Nevertheless, the two are separate disorders. A related *binge eating disorder* involves frequent binging but without subsequent fasting, exercise, or vomiting; it is the most prevalent eating disorder among American adults and is a factor in the rise in obesity (Hudson, Hiripi, Pope, & Kessler, 2007).

Bulimia and binge eating disorder are much more common than anorexia. About 3 percent of women and 0.3 percent of men have developed bulimia or binge eating disorder at some time in their lives, and much larger numbers have an occasional episode (Harvard Medical School, 2002; McGilley & Pryor, 1998). Unlike anorexia, there is little evidence of bulimia either historically or in cultures not subject to Western influence. The reasons may be that binge eating, unlike anorexia, requires an abundance of food, and purging would be difficult to hide without modern plumbing (Keel & Klump, 2003).

People with bulimia are obsessed with their weight and shape. They become overwhelmed with shame, self-contempt, and depression over their eating habits. They have low self-esteem (as do people with anorexia) and a history of wide weight fluctuation, dieting, or frequent exercise (Kendler et al., 1991).

Like anorexia, bulimia appears to be multifactorial in origin (McGilley & Pryor, 1998). Bulimia seems to be related to low levels of the brain chemical serotonin ("Eating Disorders—Part I," 1997; K. A. Smith, Fairburn, & Cowen, 1999). It may share genetic roots with major depression or with phobias and panic disorder (Keel et al., 2003). There also may be a psychoanalytic explanation: People with bulimia are thought to crave food to satisfy their hunger for love and attention ("Eating Disorders—Part I," 1997). As with anorexia, certain complications of birth or the early days of life are associated with bulimia: partial placental death, low birth weight and length, low neonatal reactivity, and early difficulties with eating (Favaro et al., 2006).

Cognitive behavioral therapy is the most effective treatment for bulimia. Patients keep daily diaries of their eating patterns and are taught ways to avoid the temptation to binge. Because these patients are at risk for depression and suicide, antidepressant drugs may be combined with psychotherapy (Harvard Medical School, 2002; McCallum & Bruton, 2003). Fluoxetine has had well-documented success in treating bulimia (Crow, 2006). Recovery rates from bulimia average 50 percent after 6 months to 5 years (Harvard Medical School, 2002). However, some 30 percent of patients quickly relapse, and as many as 40 percent have continuing symptoms (McGilley & Pryor, 1998).

Use and Abuse of Drugs

Although the great majority of adolescents do not abuse drugs, a significant minority do. **Substance abuse** is harmful use of alcohol or other drugs. It can lead to **substance dependence** (addiction), which may be physiological, psychological, or both and is likely to continue into adulthood. Addictive drugs are especially dangerous for adolescents because they stimulate parts of the brain that are changing in adolescence (Chambers et al., 2003). In 2003–2004, about 6 percent of young people ages 12 to 17 were identified as needing treatment for alcohol use and more than 5 percent as needing treatment for illicit drug use (National Survey on Drug Use and Health [NSDUH], 2006b).

bulimia nervosa Eating disorder in which a person regularly eats huge quantities of food and then purges the body by laxatives, induced vomiting, fasting, or excessive exercise.

What's your view

- Can you suggest ways to reduce the prevalence of eating disorders?

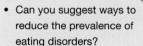

Checkpoint

Can you . . .

✔ Summarize the normal nutritional needs and typical dietary deficiencies of adolescent boys and girls?

✔ Discuss risk factors for, effects of, treatment of, and prognoses for obesity, anorexia, and bulimia?

substance abuse Repeated, harmful use of a substance, usually alcohol or other drugs.

substance dependence Addiction (physical or psychological, or both) to a harmful substance.

Figure 15-2

Trends in high school students' use of illicit drugs over the previous 12 months.

Source: Johnston, O'Malley, Bachman, & Schulenberg, Fig. 1, 2007.

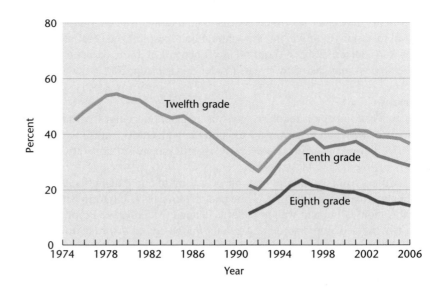

Trends in Drug Use

More than 48 percent of U.S. adolescents have tried illicit drugs by the time they leave high school. An upsurge in drug use during the mid- to late 1990s accompanied a lessening of perceptions of its dangers and a softening of peer disapproval. However, that trend has begun to reverse. Use of illicit drugs in the prior 12 months is down by about one-third among 8th graders, one-quarter among 10th graders, and about one-eighth in 12th graders since 1996 but is still well above its low point in 1992 (Johnston, O'Malley, Bachman, & Schulenberg, 2007; Figure 15-2).

These findings come from the latest in a series of annual government surveys of a nationally representative sample of 48,460 eighth, tenth, and twelfth graders in 410 schools across the United States (Johnston et al., 2007). These surveys probably underestimate adolescent drug use because they are based on self-reports and do not reach high school dropouts, who are more likely to use drugs. Continued progress in eliminating drug abuse is slow because new drugs are continually introduced or rediscovered by a new generation, and young people do not necessarily generalize the adverse consequences of one drug to another (Johnston et al., 2006).

Although illicit drug use has declined, nonmedical use of prescription drugs, such as sedatives, stimulants, tranquilizers, and narcotic pain relievers, particularly OxyContin, remains at high levels (Johnston et al., 2007). In fact, misuse of prescription drugs has been called the nation's second leading drug problem, after marijuana. Prescription drugs were used nonmedically in 2002 to 2004 by 9.9 percent of girls and 8.2 percent of boys ages 12 to 17. Most young people get the drugs from family members or friends (Colliver, Kroutil, Dai, & Gfroerer, 2006). They are widely advertised and relatively easy to obtain and are perceived as safer than street drugs (Friedman, 2006).

A new trend is the abuse of nonprescription cough and cold medications; 4.2 percent of eighth graders, 5.3 percent of tenth graders, and 6.9 percent of twelfth graders report taking medicines containing dextromethorphan (DXM), a cough suppressant, to get high within the past year. On the other hand, use of methamphetamine has dropped sharply since 2001; it is now used annually by less than 2 percent of eighth and tenth graders and 2.5 percent of twelfth graders (Johnston et al., 2007).

Risk Factors for Drug Abuse

What is the likelihood that a particular young person will abuse drugs? Risk factors include difficult temperament; poor impulse control and a tendency to seek out sensation (which may have a biochemical basis); family influences (such as a genetic predisposition to alcoholism, parental or sibling use or acceptance of drugs, poor or inconsistent parenting practices, family conflict, and troubled or distant family relationships); early and persistent behavior problems, particularly aggression; academic failure and lack of commitment to education; peer rejection; associating with drug users; alienation and rebelliousness; favorable attitudes toward drug use; and early initiation into drug use (Hawkins, Catalano, & Miller, 1992; Johnson, Hoffmann, & Gerstein, 1996; Masse & Tremblay, 1997; Pomery et al., 2005; USDHHS, 1996b). The more risk factors that are present, the greater the chance that an adolescent or young adult will abuse drugs.

Let's look more closely at alcohol, marijuana, and tobacco, the three drugs most popular with adolescents, and at influences on their use.

Alcohol, Marijuana, and Tobacco

Alcohol, marijuana, and tobacco use among U.S. teenagers has followed a trend roughly parallel to that of harder drug use, with a dramatic rise during most of the 1990s followed by a smaller, gradual decline (Johnston et al., 2006).

Alcohol is a potent, mind-altering drug with major effects on physical, emotional, and social well-being. Its use is a serious problem in many countries (Gabhainn & François, 2000). In 2006, 17.2 percent of U.S. eighth graders, 33.8 percent of tenth graders, and 45.3 percent of twelfth graders said they had consumed alcohol at least once during the past 30 days (Johnston et al., 2007).

Adolescents are more vulnerable than adults to both immediate and long-term negative effects of alcohol on learning and memory (White, 2001). In one study, 15- and 16-year-old alcohol abusers who stopped drinking showed cognitive impairments weeks later in comparison with nonabusing peers (Brown, Tapert, Granholm, & Delis, 2000).

Despite the decline in *marijuana* use since 1996, it is still by far the most widely used illicit drug in the United States. In 2006, 11.7 percent of eighth graders, 25.2 percent of tenth graders, and 31.5 percent of twelfth graders admitted to having used it in the past year (Johnston et al., 2007).

Marijuana smoke typically contains more than 400 carcinogens. Heavy use can damage the brain, heart, lungs, and immune system and cause nutritional deficiencies, respiratory infections, and other physical problems. It may lessen motivation, interfere with daily activities, and cause family problems. Marijuana use also can impede memory, thinking speed, and learning. It can cut down perception, alertness, attention span, judgment, and the motor skills needed to drive a vehicle and thus can contribute to traffic accidents (Messinis, Krypianidou, Maletaki, & Papathanasopoulos, 2006; National Institute on Drug Abuse [NIDA], 1996; Solowij et al., 2002). Both alcohol and marijuana use can harm academic performance (NSDUH, 2006a; Figure 15-3).

Contrary to common belief, marijuana use may be addictive (Tanda, Pontieri, & DiChiara, 1997) and tends to lead to hard drug use (Lynskey et al., 2003). Addictive drugs are especially dangerous for adolescents because they stimulate parts of the brain that are still changing (Chambers et al., 2003).

Adolescent *tobacco* use is a less widespread problem in the United States than in most other industrialized countries (Gabhainn & François, 2000). Smoking rates have declined by one-third to more than one-half among U.S. eighth to twelfth graders since the mid-1990s. Still, 8.7 percent of eighth graders, 14.5 percent of tenth graders, and 21.6 percent of twelfth graders are current (past-month) smokers (Johnston et al., 2007). Black youth tend to smoke less but metabolize nicotine more slowly than white youth, so their bodies take longer to get rid of it and they are quicker to become dependent (Moolchan, Franken, & Jaszyna-Gasior, 2006).

A randomized, controlled trial found nicotine replacement therapy plus behavioral skills training effective in helping adolescents stop smoking. After 10 weeks of treatment, 28 percent of teens who got a nicotine patch had quit completely. After 6 months, only 7 percent were completely smoke-free, but most cut down to a few cigarettes a day or less (Killen et al., 2004).

Dangers of Early Initiation

Drug use often begins when children enter middle school, where they become more vulnerable to peer pressure. Fourth to sixth graders may start using cigarettes, beer, and

Marijuana is the most widely used illicit drug in the United States. Aside from its own ill effects, marijuana use may lead to addiction to hard drugs.

Figure 15-3

School grades and alcohol (*a*) or marijuana use (*b*) in students ages 12–17, 2002–2004. Average last semester grades dropped with frequent use of alcohol or marijuana.

Source: National Survey on Drug Use and Health, 2006a.

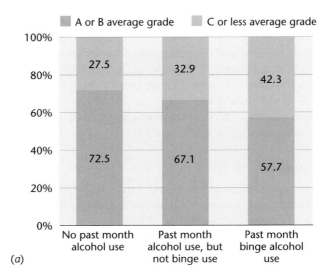

(*a*)

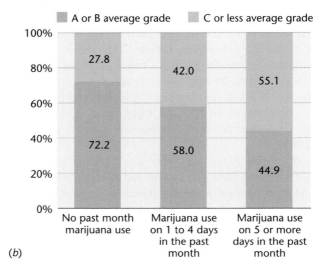

(*b*)

inhalants and, as they get older, move on to marijuana or harder drugs (National Parents' Resource Institute for Drug Education, 1999). The earlier young people start using a drug, the more frequently they are likely to use it and the greater their tendency to abuse it.

The average age for starting to drink is 13 to 14, and some children start earlier. In 2003, nearly 28 percent of underage drinkers had a drink before age 13 (Faden, 2006). Young people who begin drinking early tend to have behavior problems or to have siblings who are alcohol-dependent (Kuperman et al., 2005). Those who start drinking before age 15 are more than five times more likely to become alcohol dependent or alcohol abusers than those who do not start drinking until age 21 or later (SAMHSA, 2004).

Adolescents who begin smoking by age 11 are twice as likely as other young people to engage in risky behaviors, such as riding in a car with a drinking driver; carrying knives or guns to school; using inhalants, marijuana, or cocaine; and planning suicide. Early use of alcohol and marijuana also are associated with multiple risk behaviors (DuRant, Smith, Kreiter, & Krowchuk, 1999).

Influences on Smoking and Drinking

Peer influence on both smoking and drinking has been documented extensively (Center on Addiction and Substance Abuse at Columbia University [CASA], 1996; Cleveland & Wiebe, 2003). As with hard drugs, the influence of older siblings and their friends increases the likelihood of tobacco and alcohol use (Rende, Slomkowski, Richardson, & Niaura, 2005). Adolescents who believe that their parents disapprove of smoking are less likely to smoke (Sargent & Dalton, 2001). Rational discussions with parents can counteract harmful influences and discourage or limit drinking (Austin, Pinkleton, & Fujioka, 2000; Turrisi et al., 2000).

The omnipresence of substance use in the media is an important influence. Movies that depict smoking increase early initiation of smoking (Charlesworth & Glantz, 2005). In a national longitudinal survey, 10- to 15-year-olds who watched at least 4 or 5 hours of television each day were five to six times more likely to start smoking within the next 2 years than those who watched less than 2 hours a day (Gidwani, Sobol, DeJong, Perrin, & Gortmaker, 2002). A random sample of major motion pictures found a decline in depiction of smoking from 10.7 incidents per hour in 1950 to 4.9 in 1980–1982, but by 2002 portrayals of smoking had reverted to 1950 levels (Glantz, Kacirk, & McCulloch, 2004).

Depression

In view of the desperate situation in which Anne Frank found herself, it is not surprising that she needed to take an antidepressant. Even in normal surroundings, the prevalence of depression increases during adolescence. In 2004, 9 percent of young people ages 12 to 17 had experienced at least one episode of major depression, and only about 40 percent of them had been treated (NSDUH, 2005). Depression in young people does not necessarily appear as sadness but as irritability, boredom, or inability to experience pleasure. One reason it needs to be taken seriously is the danger of suicide (Brent & Birmaher, 2002).

Adolescent girls, especially early maturing girls, are more subject to depression than adolescent boys (Brent & Birmaher, 2002; Ge, Conger, & Elder, 2001a; NSDUH, 2005; Stice et al., 2001). This gender difference may be related to biological changes connected with puberty; studies show a correlation between advancing puberty status and depressive symptoms (Susman & Rogol, 2004). Other possible factors are the way girls are socialized (Birmaher et al., 1996) and their greater vulnerability to stress in social relationships (Ge et al., 2001a; USDHHS, 1999).

In addition to female gender, risk factors for depression include anxiety, fear of social contact, stressful life events, chronic illnesses such as diabetes or epilepsy, parent-child conflict, abuse or neglect, alcohol and drug use, sexual activity, and having a parent with a history of depression. Alcohol and drug use and sexual activity are more likely to lead to depression in girls than in boys (Brent & Birmaher, 2002; Hallfors, Waller, Bauer, Ford, & Halpern, 2005; NSDUH, 2005; Waller et al., 2006). Body-image problems and eating disturbances can aggravate depressive symptoms (Stice & Bearman, 2001).

Depressed adolescents who do not respond to outpatient treatment or who have substance dependence or psychosis or seem suicidal may need to be hospitalized. At least 1 in 5 persons who experience bouts of depression in childhood or adolescence are at risk for bipolar disorder, in which depressive episodes (low periods) alternate with manic episodes (high periods) characterized by increased energy, euphoria, grandiosity, and risk taking (Brent & Birmaher, 2002). Even adolescents with depressive symptoms not severe enough for a diagnosis of depression are at elevated risk of depression and suicidal behavior by age 25, according to a 25-year longitudinal study of 1,265 New Zealand children (Fergusson, Horwood, Ridder, & Beautrais, 2005).

SSRIs are the only type of antidepressant medication currently approved for children and adolescents. However, as with the use of SSRIs for children, there is concern about the safety of these medications for adolescents. As we mentioned in Chapter 14, the U.S. Food and Drug Administration requires a warning to accompany their distribution and sale (Leslie, Newman, Chesney, & Perrin, 2005).

The only other treatment option is psychotherapy. An analysis of all available studies found modest short-term effectiveness of psychotherapy, cognitive or noncognitive, with effects lasting no more than 1 year (Weisz, McCarty, & Valeri, 2006). In view of the greater effectiveness of antidepressant medicine, especially fluoxetine, the Society for Adolescent Medicine supports its use for adolescents when clinically warranted and closely monitored, despite the risk (Lock, Walker, Rickert, & Katzman, 2005).

> ## Checkpoint ✓
>
> Can you . . .
>
> ✔ Summarize recent trends in drug use among adolescents?
>
> ✔ Discuss risk factors and influences connected with use of drugs, specifically alcohol, marijuana, and tobacco?
>
> ✔ Tell why early initiation into substance use is dangerous?

Access to guns is a major factor in the rise in teenage suicide.

Death in Adolescence

Not every death in adolescence is as poignant as Anne Frank's. Still, death this early in life is always tragic and (unlike Anne's) usually accidental (Hoyert, Heron, Murphy, & Kung, 2006)—but not entirely so. In the United States, 71 percent of all deaths among persons 10 to 24 years old result from motor vehicle crashes, other unintentional injuries, homicide, and suicide (Eaton et al., 2006). The frequency of violent deaths in this age group reflects a violent culture as well as adolescents' inexperience and immaturity, which often lead to risk taking and carelessness.

Deaths from Vehicle Accidents and Firearms

Motor vehicle collisions are the leading cause of death among U.S. teenagers, accounting for 2 out of 5 deaths in adolescence. The risk of collision is greater among 16- to 19-year-olds than for any other age group and especially so among 16- and 17-year-olds who have recently started to drive (McCartt, 2001; Miniño, Anderson, Fingerhut, Boudreault, & Warner, 2006; National Center for Injury Prevention and Control [NCIPC], 2004). Collisions are more likely to be fatal when teenage passengers are in the vehicle, probably because adolescents tend to drive more recklessly in the presence of peers (Chen, Baker, Braver, & Li, 2000). In 2002, 29 percent of drivers ages 15 to 20 who died in motor crashes had been drinking alcohol, and 77 percent of those were not wearing seat belts (National Highway Traffic Safety Administration, 2003).

Firearm-related deaths of 15- to 19-year-olds (including homicide, suicide, and accidental deaths) are far more common in the United States than in other industrialized countries. They comprise about one-third of all injury deaths and more than 85 percent of all homicides in that age group. The chief reason for these grim statistics seems to be the ease of obtaining a gun in the United States (AAP Committee on Injury and Poison Prevention, 2000). However, youth death rates from firearms have declined since 1993 (AAP Committee on Injury and Poison Prevention, 2000; NCHS, 2005), a period during which police have been confiscating guns on the street (Cole, 1999) and fewer young people have carried them (USDHHS, 1999b).

Suicide

Ready availability of guns is also a major factor in teenage suicide, the third leading cause of death among U.S. 15- to 19-year-olds (Anderson & Smith, 2005). Firearms are used in 52 percent of completed suicides (NCIPC, 2001). A 25 percent reduction in overall suicide rates among 10- to 19-year-olds between 1992 and 2001 may in part be due to restrictions on children's access to firearms (Lubell, Swahn, Crosby, & Kegler, 2004).

Almost 17 percent of U.S. high school students report seriously considering suicide, and 8.5 percent report actually attempting it (NCHS, 2005). Although most young people who attempt suicide do it by taking pills or ingesting other substances, those who *succeed* are most likely to use firearms (Borowsky, Ireland, & Resnick, 2001). For this reason, adolescent boys, who are more apt to use guns, are five times more likely than adolescent girls to succeed in taking their lives, even though girls are more likely to consider or attempt suicide (NCHS, 2004, 2005).

Although suicide occurs in all ethnic groups, Native American boys have the highest rates and African American girls the lowest. Gay, lesbian, and bisexual youths, who have high rates of depression, also have unusually high rates of suicide and attempted suicide (AAP Committee on Adolescence, 2000; Remafedi, French, Story, Resnick, & Blum, 1998).

Young people who consider or attempt suicide tend to have histories of emotional illness. They are likely to be either perpetrators or victims of violence and to have school problems, academic or behavioral. Many have suffered from maltreatment in childhood and have severe problems with relationships. They tend to think poorly of themselves, to feel hopeless, and to have poor impulse control and low tolerance for frustration and stress. These young people are often alienated from their parents and have no one outside the family to turn to. They also tend to have attempted suicide before or to have friends or family members who did so (Borowsky et al., 2001; Brent & Mann, 2006; Garland & Zigler, 1993; Johnson et al., 2002a; NIMH, 1999; "Suicide—Part I," 1996; Swedo et al., 1991). Alcohol plays a part in half of all teenage suicides (AAP Committee on Adolescence, 2000). Perhaps the key factor is a tendency toward impulsive aggression. Postmortem and imaging studies of the brains of persons who have completed or attempted suicide have identified alterations in regions of the prefrontal cortex involved in emotion, regulation, and behavioral inhibition (Brent & Mann, 2006). Protective factors that reduce the risk of suicide include a sense of connectedness to family and school, emotional well-being, and academic achievement (Borowsky et al., 2001).

Telephone hotlines are the most common type of suicide intervention for adolescents, but their effectiveness appears to be minimal (Borowsky et al., 2001; Garland & Zigler, 1993). School-based screening programs have proliferated in recent years and have their advocates (Friedman, 2006). Although some observers worry that such programs may put ideas in young people's heads, a randomized controlled trial of 2,342 high school students in New York state found no basis for that concern (Gould et al., 2005). However, there is little evidence that such programs reduce the risk of suicide or motivate adolescents who are contemplating suicide to seek help (Harvard Medical School, 2003). Equally important is to attack the risk factors through programs to reduce substance abuse, violence, and access to guns and to strengthen families and improve parenting skills (Borowsky et al., 2001; Garland & Zigler, 1993).

Protective Factors: Health in Context

Adolescents' development, like that of younger children, does not occur in a vacuum. As we have seen, family and school environments play an important part in physical and mental health.

A study of 12,118 seventh through twelfth graders in a random sample of 134 schools across the United States (Resnick et al., 1997) looked at risk factors and protective factors affecting four major aspects of adolescent health and well-being. These were emotional distress and suicidal behavior; involvement in fighting, threats of violence, or use of weapons; use of cigarettes, alcohol, and marijuana; and sexual experience, including age of sexual initiation and any history of pregnancy. The students completed questionnaires and had 90-minute home interviews. During the sensitive portions of the interview, the young people listened to the questions through earphones and entered their answers on laptop computers. School administrators also filled out questionnaires.

The findings underline the linkage of physical, cognitive, emotional, and social development. Perceptions of connectedness to others, both at home and at school, positively affected young people's health and well-being in all domains. One important factor was parents' spending time with and being available to their adolescent children. Even more important was the sense that parents and teachers were warm and caring and had high expectations for children's achievement. These findings are clear and consistent with other research: Adolescents who are getting emotional support at home and are well-adjusted at school have the best chance of avoiding the health hazards of adolescence.

> *Checkpoint* ✔
>
> *Can you . . .*
>
> ✔ Discuss factors affecting gender differences in adolescent depression?
>
> ✔ Name the three leading causes of death among adolescents, and discuss the dangers of firearm injury?
>
> ✔ Assess risk factors and prevention programs for teenage suicide?
>
> ✔ Identify factors that tend to protect adolescents from health risks?

Refocus

Thinking back to the information about Anne Frank in the Focus vignette at the beginning of this chapter,

- What typical pubertal changes did Anne's diary describe? How did these changes affect her psychologically?

- What evidence did Anne show of cognitive maturation and moral development?

- In what ways might Anne's development have been similar and in what ways different had she lived under normal circumstances?

Despite the perils of adolescence, most young people emerge from these years with mature, healthy bodies and a zest for life. Their minds have continued to develop too, as we will see in Chapter 16.

Summary and Key Terms

Adolescence: A Developmental Transition

Guidepost 1 What is adolescence, and what opportunities and risks does it entail?

- Adolescence is the transition from childhood to adulthood. Neither its beginning nor its end is clearly marked in Western societies; it lasts about a decade, between ages 11 or 12 and the late teens or early 20s.

- In some non-Western cultures, coming of age is signified by special rites.

- Adolescence is full of opportunities for physical, cognitive, and psychosocial growth but also of risks to healthy development. Risky behavior patterns, such as drinking alcohol, abusing drugs, engaging in sexual and gang activity, and using firearms tend to be established early in adolescence. About 4 out of 5 young people experience no major problems.

  adolescence (419)   puberty (419)

Puberty: The End of Childhood

Guidepost 2 What physical changes do adolescents experience, and how do these changes affect them psychologically?

- Puberty is triggered by hormonal changes, which may affect moods and behavior. Puberty takes about 4 years, typically begins earlier in girls than in boys, and ends when a person can reproduce.

- Primary sex characteristics (the reproductive organs) enlarge and mature during puberty. Secondary sex characteristics also appear.

- During puberty, both boys and girls undergo an adolescent growth spurt. A secular trend toward earlier attainment of adult height and sexual maturity began about 100 years ago, probably because of improvements in living standards.

- The principal signs of sexual maturity are production of sperm (for males) and menstruation (for females). Spermarche typically occurs at age 13. Menarche occurs, on average, between ages 12 and 13 in the United States.

- Teenagers, especially girls, tend to be sensitive about their physical appearance. Girls who mature early tend to adjust less easily than early maturing boys.

  adrenarche (421)   gonadarche (421)   primary sex characteristics (422)   secondary sex characteristics (422)   adolescent growth spurt (423)   spermarche (424)   menarche (424)   secular trend (425)

The Adolescent Brain

Guidepost 3 What brain developments occur during adolescence, and how do they affect adolescent behavior?

- The adolescent brain is not yet fully mature. Adolescents process information about emotions with the amygdala, whereas adults use the frontal lobe. Thus, adolescents tend to make less accurate, less reasoned judgments.

- A wave of overproduction of gray matter, especially in the frontal lobes, is followed by pruning of excess dendrites. Continuing myelination of the frontal lobes facilitates maturation of cognitive processing.

- Underdevelopment of frontal cortical systems connected with motivation, impulsivity, and addiction may help explain adolescents' tendency toward risk taking.

- Because of their developing brains, adolescents are particularly vulnerable to effects of alcohol and addictive drugs.

Physical and Mental Health

Guidepost 4 What are some common health problems and health risks of adolescence, and how can they be prevented?

- For the most part, the adolescent years are relatively healthy. Health problems often are associated with poverty or a risk-taking lifestyle. Adolescents are less likely than younger children to get regular medical care.

- Many adolescents, especially girls, do not engage in regular vigorous physical activity.

- Many adolescents do not get enough sleep because the high school schedule is out of sync with their natural body rhythms.

- Three common eating disorders in adolescence are obesity, anorexia nervosa, and bulimia nervosa. All can have serious long-term effects. Anorexia and bulimia affect mostly girls. Outcomes for bulimia tend to be better than for anorexia.

- Adolescent substance abuse and dependence have lessened in recent years, but nonmedical use of prescription drugs has increased.

- Marijuana, alcohol, and tobacco are the most popular drugs with adolescents. All involve serious risks. Marijuana can be a gateway to the use of hard drugs.

- Leading causes of death among adolescents include motor vehicle accidents, firearm use, and suicide.

  anorexia nervosa (432)   bulimia nervosa (433)   substance abuse (433)   substance dependence (433)

CHAPTER SIXTEEN

16

Cognitive Development in Adolescence

I should place [the prime of a man's life] at between fifteen and sixteen. It is then, it always seems to me, that his vitality is at its highest; he has greatest sense of the ludicrous and least sense of dignity. After that time, decay begins to set in.

—Evelyn Waugh, age 16, in a school debate, 1920

Focus *Nelson Mandela, Freedom Fighter*

Nelson Mandela

Rolihlahla, the name Nelson Mandela's father gave him at his birth in 1918, means "stirring up trouble." And that is exactly what Mandela did throughout his long and finally successful struggle to topple apartheid, South Africa's rigid system of racial separation and subjugation.

Mandela's election as his country's first black president in April 1994—only 4 years after his emergence from 28 years behind bars for conspiring to overthrow the white-dominated government—was the realization of a dream formed in his youth. It was a dream kindled as Mandela sat quietly listening to his tribal elders reminisce about a bygone era of self-government more than a century earlier, before the coming of white people—an era of peace, freedom, and equality.

"The land . . . belonged to the whole tribe and there was no individual ownership whatso- ever," Mandela told the court that sentenced him to prison in 1962. "There were no classes, no rich or poor and no exploitation of man by man. . . . The council was so completely democratic that all members of the tribe could participate in its deliberations. Chief and subject, warrior and medicine man, all took part" (Meer, 1988, p. 12). Mandela recognized that his forebears' prim- itive way of life would not be viable in the modern world. But the vision of a society "in which none will be held in slavery or servitude, and in which poverty, want and insecurity shall be no more" served as a lifelong inspiration.

Mandela has royal blood: One of his ancestors ruled his Thembu tribe, and his father was chief of Mvezo, a small, isolated village in the native reservation called the Transkei where Mandela was born. Mandela seems to have inherited his "proud rebelliousness" and "stubborn sense of fairness" (Mandela, 1994, p. 6): Not long after his birth, his father, a counselor to tribal kings, was deposed for refusing to honor a summons to appear before the local British magis- trate. For standing on his traditional prerogatives and defying the magistrate's authority, Man- dela's father paid with his lands and fortune.

Mandela's mother, his father's third of four wives, moved with her baby and his three sis- ters to the nearby village of Qunu, where they lived in a compound of mud huts. At 5, Mandela became a herd boy, driving sheep and cattle through the fertile grasslands. His mother had him

The main sources of biographical information about Nelson Mandela's youth are Benson (1986), Hargrove (1989), Harwood (1987), Mandela (1994), and Meer (1988).

baptized in the Methodist church, and at 7 he became the first member of his family to go to school. It was his first teacher who gave him his English name, Nelson.

When Mandela was 9, his father died, and his mother sent him to live at the tribal head-quarters at Mqhekezweni. The acting regent, who owed his position to Mandela's father, had offered to become the boy's guardian and raise him as his own son.

As Mandela grew into adolescence, he observed tribal meetings, where any member could speak and the regent would listen quietly before summing up the consensus. This style of leadership deeply impressed Mandela and influenced his own demeanor as a leader in later years. He also watched his guardian preside over council meetings to which minor chiefs brought disputes to be tried. His fascination with the presentation of cases and the cross-examination of witnesses planted the seeds of his ambition to be a lawyer—an ambition he fulfilled as a young adult. From the visiting chiefs and headmen, Mandela heard tales about early African warriors who had fought against Western domination. These stories stirred his interest in his people's history and laid the groundwork for his political activism.

At age 16, Mandela underwent circumcision, the traditional ritual by which a boy became recognized as a man and a participant in tribal councils. At the concluding ceremony, the main speaker, Chief Meligqili, struck a discordant note. The promise of manhood, he said, was an empty one in a land where Africans were a conquered people. "Among these young men," he said, "are chiefs who will never rule because we have no power to govern ourselves; soldiers who will never fight for we have no weapons to fight with; scholars who will never teach because we have no place for them to study. The abilities, the intelligence, the promise of these young men will be squandered in their attempt to eke out a living doing the simplest, most mindless chores for the white man. These gifts [we give them] today are naught, for we cannot give them the greatest gift of all, which is freedom and independence." Although Mandela did not appreciate it at the time, that speech marked his political awakening.

● ● ●

The formative influences of Mandela's adolescent years helped shape his moral and political thinking and his life's work. The lessons he had learned about leadership and about his people's past glory stood him in good stead as he directed the resistance to an increasingly repressive regime, first in the streets and then from his island prison. Those lessons remained with him as he eventually managed to negotiate a new non-racial constitution and free elections—accomplishments for which he received the Nobel Peace Prize in 1993.

In this chapter, we examine the Piagetian stage of formal operations, which makes it possible for a young person like Nelson Mandela to visualize an ideal world. We look at adolescents' growth in information processing, including memory, knowledge, and reasoning, and in vocabulary and other linguistic skills. We note what David Elkind has identified as some immature aspects of adolescents' thought, and we examine adolescents' moral and spiritual development. Finally, we explore practical aspects of cognitive growth—issues of school and vocational choice.

After you have read and studied this chapter, you should be able to answer each of the Guidepost questions on the following page. Look for them again in the margins throughout the chapter, where they point to important concepts. To check your understanding of these Guideposts, review the end-of-chapter summary. Checkpoints located throughout the chapter will help you verify your understanding of what you have read.

1. How do adolescents' thinking and use of language differ from younger children's?

2. On what basis do adolescents make moral judgments, and how does prosocial behavior vary?

3. What influences affect adolescents' school success and their educational and vocational planning and preparation?

Guideposts
for Study

Aspects of Cognitive Maturation

Guidepost 1

How do adolescents' thinking and use of language differ from younger children's?

Adolescents not only look different from younger children; they also think and talk differently. Their speed of information processing continues to increase, though not as dramatically as in middle childhood. Although their thinking may remain immature in some ways, many adolescents are capable of abstract reasoning and sophisticated moral judgments, and they can plan more realistically for the future.

Piaget's Stage of Formal Operations

Adolescents enter what Piaget called the highest level of cognitive development—**formal operations**—when they develop the capacity for abstract thought. This development, usually around age 11, gives them a new, more flexible, way to manipulate information. No longer limited to the here and now, they can understand historical time and extraterrestrial space. They can use symbols for symbols (for example, letting the letter *X* stand for an unknown numeral) and thus can learn algebra and calculus. They can better appreciate metaphor and allegory and thus can find richer meanings in literature. They can think in terms of what *might be,* not just what *is.* They can imagine possibilities and can form and test hypotheses.

formal operations In Piaget's theory, final stage of cognitive development, characterized by the ability to think abstractly.

Like Nelson Mandela, people in the stage of formal operations can integrate what they have learned in the past with the challenges of the present and make plans for the future. The ability to think abstractly has emotional implications too. Earlier, a child could love a parent or hate a classmate. Now an adolescent like young Mandela "can love freedom or hate exploitation. . . . The possible and the ideal captivate both mind and feeling" (H. Ginsburg & Opper, 1979, p. 201).

Hypothetical-Deductive Reasoning

To appreciate the difference formal reasoning makes, let's follow the progress of a typical child in dealing with a classic Piagetian problem, the pendulum problem.* The child, Adam, is shown the pendulum, an object hanging from a string. He is then shown how he can change any of four factors: the length of the string, the weight of the object, the height from which the object is released, and the amount of force he uses to push the object. He is asked to figure out which factor or combination of factors determines how fast the pendulum swings. (Figure 16-1 depicts this and other Piagetian tasks for assessing the achievement of formal operations.)

When Adam first sees the pendulum, he is not yet 7 years old and is in the preoperational stage. He attacks the problem in a hit-or-miss manner. First he puts a light weight on a long string and pushes it; then he tries swinging a heavy weight on a short string; then he removes the weight entirely. Because his method is random, he cannot draw a logical conclusion.

---

*This description of age-related differences in the approach to the pendulum problem is adapted from H. Ginsburg and Opper (1979).

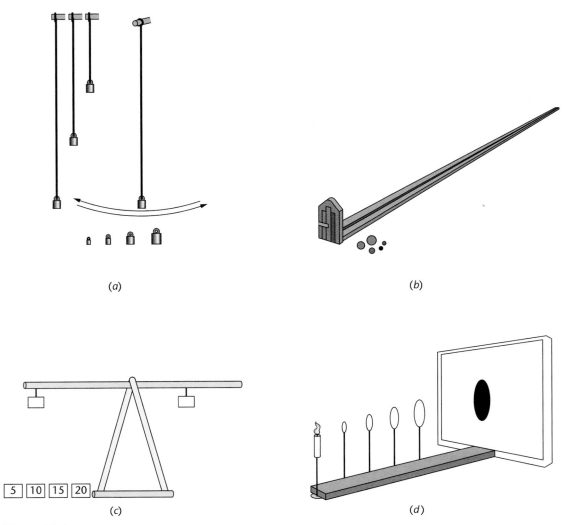

Figure 16-1

Piagetian tasks for measuring attainment of formal operations.

(a) Pendulum. The pendulum's string can be shortened or lengthened, and weights of varying sizes can be attached to it. The student must determine what variables affect the speed of the pendulum's swing. *(b)* Motion in a horizontal plane. A spring device launches balls of varying sizes that roll in a horizontal plane. The student must predict their stopping points. *(c)* Balance beam. A balance scale comes with weights of varying sizes that can be hung at different points along the crossbar. The student must determine what factors affect whether the scale will balance. *(d)* Shadows. A board containing a row of peg holes is attached perpendicularly to the base of a screen. A light source and rings of varying diameters can be placed in the holes, at varying distances from the screen. The student must produce two shadows of the same size, using different-sized rings.

Source: Adapted from Small, Fig. 8-12, 1990.

Adam next encounters the pendulum at age 10, when he is in the stage of concrete operations. This time, he discovers that varying the length of the string and the weight of the object affects the speed of the swing. However, because he varies both factors at the same time, he cannot tell which is critical or whether both are.

At age 15, when Adam is confronted with the pendulum for a third time, he goes at the problem systematically. He tests all the possible hypotheses, varying one factor at a time—first, the length of the string; next, the weight of the object; then the height from which it is released; and, finally, the amount of force used—each time holding the other three factors constant. In this way, he discovers that only one factor, the length of the string, determines the speed of the pendulum.

Adam's solution shows that he has arrived at the stage of formal operations. He is now capable of **hypothetical-deductive reasoning;** he can develop a hypothesis and can design an experiment to test it. He considers all the hypotheses he can imagine and examines them one by one to eliminate the false and arrive at the true. Hypothetical-deductive

hypothetical-deductive reasoning Ability, believed by Piaget to accompany the stage of formal operations, to develop, consider, and test hypotheses.

reasoning gives him a tool to solve problems from fixing the family car to constructing a political theory as Nelson Mandela eventually did as a leader of the anti-apartheid movement.

What brings about the shift to formal reasoning? Piaget attributed it chiefly to a combination of brain maturation and expanding environmental opportunities. Both are essential: Even if young people's neurological development has advanced enough to permit formal reasoning, they can attain it only with appropriate environmental stimulation.

As with the development of concrete operations, schooling and culture play a role, as Piaget (1972) ultimately recognized. When adolescents in New Guinea and Rwanda were tested on the pendulum problem, none was able to solve it. On the other hand, Chinese children in Hong Kong, who had been to British schools, did at least as well as U.S. or European children. Schoolchildren in Central Java and New South Wales also showed some formal operational abilities (Gardiner & Kosmitzki, 2005). Apparently, formal reasoning is a learned ability that is not equally necessary or equally valued in all cultures.

Knowing what questions to ask and what strategies work are keys to hypothetical-deductive reasoning. When 30 low-performing urban sixth graders were asked to investigate factors in earthquake risk, those who received a suggestion to focus on one variable at a time made more valid inferences than those who were not given the suggestion (Kuhn & Dean, 2005). This result demonstrates that hypothetical-deductive reasoning can be taught and learned.

Evaluating Piaget's Theory

Although adolescents do tend to think more abstractly than younger children, there is debate about the precise age at which this advance occurs (Eccles, Wigfield, & Byrnes, 2003). Piaget's writings provide many examples of children displaying aspects of scientific thinking well before adolescence. At the same time, Piaget seems to have overestimated some older children's abilities. Many late adolescents and adults—perhaps one-third to one-half—seem incapable of abstract thought as Piaget defined it (Gardiner & Kosmitzki, 2005; Kohlberg & Gilligan, 1971; Papalia, 1972), and even those who are capable of abstract thinking do not always use it.

Piaget, in most of his early writings, paid little attention to individual differences, to variations in the same child's performance on different kinds of tasks, or to social and cultural influences. In his later years, Piaget himself "came to view his earlier model of the development of children's thinking, particularly formal operations, as flawed because it failed to capture the essential *role of the situation* in influencing and constraining . . . children's thinking" (Brown, Metz, & Campione, 1996, pp. 152–153).

Piaget's concept of formal operations as the apex of mature thought may be too narrow. Neo-Piagetian research suggests that adolescent thought processes are more flexible and varied. The type of thinking young people use is closely tied to what they are thinking about, as well as to the context of a problem and the kinds of information and thought a culture considers important (Case & Okamoto, 1996; Kuhn, 2006).

Furthermore, Piaget's theory does not adequately consider such cognitive advances as gains in information-processing capacity, accumulation of knowledge and expertise in specific fields, and the role of *metacognition,* the awareness and monitoring of one's mental processes and strategies (Flavell et al., 2002). This ability to "think about what one is thinking about" and, thus, to manage one's mental processes—in other words, enhanced executive function—may be the chief advance of adolescent thought, the result of changes occurring in the adolescent brain (Kuhn, 2006).

Elkind: Immature Characteristics of Adolescent Thought

We have seen how children develop from egocentric beings whose interest extends not much farther than the nipple to persons capable of solving abstract problems and imagining ideal societies. Yet in some ways adolescents' thinking seems strangely immature. They are often rude to adults, they have trouble making up their minds what to wear each day, and they tend to act as if the whole world revolved around them.

What's your view

- How can parents and teachers help adolescents improve their reasoning ability?

Checkpoint ✔

Can you . . .

✔ Explain the difference between formal operational and concrete operational thinking, as exemplified by the pendulum problem?

✔ Cite factors influencing adolescents' development of formal reasoning?

✔ Evaluate Piaget's theory of formal operations?

Argumentativeness—usually with parents—is a typical characteristic of adolescent thought, according to David Elkind.

According to the psychologist David Elkind (1984, 1998), such behavior stems from adolescents' inexperienced ventures into formal operational thought. This new way of thinking, which fundamentally transforms the way they look at themselves and their world, is as unfamiliar to them as their reshaped bodies, and they sometimes feel just as awkward in its use. As they try out their new powers, they may sometimes stumble, like an infant learning to walk.

This immaturity of thinking, Elkind suggests, manifests itself in at least six characteristic ways:

1. *Idealism and criticalness:* As adolescents envision an ideal world, they realize how far the real world, for which they hold adults responsible, falls short. They become super-conscious of hypocrisy; with their sharpened verbal reasoning, they relish magazines and entertainers that attack public figures with satire and parody. Convinced that they know better than adults how to run the world, they frequently find fault with their parents and other authority figures.

2. *Argumentativeness:* Adolescents are constantly looking for opportunities to try out their reasoning abilities. They often become argumentative as they marshal facts and logic to build a case for, say, staying out later than their parents think they should.

3. *Indecisiveness:* Adolescents can keep many alternatives in mind at the same time yet may lack effective strategies for choosing among them. They may have trouble making up their minds even about such simple things as whether to go to the mall with a friend or to the computer to work on a school assignment.

4. *Apparent hypocrisy:* Young adolescents often do not recognize the difference between expressing an ideal, such as conserving energy, and making the sacrifices necessary to live up to it, such as driving less often.

5. *Self-consciousness:* Adolescents in the stage of formal operations can think about thinking—their own and other people's. However, in their preoccupation with their own mental state, adolescents often assume that everyone else is thinking about the same thing they are thinking about: themselves. A teenage girl may be mortified if she wears "the wrong thing" to a party, thinking that everyone else must be looking askance at her. Elkind refers to this self-consciousness as the **imaginary audience,** a conceptualized "observer" who is as concerned with a young person's thoughts and behavior as he or she is. The imaginary audience fantasy is especially strong in the early teens but persists to a lesser degree into adult life.

6. *Specialness and invulnerability:* Elkind uses the term **personal fable** to denote a belief by adolescents that they are special, that their experience is unique, and that they are not subject to the rules that govern the rest of the world ("Other people get hooked from taking drugs but not me," or, "No one has ever been as deeply in love as I am"). According to Elkind, this special form of egocentrism underlies much risky, self-destructive behavior. Like the imaginary audience, the personal fable continues in adulthood. It is the personal fable, says Elkind, that persuades people to take such everyday risks as driving a car despite statistics on highway deaths. Perhaps Elkind would say that it was in part the personal fable that led Nelson Mandela to engage in dangerous insurrectionary activities against a brutal dictatorship.

imaginary audience Elkind's term for observer who exists only in an adolescent's mind and is as concerned with the adolescent's thoughts and actions as the adolescent is.

personal fable Elkind's term for conviction that one is special, unique, and not subject to the rules that govern the rest of the world.

The concepts of the imaginary audience and the personal fable have been widely accepted, but their validity as distinct earmarks of adolescence has little independent research support. In some studies of the personal fable, adolescents were more likely than college students or adults to see themselves as vulnerable to certain risks, such as alcohol and other drug problems, rather than less likely, as the personal fable would predict (Quadrel, Fischoff, & Davis, 1993).

It has been suggested that the imaginary audience and personal fable, rather than constituting universal features of adolescents' cognitive development, may be related to specific social experiences. For example, contrary to the personal fable, in a study of 2,694 urban black adolescents treated at an outpatient clinic in Washington, D.C., about 7 percent of the boys and more than 5 percent of the girls said they believed they would die within the next 2 years. Those who reported taking health risks or being exposed to risky behavior such as weapon carrying were as much as 5.6 times more likely to hold such beliefs than those who had not seen or engaged in such behavior. It is not clear whether these adolescents take risks because, living in dangerous neighborhoods, they expect their lives to be short or whether they expect to die early because of the risks they take (Valadez-Meltzer, Silber, Meltzer, & D'Angelo, 2005).

Checkpoint ✓

Can you . . .

✔ Describe Elkind's six proposed aspects of immature adolescent thought, and explain how they may grow out of the transition to formal operational thought?

Language Development

Children's use of language reflects their level of cognitive development. School-age children are quite proficient in use of language, but adolescence brings further refinements. Vocabulary continues to grow as reading matter becomes more adult. By ages 16 to 18 the average young person knows approximately 80,000 words (Owens, 1996).

With the advent of abstract thought, adolescents can define and discuss such abstractions as *love, justice,* and *freedom.* They more frequently use such terms as *however, otherwise, anyway, therefore, really,* and *probably* to express logical relationships. They become more conscious of words as symbols that can have multiple meanings, and they take pleasure in using irony, puns, and metaphors (Owens, 1996).

Adolescents also become more skilled in *social perspective-taking,* the ability to tailor their speech to another person's knowledge level and point of view. This ability is essential for persuasion and even for polite conversation. It undoubtedly helped Nelson Mandela in his eventually successful negotiations with his country's repressive rulers.

Conscious of their audience, adolescents speak a different language with peers than with adults (Owens, 1996; Box 16-1). Teenage slang is part of the process of developing an independent identity separate from parents and the adult world. In creating such expressions as "That's sweet!" and "dabomb," young people use their newfound ability to play with words "to define their generation's unique take on values, tastes, and preferences" (Elkind, 1998, p. 29).

Changes in Information Processing in Adolescence

Changes in the way adolescents process information reflect the maturation of the brain's frontal lobes and may help explain the cognitive advances Piaget described. Which neural connections wither and which become strengthened is highly responsive to experience. Thus, progress in cognitive processing varies greatly among individual adolescents (Kuhn, 2006).

Researchers have identified two broad categories of measurable change in information processing: *structural change* and *functional change* (Eccles et al., 2003).*

Structural Change

Structural changes in adolescence may include growth of information-processing capacity and an increase in the amount of knowledge stored in long-term memory.

The capacity of working memory, which enlarges rapidly in middle childhood, may continue to increase during adolescence. The expansion of working memory enables older adolescents to deal with complex problems or decisions involving multiple pieces of information.

*Unless otherwise referenced, the discussion in these sections is indebted to Eccles et al., 2003.

"We're tight!"
"It's all good!"
"Chill!"
"Let's bounce!"

Adolescents' conversation is mainly about the people and events in their everyday world (Labov, 1992). They use slang (nonstandard speech) to label people ("player" or "hottie"), to pronounce judgments ("That's cool!"), and to describe alcohol or drug-related activity ("She's twisted" or "He's blazed").

The Canadian linguist Marcel Danesi (1994) argues that adolescent speech is more than just slang (which, of course, adults use too). Instead, it constitutes a dialect of its own: *pubilect,* "the social dialect of puberty" (p. 97). Pubilect is more than an occasional colorful expression. It is the primary mode of verbal communication among teenagers, by which they differentiate themselves from adults. As they approach puberty, youngsters absorb this dialect from slightly older peers. Like any other linguistic code, pubilect serves to strengthen group identity and to shut outsiders (adults) out. Teenage vocabulary is characterized by rapid change. Although some terms have entered common discourse, adolescents keep inventing new terms all the time.

Analyses of recorded samples of adolescent conversation reveal several key features of pubilect. First, it is an *emotive* code. Through exaggerated tone, slow and deliberate delivery, prolonged stress, accompanying gestures, and vulgar interjections, it draws attention to feelings and attitudes ("Yeah, riiight!" "Well, duuuh!"). The use of fillers, such as the word *like,* as well as the typical intonation in which each phrase or sentence seems to end with a question mark, reflects unconscious uncertainty and serves to draw the listener into the speaker's state of mind.

A second feature of pubilect is its *connotative* function. Teenagers coin descriptive words or extend the meaning of existing words to convey their view of their world and the people in it, often in highly metaphorical ways. Such terms provide a ready lexicon for quick, automatic value judgments about others.

In the United States, there is not a single youth culture but many subcultures. Vocabulary may differ by gender, ethnicity, age, geographical region, neighborhood (city, suburban, or rural) and type of school (public or private) (Labov, 1992). Also, pubilect is *clique-coded:* it varies from one clique to another. "Druggies" and "jocks" engage in different kinds of activities, which form the main subjects of their conversation. This talk, in turn, cements bonds within the clique. Males use verbal dueling to assert power. Contenders for leadership trade insults and clever retorts in an effort to gain the upper hand in front of the group.

A study of teenage speech patterns in Naples, Italy, suggests that similar features may emerge "in any culture where teenagerhood constitutes a distinct social category" (Danesi, 1994, p. 123). Neapolitan teenagers use "mmmm" much as U.S. teenagers use "like": "Devo, mmmm, dire che, mmmm, non capisco, mmmm, . . ." ("I have, mmmm, to say that, mmmm, I don't understand, mmmm, . . ."). Exaggerated tone and rising intonation at the ends of phrases are also common. The Italian young people have terms roughly equivalent to the English "cool" (*togo*), "loser" (*grasta*), and "dork" or "nerd" (*secchione*). Other investigators report that adolescents in Milan, Bologna, and other northern Italian cities speak "the language of rock and roll." This cultural borrowing—the result of wide dissemination of English-language television channels, such as MTV—may well be creating a "symbolic universe" for teenagers around the world (Danesi, 1994, p. 123).

Source: Unless otherwise referenced, the source of this discussion is Danesi, 1994.

What's your view ?

- Can you remember "pubilect" expressions from your adolescence?
- When and why did you use such expressions?
- What was their effect on others your age? On adults?

Check it out !

For more information on this topic, go to www. slanguage. com. This is a Web site called American Slanguages.

---

declarative knowledge Acquired factual knowledge stored in long-term memory.

procedural knowledge Acquired skills stored in long-term memory.

conceptual knowledge Acquired interpretive understandings stored in long-term memory.

Information stored in long-term memory can be declarative, procedural, or conceptual. **Declarative knowledge** ("knowing that . . .") consists of all the facts a person has acquired, such as knowing that $2 + 2 = 4$ and that George Washington was the first U.S. president). **Procedural knowledge** ("knowing how to . . .") consists of all the skills a person has acquired, such as being able to multiply and divide and drive a car. **Conceptual knowledge** ("knowing why . . .") is an understanding of, for example, why an algebraic equation remains true if the same amount is added or subtracted from both sides.

Functional Change

Processes for obtaining, handling, and retaining information are functional aspects of cognition. Among these are learning, remembering, and reasoning, all of which improve during adolescence.

Among the most important *functional changes* are a continued increase in processing speed (Kuhn, 2006), and further development of *executive function* (refer back to Chapter 13), which includes such skills as selective attention, decision making, inhibitory control of impulsive responses, and management of working memory. These skills seem to develop at varying rates (Blakemore & Choudbury, 2006; Kuhn, 2006). In one study, researchers tested processing speed, inhibitory control, and working memory in 245 8- to 30-year-olds by measuring their eye movements in response to cognitive tasks. For example, participants were told to remember the location of a light that appeared in their peripheral field of vision while keeping their eyes focused on the center and then, after the light went out, to look at the spot where it had been seen. Adolescents reached adult-level performance in response inhibition at age 14, processing speed at 15, and working memory at 19. Although each process appears to mature independently, each seems to aid in the development of the others (Luna et al., 2004).

However, improvements observed in laboratory situations do not necessarily carry over to real life, where behavior depends in part on motivation and emotion regulation. Many older adolescents make poorer real-world decisions than younger adolescents do. In the game Twenty Questions, the object is to ask as few yes or no questions as necessary to discover the identity of a person, place, or thing by systematically narrowing down the categories within which the answer might fall. In one study (Drumm & Jackson, 1996), high school students, especially boys, showed a greater tendency than either early adolescents or college students to jump to guessing the answer. This pattern of guesswork may reflect a penchant for impulsive, risky behavior. As we discussed in Chapter 15, adolescents' rash judgments may be related to immature brain development, which may permit feelings to override reason.

Checkpoint

Can you . . .

✔ Identify several characteristics of adolescents' language development that reflect cognitive advances?

✔ Name two major kinds of changes in adolescents' cognitive processing, and give examples of each?

Moral Development

Guidepost 2

On what basis do adolescents make moral judgments, and how does prosocial behavior vary?

As children grow older and attain higher cognitive levels, they become capable of more complex reasoning about moral issues. Their tendencies toward altruism and empathy increase as well. Adolescents are better able than younger children to take another person's perspective, to solve social problems, to deal with interpersonal relationships, and to see themselves as social beings. All of these tendencies foster moral development.

Let's look at Lawrence Kohlberg's groundbreaking theory of moral reasoning, at Carol Gilligan's influential work on moral development in women and girls, and at research on prosocial behavior in adolescence.

Kohlberg's Theory of Moral Reasoning

A woman is near death from cancer. A druggist has discovered a drug that doctors believe might save her. The druggist is charging $2,000 for a small dose—10 times what the drug costs him to make. The sick woman's husband, Heinz, borrows from everyone he knows but can scrape together only $1,000. He begs the druggist to sell him the drug for $1,000 or let him pay the rest later. The druggist refuses, saying, "I discovered the drug and I'm going to make money from it." Heinz, desperate, breaks into the man's store and steals the drug. Should Heinz have done that? Why or why not? (Kohlberg, 1969).

Heinz's problem is the most famous example of Lawrence Kohlberg's approach to studying moral development. Starting in the 1950s, Kohlberg and his colleagues posed hypothetical dilemmas like this one to 75 boys ages 10, 13, and 16 and continued to question them periodically for more than 30 years. At the heart of each dilemma was the concept of justice. By asking respondents how they arrived at their answers, Kohlberg, like Piaget, concluded that the way people look at moral issues reflects cognitive development.

Kohlberg's Levels and Stages

Moral development in Kohlberg's theory bears some resemblance to Piaget's (refer back to Chapter 13), but Kohlberg's model is more complex. On the basis of thought processes shown by responses to his dilemmas, Kohlberg (1969) described three levels of moral reasoning, each divided into two stages (Table 16-1):

- *Level I:* **Preconventional morality.** People act under external controls. They obey rules to avoid punishment or reap rewards, or act out of self-interest. This level is typical of children ages 4 to 10.

preconventional morality First level of Kohlberg's theory of moral reasoning in which control is external and rules are obeyed in order to gain rewards or avoid punishment or out of self-interest.

Table 16-1   Kohlberg's Six Stages of Moral Reasoning

Levels	Stages of Reasoning	Typical Answers to Heinz's Dilemma
Level I: Preconventional morality (ages 4 to 10)	*Stage 1: Orientation toward punishment and obedience.* "What will happen to me?" Children obey rules to avoid punishment. They ignore the motives of an act and focus on its physical form (such as the size of a lie) or its consequences (such as the amount of physical damage).	*Pro:* "He should steal the drug. It isn't really bad to take it. It isn't as if he hadn't asked to pay for it first. The drug he'd take is worth only $200; he's not really taking a $2,000 drug." *Con:* "He shouldn't steal the drug. It's a big crime. He didn't get permission; he used force and broke and entered. He did a lot of damage and stole a very expensive drug."
	Stage 2: Instrumental purpose and exchange. "You scratch my back, I'll scratch yours." Children conform to rules out of self-interest and consideration for what others can do for them. They look at an act in terms of the human needs it meets and differentiate this value from the act's physical form and consequences.	*Pro:* "It's all right to steal the drug, because his wife needs it and he wants her to live. It isn't that he wants to steal, but that's what he has to do to save her." *Con:* "He shouldn't steal it. The druggist isn't wrong or bad; he just wants to make a profit. That's what you're in business for—to make money."
Level II: Conventional morality (ages 10 to 13 or beyond)	*Stage 3: Maintaining mutual relations, approval of others, the golden rule.* "Am I a good boy or girl?" Children want to please and help others, can judge the intentions of others, and develop ideas of what a good person is. They evaluate an act according to the motive behind it or the person performing it, and they take circumstances into account.	*Pro:* "He should steal the drug. He is only doing something that is natural for a good husband to do. You can't blame him for doing something out of love for his wife. You'd blame him if he didn't love his wife enough to save her." *Con:* "He shouldn't steal. If his wife dies, he can't be blamed. It isn't because he's heartless or that he doesn't love her enough to do everything that he legally can. The druggist is the selfish or heartless one."

conventional morality (or morality of conventional role conformity) Second level in Kohlberg's theory of moral reasoning in which standards of authority figures are internalized.

postconventional morality (or morality of autonomous moral principles) Third level in Kohlberg's theory of moral reasoning in which people follow internally held moral principles and can decide among conflicting moral standards.

- *Level II:* **Conventional morality** (or **morality of conventional role conformity**). People have internalized the standards of authority figures. They are concerned about being "good," pleasing others, and maintaining the social order. This level is typically reached after age 10; many people never move beyond it, even in adulthood.
- *Level III:* **Postconventional morality** (or **morality of autonomous moral principles**). People recognize conflicts between moral standards and make judgments on the basis of principles of right, fairness, and justice, as Nelson Mandela did during adulthood. People generally do not reach this level of moral reasoning until at least early adolescence, or more commonly in young adulthood, if ever.

Kohlberg later added a transitional level between levels II and III, when people no longer feel bound by society's moral standards but have not yet reasoned out their own principles of justice. Instead, they base their moral decisions on personal feelings.

In Kohlberg's theory, it is the reasoning underlying a person's response to a moral dilemma, not the answer itself, that indicates the stage of moral development. As illustrated in Table 16-1, two people who give opposite answers may be at the same stage if their reasoning is based on similar factors.

Some adolescents and even some adults remain at Kohlberg's level I. Like young children, they seek to avoid punishment or to satisfy their needs. Most adolescents and most adults seem to be at level II, usually in stage 3. They conform to social conventions, support

Levels	Stages of Reasoning	Typical Answers to Heinz's Dilemma
	Stage 4: Social concern and conscience. "What if everybody did it?" People are concerned with doing their duty, showing respect for higher authority, and maintaining the social order. They consider an act always wrong, regardless of motive or circumstances, if it violates a rule and harms others.	*Pro:* "You should steal it. If you did nothing, you'd be letting your wife die. It's your responsibility if she dies. You have to take it with the idea of paying the druggist." *Con:* "It is a natural thing for Heinz to want to save his wife, but it's still always wrong to steal. He knows he's taking a valuable drug from the man who made it."
Level III: Postconventional morality (early adolescence, or not until young adulthood, or never)	*Stage 5: Morality of contract, of individual rights, and of democratically accepted law.* People think in rational terms, valuing the will of the majority and the welfare of society. They generally see these values as best supported by adherence to the law. While they recognize that there are times when human need and the law conflict, they believe it is better for society in the long run if they obey the law.	*Pro:* "The law wasn't set up for these circumstances. Taking the drug in this situation isn't really right, but it's justified." *Con:* "You can't completely blame someone for stealing, but extreme circumstances don't really justify taking the law into your own hands. You can't have people stealing whenever they are desperate. The end may be good, but the ends don't justify the means."
	Stage 6: Morality of universal ethical principles. People do what they as individuals think is right, regardless of legal restrictions or the opinions of others. They act in accordance with internalized standards, knowing that they would condemn themselves if they did not.	*Pro:* "This is a situation that forces him to choose between stealing and letting his wife die. In a situation where the choice must be made, it is morally right to steal. He has to act in terms of the principle of preserving and respecting life." *Con:* "Heinz is faced with the decision of whether to consider the other people who need the drug just as badly as his wife. Heinz ought to act not according to his feelings for his wife, but considering the value of all the lives involved."

Source: Adapted from Kohlberg, 1969; Lickona, 1976.

the status quo, and do the "right" thing to please others or to obey the law. Stage 4 reasoning (upholding social norms) is less common but increases from early adolescence into adulthood. (For Nelson Mandela, the event that triggered his gradual emergence from this stage was his circumcision ceremony at age 16, when he listened to the shocking speech that challenged the morality of the system into which he was being initiated.) Often adolescents show periods of apparent disequilibrium when advancing from one level to another (Eisenberg & Morris, 2004) or fall back on other ethical systems, such as religious prescriptions, rather than Kohlberg's justice-based one (Thoma & Rest, 1999).

Before people can develop a fully principled (level III) morality, Kohlberg said, they must recognize the relativity of moral standards. Many young people question their earlier moral views when they enter high school or college or the world of work and encounter people whose values, culture, and ethnic background are different from their own. Still, very few people reach a level where they can choose among differing moral standards. In fact, at one point Kohlberg questioned the validity of Stage 6, morality based on universal ethical principles, because so few people seem to attain it. Later, he proposed a seventh, "cosmic" stage, in which people consider the effect of their actions not only on other people but on the universe as a whole (Kohlberg, 1981; Kohlberg & Ryncarz, 1990).

Early adolescent girls have more intimate social relationships than early adolescent boys and are more concerned about caring for others. This may help explain why girls in this age group tend to score higher than boys on moral judgments.

Evaluating Kohlberg's Theory

Kohlberg, building on Piaget, inaugurated a profound shift in the way we look at moral development. Instead of viewing morality solely as the attainment of control over self-gratifying impulses, investigators now study how children and adults base moral judgments on their growing understanding of the social world. Kohlberg's work has influenced much additional research, including James Fowler's theory of spiritual development (Box 16-2).

Initial research supported Kohlberg's theory. The American boys whom Kohlberg and his colleagues followed through adulthood progressed through Kohlberg's stages in sequence, and none skipped a stage. Their moral judgments correlated positively with age, education, IQ, and socioeconomic status (Colby, Kohlberg, Gibbs, & Lieberman, 1983). More recent research, however, has cast doubt on the delineation of some of Kohlberg's stages (Eisenberg & Morris, 2004). A study of children's judgments about laws and lawbreaking suggests that some children can reason flexibly about such issues as early as age 6 (Helwig & Jasiobedzka, 2001).

One reason the ages attached to Kohlberg's levels are so variable is that people who have achieved a high level of cognitive development do not always reach a comparably high level of moral development. A certain level of cognitive development is *necessary* but not *sufficient* for a comparable level of moral development. Thus, other processes besides cognition must be at work. Some investigators suggest that moral activity is motivated, not only by abstract considerations of justice, but also by such emotions as empathy, guilt, and distress and the internalization of prosocial norms (Eisenberg & Morris, 2004; Gibbs, 1991, 1995; Gibbs & Schnell, 1985). It also has been argued that Kohlberg's Stages 5 and 6 cannot fairly be called the most mature stages of moral development because they restrict maturity to a select group of people given to philosophical reflection (J. C. Gibbs, 1995).

Furthermore, there is not always a clear relationship between moral reasoning and moral behavior. People at postconventional levels of reasoning do not necessarily act more morally than those at lower levels. Other factors, such as specific situations, conceptions of virtue, and concern for others contribute to moral behavior (Colby & Damon, 1992; Fischer & Pruyne, 2003). Generally speaking, however, adolescents who are more advanced in moral reasoning do tend to be more moral in their behavior as well as better adjusted and higher in social competence, whereas antisocial adolescents tend to use less mature moral reasoning (Eisenberg & Morris, 2004).

A practical problem in using Kohlberg's system is its time-consuming testing procedures. The standard dilemmas need to be presented to each person individually and then

Can spiritual belief be studied from a developmental perspective? Yes, according to James Fowler (1981, 1989). Fowler defined faith as a way of seeing or knowing the world. To find out how people arrive at this way of seeing or knowing, Fowler and his students at Harvard Divinity School interviewed more than 400 people of all ages with various ethnic, educational, and socioeconomic backgrounds and various religious or secular identifications and affiliations.

Faith, according to Fowler, can be religious or nonreligious. People may have faith in a god, in science, in humanity, or in a cause to which they attach ultimate worth and that gives meaning to their lives. Faith develops, said Fowler, as do other aspects of cognition, through interaction between the maturing person and the environment. Fowler's stages correspond roughly to those described by Piaget, Kohlberg, and Erikson. New experiences—crises, problems, or revelations—that challenge or upset a person's equilibrium may prompt a leap from one stage to the next. The ages at which these transitions occur are variable, and some people never leave a particular stage; but the first three stages normally occur during childhood and adolescence.

- *Stage 1: Primal,* or *intuitive-projective, faith* (ages 18–24 months to 7 years). The beginnings of faith, says Fowler, arise after toddlers become self-aware, begin to use language and symbolic thought, and have developed *basic trust:* the sense that their needs will be met by powerful others. As young children struggle to understand the forces that control their world, they form powerful, imaginative, often terrifying images of God, heaven, and hell, drawn from the stories adults tell. These images are often irrational; preoperational children tend to be confused about cause and effect and about the difference between reality and fantasy. Still egocentric, they may identify God's point of view with their own or their parents'. They think of God mainly in terms of obedience and punishment.
- *Stage 2: Mythic-literal faith* (ages 7 to 12 years). Children capable of concrete operations begin to develop a more coherent view of the universe. As they adopt their family's and community's beliefs and observances, they tend to take religious stories and symbols literally. They can now see God as having a perspective, beyond their own, that takes into account people's effort and intent. They believe that God is fair and that people get what they deserve.
- *Stage 3: Synthetic-conventional faith* (adolescence or beyond). Adolescents capable of abstract thought form belief systems and commitments to ideals. As they search for

identity, they seek a more personal relationship with God but look to others, usually peers, for moral authority. Their faith is unquestioning and conforms to community standards. This stage is typical of followers of organized religion; about 50 percent of adults may never move beyond it to Fowler's more advanced stages: critically examined faith and, finally, universalized faith.

As one of the first researchers to study faith systematically, Fowler has had great impact but has been criticized on several counts (Koenig, 1994). Critics say Fowler's concept of faith is at odds with conventional definitions. They challenge his emphasis on cognitive knowledge and claim that he underestimates the maturity of a simple, solid, unquestioning faith. Critics also question whether faith develops in universal stages or in those Fowler identified. Fowler's sample was not randomly selected; it consisted of paid participants who lived in or near North American cities with major colleges or universities. Thus, the findings may be more representative of people with above-average intelligence and education, and they are not representative of non-Western cultures.

Some investigators have looked more narrowly at children's understanding of prayer, one aspect of religious activity, and have come up with stages somewhat different from Fowler's. One early study using Piaget-style questioning (Goldman, 1964) noted a progression from a magical stage before age 9, in which children believe that prayers come true as if by magic, toward rational and, finally, faith-based stages.

- From your experience and observation, can faith be nonreligious?
- Can you recall having gone through any of Fowler's stages of faith? At which stage would you say you are now?

Check it out

For more information on this topic, go to http://speakingoffaith .publicradio.org/programs/childrengod/index.shtml and hear a public radio discussion of "Children and God," featuring Robert Coles, retired child psychologist at Harvard University and author of *The Spiritual Life of Children;* Diane Komp, retired pediatric oncologist at Yale University and author of *Window to Heaven: When Children See Life in Death;* and Carol Dittberner, director of religious education at St. Francis Cabrini.

---

scored by trained judges. One alternative is the Defining Issues Test (DIT), in which students rate and rank a list of statements rather than being asked to articulate the issues and arguments involved (Rest, 1975; Rest, Deemer, Barnett, & Spickelm, 1986). The DIT can be given quickly to a group and scored objectively. However, the DIT may tend to overestimate the degree of moral development (Rest et al., 1999).

Influence of Parents and Peers Neither Piaget nor Kohlberg considered parents important to children's moral development, but more recent research emphasizes parents' contribution in both the cognitive and the emotional realms. Adolescents with supportive, authoritative parents who stimulate them to question and expand on their moral reasoning tend to reason at higher levels (Eisenberg & Morris, 2004).

What's your view

- Can you think of a time when you or someone you know acted contrary to personal moral judgment? Why do you think this happened?

Peers also affect moral reasoning by talking with each other about moral conflicts. Having more close friends, spending quality time with them, and being perceived as a leader are associated with higher moral reasoning (Eisenberg & Morris, 2004).

Cross-Cultural Validity It is doubtful how accurately Kohlberg's system represents moral reasoning in non-Western cultures (Eisenberg & Morris, 2004). Older people in countries other than the United States do tend to score at higher stages than younger people. However, people in non-Western cultures rarely score above Stage 4 (Edwards, 1981; Nisan & Kohlberg, 1982; Snarey, 1985), suggesting that some aspects of Kohlberg's model may not fit the cultural values of these societies.

Gilligan's Theory: An Ethic of Care

On the basis of research on women, Carol Gilligan (1982) asserted that Kohlberg's theory is oriented toward values more important to men than to women. Gilligan claimed that women see morality not so much in terms of justice and fairness as of responsibility to show caring and avoid harm. They focus on not turning away from others rather than on not treating others unfairly (Eisenberg & Morris, 2004).

Research has not found much support for Gilligan's claim of a male bias in Kohlberg's stages (Brabeck & Shore, 2003; Jaffee & Hyde, 2000), and she has since modified her position. However, research has found small gender differences in care-related moral reasoning among adolescents in some cultures (Eisenberg & Morris, 2004). For example, early adolescent girls in the United States tend to emphasize care-related concerns more than boys do, especially when tested with open-ended questions ("How important is it to keep promises to a friend?") or self-chosen moral dilemmas related to their own experience (Garmon, Basinger, Gregg, & Gibbs, 1996). This may be because girls generally mature earlier and have more intimate social relationships (Garmon et al., 1996; Skoe & Diessner, 1994). In an analysis of 113 studies, girls and women were more likely to think in terms of care and boys and men in terms of justice, but these differences were small (Jaffee & Hyde, 2000).

Aside from possible gender differences, some researchers have studied prosocial (similar to care-oriented) moral reasoning as an alternative to Kohlberg's justice-based system. Prosocial moral reasoning is reasoning about moral dilemmas in which one person's needs or desires conflict with those of others in situations in which social rules or norms are unclear or nonexistent. In a longitudinal study that followed children into early adulthood, prosocial reasoning based on personal reflection about consequences and on internalized values and norms increased with age, whereas reasoning based on such stereotypes as "it's nice to help" decreased from childhood into the late teens (Eisenberg & Morris, 2004).

Prosocial Behavior and Volunteer Activity

Just as adolescents' moral reasoning is more sophisticated and shows more concern about others than that of younger children, prosocial behavior typically increases from childhood through adolescence (Eisenberg & Morris, 2004). Girls tend to show more prosocial behavior than boys (Eisenberg & Fabes, 1998), and this difference becomes more pronounced in adolescence (Fabes, Carlo, Kupanoff, & Laible, 1999).

Girls tend to see themselves as more empathic and prosocial than boys do, and parents of girls emphasize social responsibility more than parents of sons do (Eisenberg & Morris, 2004). In a large-scale study, this was true of 18-year-olds in seven countries—Australia, Bulgaria, Czech Republic, Hungary, Russia, Sweden, and United States, (Flannagan, Bowes, Jonsson, Csapo, & Sheblanova, 1998). As with younger children, parents who use inductive discipline are more likely to have prosocial adolescents than parents who use power-assertive techniques.

About half of all adolescents engage in some sort of community service or volunteer activity. These prosocial activities enable adolescents to become involved in adult society, to explore their potential roles as part of the community, and to link their developing sense of identity to civic involvement. Adolescent volunteers tend to be outgoing and to have a high degree of self-understanding and commitment to others. Girls tend to volunteer more than boys, and adolescents with high SES volunteer more than those with lower SES (Eisenberg & Morris, 2004). Students who engage in volunteer work outside of school tend, as adults, to be more engaged in their communities than those who do not (Eccles, 2004).

Checkpoint ✔

Can you . . .

✔ List Kohlberg's levels and stages, and discuss factors that influence how rapidly children and adolescents progress through them?

✔ Evaluate Kohlberg's theory with regard to the role of emotion and socialization, parent and peer influences, and cross-cultural validity?

✔ Explain the difference between Gilligan's and Kohlberg's standards of moral reasoning, and discuss gender effects?

✔ Discuss individual differences in prosocial behavior, such as volunteering?

Educational and Vocational Issues

Guidepost 3

What influences affect adolescents' school success and their educational and vocational planning and preparation?

School is a central organizing experience in most adolescents' lives. It offers opportunities to learn information, master new skills, and sharpen old skills; to participate in sports, the arts, and other activities; to explore vocational choices; and to be with friends. It widens intellectual and social horizons. Some adolescents, however, experience school not as an opportunity but as one more hindrance on the road to adulthood.

In the United States, as in all other industrialized countries and in some developing countries as well, more students finish high school than ever before, and many enroll in higher education (Eccles et al., 2003; OECD, 2004). In 2004, nearly 87 percent of U.S. 18- to 24-year-olds not enrolled in high school had received a high school diploma or equivalent credential (Laird, DeBell, & Chapman, 2006; Figure 16-2). Among the 30 member countries of the Organisation for Economic Cooperation and Development (OECD, 2004), average levels of educational attainment range from only 7.4 years of schooling in Mexico to 13.8 years in Norway.

The United States, with an average of 12.7 years of schooling, is on the high end of this international comparison. However, U.S. adolescents, on average, do less well on academic achievement tests than adolescents in many other countries (Lemke et al., 2004; Snyder & Hoffman, 2001). Furthermore, although fourth- and eighth-grade student achievement, as measured by the National Assessment of Educational Progress, has improved in several areas, twelfth-grade achievement generally has not (NCES, 2003, 2005b).

Let's look at influences on school achievement and then at young people who drop out of school. Then, we'll consider planning for higher education and vocations.

Influences on School Achievement

Students who like school do well in school and are likely to remain in school (Samdal & Dür, 2000). As in the elementary grades, socioeconomic status and the nature of the home environment influence school achievement in adolescence. Other factors include gender, ethnicity, parenting practices, peer influence, quality of schooling, and—perhaps first and foremost—students' motivation to learn.

Student Motivation and Self-Efficacy

In Western countries, particularly the United States, educational practices are based on the assumption that students are, or can be, motivated to learn. Educators emphasize the value of intrinsic motivation—the student's desire to learn for the sake of learning (Larson & Wilson, 2004). Unfortunately, many U.S. students are not self-motivated, and motivation often declines as they enter high school. Many are bored, some resist learning or give up easily, and some (as we will discuss later) drop out of school (Eccles, 2004; Larson & Wilson, 2004).

In these Western cultures, students high in *self-efficacy*—who believe that they can master tasks and regulate their learning—are likely to do well in school. In a study of 116 ninth and tenth graders in two U.S. high schools, students' perceived self-efficacy predicted the social studies grades they expected and achieved. Students' goals were influenced by their parents' goals for them, but students' beliefs about their own abilities were more influential (Zimmerman et al., 1992). In a longitudinal study of 140 eighth graders, students' self-discipline was twice as important as IQ in accounting for their grades and achievement test scores and for selection into a competitive high school program at the end of the year (Duckworth & Seligman, 2005).

In many cultures, education is based not on personal motivation but on such factors as duty (India), submission to authority (Islamic countries), and participation in the family and community (sub-Saharan Africa). In the countries of East Asia, students are expected to learn, not for the value of learning, but to meet family and societal expectations of perfection. Learning is expected to require intense effort, and students who fail or fall behind feel obligated to try again. This may help explain why, in international comparisons in science and math, East Asian students substantially surpass U.S. students. However, because of the heavy reliance on competitive testing to select students for continued education and careers, students tend to show high levels of anxiety, stress, and depression (Larson &

Figure 16-2

Percentages of 18- through 24-year-olds not currently in school who have not completed high school or equivalent, 1972–2004.

Source: Laird, DeBell, & Chapman, Fig. 2, 2006.

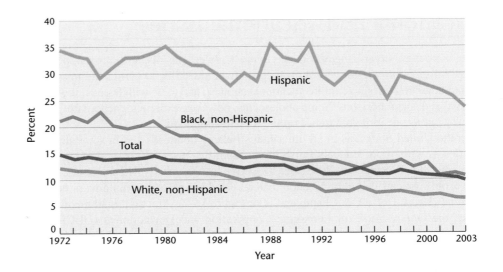

Wilson, 2004). In developing countries, issues of motivation pale in the light of social and economic barriers to education: inadequate or absent schools and educational resources, the need for child labor to support the family, barriers to schooling for girls or cultural subgroups, and early marriage (Larson & Wilson, 2004). Thus, as we discuss factors in educational success, which are drawn largely from studies in the United States and other Western countries, we need to remember that they do not apply to all cultures.

Importance of SES and Related Family Characteristics

High socioeconomic status is an important predictor of academic success, according to a study of 15-year-olds' mathematical literacy in 20 relatively high-income countries (Hampden-Thompson & Johnston, 2006). In all countries, students with at least one postsecondary-educated parent performed better than students whose parents had lower educational levels. A similar gap occurred between students whose parents had high occupational status and those whose parents were of middle or low occupational status. Having more than 200 books in the home also was associated with higher scores. All of these are indicators of socioeconomic status. Living in a two-parent family—another key predictor of math competence in all 20 countries—also was related to SES. So were the disadvantages conferred by being an immigrant and speaking a nonnative language at home, which affected math achievement in most of the countries.

Gender

Internationally, in 2000, girls were better readers than boys in all of 43 participating countries in the Organization for Economic Cooperation and Development. Boys were ahead in mathematical literacy in about half of the countries, though these gender differences were smaller (OECD, 2004). In the United States, adolescent boys and girls score about the same on standardized tests in most subject-matter areas (Freeman, 2004; Sen et al., 2005). Boys have had a slight edge on standardized tests of math and science, but this gender gap appears to be shrinking as girls take equally challenging math and science courses and do as well or better in them (Spelke, 2005). Girls do better than boys on assessments of reading and writing (Freeman, 2004; Sen et al., 2005).

Regardless of test scores, girls in the United States tend to have more confidence in their academic abilities than boys do. They like school a little better, earn better grades, and are more likely to graduate from high school and to plan to attend and finish college and graduate or professional schools. Boys are more likely than girls to be underachievers, to be assigned to special or remedial education, and to be expelled or drop out of school (Eccles et al., 2003; Freeman, 2004). Teachers tend to discipline boys more harshly than girls but give more favorable attention to high-achieving boys than to high-achieving girls. Boys are more likely than girls to be encouraged to take honors courses, to apply to top colleges, and to aim for challenging careers (Eccles et al., 2003).

Even though adolescents are more independent than younger children, the home atmosphere continues to influence school achievement. Parents help not only by monitoring homework, but also by taking an active interest in other aspects of teenagers' lives. Children of authoritative parents who discuss issues openly and offer praise and encouragement tend to do best in school.

Parenting Styles, Ethnicity, and Peer Influence

In Western cultures, the benefits of authoritative parenting continue to affect school achievement during adolescence (Baumrind, 1991). *Authoritative parents* urge adolescents to look at both sides of issues, welcome their participation in family decisions, and admit that children sometimes know more than parents. These parents strike a balance between making demands and being responsive. Their children receive praise and privileges for good grades; poor grades bring encouragement to try harder and offers of help.

Authoritarian parents, in contrast, tell adolescents not to argue with or question adults and tell them they will "know better when they are grown up." Good grades bring admonitions to do even better; poor grades may be punished by reduced allowances or grounding. *Permissive parents* seem indifferent to grades, make no rules about watching television, do not attend school functions, and neither help with nor check their children's homework. These parents may not be neglectful or uncaring; they may, in fact, be nurturant. They may simply believe that teenagers should be responsible for their own lives.

What accounts for the academic success of authoritatively raised adolescents? Authoritative parents' greater involvement in schooling may be a factor as well as their encouragement of positive attitudes toward work. A more subtle mechanism, consistent with findings on self-efficacy, may be parents' influence on how children explain success or failure. In a study of 2,353 California and Wisconsin high school students, those who saw their parents as nonauthoritative were more likely than their peers to attribute poor grades to external causes or to low ability—forces beyond their control—rather than to their own efforts. A year later, such students tended to pay less attention in class and to spend less time on homework (Glasgow et al., 1997). Thus, a sense of helplessness associated with nonauthoritative parenting may become a self-fulfilling prophecy, discouraging students from trying to succeed.

Among some ethnic groups, though, parenting styles may be less important than peer influence on motivation. In one study, Latino and African American adolescents, even those with authoritative parents, did less well in school than European American students, apparently because of lack of peer support for academic achievement (Steinberg, Dornbusch, & Brown, 1992). On the other hand, Asian American students, whose parents are sometimes described as authoritarian, get high grades and score better than European American students on math achievement tests, apparently because both parents and peers prize achievement (C. Chen & Stevenson, 1995). The strong school achievement of many young people from a variety of immigrant backgrounds reflects their families' and friends' strong emphasis on educational success (Fuligni, 1997).

Peer influence may help explain the downward trend in academic motivation and achievement that begins for many students in early adolescence. In a longitudinal study of students entering an urban middle school, motivation and grades declined, on average, during seventh grade. Students whose peer group were high achievers showed less decline in achievement and enjoyment of school, whereas those who associated with low achievers showed greater declines (Ryan, 2001).

The School

The quality of schooling strongly influences student achievement. A good middle or high school has an orderly, safe environment, adequate material resources, a stable teaching staff, and a positive sense of community. The school culture has a strong emphasis on academics and fosters the belief that all students can learn. It also offers opportunities for extracurricular activities, which keep students engaged and prevent them from getting into trouble after school. Teachers trust, respect, and care about students and have high expectations for them as well as confidence in their ability to help students succeed (Eccles, 2004).

Adolescents are more satisfied with school if they are allowed to participate in making rules and feel support from teachers and other students (Samdal & Dür, 2000) and if the curriculum and instruction are meaningful and appropriately challenging and fit their interests, skill level, and needs (Eccles, 2004). In a survey of 452 suburban sixth graders, the students' perceptions of their teachers' fairness, expectations, modeling of academic motivation, rule setting, and negative feedback explained significant variances in student motivation, behavior, and achievement. High expectations were the most consistent positive predictor of students' goals and interests, and negative feedback was the most consistent negative predictor of academic performance and classroom behavior (Wentzel, 2002).

Some big-city school systems, such as New York's, Philadelphia's, and Chicago's, are experimenting with small schools, in which students, teachers, and parents form a learning community united by a common vision of good education. The curriculum may have a special focus, such as ethnic studies. Teaching is flexible, innovative, and personalized; teachers work together closely and get to know students well (Meier, 1995; Rossi, 1996). However, some small schools that originally showed promise have closed or declined in quality due to funding problems, increased enrollment, or staff turnover (Gootman & Herszenhorn, 2005).

A decline in academic motivation and achievement often begins with the transition from the intimacy and familiarity of elementary school to the larger, more pressured, and less supportive environment of middle school or junior high school (Eccles, 2004). For this reason, some cities such as Philadelphia have tried eliminating the middle school transition by extending elementary school to eighth grade. In other places, such as New York City, some middle schools have been consolidated with small high schools where middle-schoolers can see older role models (Gootman, 2007).

The transition to college, with its higher educational standards and expectations for self-direction, can be a shock for some students. Early College High Schools—small, personalized, high-quality schools operated in cooperation with nearby colleges—are intended primarily for low-income and minority students and first-generation English language learners, groups statistically underrepresented in higher education. By combining a nurturing atmosphere with clear, rigorous standards, these schools enable students to complete high school requirements plus the first 2 years of college ("The Early College High School Initiative," n.d.).

Dropping Out of High School

Although more U.S. youths are completing high school than ever before, 5 percent of high school students dropped out during the 2003–2004 school year—this at a time when high school graduation is, for most purposes, a minimum requirement for labor force entry. Hispanic students are more likely to drop out than black students, who are more likely to drop out than white students; Asian students are the least likely to drop out. Low-income students are four times more likely to drop out than high-income students (Laird, DeBell, & Chapman, 2006; Figure 16-3).

Checkpoint ✔

Can you . . .

✔ Explain how schools in various cultures motivate students to learn?

✔ Assess the influences of personal qualities, SES, gender, ethnicity, parents, and peers on academic achievement?

✔ Give examples of educational practices that can help high school students succeed?

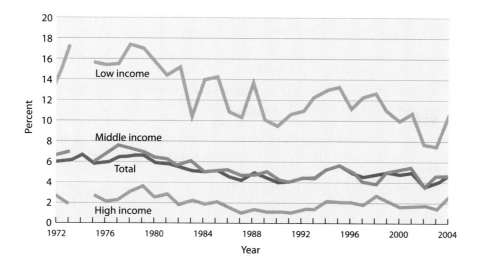

Figure 16-3

Percentage of 15- to 24-year-olds who dropped out of high school, by income, 1972–2004.

Source: Laird, DeBell, & Chapman, Fig. 1, 2006.

Why are poor and minority adolescents more likely to drop out? One reason may be ineffective schooling: low teacher expectations or differential treatment of these students; less teacher support than at the elementary level; and the perceived irrelevance of the curriculum to culturally underrepresented groups. In schools that use ability tracking, students in low-ability or noncollege tracks (where minority youth are likely to be assigned) often have inferior educational experiences. Placed with peers who are equally alienated, they tend to have feelings of incompetence and negative attitudes toward school and to engage in problem behaviors, both within and outside of school (Eccles, 2004).

Society suffers when young people do not finish school. Dropouts are more likely to be unemployed or to have low incomes, to end up on welfare, and to become involved with drugs, crime, and delinquency. They also tend to be in poorer health (Laird et al., 2006; NCES, 2001, 2003, 2004a).

A longitudinal study that followed 3,502 disadvantaged eighth graders into early adulthood points up the difference success in high school can make (Finn, 2006). Of this group, 21 percent ("successful completers") successfully completed high school, and 52 percent ("marginal completers") did so but received below average grades or test scores. The remaining 27 percent ("noncompleters") dropped out. As young adults, successful completers were most likely and noncompleters least likely to obtain postsecondary education, to have jobs, and to be consistently employed.

An important factor distinguishing the successful completers in this study was *active engagement:* the "attention, interest, investment, and effort students expend in the work of school" (Marks, 2000, p. 155). On the most basic level, active engagement means coming to class on time, being prepared, listening and responding to the teacher, and obeying school rules. A higher level of engagement consists of getting involved with the coursework—asking questions, taking the initiative to seek help when needed, or doing extra projects. Both levels of active engagement tend to pay off in positive school performance (Finn & Rock, 1997). Family encouragement, small class size, and a warm, supportive school environment promote active engagement.

Preparing for Higher Education or Vocations

Coming from an initially humble background and with a racist system stacked against him, Nelson Mandela made up his mind early to be a lawyer so he could help his people. He followed through on that ambition and the education it took to achieve it.

How do young people develop career goals? How do they decide whether to go to college and, if not, how to enter the world of work? Many factors enter in, including individual ability and personality, education, socioeconomic and ethnic background, the advice of school counselors, life experiences, and societal values. Let's look at some influences on educational and vocational aspirations. Then we'll examine provisions for young people

What's your view

- How can parents, educators, and societal institutions encourage young people to finish high school successfully?

Checkpoint ✔

Can you . . .

✔ Discuss trends in high school completion and causes and effects of dropping out?

✔ Explain the importance of active engagement in schooling?

who do not plan to go to college. We'll also discuss the pros and cons of outside work for high school students.

Influences on Students' Aspirations

About 69 percent of students finishing high school in the United States in 2004 expected to complete 4 years of college, according to an annual representative profile of high school seniors (Ingels, Planty, & Bozick, 2005). Self-efficacy beliefs—often influenced by parents' beliefs and aspirations—help shape the occupational options students consider and the way they prepare for careers (Bandura, Barbaranelli, Caprara, & Pastorelli, 2001; Bandura et al., 1996).

Parents' values with regard to academic achievement influence adolescents' values and occupational goals (Jodl, Michael, Malanchuk, Eccles, & Sameroff, 2001). This influence is especially apparent among children of East Asian immigrant families, who strongly value education. Although high school graduates from immigrant families in general are as likely to go on to college as peers from American-born families, the proportion of children of East Asian families who do so (96 percent) is much higher than among some other immigrant groups (Fuligni & Witkow, 2004).

Despite the greater flexibility in career goals today, gender—and gender-stereotyping —may influence vocational choice (Eccles et al., 2003). Girls and boys in the United States are now equally likely to plan careers in math and science; but boys are much more likely to earn college degrees in engineering, physics, and computer science (NCES, 2001), whereas girls are still more likely to go into nursing, social welfare professions, and teaching (Eccles et al., 2003). Much the same is true in other industrialized countries (OECD, 2004).

The educational system itself may act as a brake on vocational aspirations. Students who can memorize and analyze tend to do well on intelligence tests and in classrooms where teaching is geared to those abilities. Thus, as predicted by the tests, these students are achievers in a system that stresses the abilities in which they happen to excel. Students whose strength is in creative or practical thinking—areas critical to success in certain fields—never get a chance to show what they can do (Sternberg, 1997). Recognition of a broader range of intelligences (refer back to Chapter 13), combined with more flexible teaching and career counseling, could allow more students to meet their educational goals and enter the occupations they desire so as to make the contributions of which they are capable.

Guiding Students Not Bound for College

Most industrialized countries offer guidance to non-college-bound students. Germany, for example, has an apprenticeship system in which high school students go to school part-time and spend the rest of the week in paid on-the-job training supervised by an employer-mentor. About 60 percent of German high school students take advantage of this program each year, and 85 percent of those who complete it find jobs (Hopfensperger, 1996).

The United States lacks coordinated policies to help non-college-bound youth make a successful transition from high school to the labor market (Eccles, 2004). Vocational counseling is generally oriented toward college-bound youth. Whatever vocational training programs do exist for the approximately 38 percent of high school graduates who do not immediately go on to college (NCES, 2003) tend to be less comprehensive than the German system and less closely tied to the needs of businesses and industries. Most of these young people must get training on the job or in community college courses. Many, ignorant about the job market, do not obtain the skills they need. Others take jobs beneath their abilities. Some do not find work at all (NRC, 1993a).

In some communities, demonstration programs help in the school-to-work transition. The most successful ones offer instruction in basic skills, counseling, peer support, mentoring, apprenticeship, and job placement (NRC, 1993a). In 1994, Congress passed the School to Work Opportunities Act, which allocated $1.1 billion to help states and local governments develop vocational training programs. In 2000–2001 nearly half of public alternative schools and programs for at-risk youth offered vocational training (NCES, 2003).

Adolescents in the Workplace

Youth employment is not a simple issue. In much of the developing world, youth employment is an entrenched system vital to family subsistence. Working with the family in the fields or at home is part of a child's normal socialization. However, the conditions of employment for young adolescents are changing with globalization and urbanization. Young people may work as apprentices to a craftsman, as factory laborers, as live-in domestic servants, or as street vendors. Others assist parents at their jobs (Larson & Wilson, 2004). In many cases, they are bound by informal employment agreements. The United Nations International Labour Office (ILO) (2002) estimates that 5.7 million children and young adolescents are in bonded or forced labor.

This young man—one of approximately 38 percent of U.S. high school graduates who do not immediately go on to college—is learning electronics servicing and repair. Vocational training, to be effective, must be tied to the current needs of the job market.

Developmental effects of young adolescents' employment are mixed. Physical effects depend on working conditions. Worldwide, studies show that heavy work schedules interfere with schooling and may lead to dropping out. Many youths are engaged in highly repetitive, unskilled work that prepares them for nothing. However, some adolescents who work do gain useful skills. They also gain status and respect as breadwinners, fulfill filial obligations, and integrate themselves into their families and communities. When interviewed, many of these young people say that working helps them develop responsibility and self-esteem and gain economic autonomy. The costs and benefits of adolescent employment, then, depends on such factors as why adolescents are working, the conditions of employment, what skills they are acquiring, and how likely these skills are to match available jobs in a changing economy (Larson & Wilson, 2004).

In the United States, an estimated 80 to 90 percent of adolescents are employed at some time during high school, mostly in service and retail jobs (Staff, Mortimer, & Uggen, 2004). Researchers disagree over whether part-time work is beneficial to high school students (by helping them develop real-world skills and a work ethic) or detrimental (by distracting them from long-term educational and occupational goals).

Some of the alleged harmful effects of work for students may be overstated (Mortimer, 2003). In a 4-year longitudinal study of how ninth graders use their time, most of the students who worked also were heavily engaged in school and other activities (Shanahan & Flaherty, 2001). The number of hours a student worked did not seem to reduce self-esteem, mental health, or mastery motivation. Working had no effect on homework time or grades until senior year, when students who worked more than 20 hours a week tended to do less homework than other students. Even so, their grades and achievement motivation did not suffer. And students who worked fewer than 20 hours had *higher* grades than those who did not work at all.

Other research suggests that working students fall into two groups: those who are on an accelerated path to adulthood, and those who make a more leisurely transition, balancing schoolwork, paid jobs, and extracurricular activities. The "accelerators" work more than 20 hours a week during high school and spend little time on school-related leisure activities. Precocious exposure to an adult world may lead them into early alcohol and drug use, sexual activity, and delinquent behavior. Many of these adolescents have relatively low SES; they tend to look for full-time work right after high school and not to obtain college degrees. Intensive work experience in high school improves their prospects for work and income after high school, but not for long-term occupational

Checkpoint ✓

Can you . . .

✔ Discuss influences on educational and vocational aspirations and planning?

✔ Weigh factors in the value of part-time work for high school students?

attainment. The "balancers," in contrast, often come from more privileged backgrounds. For them, the effects of part-time work seem entirely benign. Work helps them to gain a sense of responsibility, independence, and self-confidence and to appreciate the value of work but does not deter them from their educational paths. These young people are more likely to earn a 4-year college degree, which opens the door to better long-term occupational prospects. If they engage in risky behaviors, they do not do so until after high school, and these activities are less likely to interfere with future attainments (Staff et al., 2004).

For high school students who must, or choose to, work outside of school, then, the effects are more likely to be positive if they try to limit working hours and remain engaged in school activities. Cooperative educational programs that enable students to work part-time as part of their school program may be especially protective (Staff et al., 2004).

Refocus

Thinking back to the information about Nelson Mandela in the Focus vignette at the beginning of this chapter,

- What signs of cognitive maturity did Mandela show as an adolescent?

- What influences played a part in his moral development? In his education? In his vocational choice?

Vocational planning is one aspect of an adolescent's search for identity. The question "What shall I do?" is very close to "Who shall I be?" People who feel they are doing something worthwhile and doing it well feel good about themselves. Those who feel that their work does not matter—or that they are not good at it—may wonder about the meaning of their lives. A prime personality issue in adolescence, which we discuss in Chapter 17, is the effort to define the self.

Summary and Key Terms

Aspects of Cognitive Maturation

Guidepost 1 How do adolescents' thinking and use of language differ from younger children's?

- People in Piaget's stage of formal operations can engage in hypothetical-deductive reasoning. They can think in terms of possibilities, deal flexibly with problems, and test hypotheses.

- Since environmental stimulation plays an important part in attaining this stage, not all people become capable of formal operations; and those who are capable do not always use it.

- Piaget's proposed stage of formal operations does not take into account such developments as accumulation of knowledge and expertise, gains in information processing, and the growth of metacognition. Piaget also paid little attention to individual differences, between-task variations, and the role of the situation.

- According to Elkind, immature thought patterns can result from adolescents' inexperience with formal thinking. These thought patterns include idealism and criticalness, argumentativeness, indecisiveness, apparent hypocrisy, self-consciousness, and an assumption of specialness and invulnerability. Research has cast doubt on the special prevalence of the latter two patterns during adolescence.

- Research has found both structural and functional changes in adolescent cognition, which reflect developments in the adolescent brain. Structural changes include increases in information-processing capacity, in the amount of knowledge in long-term memory, and in the capacity of working memory. Functional changes include progress in learning, remembering, and reasoning.

- Vocabulary and other aspects of language development, especially those related to abstract thought, such as social perspective-taking, improve in adolescence. Adolescents enjoy wordplay and create their own dialect.

  formal operations (445)   hypothetical-deductive reasoning (446)   imaginary audience (448)   personal fable (448)   declarative knowledge (450)   procedural knowledge (450)   conceptual knowledge (450)

Moral Development

Guidepost 2 On what basis do adolescents make moral judgments, and how does prosocial behavior vary?

- According to Kohlberg, moral reasoning is based on a developing sense of justice and growing cognitive abilities. Kohlberg proposed that moral development progresses from external control to internalized societal standards to personal, principled moral codes.

- Kohlberg's theory has been criticized on several grounds, including failure to credit the roles of emotion, socialization, and parental guidance. The applicability of Kohlberg's system to people in non-Western cultures has been questioned. Research has found no significant gender differences in moral reasoning as measured by Kohlbergian methods.

- Gilligan proposed an alternative theory of moral development based on an ethic of caring, rather than on justice.

- Prosocial behavior continues to increase during adolescence, especially among girls. Many adolescents engage in volunteer community service.

- According to Fowler's theory of faith development, most adolescents are in the stage of conventional faith, in which they accept established community beliefs.

  preconventional morality (451)   conventional morality (or morality of conventional role conformity) (452)   postconventional morality (or morality of autonomous moral principles) (452)

Educational and Vocational Issues

Guidepost 3   What influences affect adolescents' school success and their educational and vocational planning and preparation?

- Motivation, self-efficacy beliefs, gender, parental practices, cultural and peer influences, and quality of schooling affect educational motivation and achievement.

- Although most Americans graduate from high school, the dropout rate is higher among poor, Hispanic, and black students. Active engagement in studies is an important factor in keeping adolescents in school.

- Educational and vocational aspirations are influenced by several factors, including self-efficacy beliefs, parental values, and gender.

- High school graduates who do not immediately go on to college can benefit from vocational training.

- Part-time work seems to have both positive and negative effects on educational, social, and occupational development. The long-term effects tend to be best when working hours are limited.

CHAPTER SEVENTEEN

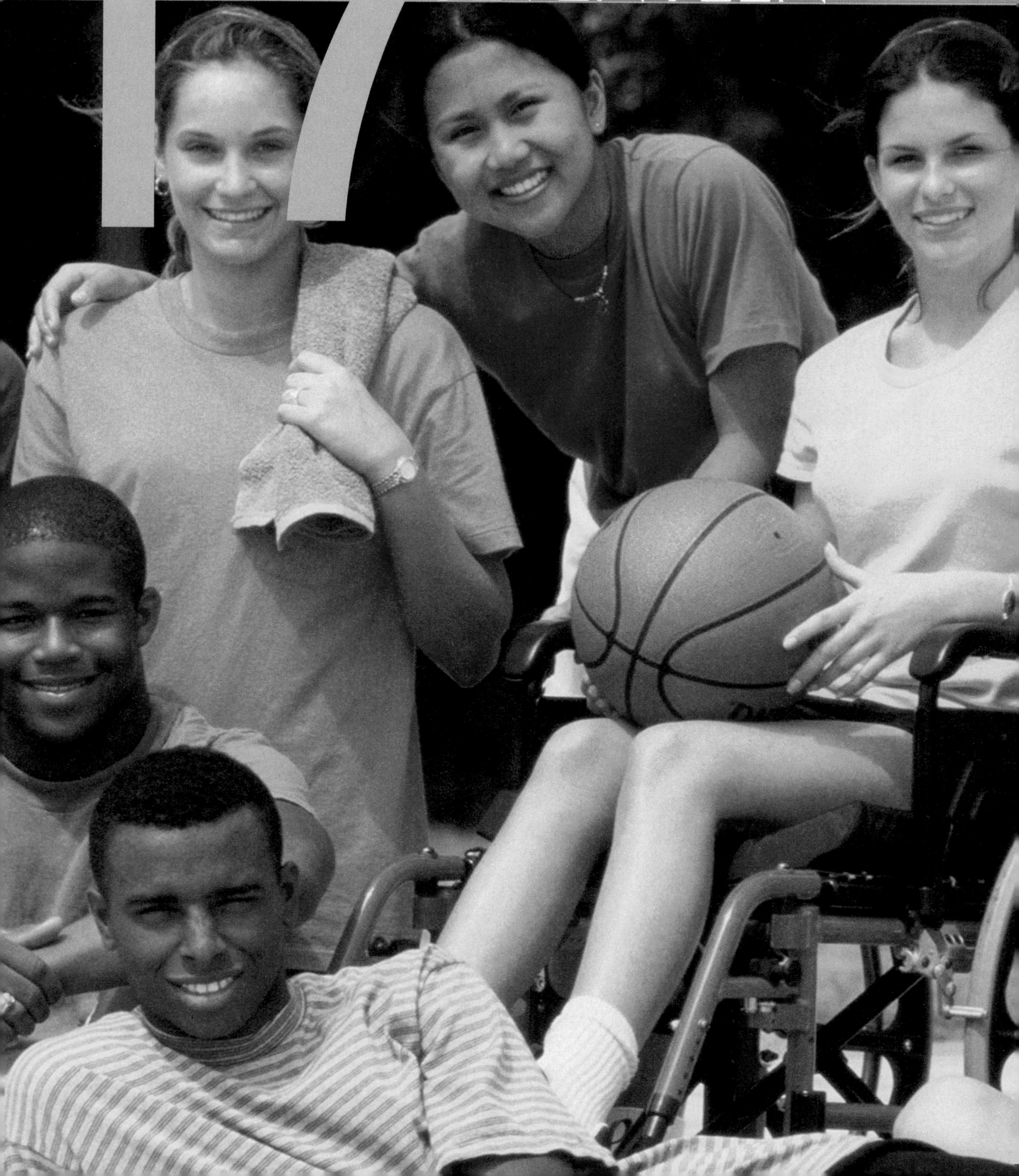

Psychosocial Development in Adolescence

This face in the mirror

stares at me

demanding Who are you? What will you become?

And taunting, You don't even know.

Chastened, I cringe and agree

and then

because I'm still young,

I stick out my tongue.

—Eve Merriam, "Conversation with Myself," 1964

Focus *Jackie Robinson, Baseball Legend*

Jackie Robinson

On April 15, 1947, when 28-year-old Jack Roosevelt ("Jackie") Robinson (1919–1972) put on a Brooklyn Dodgers uniform and strode onto Ebbets Field, he became the first African American in the 20th century to play major league baseball. By the end of a spectacular first season in which he was named Rookie of the Year, Robinson's name had become a household word. Two years later, he was voted baseball's Most Valuable Player. During his 10 years with the Dodgers, the team won six pennants, and Robinson played in six consecutive All-Star games. After his retirement, he won first-ballot election to the Hall of Fame.

His triumph did not come easily. When the Dodgers' manager, Branch Rickey, decided to bring Robinson up from the Negro Leagues, several players petitioned to keep him off the team. But Robinson's athletic prowess and dignified demeanor in the face of racist jibes, threats, hate mail, and attempts at bodily harm won the respect of the baseball world. Within the next decade, most major league teams signed African American players. Baseball had become "one of the first institutions in modern society to accept blacks on a relatively equal basis" (Tygiel, 1983).

Behind the Jackie Robinson legend is the story of a prodigiously talented boy growing up in a nation in which opportunities for black youth were extremely limited. His grandfather had been a slave. His father, a Georgia sharecropper, abandoned his wife and five children

Sources of biographical information about Jackie Robinson are Falkner (1995), Rampersad (1997), J. Robinson (1995), S. Robinson (1996), and Tygiel (1983, 1997).

---

when Jackie was 6 months old. His mother, Mallie Robinson, was a determined, deeply religious woman who imbued her children with moral strength and pride. Intent on providing them with a good education, she moved her family to Pasadena, California. But Pasadena turned out to be almost as rigidly segregated as the Deep South.

Jackie Robinson lived for sports. He idolized his older brother Mack, who won a silver medal in the 1936 Olympics. By the time Jackie was in junior high school, he was a star in his own right. He also did odd jobs after school.

Still, he had time on his hands. He joined a street gang of poor black, Mexican, and Japanese boys who seethed with "a growing resentment at being deprived of some of the advantages the white kids had" (J. Robinson, 1995, p. 6). The gang's activities—throwing rocks at cars and streetlights, smashing windows, and swiping apples from fruit stands—were serious enough to get them in trouble. But once they were taken to jail at gunpoint merely for swimming in the reservoir because they were not allowed entrance to the whites-only municipal pool.

Robinson later reflected that he "might have become a full-fledged juvenile delinquent" had it not been for the influence of two men. One was an auto mechanic, Carl Anderson, who pointed out that "it didn't take guts to follow the crowd, that courage and intelligence lay in being willing to be different" (J. Robinson, 1995, pp. 6–7). The other was a young African American minister, Karl Downs, who lured Robinson and his friends into church-sponsored athletics, listened to their worries, helped them find jobs, and got them to help build a youth center—"an alternative to hanging out on street corners" (J. Robinson, 1995, p. 8). Later, while in college, Robinson served as a volunteer Sunday school teacher at the church.

● ● ●

Adolescence is a time of both opportunities and risks. Teenagers are on the threshold of love, of life's work, and of participation in adult society. Yet adolescence is also a time when some young people engage in behavior that limits their possibilities. Today, research is increasingly focusing on how to help young people avoid hazards that can keep them from fulfilling their potential. What saved Jackie Robinson—in addition to the influence of his indomitable, hardworking mother, his older brothers, and his adult mentors—were his talent and his passion for athletics, which ultimately enabled him to channel his drive, energy, audacity, and rebellion against racism in a positive direction.

In Chapters 15 and 16 we looked at some physical and cognitive factors, such as appearance and school achievement, that contribute to an adolescent's sense of self. In this chapter, we turn our attention more directly to the quest for identity. We discuss how adolescents come to terms with their sexuality. We consider how teenagers' burgeoning individuality expresses itself in relationships with parents, siblings, and peers. We examine sources of antisocial behavior and ways of reducing the risks of adolescence so as to make it a time of positive growth and expanding possibilities. Finally, we take a cross-cultural view of late adolescence and the emerging adult.

After you have read and studied this chapter, you should be able to answer each of the Guidepost questions on the following page. Look for them again in the margins throughout the chapter, where they point to important concepts. To check your understanding of these Guideposts, review the end-of-chapter summary. Checkpoints located throughout the chapter will help you verify your understanding of what you have read.

Guideposts for Study

1. How do adolescents form an identity, and what roles do gender and ethnicity play?

2. What determines sexual orientation, what sexual practices are common among adolescents, and what leads some to engage in risky sexual behavior?

3. How do adolescents relate to parents, siblings, and peers?

4. What causes antisocial behavior, and what can be done to reduce the risk of juvenile delinquency?

5. How do various cultures define what it means to become an adult, and what markers confer adult status?

The Search for Identity

Guidepost 1

How do adolescents form an identity, and what roles do gender and ethnicity play?

The search for **identity**—according to Erikson, a coherent conception of the self made up of goals, values, and beliefs to which the person is solidly committed—comes into focus during the teenage years. Adolescents' cognitive development now enables them to construct a "theory of the self" (Elkind, 1998). As Erikson (1950) emphasized, the effort to make sense of the self is part of a healthy process that builds on the achievements of earlier stages—-on trust, autonomy, initiative, and industry—-and lays the groundwork for coping with the challenges of adult life. However, the identity crisis is seldom fully resolved in adolescence; issues concerning identity crop up again and again during adulthood.

identity In Erikson's terminology, a coherent conception of the self made up of goals, values, and beliefs to which a person is solidly committed.

Erikson: Identity versus Identity Confusion

The chief task of adolescence, said Erikson (1968), is to confront the crisis of **identity versus identity confusion** (or *identity versus role confusion*) so as to become a unique adult with a coherent sense of self and a valued role in society. His concept of the *identity crisis* was based in part on his own life experience. Growing up in Germany as the out-of-wedlock son of a Jewish woman from Denmark who had separated from her first husband, Erikson never knew his biological father. Though adopted at age 9 by his mother's second husband, a German Jewish pediatrician, he felt confusion about who he was. He floundered for some time before settling on his vocation. When he came to the United States, he needed to redefine his identity as an immigrant. All these issues found echoes in the identity crises he observed among disturbed adolescents, soldiers in combat, and members of minority groups (Erikson, 1968, 1973; L. J. Friedman, 1999).

identity versus identity confusion Erikson's fifth stage of psychosocial development, in which an adolescent seeks to develop a coherent sense of self, including the role she or he is to play in society. Also called *identity versus role confusion*.

Identity, according to Erikson, forms as young people resolve three major issues: the choice of an *occupation*, the adoption of *values* to live by, and the development of a satisfying *sexual identity*. During middle childhood, children acquire skills needed for success in their culture. As adolescents, they need to find constructive ways to use these skills. When young people have trouble settling on an occupational identity—or when their opportunities are limited, as they were for Jackie Robinson and his friends—they may engage in behavior with serious negative consequences, such as criminal activity or early pregnancy.

According to Erikson, the *psychosocial moratorium,* the time-out period that adolescence provides, allows young people to search for commitments to which they can be faithful. Jackie Robinson's commitments were to develop his athletic potential and to help improve the position of African Americans in society. Today, says the psychologist David Elkind, many adolescents "have a premature adulthood thrust upon them" (1998, p. 7). They lack the time or opportunity for a psychosocial moratorium—the protected time-out period necessary to build a stable, inner-directed self.

Adolescents who resolve the identity crisis satisfactorily, according to Erikson, develop the virtue of *fidelity:* sustained loyalty, faith, or a sense of belonging to a loved one or to friends and companions. Fidelity also can mean identification with a set of values, an ideology, a religion, a political movement, a creative pursuit, or an ethnic group (Erikson, 1982).

Mastering the challenge of a rope course may help this adolescent boy assess his abilities, interests, and desires. According to Erikson, the process of self-assessment helps adolescents resolve the crisis of identity versus identity confusion.

Fidelity is an extension of trust. In infancy, it is important for trust of others to outweigh mistrust; in adolescence, it becomes important to be trustworthy oneself. Adolescents extend their trust to mentors or loved ones. In sharing thoughts and feelings, an adolescent clarifies a tentative identity by seeing it reflected in the eyes of the beloved. However, these adolescent intimacies differ from mature intimacy, which involves greater commitment, sacrifice, and compromise.

Erikson saw the prime danger of this stage as identity, or role, confusion, which can greatly delay reaching psychological adulthood. (He did not resolve his own identity crisis until his mid-20s.) Some degree of identity confusion is normal, however. According to Erikson, it accounts for the seemingly chaotic nature of much adolescent behavior and for teenagers' painful self-consciousness. Cliquishness and intolerance of differences, both hallmarks of adolescence, are defenses against identity confusion.

Erikson's theory describes male identity development as the norm. According to Erikson, a man is not capable of real intimacy until after he has achieved a stable identity, whereas women define themselves through marriage and motherhood (something that may have been truer when Erikson developed his theory than it is today). Thus, said Erikson, women (unlike men) develop identity *through* intimacy, not before it. As we'll see, this male orientation of Erikson's theory has prompted criticism. Still, Erikson's concept of the identity crisis has inspired much valuable research.

Marcia: Identity Status—Crisis and Commitment

Caterina, Andrea, Nick, and Mark are all about to graduate from high school. Kate has considered her interests and her talents and plans to become an engineer. She has narrowed her college choices to three schools that offer good programs in this field.

Andrea knows exactly what she is going to do with her life. Her mother, a union leader at a plastics factory, has arranged for Andrea to enter an apprenticeship program there. Andrea has never considered doing anything else.

Nick is agonizing over his future. Should he attend a community college or join the army? He cannot decide what to do now or what he wants to do eventually.

Mark still has no idea what he wants to do, but he is not worried. He figures he can get some sort of a job and make up his mind about the future when he is ready.

These four young people are involved in identity formation. What accounts for the differences in the way they go about it, and how will these differences affect the outcome? According to research by the psychologist James E. Marcia (1966, 1980), these students are in four different **identity statuses,** states of ego (self) development.

Through 30-minute, semistructured *identity-status interviews* (Kroger, 2003; Table 17-1), Marcia distinguished these four types of identity status: *identity achievement, foreclosure, moratorium,* and *identity diffusion.* The four categories differ according to the presence or absence of **crisis** and **commitment,** the two elements Erikson saw as crucial to forming identity. Marcia defined *crisis* as a period of conscious decision making and *commitment* as a personal investment in an occupation or ideology (system of beliefs). He found relationships between identity status and such characteristics as anxiety, self-esteem, moral reasoning, and patterns of behavior. Building on Marcia's theory, other researchers have identified other personality and family variables related to identity status (Table 17-2). Here is a more detailed sketch of young people in each identity status:

- **Identity achievement** (*crisis leading to commitment*). Caterina has resolved her identity crisis. During the crisis period, she devoted much thought and some emotional struggle to major issues in her life. She has made choices and expresses strong commitment to them. Her parents have encouraged her to make her own decisions; they have listened to her ideas and given their opinions without pressuring her to adopt them. Caterina is thoughtful but not so introspective as to be unable to act. She

identity statuses Marcia's term for states of ego development that depend on the presence or absence of crisis and commitment.

crisis Marcia's term for period of conscious decision making related to identity formation.

commitment Marcia's term for personal investment in an occupation or system of beliefs.

identity achievement Identity status, described by Marcia, that is characterized by commitment to choices made following a crisis, a period spent in exploring alternatives.

Table 17-1   Identity-Status Interview

Sample Questions	Typical Answers for the Four Statuses
About occupational commitment: "How willing do you think you'd be to give up going into _____ if something better came along?"	*Identity achievement:* "Well, I might, but I doubt it. I can't see what 'something better' would be for me." *Foreclosure:* "Not very willing. It's what I've always wanted to do. The folks are happy with it and so am I." *Moratorium:* "I guess if I knew for sure, I could answer that better. It would have to be something in the general area—something related . . ." *Identity diffusion:* "Oh, sure. If something better came along, I'd change just like that."
About ideological commitment: "Have you ever had any doubts about your religious beliefs?"	*Identity achievement:* "Yes, I started wondering whether there is a God. I've pretty much resolved that now. The way it seems to me is . . ." *Foreclosure:* "No, not really; our family is pretty much in agreement on these things." *Moratorium:* "Yes, I guess I'm going through that now. I just don't see how there can be a God and still so much evil in the world." *Identity diffusion:* "Oh, I don't know. I guess so. Everyone goes through some sort of stage like that. But it really doesn't bother me much. I figure that one religion is about as good as another!"

Source: Adapted from Marcia, 1966.

Table 17-2   Family and Personality Factors Associated with Adolescents in Four Identity Statuses*

Factor	Identity Achievement	Foreclosure	Moratorium	Identity Diffusion
Family	Parents encourage autonomy and connection with teachers; differences are explored within a context of mutuality.	Parents are overly involved with their children; families avoid expressing differences.	Adolescents are often involved in an ambivalent struggle with parental authority.	Parents are laissez-faire in child-rearing attitudes; are rejecting or not available to children.
Personality	High levels of ego development, moral reasoning, self-certainty, self-esteem, performance under stress, and intimacy.	Highest levels of authoritarianism and stereotypical thinking, obedience to authority, dependent relationships, low level of anxiety.	Most anxious and fearful of success; high levels of ego development, moral reasoning, and self-esteem.	Mixed results, with low levels of ego development, moral reasoning, cognitive complexity, and self-certainty; poor cooperative abilities.

*These associations have emerged from a number of separate studies. Because the studies have all been correlational rather than longitudinal, it is impossible to say that any factor caused placement in any identity status.

Source: Kroger, 1993.

has a sense of humor, functions well under stress, is capable of intimate relationships, and holds to her standards while being open to new ideas. Research in a number of cultures has found people in this category to be more mature and more socially competent than people in the other three (Marcia, 1993).

- **Foreclosure** (*commitment without crisis*). Andrea has made commitments, not as a result of exploring possible choices, but by accepting someone else's plans for her life. She is happy and self-assured, perhaps even smug and self-satisfied, and she becomes dogmatic when her opinions are questioned. She has close family ties, is obedient, and tends to follow a powerful leader, like her mother, who accepts no disagreement.
- **Moratorium** (*crisis with no commitment yet*). Nick is in crisis, struggling with decisions. He is lively, talkative, self-confident, and scrupulous but also anxious and fearful. He is close to his mother but resists her authority. He wants to have a

foreclosure Identity status, described by Marcia, in which a person who has not spent time considering alternatives (that is, has not been in crisis) is committed to other people's plans for his or her life.

moratorium Identity status, described by Marcia, in which a person is considering alternatives (in crisis) and seems headed for commitment.

What's your view

- Which of Marcia's identity statuses do you think you fit into as an adolescent?
- Has your identity status changed since then? If so, how?

girlfriend but has not yet developed a close relationship. He will probably come out of his crisis eventually with the ability to make commitments and achieve identity.

- **Identity diffusion** (*no commitment, no crisis*). Mark has not seriously considered options and has avoided commitments. He is unsure of himself and tends to be uncooperative. His parents do not discuss his future with him; they say it's up to him. People in this category tend to be unhappy and often lonely.

These categories are not stages; they represent the status of identity development at a particular time, and they are likely to change in any direction as young people continue to develop (Marcia, 1979). When middle-aged people look back on their lives, they most commonly trace a path from foreclosure to moratorium to identity achievement (Kroger & Haslett, 1991). From late adolescence on, as Marcia proposed, more and more people are in moratorium or achievement: seeking or finding their identity. About half of late adolescents remain in foreclosure or diffusion, but when development does occur, it is typically in the direction Marcia described (Kroger, 2003). Furthermore, although people in foreclosure seem to have made final decisions, that is often not so.

Gender Differences in Identity Formation

Much research supports Erikson's view that, for women, identity and intimacy develop together. Rather than view this pattern as a departure from a male norm, however, some researchers see it as pointing to a weakness in Erikson's theory, which, they claim, is based on male-centered Western concepts of individuality, autonomy, and competitiveness. According to Carol Gilligan (1982, 1987a, 1987b; L. M. Brown & Gilligan, 1990), the female sense of self develops not so much through achieving a separate identity as through establishing relationships. Girls and women, says Gilligan, judge themselves on their handling of their responsibilities and on their ability to care for others as well as for themselves.

Some developmental scientists question how different the male and female paths to identity really are—-especially today—-and suggest that individual differences may be more important than gender differences (Archer, 1993; Marcia, 1993). Indeed, Marcia (1993) argues that an ongoing tension between independence and connectedness is at the heart of all of Erikson's psychosocial stages for *both* men and women. In research on Marcia's identity statuses, few gender differences have appeared (Kroger, 2003).

 However, the development of self-esteem during adolescence seems to support Gilligan's view. Male self-esteem tends to be linked with striving for individual achievement, whereas female self-esteem depends more on connections with others (Thorne & Michaelieu, 1996).

The preponderance of evidence suggests that adolescent girls have lower self-esteem, on average, than adolescent boys, though this finding has been controversial. Several large, recent studies find that self-esteem drops during adolescence, more rapidly for girls than for boys, and then rises gradually into adulthood. These changes may be due in part to body image and other anxieties associated with puberty and with the transitions to junior high or middle school and high school (Robins & Trzesniewski, 2005). As we will see, the pattern seems to be different among minorities,

Ethnic Factors in Identity Formation

For many young people in minority groups, race or ethnicity is central to identity formation. Following Marcia's model, some research has identified four ethnic identity statuses (Phinney, 1998):

- *Diffuse:* Juanita has done little or no exploration of her ethnicity and does not clearly understand the issues involved.
- *Foreclosed:* Kwame has done little or no exploration of his ethnicity but has clear feelings about it. These feelings may be positive or negative, depending on the attitudes he absorbed at home.
- *Moratorium:* Cho-san has begun to explore her ethnicity but is confused about what it means to her.
- *Achieved:* Diego has explored his identity and understands and accepts his ethnicity.

Table 17-3	Representative Quotations from Each Status of Ethnic Identity Development

Diffusion

"Why do I need to learn about who was the first black woman to do this or that? I'm just not too interested." (African American female)

Foreclosure

"I don't go looking for my culture. I just go by what my parents say and do, and what they tell me to do, the way they are." (Mexican American male)

Moratorium

"There are a lot of non-Japanese people around and it gets pretty confusing to try and decide who I am." (Asian American male)

Achieved

"People put me down because I'm Mexican, but I don't care anymore. I can accept myself more." (Mexican American female)

Source: Phinney, 1998, Table 2, p. 277.

Identity development can be especially complicated for young people from minority groups. Ethnicity may play a central part in their self-concept.

Table 17-3 quotes representative statements by minority young people in each status.

A study of 940 African American adolescents, college students, and adults found evidence of all four identity statuses in each age group. Only 27 percent of the adolescents were in the achieved group, as compared with 47 percent of the college students and 56 percent of the adults. Instead, adolescents were more likely to be in moratorium (42 percent), still exploring what it means to be African American. Some 25 percent of the adolescents were in foreclosure, with feelings about African American identity based on their family upbringing. All three of these groups (achieved, moratorium, and foreclosed) reported more positive regard for being African American than the 6 percent of adolescents who were diffused (neither committed nor exploring). Those of any age who were in the achieved status were most likely to view race as central to their identity (Yip, Seaton, & Sellers, 2006).

Another model focuses on three aspects of racial/ethnic identity: *connectedness* to one's own racial/ethnic group, *awareness of racism,* and *embedded achievement,* the belief that academic achievement is a part of group identity. A longitudinal study of low-income minority youth found that all three aspects of identity appear to stabilize and even to increase slightly by midadolescence. Thus racial/ethnic identity may buffer tendencies toward a drop in grades and connection to school during the transition from middle school to high school (Altschul, Oyserman, & Bybee, 2006). On the other hand, perceived discrimination during the transition to adolescence can interfere with positive identity formation and lead to conduct problems or depression. Protective factors are nurturant, involved parenting, prosocial friends, and strong academic performance (Brody et al., 2006).

A 3-year longitudinal study of 420 African American, Latino American, and European American adolescents looked at two dimensions of ethnic identity: *group esteem* (feeling good about one's ethnicity) and *exploration of the meaning of ethnicity* in one's life. Group esteem rose during both early and middle adolescence, especially for African Americans and Latinos, whose group esteem was lower to begin with. Exploration of the meaning of ethnicity increased only in middle adolescence, perhaps reflecting the transition from relatively homogeneous neighborhood elementary or junior high schools into more ethnically diverse high schools. Interactions with members of other ethnic groups may stimulate young people to curiosity about their ethnic identity (French, Seidman, Allen, & Aber, 2006).

Contrary to the pattern among the general population, minority adolescents—both boys and girls—often gain in self-esteem with age, according to self-reports of students at a New York public high school. Family support was the strongest factor in self-esteem, followed by a positive school climate (Greene & Way, 2005).

The term **cultural socialization** refers to parental practices that teach children about their racial or ethnic heritage, promote cultural customs and traditions, and promote racial/ethnic and cultural pride. Adolescents who have experienced cultural socialization tend to have stronger and more positive ethnic identity than those who have not (Hughes et al., 2006).

cultural socialization Parental practices that teach children about their racial/ethnic heritage and promote cultural practices and cultural pride.

Checkpoint ✔

Can you . . .

✔ List the three major issues involved in identity formation, according to Erikson?

✔ Describe four types of identity status found by Marcia?

✔ Discuss how gender and ethnicity affect identity formation?

What determines sexual orientation, what sexual practices are common among adolescents, and what leads some to engage in risky sexual behavior?

Sexuality

Seeing oneself as a sexual being, recognizing one's sexual orientation, coming to terms with sexual stirrings, and forming romantic or sexual attachments all are parts of achieving *sexual identity*. Awareness of sexuality is an important aspect of identity formation, profoundly affecting self-image and relationships. Although this process is biologically driven, its expression is in part culturally defined.

During the 20th century a major change in sexual attitudes and behavior in the United States and other industrialized countries brought more widespread acceptance of premarital sex, homosexuality, and other previously disapproved forms of sexual activity. With widespread access to the Internet, casual sex with fleeting cyber-acquaintances who hook up through online chat rooms or singles' meeting sites has become common. Cell phones, e-mail, and instant messaging make it easy for adolescents to arrange hookups with disembodied strangers, insulated from adult scrutiny. These changes have brought increased concerns about sexual risk taking. On the other hand, the AIDS epidemic has led many young people to abstain from sexual activity outside of committed relationships or to engage in safer sexual practices.

Sexual Orientation and Identity

sexual orientation Gender focus of consistent sexual, romantic, and affectionate interest, either heterosexual, homosexual, or bisexual.

Although present in younger children, it is in adolescence that a person's **sexual orientation** generally becomes a pressing issue: whether that person will consistently be sexually attracted to persons of the other sex (*heterosexual*), of the same sex (*homosexual*), or of both sexes (*bisexual*). Heterosexuality predominates in nearly every known culture throughout the world. The prevalence of homosexual orientation varies widely, depending on how it is defined and measured. Depending on whether it is measured by sexual, or romantic, *attraction or arousal*, or by sexual *behavior*, or by sexual *identity*, the rate of homosexuality in the U.S. population ranges from 1 to 21 percent (Savin-Williams, 2006).

Many young people have one or more homosexual experiences as they are growing up, but isolated experiences or even occasional homosexual attractions or fantasies do not determine sexual orientation. In a national survey, 4.5 percent of 15- to 19-year-old boys and 10.6 percent of 15- to 19-year-old girls reported ever having had same-sex sexual contact, but only 2.4 percent of the boys and 7.7 percent of the girls reported having done so in the past year (Mosher, Chandra, & Jones, 2005). Social stigma may bias such self-reports, underestimating the prevalence of homosexuality and bisexuality.

Origins of Sexual Orientation

Much research on sexual orientation has focused on efforts to explain homosexuality. Although it once was considered a mental illness, several decades of research have found no association between homosexual orientation and emotional or social problems—apart from those apparently caused by societal treatment of homosexuals, such as a tendency to depression (American Psychological Association (APA), n. d.; C. J. Patterson, 1992, 1995a, 1995b). These findings led the psychiatric profession in 1973 to stop classifying homosexuality as a mental disorder.

Sexual orientation seems to be partly genetic (Diamond & Savin-Williams, 2003). The first full genome-wide scan for male sexual orientation has identified three stretches of DNA on chromosomes 7, 8, and 10 that appear to be involved (Mustanski et al., 2005). However, because identical twins are not perfectly concordant for sexual orientation, nongenetic factors also must play a part. Different combinations of causes may operate in different individuals, and this may also account for individual differences in the age at which same-sex attraction first appears (Diamond & Savin-Williams, 2003).

The more older brothers a man has, the more likely he is to be gay—but only if they are biological brothers. In an analysis of 905 men and their biological, adoptive, half-, or stepsiblings, the only significant factor in whether a man was heterosexual or homosexual was the number of times his mother had previously given birth to boys. Each older biological brother increased the chances of homosexuality in a younger brother by 33 percent. This phenomenon may be a cumulative immunelike response to the presence of successive "foreign" male fetuses in the womb (Bogaert, 2006).

One researcher has reported a difference in the size of the hypothalamus, a brain structure that governs sexual activity, in heterosexual and gay men. However, it is not known whether this difference arises before birth or later (LeVay, 1991). In brain-imaging studies on the effects of pheromones, odors that attract mates, the odor of male sweat activated the hypothalamus in gay men much as it did in heterosexual women. Similarly, lesbian women, like straight men, reacted more positively to female than to male pheromones, though the effect was smaller (Savic, Berglund, & Lindström, 2005; Savic, Berglund, & Lindström, 2006). However, we do not know whether these differences are a cause of homosexuality or an effect of it.

Although sexual orientation may be shaped before birth or very early in life, it is in adolescence that it becomes a pressing issue. Here, a Massachusetts high school girl who came out as a lesbian sits in front of a banner for a student support group.

Homosexual and Bisexual Identity Development

Despite the increased acceptance of homosexuality in the United States, many adolescents who openly identify as gay, lesbian, or bisexual feel isolated in a hostile environment. They may be subject to discrimination and even violence. Others may be reluctant to disclose their sexual orientation, even to their parents, for fear of strong disapproval or a rupture in the family (Hillier, 2002; C. J. Patterson, 1995b). They may find it difficult to meet and identify potential same-sex partners. Thus, homosexuals' recognition and expression of their sexual identity are more complex and follow a less defined timetable than heterosexuals' do (Diamond & Savin-Williams, 2003).

There is no single route to the development of gay, lesbian, or bisexual identity and behavior. Because of the lack of socially sanctioned ways to explore their sexuality, many gay and lesbian adolescents experience identity confusion (Sieving, Oliphant, & Blum, 2002). Gay, lesbian, and bisexual youth who are unable to establish peer groups that share their sexual orientation may struggle with the recognition of same-sex attractions (Bouchey & Furman, 2003; Furman & Wehner, 1997).

One model for the development of gay or lesbian sexual identity proposes the following sequence: (1) awareness of same-sex attraction (beginning at ages 8 to 11); (2) same-sex sexual behaviors (ages 12 to 15); (3) identification as gay or lesbian (ages 15 to 18); (4) disclosure to others (ages 17 to 19); and (5) development of same-sex romantic relationships (ages 18 to 20). However, this model may not accurately reflect the experience of younger gay men, many of whom feel freer than in the past to openly declare their sexual orientation; of lesbian and bisexual women, whose sexual identity development may be slower, more flexible, and more tied to emotional and situational factors than that of homosexual men; and of ethnic minorities, whose traditional communities and cultures may espouse strong religious beliefs or sterotypical gender roles, leading to internal and family conflict (Diamond, 1998, 2000; Diamond & Savin-Williams, 2003; Dubé & Savin-Williams, 1999).

Sexual Behavior

Internationally, there are wide variations in timing of heterosexual initiation. The percentage of women who report having first intercourse by age 17 is about 10 times greater in Mali (72 percent) than in Thailand (7 percent) or the Philippines (6 percent). Similar differences exist for men. Although earlier male initiation is the norm in most cultures, in Mali and Ghana more women than men become sexually active at an early age (Singh et al., 2000).

In the United States, according to national surveys, 77 percent of young people have had sex by age 20. This proportion has been roughly the same since the mid-1960s and the advent of the pill (Finer, 2007). The average girl has her first sexual intercourse at 17, the average boy at 16, and approximately 25 percent of boys and girls report having had intercourse by 15 (Klein & Committee on Adolescence, 2005). Blacks and Latinos tend to begin

Checkpoint ✔

Can you . . .

✔ Discuss theories and research regarding origins of sexual orientation?

✔ Discuss homosexual identity and relationship formation?

Table 17-4   Adolescents* Attitudes about Sexual Activity

Percent of 15- to 17-Year-Olds Who Say They "Strongly" or "Somewhat" Agree with Each of the Following

	Male	Female	Sexually Active	Not Sexually Active
Waiting to have sex is a nice idea but nobody really does.	66%	60%	69%	59%
There is pressure to have sex by a certain age.	59%	58%	58%	59%
Once you have had sex it is harder to say no the next time.	56%	47%	54%	50%
If you have been seeing someone for a while it is expected that you will have sex.	50%	27%	52%	31%
Oral sex is not as big of a deal as sexual intercourse.	54%	38%	52%	42%

Source: Adapted from Kaiser Family Foundation et al., 2003, Table 8, p. 12, and Table 33, p. 39.

sexual activity earlier than white youth (Kaiser Family Foundation, Hoff, Greene, & Davis, 2003). Whereas teenage boys in previous years were more likely to be sexually experienced than teenage girls, that is no longer true: In 2002, 49 percent of 15- to 19-year-old boys and 53 percent of girls in that age group reported having had vaginal intercourse (Mosher et al., 2005).

In a study of gay and bisexual males, the first reported male-to-male sexual encounters among Asian American youths took place about three years later than among white, African American, and Latino men. This pattern of delayed sexual activity has also been found among Asian American heterosexuals, which may reflect strong cultural pressures to save sex for marriage or adulthood and then to have children who will carry on the family name (Dubé & Savin-Williams, 1999).

Sexual Risk Taking

Two major concerns about adolescent sexual activity are the risks of contracting sexually transmitted diseases (STDs) and, for heterosexual activity, of pregnancy. Most at risk are young people who start sexual activity early, have multiple partners, do not use contraceptives regularly, and have inadequate information—or misinformation—about sex (Abma et al., 1997). Other risk factors are living in a socioeconomically disadvantaged community, substance use, antisocial behavior, and association with deviant peers. Parental monitoring can help reduce these risks (Baumer & South, 2001; Capaldi, Stoolmiller, Clark, & Owen, 2002).

Why do some adolescents become sexually active at an early age? Various factors, including early entrance into puberty, poverty, poor school performance, lack of academic and career goals, a history of sexual abuse or parental neglect, and cultural or family patterns of early sexual experience, may play a part (Klein & Committee on Adolescence, 2005). The absence of a father, especially early in life, is a strong factor (Ellis et al., 2003). Teenagers who have close, warm relationships with their mothers are more likely to delay sexual activity. So are those who perceive that their mothers disapprove of such activity (Jaccard & Dittus, 2000; Sieving, McNeely, & Blum, 2000). Other reasons teenagers give for not yet having had sex are that it is against their religion or morals and that they do not want to get (or get a girl) pregnant (Abma, Martinez, Mosher, & Dawson, 2004).

One of the most powerful influences is perception of peer group norms. Young people often feel under pressure to engage in activities they do not feel ready for. In a nationally representative survey, nearly one-third of 15- to 17-year-olds, especially boys, said they had experienced pressure to have sex (Kaiser Family Foundation et al., 2003; Table 17-4).

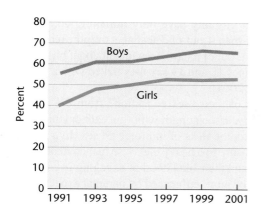

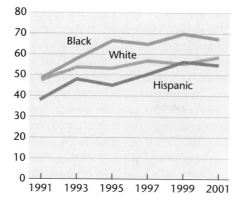

Figure 17-1

Percentage of high school students who report using a condom the last time they had sexual intercourse, by gender and race/ethnicity.

Source: Bernstein, 2004. Based on data from Centers for Disease Control and Prevention, Alan Guttmacher Institute, and Child Trends Databank.

As U.S. adolescents have become more aware of the risks of sexual activity, the percentage who have ever had intercourse has declined, especially among boys (Abma et al., 2004). However, noncoital forms of genital sexual activity, such as oral and anal sex and mutual masturbation, are common. Many heterosexual teens do not regard these activities as sex but as substitutes for, or precursors of, sex, or even as abstinence (Remez, 2000). In one national survey, just over half of teenage boys and girls reported having given or received oral sex, more than had had vaginal intercourse (Mosher et al., 2005).

What's your view

• How can adolescents be helped to avoid or change risky sexual behavior?

Use of Contraceptives

The use of contraceptives among teenagers has increased since 1990 (Abma et al., 2004). About 83 percent of girls and 91 percent of boys in one survey said they had used contraception the most recent time they had sex (Abma et al., 2004). Teens who, in their first relationship, delay intercourse, discuss contraception before having sex, or use more than one method of contraception are more likely to use contraceptives consistently throughout that relationship (Manlove, Ryan, & Franzetta, 2003).

The best safeguard for sexually active teens is regular use of condoms, which give some protection against STDs as well as against pregnancy. Condom use has increased in recent years (Figure 17-1), as has use of the pill and new hormonal and injectable methods of contraception or combinations of methods (Abma et al., 2004). Still, in 2003, only 63 percent of sexually active high school students reported having used condoms the last time they had intercourse (Klein & Committee on Adolescence, 2005). Adolescents who start using prescription contraceptives often stop using condoms, not realizing that they leave themselves unprotected against STDs (Klein & Committee on Adolescence, 2005).

Where Do Teenagers Get Information about Sex?

Adolescents get their information about sex primarily from friends, parents, sex education in school, and the media (Kaiser Family Foundation et al., 2003). Adolescents who can talk about sex with older siblings as well as with parents are more likely to have positive attitudes toward safer sexual practices (Kowal & Pike, 2004).

Since 1998, federal- and state-funded sex education programs stressing abstinence from sex until marriage as the best or only option have become common (Devaney, Johnson, Maynard, & Trenholm, 2002). Programs that encourage abstinence but also discuss STD prevention and safer sexual practices for the sexually active have been found to delay sexual initiation and increase contraceptive use (AAP Committee on Psychosocial Aspects of Child and Family Health and Committee on Adolescence, 2001).

However, some school programs promote abstinence as the only option, even though abstinence-only courses have not been shown to delay sexual activity (AAP Committee on Psychosocial Aspects of Child and Family Health and Committee on Adolescence, 2001;

Checkpoint ✔

Can you . . .

✔ Cite trends in sexual activity among adolescents?

✔ Identify factors that increase or decrease the risks of sexual activity?

sexually transmitted diseases (STDs) Diseases spread by sexual contact.

Satcher, 2001). Likewise, pledges to maintain virginity have only limited effectiveness (Bearman & Bruckner, 2001). Although more than 4 out of 5 teenagers report receiving formal instruction in how to say no to sex, only 2 out of 3 have been taught about birth control. Only 1 out of 2 girls and 1 out of 3 boys ages 18 and 19 say they talked with a parent about birth control before age 18 (Abma et al., 2004).

Unfortunately, many teenagers get much of their "sex education" from the media, which present a distorted view of sexual activity, associating it with fun, excitement, competition, danger, or violence and rarely showing the risks of unprotected sex. In a 2-year longitudinal survey of 12- to 14-year-olds, exposure to a heavy diet of sexual content in the media accelerated white teens' sexual activity and their likelihood of engaging in early intercourse. Black teens, in contrast, appeared to be more influenced by parental expectations and their friends' behavior (Brown et al., 2006).

Sexually Transmitted Diseases (STDs)

Sexually transmitted diseases (STDs) are diseases spread by sexual contact. Table 17-5 summarizes some common STDs: their causes, most frequent symptoms, treatment, and consequences.

About 1 in 4 new cases of STDs in the United States occurs in 15- to 19-year-olds. The chief reasons for the prevalence of STDs among teenagers are early sexual activity, which increases the likelihood of having multiple high-risk partners, failure to use condoms or to use them regularly and correctly, and, for women, the tendency to have sex with older partners (CDC, 2000b).

STDs are most likely to develop undetected in adolescent girls. In a *single* unprotected sexual encounter with an infected partner, a girl runs a 1 percent risk of acquiring HIV, a 30 percent risk of acquiring genital herpes, and a 50 percent risk of acquiring gonorrhea (AGI, 1999). Although teenagers tend to view oral sex as less risky than intercourse, a number of STDs, especially pharyngeal gonorrhea, can be transmitted in that way (Remez, 2000).

The most common STD is human papilloma virus (HPV), which sometimes produces warts on the genitals. It is the leading cause of cervical cancer in women. A new vaccine for HPV is highly effective when given routinely to 11- and 12-year-old girls (CDC Divison of Media Relations, 2006). Also common among young people is trichomoniasis, a parasitic infection that may be passed along by moist towels and bathing suits (Weinstock, Berman, & Cates, Jr., 2004).

Genital herpes simplex is a chronic, recurring, often painful, and highly contagious disease caused by a virus. This condition can be fatal to a person with a deficiency of the immune system or to the newborn infant of a mother who has an outbreak at the time of delivery. There is no cure, but the antiviral drug acyclovir can prevent active outbreaks. The incidence of genital herpes has increased dramatically during the past 3 decades. Hepatitis B remains a prominent STD despite the availability of a preventive vaccine for more than 20 years (Weinstock et al., 2004).

The most common curable STDs are chlamydia and gonorrhea. These diseases, if undetected and untreated, can lead to severe health problems, including, in women, to pelvic inflammatory disease (PID), a serious abdominal infection. In the United States, more than 1 in 10 teenage girls and 1 in 5 boys are affected (CDC, 2000b).

The human immunodeficiency virus (HIV), which causes AIDS, is transmitted through bodily fluids (mainly blood and semen), usually by sharing of intravenous drug needles or by sexual contact with an infected partner. The virus attacks the body's immune system, leaving a person vulnerable to a variety of fatal diseases. Symptoms of AIDS, which include extreme fatigue, fever, swollen lymph nodes, weight loss, diarrhea, and night sweats, may not appear until 6 months to 10 or more years after initial infection.

Worldwide, of the 4.1 million new HIV infections each year, about half are in young people ages 15 to 24 (UNAIDS, 2006). In the United States, more than 1 out of 4 persons living with HIV or AIDS were infected in their teens (Kaiser Family Foundation et al., 2003). As of now, AIDS is incurable, but increasingly the related infections

Table 17-5   Common Sexually Transmitted Diseases

Disease	Cause	Symptoms: Male	Symptoms: Female	Treatment	Consequences If Untreated
Chlamydia	Bacterial infection	Pain during urination, discharge from penis	Vaginal discharge, abdominal discomfort†	Tetracycline or erythromycin	Can cause pelvic inflammatory disease or eventual sterility
Trichomoniasis	Parasitic infection, sometimes passed on in moist objects such as towels and bathing suits	Often absent	Absent or may include vaginal discharge, discomfort during intercourse, odor, painful urination	Oral antibiotic	May lead to abnormal growth of cervical cells
Gonorrhea	Bacterial infection	Discharge from penis, pain during urination*	Discomfort when urinating, vaginal discharge, abnormal menses†	Penicillin or other antibiotics	Can cause pelvic inflammatory disease or eventual sterility; can also cause arthritis, dermatitis, and meningitis
HPV (genital warts)	Human papilloma virus	Painless growth that usually appear on penis but may also appear on urethra or in rectal area*	Small, painless growths on genitals and anus; may also occur inside the vagina without external symptoms*	Removal of warts; but infection often reappears	May be associated with cervical cancer; in pregnancy, warts enlarge and may obstruct birth canal
Herpes	Herpes simplex virus	Painful blisters anywhere on the genitalia, usually on the penis*	Painful blisters on the genitalia, sometimes with fever and aching muscles; women with sores on cervix may be unaware of outbreaks*	No known cure but controlled with an antiviral drug, such as acyclovir	Possible increased risk of cervical cancer
Hepatitis B	Hepatitis B virus	Skin and eyes become yellow	Skin and eyes become yellow	No specific treatment; no alcohol	Can cause liver damage, chronic hepatitis
Syphilis	Bacterial infection	In first stage, reddish-brown sores on the mouth or genitalia or both, which may disappear, though the bacteria remain; in the second, more infectious stage, a widespread skin rash*	In first stage, reddish-brown sores on the mouth or genitalia or both, which may disappear, though the bacteria remain; in the second, more infectious stage, a widespread skin rash*	Penicillin or other antibiotics	Paralysis, convulsions, brain damage, and sometimes death
AIDS (acquired immune deficiency syndrome)	Human immunodeficiency virus (HIV)	Extreme fatigue, fever, swollen lymph nodes, weight loss, diarrhea, night sweats, susceptibility to other diseases*	Extreme fatigue, fever, swollen lymph nodes, weight loss, diarrhea, night sweats, susceptibility to other diseases*	No known cure; protease inhibitors and other drugs appear to extend life	Death, usually due to other diseases, such as cancer

*May be asymptomatic.
†Is often asymptomatic.

Checkpoint ✔

Can you . . .

✔ Identify and describe the most common sexually transmitted diseases?

✔ List risk factors for developing an STD during adolescence, and describe effective prevention methods?

that kill people are being stopped with antiviral therapy, including protease inhibitors (Palella et al., 1998; Weinstock et al., 2004). A Danish study found the young patients diagnosed with HIV have an estimated median survival of more than 35 years (Lohse et al., 2007).

Because symptoms may not appear until a disease has progressed to the point of causing serious long-term complications, early detection is important. Regular, school-based screening and treatment, together with programs that promote abstention from or postponement of sexual activity, responsible decision making, and ready availability of condoms for those who are sexually active may have some effect in controlling the spread of STDs (AAP Committee on Adolescence, 1994; AGI, 1994; Cohen, Nsuami, Martin, & Farley, 1999; Rotheram-Borus & Futterman, 2000). There is no evidence that education about condom use and availability contributes to increased sexual activity (Klein & Committee on Adolescence, 2005).

Teenage Pregnancy and Childbearing

A dramatic drop in teenage pregnancy and birthrates has accompanied the steady decreases in early intercourse and in sex with multiple partners and the increase in contraceptive use. Birthrates for U.S. 15- to 19-year-old girls fell by 33 percent between 1991 and 2004 to a record low of 41.1 births per 1,000 girls. Teen pregnancy rates in that age group fell almost as rapidly—27 percent between 1990 and 2000, to 84.5 pregnancies per 1,000 girls, the lowest reported rate since 1976 (Martin, Hamilton, Sutton, Ventura, Menacker, & Kirmeyer, 2006).

Nevertheless, more than 40 percent of adolescent girls have been pregnant at least once before age 20 (Klein & Committee on Adolescence, 2005). More than half, 51 percent, of pregnant teenagers have their babies, and 35 percent choose to abort. Another 14 percent of teen pregnancies end in miscarriage or stillbirth (Klein & Committee on Adolescence, 2005).

Although declines in teenage childbearing have occurred among all population groups, birthrates have fallen most sharply among black teenagers. Still, black and Hispanic girls are more likely to have babies than white, Native American, or Asian American girls (Martin, Hamilton, et al., 2006). U.S. teens are more likely to become pregnant and give birth than teenagers in most other industrialized countries (Martin et al., 2005; Box 17-1).

More than 90 percent of pregnant teenagers describe their pregnancies as unintended, and 50 percent of teen pregnancies occur within 6 months of sexual initiation (Klein & the Committee on Adolescence, 2005). Many of these girls grew up fatherless (Ellis et al., 2003). Among 9,159 women at a California primary care clinic, those who had become pregnant in adolescence were likely, as children, to have been physically, emotionally, or sexually abused and/or exposed to parental divorce or separation, domestic violence, substance abuse, or a household member who was mentally ill or engaged in criminal behavior (Hillis et al., 2004). Teenage fathers, too, tend to have limited financial resources, poor academic performance, and high dropout rates. At least one-third of teenage parents are themselves products of adolescent pregnancy (Klein & Committee on Adolescence, 2005).

Teenage pregnancies often have poor outcomes. Many of the mothers are impoverished and poorly educated, and some are drug users. Many do not eat properly, do not gain enough weight, and get inadequate prenatal care or none at all. Their babies are likely to be premature or dangerously small and are at heightened risk of other birth complications; late fetal, neonatal, or infant death; health and academic problems; abuse and neglect; and developmental disabilities that may continue into adolescence (AAP Committee on Adolescence, 1999; AAP Committee on Adolescence and Committee on Early Childhood, Adoption, and Dependent Care, 2001; AGI, 1999; Children's Defense Fund, 1998, 2004; Klein & Committee on Adolescence, 2005; Menacker et al., 2004).

Box 17-1 *Preventing Teenage Pregnancy*

Although teenage pregnancy and birthrates in the United States dropped dramatically during the 1990s, they remain many times higher than in other industrialized countries, where adolescents begin sexual activity just as early or earlier (Darroch, Singh, Frost, & the Study Team, 2001). Teenage birthrates in recent years have been nearly five times as high in the United States as in Denmark, Finland, France, Germany, Italy, the Netherlands, Spain, Sweden, and Switzerland and twelve times as high as in Japan (Ventura, Mathews, & Hamilton, 2001). Some 22 percent of American girls have had children before age 20, as compared with 15 percent of British girls, 11 percent of Canadian girls, 6 percent of French girls, and 4 percent of Swedish girls (Darroch et al., 2001) (Figure 17-2).

Why are U.S. rates so high? Some observers point to such factors as the reduced stigma on unwed motherhood, media glorification of sex, the lack of a clear message that sex and parenthood are for adults, the influence of childhood sexual abuse, and failure of parents to communicate with children. Comparisons with the European experience suggest the importance of other factors: U.S. girls are more likely to have multiple sex partners and less likely to use contraceptives (Darroch et al., 2001).

Europe's industrialized countries have provided universal, comprehensive sex education for a much longer time than the United States. Comprehensive programs encourage young teenagers to delay intercourse but also aim to improve contraceptive use among sexually active adolescents. Such programs include education about sexuality and acquisition of skills for making responsible sexual decisions and communicating with partners. They provide information about risks and consequences of teenage pregnancy, about birth control methods, and about where to get medical and contraceptive help (AAP Committee on Psychosocial Aspects of Child and Family Health and Committee on Adolescence, 2001; AGI, 1994; Kirby, 1997; I. C. Stewart, 1994). Programs aimed at adolescent boys emphasize the wisdom of delaying fatherhood and the need to take responsibility when it occurs (Children's Defense Fund, 1998).

In the United States the provision and content of sex education programs are political issues. Some critics claim that community- and school-based sex education leads to more or earlier sexual activity, even though evidence shows otherwise (AAP Committee on Adolescence, 2001; Children's Defense Fund, 1998; Satcher, 2001).

An important component of pregnancy prevention in European countries is access to reproductive services. Contraceptives are provided free to adolescents in Britain, France, Sweden, and, in many cases, the Netherlands. Sweden showed a fivefold reduction in the teenage birthrate following introduction of birth control education, free access to contraceptives, and free abortion on demand (Bracher & Santow, 1999). Indeed, U.S. teens who use contraception in their first sexual experience are much less likely to bear a child by age 20 (Abma et al., 2004).

The problem of teenage pregnancy requires a multifaceted solution. It must include programs and policies to encourage postponing or refraining from sexual activity, but it also must recognize that many young people do become sexually active and need education and information to prevent pregnancy and

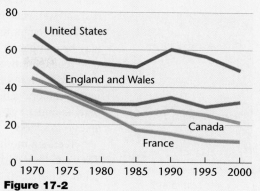

Figure 17-2

Trends in teenage birthrates per 1,000 girls ages 15 to 19 in selected Western countries. The U.S. teenage birthrate has fallen since 1990, but it remains significantly higher than in England and Wales, Canada, and France.

infection. It requires attention to underlying factors that put teenagers and families at risk—reducing poverty, school failure, behavioral and family problems, and expanding employment, skills training, and family life education (AGI, 1994; Children's Defense Fund, 1998; Kirby, 1997)—and it should target young people at highest risk (Klein & Committee on Adolescence, 2005). Comprehensive early intervention programs for preschoolers and elementary school students have reduced teenage pregnancy (Lonczak et al., 2002; Hawkins et al., 1999; Schweinhart, Barnes, & Weikart, 1993).

Because adolescents with high aspirations are less likely to become pregnant, programs that motivate young people to achieve and raise their self-esteem have had some success. Teen Outreach Program (TOP), which began in 1978, helps teenagers make decisions, handle emotions, and deal with peers and adults. The program also includes community service. By encouraging students to select a volunteer activity, the program helps them see themselves as autonomous and competent. Among 1,600 students in TOP and 1,600 in a control group, TOP participants had about 50 percent the risk of pregnancy or school suspension and 60 percent of the risk of failure of nonparticipants (Allen & Philliber, 2001). This is evidence that teenage pregnancy and school failure are not isolated problems but are part of a larger developmental picture.

What's your view ?

If you were designing a school-based or community-based sexuality education program, what would you include? Do you favor or oppose programs that provide contraceptives to teenagers?

Check it out !

For more information on this topic, go to www.teenwire.com/topics/birth-control-and-safer-sex.php. This site is from teenwire.com, the Planned Parenthood Web site for teens. Or visit www.teenpregnancy.org, the Web site of the National Campaign to Prevent Teen Pregnancy.

Babies of more affluent teenage mothers also may be at risk. Among more than 134,000 white, largely middle-class girls and women, 13- to 19-year-olds were more likely than 20- to 24-year-olds to have low-birth-weight babies, even when the mothers were married and well educated and had adequate prenatal care. Prenatal care apparently cannot always overcome the biological disadvantage of being born to a still-growing girl whose own body may be competing for vital nutrients with the developing fetus (Fraser et al., 1995).

Teenage unwed mothers and their families are likely to suffer financially. Child support laws are spottily enforced, court-ordered payments are often inadequate, and many young fathers cannot afford them (AAP Committee on Adolescence, 1999). Unmarried parents under age 18 are eligible for public assistance only if they live with their parents and go to school.

Teenage mothers are likely to drop out of school and to have repeated pregnancies. They and their partners may lack the maturity, skills, and social support to be good parents. Their children, in turn, are likely to have developmental and academic problems, to be depressed, to engage in substance abuse and early sexual activity, and to become adolescent parents themselves (Klein & Committee on Adolescence, 2005). However, these outcomes are far from inevitable. Several long-term studies find that, 20 years after giving birth, most former adolescent mothers are not on welfare; many have finished high school and secured steady jobs, and do not have large families. Comprehensive adolescent pregnancy and home visitation programs seem to contribute to good outcomes (Klein & Committee on Adolescence, 2005).

Checkpoint

Can you . . .

✔ Summarize trends in teenage pregnancy and birthrates?

✔ Cite ways to prevent teenage pregnancy?

✔ Discuss risk factors, problems, and outcomes connected with teenage pregnancy?

Guidepost 3

How do adolescents relate to parents, siblings, and peers?

Relationships with Family and Peers

Age becomes a powerful bonding agent in adolescence. Adolescents spend more time with peers and less with family. However, most teenagers' fundamental values (like Jackie Robinson's) remain closer to their parents' than is generally realized (Offer & Church, 1991). Even as adolescents turn to peers for role models, companionship, and intimacy, they—much like toddlers beginning to explore a wider world—look to parents for a secure base from which they can try their wings. The most secure adolescents have strong, supportive relationships with parents who are attuned to the way the young people see themselves, who permit and encourage their strivings for independence, and who provide a safe haven in times of emotional stress (Allen et al., 2003; Laursen, 1996).

Is Adolescent Rebellion a Myth?

The teenage years have been called a time of **adolescent rebellion,** involving emotional turmoil, conflict within the family, alienation from adult society, reckless behavior, and rejection of adult values. Yet school-based research on adolescents the world over suggests that only about 1 in 5 teenagers fits this pattern (Offer & Schonert-Reichl, 1992).

The idea of adolescent rebellion may have been born in the first formal theory of adolescence, that of the psychologist G. Stanley Hall. Hall (1904/1916) believed that young people's efforts to adjust to their changing bodies and to the imminent demands of adulthood usher in a period of "storm and stress" that produces conflict between the generations. Sigmund Freud (1935/1953) and his daughter Anna Freud (1946) described this storm and stress as universal and inevitable, growing out of a resurgence of early sexual drives toward the parents.

However, the anthropologist Margaret Mead (1928, 1935; see Chapter 2 Focus), who studied growing up in Samoa and other South Pacific islands, concluded that when a culture provides a gradual, serene transition from childhood to adulthood, storm and stress is not typical. Although her research in Samoa was later challenged (Freeman, 1983), her observation was eventually supported by research in 186 preindustrial societies (Schlegel & Barry, 1991).

Full-fledged rebellion now appears to be relatively uncommon even in Western societies, at least among middle-class adolescents who are in school. Most young people feel close to and positive about their parents, share similar opinions on major issues, and value

adolescent rebellion Pattern of emotional turmoil, characteristic of a minority of adolescents that may involve conflict with family, alienation from adult society, reckless behavior, and rejection of adult values.

What's your view

• Can you think of values you hold that are different from those of your parents? How did you come to develop these values?

their parents' approval (J. P. Hill, 1987; Offer et al., 1989; Offer, Ostrov, Howard, & Atkinson, 1988). Furthermore, contrary to a popular belief, apparently well-adjusted adolescents are not ticking time bombs set to explode later in life. In a 34-year longitudinal study of 67 14-year-old suburban boys, the vast majority adapted well to their life experiences (Offer, Offer, & Ostrov, 2004). The relatively few deeply troubled adolescents tended to come from disrupted families and, as adults, continued to have unstable family lives and to reject cultural norms. Those raised in intact two-parent homes with a positive family atmosphere tended to sail through adolescence with no serious problems and, as adults, to have solid marriages and lead well-adjusted lives (Offer, Kaiz, Ostrov, & Albert, 2002).

Still, adolescence can be a tough time for young people and their parents. Family conflict, depression, and risky behavior are more common than during other parts of the life span (Arnett, 1999; Petersen et al., 1993). Negative emotionality and mood swings are most intense during early adolescence, perhaps due to the stress connected with puberty. By late adolescence, emotionality tends to become more stable (Larson, Moneta, Richards, & Wilson, 2002).

Recognizing that adolescence may be a difficult time can help parents and teachers put trying behavior in perspective. But adults who assume that storm and stress is normal and necessary may fail to heed the signals of the relatively few young persons who need special help.

Changing Time Use and Changing Relationships

One way to assess changes in adolescents' relationships with the important people in their lives is to see how they spend their discretionary time. The amount of time U.S. adolescents spend with families declines dramatically between ages 10 and 18, from 35 percent to 14 percent of waking hours (Larson, Richards, Moneta, Holmbeck, & Duckett, 1996).

Disengagement is not a rejection of the family but a response to developmental needs. Early adolescents often retreat to their rooms; they seem to need time alone to step back from the demands of social relationships, regain emotional stability, and reflect on identity issues (Larson, 1997).

Cultural variations in time use reflect varying cultural needs, values, and practices (Verma & Larson, 2003). Young people in tribal or peasant societies spend most of their time producing bare necessities of life and have much less time for socializing than adolescents in technologically advanced societies (Larson & Verma, 1999). In some postindustrial societies such as Korea and Japan, where the pressures of schoolwork and family obligations are strong, adolescents have relatively little free time. To relieve stress, they spend their time in passive pursuits, such as watching television and "doing nothing" (Verma & Larson, 2003). In India's family-centered culture, on the other hand, middle-class urban eighth graders spend 39 percent of their waking hours with family, compared with 23 percent for U.S. eighth graders, and report being happier when with their families than U.S. eighth graders do. For these young people, the task of adolescence is not to separate from the family but to become more integrated with it. Similar findings have been reported in Indonesia, Bangladesh, Morocco, and Argentina (Larson & Wilson, 2004).

In comparison, U.S. adolescents have a good deal of discretionary time, most of which they spend with peers, increasingly of the other sex (Juster et al., 2004; Larson & Seepersad, 2003; Verma & Larson, 2003). Black teenagers, who may look on their families as havens in a hostile world, tend to maintain more intimate family relationships and less intense peer relations than white teenagers (Giordano, Cernkovich, & DeMaris, 1993). Mexican American boys, but not girls, tend to become closer to their parents during puberty. This may reflect the especially close-knit nature of Mexican American families as well as the importance these families place on the traditional male role (Molina & Chassin, 1996). For Chinese American youth from immigrant families, the need to adapt to U.S. society often conflicts with the pull of traditional family obligations (Fuligni, Yip, & Tseng, 2002).

With such cultural variations in mind, let's look more closely at relationships with parents, and then with siblings and peers.

> ### Checkpoint ✔
>
> *Can you . . .*
>
> ✔ Assess the extent of storm and stress during the teenage years?
>
> ✔ Identify age and cultural differences in how young people spend their time, and discuss their significance?

Adolescents and Parents

Just as adolescents feel tension between dependency on their parents and the need to break away, parents often have mixed feelings too. They want their children to be independent, yet they find it hard to let go. Parents have to walk a fine line between giving adolescents enough independence and protecting them from immature lapses in judgment. Tensions can lead to family conflict, and parenting styles can influence its shape and outcome. Effective parental monitoring depends on how much adolescents let parents know about their daily lives, and this may depend on the atmosphere parents have established. Also, as with younger children, teenagers' relationships with parents are affected by the parents' life situation—their work and marital and socioeconomic status.

Family Conflict and Individuation

Most arguments between adolescents and parents concern mundane personal matters—chores, schoolwork, dress, money, curfews, dating, and friends—rather than issues of health and safety or right and wrong (Adams & Laursen, 2001; Steinberg, 2005). The emotional intensity of these conflicts—out of all proportion with the subject matter—may reflect the underlying process of **individuation,** the adolescent's struggle for autonomy and differentiation, or personal identity. An important aspect of individuation is carving out boundaries of control between the self and others (Nucci, Hasebe, & Lins-Dyer, 2005).

Family conflict is most frequent during early adolescence but most intense in midadolescence (Laursen, Coy, & Collins, 1998). The frequency of strife in early adolescence may be related to the strains of puberty and the need to assert autonomy. The more highly charged arguments in midadolescence and, to a lesser extent, in late adolescence may reflect the emotional stress that occurs as adolescents try their wings. The reduced frequency of conflict in late adolescence may signify adjustment to the momentous changes of the teenage years and a renegotiation of the balance of authority between parent and child (Fuligni & Eccles, 1993; Laursen et al., 1998; Molina & Chassin, 1996), enlarging the boundaries of what is considered the adolescent's own business (Steinberg, 2005).

The level of family discord may depend largely on family atmosphere. Among 335 two-parent rural midwestern families with teenagers, conflict declined during early to middle adolescence in warm, supportive families but worsened in hostile, coercive, or critical families (Rueter & Conger, 1995).

Parenting Styles and Parental Authority

As we mentioned in Chapter 16, authoritative parenting continues to foster healthy development (Baumrind, 1991, 2005). Parents who show disappointment in teenagers' misbehavior are more effective in motivating responsible behavior than parents who punish harshly (Krevans & Gibbs, 1996). Overly strict, authoritarian parenting may lead an adolescent to reject parental influence and to seek peer support and approval at all costs (Fuligni & Eccles, 1993).

Authoritative parents insist on important rules, norms, and values but are willing to listen, explain, and negotiate (Lamborn, Mounts, Steinberg, & Dornbusch, 1991). They exercise appropriate control over a child's conduct (*behavioral control*) but not over the child's feelings, beliefs, and sense of self (*psychological control*) (Steinberg & Darling, 1994). Psychological control, exerted through such emotionally manipulative techniques as withdrawal of love, can harm adolescents' psychosocial development and mental health (Steinberg, 2005). (Table 17-6 is a checklist used for adolescents' self-reports on parents' use of psychological control.) Parents who are psychologically controlling tend to be unresponsive to their children's growing need for *psychological autonomy,* the right to their own thoughts and feelings (Steinberg, 2005).

Authoritative parenting seems to bolster an adolescent's self-image. A survey of 8,700 ninth to twelfth graders concluded that "the more involvement, autonomy granting, and structure that adolescents perceive from their parents, the more positively teens evaluate their own general conduct, psychosocial development, and mental health" (Gray & Steinberg, 1999, p. 584). When adolescents thought their parents were trying to dominate their psychological experience, their emotional health suffered more than when they thought their

individuation Adolescent's struggle for autonomy and differentiation, or personal identity.

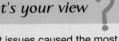

What's your view

- What issues caused the most conflict in your family when you were a teenager, and how were they resolved?

- If you lived with both parents, were your conflicts more with one parent than with the other? Did your mother and father handle such issues similarly or differently?

Table 17-6	Psychological Control Scale—Youth Self-Report

Ratings:
1 = Not like her (him); 2 = Somewhat like her (him); 3 = A lot like her (him)

My Mother (Father) is a person who . . .

1. changes the subject, whenever I have something to say.
2. finishes my sentences whenever I talk.
3. often interrupts me.
4. acts like she (he) knows what I'm thinking or feeling.
5. would like to be able to tell me how to feel or think about things all the time.
6. is always trying to change how I feel or think about things.
7. blames me for other family members' problems.
8. brings up my past mistakes when she (he) criticizes me.
9. tells me that I am not a loyal or good member of the family.
10. tells me of all the things she (he) had done for me.
11. says, if I really cared for her (him), I would not do things that cause her (him) to worry.
12. is less friendly with me, if I do not see things her (his) way.
13. will avoid looking at me when I have disappointed her (him).
14. if I have hurt her (his) feelings, stops talking to me until I please her (him) again.
15. often changes her (his) moods when with me.
16. goes back and forth between being warm and critical toward me.

Source: Adapted from Barber, 1996.

parents were trying to control their behavior. Teens whose parents were firm in enforcing behavioral rules had more self-discipline and fewer behavior problems than those with more permissive parents. Those whose parents granted them psychological autonomy tended to become self-confident and competent in both the academic and social realms.

Problems arise when parents overstep what adolescents perceive as appropriate bounds of legitimate parental authority. The existence of a mutually agreed personal domain in which authority belongs to the adolescent has been found in various cultures and social classes from Japan to Brazil. This domain expands as parents and adolescents continually renegotiate its boundaries (Nucci et al., 2005).

Parental Monitoring and Adolescents' Self-Disclosure

Young people's growing autonomy and the shrinking areas of perceived parental authority redefine the types of behavior adolescents are expected to disclose to parents (Smetana, Crean, & Campione-Barr, 2005; Table 17-7). In a study of 276 ethnically diverse suburban ninth and twelfth graders, both adolescents and parents saw *prudential* behavior related to health and safety (such as smoking, drinking, and drug use) as most subject to disclosure; followed by *moral* issues (such as lying); *conventional* issues (such as bad manners or swearing); and *multifaceted,* or borderline, issues (such as seeing an R-rated movie), which lie at the boundary between personal matters and one of the other categories. Both adolescents and parents saw *personal* issues (such as how teens spend their time and money) as least subject to disclosure. However, for each type of behavior parents were more inclined to expect disclosure than adolescents were to do it. This discrepancy diminished between ninth and twelfth grades as parents modified their expectations to fit adolescents' growing maturity (Smetana, Metzger, Gettman, & Campione-Barr, 2006).

In a study of 690 Belgian adolescents, young people were more willing to disclose information about themselves when parents maintained a warm, responsive family climate in which adolescents were encouraged to speak openly and when parents provided clear expectations without being overly controlling (Soenens, Vansteenkiste, Luyckx, & Goossens, 2006)—in other words, when parenting was authoritative. Adolescents, especially girls, tend to have closer, more supportive relationships with their mothers than with their fathers, and girls confide more in their mothers (Smetana et al., 2006).

Table 17-7   Items Used to Assess Perceived Areas of Parental vs. Adolescent Authority

Moral Items	Conventional Items	Prudential Items	Multifaceted Items	Multifaceted Friendship	Personal Items
Stealing money from parents	Not doing assigned chores	Smoking cigarettes	Not cleaning bedroom	When to start dating	Sleeping late on weekends
Hitting siblings	Talking back to parents	Drinking beer or wine	Getting ears pierced with multiple holes	Staying over at a friend's house	Choosing how to spend allowance money
Lying to parents	Using bad manners	Doing drugs	Staying out late	Seeing friends whom parents don't like	Choosing own clothes or hairstyles
Breaking a promise to parents	Cursing	Having sex	Watching cable TV	Seeing friends rather than going out with family	Choice of music

Source: Adapted from Smetana, Crean, & Campione-Barr, 2005.

Family Structure and Family Atmosphere

Many adolescents today live in families that are very different from families a few decades ago. Many households, like Jackie Robinson's was, are fatherless, many parents are divorced or cohabiting, and many mothers, as his did, work outside the home. How do these family situations affect adolescents?

Adolescents, like younger children, are sensitive to the atmosphere in the family home. In a longitudinal study of 451 adolescents and their parents, changes in marital distress or marital conflict—either for better or worse—predicted corresponding changes in adolescents' adjustment (Cui, Conger, & Lorenz, 2005). In other studies, adolescent boys and girls whose parents later divorced showed more academic, psychological, and behavioral problems *before* the breakup than peers whose parents did not later divorce (Sun, 2001).

Adolescents living with their continuously married parents tend to have significantly less behavioral problems than those in any other family structure (single-parent, cohabiting, or stepfamilies), according to data from a major national longitudinal study. An important factor is father involvement. High-quality involvement of a nonresident father helps a great deal, but not as much as the involvement of a father living in the home (Carlson, 2006).

Adolescents in cohabiting families, like younger children, tend to have greater behavioral and emotional problems than adolescents in married families; and, when one of the cohabiting parents is not the biological parent, school engagement suffers as well. For adolescents, unlike younger children, these effects are independent of economic resources, parental well-being, or effectiveness of parenting, suggesting that parental cohabitation itself may be more troublesome for adolescents than for younger children (Brown, 2004).

On the other hand, a multiethnic study of 12- and 13-year-old children of single mothers—first assessed when the children were 6 and 7 years old—found no negative effects of single parenting on school performance and no greater risk of problem behavior. What mattered most were the mother's educational level and ability, family income, and the quality of the home environment (Ricciuti, 2004). This finding suggests that negative effects of living in a single-parent home can be offset by positive factors.

Mothers' Employment and Economic Stress

The impact of a mother's work outside the home may depend on whether there are two parents or only one in the household. Often a single mother like Mallie Robinson must work to stave off economic disaster; how her working affects her teenage children may hinge on how much time and energy she has left over to spend with them, how well she keeps track of their whereabouts, and what kind of role model she provides. A longitudinal study of 819 10- to 14-year-olds from low-income urban families points up the importance of the type of care and supervisions adolescents receive after school. Those who are on their own, away from home, tend to become involved in alcohol and drug use and in misconduct in school, especially if they have an early history of problem behavior. However, this is less likely to happen when parents monitor their children's activities and neighbors are actively involved (Coley, Morris, & Hernandez, 2004).

As we have discussed earlier, a major problem in many single-parent families is lack of money. In a national longitudinal study, adolescent children of low-income single mothers were negatively affected by their mother's unstable employment or being out of work for 2 years. The adolescents were more likely to drop out of school and to experience declines in self-esteem and mastery (Kalil & Ziol-Guest, 2005). Furthermore, family economic hardship during adolescence can affect adult well-being.

Sibling relationships become more equal as the younger sibling approaches or reaches adolescence and the relative difference in age diminishes. Even so, this younger sister still looks up to her big sister and may try to emulate her.

The degree of risk depends on whether parents see their situation as stressful, whether that stress interferes with family relationships, and how much it affects children's educational and occupational attainments (Sobolewski & Amato, 2005).

Many adolescents in economically distressed families may benefit from accumulated social capital—the support of kin and community. In 51 poor, urban African American families in which teenagers were living with their mothers, grandmothers, or aunts, women who had strong kinship networks exercised firmer control and closer monitoring while granting appropriate autonomy, and their teenage charges were more self-reliant and had fewer behavior problems (R. D. Taylor & Roberts, 1995).

Adolescents and Siblings

As adolescents spend more time with peers, they have less time and less need for the emotional gratification they used to get from the sibling bond. Adolescents are less close to siblings than to either parents or friends, are less influenced by them, and become even more distant as they move through adolescence (Laursen, 1996).

Changes in sibling relationships may well precede similar changes in the relationship between adolescents and parents: more independence on the part of the younger person and less authority exerted by the older person. As children approach high school, their relationships with their siblings become progressively more equal. Older siblings exercise less power over younger ones, and younger siblings no longer need as much supervision. As relative age differences shrink, so do differences in competence and independence (Buhrmester & Furman, 1990).

Older and younger siblings tend to have different feelings about their changing relationship. As the younger sibling grows up, the older one may look on a newly assertive younger brother or sister as a pesky annoyance. Younger siblings still tend to look up to older ones—as Jackie Robinson looked up to his brother Mack—and try to feel more grown-up by identifying with and emulating them (Buhrmester & Furman, 1990).

In a 5-year longitudinal study of 227 Latino and African American families, sibling relationships under certain circumstances had important effects on the younger sibling. In single-mother homes, a warm and nurturing relationship with an older sister tended to prevent a younger sister from engaging in substance use and risky sexual behavior. However, having a domineering older sister tended to increase a younger sibling's high-risk sexual behavior (East & Khoo, 2005). As we mentioned in Chapter 15, older siblings may influence a younger one to smoke, drink, or use drugs (Pomery et al., 2005; Rende et al., 2005). In a longitudinal study of 206 boys and their younger siblings, younger siblings hanging out with an antisocial older brother were at serious risk for adolescent antisocial behavior, drug use, sexual behavior, and violence, regardless of parental discipline (Snyder, Bank, & Burraston, 2005).

Checkpoint ✔

Can you . . .

✔ Identify factors that affect conflict with parents and adolescents' self-disclosure?

✔ Discuss the impact on adolescents of parenting styles and of marital status, mothers' employment, and economic stress?

What's your view

• If you have one or more brothers or sisters, did your relationships with them change during adolescence?

Peers and Friends

As Jackie Robinson found, an important source of emotional support during the complex transition of adolescence—as well as a source of pressure for behavior that parents may deplore—is the peer group. The peer group is a source of affection, sympathy, understanding, and moral guidance; a place for experimentation; and a setting for achieving autonomy and independence from parents. It is a place to form intimate relationships that serve as - rehearsals for adult intimacy.

The influence of peers normally peaks at ages 12 to 13 and declines during middle and late adolescence. At age 13 or 14, popular adolescents may engage in mildly antisocial behaviors, such as trying drugs or sneaking into a movie without paying, so as to demonstrate to their peers their independence from parental rules (Allen, Porter, McFarland, Marsh, & McElhaney, 2005). However, attachment to peers in early adolescence is not likely to forecast real trouble unless the attachment is so strong that the young person is willing to give up obeying household rules, doing schoolwork, and developing his or her own talents in order to win peer approval and popularity (Fuligni et al., 2001).

In one study that demonstrated the influence of peers on risk-taking, 306 adolescents, college-age youth, and young adults played a video game called "Chicken." The younger participants were more likely to take risks and make risky decisions than the older ones. For all ages groups, risk-taking was higher in the company of peers than alone, but this was more true of younger participants than of adults (Gardner & Steinberg, 2005).

In childhood, most peer interactions are *dyadic,* or one-to-one, though somewhat larger groupings begin to form in middle childhood. As children move into adolescence, *cliques*—structured groups of friends who do things together—become more important. A larger type of grouping, *crowds,* which does not normally exist before adolescence, is based not on personal interactions but on reputation, image, or identity. Crowd membership is a social construction, a set of labels by which young people divide the social map based on neighborhood, ethnicity, socioeconomic status, or other factors. All three levels of peer groupings may exist simultaneously, and some may overlap in membership, which may change over time (Brown & Klute, 2003).

Friendships

The intensity and importance of friendships and the amount of time spent with friends are probably greater in adolescence than at any other time in the life span. Friendships tend to become more reciprocal, more equal, and more stable; those that are not may lose importance or be abandoned.

Adolescents, like younger children, tend to choose friends who are like them in gender, race/ethnicity, and other respects. Friends tend to have similar academic attitudes and performance and similar levels of drug use (Hamm, 2000), and they may influence each other either toward prosocial activity (Barry & Wentzel, 2005) or toward risky or problem behavior. Alternatively, the qualities that lead friends to choose each other may lead them to develop in similar directions. By controlling for these selection effects, a 1-year longitudinal study of 1,700 adolescent friendship pairs found that friends' influence on binge drinking and sexual activity was fairly weak (Jaccard, Blanton, & Dodge, 2005).

A stress on intimacy, loyalty, and sharing marks a transition toward adultlike friendships. Adolescents begin to rely more on friends than on parents for intimacy and support, and they share confidences more than younger friends do (Berndt & Perry, 1990; Buhrmester, 1990, 1996; Hartup & Stevens, 1999; Laursen, 1996). Girls' friendships tend to be more intimate than boys', with frequent sharing of confidences (Brown & Klute, 2003). Intimacy with same-sex friends increases during early to midadolescence, after which it typically declines as intimacy with the other sex grows (Laursen, 1996).

The increased intimacy of adolescent friendship reflects cognitive as well as emotional development. Adolescents are now better able to express their private thoughts and feelings. They can more readily consider another person's point of view, and so it is easier for them to understand a friend's thoughts and feelings. Increased intimacy reflects early adolescents' concern with getting to know themselves. Confiding in a friend helps young people explore their feelings, define their identity, and validate their self-worth (Buhrmester, 1996).

The capacity for intimacy is related to psychological adjustment and social competence. Adolescents who have close, stable, supportive friendships generally have a high opinion of themselves, do well in school, are sociable, and are unlikely to be hostile, anxious, or depressed (Berndt & Perry, 1990; Buhrmester, 1990; Hartup & Stevens, 1999). They also tend to have established strong bonds with parents (Brown & Klute, 2003). A bidirectional process seems to be at work: Good relationships foster adjustment, which in turn fosters good friendships.

Cliques

Cliques may exist among preadolescent children but are a more prominent feature of early adolescence. As expanded circles of friends, they usually consist of young people of the same age, gender, and ethnicity. However, membership in cliques tends to be based not only on personal affinity but also on popularity, or social status. A person may belong to more than one clique or to no clique, and the membership of a clique may be stable or shifting (Brown & Klute, 2003).

The dynamics of clique membership in preadolescence are highly status-based, especially among girls. The members with highest status are acknowledged leaders with the ultimate say over who is in and who is out. Cliques themselves form a hierarchy; higher-status cliques are most desirable to outsiders but maintain the tightest control over membership (Adler & Adler, 1995). In early adolescence this social control may become somewhat less rigid (Brown & Klute, 2003).

The clique structure can seem harsh to outsiders, but it effectively serves the purpose of "redirecting young people's priorities from childhood to adolescent social norms. It sends a blunt message as to who is in charge of the peer social system (peers, rather than adults) and provides unequivocal information about how to proceed within that system" (Brown & Klute, 2003, p. 341). It also can create emotional distress among those who are less than successful in negotiating the system (Brown & Klute, 2003).

Crowds

Leonard Bernstein's musical *West Side Story* vividly illustrates the power of adolescent crowds. Crowd labels are cognitive designations for a feature that members of the crowd have in common, such as neighborhood (west siders or south siders), ethnic background (Puerto Ricans or Italians), peer status (snobs or nobodies), or abilities, interests, or lifestyle (brains, jocks, druggies). The specific categories by which adolescents describe their social landscape may vary from one community to another.

Crowds serve several purposes. They help adolescents establish their identity and reinforce allegiance to the behavioral norms of ethnic or socioeconomic groups. As *West Side Story* dramatizes, being part of a crowd makes it easier to establish relationships with peers in the same crowd and harder with outsiders. As with cliques, crowd affiliation tends to become looser as adolescence progresses (Brown & Klute, 2003).

What's your view

- As an adolescent, were you part of a clique or crowd? If so, how did it affect your social relationships and attitudes?

Romantic Relationships

Romantic relationships are a central part of most adolescents' social worlds. They contribute to the development of both intimacy and identity. Because they tend to involve sexual contact, they also entail risks of pregnancy, STDs, and sometimes of sexual victimization. Nearly 1 out of 11 U.S. high school students—as many boys as girls—are subjected to dating violence each year (CDC, 2006f). Breakups with romantic partners are among the strongest predictors of depression and suicide (Bouchey & Furman, 2003).

With the onset of puberty, most heterosexual boys and girls begin to think about and interact more with members of the other sex. Typically they move from mixed groups or group dates to one-on-one romantic relationships that involve passion and a sense of commitment (Bouchey & Furman, 2003; Furman & Wehner, 1997).

Romantic relationships tend to become more intense and more intimate across adolescence (Bouchey & Furman, 2003). Early adolescents think primarily about how a romantic relationship may affect their status in the peer group (Bouchey & Furman, 2003). They

Checkpoint ✔

Can you . . .

✔ Describe typical changes in sibling relationships during adolescence?

✔ List several functions of the peer group in adolescence?

✔ Discuss important features of adolescent friendships, cliques, and crowds?

✔ Describe developmental changes in romantic relationships?

pay little or no attention to attachment or support needs, such as help, caring, and nurturance, and their attention to sexual needs is limited to how to engage in sexual activity and which activities to engage in (Bouchey & Furman, 2003; Furman & Wehner, 1997).

In midadolescence, most young people have at least one exclusive partner lasting for several months to about a year, and the effect of the choice of partner on peer status tends to become less important (Furman & Wehner, 1997). In interviews with 1,316 junior high and high school students, boys revealed less confidence than girls about these early romantic relationships. Girls' greater ease in romantic relationships may be an extension of their greater intimacy in same-sex friendships (Giordano, Longmore, & Manning, 2006).

By age 16, adolescents interact with and think about romantic partners more than about parents, friends, or siblings (Bouchey & Furman, 2003). Not until late adolescence or early adulthood, though, do romantic relationships begin to meet the full gamut of emotional needs that such relationships can serve and then only in relatively long-term relationships (Furman & Wehner, 1997).

Relationships with parents and peers may affect the quality of romantic relationships. The parents' marriage or romantic relationship may serve as a model for their adolescent child. The peer group forms the context for most romantic relationships and may affect an adolescent's choice of a partner and the way the relationship develops (Bouchey & Furman, 2003).

Antisocial Behavior and Juvenile Delinquency

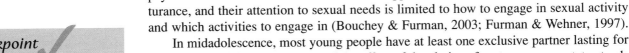

Guidepost 4

What causes antisocial behavior, and what can be done to reduce the risk of juvenile delinquency?

What influences young people to engage in—or refrain from—violence (Box 17-2) or other antisocial acts? By what processes do antisocial tendencies develop? How do problem behaviors escalate into chronic delinquency—an outcome Jackie Robinson managed to avoid? What determines whether a juvenile delinquent will grow up to be a hardened criminal? As we mentioned in Chapter 14, an interaction between environmental and genetic or biological risk factors may underlie much antisocial behavior (van Goozen, Fairchild, Snoek, & Harold, 2007).

Becoming a Delinquent: Genetic and Neurological Factors

Antisocial behavior tends to run in families. Analyses of many studies have concluded that genes influence 40 to 50 percent of the variation in antisocial behavior within a population and 60 to 65 percent of the variation in aggressive antisociality (Rhee & Waldman, 2002; Tackett, Krueger, Iacono, & McGue, 2005).

Neurobiological deficits, particularly in the portions of the brain that regulate reactions to stress, may help explain why some children become antisocial children and adolescents. As a result of these neurological deficits, which may result from the interaction of genetic factors or difficult temperament with adverse early environments, children may not receive or heed normal warning signals to restrain impulsive or reckless behavior (van Goozen et al., 2007).

Becoming a Delinquent: How Family, Peer, and Community Influences Interact

As Bronfenbrenner's theory would suggest, antisocial behavior is influenced by multileveled, interacting factors ranging from microsystem influences—such as parent-child hostility, poor parenting practices, and peer deviance—to macrosystem influences—such as community structure and neighborhood social support (Buehler, 2006; Tolan, Gorman-Smith, & Henry, 2003). This network of interacting influences begins to be woven early in childhood.

Parents shape prosocial or antisocial behavior through their responses to children's basic emotional needs (Krevans & Gibbs, 1996; Staub, 1996). Parents of children who become antisocial may have failed to reinforce good behavior in early childhood and may

Box 17-2 *The Youth Violence Epidemic*

On April 20, 1999, 18-year-old Eric Harris and 17-year-old Dylan Klebold entered Columbine High School in Littleton, Colorado, wearing black trench coats and carrying a rifle, a semiautomatic pistol, two sawed-off shotguns, and more than 30 homemade bombs. Laughing and taunting, they sprayed bullets at fellow students, killing 12 classmates and 1 teacher before fatally shooting themselves.

The massacre in Littleton was not an isolated event. In 2004–2005, 21 young people ages 5 to 18 were victims of school killings. But while the occasional youth killing may make the headlines, such crimes as forcible rape, robbery, and assault are much more prevalent. In 2004 students ages 12 to 18 were victims of about 1.4 million nonfatal crimes at school, 107,000 of them serious. In 2005, 10 percent of male high school students and 6 percent of female students reported being threatened or injured by a weapon on school property; 6 percent of the students, including 10 percent of boys, admitted carrying weapons on school property (Dinkes, Forrest Cataldi, Kena, & Baum, 2006). A high proportion of delinquent youth, who are disproportionately ethnic/racial minorities, die violent deaths (Teplin, McClelland, Abram, & Mileusnic, 2005).

School violence is not a peculiarly U.S. phenomenon. In a Japanese elementary school in June 2004, an 11-year-old girl stabbed a 12-year-old classmate to death after an argument over messages sent each other over the Internet—one of several such incidents in recent years ("Japan in shock at school murder," 2004). In a survey of 161,082 students in 35 Western countries, 37 to 69 percent of the boys and 13 to 32 percent of the girls reported fighting, usually with friends or relatives. The lowest prevalence of fighting for both boys and girls was in Finland; the highest prevalence was in eastern or central European countries. Although fighting was less common in the United States than in many other countries, it had the highest proportion of weapon carrying: 22 percent of boys and 5 percent of girls. In all countries, fighting and weapon carrying were associated with risks of serious injury (Pickett et al., 2005).

Why do some young people engage in such destructive behavior? One answer lies in the immaturity of the adolescent brain, particularly the prefrontal cortex, which is critical to judgment and impulse suppression (refer back to Chapter 15). Another answer is ready access to guns in a culture that "romanticizes gunplay" (Weinberger, 2001, p. 2).

Youth violence is strongly related to the presence of gangs at school (NCES, 2003; "Youth Violence," 2001). For many adolescents, gangs satisfy unfulfilled needs for identity, connection, and a sense of power and control. For young people who lack positive family relationships, a gang can become a substitute family. Gangs promote a sense of "us-versus-them." Violence against outsiders strengthens bonds of loyalty and support within the gang (Staub, 1996).

Teenage violence and antisocial behavior have roots in childhood. Children, especially boys, who are aggressive in elementary school tend to be violently antisocial in adolescence (Broidy et al., 2003). Children raised in a rejecting or coercive atmosphere or in an overly permissive or chaotic one tend to behave aggressively, and the hostility they evoke in others increases their aggression. Their negative self-image prevents them from succeeding at school or developing other constructive interests, and they generally associate with peers who reinforce their antisocial attitudes and behavior (Staub, 1996). Boys in poor, unstable inner-city neighborhoods with high crime rates and low community involvement and neighborhood support are most likely to become involved in violence (Tolan et al., 2003), but the shootings at Columbine show that even middle-class students in a suburban school are not immune.

Adolescents are more likely to commit violence if they have witnessed or have been victims of neighborhood violence or have been exposed to media violence (Brookmeyer, Henrich, & Stone, 2005; Pearce, Jones, Schwab-Stone, & Ruchkin, 2003). As we discussed in Chapter 14, a steady diet of media violence can breed aggression, and adolescents are no exception (Johnson, Cohen, Smailes, Kasen, & Brook, 2002). Parental support tends to buffer

Five Myths about Youth Violence

Myth	Fact
Most future offenders can be identified in early childhood.	Children with conduct disorders or uncontrolled behavior do not necessarily turn out to be violent adolescents.
African American and Hispanic youth are more likely than other ethnic youth to become involved in violence.	Although arrest rates differ, self-reports suggest that race and ethnicity have little effect on the overall proportion of nonfatal violent behavior.
A new breed of super-predators, who grew to adolescence in the 1990s, threatens to make the United States an even more violent place than it is.	There is no evidence that young people involved in violence during the 1990s were more violent or more vicious than youths in earlier years.
Trying young offenders in tough adult criminal courts makes them less likely to commit more violent crimes.	Juveniles handled in adult courts have significantly higher rates of repeat offenses and of later felonies than young offenders handled in juvenile courts.
Most violent youths will end up being arrested for violent crimes.	Most youths involved in violent behavior will never be arrested for a violent crime.

Source: Based on data from "Youth Violence," 2001.

(continued)

Box 17-2 *The Youth Violence Epidemic (continued)*

the negative effects of exposure to violence, especially for boys; girls' own prosocial tendencies have a buffering effect (Brookmeyer et al., 2005; Pearce et al., 2003).

Psychologists point to potential warning signs. Adolescents likely to commit violence often refuse to listen to parents and teachers; ignore the feelings and rights of others; mistreat people; rely on violence or threats to solve problems; and believe that life has treated them unfairly. They tend to do poorly in school; to cut classes or play truant; to be held back or suspended or to drop out; to be victims of bullying; to use alcohol, inhalants, and/or drugs; to engage in early sexual activity; to join gangs; and to fight, steal, or destroy property (APA and AAP, 1996; Resnick et al., 1997; Smith-Khuri et al., 2004; "Youth Violence," 2001). Harris and Klebold showed several of these characteristics.

A report by the Surgeon General of the United States challenges some myths, or stereotypes, about youth violence ("Youth Violence," 2001; see table). One of the worst is the myth that nothing can be done to prevent or treat violent behavior. School-based programs designed to prevent violent behavior by promoting social competence and emotional awareness and control have been modestly successful (Henrich, Brown, & Aber, 1999). A program in Galveston, Texas, that addressed specific risk factors led to a drop in arrests for juvenile crime (Thomas, Holzer, & Wall, 2002). Unfortunately, about half of the hundreds of programs being used in schools and communities fall short when rigorously evaluated.

What's your view

What methods for controlling youth violence seem to you most likely to work?

Check it out

For more information on this topic, go to http://www.search-institute.org/. The Search Institute is an organization dedicated to "raising caring and responsible children and teenagers" by providing "developmental assets" and creating health communities.

These 16-year-old girls console each other at a vigil service for victims of a shooting spree by teenage gunmen at Columbine High School in Littleton, Colorado, on April 20, 1999. This and other school shootings are part of what has been called an epidemic of youth violence.

have been harsh or inconsistent—or both—in punishing misbehavior (Coie & Dodge, 1998; Snyder, Cramer, Afrank, & Patterson, 2005). Through the years these parents may not have been closely and positively involved in their children's lives (G. R. Patterson, DeBaryshe, & Ramsey, 1989). The children may get payoffs for antisocial behavior: When they act up, they may gain attention or get their way. These early negative patterns pave the way for negative peer influences that promote and reinforce antisocial behavior (Collins et al., 2000; B. B. Brown, Mounts, Lamborn, & Steinberg, 1993).

By early adolescence, open hostility may exist between parent and child. When constant criticism, angry coercion, or rude, uncooperative behavior characterizes parent-child interactions, the child tends to show aggressive behavior problems, which worsen the parent-child relationship (Buehler, 2006). Ineffective parenting can leave younger siblings to the powerful influence of a deviant older brother, especially if the siblings are close in age (Snyder, Bank, & Burraston, 2005).

The choice of antisocial peers is affected mainly by environmental factors (Iervolino et al., 2002). Young people gravitate to others brought up like themselves who are similar in school achievement, adjustment, and prosocial or antisocial tendencies (Collins et al., 2000; B. B. Brown, Mounts, Lamborn, & Steinberg, 1993). As in childhood, antisocial adolescents tend to have antisocial friends, and their antisocial behavior increases when they associate with each other (Dishion, McCord, & Poulin, 1999; Hartup & Stevens, 1999; Vitaro, Tremblay, Kerr, Pagani, & Bukowski, 1997). The way antisocial teenagers talk, laugh, or smirk about rule breaking and nod knowingly among themselves seems to constitute a sort of "deviancy training" (Dishion et al., 1999). These "problem children" continue to elicit ineffective parenting, which predicts delinquent behavior and association with deviant peer groups or gangs (Simons, Chao, Conger, & Elder, 2001; Tolan et al., 2003).

Authoritative parenting can help young people internalize standards that may insulate them against negative peer influences and open them to positive ones (Collins et al., 2000;

Mounts & Steinberg, 1995). Improved parenting during adolescence can reduce delinquency by discouraging association with deviant peers (Simons et al., 2001). Adolescents whose parents know where they are and what they are doing are less likely to engage in delinquent acts (Laird, Pettit, Bates, & Dodge, 2003) or to associate with deviant peers (Lloyd & Anthony, 2003).

Family economic circumstances may influence the development of antisocial behavior. Persistent economic deprivation can undermine sound parenting by depriving the family of social capital. Poor children are more likely than other children to commit antisocial acts, and those whose families are continuously poor tend to become more antisocial with time. Conversely, when families rise from poverty while a child is still young, the child is no more likely to develop behavior problems than a child whose family was never poor (Macmillan, McMorris, & Kruttschnitt, 2004).

Weak neighborhood social organization in a disadvantaged community can influence delinquency through its effects on parenting behavior and peer deviance (Chung & Steinberg, 2006). *Collective efficacy*—the strength of social connections within a neighborhood and the extent to which residents monitor or supervise each other's children—can influence outcomes in a positive direction (Sampson, 1997). A combination of nurturant, involved parenting and collective efficacy can discourage adolescents from association with deviant peers (Brody et al., 2001).

Long-Term Prospects

Many adolescents, like Jackie Robinson and his friends, at some point engage in antisocial behavior or even in violence. The vast majority of these young people do not become adult criminals (Kosterman, Graham, Hawkins, Catalano, & Herrenkohl, 2001; Moffitt, 1993). Delinquency peaks at about age 15 and then declines as most adolescents and their families come to terms with young people's need to assert independence.

Teenagers who do not see positive alternatives are more likely to adopt a permanently antisocial lifestyle (Elliott, 1993). Those most likely to persist in violence are boys who had early antisocial influences. Least likely to persist are boys and girls who were early school achievers and girls who showed early prosocial development (Kosterman et al., 2001). Because adolescents' character is still in flux, many developmental psychologists deplore the current trend toward transferring juvenile offenders from the juvenile court system, which is aimed at rehabilitation, to criminal courts where they are tried and sentenced as adults (Steinberg, 2000; Steinberg & Scott, 2003).

What's your view

- How should society deal with youthful offenders?

Preventing and Treating Delinquency

Because juvenile delinquency has roots early in childhood, so should preventive efforts. To be most successful, interventions should attack the multiple factors that can lead to delinquency.

Adolescents who have taken part in certain early childhood intervention programs are less likely to get in trouble than their equally underprivileged peers who did not have these early experiences (Yoshikawa, 1994; Zigler, Taussig, & Black, 1992). Effective programs are those that target high-risk urban children and last at least 2 years during the child's first 5 years of life. They influence children directly, through high-quality day care or education, and at the same time indirectly, by offering families assistance and support geared to their needs (Berrueta-Clement et al., 1985; Berrueta-Clement, Schweinhart, Barnett, & Weikart, 1987; Schweinhart et al., 1993; Seitz, 1990; Yoshikawa, 1994; Zigler et al., 1992).

These programs operate on Bronfenbrenner's mesosystem by affecting interactions between the home and the school and/or child care center. The programs also go one step further to the exosystem by creating supportive parent networks and linking parents with such community services as prenatal and postnatal care and educational and vocational counseling (Yoshikawa, 1994; Zigler et al., 1992). Through their multipronged approach, these interventions have an impact on several early risk factors for delinquency.

Table 17-8	Effective Measures to Discourage Deviant Behavior

Mental Health

1. Individually administered treatment
2. Family-based interventions
3. Mentoring programs such as Big Brothers/Big Sisters

Education

1. Universal, environment-centered programs that focus on school-wide reform, including
   a. Clearly explicated expectations for student and staff behavior
   b. Consistent utilization of proactive school discipline strategies
   c. Active monitoring of "hot spots" for behavior problems
   d. Improved systems to monitor student achievement and behavior
2. Universal classroom programs to build social competence
3. School-wide positive behavior support
4. Individual behavior support plan for each student
5. Improved training in behavior management practices for classroom teachers
6. Consultation and support for classroom teachers
7. Matching deviant youth with well-adjusted peers (e.g., coaching)
8. Proactive prevention programs that shape student morals and encourage responsible decision-making

Juvenile Justice and Child Welfare

1. Multidimensional Treatment Foster Care
2. Intensive Protective Supervision Project

3. Sending delinquent youth to programs that serve the general population of youth in their neighborhoods (e.g., Boys and Girls Clubs)
4. Community rather than custodial settings
5. Interpersonal skills training
6. Individual counseling
7. Treatment administered by mental health professionals
8. Early diversion programs
9. Victim-Offender Mediation programs
10. Teen Court programs

Community Programming

1. Public or private organizations, open to all youth, that provide structure and adult involvement (e.g., religious groups, service clubs, Scouts, Boys and Girls Clubs)
2. School-based extracurricular activities
3. Encouragement of commitments outside of gangs (e.g., to jobs, family roles, military service, mentors)
4. Early childhood interventions such as the Perry Preschool program
5. Job Corps
6. Policing programs that target high-crime neighborhoods where high-risk youth congregate
7. Community efforts to reduce marginalization of specific groups of youth

Source: Adapted from Dodge, Dishion, & Lansford (2006).

The Chicago Child-Parent Centers is a preschool program for disadvantaged children in the Chicago public schools. The program offers follow-up services through age 9. Participants studied at age 20 had better educational and social outcomes and fewer juvenile arrests than a comparison group who had received less extensive early interventions (Reynolds et al., 2001).

Once children reach adolescence, especially in poor, crime-ridden neighborhoods, interventions need to focus on spotting troubled adolescents and preventing gang recruitment (Tolan et al., 2003). Successful programs boost parenting skills through better monitoring, behavioral management, and neighborhood social support.

Programs such as teen hangouts and summer camps for behaviorally disturbed youth can be counterproductive because they bring together groups of deviant youth who tend to reinforce each other's deviancy. More effective programs—Scouts, sports, and church activities—integrate deviant youth into the nondeviant mainstream. Structured, adult-monitored, or school-based activities after school, on weekend evenings, and in summer, when adolescents are most likely to be idle and to get in trouble, can reduce their exposure to settings that encourage antisocial behavior (Dodge, Dishion, & Lansford, 2006).

As Jackie Robinson's experience shows, getting teenagers involved in constructive activities or job skills programs during their free time can pay long-range dividends. Participation in extracurricular school activities tends to cut down on dropout and criminal arrest rates among high-risk boys and girls (Mahoney, 2000). Table 17-8 lists examples of effective programs to discourage deviancy.

Fortunately, the great majority of adolescents do not get into serious trouble. Those who show disturbed behavior can—and should—be helped. With love, guidance, and support, adolescents can avoid risks, build on their strengths, and explore their possibilities as they approach adult life.

Checkpoint ✔

Can you . . .

✔ Explain how family, peer, and community influences may interact to promote antisocial behavior and delinquency?

✔ Give examples of types of programs that have been successful in preventing or stopping delinquency and other antisocial behavior?

Emerging Adulthood

Guidepost 5

How do various cultures define what it means to become an adult, and what markers confer adult status?

In modern Western societies, entrance into adulthood takes longer and follows more varied routes than in the past. Before the mid-20th century, a young man just out of high school could, in short order, obtain a stable job, marry, and start a family. For a young woman, the chief route to adulthood was marriage, which occurred as soon as she could find a suitable mate. Now, the technological revolution has made higher education or specialized training increasingly essential. The gender revolution has brought more women into the workforce and broadened female roles (Furstenberg, Rumbaut, & Settersten, Jr., 2005; Fussell & Furstenberg, 2005). Today the road to adulthood may be marked by multiple milestones—entering college (full- or part-time), working (full- or part-time), moving away from home, getting married, and having children—and the order and timing of these transitions varies (Schulenberg, O'Malley, Bachman, & Johnston, 2005). Thus, some developmental scientists suggest that the period from the late teens through the mid- to late 20s has become a distinct period of the life course: **emerging adulthood**—a time when young people are no longer adolescents but have not yet become fully adult (Arnett, 2000, 2004; Furstenberg et al., 2005).

emerging adulthood Proposed transitional period between adolescence and adulthood, usually extending from the late teens through the mid-20s.

In the minds of many people today, the onset of adulthood is marked, not so much by external criteria such as driving, voting, and work, as by such internal indicators as a sense of autonomy, self-control, and personal responsibility. It is more a state of mind than a discrete event (Shanahan, Porfeli, & Mortimer, 2005).

Since the 1990s, surveys of emerging adult Americans (mostly white, urban, and middle class) have repeatedly come up with three top criteria for adulthood: "accepting responsibility for oneself, making independent decisions, and becoming financially independent"—criteria that reflect their society's values of individualism and self-sufficiency (Arnett & Galambos, 2003, p. 92). In similar studies of Israelis, Argentinians, U.S. minority groups, and Mormons, those same criteria were most widely expressed. However, emerging adults in those cultures also mentioned criteria reflecting collectivistic values. In Israel, universal military service is an important marker of adulthood (Mayseless & Scharf, 2003). Young Argentines, who have experienced severe economic crises and high unemployment in recent years, emphasize family responsibilities more than work (Facio & Micocci, 2003). Mormons cite religious rites of passage, such as being admitted to men's or women's organizations of their church (Nelson, 2003).

What's your view

- What criteria for adulthood do you consider most relevant?
- Do you think those criteria are influenced by the culture in which you live or grew up?

African Americans, Latinos, and Asian Americans are more likely than European Americans to mention criteria involving obligations to others (such as supporting one's family), recognized role transitions (such as marriage), and complying with social norms (such as avoiding illegal drug use). African Americans and Latinos who come from lower-SES families tend to believe they have reached adulthood at an earlier age than do European Americans and Asian Americans, probably because of greater and earlier family responsibilities (Arnett, 2003).

As research on this topic continues, it will be interesting to see what adulthood means in rural, non-Westernized cultures, which tend to hold more strongly collectivist values.

Checkpoint ✓

Can you . . .

✔ Explain the concept of emerging adulthood, and tell why it applies to modern Westernized societies?

✔ Discuss cultural conceptions of what it means to be an adult?

Refocus

Thinking back to the Focus vignette about Jackie Robinson at the beginning of this chapter,

- What evidence suggests that Jackie Robinson may have gone through Erikson's stage of identity versus identity confusion?
- Which of Marcia's identity statuses did Robinson seem to fall into, both with regard to his identity in general and his ethnicity in particular?

- Did Robinson's relationships with his mother and his peers seem consistent with the findings reported in this chapter?
- Would you say that Robinson showed adolescent rebellion?
- Based on the material in this chapter, why do you think Robinson did not become a juvenile delinquent?

The normal developmental changes in the early years of life are obvious and dramatic signs of growth. The infant lying in the crib becomes an active, exploring toddler. The young child enters and embraces the worlds of school and society. The adolescent, with a new body and new awareness, prepares to step into adulthood.

Growth and development do not screech to a stop even then. People change in important ways throughout adulthood. They continue to shape their development, as they have been doing since birth. What occurs in a child's world is significant, but it is not the whole story. We each continue to write the story of human development for ourselves and our society for as long as we live.

Summary and Key Terms

The Search for Identity

Guidepost 1 How do adolescents form an identity, and what roles do gender and ethnicity play?

- A central concern during adolescence is the search for identity, which has occupational, sexual, and values components. Erik Erikson described the psychosocial crisis of adolescence as the crisis of identity versus identity confusion. The virtue that should arise from this crisis is *fidelity*.

- James Marcia, in research based on Erikson's theory, described four identity statuses with differing combinations of crisis and commitment: identity achievement, foreclosure, moratorium, and identity diffusion.

- Self-esteem tends to fall during adolescence, especially for girls, but not for minority youth.

- Ethnicity is an important part of identity. Minority adolescents seem to go through stages of ethnic identity development much like Marcia's identity statuses.

    identity (469) **identity versus identity confusion (469)**
    identity statuses (470) **crisis (470)** **commitment (470)**
    identity achievement (470) **foreclosure (471)** **moratorium (471)**
    identity diffusion (472) **cultural socialization (473)**

Sexuality

Guidepost 2 What determines sexual orientation, what sexual attitudes and practices are common among adolescents, and what leads some to engage in risky sexual behavior?

- Sexual orientation appears to be influenced by an interaction of biological and environmental factors and may be at least partly genetic.

- Teenage sexual activity is more prevalent and more accepted than in the past, but it involves risks of pregnancy and sexually transmitted diseases (STDs). Adolescents at greatest risk are those who begin sexual activity early, have multiple partners, do not use contraceptives, and are ill-informed about sex.

- The course of homosexual identity and relationship development may vary with cohort, gender, and ethnicity.

- Rates of STDs in the United States are the highest in the world, and especially high among adolescents. STDs are more likely to develop undetected in girls than in boys.

- Teenage pregnancy and birthrates in the United States have declined. Most of these births are to unmarried mothers.

- Teenage pregnancy and childbearing often have negative outcomes. Teenage mothers and their families tend to suffer ill health and financial hardship, and the children often suffer from ineffective parenting.

    sexual orientation (474)
    sexually transmitted diseases (STD's) (478)

Relationships with Family and Peers

Guidepost 3 How do adolescents relate to parents, siblings, and peers?

- Although relationships between adolescents and their parents are not always smooth, full-scale adolescent rebellion is unusual. For the majority of teens, adolescence is a fairly smooth transition. For the minority who seem more deeply troubled, it can predict a troubled adulthood.

- Adolescents spend an increasing amount of time with peers, but relationships with parents continue to be close and influential.

- Conflict with parents tends to be most frequent during early adolescence and most intense during middle adolescence. The intensity of minor conflicts may reflect the process of individuation.

- Authoritative parenting is associated with the most positive outcomes. Behavioral control normally diminishes across adolescence; psychological control, which suppresses a young person's emotional autonomy, does not.

- Effective parental monitoring depends on adolescents' self-disclosure, which is influenced by the quality of the parent-child relationship.

- Effects of divorce, single parenting, and maternal employment on adolescents' development depend on such factors as how closely parents monitor adolescents' activity and the quality of the home environment.

- Economic stress affects relationships in both single-parent and two-parent families.

- Relationships with siblings tend to become more distant during adolescence, and the balance of power between older and younger siblings becomes more equal.

- The influence of the peer group is strongest in early adolescence. Adolescents who are rejected by peers tend to have the greatest adjustment problems. Peer relationships fall into three categories: friendships, cliques, and crowds.

- Friendships, especially among girls, become more intimate and supportive in adolescence. Cliques are highly status-based; crowds are based on common features, such as ethnicity or SES.

- Romantic relationships involve several roles and develop with age and experience.

    adolescent rebellion (482) **individuation (484)**

Guidepost 4 What causes antisocial behavior, and what can be done to reduce the risk of juvenile delinquency?

- Antisocial behavior is associated with multiple interacting risk factors, including genes, neurological deficits, ineffective parenting, school failure, peer influence, and low socioeconomic status.

- Programs that attack environmental risk factors from an early age have had success in preventing juvenile delinquency.

Emerging Adulthood

Guidepost 5 How do various cultures define what it means to become an adult, and what markers confer adult status?

- A transitional period called emerging adulthood has developed in Westernized cultures in recent years.

- Emerging adults in various Westernized cultures hold similar views of what defines entrance into adulthood. The most widely accepted criteria are individualistic ones having to do with self-sufficiency and independence. However, some cultures also embrace collectivistic criteria, such as family responsibilities and conformity with social norms.

emerging adulthood (495)

Glossary

A, not-B error Tendency for 8- to 12-month-old infants to search for a hidden object in a place where they previously found it rather than in the place where they most recently saw it being hidden.

acceleration Approach to educating the gifted that moves them through the curriculum at an unusually rapid pace.

accommodation Piaget's term for changes in a cognitive structure to include new information.

acquired immune deficiency syndrome (AIDS) Viral disease that undermines effective functioning of the immune system.

acute medical conditions Occasional illnesses that last a short time.

adaptation Piaget's term for adjustment to new information about the environment.

adolescence Developmental transition between childhood and adulthood entailing major physical, cognitive, and psychosocial changes.

adolescent growth spurt Sharp increase in height and weight that precedes sexual maturity.

adolescent rebellion Pattern of emotional turmoil, characteristic of a minority of adolescents that may involve conflict with family, alienation from adult society, reckless behavior, and rejection of adult values.

adrenarche Maturation of adrenal glands.

affordance In the Gibsons' ecological theory of perception, the fit between a person's physical attributes and capabilities and characteristics of the environment.

alleles Two or more alternative forms of a gene that can occupy the same position on paired chromosomes and affect the same trait.

altruism Motivation to help others without expectation of reward; may involve self-denial or self-sacrifice.

ambivalent (resistant) attachment Pattern in which an infant becomes anxious before the primary caregiver leaves, is extremely upset during his or her absence, and both seeks and resists contact on his or her return.

animism Tendency to attribute life to objects that are not alive.

anorexia nervosa Eating disorder characterized by self-starvation and extreme weight loss.

anoxia Lack of oxygen, which may cause brain damage.

Apgar scale Standard measurement of a newborn's condition; it assesses appearance, pulse, grimace, activity, and respiration.

art therapy Therapeutic approach that allows a child to express troubled feelings without words, using art materials and media.

assimilation Piaget's term for incorporation of new information into an existing cognitive structure.

asthma A chronic respiratory disease characterized by sudden attacks of coughing, wheezing, and difficulty in breathing.

attachment Reciprocal, enduring tie between two people—especially between infant and caregiver—each of whom contributes to the quality of the relationship.

attention-deficit/hyperactivity disorder (ADHD) Syndrome characterized by persistent inattention and distractibility, impulsivity, low tolerance for frustration, and inappropriate overactivity.

authoritarian In Baumrind's terminology, parenting style emphasizing control and obedience.

authoritative In Baumrind's terminology, parenting style blending respect for a child's individuality with an effort to instill social values.

autobiographical memory Memory of specific events in one's own life; a type of episodic memory.

autonomy versus shame and doubt Erikson's second stage in psychosocial development, in which children achieve a balance between self-determination and control by others.

autosomes In humans, the 22 pairs of chromosomes not related to sexual expression.

avoidant attachment Pattern in which an infant rarely cries when separated from the primary caregiver and avoids contact on his or her return.

B

basic trust versus basic mistrust Erikson's first stage in psychosocial development, in which infants develop a sense of the reliability of people and objects.

Bayley Scales of Infant and Toddler Development Standardized test of infants' and toddlers' mental and motor development.

behavior therapy Therapeutic approach using principles of learning theory to encourage desired behaviors or eliminate undesired ones; also called *behavior modification*.

behavioral genetics Quantitative study of relative hereditary and environmental influences on behavior.

behaviorism Learning theory that emphasizes the predictable role of environment in causing observable behavior.

behaviorist approach Approach to the study of cognitive development that is concerned with the basic mechanics of learning.

bilingual Fluent in two languages.

bilingual education System of teaching non-English-speaking children in their native language while they learn English and later switching to all-English instruction.

bioecological theory Bronfenbrenner's approach to understanding processes and contexts of child development.

body image Descriptive and evaluative beliefs about one's appearance.

brain growth spurts Periods of rapid brain growth and development.

Brazelton Neonatal Behavioral Assessment Scale (NBAS) Neurological and behavioral test to measure a neonate's responses to the environment.

bulimia nervosa Eating disorder in which a person regularly eats huge quantities of food and then purges the body by laxatives, induced vomiting, fasting, or excessive exercise.

bullying Aggression deliberately and persistently directed against a particular target, or victim, typically one who is weak, vulnerable, and defenseless.

C

canalization Limitation on variance of expression of certain inherited characteristics.

case study Study of a single subject, such as an individual or family.

cell death In brain development, normal elimination of excess cells to achieve more efficient functioning.

central executive In Baddeley's model, element of working memory that controls the processing of information.

central nervous system Brain and spinal cord.

centration In Piaget's theory, tendency of preoperational children to focus on one aspect of a situation and neglect others.

cephalocaudal principle Principle that development proceeds in a head-to-tail direction; that is, that upper parts of the body develop before lower parts of the trunk.

cesarean delivery Delivery of a baby by surgical removal from the uterus.

child development Processes of change and stability in children from conception through adolescence.

child-directed speech (CDS) Form of speech often used in talking to babies or toddlers; includes slow, simplified speech, a high-pitched tone, exaggerated vowel sounds, short words and sentences, and much repetition; also called *parentese*.

childhood depression Mood disorder characterized by such symptoms as a prolonged sense of friendlessness, inability to have fun or concentrate, fatigue, extreme activity or apathy, feelings of worthlessness, weight change, physical complaints, and thoughts of death or suicide.

chromosomes Coils of DNA that consist of genes.

chronic medical conditions Physical, developmental, behavioral, and/or emotional conditions that require special health services.

chronosystem Bronfenbrenner's term for effects of time on other developmental systems.

circular reactions Piaget's term for processes by which an infant learns to reproduce desired occurrences originally discovered by chance.

class inclusion Understanding of the relationship between a whole and its parts.

classical conditioning Learning based on association of a stimulus that does not ordinarily elicit a particular response with another stimulus that does elicit the response.

code mixing Use of elements of two languages, sometimes in the same utterance, by young children in households where both languages are spoken.

code switching Changing one's speech to match the situation, as in people who are bilingual.

cognitive development Pattern of change in mental abilities, such as learning, attention, memory, language, thinking, reasoning, and creativity.

cognitive neuroscience Approach to the study of cognitive development that links brain processes with cognitive ones.

cognitive perspective View that thought processes are central to development.

cognitive-stage theory Piaget's theory that children's cognitive development advances in a series of four stages involving qualitatively distinct types of mental operations.

cohort A group of people born at about the same time.

commitment Marcia's term for personal investment in an occupation or system of beliefs.

committed compliance Kochanska's term for wholehearted obedience of a parent's orders without reminders or lapses.

componential element Sternberg's term for the analytic aspect of intelligence.

conceptual knowledge Acquired interpretive understandings stored in long-term memory.

concordant Term describing tendency of twins to share the same trait or disorder.

concrete operations Third stage of Piagetian cognitive development (approximately from age 7 to 12), during which children develop logical but not abstract thinking.

conduct disorder (CD) Persistent, repetitive pattern of aggressive, antisocial behavior

violating societal norms or the rights of others.

conscience Internal standards of behavior, which usually control one's conduct and produce emotional discomfort when violated.

conservation Piaget's term for awareness that two objects that are equal according to a certain measure remain equal in the face of perceptual alteration so long as nothing has been added to or taken away from either object.

constructive play In Smilansky's terminology, second cognitive level of play, involving use of objects or materials to make something; also called *object play*.

contextual element Sternberg's term for the practical aspect of intelligence.

contextual perspective View of child development that sees the individual as inseparable from the social context.

control group In an experiment, a group of people, similar to those in the experimental group, who do not receive the treatment under study.

conventional morality (or morality of conventional role conformity) Second level in Kohlberg's theory of moral reasoning in which standards of authority figures are internalized.

convergent thinking Thinking aimed at finding the one right answer to a problem.

coregulation Transitional stage in the control of behavior in which parents exercise general supervision and children exercise moment-to-moment self-regulation.

corporal punishment Use of physical force with the intention of causing pain but not injury so as to correct or control behavior.

correlational study Research design intended to discover whether a statistical relationship between variables exists.

crisis Marcia's term for period of conscious decision making related to identity formation.

critical period Specific time when a given event or its absence has a specific impact on development.

cross-modal transfer Ability to use information gained by one sense to guide another.

cross-sectional study Study designed to assess age-related differences, in which people of different ages are assessed on one occasion.

cultural bias Tendency of intelligence tests to include items calling for knowledge or skills more familiar or meaningful to some cultural groups than to others.

cultural socialization Parental practices that teach children about their racial/ethnic heritage and promote cultural practices and cultural pride.

culture A society's or group's total way of life, including customs, traditions, beliefs, values, language, and physical products— all learned behavior passed on from parents to children.

culture-fair Describing an intelligence test that deals with experiences common to various cultures, in an attempt to avoid cultural bias.

culture-free Describing an intelligence test that, if it were possible to design, would have no culturally linked content.

culture-relevant Describing an intelligence test that takes into account the adaptive tasks children face in their culture.

D

decenter In Piaget's terminology, to think simultaneously about several aspects of a situation.

declarative knowledge Acquired factual knowledge stored in long-term memory.

decoding Process of phonetic analysis by which a printed word is converted to spoken form before retrieval from long-term memory.

deductive reasoning Type of logical reasoning that moves from a general premise about a class to a conclusion about a particular member or members of the class.

deferred imitation Piaget's term for reproduction of an observed behavior after the passage of time by calling up a stored symbol of it.

Denver Developmental Screening Test Screening test given to children 1 month to 6 years old to determine whether they are developing normally.

deoxyribonucleic acid (DNA) Chemical that carries inherited instructions for the development of all cellular forms of life.

dependent variable In an experiment, the condition that may or may not change as a result of changes in the independent variable.

depth perception Ability to perceive objects and surfaces in three dimensions.

differentiation Process by which cells acquire specialized structure and function.

difficult children Children with irritable temperament, irregular biological rhythms, and intense emotional responses.

discipline Methods of molding children's character and of teaching them to exercise self-control and engage in acceptable behavior.

dishabituation Increase in responsiveness after presentation of a new stimulus.

disorganized-disoriented attachment Pattern in which an infant, after separation from the primary caregiver, shows contradictory behaviors on his or her return.

divergent thinking Thinking that produces a variety of fresh, diverse possibilities.

dominant inheritance Pattern of inheritance in which, when a child receives different alleles, only the dominant one is expressed.

Down syndrome Chromosomal disorder characterized by moderate-to-severe mental retardation and by such physical signs as a downward-sloping skin fold at the inner corners of the eyes.

dramatic play Play involving imaginary people or situations; also called *fantasy play*, *pretend play*, or *imaginative play*.

drug therapy Administration of drugs to treat emotional disorders.

dual representation hypothesis Proposal that children under age 3 have difficulty grasping spatial relationships because of the need to keep more than one mental representation in mind at the same time.

dynamic systems theory (DST) Thelen's theory, which holds that motor development is a dynamic process of active coordination of multiple systems within the infant in relation to the environment.

dyslexia Developmental disorder in which reading achievement is substantially lower than predicted by IQ or age.

E

early intervention Systematic process of providing services to help families meet young children's developmental needs.

easy children Children with a generally happy temperament, regular biological rhythms, and a readiness to accept new experiences.

ecological theory of perception Theory developed by Eleanor and James Gibson, which describes developing motor and perceptual abilities as interdependent parts of a functional system that guides behavior in varying contexts.

egocentrism Piaget's term for inability to consider another person's point of view; a characteristic of young children's thought.

elaboration Mnemonic strategy of making mental associations involving items to be remembered.

electronic fetal monitoring Mechanical monitoring of fetal heartbeat during labor and delivery.

elicited imitation Research method in which infants or toddlers are induced to imitate a specific series of actions they have seen but not necessarily done before.

embryonic stage Second stage of prenatal development (2 to 8 weeks), characterized by rapid growth and development of major body systems and organs.

emergent literacy Preschoolers' development of skills, knowledge, and attitudes that underlie reading and writing.

emerging adulthood Proposed transitional period between adolescence and adulthood, usually extending from the late teens through the mid-20s.

emotional maltreatment Action or inaction that may cause behavioral, cognitive, emotional, or mental disorders.

emotions Subjective reactions to experience that are associated with physiological and behavioral changes.

empathy Ability to put oneself in another person's place and feel what the other person feels.

encoding Process by which information is prepared for long-term storage and later retrieval.

English-immersion Approach to teaching English as a second language in which instruction is presented only in English.

enrichment Approach to educating the gifted that broadens and deepens knowledge and skills through extra activities, projects, field trips, or mentoring.

enuresis Repeated urination in clothing or in bed.

environment Totality of nonhereditary, or experiential, influences on development.

epigenesis Mechanism that turns genes on or off and determines functions of body cells.

episodic memory Long-term memory of specific experiences or events, linked to time and place.

equilibration Piaget's term for the tendency to seek a stable balance among cognitive elements.

ethnic gloss Overgeneralization about an ethnic or cultural group that blurs or obscures variations within the group or overlaps with other such groups.

ethnic group A group united by ancestry, race, religion, language, and/or national origins, which contribute to a sense of shared identity.

ethnographic study In-depth study of a culture, which uses a combination of methods including participant observation.

ethology Study of distinctive adaptive behaviors of species of animals that have evolved to increase survival of the species.

evolutionary psychology Application of Darwinian principles of natural selection and survival of the fittest to individual behavior.

evolutionary/sociobiological perspective View of human development that focuses on evolutionary and biological bases of social behavior.

executive function Conscious control of thoughts, emotions, and actions to accomplish goals or solve problems.

exosystem Bronfenbrenner's term for linkages between two or more settings, one of which does not contain the child.

experiential element Sternberg's term for the insightful aspect of intelligence.

experiment Rigorously controlled, replicable procedure in which the researcher manipulates variables to assess the effect of one on the other.

experimental group In an experiment, the group receiving the treatment under study.

explicit memory Intentional and conscious memory, generally of facts, names, and events; sometimes called *declarative memory*.

extended family Multigenerational kinship network of parents, children, and other relatives, sometimes living together in an extended-family household.

external memory aids Mnemonic strategies using something outside the person.

F

family therapy Psychological treatment in which a therapist sees the whole family together to analyze patterns of family functioning.

fast mapping Process by which a child absorbs the meaning of a new word after hearing it once or twice in conversation.

fertilization Union of sperm and ovum to produce a zygote; also called *conception*.

fetal alcohol syndrome (FAS) Combination of mental, motor, and developmental abnormalities affecting the offspring of some women who drink during pregnancy.

fetal stage Final stage of prenatal development (from 8 weeks to birth), characterized by increased differentiation of body parts and greatly enlarged body size.

fine motor skills Physical skills that involve the small muscles and eye-hand coordination.

foreclosure Identity status, described by Marcia, in which a person who has not spent time considering alternatives (that is, has not been in crisis) is committed to other people's plans for his or her life.

formal games with rules Organized games with known procedures and penalties.

formal operations In Piaget's theory, final stage of cognitive development, characterized by the ability to think abstractly.

functional play In Smilansky's terminology, lowest cognitive level of play, involving repetitive muscular movements; also called *locomotor play*.

G

gender Significance of being male or female.

gender constancy Awareness that one will always be male or female. Also called *sex-category constancy*.

gender identity Awareness, developed in early childhood, that one is male or female.

gender roles Behaviors, interests, attitudes, skills, and traits that a culture considers appropriate for each sex; differs for males and females.

gender-schema theory Theory, proposed by Bem, that children socialize themselves in their gender roles by developing a mentally organized network of information about what it means to be male or female in a particular culture.

gender stereotypes Preconceived generalizations about male or female role behavior.

gender-typing Socialization process by which children, at an early age, learn appropriate gender roles.

generalized anxiety disorder Anxiety not focused on any single aspect of title.

generic memory Memory that produces scripts of familiar routines to guide behavior.

genes Small segments of DNA located in definite positions on particular chromosomes; functional units of heredity.

genetic code Sequence of bases within the DNA molecule; governs the formation of proteins that determine the structure and functions of living cells.

genetic counseling Clinical service that advises couples of their probable risk of having children with hereditary defects.

genotype Genetic makeup of a person, containing both expressed and unexpressed characteristics.

genotype-environment correlation Tendency of certain genetic and environmental influences to reinforce each other; may be passive, reactive (evocative), or active. Also called *genotype-environment covariance.*

genotype-environment interaction The portion of phenotypic variation that results from the reactions of genetically different individuals to similar environmental conditions.

germinal stage First 2 weeks of prenatal development, characterized by rapid cell division, increasing complexity and differentiation, and implantation in the wall of the uterus.

gonadarche Maturation of testes or ovaries.

goodness of fit Appropriateness of environmental demands and constraints to a child's temperament.

gross motor skills Physical skills that involve the large muscles.

guided participation Participation of an adult in a child's activity in a manner that helps to structure the activity and to bring the child's understanding of it closer to that of the adult.

H

habituation Type of learning in which familiarity with a stimulus reduces, slows, or stops a response.

handedness Preference for using a particular hand.

haptic perception Ability to acquire information about properties of objects, such as size, weight, and texture, by handling them.

heredity Inborn characteristics inherited from the biological parents.

heritability Statistical estimate of contribution of heredity to individual differences in a specific trait within a given population.

heterozygous Possessing differing alleles for a trait.

historical generation A group of people strongly influenced by a major historical event during their formative period.

holophrase Single word that conveys a complete thought.

Home Observation for Measurement of the Environment (HOME) Instrument to measure the influence of the home environment on children's cognitive growth.

homozygous Possessing two identical alleles for a trait.

horizontal décalage Piaget's term for inability to transfer learning about one type of conservation to other types, which causes a child to master different types of conservation tasks at different ages.

hostile aggression Aggressive behavior intended to hurt another person.

hostile attribution bias Tendency for someone to perceive others as trying to hurt him or her and to strike out in retaliation or self-defense.

hypertension High blood pressure.

hypotheses Possible explanations for phenomena, used to predict the outcome of research.

hypothetical-deductive reasoning Ability, believed by Piaget to accompany the stage of formal operations, to develop, consider, and test hypotheses.

I

ideal self Self one would like to be.

identification In Freudian theory, process by which a young child adopts characteristics, beliefs, attitudes, values, and behaviors of the parent of the same sex.

identity In Erikson's terminology, a coherent conception of the self made up of goals, values, and beliefs to which a person is solidly committed.

identity achievement Identity status, described by Marcia, that is characterized by commitment to choices made following a crisis, a period spent in exploring alternatives.

identity diffusion Identity status, described by Marcia, that is characterized by absence of commitment and lack of serious consideration of alternatives.

identity statuses Marcia's term for states of ego development that depend on the presence or absence of crisis and commitment.

identity versus identity confusion Erikson's fifth stage of psychosocial development, in which an adolescent seeks to develop a coherent sense of self, including the role she or he is to play in society. Also called *identity versus role confusion.*

imaginary audience Elkind's term for observer who exists only in an adolescent's mind and is as concerned with the adolescent's thoughts and actions as the adolescent is.

implicit memory Unconscious recall, generally of habits and skills; sometimes called *procedural memory.*

imprinting Instinctive form of learning in which, during a critical period in early development, a young animal forms an attachment to the first moving object it sees, usually the mother.

incomplete dominance Pattern of inheritance in which a child receives two different alleles, resulting in partial expression of a trait.

independent variable In an experiment, the condition over which the experimenter has direct control.

individual differences Differences among children in characteristics, influences, or developmental outcomes.

individual psychotherapy Psychological treatment in which a therapist sees a troubled person one-on-one.

individuation Adolescent's struggle for autonomy and differentiation, or personal identity.

inductive reasoning Type of logical reasoning that moves from particular observations about members of a class to a general conclusion about that class.

inductive techniques Disciplinary techniques designed to induce desirable behavior by appealing to a child's sense of reason and fairness.

industry versus inferiority Erikson's fourth crisis of psychosocial development, in which children must learn the productive skills their culture requires or else face feelings of inferiority.

infant mortality rate Proportion of babies born alive who die within the first year.

infertility Inability to conceive after 12 months of trying.

information-processing approach Approach to the study of cognitive development by observing and analyzing the mental processes involved in perceiving and handling information.

initiative versus guilt Erikson's third stage in psychosocial development, in which children balance the urge to pursue goals with moral reservations that may prevent carrying them out.

instrumental aggression Aggressive behavior used as a means of achieving a goal.

integration Process by which neurons coordinate the activities of muscle groups.

intelligent behavior Behavior that is goal oriented and adaptive to circumstances and conditions of life.

internalization During socialization, process by which children accept societal standards of conduct as their own.

invisible imitation Imitation with parts of one's body that one cannot see.

IQ (intelligence quotient) tests Psychometric tests that seek to measure intelligence by comparing a test-taker's performance with standardized norms.

irreversibility Piaget's term for a preoperational child's failure to understand that an operation can go in two or more directions.

L

laboratory observation Research method in which all participants are observed under the same controlled conditions.

language Communication system based on words and grammar.

language acquisition device (LAD) In Chomsky's terminology, an inborn mechanism that enables children to infer linguistic rules from the language they hear.

lateralization Tendency of each of the brain's hemispheres to have specialized functions.

learning disabilities (LDs) Disorders that interfere with specific aspects of learning and school achievement.

learning perspective View of human development that holds that changes in behavior result from experience or adaptation to the environment.

linguistic speech Verbal expression designed to convey meaning.

literacy Ability to read and write.

longitudinal study Study designed to assess changes in a sample over time.

long-term memory Storage of virtually unlimited capacity that holds information for very long periods.

low birth weight Weight of less than 5½ pounds (2,500 grams) at birth because of prematurity or being small-for-date.

M

macrosystem Bronfenbrenner's term for a society's overall cultural patterns, including values, customs, and social systems.

maturation Unfolding of a universal natural sequence of physical and behavioral changes, including readiness to master new abilities.

mechanistic model Model that views human development as a series of passive, predictable responses to stimuli.

menarche Girl's first menstruation.

mental retardation Significantly subnormal cognitive functioning.

mesosystem Bronfenbrenner's term for linkages between two or more microsystems.

metacognition Awareness of one's own mental processes.

metamemory Understanding of processes of memory.

microgenetic study Study design that enables researchers to directly observe change by repeated testing over a short time.

microsystem Bronfenbrenner's term for a setting in which a child interacts with others on an everyday, face-to-face basis.

mnemonic strategies Techniques to aid memory.

moratorium Identity status, described by Marcia, in which a person is considering alternatives (in crisis) and seems headed for commitment.

mother-infant bond Mother's feeling of close, caring connection with her newborn.

multifactorial transmission Combination of genetic and environmental factors to produce certain complex traits.

mutations Permanent alterations in genes or chromosomes that may produce harmful characteristics.

mutual regulation Process by which infant and caregiver communicate emotional states to each other and respond appropriately.

myelination Process of coating neurons with myelin, a fatty substance that enables faster communication between cells.

N

nativism Theory that human beings have an inborn capacity for language acquisition.

natural, or prepared, childbirth Methods of childbirth that seek to reduce or eliminate use of drugs, enable both parents to participate fully, and control perceptions of pain.

naturalistic observation Research method in which behavior is studied in natural settings without intervention or manipulation.

neglect Failure to meet a dependent's basic needs.

neonatal jaundice Condition, in many newborn babies, caused by immaturity of the liver and evidenced by yellowish appearance; can cause brain damage if not treated promptly.

neonatal period First 4 weeks of life, a time of transition from intrauterine dependency to independent existence.

neonate Newborn baby, up to 4 weeks old.

neurons Nerve cells.

nonnormative Characteristic of an unusual event that happens to a particular person or a typical event that happens at an unusual time of life.

nonshared environmental effects The unique environment in which each child grows up, consisting of distinctive influences or influences that affect one child differently than another.

normative Characteristic of an event that occurs in a similar way for most people in a group.

nuclear family Two-generational kinship, economic, and household unit consisting of one or two parents and their biological children, adopted children, or stepchildren.

O

obesity Extreme overweight in relation to age, sex, height, and body type.

object permanence Piaget's term for the understanding that a person or object still exists when out of sight.

observational learning Learning through watching the behavior of others.

obsessive-compulsive disorder Anxiety aroused by repetitive, intrusive thoughts, images, or impulses, often leading to compulsive ritual behaviors.

operant conditioning (1) Learning based on association of behavior with its consequences. (2) Learning based on reinforcement or punishment.

operational definition Definition stated solely in terms of the operations or procedures used to produce or measure a phenomenon.

oppositional defiant disorder (ODD) Pattern of behavior, persisting into middle childhood, marked by negativity, hostility, and defiance.

organismic model Model that views human development as internally initiated by an active organism, and as occurring in a sequence of qualitatively different stages.

organization (1) Mnemonic strategy of categorizing material to be remembered. (2) Piaget's term for the creation of systems of knowledge.

Otis-Lennon School Ability Test (OLSAT8) Group intelligence test for kindergarten through twelfth grade.

overt, or direct, aggression Aggression that is openly directed at its target.

P

participant observation Research method in which the observer lives with the people or participates in the activity being observed.

parturition Process of uterine, cervical, and other changes, usually lasting about 2 weeks, preceding childbirth.

permissive In Baumrind's terminology, parenting style emphasizing self-expression and self-regulation.

personal fable Elkind's term for conviction that one is special, unique, and not subject to the rules that govern the rest of the world.

phenotype Observable characteristics of a person.

phonetic, or code-emphasis, approach Approach to teaching reading that emphasizes decoding of unfamiliar words.

physical abuse Action taken deliberately to endanger another person, involving potential bodily injury.

physical development Growth of body and brain, including patterns of change in sensory capacities, motor skills, and health.

Piagetian approach Approach to the study of cognitive development that describes qualitative stages in cognitive functioning.

plasticity (1) Modifiability of performance. (2) Modifiability of the brain through experience.

play therapy Therapeutic approach in which a child plays freely while a therapist observes and occasionally comments, asks questions, or makes suggestions.

polygenic inheritance Pattern of inheritance in which multiple genes at different sites on chromosomes affect a complex trait.

postconventional morality (or morality of autonomous moral principles) Third level in Kohlberg's theory of moral reasoning in which people follow internally held moral principles and can decide among conflicting moral standards.

postmature A fetus not yet born as of 42 weeks' gestation.

power assertion Disciplinary strategy designed to discourage undesirable behavior through physical or verbal enforcement of parental control.

pragmatics Practical knowledge needed to use language for communicative purposes.

preconventional morality First level of Kohlberg's theory of moral reasoning in which control is external and rules are obeyed in order to gain rewards or avoid punishment or out of self-interest.

prejudice Unfavorable attitude toward members of certain groups outside one's own, especially racial or ethnic groups.

prelinguistic speech Forerunner of linguistic speech; utterance of sounds that are not words. Includes crying, cooing, babbling, and accidental and deliberate imitation of sounds without understanding their meaning.

preoperational stage In Piaget's theory, the second major stage of cognitive development, in which children become more sophisticated in their use of symbolic thought but are not yet able to use logic.

pretend play Play involving imaginary people or situations; also called *fantasy play, dramatic play,* or *imaginary play.*

preterm (premature) infants Infants born before completing the 37th week of gestation.

primary sex characteristics Organs directly related to reproduction, which enlarge and mature during adolescence.

private speech Talking aloud to oneself with no intent to communicate with others.

procedural knowledge Acquired skills stored in long-term memory.

prosocial behavior Any voluntary behavior intended to help others.

protective factors Factors that reduce the impact of early stress or potentially negative influences and tend to predict positive outcomes.

proximodistal principle Principle that development proceeds from within to without; that is, that parts of the body near the center develop before the extremities.

psychoanalytic perspective View of human development as being shaped by unconscious forces.

psychological aggression Verbal attack by a parent that may result in psychological harm to a child.

psychometric approach Approach to the study of cognitive development that seeks to measure the quantity of intelligence a person possesses.

psychosexual development In Freudian theory, an unvarying sequence of stages of personality development during infancy, childhood, and adolescence, in which gratification shifts from the mouth to the anus and then to the genitals.

psychosocial development (1) In Erikson's eight-stage theory, the socially and culturally influenced process of development of the ego, or self. (2) Pattern of change in emotions, personality, and social relationships.

puberty Process by which a person attains sexual maturity and the ability to reproduce.

punishment In operant conditioning, a process that weakens and discourages repetition of a behavior.

Q

qualitative change Change in kind, structure, or organization, such as the change from nonverbal to verbal communication.

qualitative research Research that involves the interpretation of nonnumerical data, such as subjective experiences, feelings, or beliefs.

quantitative change Change in number or amount, such as in height, weight, or size of vocabulary.

quantitative research Research that deals with objectively measurable data.

R

random assignment Assignment of participants in an experiment to groups in such a way that each person has an equal chance of being placed in any group.

random selection Selection of a sample in such a way that each person in a population has an equal and independent chance of being chosen.

reaction range Potential variability, depending on environmental conditions, in the expression of a hereditary trait.

real self Self one actually is.

recall Ability to reproduce material from memory.

receptive cooperation Kochanska's term for eager willingness to cooperate harmoniously with a parent in daily interactions, including routines, chores, hygiene, and play.

recessive inheritance Pattern of inheritance in which a child receives identical recessive alleles, resulting in expression of a nondominant trait.

reciprocal determinism Bandura's concept that behavior is determined bidirectionally, by the child and the environment acting on each other.

recognition Ability to identify a previously encountered stimulus.

reflex behavior Automatic, involuntary, innate response to stimulation.

rehearsal Mnemonic strategy to keep an item in working memory through conscious repetition.

reinforcement In operant conditioning, a process that strengthens and encourages repetition of a desired behavior.

relational, or social, aggression Aggression aimed at damaging or interfering with another person's relationships, reputation, or psychological well-being; can be overt or covert.

representational ability Piaget's term for capacity to store mental images or symbols of objects and events.

representational mappings In neo-Piagetian terminology, second stage in development of self-definition, in which a child makes logical connections between aspects of the self but still sees these characteristics in all-or-nothing terms.

representational systems In neo-Piagetian terminology, the third stage in development of self-definition, characterized by breadth, balance, and the integration and assessment of various aspects of the self.

resilient children Children who weather adverse circumstances, function well despite challenges or threats, or bounce back from traumatic events.

retrieval Process by which information is accessed or recalled from memory storage.

risk factors Conditions that increase the likelihood of a negative developmental outcome.

rough-and-tumble play Vigorous play involving wrestling, hitting, and chasing, often accompanied by laughing and screaming.

S

sample Group of participants chosen to represent the entire population under study.

scaffolding Temporary support to help a child master a task.

schemes Piaget's term for organized patterns of thought and behavior used in particular situations.

schizophrenia Neurological disorder marked by loss of contact with reality; symptoms include hallucinations and delusions.

school phobia Unrealistic fear of going to school; may be a form of *separation anxiety disorder* or *social phobia.*

scientific method System of established principles and processes of scientific inquiry, which includes identifying a problem to be studied, formulating a hypothesis to be tested by research, collecting data, analyzing the data, and disseminating findings.

script General remembered outline of a familiar, repeated event, used to guide behavior.

secondary sex characteristics Physiological signs of sexual maturation (such as breast development and growth of body hair) that do not involve the sex organs.

secular trend Trend that can be seen only by observing several generations, such as the trend toward earlier attainment of adult height and sexual maturity, which began a century ago.

secure attachment Pattern in which an infant cries or protests when the primary caregiver leaves and actively seeks out the caregiver on his or her return.

self-awareness Realization that one's existence and functioning are separate from those of other people and things.

self-concept Sense of self; descriptive and evaluative mental picture of one's abilities and traits.

self-conscious emotions Emotions, such as embarrassment, empathy, and envy, that depend on self-awareness.

self-definition Cluster of characteristics used to describe oneself.

self-efficacy Sense of one's capability to master challenges and achieve goals.

self-esteem Judgment a person makes about his or her self-worth.

self-evaluative emotions Emotions, such as pride, shame, and guilt, that depend on both self-awareness and knowledge of socially accepted standards of behavior.

self-regulation A person's independent control of behavior to conform to understood social expectations.

sensitive periods Times in development when a person is particularly open to certain kinds of experiences.

sensorimotor stage In Piaget's theory, first stage in cognitive development, during which infants learn through senses and motor activity.

sensory memory Initial, brief, temporary storage of sensory information.

separation anxiety Distress shown by someone, typically an infant, when a familiar caregiver leaves.

separation anxiety disorder Condition involving excessive, prolonged anxiety concerning separation from home or from people to whom a child is attached.

sequential study Study design that combines cross-sectional and longitudinal techniques.

seriation Ability to order items along a dimension.

sex chromosomes Pair of chromosomes that determines sex: XX in the normal human female, XY in the normal human male.

sex-linked inheritance Pattern of inheritance in which certain characteristics carried on the X chromosome inherited from the mother are transmitted differently to her male and female offspring.

sexual abuse Physical or psychologically harmful sexual activity, or any sexual activity involving a child and an older person.

sexual orientation Gender focus of consistent sexual, romantic, and affectionate interest, either heterosexual, homosexual, or bisexual.

sexually transmitted diseases (STDs) Diseases spread by sexual contact.

single representations In neo-Piagetian terminology, first stage in development of self-definition, in which children describe themselves in terms of individual, unconnected characteristics and in all-or-nothing terms.

situational compliance Kochanska's term for obedience of a parent's orders only in the presence of signs of ongoing parental control.

slow-to-warm-up children Children whose temperament is generally mild but who are hesitant about accepting new experiences.

small-for-date (small-for-gestational-age) infants Infants whose birth weight is less than that of 90 percent of babies of the same gestational age, as a result of slow fetal growth.

social capital Family and community resources on which a person or family can draw.

social cognition Ability to understand that other people have mental states and to gauge their feelings and intentions.

social cognitive theory Albert Bandura's expansion of social learning theory; holds that children learn gender roles through socialization.

social construction Concept about the nature of reality based on societally shared perceptions or assumptions.

social-contextual approach Approach to the study of cognitive development by focusing on environmental influences, particularly parents and other caregivers.

social interaction model Model, based on Vygotsky's sociocultural theory, which proposes that children construct autobiographical memories through conversation with adults about shared events.

social learning theory Theory that behaviors are learned by observing and imitating models. Also called *social cognitive theory.*

social phobia Extreme fear and/or avoidance of social situations.

social promotion Policy of automatically promoting children even if they do not meet academic standards.

social referencing Understanding an ambiguous situation by seeking out another person's perception of it.

social speech Speech intended to be understood by a listener.

socialization Development of habits, skills, values, and motives shared by responsible, productive members of a society.

sociocultural theory Vygotsky's theory of how contextual factors affect children's development.

socioeconomic status (SES) Combination of economic and social factors, including income, education, and occupation, that describe an individual or family.

spermarche Boy's first ejaculation.

spontaneous abortion Natural expulsion from the uterus of a embryo that cannot survive outside the womb; also called *miscarriage.*

Stanford-Binet Intelligence Scales Individual intelligence test for ages 2 and up, used to measure knowledge, quantitative reasoning, visual-spatial processing, and working memory.

state of arousal Infant's physiological and behavioral status at a given moment in the periodic daily cycle of wakefulness, sleep, and activity.

stillbirth Death of a fetus at or after the 20th week of gestation.

"still-face" paradigm Research procedure used to measure mutual regulation in infants 2 to 9 months old.

storage Retention of information in memory for future use.

Strange Situation Laboratory technique used to study infant attachment.

stranger anxiety Wariness of strange people and places, shown by some infants from age 6 to 12 months.

stuttering Involuntary, frequent repetition or prolongation of sounds or syllables.

substance abuse Repeated, harmful use of a substance, usually alcohol or other drugs.

substance dependence Addiction (physical or psychological, or both) to a harmful substance.

sudden infant death syndrome (SIDS) Sudden and unexplained death of an apparently healthy infant.

symbolic function Piaget's term for ability to use mental representations (words, numbers, or images) to which a child has attached meaning.

syntax Rules for forming sentences in a particular language.

systems of action Increasingly complex combinations of motor skills that permit a wider or more precise range of movement and more control of the environment.

T

tacit knowledge Sternberg's term for information that is not formally taught or openly expressed but is necessary to get ahead.

telegraphic speech Early form of sentence use consisting of only a few essential words.

temperament Characteristic disposition or style of approaching and reacting to situations.

teratogenic Capable of causing birth defects.

theory Coherent set of logically related concepts that seeks to organize, explain, and predict data.

theory of mind Awareness and understanding of mental processes.

theory of multiple intelligences Gardner's theory that each person has several distinct forms of intelligence.

theory of sexual selection Darwinian theory, which holds that selection of sexual partners is influenced by the differing reproductive pressures that early men and women confronted in the struggle for survival of the species.

transduction In Piaget's terminology, preoperational child's tendency to mentally link particular experiences, whether or not there is logically a causal relationship.

transitive inference Understanding of the relationship between two objects by knowing the relationship of each to a third object.

triarchic theory of intelligence Sternberg's theory describing three types of intelligence: componential (analytical ability), experiential (insight and originality), and contextual (practical thinking).

two-way, or dual-language, learning Approach to second-language education in which English speakers and non-English speakers learn together in their own and each other's languages.

U

ultrasound Prenatal medical procedure using high-frequency sound waves to detect the outline of a fetus and its movements, so as to determine whether a pregnancy is progressing normally.

V

violation-of-expectations Research method in which dishabituation to a stimulus that conflicts with experience is taken as evidence that an infant recognizes the new stimulus as surprising.

visible imitation Imitation with parts of one's body that one can see.

visual cliff Apparatus designed to give an illusion of depth and used to assess depth perception in infants.

visual guidance Use of the eyes to guide movements of the hands or other parts of the body.

visual preference Tendency of infants to spend more time looking at one sight than another.

visual recognition memory Ability to distinguish a familiar visual stimulus from an unfamiliar one when shown both at the same time.

visually based retrieval Process of retrieving the sound of a printed word on seeing the word as a whole.

W

Wechsler Intelligence Scale for Children (WISC-III) Individual intelligence test for schoolchildren that yields verbal and performance scores as well as a combined score.

Wechsler Preschool and Primary Scale of Intelligence, Revised (WPPSI-III) Individual intelligence test for children ages 2½ to 7 that yields verbal and performance scores as well as a combined score.

whole-language approach Approach to teaching reading that emphasizes visual retrieval and use of contextual clues.

withdrawal of love Disciplinary strategy that involves ignoring, isolating, or showing dislike for a child.

working memory Short-term storage of information being actively processed.

Z

zone of proximal development (ZPD) Vygotsky's term for the difference between what a child can do alone and what the child can do with help.

zygote One-celled organism resulting from fertilization.

Bibliography

Aaron, V., Parker, K. D., Ortega, S., & Calhoun, T. (1999). The extended family as a source of support among African Americans. *Challenge: A Journal of Research on African American Men, 10*(2), 23–36.

Abbey, A., Andrews, F. M., & Halman, J. (1992). Infertility and subjective well-being: The mediating roles of self-esteem, internal control, and interpersonal conflict. *Journal of Marriage and the Family, 54,* 408–417.

Aber, J. L., Brown, J. L., & Jones, S. M. (2003). Developmental trajectories toward violence in middle childhood: Course, demographic differences, and response to school-based intervention. *Developmental Psychology, 39,* 324–348.

Abma, J. C., Chandra, A., Mosher, W. D., Peterson, L., & Piccinino, L. (1997). Fertility, family planning, and women's health: New data from the 1995 National Survey of Family Growth. *Vital Health Statistics, 23*(19). Washington, DC: National Center for Health Statistics.

Abma, J. C., Martinez, G. M., Mosher, W. D., & Dawson, B. S. (2004). Teenagers in the United States: Sexual activity, contraceptive use, and childbearing, 2002. *Vital Health Statistics, 23*(24). Washington, DC: National Center for Health Statistics.

Abramovitch, R., Corter, C., & Lando, B. (1979). Sibling interaction in the home. *Child Development, 50,* 997–1003.

Abramovitch, R., Corter, C., Pepler, D., & Stanhope, L. (1986). Sibling and peer interactions: A final follow-up and comparison. *Child Development, 57,* 217–229.

Abramovitch, R., Pepler, D., & Corter, C. (1982). Patterns of sibling interaction among preschool-age children. In M. E. Lamb (Ed.), *Sibling relationships: Their nature and significance across the lifespan.* Hillsdale, NJ: Erlbaum.

Achter, J. A., & Lubinski, D. (2003). Fostering exceptional development in intellectually talented populations. In W. B. Walsh (Ed.), *Counseling psychology and optimal human functioning* (pp. 279–296). Mahwah, NJ: Erlbaum.

Ackerman, B. P., Kogos, J., Youngstrom, E., Schoff, K., & Izard, C. (1999). Family instability and the problem behaviors of children from economically disadvantaged families. *Developmental Psychology, 35*(1), 258–268.

Ackerman, M. J., Siu, B. L., Sturner, W. Q., Tester, D. J., Valdivia, C. R., Makielski, J. C., et al. (2001). Postmortem molecular analysis of SCN5A defects in sudden infant death syndrome. *Journal of the American Medical Association, 286,* 2264–2269.

Acosta, M. T., Arcos-Burgos, M., & Muenke, M. (2004). Attention deficit/hyperactivity disorder (ADHD): Complex phenotype, simple genotype? *Genetics in Medicine, 6,* 1–15.

ACT for Youth Upstate Center of Excellence. (2002). *Adolescent brain development. Research facts and findings* [A collaboration of Cornell University, University of Rochester, and the NYS Center for School Safety]. Retrieved March 23, 2004, from http://www.human.cornell.edu/actforyouth

Adam, E. K., Gunnar, M. R., & Tanaka, A. (2004). Adult attachment, parent emotion, and observed parenting behavior: Mediator and moderator models. *Child Development, 75,* 110–122.

Adams, L. A., & Rickert, V. I. (1989). Reducing bedtime tantrums: Comparison between positive routines and graduated extinction. *Pediatrics, 84,* 756–761.

Adams, R., & Laursen, B. (2001). The organization and dynamics of adolescent conflict with parents and friends. *Journal of Marriage and the Family, 63,* 97–110.

Adler, P. A., & Adler, P. (1995). Dynamics of inclusion and exclusion in preadolescent cliques. *Social Psychology Quarterly, 58,* 145–162.

Adolph, K. E. (1997). Learning in the development of infant locomotion. *Monographs of the Society for Research in Child Development, 62*(3, Serial No. 251).

Adolph, K. E. (2000). Specificity of learning: Why infants fall over a veritable cliff. *Psychological Science, 11,* 290–295.

Adolph, K. E., & Eppler, M. A. (2002). Flexibility and specificity in infant motor skill acquisition. In J. Fagen & H. Hayne (Eds.), *Progress in infancy research* (Vol. 2, pp. 121–167). Mahwah, NJ: Erlbaum.

Adolph, K. E., Vereijken, B., & Shrout, P. E. (2003). What changes in infant walking and why. *Child Development, 74,* 475–497.

Agosin, M. (1999). Pirate, conjurer, feminist. In J. Rodden (Ed.), *Conversations with Isabel Allende* (pp. 35–47). Austin: University of Texas Press.

Ahnert, L., Gunnar, M. R., Lamb, M. E., & Barthel, M. (2004). Transition to child care: Associations with infant-mother attachment, infant negative emotion and corticol elevation. *Child Development, 75,* 639–650.

Ahnert, L., Pinquart, M., & Lamb, M. E. (2006). Security of children's relationships with nonparental care providers: A meta-analysis. *Child Development, 74,* 664–679.

Ahrons, C. R., & Tanner, J. L. (2003). Adult children and their fathers: Relationship changes 20 years after parental divorce. *Family Relations, 52,* 340–351.

Ainsworth, M. D. S. (1967). *Infancy in Uganda: Infant care and the growth of love.* Baltimore: Johns Hopkins University Press.

Ainsworth, M. D. S., Blehar, M. C., Waters, E., & Wall, S. (1978). *Patterns of attachment: A psychological study of the strange situation.* Hillsdale, NJ: Erlbaum.

Akinbami, L. (2006). The state of childhood asthma, United States, 1980–2005. *Advance Data from Vital and Health Statistics, 381.* Hyattsville, MD: National Center for Health Statistics.

Alaimo, K., Olson, C. M., & Frongillo, E. A. (2001). Food insufficiency and American school-aged children's cognitive, academic, and psychosocial development. *Pediatrics, 108,* 44–53.

Alan Guttmacher Institute (AGI). (1994). *Sex and America's teenagers.* New York: Author.

Alan Guttmacher Institute (AGI). (1999). *Facts in brief: Teen sex and pregnancy.* Retrieved January 31, 2000, from http://www.agi_usa. org/pubs/ fb_teen_sex.html#sfd

Alati, R., Al Mamun, A., Williams, G. M., O'Callaghan, M., Najman, J. M., & Bor, W. (2006). In utero alcohol exposure and prediction of alcohol disorders in early adulthood: A birth cohort study. *Archives of General Psychiatry, 63*(9), 1009–1016.

Albanese, A., & Stanhope, R. (1993). Growth and metabolic data following growth hormone treatment of children with intrauterine growth retardation. *Hormone Research, 39,* 8–12.

Alexander, K. L., Entwisle, D. R., & Dauber, S. L. (1993). First-grade classroom behavior: Its short- and long-term consequences for school performance. *Child Development, 64,* 801–814.

Allen, G. L., & Ondracek, P. J. (1995). Age-sensitive cognitive abilities related to children's acquisition of spatial knowledge. *Developmental Psychology, 31,* 934–945.

Allen, J. P., McElhaney, K. B., Land, D. J., Kuperminc, G. P., Moore, C. W., O'Beirner-Kelly, H., et al. (2003). A secure base in adolescence: Markers of attachment security in the mother-adolescent relationship. *Child Development, 74,* 292–307.

Allen, J. P., & Philliber, S. (2001). Who benefits most from a broadly targeted prevention program? Differential efficacy across populations in the Teen Outreach Program. *Journal of Community Psychology, 29,* 637–655.

Allen, K. R., Blieszner, R., & Roberto, K. A. (2000). Families in the middle and later years: A review and critique of research in the 1990s. *Journal of Marriage and the Family, 62,* 911–926.

Allende, I. (1995). *Paula* (M. S. Peden, Trans.). New York: HarperCollins.

Al-Oballi Kridli, S. (2002). Health beliefs and practices among Arab women. *MCN, The American Journal of Maternal/Child Nursing, 27,* 178–182.

Als, H., Duffy, F. H., McAnulty, G. B., Rivkin, M. J., Vajapeyam, S., Mulkern, R. V., et al. (2004). Early experience alters brain function and structure. *Pediatrics, 113,* 846–857.

Alsaker, F. D. (1992). Pubertal timing, overweight, and psychological adjustment. *Journal of Early Adolescence, 12*(4), 396–419.

Altschul, I., Oyserman, D., & Bybee, D. (2006). Racial-ethnic identity in mid-adolescence: Content and change as predictors of academic achievement. *Child Development, 77,* 1155–1169.

Amato, P. R. (2003). Reconciling divergent perspectives: Judith Wallerstein, quantitative family research, and children of divorce. *Family Relations, 52,* 332–339.

Amato, P. R. (2005). The impact of family formation change on the cognitive, social, and emotional well-being of the next generation. *Future of Children, 15,* 75–96.

Amato, P. R., & Booth, A. (1997). *A generation at risk: Growing up in an era of family upheaval.* Cambridge, MA: Harvard University Press.

Amato, P. R., & Cheadle, J. (2005). The long reach of divorce: Divorce and child well-being across three generations. *Journal of Marriage and Family, 67,* 191–206.

Amato, P. R., & Gilbreth, J. G. (1999). Non-resident fathers and children's well-being: A meta-analysis. *Journal of Marriage and the Family, 61,* 557–573.

American Academy of Child and Adolescent Psychiatry (AACAP). (1997). *Children's sleep problems.* Fact sheet no. 34. Retrieved from http://www.aacap.org/cs/root/facts_for_families/childrens_sleep_problems

American Academy of Child and Adolescent Psychiatry (AACAP). (2002). Children and the news. *Facts for Families* #67. Retrieved April 24, 2005, from http://www.aacap.org/publications/ factsfam/67.htm

American Academy of Child and Adolescent Psychiatry (AACAP). (2003). Talking to children about terrorism and war. *Facts for Families* #87. [Online]. Retrieved April 22, 2005, from http://www.aacap.org/publications/factsfam/87.htm

American Academy of Pediatrics (AAP). (1986). *Positive approaches to day care dilemmas: How to make it work.* Elk Grove Village, IL: Author.

American Academy of Pediatrics (AAP). (1992, Spring). Bedtime doesn't have to be a struggle. *Healthy Kids,* pp. 4–10.

American Academy of Pediatrics (AAP). (2000). Shaken baby syndrome. Retrieved February 17, 2007, from http://www.medem.com/search/article_display.cfm?path=\\TANQUERAY\M_ContentItem&mstr=/M_ContentItem/ZZZM8JMMH4C.html&soc=AAP&srch_typ=NAV_SERCH

American Academy of Pediatrics (AAP). (2004, September 30). American Academy of Pediatrics (AAP) supports Institute of Medicine's (IOM) childhood obesity recommendations. Press release.

American Academy of Pediatrics (AAP) & Canadian Paediatric Society. (2000). Prevention and management of pain and stress in the neonate. *Pediatrics, 105*(2), 454–461.

American Academy of Pediatrics (AAP) & Center to Prevent Handgun Violence. (1994). *Keep your family safe from firearm injury.* Washington, DC: Center to Prevent Handgun Violence.

American Academy of Pediatrics (AAP) Committee on Accident and Poison Prevention. (1988). Snowmobile statement. *Pediatrics, 82,* 798–799.

American Academy of Pediatrics (AAP) Committee on Adolescence. (1994). Sexually transmitted diseases. *Pediatrics, 94,* 568–572.

American Academy of Pediatrics (AAP) Committee on Adolescence. (1999). Adolescent pregnancy—Current trends and issues: 1998. *Pediatrics, 103,* 516–520.

American Academy of Pediatrics (AAP) Committee on Adolescence. (2000). Suicide and suicide attempts in adolescents. *Pediatrics, 105*(4), 871–874.

American Academy of Pediatrics (AAP) Committee on Adolescence. (2001). Condom use by adolescents. *Pediatrics, 107*(6), 1463–1469.

American Academy of Pediatrics (AAP) Committee on Adolescence. (2003). Policy statement: Identifying and treating eating disorders. *Pediatrics, 111,* 204–211.

American Academy of Pediatrics (AAP) Committee on Adolescence & Committee on Early Childhood, Adoption, and Dependent Care. (2001). Care of adolescent parents and their children. *Pediatrics, 107,* 429–434.

American Academy of Pediatrics (AAP) Committee on Bioethics. (1992, July). Ethical issues in surrogate motherhood. *AAP News,* 14–15.

American Academy of Pediatrics (AAP) Committee on Bioethics. (2001). Ethical issues with genetic testing in pediatrics. *Pediatrics, 107*(6), 1451–1455.

American Academy of Pediatrics (AAP) Committee on Child Abuse and Neglect. (2001). Shaken baby syndrome: Rotational cranial injuries—Technical report. *Pediatrics, 108,* 206–210.

American Academy of Pediatrics (AAP) Committee on Children with Disabilities. (2001). The pediatrician's role in the diagnosis and management of autistic spectrum disorder in children. *Pediatrics, 107*(5), 1221–1226.

American Academy of Pediatrics (AAP) Committee on Children with Disabilities & Committee on Drugs (1996). Medication for children with attentional disorders. *Pediatrics, 98,* 301–304.

American Academy of Pediatrics (AAP) Committee on Community Health Services. (1996). Health needs of homeless children and families. *Pediatrics, 88,* 789–791.

American Academy of Pediatrics (AAP) Committee on Drugs. (1994). The transfer of drugs and other chemicals into human milk. *Pediatrics, 93,* 137–150.

American Academy of Pediatrics (AAP) Committee on Drugs. (2000). Use of psychoactive medication during pregnancy and possible effects on the fetus and newborn. *Pediatrics, 105,* 880–887.

American Academy of Pediatrics (AAP) Committee on Environmental Health. (1998). Screening for elevated blood lead levels. *Pediatrics, 101,* 1072–1078.

American Academy of Pediatrics (AAP) Committee on Environmental Health. (2005). Lead exposure in children: Prevention, detection, and management. *Pediatrics, 116,* 1036–1046.

American Academy of Pediatrics (AAP) Committee on Fetus and Newborn & American College of Obstetricians and Gynecologists (ACOG) Committee on Obstetric Practice. (1996). Use and abuse of the Apgar score. *Pediatrics, 98,* 141–142.

American Academy of Pediatrics (AAP) Committee on Fetus and Newborn & American College of Obstetricians and Gynecologists (ACOG) Committee on Obstetric Practice. (2006). The Apgar score. *Pediatrics, 117,* 1444–1447.

American Academy of Pediatrics (AAP) Committee on Genetics. (1999). Folic acid for the prevention of neural tube defects. *Pediatrics, 104,* 325–327.

American Academy of Pediatrics (AAP) Committee on Infectious Diseases. (2000). Recommended childhood immunization schedule—United States, January–December, 2000. *Pediatrics, 105,* 148–151.

American Academy of Pediatrics (AAP) Committee on Injury and Poison Prevention. (1995). Bicycle helmets. *Pediatrics, 95,* 609–610.

American Academy of Pediatrics (AAP) Committee on Injury and Poison Prevention. (2000). Firearm-related injuries affecting the pediatric population. *Pediatrics, 105*(4), 888–895.

American Academy of Pediatrics (AAP) Committee on Injury and Poison Prevention. (2001a). Bicycle helmets. *Pediatrics, 108*(4), 1030–1032.

American Academy of Pediatrics (AAP) Committee on Injury and Poison Prevention. (2001b). Injuries associated with infant walkers. *Pediatrics, 108*(3), 790–792.

American Academy of Pediatrics (AAP) Committee on Injury and Poison Prevention & Committee on Sports Medicine and Fitness. (1999). Policy statement: Trampolines at home, school, and recreational centers. *Pediatrics, 103*, 1053–1056.

American Academy of Pediatrics (AAP) Committee on Nutrition. (1992). Statement on cholesterol. *Pediatrics, 90*, 469–473.

American Academy of Pediatrics (AAP) Committee on Nutrition. (2003). Prevention of pediatric overweight and obesity. *Pediatrics, 112*, 424–430.

American Academy of Pediatrics (AAP) Committee on Pediatric AIDS. (2000). Education of children with human immunodeficiency virus infection. *Pediatrics, 105*, 1358–1360.

American Academy of Pediatrics (AAP) Committee on Pediatric Research. (2000). Race/ethnicity, gender, socioeconomic status—Research exploring their effects on child health: A subject review. *Pediatrics, 105*, 1349–1351.

American Academy of Pediatrics (AAP) Committee on Practice and Ambulatory Medicine and Section on Ophthalmology. (1996). Eye examination and vision screening in infants, children, and young adults. *Pediatrics, 98*, 153–157.

American Academy of Pediatrics (AAP) Committee on Practice and Ambulatory Medicine and Section on Ophthalmology. (2002). Use of photoscreening for children's vision screening. *Pediatrics, 109*, 524–525.

American Academy of Pediatrics (AAP) Committee on Psychosocial Aspects of Child and Family Health. (1998). Guidance for effective discipline. *Pediatrics, 101*, 723–728.

American Academy of Pediatrics (AAP) Committee on Psychosocial Aspects of Child and Family Health. (2002). Coparent or second-parent adoption by same-sex parents. *Pediatrics, 109*(2), 339–340.

American Academy of Pediatrics (AAP) Committee on Psychosocial Aspects of Child and Family Health & Committee on Adolescence. (2001). Sexuality education for children and adolescence. *Pediatrics, 108*(2), 498–502.

American Academy of Pediatrics (AAP) Committee on Public Education. (2001). Policy statement: Children, adolescents, and television. *Pediatrics, 107*, 423–426.

American Academy of Pediatrics (AAP) Committee on Quality Improvement. (2002). *Making advances against jaundice in infant care (MAJIC)*. Retrieved October 25, 2002, from http://www/ aap.org/ visit/majic.htm

American Academy of Pediatrics (AAP) Committee on Sports Medicine and Fitness.

(1992). Fitness, activity, and sports participation in the preschool child. *Pediatrics, 90*, 1002–1004.

American Academy of Pediatrics (AAP) Committee on Sports Medicine and Fitness. (1997). Participation in boxing by children, adolescents, and young adults. *Pediatrics, 99*, 134–135.

American Academy of Pediatrics (AAP) Committee on Sports Medicine and Fitness. (1999). Human immunodeficiency virus and other blood-borne viral pathogens in the athletic setting. *Pediatrics, 104*(6), 1400–1403.

American Academy of Pediatrics (AAP) Committee on Sports Medicine and Fitness. (2000). Injuries in youth soccer: A subject review. *Pediatrics, 105*(3), 659–660.

American Academy of Pediatrics (AAP) Committee on Sports Medicine and Fitness. (2001). Risk of injury from baseball and softball in children. *Pediatrics, 107*(4), 782–784.

American Academy of Pediatrics (AAP) Committee on Substance Abuse. (2001). Tobacco's toll: Implications for the pediatrician. *Pediatrics, 107*, 794–798.

American Academy of Pediatrics (AAP) Committee on Substance Abuse & Committee on Children with Disabilities. (1993). Fetal alcohol syndrome and fetal alcohol effects. *Pediatrics, 91*, 1004–1006.

American Academy of Pediatrics (AAP) Newborn Screening Task Force (2000). Serving the family from birth to the medical home. A report from the Newborn Screening Task Force convened in Washington, DC, May 10–11, 1999. *Pediatrics, 106*(2), Part 2 of 3.

American Academy of Pediatrics (AAP) Section on Breastfeeding. (2005). Breastfeeding and the use of human milk. *Pediatrics, 115*, 496–506.

American Academy of Pediatrics (AAP) Task Force on Infant Sleep Position and Sudden Infant Death Syndrome. (2000). Changing concepts of sudden infant death syndrome: Implications for infant sleeping environment and sleep position. *Pediatrics, 105*, 650–656.

American Academy of Pediatrics (AAP) Task Force on Sudden Infant Death Syndrome. (2005). The changing concept of sudden infant death syndrome: Diagnostic coding shifts, controversies regarding sleeping environment, and new variables to consider in reducing risk. *Pediatrics, 116*, 1245–1255.

American College of Obstetrics and Gynecology (ACOG). (1994). *Exercise during pregnancy and the postpartum pregnancy* (Technical Bulletin No. 189). Washington DC: Author.

American Heart Association, Gidding, S. S., Dennison, B. A., Birch, L. L., Daniels, S. R., Gilman, M. W., et al. (2006). Dietary recommendations for children and adolescents: A guide for practitioners. *Pediatrics, 117*, 544–559.

American Psychiatric Association (APA). (1994). *Diagnostic and statistical manual of mental disorders* (4th ed.). Washington, DC: Author.

American Psychiatric Association (APA). (2000). *Diagnostic and statistical manual of mental disorders* (4th ed., Text Revision). Washington, DC: Author.

American Psychological Association. (undated). *Answers to your questions about sexual orientation and homosexuality* [Brochure]. Washington, DC: Author.

American Psychological Association (APA). (2002). Ethical principles of psychologists and code of conduct. *American Psychologist, 57*, 1060–1073.

American Psychological Association (APA). (2004, July). *Resolution on sexual orientation, parents, and children*. Retrieved January 23, 2007, from http://www.apa.org/ pi/lgbc/policy/parents.html

American Psychological Association (APA) & American Academy of Pediatrics (AAP). (1996). *Raising children to resist violence: What you can do* [Brochure]. Retrieved from http://www.apa.org/ pubinfo/apaaap.html

American Public Health Association. (2004). Disparities in infant mortality. Fact sheet. [Online]. Retrieved from: http://www .medscape.com/viewarticle/472721.

Ames, E. W. (1997). *The development of Romanian orphanage children adopted to Canada: Final report* (National Welfare Grants Program, Human Resources Development, Canada). Burnaby, BC, Canada: Simon Fraser University, Psychology Department.

Amsel, E., Goodman, G., Savoie, D., & Clark, M. (1996). The development of reasoning about causal and noncausal influences on levers. *Child Development, 67*, 1624–1646.

Ananth, C. V., Liu, S., Kinzler, W. L., & Kramer, M. S. (2005). Stillbirths in the United States, 1981–2000: An age, period, and cohort analysis. *American Journal of Public Health, 95*, 2213–2217.

Anastasi, A. (1988). *Psychological testing* (6th ed.). New York: Macmillan.

Anastasi, A., & Schaefer, C. E. (1971). Note on concepts of creativity and intelligence. *Journal of Creative Behavior, 3*, 113–116.

Andersen, A. E. (1995). Eating disorders in males. In K. D. Brownell & C. G. Fairburn (Eds.), *Eating disorders and obesity: A comprehensive handbook* (pp. 177–187). New York: Guilford.

Anderson, A. H., Clark, A., & Mullin, J. (1994). Interactive communication between children: Learning how to make language work in dialog. *Journal of Child Language, 21*, 439–463.

Anderson, A. M., Wohlfahrt, J., Christens, P., Olsen, J., & Melbye, M. (2000). Maternal age and fetal loss: Population based register linkage study. *British Medical Journal, 320*, 1708–1712.

Anderson, C. (2000). *The impact of interactive violence on children.* Statement before the Senate Committee on Commerce, Science, and Transportation, 106th Congress, 1st session.

Anderson, C. A., Berkowitz, L., Donnerstein, E., Huesmann, L. R., Johnson, J. D., Linz, D., et al. (2003). The influence of media violence on youth. *Psychological Science in the Public Interest, 4,* 81–110.

Anderson, D., & Anderson, R. (1999). The cost-effectiveness of home birth. *Journal of Nurse-Midwifery, 44*(1), 30–35.

Anderson, D. A., & Hamilton, M. (2005). Gender role stereotyping of parents in children's picture books: The invisible father. *Sex Roles, 52,* 145–151.

Anderson, D. R., Huston, A. C., Schmitt, K. L., Linebarger, D. L., & Wright, J. C. (2001). Early childhood television viewing and adolescent behavior. *Monographs of the Society for Research in Child Development,* Serial No. 264, *66*(1).

Anderson, M. (1992). *My Lord, what a morning.* Madison, WI: University of Wisconsin Press.

Anderson, M., Kaufman, J., Simon, T. R., Barrios, L., Paulozzi, L., Ryan, G., et al., & the School-Associated Violent Deaths Study Group. (2001). School-associated violent deaths in the United States, 1994–1999. *Journal of the American Medical Association, 286*(21), 2695–2702.

Anderson, P., Doyle, L. W., & the Victorian Infant Collaborative Study Group. (2003). *Journal of the American Medical Association, 289,* 3264–3272.

Anderson, R. N., & Smith, B. L. (2003). Deaths: Leading causes for 2001. *National Vital Statistics Reports, 52*(9). Hyattsville, MD: National Center for Health Statistics.

Anderson, R. N., & Smith, B. L. (2005). Deaths: Leading causes for 2002. *National Vital Statistics Reports, 53*(17). Hyattsville, MD: National Center for Health Statistics.

Anderson, S. E., Dallal, G. E., & Must, A. (2003). Relative weight and race influence average age at menarche: Results from two nationally representative surveys of U.S. girls studied 25 years apart. *Pediatrics 2003, 111,* 844–850.

Anderson, W. F. (1998). Human gene therapy. *Nature, 392*(Suppl.), 25–30.

Anderssen, N., Amlie, C., & Ytteroy, E. A. (2002). Outcomes for children with lesbian or gay parents: A review of studies from 1978 to 2000. *Scandinavian Journal of Psychology, 43*(4), 335–351.

Andrade, S. E., Gurwitz, J. H., Davis, R. L., Chan, K. A., Finkelstein, J. A., Fortman, K., et al. (2004). Prescription drug use in pregnancy. *American Journal of Obstetrics and Gynecology, 191,* 398–407.

Ann Bancroft, 1955–. (1998). National Women's Hall of Fame. Retrieved April 4, 2002, from http://www.jerseycity.k12.nj.us/womenshistory/bancroft.htm

Ann Bancroft (1955–), explorer. (1999). Women in American history by Encyclopedia Britannica. Retrieved April 4, 2002, from http://www.britannica.com/women/articles/Bancroft_Ann.html

Ann Bancroft, explorer. (undated). Retrieved April 4, 2002, from http://www.people.memphis.edu/~cbburr/g old/bancroft.htm

Antonarakis, S. E., & Down Syndrome Collaborative Group. (1991). Parental origin of the extra chromosome in trisomy 21 as indicated by analysis of DNA polymorphisms. *New England Journal of Medicine, 324,* 872–876.

Apgar, V. (1953). A proposal for a new method of evaluation of the newborn infant. *Current Research in Anesthesia and Analgesia, 32,* 260–267.

Archer, J. (2004). Sex differences in aggression in real-world settings: A meta-analytic review. *Review of General Psychology, 8,* 291–322.

Archer, S. L. (1993). Identity in relational contexts: A methodological proposal. In J. Kroger (Ed.), *Discussions on ego identity* (pp. 75–99). Hillsdale, NJ: Erlbaum.

Arcus, D., & Kagan, J. (1995). Temperament and craniofacial variation in the first two years. *Child Development, 66,* 1529–1540.

Arend, R., Gove, F., & Sroufe, L. A. (1979). Continuity of individual adaptation from infancy to kindergarten: A predictive study of ego-resiliency and curiosity in preschoolers. *Child Development, 50*(4), 950–959.

Arias, E., MacDorman, M. F., Strobino, D. M., & Guyer, B. (2003). Annual summary of vital statistics—2002. *Pediatrics, 112,* 1215–1230.

Ariès, P. (1962). *Centuries of childhood.* New York: Random House.

Arnestad, M., Crotti, L., Rognum, T. O., Insolia, R., Pedrazzini, M., Ferrandi, C., et al. (2007). Prevalence of long-qt syndrome gene variants in sudden infant death syndrome. *Circulation, 115,* 361–367.

Arnett, J. J. (1999). Adolescent storm and stress, reconsidered. *American Psychologist, 54,* 317–326.

Arnett, J. J. (2000). Emerging adulthood: A theory of development from the late teens through the twenties. *American Psychologist, 55,* 469–480.

Arnett, J. J. (2003). Conceptions of the transition to adulthood among emerging adults in American ethnic groups. In J. J. Arnett & N. L. Galambos (Eds.), *Exploring cultural conceptions of the transition to adulthood. New Directions for Child and Adolescent Development, 100,* 63–75.

Arnett, J. J., & Galambos, N. L. (2003). Culture and conceptions of adulthood. In J. J. Arnett & N. L. Galambos (Eds.), *Exploring cultural conceptions of the transition to adulthood. New Directions for Child and Adolescent Development, 100,* 91–98.

Asher, M. I., Montefort, S., Björkstén, B., Lai, C. K., Strachan, D. P., Weiland, S. K., et al., & the ISAAC Phase Three Study Group. (2006). Worldwide time trends in the prevalence of symptoms of asthma, allergic rhinoconjunctivitis, and eczema in childhood: ISAAC phases one and three repeat multicountry cross-sectional surveys. *Lancet, 368*(9537), 733–743.

Ashman, S. B., & Dawson, G. (2002). Maternal depression, infant psychobiological development, and risk for depression. In S. H. Goodman & I. H. Gotlib (Eds.), *Children of depressed parents: Mechanisms of risk and implications for treatment* (pp. 37–58). Washington, DC: American Psychological Association.

Associated Press. (2004a, November 22). Boys have no place in politics: 4-year-old. AP Newswire.

Associated Press. (2004b, April 29). *Mom in C-section case received probation: Woman originally charged with murder for delaying operation.* Retrieved June 8, 2004, from http://www.msnbc.msn.com/id/4863415/

Associated Press. (2007, January 15). *Louise Brown, world's first "test-tube" baby, gives birth.* AP Newswire.

Astington, J. W. (1993). *The child's discovery of the mind.* Cambridge, MA: Harvard University Press.

Athansiou, M. S. (2001). Using consultation with a grandmother as an adjunct to play therapy. *Family Journal—Consulting and Therapy for Couples and Families, 9,* 445–449.

Aunola, K., & Nurmi, J.-E. (2005). The role of parenting styles in children's problem behavior. *Child Development, 76,* 1144–1159.

Austin, E. W., Pinkleton, B. E., & Fujioka, Y. (2000). The role of interpretation processes and parental discussion in the media's effects on adolescents' use of alcohol. *Pediatrics, 105*(2), 343–349.

Autism and Developmental Disabilities Monitoring Network Surveillance Year 2002 Principal Investigators. (2007, February 9). Prevalence of autism spectrum disorders—Autism and Developmental Disabilities Monitoring Network, 14 sites, United States, 2002. *Morbidity and Mortality Weekly Report, Surveillance Summaries, 56*(SS01), 12–28.

Autism-Part II. (2001, July). *The Harvard Mental Health Letter, 18*(1), 1–4.

Autism Society of America. (n.d.). *List of characteristics of autism.* Retrieved May 17, 2006, from http://www.unc.edu/~cory/autism-info/autism-info.html

Azar, B. (2002, January). At the frontier of science. *Monitor on Psychology,* 40–41.

Babu, A., & Hirschhorn, K. (1992). *A guide to human chromosome defects* (Birth Defects: Original Article Series, 28[2]). White Plains, NY: March of Dimes Birth Defects Foundation.

Bada, H. S., Das, A., Bauer, C. R., Shankaran, S., Lester, B., LaGasse, L., et al. (2007). Impact of prenatal cocaine exposure on child behavior problems through school age. *Pediatrics, 119,* e348–e359.

Baddeley, A. (1996). Exploring the central executive. *Quarterly Journal of Experimental Psychology: Human Experimental Psychology* (Special Issue: Working Memory), *49A,* 5–28.

Baddeley, A. (1998). Recent developments in working memory. *Current Opinion in Neurobiology, 8,* 234–238.

Baddeley, A. D. (1981). The concept of working memory: A view of its current state and probable future development. *Cognition, 10,* 17–23.

Baddeley, A. D. (1986). *Working memory.* London: Oxford University Press.

Baddeley, A. D. (1992). Working memory. *Science, 255,* 556–559.

Baddock, S. A., Galland, B. C., Bolton, D. P. G., Williams, S. M., & Taylor, B. J. (2006). Differences in infant and parent behaviors during routine bed sharing compared with cot sleeping in the home setting. *Pediatrics, 117,* 1599–1607.

Baer, J. S., Sampson, P. D., Barr, H. M., Connor, P. D., & Streissguth, A. P. (2003). A 21-year longitudinal analysis of the effects of prenatal alcohol exposure on young adult drinking. *Archives of General Psychiatry, 60,* 377–385.

Bagwell, C. L., Newcomb, A. F., & Bukowski, W. M. (1998). Preadolescent friendship and peer rejection as predictors of adult adjustment. *Child Development, 69,* 140–153.

Baillargeon, R. (1994). How do infants learn about the physical world? *Current Directions in Psychological Science, 3,* 133–140.

Baillargeon, R. (1999). Young infants' expectations about hidden objects. *Developmental Science, 2,* 115–132.

Baillargeon, R., & DeVos, J. (1991). Object permanence in young infants: Further evidence. *Child Development, 62,* 1227–1246.

Baillargeon, R. H., Zoccolillo, M., Keenan, K., Côté, S., Pérusse, D., Wu, H.-X., et al. (2007). Gender differences in physical aggression: A prospective population-based survey of children before and after 2 years of age. *Developmental Psychology, 43,* 13–26.

Baird, A. A., Gruber, S. A., Fein, D. A., Maas, L. C., Steingard, R. J., Renshaw, P. F., et al. (1999). Functional magnetic resonance imaging of facial affect recognition in children and adolescents. *Journal of the American Academy of Child and Adolescent Psychiatry, 38,* 195–199.

Baldwin, J. (1972). *No name in the street.* New York: Dial Press.

Balercia, G., Mosca, F., Mantero, F., Boscaro, M., Mancini, A., Ricciardo-Lamonica, G., et al. (2004). Coenzyme q(10) supplementation in infertile men with idiopathic asthenozoospermia: An open, uncontrolled pilot study. *Fertility and Sterility, 81,* 93–98.

Bandura, A. (1977). *Social learning theory.* Englewood Cliffs, NJ: Prentice-Hall.

Bandura, A. (1986). *Social foundations of thought and action: A social cognitive theory.* Englewood Cliffs, NJ: Prentice-Hall.

Bandura, A. (1989). Social cognitive theory. In R. Vasta (Ed.), *Annals of child development: Vol. 6* (pp. 1–60). Greenwich, CT: JAI.

Bandura, A. (1994). Self-efficacy. In V. S. Ramachandran (Ed.), *Encyclopedia of human behavior* (Vol. 4, pp. 71–81). New York: Academic Press.

Bandura, A., Barbaranelli, C., Caprara, G. V., & Pastorelli, C. (1996). Multifaceted impact of self-efficacy beliefs on academic functioning. *Child Development, 67,* 1206–1222.

Bandura, A., Barbaranelli, C., Caprara, G. V., & Pastorelli, C. (2001). Self-efficacy beliefs as shapers of children's aspirations and career trajectories. *Child Development 72*(1), 187–206.

Bandura, A., Ross, D., & Ross, S. A. (1961). Transmission of aggression through imitation of aggressive models. *Journal of Abnormal and Social Psychology, 63,* 575–582.

Bandura, A., & Walters, R. H. (1963). *Social learning and personality development.* New York: Holt, Rinehart, & Winston.

Banks, E. (1989). Temperament and individuality: A study of Malay children. *American Journal of Orthopsychiatry, 59,* 390–397.

Barber, B. K. (1996). Parental psychological control: Revisiting a neglected construct. *Child Development, 67,* 3296–3319.

Barber, B. L., & Eccles, J. S. (1992). Longterm influence of divorce and single parenting on adolescent, family and work related values, behaviors, and aspirations. *Psychological Bulletin, 111*(1), 108–126.

Barker, D. J., & Lackland, D. T. (2003). Prenatal influences on stroke mortality in England and Wales. *Stroke: A Journal of Cerebral Circulation, 34,* 1598–1602.

Barkley, R. A. (1998a, February). How should attention deficit disorder be described? *Harvard Mental Health Letter,* p. 8.

Barkley, R. A. (1998b, September). Attention-deficit hyperactivity disorder. *Scientific American,* pp. 66–71.

Barkley, R. A., Murphy, K. R., & Kwasnik, D. (1996). Motor vehicle competencies and risks in teens and young adults with attention deficit hyperactivity disorder. *Pediatrics, 98,* 1089–1095.

Barlow, S. E., & Dietz, W. H. (1998). Obesity evaluation and treatment: Expert committee recommendations. *Pediatrics, 102*(3), e29. Retrieved from http://www.pediatrics.org/cgi/content/full/102/3/e29

Barnes, J., Sutcliffe, A., Ponjaert, I., Loft, A., Wennerholm, U., Tarlatzis, V., et al. (2003, July). *The European study of 1,523 ICSI/IVF versus naturally conceived 5-year-old children and their families:*
Family functioning and socioemotional development. Paper presented at conference of European Society of Human Reproduction and Embryology, Madrid.

Baron-Cohen, S. (2005). The essential difference: The male and female brain. *Phi Kappa Phi Forum, 85*(1), 23–26.

Barry, C. M., & Wentzel, K. R. (2006). Friend influence on prosocial behavior: The role of motivational factors and friendship characteristics. *Developmental Psychology, 42,* 153–163.

Barthel, J. (1982, May). Just a normal, naughty three-year-old. *McCall's,* pp. 78, 136–144.

Bartoshuk, L. M., & Beauchamp, G. K. (1994). Chemical senses. *Annual Review of Psychology, 45,* 419–449.

Basso, O., & Baird, D. D. (2003). Infertility and preterm delivery, birth weight, and Caesarean section: A study within the Danish National Birth Cohort. *Human Reproduction, 18,* 2478–2484.

Bassuk, E. L. (1991). Homeless families. *Scientific American, 265*(6), 66–74.

Bates, E., Bretherton, I., & Snyder, L. (1988). *From first words to grammar: Individual differences and dissociable mechanisms.* New York: Cambridge University Press.

Bates, E., O'Connell, B., & Shore, C. (1987). Language and communication in infancy. In J. D. Osofsky (Ed.), *Handbook of infant development* (2d ed.). New York: Wiley.

Bateson, M. C. (1984). *With a daughter's eye: A memoir of Margaret Mead and Gregory Bateson.* New York: William Morrow & Co.

Bauer, P. J. (1993). Memory for gender-consistent and gender-inconsistent event sequences by twenty-five-month-old children. *Child Development, 64,* 285–297.

Bauer, P. J. (1996). What do infants recall of their lives? Memory for specific events by 1- to 2-year-olds. *American Psychologist, 51,* 29–41.

Bauer, P. J. (2002). Long-term recall memory: Behavioral and neurodevelopmental changes in the first 2 years of life. *Current Directions in Psychological Science, 11,* 137–141.

Bauer, P. J., Wenner, J. A., Dropik, P. L., & Wewerka, S. S. (2000). Parameters of remembering and forgetting in the transition from infancy to early childhood. *Monographs of the Society for Research in Child Development,* Serial No. 263, *65*(4). Malden, MA: Blackwell.

Bauer, P. J., Wiebe, S. A., Carver, L. J., Waters, J. M., & Nelson, C. A. (2003). Developments in long-term explicit memory late in the first year of life: Behavioral and electrophysiological indices. *Psychological Science, 14,* 629–635.

Bauman, L. J., Silver, E. J., & Stein, R. E. K. (2006). Cumulative social disadvantage and child health. *Pediatrics, 117,* 1321–1328.

Baumer, E. P., & South, S. J. (2001). Community effects on youth sexual activity. *Journal of Marriage and the Family, 63,* 540–554.

Baumrind, D. (1971). Harmonious parents and their preschool children. *Developmental Psychology, 41,* 92–102.

Baumrind, D. (1989). Rearing competent children. In W. Damon (Ed.), *Child development today and tomorrow* (pp. 349–378). San Francisco: Jossey-Bass.

Baumrind, D. (1991). Parenting styles and adolescent development. In J. Brooks-Gunn, R. Lerner, & A. C. Peterson (Eds.), *The encyclopedia of adolescence* (pp. 746–758). New York: Garland.

Baumrind, D. (1996a). A blanket injunction against disciplinary use of spanking is not warranted by the data. *Pediatrics, 88,* 828–831.

Baumrind, D. (1996b). The discipline controversy revisited. *Family Relations, 45,* 405–414.

Baumrind, D. (2005). Patterns of parental authority and adolescent autonomy. In J. Smetana (Ed.), *Changing boundaries of parental authority during adolescence: New directions for child and adolescent development, 108* (pp. 61–70). San Francisco: Jossey-Bass.

Baumrind, D., & Black, A. E. (1967). Socialization practices associated with dimensions of competence in preschool boys and girls. *Child Development, 38,* 291–327.

Baumrind, D., Larzelere, R. E., & Cowan, P. A. (2002). Ordinary physical punishment: Is it harmful? Comment on Gershoff (2002). *Psychological Bulletin, 128,* 580–589.

Bauserman, R. (2002). Child adjustment in joint-custody versus sole-custody arrangements: A meta-analytic review. *Journal of Family Psychology, 16,* 91–102.

Baydar, N., Greek, A., & Brooks-Gunn, J. (1997). A longitudinal study of the effects of the birth of a sibling during the first 6 years of life. *Journal of Marriage and the Family, 59,* 939–956.

Baydar, N., Hyle, P., & Brooks-Gunn, J. (1997). A longitudinal study of the effects of the birth of a sibling during preschool and early grade school years. *Journal of Marriage and the Family, 59,* 957–965.

Bayliss, D. M., Jarrold, C., Baddeley, A. D., Gunn, D. M., & Leigh, E. (2005). Mapping the developmental constraints on working memory span performance. *Developmental Psychology, 41*(4), 579–597.

Bayley, N. (1969). *Bayley Scales of Infant Development.* New York: Psychological Corporation.

Bayley, N. (1993). *Bayley Scales of Infant Development: II.* New York: Psychological Corporation.

Bayley, N. (2005). *Bayley Scales of Infant Development, Third Ed.* (Bayley-III). New York: Harcourt Brace.

Bearman, P. S., & Bruckner, H. (2001). Promising the future: Virginity pledges and first intercourse. *American Journal of Sociology, 106,* 859–913.

Bech, B. H., Nohr, E. A., Vaeth, M., Henriksen, T. B., & Olsen, J. (2005). Coffee and fetal death: A cohort study with prospective data. *American Journal of Epidemiology, 162*(10), 983–990.

Beckett, C., Maughan, B., Rutter, M., Castle, J., Colvert, E., Groothues, C., et al. (2006). Do the effects of severe early deprivation on cognition persist into early adolescence? Findings from the English and Romanian adoptees study. *Child Development, 77,* 696–711.

Behne, R., Carpenter, M., Call, J., & Tomasello, M. (2005). Unwilling versus unable: Infants' understanding of intentional action. *Developmental Psychology, 41,* 328–337.

Behrman, R. E. (1992). *Nelson textbook of pediatrics* (13th ed.). Philadelphia: Saunders.

Beidel, D. C., & Turner, S. M. (1998). *Shy children, phobic adults: Nature and treatment of social phobia.* Washington, DC: American Psychological Association.

Bekedam, D. J., Engelsbel, S., Mol, B. W., Buitendijk, S. E., & van der Pal-de Bruin, K. M. (2002). Male predominance in fetal distress during labor. *American Journal of Obstetrics and Gynecology, 187,* 1605–1607.

Belizzi, M. (2002, May). *Obesity in children—What kind of future are we creating?* Presentation at the Fifty-Fifth World Health Assembly Technical Briefing, Geneva.

Bell, M. A., & Fox, N. A. (1992). The relations between frontal brain electrical activity and cognitive development during infancy. *Child Development, 63,* 1142–1163.

Bellinger, D. (2004). Lead. *Pediatrics, 113,* 1016–1022.

Belsky, J. (1984). Two waves of day care research: Developmental effects and conditions of quality. In R. Ainslie (Ed.), *The child and the day care setting.* New York: Praeger.

Belsky, J., Fish, M., & Isabella, R. (1991). Continuity and discontinuity in infant negative and positive emotionality: Family antecedents and attachment consequences. *Developmental Psychology, 27,* 421–431.

Belsky, J., Vandell, D. L., Burchinal, M., Clarke-Stewart, K. A., McCartney, K., Owen, M. T., & the NICHD Early Child Care Research Network. (2007). Are there long-term effects of early child care? *Child Development, 78,* 681–701.

Bem, S. L. (1983). Gender schema theory and its implications for child development: Raising gender-aschematic children in a gender-schematic society. *Signs, 8,* 598–616.

Bem, S. L. (1985). Androgyny and gender schema theory: A conceptual and empirical integration. In T. B. Sondregger (Ed.),

Nebraska symposium on motivation, 1984: Psychology and gender. Lincoln, NE: University of Nebraska Press.

Bem, S. L. (1993). *The lenses of gender: Transforming the debate on sexual inequality.* New Haven, CT: Yale University Press.

Benenson, J. F. (1993). Greater preference among females than males for dyadic interaction in early childhood. *Child Development, 64,* 544–555.

Benson, E. (2003). Intelligent intelligence testing. *Monitor on Psychology, 43*(2), 48–51.

Benson, M. (1986). *Nelson Mandela: The man and the movement.* New York: Norton.

Bergeman, C. S., & Plomin, R. (1989). Genotype-environment interaction. In M. Bornstein & J. Bruner (Eds.), *Interaction in human development* (pp. 157–171). Hillsdale, NJ: Erlbaum.

Bergen, D. (2002). The role of pretend play in children's cognitive development. *Early Childhood Research & Practice, 4*(1). Retrieved from http://ecrp.uiuc.edu/v4n1/bergen.html

Bergen, D., Reid, R., & Torelli, L. (2000). *Educating and caring for very young children: The infant-toddler curriculum.* Washington, DC: National Association for the Education of Young Children.

Berk, L. E. (1986a). Development of private speech among preschool children. *Early Child Development and Care, 24,* 113–136.

Berk, L. E. (1986b). Private speech: Learning out loud. *Psychology Today, 20*(5), 34–42.

Berk, L. E. (1992). Children's private speech: An overview of theory and the status of research. In R. M. Diaz & L. E. Berk (Eds.), *Private speech: From social interaction to self-regulation* (pp. 17–53). Hillsdale, NJ: Erlbaum.

Berk, L. E., & Garvin, R. A. (1984). Development of private speech among low income Appalachian children. *Developmental Psychology, 20,* 271–286.

Berkowitz, G. S., Skovron, M. L., Lapinski, R. H., & Berkowitz, R. L. (1990). Delayed childbearing and the outcome of pregnancy. *New England Journal of Medicine, 322,* 659–664.

Berkowitz, R. I., Stallings, V. A., Maislin, G., & Stunkard, A. J. (2005). Growth of children at high risk of obesity during the first 6 years of life: Implications for prevention. *American Journal of Clinical Nutrition, 81,* 140–146.

Berkowitz, R. I., Wadden, T. A., Tershakovec, A. M., & Cronquist, J. L. (2003). Behavior therapy and sibutramine for the treatment of adolescent obesity: A randomized controlled trial. *Journal of the American Medical Association, 289,* 1805–1812.

Berndt, T. J., & Perry, T. B. (1990). Distinctive features and effects of early adolescent friendships. In R. Montemayor, G. R. Adams, & T. P. Gullotta (Eds.), *From childhood to adolescence: A transitional period?*

(Vol. 2, pp. 269–287). Newbury Park, CA: Sage.

Bernstein, J. (1973). *Einstein.* New York: Viking.

Bernstein, N. (2004, March 7). Behind fall in pregnancy, a new teenage culture of restraint. *New York Times,* pp. 1, 36–37.

Bernstein, P. S. (2003). Achieving equity in women's and perinatal health. *Medscape Ob/Gyn & Women's Health, 8.* Posted 12/12/03.

Berrick, J. D. (1998). When children cannot remain home: Foster family care and kinship care. *The Future of Children, 8,* 72–87.

Berrueta-Clement, J. R., Schweinhart, L. J., Barnett, W. S., Epstein, A. S., & Weikart, D. P. (1985). *Changed lives: The effects of the Perry Preschool Program on youths through age 19.* Ypsilanti, MI: High/Scope.

Berrueta-Clement, J. R., Schweinhart, L. J., Barnett, W. S., & Weikart, D. P. (1987). The effects of early educational intervention on crime and delinquency in adolescence and early adulthood. In J. D. Burchard & S. N. Burchard (Eds.), *Primary prevention of psychopathology: Vol. 10. Prevention of delinquent behavior* (pp. 220–240). Newbury Park, CA: Sage.

Berry, M., Dylla, D. J., Barth, R. P., & Needell, B. (1998). The role of open adoption in the adjustment of adopted children and their families. *Children and Youth Services Review, 20,* 151–171.

Berry, N., Jobanputra, V., & Pal, H. (2003). Molecular genetics of schizophrenia: A critical review. *Journal of Psychiatry and Neuroscience, 28,* 415–429.

Berry, R. J., Li, Z., Erickson, J. D., Li, S., Moore, C. A., Wang, H., et al. for the China-U.S. Collaborative Project for Neural Tube Defect Prevention. (1999). Prevention of neural-tube defects with folic acid in China. *New England Journal of Medicine, 341,* 1485–1490.

Bertenthal, B. I., & Campos, J. J. (1987). New directions in the study of early experience. *Child Development, 58,* 560–567.

Bertenthal, B. I., Campos, J. J., & Barrett, K. C. (1984). Self-produced locomotion: An organizer of emotional, cognitive, and social development in infancy. In R. N. Emde & R. J. Harmon (Eds.), *Continuities and discontinuities in development.* New York: Plenum.

Bertenthal, B. I., Campos, J. J., & Kermoian, R. (1994). An epigenetic perspective on the development of self-produced locomotion and its consequences. *Current Directions in Psychological Science, 3*(5), 140–145.

Bertenthal, B. I., & Clifton, R. K. (1998). Perception and action. In W. Damon (Ed.-in-Chief), D. Kuhn & R. S. Siegler (Vol. Eds.), *Handbook of child psychology: Vol. 2. Cognition perception, and language* (pp. 51–102). New York: Wiley.

Bertin, E., & Striano, T. (2006). The still face response in newborn, 1.5-, and 3-month-old infants. *Infant Behavior and Development, 29,* 294–297.

Berz, J. B., Murdock, K. K., & Mitchell, D. K. (2005). Children's asthma, internalizing problems, and social functioning: An urban perspective. *Journal of Child and Adolescent Psychiatric Nursing, 18*(4), 181–197.

Bespalova, I. N., & Buxbaum, J. D. (2003). Disease susceptibility genes for autism. *Annals of Medicine, 35,* 274–281.

Bethell, C. D., Read, D. D., & Blumberg, S. J. (2005). Mental health in the United States: Health care and well-being of children with chronic emotional, behavioral, or developmental problems—United States, 2001. *Morbidity and Mortality Weekly Report, 54,* 985–989.

Bethell, T. N. (2005, April). What's the big idea? There's more than one solution for Social Security. Here are nine ways to keep the system solvent. *AARP Bulletin,* pp. 22–26.

Beversdorf, D. Q., Manning, S. E., Anderson, S. L., Nordgren, R. E., Walters, S. E., Cooley, W. C., et al. (2001, November 10–15). *Timing of prenatal stressors and autism.* Presentation at the 31st Annual Meeting of the Society for Neuroscience, San Diego.

Bialystok, E., & Senman, L. (2004). Executive processes in appearance-reality tasks: The role of inhibition of attention and symbolic representation. *Child Development, 75,* 562–579.

Biason-Lauber, A., Konrad, D., Navratil, F., & Schoenle, E. J. (2004). A WNT4 mutation associated with Mullerian-duct regression and virilization in a 46, XX woman. *New England Journal of Medicine, 351,* 792–798.

Bierman, K. L., Smoot, D. L., & Aumiller, K. (1993). Characteristics of aggressive rejected, aggressive (nonrejected), and rejected (non-aggressive) boys. *Child Development, 64,* 139–151.

Bjork, J. M., Knutson, B., Fong, G. W., Caggiano, D. M., Bennett, S. M., & Hommer, D. W. (2004). Incentive-elicited brain activities in adolescents: Similarities and differences from young adults. *The Journal of Neuroscience, 24,* 1793–1802.

Bjorklund, D. F. (1997). The role of immaturity in human development. *Psychological Bulletin, 122,* 153–169.

Bjorklund, D. F., & Harnishfeger, K. K. (1990). The resources construct in cognitive development: Diverse sources of evidence and a theory of inefficient inhibition. *Developmental Review, 10,* 48–71.

Bjorklund, D. F., & Pellegrini, A. D. (2000). Child development and evolutionary psychology. *Child Development, 71,* 1687–1708.

Bjorklund, D. F., & Pellegrini, A. D. (2002). *The origins of human nature: Evolutionary developmental psychology.* Washington, DC: American Psychological Association.

Bickham, D., & Rich, M. (2006). Is television viewing associated with social isolation? Roles of exposure time, viewing context, and violent content. *Archives of Pediatrics and Adolescent Medicine, 160,* 387–392.

Birmaher, B. (1998). Should we use antidepressant medications for children and adolescents with depressive disorders? *Psychopharmacology Bulletin, 34,* 35–39.

Birmaher, B., Ryan, N. D., Williamson, D. E., Brent, D. A., Kaufman, J., Dahl, R. E., et al. (1996). Childhood and adolescent depression: A review of the past 10 years. *Journal of the American Academy of Child and Adolescent Psychiatry, 35,* 1427–1440.

Black, J. E. (1998). How a child builds its brain: Some lessons from animal studies of neural plasticity. *Preventive Medicine, 27,* 168–171.

Black, M. M., & Krishnakumar, A. (1998). Children in low-income, urban settings: Interventions to promote mental health and well-being. *American Psychologist, 53,* 636–646.

Black, R. E., Morris, S. S., & Bryce, J. (2003). Where and why are 10 million children dying each year? *The Lancet, 361,* 2226–2234.

Blair, C. (2002). School readiness: Integrating cognition and emotion in a neurobiological conceptualization of children's functioning at school entry. *American Psychologist, 57,* 111–127.

Blakemore, S., & Choudhury, S. (2006). Development of the adolescent brain: Implications for executive function and social cognition. *Journal of Child Psychology and Psychiatry, 47*(3), 296–312.

Blakeslee, S. (1997, April 17). Studies show talking with infants shapes basis of ability to think. *New York Times,* p. D21.

Bleske-Rechek, A., Lubinski, D., & Benbow, C. P. (2004). Meeting the educational needs of special populations. Advanced placement's role in developing exceptional human capital. *Psychological Sciences, 15,* 217–224.

Block, R. W., Krebs, N. F., the Committee on Child Abuse and Neglect & the Committee on Nutrition. (2005). *Pediatrics, 116*(5), 1234–1237.

Bloom, B. (1985). *Developing talent in young people.* New York: Ballantine.

Bloom, B., Cohen, R. A., Vickerie, J. L., & Wondimu, E. A. (2003). Summary health statistics for U.S. children: National Health Interview Survey, 2001. *Vital and Health Statistics, 10*(216). Hyattsville, MD: National Center for Health Statistics.

Bloom, H. (Ed.). (1999). *A scholarly look at The Diary of Anne Frank.* Philadelphia: Chelsea.

Blum, N. J., Taubman, B., & Nemeth, N. (2003). Relationship between age at initiation of toilet training and duration of training: A prospective study. *Pediatrics, 111,* 810–814.

Boatman, D., Freeman, J., Vining, E., Pulsifer, M., Miglioretti, D., Minahan, R., et al. (1999). Language recovery after left hemispherectomy in children with late onset seizures. *Annals of Neurology, 46*(4), 579–586.

Bocskay, K. A., Tang, D., Orjuela, M. A., Liu, X., Warburton, D. P., & Perera, F. P. (2005). Chromosomal aberrations in cord blood are associated with prenatal exposure to carcinogenic polycyclic aromatic hydrocarbons. *Cancer Epidemiology Biomarkers and Prevention, 14*, 506–511.

Bodrova, E., & Leong, D. J. (1998). Adult influences on play: The Vygotskian approach. In D. P. Fromberg & D. Bergen (Eds.), *Play from birth to twelve and beyond: Contexts, perspectives, and meanings* (pp. 277–282). New York: Garland.

Bogaert, A. F. (2006). Biological versus nonbiological older brothers and men's sexual orientation. *Proceedings of the National Academy of Sciences, 103*, 10771–10774.

Bogard, K., & Takaneshi, R. (2005). PK-3: An aligned and coordinated approach to education for children 3 to 8 years old. *Social Policy Report, 19*, 3–23.

Bojczyk, K. E., & Corbetta, D. (2004). Object retrieval in the 1st year of life: Learning effects of task exposure and box transparency. *Developmental Psychology, 40*, 54–66.

Bollinger, M. B. (2003). Involuntary smoking and asthma severity in children: Data from the Third National Health and Nutrition Examination Survey (NHANES III). *Pediatrics, 112*, 471.

Bond, C. A. (1989, September). A child prodigy from China wields a magical brush. *Smithsonian*, pp. 70–79.

Bonham, V. L., Warshauer-Baker, E., & Collins, F. S. (2005). Race and ethnicity in the genome era. *American Psychologist, 60*, 9–15.

Booth, A. E., & Waxman, S. (2002). Object names and object functions serve as cues to categories for infants. *Developmental Psychology, 38*, 948–957.

Booth, J. L., & Siegler, R. S. (2006). Developmental and individual differences in pure numerical estimation. *Developmental Psychology, 41*, 189–201.

Booth, J. R., Perfetti, C. A., & MacWhinney, B. (1999). Quick, automatic, and general activation of orthographic and phonological representations in young readers. *Developmental Psychology, 35*(1), 3–19.

Borman, G., Boulay, M., Kaplan, J., Rachuba, L., & Hewes, G. (1999, December 13). *Evaluating the longterm impact of multiple summer interventions on the reading skills of low-income, early elementary students.* Preliminary report, Year 1. Baltimore, MD: Center for Social Organization of Schools, Johns Hopkins University.

Bornstein, M., Kessen, W., & Weiskopf, S. (1976). The categories of hue in infancy. *Science, 191*, 201–202.

Bornstein, M. H. & Cote, L. R. with Maital, S., Painter, K., Park, S. Y., Pascual, L., et al. (2004). Cross-linguistic analysis of vocabulary in young children: Spanish, Dutch, French, Hebrew, Italian, Korean, and American English. *Child Development, 75*, 1115–1139.

Bornstein, M. H., & Sigman, M. D. (1986). Continuity in mental development from infancy. *Child Development, 57*, 251–274.

Bornstein, M. H., & Tamis-LeMonda, C. S. (1994). Antecedents of information processing skills in infants: Habituation, novelty responsiveness, and cross-modal transfer. *Infant Behavior and Development, 17*, 371–380.

Borowsky, I. A., Ireland, M., & Resnick, M. D. (2001). Adolescent suicide attempts: Risks and protectors. *Pediatrics, 107*(3), 485–493.

Bosch, J., Sullivan, S.,Van Dyke, D. C., Su, H., Klockau, L., Nissen, K., et al. (2003). Promoting a healthy tomorrow here for children adopted from abroad. *Contemporary Pediatrics, 20*(2), 69–86.

Botkin, J. R., Clayton, E. W., Fost, N. C., Burke, W., Murray, T. H., Baily, M. A., et al. (2006). Newborn screening technology: Proceed with caution. *Pediatrics, 117*, 1793–1799.

Bouchard, T. J. (1994). Genes, environment, and personality. *Science, 264*, 1700–1701.

Bouchard, T. J. (2004). Genetic influence on human psychological traits: A survey. *Current Directions in Psychological Science, 13*, 148–154.

Bouchey, H. A., & Furman, W. (2003). Dating and romantic experiences in adolescence. In G. R. Adams & M.D. Berzonsky (Eds.), *Blackwell handbook of adolescence* (pp. 313–329). Oxford, UK: Blackwell.

Boulton, M. J. (1995). Playground behaviour and peer interaction patterns of primary school boys classified as bullies, victims and not involved. *British Journal of Educational Psychology, 65*, 165–177.

Boulton, M. J., & Smith, P. K. (1994). Bully/victim problems in middle school children: Stability, self perceived competence, peer perception, and peer acceptance. *British Journal of Developmental Psychology, 12*, 315–329.

Boutin, P., Dina, C., Vasseur, F., Dubois, S. S., Corset, L., Seron, K., et al. (2003). GAD2 on chromosome 10p12 is a candidate gene for human obesity. *Public Library of Science Biology, 1*(3), E68.

Bower, T. G. R. (1966). The visual world of infants. *Scientific American, 215*, 80–92.

Bowlby, J. (1951). Maternal care and mental health. *Bulletin of the World Health Organization, 3*, 355–534.

Bowlby, J. (1969). *Attachment and loss: Vol. I. Attachment.* London: Hogarth Press & the Institute of Psychoanalysis.

Bowman, S. A., Gortmaker, S. L., Ebbeling, C. B., Pereira, M. A., & Ludwig, D. S. (2004). Effects of fast food consumption on energy intake and diet quality among children in a national household survey. *Pediatrics, 113*, 112–118.

Boyles, S. (2002, January 27). Toxic landfills may boost birth defects. *WebMD Medical News.* Retrieved February 5, 2007, from http://www.webmd.com/content/article/25/3606_1181.htm

Boyum, L. A., & Parke, R. D. (1995). The role of family emotional expressiveness in the development of children's social competence. *Journal of Marriage and the Family, 57*, 593–608.

Brabeck, M. M., & Shore, E. L. (2003). Gender differences in intellectual and moral development? The evidence refutes the claims. In J. Demick & C. Andreoletti (Eds.), *Handbook of adult development* (pp. 351–368). New York: Plenum Press.

Bracher, G., & Santow, M. (1999). Explaining trends in teenage childbearing in Sweden. *Studies in Family Planning, 30*, 169–182.

Bradley, R., & Caldwell, B. (1982). The consistency of the home environment and its relation to child development. *International Journal of Behavioral Development, 5*, 445–465.

Bradley, R., Caldwell, B., & Rock, S. (1988). Home environment and school performance: A ten-year follow-up and examination of three models of environmental action. *Child Development, 59*, 852–867.

Bradley, R. H. (1989). Home measurement of maternal responsiveness. In M. H. Bornstein (Ed.), *Maternal responsiveness: Characteristics and consequences* (New Directions for Child Development No. 43). San Francisco: Jossey-Bass.

Bradley, R. H., Caldwell, B. M., Rock, S. L., Ramey, C. T., Barnard, K. E., Gray, C., et al. (1989). Home environment and cognitive development in the first 3 years of life: A collaborative study involving six sites and three ethnic groups in North America. *Developmental Psychology, 25*, 217–235.

Bradley, R. H., Corwyn, R. F., Burchinal, M., McAdoo, H. P., & Coll, C. G. (2001). The home environment of children in the United States: Part II. Relations with behavioral development through age thirteen. *Child Development, 72*(6), 1868–1886.

Bradley, R. H., Corwyn, R. F., McAdoo, H. P., & Coll, C. G. (2001). The home environment of children in the United States: Part I. Variation by age, ethnicity, and poverty status. *Child Development, 72*(6), 1844–1867.

Bradley, S. J., Oliver, G. D., Chernick, A. B., & Zuker, K. J. (1998). Experiment of nurture: Ablatio penis at 2 months, sex reassignment at 7 months, and a psychosexual follow-up in young adulthood. *Pediatrics, 102*(1), e9.

Braine, M. (1976). Children's first word combinations. *Monographs of the Society for Research in Child Development, 41*(1, Serial No. 164).

Brambati, S. M., Termine, C., Ruffino, M., Stella, G., Fazio, F., Cappa, S. F., et al. (2004). Regional reductions of gray matter volume in familial dyslexia. *Neurology, 63,* 742–745.

Brass, L. M., Isaacsohn, J. L., Merikangas, K. R., & Robinette, C. D. (1992). A study of twins and stroke. *Stroke, 23*(2), 221–223.

Bratton, S. C., & Ray, D. (2002). Humanistic play therapy. In D. J. Cain (Ed.), *Humanistic psychotherapies: Handbook of research and practice* (pp. 369–402). Washington, DC: American Psychological Association.

Braun, H., Jenkins, F., & Grigg, W. (2006). *A closer look at charter schools using hierarchical linear modeling* (NCES 2006-460). Washington, DC: U.S. Government Printing Office.

Braungart, J. M., Plomin, R., DeFries, J. C., & Fulker, D. W. (1992). Genetic influence on tester-rated infant temperament as assessed by Bayley's Infant Behavior Record: Nonadoptive and adoptive siblings and twins. *Developmental Psychology 28,* 40–47.

Braungart-Rieker, J., Garwood, M. M., Powers, B. P., & Notaro, P. C. (1998). Infant affect and affect regulation during the still-face paradigm with mothers and fathers: The role of infant characteristics and parental sensitivity. *Developmental Psychology, 34*(6), 1428–1437.

Braungart-Rieker, J. M., Garwood, M. M., Powers, B. P., & Wang, X. (2001). Parental sensitivity, infant affect, and affect regulation: Predictors of later attachment. *Child Development, 72,* 252–270.

Bray, J. H., & Hetherington, E. M. (1993). Families in transition: Introduction and overview. *Journal of Family Psychology, 7,* 3–8.

Brazelton, T. B. (1973). *Neonatal Behavioral Assessment Scale.* Philadelphia: Lippincott.

Brazelton, T. B. (1984). *Neonatal Behavioral Assessment Scale.* Philadelphia: Lippincott.

Brazelton, T. B., & Nugent, J. K. (1995). *Neonatal Behavioral Assessment Scale* (3rd ed.). Cambridge, England: Cambridge University Press.

Breastfeeding and HIV International Transmission Study Group. (2004). Late postnatal transmission of HIV-1 in breastfed children: An individual patient data meta-analysis. *Journal of Infectious Diseases, 189,* 2154–2166.

Breier, J. I., Simos, P. G., Fletcher, J. M., Castillo, E. M., Zhang, W., & Papanicolaou, A. C. (2003). Abnormal activation of temporoparietal language areas during phonetic analysis in children with dyslexia. *Neuropsychology, 17,* 610–621.

Brendgen, M., Dionne, G., Girard, A., Boivin, M., Vitaro, F., & Perusse, D. (2005). Examining genetic and environmental effects on social aggression: A study of 6-year-old twins. *Child Development, 76,* 930–946.

Brenneman, K., Massey, C., Machado, S. F., & Gelman, R. (1996). Young children's plans differ for writing and drawing. *Cognitive Development, 11,* 397–419.

Brenner, R. A., Sismons-Morton, B. G., Bhaskar, B., Revenis, M., Das, A., & Clemens, J. D. (2003). Infant-parent bed sharing in an inner-city population. *Archives of Pediatrics and Adolescent Medicine, 57,* 33–39.

Brent, D. A., & Birmaher, B. (2002). Adolescent depression. *New England Journal of Medicine, 347,* 667–671.

Brent, D. A., & Mann, J. J. (2006). Familial pathways to suicidal behavior—Understanding and preventing suicide among adolescents. *New England Journal of Medicine, 355,* 2719–2721.

Brent, R. L., & Weitzman, M. (2004). The current state of knowledge about the effects, risks, and science of children's environmental exposures. *Pediatrics, 113,* 1158–1166.

Bretherton, I. (1990). Communication patterns, internal working models, and the intergenerational transmission of attachment relationships. *Infant Mental Health Journal, 11*(3), 237–252.

Brewaeys, A., Ponjaert, I., Van Hall, V. E., & Golombok, S. (1997). Donor insemination: Child development and family functioning in lesbian mother families. *Human Reproduction, 12,* 1349–1359.

Brezina, T. (1999). Teenage violence toward parents as an adaptation to family strain: Evidence from a national survey of male adolescents. *Youth and Society, 30,* 416–444.

Brian, D. (1996). *Einstein: A life.* New York: Wiley.

Brin, D. J. (2004). The use of rituals in grieving for a miscarriage or stillbirth. *Women and Therapy, 27,* 123–132.

Brody, G. H. (1998). Sibling relationship quality: Its causes and consequences. *Annual Review of Psychology, 49,* 1–24.

Brody, G. H. (2004). Siblings' direct and indirect contributions to child development. *Current Directions in Psychological Science, 13,* 124–126.

Brody, G. H., Chen, Y.-F., Murry, V. M., Ge, X., Simons, R. L., Gibbons, F. X., et al. (2006). Perceived discrimination and the adjustment of African American youths: A five-year longitudinal analysis with contextual moderation effects. *Child Development, 77*(5), 1170–1189.

Brody, G. H., Flor, D. L., & Gibson, N. M. (1999). Linking maternal efficacy beliefs, developmental goals, parenting practices, and child competence in rural single-parent African American families. *Child Development, 70*(5), 1197–1208.

Brody, G. H., Ge, X., Conger, R., Gibbons, F. X., Murry, V. M., Gerrard, M., et al. (2001). The influence of neighborhood disadvantage, collective socialization, and parenting on African American children's affiliation with deviant peers. *Child Development, 72*(4),1231–1246.

Brody, G. H., Kim, S., Murry, V. M., & Brown, A. C. (2004). Protective longitudinal paths linking child competence to behavioral problems among African American siblings. *Child Development, 75,* 455–467.

Brody, G. H., Stoneman, Z., & Flor, D. (1995). Linking family processes and academic competence among rural African American youths. *Journal of Marriage and the Family, 57,* 567–579.

Brody, J. E. (1995, June 28). Preventing birth defects even before pregnancy. *New York Times,* p. C10.

Brody, L. R., Zelazo, P. R., & Chaika, H. (1984). Habituation-dishabituation to speech in the neonate. *Developmental Psychology, 20,* 114–119.

Broidy, L. M., Tremblay, R. E., Brame, B., Fergusson, D., Horwood, J. L., Laird, R., et al. (2003). Developmental trajectories of childhood disruptive behaviors and adolescent delinquency: A six-site cross-national study. *Developmental Psychology, 39,* 222–245.

Bronfenbrenner, U. (1979). *The ecology of human development.* Cambridge, MA: Harvard University Press.

Bronfenbrenner, U. (1986). Ecology of the family as a context for human development: Research perspectives. *Developmental Psychology, 22,* 723–742.

Bronfenbrenner, U. (1994). Ecological models of human development. In T. Husen & T. N. Postlethwaite (Eds.), *International encyclopedia of education* (2nd ed., Vol. 3, pp. 1643–1647). Oxford, UK: Pergamon Press/Elsevier Science.

Bronfenbrenner, U., & Morris, P. A. (1998). The ecology of developmental processes. In W. Damon (Series Ed.) & R. Lerner (Vol. Ed.), *Handbook of child psychology: Vol. I. Theoretical models of human development* (5th ed., pp. 993–1028). New York: Wiley.

Bronner, E. (1999, January 22). Social promotion is bad; repeating a grade may be worse. *New York Times.* Retrieved from http://search.nytimes.com/search/daily/bin/fastweb?getdocPsitePsiteP13235POPwAAAPsocial%7Epromotion

Bronstein, P. (1988). Father-child interaction: Implications for gender role socialization. In P. Bronstein & C. P. Cowan (Eds.), *Fatherhood today: Men's changing role in the family.* New York: Wiley.

Bronstein, P., Clauson, J., Stoll, M. F., & Abrams, C. L. (1993). Parenting behavior and children's social, psychological, and academic adjustment in diverse family structures. *Family Relations, 42,* 268–276.

Brookmeyer, K. A., Henrich, C. C., & Schwab-Stone, M. (2005). Adolescents who witness community violence: Can parent support and prosocial cognitions protect them from committing violence? *Child Development, 76,* 917–929.

Brooks, R., & Meltzoff, A. N. (2002). The importance of eyes: How infants interpret adult looking behavior. *Developmental Psychology, 38,* 958–966.

Brooks, R., & Meltzoff, A. N. (2005). The development of gaze following and its relation to language. *Developmental Science, 8*, 535–543.

Brooks-Gunn, J. (2003). Do you believe in magic? What can we expect from early childhood intervention programs? *SRCD Social Policy Report, 17*(1).

Brooks-Gunn, J., Britto, P. R., & Brady, C. (1998). Struggling to make ends meet: Poverty and child development. In M. E. Lamb (Ed.), *Parenting and child development in "non-traditional" families* (pp. 279–304). Mahwah, NJ: Erlbaum.

Brooks-Gunn, J., & Duncan, G. J. (1997). The effects of poverty on children. *The Future of Children, 7*, 55–71.

Brooks-Gunn, J., Han, W.-J., & Waldfogel, J. (2002). Maternal employment and child cognitive outcomes in the first three years of life: The NICHD study of early child care. *Child Development, 73*, 1052–1072.

Brooks-Gunn, J., Klebanov, P. K., Liaw, F., & Spiker, D. (1993). Enhancing the development of low birth weight, premature infants: Changes in cognition and behavior over the first three years. *Child Development, 64*, 736–753.

Brooks-Gunn, J., McCarton, C. M., Casey, P. H., McCormick, M. C., Bauer, C. R., Bernbaum, J. C., et al. (1994). Early intervention in low-birth weight premature infants: Results through age 5 years from the Infant Health Development Program. *Journal of the American Medical Association, 272*, 1257–1262.

Broude, G. J. (1995). *Growing up: A cross-cultural encyclopedia.* Santa Barbara, CA: ABC-CLIO.

Brousseau, E. (2006, May). *The effect of maternal body mass index on efficacy of dinoprostone vaginal insert for cervical ripening.* Paper presented at the annual meeting of the American College of Obstetricians and Gynecologists, Washington, DC.

Brown, A. L., Metz, K. E., & Campione, J. C. (1996). Social interaction and individual understanding in a community of learners: The influence of Piaget and Vygotsky. In A. Tryphon & J. Voneche (Eds.), *Piaget-Vygotsky: The social genesis of thought* (pp. 145–170). Hove, England: Psychology/Erlbaum (UK) Taylor & Francis.

Brown, A. S., Begg, M. D., Gravenstein, S., Schaefer, C. A., Wyatt, R. J., Bresnahan, M., et al. (2004). Serologic evidence of prenatal influence in the etiology of schizophrenia. *Archives of General Psychiatry, 61*, 774–780.

Brown, A. S., Tapert, S. F., Granholm, E., & Delis, D. C. (2000) Neurocognitive functioning of adolescents: Effects of protracted alcohol use. *Alcoholism: Clinical and Experimental Research, 24*, 164–171.

Brown, B. B., & Klute, C. (2003). Friendships, cliques, and crowds. In G. R. Adams & M. D. Berzonsky (Eds.), *Blackwell handbook of adolescence* (pp. 330–348). Malden, MA: Blackwell.

Brown, B. B., Mounts, N., Lamborn, S. D., & Steinberg, L. (1993). Parenting practices and peer group affiliation in development. *Child Development, 64*, 467–482.

Brown, J. D., L'Engle, K. L., Pardun, C. J., Guo, G., Kenneavy, K., & Jackson, C. (2006). Sexy media matter: Exposure to sexual content in music, movies, television, and magazines predicts black and white adolescents' sexual behavior. *Pediatrics, 117*, 1018–1027.

Brown, J. L. (1987). Hunger in the U.S. *Scientific American, 256*(2), 37–41.

Brown, J. R., & Dunn, J. (1996). Continuities in emotion understanding from three to six years. *Child Development, 67*, 789–802.

Brown, L. J., Kaste, L. M., Selwitz, R. H., & Furman, L. J. (1996). Dental caries and sealant usage in U.S. children, 1988–1991. *Journal of the American Dental Association, 127*, 335–343.

Brown, L. J., Wall, T. P., & Lazar, V. (1999). Trends in untreated caries in permanent teeth of children 6 to 18 years old. *Journal of the American Dental Association, 130*, 1637–1644.

Brown, L. J., Wall, T. P., & Lazar, V. (2000). Trends in untreated caries in primary teeth of children 2 to 10 years old. *Journal of the American Dental Association, 131*, 93–100.

Brown, L. M., & Gilligan, C. (1990, April). *The psychology of women and the development of girls.* Paper presented at the Laurel-Harvard Conference on the Psychology of Women and the Education of Girls, Cleveland, OH.

Brown, N. M. (1990). Age and children in the Kalahari. *Health and Human Development Research, 1*, 26–30.

Brown, P. (1993, April 17). Motherhood past midnight. *New Scientist*, 4–8.

Brown, S. L. (2004). Family structure and child well-being: The significance of parental cohabitation. *Journal of Marriage and Family, 66*, 351–367.

Brown, S. S. (1985). Can low birth weight be prevented? *Family Planning Perspectives, 17*(3), 112–118.

Browne, A., & Finkelhor, D. (1986). Impact of child sexual abuse: A review of research. *Psychological Bulletin, 99*(1), 66–77.

Brownell, C. A., Ramani, G. B., & Zerwas, S. (2006). Becoming a social partner with peers: Cooperation and social understanding in one- and two-year-olds. *Child Development, 77*, 803–821.

Browning, E. B. (1857). *Aurora Leigh, a poem.* London: J. Miller.

Bruer, J. T. (2001). A critical and sensitive period primer. In D. B. Bailey, J. T. Bruer, F. J. Symons, & J. W. Lichtman (Eds.), *Critical thinking about critical periods: A series from the National Center for Early Development and Learning* (pp. 289–292). Baltimore: Brookes.

Bruner, A. B., Joffe, A., Duggan, A. K., Casella, J. F., & Brandt, J. (1996). Randomised study of cognitive effects of iron supplementation in non-anaemic iron deficient adolescent girls. *Lancet, 348*, 992–996.

Brunson, K. L., Kramar, E., Lin, B., Chen, Y., Colgin, L. L., Yanagihara, T. K., et al. (2005). Mechanisms of late-onset cognitive decline after early-life stress. *Journal of Neuroscience, 25*(41), 9328–9338.

Bryant, B. K. (1987). Mental health, temperament, family, and friends: Perspectives on children's empathy and social perspective taking. In N. Eisenberg & J. Strayer (Eds.), *Empathy and its development* (pp. 245–270). New York: Cambridge University Press.

Bryce, J., Boschi-Pinto, C., Shibuya, K., & The WHO Child Health Epidemiology Reference Group. (2005). WHO estimates of the causes of death in children. *Lancet, 365*, 1147–1152.

Buchanan, C. M., Eccles, J. S., & Becker, J. B. (1992). Are adolescents the victims of raging hormones? Evidence for activational effects of hormones on moods and behavior at adolescence. *Psychological Bulletin, 111*(1), 62–107.

Büchel, C., & Sommer, M. (2004). Unsolved mystery: What causes stuttering? *PLoS Biology, 2*, 0159–0163.

Buckner, J. C., Bassuk, E. L., Weinreb, L. F., & Brooks, M. G. (1999). Homelessness and its relation to the mental health and behavior of low-income school-age children. *Developmental Psychology, 35*(1), 246–257.

Buehler, C. (2006). Parents and peers in relation to early adolescent problem behavior. *Journal of Marriage and Family, 68*, 109–124.

Buhrmester, D. (1990). Intimacy of friendship, interpersonal competence, and adjustment during preadolescence and adolescence. *Child Development, 61*, 1101–1111.

Buhrmester, D. (1996). Need fulfillment, interpersonal competence, and the developmental contexts of early adolescent friendship. In W. M. Bukowski, A. F. Newcomb, & W. W. Hartup (Eds.), *The company they keep: Friendship in childhood and adolescence* (pp. 158–185). New York: Cambridge University Press.

Buhrmester, D., & Furman, W. (1990). Perceptions of sibling relationships during middle childhood and adolescence. *Child Development, 61*, 138–139.

Bulik, C. M., Sullivan, P. F., Tozzi, F., Furberg, H., Lichenstein, P., & Petersen, N. L. (2006). Prevalence, heritability, and prospective risk factors for anorexia nervosa. *Archives of General Psychiatry, 63*, 305–312.

Bulkley, K., & Fisler, J. (2002). *A decade of charter schools: From theory to practice.* Philadelphia: Consortium for Policy

Research in Education, Graduate School of Education. University of Pennsylvania.

Bunikowski, R., Grimmer, I., Heiser, A., Metze, B., Schafer, A., & Obladen, M. (1998). Neurodevelopmental outcome after prenatal exposure to opiates. *European Journal of Pediatrics, 157,* 724–730.

Burchinal, M. R., Campbell, F. A., Bryant, D. M., Wasik, B. H., & Ramey, C. T. (1997). Early intervention and mediating processes in cognitive performance of children of low-income African American families. *Child Development, 68,* 935–954.

Burchinal, M. R., Roberts, J. E., Nabors, L. A., & Bryant, D. M. (1996). Quality of center child care and infant cognitive and language development. *Child Development, 67,* 606–620.

Bureau of Labor Statistics. (2005). *Women in the labor force: A databook.* Retrieved May 19, 2005, from http://www.bls.gov/cps/wlf-databook2005.htm

Bureau of Labor Statistics. (2006, April 27). Employment characteristics of families in 2005 [News release]. Washington, DC: Author.

Burhans, K. K., & Dweck, C. S. (1995). Helplessness in early childhood: The role of contingent worth. *Child Development, 66,* 1719–1738.

Burns, B. J., Phillips, S. D., Wagner, H. R., Barth, R. P., Kolko, D. J., Campbell, Y., et al. (2004). Mental health need and access to mental health services by youths involved with child welfare: A national survey. *Journal of the American Academy of Child and Adolescent Psychiatry, 43,* 960–970.

Burt, A., Annest, J. L., Ballesteros, M. F., & Budnitz, D. S. (2006). Nonfatal, unintentional medication exposures among young children—United States, 2001–2003. *Morbidity and Mortality Weekly Report, 55,* 1–5.

Bushnell, E. W., & Boudreau, J. P. (1993). Motor development and the mind: The potential role of motor abilities as a determinant of aspects of perceptual development. *Child Development, 64,* 1005–1021.

Bussey, K., & Bandura, A. (1992). Self-regulatory mechanisms governing gender development. *Child Development, 63,* 1236–1250.

Bussey, K., & Bandura, A. (1999). Social cognitive theory of gender development and differentiation. *Psychological Review, 106,* 676–713.

Byrne, M., Agerbo, E., Ewald, H., Eaton, W. W., & Mortensen, P. B. (2003). Parental age and risk of schizophrenia. *Archives of General Psychiatry, 60,* 673–678.

Byrnes, J. P., & Fox, N. A. (1998). The educational relevance of research in cognitive neuroscience. *Educational Psychology Review, 10,* 297–342.

Bystron, I., Rakic, P., Molnar, Z., & Blakemore, C. (2006). The first neurons of the human cerebral cortex. *Nature Neuroscience, 9*(7), 880–886.

Cabrera, N. J., Tamis-LeMonda, C. S., Bradley, R. H., Hofferth, S., & Lamb, M. E. (2000). Fatherhood in the twenty-first century. *Child Development, 71,* 127–136.

Caelli, K., Downie, J., & Letendre, A. (2002). Parents' experiences of midwife-managed care following the loss of a baby in a previous pregnancy. *Journal of Advanced Nursing, 39,* 127–136.

Caldji, C., Diorio, J., & Meaney, M. J. (2003). Variations in maternal care alter GABA(A) receptor subunit expression in brain regions associated with fear. *Neuropsychopharmacology, 28,* 1950–1959.

Caldwell, B. M., & Bradley, R. H. (1984). *Home observation for measurement of the environment.* Unpublished manuscript, University of Arkansas at Little Rock.

Calkins, S. D., & Fox, N. A. (1992). The relations among infant temperament, security of attachment, and behavioral inhibition at twenty-four months. *Child Development, 63,* 1456–1472.

Camarata, S., & Woodcock, R. (2006). Sex differences in processing speed: Developmental effects in males and females. *Intelligence, 34*(3), 231–252.

Campbell, A., Shirley, L., & Candy, J. (2004). A longitudinal study of gender-related cognition and behaviour. *Developmental Science, 7,* 1–9.

Campbell, A., Shirley, L., Heywood, C., & Crook, C. (2000). Infants' visual preference for sex-congruent babies, children, toys, and activities: A longitudinal study. *British Journal of Developmental Psychology, 18,* 479–498.

Campbell, D. B., Sutcliffe, J. S., Ebert, P. J., Militerni, R., Bravaccio, C., Trillo, S., et al. (2006). A genetic variant that disrupts MET transcription is associated with autism. *Proceedings of the National Academy of Sciences of the United States of America, 103*(45), 16834–16839.

Campbell, F. A., Pungello, E. P., Miller-Johnson, S., Burchinal, M., & Ramey, C. T. (2001). The development of cognitive and academic abilities: Growth curves from an early childhood education experiment. *Developmental Psychology, 37*(2), 231–242.

Campos, J., Bertenthal, B., & Benson, N. (1980, April). *Self-produced locomotion and the extraction of form invariance.* Paper presented at the meeting of the International Conference on Infant Studies, New Haven, CT.

Canfield, R. L., Henderson, C. R., Cory-Slechta, D. A., Cox, C., Jusko, T. A., & Lanphear, B. P. (April 17, 2003). Intellectual impairment in children with blood lead concentrations below 10 adolescence to young adulthood: Prevalence, prediction, and association with STD contraction. *Developmental Psychology, 38,* 394–406.

Cannon, T. D., Hennah, W., van Erp, T. G. M., Thompson, P. M., Lonnqvistt, J., Huttenen, M., et al. (2005). Association of DISC1/TRAX haplotypes with schizophrenia, reduced prefrontal gray matter, and impaired short- and long-term memory. *Archives of General Psychiatry, 62,* 1205–1213.

Cantor, J. (1994). Confronting children's fright responses to mass media. In D. Zillman, J. Bryant, & A. C. Huston (Eds.), *Media, children, and the family: Social scientific, psychoanalytic, and clinical perspectives* (pp. 139–150). Hillsdale, NJ: Erlbaum.

Cao, A., Saba, L., Galanello, R., & Rosatelli, M. C. (1997). Molecular diagnosis and carrier screening for thalassemia. *Journal of the American Medical Association, 278,* 1273–1277.

Capaldi, D. M., Stoolmiller, M., Clark, S., & Owen, L. D. (2002). Heterosexual risk behaviors in at-risk young men from early adolescence to young adulthood: Prevalence, prediction, and STD contraction. *Developmental Psychology, 38,* 394–406.

Caplan, M., Vespo, J., Pedersen, J., & Hay, D. F. (1991). Conflict and its resolution in small groups of one- and two-year olds. *Child Development, 62,* 1513–1524.

Capute, A. J., Shapiro, B. K., & Palmer, F. B. (1987). Marking the milestones of language development. *Contemporary Pediatrics, 4*(4), 24.

Carlson, E. A. (1998). A prospective longitudinal study of attachment disorganization/disorientation. *Child Development, 69*(4), 1107–1128.

Carlson, E. A., Sroufe, L. A., & Egeland, B. (2004). The construction of experience: A longitudinal study of representation and behavior. *Child Development, 75,* 66–83.

Carlson, M. J. (2006). Family structure, father involvement, and adolescent behavioral outcomes. *Journal of Marriage and Family, 68,* 137–154.

Carlson, S. M., Moses, L. J., & Hix, H. R. (1998). The role of inhibitory processes in young children's difficulties with deception and false belief. *Child Development, 69*(3), 672–691.

Carlson, S. M., & Taylor, M. (2005). Imaginary companions and impersonated characters: Sex differences in children's fantasy play. *Merrill-Palmer Quarterly, 51*(1), 93–118.

Carlson, S. M., Wong, A., Lemke, M., & Cosser, C. (2005). Gesture as a window in children's beginning understanding of false belief. *Child Development, 76,* 73–86.

Carmichael, M. (2004, January 26). In parts of Asia, sexism is ingrained and gender selection often means murder. No girls, please. *Newsweek,* p. 50.

Carnethon, M. R., Gulati, M., & Greenland, P. (2005). Prevalence and cardiovascular disease correlates of low cardiorespiratory fitness in adolescents and adults. *Journal of the American Medical Association, 294,* 2981–2988.

Carraher, T. N., Schliemann, A. D., & Carraher, D. W. (1988). Mathematical concepts in everyday life. In G. B. Saxe & M. Gearhart (Eds.), *Children's mathematics: New Directions in Child Development, 41,* 71–87.

Carrel, L., & Willard, B. F. (2005). X-inactivation profile reveals extensive variability in X-linked gene expression in females. *Nature, 434,* 400–404.

Carskadon, M. A., Acebo, C., Richardson, G. S., Tate, B. A., & Seifer, R. (1997). Long nights protocol: Access to circadian parameters in adolescents. *Journal of Biological Rhythms, 12,* 278–289.

Carter, R. C., Jacobson, S. W., Molteno, C. D., Chiodo, L. M., Viljoen, D., & Jacobson, J. L. (2005). Effects of prenatal alcohol exposure on infant visual acuity. *The Journal of Pediatrics, 147*(4), 473–479.

Carver, P. R., & Iruka, I. U. (2006). *After-school programs and activities: 2005* (NCES 2006-076). Washington, DC: National Center for Education Statistics.

Casaer, P. (1993). Old and new facts about perinatal brain development. *Journal of Child Psychology and Psychiatry, 34*(1), 101–109.

Casanova, M. F., Christensen, J. D., Giedd, J., Rumsey, J. M., Garver, D. L., & Postel, G. C. (2005). Magnetic response imaging of brain asymmetries in dyslexic patients. *Journal of Child Neurology, 20,* 842–847.

Case, R. (1985). *Intellectual development: Birth to adulthood.* Orlando, FL: Academic Press.

Case, R. (1992). Neo-Piagetian theories of child development. In R. Sternberg & C. Berg (Eds.), *Intellectual development* (pp. 161–196). New York: Cambridge University Press.

Case, R., & Okamoto, Y. (1996). The role of central conceptual structures in the development of children's thought. *Monographs of the Society for Research in Child Development, 61*(1–2, serial no. 246).

Casey, B. M., McIntire, D. D., & Leveno, K. J. (2001). The continuing value of the Apgar score for the assessment of newborn infants. *New England Journal of Medicine, 344,* 467–471.

Casper, L. M. (1997). My daddy takes care of me: Fathers as care providers. *Current Population Reports* (P70–59). Washington, DC: U.S. Bureau of the Census.

Casper, L. M., & Bryson, K. R. (1998). *Coresident grandparents and their grandchildren: Grandparent maintained families* (Population Division Working Paper No. 26). Washington, DC: U.S. Bureau of the Census.

Caspi, A. (2000). The child is father of the man: Personality continuity from childhood to adulthood. *Journal of Personality and Social Psychology, 78,* 158–172.

Caspi, A., McClay, J., Moffitt, T. E., Mill, J., Martin, J., Craig, I. W., et al. (2002). Role of genotype in the cycle of violence in maltreated children. *Science, 297,* 851–854.

Caspi, A., & Silva, P. (1995). Temperamental qualities at age 3 predict personality traits in young adulthood: Longitudinal evidence from a birth cohort. *Child Development, 66,* 486–498.

Caspi, A., Sugden, K., Moffitt, T. E., Taylor, A., Craig, I. W., Harrington, H., et al. (2003). Influence of life stress on depression: Moderation by a polymorphism in the 5-HTT gene. *Science, 301,* 386–389.

Caspi, A. M., Lyman, D., Moffitt, T. E., & Silva, P. A. (1993). Unraveling girls' delinquency: Biological, dispositional, and contextual contributions to adolescent misbehavior. *Developmental Psychology, 29,* 19–30.

Cassidy, K. W., Werner, R. S., Rourke, M., Zubernis, L. S., & Balaraman, G. (2003). The relationship between psychological understanding and positive social behaviors. *Social Development, 12,* 198–221.

Cattanach, B. M., & Kirk, M. (1985). Differential activity of maternally and paternally derived chromosome regions in mice. *Nature, 315,* 496–498.

Caughey, A. B., Hopkins, L. M., & Norton, M. E. (2006). Chorionic villus sampling compared with amniocentesis and the difference in the rate of pregnancy loss. *Obstetrics and Gynecology, 108,* 612–616.

Cavazanna-Calvo, M., Hacein-Bey, S., de Saint Basile, G., Gross, F., Yvon, E., Nusbaum, P., et al. (2000). Gene therapy of human severe combined immunodeficiency (SCID)-X1 disease. *Science, 288,* 669–672.

CBS News. (2004). *Becoming Barbie: Living dolls.* Retrieved December 5, 2004, from http://www.cbsnews.com/stories/2004/07/29/48hours/main632909.shtml

Ceci, S. J. (1991). How much does schooling influence general intelligence and its cognitive components? A reassessment of the evidence. *Developmental Psychology, 27,* 703–722.

Ceci, S. J., & Williams, W. M. (1997). Schooling, intelligence, and income. *American Psychologist, 52*(10), 1051–1058.

Celis, W. (1990). More states are laying school paddle to rest. *New York Times,* pp. A1, B12.

Center for Autism Research. (n.d.). *MRI research.* Retrieved May 10, 2006, from http://www.courchesneautismlab.org/mri.html

Center for Education Reform. (2004, August 17). *Comprehensive data discounts* New York Times *account; reveals charter schools performing at or above traditional schools* (CER press release). Retrieved September 17, 2004, from http://edreform.com/index.cfm?fuseAction =document&documentID=1806

Center for Education Reform. (2005). *Charter schools. CER quick facts.* Retrieved April 14, 2006, from http://209.183.221.111/index.cfm?fuseAction=document&document ID=1965

Center for Effective Discipline. (2005). *Facts about corporal punishment in Canada.* Retrieved April 20, 2005, from http://www.stophitting.com/news

Center for Weight and Health. (2001). *Pediatric overweight: A review of the literature: Executive summary.* Berkeley, CA: University of California at Berkeley.

Center on Addiction and Substance Abuse at Columbia University (CASA). (1996, June). *Substance abuse and the American woman.* New York: Author.

Centers for Disease Control and Prevention (CDC). (2000a). *CDC's guidelines for school and community programs: Promoting lifelong physical activity.* Retrieved May 26, 2000, from http://www.cdc.gov/nccdphp/dash/phactaag.htm

Centers for Disease Control and Prevention (CDC). (2000b). *Tracking the hidden epidemic: Trends in STDs in the U.S., 2000.* Washington, DC: Author.

Centers for Disease Control and Prevention (CDC). (2002). Youth risk behavior surveillance—United States, 2001. *Morbidity and Mortality Weekly Report, 51*(4). Atlanta, GA: Author.

Centers for Disease Control and Prevention.(CDC) (2003). *Second National Report on Human Exposure to Environmental Chemicals.* Atlanta, GA: Author.

Centers for Disease Control and Prevention (CDC). (2004). National, state, and urban area vaccination coverage among children aged 19–36 months—United States, 2003. *Morbidity and Mortality Weekly Report, 53,* 658–661.

Centers for Disease Control and Prevention (CDC). (2005). *Assisted reproductive technology: Home.* Retrieved January 25, 2006, from http://www.cdc.gov/ART/

Centers for Disease Control and Prevention (CDC). (2006a). Achievements in public health: Reduction in perinatal transmission of HIV infection—United States, 1985–2005. *Morbidity and Mortality Weekly Report, 55*(21), 592–597.

Centers for Disease Control and Prevention (CDC). (2006b). Improved national prevalence estimates for 18 selected major birth defects—United States, 1999–2001. *Morbidity and Mortality Weekly Report, 54*(51 & 52), 1301–1305.

Centers for Disease Control and Prevention (CDC). (2006c). National, state, and urban area vaccination coverage among children aged 19-35 months—United States, 2005. *Morbidity and Mortality Weekly Report, 55*(36), 988–993.

Centers for Disease Control and Prevention (CDC). (2006d). QuickStats: Infant mortality rates, by maternal race/ethnicity—United States, 1995 and 2003. *Morbidity and Mortality Weekly Report, 55*(24), 683.

Centers for Disease Control and Prevention (CDC). (2006e). Recommendations to improve preconception health and health care—United States. *Morbidity and Mortality Weekly Report, 55*(RR06), 1–23.

Centers for Disease Control and Prevention (CDC). (2006f). Youth risk behavior surveillance—United States, 2005. *Morbidity and Mortality Weekly Report, 55*(SS-5).

Centers for Disease Control and Prevention (CDC) Office of Media Relations. (2006, June 29). *CDC's advisory committee recommends human papillomavirus virus vaccination.* (Press release). Atlanta, GA: Author.

Chambers, C. D., Hernandez-Diaz, S., Van Marter, L. J., Werler, M. M., Louik, C., Jones, K. L., & Mitchell, A. A. (2006). Selective serotonin-reuptake inhibitors and risk of persistent pulmonary hypertension of the newborn. *New England Journal of Medicine, 354,* 579–587.

Chambers, R. A., Taylor, J. R., & Potenza, M. N. (2003). Developmental neurocircuitry of motivation in adolescence: A critical period of addiction vulnerability. *American Journal of Psychiatry, 160,* 1041–1052.

Chan, R. W., Raboy, B., & Patterson, C. J. (1998). Psychosocial adjustment among children conceived via donor insemination by lesbian and heterosexual mothers. *Child Development, 69,* 443–457.

Chao, R. (1996). Chinese and European American mothers' beliefs about the role of parenting in children's school success. *Journal of Cross-Cultural Psychology, 27,* 403–423.

Chao, R. K. (1994). Beyond parental control and authoritarian parenting style: Understanding Chinese parenting through the cultural notion of training. *Child Development, 65,* 1111–1119.

Chao, R. K. (2001). Extending research on the consequences of parenting style for Chinese Americans and European Americans. *Child Development, 72,* 1832–1843.

Chapman, M., & Lindenberger, U. (1988). Functions, operations, and décalage in the development of transitivity. *Developmental Psychology, 24,* 542–551.

Charlesworth, A., & Glantz, S. A. (2005). Smoking in the movies increases adolescent smoking: A review. *Pediatrics, 116,* 1516–1528.

Chase-Lansdale, P. L., Moffitt, R. A., Lohman, B. J., Cherlin, A. J., Coley, R. L., Pittman, L. D., et al. (2003). Mothers' transitions from welfare to work and the well-being of preschoolers and adolescents. *Science, 299*(5612), 1548–1552.

Chehab, F. F., Mounzih, K., Lu, R., & Lim, M. E. (1997, January 3). Early onset of reproductive function in normal female mice treated with leptin. *Science, 275,* 88–90.

Chen, A., & Rogan, W. J. (2004). Breastfeeding and the risk of postneonatal death in the United States. *Pediatrics, 113,* e435–e439.

Chen, C., & Stevenson, H. W. (1995). Motivation and mathematics achievement: A comparative study of Asian-American, Caucasian-American, and East Asian high school students. *Child Development, 66,* 1215–1234.

Chen, E., Matthews, K. A., & Boyce, W. T. (2002). Socioeconomic differences in children's health: How and why do these relationships change with age? *Psychological Bulletin, 128,* 295–329.

Chen, L., Baker, S. B., Braver, E. R., & Li, G. (2000). Carrying passengers as a risk factor for crashes fatal to 16- and 17-year-old drivers. *Journal of the American Medical Association, 283*(12), 1578–1582.

Chen, W., Li, S., Cook, N. R., Rosner, B. A., Srinivasan, S. R., Boerwinkle, E., et al. (2004). An autosomal genome scan for loci influencing longitudinal burden of body mass index from childhood to young adulthood in white sibships: The Bogalusa Heart Study. *International Journal of Obesity, 28,* 462–469.

Chen, X., Cen, G., Li, D., & He, Y. (2005). Social functioning and adjustment in Chinese children: The imprint of historical time. *Child Development, 76,* 182–195.

Chen, X., Rubin, K. H., & Li, D. (1995). Social functioning and adjustment in Chinese children: A longitudinal study. *Developmental Psychology, 31,* 531–539.

Chen, X., Rubin, K. H., & Sun, Y. (1992). Social reputation and peer relationships in Chinese and Canadian children: A cross-cultural study. *Child Development, 63,* 1336–1343.

Cheruku, S. R., Montgomery-Downs, H. E., Farkas, S. L., Thoman, E. B., Lammi-Keefe, C. J. (2002). Higher maternal plasma docosahexaenoic acid during pregnancy is associated with more mature neonatal sleep-state patterning. *American Journal of Clinical Nutrition, 76,* 608–613.

Chess, S., & Thomas, A. (1982). Infant bonding: Mystique and reality. *American Journal of Orthopsychiatry, 52*(2), 213–222.

Chia, S. E., Shi, L. M., Chan, O. Y., Chew, S. K., & Foong, B. H. (2004). A population-based study on the association between parental occupations and some common birth defects in Singapore (1994–1998). *Journal of Occupational and Environmental Medicine, 46*(9), 916–923.

Children's Defense Fund. (1998). *The state of America's children yearbook, 1998.* Washington, DC: Author.

Children's Defense Fund. (2004). *The state of America's children 2004.* Washington, DC: Author.

Chiriboga, C. A., Brust, J. C. M., Bateman, D., & Hauser, W. A. (1999). Dose-response effect of fetal cocaine exposure on newborn neurologic function. *Pediatrics, 103,* 79–85.

Chodirker, B. N., Cadrin, C., Davies, G. A. L., Summers, A. M., Wilson, R. D., Winsor, E. J. T., et al. (2001, July). Canadian guidelines for prenatal diagnosis: Techniques of prenatal diagnosis. *JOGC Clinical Practice Guidelines,* No. 105.

Chomitz, V. R., Cheung, L. W. Y., & Lieberman, E. (1995). The role of lifestyle in preventing low birth weight. *The Future of Children, 5*(1), 121–138.

Chomsky, C. S. (1969). *The acquisition of syntax in children from five to ten.* Cambridge, MA: MIT Press.

Chomsky, N. (1957). *Syntactic structures.* The Hague, Netherlands: Mouton.

Chomsky, N. (1972). *Language and mind* (2nd ed.). New York: Harcourt Brace Jovanovich.

Chomsky, N. (1995). *The minimalist program.* Cambridge, MA: MIT Press.

Chorpita, B. P., & Barlow, D. H. (1998). The development of anxiety: The role of control in the early environment. *Psychological Bulletin, 124,* 3–21.

Christakis, D. A., Zimmerman, F. J., DiGiuseppe, D. L., & McCarty, C. A. (2004). Early television exposure and subsequent attentional problems in children. *Pediatrics, 113,* 708–713.

Christian, M. S., & Brent, R. L. (2001). Teratogen update: Evaluation of the reproductive and developmental risks of caffeine. *Teratology, 64*(1), 51–78.

Christie, J. F. (1991). *Psychological research on play: Connections with early literacy development.* Albany, NY: State University of New York Press.

Christie, J. F. (1998). Play as a medium for literacy development. In D. P. Fromberg & D. Bergen (Eds.), *Play from birth to 12 and beyond: Contexts, perspectives, and meanings* (pp. 50–55). New York: Garland.

Chung. H. L., & Steinberg, L. (2006). Relations between neighborhood factors, parenting behaviors, peer deviance, and delinquency among serious juvenile offenders. *Developmental Psychology, 42,* 319–331.

Cicchetti, D., & Toth, S. L. (1998). The development of depression in children and adolescents. *American Psychologist, 53,* 221–241.

Cicero, S., Curcio, P., Papageorghiou, A., Sonek, J., & Nicolaides, K. (2001). Absence of nasal bone in fetuses with trisomy 21 at 11–14 weeks of gestation: An observational study. *Lancet, 358,* 1665–1667.

Cicirelli, V. G. (1976). Family structure and interaction: Sibling effects on socialization. In M. F. McMillan & S. Henao (Eds.), *Child psychiatry: Treatment and research.* New York: Brunner/Mazel.

Cicirelli, V. G. (1994). Sibling relationships in cross-cultural perspective. *Journal of Marriage and the Family, 56,* 7–20.

Cicirelli, V. G. (1995). *Sibling relationships across the life span.* New York: Plenum Press.

Cillessen, A. H. N., & Mayeux, L. (2004). From censure to reinforcement: Developmental changes in the association between aggression and social status. *Child Development, 75,* 147–163.

Clark, A. G., Glanowski, S., Nielsen, R., Thomas, P. D., Kejariwal, A., Todd, M. A., et al. (2003). Inferring non-neutral evolution from human-chimp-mouse orthologous gene trios. *Science, 302,* 1960–1963.

Clarke-Stewart, K. A. (1987). Predicting child development from day care forms and features: The Chicago study. In D. A. Phillips (Ed.), *Quality in child care: What does the research tell us?* (Research Monographs of the National Association for the Education of Young Children). Washington, DC: National Association for the Education of Young Children.

Clausen, J. A. (1993). *American lives.* New York: Free Press.

Clayton, E. W. (2003). Ethical, legal, and social implications of genomic medicine. *New England Journal of Medicine, 349,* 562–569.

Clayton, R., & Heard, D. (Eds.). (1994). *Elvis up close: In the words of those who knew him best.* Atlanta, GA: Turner.

Clearfield, M. W., & Mix, K. S. (1999). Number versus contour length in infants' discrimination of small visual sets. *Current Directions in Psychological Science, 10,* 408–411.

Clément, K., Vaisse, C., Lahlou, N., Cabrol, S., Pelloux, V., Cassuto, D., et al. (1998). A mutation in the human leptin receptor gene causes obesity and pituitary dysfunction. *Nature, 392,* 398–401.

Cleveland, E., & Reese, E. (2005). Maternal structure and autonomy support in conversations about the past: Contributions to children's autobiographical memory. *Development Psychology, 41,* 376–388.

Cleveland, H. H., & Wiebe, R. P. (2003). The moderation of adolescent-to-peer similarity in tobacco and alcohol use by school level of substance use. *Child Development, 74,* 279–291.

Clifton, R. K., Muir, D. W., Ashmead, D. H., & Clarkson, M. G. (1993). Is visually guided reaching in early infancy a myth? *Child Development, 64,* 1099–1110.

Cnattingius, S., Bergström, R., Lipworth, L., & Kramer, M. S. (1998). Prepregnancy weight and the risk of adverse pregnancy outcomes. *New England Journal of Medicine, 338,* 147–152.

Cnattingius, S., Signorello, L. B., Anneré, G., Clausson, B., Ekbom, A., Ljunger, E., et al. (2000). Caffeine intake and the risk of first-trimester spontaneous abortion. *New England Journal of Medicine, 343*(25), 1839–1845.

Cohen, D. A., Nsuami, M., Martin, D. H., & Farley, T. A. (1999). Repeated schoolbased screening for sexually transmitted diseases: A feasible strategy for reaching adolescents. *Pediatrics, 104*(6), 1281–1285.

Cohen, L. B., & Amsel, L. B. (1998). Precursors to infants' perception of the causality of a simple event. *Infant Behavior and Development, 21,* 713–732.

Cohen, L. B., & Oakes, L. M. (1993). How infants perceive a simple causal event. *Developmental Psychology, 29,* 421–433.

Cohen, L. B., Rundell, L. J., Spellman, B. A., & Cashon, C. H. (1999). Infants' perception of causal chains. *Current Directions in Psychological Science, 10,* 412–418.

Cohn, J. F., & Tronick, E. Z. (1983). Three-month-old infants' reaction to simulated maternal depression. *Child Development, 54,* 185–193.

Coie, J. D., & Dodge, K. A. (1998). Aggression and antisocial behavior. In W. Damon (Series Ed.) & N. Eisenberg (Vol. Ed.), *Handbook of child psychology: Vol. 3. Social, emotional, and personality development* (5th ed., pp. 780–862). New York: Wiley.

Colby, A., & Damon, W. (1992). *Some do care: Contemporary lives of moral commitment.* New York: Free Press.

Colby, A., Kohlberg, L., Gibbs, J., & Lieberman, M. (1983). A longitudinal study of moral development. *Monographs of the Society for Research in Child Development, 48*(1–2, Serial No. 200).

Cole, M. (1998). *Cultural psychology: A once and future discipline.* Cambridge, MA: Belknap.

Cole, P. M., Barrett, K. C., & Zahn-Waxler, C. (1992). Emotion displays in two-year-olds during mishaps. *Child Development, 63,* 314–324.

Cole, P. M., Bruschi, C. J., & Tamang, B. L. (2002). Cultural differences in children's emotional reactions to difficult situations. *Child Development, 73*(3), 983–996.

Cole, P. M., Tamang, B. L., & Shrestha, S. (2006). Cultural variations in the socialization of young children's anger and shame. *Child Development, 77*(5), 1237–1251.

Cole, T. B. (1999). Ebbing epidemic: Youth homicide rate at a 14-year low. *Journal of the American Medical Association, 281,* 25–26.

Coleman, J. S. (1988). Social capital in the creation of human capital. *American Journal of Sociology, 94*(Suppl. 95), S95–S120.

Colen, C. G., Geronimus, A. T., Bound, J., & James, S. A. (2006). Maternal upward socioeconomic mobility and black-white disparities in infant birthweight. *American Journal of Public Health, 96,* 2032–2039.

Coley, R. L., Morris, J. E., & Hernandez, D. (2004). Out-of-school care and problem behavior trajectories among low-income adolescents: Individual, family, and neighborhood characteristics as added risks. *Child Development, 75,* 948–965.

Collier, V. P. (1995). Acquiring a second language for school. *Directions in Language and Education, 1*(4), 1–11.

Collins, J. G., & LeClere, F. B. (1997). *Health and selected socioeconomic characteristics of the family: United States, 1988–90* (DHHS No. PHS 97–1523). Washington, DC: U.S. Government Printing Office.

Collins, W. A., Maccoby, E. E., Steinberg, L., Hetherington, E. M., & Bornstein, M. H. (2000). Contemporary research in parenting: The case for nature and nurture. *American Psychologist, 55,* 218–232.

Colliver, J. D., Kroutil, L. A., Dai, L., & Gfroerer, J. C. (2006). *Misuse of prescription drugs: Data from the 2002, 2003, and 2004 National Surveys on Drug Use and Health* (DHHS Publication No. SMA 06-4192, Analytic Series A-28). Rockville, MD: Substance Abuse and Mental Health Services Administration, Office of Applied Studies.

Colombo, J. (1993). *Infant cognition: Predicting later intellectual functioning.* Thousand Oaks, CA: Sage.

Colombo, J. (2001). The development of visual attention in infancy. *Annual Review of Psychology, 52,* 337–367.

Colombo, J. (2002). Infant attention grows up: The emergence of a developmental cognitive neuroscience perspective. *Current Directions in Psychological Science, 11,* 196–200.

Colombo, J., & Janowsky, J. S. (1998). A cognitive neuroscience approach to individual differences in infant cognition. In J. E. Richards (Ed.), *Cognitive neuroscience of attention* (pp. 363–391). Mahwah, NJ: Erlbaum.

Colombo, J., Kannass, K. N., Shaddy, J., Kundurthi, S., Maikranz, J. M., Anderson, C. J., et al. (2004). Maternal DHA and the development of attention in infancy and toddlerhood. *Child Development, 75,* 1254–1267.

Comings, D. E., Muhleman, D., Johnson, J. P., & MacMurray, J. P. (2002). Parent-daughter transmission of the androgen receptor gene as an explanation of the effect of father absence on age of menarche. *Child Development, 73*(4), 1046–1051.

Commissioner's Office of Research and Evaluation and Head Start Bureau, Department of Health and Human Services. (2001). *Building their futures: How Early Head Start programs are enhancing the lives of infants and toddlers in low-income families. Summary report.* Washington, DC: Author.

Committee on Obstetric Practice. (2002). ACOG committee opinion: Exercise during pregnancy and the postpartum period. *International Journal of Gynaecology and Obstetrics, 77*(1), 79–81.

Community Paediatrics Committee, Canadian Paediatrics Society. (2005). Management of primary nocturnal enuresis. *Paediatrics and Child Health, 10,* 611–614.

Conde-Agudelo, A., Rosas-Bermúdez, A., & Kafury-Goeta, A. C. (2006). Birth spacing and risk of adverse perinatal outcomes: A meta-analysis. *Journal of the American Medical Association, 295,* 1809–1823.

Conel, J. L. (1959). *The postnatal development of the human cerebral cortex.* Cambridge, MA: Harvard University Press.

Conger, R. D., Conger, K. J., Elder, G. H., Jr., Lorenz, F. O., Simons, R. L., & Whitbeck,

L. B. (1993). Family economic stress and adjustment of early adolescent girls. *Developmental Psychology, 29,* 206–219.

Conger, R. D., & Elder, G. H., Jr. (1994). *Families in troubled times: Adapting to change in rural America.* New York: Aldine de Gruyter.

Constantino, J. N. (2003). Autistic traits in the general population: A twin study. *Archives of General Psychiatry, 60,* 524–530.

Constantino, J. N., Grosz, D., Saenger, P., Chandler, D. W., Nandi, R., & Earls, F. J. (1993). Testosterone and aggression in children. *Journal of the Academy of Child and Adolescent Psychiatry, 32,* 1217–1222.

Cooper, H. (1989, November). Synthesis of research on homework. *Educational Leadership,* 85–91.

Cooper, R. P., & Aslin, R. N. (1990). Preference for infant-directed speech in the first month after birth. *Child Development, 61,* 1584–1595.

Cooper, W. O., Hernandez-Diaz, S., Arbogast, P. G., Dudley, J. A., Dyer, S., Gideon, P. S., et al. (2006). Major congenital formations after first-trimester exposure to ACE inhibitors. *New England Journal of Medicine, 354,* 2443–2451.

Coplan, R. J., Gavinski-Molina, M., Lagacè-Sèguin, D. G., & Wichman, C. (2001). When girls versus boys play alone: Nonsocial play and adjustment in kindergarten. *Developmental Psychology, 37*(4), 464–474.

Coplan, R. J., Prakash, K., O'Neil, K., & Armer, M. (2004). Do you "want" to play? Distinguishing between conflicted-shyness and social disinterest in early childhood. *Developmental Psychology, 40,* 244–258.

Corbet, A., Long, W., Schumacher, R., Gerdes, J., Cotton, R., & the American Exosurf Neonatal Study Group 1. (1995). Double-blind developmental evaluation at 1-year corrected age of 597 premature infants with birth weight from 500 to 1,350 grams enrolled in three placebo-controlled trials of prophylactic synthetic surfactant. *Journal of Pediatrics, 126,* S5–S12.

Corbin, C. (1973). *A textbook of motor development.* Dubuque, IA: Brown.

Correa, A., Botto, L., Liu, V., Mulinare, J., & Erickson, J. D. (2003). Do multivitamin supplements attenuate the risk for diabetes-associated birth defects? *Pediatrics, 111,* 1146–1151.

Costello, E. J., Compton, S. N., Keeler, G., & Angold, A. (2003). Relationship between poverty and psychopathology: A natural experiment. *Journal of the American Medical Association, 290,* 2023–2029.

Costello, S. (1990, December). Yani's monkeys: Lessons in form and freedom. *School Arts,* pp. 10–11.

Council on Sports Medicine and Fitness & Council on School Health. (2006). Active healthy living: Prevention of childhood obesity through increased physical activity. *Pediatrics, 117,* 1834–1842.

Cowan, N., Nugent, L. D., Elliott, E. M., Ponomarev, I., & Saults, J. S. (1999). The role of attention in the development of short-term memory: Age differences in the verbal span of apprehension. *Child Development, 70,* 1082–1097.

Coyle, T. R., & Bjorklund, D. F. (1997). Age differences in, and consequences of, multiple- and variable-strategy use on a multitrial sort-recall task. *Developmental Psychology, 33,* 372–380.

Crain-Thoreson, C., & Dale, P. S. (1992). Do early talkers become early readers? Linguistic precocity, preschool language, and emergent literacy. *Developmental Psychology, 28,* 421–429.

Crary, D. (2007, January 6). *After years of growth, foreign adoptions by Americans decline sharply.* Associated Press.

Cratty, B. J. (1986). *Perceptual and motor development in infants and children* (3rd ed.). Englewood Cliffs, NJ: Prentice-Hall.

Crawford, C. (1998). Environments and adaptations: Then and now. In C. Crawford & D. L. Krebs (Eds.), *Handbook of evolutionary psychology: Ideas, issues, and applications* (pp. 275-302). Mahwah, NJ: Erlbaum.

Crawford, J. (2002). Obituary: The Bilingual Ed Act, 1968–2002. *Rethinking Schools Online.* Retrieved August 26, 2006, from http://www.rethinkingschool.org/specialreports/bilingual/Bill64.shtml

Crawford, J. (2007). The decline of bilingual education: How to reverse a troubling trend? *International Multilingual Research Journal, 1,* 33–37.

Crick, N. R., Casas, J. F., & Nelson, D. A. (2002). Toward a more comprehensive understanding of peer maltreatment: Studies of relational victimization. *Current Directions in Psychological Science, 11*(3), 98–101.

Crick, N. R., & Dodge, K. A. (1994). A review and reformulation of social information-processing mechanisms in children's social adjustment. *Psychological Bulletin, 115,* 74–101.

Crick, N. R., & Dodge, K. A. (1996). Social information-processing mechanisms in reactive and proactive aggression. *Child Development, 67,* 993–1002.

Crick, N. R., & Grotpeter, J. K. (1995). Relational aggression, gender, and social psychological adjustment. *Child Development, 66,* 710–722.

Crisp, J., Ungerer, J. A., & Goodnow, J. J. (1996). The impact of experience on children's understanding of illness. *Journal of Pediatric Psychology, 21,* 57–72.

Crockenberg, S., & Lourie, A. (1996). Parents' conflict strategies with children and children's conflict strategies with peers. *Merrill-Palmer Quarterly, 42,* 495–518.

Crockenberg, S. C. (2003). Rescuing the baby from the bathwater: How gender and temperament influence how child care affects child development. *Child Development, 74,* 1034–1038.

Cronk, L. B., Ye, B., Tester, D. J., Vatta, M., Makielski, J. C., & Ackerman, M. J. (2006, May). *Identification of CAV3-encoded caveolin-3 mutations in sudden infant death syndrome.* Presentation at Heart Rhythm 2006, the 27th Annual Scientific Sessions of the Heart Rhythm Society, Boston.

Crouter, A., & Larson, R. (Eds.). (1998). *Temporal rhythms in adolescence: Clocks, calendars, and the coordination of daily life* (New Directions in Child and Adolescent Development, No. 82). San Francisco: Jossey-Bass.

Crouter, A. C., MacDermid, S. M., McHale, S. M., & Perry-Jenkins, M. (1990). Parental monitoring and perception of children's school performance and conduct in dual- and single-earner families. *Developmental Psychology, 26,* 649–657.

Crow, S. J. (2006). Fluoxetine treatment of anorexia nervosa: Important but disappointing results. *Journal of the American Medical Association, 295,* 2659–2660.

Crowley, S. L. (1993, October). Grandparents to the rescue. *AARP Bulletin,* pp. 1, 16–17.

Cui, M., Conger, R. D., & Lorenz, F. O. (2005). Predicting change in adolescent adjustment from change in marital problems. *Developmental Psychology, 41,* 812–823.

Cummings, E. M., Iannotti, R. J., & Zahn-Waxler, C. (1989). Aggression between peers in early childhood: Individual continuity and developmental change. *Child Development, 60,* 887–895.

Cunniff, C., & the Committee on Genetics. (2004). Prenatal screening and diagnosis for pediatricians. *Pediatrics, 114,* 889–894.

Cunningham, F. G., & Leveno, K. J. (1995). Childbearing among older women: The message is cautiously optimistic. *New England Journal of Medicine, 333,* 1002–1004.

Curtiss, S. (1977). *Genie.* New York: Academic Press.

Czikszentmihalyi, M. (1996*). Creativity: Flow and the psychology of discovery and invention.* New York: HarperCollins.

Daiute, C., Hartup, W. W., Sholl, W., & Zajac, R. (1993, March). *Peer collaboration and written language development: A study of friends and acquaintances.* Paper presented at the meeting of the Society for Research in Child Development, New Orleans, LA.

Dale, P. S., Price, T. S., Bishop, D. V. M., & Plomin, R. (2003). Outcomes of early language delay: I. Predicting persistent and transient language difficulties at 3 and 4 years. *Journal of Speech, Language, and Hearing Research, 46,* 544–560.

Dale, P. S., Simonoff, E., Bishop, D. V. M., Eley, T. C., Oliver, B., Price, T. S., et al. (1998). Genetic influence on language delay in two-year-old children. *Nature Neuroscience, 1,* 324–328.

Daley, P. (2003, July 19). "Miracle baby" speaks of life after the test tube. *The Age*. Retrieved December 30, 2003, from http://www.theage.com.au/articles/2003/07/18/1058035200790.html

Daly, R. (2005). Drop in youth antidepressant use prompts call for FDA monitoring. *Psychiatric News, 40*(19), 18.

Danesi, M. (1994). *Cool: The signs and meanings of adolescence*. Toronto: University of Toronto Press.

Daniel, I., Berg, C., Johnson, C. H., & Atrash, H. (2003). Magnitude of maternal morbidity during labor and delivery: United States, 1993–1997. *American Journal of Public Health, 93*, 633–634.

Daniel, M. H. (1997). Intelligence testing: Status and trends. *American Psychologist, 52*, 1038–1045.

Darling, N., & Steinberg, L. (1993). Parenting style as context: An integrative model. *Psychological Bulletin, 113*, 487–496.

Darroch, J. E., Singh, S., Frost, J. J., & the Study Team. (2001). Differences in teenage pregnancy rates among five developed countries: The roles of sexual activity and contraceptive use. *Family Planning Perspectives, 33*, 244–250, 281.

Darwin, C. R. (1871). *The descent of man and selection in relation to sex*. London: John Murray.

Darwin, C. R. (1995). *The origin of species*. New York: Gramercy. (Original work published 1859.)

Datar, A., & Sturm, R. (2004a). Childhood overweight and parent- and teacher-reported behavior problems. *Archives of Pediatric and Adolescent Medicine, 158*, 804–810.

Datar, A., & Sturm, R. (2004b). Duke physical education in elementary school and body mass index: Evidence from the Early Childhood Longitudinal Study. *American Journal of Public Health, 94*, 1501–1507.

Datar, A., Sturm, R., & Magnabosco, J. L. (2004). Childhood overweight and academic performance: National study of kindergartners and first-graders. *Obesity Research, 12*, 58–68.

David and Lucile Packard Foundation. (2004). Children, families, and foster care: Executive summary. *The Future of Children, 14*(1). Retrieved from http://www.futureofchildren.org

Davidson, J. I. F. (1998). Language and play: Natural partners. In D. P. Fromberg & D. Bergen (Eds.), *Play from birth to 12 and beyond: Contexts, perspectives, and meanings* (pp. 175–183). New York: Garland.

Davidson, R. J., & Fox, N. A. (1989). Frontal brain asymmetry predicts infants' response to maternal separation. *Journal of Abnormal Psychology, 948*(2), 58–64.

Davis, M., & Emory, E. (1995). Sex differences in neonatal stress reactivity. *Child Development, 66*, 14–27.

Davison, K. K., & Birch, L. L. (2001). Weight status, parent reaction, and self-concept in 5-year-old girls. *Pediatrics, 107*, 46–53.

Davison, K. K., Susman, E. J., & Birch, L. L. (2003). Percent body fat at age 5 predicts earlier pubertal development among girls at age 9. *Pediatrics, 111*, 815–821.

Dawson, D. A. (1991). Family structure and children's health and well-being. Data from the 1988 National Health Interview Survey on child health. *Journal of Marriage and the Family, 53*, 573–584.

Dawson, G., Frey, K., Panagiotides, H., Yamada, E., Hessl, D., & Osterling, J. (1999). Infants of depressed mothers exhibit atypical frontal electrical brain activity during interactions with mother and with a familiar nondepressed adult. *Child Development, 70*, 1058–1066.

Dawson, G., Klinger, L. G., Panagiotides, H., Hill, D., & Spieker, S. (1992). Frontal lobe activity and affective behavior of infants of mothers with depressive symptoms. *Child Development, 63*, 725–737.

Day, J. C., Janus, A., & Davis, J. (2005). Computer and Internet use in the United States: 2003. *Current Population Reports* (P23-208). Washington, DC: U.S. Census Bureau.

Deardorff, J., Gonzales, N. A., Christopher, S., Roosa, M. W., & Millsap, R. E. (2005). Early puberty and adolescent pregnancy: The influence of alcohol use. *Pediatrics, 116*, 1451–1456.

DeBell, M., & Chapman, C. (2006). *Computer and Internet use by students in 2003: Statistical analysis report* (NCES 2006-065). Washington, DC: National Center for Education Statistics.

De Bellis, M. D., Keshavan, M. S., Beers, S. R., Hall, J., Frustaci, K., Masalehdan, A., et al. (2001). Sex differences in brain maturation during childhood and adolescence. *Cerebral Cortex, 11*, 552–557.

DeCasper, A. J., & Fifer, W. P. (1980). Of human bonding: Newborns prefer their mothers' voices. *Science, 208*, 1174–1176.

DeCasper, A. J., Lecanuet, J. P., Busnel, M. C., Granier-Deferre, C., & Maugeais, R. (1994). Fetal reactions to recurrent maternal speech. *Infant Behavior and Development, 17*, 159–164.

DeCasper, A. J., & Spence, M. J. (1986). Prenatal maternal speech influences newborns' perceptions of speech sounds. *Infant Behavior and Development, 9*, 133–150.

de Castro, B. O., Veerman, J. W., Koops, W., Bosch, J. D., & Monshouwer, H. J. (2002). Hostile attribution of intent and aggressive behavior: A meta-analysis. *Child Development, 73*, 916–934.

Dekovic, M., & Janssens, J. (1992). Parents' child-rearing style and child's sociometric status. *Developmental Psychology, 28*, 925–932.

Del Carmen, R. D., Pedersen, F. A., Huffman, L. C., & Bryan, V. E. (1993). Dyadic

distress management predicts subsequent security of attachment. *Infant Behavior and Development, 16*, 131–147.

DeLoache, J., & Gottlieb, A. (2000). If Dr. Spock were born in Bali: Raising a world of babies. In J. DeLoache & A. Gottlieb (Eds.), *A world of babies: Imagined childcare guides for seven societies* (pp. 1–27). New York: Cambridge University Press.

DeLoache, J. S. (2000). Dual representation and young children's use of scale models. *Child Development, 71*, 329–338.

DeLoache, J. S. (2004). Becoming symbol-minded. *Trends in Cognitive Science, 8*, 66–70.

DeLoache, J. S. (2006). Mindful of symbols. *Scientific American Mind, 17*, 70–75.

DeLoache, J. S., Miller, K. F., & Pierroutsakos, S. L. (1998). Reasoning and problem solving. In D. Kuhn & R. S. Siegler (Eds.), *Handbook of child psychology: Vol. 2. Cognition, perception, and language* (5th ed., pp. 801–850). New York: Wiley.

DeLoache, J. S., Miller, K. F., & Rosengren, K. S. (1997). The credible shrinking room: Very young children's performance with symbolic and nonsymbolic relations. *Psychological Science, 8*, 308–313.

DeLoache, J. S., Pierroutsakos, S. L., & Uttal, D. H. (2003). The origins of pictorial competence. *Current Directions in Psychological Science, 12*, 114–118.

DeLoache, J. S., Pierroutsakos, S. L., Uttal, D. H., Rosengren, K. S., & Gottlieb, A. (1998). Grasping the nature of pictures. *Psychological Science, 9*, 205–210.

DeLoache, J. S., Uttal, D. H., & Rosengren, K. S. (2004). Scale errors offer evidence for a perception-action dissociation early in life. *Science, 304*, 1027–1029.

Dennis, T. (2006). Emotional self-regulation in preschoolers: The interplay of child approach reactivity, parenting, and control capacities. *Developmental Psychology, 42*, 84–97.

Dennis, W. (1936). A bibliography of baby biographies. *Child Development, 7*, 71–73.

Dennison, B. A., Erb, T. A., & Jenkins, P. L. (2002). Television viewing and television in bedroom associated with overweight risk among low-income preschool children. *Pediatrics, 109*, 1028–1035.

Denham, S. A., Blair, K. A., DeMulder, E., Levitas, J., Sawyer, K., Auerbach-Major, S., et al. (2003). Preschool emotional competence: Pathway to social competence? *Child Development, 74*, 238–256.

Denton, K., West, J., & Walston, J. (2003). *Reading—young children's achievement and classroom experiences: Findings from The Condition of Education 2003*. Washington, DC: National Center for Education Statistics.

Department of Immunization, Vaccines, and Biologicals, World Health Organization; United Nations Children's Fund; Global Immunization Division, National Center for Immunization and Respiratory Diseases (proposed); & McMorrow, M. (2006). Vaccine preventable deaths and the global immunization vision and strategy, 2006–2015. *Morbidity and Mortality Weekly Report, 55,* 511–515.

Detrich, R., Phillips, R., & Durett, D. (2002). Critical issue: Dynamic debate—determining the evolving impact of charter schools. North Central Regional Educational Laboratory. Retrieved from http://www.ncrel.org/sdrs/areas/issues/envrnmnt/go/go800.htm

Devaney, B., Johnson, A., Maynard, R., & Trenholm, C. (2002). *The evaluation of abstinence education programs funded under Title V, Section 510: Interim report.* Washington, DC: U.S. Department of Health and Human Services.

Devlin, B., Scherer, S., & the Autism Genome Project Consortium. (2007, February 18). Mapping autism risk loci using genetic linkage and chromosomal rearrangements. Article doi10.1038/ng1985. Retrieved February 20, 2007, from http://www.nature.com/ng/journal/vaop/ncurrent/abs/ng1985.html

DeVoe, J. F., Peter, K., Kaufman, P., Miller, A., Noonan, M., Snyder, T. D., & Baum, K. (2004). *Indicators of school crime and safety: 2004* (NCES 2005-002/NCJ 205290). Washington, DC: U.S. Departments of Education and Justice.

DeVoe, J. F., Peter, K., Noonan, M., Snyder, T. D., Baum, K., & U. S. Departments of Education and Justice. (2005). *Indicators of school crime and safety: 2005* (NCES 2006-001/NCJ210697). Washington, DC: U.S. Government Printing Office.

Dewing, P., Shi, T., Horvath, S., & Vilain, E. (2003). Sexually dimorphic gene expression in mouse brain precedes gonadal differentiation. *Molecular Brain Research, 118,* 82–90.

De Wolff, M. S., & van IJzendoorn, M. H. (1997). Sensitivity and attachment: A meta-analysis on parental antecedents of infant attachment. *Child Development, 68,* 571–591.

Dey, A. N., Schiller, J. S., & Tai, D. A. (2004). Summary health statistics for U.S. children: National Health Interview Survey, 2002. *Vital Health Statistics 10* (221). Bethesda, MD: National Center for Health Statistics.

Diamond, A. (1991). Neuropsychological insights into the meaning of object concept development. In S. Carey & R. Gelman (Eds.), *Epigenesis of mind* (pp. 67–110). Hillsdale, NJ: Erlbaum.

Diamond, A. (2007). Interrelated and interdependent. *Developmental Science, 10,* 152–158.

Diamond, L. M. (1998). Development of sexual orientation among adolescent and young adult women. *Developmental Psychology, 34*(5), 1085–1095.

Diamond, L. M. (2000). Sexual identity, attractions, and behavior among young sexual-minority women over a 2-year period. *Developmental Psychology, 36,* 241–250.

Diamond, L. M., & Savin-Williams, R. C. (2003). The intimate relationships of sexual-minority youths. In G. R. Adams & M. D. Berzonsky (Eds.), *Blackwell handbook of adolescence* (pp. 393–412). Malden, MA: Blackwell.

Diamond, M., & Sigmundson, H. K. (1997). Sex reassignment at birth: Longterm review and clinical implications. *Archives of Pediatric and Adolescent Medicine, 151,* 298–304.

Dick, D. M., Rose, R. J., Kaprio, J., & Viken, R. (2000). Pubertal timing and substance use: Associations between and within families across late adolescence. *Developmental Psychology, 36,* 180–189.

Dickens, W. T., & Flynn, J. R. (2006). Black Americans reduce the racial IQ gap: Evidence from standardization samples. *Psychological Science, 17,* 913–920.

Dietert, R. R. (2005). Developmental immunotoxicology (DIT): Is DIT testing necessary to ensure safety? *Proceedings of the 14th Immunotoxicology Summer School, Lyon, France, October 2005,* 246–257.

DiFranza, J. R., Aligne, C. A., & Weitzman, M. (2004). Prenatal and postnatal environmental tobacco smoke exposure and children's health. *Pediatrics, 113,* 1007–1015.

Dilworth-Bart, J. E., & Moore, C. F. (2006). Mercy mercy me: Social injustice and the prevention of environmental pollutant exposures among ethnic minority and poor children. *Child Development, 77*(2), 247–265.

DiMarco, M. A., Menke, E. M., & McNamara, T. (2001). Evaluating a support group for perinatal loss. *MCN American Journal of Maternal and Child Nursing, 26,* 135–140.

Dingfelder, S. (2004). Programmed for psychopathology? Stress during pregnancy may increase children's risk for mental illness, researchers say. *Monitor on Psychology, 35*(2), 56–57.

Dinkes, R., Forrest Cataldi, E., Kena, G., & Baum, K. (2006). *Indicators of school crime and safety: 2006* (NCES 2007003). National Center for Education Statistics. Retrieved January 30, 2007, from http://nces.ed.gov/pubsearch/pubsinfo.asp?pubid=2007003

DiPietro, J. A. (2004). The role of prenatal maternal stress in child development. *Current Directions in Psychological Science, 13*(2), 71–74.

DiPietro, J. A., Caulfield, L. E., Costigan, K. A., Merialdi, M., Nguyen, R. H. N., Zavaleta, N., & Gurewitsch, E. D. (2004). Fetal neurobehavioral development: A tale of two cities. *Developmental Psychology, 40,* 445–456.

DiPietro, J., Hilton, S., Hawkins, M., Costigan, K., & Pressman, E. (2002). Maternal stress and affect influences fetal neurobehavioral development. *Developmental Psychology, 38,* 659–668.

DiPietro, J. A., Hodgson, D. M., Costigan, K. A., Hilton, S. C., & Johnson, T. R. B. (1996). Development of fetal movement fetal heart rate coupling from 20 weeks through term. *Early Human Development, 44,* 139–151.

DiPietro, J. A., Novak, M. F. S. X., Costigan, K. A., Atella, L. D., & Reusing, S. P. (2006). Maternal psychological distress during pregnancy in relation to child development at age 2. *Child Development, 77,* 573–587.

Dishion, T. J., McCord, J., & Poulin, F. (1999). When intervention harms. *American Psychologist, 54,* 755–764.

Dittmar, H., Halliwell, E., & Ive, S. (2006). Does Barbie make girls want to be thin? The effect of experimental exposure to images of dolls on the body image of 5- to 8-year-old girls. *Developmental Psychology, 42,* 283–292.

Dlugosz, L., Belanger, K., Helienbrand, K., Holfard, T. R., Leaderer, B., & Bracken, M. B. (1996). Maternal caffeine consumption and spontaneous abortion: A prospective cohort study. *Epidemiology, 7,* 250–255.

Dodge, K. A., Coie, J. D., Pettit, G. S., & Price, J. M. (1990). Peer status and aggression in boys' groups: Developmental and contextual analysis. *Child Development, 61,* 1289–1309.

Dodge, K. A., Dishion, T. J., & Lansford, J. E. (2006). Deviant peer influences in intervention and public policy for youth. *Social Policy Report, XX,* 3–19.

Dodge, K. A., Pettit, G. S., & Bates, J. E. (1994). Socialization mediators of the relation between socioeconomic status and child conduct problems. *Child Development, 65,* 649–665.

Donovan, W. L., Leavitt, L. A., & Walsh, R. O. (1998). Conflict and depression predict maternal sensitivity to infant cries. *Infant Behavior and Development, 21,* 505–517.

Dorris, M. (1989). *The broken cord.* New York: Harper & Row.

Dorsey, M. J., & Schneider, L. C. (2003). Improving asthma outcomes and self-management behaviors of inner-city children. *Pediatrics, 112,* 474.

Dougherty, T. M., & Haith, M. M. (1997). Infant expectations and reaction time as predictors of childhood speed of processing and IQ. *Developmental Psychology, 33,* 146–155.

Downey, D. B., & Condron, D. J. (2004). Playing well with others in kindergarten: The benefit of siblings at home. *Journal of Marriage and Family, 66,* 333–350.

Dowshen, S., Crowley, J., & Palusci, V. J. (2004). *Shaken baby/shaken impact syndrome.* Retrieved February 17, 2007, from http://www.kidshealth.org/parent/medical/brain/shaken.html

Dozier, M., Stovall, K. C., Albus, K. E., & Bates, B. (2001). Attachment for infants in foster care: The role of caregiver state of mind. *Child Development, 72,* 1467–1477.

Drug Policy Alliance. (2004, June 23). *South Carolina v. McKnight*. Retrieved April 6, 2005, from http://www.drugpolicy.org/law/womenpregnan/mcknight.cfm

Drumm, P., & Jackson, D. W. (1996). Developmental changes in questioning strategies during adolescence. *Journal of Adolescent Research, 11,* 285–305.

Dubé, E. M., & Savin-Williams, R. C. (1999). Sexual identity development among ethnic sexual-minority youths. *Developmental Psychology, 35*(6), 1389–1398.

Dube, S. R., Anda, R. F., Felitti, V. J., Chapman, D. P., Williamson, D. F., & Giles, W. H. (2001). Childhood abuse, household dysfunction, and the risk of attempted suicide throughout the life span: Findings from the Adverse Childhood Experiences Study. *Journal of the American Medical Association, 286*(24), 3089–3096.

Dube, S. R., Felitti, V. J., Dong, M., Chapman, D. P., Giles, W. H., & Anda, R. F. (2003, March). Childhood abuse, neglect, and household dysfunction and the risk of illicit drug use: The Adverse Childhood Experiences Study. *Pediatrics, 111*(3), 564–572.

Dubowitz, H. (1999). The families of neglected children. In M. E. Lamb (Ed.), *Parenting and child development in "nontraditional" families* (pp. 372–345). Mahwah, NJ: Erlbaum.

Duckworth, A., & Seligman, M. E. P. (2005). Self-discipline outdoes IQ in predicting academic performance of adolescents. *Psychological Science, 26,* 939–944.

Duenwald, M. (2003, July 15). After 25 years, new ideas in the prenatal test tube. *New York Times.* Retrieved from http://www.nytimes.com/2003/07/15/health/15IVF.html?ex

Duke, J., Huhman, M., & Heitzler, C. (2003). Physical activity levels among children aged 9–13 years—United States, 2002. *Morbidity and Mortality Weekly Report, 52,* 785–788.

Duncan, G. J., & Brooks-Gunn, J. (1997). Income effects across the life span: Integration and interpretation. In G. J. Duncan & J. Brooks-Gunn (Eds.), *Consequences of growing up poor* (pp. 596–610). New York: Russell Sage Foundation.

Dundy, E. (1985). *Elvis and Gladys.* New York: Dell.

Dunn, J. (1985). *Sisters and brothers.* Cambridge, MA: Harvard University Press.

Dunn, J. (1991). Young children's understanding of other people: Evidence from observations within the family. In D. Frye & C. Moore (Eds.), *Children's theories of mind: Mental states and social understanding.* Hillsdale, NJ: Erlbaum.

Dunn, J. (1996). Sibling relationships and perceived self-competence: Patterns of stability between childhood and early adolescence. In A. J. Sameroff & M. M. Haith (Eds.), *The five to seven year shift: The age of reason and responsibility* (pp. 253–269). Chicago: University of Chicago Press.

Dunn, J. (1999). Siblings, friends, and the development of social understanding. In W.A. Collins & B. Laursen (Eds.), *The Minnesota Symposia on Child Psychology: Vol. 30. Relationships as developmental contexts* (pp. 263–279). Mahwah, NJ: Erlbaum.

Dunn, J., Brown, J., Slomkowski, C., Tesla, C., & Youngblade, L. (1991). Young children's understanding of other people's feelings and beliefs: Individual differences and antecedents. *Child Development, 62,* 1352–1366.

Dunn, J., & Hughes, C. (2001). "I got some swords and you're dead!": Violent fantasy, antisocial behavior, friendship, and moral sensibility in young children. *Child Development, 72,* 491–505.

Dunn, J., & Kendrick, C. (1982). *Siblings: Love, envy and understanding.* Cambridge, MA: Harvard University Press.

Dunn, J., & Munn, P. (1985). Becoming a family member: Family conflict and the development of social understanding in the second year. *Child Development, 56,* 480–492.

Dunson, D. (2002). *Late breaking research session. Increasing infertility with increasing age: Good news and bad news for older couples.* Paper presented at 18th Annual Meeting of the European Society of Human Reproduction and Embryology, Vienna.

Dunson, D. B., Colombo, B., & Baird, D. D. (2002). Changes with age in the level and duration of fertility in the menstrual cycle. *Human Reproduction, 17,* 1399–1403.

DuPont, R. L. (1983). Phobias in children. *Journal of Pediatrics, 102,* 999–1002.

Durand, A. M. (1992). The safety of home birth: The Farm Study. *American Journal of Public Health, 82,* 450–452.

DuRant, R. H., Smith, J. A., Kreiter, S. R., & Krowchuk, D. P. (1999). The relationship between early age of onset of initial substance use and engaging in multiple health risk behaviors among young adolescents. *Archives of Pediatrics and Adolescent Medicine, 153,* 286–291.

Dwyer, T., Ponsonby, A. L., Blizzard, L., Newman, N. M., & Cochrane, J. A. (1995). The contribution of changes in the prevalence of prone sleeping position to the decline in sudden infant death syndrome in Tasmania. *Journal of the American Medical Association, 273,* 783–789.

Dyl, J., Kittler, J., Phillips, K. A., & Hunt, J. I. (2006). Body dysmorphic disorder and other clinically significant body image concerns in adolescent psychiatric inpatients: Prevalence and clinical characteristics. *Child Psychiatry and Human Development, 36*(4), 369–382.

Early College High School Initiative. (undated). Retrieved March 31, 2004, from http://www.earlycolleges.org

East, P. L., & Khoo, S. T. (2005). Longitudinal pathways linking family factors and sibling relationship qualities to adolescent substance use and sexual risk behaviors. *Journal of Family Psychology, 19,* 571–580.

Eating disorders—Part I. (1997, October). *The Harvard Mental Health Letter,* pp. 1–5.

Eating disorders—Part II. (1997, November). *The Harvard Mental Health Letter,* pp. 1–5.

Eaton, D. K., Kann, L., Kinchen, S., Ross, J., Hawkins, J., Harris, W. A., et al. (2006). Youth risk behavior surveillance—United States, 2005. *Morbidity and Mortality Weekly Report, 55*(SS-5).

Eccles, A. (1982). *Obstetrics and gynaecology in Tudor and Stuart England.* Kent, OH: Kent State University Press.

Eccles, J. S. (2004). Schools, academic motivation, and stage-environment fit. In R. M. Lerner & L. Steinberg (Eds), *Handbook of adolescent development* (2nd ed., pp. 125–153). Hoboken, NJ: Wiley.

Eccles, J. S., Wigfield, A., & Byrnes, J. (2003). Cognitive development in adolescence. In I. B. Weiner (Ed.) & R. M. Lerner, M. A. Easterbrooks, & J. Mistry (Vol. Eds.), *Handbook of psychology: Vol. 6. Developmental psychology.* New York: Wiley.

Echeland, Y., Epstein, D. J., St-Jacques, B., Shen, L., Mohler, J., McMahon, J. A., et al. (1993). Sonic hedgehog, a member of a family of putative signality molecules, is implicated in the regulation of CNS polarity. *Cell, 75,* 1417–1430.

Eckerman, C. O., Davis, C. C., & Didow, S. M. (1989). Toddlers' emerging ways of achieving social coordination with a peer. *Child Development, 60,* 440–453.

Eckerman, C. O., & Didow, S. M. (1996). Nonverbal imitation and toddlers' mastery of verbal means of achieving coordinated action. *Developmental Psychology, 32,* 141–152.

Eckerman, C. O., & Stein, M. R. (1982). The toddler's emerging interactive skills. In K. H. Rubin & H. S. Ross (Eds.), *Peer relationships and social skills in childhood.* New York: Springer-Verlag.

Eddleman, K. A., Malone, F. D., Sullivan, L., Dukes, K., Berkowitz, R. L., Kharbutli, Y., et al. (2006). Pregnancy loss rates after midtrimester amniocentesis. *Obstetrics and Gynecology, 108*(5), 1067–1072.

Eden, G. F., Jones, K. M., Cappell, K., Gareau, L., Wood, F. B., Zeffiro, T. A., et al. (2004). Neural changes following remediation in adult developmental dyslexia. *Neuron, 44,* 411–422.

Eder, W., Ege, M. J., & von Mutius, E. (2006). The asthma epidemic. *New England Journal of Medicine, 355,* 2226–2235.

Edwards, C. P. (1981). The comparative study of the development of moral judgment and reasoning. In R. H. Monroe, R. L. Monroe, & B. B. Whiting (Eds.), *Handbook of cross-cultural human development.* New York: Garland.

Edwards, C. P. (1994, April). *Cultural relativity meets best practice, or, anthropology and early education, a promising friendship.* Paper presented at the meeting of the American Educational Research Association, New Orleans.

Egan, M. F., Straub, R. E., Goldberg, T. E., Yakub, I., Callicott, J. H., Hariri, A. R., et al. (2004). Variation in GRM3 affects cognition, prefrontal glutamate, and risk for schizophrenia. *Proceedings of the National Academy of Sciences (USA), 101*(34), 12604–12609.

Eiberg, H. (1995). Nocturnal enuresis is linked to a specific gene. *Scandinavian Journal of Urology and Nephrology, 173*(Supplement), 15–17.

Eiberg, H., Berendt, I., & Mohr, J. (1995). Assignment of dominant inherited nocturnal enuresis (ENUR1) to chromosome 13q. *Nature Genetics, 10*, 354–356.

Eiger, M. S., & Olds, S. W. (1999). *The complete book of breastfeeding* (3rd ed.). New York: Workman.

Eimas, P. (1985). The perception of speech in early infancy. *Scientific American, 252*(1), 46–52.

Eimas, P., Siqueland, E., Jusczyk, P., & Vigorito, J. (1971). Speech perception in infants. *Science, 171*, 303–306.

Eisenberg, A. R. (1996). The conflict talk of mothers and children: Patterns related to culture, SES, and gender of child. *Merrill-Palmer Quarterly, 42*, 438–452.

Eisenberg, N. (1992). *The caring child.* Cambridge, MA: Harvard University Press.

Eisenberg, N. (2000). Emotion, regulation, and moral development. *Annual Review of Psychology, 51*, 665–697.

Eisenberg, N., & Fabes, R. A. (1998). Prosocial development. In W. Damon (Series Ed.) & N. Eisenberg (Vol. Ed.), *Handbook of child psychology: Vol. 3. Social, emotional, and personality development* (5th ed., pp. 701–778). New York: Wiley.

Eisenberg, N., Fabes, R. A., & Murphy, B. C. (1996). Parents' reactions to children's negative emotions: Relations to children's social competence and comforting behavior. *Child Development, 67*, 2227–2247.

Eisenberg, N., Fabes, R. A., Nyman, M., Bernzweig, J., & Pinuelas, A. (1994). The relations of emotionality and regulation to children's anger-related reactions. *Child Development, 65*, 109–128.

Eisenberg, N., Fabes, R. A., Shepard, S. A., Guthrie, I. K., Murphy, B. C., & Reiser, M. (1999). Parental reactions to children's negative emotions: Longitudinal relations to quality of children's social functioning. *Child Development, 70*(2), 513–534.

Eisenberg, N., Guthrie, I. K., Fabes, R. A., Reiser, M., Murphy, B. C., Holgren, R., et al. (1997). The relations of regulation and emotionality to resiliency and competent social functioning in elementary school children. *Child Development, 68*, 295–311.

Eisenberg, N., Guthrie, I. K., Murphy, B. C., Shepard, S. A., Cumberland, A., & Carlo, G. (1999). Consistency and development of prosocial dispositions: A longitudinal study. *Child Development, 70*(6), 1360–1372.

Eisenberg, N., & Morris, A. D. (2004). Moral cognitions and prosocial responding in adolescence. In R. M. Lerner & L. Steinberg (Eds.), *Handbook of adolescent psychology* (2nd ed., pp. 155–188). Hoboken, NJ: Wiley.

Eisenberg, N., Spinrad, T. L., Fabes, R. A., Reiser, M., Cumberland, A., Shepard, S. A., et al. (2004). The relations of effortful control and impulsivity to children's resiliency and adjustment. *Child Development, 75*, 25–46.

Elder, G. H., Jr. (1974). *Children of the Great Depression: Social change in life experience.* Chicago: University of Chicago Press.

Elder, G. H., Jr. (1998). The life course and human development. In W. Damon (Series Ed.) & R. M. Lerner (Vol. Ed.), *Handbook of child psychology: Vol. 1. Theoretical models of human development* (5th ed., pp. 939–992). New York: Wiley.

Elia, J., Ambrosini, P. J., & Rapoport, J. L. (1999). Treatment of attention-deficit hyperactivity disorder. *New England Journal of Medicine, 340*, 780–788.

Elicker, J., Englund, M., & Sroufe, L. A. (1992). Predicting peer competence and peer relationships in childhood from early parent-child relationships. In R. Parke & G. Ladd (Eds.), *Family peer relationships: Modes of linkage* (pp. 77–106). Hillsdale, NJ: Erlbaum.

Elkind, D. (1981). *The hurried child.* Reading, MA: Addison-Wesley.

Elkind, D. (1984). *All grown up and no place to go.* Reading, MA: Addison-Wesley.

Elkind, D. (1986). *The miseducation of children: Superkids at risk.* New York: Knopf.

Elkind, D. (1997). *Reinventing childhood: Raising and educating children in a changing world.* Rosemont, NJ: Modern Learning Press.

Elkind, D. (1998). *Teenagers in crisis: All grown up and no place to go.* Reading, MA: Perseus Books.

Elliott, D. S. (1993). Health enhancing and health compromising lifestyles. In S. G. Millstein, A. C. Petersen, & E. O. Nightingale (Eds.), *Promoting the health of adolescents: New directions for the twenty-first century* (pp. 119–145). New York: Oxford University Press.

Elliott, V. S. (2000, November 20). Doctors caught in middle of ADHD treatment controversy: Critics charge that medications are being both under- and overprescribed. *AMNews.* Retrieved April 21, 2005, from http://www.ama-assn.org/amednews/2000/11/20/hlsb1120.htm

Ellis, B. J., Bates, J. E., Dodge, K. A., Fergusson, D. M., Horwood, L. J., Pettit, G. S., et al. (2003). Does father-absence place daughters at special risk for early sexual activity and teenage pregnancy? *Child Development, 74*, 801–821.

Ellis, B. J., & Garber, J. (2000). Psychosocial antecedents of variation in girls' pubertal timing: Maternal depression, stepfather presence, and marital family stress. *Child Development, 71*(2), 485–501.

Ellis, B. J., McFadyen-Ketchum, S., Dodge, K. A., Pettit, G. S., & Bates, J. E. (1999). Quality of early family relationships and individual differences in the timing of pubertal maturation in girls: A longitudinal test of an evolutionary model. *Journal of Personality and Social Psychology, 77*, 387–401.

Ellis, K. J., Abrams, S. A., & Wong, W. W. (1997). Body composition of a young, multiethnic female population. *American Journal of Clinical Nutrition, 65*, 724–731.

Else-Quest, N. M., Hyde, J. S., Goldsmith, H. H., & Van Hulle, C. A. (2006). Gender differences in temperament: A meta-analysis. *Psychological Bulletin, 132*, 33–72.

Eltzschig, H. K., Lieberman, E. S., & Camann, W. R. (2003). Regional anesthesia and analgesia for labor and delivery. *New England Journal of Medicine, 348*, 319–332.

Emde, R. N., Plomin, R., Robinson, J., Corley, R., DeFries, J., Fulker, D. W., et al. (1992). Temperament, emotion, and cognition at 14 months: The MacArthur longitudinal twin study. *Child Development, 63*, 1437–1455.

Engle, P. L., & Breaux, C. (1998). Fathers' involvement with children: Perspectives from developing countries. *Social Policy Report, 12*(1), 1–21.

Enloe, C. F. (1980). How alcohol affects the developing fetus. *Nutrition Today, 15*(5), 12–15.

Eogan, M. A., Geary, M. P., O'Connell, M. P., & Keane, D. P. (2003). Effect of fetal sex on labour and delivery: Retrospective review. *British Medical Journal, 326*, 137.

Erdley, C. A., Cain, K. M., Loomis, C. C., Dumas-Hines, F., & Dweck, C. S. (1997). Relations among children's social goals, implicit personality theories, and responses to social failure. *Developmental Psychology, 33*, 263–272.

Erdrich, L. (2000, March 1). Personal communication.

Erikson, E. H. (1950). *The life cycle completed.* New York: Norton.

Erikson, E. H. (1968). *Identity: Youth and crisis.* New York: Norton.

Erikson, E. H. (1973). The wider identity. In K. Erikson (Ed.), *In search of common ground: Conversations with Erik H. Erikson and Huey P. Newton.* New York: Norton.

Erikson, E. H. (1982). *The life cycle completed.* New York: Norton.

Erikson, E. H., Erikson, J. M., & Kivnick, H. Q. (1986). *Vital involvement in old age: The experience of old age in our time.* New York: Norton.

Eriksson, P. S., Perfilieva, E., Björk-Eriksson, T., Alborn, A., Nordborg, C., Peterson, D. A., et al. (1998). Neurogenesis in the adult human hippocampus. *Nature Medicine, 4*, 1313–1317.

Eron, L. D. (1980). Prescription for reduction of aggression. *American Psychologist, 35*, 244–252.

Eron, L. D. (1982). Parent-child interaction, television violence, and aggression in children. *American Psychologist, 37,* 197–211.

Eron, L. D., & Huesmann, L. R. (1986). The role of television in the development of prosocial and antisocial behavior. In D. Olweus, J. Block, & M. Radke-Yarrow (Eds.), *The development of antisocial and prosocial behavior: Research, theories, and issues.* New York: Academic.

Etzel, R. A. (2003). How environmental exposures influence the development and exacerbation of asthma. *Pediatrics, 112*(1): 233–239.

European Collaborative Study. (1994). Natural history of vertically acquired human immunodeficiency virus-1 infection. *Pediatrics, 94,* 815–819.

Evans, G. W. (2004). The environment of childhood poverty. *American Psychologist, 59,* 77–92.

Evans, G. W., & English, K. (2002). The environment of poverty: Multiple stressor exposure, psychophysiological stress and socioemotional adjustment. *Child Development, 73*(4), 1238–1248.

Fabes, R. A., Carlo, G., Kupanoff, K., & Laible, D. (1999). Early adolescence and prosocial/moral behavior: I. The role of individual processes. *Journal of Early Adolescence, 19,* 5–16.

Fabes, R. A., & Eisenberg, N. (1992). Young children's coping with interpersonal anger. *Child Development, 63,* 116–128.

Fabes, R. A., Eisenberg, N., Smith, M. C., & Murphy, B. C. (1996). Getting angry at peers: Associations with liking of the provocateur. *Child Development, 67,* 942–956.

Fabes, R. A., Leonard, S. A., Kupanoff, K., & Martin, C. L. (2001). Parental coping with children's negative emotions: Relations with children's emotional and social responding. *Child Development, 72,* 907–920.

Fabes, R. A., Martin, C. L., & Hanish, L. D. (2003, May). Young children's play qualities in same-, other-, and mixed-gender peer groups. *Child Development, 74*(3), 921–932.

Fabricius, W. V. (2003). Listening to children of divorce: New findings that diverge from Wallerstein, Lewis, and Blakeslee. *Family Relations, 52,* 385–394.

Facio, A., & Micocci, F. (2003). Emerging adulthood in Argentina. In J. J. Arnett & N. L. Galambos (Eds.), *Exploring cultural conceptions of the transition to adulthood. New Directions for Child and Adolescent Development, 100,* 21–32.

Faden, V. B. (2006). Trends in initiation of alcohol use in the United States: 1975–2003. *Alcoholism: Clinical and Experimental Research. 30*(6), 1011–1022.

Fagot, B. I. (1997). Attachment, parenting, and peer interactions of toddler children. *Developmental Psychology, 33,* 489–499.

Fagot, B. I., & Leinbach, M. D. (1995). Gender knowledge in egalitarian and traditional families. *Sex Roles, 32,* 513–526.

Faith, M. S., Berman, N., Heo, M., Pietrobelli, A., Gallagher, D., Epstein, L. H., et al. (2001). Effects of contingent television on physical activity and television viewing in obese children. *Pediatrics, 107,* 1043–1048.

Falbo, T. (2006). *Your one and only: Educational psychologist dispels myths surrounding only children.* Retrieved July 20, 2006, from http://www.utexas.edu/features/archive/2004/single.htm

Falbo, T., & Polit, D. F. (1986). Quantitative review of the only child literature: Research evidence and theory development. *Psychological Bulletin, 100*(2), 176–189.

Falbo, T., & Poston, D. L. (1993). The academic, personality, and physical outcomes of only children in China. *Child Development, 64,* 18–35.

Falkner, D. (1995). *Great time coming: The life of Jackie Robinson, from baseball to Birmingham.* New York: Simon & Schuster.

Faltermayer, C., Horowitz, J. M., Jackson, D., Lofaro, L., Maroney, T., Morse, J., et al. (1996, August 5). Where are they now? *Time,* p. 18.

Fantz, R. L. (1963). Pattern vision in newborn infants. *Science, 140,* 296–297.

Fantz, R. L. (1964). Visual experience in infants: Decreased attention to familiar patterns relative to novel ones. *Science, 146,* 668–670.

Fantz, R. L. (1965). Visual perception from birth as shown by pattern selectivity. In H. E. Whipple (Ed.), *New issues in infant development. Annals of the New York Academy of Sciences, 118,* 793–814.

Fantz, R. L., Fagen, J., & Miranda, S. B. (1975). Early visual selectivity. In L. Cohen & P. Salapatek (Eds.), *Infant perception: From sensation to cognition: Vol. 1. Basic visual processes* (pp. 249–341). New York: Academic Press.

Fantz, R. L., & Nevis, S. (1967). Pattern preferences and perceptual-cognitive development in early infancy. *Merrill-Palmer Quarterly, 13,* 77–108.

Farver, J. A. M., Kim, Y. K., & Lee, Y. (1995). Cultural differences in Korean and Anglo-American preschoolers' social interaction and play behavior. *Child Development, 66,* 1088–1099.

Farver, J. A. M., Xu, Y., Eppe, S., Fernandez, A., & Schwartz, D. (2005). Community violence, family conflict, and preschoolers' socioemotional functioning. *Developmental Psychology, 41,* 160–170.

Favaro, A., Tenconi, E., & Santonastaso, P. (2006). Perinatal factors and the risk of developing anorexia nervosa and bulimia nervosa. *Archives of General Psychiatry, 63,* 82–88.

Fearon, P., O'Connell, P., Frangou, S., Aquino, P., Nosarti, C., Allin, M., et al. (2004). Brain volume in adult survivors of very low birth weight: A sibling-controlled study. *Pediatrics, 114,* 367–371.

Federal Interagency Forum on Child and Family Statistics. (2005). *America's children: Key national indicators of well-being, 2005.* Washington, DC: U.S. Government Printing Office.

Federal Interagency Forum on Child and Family Statistics. (2006). *America's children in brief: Key national indicators of well-being, 2006.* Washington, DC: U.S. Government Printing Office.

Feingold, A., & Mazzella, R. (1998). Gender differences in body image are increasing. *Psychological Science, 9*(3), 190–195.

Feinstein, L., & Bynner, J. (2004). The importance of cognitive development in middle childhood for adult socioeconomic status, mental health, and problem behavior. *Child Development, 75,* 1329–1339.

Feldman, R., & Eidelman, A. I. (2005). Does a triplet birth pose a special risk for infant development? Assessing cognitive development in relation to intrauterine growth and mother-infant interaction across the first 2 years. *Pediatrics, 114,* 443–452.

Felner, R. D., Brand, S., DuBois, D. L., Adan, A. M., Mulhall, P. F., & Evans, E. G. (1995). Socioeconomic disadvantage, proximal environmental experiences, and socioemotional and academic adjustment in early adolescence: Investigation of a mediated effect. *Child Development, 66,* 774–792.

Ferber, R. (1985). *Solve your child's sleep problems.* New York: Simon & Schuster.

Ferber, S. G. & Makhoul, I. R. (2004). The effect of skin-to-skin contact (Kangaroo Care) shortly after birth on the neurobehavioral responses of the term newborn: A randomized, controlled trial. *Pediatrics, 113,* 858–865.

Fergusson, D. M., Horwood, L. J., Ridder, E. M., & Beautrais, A. L. (2005). Subthreshold depression in adolescence and mental health outcomes in adulthood. *Archives of General Psychiatry, 62*(1), 66–72.

Fergusson, D. M., Horwood, L. J., & Shannon, F. T. (1986). Factors related to the age of attainment of nocturnal bladder control: An 8-year longitudinal study. *Pediatrics, 78,* 884–890.

Fernald, A., & O'Neill, D. K. (1993). Peekaboo across cultures: How mothers and infants play with voices, faces, and expectations. In K. MacDonald (Ed.), *Parent-child play* (pp. 259–285). Albany, NY: State University of New York Press.

Fernald, A., Perfors, A., & Marchman, V. A. (2006). Picking up speed in understanding: Speech processing efficiency and vocabulary growth across the second year. *Developmental Psychology, 42,* 98–116.

Fernald, A., Pinto, J. P., Swingley, D., Weinberg, A., & McRoberts, G. W. (1998). Rapid gains in speed of verbal processing by infants in the 2nd year. *Psychological Science, 9*(3), 228–231.

Fernald, A., Swingley, D., & Pinto, J. P. (2001). When half a word is enough: Infants can recognize spoken words using partial phonetic information. *Child Development, 72*(4), 1003–1015.

Field, A. E., Austin, S. B., Taylor, C. B., Malspeis, S., Rosner, B., Rockett, H. R., et al. (2003). Relation between dieting and weight change among preadolescents and adolescents. *Pediatrics, 112*(4), 900–906.

Field, A. E., Camargo, C. A., Taylor, B., Berkey, C. S., Roberts, S. B., & Colditz, G. A. (2001). Peer, parent, and media influence on the development of weight concerns and frequent dieting among preadolescent and adolescent girls and boys. *Pediatrics, 107*(1), 54–60.

Field, A. E., Cook, N. R., & Gillman, M. W. (2005). Weight status in childhood as a predictor of becoming overweight or hypertensive in early adulthood. *Obesity Research, 13*, 163–169.

Field, T. (1995). Infants of depressed mothers. *Infant Behavior and Development, 18*, 1–13.

Field, T. (1998a). Emotional care of the at-risk infant: Early interventions for infants of depressed mothers. *Pediatrics, 102*, 1305–1310.

Field, T. (1998b). Massage therapy effects. *American Psychologist, 53*, 1270–1281.

Field, T. (1998c). Maternal depression effects on infants and early intervention. *Preventive Medicine, 27*, 200–203.

Field, T., Diego, M., & Hernandez-Reif, M. (2007). Massage therapy research. *Developmental Review, 27*, 75–89.

Field, T., Diego, M., Hernandez-Reif, M., Schanberg, S., & Kuhn, C. (2003). Depressed mothers who are "good interaction" partners versus those who are withdrawn or intrusive. *Infant Behavior & Development, 26*, 238–252.

Field, T., Fox, N. A., Pickens, J., Nawrocki, T., & Soutollo, D. (1995). Right frontal EEG activation in 3- to 6-month-old infants of depressed mothers. *Developmental Psychology, 31*, 358–363.

Field, T., Grizzle, N., Scafidi, F., Abrams, S., Richardson, S., Kuhn, C., et al. (1996). Massage therapy for infants of depressed mothers. *Infant Behavior and Development, 19*, 107–112.

Field, T., Hernandez-Reif, M., & Freedman, J. (2004). Stimulation programs for preterm infants. *Social Policy Report, 18*(1), 1–19.

Field, T. M. (1986). Interventions for premature infants. *Journal of Pediatrics, 109*(1), 183–190.

Field, T. M. (1978). Interaction behaviors of primary versus secondary caretaker fathers. *Developmental Psychology, 14*, 183–184.

Field, T. M., & Roopnarine, J. L. (1982). Infant-peer interaction. In T. M. Field, A. Huston, H. C. Quay, L. Troll, & G. Finley (Eds.), *Review of human development*. New York: Wiley.

Field, T. M., Sandberg, D., Garcia, R., Vega-Lahr, N., Goldstein, S., & Guy, L. (1985). Pregnancy problems, postpartum depression, and early infant-mother interactions. *Developmental Psychology, 21*, 1152–1156.

Fields, J. (2003). Children's living arrangements and characteristics: March 2002. *Current Population Reports* (P20-547). Washington, DC: U.S. Bureau of the Census.

Fields, J. (2004). America's families and living arrangements: 2003. *Current Population Reports* (P20–553). Washington, DC: U.S. Census Bureau.

Fields, J. M., & Smith, K. E. (1998, April). *Poverty, family structure, and child well-being: Indicators from the SIPP* (Population Division Working Paper No. 23, U.S. Bureau of the Census). Paper presented at the Annual Meeting of the Population Association of America, Chicago, IL.

Fifer, W. P., & Moon, C. M. (1995). The effects of fetal experience with sound. In J. P. Lecanuet, W. P. Fifer, N. A. Krasnegor, & W. P. Smotherman (Eds.), *Fetal development: A psychobiological perspective* (pp. 351–366). Hillsdale, NJ: Erlbaum.

Finn, J. D. (2006). *The adult lives of at-risk students: The roles of attainment and engagement in high school* (NCES 2006-328). Washington, DC: U. S. Department of Education, National Center for Education Statistics.

Finn, J. D., Gerber, S. B., & Boyd-Zaharias, J. (2005). Small classes in the early grades, academic achievement, and graduating from high school. *Journal of Educational Psychology, 97*, 214–223.

Finn, J. D., & Rock, D. A. (1997). Academic success among students at risk for dropout. *Journal of Applied Psychology, 82*, 221–234.

First test-tube baby. (1978, July 31). *Time*, 58–70.

First woman to both poles—Ann Bancroft. (1997). Retrieved April 4, 2002, from http://www. zplace.com/rhonda/abancroft/

Fiscella, K., Kitzman, H. J., Cole, R. E., Sidora, K. J., & Olds, D. (1998). Does child abuse predict adolescent pregnancy? *Pediatrics, 101*, 620–624.

Fischer, K. (1980). A theory of cognitive development: The control and construction of hierarchies of skills. *Psychological Review, 87*, 477–531.

Fischer, K. W., & Pruyne, E. (2003). Reflective thinking in adulthood. In J. Demick & C. Andreoletti (Eds.), *Handbook of adult development*. New York: Plenum Press.

Fischer, K. W., & Rose, S. P. (1994). Dynamic development of coordination of components in brain and behavior: A framework for theory and research. In G. Dawson & K. W. Fischer (Eds.), *Human behavior and the developing brain* (pp. 3–66). New York: Guilford.

Fischer, K. W., & Rose, S. P. (1995, Fall). Concurrent cycles in the dynamic development of brain and behavior. *SCRD Newsletter*, pp. 3–4, 15–16.

Fisher, C. B., Hoagwood, K., Boyce, C., Duster, T., Frank, D. A., Grisso, T., et al. (2002). Research ethics for mental health science involving ethnic minority children and youth. *American Psychologist, 57*, 1024–1040.

Fivush, R., & Nelson, K. (2004). Culture and language in the emergence of autobiographical memory. *Psychological Science, 15*, 573–577.

Fivush, R., & Schwarzmueller, A. (1998). Children remember childhood: Implications for childhood amnesia. *Applied Cognitive Psychology, 12*, 455–473.

Flannagan, C. A., Bowes, J. M., Jonsson, B., Csapo, B., & Sheblanova, E. (1998). Ties that bind: Correlates of adolescents' civic commitment in seven countries. *Journal of Social Issues, 54*, 457–475.

Flavell, J. (1963). *The developmental psychology of Jean Piaget*. New York: Van Nostrand.

Flavell, J. H. (1970). Developmental studies of mediated memory. In H. W. Reese & L. P. Lipsitt (Eds.), *Advances in child development and behavior* (Vol. 5, pp. 181–211). New York: Academic.

Flavell, J. H. (1993). Young children's understanding of thinking and consciousness. *Current Directions in Psychological Science, 2*, 40–43.

Flavell, J. H., Green, F. L., & Flavell, E. R. (1986). Development of knowledge about the appearance-reality distinction. *Monographs of the Society for Research in Child Development, 51*(1, Serial No. 212).

Flavell, J. H., Green, F. L., & Flavell, E. R. (1995). Young children's knowledge about thinking. *Monographs of the Society for Research in Child Development, 60*(1, serial no. 243).

Flavell, J. H., Green, F. L., Flavell, E. R., & Grossman, J. B. (1997). The development of children's knowledge about inner speech. *Child Development, 68*, 39–47.

Flavell, J. H., Miller, P. H., & Miller, S. A. (2002). *Cognitive development*. Englewood Cliffs, NJ: Prentice-Hall.

Flinn, M. V., & Ward, C. V. (2005). Ontogeny and the evolution of the social child. In B. J. Ellis & D. F. Bjorklund (Eds.), *Origins of the social mind: Evolutionary psychology and child development* (pp. 19-44). London: Guilford.

Flook, L., Repetti, R. L., & Ullman, J. B. (2005). Classroom social experiences as predictors of academic performance. *Developmental Psychology, 41*, 319–327.

Flores, G., Fuentes-Afflick, E., Barbot, O., Carter-Pokras, O., Claudio, L., Lara, M., et al. (2002). The health of Latino children: Urgent priorities, unanswered questions, and a research agenda. *Journal of the American Medical Association, 288*, 82–90.

Flores, G., Olson, L., & Tomany-Korman, S. C. (2005). Racial and ethnic disparities in early childhood health and health care. *Pediatrics, 115*, e183–e193.

Flynn, J. R. (1984). The mean IQ of Americans: Massive gains 1932 to 1978. *Psychological Bulletin, 95,* 29–51.

Flynn, J. R. (1987). Massive IQ gains in 14 nations: What IQ tests really measure. *Psychological Bulletin, 101,* 171–191.

Fontanel, B., & d'Harcourt, C. (1997). *Babies, history, art and folklore.* New York: Abrams.

Ford, D. Y., & Harris, J. J., III. (1996). Perceptions and attitudes of black students toward school, achievement, and other educational variables. *Child Development, 67,* 1141–1152.

Ford, R. P., Schluter, P. J., Mitchell, E. A., Taylor, B. J., Scragg, R., & Stewart, A. W. (1998). Heavy caffeine intake in pregnancy and sudden infant death syndrome (New Zealand Cot Death Study Group). *Archives of Disease in Childhood, 78*(1), 9–13.

Foster, D. (1999). Isabel Allende unveiled. In J. Rodden (Ed.), *Conversations with Isabel Allende* (pp. 105–113). Austin: University of Texas Press.

Fowler, J. (1981). *Stages of faith: The psychology of human development and the quest for meaning.* New York: Harper & Row.

Fowler, J. W. (1989). Strength for the journey: Early childhood development in selfhood and faith. In D. A. Blazer, J. W. Fowler, K. J. Swick, A. S. Honig, P. J. Boone, B. M. Caldwell, et al. (Eds.), *Faith development in early childhood* (pp. 1–63). New York: Sheed & Ward.

Fox, M. K., Pac, S., Devaney, B., & Jankowski, L. (2004). Feeding Infants and Toddlers Study: What foods are infants and toddlers eating? *Journal of the American Dietetic Association, 104,* 22–30.

Fox, N., Nelson, C. A., Zeanah, C., & Johnson, D. (2006, February 17). *Effects of social deprivation: The Bucharest early intervention project.* Presentation at the annual meeting of the American Association for the Advancement of Science, St. Louis, MO.

Fox, N. A., Kimmerly, N. L., & Schafer, W. D. (1991). Attachment to mother/attachment to father: A meta-analysis. *Child Development, 62,* 210–225.

Fraga, M. F., Ballestar, E., Paz, M. F., Ropero, S., Setien, F., Ballestar, M. L., et al. (2005). Epigenetic differences arise during the lifetime of monozygotic twins. *Proceedings of the National Academy of Sciences, USA, 102,* 10604–10609.

Frank, A. (1958). *The diary of a young girl* (B. M. Mooyaart-Doubleday, Trans.). New York: Pocket.

Frank, A. (1995). *The diary of a young girl: The definitive edition* (O. H. Frank & M. Pressler, Eds.; S. Massotty, Trans.). New York: Doubleday.

Frank, D. A., Augustyn, M., Knight, W. G., Pell, T., & Zuckerman, B. (2001). Growth, development, and behavior in early childhood following prenatal cocaine exposure. *Journal of the American Medical Association, 285,* 1613–1625.

Frankenburg, W. K., Dodds, J., Archer, P., Bresnick, B., Maschka, P., Edelman, N., et al. (1992). *Denver II training manual.* Denver: Denver Developmental Materials.

Frankenburg, W. K., Dodds, J. B., Fandal, A. W., Kazuk, E., & Cohrs, M. (1975). *The Denver Developmental Screening Test: Reference manual.* Denver: University of Colorado Medical Center.

Fraser, A. M., Brockert, J. F., & Ward, R. H. (1995). Association of young maternal age with adverse reproductive outcomes. *New England Journal of Medicine, 332*(17), 1113–1117.

Frazier, J. A., & Morrison, F. J. (1998). The influence of extended-year schooling on growth of achievement and perceived competence in early elementary school. *Child Development, 69,* 495–517.

Fredricks, J. A., & Eccles, J. S. (2002). Children's competence and value beliefs from childhood through adolescence: Growth trajectories in two male-sex-typed domains. *Developmental Psychology, 38,* 519–533.

Fredriksen, K., Rhodes, J., Reddy, R., & Way, N. (2004). Sleepless in Chicago: Tracking the effects of adolescent sleep loss during the middle-school years. *Child Development, 75,* 84–95.

Freeark, K., Rosenberg, E. B., Bornstein, J., Jozefowicz-Simbeni, D., Linkevich, M., & Lohnes, K. (2005). Gender differences and dynamics shaping the adoption life cycle: Review of the literature and recommendations. *American Journal of Orthopsychiatry, 75,* 86–101.

Freedman, R. (2004). *The voice that challenged a nation: Marian Anderson and the struggle for equal rights.* New York: Clarion.

Freeman, C. (2004). *Trends in educational equity of girls and women: 2004* (NCES 2005016). Washington, DC: National Center for Education Statistics.

Freeman, D. (1983). *Margaret Mead and Samoa: The making and unmaking of an anthropological myth.* Cambridge, MA: Harvard University Press.

French, A. P. (Ed.). (1979). *Einstein: A centenary volume.* Cambridge, MA: Harvard University Press.

French, S. A., Story, M., & Jeffery, R. W. (2001). Environmental influences on eating and physical activity. *Annual Review of Public Health, 22,* 309–335.

French, S. E., Seidman, E., Allen, L., & Aber, J. L. (2006). The development of ethnic identity during adolescence. *Developmental Psychology, 42,* 1–10.

Freud, A. (1946). *The ego and the mechanisms of defense.* New York: International Universities Press.

Freud, S. (1953). *A general introduction to psychoanalysis* (J. Rivière, Trans.) New York: Perma-books. (Original work published 1935)

Freud, S. (1964a). New introductory lectures on psychoanalysis. In J. Strachey (Ed. & Trans.), *The standard edition of the complete psychological works of Sigmund Freud* (Vol. 22). London: Hogarth. (Original work published 1933)

Freud, S. (1964b). An outline of psychoanalysis. In J. Strachey (Ed. & Trans.), *The standard edition of the complete psychological works of Sigmund Freud* (Vol. 23). London: Hogarth. (Original work published 1940)

Frey, K. S., Hirschstein, M. K., Snell, J. L., Edstrom, L. V. S., MacKenzie, E P., & Broderick, C. J. (2005). Reducing playground bullying and supporting beliefs: An experimental trial of the Steps to Respect program. *Developmental Psychology, 41,* 479–491.

Fried, P. A., & Smith, A. M. (2001). A literature review of the consequences of prenatal marijuana exposure: An emerging theme of a deficiency in aspects of executive function. *Neurotoxicology and Teratology, 23,* 1–11.

Fried, P. A., Watkinson, B., & Willan, A. (1984). Marijuana use during pregnancy and decreased length of gestation. *American Journal of Obstetrics and Gynecology, 150,* 23–27.

Friedman, L. J. (1999). *Identity's architect.* New York: Scribner.

Friedman, R. A. (2006). The changing face of teenage drug abuse—The trend toward prescription drugs. *New England Journal of Medicine, 354,* 1448–1450.

Friend, M., & Davis, T. L. (1993). Appearance-reality distinction: Children's understanding of the physical and affective domains. *Developmental Psychology, 29,* 907–914.

Fries, A. B. W., Ziegler, T. E., Kurian, J. R., Jacoris, S., & Pollak, S. D. (2005). Early experiences in humans is associated with changes in neuropeptides critical for regulating social behavior. *Proceedings of the National Academy of Sciences, USA, 102,* 17237–17240.

Frith, U. (1989). *Autism: Explaining the enigma.* Oxford, UK: Blackwell.

Froehlich, T. E., Lamphear, B. P., Dietrich, K. N., Cory-Slechta, D. A., & Kahn, R. S. (2006, May). *Effects of DRD4, lead, and sex on ADHD-related executive function.* Paper presented at the annual meeting of the Pediatric Academic Societies, San Francisco.

Fromkin, V., Krashen, S., Curtiss, S., Rigler, D., & Rigler, M. (1974). The development of language in Genie: Acquisition beyond the "critical period." *Brain and Language, 15*(9), 28–34.

Fuligni, A. J. (1997). The academic achievement of adolescents from immigrant families: The roles of family background, attitudes, and behavior. *Child Development, 68,* 351–363.

Fuligni, A. J., & Eccles, J. S. (1993). Perceived parent-child relationships and early adolescents' orientation toward peers. *Developmental Psychology, 29,* 622–632.

Fuligni, A. J., Eccles, J. S., Barber, B. L., & Clements, P. (2001). Early adolescent peer orientation and adjustment during high school. *Developmental Psychology, 37*(1), 28–36.

Fuligni, A. J., & Stevenson, H. W. (1995). Time use and mathematics achievement among American, Chinese, and Japanese high school students. *Child Development, 66,* 830–842.

Fuligni, A. J., & Witkow, M. (2004). The postsecondary educational progress of youth from immigrant families. *Journal of Research on Adolescence, 14,* 159–183.

Fuligni, A. J., Yip, T., & Tseng, V. (2002). The impact of family obligation on the daily activities and psychological well-being of Chinese American adolescents. *Child Development, 73*(1), 302–314.

Furman, L. (2005). What is attention-deficit hyperactivity disorder (ADHD)? *Journal of Child Neurology, 20,* 994–1003.

Furman, L., Taylor, G., Minich, N., & Hack, M. (2003). The effect of maternal milk on neonatal morbidity of very low birth-weight infants. *Archives of Pediatrics and Adolescent Medicine, 157,* 66–71.

Furman, W. (1982). Children's friendships. In T. M. Field, A. Huston, H. C. Quay, L. Troll, & G. E. Finley (Eds.), *Review of human development.* New York: Wiley.

Furman, W., & Bierman, K. L. (1983). Developmental changes in young children's conception of friendship. *Child Development, 54,* 549–556.

Furman, W., & Buhrmester, D. (1985). Children's perceptions of the personal relationships in their social networks. *Developmental Psychology, 21,* 1016–1024.

Furman, W., & Wehner, E. A. (1997). Adolescent romantic relationships: A developmental perspective. In S. Shulman & A. Collins (Eds.), *Romantic relationships in adolescence: Developmental perspectives. New Directions for Child and Adolescent Development, 78,* 21–36.

Furrow, D. (1984). Social and private speech at two years. *Child Development, 55,* 355–362.

Furstenberg, F. F., Jr., Rumbaut, R. G., & Settersten, R. A., Jr., (2005). On the frontier of adulthood: Emerging themes and new directions. In R. A. Settersten, Jr., F. F. Furstenberg, Jr., & R. G. Rumbaut (Eds.), *On the frontier of adulthood: Theory, research, and public policy* (pp. 3–25). (John D. and Catherine T. MacArthur Foundation Series on Mental Health and Development, Research Network on Transitions to Adulthood and Public Policy.) Chicago: University of Chicago Press.

Fussell, E., & Furstenberg, F. (2005). The transition to adulthood during the twentieth century: Race, nativity, and gender. In R. A. Settersten, Jr., F. F. Furstenberg, Jr., & R. G. Rumbaut (Eds.), *On the frontier of adulthood: Theory, research, and public policy* (pp. 29–75). (John D. and Catherine T. MacArthur Foundation Series on Mental Health and Development, Research Network on Transitions to Adulthood and Public Policy.) Chicago: University of Chicago Press.

Gabbard, C. P. (1996). *Lifelong motor development* (2nd ed.). Madison, WI: Brown & Benchmark.

Gabhainn, S., & François, Y. (2000). Substance use. In C. Currie, K. Hurrelmann, W. Settertobulte, R. Smith, & J. Todd (Eds.), *Health behaviour in schoolaged children: A WHO cross-national study (HBSC) international report* (pp. 97–114). WHO Policy Series: Healthy Policy for Children and Adolescents, Series No. 1. Copenhagen, Denmark: World Health Organization Regional Office for Europe.

Gabriel, T. (1996, January 7). High-tech pregnancies test hope's limit. *New York Times,* pp. 1, 18–19.

Gaffney, M., Gamble, M., Costa, P., Holstrum, J., & Boyle, C. (2003). Infants tested for hearing loss—United States, 1999–2001. *Morbidity and Mortality Weekly Report, 51,* 981–984.

Galotti, K. M., Komatsu, L. K., & Voelz, S. (1997). Children's differential performance on deductive and inductive syllogisms. *Developmental Psychology, 33,* 70–78.

Ganger, J., & Brent, M. R. (2004). Reexamining the vocabulary spurt. *Developmental Psychology, 40,* 621–632.

Gannon, P. J., Holloway, R. L., Broadfield, D. C., & Braun, A. R. (1998). Asymmetry of chimpanzee planum temporale: Humanlike pattern of Wernicke's brain language homlog. *Science, 279,* 220–222.

Gans, J. E. (1990). *America's adolescents: How healthy are they?* Chicago: American Medical Association.

Garbarino, J., Dubrow, N., Kostelny, K., & Pardo, C. (1992). *Children in danger: Coping with the consequences of community violence.* San Francisco: Jossey-Bass.

Garbarino, J., & Kostelny, K. (1993). Neighborhood and community influences on parenting. In T. Luster & L. Okagaki (Eds.), *Parenting: An ecological perspective* (pp. 203–226). Hillsdale, NJ: Erlbaum.

Gardiner, H. W., & Kosmitzki, C. (2005). *Lives across cultures: Cross-cultural human development.* Boston: Allyn & Bacon.

Gardner, H. (1993). *Frames of mind: The theory of multiple intelligences.* New York: Basic. (Original work published 1983)

Gardner, H. (1995). Reflections on multiple intelligences: Myths and messages. *Phi Delta Kappan,* 200–209.

Gardner, H. (1998). Are there additional intelligences? In J. Kane (Ed.), *Education,* *information, and transformation: Essays on learning and thinking.* Englewood Cliffs, NJ: Prentice-Hall.

Gardner, M., & Steinberg, L. (2005). Peer influence on risk taking, risk preference, and risky decision making in adolescence and adulthood: An experimental study. *Developmental Psychology, 41,* 625–635.

Garland, A. F., & Zigler, E. (1993). Adolescent suicide prevention: Current research and social policy implications. *American Psychologist, 48*(2), 169–182.

Garlick, D. (2003). Integrating brain science research with intelligence research. *Current Directions in Psychological Science, 12,* 185–192.

Garmon, L. C., Basinger, K. S., Gregg, V. R., & Gibbs, J. C. (1996). Gender differences in stage and expression of moral judgment. *Merrill-Palmer Quarterly, 42,* 418–437.

Garner, P. W., & Power, T. G. (1996). Preschoolers' emotional control in the disappointment paradigm and its relation to temperament, emotional knowledge, and family expressiveness. *Child Development, 67,* 1406–1419.

Gartrell, N., Deck, A., Rodas, C., Peyser, H., & Banks, A. (2005). The National Lesbian Family Study: Interviews with the 10-year-old children. *American Journal of Orthopsychiatry, 75,* 518–524.

Gartstein, M. A., & Rothbart, M. K. (2003). Studying infant temperament via the Revised Infant Behavior Questionnaire. *Infant Behavior and Development, 26,* 64–86.

Gatewood, J. D., Wills, A., Shetty, S., Xu, J., Arnold, A. P., Burgoyne, P. S., et al. (2006). Sex chromosome complement and gonadal sex influence aggressive and parental behaviors in mice. *Journal of Neuroscience, 26,* 2335–2342.

Gauvain, M. (1993). The development of spatial thinking in everyday activity. *Developmental Review, 13,* 92–121.

Gauvain, M., & Perez, S. M. (2005). Parent-child participation in planning children's activities outside of school in European American and Latino families. *Child Development, 76,* 371–383.

Gazzaniga, M. S. (Ed.). (2000). *The new cognitive neurosciences* (2nd ed.). Cambridge, MA: The MIT Press.

Ge, X., Brody, G. H., Conger, R. D., Simons, R. L., & Murry, V. (2002). Contextual amplification of pubertal transitional effect on African American children's problem behaviors. *Developmental Psychology, 38,* 42–54.

Ge, X., Conger, R. D., & Elder, G. H., Jr., (1996). Coming of age too early: Pubertal influences on girls' vulnerability to psychological distress. *Child Development, 67,* 3386–3400.

Ge, X., Conger, R. D., & Elder, G. H. (2001a). Pubertal transition, stressful life events, and the emergence of gender differences in adolescent depressive symptoms. *Developmental Psychology, 37*(3), 404–417.

Ge, X., Conger, R. D., & Elder, G. H. (2001b). The relation between puberty and psychological distress in adolescent boys. *Journal of Research on Adolescence, 11,* 49–70.

Geary, D. C. (1993). Mathematical disabilities: Cognitive, neuropsychological, and genetic components. *Psychological Bulletin, 114,* 345–362.

Geary, D. C. (1999). Evolution and developmental sex differences. *Current Directions in Psychological Science, 8*(4), 115–120.

Geen, R. (2004). The evolution of kinship care: Policy and practice. In David and Lucile Packard Foundation, Children, families, and foster care. *The Future of Children, 14*(1). Retrieved from http://www.futureofchildren.org

Geier, D. A., & Geier, M. R. (2006). Early downward trends in neurodevelopmental disorders following removal of thimerosal-containing vaccines. *Journal of American Physicians and Surgeons, 11*(1), 8–13.

Gelfand, D. M., & Teti, D. M. (1995, November). How does maternal depression affect children? *The Harvard Mental Health Letter,* p. 8.

Gélis, J. (1991). *History of childbirth: Fertility, pregnancy, and birth in early modern Europe.* Boston: Northeastern University Press.

Gelman, R. (n.d.). *Young natural number arithmeticians.* Unpublished manuscript.

Gelman, R., Spelke, E. S., & Meck, E. (1983). What preschoolers know about animate and inanimate objects. In D. R. Rogers & J. S. Sloboda (Eds.), *The acquisition of symbolic skills* (pp. 297–326). New York: Plenum.

Genbacev, O. D., Prakobphol, A., Foulk, R. A., Krtolica, A. R., Ilic, D., Singer, M. S., et al. (2003). Trophoblast L-selectin-mediated adhesion at the maternal-fetal interface. *Science, 299,* 405–408.

Genesee, F., Nicoladis, E., & Paradis, J. (1995). Language differentiation in early bilingual development. *Journal of Child Language, 22,* 611–631.

George, C., Kaplan, N., & Main, M. (1985). *The Berkeley Adult Attachment Interview.* Unpublished protocol, Department of Psychology, University of California, Berkeley, CA.

George, T. P., & Hartmann, D. P. (1996). Friendship networks of unpopular, average, and popular children. *Child Development, 67,* 2301–2316.

Gershoff, E. T. (2002). Corporal punishment by parents and associated child behaviors and experiences: A meta-analytic and theoretical review. *Psychological Bulletin, 128,* 539–579.

Gesell, A. (1929). Maturation and infant behavior patterns. *Psychological Review, 36,* 307–319.

Getzels, J. W. (1964). Creative thinking, problem-solving, and instruction. In *Yearbook of the National Society for the Study of Education* (Pt. 1, pp. 240–267). Chicago: University of Chicago Press.

Getzels, J. W. (1984, March). *Problem finding in creativity in higher education.* The Fifth Rev. Charles F. Donovan, S. J., Lecture, Boston College, School of Education, Boston, MA.

Getzels, J. W., & Jackson, P. W. (1962). *Creativity and intelligence: Explorations with gifted students.* New York: Wiley.

Getzels, J. W., & Jackson, P. W. (1963). The highly intelligent and the highly creative adolescent: A summary of some research findings. In C. W. Taylor & F. Baron (Eds.), *Scientific creativity: Its recognition and development* (pp. 161–172). New York: Wiley.

Gibbs, J. C. (1991). Toward an integration of Kohlberg's and Hoffman's theories of moral development. In W. M. Kurtines & J. L. Gewirtz (Eds.), *Handbook of moral behavior and development: Advances in theory, research, and application* (Vol. 1). Hillsdale, NJ: Erlbaum.

Gibbs, J. C. (1995). The cognitive developmental perspective. In W. M. Kurtines & J. L. Gewirtz (Eds.), *Moral development: An introduction.* Boston: Allyn & Bacon.

Gibbs, J. C., & Schnell, S. V. (1985). Moral development "versus" socialization. *American Psychologist, 40*(10),1071–1080.

Gibson, E. J. (1969). *Principles of perceptual learning and development.* New York: Appleton-Century-Crofts.

Gibson, E. J., & Pick, A. D. (2000). *An ecological approach to perceptual learning and development.* New York: Oxford University Press.

Gibson, E. J., & Walk, R. D. (1960). The "visual cliff." *Scientific American, 202,* 64–71.

Gibson, E. J., & Walker, A. S. (1984). Development of knowledge of visual tactual affordances of substance. *Child Development, 55,* 453–460.

Gibson, J. J. (1979). *The ecological approach to visual perception.* Boston: Houghton-Mifflin.

Gidwani, P. P., Sobol, A., DeJong, W., Perrin, J. M., & Gortmaker, S. L. (2002). Television viewing and initiation of smoking among youth. *Pediatrics, 110,* 505–508.

Giedd, J. N., Blumenthal, J., Jeffries, N. O., Castellanos, F. X., Zijdenbos, A., Paus, T., et al. (1999). Brain development during childhood and adolescence: A longitudinal MRI study. *Nature Neuroscience, 2,* 861–863.

Gilbert, W. M., Nesbitt, T. S., & Danielsen, B. (1999). Childbearing beyond age 40: Pregnancy outcome in 24,032 cases. *Obstetrics and Gynecology, 93,* 9–14.

Gill, B., & Schlossman, S. (1996). "A sin against childhood": Progressive education and the crusade to abolish homework, 1897–1941. *American Journal of Education, 105,* 27–66.

Gilligan, C. (1982). *In a different voice: Psychological theory and women's development.* Cambridge, MA: Harvard University Press.

Gilligan, C. (1987a). Adolescent development reconsidered. In E. E. Irwin (Ed.), *Adolescent social behavior and health.* San Francisco: Jossey-Bass.

Gilligan, C. (1987b). Moral orientation and moral development. In E. F. Kittay & D. T. Meyers (Eds.), *Women and moral theory* (pp. 19–33). Totowa, NJ: Rowman & Littlefield.

Gilmore, J., Lin, W., Prastawa, M. W., Looney, C. B., Vetsa, Y. S. K., Knickmeyer, R. C., et al. (2007). Regional gray matter growth, sexual dimorphism, and cerebral asymmetry in the neonatal brain. *Journal of Neuroscience, 27*(6), 1255–1260.

Ginsburg, G. S., & Bronstein, P. (1993). Family factors related to children's intrinsic/extrinsic motivational orientation and academic performance. *Child Development, 64,* 1461–1474.

Ginsburg, H., & Opper, S. (1979). *Piaget's theory of intellectual development* (2nd ed.). Englewood Cliffs, NJ: Prentice-Hall.

Ginsburg, H. P. (1997). Mathematics learning disabilities: A view from developmental psychology. *Journal of Learning Disabilities, 30,* 20–33.

Ginsburg, K., & Committee on Communications & the Committee on Psychosocial Aspects of Child and Family Health, American Academy of Pediatrics (AAP). (2007). The importance of play in promoting healthy child development and maintaining strong parent-child bonds. *Pediatrics, 119,* 182–191.

Ginzburg, N. (1985). *The little virtues* (D. Davis, Trans.). Manchester, England: Carcanet.

Ginsburg-Block, M. D., & Fantuzzo, J. W. (1998). An evaluation of the relative effectiveness of NCTM standards-based interventions for low-achieving urban elementary students. *Journal of Educational Psychology, 90,* 560–569.

Giordano, P. C., Cernkovich, S. A., & DeMaris, A. (1993). The family and peer relations of black adolescents. *Journal of Marriage and the Family, 55,* 277–287.

Giordano, P. C., Longmore, M. A., & Manning, W. D. (2006). Gender and the meanings of adolescent romantic relationships: A focus on boys. *American Sociological Review, 71*(2), 260–287.

Giscombé, C. L., & Lobel, M. (2005). Explaining disproportionately high rates of adverse birth outcomes among African Americans: The impact of stress, racism, and related factors in pregnancy. *Psychological Bulletin, 131,* 662–683.

Giusti, R. M., Iwamoto, K., & Hatch, E. E. (1995). Diethylstilbestrol revisited: A review of the long-term health effects. *Annals of Internal Medicine, 122,* 778–788.

Gjerdingen, D. (2003). The effectiveness of various postpartum depression treatments and the impact of antidepressant drugs on nursing infants. *Journal of American Board of Family Practice, 16,* 372–382.

Glantz, S. A., Kacirk, K. W., & McCulloch, C. (2004). Back to the future: Smoking in movies in 2002 compared with 1950 levels.

American Journal of Public Health, 94, 261–263.

Glaser, D. (2000). Child abuse and neglect and the brain: A review. *Journal of Child Psychiatry, 41,* 97–116.

Glasgow, K. L., Dornbusch, S. M., Troyer, L., Steinberg, L., & Ritter, P. L. (1997). Parenting styles, adolescents' attributions, and educational outcomes in nine heterogeneous high schools. *Child Development, 68,* 507–529.

Glassbrenner, D., Carra, J. S., & Nichols, J. (2005). Recent estimates of safety belt use. *Journal of Safety Research, 35*(2), 237–244.

Glasson, E. J., Bower, C., Petterson, B., de Klerk, N., Chaney, G., & Hallmayer, J. F. (2004). Perinatal factors and the development of autism: A population study. *Archives of General Psychiatry, 61,* 618–627.

Gleason, T. R., Sebanc, A. M., & Hartup, W. W. (2000). Imaginary companions of preschool children. *Developmental Psychology, 36,* 419–428.

Gleitman, L. R., Newport, E. L., & Gleitman, H. (1984). The current status of the motherese hypothesis. *Journal of Child Language, 11,* 43–79.

Glenn, N., & Marquardt, E. (2001). *Hooking up, hanging out, and hoping for Mr. Right: College women on dating and mating today.* New York: Institute for American Values.

Goetz, P. J. (2003). The effects of bilingualism on theory of mind development. *Bilingualism: Language and Cognition, 6,* 1–15.

Gogtay, N., Giedd, J. N., Lusk, L., Hayashi, K. M., Greenstein, D., Vaituzis, A. C., et al. (2004). Dynamic mapping of human cortical development during childhood through early adulthood. *Proceedings of the National Academy of Sciences, USA, 101,* 8174–8179.

Goldberg, W. A., Greenberger, E., & Nagel, S. K. (1996). Employment and achievement: Mothers' work involvement in relation to children's achievement behaviors and mothers' parenting behaviors. *Child Development, 67,* 1512–1527.

Goldenberg, R. L., & Rouse, D. J. (1998). Prevention of premature labor. *New England Journal of Medicine, 339,* 313–320.

Goldenberg, R. L., & Tamura, T. (1996). Prepregnancy weight and pregnancy outcome. *Journal of the American Medical Association, 275,* 1127–1128.

Goldenberg, R. L., Tamura, T., Neggers, Y., Copper, R. L., Johnston, K. E., DuBard, M. B., et al. (1995). The effect of zinc supplementation on pregnancy outcome. *Journal of the American Medical Association, 274,* 463–468.

Goldin-Meadow, S., & Mylander, C. (1998). Spontaneous sign systems created by deaf children in two cultures. *Nature, 391,* 279–281.

Goldman, A. (1981). *Elvis.* New York: McGraw-Hill.

Goldman, L., Falk, H., Landrigan, P. J., Balk, S. J., Reigart, J. R., & Etzel, R. A. (2004). Environmental pediatrics and its impact on government health policy. *Pediatrics, 113,* 1146–1157.

Goldman, R. (1964). *Religious thinking from childhood to adolescence.* London: Routledge & Kegan Paul.

Goldsmith, M., Mackay, A., & Woudhuysen, J. S. (Eds.). (1980). *Einstein: The first hundred years.* Oxford, UK: Pergamon.

Goldstein, M., King, A., & West, M. (2003). Social interaction shapes babbling: Testing parallels between birdsong and speech. *Proceedings of the National Academy of Sciences, USA, 100,* 8030–8035.

Goleman, D. (1995, July 1). A genetic clue to bed-wetting is located: Researchers say discovery shows the problem is not emotions! *New York Times,* p. 8.

Golinkoff, R. M., Jacquet, R. C., Hirsh-Pasek, K., & Nandakumar, R. (1996). Lexical principles may underlie the learning of verbs. *Child Development, 67,* 3101–3119.

Golomb, C., & Galasso, L. (1995). Make believe and reality: Explorations of the imaginary realm. *Developmental Psychology, 31,* 800–810.

Golombok, S., MacCallum, F., & Goodman, E. (2001). The "test-tube" generation: Parent-child relationships and the psychological well-being of in vitro fertilization children at adolescence. *Child Development, 72,* 599–608.

Golombok, S., MacCallum, F., Goodman, E., & Rutter, M. (2002). Families with children conceived by donor insemination: A follow-up at age twelve. *Child Development, 73,* 952–968.

Golombok, S., Murray, C., Jadva, V., MacCallum, F., & Lycett, E. (2004). Families created through surrogacy arrangements: Parent-child relationships in the 1st year of life. *Developmental Psychology, 40,* 400–411.

Golombok, S., Perry, B., Burston, A., Murray, C., Mooney-Summers, J., Stevens, M., et al. (2003). Children with lesbian parents: A community study. *Developmental Psychology, 39,* 20–33.

Gonzales, N. A., Cauce, A. M., & Mason, C. A. (1996). Interobserver agreement in the assessment of parental behavior and parent-adolescent conflict: African American mothers, daughters, and independent observers. *Child Development, 67,* 1483–1498.

Gonzales, P., Guzman, J. C., Partelow, L., Pahlke, E., Jocelyn, L., Kastberg, D., et al. (2004). *Highlights from the Trends in International Mathematics and Science Study (TIMSS) 2003* (NCES 2005-205). Washington, DC: National Center for Education Statistics, U.S. Department of Education, Institute of Education Sciences.

Gooden, A. M. (2001). Gender representation in notable children's picture books: 1995–1999. *Sex Roles: A Journal of Research.* Retrieved April 20, 2005, from http://www.?ndarticles.com/p/articles/ mi m2294/is_2001_July/ ai_81478076

Goodwin, J. (1994). *Akira Kurosawa and intertextual cinema.* Baltimore, MD: Johns Hopkins University Press.

Goodwyn, S. W., & Acredolo, L. P. (1998). Encouraging symbolic gestures: A new perspective on the relationship between gesture and speech. In J. M. Iverson & S. Goldin-Meadow (Eds.), *The nature and functions of gesture in children's communication* (pp. 61–73). San Francisco: Jossey-Bass.

Gootman, E. (2007, January 22). Taking middle schoolers out of the middle. *New York Times,* p. A1.

Gootman, E., & Herszenhorn, D. M. (2005, May 3). Getting smaller to improve the big picture. *New York Times.* Retrieved May 3, 2005, from http://www.nytimes.com/ 1005/05/03/nyregion/03small.html

Gopnik, A., Sobel, D. M., Schulz, L. E., & Glymour, C. (2001). Causal learning mechanisms in very young children: Two-, three-, and four-year-olds infer causal relations from patterns of variation and covariation. *Developmental Psychology, 37*(5), 620–629.

Gordon, I., Lask, B., Bryantwaugh, R., Christie, D., & Timini, S. (1997). Childhood onset anorexia nervosa: Towards identifying a biological substrate. *International Journal of Eating Disorders, 22*(2), 159–165.

Gorman, M. (1993). Help and self-help for older adults in developing countries. *Generations, 17*(4), 73–76.

Gormley, W. T., Gayer, T., Phillips, D., & Dawson, B. (2005). The effects of universal pre-K on cognitive development. *Developmental Psychology, 41,* 872–884.

Gortmaker, S. L., Hughes, M., Cervia, J., Brady, M., Johnson, G. M., Seage, G. R., et al. for the Pediatric AIDS Clinical Trials Group Protocol 219 Team. (2001). Effect of combination therapy including protease inhibitors on mortality among children and adolescents infected with HIV-1. *New England Journal of Medicine, 345*(21), 1522–1528.

Gortmaker, S. L., Must, A., Perrin, J. M., Sobol, A. M., & Dietz, W. H. (1993). Social and economic consequences of overweight in adolescence and young adulthood. *New England Journal of Medicine, 329,* 1008–1012.

Gosden, R. G., & Feinberg, A. P. (2007). Genetics and epigenetics—nature's pen-and-pencil set. *New England Journal of Medicine, 356,* 731–733.

Gottfried, A. E., Fleming, J. S., & Gottfried, A. W. (1998). Role of cognitively stimulating home environment in children's academic intrinsic motivation: A longitudinal study. *Child Development, 69,* 1448–1460.

Gottlieb, G. (1991). Experiential canalization of behavioral development theory. *Developmental Psychology, 27*(1), 4–13.

Gottlieb, G. (2007). Probabilistic epigenesis. *Developmental Science, 10,* 1–11.

Gottman, J. M., & Notarius, C. I. (2000). Decade review: Observing marital interaction. *Journal of Marriage and the Family, 62,* 927–947.

Goubet, N., & Clifton, R. K. (1998). Object and event representation in 6 1/2-month-old infants. *Developmental Psychology, 34,* 63–76.

Gould, E., Reeves, A. J., Graziano, M. S. A., & Gross, C. G. (1999). Neurogenesis in the neocortex of adult primates. *Science, 286,* 548–552.

Gould, M. S., Marrocco, F. A., Kleinman, M., Thomas, J. G., Mostkoff, K., Cote, J., et al. (2005). Evaluating iatrogenic risk of youth suicide screening programs: A randomized controlled trial. *Journal of the American Medical Association, 293,* 1635–1643.

Graber, J. A., Brooks-Gunn, J., & Warren, M. P. (1995). The antecedents of menarcheal age: Heredity, family environment, and stressful life events. *Child Development, 66,* 346–359.

Graber, J. A., Lewinsohn, P. M., Seeley, J. R., & Brooks-Gunn, J. (1997). Is psychopathology associated with the timing of pubertal development? *Journal of the American Academy of Child and Adolescent Psychiatry, 36,* 1768–1776.

Grady, B. (2002, December). *Miscarriage: The need to grieve.* Retrieved April 9, 2006, from http://www.parenting-plus.com/newsletter_0212.htm

Grantham-McGregor, S., Powell, C., Walker, S., Chang, S., & Fletcher, P. (1994). The long-term follow-up of severely malnourished children who participated in an intervention program. *Child Development, 65,* 428–439.

Gray, J. R., & Thompson, P. M. (2004). Neurobiology of intelligence: Science and ethics. *Neuroscience, 5,* 471–492.

Gray, M. R., & Steinberg, L. (1999). Unpacking authoritative parenting: Reassessing a multidimensional construct. *Journal of Marriage and the Family, 61,* 574–587.

Graziano, A. M., & Mooney, K. C. (1982). Behavioral treatment of "nightfears" in children: Maintenance and improvement at 2 1/2- to 3-year follow-up. *Journal of Counseling and Clinical Psychology, 50,* 598–599.

Greene, M. F. (2002). Outcomes of very low birth weight in young adults. *New England Journal of Medicine, 346*(3), 146–148.

Greene, M. L., & Way, N. (2005). Self-esteem trajectories among ethnic minority adolescents: A growth curve analysis of the patterns and predictors of change. *Journal of Research on Adolescence, 15,* 151–178.

Greenfield, P. M., & Childs, C. P. (1978). Understanding sibling concepts: A developmental study of kin terms in Zinacanten. In P. R. Dasen (Ed.), *Piagetian psychology* (pp. 335–358). New York: Gardner.

Greenhouse, L. (2000a, February 29). Program of drug-testing pregnant women draws review by the Supreme Court. *New York Times,* p. A12.

Greenhouse, L. (2000b, September 9). Should a fetus's well-being override a mother's rights? *New York Times,* pp. B9, B11.

Greenstone, M., & Chay, K. (2003). The impact of air pollution on infant mortality: Evidence from geographic variation in pollution shocks induced by a recession. *Quarterly Journal of Economics, 118,* 1121–1167.

Grigorenko, E. L., Meier, E., Lipka, J., Mohatt, G., Yanez, E., & Sternberg, R. J. (2004). Academic and practical intelligence: A case study of the Yup'ik in Alaska. *Learning and Individual Differences, 14*(4), 183–207.

Grigorenko, E. L., & Sternberg, R. J. (1998). Dynamic testing. *Psychological Bulletin, 124,* 75–111.

Groce, N. E., & Zola, I. K. (1993). Multiculturalism, chronic illness, and disability. *Pediatrics, 91,* 1048–1055.

Groos, K. (1898). *The play of animals.* New York: Appleton.

Groos, K. (1901). *The play of man.* New York: Appleton.

Gross, R. T., & Duke, P. (1980). The effect of early versus late physical maturation on adolescent behavior. [Special issue: I. Litt (Ed.), Symposium on adolescent medicine.] *Pediatric Clinics of North America, 27,* 71–78.

Grotevant, H. D., McRoy, R. G., Eide, C. L., & Fravel, D. L. (1994). Adoptive family system dynamics: Variations by level of openness in the adoption. *Family Process, 33*(2), 125–146.

Gruber, H. (1981). *Darwin on man: A psychological study of scientific creativity* (2nd ed.). Chicago: University of Chicago Press.

Grubman, S., Gross, E., Lerner-Weiss, N., Hernandez, M., McSherry, G. D., Hoyt, L. G., et al. (1995). Older children and adolescents living with perinatally acquired human immunodeficiency virus. *Pediatrics, 95,* 657–663.

Grusec, J. E., & Goodnow, J. J. (1994). Impact of parental discipline methods on the child's internalization of values: A reconceptualization of current points of view. *Developmental Psychology, 30,* 4–19.

Guberman, S. R. (1996). The development of everyday mathematics in Brazilian children with limited formal education. *Child Development, 67,* 1609–1623.

Guerino, P., Hurwitz, M. D., Noonan, M. E., & Kaffenberger, S. M. (2006). *Crime, violence, discipline, and safety in U.S. public schools: Findings from the School Survey on Crime and Safety: 2003–2004* (NCES 2007-303). Washington, DC: National Center for Education Statistics.

Guilford, J. P. (1956). Structure of intellect. *Psychological Bulletin, 53,* 267–293.

Guilford, J. P. (1959). Three faces of intellect. *American Psychologist, 14,* 469–479.

Guilford, J. P. (1960). Basic conceptual problems of the psychology of thinking. *Proceedings of the New York Academy of Sciences, 91,* 6–21.

Guilford, J. P. (1967). *The nature of human intelligence.* New York: McGraw-Hill.

Guilford, J. P. (1986). *Creative talents: Their nature, uses and development.* Buffalo, NY: Bearly.

Guilleminault, C., Palombini, L., Pelayo, R., & Chervin, R. D. (2003). Sleeping and sleep terrors in prepubertal children: What triggers them? *Pediatrics, 111,* e17–e25.

Guillette, E. A., Meza, M. M., Aquilar, M. G., Soto, A. D., & Garcia, I. E. (1998). An anthropological approach to the evaluation of pre-school children exposed to pesticides in Mexico. *Environmental Health Perspectives, 106,* 347–353.

Gullone, E. (2000). The development of normal fear: A century of research. *Clinical Psychology Review, 20,* 429–451.

Gunnar, M. R., Larson, M. C., Hertsgaard, L., Harris, M. L., & Brodersen, L. (1992). The stressfulness of separation among 9-month-old infants: Effects of social context variables and infant temperament. *Child Development, 63,* 290–303.

Gunnoe, M. L., & Hetherington, E. M. (2004). Stepchildren's perceptions of non-custodial mothers and noncustodial fathers: Differences in socioemotional involvement and associations with adolescent adjustment problems. *Journal of Family Psychology, 18,* 555–563.

Gunnoe, M. L., & Mariner, C. L. (1997). Toward a developmental-contextual model of the effects of parental spanking on children's aggression. *Archives of Pediatric and Adolescent Medicine, 151,* 768–775.

Guralnick, P. (1994). *Last train to Memphis: The rise of Elvis Presley.* Boston: Little, Brown.

Guyer, B., Hoyert, D. L., Martin, J. A., Ventura, S. J., MacDorman, M. F., & Strobino, D. M. (1999). Annual summary of vital statistics—1998. *Pediatrics, 104,* 1229–1246.

Guyer, B., Strobino, D. M., Ventura, S. J., & Singh, G. K. (1995). Annual summary of vital statistics—1994. *Pediatrics, 96,* 1029–1039.

Guzell, J. R., & Vernon-Feagans, L. (2004). Parental perceived control over caregiving and its relationship to parent-infant interaction. *Child Development, 75,* 134–146.

Guzick, D. S., Carson, S. A., Coutifaris, C., Overstreet, J. W., Factor-Litvak, P., Steinkampf, M. P., et al. (1999). Efficacy of superovulation and intrauterine insemination in the treatment of infertility. *New England Journal of Medicine, 340,* 177–183.

Hack, M., Flannery, D. J., Schluchter, M., Cartar, L., Borawski, E., & Klein, N. (2002). Outcomes in young adulthood for very-low-birth-weight infants. *New England Journal of Medicine, 346*(3), 149–157.

Hack, M., Youngstrom, E. A., Cartar, L., Schluchter, M., Taylor, H. G., Flannery, D., et al. (2004). Behavioral outcomes and evidence of psychopathology among very low birth weight infants at age 20 years. *Pediatrics, 114,* 932–940.

Haddow, J. E., Palomaki, G. E., Allan, W. C., Williams, J. R., Knight, G. J., Gagnon, J., et al. (1999). Maternal thyroid deficiency during pregnancy and subsequent neuropsychological development of the child. *New England Journal of Medicine, 341,* 549–555.

Haden, C. A., & Fivush, F. (1996). Contextual variation in maternal conversational styles. *Merrill-Palmer Quarterly, 42,* 200–227.

Haden, C. A., Haine, R. A., & Fivush, R. (1997). Developing narrative structure in parent-child reminiscing across the preschool years. *Developmental Psychology, 33,* 295–307.

Haden, C. A., Ornstein, P. A., Eckerman, C. O., & Didow, S. M. (2001). Mother-child conversational interactions as events unfold: Linkages to subsequent remembering. *Child Development, 72*(4), 1016–1031.

Hagan, J. F., Committee on Psychosocial Aspects of Child and Family Health, & Task Force on Terrorism. (2005). Psychosocial implications of disaster or terrorism on children: A guide for pediatricians. *Pediatrics, 116,* 787–796.

Haig, D. (1993). Genetic conflicts in human pregnancy. *Quarterly Review of Biology, 68,* 495–532.

Haig, D., & Westoby, M. (1989). Parent-specific gene expression and the triploid endosperm. *American Naturalist, 134,* 147–155.

Haith, M. M. (1986). Sensory and perceptual processes in early infancy. *Journal of Pediatrics, 109*(1), 158–171.

Haith, M. M. (1998). Who put the cog in infant cognition? Is rich interpretation too costly? *Infant Behavior and Development, 21*(2), 167–179.

Haith, M. M., & Benson, J. B. (1998). Infant cognition. In D. Kuhn & R. S. Siegler (Eds.), *Handbook of child psychology: Vol. 2. Cognition, perception, and language* (5th ed., pp. 199–254). New York: Wiley.

Hala, S., & Chandler, M. (1996). The role of strategic planning in accessing false-belief understanding. *Child Development, 67,* 2948–2966.

Hall, D. G., & Graham, S. A. (1999). Lexical form class information guides word-to-object mapping in preschoolers. *Child Development, 70,* 78–91.

Hall, G. S. (1916). *Adolescence.* New York: Appleton. (Original work published 1904)

Hallfors, D. D., Waller, M. W., Bauer, D., Ford, C. A., & Halpern, C. T. (2005). Which comes first in adolescence—sex and drugs or depression? *American Journal of Preventive Medicine, 29,* 163–170.

Halpern, D. F. (1997). Sex differences in intelligence: Implications for education. *American Psychologist, 52*(10), 1091–1102.

Halterman, J. S., Aligne, A., Auinger, P., McBride, J. T., & Szilagyi, P. G. (2000). Inadequate therapy for asthma among children in the United States. *Pediatrics, 105*(1), 272–276.

Hamilton, B. E., Martin, J. A., & Sutton, P. D. (2004). Births: Preliminary data for 2003. *National Vital Statistics Reports, 53*(9). Hyattsville, MD: National Center for Health Statistics.

Hamilton, B. E., Miniño, A. M., Martin, J. A., Kochanek, K. D., Strobino, D. M., & Guyer, B. (2007). Annual summary of vital statistics, 2005. *Pediatrics, 119,* 345–360.

Hamilton, L., Cheng, S., & Powell, B. (2007). Adoptive parents, adaptive parents: Evaluating the importance of biological ties for parental investment. *American Sociological Review, 72,* 95–116.

Hamm, J. V. (2000). Do birds of a feather flock together? The variable bases for African American, Asian American, and European American adolescents' selection of similar friends. *Developmental Psychology, 36*(2), 209–219.

Hammad, T. A., Laughren, T., & Racoosin, J. (2006). Suicidality in pediatric patients treated with antidepressant drugs. *Archives of General Psychiatry, 63,* 332–339.

Hampden-Thompson, G., & Johnston, J. S. (2006). *Variation in the relationship between nonschool factors and student achievement on international assessments* (NCES 2006-014). Washington, DC: U. S. Department of Education, National Center for Education Statistics.

Hampson, J. G., Money, J., & Hampson, J. L. (1956). Hermaphrodism: Recommendations concerning case management. *Journal of Clinical Endocrinology and Metabolism, 16*(4), 547–556.

Hamre, B. K., & Pianta, R. C. (2005). Can instructional and emotional support in the first-grade classroom make a difference for children at risk of school failure? *Child Development, 76,* 949–967.

Handmaker, N. S., Rayburn, W. F., Meng, C., Bell, J. B., Rayburn, B. B., & Rappaport, V. J. (2006). Impact of alcohol exposure after pregnancy recognition on ultrasonographic fetal growth measures. *Alcoholism: Clinical and Experimental Research, 30,* 892–898.

Hansen, D., Lou, H. C., & Olsen, J. (2000). Serious life events and congenital malformations: A national study with complete follow-up. *Lancet, 356,* 875–880.

Hansen, M., Janssen, I., Schiff, A., Zee, P. C., & Dubocovich, M. L. (2005). The impact of school daily schedule on adolescent sleep. *Pediatrics, 115,* 1555–1561.

Hara, H. (2002). Justifications for bullying among Japanese school children. *Asian Journal of Social Psychology, 5,* 197–204.

Hardy, R., Kuh, D., Langenberg, C., & Wadsworth, M. E. (2003). Birth weight, childhood social class, and change in adult blood pressure in the 1946 British birth cohort. *Lancet, 362,* 1178–1183.

Hardy-Brown, K., & Plomin, R. (1985). Infant communicative development: Evidence from adoptive and biological families for genetic and environmental influences on rate differences. *Developmental Psychology, 21,* 378–385.

Hardy-Brown, K., Plomin, R., & DeFries, J. C. (1981). Genetic and environmental influences on rate of communicative development in the first year of life. *Developmental Psychology, 17,* 704–717.

Hargrove, J. (1989). *Nelson Mandela: South Africa's silent voice of protest.* Chicago: Children's Press.

Harlow, H. F., & Harlow, M. K (1962). The effect of rearing conditions on behavior. *Bulletin of the Menninger Clinic, 26,* 213–224.

Harlow, H. F., & Zimmerman, R. R. (1959). Affectional responses in the infant monkey. *Science, 130,* 421–432.

Harmon, A. (2005, November 20). The problem with an almost-perfect genetic world. *New York Times.* Retrieved November 20, 2005, from http://www.nytimes.com/2005/11/20/weekinreview/20harmon.html?ex=1142053200&en=c6c3a9ec0867ef48&ei=5070

Harnishfeger, K. K., & Bjorklund, D. F. (1993). The ontogeny of inhibition mechanisms: A renewed approach to cognitive development. In M. L. Howe & R. P. Pasnak (Eds.), *Emerging themes in cognitive development* (Vol. 1, pp. 28–49). New York: Springer-Verlag.

Harnishfeger, K. K., & Pope, R. S. (1996). Intending to forget: The development of cognitive inhibition in directed forgetting. *Journal of Experimental Psychology, 62,* 292–315.

Harris, G. (1997). Development of taste perception and appetite regulation. In G. Bremner, A. Slater, & G. Butterworth (Eds.), *Infant development: Recent advances* (pp. 9–30). East Sussex, UK: Psychology Press.

Harris, G. (2005, March 3). Gene therapy is facing a crucial hearing. *New York Times.* Retrieved March 3, 2005, from http://www.nytimes.com/2005/03/03/politics/03gene.html

Harris, L. H., & Paltrow, L. (2003). The status of pregnant women and fetuses in U.S. criminal law. *Journal of the American Medical Association, 289,* 1697–1699.

Harris, P. L., Brown, E., Marriott, C., Whittall, S., & Harmer, S. (1991). Monsters, ghosts, and witches: Testing the limits of the fantasy-reality distinction in young children. In G. E. Butterworth, P. L. Harris, A. M. Leslie, & H. M. Wellman (Eds.), *Perspective on the child's theory of mind.* Oxford, UK: Oxford University Press.

Harris, P. L., Olthof, T., Meerum Terwogt, M., & Hardman, C. (1987). Children's knowledge of situations that provoke emotion. *International Journal of Behavioral Development, 10,* 319–343.

Harrist, A. W., & Waugh, R. M. (2002). Dyadic synchrony: Its structure and function in children's development. *Developmental Review, 22,* 555–592.

Harrist, A. W., Zain, A. F., Bates, J. E., Dodge, K. A., & Pettit, G. S. (1997). Subtypes of social withdrawal in early childhood: Sociometric status and social-cognitive differences across four years. *Child Development, 68,* 278–294.

Hart, C. H., DeWolf, M., Wozniak, P., & Burts, D. C. (1992). Maternal and paternal disciplinary styles: Relations with preschoolers' playground behavioral orientation and peer status. *Child Development, 63,* 879–892.

Hart, C. H., Ladd, G. W., & Burleson, B. R. (1990). Children's expectations of the outcome of social strategies: Relations with sociometric status and maternal disciplinary style. *Child Development, 61,* 127–137.

Harter, S. (1990). Causes, correlates, and the functional role of global self-worth: A life-span perspective. In J. Kolligan & R. Sternberg (Eds.), *Competence considered: Perceptions of competence and incompetence across the life-span* (pp. 67–97). New Haven, CT: Yale University Press.

Harter, S. (1993). Developmental changes in self-understanding across the 5 to 7 shift. In A. Sameroff & M. Haith (Eds.), *Reason and responsibility: The passage through childhood.* Chicago: University of Chicago Press.

Harter, S. (1996). Developmental changes in self-understanding across the 5 to 7 shift. In A. J. Sameroff & M. M. Haith (Eds.), *The five to seven year shift: The age of reason and responsibility* (pp. 207–235). Chicago: University of Chicago Press.

Harter, S. (1998). The development of self-representations. In W. Damon (Series Ed.) & N. Eisenberg (Vol. Ed.), *Handbook of child psychology: Vol. 3. Social, emotional, and personality development* (5th ed., pp. 553–617). New York: Wiley.

Hartford, J. (1971). *Life prayer.*

Hartshorn, K., Rovee-Collier, C., Gerhardstein, P., Bhatt, R. S., Wondoloski, R. L., Klein, P., et al. (1998). The ontogeny of long-term memory over the first year-and-a-half of life. *Developmental Psychobiology, 32,* 69–89.

Hartup, W. W. (1992). Peer relations in early and middle childhood. In V. B. Van Hasselt & M. Hersen (Eds.), *Handbook of social development: A lifespan perspective* (pp. 257–281). New York: Plenum.

Hartup, W. W. (1996a). The company they keep: Friendships and their developmental significance. *Child Development, 67,* 1–13.

Hartup, W. W. (1996b). Cooperation, close relationships, and cognitive development. In W. M. Bukowski, A. F. Newcomb, & W. W. Hartup (Eds.), *The company they keep: Friendship in childhood and adolescence* (pp. 213–237). New York: Cambridge University Press.

Hartup, W. W., & Stevens, N. (1999). Friendships and adaptation across the life span. *Current Directions in Psychological Science, 8,* 76–79.

Harvard Medical School. (2002, July). Treatment of bulimia and binge eating. *Harvard Mental Health Letter, 19*(1), 1–4.

Harvard Medical School. (2003, June). Confronting suicide: Part II. *Harvard Mental Health Letter, 19*(12), 1–5.

Harvard Medical School. (2004, December). Children's fears and anxieties. *Harvard Mental Health Letter, 21*(6), 1–3.

Harvey, J. H., & Pauwels, B. G. (1999). Recent developments in close relationships theory. *Current Directions in Psychological Science, 8*(3), 93–95.

Harwood, R. (1987). *Mandela.* New York: New American Library.

Harwood, R. L., Schoelmerich, A., Ventura-Cook, E., Schulze, P. A., & Wilson, S. P. (1996). Culture and class influences on Anglo and Puerto Rican mothers' beliefs regarding long-term socialization goals and child behavior. *Child Development, 67,* 2446–2461.

Haswell, K., Hock, E., & Wenar, C. (1981). Oppositional behavior of preschool children: Theory and prevention, *Family Relations, 30,* 440–446.

Hatano, G., Siegler, R. S., Richards, D. D., Inagaki, K., Stavy, R., & Wax, N. (1993). The development of biological knowledge: A multinational study. *Cognitive Development, 8,* 47–62.

Hatcher, P. J., Hulme, C., & Ellis, A. W. (1994). Ameliorating early reading failure by integrating the teaching of reading and phonological skills: The phonological linkage hypotheses. *Child Development, 65,* 41–57.

Hauck, F. R., Herman, S. M., Donovan, M., Iyasu, S., Moore, C. M., Donoghue, E., et al. (2003). Sleep environment and the risk of sudden infant death syndrome in an urban population: The Chicago Infant Mortality Study. *Pediatrics, 111,* 1207–1214.

Hauck, F. R., Omojokun, O. O., & Siadaty, M. S. (2005). Do pacifiers reduce the risk of sudden infant death syndrome? A meta-analysis. *Pediatrics, 116,* e716-e723.

Haugaard, J. J. (1998). Is adoption a risk factor for the development of adjustment problems? *Clinical Psychology Review, 18,* 47–69.

Hawes, A. (1996). Jungle gyms: The evolution of animal play. *ZooGoer, 25*(1). Retrieved July 18, 2006, from http://nationalzoo.si.edu/Publications/ZooGoer.1996/1/junglegyms.cfm

Hawkins, J. D., Catalano, R. F., Kosterman, R., Abbott, R., & Hill, K. G. (1999). Preventing adolescent health-risk behaviors by strengthening protection during childhood. *Archives of Pediatrics and Adolescent Medicine, 153,* 226–234.

Hawkins, J. D., Catalano, R. F., & Miller, J. Y. (1992). Risk and protective factors for alcohol and other drug problems in adolescence and early adulthood: Implications for substance abuse programs. *Psychological Bulletin, 112*(1), 64–105.

Hay, D. (2003). Pathways to violence in the children of mothers who were depressed post partum. *Developmental Psychology, 39,* 1083–1094.

Hay, D. F., Pedersen, J., & Nash, A. (1982). Dyadic interaction in the first year of life. In K. H. Rubin & H. S. Ross (Eds.), *Peer relationships and social skills in children.* New York: Springer.

Hayes, A., & Batshaw, M. L. (1993). Down syndrome. *Pediatric Clinics of North America, 40,* 523–535.

Hayne, H., Barr, R., & Herbert, J. (2003). The effect of prior practice on memory reactivation and generalization. *Child Development, 74,* 1615–1627.

Healy, A. J., Malone, F. D., Sullivan, L. M., Porter, T. F., Luthy, D. A., Comstock, C. H., et al. (2006). Early access to prenatal care: Implications for racial disparity in perinatal mortality. *Obstetrics and Gynecology, 107,* 625–631.

Heath, S. B. (1989). Oral and literate tradition among black Americans living in poverty. *American Psychologist, 44,* 367–373.

Heffner, L. J. (2004). Advanced maternal age—how old is too old? *New England Journal of Medicine, 351,* 1927–1929.

Heilbut, A. (1993, April 26). Marian Anderson: Postscript. *New Yorker,* pp. 82–83.

Helms, J. E. (1992). Why is there no study of cultural equivalence in standardized cognitive ability testing? *American Psychologist, 47,* 1083–1101.

Helms, J. E., Jernigan, M., & Mascher, J. (2005).The meaning of race in psychology and how to change it: A methodological perspective. *American Psychologist, 60,* 27–36.

Helwig, C. C., & Jasiobedzka, U. (2001). The relation between law and morality: Children's reasoning about socially beneficial and unjust laws. *Child Development, 72,* 1382–1393.

Henderson, H. A., Marshall, P. J., Fox, N. A., & Rubin, K. H. (2004). Psychophysiological and behavioral evidence for varying forms and functions of nonsocial behavior in preschoolers. *Child Development, 75,* 251–263.

Henrich, C. C., Brown, J. L., & Aber, J. L. (1999). Evaluating the effectiveness of school-based violence prevention: Developmental approaches. *Social Policy Report, SRCD, 13*(3).

Hernandez, D. J. (1997). Child development and the social demography of childhood. *Child Development, 68,* 149–169.

Hernandez, D. J. (2004, Summer). Demographic change and the life circumstances of immigrant families. *The Future of Children, 14*(2). Retrieved October 7, 2004, from http://www.futureofchildren.org

Herrmann, D. (1999). *Helen Keller: A life.* Chicago: University of Chicago Press.

Herrmann, H. J., & Roberts, M. W. (1987). Preventive dental care: The role of the pediatrician. *Pediatrics, 80,* 107–110.

Herrnstein, R. J., & Murray, C. (1994). *The bell curve: Intelligence and class structure in American life.* New York: Free Press.

Hertenstein, M. J., & Campos, J. J. (2004). The retention effects of an adult's emotional displays on infant behavior. *Child Development, 75,* 595–613.

Hertz-Pannier, L., Chiron, C., Jambaque, I., Renaux-Kieffer, V., Van de Moortele, P., Delalande, O., et al. (2002). Late plasticity for language in a child's non-dominant hemisphere. A pre- and post-surgery fMRI study. *Brain, 125*(2), 361–372.

Hesketh, T., Lu, L., & Xing, Z. W. (2005). The effect of China's one-child policy after 25 years. *New England Journal of Medicine, 353,* 1171–1176.

Hesso, N. A., & Fuentes, E. (2005). Ethnic differences in neonatal and postneonatal mortality. *Pediatrics, 115,* e44–e51.

Hetherington, E. M. (1987). Family relations six years after divorce. In K. Pasley & M. Ihinger-Tallman (Eds.), *Remarriage and parenting today: Research and theory.* New York: Guilford.

Hetherington, E. M., Bridges, M., & Insabella, G. M. (1998). What matters? What does not? Five perspectives on the association between marital transitions and children's adjustment. *American Psychologist, 53,* 167–184.

Hetherington, E. M., & Kelly, J. (2002). *For better or worse: Divorce reconsidered.* New York: Norton.

Hetherington, E. M., Stanley-Hagan, M., & Anderson, E. (1989). Marital transitions: Child's perspective. *American Psychologist, 44,* 303–312.

Hewlett, B. S. (1987). Intimate fathers: Patterns of paternal holding among Aka pygmies. In M. E. Lamb (Ed.), *The father's role: Cross-cultural perspectives* (pp. 295–330). Hillsdale, NJ: Erlbaum.

Hewlett, B. S. (1992). Husband-wife reciprocity and the father-infant relationship among Aka pygmies. In B. S. Hewlett (Ed.), *Father-child relations: Cultural and biosocial contexts* (pp. 153–176). New York: de Gruyter.

Hewlett, B. S., Lamb, M. E., Shannon, D., Leyendecker, B., & Schölmerich, A. (1998). Culture and early infancy among central African foragers and farmers. *Developmental Psychology, 34*(4), 653–661.

Hickling, A. K., & Wellman, H. M. (2001). The emergence of children's causal explanations and theories: Evidence from everyday conversations. *Developmental Psychology, 37*(5), 668–683.

Hickman, M., Roberts, C., & de Matos, M. G. (2000). Exercise and leisure time activities. In C. Currie, K. Hurrelmann, W. Settertobulte, R. Smith, & J. Todd (Eds.), *Health and health behaviour among young people: A WHO crossnational study (HBSC) international report* (pp. 73–82.). WHO Policy Series: Health Policy for Children and Adolescents, Series No. 1. Copenhagen, Denmark: World Health Organization Regional Office for Europe.

Hill, D. A., Gridley, G., Cnattingius, S., Mellemkjaer, L., Linet, M., Adami, H.-O., et al. (2003). Mortality and cancer incidence among individuals with Down syndrome. *Archives of Internal Medicine, 163,* 705–711.

Hill, J. L., Waldfogel, J., Brooks-Gunn, J., & Han, W.-J. (2005). Maternal employment and child development: A fresh look using newer methods. *Developmental Psychology, 41,* 833–850.

Hill, J. P. (1987). Research on adolescents and their families: Past and prospect. In E. E. Irwin (Ed.), *Adolescent social behavior and health.* San Francisco: Jossey-Bass.

Hill, N. E., & Taylor, L. C. (2004). Parental school involvement and children's academic achievement: Pragmatics and issues. *Current Directions in Psychological Science, 13,* 161–168.

Hillier, L. (2002). "It's a catch-22": Same-sex-attracted young people on coming out to parents. In S. S. Feldman & D. A. Rosenthal (Eds.), *Talking sexuality. New Directions for Child and Adolescent Development, 97,* 75–91.

Hillis, S. D., Anda, R. F., Dubé, S. R., Felitti, V. J., Marchbanks, P. A., & Marks, J. S. (2004). The association between adverse childhood experiences and adolescent pregnancy, long-term psychosocial consequences, and fetal death. *Pediatrics, 113,* 320–327.

Hinckley, A. F., Bachard, A. M., & Reif, J. S. (2005). Late pregnancy exposures to disinfection by-products and growth-related birth outcomes. *Environmental Health Perspectives, 113,* 1808–1813.

Hinds, T. S., West, W. L., Knight, E. M., & Harland, B. F. (1996). The effect of caffeine on pregnancy outcome variables. *Nutrition Reviews, 54,* 203–207.

Hines, A. M. (1997). Divorce-related transitions, adolescent development, and the role of the parent-child relationship: A review of the literature. *Journal of Marriage and the Family, 59,* 375–388.

Hines, M., Chiu, L., McAdams, L. A., Bentler, M. P., & Lipcamon, J. (1992). Cognition and the corpus callosum: Verbal fluency, visual-spatial ability, language lateralization related to midsagittal surface areas of the corpus callosum. *Behavioral Neuroscience, 106,* 3–14.

Hitchins, M. P., & Moore, G. E. (2002, May 9). Genomic imprinting in fetal growth and development. *Expert Reviews in Molecular Medicine.* Retrieved November 21, 2006, from http://www.expertreviews.org/0200457Xh.htm

Hitlin, S., Brown, J. S., & Elder, G. H. (2006). Racial self-categorization in adolescence: Multiracial development and social pathways. *Child Development, 77,* 1298–1308.

Ho, W. C. (1989). *Yani: The brush of innocence.* New York: Hudson Hills.

Hoban, T. F. (2004). Sleep and its disorders in children. *Seminars in Neurology, 24,* 327–340.

Hobson, J. A., & Silvestri, L. (1999, February). Parasomnias. *Harvard Mental Health Letter,* pp. 3–5.

Hodges, E. V. E., Boivin, M., Vitaro, F., & Bukowski, W. M. (1999). The power of friendship: Protection against an escalating cycle of peer victimization. *Developmental Psychology, 35,* 94–101.

Hoff, E. (2003). The specificity of environmental influence: Socioeconomic status affects early vocabulary development via maternal speech. *Child Development, 74,* 1368–1378.

Hofferth, S. L., & Jankuniene, Z. (2000, April 2). *Children's after-school activities.* Paper presented at biennial meeting of the Society for Research on Adolescence, Chicago, IL.

Hoffman, H. J., & Hillman, L. S. (1992). Epidemiology of the sudden infant death syndrome: Maternal, neonatal, and postneonatal risk factors. *Clinics in Perinatology, 19,* 717–737.

Hoffman, M. L. (1970a). Conscience, personality, and socialization techniques. *Human Development, 13,* 90–126.

Hoffman, M. L. (1970b). Moral development. In P. H. Mussen (Ed.), *Carmichael's manual of child psychology* (Vol. 2, 3rd ed., pp. 261–360). New York: Wiley.

Hoffrage, U., Weber, A., Hertwig, R., & Chase, V. M. (2003). How to keep children safe in traffic: Find the daredevils early. *Journal of Experimental Psychology: Applied, 9,* 249–260.

Hofman, P. L., Regan, F., Jackson, W. E., Jefferies, C., Knight, D. B., Robinson, E. M., et al. (2004). Premature birth and later insulin resistance. *New England Journal of Medicine, 351,* 2179–2186.

Holden, C. (2000). Asia stays on top, U.S. in middle in new global rankings. *Science, 290,* 1866.

Holden, G. W., & Miller, P. C. (1999). Enduring and different: A meta-analysis of the similarity in parents' child rearing. *Psychological Bulletin, 125,* 223–254.

Holowka, S., & Petitto, L. A. (2002). Left hemisphere cerebral specialization for babies while babbling. *Science, 297,* 1515.

Holtzman, N. A., Murphy, P. D., Watson, M. S., & Barr, P. A. (1997). Predictive genetic testing: From basic research to clinical practice. *Science, 278,* 602–605.

Honein, M. A., Paulozzi, L. J., Mathews, T. J., Erickson, J. D., & Wong, L.-Y. C. (2001). Impact of folic acid fortification of the U.S. food supply on the occurrence of neural tube defects. *Journal of the American Medical Association, 285*, 2981–2986.

Hopfensperger, J. (1996, April 15). Germany's fast track to a career. *Minneapolis Star-Tribune*, pp. A1, A6.

Hopkins, B., & Westra, T. (1988). Maternal handling and motor development: An intracultural study. *Genetic, Social and General Psychology Monographs, 14*, 377–420.

Hopkins, B., & Westra, T. (1990). Motor development, maternal expectations and the role of handling. *Infant Behavior and Development, 13*, 117–122.

Horbar, J. D., Wright, E. C., Onstad, L., & the Members of the National Institute of Child Health and Human Development Neonatal Research Network. (1993). Decreasing mortality associated with the introduction of surfactant therapy: An observational study of neonates weighing 601 to 1300 grams at birth. *Pediatrics, 92*, 191–196.

Houk, C. P., Hughes, I. A., Ahmed, S. F., Lee, P. A., & Writing Committee for the International Intersex Consensus Conference Participants. (2006). Summary of consensus statement on intersex disorders and their management. *Pediatrics, 118*, 753–757.

Howe, M. L. (2003). Memories from the cradle. *Current Directions in Psychological Science, 12*, 62–65.

Howe, M. L., & Courage, M. L. (1993). On resolving the enigma of infantile amnesia. *Psychological Bulletin, 113*, 305–326.

Howe, M. L., & Courage, M. L. (1997). The emergence and early development of autobiographical memory. *Psychological Review, 104*, 499–523.

Howe, N., Petrakos, H., Rinaldi, C. M., & LeFebvre, R. (2005). "This is a bad dog, you know . . .": Constructing shared meanings during sibling pretend play. *Child Development, 76*, 783–794.

Howell, R. R. (2006). We need expanded newborn screening. *Pediatrics, 117*, 1800–1805.

Howes, C., & Matheson, C. C. (1992). Sequences in the development of competent play with peers: Social and social pretend play. *Developmental Psychology, 28*, 961–974.

Hoxby, C. (2004). *Achievement in charter schools and regular public schools in the United States: Understanding the difference.* Cambridge, MA: Harvard University and National Bureau of Economic Research.

Hoyert, D. L., Heron, M. P., Murphy, S. L., & Kung, H. C. (2006). Deaths: Final data for 2003. *National Vital Statistics Reports, 54*(13). Hyattsville, MD: National Center for Health Statistics.

Hoyert, D. L., Kung, H.-C., & Smith, B. L. (2005). Deaths: Preliminary data for 2003.

National Vital Statistics Reports, 53(15). Hyattsville, MD: National Center for Health Statistics.

Hoyert, D. L., Mathews, T. J., Menacker, F., Strobino, D. M., & Guyer, B. (2006). Annual summary of vital statistics: 2004. *Pediatrics, 117*, 168–183.

Hubbard, F. O. A., & van IJzendoorn, M. H. (1991). Maternal unresponsiveness and infant crying across the first 9 months: A naturalistic longitudinal study. *Infant Behavior and Development, 14*, 299–312.

Hudnall, C. E. (2001, November). "Grand" parents get help: Programs aid aging caregivers and youngsters. *AARP Bulletin,* 9, 12–13.

Hudson, J. I., Hiripi, E., Pope, H. G., Jr., & Kessler, R. C. (2007). The prevalence and correlates of eating disorders in the national comorbidity survey replication. *Biological Psychiatry, 61*(3), 348–358.

Hudson, V. M., & den Boer, A. M. (2004). *Bare branches: Security implications of Asia's surplus male population.* Cambridge, MA: MIT Press.

Huebner, C. E., & Meltzoff, A. N. (2005). Intervention to change parent-child reading style: A comparison of instructional methods. *Applied Developmental Psychology, 26*, 296–313.

Huesmann, L. R. (1986). Psychological processes promoting the relation between exposure to media violence and aggressive behavior by the viewer. *Journal of Social Issues, 42*, 125–139.

Huesmann, L. R., & Eron, L. D. (1984). Cognitive processes and the persistence of aggressive behavior. *Aggressive Behavior, 10*, 243–251.

Huesmann, L. R., Moise-Titus, J., Podolski, C. L., & Eron, L. (2003). Longitudinal relations between children's exposure to TV violence and their aggressive and violent behavior in young adulthood: 1977–1992. *Developmental Psychology, 39*, 201–221.

Hughes, D., Rodriguez, J., Smith, E. P., Johnson, D. J., Stevenson, H. C., & Spicer, P. (2006). Parents' ethnic-racial socialization practices: A review of research and directions for future study. *Developmental Psychology, 42*, 747–770.

Hughes, I. A. (2004). Female development—all by default? *New England Journal of Medicine, 351*, 748–750.

Hughes, M. (1975). *Egocentrism in preschool children.* Unpublished doctoral dissertation, Edinburgh University, Edinburgh, Scotland.

Huizink, A., Robles de Medina, P., Mulder, E., Visser, G., & Buitelaar, J. (2002). Psychological measures of prenatal stress as predictors of infant temperament. *Journal of the American Academy of Child and Adolescent Psychiatry, 41*, 1078–1085.

Huizink, A. C., Mulder, E. J. H., & Buitelaar, J. K. (2004). Prenatal stress and risk for psychopathology: Specific effects or induction of general susceptibility? *Psychological Bulletin 130*, 80–114.

Hujoel, P. P., Bollen, A.-M., Noonan, C. J., & del Aguila, M. A. (2004). Antepartum dental radiography and infant low birth weight. *Journal of the American Medical Association, 291*, 1987–1993.

Humphreys, A. P., & Smith, P. K. (1984). Rough-and-tumble in preschool and playground. In P. K. Smith (Ed.), *Play in animals and humans.* Oxford, UK: Blackwell.

Humphreys, G. W. (2002). Cognitive neuroscience. In H. Pashler & D. Medin (Eds.), *Steven's handbook of experimental psychology: Vol. 2. Memory and cognitive processes* (3rd. ed., pp. 77–112). New York: Wiley.

Hunt, C. E. (1996). Prone sleeping in healthy infants and victims of sudden infant death syndrome. *Journal of Pediatrics, 128*, 594–596.

Huntsinger, C. S., & Jose, P. E. (1995). Chinese American and Caucasian American family interaction patterns in spatial rotation puzzle solutions. *Merrill-Palmer Quarterly, 41*, 471–496.

Huston, A. C., & Aronson, S. R. (2005). Mothers' time with infant and time in employment as predictors of mother-child relationships and children's early development. *Child Development, 76*, 467–482.

Huston, A. C., Duncan, G. J., McLoyd, V. C., Crosby, D. A., Ripke, M. N., Weisner, T. S., et al. (2005). Impacts on children of a policy to promote employment and reduce poverty for low-income parents: New hope after 5 years. *Developmental Psychology, 41*, 902–918.

Huston, H. C., Duncan, G. J., Granger, R., Bos, J., McLoyd, V., Mistry, R., et al. (2001). Work-based antipoverty programs for parents can enhance the performance and social behavior of children. *Child Development, 72*(1), 318–336.

Huttenlocher, J. (1998). Language input and language growth. *Preventive Medicine, 27*, 195–199.

Huttenlocher, J., Haight, W., Bryk, A., Seltzer, M., & Lyons, T. (1991). Early vocabulary growth: Relation to language input and gender. *Developmental Psychology, 27*, 236–248.

Huttenlocher, J., Levine, S., & Vevea, J. (1998). Environmental input and cognitive growth: A study using time period comparisons. *Child Development, 69*, 1012–1029.

Huttenlocher, J., Vasilyeva, M., Cymerman, E., & Levine, S. (2002). Language input and child syntax. *Cognitive Psychology, 45*, 337–374.

Huxley, A. (1932). *Brave new world.* Toronto: Granada.

Hwang, S. J., Beaty, T. H., Panny, S. R., Street, N. A., Joseph, J. M., Gordon, S., et al. (1995). Association study of transforming growth factor alpha (TGFa) TaqI polymorphism and oral clefts: Indication of gene-environment interaction in a population-based sample of infants with birth defects. *American Journal of Epidemiology, 141*, 629–636.

Hyde, J. S. (2005). The gender similarity hypothesis. *American Psychologist, 60,* 581–592.

Ialongo, N. S., Edelsohn, G., & Kellam, S. G. (2001). A further look at the prognostic power of young children's reports of depressed mood and feelings. *Child Development, 72,* 736–747.

Iervolino, A. C., Hines, M., Golombok, S. E., Rust, J., & Plomin, R. (2005). Genetic and environmental influences on sex-types behavior during the preschool years. *Child Development, 76,* 826–840.

Iervolino, A. C., Pike, A., Manke, B., Reiss, D., Hetherington, E. M., & Plomin, R. (2002). Genetic and environmental influences in adolescent peer socialization: Evidence from two genetically sensitive designs. *Child Development, 73*(1), 162–174.

Iglowstein, I., Jenni, O. G., Molinari, L., & Largo, R. H. (2003). Sleep duration from infancy to adolescence: Reference values and generational trends. *Pediatrics, 111,* 302–307.

Impagnatiello, F., Guidotti, A. R., Pesold, C., Dwivedi, Y., Caruncho, H., Pisu, M. G., et al. (1998). A decrease of reelin expression as a putative vulnerability factor in schizophrenia. *Proceedings of the National Academy of Sciences, USA, 95,* 15718–15723.

Infant Health and Development Program (IHDP). (1990). Enhancing the outcomes of low-birth-weight, premature infants. *Journal of the American Medical Association, 263*(22), 3035–3042.

Infante-Rivard, C., Fernandez, A., Gauthier, R., David, M., & Rivard, G. E. (1993). Fetal loss associated with caffeine intake before and after pregnancy. *Journal of the American Medical Association, 270,* 2940–2943.

Ingels, S. J., Planty, M., & Bozick, R. (2005). *A profile of the American high school senior in 2004: A first look. Initial results from the first follow-up of the Education Longitudinal Study of 2002 (ELS:2002)* (NCES 2006348). Jessup, MD: National Center for Education Statistics.

Ingersoll, E. W., & Thoman, E. B. (1999). Sleep/wake states of preterm infants: Stability, developmental change, diurnal variation, and relation with care giving activity. *Child Development, 70,* 1–10.

Ingram, J. L., Stodgell, C. S., Hyman, S. L., Figlewicz, D. A., Weitkamp, L. R., & Rodier, P. M. (2000). Discovery of allelic variants of HOXA1 and HOXB1: Genetic susceptibility to autism spectrum disorders. *Teratology, 62,* 393–406.

Institute of Medicine (IOM), National Academy of Sciences. (1993, November). *Assessing genetic risks: Implications for health and social policy.* Washington, DC: National Academy of Sciences.

Institute of Medicine of the National Academies. (2005). *Preventing childhood obesity: Health in the balance.* Washington, DC: Author.

International Cesarean Awareness Network. (2003, March 5). *Statistics: International cesarean and VBAC rates.* Retrieved January 20, 2004, from http://www .icanonline.org/resources. statistics3.htm

International Committee for Monitoring Assisted Reproductive Technologies (ICMART). (2006, June). *2002 World report on ART.* Report released at meeting of the European Society of Human Reproduction and Embryology, Prague.

International Human Genome Sequencing Consortium. (2004). Finishing the euchromatic sequence of the human genome. *Nature, 431,* 931–945.

International Labour Office (ILO). (2002). *Every child counts: New global estimates on child labour.* Geneva, Switzerland: Author.

Ionesco, E. (1990). *Fragments of a journal* (J. Stewart, Trans.). New York: Paragon House.

Iruka, I. U., & Carver, P. R. (2006). *Initial results from the 2005 NHDS Early Childhood Program_Participation Survey* (NCES 2006-075). Washington, DC: National Center for Education Statistics.

Isabella, R. A. (1993). Origins of attachment: Maternal interactive behavior across the first year. *Child Development, 64,* 605–621.

Isley, S., O'Neil, R., & Parke, R. (1996). The relation of parental affect and control behaviors to children's classroom acceptance: A concurrent and predictive analysis. *Early Education and Development, 7,* 7–23.

Iverson, J. M., & Goldin-Meadow, S. (1998). Why people gesture when they speak. *Nature, 396,* 228.

Iverson, J. M., & Goldin-Meadow, S. (2005). Gesture paves the way for language development. *Psychological Science, 16,* 367–371.

Izard, C. E., Huebner, R. R., Resser, D., McGinness, G. C., & Dougherty, L. M. (1980). The young infant's ability to produce discrete emotional expressions. *Developmental Psychology, 16,* 132–140.

Izard, C. E., Porges, S. W., Simons, R. F., Haynes, O. M., & Cohen, B. (1991). Infant cardiac activity: Developmental changes and relations with attachment. *Developmental Psychology, 27,* 432–439.

Jaccard, J., Blanton, H., & Dodge, T. (2005). Peer influences on risk behavior: An analysis of the effects of a close friend. *Developmental Psychology, 41,* 135–147.

Jaccard, J., & Dittus, P. J. (2000). Adolescent perceptions of maternal approval of birth control and sexual risk behavior. *American Journal of Public Health, 90,* 1426–1430.

Jackson, A. (1997a). The math wars: California battles it out over mathematics education reform (Part I). *Notices of the American Mathematical Society.* Retrieved January 22, 1999, from http://www.ams.org/ notices/199706/commcalif.html

Jackson, A. (1997b). The math wars: California battles it out over mathematics education reform (Part II). *Notices of the American Mathematical Society.* Retrieved January 22, 1999, from http://www.ams.org/ notices/199708/commcalif2.html

Jacobsen, T., & Hofmann, V. (1997). Children's attachment representations: Longitudinal relations to school behavior and academic competency in middle childhood and adolescence. *Developmental Psychology, 33,* 703–710.

Jacobson, J. L., & Wille, D. E. (1986). The influence of attachment pattern on developmental changes in peer interaction from the toddler to the preschool period. *Child Development, 57,* 338–347.

Jaffee, S. R., Caspi, A., Moffitt, T. E., Dodge, K. A., Rutter, M., Taylor, A., et al. (2005). Nature X nature: Genetic vulnerabilities interact with physical maltreatment to promote conduct problems. *Developmental Psychopathology, 17,* 67–84.

Jaffee, S. R., Caspi, A., Moffitt, T. E., Polo-Tomas, M., Price, T. S., & Taylor, A. (2004). The limits of child effects: Evidence for genetically mediated child effects on corporal punishment but not on physical maltreatment. *Developmental Psychology, 40,* 1047–1058.

Jaffee, S., & Hyde, J. S. (2000). Gender differences in moral orientation: A meta-analysis. *Psychological Bulletin, 126,* 703–726.

Jagers, R. J., Bingham, K., & Hans, S. L. (1996). Socialization and social judgments among inner-city African-American kindergartners. *Child Development, 67,* 140–150.

Jain, T., Missmer, S. A., & Hornstein, M. D. (2004). Trends in embryo-transfer practice and in outcomes of the use of assisted reproductive technology in the United States. *New England Journal of Medicine, 350,* 1639–1645.

Jankowiak, W. (1992). Father-child relations in urban China. In B. S. Hewlett (Ed.), *Father-child relations: Cultural and biosocial contexts* (pp. 345–363). New York: de Gruyter.

Jankowski, J. J., Rose, S. A., & Feldman, J. F. (2001). Modifying the distribution of attention in infants. *Child Development, 72,* 339–351.

Janowsky, J. S., & Carper, R. (1996). Is there a neural basis for cognitive transitions in school-age children? In A. J. Sameroff & M. M. Haith (Eds.), *The five to seven year shift: The age of reason and responsibility* (pp. 33–56). Chicago: University of Chicago Press.

Janssen, I., Craig, W. M., Boyce, W. F., & Pickett, W. (2004). Associations between overweight and obesity with bullying behaviors in school-aged children. *Pediatrics, 113,* 1187–1194.

Japan in shock at school murder. (2004, June 2). BBC News. Retrieved June 2, 2004, from http://news.bbc.co.uk/go/pr/fr/-/1/hi/world/ asia-pacific/3768983.stm

Javaid, M. K., Crozier, S. R., Harvey, N. C., Gale, C. R., Dennison, E. M., Boucher, B. J., et al., & Princess Anne Hospital Study Group. (2006). Maternal vitamin D status during pregnancy and childhood bone mass at age 9 years: A longitudinal study. *Lancet, 367*(9504), 36–43.

Jeffery, H. E., Megevand, M., & Page, M. (1999). Why the prone position is a risk factor for sudden infant death syndrome. *Pediatrics, 104,* 263–269.

Jeffords, J. M., & Daschle, T. (2001). Political issues in the genome era. *Science, 291,* 1249–1251.

Jensen, A. R. (1969). How much can we boost IQ and scholastic achievement? *Harvard Educational Review, 39,* 1–123.

Jeynes, W. H., & Littell, S. W. (2000). A meta-analysis of studies examining the effect of whole language instruction on the literacy of low-SES students. *Elementary School Journal, 101*(1), 21–33.

Ji, B. T., Shu, X. O., Linet, M. S., Zheng, W., Wacholder, S., Gao, Y. T., et al. (1997). Paternal cigarette smoking and the risk of childhood cancer among offspring of non-smoking mothers. *Journal of the National Cancer Institute, 89,* 238–244.

Jiao, S., Ji, G., & Jing, Q. (1996). Cognitive development of Chinese urban only children and children with siblings. *Child Development, 67,* 387–395.

Jodl, K. M., Michael, A., Malanchuk, O., Eccles, J. S., & Sameroff, A. (2001). Parents' roles in shaping early adolescents' occupational aspirations. *Child Development, 72*(4), 1247–1265.

Johnson, D. J., Jaeger, E., Randolph, S. M., Cauce, A. M., Ward, J., & National Institute of Child Health and Human Development Early Child Care Research Network. (2003). Studying the effects of early child care experiences on the development of children of color in the United States: Toward a more inclusive research agenda. *Child Development, 74,* 1227–1244.

Johnson, J., Canning, J., Kaneko, T., Pru, J. K., & Tilly, J. L. (2004). Germline stem cells and follicular renewal in the postnatal mammalian ovary. *Nature, 428*(6979), 145–150.

Johnson, J. E. (1998). Play development from ages four to eight. In D. P. Fromberg & D. Bergen (Eds.), *Play from birth to twelve and beyond: Contexts, perspectives, and meanings* (pp. 145–153). New York: Garland.

Johnson, J. G., Cohen, P., Gould, M. S., Kasen, S., Brown, J., & Brook, J. S. (2002). Childhood adversities, interpersonal difficulties, and risk for suicide attempts during late adolescence and early adulthood. *Archives of General Psychiatry, 59,* 741–749.

Johnson, J. G., Cohen, P., Smailes, E. M., Kasen, S., & Brook, J. S. (2002). Television viewing and aggressive behavior during adolescence and adulthood. *Science, 295,* 2468–2471.

Johnson, J. O. (2005). Who's minding the kids? Child care arrangements: Winter 2002. *Current Population Report, October, 2005* (P70-101). Washington, DC: U.S. Census Bureau.

Johnson, K. (2004, March 27). Harm to fetuses becomes issue in Utah and elsewhere. *New York Times.* Retrieved March 29, 2004, from http://www.nytimes.com/2004/03027//national/27FETU.html?ex=1081399221&eu=1&en=ede725fc158cb2bd

Johnson, K. E., Scott, P., & Mervis, C. B. (1997). Development of children's understanding of basic-subordinate inclusion relations. *Developmental Psychology, 33,* 745–763.

Johnson, M. H. (1998). The neural basis of cognitive development. In D. Kuhn & R. S. Siegler (Eds.), *Handbook of child psychology: Vol. 2. Cognition, perception, and language* (5th ed., pp. 1–49). New York: Wiley.

Johnson, M. H. (1999). Developmental cognitive neuroscience. In M. Bennett (Ed.), *Developmental psychology: Achievements and prospects* (pp. 147–164). Philadelphia, PA: Psychology Press/Taylor & Francis.

Johnson, M. H. (2001). Functional brain development during infancy. In G. Bremner & A. Fogel (Eds.), *Handbooks of developmental psychology: Blackwell handbook of infant development* (pp. 169–190). Malden, MA: Blackwell.

Johnson, R. A., Hoffmann, J. P., & Gerstein, D. R. (1996). *The relationship between family structure and adolescent substance use* (DHHS Publication No. SMA 96–3086). Washington, DC: U.S. Department of Health and Human Services.

Johnson, S. L. (2000). Improving preschoolers' self-regulation of energy intake. *Pediatrics, 106,* 1429–1435.

Johnson, S. L., & Birch, L. L. (1994). Parents' and children's adiposity and eating styles. *Pediatrics, 94,* 653–661.

Johnston, L. D., O'Malley, P. M., Bachman, J. G., & Schulenberg, J. E. (2006). *Monitoring the Future national results on adolescent drug use: Overview of key findings, 2005* (NIH Publication No. 06-5882). Bethesda, MD: National Institute on Drug Abuse.

Johnston, L. D., O'Malley, P. M., Bachman, J. G., & Schulenberg, J. E. (2007). *Monitoring the Future national results on adolescent drug use: Overview of key findings, 2006* (NIH Publication No. 07-6202). Bethesda, MD: National Institute on Drug Abuse.

Jones, H. W., & Toner, J. P. (1993). The infertile couple. *New England Journal of Medicine, 329,* 1710–1715.

Jones, N. A., Field, T., Fox, N. A., Davalos, M., Lundy, B., & Hart, S. (1998). Newborns of mothers with depressive symptoms are physiologically less developed. *Infant Behavior and Development, 21*(3), 537–541.

Jones, N. A., Field, T., Fox, N. A., Lundy, B., & Davalos, M. (1997). EEG activation in one-month-old infants of depressed mothers. *Development and Psychopathology, 9,* 491–505.

Jones, R. L. (2004). Biographies: Marian Anderson (1897–1993). *Afrocentric Voices in "Classical" Music.* [Online]. Retrieved November 18, 2004 from http://www.afrovoices.com/anderson.html

Jones, S. S. (1996). Imitation or exploration? Young infants' matching of adults' oral gestures. *Child Development, 67,* 1952–1969.

Jordan, B. (1993). *Birth in four cultures: A cross-cultural investigation of childbirth in Yucatan, Holland, Sweden, and the United States* (4th ed.). Prospect Heights, IL: Waveland Press. (Original work published 1978)

Jordan, N. C., Kaplan, D., Olah, L. N., & Locuniak, M. N. (2006). Number sense growth in kindergarten: A longitudinal investigation of children at risk for mathematics difficulties. *Child Development, 77,* 153–175.

Jusczyk, P. W. (2003). The role of speech perception capacities in early language acquisition. In M. T. Banich & M. Mack (Eds.), *Mind, brain, and language: Multidisciplinary perspectives.* Mahwah, NJ: Erlbaum.

Jusczyk, P. W., & Hohne, E. A. (1997). Infants' memory for spoken words. *Science, 277,* 1984–1986.

Just, M. A., Cherkassky, V. L., Keller, T. A., Kana, R. K., & Minshew, N. J. (2007). Functional and anatomical cortical underconnectivity in autism: Evidence from an fMRI study of an executive function task and corpus callosum morphometry. *Cerebral Cortex, 17,* 951–961.

Just, M. A., Cherkassky, V. L., Keller, T. A., & Minshew, N. J. (2004). Cortical activation and synchronization during sentence comprehension in high-functioning autism: Evidence of underconnectivity. *Brain, 127,* 1811–1821.

Juster, F. T., Ono, H., & Stafford, F. P. (2004). *Changing times of American youth: 1981–2003* (Child Development Supplement). Ann Arbor, MI: University of Michigan Institute for Social Research.

Juul-Dam, N., Townsend, J., & Courchesne, E. (2001). Prenatal, perinatal, and neonatal factors in autism, pervasive developmental disorder—not otherwise specified, and the general population. *Pediatrics, 107*(4), e63.

Kaback, M., Lim-Steele, J., Dabholkar, D., Brown, D., Levy, N., & Zeiger, K., for the International TSD Data Collection Network. (1993). Tay-Sachs disease—Carrier screening, prenatal diagnosis, and the molecular era. *Journal of the American Medical Association, 270,* 2307–2315.

Kagan, J. (1997). Temperament and the reactions to unfamiliarity. *Child Development, 68,* 139–143.

Kagan, J., & Snidman, N. (1991a). Infant predictors of inhibited and uninhibited behavioral profiles. *Psychological Science, 2,* 40–44.

Kagan, J., & Snidman, N. (1991b). Temperamental factors in human development. *American Psychologist, 46,* 856–862.

Kagan, J., & Snidman, N. (2004). *The long shadow of temperament.* Cambridge, MA: Belknap.

Kaiser Family Foundation, Hoff, T., Greene, L., & Davis, J. (2003). *National survey of adolescents and young adults: Sexual health knowledge, attitudes and experiences.* Menlo Park, CA: Kaiser Family Foundation.

Kalil, A., & Ziol-Guest, K. M. (2005). Single mothers' employment dynamics and adolescent well-being. *Child Development, 76,* 196–211.

Kalish, C. W. (1998). Young children's predictions of illness: Failure to recognize probabilistic cause. *Developmental Psychology, 34*(5), 1046–1058.

Kanaya, T., Scullin, M. H., & Ceci, S. J. (2003). The Flynn effect and U.S. policies: The impact of rising IQ scores on American society via mental retardation diagnoses. *American Psychologist, 58,* 778–790.

Kanetsuna, T., & Smith, P. K. (2002). Pupil insight into bullying and coping with bullying: A bi-national study in Japan and England. *Journal of School Violence, 1,* 5–29.

Kaplan, H., & Dove, H. (1987). Infant development among the Ache of East Paraguay. *Developmental Psychology, 23,* 190–198.

Kaplowitz, P. B., Oberfield, S. E., & the Drug and Therapeutics and Executive Committees of the Lawson Wilkins Pediatric Endocrine Society. (1999). Reexamination of the age limit for defining when puberty is precocious in girls in the United States: Implications for evaluation and treatment. *Pediatrics, 104,* 936–941.

Katzman, R. (1993). Education and prevalence of Alzheimer's disease. *Neurology, 43,* 13–20.

Kaufman, A. S., & Kaufman, N. L. (1983). *Kaufman Assessment Battery for Children: Administration and scoring manual.* Circle Pines, MN: American Guidance Service.

Kaufman, A. S., & Kaufman, N. L. (2003). *Kaufman Assessment Battery for Children* (2nd ed.). Circle Pines, MN: American Guidance Service.

Kazdin, A. E., & Benjet, C. (2003). Spanking children: Evidence and issues. *Current Directions in Psychological Science, 12,* 99–103.

Keegan, R. T. (1996). Creativity from childhood to adulthood: A difference of degree and not of kind. *New Directions for Child Development, 72,* 57–66.

Keegan, R. T., & Gruber, H. E. (1985). Charles Darwin's unpublished "Diary of an Infant": An early phase in his psychological work. In G. Eckardt, W. G. Bringmann, & L. Sprung (Eds.), *Contributions to a history of developmental psychology: International William T. Preyer Symposium* (pp.127–145). Berlin, Germany: de Gruyter.

Keel, P. K., Dorer, D. J., Eddy, K. T., Franko, D., Charatan, D. L., & Herzog, D. B. (2003). Predictors of mortality in eating disorders. *Archives of General Psychiatry, 60*(2), 179–183.

Keel, P. K., & Klump, K. L. (2003). Are eating disorders culture-bound syndromes? Implications for conceptualizing their etiology. *Psychological Bulletin, 129,* 747–769.

Keenan, K., & Shaw, D. (1997). Developmental and social influences on young girls' early problem behavior. *Psychological Bulletin, 121*(1), 95–113.

Kelleher, K. J., Casey, P. H., Bradley, R. H., Pope, S. K., Whiteside, L., Barrett, K. W., et al. (1993). Risk factors and outcomes for failure to thrive in low birth weight preterm infants. *Pediatrics, 91,* 941–948.

Keller, B. (1999, February 24). A time and place for teenagers. *Education Week on the WEB.* Retrieved March 11, 2004, from http://www.edweek.org/ew/vol-18/24studen.h18

Keller, H. (1905). *The story of my life.* New York: Grosset & Dunlap. (Original work published 1903)

Keller, H. (1920). *The world I live in.* New York: Century. (Original work published 1908)

Keller, H. (1929). *The bereaved.* New York: Leslie Fulenwider.

Keller, H. (2003). *The story of my life: The restored edition* (J. Berger, Ed.). New York: Norton.

Kelley, M. L., Smith, T. S., Green, A. P., Berndt, A. E., & Rogers, M. C. (1998). Importance of fathers' parenting to African-American toddler's social and cognitive development. *Infant Behavior and Development, 21,* 733–744.

Kellman, P. J., & Arterberry, M. E. (1998). *The cradle of knowledge: Development of perception in infancy.* Cambridge, MA: MIT.

Kellman, P. J., & Banks, M. S. (1998). Infant visual perception. In W. Damon (Ed.-in-Chief), D. Kuhn, & R. S. Siegler (Vol. Eds.), *Handbook of child psychology: Vol. 2. Cognition, perception, and language* (5th ed., pp. 103–146). New York: Wiley.

Kelly, A. M., Wall, M., Eisenberg, M., Story, M., & Neumark-Sztainer, D. (2004). High body satisfaction in adolescent girls: Association with demographic, socio-environmental, personal, and behavioral factors. *Journal of Adolescent Health, 34,* 129.

Kelly, J. B., & Emery, R. E. (2003). Children's adjustment following divorce: Risk and resiliency perspectives. *Family Relations, 52,* 352–362.

Kellogg, N., & the Committee on Child Abuse and Neglect. (2005). The evaluation of sexual abuse in children. *Pediatrics, 116*(2), 506–512.

Kellogg, R. (1970). Understanding children's art. In P. Cramer (Ed.), *Readings in developmental psychology today.* Delmar, CA: CRM.

Kendler, K. S., MacLean, C., Neale, M., Kessler, R., Heath, A., & Eaves, L. (1991). The genetic epidemiology of bulimia nervosa. *American Journal of Psychiatry, 148,* 1627–1637.

Kenney-Benson, G. A., Pomerantz, E. M., Ryan, A. M., & Patrick, H. (2006). Sex differences in math performance: The role of children's approach to schoolwork. *Developmental Psychology, 42,* 11–26.

Kere, J., Hannula-Jouppi, K., Kaminen-Ahola, N., Taipale, M., Eklund, R., Nopola-Hemmi, J., et al. (2005, October). *Identification of the dyslexia susceptibility gene for DYX5 on chromosone 3.* Paper presented at the American Society of Human Genetics meeting, Salt Lake City, UT.

Kernan, M. (1993, June). The object at hand. *Smithsonian,* 14–16.

Kerns, K A., Don, A., Mateer, C. A., & Streissguth, A. P. (1997). Cognitive deficits in nonretarded adults with fetal alcohol syndrome. *Journal of Learning Disabilities, 30,* 685–693.

Kessler, R. C., Berglund, P., Demler, O., Jin, R., Merikangas, K. R., & Walters, E. E. (2005). Lifetime prevalence and age-of-onset distributions of *DSM-IV* disorders in the National Comorbidity Survey Replication. *Archives of General Psychiatry, 62,* 593–602.

Kestenbaum, R., & Gelman, S. A. (1995). Preschool children's identification and understanding of mixed emotions. *Cognitive Development, 10,* 443–458.

Khoury, M. J., McCabe, L. L., & McCabe, E. R. B. (2003). Population screening in the age of genomic medicine. *New England Journal of Medicine, 348,* 50–58.

Kier, C., & Lewis, C. (1998). Preschool sibling interaction in separated and married families: Are same-sex pairs or older sisters more sociable? *Journal of Child Psychology and Psychiatry, 39,* 191–201.

Killen, J. D., Robinson, T. N., Ammerman, S., Hayward, C., Rogers, J., Stone, C., et al. (2004). Randomized clinical trial of the efficacy of bupropion combined with nicotine patch in the treatment of adolescent smokers. *Journal of Consulting and Clinical Psychology, 72,* 729–735.

Kim, J., Peterson, K. E., Scanlon, K. S., Fitzmaurice, G. M., Must, A., Oken, E., et al. (2006). Trends in overweight from 1980 through 2001 among preschool-aged children enrolled in a health maintenance organization. *Obesity, 14*(7), 1107–1112.

Kim, K. J., Conger, R. D., Elder, G. H., & Lorenz, F. O. (2003). Reciprocal influences between stressful life events and adolescent internalizing and externalizing problems. *Child Development, 74*(1), 127–143.

Kim, Y. S., Koh, Y.-J., & Leventhal, B. (2005). School bullying and suicidal risk in Korean middle school students. *Pediatrics, 115,* 357–363.

Kim-Cohen, J., Caspi, A., Moffitt, T. E., Harrington, H., Milne, B. J., & Poulton,

R. (2003). Prior juvenile diagnoses in adults with mental disorder: Developmental follow-back of a prospective-longitudinal cohort. *Archives of General Psychiatry, 60,* 709–717.

Kim-Cohen, J., Moffitt, T. E., Caspi, A., & Taylor, A. (2004). Genetic and environmental processes in young children's resilience and vulnerability to socioeconomic deprivation. *Child Development, 75,* 651–668.

Kimball, M. M. (1986). Television and sex-role attitudes. In T. M. Williams (Ed.), *The impact of television: A natural experiment in three communities* (pp. 265–301). Orlando, FL: Academic Press.

King, B. M. (1996). *Human sexuality today* (2nd ed.). Upper Saddle River, NJ: Prentice-Hall.

King, W. J., MacKay, M., Sirnick, A., & the Canadian Shaken Baby Study Group. (2003). Shaken baby syndrome in Canada: Clinical characteristics and outcomes of hospital cases. *Canadian Medical Association Journal, 168,* 155–159.

Kinney, H. C., Filiano, J. J., Sleeper, L. A., Mandell, F., Valdes-Dapena, M., & White, W. F. (1995). Decreased muscarinic receptor binding in the arcuate nucleus in sudden infant death syndrome. *Science, 269,* 1446–1450.

Kinsella, K., & Velkoff, V. A. (2001). *An aging world: 2001.* U.S. Census Bureau, Series P95/01–1. Washington, DC: U.S. Government Printing Office.

Kirby, D. (1997). *No easy answers: Research findings on programs to reduce teen pregnancy.* Washington, DC: National Campaign to Prevent Teen Pregnancy.

Kisilevsky, B. S., Hains, S. M. J., Lee, K., Muir, D. W., Xu, F., Fu, G., et al. (1998). The still-face effect in Chinese and Canadian 3- to 6-month-old infants. *Developmental Psychology, 34*(4), 629–639.

Kisilevsky, B. S., Hains, S. M. J., Lee, K., Xie, X., Huang, H., Ye, H. H., et al. (2003). Effects of experience on fetal voice recognition. *Psychological Science, 14,* 220–224.

Kisilevsky, B. S., Muir, D. W., & Low, J. A. (1992). Maturation of human fetal responses to vibroacoustic stimulation. *Child Development, 63,* 1497–1508.

Klar, A. J. S. (1996). A single locus, RGHT, specifies preference for hand utilization in humans. *Cold Spring Harbor Symposia on Quantitative Biology 61,* 59–65. Cold Spring Harbor, NY: Cold Spring Harbor Laboratory Press.

Klaus, M. H., & Kennell, J. H. (1982). *Parent-infant bonding* (2nd ed.). St. Louis, MO: Mosby.

Klaus, M. H., & Kennell, J. H. (1997). The doula: An essential ingredient of childbirth rediscovered. *Acta Paediatrica, 86,* 1034–1036.

Klebanoff, M. A., Levine, R. J., DerSimonian, R., Clemens, J. D., & Wilkins, D. G. (1999). Maternal serum paraxanthine, a caffeine metabolite, and the risk of spontaneous abortion. *New England Journal of Medicine, 341,* 1639–1644.

Klebanov, P. K., Brooks-Gunn, J., & McCormick, M. C. (2001). Maternal coping strategies and emotional distress: Results of an early intervention program for low birth weight young children. *Developmental Psychology, 37*(5), 654–667.

Klein, J. D., & the American Academy of Pediatrics Committee on Adolescence. (2005). Adolescent pregnancy: Current trends and issues. *Pediatrics, 116,* 281–286.

Kleiner, B., Nolin, M. J., & Chapman, C. (2004). *Before- and after-school care, programs, and activities of children in kindergarten through eighth grade: 2001. Statistical analysis report* (NCES 2004–008). Washington, DC: National Center for Education Statistics.

Klibanoff, R. S., Levine, S. C., Huttenlocher, J., Vasilyeva, M., & Hedges, L. V. (2006). Preschool children's mathematical knowledge: The effect of teacher "math talk." *Developmental Psychology, 42,* 59–69.

Knafo, A., & Plomin, R. (2006). Parental discipline and affection and children's prosocial behavior: Genetic and environmental links. *Journal of Personality and Social Psychology, 90,* 147–164.

Knickmeyer, R., Baron-Cohen, S., Raggatt, P., & Taylor, K. (2005). Foetal testosterone, social relationships, and restricted interests in children. *Journal of Child Psychology and Psychiatry, 46,* 198–210.

Knudsen, E. I. (1999). Early experience and critical periods. In M. J. Zigmond (Ed.), *Fundamental neuroscience* (pp. 637–654). San Diego, CA: Academic.

Kochanek, K. D., Murphy, S. L., Anderson, R. N., & Scott, C. (2004). Deaths: Final data for 2002. *National Vital Statistics Reports, 53*(5). Hyattsville, MD: National Center for Health Statistics.

Kochanek, K. D., & Smith, B. L. (2004). Deaths: Preliminary data for 2002. *National Vital Statistics Reports, 52*(13). Hyattsville, MD: National Center for Health Statistics.

Kochanska, G. (1992). Children's interpersonal influence with mothers and peers. *Developmental Psychology, 28,* 491–499.

Kochanska, G. (1993). Toward a synthesis of parental socialization and child temperament in early development of conscience. *Child Development, 64,* 325–347.

Kochanska, G. (1995). Children's temperament, mothers' discipline, and security of attachment: Multiple pathways to emerging internalization. *Child Development, 66,* 597–615.

Kochanska, G. (1997a). Multiple pathways to conscience for children with different temperaments: From toddlerhood to age 5. *Developmental Psychology, 33,* 228–240.

Kochanska, G. (1997b). Mutually responsive orientation between mothers and their young children: Implications for early socialization. *Child Development, 68,* 94–112.

Kochanska, G. (2001). Emotional development in children with different attachment histories: The first three years. *Child Development, 72,* 474–490.

Kochanska, G. (2002). Mutually responsive orientation between mothers and their young children: A context for the early development of conscience. *Current Directions in Psychological Science, 11,* 191–195.

Kochanska, G., & Aksan, N. (1995). Mother-child positive affect, the quality of child compliance to requests and prohibitions, and maternal control as correlates of early internalization. *Child Development, 66,* 236–254.

Kochanska, G., Aksan, N., & Carlson, J. J. (2005). Temperament, relationships, and young children's receptive cooperation with their parents. *Developmental Psychology, 41,* 648–660.

Kochanska, G., Aksan, N., & Joy, M. E. (2007). Children's fearfulness as a moderator of parenting in early socialization: Two longitudinal studies. *Developmental Psychology, 43,* 222–237.

Kochanska, G., Aksan, N., Knaack, A., & Rhines, H. M. (2004). Maternal parenting and children's conscience: Early security as moderator. *Child Development, 75,* 1229–1242.

Kochanska, G., Coy, K. C., & Murray, K. T. (2001). The development of self-regulation in the first four years of life. *Child Development, 72*(4), 1091–1111.

Kochanska, G., Murray, K., & Coy, K. C. (1997). Inhibitory control as a contributor to conscience in childhood: From toddler to early school age. *Child Development, 68,* 263–277.

Kochanska, G., Tjebkes, T. L., & Forman, D. R. (1998). Children's emerging regulation of conduct: Restraint, compliance, and internalization from infancy to the second year. *Child Development, 69*(5), 1378–1389.

Kochenderfer, B. H., & Ladd, G. W. (1996). Peer victimization: Cause or consequence of school maladjustment? *Child Development, 67,* 1305–1317.

Koenig, H. G. (1994). *Aging and God.* New York: Haworth.

Koenig, L. B., McGue, M., Krueger, R. F., & Bouchard, T. J. (2005). Genetic and environmental influences on religiousness: Findings for retrospective and current religiousness ratings. *Journal of Personality, 73,* 471–488.

Kogan, M. D., Newacheck, P. W., Honberg, L., & Strickland, B. (2005). Association between underinsurance and access to care among children with special health care needs in the United States. *Pediatrics, 116,* 1162-1169.

Kohlberg, L. (1966). A cognitive developmental analysis of children's sex role concepts and attitudes. In E. E. Maccoby (Ed.), *The development of sex differences.* Stanford, CA: Stanford University Press.

Kohlberg, L. (1969). Stage and sequence: The cognitive-developmental approach to socialization. In D. A. Goslin (Ed.), *Handbook of socialization theory and research.* Chicago: Rand McNally.

Kohlberg, L. (1981). *Essays on moral development.* San Francisco: Harper & Row.

Kohlberg, L., & Gilligan, C. (1971, Fall). The adolescent as a philosopher: The discovery of the self in a postconventional world. *Daedalus, 1051–1086.*

Kohlberg, L., & Ryncarz, R. A. (1990). Beyond justice reasoning: Moral development and consideration of a seventh stage. In C. N. Alexander & E. J. Langer (Eds.), *Higher stages of human development* (pp. 191–207). New York: Oxford University Press.

Kohlberg, L., Yaeger, J., & Hjertholm, E. (1968). Private speech: Four studies and a review of theories. *Child Development, 39,* 691–736.

Kolata, G. (2003, February 18). Using genetic tests, Ashkenazi Jews vanquish a disease. *The New York Times.* pp. D1, D6.

Kolbert, E. (1994, January 11). Canadians curbing TV violence. *New York Times,* pp. C15–C19.

Kopp, C. B. (1982). Antecedents of self-regulation. *Developmental Psychology, 18,* 199–214.

Koren, G., Pastuszak, A., & Ito, S. (1998). Drugs in pregnancy. *New England Journal of Medicine, 338,* 1128–1137.

Korner, A. (1996). Reliable individual differences in preterm infants' excitation management. *Child Development, 67,* 1793–1805.

Korner, A. F., Zeanah, C. H., Linden, J., Berkowitz, R. I., Kraemer, H. C., & Agras, W. S. (1985). The relationship between neonatal and later activity and temperament. *Child Development, 56,* 38–42.

Korte, D., & Scaer, R. (1984). *A good birth, a safe birth.* New York: Bantam.

Kosterman, R., Graham, J. W., Hawkins, J. D., Catalano, R. F., & Herrenkohl, T. I. (2001). Childhood risk factors for persistence of violence in the transition to adulthood: A social development perspective. *Violence and Victims. Special Issue: Developmental Perspectives on Violence and Victimization, 16*(4), 355–369.

Kowal, A. K., & Pike, L. B. (2004). Sibling influences on adolescents' attitudes toward safe sex practices. *Family Relations, 53,* 377–384.

Kozlowska, K., & Hanney, L. (1999). Family assessment and intervention using an interactive art exercise. *Australia and New Zealand Journal of Family Therapy, 20*(2), 61–69.

Kralovec, E., & Buell, J. (2000). *The end of homework.* Boston: Beacon.

Kramer, L., & Kowal, A. K. (2005). Sibling relationship quality from birth to adolescence: The enduring contributions of

friends. *Journal of Family Psychology, 19,* 503–511.

Kramer, M. S., Chalmers, B., Hodnett, E. D., Sevkovskaya, Z., Dzikovich, I., Shapiro, S., et al., for the PROBIT Study Group. (2001). Promotion of Breastfeeding Intervention Trial (PROBIT): A randomized trial in the Republic of Belarus. *Journal of the American Medical Association, 285,* 413–420.

Krashen, S., & McField, G. (2005, November/ December). What works? Reviewing the latest evidence on bilingual education. *Language Learner, 1*(2), 7–10, 34.

Krauss, S., Concordet, J. P., & Ingham, P. W. (1993). A functionally conserved homolog of the Drosophila segment polarity gene hh is expressed in tissues with polarizing activity in zebrafish embryos. *Cell, 75,* 1431–1444.

Kravetz, J. D., & Federman, D. G. (2002). Cat-associated zoonoses. *Archives of Internal Medicine, 162,* 1945–1952.

Kreider, R. M. (2003). Adopted children and stepchildren: 2000. *Census 2000 Special Reports.* Washington, DC: U.S. Bureau of the Census.

Kreider, R. M. (2005). Number, timing, and duration of marriages and divorces: 2001. *Household economic studies* (P70–97). Washington, DC: U.S. Census Bureau.

Kreider, R. M., & Fields, J. (2005). Living arrangements of children: 2001. *Current Population Reports* (P70-104). Washington, DC: U.S. Census Bureau.

Kreutzer, M., Leonard, C., & Flavell, J. (1975). An interview study of children's knowledge about memory. *Monographs of the Society for Research in Child Development, 40*(1), Serial No. 159.

Krevans, J., & Gibbs, J. C. (1996). Parents' use of inductive discipline: Relations to children's empathy and prosocial behavior. *Child Development, 67,* 3263–3277.

Krishnamoorthy, J. S., Hart, C., & Jelalian, E. (2006). The epidemic of childhood obesity: Review of research and implications for public policy. *Society for Research in Child Development (SRCD) Social Policy Report, 20*(2).

Kroger, J. (1993). Ego identity: An overview. In J. Kroger (Ed.), *Discussions on ego identity* (pp. 1–20). Hillsdale, NJ: Erlbaum.

Kroger, J. (2003). Identity development during adolescence. In G. R. Adams & M. D. Berzonsky (Eds.), *Blackwell handbook of adolescence* (pp. 205–226). Malden, MA: Blackwell.

Kroger, J., & Haslett, S. J. (1991). A comparison of ego identity status transition pathways and change rates across five identity domains. *International Journal of Aging and Human Development, 32,* 303–330.

Krueger, A. B. (2003, February). Economic, considerations and class size. *Economic Journal, 113,* F34–F63.

Krueger, A. B., & Whitmore, D. M. (2000, April). *The effect of attending a small class

in the early grades on college-test taking and middle school test results: Evidence from Project STAR* (NBER Working Paper No. W7656)

Kruse, D. L., & Mahony, D. (2000). Illegal child labor in the United States: Prevalence and characteristics. *Industrial and Labor Relations Review, 54,* 17–40.

Kuczmarski, R. J., Ogden, C. L., Grummer-Strawn, L. M., Flegal, K. M., Guo, S. S., Wei, R., et al. (2000). CDC growth charts: United States. *Advance Data, No. 314.* Hyattsville, MD: U.S. Department of Health and Human Services.

Kuczynski, L., & Kochanska, G. (1995). Function and content of maternal demands: Developmental significance of early demands for competent action. *Child Development, 66,* 616–628.

Kuhl, P. K. (2004). Early language acquisition: Cracking the speech code. *Nature Reviews Neuroscience, 5,* 831–843.

Kuhl, P. K., Andruski, J. E., Chistovich, I. A., Chistovich, L. A., Kozhevnikova, E. V., Ryskina, V. L., et al. (1997). Cross-language analysis of phonetic units in language addressed to infants. *Science, 277,* 684–686.

Kuhl, P. K., Conboy, B. T., Padden, D., Nelson, T., & Pruitt, J. (2005). Early speech perception and later language development: Implications for the "critical period." *Language Learning and Development, 1,* 237–264.

Kuhl, P. K., Williams, K. A., Lacerda, F., Stevens, K. N., & Lindblom, B. (1992). Linguistic experience alters phonetic perception in infants by 6 months of age. *Science, 255,* 606–608.

Kuhn, D. (2006). Do cognitive changes accompany developments in the adolescent brain? *Perspectives on Psychological Science, 1,* 59–67.

Kuhn, D., & Dean, D. (2005). Is developing scientific thinking all about learning to control variables? *Psychological Science, 16,* 866–870.

Kuperman, S., Chan, G., Kramer, J. R., Bierut, L., Buckholz, K. K., Fox, L., et al. (2005). Relationship of age of first drink to child behavioral problems and family psychopathology. *Alcoholism: Clinical and Experimental Research, 29*(10),1869–1876.

Kupersmidt, J. B., & Coie, J. D. (1990). Preadolescent peer status, aggression, and school adjustment as predictors of externalizing problems in adolescence. *Child Development, 61,* 1350–1362.

Kurjak, A., Kupesic, S., Matijevic, R., Kos, M., & Marton, U. (1999). First trimester malformation screening. *European Journal of Obstetrics, Gynecology, and Reproductive Biology (E4L), 85,* 93–96.

Kurosawa, A. (1983). *Something like an autobiography* (A. E. Bock, Trans.). New York: Vintage.

Kuther, T., & McDonald, E. (2004). Early adolescents' experiences with, and views of, Barbie. *Adolescence, 39,* 39–51.

Kye, C., & Ryan, N. (1995). Pharmacologic treatment of child and adolescent depression. *Child and Adolescent Psychiatric Clinics of North America, 4,* 261–281.

Labarere, J., Gelbert-Baudino, N., Ayral, A. S., Duc, C., Berchotteau, M., et al. (2005). Efficacy of breast-feeding support provided by trained clinicians during an early, routine, preventive visit: A prospective, randomized, open trial of 226 mother-infant pairs. *Pediatrics, 115,* e139–e146.

Laberge, L., Tremblay, R. E., Vitaro, F., & Montplaisir, J. (2000). Development of parasomnias from childhood to early adolescence. *Pediatrics, 106,* 67–74.

Labov. T. (1992). Social and language boundaries among adolescents. *American Speech, 67,* 339–366.

Ladd, G. W. (1996). Shifting ecologies during the 5- to 7-year period: Predicting children's adjustment during the transition to grade school. In A. J. Sameroff & M. M. Haith (Eds.), *The five to seven year shift: The age of reason and responsibility* (pp. 363–386). Chicago: University of Chicago Press.

Ladd, G. W., Kochenderfer, B. J., & Coleman, C. C. (1996). Friendship quality as a predictor of young children's early school adjustment. *Child Development, 67,* 1103–1118.

LaFontana, K. M., & Cillessen, A. H. N. (2002). Children's perceptions of popular and unpopular peers: A multi-method assessment. *Developmental Psychology, 38,* 635–647.

Lagattuta, K. H. (2005). When you shouldn't do what you want to do: Young children's understanding of desires, rules, and emotions. *Child Development, 76,* 713–733.

Lagercrantz, H., & Slotkin, T. A. (1986). The "stress" of being born. *Scientific American, 254*(4), 100–107.

Laible, D. J., & Thompson, R. A. (1998). Attachment and emotional understanding in preschool children. *Developmental Psychology, 34*(5), 1038–1045.

Laible, D. J., & Thompson, R. A. (2002). Mother-child conflict in the toddler years: Lessons in emotion, morality, and relationships. *Child Development, 73,*1187–1203.

Laird, J., Lew, S., DeBell, M., & Chapman, C. (2006). *Dropout rates in the United States: 2002 and 2003* (NCES 2006-062). Washington, DC: U. S. Department of Education, National Center for Education Statistics.

Laird, R. D., Pettit, G. S., Bates, J. E., & Dodge, K. A. (2003). Parents' monitoring relevant knowledge and adolescents' delinquent behavior: Evidence of correlated developmental changes and reciprocal influences. *Child Development, 74,* 752–768.

Lalonde, C. E., & Werker, J. F. (1995). Cognitive influences on cross-language speech perception in infancy. *Infant Behavior and Development, 18,* 459–475.

Lamason, R. L., Mohideen, M.-A. P. K., Mest, J. R., Wong, A, C., Norton, H. L., et al. (2005). SLC24A5, a putative cation exchanger, affects pigmentation in zebrafish and humans. *Science, 310,* 1782–1786.

Lamb, M. E. (1981). The development of father-infant relationships. In M. E. Lamb (Ed.), *The role of the father in child development* (2nd ed.). New York: Wiley.

Lamb, M. E. (1983). Early mother-neonate contact and the mother-child relationship. *Journal of Child Psychology and Psychiatry and Allied Disciplines, 24,* 487–494.

Lamb, M. E., Frodi, A. M., Frodi, M., & Hwang, C. P. (1982). Characteristics of maternal and paternal behavior in traditional and non-traditional Swedish families. *International Journal of Behavior Development, 5,* 131–151.

Lamborn, S. D., Mounts, N. S., Steinberg, L., & Dornbusch, S. M. (1991). Patterns of competence and adjustment among adolescents from authoritative, authoritarian, indulgent, and neglectful families. *Child Development, 62,* 1049–1065.

Lamm, C., Zelazo, P. D., & Lewis, M. D. (2006). Neural correlates of cognitive control in childhood and adolescence: Disentangling the contributions of age and executive function. *Neuropsychologia, 44,* 2139–2148.

Landon, M. B., Hauth, J. C., Leveno, K. J., Spong, C. Y., Leindecker, S., Varner, M. W., et al., for the National Institute of Child Health and Human Development Maternal-Fetal Medicine Units Network. (2004). Maternal and perinatal outcomes associated with a trial of labor after prior cesarean delivery. *New England Journal of Medicine, 351,* 2581–2589.

Landry, S. H., Smith, K. E., Swank, P. R., & Miller Loncar, C. L. (2000). Early maternal and child influences on children's later independent cognitive and social functioning. *Child Development, 71,* 358–375.

Lane, H. (1976). *The wild boy of Aveyron.* Cambridge, MA: Harvard University Press.

Lange, G., MacKinnon, C. E., & Nida, R. E. (1989). Knowledge, strategy, and motivational contributions to preschool children's object recall. *Developmental Psychology, 25,* 772–779.

Lanphear, B. P., Aligne, C. A., Auinger, P., Weitzman, M., & Byrd, R. S. (2001). Residential exposure associated with asthma in U.S. children. *Pediatrics, 107,* 505–511.

Lansford, J. E., Chang, L., Dodge, K. A., Malone, P. S., Oburu, P., Palmérus, K., et al. (2005). Physical discipline and children's adjustment: Cultural normativeness as a moderator. *Child Development, 76,* 1234–1246.

Lansford, J. E., Dodge, K. A., Pettit, G. S., Bates, J. E., Crozier, J., & Kaplow, J.

(2002). A 12-year prospective study of the long-term effects of early child physical maltreatment on psychological, behavioral, and academic problems in adolescence. *Archives of Pediatric and Adolescent Medicine, 156*(8), 824–830.

Lanting, C. I., Fidler, V., Huisman, M., Touwen, B. C. L., & Boersma, E. R. (1994). Neurological differences between 9-year-old children fed breastmilk or formula-milk as babies. *Lancet, 334,* 1319–1322.

Lapham, E. V., Kozma, C., & Weiss, J. O. (1996). Genetic discrimination: Perspectives of consumers. *Science, 274,* 621–624.

Larsen, D. (1990, December–1991, January). Unplanned parenthood. *Modern Maturity,* 32–36.

Larson, R., & Seepersad, S. (2003). Adolescents' leisure time in the United States: Partying, sports, and the American experiment. In S. Verma & R. Larson (Eds.), *Examining adolescent leisure time across cultures: Developmental opportunities and risks. New Directions for Child and Adolescent Development, 99,* 53–64.

Larson, R., & Wilson, S. (2004). Adolescents across place and time: Globalization and the changing pathways to adulthood. In R. M. Lerner & L. Steinberg (Eds.), *Handbook of adolescent psychology* (2nd ed., pp. 299–331). Hoboken, NJ: Wiley.

Larson, R. W. (1997). The emergence of solitude as a constructive domain of experience in early adolescence. *Child Development, 68,* 80–93.

Larson, R. W., Moneta, G., Richards, M. H., & Wilson, S. (2002). Continuity, stability, and change in daily emotional experience across adolescence. *Child Development, 73,* 1151–1165.

Larson, R. W., Richards, M. H., Moneta, G., Holmbeck, G., & Duckett, E. (1996). Changes in adolescents' daily interactions with their families from ages 10 to 18: Disengagement and transformation. *Developmental Psychology, 32,* 744–754.

Larson, R. W., & Verma, S. (1999). How children and adolescents spend time across the world: Work, play, and developmental opportunities. *Psychological Bulletin, 125,* 701–736.

Larzalere, R. E. (2000). Child outcomes of nonabusive and customary physical punishment by parents: An updated literature review. *Clinical Child and Family Psychology Review, 3,* 199–221.

Lash, J. P. (1980). *Helen and teacher: The story of Helen Keller and Anne Sullivan Macy.* New York: Delacorte.

Laucht, M., Esser, G., & Schmidt, M. H. (1994). Contrasting infant predictors of later cognitive functioning. *Journal of Child Psychology and Psychiatry, 35,* 649–652.

Laursen, B. (1996). Closeness and conflict in adolescent peer relationships: Interdependence with friends and romantic partners.

In W. M. Bukowski, A. F. Newcomb, & W. W. Hartup (Eds.), *The company they keep: Friendship in childhood and adolescence* (pp. 186–210). New York: Cambridge University Press.

Laursen, B., Coy, K. C., & Collins, W. A. (1998). Reconsidering changes in parent-child conflict across adolescence: A meta-analysis. *Child Development, 69,* 817–832.

Lavelli, M., & Fogel, A. (2005). Developmental changes in the relationship between the infant's attention and emotion during early face-to-face communication: The 2-month transition. *Developmental Psychology, 41,* 265–280.

Law, K. L., Stroud, L. R., LaGasse, L. L., Niaura, R., Liu, J., & Lester, B. (2003). Smoking during pregnancy and newborn neurobehavior. *Pediatrics, 111,* 1318–1323.

Lawn, J. E., Cousens, S., & Zupan, J., for the Lancet Neonatal Survival Steering Team. (2005). 4 million neonatal deaths: When? Where? Why? *The Lancet, 365,* 891–900.

Lawson, C. (1993, October 4). Celebrated birth aside, teen-ager is typical now. *New York Times,* p. A18.

Leaper, C., Anderson, K. J., & Sanders, P. (1998). Moderators of gender effects on parents' talk to their children: A meta-analysis. *Developmental Psychology, 34*(1), 3–27.

Leaper, C., & Smith, T. E. (2004). A meta-analytic review of gender variations in children's language use: Talkativeness, affiliative speech, and assertive speech. *Developmental Psychology, 40,* 993–1027.

Leblanc, M., & Ritchie, M. (2001). A meta-analysis of play therapy outcomes. *Counseling Psychology Quarterly, 14,* 149–163.

Lecanuet, J. P., Granier-Deferre, C., & Busnel, M.-C. (1995). Human fetal auditory perception. In J. P. Lecanuet, W. P. Fifer, N. A. Krasnegor, & W. P. Smotherman (Eds.), *Fetal development: A psychobiological perspective* (pp. 239–262). Hillsdale, NJ: Erlbaum.

Lee, F. R. (2004, July 3). Engineering more sons than daughters: Will it tip the scales toward war? *New York Times,* pp. A17, A19.

Lee, G. M., Gortmaker, S. L., McIntosh, K., Hughes, M. D., Oleske, J. M., & Pediatric AIDS Clinical Trials Group Protocol 219C Team. (2006). Quality of life for children and adolescents: Impact of HIV infection and antiretroviral treatment. *Pediatrics, 117,* 273–283.

Lee, M. M. (2006). Idiopathic short stature. *New England Journal of Medicine, 354,* 2576–2582.

Lee, S. J., Ralston, H. J. P., Drey, E. A., Partridge, J. C., & Rosen, M. A. (2005). Fetal pain: A systematic multidisciplinary review of the evidence. *Journal of the American Medical Association, 294,* 947–954.

Legerstee, M., & Varghese, J. (2001). The role of maternal affect mirroring on social

expectancies in three-month-old infants. *Child Development, 72,* 1301–1313.

Leibel, R. L. (1997). And finally, genes for human obesity. *Nature Genetics, 16,* 218–220.

Leman, P. J., Ahmed, S., & Ozarow, L. (2005). Gender, gender relations, and the social dynamics of children's conversations. *Developmental Psychology, 41,* 64–74.

Lemke, M., Sen, A., Pahlke, E., Partelow, L., Miller, D., Williams, T., et al. (2004). *International outcomes of learning in mathematics literacy and problem solving: PISA 2003. Results from the U.S. perspective* (NCES 2005–003). Washington, DC: National Center for Education.

Lenneberg, E. H. (1967). *Biological functions of language.* New York: Wiley.

Lenneberg, E. H. (1969). On explaining language. *Science, 164*(3880), 635–643.

Leonard, W. E. (1925). *Two lives: A poem.* New York: Huebsch.

Lesch, K. P., Bengel, D., Heils, A., Sabol, S. Z., Greenberg, B. D., Petri, S., et al. (1996). Association of anxiety-related traits with a polymorphism in the serotonin transporter gene regulatory region. *Science, 274,* 1527–1531.

Leslie, A. M. (1982). The perception of causality in infants. *Perception, 11,* 173–186.

Leslie, A. M. (1984). Spatiotemporal continuity and the perception of causality in infants. *Perception, 13,* 287–305.

Leslie, L. K., Newman, T. B., Chesney, J., & Perrin, J. M. (2005). The Food and Drug Administration's deliberations on antidepressant use in pediatric patients. *Pediatrics, 116,* 195–204.

Lester, B. M., & Boukydis, C. F. Z. (1985). *Infant crying: Theoretical and research perspectives.* New York: Plenum.

Lewis, M., & Brooks, J. (1974). Self, other, and fear: Infants' reaction to people. In H. Lewis & L. Rosenblum (Eds.), *The origins of fear: The origins of behavior* (Vol. 2). New York: Wiley.

LeVay, S. (1991). A difference in hypothalamic structure between heterosexual and homosexual men. *Science, 253,* 1034–1037.

LeVine, R. A. (1974). Parental goals: A cross-cultural view. *Teacher College Record, 76,* 226–239.

LeVine, R. A. (1989). Human parental care: Universal goals, cultural strategies, individual behavior. In R. A. LeVine, P. M. Miller, & M. M. West (Eds.), *Parental behavior in diverse societies* (pp. 3–12). San Francisco: Jossey-Bass.

LeVine, R. A. (1994). *Child care and culture: Lessons from Africa.* Cambridge, England: Cambridge University Press.

Levine, S. C., Vasilyeva, M., Lourenco, S. E., Newcombe, N. S., & Huttenlocher, J. (2005). Socioeconomic status modifies the sex differences in spatial skills. *Psychological Science, 16,* 841–845.

Leviton, A., & Cowan, L. (2002). A review of the literature relating caffeine consumption by women to their risk of reproductive hazards. *Food and Chemical Toxicology, 40*(9), 1271–1310.

Levron, J., Aviram, A., Madgar, I., Livshits, A., Raviv, G., Bider, D., et al. (1998, October). *High rate of chromosomal aneuploidies in testicular spermatozoa retrieved from azoospermic patients undergoing testicular sperm extraction for in vitro fertilization.* Paper presented at the 16th World Congress on Fertility and Sterility and the 54th annual meeting of the American Society for Reproductive Medicine, San Francisco, CA.

Levy-Shiff, R., Zoran, N., & Shulman, S. (1997). International and domestic adoption: Child, parents, and family adjustment. *International Journal of Behavioral Development, 20,* 109–129.

Lewinsohn, P. M., Gotlib, I. H., Lewinsohn, M., Seeley, J. R., & Allen, N. B. (1998). Gender differences in anxiety disorders and anxiety symptoms in adolescence. *Journal of Abnormal Psychology, 107,* 109–117.

Lewis, M. (1995). Self-conscious emotions. *American Scientist, 83,* 68–78.

Lewis, M. (1997). The self in self-conscious emotions. In S. G. Snodgrass & R. L. Thompson (Eds.), *Annals of the New York Academy of Sciences: Vol. 818. The self across psychology: Self-recognition, self-awareness, and the self-concept.* New York: The New York Academy of Sciences.

Lewis, M. (1998). Emotional competence and development. In D. Pushkar, W. Bukowski, A. E. Schwartzman, D. M. Stack, & D. R. White (Eds.), *Improving competence across the lifespan* (pp. 27–36). New York: Plenum.

Lewit, E., & Kerrebrock, N. (1997). Population-based growth stunting. *The Future of Children, 7*(2), 149–156.

Li, R., Chase, M., Jung, S., Smith, P. J. S., & Loeken, M. R. (2005). Hypoxic stress in diabetic pregnancy contributes to impaired embryo gene expression and defective development by inducing oxidative stress. *American Journal of Physiology: Endocrinology and Metabolism, 289,* 591–599.

Li, R., Darling, N., Maurice, E., Barker, L., & Grummer-Strawn, L. M. (2005). Breast-feeding rates in the United States by characteristics of the child, mother, or family: The 2002 National Immunization Survey. *Pediatrics, 115,* e31–e37.

Li, X., Li, S., Ulusoy, E., Chen, W., Srinivasan, S. R., & Berenson, G. S. (2004). Childhood adiposity as a predictor of cardiac mass in adulthood. *Circulation, 110,* 3488–3492.

Liaw, F., & Brooks-Gunn, J. (1993). Patterns of low-birth-weight children's cognitive development. *Developmental Psychology, 29,* 1024–1035.

Liberman, I. Y., & Liberman, A. M. (1990). Whole language vs. code emphasis: Underlying assumptions and their implications for reading instruction. *Annals of Dyslexia, 40,* 51–76.

Lickliter, R., & Honeycutt, H. (2003). Developmental dynamics: Toward a biologically plausible evolutionary psychology. *Psychological Bulletin, 129,* 819–835.

Lickona, T. (Ed.). (1976). *Moral development and behavior.* New York: Holt.

Lillard, A., & Curenton, S. (1999). Do young children understand what others feel, want, and know? *Young Children, 54*(5), 52–57.

Lillard, A., & Else-Quest, N. (2006). The early years: Evaluating Montessori education. *Science, 313,* 1893–1894.

Lin, S., Hwang, S. A., Marshall, E. G., & Marion, D. (1998). Does paternal occupational lead exposure increase the risks of low birth weight or prematurity? *American Journal of Epidemiology, 148,* 173–181.

Lin, S. S., & Kelsey, J. L. (2000). Use of race and ethnicity in epidemiological research: Concepts, methodological issues, and suggestions for research. *Epidemiologic Reviews, 22*(2), 187–202.

Lindwer, W. (1991). *The last seven months of Anne Frank* (A. Meersschaert, Trans.). New York: Pantheon.

Linnet, K. M., Wisborg, K., Obel, C., Secher, N. J., Thomsen, P. H., Agerbo, E., et al. (2005). Smoking during pregnancy and the risk of hyperkinetic disorder in offspring. *Pediatrics, 116,* 462–467.

Lissau, I., Overpeck, M. D., Ruan, J., Due, P., Holstein, B. E., Hediger, M. L., & Health Behaviours in School-Aged Children Obesity Working Group. (2004). Body mass index and overweight in adolescents in 13 European countries, Israel, and the United States. *Archives of Pediatric and Adolescent Medicine, 158,* 27–33.

Littleton, H., Breitkopf, C., & Berenson, A. (2006, August 13). *Correlates of anxiety symptoms during pregnancy and association with perinatal outcomes: A meta-analysis.* Presentation at the 114th annual convention of the American Psychological Association, New Orleans.

Liu, J., Raine, A., Venables, P. H., Dalais, C., & Mednick, S. A. (2003). Malnutrition at age 3 years and lower cognitive ability at age 11 years. *Archives of Pediatric and Adolescent Medicine, 157,* 593–600.

Livson, N., & Peskin, H. (1980). Perspectives on adolescence from longitudinal research. In J. Adelson (Ed.), *Handbook of adolescent psychology.* New York: Wiley.

Lloyd, J. J., & Anthony, J. C. (2003). Hanging out with the wrong crowd: How much difference can parents make in an urban environment? *Journal of Urban Health, 80,* 383–399.

Lloyd, T., Andon, M. B., Rollings, N., Martel, J. K., Landis, J. R., Demers, L. M., et al. (1993). Calcium supplementation and bone mineral density in adolescent girls. *Journal of the American Medical Association, 270,* 841–844.

Lock, A., Young, A., Service, V., & Chandler, P. (1990). Some observations on the origin of the pointing gesture. In V. Volterra & C. J. Erting (Eds.), *From gesture to language in hearing and deaf children.* New York: Springer.

Lock, J., Walker, L. R., Rickert, V. I., & Katzman, D. K. (2005). Suicidality in adolescents being treated with antidepressant medications and the black box label: Position paper of the Society for Adolescent Medicine. *Journal of Adolescent Health, 36,* 92–93.

Lockwood, C. J. (2002). Predicting premature delivery—no easy task. *New England Journal of Medicine, 346,* 282–284.

Loeb, S., Bridges, M., Bassok, D., Fuller, B. & Rumberger, R.W. (2007). How much is too much? The influence of preschool centers on children's social and cognitive development. *Economics of Education Review, 26,* 52.

Loeb, S., Fuller, B., Kagan, S. L., & Carrol, B. (2004). Child care in poor communities: Early learning effects of type, quality, and stability. *Child Development, 75,* 47–65.

Loewen, N., & Bancroft, A. (2001). *Four to the Pole: The American Women's Expedition to Antarctica, 1992–1993.* North Haven, CT: Shoestring Press.

Lohse, N., Hansen, A. E., Pedersen, G., Kronborg, G., Gerstoft, J., Sørensen, H. T., et al. (2007). Survival of persons with and without HIV infection in Denmark, 1995–2005. *Annals of Internal Medicine, 146,* 87–95.

Lonczak, H. S., Abbott, R. D., Hawkins, J. D., Kosterman, R., & Catalano, R. F. (2002). Effects of the Seattle Social Development Project on sexual behavior, pregnancy, birth, and sexually transmitted disease. *Archives of Pediatric and Adolescent Medicine, 156,* 438–447.

Longnecker, M. P., Klebanoff, M. A., Zhou, H., & Brock, J. W. (2001). Association between maternal serum concentration of the DDT metabolite DDE and preterm and small-for-gestational-age babies at birth. *Lancet, 358,* 110–114.

Lonigan, C. J., Burgess, S. R., & Anthony, J. L. (2000). Development of emergent literacy and early reading skills in preschool children: Evidence from a latent-variable longitudinal study. *Developmental Psychology, 36,* 593–613.

Lorenz, K. (1957). Comparative study of behavior. In C. H. Schiller (Ed.), *Instinctive behavior.* New York: International Universities Press.

Lorsbach, T. C., & Reimer, J. F. (1997). Developmental changes in the inhibition of previously relevant information. *Journal of Experimental Child Psychology, 64,* 317–342.

Louise Brown: From miracle baby to regular teen. (1994, February 7). *People Weekly,* p. 12.

Louise Brown: The world's first "test-tube baby" ushered in a revolution in fertility. (1984, March). *People Weekly,* p. 82.

Love, J. M., Kisker, E. E., Ross, C., Raikes, H., Constantine, J., Boller, K., et al. (2005). The effectiveness of Early Head Start for 3-year-old children and their parents: Lessons for policy and programs. *Developmental Psychology, 41,* 885–901.

Love, J. M., Kisker, E. E., Ross, C. M., Schochet, P. Z., Brooks-Gunn, J., Paulsell, D., et al. (2002). *Making a difference in the lives of infants and toddlers and their families: The impacts of Early Head Start: Executive Summary.* Washington, DC: U.S. Department of Health and Human Services.

Love, K. M., & Murdock, B. (2004). Attachment to parents and psychological well-being: An examination of young adult college students in intact families and stepfamilies. *Journal of Family Psychology, 18,* 600–608.

Lubell, K. M., Swahn, M. H., Crosby, A. E., & Kegler, S. R. (2004). Methods of suicide among persons aged 10–19 years—United States, 1992–2001. *Morbidity and Mortality Weekly Report, 53,* 471–474.

Lubinski, D., & Benbow, C. P. (2006). Study of Mathematically Precocious Youth (SMPY) after 35 years: Uncovering antecedents for the development of math-science expertise. *Perspectives on Psychological Science, 1,* 316–343.

Lubinski, D., Benbow, C. P., Webb, R. M., & Bleske-Reckek, A. (2006). Tracking exceptional human capital over two decades. *Psychological Sciences, 17,* 104–109.

Lubinski, D., Webb, M. R., Morelock, M. J., & Benbow, C. P. (2001). Top 1 in 10,000: A 10-year follow-up of the profoundly gifted. *Journal of Applied Psychology, 86,* 718–729.

Lugaila, T. A. (2003). A child's day: 2000 (Selected indicators of child well-being). *Current Population Reports* (P70-89). Washington, DC: U.S. Census Bureau.

Luke, B., & Brown, M. B. (2006). The changing risk of infant mortality by gestation, plurality, and race: 1989–1991 versus 1999–2001. *Pediatrics, 118,* 2488–2497.

Luke, B., Mamelle, N., Keith, L., Munoz, F., Minogue, J., Papiernik, E., et al. (1995). The association between occupational factors and preterm birth: A United States nurses' study. *American Journal of Obstetrics and Gynecology, 173,* 849–862.

Luna, B., Garver, K. E., Urban, T. A., Lazar, N. A., & Sweeney, J. A. (2004). Maturation of cognitive processes from late childhood to adulthood. *Child Development, 75,* 1357–1372.

Lundy, B. L. (2003). Father- and mother-infant face-to-face interactions: Differences in mind-related comments and infant attachment? *Infant Behavior and Development, 26,* 200–212.

Lundy, B. L., Jones, N. A., Field, T., Nearing, G., Davalos, M., Pietro, P. A., et al. (1999). Prenatal depression effects on neonates. *Infant Behavior and Development, 22,* 119–129.

Luthar, S. S., & Latendresse, S. J. (2005). Children of the affluence: Challenges to well-being. *Current Directions in Psychological Science, 14,* 49–53.

Lyman, R. (1997, April 15). Michael Dorris dies at 52: Wrote of his son's suffering. *New York Times,* p. C24.

Lynskey, M. T., Heath, A. C., Bucholz, K. K., Slutske, W. S., Madden, P. A. F., Nelson, E. C., et al. (2003). Escalation of drug use in early-onset cannabis users versus co-twin controls. *Journal of the American Medical Association, 289,* 427–433.

Lyons-Ruth, K., Alpern, L., & Repacholi, B. (1993). Disorganized infant attachment classification and maternal psychosocial problems as predictors of hostile-aggressive behavior in the preschool classroom. *Child Development, 64,* 572–585.

Lytton, H., & Romney, D. M. (1991). Parents' differential socialization of boys and girls: A meta-analysis. *Psychological Bulletin, 109*(2), 267–296.

Lyytinen, P., Poikkeus, A., Laakso, M., Eklund, K., & Lyytinen, H. (2001). Language development and symbolic play in children with and without familial risk for dyslexia. *Journal of Speech, Language, and Hearing Research, 44,* 873–885.

Maccoby, E. (1980). *Social development.* New York: Harcourt Brace Jovanovich.

Maccoby, E. E. (1984). Middle childhood in the context of the family. In W. A. Collins (Ed.), *Development during middle childhood.* Washington, DC: National Academy.

Maccoby, E. E. (1992). The role of parents in the socialization of children: An historical overview. *Developmental Psychology, 28,* 1006–1017.

Maccoby, E. E. (2002). Gender and group process: A developmental perspective. *Current Directions in Psychological Science, 11,* 54–58.

Maccoby, E. E., & Lewis, C. C. (2003). Less day care or different day care? *Child Development, 74,* 1069–1075.

Maccoby, E. E., & Martin, J. A. (1983). Socialization in the context of the family: Parent-child interaction. In P. H. Mussen (Series Ed.) & E. M. Hetherington (Vol. Ed.), *Handbook of child psychology: Vol. 4. Socialization, personality, and social development* (pp. 1–101). New York: Wiley.

MacDonald, K. (1988). The interfaces between developmental psychology and evolutionary biology. In K. MacDonald (Ed.), *Sociobiological perspectives on human development* (pp. 3–23). New York: Springer-Verlag.

MacDonald, K. (1998). Evolution and development. In A. Campbell & S. Muncer (Eds.), *Social development* (pp. 21–49). London: UCL Press.

MacKinnon-Lewis, C., Starnes, R., Volling, B., & Johnson, S. (1997). Perceptions of parenting as predictors of boys' sibling and peer relations. *Developmental Psychology, 33,* 1024–1031.

Macmillan, C., Magder, L. S., Brouwers, P., Chase, C., Hittelman, J., Lasky, T., et al. (2001). Head growth and neurodevelopment of infants born to HIV-1–infected drug-using women. *Neurology, 57,* 1402–1411.

MacMillan, H. M., Boyle, M. H., Wong, M.Y.-Y., Duku, E. K., Fleming, J. E., & Walsh, C. A. (1999). Slapping and spanking in childhood and its association with lifetime prevalence of psychiatric disorders in a general population sample. *Canadian Medical Association Journal, 161,* 805–809.

Macmillan, R., McMorris, B. J., & Kruttschnitt, C. (2004). Linked lives: Stability and change in maternal circumstances and trajectories of antisocial behavior in children. *Child Development, 75,* 205–220.

MacWhinney, B. (2005). Language evolution and human development. In B. J. Ellis & D. F. Bjorklund (Eds.), *Origins of the social mind: Evolutionary psychology and child development* (pp. 383–410). New York: Guilford.

Maestripieri, D., Higley, J. D., Lindell, S. G., Newman, T. K., McCormack, K. M., & Sanchez, M. M. (2006). Early maternal rejection affects the development of monoaminergic systems and adult abusive parenting in rhesus macaques. *Behavioral Neuroscience, 120*(5), 1017–1024.

Mahoney, J. L. (2000). School extracurricular activity participation as a moderator in the development of antisocial patterns. *Child Development, 71*(2), 502–516.

Main, M. (1983). Exploration, play, and cognitive functioning related to infant-mother attachment. *Infant Behavior and Development, 6,* 167–174.

Main, M., Kaplan, N., & Cassidy, J. (1985). Security in infancy, childhood and adulthood: A move to the level of representation. In I. Bretherton & E. Waters (Eds.), Growing points in attachment. *Monographs of the Society for Research in Child Development, 50*(1–20), 66–104.

Main, M., & Solomon, J. (1986). Discovery of an insecure, disorganized/disoriented attachment pattern: Procedures, findings, and implications for the classification of behavior. In M. Yogman & T. B. Brazelton (Eds.), *Affective development in infancy.* Norwood, NJ: Ablex.

Makino, M., Tsuboi, K., & Dennerstein, L. (2004). Prevalence of eating disorders: A comparison of Western and non-Western countries. *Medscape General Medicine, 6*(3). Retrieved September 27, 2004, from http://www.medscape.com/viewarticle/487413

Makrides, M., Neumann, M., Simmer, K., Pater, J., & Gibson, R. (1995). Are longchain polyunsaturated fatty acids essential nutrients in infancy? *Lancet, 345,*1463–1468.

Malaspina, D., Harlap, S., Fennig, S., Heiman, D., Nahon, D., Feldman, D., et al. (2001). Advancing paternal age and the risk of schizophrenia. *Archives of General Psychiatry, 58,* 361–371.

Malone, F. D., Canick, J. A., Ball, R. H., Nyberg, D. A., Comstock, C. H., Bukowski, R., et al. (2005). First-trimester or second-trimester screening, or both, for Down's syndrome. *New England Journal of Medicine, 353,* 2001–2011.

Malone, L. M., West, J., Flanagan, K. D., & Park, J. (2006). *Statistics in brief: The early reading and mathematics achievement of children who repeated kindergarten or who began school a year late* (NCES 2006-064). Washington, DC: National Center for Education Statistics.

Mandela, N. (1994). *Long walk to freedom: The autobiography of Nelson Mandela.* Boston: Little, Brown.

Mandler, J. M. (1998a). Representation. In D. Kuhn & R. S. Siegler (Eds.), *Handbook of child psychology: Vol. 2: Cognition, perception, and language* (5th ed., pp. 255–308). New York: Wiley.

Mandler, J. M., & McDonough, L. (1993). Concept formation in infancy. *Cognitive Development, 8,* 291–318.

Mandler, J. M., & McDonough, L. (1996). Drinking and driving don't mix: Inductive generalization in infancy. *Cognition, 59,* 307–335.

Mandler, J. M., & McDonough, L. (1998). Cognition across the life span: On developing a knowledge base in infancy. *Developmental Psychology, 34,* 1274–1288.

Manlove, J., Ryan, S., & Franzetta, K. (2003). Patterns of contraceptive use within teenagers' first sexual relationships. *Perspectives on Sexual and Reproductive Health, 35,* 246–255.

March of Dimes Birth Defects Foundation. (1987). *Genetic counseling: A public health information booklet* (Rev. ed.). White Plains, NY: Author.

March of Dimes Birth Defects Foundation. (2004a). *Cocaine use during pregnancy.* Fact sheet. Retrieved October 29, 2004, from marchofdimes.com/professionals/681_1169.asp

March of Dimes Birth Defects Foundation. (2004b). *Marijuana: What you need to know.* Retrieved October 29, 2004, from http://www.marchofdimes.com/pnhec/159_4427.asp

March of Dimes Foundation. (2002). *Toxoplasmosis.* (Fact Sheet). Wilkes-Barre, PA: Author.

Marcia, J. E. (1966). Development and validation of ego identity status. *Journal of Personality and Social Psychology, 3*(5), 551–558.

Marcia, J. E. (1979, June). *Identity status in late adolescence: Description and some clinical implications.* Address given at symposium on identity development, Rijksuniversitat Groningen, Netherlands.

Marcia, J. E. (1980). Identity in adolescence. In J. Adelson (Ed.), *Handbook of adolescent psychology*. New York: Wiley.

Marcia, J. E. (1993). The relational roots of identity. In J. Kroger (Ed.), *Discussions on ego identity* (pp. 101–120). Hillsdale, NJ: Erlbaum.

Marcon, R. A. (1999). Differential impact of preschool models on development and early learning of inner-city children: A three-cohort study. *Developmental Psychology, 35*(2), 358–375.

Marcus, G. F., Vijayan, S., Rao, S. B., & Vishton, P. M. (1999). Rule learning by seven-month-old infants. *Science, 283,* 77–80.

Marian Anderson plans move to Portland, Oregon with her nephew, James DePriest. (1992, July 13). *Jet,* 33.

Markoff, J. (1992, October 12). Miscarriages tied to chip factories. *New York Times,* pp. A1, D2.

Marks, H. (2000). Student engagement in instructional activity: Patterns in the elementary, middle, and high school years. *American Education Research Journal, 37,* 153–184.

Marlier, L., & Schaal, B. (2005). Human newborns prefer human milk: Conspecific milk odor is attractive without postnatal exposure. *Child Development, 76,* 155–168.

Marling, K. A. (1996). *Graceland: Going home with Elvis.* Cambridge, MA: Harvard University Press.

Marlow, N., Wolke, D., Bracewell, M. A., & Samara, M., for the EPICure Study Group. (2005). Neurologic and developmental disability at six years of age after extremely preterm birth. *New England Journal of Medicine, 352,* 9–19.

Marshall, N. L. (2004). The quality of early child care and children's development. *Current Directions in Psychological Science, 13,* 165–168.

Marshall, T. A., Levy, S. M., Broffitt, B., Warren, J. J., Eichenberger-Gilmore, J. M., Burns, T. L., et al. (2003) Dental caries and beverage consumption in young children. *Pediatrics, 112,* e184–e191.

Martin, C. L., Eisenbud, L., & Rose, H. (1995). Children's gender-based reasoning about toys. *Child Development, 66,* 1453–1471.

Martin, C. L., & Fabes, R. A. (2001). The stability and consequences of young children's same-sex peer interactions. *Developmental Psychology, 37,* 431–446.

Martin, C. L., & Halverson, C. F. (1981). A schematic processing model of sex typing and stereotyping in children. *Child Development, 52,* 1119–1134.

Martin, C. L., & Ruble, D. (2004). Children's search for gender cues: Cognitive perspectives on gender development. *Current Directions in Psychological Science, 13,* 67–70.

Martin, C. L., Ruble, D. N., & Szkrybalo, J. (2002). Cognitive theories of early gender development. *Psychological Bulletin, 128,* 903–933.

Martin, J. A., Hamilton, B. E., Sutton, P. D., Ventura, S. J., Menacker, F., & Kirmeyer, S. (2006). Births: Final data for 2004. *National Vital Statistics Reports, 55*(1). Hyattsville, MD: National Center for Health Statistics.

Martin, J. A., Hamilton, B. E., Sutton, P. D., Ventura, S. J., Menacker, F., & Munson, M. L. (2003). Births: Final data for 2002. *National Vital Statistics Reports, 52*(10). Hyattsville, MD: National Center for Health Statistics.

Martin, J. A., Hamilton, B. E., Sutton, P. D., Ventura, S. J., Menacker, F., & Munson, M. L. (2005). Births: Final data for 2003. *National Vital Statistics Reports, 54*(2). Hyattsville, MD: National Center for Health Statistics.

Martin, J. A., Hamilton, B. E., Ventura, S. J., Menacker, F., & Park, M. M. (2002). Births: Final data for 2000. *National Vital Statistics Reports, 50*(5). Hyattsville, MD: National Center for Health Statistics.

Martin, N., & Montgomery, G. (2002, March 18). *Is having twins, either identical or fraternal, in someone's genes? Is there a way to increase your chances of twins or is having twins just luck?* Retrieved March 7, 2006, from http://genepi.qimr.edu.au/ScientificAmericanTwins.html

Martin, R., Noyes, J., Wisenbaker, J., & Huttunen, M. (2000). Prediction of early childhood negative emotionality and inhibition from maternal distress during pregnancy. *Merrill-Palmer Quarterly, 45,* 370–391.

Martínez-González, M. A., Gual, P., Lahortiga, F., Alonso, Y., de Irala-Estévez, J., & Cervera, S. (2003). Parental factors, mass media influences, and the onset of eating disorders in a prospective population-based cohort. *Pediatrics, 111,* 315–320.

Marwick, C. (1997). Health care leaders from drug policy group. *Journal of the American Medical Association, 278,* 378.

Marwick, C. (1998). Physician leadership on national drug policy finds addiction treatment works. *Journal of the American Medical Association, 279,* 1149–1150.

Masse, L. C., & Tremblay, R. E. (1997). Behavior of boys in kindergarten and the onset of substance use during adolescence. *Archives of General Psychiatry, 54,* 62–68.

Masten, A. S. (2001). Ordinary magic: Resilience processes in development. *American Psychologist, 56,* 227–238.

Masten, A., Best, K., & Garmezy, N. (1990). Resilience and development: Contributions from the study of children who overcome adversity. *Development and Psychopathology, 2,* 425–444.

Masten, A. S., & Coatsworth, J. D. (1998). The development of competence in favorable and unfavorable environments: Lessons from research on successful children. *American Psychologist, 53,* 205–220.

Mathews, T. J., & MacDorman, M. F. (2006). Infant mortality statistics from the 2003 period linked birth/infant death data set. *National Vital Statistics Reports, 54*(16). Hyattsville, MD: National Center for Health Statistics.

May, K. A., & Perrin, S. P. (1985). Prelude: Pregnancy and birth. In S. M. H. Hanson & F. W. Bozett (Eds.), *Dimensions of fatherhood.* Beverly Hills, CA: Sage.

Mayer, D. P. (1998). Do new teaching standards undermine performance on old tests? *Educational Evaluation and Policy Analysis, 20,* 53–73.

Mayo Clinic. (2005, December 7). *Infertility.* Retrieved May 5, 2006, from http://www.mayoclinic.com/health/infertility/DS00310

Mayseless, O., & Scharf, M. (2003). What does it mean to be an adult? The Israeli experience. In J. J. Arnett & N. L. Galambos (Eds.), *Exploring cultural conceptions of the transition to adulthood. New Directions for Child and Adolescent Development, 100,* 5–20.

McCall, R. B., & Carriger, M. S. (1993). A meta-analysis of infant habituation and recognition memory performance as predictors of later IQ. *Child Development, 64,* 57–79.

McCallum, K. E., & Bruton, J. R. (2003). The continuum of care in the treatment of eating disorders. *Primary Psychiatry, 10*(6), 48–54.

McCarton, C. M., Brooks-Gunn, J., Wallace, I. F., Bauer, C. R., Bennett, F. C., Bernbaum, J. C., et al., for the Infant Health and Development Program Research Group. (1997). Results at age 8 years of early intervention for low-birth-weight premature infants. *Journal of the American Medical Association, 277,* 126–132.

McCartt, A. T. (2001). Graduated driver licensing systems: Reducing crashes among teenage drivers. *Journal of the American Medical Association, 286,* 1631–1632.

McCarty, M. E., Clifton, R. K., Ashmead, D. H., Lee, P., & Goubet, N. (2001). How infants use vision for grasping objects. *Child Development, 72,* 973–987.

McClearn, G. E., Johansson, B., Berg, S., Pedersen, N. L., Ahern, F., Petrill, S. A., et al. (1997). Substantial genetic influence on cognitive abilities in twins 80 or more years old. *Science, 276,* 1560–1563.

McClintock, M. K., & Herdt, G. (1996). Rethinking puberty: The development of sexual attraction. *Current Directions in Psychological Science, 5*(6), 178–183.

McCord, J. (1996). Unintended consequences of punishment. *Pediatrics, 88,* 832–834.

McCormick, M. C., Brooks-Gunn, J., Buka, S. L., Goldman, J., Yu, J., Salganik, M., et al. (2006). Early intervention in low birth weight premature infants: Results at 18 years of age for the Infant Health and Development Program. *Pediatrics, 117,* 771–780.

McCormick, M. C., McCarton, C., Brooks-Gunn, J., Belt, P., & Gross, R. T. (1998). The infant health and development program: Interim summary. *Journal of Developmental and Behavioral Pediatrics, 19*, 359–371.

McCoy, A. R., & Reynolds, A. J. (1999). Grade retention and school performance: An extended investigation. *Journal of School Psychology, 37*, 273–298.

McCrink, K., & Wynn, K. (2004). Large-number addition and subtraction by 9-month-old infants. *Psychological Science, 15*, 776–781.

McDaniel, M., Paxson, C., & Waldfogel, J. (2006). Racial disparities in childhood asthma in the United States: Evidence from the National Health Interview Survey, 1997 to 2003. *Pediatrics, 117*, 868–877.

McElwain, N. L., & Volling, B. L. (2005). Preschool children's interactions with friends and older siblings: Relationship specificity and joint contributions to problem behavior. *Journal of Family Psychology, 19*, 486–496.

McGee, R., Partridge, F., Williams, S., & Silva, P. A. (1991). A twelve-year followup of preschool hyperactive children. *Journal of the American Academy of Child and Adolescent Psychiatry, 30*, 224–232.

McGilley, B. M., & Pryor, T. L. (1998). Assessment and treatment of bulimia nervosa. *American Family Physician, 57*(11), 2743–2750.

McGue, M. (1997). The democracy of the genes. *Nature, 388*, 417–418.

McGuffin, P., Owen, M. J., & Farmer, A. E. (1995). Genetic basis of schizophrenia. *Lancet, 346*, 678–682.

McGuffin, P., Riley, B., & Plomin, R. (2001). Toward behavioral genomics. *Science, 291*, 1232–1249.

McGuigan, F., & Salmon, K. (2004). The time to talk: The influence of the timing of adult-child talk on children's event memory. *Child Development, 75*, 669–686.

McHale, S. M., Kim, J., Whiteman, S., & Crouter, A. C. (2004). Links between sex-typed time use in middle childhood and gender development in early adolescence. *Developmental Psychology, 40*, 868–881.

McHale, S. M., Updegraff, K. A., Helms-Erikson, H., & Crouter, A. C. (2001). Sibling influences on gender development in middle childhood and early adolescence: A longitudinal study. *Developmental Psychology, 37*, 115–125.

McKay, N. Y. (1992). Introduction. In M. Anderson, *My Lord, what a morning* (pp. ix–xxxiii). Madison, WI: University of Wisconsin Press.

McKenna, J. J., & Mosko, S. (1993). Evolution and infant sleep: An experimental study of infant-parent cosleeping and its implications for SIDS. *Acta Paediatrica, 389*(Suppl.), 31–36.

McKenna, J. J., Mosko, S. S., & Richard, C. A. (1997). Bedsharing promotes breastfeeding. *Pediatrics, 100*, 214–219.

McKusick, V. A. (2001). The anatomy of the human genome. *Journal of the American Medical Association, 286*(18), 2289–2295.

McLanahan, S., & Sandefur, G. (1994). *Growing up with a single parent.* Cambridge, MA: Harvard University Press.

McLeod, R., Boyer, K., Karrison, T., Kasza, K., Swisher, C., Roizen, N., et al., & Toxoplasmosis Study Group. (2006). Outcome of treatment for congenital toxoplasmosis, 1981–2004: The national collaborative Chicago-based, congenital toxoplasmosis study. *Clinical Infectious Diseases: An Official Publication of the Infectious Diseases Society of America, 42*(10), 1383–1394.

McLeskey, J., Lancaster, M., & Grizzle, K. L. (1995). Learning disabilities and grade retention: A review of issues with recommendations for practice. *Learning Disabilities Research and Practice, 10*, 120–128.

McLoyd, V. C. (1990). The impact of economic hardship on black families and children: Psychological distress, parenting, and socioemotional development. *Child Development, 61*, 311–346.

McLoyd, V. C. (1998). Socioeconomic disadvantage and child development. *American Psychologist, 53*, 185–204.

McLoyd, V. C., & Smith, J. (2002). Physical discipline and behavior problems in African American, European American, and Hispanic children: Emotional support as a moderator. *Journal of Marriage and Family, 64*, 40–53.

McNeilly-Choque, M. K., Hart, C. H., Robinson, C. C., Nelson, L. J., & Olsen, S. F. (1996). Overt and relational aggression on the playground. Correspondence among different informants. *Journal of Research in Childhood Education, 11*, 47–67.

McQuillan, J., Greil, A. L., White, L., & Jacob, M. C. (2003). Frustrated fertility: Infertility and psychological distress among women. *Journal of Marriage and Family, 65*, 1007–1018.

Mead, M. (1928). *Coming of age in Samoa.* New York: Morrow.

Mead, M. (1930). *Growing up in New Guinea.* New York: Blue Ribbon.

Mead, M. (1935). *Sex and temperament in three primitive societies.* New York: Morrow.

Mead, M. (1972). *Blackberry winter: My earlier years.* New York: Morrow.

Mears, B. (2005, March 1). *High court: Juvenile death penalty unconstitutional: Slim majority cites "evolving standards" in American society.* Retrieved March 30, 2005, from http://cnn.com/2005/LAW/03/01/scotus.death.penalty

Meeks, J. J., Weiss, J., & Jameson, J. L. (2003, May). Dax1 is required for testis formation. *Nature Genetics, 34*, 32–33.

Meer, F. (1988). *Higher than hope: The authorized biography of Nelson Mandela.* New York: Harper & Row.

Meezan, W., & Rauch, J. (2005). Gay marriage, same-sex parenting, and America's children. *Future of Children, 15*, 97–115.

Meier, D. (1995). *The power of their ideas.* Boston: Beacon.

Meier, R. (1991, January–February). Language acquisition by deaf children. *American Scientist, 79*, 60–70.

Meins, E. (1998). The effects of security of attachment and maternal attribution of meaning on children's linguistic acquisitional style. *Infant Behavior and Development, 21*, 237–252.

Meis, P. J., Klebanoff, M., Thom, E., Dombrowski, M. P., Sibai, B., Moawad, A. H., et al., & National Institute of Child Health and Human Development Maternal-Fetal Medicine Units Network. (2003). Prevention of recurrent preterm delivery by 17 alpha-hydroxyprogesterone caproate. *New England Journal of Medicine, 348*, 2379–2385.

Meltzoff, A. N., & Gopnik, A. (1993). The role of imitation in understanding persons and developing a theory of mind. In S. Baron-Cohen, H. Tager-Flusberg, & D. J. Cohen (Eds.), *Understanding other minds: Perspectives from autism* (pp. 335–366). New York: Oxford University Press.

Meltzoff, A. N., & Moore, M. K. (1983). Newborn infants imitate adult facial gestures. *Child Development, 54*, 702–709.

Meltzoff, A. N., & Moore, M. K. (1989). Imitation in newborn infants: Exploring the range of gestures imitated and the underlying mechanisms. *Developmental Psychology, 25*, 954–962.

Meltzoff, A. N., & Moore, M. K. (1994). Imitation, memory, and the representation of persons. *Infant Behavior and Development, 17*, 83–99.

Meltzoff, A. N., & Moore, M. K. (1998). Object representation, identity, and the paradox of early permanence: Steps toward a new framework. *Infant Behavior and Development, 21*, 201–235.

Menacker, F., Martin, J. A., MacDorman, M. F., & Ventura, S. J. (2004). Births to 10–14 year-old mothers, 1990–2002: Trends and health outcomes. *National Vital Statistics Reports, 53*(7). Hyattsville, MD: National Center for Health Statistics.

Mendle, J., Turkheimer, E., D'Onofrio, B. M., Lynch, S. K., Emery, R. E., Slutske, W. S., et al. (2006). Family structure and age at menarche: A children-of-twins approach. *Developmental Psychology, 42*, 533–542.

Menegaux, F., Baruchel, A., Bertrand, Y., Lescoeur, B., Leverger, G., Nelken, B., et al. (2006). Household exposure to pesticides and risk of childhood acute leukaemia. *Occupational and Environmental Medicine, 63*(2), 131–134.

Meng, H., Smith, S. D., Hager, K., Held, M., Liu, J., Olson, R. K., et al. (2005, October). *A deletion in DCDC2 on 6p22 is associated with reading disability.* Paper presented at the American Society of Human Genetics meeting, Salt Lake City, UT.

Menken, J., Trussell, J., & Larsen, U. (1986). Age and infertility. *Science, 233,* 1389–1394.

Mennella, J. A., & Beauchamp, G. K. (1996a). The early development of human flavor preferences. In E. D. Capaldi (Ed.), *Why we eat what we eat: The psychology of eating* (pp. 83–112). Washington, DC: American Psychological Association.

Mennella, J. A., & Beauchamp, G. K. (1996b). The human infants' response to vanilla flavors in mother's milk and formula. *Infant Behavior and Development, 19,* 13–19.

Mennella, J. A., & Beauchamp, G. K. (2002). Flavor experiences during formula feeding are related to preferences during childhood. *Early Human Development, 68,* 71–82.

Ment, L. R., Vohr, B., Allan, W., Katz, K. H., Schneider, K. C., Westerveld, M., et al. (2003). Changes in cognitive function over time in very low-birth-weight infants. *Journal of the American Medical Association, 289,* 705–711.

Merewood, A., Mehta, S. D., Chamberlain, L. B., Philipp, B. L., & Bauchner, H. (2005). Breastfeeding rates in US baby-friendly hospitals: Results of a national survey. *Pediatrics, 116,* 628–634.

Messinger, D. S., Bauer, C. R., Das, A., Seifer, R., Lester, B. M., Lagasse, L. L., et al. (2004). The maternal lifestyle study: Cognitive, motor, and behavioral outcomes of cocaine-exposed and opiate-exposed infants through three years of age. *Pediatrics, 113,* 1677–1685.

Messinis, L., Krypianidou, A., Maletaki, S., & Papathanasopoulos, P. (2006). Neuropsychological deficits in long-term cannabis users. *Neurology, 66,* 737–739.

Michelmore, P. (1962). *Einstein: Profile of the man.* London: Frederick Muller, Ltd.

Miech, R. A., Kumanyika, S. K., Stettler, N., Link, B., Phelan, J. C., & Chang, V. W. (2006). Trends in the association of poverty with overweight among US adolescents, 1971–2004. *Journal of the American Medical Association, 295,* 2385–2393.

Miedzian, M. (1991). *Boys will be boys: Breaking the link between masculinity and violence.* New York: Doubleday.

Migeon, B. R. (2006). The role of X inactivation and cellular mosaicism in women's health and sex-specific disorders. *Journal of the American Medical Association, 295,* 1428–1433.

Mikkola, K., Ritari, N., Tommiska, V., Salokorpi, T., Lehtonen, L., Tammela, O., et al. for the Finnish ELBW Cohort Study Group. (2005). Neurodevelopmental outcome at 5 years of age of a national cohort of extremely low birth weight infants who were born in 1996–1997. *Pediatrics, 116,* 1391–1400.

Milberger, S., Biederman, J., Faraone, S. V., Chen, L., & Jones, J. (1996). Is maternal smoking during pregnancy a risk factor for attention hyperactivity disorder in children? *American Journal of Psychiatry, 153,* 1138–1142.

Miles, S. B., & Stipek, D. (2006). Contemporaneous and longitudinal associations between social behavior and literacy achievement in a sample of low-income elementary school children. *Child Development, 77,* 103–117.

Miller, V., Onotera, R. T., & Deinard, A. S. (1984). Denver Developmental Screening Test: Cultural variations in Southeast Asian children. *Journal of Pediatrics, 104*(3), 481–482.

Miller-Kovach, K. (2003). *Childhood and adolescent obesity: A review of the scientific literature.* Unpublished manuscript, Weight Watchers International.

Millman, R. P., Working Group on Sleepiness in Adolescents/Young Adults, & AAP Committee on Adolescents. (2005). Excessive sleepiness in adolescents and young adults: Causes, consequences, and treatment strategies. *Pediatrics, 115,* 1774–1786.

Mills, J. L., & England, L. (2001). Food fortification to prevent neural tube defects: Is it working? *Journal of the American Medical Association, 285,* 3022–3033.

Mills, J. L., Holmes, L. B., Aarons, J. H., Simpson, J. L., Brown, Z. A., Jovanovic-Peterson, L. G., et al. (1993). Moderate caffeine use and the risk of spontaneous abortion and intrauterine growth retardation. *Journal of the American Medical Association, 269,* 593–597.

Milunsky, A. (1992). *Heredity and your family's health.* Baltimore: Johns Hopkins University Press.

Miniño, A. M., Anderson, R. N., Fingerhut, L. A., Boudreault, M. A., & Warner, M. (2006). Deaths: Injuries, 2002. *National Vital Statistics Reports, 54*(10). Hyattsville MD: National Center for Health Statistics.

Minkler, M., & Fuller-Thomson, E. (2005). African American grandparents raising grandchildren: A national study using the Census 2000 American Community Survey. *Journal of Gerontology: Social Sciences, 60B,* S82–S92.

Minnesota explorer Ann Bancroft. (2002). Minnesota Public Radio. Retrieved February 20, 2002, from http://news.mpr.org/programs/midmorning/

Mintz, T. H. (2005). Linguistic and conceptual influences on adjective acquisition in 24- to 36-month-olds. *Developmental Psychology, 41,* 17–29.

Mischel, W. (1966). A social learning view of sex differences in behavior. In E. Maccoby (Ed.), *The development of sex differences* (pp. 57–81). Stanford, CA: Stanford University Press.

Miserandino, M. (1996). Children who do well in school: Individual differences in perceived competence and autonomy in above-average children. *Journal of Educational Psychology, 88*(2), 203–214.

Mistry, R. S., Vandewater, E. A., Huston, A. C., & McLoyd, V. (2002). Economic well-being and children's social adjustment: The role of family process in an ethnically diverse low income sample. *Child Development, 73,* 935–951.

Mitchell, E. A., Blair, P. S., & L'Hoir, M. P. (2006). Should pacifiers be recommended to prevent sudden infant death syndrome? *Pediatrics, 117,* 1755–1758.

Mix, K. S., Huttenlocher, J., & Levine, S. C. (2002). Multiple cues for quantification in infancy: Is number one of them? *Psychological Bulletin, 128,* 278–294.

Mix, K. S., Levine, S. C., & Huttenlocher, J. (1999). Early fraction calculation ability. *Developmental Psychology, 35,* 164–174.

Miyake, K., Chen, S., & Campos, J. (1985). Infants' temperament, mothers' mode of interaction and attachment in Japan: An interim report. In I. Bretherton & E. Waters (Eds.), *Growing points of attachment theory and research. Monographs of the Society for Research in Child Development, 50*(1–2, Serial No. 109), 276–297.

Mlot, C. (1998). Probing the biology of emotion. *Science, 280,* 1005–1007.

Moffitt, T. E. (1993). Adolescent-limited and life-course persistent antisocial behavior: A developmental taxonomy. *Psychological Review, 100,* 674–701.

Moffitt, T. E., Caspi, A., Belsky, J., & Silva, P. A. (1992). Childhood experience and the onset of menarche: A test of a sociobiological model. *Child Development, 63,* 47–58.

Molina, B. S. G., & Chassin, L. (1996). The parent-adolescent relationship at puberty: Hispanic ethnicity and parent alcoholism as moderators. *Developmental Psychology, 32,* 675–686.

Molina, B. S. G., & Pelham, W. E., Jr. (2003). Childhood predictors of adolescent substance use in a longitudinal study of children with ADHD. *Journal of Abnormal Psychology, 112,* 497–507.

Mondschein, E. R., Adolph, K. E., & Tamis-Lemonda, C. S. (2000). Gender bias in mothers' expectations about infant crawling. *Journal of Experimental Child Psychology. Special Issue on Gender, 77,* 304–316.

Money, J., & Ehrhardt, A. A. (1972). *Man and woman/Boy and girl.* Baltimore, MD: Johns Hopkins University Press.

Money, J., Hampson, J. G., & Hampson, J. L. (1955). Hermaphroditism recommendations concerning assignment of sex, change of sex, and psychotic management. *Bulletin of Johns Hopkins Hospital, 97,* 284–300.

Montague, D. P. F., & Walker-Andrews, A. S. (2001). Peekaboo: A new look at infants' perception of emotion expressions. *Developmental Psychology, 37,* 826–838.

Montaldo, C. (2005). *About death penalty for juveniles.* Retrieved May 5, 2005, from http://crime.about.com/od/juvenile/i/juvenile death 2.htm

Moolchan, E. T., Franken, F. H., & Jaszyna-Gasior, M. (2006). Adolescent nicotine metabolism: Ethnoracial differences among dependent smokers. *Ethnicity and Disease, 16*(1), 239–243.

Moon, C., Cooper, R. P., & Fifer, W. P. (1993). Two-day-olds prefer their native language. *Infant Behavior and Development, 16*, 495–500.

Moon, C., & Fifer, W. P. (1990, April). *Newborns prefer a prenatal version of mother's voice.* Paper presented at the biannual meeting of the International Society of Infant Studies, Montreal, Canada.

Moon, R. Y., Sprague, B. M., & Patel, K. M. (2005). Stable prevalence but changing risk factors for sudden infant death syndrome in child care settings in 2001. *Pediatrics, 116*, 972–977.

Mooney-Somers, J., & Golombok, S. (2000). Children of lesbian mothers: From the 1970s to the new millennium. *Sexual and Relationship Therapy 15*(2), 121–126.

Moore, M. K., & Meltzoff, A. N. (2004). Object permanence after a 24-hr delay and leaving the locale of disappearance: The role of memory, space, and identity. *Developmental Psychology, 40*, 606–620.

Moore, S. E., Cole, T. J., Poskitt, E. M. E., Sonko, B. J., Whitehead, R. G., McGregor, I. A., et al. (1997). Season of birth predicts mortality in rural Gambia. *Nature, 388*, 434.

Morelli, G. A., Rogoff, B., Oppenheim, D., & Goldsmith, D. (1992). Cultural variation in infants' sleeping arrangements: Questions of independence. *Developmental Psychology, 28*, 604–613.

Morgan, B., Maybery, M., & Durkin, K. (2003). Weak central coherence, poor joint attention, and low verbal ability: Independent deficits in early autism. *Developmental Psychology, 39*, 646–656.

Morgan, W. J., Crain, E. F., Gruchalla, R. S., O'Connor, G. T., Kattan, M., Evans, R., et al. for the Inner-City Asthma Study Group. (2004). Results of a home-based environmental intervention among urban children with asthma. *New England Journal of Medicine, 351*, 1068–1080.

Morison, P., & Masten, A. S. (1991). Peer reputation in middle childhood as a predictor of adaptation in adolescence: A seven-year follow-up. *Child Development, 62*, 991–1007.

Morris, R., & Kratochwill, T. (1983). *Treating children's fears and phobias: A behavioral approach.* Elmsford, NY: Pergamon.

Morris, R. D., Stuebing, K. K., Fletcher, J. M., Shaywitz, S. E., Lyon, G. R., Shankweiler, D. P., et al. (1998). Subtypes of reading disability: Variability around a phonological core. *Journal of Educational Psychology, 90*, 347–373.

Morrison, J. A., Friedman, L. A., Harlan, W. R., Harlan, L. C., Barton, B. A., Schreiber, G. B., et al. (2005). Development of the metabolic syndrome in black and white adolescent girls. *Pediatrics, 116*, 1178–1182.

Morse, J. M., & Field, P. A. (1995). *Qualitative research methods for health professionals.* Thousand Oaks, CA: Sage.

Mortensen, E. L., Michaelson, K. F., Sanders, S. A., & Reinisch, J. M. (2002). The association between duration of breastfeeding and adult intelligence. *Journal of the American Medical Association, 287*, 2365–2371.

Mortimer, J. (2003). *Working and growing up in America.* Cambridge, MA: Harvard University Press.

Moses, L. J., Baldwin, D. A., Rosicky, J. G., & Tidball, G. (2001). Evidence for referential understanding in the emotions domain at twelve and eighteen months. *Child Development, 72*, 718–735.

Mosher, W. D., Chandra, A., & Jones, J. (2005). *Sexual behavior and selected health measures: Men and women 15–44 years of age, United States, 2002. Advance data from vital and health statistics; no. 362.* Hyattsville, MD: Centers for Disease Control and Prevention, National Center for Health Statistics.

Mosier, C. E., & Rogoff, B. (2003). Privileged treatment of toddlers: Cultural aspects of individual choice and responsibility. *Developmental Psychology, 39*, 1047–1060.

Moss, E., & St-Laurent, D. (2001). Attachment at school age and academic performance. *Developmental Psychology, 37*, 863–874.

Mounts, N. S., & Steinberg, L. (1995). An ecological analysis of peer influence on adolescent grade point average and drug use. *Developmental Psychology, 31*, 915–922.

Msall, M. S. E. (2004). Developmental vulnerability and resilience in extremely preterm infants. *Journal of the American Medical Association, 292*, 2399–2401.

MTA Cooperative Group. (1999). A 14-month randomized clinical trial of treatment strategies for attention deficit/hyperactivity disorder. *Archives of General Psychiatry, 56*, 1073–1986.

MTA Cooperative Group. (2004a). National Institute of Mental Health multimodal treatment study of ADHD follow-up: Changes in effectiveness and growth after the end of treatment. *Pediatrics, 113*, 762–769.

MTA Cooperative Group. (2004b). National Institute of Mental Health multimodal treatment study of ADHD follow-up: 24-month outcomes of treatment strategies for attention-deficit/hyperactivity disorder. *Pediatrics, 113*, 754–769.

Mullan, D., & Currie, C. (2000). Socioeconomic equalities in adolescent health. In C. Currie, K. Hurrelmann, W. Settertobulte, R. Smith, & J. Todd (Eds.), *Health and health behaviour among young people: A WHO crossnational study (HBSC) international report* (pp. 65–72). WHO Policy Series: Healthy Policy for Children and Adolescents, Series No. 1. Copenhagen, Denmark: World Health Organization Regional Office for Europe.

Müller, M. (1998). *Anne Frank: The biography.* New York: Holt.

Mulrine, A. (2004, February 2). Coming of age in ancient times. *U.S. News & World Report.* Retrieved March 31, 2004, from http://www.usnews.com/usnews/culture/articles/040202/2child.htm

Mumme, D. L., & Fernald, A. (2003). The infant as onlooker: Learning from emotional reactions observed in a television scenario. *Child Development, 74*, 221–237.

Munakata, Y. (2001). Task-dependency in infant behavior: Toward an understanding of the processes underlying cognitive development. In F. Lacerda, C. von Hofsten, & M. Heimann (Eds.), *Emerging cognitive abilities in early infancy.* Hillsdale, NJ: Erlbaum.

Munakata, Y., McClelland, J. L., Johnson, M. J., & Siegler, R. S. (1997). Rethinking infant knowledge: Toward an adaptive process account of successes and failures in object permanence tasks. *Psychological Review, 104*, 686–714.

Munk-Olsen, T., Laursen, T. M., Pedersen, C. B., Mors, O., & Mortensen, P. B. (2006). New parents and mental disorders: A population-based register study. *Journal of the American Medical Association, 296*, 2582–2589.

Munson, M. L., & Sutton, P. D. (2004). Births, marriages, divorces, and deaths: Provisional data for November 2003. *National Vital Statistics Reports, 52*(20). Hyattsville, MD: National Center for Health Statistics.

Muntner, P., He, J., Cutler, J. A., Wildman, R. P., & Whelton, P. K. (2004, May 5). Trends in blood pressure among children and adolescents. *Journal of the American Medical Association, 291*, 2107–2113.

Murachver, T., Pipe, M., Gordon, R., Owens, J. L., & Fivush, R. (1996). Do, show, and tell: Children's event memories acquired through direct experience, observation, and stories. *Child Development, 67*, 3029–3044.

Murchison, C., & Langer, S. (1927). Tiedemann's observations on the development of the mental facilities of children. *Journal of Genetic Psychology, 34*, 204–230.

Muris, P., Merckelbach, H., & Collaris, R. (1997). Common childhood fears and their origins. *Behaviour Research and Therapy, 35*, 929–937.

Murphy, C. M., & Bootzin, R. R. (1973). Active and passive participation in the contact desensitization of snake fear in children. *Behavior Therapy, 4*, 203–211.

Murray, B. (1998, June). Dipping math scores heat up debate over math teaching: Psychologists differ over the merits of teaching children "whole math." *APA Monitor, 29*(6), 34–35.

Murray, M. L., deVries, C. S., & Wong, I. C. K. (2004). A drug utilisation study of anti-depressants in children and adolescents using the General Practice Research data base. *Archives of the Diseases of Children, 89*, 1098–1102.

Mussen, P. H., & Jones, M. C. (1957). Self-conceptions, motivations, and interpersonal attitudes of late- and early-maturing boys. *Child Development, 28*, 243–256.

Must, A., Jacques, P. F., Dallal, G. E., Bajema, C. J., & Dietz, W. H. (1992). Long-term morbidity and mortality of overweight adolescents: A follow-up of the Harvard Growth Study of 1922 to 1935. *New England Journal of Medicine, 327*(19), 1350–1355.

Must, A., Naumova, E. N., Phillips, S. M., Blum, M., Dawson-Hughes, B., & Rand, W. M. (2005). Childhood overweight and maturational timing in the development of adult overweight and fatness: The Newton Girls Study and its follow-up. *Pediatrics, 116*, 620–627.

Mustanski, B. S., DuPree, M. G., Nievergelt, C. M., Bocklandt, S., Schork, N. J., & Hamer, D. H. (2005). A genomewide scan of male sexual orientation. *Human Genetics, 116*, 272–278.

Mustillo, S., Worthman, C., Erkanli, A., Keeler, G., Angold, A., & Costello, E. J. (2003). Obesity and psychiatric disorder: Developmental trajectories. *Pediatrics, 111*, 851–859.

Muter, V., Hulme, C., Snowling, M. J., & Stevenson, J. (2004). Phonemes, rimes, vocabulary, and grammatical skill as foundations of early reading development: Evidence from a longitudinal study. *Developmental Psychology, 40*, 665–681.

Naeye, R. L., & Peters, E. C. (1984). Mental development of children whose mothers smoked during pregnancy. *Obstetrics and Gynecology, 64*, 601.

Nagaoka, J., & Roderick, M. (2004, April). *Ending social promotion: The effects of retention.* Chicago: Consortium on Chicago School Research.

Nagaraja, J., Menkedick, J., Phelan, K. J., Ashley, P., Zhang, X., & Lanphear, B. P. (2005). Deaths from residential injuries in US children and adolescents, 1985–1997. *Pediatrics, 116*, 454–461.

Naito, M., & Miura, H. (2001). Japanese childrens' numerical competencies: Age and school-related influences on the development of number concepts and addition skills. *Developmental Psychology, 37*, 217–230.

Nansel, T. R., Overpeck, M., Pilla, R. S., Ruan, W. J., Simons-Morton, B., & Scheidt, P. (2001). Bullying behaviors among U.S. youth: Prevalence and association with psychosocial adjustment. *Journal of the American Medical Association, 285*, 2094–2100.

Nash, J. M. (1997, February 3). Fertile minds. *Time*, pp. 49–56.

Nash, O. (1957). *You can't get there from here.* New York: Little, Brown.

Nathanielsz, P. W. (1995). The role of basic science in preventing low birth weight. *The Future of Our Children, 5*(1), 57–70.

National Assessment of Educational Progress: The Nation's Report Card. (2004). *America's charter schools: Results from the NAEP 2003 Pilot Study* (NCES 2005-456). Jessup, MD: U.S. Department of Education.

National Association for Gifted Children (NAGC). (undated). *Frequently asked questions.* Retrieved April 22, 2006, from http://www.nagc.org/index.aspx?id=548

National Association of State Boards of Education. (2000). *Fit, healthy, and ready to learn: A school health policy guide.* Alexandria, VA: Author.

National Center for Education Statistics (NCES). (2001). *The condition of education 2001* (Publication No. 2001–072). Washington, DC: U.S. Government Printing Office.

National Center for Education Statistics (NCES). (2003). *The condition of education, 2003* (Publication No. 2003–067). Washington, DC: Author.

National Center for Education Statistics (NCES). (2004a). *The condition of education 2004* (NCES 2004–077). Washington, DC: U.S. Government Printing Office.

National Center for Education Statistics (NCES). (2004b). *National assessment of educational progress: The nation's report card. Mathematics highlights 2003* (NCES 2004–451). Washington, DC: U.S. Department of Education.

National Center for Education Statistics (NCES). (2004c). *National assessment of educational progress: The nation's report card. Reading highlights 2003* (NCES 2004–452). Washington, DC: U.S. Department of Education.

National Center for Education Statistics (NCES). (2005a). *Children born in 2001—First results from the base year of Early Childhood Longitudinal Study, Birth Cohort* (ECLS-B). Retrieved November 19, 2004, from http://nces. ed.gov/pubs2005/children/index.asp

National Center for Education Statistics (NCES). (2005b). *The condition of education 2005* (NCES 2005-094). Washington, DC: U.S. Government Printing Office.

National Center for Education Statistics (NCES). (2006). *Calories in, calories out: Food and exercise in public elementary schools, 2005* (NCES 2006-057). Washington, DC: Author.

National Center for Health Statistics (NCHS). (1999). Abstract adapted from *Births: Final data for 1999* by Mid Atlantic Parents of Multiples. Retrieved March 7, 2006, from http://www.orgsites.com/va/mapom/_pgg1.php3

National Center for Health Statistics (NCHS). (2004). *Health, United States, 2004 with chart-book on trends in the health of Americans* (DHHS Publication No. 2004-1232). Hyattsville, MD: National Center for Health Statistics.

National Center for Health Statistics (NCHS). (2005). *Health, United States, 2005* (DHHS Publication No. 2005-1232). Hyattsville, MD: Author.

National Center for Injury Prevention and Control (NCIPC). (2001). *2001 United States suicide: Ages 15–19, all races, both sexes* (Web-based injury statistics query and reporting system). Retrieved May 2, 2004, from http://www.cdc.gov/ncipc

National Center for Injury Prevention and Control (NCIPC). (2004). *Fact sheet: Teen drivers.* Retrieved May 7, 2004, from http://www.cdc.gov/ncip

National Center for Learning Disabilities. (2004a). *Dyslexia: Learning disabilities in reading.* Fact sheet.Retrieved May 30, 2004, from http://www.ld.org/LDInfoZone/InfoZone_ FactSheet_Dyslexia.cfm

National Center for Learning Disabilities. (2004b). *LD at a glance.* Fact sheet. Retrieved May 30, 2004, from http://www.ld.org/LDInfoZone/InfoZone_ FactSheet_LD.cfm

National Center on Shaken Baby Syndrome. (2000). *SBS questions.* Retrieved from http://www.dontshake.com/sbsquestions.html

National Children's Study. (2004, November 16). *National Children's Study releases study plan and locations.* Retrieved April 3, 2005, from http://www.nationalchild-rensstudy.gov/research/study plan/index.cfm

National Clearinghouse on Child Abuse and Neglect Information (NCCANI). (2004). *Long-term consequences of child abuse and neglect.* Washington, DC: Retrieved October, 5, 2004, from http://nccanch.acf.hhs.gov/pubs/factsheets/long term consequences.cfm

National Coalition for the Homeless. (2004, May). *Who is homeless?* NCH Fact Sheet 3. Washington, DC: Author.

National Commission for the Protection of Human Subjects of Biomedical and Behavioral Research. (1978). *Report.* Washington, DC: Author.

National Council of Teachers of Mathematics (NCTM). (2006). *Curriculum focal points for prekindergarten through grade 8 mathematics.* Reston, VA: Author.

National Enuresis Society. (1995). *Enuresis.* [Fact sheet].

National High Blood Pressure Education Program Working Group on High Blood Pressure in Children and Adolescents. (2004). The fourth report on the diagnosis, evaluation, and treatment of high blood pressure in children and adolescents. *Pediatrics, 114*(2, Supp.), 555–576.

National Highway Traffic Safety Administration. (2003). *Traffic safety facts 2002: Young drivers.* Washington, DC: Author.

National Institute of Mental Health (NIMH). (1999, April). *Suicide facts.* Washington, DC: Author. Retrieved from http://www.nimh.nih.gov/research/suifact.htm

National Institute of Mental Health (NIMH). (2001a). *Helping children and adolescents cope with violence and disasters: Fact sheet* (NIH Publication No. 01-3518). Bethesda, MD: Author.

National Institute of Mental Health (NIMH). (2001b). *Teenage brain: A work in progress.* Retrieved March 11, 2004, from http://www.nimh.gov/publicat/teenbrain.cfm

National Institute of Neurological Disorders and Stroke (NINDS). (2006, January 25). NINDS *Shaken baby syndrome information page.* Retrieved June 20, 2006, from http://www.ninds.nih.gov/disorders/shakenbaby/shakenbaby.htm

National Institute of Neurological Disorders and Stroke (NINDS). (2007). *Asperger syndrome information page.* Retrieved May 24, 2007, from http://www.ninds.nih.gov/disorders/asperger/asperger.htm

National Institute on Drug Abuse (NIDA). (1996). *Monitoring the future.* Washington, DC: National Institutes of Health.

National Institutes of Health Consensus Development Panel. (2001). *National Institutes of Health Consensus Development conference statement: Phenylketonuria screening and management. October 16–18, 2000. Pediatrics, 108*(4), 972–982.

National Library of Medicine. (2003). *Medical encyclopedia: Conduct disorder.* Retrieved April 23, 2005, from http://www.nlm.nih.gov/medlineplus/ency/article/000919.htm

National Library of Medicine. (2004). *Medical encyclopedia: Oppositional defiant disorder.* Retrieved April 23, 2005, from http://www.nlm.nih.gov/medlineplus/ency/article/001537.htm

National Parents' Resource Institute for Drug Education. (1999, September 8). *PRIDE surveys, 1998–99 national summary: Grades 6–12.* Bowling Green, KY: Author.

National Reading Panel. (2000). *Report of the National Reading Panel: Teaching children to read: An evidence-based assessment of the scientific research literature on reading and its implications for reading instruction: Reports of the subgroups.* Washington, DC: National Institute of Child Health and Human Development.

National Research Council (NRC). (1993a). *Losing generations: Adolescents in high risk settings.* Washington, DC: National Academy Press.

National Research Council (NRC). (1993b). *Understanding child abuse and neglect.* Washington, DC: National Academy Press.

National Sleep Foundation. (2004). *Sleep in America.* Washington, DC: Author.

National Survey on Drug Use and Health (NSDUH). (2005, December 30). *Depression among adolescents. The NSDUH Report.* Rockville, MD: Office of Applied Statistics, Substance Abuse and Mental Health Services, U. S. Department of Health and Human Services.

National Survey on Drug Use and Health (NSDUH). (2006a). *Academic performance and substance use among students aged 12 to 17: 2002, 2003, and 2004. The NSDUH Report (Issue 18).* Rockville, MD: Office of Applied Statistics, Substance Abuse and Mental Health Services, U. S. Department of Health and Human Services.

National Survey on Drug Use and Health (NSDUH). (2006b). *Substance use treatment need among adolescents: 2003–2004. The NSDUH Report (Issue 24).* Rockville, MD: Office of Applied Statistics, Substance Abuse and Mental Health Services, U. S. Department of Health and Human Services.

Nef, S., Verma-Kurvari, S., Merenmies, J., Vassallt, J.-D., Efstratiadis, A., Accili, D., et al. (2003). Testis determination requires insulin receptor family function in mice. *Nature, 426,* 291–295.

Neisser, U., Boodoo, G., Bouchard, T. J., Jr., Boykin, A. W., Brody, N., Ceci, S. J., et al. (1996). Intelligence: Knowns and unknowns. *American Psychologist, 51*(2), 77–101.

Neitzel, C., & Stright, A. D. (2003). Relations between parents' scaffolding and children's academic self-regulation: Establishing a foundation of self-regulatory competence. *Journal of Family Psychology, 17,* 147–159.

Nelson, C. A. (1995). The ontogeny of human memory: A cognitive neuroscience perspective. *Developmental Psychology, 31,* 723–738.

Nelson, C. A., Monk, C. S., Lin, J., Carver, L. J., Thomas, K. M., & Truwit, C. L. (2000). Functional neuroanatomy of spatial working memory in children. *Developmental Psychology, 36,* 109–116.

Nelson, K. (1992). Emergence of autobiographical memory at age 4. *Human Development, 35,* 172–177.

Nelson, K. (1993a). Events, narrative, memory: What develops? In C. Nelson (Ed.), *Memory and affect in development: The Minnesota Symposia on Child Psychology* (Vol. 26, pp. 1–24). Hillsdale, NJ: Erlbaum.

Nelson, K. (1993b). The psychological and social origins of autobiographical memory. *Psychological Science, 47,* 7–14.

Nelson, K. (2005). Evolution and development of human memory systems. In B. J. Ellis & D. F. Bjorklund (Eds.), *Origins of the social mind: Evolutionary psychology and child development* (pp. 319–345). New York: Guilford.

Nelson, K. B., Dambrosia, J. M., Ting, T. Y., & Grether, J. K. (1996). Uncertain value of electronic fetal monitoring in predicting cerebral palsy. *New England Journal of Medicine, 334,* 613–618.

Nelson, L. J. (2003). Rites of passage in emerging adulthood: Perspectives of young Mormons. In J. J. Arnett & N. L. Galambos (Eds.), *Exploring cultural conceptions of the transition to adulthood. New Directions for Child and Adolescent Development, 100,* 33–49.

Nelson, L. J., & Marshall, M. F. (1998). *Ethical and legal analyses of three coercive policies aimed at substance abuse by pregnant women.* Report published by the Robert Wood Johnson Substance Abuse Policy Research Foundation.

Nelson, M. C., & Gordon-Larsen, P. (2006). Physical activity and sedentary behavior patterns are associated with selected adolescent risk behaviors. *Pediatrics, 117,* 1281–1290.

Netherlands State Institute for War Documentation. (1989). *The diary of Anne Frank: The critical edition* (D. Barnouw & G. van der Stroom, Eds.; A. J. Pomerans & B. M. Mooyaart-Doubleday, Trans.). New York: Doubleday.

Neugebauer, R., Hoek, H. W., & Susser, E. (1999). Prenatal exposure to wartime famine and development of antisocial personality disorder in early adulthood. *Journal of the American Medical Association, 282,* 455–462.

Neville, A. (undated). *The emotional and psychological effects of miscarriage.* Retrieved April 9, 2006, from http://www.opendoors.com.au/EffectsMiscarriage/EffectsMiscarriage.htm

Neville, H. J., & Bavelier, D. (1998). Neural organization and plasticity of language. *Current Opinion in Neurobiology, 8*(2), 254–258.

Newacheck, P. W., & Halfon, N. (2000). Prevalence, impact, and trends in childhood disability due to asthma. *Archives of Pediatrics and Adolescent Medicine, 154,* 287–293.

Newacheck, P. W., Stoddard, J. J., & McManus, M. (1993). Ethnocultural variations in the prevalence and impact of childhood chronic conditions. *Pediatrics, 91,* 1031–1047.

Newacheck, P. W., Strickland, B., Shonkoff, J. P., Perrin, J. M., McPherson, M., McManus, M., et al. (1998). An epidemiologic profile of children with special health care needs. *Pediatrics, 102,* 117–123.

Newcomb, A. F., & Bagwell, C. L. (1995). Children's friendship relations: A meta-analytic review. *Psychological Bulletin, 117*(2), 306–347.

Newcomb, A. F., Bukowski, W. M., & Pattee, L. (1993). Children's peer relations: A meta-analytic review of popular, rejected, neglected, controversial, and average sociometric status. *Psychological Bulletin, 113,* 99–128.

Newman, A. J., Bavelier, D., Corina, D., Jezzard, P., & Neville, H. J. (2002). A critical period for right hemisphere recruitment in American Sign Language processing. *Nature Neuroscience, 5*(1), 76–80.

Newman, D. L., Caspi, A., Moffitt, T. E., & Silva, P. A. (1997). Antecedents of adult interpersonal functioning: Effects of individual differences in age 3 temperament. *Developmental Psychology, 33,* 206–217.

Newman, R. S. (2005). The cocktail party effect in infants revisited: Listening to one's name in noise. *Developmental Psychology, 41*, 352–362.

Newport, E. L. (1991). Contrasting conceptions of the critical period for language. In S. Carey & R. Gelman (Eds.), *The epigenesis of mind: Essays on biology and cognition.* Hillsdale, NJ: Erlbaum.

Newport, E. L., Bavelier, D., & Neville, H. J. (2001). Critical thinking about critical periods: Perspectives on a critical period for language acquisition. In E. Dupoux (Ed.), *Language, brain, and cognitive development: Essays in honor of Jacques Mehler* (pp. 481–502). Cambridge, MA: The MIT Press.

Newport, E., & Meier, R. (1985). The acquisition of American Sign Language. In D. Slobin (Ed.), *The crosslinguistic study of language acquisition* (Vol. 1, pp. 881–938). Hillsdale, NJ: Erlbaum.

Newschaffer, C. J., Falb, M. D., & Gurney, J. G. (2005). National autism prevalence trends from United States special education data. *Pediatrics, 115*, e277–e282.

NICHD Early Child Care Research Network. (1996). Characteristics of infant child care: Factors contributing to positive caregiving. *Early Childhood Research Quarterly, 11*, 269–306.

NICHD Early Child Care Research Network. (1997). The effects of infant child care on infant-mother attachment security: Results of the NICHD study of early child care. *Child Development, 68*, 860–879.

NICHD Early Child Care Research Network. (1998a). Early child care and self-control, compliance and problem behavior at 24 and 36 months. *Child Development, 69*, 1145–1170.

NICHD Early Child Care Research Network. (1998b). Relations between family predictors and child outcomes: Are they weaker for children in child care? *Developmental Psychology, 34*, 1119–1127.

NICHD Early Child Care Research Network. (1998c, November). *When childcare classrooms meet recommended guidelines for quality.* Paper presented at the meeting of the National Association for the Education of Young People.

NICHD Early Child Care Research Network. (1999a). Child outcomes when child care center classes meet recommended standards for quality. *American Journal of Public Health, 89*, 1072–1077.

NICHD Early Child Care Research Network. (1999b). Chronicity of maternal depressive symptoms, maternal sensitivity, and child functioning at 36 months. *Developmental Psychology, 35*, 1297–1310.

NICHD Early Child Care Research Network. (2000). The relation of child care to cognitive and language development. *Child Development, 71*, 960–980.

NICHD Early Child Care Research Network. (2001a). Child care and children's peer interaction at 24 and 36 months: The NICHD Study of Early Child Care. *Child Development, 72*, 1478–1500.

NICHD Early Child Care Research Network. (2001b). Child-care and family predictors of preschool attachment and stability from infancy. *Developmental Psychology, 37*, 847–862.

NICHD Early Child Care Research Network. (2002). Child-care structure "process" outcome: Direct and indirect effects of child-care quality on young children's development. *Psychological Science, 13*, 199–206.

NICHD Early Child Care Research Network. (2003). Does amount of time spent in child care predict socioemotional adjustment during the transition to kindergarten? *Child Development, 74*, 976–1005.

NICHD Early Child Care Research Network (2004a). Are child developmental outcomes related to before- and afterschool care arrangement? Results from the NICHD Study of Early Child Care. *Child Development 75*, 280–295.

NICHD Early Child Care Research Network. (2004b). Does class size in first grade relate to children's academic and social performance or observed classroom processes? *Developmental Psychology, 40*, 651–664.

NICHD Early Child Care Research Network. (2005a). Duration and developmental timing of poverty and children's cognitive and social development from birth through third grade. *Child Development, 76*, 795–810.

NICHD Early Child Care Research Network. (2005b). Early child care and children's development in the primary grades: Follow-up results from the NICHD study of early child care. *American Educational Research Journal, 42*(3), 537–570.

NICHD Early Child Care Research Network. (2005c). Predicting individual differences in attention, memory, and planning in first graders from experiences at home, child care, and school. *Developmental Psychology, 41*, 99–114.

NICHD Early Child Care Research Network. (2005d). Pathways to reading: The role of oral language in the transition to reading. *Developmental Psychology, 41*, 428–442.

NICHD Early Child Care Research Network. (2006a). Child-care effect sizes for the NICHD study of early child care and youth development. *American Psychologist, 61*, 99–116.

NICHD Early Child Care Research Network. (2006b). Infant-mother attachment classification: Risk and protection in relation to changing maternal caregiving quality. *Developmental Psychology, 42*, 38–58.

NICHD Early Child Care Research Network & Duncan, G. J. (2003). Modeling the impacts of child care quality on children's preschool cognitive development. *Child Development, 74*, 1454–1475.

Nielsen, K., McSherry, G., Petru, A., Frederick, T., Wara, D., Bryson, Y., et al. (1997). A descriptive survey of pediatric human immunodeficiency virus-infected, long-term survivors. *Pediatrics, 99.* Retrieved from http://www.pediatrics.org/cgi/content/full/99/4/e4

Nielsen, M., Dissanayake, C., & Kashima, Y. (2003). A longitudinal investigation of self-other discrimination and the emergence of mirror self-recognition. *Infant Behavior* and *Development, 26*, 213–226.

Nielsen, M., Suddendorf, T., & Slaughter, V. (2006). Mirror self-recognition beyond the face. *Child Development, 77*, 176–185.

Nin, A. (1971). *The diaries of Anaïs Nin* (Vol. 4). New York: Harcourt.

Nisan, M., & Kohlberg, L. (1982). Universality and variation in moral judgment: A longitudinal and cross sectional study in Turkey. *Child Development, 53*, 865–876.

Nisbett, R. E. (1998). Race, genetics, and IQ. In C. Jencks & M. Phillips (Eds.), *The Black-White test score gap* (pp. 86–102). Washington, DC: Brookings Institution.

Nisbett, R. E. (2005). Heredity, environment, and race differences in IQ: A commentary on Rushton and Jensen (2005). *Psychology, Public Policy, and Law, 11*, 302–310.

Niskar, A. S., Kieszak, S. M., Holmes, A., Esteban, E., Rubin, C., & Brody D. J. (1998). Prevalence of hearing loss among children 6 to 19 years of age: The Third National Health and Nutrition Examination Survey. *Journal of the American Medical Association, 279*, 1071–1075.

Nissen, S. E. (2006). ADHD drugs and cardiovascular risk. *New England Journal of Medicine, 354*, 1445–1448.

Nitschke, M., Pilotto, L. S., Attewell, R. G., Smith, B. J., Pisaniello, D., Martin, J., et al. (2006). Cohort study of indoor nitrogen dioxide and house dust mite exposure in asthmatic children. *Journal of Occupational and Environmental Medicine, 48*(5), 462–469.

Nix, R. L., Pinderhughes, E. E., Dodge, K. A., Bates, J. E., Pettit, G. S., & McFadyen-Ketchum, S. A. (1999). The relation between mothers' hostile attribution tendencies and children's externalizing behavior problems: The mediating role of mothers' harsh discipline practices. *Child Development, 70*(4), 896–909.

Nobre, A. C., & Plunkett, K. (1997). The neural system of language: Structure and development. *Current Opinion in Neurobiology, 7*, 262–268.

Noirot, E., & Algeria, J. (1983). Neonate orientation towards human voice differs with type of feeding. *Behavioral Processes, 8*, 65–71.

Noone, K. (2000). Ann Bancroft, polar explorer. *My Prime Time.* Retrieved April 4, 2002, from http://www.myprimetime.com/misc/bae_abpro/index.shtml

Norwitz, E. R., Schust, D. J., & Fisher, S. J. (2001). Implantation and the survival of early pregnancy. *New England Journal of Medicine, 345*(19), 1400–1408.

Notzon, F. C. (1990). International differences in the use of obstetric interventions. *Journal of the American Medical Association, 263*(24), 3286–3291.

Nourot, P. M. (1998). Sociodramatic play: Pretending together. In D. P. Fromberg & D. Bergen (Eds.), *Play from birth to twelve and beyond: Contexts, perspectives, and meanings* (pp. 378–391). New York: Garland.

Nozyce, M., Hittelman, J., Muenz, L., Durako, S. J., Fischer, M. L., & Willoughby, A. (1994). Effect of perinatally acquired human immunodeficiency virus infection on neurodevelopment in children during the first two years of life. *Pediatrics, 94,* 883–891.

Nucci, L., Hasebe, Y., & Lins-Dyer, M. T. (2005). Adolescent psychological well-being and parental control. In J. Smetana (Ed.), *Changing boundaries of parental authority during adolescence: New directions for child and adolescent development, 108,* 17–30.

Nugent, J. K., Keefer, C., O'Brien, S., Johnson, L., & Blanchard, Y. (2005). *The Newborn Behavioral Observation System.* Boston: Brazelton Institute, Children's Hospital.

Nugent, J. K., Lester, B. M., Greene, S. M., Wieczorek-Deering, D., & O'Mahony, P. (1996). The effects of maternal alcohol consumption and cigarette smoking during pregnancy on acoustic cry analysis. *Child Development, 67,* 1806–1815.

Nugent, T. (1999, September). At risk: 4 million students with asthma: Quick access to rescue inhalers critical for schoolchildren. *AAP News, 1,* 10.

Oakes, L. M. (1994). Development of infants' use of continuity cues in their perception of causality. *Developmental Psychology, 30,* 869–879.

Oakes, L. M., Coppage, D. J., & Dingel, A. (1997). By land or by sea: The role of perceptual similarity in infants' categorization of animals. *Developmental Psychology, 33,* 396–407.

O'Brien, C. M., & Jeffery, H. E. (2002). Sleep deprivation, disorganization and fragmentation during opiate withdrawal in newborns. *Pediatric Child Health, 38,* 66–71.

Ochsner, K. N., & Lieberman, M. D. (2001). The emergence of social cognitive neuroscience. *American Psychologist, 56,* 717–734.

O'Connor, T., Heron, J., Golding, J., Beveridge, M., & Glover, V. (2002). Maternal antenatal anxiety and children's behavioural/emotional problems at 4 years. *British Journal of Psychiatry, 180,* 502–508.

Offer, D., & Church, R. B. (1991). Generation gap. In R. M. Lerner, A. C. Petersen, & J. Brooks-Gunn (Eds.), *Encyclopedia of adolescence* (pp. 397–399). New York: Garland.

Offer, D., Kaiz, M., Ostrov, E., & Albert, D. B. (2002). Continuity in family constellation. *Adolescent and Family Health, 3,* 3–8.

Offer, D., Offer, M. K., & Ostrov, E. (2004). *Regular guys: 34 years beyond adolescence.* Dordrecht, Netherlands: Kluwer Academic.

Offer, D., Ostrov, E., & Howard, K. I. (1989). Adolescence: What is normal? *American Journal of Diseases of Children, 143,* 731–736.

Offer, D., Ostrov, E., Howard, K. I., & Atkinson, R. (1988). *The teenage world: Adolescents' self-image in ten countries.* New York: Plenum.

Offer, D., & Schonert-Reichl, K. A. (1992). Debunking the myths of adolescence: Findings from recent research. *Journal of the American Academy of Child and Adolescent Psychiatry, 31,* 1003–1014.

Office on Smoking and Health, Centers for Disease Control and Prevention. (2006). *The health consequences of involuntary exposure to tobacco smoke: A report of the surgeon-general* (No. 017-024-01685-3). Washington, DC: U. S. Department of Health and Human Services.

Offit, P. A., Quarles, J., Gerber, M. A., Hackett, C. J., Marcuse, E. K., Kollman, T. R., et al. (2002). Addressing parents' concerns: Do multiple vaccines overwhelm or weaken the infant's immune system? *Pediatrics, 109,* 124–129.

Ofori, B., Oraichi, D., Blais, L., Rey, E., & Berard, A. (2006). Risk of congenital anomalies in pregnant users of non-steroidal anti-inflammatory drugs: A nested case-control study. *Birth Defects Research: Part B. Developmental and Reproductive Toxicology, 77*(4), 268–279.

Ogden, C. L., Carroll, M. D., Curtin, L. R., McDowell, M. A., Tabak, C. J., & Flegal, K. M. (2006). Prevalence of overweight and obesity in the United States, 1999–2004. *Journal of the American Medical Association, 295,* 1549–1555.

Ogden, C. L., Fryar, C. D., Carroll, M. D., & Flegal, K. M. (2004). Mean body weight, height, and body mass index, United States 1960–2002. Advance data from *Vital and Health Statistics,* No. 347. Hyattsville, MD: National Center for Health Statistics.

Ojito, M. (2003, July 28). A writer's heartbeats answer two calls. *New York Times,* p. E1.

Oken, E., Wright, R. O., Kleinman, K. P., Bellinger, D., Amarasiriwardena, C. J., Hu, H., et al. (2005). Maternal fish consumption, hair mercury, and infant cognition in a U.S. cohort. *Environmental Health Perspectives, 113*(10), 1376–1380.

Olds, D. L., Henderson, C. R., & Tatelbaum, R. (1994a). Intellectual impairment in children of women who smoke cigarettes during pregnancy. *Pediatrics, 93,* 221–227.

Olds, D. L., Henderson, C. R., & Tatelbaum, R. (1994b). Prevention of intellectual impairment in children of women who smoke cigarettes during pregnancy. *Pediatrics, 93,* 228–233.

Olds, S. W. (1989). *The working parents' survival guide.* Rocklin, CA: Prima.

Olds, S. W. (2002). *A balcony in Nepal: Glimpses of a Himalayan village.* Lincoln, NE: ASJA Books, an imprint of iUniverse.

Olfson, M., Blanco, C., Liu, L., Moreno, C., & Laje, G. (2006). National trends in the outpatient treatment of children and adolescents with antipsychotic drugs. *Archives of General Psychiatry, 63,* 679–685.

Oliver, B. R., Dale, P. S., & Plomin, R. (2005). Predicting literacy at age 7 from preliteracy at age 4: A longitudinal genetic analysis. *Psychological Science, 16,* 861–865.

Ollendick, T. H., Yang, B., King, N. J., Dong, Q., & Akande, A. (1996). Fears in American, Australian, Chinese, and Nigerian children and adolescents: A crosscultural study. *Journal of Child Psychology and Psychiatry, 37,* 213–220.

Olthof, T., Schouten, A., Kuiper, H., Stegge, H., & Jennekens-Schinkel, A. (2000). Shame and guilt in children: Differential situational antecedents and experiential correlates. *British Journal of Developmental Psychology, 18,* 51–64.

Olweus, D. (1995). Bullying or peer abuse at school: Facts and intervention. *Current Directions in Psychological Science, 4,* 196–200.

Opdal, S. H., & Rognum, T. O. (2004). The sudden infant death syndrome gene: Does it exist? *Pediatrics, 114,* e506–e512.

O'Rahilly, S. (1998). Life without leptin. *Nature, 392,* 330–331.

Orenstein, P. (2002, April 21). *Mourning my miscarriage.* Retrieved from http://newyorktimes.com

Organization for Economic Cooperation and Development (OECD). (2004). Education at a glance: OECD indicators—2004. *Education and Skills, 2004*(14), 1–456.

Orr, D. P., & Ingersoll, G. M. (1995). The contribution of level of cognitive complexity and pubertal timing behavioral risk in young adolescents. *Pediatrics, 95*(4), 528–533.

Oshima-Takane, Y., Goodz, E., & Derevensky, J. L. (1996). Birth order effects on early language development: Do secondborn children learn from overheard speech? *Child Development, 67,* 621–634.

Ossorio, P., & Duster, T. (2005). Race and genetics: Controversies in biomedical, behavioral, and forensic sciences. *American Psychologist, 60,* 115–128.

Owen, C. G., Martin, R. M., Whincup, P. H., Smith, G. D., & Cook, D. G. (2005). Effects of infant feeding on the risk of obesity across the life course: A quantitative review of published evidence. *Pediatrics, 115,* 1367–1377.

Owen, C. G., Whincup, P. H., Odoki, K., Gilg, J. A., & Cook, D. G. (2002). Infant feeding and blood cholesterol: A study in adolescents and a systematic review. *Pediatrics, 110,* 597–608.

Owens, J., Maxim, R., McGuinn, M., Nobile, C., Msall, M., & Alario, A. (1999). Television-viewing habits and sleep disturbances in school children. *Pediatrics, 104*(3), e27.

Owens, J., Spirito, A., McGuinn, N., & Nobile, C. (2000). Sleep habits and sleep disturbance in elementary school children. *Developmental and Behavioral Pediatrics, 21,* 27-36.

Owens, R. E. (1996). *Language development* (4th ed.). Boston: Allyn & Bacon.

Ozick, C. (2003, June 16 & 23). What Helen Keller saw: The making of a writer. *New Yorker,* pp. 188–196.

Padden, C. A. (1996). Early bilingual lives of deaf children. In I. Parasnis (Ed.), *Cultural and language diversity and the deaf experience* (pp. 99–116). New York: Cambridge University Press.

Padilla, A. M., Lindholm, K. J., Chen, A., Duran, R., Hakuta, K., Lambert, W., et al. (1991). The English-only movement: Myths, reality, and implications for psychology. *American Psychologist, 46*(2), 120–130.

Palella, F. J., Delaney, K. M., Moorman, A. C., Loveless, M. O., Fuhrer, J., Satten, G. A., et al., & the HIV Outpatient Study investigators. (1998). Declining morbidity and mortality among patients with advanced human immunodeficiency virus infection. *New England Journal of Medicine, 358,* 853–860.

Palkovitz, R. (1985). Fathers' birth attendance, early contact, and extended contact with their newborns: A critical review. *Child Development, 56,* 392–406.

Palmer, J. R., Wise, L. A., Hatch, E. E., Troisi, R., Titus-Ernstoff, L., Strohsnitter, W., et al. (2006). Prenatal diethylstilbestrol exposure and risk of breast cancer. *Cancer Epidemiology, Biomarkers and Prevention: A Publication of the American Association for Cancer Research, Cosponsored by the American Society of Preventive Oncology, 15*(8), 1509–1514.

Pan, B. A., Rowe, M. L., Singer, J. D., & Snow, C. E. (2005). Maternal correlates of growth in toddler vocabulary production in low-income families. *Child Development, 76,* 763–782.

Panigrahy, A., Filiano, J., Sleeper, L. A., Mandell, F., Valdes-Dapena, M., Krous, H. F., et al. (2000). Decreased serotonergic receptor binding in rhombic lip-derived regions of the medulla oblongata in the sudden infant death syndrome. *Journal of Neuropathology and Experimental Neurology, 59,* 377–384.

Papalia, D. (1972). The status of several conservation abilities across the lifespan. *Human Development, 15,* 229–243.

Park, S., Belsky, J., Putnam, S., & Crnic, K. (1997). Infant emotionality, parenting, and 3-year inhibition: Exploring stability and lawful discontinuity in a male sample. *Developmental Psychology, 33,* 218–227.

Parke, R. D. (2004). The Society for Research in Child Development at 70: Progress and promise. *Child Development, 75,* 1–24.

Parke, R. D., & Buriel, R. (1998). Socialization in the family: Ethnic and ecological perspectives. In W. Damon (Series Ed.) & N. Eisenberg (Vol. Ed.), *Handbook of child psychology: Vol. 3. Social, emotional, and personality development* (5th ed., pp. 463–552). New York: Wiley.

Parke, R. D., Grossman, K., & Tinsley, R. (1981). Father-mother-infant interaction in the newborn period: A German-American comparison. In T. M. Field, A. M. Sostek, P. Viete, & P. H. Leideman (Eds.), *Culture and early interaction.* Hillsdale, NJ: Erlbaum.

Parke, R. D., Ornstein, P. A., Rieser, J. J., & Zahn-Waxler, C. (1994). The past as prologue: An overview of a century of developmental psychology. In R. D. Parke, P. A. Ornstein, J. J. Rieser, & C. Zahn-Waxler (Eds.), *A century of developmental psychology* (pp. 1–70). Washington, DC: American Psychological Association.

Parker, J. D., Woodruff, T. J., Basu, R., & Schoendorf, K. C. (2005). Air pollution and birth weight among term infants in California. *Pediatrics, 115,* 121–128.

Parker, L., Pearce, M. S., Dickinson, H. O., Aitkin, M., & Craft, A. W. (1999). Stillbirths among offspring of male radiation workers at Sellafield Nuclear Reprocessing Plant. *Lancet, 354,* 1407–1414.

Parten, M. B. (1932). Social play among preschool children. *Journal of Abnormal and Social Psychology, 27,* 243–269.

Patenaude, A. F., Guttmacher, A. E., & Collins, F. S. (2002). Genetic testing and psychology: New roles, new responsibilities. *American Psychologist, 57,* 271–282.

Paterson, D. S., Trachtenberg, F. L., Thompson, E. G., Belliveau, R. A., Beggs, A. H., Darnell, R., et al. (2006). Multiple serotogenic brainstem abnormalities in sudden infant death syndrome. *Journal of the American Medical Association, 296,* 2124–2132.

Patrick, K., Norman, G. J., Calfas, K. J., Sallis, J. F., Zabinski, M. F., Rupp, J., et al. (2004). Diet, physical activity, and sedentary behaviors as risk factors for overweight in adolescence. *Archives of Pediatric Adolescent Medicine, 158,* 385–390.

Patterson, C. J. (1992). Children of lesbian and gay parents. *Child Development, 63,* 1025–1042.

Patterson, C. J. (1995a). Lesbian mothers, gay fathers, and their children. In A. R. D'Augelli & C. J. Patterson (Eds.), *Lesbian, gay, and bisexual identities over the lifespan: Psychological perspectives* (pp. 293–320). New York: Oxford University Press.

Patterson, C. J. (1995b). Sexual orientation and human development: An overview. *Developmental Psychology, 31,* 3–11.

Patterson, G. R., DeBaryshe, B. D., & Ramsey, E. (1989). A developmental perspective on antisocial behavior. *American Psychologist, 44*(2), 329–335.

Pauen, S. (2002). Evidence for knowledge-based category discrimination in infancy. *Child Development, 73,* 1016–1033.

Paus, T., Zijdenbos, A., Worsley, K., Collins, D. L., Blumenthal, J., Giedd, J. N., et al. (1999). Structural maturation of neural pathways in children and adolescents: In vivo study. *Science, 283,* 1908–1911.

Pawelski, J. G., Perrin, E. C., Foy, J. M., Allen, C. E., Crawford, J. E., Del Monte, M., et al. (2006). The effects of marriage, civil union, and domestic partnership laws on the health and well-being of children. *Pediatrics, 118,* 349–364.

Pearce, M. J., Jones, S. M., Schwab-Stone, M. E., & Ruchkin, V. (2003). The protective effects of religiousness and parent involvement on the development of conduct problems among youth exposed to violence. *Child Development, 74,* 1682–1696.

Peirce, C. S. (1931). In C. Hartshorne, P. Weiss, & A. Burks (Eds.), *The collected papers of Charles Sanders Peirce.* Cambridge, MA: Harvard University Press.

Pellegrini, A. D., & Archer, J. (2005). Sex differences in competitive and aggressive behavior: A view from sexual selection theory. In B. J. Ellis & D. F. Bjorklund (Eds.), *Origins of the social mind: Evolutionary psychology and child development* (pp. 219–244). New York: Guilford.

Pellegrini, A. D., & Gustafson, K. (2005). Boys' and girls' uses of objects for exploration, play, and tools in early childhood. In A. D. Pellegrini & P. K. Smith (Eds.), *The nature of play* (pp. 113–135). New York: Guilford.

Pellegrini, A. D., Kato, K., Blatchford, P., & Baines, E. (2002). A short-term longitudinal study of children's playground games across the first year of school: Implications for social competence and adjustment to school. *American Educational Research Journal, 39,* 991–1015.

Pellegrini, A. D., & Long, J. D. (2002). A longitudinal study of bullying, dominance, and victimization during the transition from primary school through secondary school. *British Journal of Developmental Psychology, 20,* 259–280.

Pennington, B. F., Moon, J., Edgin, J., Stedron, J., & Nadel, L. (2003). The neuropsychology of Down Syndrome: Evidence for hippocampal dysfunction. *Child Development, 74,* 75–93.

Pepper, S. C. (1942/1961). *World hypotheses.* Berkeley: University of California Press.

Perera, F. P., Rauh, V., Whyatt, R. M., Tsai, W.-Y., Bernert, J. T., Tu, Y.-H., et al. (2004). Molecular evidence of an interaction between prenatal environmental exposures and birth outcomes in a multiethnic population. *Environmental Health Perspectives, 112,* 626–630.

Perera, V. (1995). *Surviving affliction.* Retrieved April 1, 2002, from http://www.metroactive.com/papers/metro/12.14.95/all ende-9550.html

Perozynski, L., & Kramer, L. (1999). Parental beliefs about managing sibling conflict. *Developmental Psychology, 35,* 489–499.

Perrin, E. C., & the Committee on Psychosocial Aspects of Child and Family Health. (2002). Technical report: Coparent or second-parent adoption by same-sex parents. *Pediatrics, 109*(2), 341–344.

Pesonen, A., Raïkkönen, K., Keltikangas-Järvinen, L., Strandberg, T., & Järvenpää, A. (2003). Parental perception of infant temperament: Does parents' joint attachment matter? *Infant Behavior* and *Development, 26,* 167–182.

Petersen, A. C. (1993). Presidential address: Creating adolescents: The role of context and process in developmental transitions. *Journal of Research on Adolescents, 3*(1), 1–18.

Petersen, A. C., Compas, B. E., Brooks-Gunn, J., Stemmler, M., Ey, S., & Grant, K. E. (1993). Depression in adolescence. *American Psychologist, 48*(2), 155–168.

Peterson, C., & McCabe, A. (1994). A social interactionist account of developing decontextualized narrative skill. *Developmental Psychology, 30,* 937–948.

Petitto, L. A., Holowka, S., Sergio, L., & Ostry, D. (2001). Language rhythms in babies' hand movements. *Nature, 413,* 35–36.

Petitto, L. A., Katerelos, M., Levy, B., Gauna, K., Tetrault, K., & Ferraro, V. (2001). Bilingual signed and spoken language acquisition from birth: Implications for mechanisms underlying bilingual language acquisition. *Journal of Child Language, 28,* 1–44.

Petitto, L. A., & Kovelman, I. (2003). The bilingual paradox: How signing-speaking bilingual children help us to resolve it and teach us about the brain's mechanisms underlying all language acquisition. *Learning Languages, 8,* 5–18.

Petitto, L. A., & Marentette, P. F. (1991). Babbling in the manual mode: Evidence for the ontogeny of language. *Science, 251,* 1493–1495.

Petrill, S. A., Lipton, P. A., Hewitt, J. K., Plomin, R., Cherny, S. S., Corley, R., et al. (2004). Genetic and environmental contributions to general cognitive ability through the first 16 years of life. *Developmental Psychology, 40,* 805–812.

Pettit, G. S., Bates, J. E., & Dodge, K. A. (1997). Supportive parenting, ecological context, and children's adjustment: A seven-year longitudinal study. *Child Development, 68,* 908–923.

Pharaoh, P. D. P., Antoniou, A., Bobrow, M., Zimmern, R. L., Easton, D. F., & Ponder, B. A. J. (2002). Polygenic susceptibility to breast cancer and implications for prevention. *Nature Genetics, 31,* 33–36.

Phillips, D. F. (1998). Reproductive medicine experts till an increasingly fertile field. *Journal of the American Medical Association, 280,* 1893–1895.

Phinney, J. S. (1998). Stages of ethnic identity development in minority group adolescents. In R. E. Muuss & H. D. Porton (Eds.), *Adolescent behavior and society: A book of readings* (pp. 271–280). Boston: McGraw-Hill.

Piaget, J. (1929). *The child's conception of the world.* New York: Harcourt Brace.

Piaget, J. (1932). *The moral judgment of the child.* New York: Harcourt Brace.

Piaget, J. (1952). *The origins of intelligence in children.* New York: International Universities Press. (Original work published 1936.)

Piaget, J. (1962). *The language and thought of the child* (M. Gabain, Trans.). Cleveland, OH: Meridian. (Original work published 1923).

Piaget, J. (1964). *Six psychological studies.* New York: Vintage.

Piaget, J. (1969). *The child's conception of time* (A. J. Pomerans, Trans.). London: Routledge & Kegan Paul.

Piaget, J. (1972). Intellectual evolution from adolescence to adulthood. *Human Development, 15,* 1–12.

Piaget, J., & Inhelder, B. (1967). *The child's conception of space.* New York: Norton.

Piaget, J., & Inhelder, B. (1969). *The psychology of the child.* New York: Basic Books.

Picker, J. (2005). The role of genetic and environmental factors in the development of schizophrenia. *Psychiatric Times, 22,* 1–9.

Pickett, W., Craig, W., Harel, Y., Cunningham, J., Simpson, K., Molcho, M., et al. on behalf of the HBSC Violence and Injury Writing Group. (2005). Cross-national study of fighting and weapon carrying as determinants of adolescent injury. *Pediatrics, 116,* 855–863.

Pickett, W., Streight, S., Simpson, K., & Brison, R. J. (2003). Injuries experienced by infant children: A population-based epidemiological analysis. *Pediatrics, 111,* e365–e370.

Pierce, K. M., Hamm, J. V., & Vandell, D. L. (1999). Experiences in afterschool programs and children's adjustment in first-grade classrooms. *Child Development, 70*(3), 756–767.

Pierroutsakos, S. L., & DeLoache, J. S. (2003). Infants' manual exploration of pictorial objects varying in realism. *Infancy, 4,* 141–156.

Pike, A., Coldwell, J., & Dunn, J. F. (2005). Sibling relationships in early/middle childhood: Links with individual adjustment. *Journal of Family Psychology, 19,* 523–532.

Pillow, B. H., & Henrichon, A. J. (1996). There's more to the picture than meets the eye: Young children's difficulty understanding biased interpretation. *Child Development, 67,* 803–819.

Piña, J. A. (1999). The "uncontrollable" rebel. In J. Rodden (Ed.), *Conversations with Isabel Allende* (pp. 167–200). Austin: University of Texas Press.

Pines, M. (1981). The civilizing of Genie. *Psychology Today, 15*(9), 28–34.

Plant, L. D., Bowers, P. N., Liu, Q., Morgan, T., Zhang, T., State, M. W., et al. (2006). A common cardiac sodium channel variant associated with sudden infant death in African Americans, SCN5A S1103Y. *The Journal of Clinical Investigation, 116*(2), 430–435.

Pleck, J. H. (1997). Paternal involvement: Levels, sources, and consequences. In M. E. Lamb (Ed.), *The role of the father in child development* (3rd ed., pp. 66–103). New York: Wiley.

Plomin, R. (1989). Environment and genes: Determinants of behavior. *American Psychologist, 44*(2), 105–111.

Plomin, R. (1990). The role of inheritance in behavior. *Science, 248,* 183–188.

Plomin, R. (1996). Nature and nurture. In M. R. Merrens & G. G. Brannigan (Eds.), *The developmental psychologist: Research adventures across the life span* (pp. 3–19). New York: McGraw-Hill.

Plomin, R. (2001). Genetic factors contributing to learning and language delays and disabilities. *Child and Adolescent Psychiatric Clinics of North America, 10*(2), 259–277.

Plomin, R., & Daniels, D. (1987). Why are children in the same family so different from one another? *Behavioral and Brain Sciences, 10,* 1–16.

Plomin, R., & DeFries, J. C. (1999). The genetics of cognitive abilities and disabilities. In S. J. Ceci & W. M. Williams (Eds.), *The nature nurture debate: The essential readings* (pp. 178–195). Malden, MA: Blackwell.

Plomin, R., & Kovas, Y. (2005). Generalist genes and learning disabilities. *Psychological Bulletin, 131,* 592–617.

Plomin, R., Owen, M. J., & McGuffin, P. (1994). The genetic bases of behavior. *Science, 264,* 1733–1739.

Plomin, R., & Rutter, M. (1998). Child development, molecular genetics, and what to do with genes once they are found. *Child Development, 69*(4), 1223–1242.

Plomin, R., & Spinath, F. M. (2004). Intelligence: Genetics, genes, and genomics. *Journal of Personality and Social Psychology, 86,* 112–129.

Plotkin, S. A., Katz, M., & Cordero, J. F. (1999). The eradication of rubella. *Journal of the American Medical Association, 281,* 561–562.

Polit, D. F., & Falbo, T. (1987). Only children and personality development: A quantitative review. *Journal of Marriage and the Family, 49,* 309–325.

Pollock, L. A. (1983). *Forgotten children.* Cambridge, England: Cambridge University Press.

Pomerantz, E. M., & Eaton, M. M. (2001). Maternal intrusive support in the academic context: Transactional socialization processes. *Developmental Psychology, 37,* 174–186.

Pomerantz, E. M., & Saxon, J. L. (2001). Conceptions of ability as stable and self-evaluative processes: A longitudinal examination. *Child Development, 72,* 152–173.

Pomerantz, E. M., Wang, Q., & Ng, F. (2005). Mothers' affect in the homework context: The importance of staying positive. *Developmental Psychology, 41,* 414–427.

Pomery, E. A., Gibbons, F. X., Gerrard, M., Cleveland, M. J., Brody, G. H., & Wills, T. A. (2005). Families and risk: Prospective analyses of familial and social influences on adolescent substance use. *Journal of Family Psychology, 19,* 560–570.

Pong, S., Dronkers, J., & Hampden-Thompson, G. (2003). Family policies and children's school achievement in single-versus two-parent families. *Journal of Marriage and the Family, 65,* 681–699.

Pope, A. W., Bierman, K. L., & Mumma, G. H. (1991). Aggression, hyperactivity, and inattention-immaturity: Behavior dimensions associated with peer rejection in elementary school boys. *Developmental Psychology, 27,* 663–671.

Population Reference Bureau. (2005). *Human population: Fundamentals of growth; world health.* Retrieved April 11, 2005, from http://www.prb.org/Content/ NavigationMenu/PRB/Educators/Human Population/Health2/World Health1.htm

Posada, G., Gao, Y., Wu, F., Posada, R., Tascon, M., Schoelmerich, A., et al. (1995). The secure-base phenomenon across cultures: Children's behavior, mothers' preferences, and experts' concepts. In E. Waters, B. E. Vaughn, G. Posada, & K. Kondo-Ikemura (Eds.), *Care-giving, cultural, and cognitive perspectives on secure-base behavior and working models: New growing points of attachment theory and research. Monographs of the Society for Research in Child Development, 60*(2–3, Serial No. 244, 27–48).

Posner, J. K., & Vandell, D. L. (1999). After-school activities and the development of low-income urban children: A longitudinal study. *Developmental Psychology, 35*(3), 868–879.

Posner, M. L., & DiGirolamo, G. J. (2000). Cognitive neuroscience: Origins and promise. *Psychological Bulletin, 126*(6), 873–889.

Post, S. G. (1994). Ethical commentary: Genetic testing for Alzheimer's disease. *Alzheimer Disease and Associated Disorders, 8,* 66–67.

Posthuma, D., & de Gues, E. J. C. (2006). Progress in the molecular-genetic study of intelligence. *Current Directions in Psychological Science, 15,* 151–155.

Povinelli, D. J., & Giambrone, S. (2001). Reasoning about beliefs: A human specialization? *Child Development, 72,* 691–695.

Power, T. G., & Chapieski, M. L. (1986). Childrearing and impulse control in toddlers: A naturalistic investigation. *Developmental Psychology, 22,* 271–275.

Powlishta, K. K., Serbin, L. A., Doyle, A. B., & White, D. R. (1994). Gender, ethnic, and body type biases: The generality of prejudice in childhood. *Developmental Psychology, 30,* 526–536.

Prechtl, H. F. R., & Beintema, D. J. (1964). The neurological examination of the fullterm newborn infant. *Clinics in Developmental Medicine* (No. 12). London: Heinemann.

Princiotta, D., Bielick, S., & Chapman, C. (2004). *1.1 million homeschooled students in the United States in 2003* (NCES 2004–115). Washington, DC: National Center for Education Statistics.

Princiotta, D., & Chapman, C. (2006). *Homeschooling in the United States: 2003* (NCES 2006-042). Washington, DC: National Center for Education Statistics, U.S. Department of Education.

Pruden, S. M., Hirsh-Pasek, K., Golinkoff, R. M., & Hennon, E. A. (2006). The birth of words: Ten-month-olds learn words through perceptual salience. *Child Development, 77,* 266–280.

Putallaz, M., & Bierman, K. L. (Eds.). (2004). *Aggression, antisocial behavior, and violence among girls: A developmental perspective.* New York: Guilford.

Quadrel, M. J., Fischoff, B., & Davis, W. (1993). Adolescent (in) vulnerability. *American Psychologist, 48,* 102–116.

Quasha, S. (1980). *Albert Einstein: An intimate portrait.* Larchmont, NY: Forest.

Quattrin, T., Liu, E., Shaw, N., Shine, B., & Chiang, E. (2005). Obese children who are referred to the pediatric oncologist: Characteristics and outcome. *Pediatrics, 115,* 348–351.

Quinn, P. C., Eimas, P. D., & Rosenkrantz, S. L. (1993). Evidence for representations of perceptually similar natural categories by 3-month-old and 4-month-old infants. *Perception, 22,* 463–475.

Quinn, P. C., Westerlund, A., & Nelson, C. A. (2006). Neural markers of categorization in 6-month-old infants. *Psychological Science, 17,* 59–66.

Rabiner, D., & Coie, J. (1989). Effect of expectancy induction on rejected peers' acceptance by unfamiliar peers. *Developmental Psychology, 25,* 450–457.

Rafferty, Y., & Shinn, M. (1991). Impact of homelessness on children. *American Psychologist, 46*(11), 1170–1179.

Raine, A., Mellingen, K., Liu, J., Venables, P., & Mednick, S. (2003). Effects of environmental enrichment at ages 3–5 years in schizotypal personality and antisocial behavior at ages 17 and 23 years. *American Journal of Psychiatry, 160,* 1627–1635.

Rakison, D. H. (2005). Infant perception and cognition. In B. J. Ellis & D. F. Bjorklund (Eds.), *Origins of the social mind* (pp. 317–353). New York: Guilford.

Rakoczy, H., Tomasello, M., & Striano, T. (2004). Young children know that trying is not pretending: A test of the "behaving-as-if" construal of children's early concept of pretense. *Developmental Psychology, 40,* 388–399.

Rakyan, V. K., & Beck, S. (2006). Epigenetic variation and inheritance in mammals. *Current Opinion in Genetics and Development, 16,* 573–577.

Ram, A., & Ross, H. S. (2001). Problem solving, contention, and struggle: How siblings resolve a conflict of interests. *Child Development, 72,* 1710–1722.

Ramey, C. T., & Campbell, F. A. (1991). Poverty, early childhood education, and academic competence. In A. Huston (Ed.), *Children reared in poverty* (pp. 190–221). Cambridge, England: Cambridge University Press.

Ramey, C. T., Campbell, F. A., Burchinal, M., Skinner, M. L., Gardner, D. M., & Ramey, S. L. (2000). Persistent effects of early childhood education on high-risk children and their mothers. *Applied Developmental Science, 4*(1), 2–14.

Ramey, C. T., & Ramey, S. L. (1996). Early intervention: Optimizing development for children with disabilities and risk conditions. In M. Wolraich (Ed.), *Disorders of development and learning: A practical guide to assessment and management* (2nd ed., pp. 141–158). Philadelphia: Mosby.

Ramey, C. T., & Ramey, S. L. (1998a). Early intervention and early experience. *American Psychologist, 53,* 109–120.

Ramey, C. T., & Ramey, S. L. (1998b). Prevention of intellectual disabilities: Early interventions to improve cognitive development. *Preventive Medicine, 21,* 224–232.

Ramey, C. T., & Ramey, S. L. (2003, May). *Preparing America's children for success in school.* Paper prepared for an invited address at the White House Early Childhood Summit on Ready to Read, Ready to Learn, Denver, CO.

Ramey, S. L. (1999). Head Start and preschool education: Toward continued improvement. *American Psychologist, 54,* 344–346.

Ramey, S. L., & Ramey, C. T. (1992). Early educational intervention with disadvantaged children—To what effect? *Applied and Preventive Psychology, 1,* 131–140.

Ramoz, N., Reichert, J. G., Smith, C. J., Silverman, J. M., Bespalova, I. N., Davis, K. L., et al. (2004). Linkage and association of the mitochondrial aspartate/glutamate carrier SLC25A12 gene with autism. *American Journal of Psychiatry, 161,* 662–669.

Rampersad, A. (1997). *Jackie Robinson: A biography.* New York: Knopf.

Ramsey, P. G., & Lasquade, C. (1996). Preschool children's entry attempts. *Journal of Applied Developmental Psychology, 17,* 135–150.

Randall, D. (2005). *Corporal punishment in school.* Retrieved April 20, 2005, from http://www.familyeducation.com/article/ 0,1120,1–3980,00. html

Rapoport, J. L., Addington, A. M., & Frangou, S. (2005). The neurodevelopmental model of schizophrenia: Update 2005. *Molecular Psychiatry, 10,* 434–449.

Rask-Nissilä, L., Jokinen, E., Terho, P., Tammi, A., Lapinleimu, H., Ronnemaa, T., et al. (2000). Neurological development of 5-year-old children receiving a low-saturated-fat, low-cholesterol diet since infancy. *Journal of the American Medical Association, 284*(8), 993–1000.

Rathbun, A., West, J., & Germino-Hausken, E. (2004). From kindergarten through third grade: Children's beginning school experiences (NCES 2004–007). Washington, DC: National Center for Education Statistics.

Rauh, V. A., Whyatt, R. M., Garfinkel, R., Andrews, H., Hoepner, L., Reyes, A., et al. (2004). Developmental effects of exposure to environmental tobacco smoke and material hardship among inner-city children. *Neurotoxicology and Teratology, 26,* 373–385.

Raver, C. C. (2002). Emotions matter: Making the case for the role of young children's emotional development for early school readiness. *Social Policy Report, 16*(3).

Reaney, P. (2006, June 21). Three million babies born after fertility treatment. *Medscape.* Retrieved January 29, 2007, from http://www.medscape.com/viewarticle/537128

Reese, E. (1995). Predicting children's literacy from mother-child conversations. *Cognitive Development, 10,* 381–405.

Reese, E., & Cox, A. (1999). Quality of adult book reading affects children's emergent literacy. *Developmental Psychology, 35,* 20–28.

Reese, E., & Fivush, R. (1993). Parental styles of talking about the past. *Developmental Psychology, 29,* 596–606.

Reese, E., Haden, C., & Fivush, R. (1993). Mother-child conversations about the past: Relationships of style and memory over time. *Cognitive Development, 8,* 403–430.

Reese, E., & Newcombe, R. (2007). Training mothers in elaborative reminiscing enhances children's autobiographical memory and narrative. *Child Development, 78,* 1153–1170.

Reichenberg, A., Gross, R., Weiser, M., Bresnahan, M., Silverman, J., Harlap, S., et al. (2006). Advancing paternal age and autism. *Archives of General Psychiatry, 63*(9), 1026–1032.

Reijo, R., Alagappan, R. K., Patrizio, P., & Page, D. C. (1996). Severe oligozoospermia resulting from deletions of azoospermia factor gene on Y chromosome. *Lancet, 347,* 1290–1293.

Reilly, J. J., Jackson, D. M., Montgomery, C., Kelly, L. A., Slater, C., Grant, S., et al. (2004). Total energy expenditure and physical activity in young Scottish children: Mixed longitudinal study. *Lancet, 363,* 211–212.

Reiss, A. L., Abrams, M. T., Singer, H. S., Ross, J. L., & Denckla, M. B. (1996). Brain development, gender and IQ in children: A volumetric imaging study. *Brain, 119,* 1763–1774.

Remafedi, G., French, S., Story, M., Resnick, M. D., & Blum, R. (1998). The relationship between suicide risk and sexual orientation: Results of a population-based study. *American Journal of Public Health, 88,* 57–60.

Remez, L. (2000). Oral sex among adolescents: Is it sex or is it abstinence? *Family Planning Perspectives, 32,* 298–304.

Rende, R., Slomkowski, C., Lloyd-Richardson, E., & Niaura, R. (2005). Sibling effects on substance use in adolescence: Social contagion and genetic relatedness. *Journal of Family Psychology, 19,* 611–618.

Resnick, L. B. (1989). Developing mathematical knowledge. *American Psychologist, 44,* 162–169.

Resnick, M. D., Bearman, P. S., Blum, R.W., Bauman, K. E., Harris, K. M., Jones, J., et al. (1997). Protecting adolescents from harm: Findings from the National Longitudinal Study on Adolescent Health. *Journal of the American Medical Association, 278,* 823–832.

Rest, J., Narvaez, D., Bebeau, M. J., & Thoma, S. J. (1999). *Postconventional moral thinking.* Mahwah, NJ: Erlbaum.

Rest, J. R. (1975). Longitudinal study of the Defining Issues Test of moral judgment: A strategy for analyzing developmental change. *Developmental Psychology, 11,* 738–748.

Rest, J. R., Deemer, D., Barnett, R., Spickelmier, J., & Volker, J. (1986). Life experiences and developmental pathways. In J. R. Rest (Ed.), *Moral development: Advances in theory and research.* New York: Praeger.

Reuters. (2004a). *Canada first country to ban sale of baby walkers.*

Reuters. (2004b). Senate passes unborn victims bill. *New York Times.* Retrieved March 29, 2004, from http://www.nytimes.com/reuters/politics/politics-congress-unborn.html?ex=1081399302&ei=1&en=636394338d275008

Reynolds, A. J., & Temple, J. A. (1998). Extended early childhood intervention and school achievement: Age thirteen findings from the Chicago Longitudinal Study. *Child Development, 69,* 231–246.

Reynolds, A. J., Temple, J. A., Robertson, D. L., & Mann, E. A. (2001). Long-term effects of an early childhood intervention on educational achievement and juvenile arrest: A 15-year follow-up of low-income children in public schools. *Journal of American Medical Association, 285*(18), 2339–2346.

Rhee, S. H., & Waldman, I. D. (2002). Genetic and environmental influences on antisocial behavior: A meta-analysis of twin and adoption studies. *Psychological Bulletin, 128,* 490–529.

Ricciuti, H. N. (1999). Single parenthood and school readiness in white, black, and Hispanic 6- and 7-year-olds. *Journal of Family Psychology, 13,* 450–465.

Ricciuti, H. N. (2004). Single parenthood, achievement, and problem behavior in white, black, and Hispanic children. *Journal of Educational Research, 97,* 196–206.

Rice, C., Koinis, D., Sullivan, K., Tager-Flusberg, H., & Winner, E. (1997). When 3-year-olds pass the appearance-reality test. *Developmental Psychology, 33,* 54–61.

Rice, M., Oetting, J. B., Marquis, J., Bode, J., & Pae, S. (1994). Frequency of input effects on SLI children's word comprehension. *Journal of Speech and Hearing Research, 37,* 106–122.

Rice, M. L. (1982). Child language: What children know and how. In T. M. Field, A. Huston, H. C. Quay, L. Troll, & G. E. Finley (Eds.), *Review of human development research.* New York: Wiley.

Rice, M. L. (1989). Children's language acquisition. *American Psychologist, 44*(2), 149–156.

Rice, M. L., Huston, A. C., Truglio, R., & Wright, J. (1990). Words from "Sesame Street": Learning vocabulary while viewing. *Developmental Psychology, 26,* 421–428.

Richardson, J. (1995). *Achieving gender equality in families: The role of males.* Innocenti Global Seminar, Summary Report. Florence, Italy: UNICEF International Child Development Centre, Spedale degli Innocenti.

Richie, D. (1984). *The films of Akira Kurosawa.* Berkeley, CA: University of California Press.

Riddle, R. D., Johnson, R. L., Laufer, E., & Tabin, C. (1993). Sonic hedgehog mediates the polarizing activity of the ZPA. *Cell, 75,* 1401–1416.

Rideout, V. J., Vandewater, E. A., & Wartella, E. A. (2003). *Zero to six: Electronic media in the lives of infants, toddlers and preschoolers.* Menlo Park, CA: Kaiser Family Foundation.

Riemann, M. K., & Kanstrup Hansen, I. L. (2000). Effects on the fetus of exercise in pregnancy. *Scandinavian Journal of Medicine and Science in Sports. 10*(1), 12–19.

Rifkin, J. (1998, May 5). Creating the "perfect" human. *Chicago Sun-Times,* p. 29.

Rios-Ellis, B., Bellamy, L., & Shoji, J. (2000). An examination of specific types of *ijime* within Japanese schools. *School Psychology International, 21,* 227–241.

Ripple, C. H., Gilliam, W. S., Chanana, N., & Zigler, E. (1999). Will fifty cooks spoil the broth? The debate over entrusting Head Start to the states. *American Psychologist, 54,* 327–343.

Ritchie, L., Crawford, P., Woodward-Lopez, G., Ivey, S., Masch, M., & Ikeda, J. (2001). *Prevention of childhood overweight: What should be done?* Berkeley, CA: Center for Weight and Health, U.C. Berkeley.

Ritter, J. (1999, November 23). Scientists close in on DNA code. *Chicago Sun-Times,* p. 7.

Rivara, F. P. (1999). Pediatric injury control in 1999: Where do we go from here? *Pediatrics, 103*(4), 883–888.

Rivera, J. A., Sotres-Alvarez, D., Habicht, J. P., Shamah, T., & Villalpando, S. (2004). Impact of the Mexican Program for Education, Health and Nutrition (Progresa) on rates of growth and anemia in infants and young children. *Journal of the American Medical Association, 291,* 2563–2570.

Rivera, S. M., Wakeley, A., & Langer, J. (1999). The drawbridge phenomenon: Representational reasoning or perceptual preference? *Developmental Psychology, 35*(2), 427–435.

Roberts, G. C., Block, J. H., & Block, J. (1984). Continuity and change in parents' child-rearing practices. *Child Development, 55,* 586–597.

Robin, D. J., Berthier, N. E., & Clifton, R. K. (1996). Infants' predictive reaching for moving objects in the dark. *Developmental Psychology, 32,* 824–835.

Robins, R. W., & Trzesniewski, K. H. (2005). Self-esteem development across the lifespan. *Current Directions in Psychological Science, 14*(3), 158–162.

Robinson, J. (as told to A. Duckett). (1995). *I never had it made.* Hopewell, NJ: Ecco.

Robinson, S. (1996). *Stealing home.* New York: HarperCollins.

Robinson, T. N., Wilde, M. L., Navacruz, L. C., Haydel, K. F., & Varady, A. (2001). Effects of reducing children's television and video game use on aggressive behavior: A randomized controlled trial. *Archives of Pediatric and Adolescent Medicine, 155,* 17–23.

Rochat, P., Querido, J. G., & Striano, T. (1999). Emerging sensitivity to the timing and structure of proto conversations in early infancy. *Developmental Psychology, 35,* 950–957.

Rochat, P., & Striano, T. (2002). Who's in the mirror? Self-other discrimination in specular images by 4- and 9-month-old infants. *Child Development, 73,* 35–46.

Rodden, J. (Ed.). (1999). *Conversations with Isabel Allende.* Austin: University of Texas Press.

Roderick, M., Engel, M., & Nagaoka, J. (2003). *Ending social promotion: Results from Summer Bridge.* Chicago: Consortium on Chicago School Research.

Rodier, P. M. (2000, February). The early origins of autism. *Scientific American,* 56–63.

Rodkin, P. C., Farmer, T. W., Pearl, R., & Van Acker, R. (2000). Heterogeneity of popular boys: Antisocial and prosocial configurations. *Developmental Psychology, 36*(1), 14–24.

Rogan, W. J, Dietrich, K. N., Ware, J. H., Dockery, D. W., Salganik, M., Radcliffe, J., et al., for the Treatment of Lead-Exposed Children Trial Group. (2001). The effect of chelation therapy with succimer on neuropsychological development in children exposed to lead. *New England Journal of Medicine, 344,* 1421–1426.

Rogler, L. H. (2002). Historical generations and psychology: The case of the Great Depression and World War II. *American Psychologist, 57*(12), 1013–1023.

Rogoff, B., Mistry, J., Göncü, A., & Mosier, C. (1993). Guided participation in cultural activity by toddlers and caregivers. *Monographs of the Society for Research in Child Development, 58* (8, Serial No. 236).

Rogoff, B., & Morelli, G. (1989). Perspectives on children's development from cultural psychology. *American Psychologist, 44,* 343–348.

Rolls, B. J., Engell, D., & Birch, L. L. (2000). Serving portion size influences 5-year-old but not 3-year-old children's food intake. *Journal of the American Dietetic Association, 100,* 232–234.

Rome-Flanders, T., Cronk, C., & Gourde, C. (1995). Maternal scaffolding in mother-infant games and its relationship to language development: A longitudinal study. *First Language, 15,* 339–355.

Ronca, A. E., & Alberts, J. R. (1995). Maternal contributions to fetal experience and the transition from prenatal to postnatal life. In J. P. Lecanuet, W. P. Fifer, N. A. Krasnegor, & W. P. Smotherman (Eds.), *Fetal development: A psychobiological perspective* (pp. 331–350). Hillsdale, NJ: Erlbaum.

Roopnarine, J., & Honig, A. S. (1985, September). The unpopular child. *Young Children,* 59–64.

Roopnarine, J. L., Hooper, F. H., Ahmeduzzaman, M., & Pollack, B. (1993). Gentle play partners: Mother-child and father-child play in New Delhi, India. In K. MacDonald (Ed.), *Parent-child play* (pp. 287–304). Albany: State University of New York Press.

Roopnarine, J. L., Talokder, E., Jain, D., Josh, P., & Srivastav, P. (1992). Personal well-being, kinship ties, and mother-infant and father-infant interactions in single-wage and dual-wage families in New Delhi, India. *Journal of Marriage and the Family, 54,* 293–301.

Rose, A. J., & Rudolph, K. D. (2006). A review of sex differences in peer relationship processes: Potential trade-offs for the emotional and behavioral development of girls and boys. *Psychological Bulletin, 132,* 98–131.

Rose, S. A. (1994). Relation between physical growth and information processing in infants born in India. *Child Development, 65,* 889–902.

Rose, S. A., & Feldman, J. F. (1995). Prediction of IQ and specific cognitive abilities at 11 years from infancy measures. *Developmental Psychology, 31,* 685–696.

Rose, S. A., & Feldman, J. F. (1997). Memory and speed: Their role in the relation of infant information processing to later IQ. *Child Development, 68,* 630–641.

Rose, S. A., & Feldman, J. F. (2000). The relation of very low birth weight to basic cognitive skills in infancy and childhood. In C. A. Nelson (Ed.), *The effects of early adversity on neurobehavioral development.*

The Minnesota Symposia on Child Psychology (Vol. 31, pp. 31–59). Mahwah, NJ: Erlbaum.

Rose, S. A., Feldman, J. F., & Jankowski, J. J. (2001). Attention and recognition memory in the 1st year of life: A longitudinal study of preterm and full-term infants. *Developmental Psychology, 37,* 135–151.

Rose, S. A., Feldman, J. F., & Jankowski, J. J. (2002). Processing speed in the 1st year of life: A longitudinal study of preterm and full-term infants. *Developmental Psychology, 38,* 895–902.

Rosenblum, G. D., & Lewis, M. (1999). The relations among body image, physical attractiveness, and body mass in adolescence. *Child Development, 70,* 50–64.

Rosengren, K. S., Gelman, S. A., Kalish, C. W., & McCormick, M. (1991). As time goes by: Children's early understanding of growth in animals. *Child Development, 62,* 1302–1320.

Rosenthal, E. (2003, July 20). Bias for boys leads to sale of baby girls in China. *New York Times,* sec. 1, p. 6, col. 3.

Ross, H. S. (1996). Negotiating principles of entitlement in sibling property disputes. *Developmental Psychology, 32,* 90–101.

Rossi, R. (1996, August 30). Small schools under microscope. *Chicago Sun-Times,* p. 24.

Rotenberg, K. J., & Eisenberg, N. (1997). Developmental differences in the understanding of and reaction to others' inhibition of emotional expression. *Developmental Psychology, 33,* 526–537.

Rothbart, M. K., Ahadi, S. A., & Evans, D. E. (2000). Temperament and personality: Origins and outcomes. *Journal of Personality and Social Psychology, 78,* 122–135.

Rothbart, M. K., Ahadi, S. A., Hershey, K. L., & Fisher, P. (2001). Investigations of temperament at three to seven years: The Children's Behavior Questionnaire. *Child Development, 72,* 1394–1408.

Rothbart, M. K., & Hwang, J. (2002). Measuring infant temperament. *Infant Behavior and Development, 130,* 1–4.

Rotheram-Borus, M., & Futterman, D. (2000). Promoting early detection of HIV among adolescents. *Archives of Pediatrics and Adolescent Medicine, 154,* 435–439.

Rouse, C., Brooks-Gunn, J., & McLanahan, S. (2005). Introducing the issue. *The Future of Children, 15*(1), 5–14.

Roush, W. (1995). Arguing over why Johnny can't read. *Science, 267,* 1896–1898.

Rovee-Collier, C. (1996). Shifting the focus from what to why. *Infant Behavior and Development, 19,* 385–400.

Rovee-Collier, C. (1999). The development of infant memory. *Current Directions in Psychological Science, 8,* 80–85.

Rovee-Collier, C., & Boller, K. (1995). Current theory and research on infant learning and memory: Application to early intervention. *Infants and Young Children, 7*(3), 1–12.

Rowland, A. S., Umbach, D. M., Stallone, L., Naftel, J., Bohlig, E. M., & Sandler, D. P. (2002). Prevalence of medication treatment for attention-deficit hyperactivity disorder among elementary school children in Johnston County, North Carolina. *American Journal of Public Health, 92*, 231–234.

Rozen, S., Skaletsky, H., Marszalek, J. D, Minx, P. J., Cordum, H. S., Waterston, R. H., et al. (2003). Abundant gene conversion between arms of palindromes in human and ape Y chromosomes. *Nature, 423*, 810–811, 813.

Rubin, D. H., Erickson, C. J., San Agustin, M., Cleary, S. D., Allen, J. K., & Cohen, P. (1996). Cognitive and academic functioning of homeless children compared with housed children. *Pediatrics, 97*, 289–294.

Rubin, D. H., Krasilnikoff, P. A., Leventhal, J. M., Weile, B., & Berget, A. (1986, August 23). Effect of passive smoking on birth weight. *Lancet*, 415–417.

Rubin, K. (1982). Nonsocial play in preschoolers: Necessary evil? *Child Development, 53*, 651–657.

Rubin, K. H., Bukowski, W., & Parker, J. G. (1998). Peer interactions, relationships, and groups. In W. Damon (Series Ed.) & N. Eisenberg (Vol. Ed.), *Handbook of child psychology: Vol. 3. Social, emotional, and personality development* (5th ed., pp. 619–700). New York: Wiley.

Ruble, D. N., & Brooks-Gunn, J. (1982). The experience of menarche. *Child Development, 53*, 1557–1566.

Ruble, D. N., & Dweck, C. S. (1995). Self-conceptions, person conceptions, and their development. In N. Eisenberg, (Ed.), *Social development: Review of personality and social psychology* (pp. 109–139). Thousand Oaks, CA: Sage.

Ruble, D. N., & Martin, C. L. (1998). Gender development. In W. Damon (Series Ed.) & N. Eisenberg (Vol. Ed.), *Handbook of child psychology: Vol. 3. Social, emotional, and personality development* (5th ed., pp. 933–1016). New York: Wiley.

Rudolph, K. D., Lambert, S. F., Clark, A. G., & Kurlakowsky, K. D. (2001). Negotiating the transition to middle school: The role of self-regulatory processes. *Child Development, 72*(3), 929–946.

Rueter, M. A., & Conger, R. D. (1995). Antecedents of parent-adolescent disagreements. *Journal of Marriage and the Family, 57*, 435–448.

Ruffman, T., Slade, L., & Crowe, E. (2002). The relation between children's and mothers' mental state language and theory-of-mind understanding. *Child Development, 73*, 734–751.

Ruiz, F., & Tanaka, K. (2001). The *ijime* phenomenon and Japan: Overarching consideration for cross-cultural studies. *Psychologia: An International Journal of Psychology in the Orient, 44*, 128–138.

Rushton, J. P., & Jensen, A. R. (2005). Thirty years of research on race differences in cognitive ability. *Psychology, Public Policy, and Law, 11*, 235–294.

Rutland, A. F., & Campbell, R. N. (1996). The relevance of Vygotsky's theory of the "zone of proximal development" to the assessment of children with intellectual disabilities. *Journal of Intellectual Disability Research, 40*, 151–158.

Rutter, M. (2002). Nature, nurture, and development: From evangelism through science toward policy and practice. *Child Development, 73*, 1–21.

Rutter, M. (2007). Gene-environment interdependence. *Developmental Science, 10*, 12–18.

Rutter, M., & the English and Romanian Adoptees (ERA) Study Team. (1998). Developmental catch-up, and deficit, following adoption after severe global early privation. *Journal of Child Psychology and Psychiatry, 39*, 465–476.

Rutter, M., O'Connor, T. G., and the English and Romanian Adoptees (ERA) Study Team. (2004). Are there biological programming effects for psychological development? Findings from a study of Romanian adoptees. *Developmental Psychology, 40*, 81–94.

Ryan, A. (2001). The peer group as a context for the development of young adolescent motivation and achievement. *Child Development, 72*(4), 1135–1150.

Ryan, A. S. (1997). The resurgence of breast-feeding in the United States. *Pediatrics, 99*. Retrieved from http://www.pediatrics.org/cgi/content/full/99/4/e12

Ryan, A. S., Wenjun, Z., & Acosta, A. (2002). Breastfeeding continues to increase into the new millennium. *Pediatrics, 110*, 1103–1109.

Ryan, V., & Needham, C. (2001). Nondirective play therapy with children experiencing psychic trauma. *Clinical Child Psychology and Psychiatry* (special issue), *6*, 437–453.

Rymer, R. (1993). *An abused child: Flight from silence.* New York: HarperCollins.

Saarni, C., Mumme, D. L., & Campos, J. J. (1998). Emotional development: Action, communication, and understanding. In W. Damon (Series Ed.) & N. Eisenberg (Vol. Ed.), *Handbook of child psychology: Vol. 3. Social, emotional, and personality development* (5th ed., pp. 237–309). New York: Wiley.

Sachs, B. P., Kobelin, C., Castro, M. A., & Frigoletto, F. (1999). The risks of lowering the cesarean-delivery rate. *New England Journal of Medicine, 340*, 54–57.

Sadeh, A., Raviv, A., & Gruber, R. (2000). Sleep patterns and sleep disruptions in school age children. *Developmental Psychology, 36*(3), 291–301.

Saffran, J. R. & Thiessen, E.D. (2003). Pattern induction by infant language learners. *Developmental Psychology, 39*, 484–494.

Saigal, S., Hoult, L. A., Streiner, D. L., Stoskopf, B. L., & Rosenbaum, P. L. (2000). School difficulties at adolescence in a regional cohort of children who were extremely low birth weight. *Pediatrics, 105*, 325–331.

Saigal, S., Stoskopf, B., Streiner, D., Boyle, M., Pinelli, J., Paneth, N., et al. (2006). Transition of extremely low-birth-weight infants from adolescence to young adulthood: Comparison with normal birth-weight controls. *Journal of the American Medical Association, 295*, 667–675.

Saigal, S., Stoskopf, B. L., Streiner, D. L., & Burrows, E. (2001). Physical growth and current health status of infants who were of extremely low birth weight and controls at adolescence. *Pediatrics, 108*(2), 407–415.

Salihu, H. M., Shumpert, M. N., Slay, M., Kirby, R. S., &Alexander, G. R. (2003). Childbearing beyond maternal age 50 and fetal outcomes in the United States. *Obstetrics and Gynecology, 102*, 1006–1014.

Salisbury, A., Law, K., LaGasse, L., & Lester, B. (2003). Maternal-fetal attachment. *Journal of the American Medical Association, 289*, 1701.

Samdal, O., & Dür, W. (2000). The school environment and the health of adolescents. In C. Currie, K. Hurrelmann, W. Settertobulte, R. Smith, & J. Todd (Eds.), *Health and health behaviour among young people: A WHO cross-national study (HBSC) international report* (pp. 49–64). WHO Policy Series: Health Policy for Children and Adolescents, Series No. 1. Copenhagen, Denmark: World Health Organization Regional Office for Europe.

Sampson, R. J. (1997). The embeddedness of child and adolescent development: A community-level perspective on urban violence. In J. McCord (Ed.), *Violence and childhood in the inner city* (pp. 31–77). Cambridge, England: Cambridge University Press.

Samuelsson, M., Radestad, I., & Segesten, K. (2001). A waste of life: Fathers' experience of losing a child before birth. *Birth, 28*, 124–130.

Sandberg, S., Järvenpää, S., Penttinen, A., Paton, J. Y., & McCann, D. C. (2004). Asthma exacerbations in children immediately following stressful life events: A Cox's hierarchical regression. *Thorax, 59*, 1046–1051.

Sandler, D. P., Everson, R. B., Wilcox, A. J., & Browder, J. P. (1985). Cancer risk in adulthood from early life exposure to parents' smoking. *American Journal of Public Health, 75*, 487–492.

Sandler, W., Meir, I., Padden, C., & Aronoff, M. (2005). The emergence of grammar: Systematic structure in a new language. *Proceedings of the National Academy of Sciences, 102*, 2661–2665.

Sandnabba, H. K., & Ahlberg, C. (1999). Parents' attitudes and expectations about children's cross-gender behavior. *Sex Roles, 40*, 249–263.

Sandstrom, M. J., & Coie, J. D. (1999). A developmental perspective on peer rejection: Mechanisms of stability and change. *Child Development, 70*(4), 955–966.

Santos, F., & Ingrassia, R. (2002, August 18). The face of homelessness has changed: Family surge at shelters. *New York Daily News.* Retrieved from www.nationalhome-less.org/housing/familiesarticle.html

Santos, I. S., Victora, C. G., Huttly, S., & Carvalhal, J. B. (1998). Caffeine intake and low birthweight: A population-based case-control study. *American Journal of Epidemiology, 147,* 620–627.

Sapp, F., Lee, K., & Muir, D. (2000). Three-year-olds' difficulty with the appearance-reality distinction: Is it real or apparent? *Developmental Psychology, 36,* 547–560.

Sargent, J. D., & Dalton, M. (2001). Does parental disapproval of smoking prevent adolescents from becoming established smokers? *Pediatrics, 108*(6), 1256–1262.

Satchell, M., & Pati, S. (2005). Insurance gaps among vulnerable children in the United States, 1999–2001. *Pediatrics, 116,* 1155–1161.

Satcher, D. (2001). *Women and smoking: A report of the Surgeon General.* Washington, DC: Department of Health and Human Services.

Saudino, K. J. (2003a). Parent ratings of infant temperament: Lessons from twin studies. *Infant Behavior and Development, 26,* 100–107.

Saudino, K. J. (2003b). The need to consider contrast effects in parent-rated temperament *Infant Behavior and Development, 26,* 118–120.

Saudino, K. J., Wertz, A. E., Gagne, J. R., & Chawla, S. (2004). Night and day: Are siblings as different in temperament as parents say they are? *Journal of Personality and Social Psychology, 87,* 698–706.

Saunders, N. (1997, March). Pregnancy in the 21st century: Back to nature with a little assistance. *Lancet, 349,* s17–s19.

Savage, S. L., & Au, T. K. (1996). What word learners do when input contradicts the mutual exclusivity assumption. *Child Development, 67,* 3120–3134.

Savic, I., Berglund, H., & Lindström, P. (2005). Brain response to putative pheromones in homosexual men. *Proceedings of the National Academy of Sciences, 102,* 7356–7361.

Savin-Williams, R. C. (2006). Who's gay? Does it matter? *Current Directions in Psychological Science, 15,* 40–44.

Saxe, R., Tenenbaum, J. B., & Carey, S. (2005). Secret agents: Inferences about hidden causes by 10- and 12-month old infants. *Psychological Science, 16,* 995–1001.

Scarr, S. (1992). Developmental theories for the 1990s: Development and individual differences. *Child Development, 63,* 1–19.

Scarr, S. (1997). Why child care has little impact on most children's development. *Current Directions in Psychological Science, 6*(5), 143–148.

Scarr, S. (1998). American child care today. *American Psychologist, 53,* 95–108.

Scarr, S., & McCartney, K. (1983). How people make their own environments: A theory of genotype-environment effects. *Child Development, 54,* 424–435.

Schacter, D. L. (1999). The seven sins of memory: Insights from psychology and cognitive neuroscience. *American Psychologist, 54,* 182–203.

Schanberg, S. M., & Field, T. M. (1987). Sensory deprivation illness and supplemental stimulation in the rat pup and preterm human neonate. *Child Development, 58,* 1431–1447.

Scheers, N. J., Rutherford, G. W., & Kemp, J. S. (2003). Where should infants sleep? A comparison of risk for suffocation of infants sleeping in cribs, adult beds, and other sleeping locations. *Pediatrics, 112,* 883–889.

Scheidt, P., Overpeck, M. D., Whatt, W., & Aszmann, A. (2000). In C. Currie, K. Hurrelmann, W. Settertobulte, R. Smith, & J. Todd (Eds.), *Health and health behaviour among young people: A WHO crossnational study (HBSC) international report* (pp. 24–38). WHO Policy Series: Healthy Policy for Children and Adolescents, Series No. 1. Copenhagen, Denmark: World Health Organization Regional Office for Europe.

Schellenberg, G., Dawson, G., Sung, Y. J., Estes, A., Munson, J., Rosenthal, E., et al. (2006). Evidence for multiple loci from a genome scan of autism kindreds. *Molecular Psychiatry, 11,* 1049–1060.

Schemo, D. J. (2004, August 19). Charter schools lagging behind, test scores show. *New York Times,* pp. A1, A16.

Scher, M. S., Richardson, G. A., & Day, N. L. (2000). Effects of prenatal crack/cocaine and other drug exposure on electroencephalographic sleep studies at birth and one year. *Pediatrics, 105,* 39–48.

Schieve, L. A., Meikle, S. F., Ferre, C., Peterson, H. B., Jeng, G., & Wilcox, L. S. (2002). Low and very low birth weight in infants conceived with use of assisted reproductive technology. *New England Journal of Medicine, 346,* 731–737.

Schieve, L. A., Rice, C., Boyle, C., Visser, M. S., & Blumberg, S. J. (2006). Mental health in the United States: Parental report of diagnosed autism in children aged 4–17 years—United States, 2003–2004. *Morbidity and Mortality Weekly Report, 55*(17), 481–486.

Schilpp, P. A. (1970). *Albert Einstein: Philosopher-scientist* (3rd ed.). La Salle, IL: Open Court. (Original work published 1949)

Schlegel, A., & Barry, H. (1991). *Adolescence: An anthropological inquiry.* New York: Free Press.

Schmitt, B. D. (1997). Nocturnal enuresis. *Pediatrics in Review, 18,* 183–190.

Schmitz, S., Saudino, K. J., Plomin, R., Fulker, D. W., & DeFries, J. C. (1996). Genetic and environmental influences on temperament in middle childhood: Analyses of teacher and tester ratings. *Child Development, 67,* 409–422.

Schnaas, L., Rothenberg, S. J., Flores, M., Martinez, S., Hernandez, C., Osorio, E., et al. (2006). Reduced intellectual development in children with prenatal lead exposure. *Environmental Health Perspectives, 114*(5), 791–797.

Schneider, B. H., Atkinson, L., & Tardif, C. (2001). Child-parent attachment and children's peer relations: A quantitative review. *Developmental Psychology, 37,* 86–100.

Schneider, H., & Eisenberg, D. (2006). Who receives a diagnosis of attention-deficit hyperactivity disorder in the United States elementary school population? *Pediatrics, 117,* 601–609.

Schneider, M. (2002). *Do school facilities affect academic outcomes?* Washington, DC: National Clearinghouse for Educational Facilities.

Scholten, C. M. (1985). *Childbearing in American society: 1650–1850.* New York: New York University Press.

Schore, A. N. (1994). *Affect regulation and the origin of the self: The neurobiology of emotional development.* Hillsdale, NJ: Erlbaum.

Schulenberg, J., O'Malley, P., Backman, J., & Johnston, L. (2005). Early adult transitions and their relation to well-being and substance use. In R. A. Settersten, Jr., F. F. Furstenberg, Jr., & R. G. Rumbaut (Eds.), *On the frontier of adulthood: Theory, research, and public policy* (pp. 417–453). (John D. and Catherine T. MacArthur Foundation Series on Mental Health and Development, Research Network on Transitions to Adulthood and Public Policy.) Chicago: University of Chicago Press.

Schulting, A. B., Malone, P. S., & Dodge, K. A. (2005). The effect of school-based kindergarten transition policies and practices on child academic outcomes. *Developmental Psychology, 41,* 860–871.

Schumann, C. M., & Amaral, D. G. (2006). Stereological analysis of amygdala neuron number in autism. *The Journal of Neuroscience, 26*(29), 7674–7679.

Schumann, J. (1997). The view from elsewhere: Why there can be no best method for teaching a second language. *The Clarion: Magazine of the European Second Language Acquisition, 3*(1), 23–24.

Schwartz, D., Chang, L., & Farver, J. M. (2001). Correlates of victimization in Chinese children's peer groups. *Developmental Psychology, 37*(4), 520–532.

Schwartz, D., Dodge, K. A., Pettit, G. S., Bates, J. E., & the Conduct Problems Prevention Research Group. (2000). Friendship as a moderating factor in the pathway between early harsh home environment and later victimization in the peer group. *Developmental Psychology, 36,* 646–662.

Schwartz, D., McFadyen-Ketchum, S. A., Dodge, K. A., Pettit, G. S., & Bates, J. E. (1998). Peer group victimization as a predictor of children's behavior problems at home and in school. *Developmental and Psychopathology, 10,* 87–99.

Schwartz, J. (2004). Air pollution and children's health. *Pediatrics, 113,* 1037–1043.

Schweinhart, L. J., Barnes, H. V., & Weikart, D. P. (1993). *Significant benefits: The High/Scope Perry Preschool Study through age 27* (Monographs of the High/Scope Educational Research Foundation No. 10). Ypsilanti, MI: High/Scope.

Schwimmer, J. B., Burwinkle, T. M., & Varni, J. W. (2003, April). Health-related quality of life of severely obese children and adolescents. *Journal of the American Medical Association, 289*(14), 1813–1819.

Scott, G., & Ni, H. (2004). Access to health care among Hispanic/Latino children: United States, 1998–2001. *Advance Data from Vital and Health Statistics,* No. 344. Hyattsville, MD: National Center for Health Statistics.

Sedlak, A. J., & Broadhurst, D. D. (1996). *Executive summary of the third national incidence study of child abuse and neglect* (NIS-3). Washington, DC: U.S. Department of Health and Human Services.

Seifer, R. (2003). Twin studies, biases of parents, and biases of researchers. *Infant Behavior and Development, 26,* 115–117.

Seifer, R., Schiller, M., Sameroff, A. J., Resnick, S., & Riordan, K. (1996). Attachment, maternal sensitivity, and infant temperament during the first year of life. *Developmental Psychology, 32,* 12–25.

Seiner, S. H., & Gelfand, D. M. (1995). Effects of mother's simulated withdrawal and depressed affect on mother-toddler interactions. *Child Development, 60,* 1519–1528.

Seitz, V. (1990). Intervention programs for impoverished children: A comparison of educational and family support models. *Annals of Child Development, 7,* 73–103.

Selman, R. L. (1980). *The growth of interpersonal understanding: Developmental and clinical analyses.* New York: Academic.

Selman, R. L., & Selman, A. P. (1979, April). Children's ideas about friendship: A new theory. *Psychology Today,* pp. 71–80.

Seltzer, J. A. (2000). Families formed outside of marriage. *Journal of Marriage and the Family, 62,* 1247–1268.

Seminara, S. B., Messager, S., Chatzidaki, E. E., Thresher, R. R., Acierno, J. S., Jr., Shagoury, J. K., et al. (2003). The GPR54 gene as a regulator of puberty. *New England Journal of Medicine, 349,* 1614–1627.

Sen, A., Partelow, L., & Miller, D. C. (2005). *Comparative indicators of education in the United States and other G8 countries: 2004* (NCES 2005-021). Washington, DC: National Center for Education Statistics.

Sen, M., & Bauer, P. (2001). *Correlates of gender-based schematic processing in 24- and 30-month-old children.* Manuscript submitted for publication.

Senghas, A., & Coppola, M. (2001). Children creating language: How Nicaraguan sign language acquired a spatial grammar. *Psychological Science, 12,* 323–328.

Senghas, A., Kita, S., & Ozyürek, A. (2004). Children creating core properties of language: Evidence from an emerging sign language in Nicaragua. *Science, 305,* 1779–1782.

Serbin, L., Poulin-Dubois, D., Colburne, K. A., Sen, M., & Eichstedt. J. A. (2001). Gender stereotyping in infancy: Visual preferences for knowledge of gender-stereotyped toys in the second year. *International Journal of Behavioral Development, 25,* 7–15.

Serbin, L. A., Moller, L. C., Gulko, J., Powlishta, K. K., & Colburne, K. A. (1994). The emergence of gender segregation in toddler playgroups. In C. Leaper (Ed.), *Childhood gender segregation: Causes and consequences* (New Directions for Child Development No. 65, pp. 7–17). San Francisco: Jossey-Bass.

Serres, L. (2001). Morphological changes of the human hippocampal formation from midgestation to early childhood. In C. A. Nelson & M. Luciana (Eds.), *Handbook of developmental cognitive neuroscience* (pp. 45–58). Cambridge, MA: MIT Press.

Sethi, A., Mischel, W., Aber, J. L., Shoda, Y., & Rodriguez, M. L. (2000). The role of strategic attention deployment in development of self-regulation: Predicting preschoolers' delay of gratification from mother-toddler interactions. *Developmental Psychology, 36,* 767–777.

Sexton, A. (1966). Little girl, my string bean, my lovely woman. *The complete poems: Anne Sexton.* New York: Houghton Mifflin, 1981.

Shah, T., Sullivan, K., & Carter, J. (2006). Sudden infant death syndrome and reported maternal smoking during pregnancy. *American Journal of Public Health, 96*(10), 1757–1759.

Shanahan, M. J., & Flaherty, B. P. (2001). Dynamic patterns of time use in adolescence. *Child Development, 72*(2), 385–401.

Shanahan, M., Porfeli, E., & Mortimer, J. (2005). Subjective age identity and the transition to adulthood: When do adolescents become adults? In R. A. Settersten, Jr., F. F. Furstenberg, Jr., & R. G. Rumbaut (Eds.), *On the frontier of adulthood: Theory, research, and public policy* (pp. 225–255). (John D. and Catherine T. MacArthur Foundation Series on Mental Health and Development, Research Network on Transitions to Adulthood and Public Policy.) Chicago: University of Chicago Press.

Shankaran, S., Das, A., Bauer, C. R., Bada, H. S., Lester, B., Wright, L. L., et al. (2004). Association between patterns of maternal substance use and infant birth weight, length, and head circumference. *Pediatrics, 114,* e226–e234.

Shannon, J. D., Tamis-LeMonda, C. S., London, K., & Cabrera, N. (2002). Beyond rough and tumble: Low income fathers' interactions and children's cognitive development at 24 months. *Parenting: Science and Practice, 2*(2), 77–104.

Shannon, M. (2000). Ingestion of toxic substances by children. *New England Journal of Medicine, 342,* 186–191.

Sharma, A. R., McGue, M. K., & Benson, P. L. (1996a). The emotional and behavioral adjustment of United States adopted adolescents: Part I. An overview. *Children and Youth Services Review, 18,* 83–100.

Sharma, A. R., McGue, M. K., & Benson, P. L. (1996b). The emotional and behavioral adjustment of United States adopted adolescents: Part II. Age at adoption. *Children and Youth Services Review, 18,* 101–114.

Shatz, M., & Gelman, R. (1973). The development of communication skills: Modifications in the speech of young children as a function of listener. *Monographs of the Society for Research in Child Development, 38*(5, Serial No. 152).

Shaw, G. M., Velie, E. M., & Schaffer, D. (1996). Risk of neural tube defect affected pregnancies among obese women. *Journal of the American Medical Association, 275,* 1093–1096.

Shaw, P., Greenstein, D., Lerch, J., Clasen, L., Lenroot, R., Gogtay, N., et al. (2006). Intellectual ability and cortical development in children and adolescents. *Nature, 440,* 676–679.

Shayer, M., Ginsburg, D., & Coe, R. (2007). Thirty years on—a large anti-Flynn effect? The Piagetian test Volume and Heaviness norms 1975–2003. *British Journal of Educational Psychology, 77,* 25–41.

Shaywitz, S. (2003). *Overcoming dyslexia: A new and complete science-based program for overcoming reading problems at any level.* New York: Knopf.

Shaywitz, S. E. (1998). Current concepts: Dyslexia. *New England Journal of Medicine, 338,* 307–312.

Shea, K. M., Little, R. E., & the ALSPAC Study Team (1997). Is there an association between preconceptual paternal X-ray exposure and birth outcome? *American Journal of Epidemiology, 145,* 546–551.

Shea, S., Basch, C. E., Stein, A. D., Contento, I. R., Irigoyen, M., & Zybert, P. (1993). Is there a relationship between dietary fat and stature or growth in children 3 to 5 years of age? *Pediatrics, 92,* 579–586.

Shevell, T., Malone, F. D., Vidaver, J., Porter, T. F., Luthy, D. A., Comstock, C. H., et al. for the FASTER Research Consortium. (2005). Assisted reproductive technology and pregnancy outcome. *Obstetrics and Gynecology, 106,* 1039–1045.

Shields. A. E., Comstock, C., & Weiss, K. B. (2004). Variations in asthma by race/ethnicity among children enrolled in a state Medicaid program. *Pediatrics, 113,* 496–504.

Shields, B. J., & Smith, G. A. (2006). Success in the prevention of infant walker-related injuries: An analysis of national data, 1990–2001. *Pediatrics, 117,* 452–459.

Shields, M. K., & Behrman, R. E. (2004). Children of immigrant families: Analysis and recommendations. *The Future of Children, 14*(2), 4–15. Retrieved October 8, 2004, from http://www.futureofchildren.org

Shiono, P. H., & Behrman, R. E. (1995). Low birth weight: Analysis and recommendations. *The Future of Children, 5*(1), 4–18.

Shonkoff, J., & Phillips, D. (2000). Growing up in child care. In I. Shonkoff & D. Phillips (Eds.), *From neurons to neighborhoods* (pp. 297–327). Washington, DC: National Research Council/Institute of Medicine.

Shulman, S., Scharf, M., Lumer, D., & Maurer, O. (2001). Parental divorce and young adult children's romantic relationships: Resolution of the divorce experience. *American Journal of Orthopsychiatry, 71*, 473–478.

Shurkin, J. N. (1992). *Terman's kids: The groundbreaking study of how the gifted grow up*. Boston: Little, Brown.

Shwe, H. I., & Markman, E. M. (1997). Young children's appreciation of the mental impact of their communicative signals. *Developmental Psychology, 33*(4), 630–636.

Sick, W. T., Perfetti, C. A., Jin, Z., & Tan, L. H. (2004). Biological abnormality of impaired reading is constrained by culture. *Nature, 431*, 71–76.

Siegal, M., & Peterson, C. C. (1998). Preschoolers' understanding of lies and innocent and negligent mistakes. *Developmental Psychology, 34*(2), 332–341.

Siegel, A. C., & Burton, R. V. (1999). Effects of baby walkers on motor and mental development in human infants. *Journal of Developmental and Behavioral Pediatrics, 20*, 355–361.

Siegler, R. S. (1998). *Children's thinking* (3rd ed.). Upper Saddle River, NJ: Prentice Hall.

Siegler, R. S., & Booth, J. L. (2004). Development of numerical estimation in young children. *Child Development, 75*, 428–444.

Siegler, R. S., & Opfer, J. E. (2003). The development of numerical estimation: Evidence for multiple representations of numerical quantity. *Psychological Science, 14*, 237–243.

Siegler, R. S., & Richards, D. (1982). The development of intelligence. In R. Sternberg (Ed.), *Handbook of human intelligence*. London: Cambridge University Press.

Sieving, R. E., McNeely, C. A., & Blum, R. W. (2000). Maternal expectations, mother-child connections, and adolescent sexual debut. *Archives of Pediatric Adolescent Medicine, 154*, 809–816.

Sieving, R. E., Oliphant, J. A., & Blum, R. W. (2002). Adolescent sexual behavior and sexual health. *Pediatrics in Review, 23*, 407–416.

Sigman, M., Cohen, S. E., & Beckwith, L. (1997). Why does infant attention predict adolescent intelligence? *Infant Behavior and Development, 20*, 133–140.

Signorello, L. B., Nordmark, A., Granath, F., Blot, W. J., McLaughlin, J. K., Anneren, G., et al. (2001). Caffeine metabolism and the risk of spontaneous abortion of normal karyotype fetuses. *Obstetrics and Gynecology, 98*(6), 1059–1066.

Silver, R. M., Landon, M. D., Rouse, D. J., Leveno, K. J., Spong, C. Y., Thom, E. A., et al., & National Institute of Child Health and Human Development Maternal-Fetal Medicine Units Network. (2006). Maternal morbidity associated with multiple repeat cesarean deliveries. *Obstetrics and Gynecology, 107*(6), 1226–1232.

Silverman, W. K., La Greca, A. M., & Wasserstein, S. (1995). What do children worry about? Worries and their relation to anxiety. *Child Development, 66*, 671–686.

Simmons, R. G., Blyth, D. A., & McKinney, K. L. (1983). The social and psychological effect of puberty on white females. In J. Brooks-Gunn & A. C. Petersen (Eds.), *Girls at puberty: Biological and psychological perspectives*. New York: Plenum.

Simmons, R. G., Blyth, D. A., Van Cleave, E. F., & Bush, D. M. (1979). Entry into early adolescence: The impact of school structure, puberty, and early dating on self-esteem. *American Sociological Review, 44*(6), 948–967.

Simon, G. E. (2006). The antidepressant quandary—Considering suicide risk when treating adolescent depression. *New England Journal of Medicine, 355*, 2722–2723.

Simon, G. E., Savarino, J., Operskalski, B., & Wang, P. S. (2006). Suicide risk during antidepressant treatment. *American Journal of Psychiatry, 163*, 41–47.

Simons, R. L., Chao, W., Conger, R. D., & Elder, G. H. (2001). Quality of parenting as mediator of the effect of childhood defiance on adolescent friendship choices and delinquency: A growth curve analysis. *Journal of Marriage and the Family, 63*, 63–79.

Simons, R. L., Lin, K.-H., & Gordon, L. C. (1998). Socialization in the family of origin and male dating violence: A prospective study. *Journal of Marriage and the Family, 60*, 467–478.

Simonton, D. K. (1990). Creativity and wisdom in aging. In J. E. Birren & K. W. Schaie (Eds.), *Handbook of the psychology of aging* (pp. 320–329). New York: Academic Press.

Simpson, J. E. (2005). Choosing the best prenatal screening protocol. *New England Journal of Medicine, 353*, 2068–2070.

Simpson, K. (2001). The role of testosterone in aggression. *McGill Journal of Medicine, 6*, 32–40.

Singer, D. G., & Singer, J. L. (1990). *The house of make-believe: Play and the developing imagination*. Cambridge, MA: Harvard University Press.

Singer, J. L., & Singer, D. G. (1981). *Television, imagination, and aggression: A study of preschoolers*. Hillsdale, NJ: Erlbaum.

Singer, J. L., & Singer, D. G. (1998). *Barney and Friends* as entertainment and education: Evaluating the quality and effectiveness of a television series for preschool children. In J. K. Asamen & G. L. Berry (Eds.), *Research paradigms, television, and social behavior* (pp. 305–367). Thousand Oaks, CA: Sage.

Singer, L. T., Minnes, S., Short, E., Arendt, K., Farkas, K., Lewis, B., et al. (2004). Cognitive outcomes of preschool children with prenatal cocaine exposure. *Journal of the American Medical Association, 291*, 2448–2456.

Singh, K. K., Barroga, C. F., Hughes, M. D., Chen, J., Raskino, C., McKinney, R. E., et al. (2003, November 15). Genetic influence of CCR5, CCR2, and SDF1 variants on human immunodeficiency virus 1 (HIV-1)-related disease progression and neurological impairment, in children with symptomatic HIV-1 infection. *Journal of Infectious Disease, 188*(10), 1461–1472.

Singh, S., Wulf, D., Samara, R., & Cuca, Y. P. (2000). Gender differences in the timing of first intercourse: Data from 14 countries. *International Family Planning Perspectives, Part 1, 26*, 21–28.

Singhal, A., Cole, T. J., Fewtrell, M., & Lucas, A. (2004). Breastmilk feeding and lipoprotein profile in adolescents born preterm: Follow-up of a prospective randomised study. *Lancet, 363*, 1571–1578.

Sipos, A., Rasmussen, F., Harrison, G., Tynelius, P., Lewis, G., Leon, D. A., et al. (2004). Paternal age and schizophrenia: A population based cohort study. *British Medical Journal, 329*, 1070–1073.

Skadberg, B. T., Morild, I., & Markestad, T. (1998). Abandoning prone sleeping: Effects on the risk of sudden infant death syndrome. *Journal of Pediatrics, 132*, 234–239.

Skinner, B. F. (1938). *The behavior of organisms: An experimental approach*. New York: Appleton-Century.

Skinner, B. F. (1957). *Verbal behavior*. New York: Appleton-Century-Crofts.

Skinner, D. (1989). The socialization of gender identity: Observations from Nepal. In J. Valsiner (Ed.), *Child development in cultural context* (pp. 181–192). Toronto: Hogrefe & Huber.

Skoe, E. E., & Diessner, R. E. (1994). Ethic of care, justice, identity, and gender: An extension and replication. *Merrill-Palmer Quarterly, 40*, 272–289.

Skolnick, A. A. (1993). "Female athlete triad" risk for women. *Journal of the American Medical Association, 270*, 921–923.

Slade, A., Belsky, J., Aber, J. L., & Phelps, J. L. (1999). Mothers' representation of their relationships with their toddlers: Links to adult attachment and observed mothering. *Developmental Psychology, 35*, 611–619.

Slobin, D. (1971). Universals of grammatical development in children. In W. Levitt & G. B. Flores d' Arcais (Eds.), *Advances in psycholinguistic research*. Amsterdam: New Holland.

Slobin, D. (1973). Cognitive prerequisites for the acquisition of language. In C. Ferguson & D. Slobin (Eds.), *Studies of child language development*. New York: Holt, Rinehart, & Winston.

Slobin, D. (1983). Universal and particular in the acquisition of grammar. In E. Wanner

& L. Gleitman (Eds.), *Language acquisition: The state of the art.* Cambridge, England: Cambridge University Press.

Sly, R. M. (2000). Decreases in asthma mortality in the United States. *Annal of Allergy, Asthma, and Immunology, 85,* 121–127.

Slyper, A. H. (2006). The pubertal timing controversy in the USA, and a review of possible causative factors for the advance in timing of onset of puberty. *Clinical Endocrinology, 65,* 1–8.

Small, M. Y. (1990). *Cognitive development.* New York: Harcourt Brace.

Smedje, J., Broman, J. E., & Hetta, J. (1999). Parents' reports of disturbed sleep in 5–7-year-old Swedish children. *Acta Paediatrica, 88,* 858–865.

Smedley, A., & Smedley, B. D. (2005). Race as biology is fiction, racism as a social problem is real: Anthropological and historical perspectives on the social construction of race. *American Psychologist, 60,* 16–26.

Smetana, J., Crean, H., & Campione-Barr, N. (2005). Adolescents' and parents' changing conceptions of parental authority. In J. Smetana (Ed.), *Changing boundaries of parental authority during adolescence: New directions for child and adolescent development, no. 108* (pp. 31–46). San Francisco: Jossey-Bass.

Smetana, J. G., Metzger, A., Gettman, D. C., & Campione-Barr, N. (2006). Disclosure and secrecy in adolescent-parent relationships. *Child Development, 77,* 201–217.

Smilansky, S. (1968). *The effects of sociodramatic play on disadvantaged preschool children.* New York: Wiley.

Smith, B. A., & Blass, E. M. (1996). Taste mediated calming in premature, preterm, and full-term human infants. *Developmental Psychology, 32,* 1084–1089.

Smith, G. C., Wood, A. M., Pell, J. P., & Dobbie, R. (2005). Sudden infant death syndrome and complications in other pregnancies. *Lancet, 366*(9503), 2107–2111.

Smith, G. C. S., Pell, J. P., Cameron, A. D., & Dobbie, R. (2002). Risk of perinatal death associated with labor after previous cesarean delivery in uncomplicated term pregnancies. *Journal of the American Medical Association, 287,* 2684–2690.

Smith, G. C. S., Wood, A. M., Pell, J. P., White, I. R., Crossley, J. A., & Dobbie, R. (2004). Second-trimester maternal serum levels of alpha-fetoprotein and the subsequent risk of Sudden Infant Death Syndrome. *New England Journal of Medicine, 351,* 978–986.

Smith, K. A., Fairburn, C. G., & Cowen, P. J. (1999). Symptomatic release in bulimia nervosa following acute tryptophan depletion. *Archives of General Psychiatry (72C), 56*(2), 171–176.

Smith, L. B., & Thelen, E. (2003). Development as a dynamic system. *Trends in Cognitive Sciences, 7,* 343–348.

Smith, L. M., LaGasse, L. L., Derauf, C., Grant, P., Shah, R., Arria, A., et al. (2006). The infant development, environment, and lifestyle study: Effects of prenatal methamphetamine exposure, polydrug exposure, and poverty on intrauterine growth. *Pediatrics, 118,* 1149–1156.

Smith, M. (1998, February 25). U.S. 12th graders trail students of other nations in math, science. *Minneapolis Star-Tribune,* p. A5.

Smith, P. K. (2005a). Play: Types and functions in human development. In A. D. Pellegrini & P. K. Smith (Eds.), *The nature of play* (pp. 271–291). New York: Guilford.

Smith, P. K. (2005b). Social and pretend play in children. In A. D. Pellegrini & P. K. Smith (Eds.), *The nature of play* (pp. 173–209). New York: Guilford.

Smith, P. K., & Levan, S. (1995). Perceptions and experiences of bullying in younger pupils. *British Journal of Educational Psychology, 65,* 489–500.

Smith, R. (1999, March). The timing of birth. *Scientific American,* 68–75.

Smith, R. (2007). Parturition. *New England Journal of Medicine, 356,* 271–283.

Smith, V. K., & Rousseau, D. M. (2005). *SCHIP enrollment in 50 states.* Washington, DC: Kaiser Commission on Medicaid and the Uninsured.

Smith-Khuri, E., Iachan, R., Scheidt, P. C., Overpeck, M. D., Gabhainn, S. N., Pickett, W., et al. (2004). A crossnational study of violence-related behaviors in adolescents. *Archives of Pediatrics and Adolescent Medicine, 158,* 539–544.

Smotherman, W. P., & Robinson, S. R. (1995). Tracing developmental trajectories into the prenatal period. In J. P. Lecanuet, W. P. Fifer, N. A. Krasnegor, & W. P. Smotherman (Eds.), *Fetal development: A psychobiological perspective* (pp. 15–32). Hillsdale, NJ: Erlbaum.

Smotherman, W. P., & Robinson, S. R. (1996). The development of behavior before birth. *Developmental Psychology, 32,* 425–434.

Snarey, J. R. (1985). Cross-cultural universality of social-moral development: A critical review of Kohlbergian research. *Psychological Bulletin, 97,* 202–232.

Snow, C. E. (1990). The development of definitional skill. *Journal of Child Language, 17,* 697–710.

Snow, C. E. (1993). Families as social contexts for literacy development. In C. Daiute (Ed.), *The development of literacy through social interaction* (New Directions for Child Development No. 61, pp. 11–24). San Francisco: Jossey-Bass.

Snow, M. E., Jacklin, C. N., & Maccoby, E. E. (1983). Sex-of-child differences in father-child interaction at one year of age. *Child Development, 54,* 227–232.

Snyder, J., Bank, L., & Burraston, B. (2005). The consequences of antisocial behavior in older male siblings for younger brothers and sisters. *Journal of Family Psychology, 19,* 643–653.

Snyder, J., Cramer, A., Afrank, J., & Patterson, G. R. (2005). The contributions of ineffective discipline and parental hostile attributions of child misbehavior to the development of conduct problems at home and school. *Developmental Psychology, 41,* 30–41.

Snyder, J., West, L., Stockemer, V., Gibbons, S., & Almquist-Parks, L. (1996). A social learning model of peer choice in the natural environment. *Journal of Applied Developmental Psychology, 17,* 215–237.

Snyder, T. D., & Hoffman, C. M. (2001). *Digest of education statistics: 2000.* Washington, DC: National Center for Education Statistics.

Snyder, T. D., & Hoffman, C. M. (2002). *Digest of education statistics: 2001.* Washington, DC: National Center for Education Statistics.

Snyder, T. D., & Hoffman, C. M. (2003). *Digest of education statistics: 2002* (Publication No. NCES 2003–060). Washington, DC: National Center for Education Statistics.

Sobolewski, J. M., & Amato, P. J. (2005). Economic hardship in the family of origin and children's psychological well-being in adulthood. *Journal of Marriage and Family, 67,* 141–156.

Sobolewski, J. M., & King, V. (2005). The importance of the coparental relationship for nonresident fathers' ties to children. *Journal of Marriage and Family, 67,* 1196–1212.

Society for Assisted Reproductive Technology & the American Fertility Society. (1993). Assisted reproductive technology in the United States and Canada: 1991 results from the Society for Assisted Reproductive Technology generated from the American Fertility Society Registry. *Fertility and Sterility, 59,* 956–962.

Society for Assisted Reproductive Technology & the American Society for Reproductive Medicine. (2002). Assisted reproductive technology in the United States: 1998 results generated from the American Society for Reproductive Medicine/Society for Assisted Reproductive Technology Registry. *Fertility & Sterility, 77*(1), 18–31.

Society for Neuroscience. (2005). *Brain facts: A primer on the brain and nervous system.* Washington, DC: Author.

Society for Research in Child Development. (1996). Ethical standards for research with children. In *Directory of members* (pp. 337–339). Ann Arbor, MI: Author.

Soenens, B., Vansteenkiste, M., Luyckx, K., & Goossens, L. (2006). Parenting and adolescent problem behavior: An integrated model with adolescent self-disclosure and perceived parental knowledge as intervening variables. *Developmental Psychology, 42,* 305–318.

Sokol, R. J., Delaney-Black, V., & Nordstrom, B. (2003). Fetal alcohol spectrum disorder. *Journal of the American Medical Association, 209,* 2996–2999.

Sokol, R. Z., Kraft, P., Fowler, I. M., Mamet, R., Kim, E., & Berhane, K. T. (2006).

Exposure to environmental ozone alters semen quality. *Environmental Health Perspectives, 114*(3), 360–365.

Solowij, N., Stephens, R. S., Roffman, R. A., Babor, T., Kadden, R., Miller, M., et al., for the Marijuana Treatment Research Group. (2002). Cognitive functioning of long-term heavy cannabis users seeking treatment. *Journal of the American Medical Association, 287*, 1123–1131.

Sondergaard, C., Henriksen, T. B., Obel, C., & Wisborg, K. (2001). Smoking during pregnancy and infantile colic. *Pediatrics, 108*(2), 342–346.

Sood, B., Delaney-Black, V., Covington, C., Nordstrom-Klee, B., Ager, J., Templin, T., et al. (2001). Prenatal alcohol exposure and childhood behavior at age 6 to 7 years: I. Dose-response effect. *Pediatrics, 108*(8), e461–e462.

Sophian, C., Garyantes, D., & Chang, C. (1997). When three is less than two: Early developments in children's understanding of fractional quantities. *Developmental Psychology, 33*, 731–744.

Sophian, C., & Wood, A. (1997). Proportional reasoning in young children: The parts and the whole of it. *Journal of Educational Psychology, 89*, 309–317.

Sophian, C., Wood, A., & Vong, K. I. (1995). Making numbers count: The early development of numerical inferences. *Developmental Psychology, 31*, 263–273.

Sorensen, T., Nielsen, G., Andersen, P., & Teasdale, T. (1988). Genetic and environmental influence of premature death in adult adoptees. *New England Journal of Medicine, 318*, 727–732.

Sorof, J. M., Lai, D., Turner, J., Poffenbarger, T., & Portman, R. J. (2004). Overweight, ethnicity, and the prevalence of hypertension in school-aged children. *Pediatrics, 113*, 475–482.

Sowell, E. R., Thompson, P. M., Welcome, S. E., Henkenius, A. L., Toga, A. W., & Peterson, B. S. (2003). Cortical abnormalities in children and adolescents with attention-deficit hyperactivity disorder. *Lancet, 362*, 1699–1701.

Spady, D. W., Saunders. D. L., Schopflocher, D. P., & Svenson, L. W. (2004). Patterns for injury in childhood: A population-based approach. *Pediatrics, 113*, 522–529.

Spelke, E. (1994). Initial knowledge: Six suggestions. *Cognition, 50*, 431–445.

Spelke, E. S. (1998). Nativism, empiricism, and the origins of knowledge. *Infant Behavior and Development, 21*(2), 181–200.

Spelke, E. S. (2005). Sex differences in intrinsic aptitude for mathematics and science? A critical review. *American Psychologist, 60*, 950–958.

Spencer, H. (1898). *The principles of psychology.* New York: Appleton. (Original work published 1878.)

Spencer, J. P., Clearfield, M., Corbetta. D., Ulrich, B., Buchanan, P., & Schöner, G. (2006). Moving toward a grand theory of development: In memory of Esther Thelen. *Child Development, 77*, 1521–1538.

Spencer, J. P., Smith, L. B., & Thelen, E. (2001). Tests of a dynamic systems account of the A-not-B error: The influence of prior experience on the spatial memory abilities of two-year-olds. *Child Development, 72*, 1327–1346.

Sperling, M. A. (2004). Prematurity—A window of opportunity? *New England Journal of Medicine, 351*, 2229–2231.

Spieker, S. J., Nelson, D. C., Petras, A., Jolley, S. N., & Barnard, K. E. (2003). Joint influence of child care and infant attachment security for cognitive and language outcomes of low-income toddlers. *Infant Behavior and Development, 26*, 326–344.

Spinath, F. M., Price, T. S., Dale, P. S., & Plomin, R. (2004). The genetic and environmental origins of language disability and ability. *Child Development, 75*, 445–454.

Spinrad, T. L., Eisenberg, N., Harris, E., Hanish, L., Fabes, R. A., Kupanoff, K., et al. (2004). The relation of children's everyday nonsocial peer play behavior to their emotionality, regulation, and social functioning. *Developmental Psychology, 40*, 67–80.

Spira, E. G., Brachen, S. S., & Fischel, J. E. (2005). Predicting improvement after first-grade reading difficulties: The effects of oral language, emergent literacy, and behavior skills. *Developmental Psychology, 41*, 225–234.

Spitz, R. A. (1945). Hospitalism: An inquiry into the genesis of psychiatric conditioning in early childhood. In D. Fenschel et al. (Eds.), *Psychoanalytic studies of the child* (Vol. 1, pp. 53–74). New York: International Universities Press.

Spitz, R. A. (1946). Hospitalism: A followup report. In D. Fenschel et al. (Eds.), *Psychoanalytic studies of the child* (Vol. 1, pp. 113–117). New York: International Universities Press.

Spohr, H. L., Willms, J., & Steinhausen, H. C. (1993). Prenatal alcohol exposure and long-term developmental consequences. *Lancet, 341*, 907–910.

Squire, L. R. (1992). Memory and the hippocampus: A synthesis of findings with rats, monkeys, and humans. *Psychological Review, 99*, 195–231.

Sroufe, L. A. (1979). Socioemotional development. In J. Osofsky (Ed.), *Handbook of infant development.* New York: Wiley.

Sroufe, L. A. (1997). *Emotional development.* Cambridge, England: Cambridge University Press.

Sroufe, L. A., Bennett, C., Englund, M., Urban, J., & Shulman, S. (1993). The significance of gender boundaries in preadolescence: Contemporary correlates and antecedents of boundary violation and maintenance. *Child Development, 64*, 455–466.

Sroufe, L. A., Carlson, E., & Shulman, S. (1993). Individuals in relationships: Development from infancy through adolescence. In D. C. Funder, R. D. Parke,

C. Tomlinson-Keasey, & K. Widaman (Eds.), *Studying lives through time: Personality and development* (pp. 315–342). Washington, DC: American Psychological Association.

Staff, J., Mortimer, J. T., & Uggen, C. (2004). Work and leisure in adolescence. In R. M. Lerner & L. Steinberg (Eds.). *Handbook of adolescent development* (2nd ed., pp. 429–450). Hoboken, NJ: Wiley.

Stahl, S. A., McKenna, M. C., & Pagnucco, J. R. (1994). The effects of whole-language instruction: An update and a reappraisal. *Educational Psychologist, 29*, 175–185.

Standley, J. M. (1998). Strategies to improve outcomes in critical care—The effect of music and multimodal stimulation on responses of premature infants in neonatal intensive care. *Pediatric Nursing, 24*, 532–538.

Stapleton, S. (1998, May 11). Asthma rates hit epidemic numbers; experts wonder why. *American Medical News, 41*(18). Retrieved from http://www. amaassn.org/special/ asthma/newsline/special/ep idem.htm

Starr, J. M., Deary, I. J., Lemmon, H., & Whalley, L. J. (2000). Mental ability age 11 years and health status age 77 years. *Age and Ageing, 29*, 523–528.

Staub, E. (1996). Cultural-societal roots of violence: The examples of genocidal violence and of contemporary youth violence in the United States. *American Psychologist, 51*, 117–132.

Stauder, J. E. A., Molenaar, P. C. M., & Van der Molen, M. W. (1993). Scalp topography of event-related brain potentials and cognitive transition during childhood. *Child Development, 64*, 769–788.

St. Clair, D., Xu, M., Wang, P., Yu, Y., Fang, Y., Zhang, F., et al. (2005). Rates of adult schizophrenia following prenatal exposure to the Chinese famine of 1959–1961. *Journal of the American Medical Association, 294*, 557–562.

Stein, M. A., Mendelsohn, J., Obermeyer, W. H., Amromin, J., & Benca, R. (2001). Sleep and behavior problems in school-aged children. *Pediatrics, 107*, 1–9.

Steinberg, L. (2000, January 19). *Should juvenile offenders be tried as adults? A developmental perspective on changing legal policies.* Paper presented as part of a Congressional Research Briefing entitled "Juvenile Crime: Causes and Consequences." Washington, DC.

Steinberg, L. (2005). Psychological control: Style or substance? In J. Smetana (Ed.), *Changing boundaries of parental authority during adolescence: New directions for child and adolescent development, no. 108* (pp. 71–78). San Francisco: Jossey-Bass.

Steinberg, L., & Darling, N. (1994). The broader context of social influence in adolescence. In R. Silberstein & E. Todt (Eds.), *Adolescence in context.* New York: Springer.

Steinberg, L., Dornbusch, S. M., & Brown, B. B. (1992). Ethnic differences in adolescent achievement: An ecological perspective. *American Psychologist, 47,* 723–729.

Steinberg, L., & Scott, E. S. (2003). Less guilty by reason of adolescence: Developmental immaturity, diminished responsibility, and the juvenile death penalty. *American Psychologist, 58,* 1009–1018.

Steinman, G. (2006). Mechanisms of twinning: VII. Effect of diet and heredity on the human twinning rate. *The Journal of Reproductive Medicine, 51*(5), 405–410.

Stennes, L. M., Burch, M. M., Sen, M. G., & Bauer, P. J. (2005). A longitudinal study of gendered vocabulary and communicative action in young children. *Developmental Psychology, 41,* 75–88.

Stephens, J. C., Schneider, J. A., Tanguay, D. A., Choi, J., Acharya, T., Stanley, S. E., et al. (2001). Haplotype variation and linkage disequilibrium in 313 human genes. *Science, 293,* 489–493.

Sternberg, R. J. (1985). *Beyond IQ: A triarchic theory of human intelligence.* New York: Cambridge University Press.

Sternberg, R. J. (1987, September 23). The use and misuse of intelligence testing: Misunderstanding meaning, users over-rely on scores. *Education Week,* pp. 22, 28.

Sternberg, R. J. (1993). *Sternberg Triarchic Abilities Test.* Unpublished manuscript.

Sternberg, R. J. (1997). The concept of intelligence and its role in lifelong learning and success. *American Psychologist, 52,* 1030–1037.

Sternberg, R. J. (2004). Culture and intelligence. *American Psychologist, 59,* 325–338.

Sternberg, R. J. (2005). There are no public policy implications: A reply to Rushton and Jensen (2005). *Psychology, Public Policy, and Law, 11,* 295–301.

Sternberg, R. J., & Clinkenbeard, P. (1995). A triarchic view of identifying, teaching, and assessing gifted children. *Roeper Review, 17,* 255–260.

Sternberg, R. J., Grigorenko, E. L., & Kidd, K. K. (2005). Intelligence, race, and genetics. *American Psychologist, 60,* 46–59.

Sternberg, R. J., Grigorenko, E. L., & Oh, S. (2001). The development of intelligence at midlife. In M. E. Lachman (Ed.), *Handbook of midlife development* (pp. 217–247). New York: Wiley.

Sternberg, R. J., Torff, B., & Grigorenko, E. L. (1998). Teaching triarchically improves school achievement. *Journal of Educational Psychology, 90*(3), 374–384.

Stevens, J. H., & Bakeman, R. (1985). A factor analytic study of the HOME scale for infants. *Developmental Psychology, 21,* 1106–1203.

Stevenson, H. W. (1995). Mathematics achievement of American students: First in the world by the year 2000? In C. A. Nelson (Ed.), *The Minnesota Symposia on Child Psychology: Vol. 28. Basic and applied perspectives on learning, cognition, and development* (pp. 131–149). Mahwah, NJ: Erlbaum.

Stevenson, H. W., Chen, C., & Lee, S. Y. (1993). Mathematics achievement of Chinese, Japanese, and American children: Ten years later. *Science, 258*(5081), 53–58.

Stevenson, H. W., Lee, S., Chen, C., & Lummis, M. (1990). Mathematics achievement of children in China and the United States. *Child Development, 61,* 1053–1066.

Stevenson, H. W., Lee, S. Y., Chen, C., Stigler, J. W., Hsu, C. C., & Kitamura, S. (1990). Contexts of achievement: A study of American, Chinese, and Japanese children. *Monographs of the Society for Research in Child Development, 55*(1–2, Serial No. 221).

Stevenson-Hinde, J., & Shouldice, A. (1996). Fearfulness: Developmental consistency. In A. J. Sameroff & M. M. Haith (Eds.), *The five- to seven-year shift: The age of reason and responsibility* (pp. 237–252). Chicago: University of Chicago Press.

Stewart, I. C. (1994, January 29). Two part message [Letter to the editor]. *New York Times,* p. A18.

Stice, E., & Bearman, K. (2001). Body image and eating disturbances prospectively predict increases in depressive symptoms in adolescent girls: A growth curve analysis. *Developmental Psychology, 37*(5), 597–607.

Stice, E., Presnell, K., & Bearman, S. K. (2001). Relation of early menarche to depression, eating disorders, substance abuse, and comorbid psychopathology among adolescent girls. *Developmental Psychology, 37,* 608–619.

Stice, E., Presnell, K., Shaw, H., & Rohde, P. (2005). Psychological and behavioral risk factors for obesity onset in adolescent girls: A prospective study. *Journal of Consulting and Clinical Psychology, 73,* 195–202.

Stick, S. M., Burton, P. B., Gurrin, L., Sly, P. D., & LeSouîf, P. N. (1996). Effects of maternal smoking during pregnancy and a family history of asthma on respiratory function in newborn infants. *The Lancet, 348,* 1060–1064.

Stipek, D. (2002). At what age should children enter kindergarten? A question for policy makers and parents. *SRCD Social Policy Report, 16*(2), 1–16.

Stipek, D., & Byler, P. (2001). Academic achievement and social behaviors associated with age of entry into kindergarten. *Journal of Applied Developmental Psychology, 22,* 175–189.

Stipek, D. J., Gralinski, H., & Kopp, C. B. (1990). Self-concept development in the toddler years. *Developmental Psychology, 26,* 972–977.

Stoecker, J. J., Colombo, J., Frick, J. E., & Allen, J. R. (1998). Long- and short-looking infants' recognition of symmetrical and asymmetrical forms. *Journal of Experimental Child Psychology, 71,* 63–78.

Stoelhorst, M. S. J., Rijken, M., Martens, S. E., Brand, R., den Ouden, A. L., Wit, J.-M., et al., on behalf of the Leiden Follow-up Project on Prematurity. (2005). Changes in neonatology: Comparison of two cohorts of very preterm infants (gestational age < 32 weeks): The Project on Preterm and Small for Gestational Age Infants 1983 and the Leiden Follow-up Project on Prematurity 1996–1997. *Pediatrics, 115,* 396–405.

Stoll, B. J., Hansen, N. I., Adams-Chapman, I., Fanaroff, A. A., Hintz, S. R., Vohr, B., et al., for the National Institute of Child Health and Human Development Neonatal Research Network. (2004). Neurodevelopmental and growth impairment among extremely low-birth-weight infants with neonatal infection. *Journal of the American Medical Association, 292,* 2357–2365.

Strassberg, Z., Dodge, K. A., Pettit, G. S., & Bates, J. E. (1994). Spanking in the home and children's subsequent aggression toward kindergarten peers. *Development and Psychopathology, 6,* 445–461.

Straus, M. A. (1994a). *Beating the devil out of them: Corporal punishment in American families.* San Francisco, CA: Jossey-Bass.

Straus, M. A. (1994b). Should the use of corporal punishment by parents be considered child abuse? In M. A. Mason & E. Gambrill (Eds.), *Debating children's lives: Current controversies on children and adolescents* (pp. 196–222). Newbury Park, CA: Sage.

Straus, M.A. (1999). *The benefits of avoiding corporal punishment: New and more definitive evidence.* Paper presented at the Changing Family and Child Development Conference, Banff, Alberta, Canada.

Straus, M.A., & Field, C. J. (2003). Psychological aggression by American parents: National data on prevalence, chronicity, and severity. *Journal of Marriage and Family, 65,* 795–808.

Straus, M.A., & Paschall, M. J. (1999, July). *Corporal punishment by mothers and children's cognitive development: A longitudinal study of two age cohorts.* Paper presented at the Sixth International Family Violence Research Conference, University of New Hampshire, Durham, NH.

Straus, M.A., & Stewart, J. H. (1999). Corporal punishment by American parents: National data on prevalence, chronicity, severity, and duration, in relation to child and family characteristics. *Clinical Child and Family Psychology Review, 2*(21), 55–70.

Straus, M.A., Sugarman, D. B., & Giles- Sims, J. (1997). Spanking by parents and subsequent antisocial behavior of children. *Archives of Pediatric and Adolescent Medicine, 151,* 761–767.

Streissguth, A. P., Aase, J. M., Clarren, S. K., Randels, S. P., LaDue, R. A., & Smith, D. F. (1991). Fetal alcohol syndrome in adolescents and adults. *Journal of the American Medical Association, 265,* 1961–1967.

Streissguth, A. P., Bookstein, F. L., Barr, H. M., Sampson, P. D., O'Malley, K., & Young, J. K. (2004). Risk factors for adverse life outcomes in fetal alcohol syndrome and fetal alcohol effects. *Journal of Developmental and Behavioral Pediatrics, 25,* 228–238.

Striano, T. (2004). Direction of regard and the still-face effect in the first year: Does intention matter? *Child Development, 75,* 468–479.

Striegel-Moore, R. H., & Bulik, C. M. (2007). Risk factors for eating disorders. *American Psychologist, 62,* 181–198.

Strobel, A., Camoin, T. I. L., Ozata, M., & Strosberg, A. D. (1998). A leptin missense mutation associated with hypogonadism and morbid obesity. *Nature Genetics, 18,* 213–215.

Strohschein, L. (2005). Parental divorce and child mental health trajectories. *Journal of Marriage and Family, 67,* 1286–1300.

Strömland, K., & Hellström, A. (1996). Fetal alcohol syndrome—An ophthalmological and socioeducational prospective study. *Pediatrics, 97,* 845–850.

Stuart, J. (1991). Introduction. In Z. Zhensun & A. Low, *A young painter: The life and paintings of Wang Yani—China's extraordinary young artist* (pp. 6–7). New York: Scholastic.

Stubbs, M. L., Rierdan, J., & Koff, E. (1989). Developmental differences in menstrual attitudes. *Journal of Early Adolescence, 9*(4), 480–498.

Stuebe, A. M., Rich-Edwards, J. W., Willett, W. C., Manson, J. E., & Michels, K. B. (2005). Duration of lactation and incidence of type 2 diabetes. *Journal of the American Medical Association, 294,* 2601–2610.

Sturges, J. W., & Sturges, L. V. (1998). In vivo systematic desensitization in a single-session treatment of an 11-year-old girl's elevator phobia. *Child and Family Behavior Therapy, 20,* 55–62.

Stuttering Foundation. (2006). *Stuttering: Straight talk for teachers* (Pub. No. 0125). Memphis, TN: Author.

Substance Abuse and Mental Health Services Administration (SAMHSA). (2004, October 22). Alcohol dependence or abuse and age at first use. *The NSDUH Report.* Retrieved December 18, 2004, from http://oas.samhsa.gov/2k4/ageDependence/ageDependence.htm

Suddendorf, T. (2003). Early representational insight: 24-month-olds can use a photo to find an object in the world. *Child Development, 74,* 896–904.

Sue, S., & Okazaki, S. (1990). Asian-American educational achievements: A phenomenon in search of an explanation. *American Psychologist, 45*(8), 913–920.

Suicide—Part I. (1996, November). *The Harvard Mental Health Letter,* pp. 1–5.

Sun, Y. (2001). Family environment and adolescents' well-being before and after parents' marital disruption. *Journal of Marriage and the Family, 63,* 697–713.

Suomi, S., & Harlow, H. (1972). Social rehabilitation of isolate-reared monkeys. *Developmental Psychology, 6,* 487–496.

Surkan, P. J., Stephansson, O., Dickman, P. W., & Cnattingius, S. (2004). Previous preterm and small-for-gestational-age births and the subsequent risk of stillbirth. *New England Journal of Medicine, 350,* 777–785.

Susman, E. J., & Rogol, A. (2004). Puberty and psychological development. In R. M. Lerner & L. Steinberg (Eds.)., *Handbook of adolescent psychology* (2nd ed., pp. 15–44). Hoboken, NJ: Wiley.

Susman-Stillman, A., Kalkoske, M., Egeland, B., & Waldman, I. (1996). Infant temperament and maternal sensitivity as predictors of attachment security. *Infant Behavior and Development, 19,* 33–47.

Susser, E. S., & Lin, S. P. (1992). Schizophrenia after prenatal exposure to the Dutch hunger winter of 1944–1945. *Archives of General Psychiatry, 49,* 983–988.

Sutcliffe, A., Loft, A., Wennerholm, U. B., Tarlatzis, V., & Bonduelle, M. (2003, July). *The European study of 1,523 ICSI/IVF versus naturally conceived 5-year-old children and their families: Physical development at five years.* Paper presented at conference of European Society of Human Reproduction and Embryology, Madrid.

Suzuki, L. A., & Valencia, R. R. (1997). Race-ethnicity and measured intelligence: Educational implications. *American Psychologist, 52,* 1103–1114.

Swain, I. U., Zelazo, P. R., & Clifton, R. K. (1993). Newborn infants' memory for speech sounds retained over 24 hours. *Developmental Psychology, 29,* 312–323.

Swallen, K. C., Reither, E. N., Haas, S. A., & Meier, A. M. (2005). Overweight, obesity, and health-related quality of life among adolescents: The National Longitudinal Study of Adolescent Health. *Pediatrics, 115,* 340–347.

Swan, S. H. (2000). Intrauterine exposure to diethylstilbestrol: Long-term effects in humans. *APMIS, 108,* 793–804.

Swan, S. H., Kruse, R. L., Liu, F., Barr, D. B., Drobnis, E. Z., Redmon, J. B., et al., & Study for Future Families Research Group. (2003). Semen quality in relation to biomarkers of pesticide exposure. *Environmental Health Perspectives, 111,* 1478–1484.

Swanston, H. Y., Tebbutt, J. S., O'Toole, B. I., & Oates, R. K. (1997). Sexually abused children 5 years after presentation: A case-control study. *Pediatrics, 100,* 600–608.

Swarr, A. E., & Richards, M. H. (1996). Longitudinal effects of adolescent girls' pubertal development, perceptions of pubertal timing, and parental relations on eating problems. *Developmental Psychology, 32,* 636–646.

Swedo, S., Rettew, D. C., Kuppenheimer, M., Lum, D., Dolan, S., & Goldberger, E. (1991). Can adolescent suicide attemptors be distinguished from at-risk adolescents? *Pediatrics, 88*(3), 620–629.

Swingley, D., & Fernald, A. (2002). Recognition of words referring to present and absent objects by 24-month olds. *Journal of Memory and Language, 46,* 39–56.

Szaflarski, J. P., Holland, S. K., Schmithorst, V. J., & Weber-Byars, A. (2004). *An fMRI study of cerebral language lateralization in 121 children and adults.* Paper presented at the 56th Annual Meeting of the American Academy of Neurology, San Francisco, CA.

Szatmari, P., Paterson, A. D., Zwaigenbaum, L., Roberts, W., Brian, J., Liu, X.-Q., et al. (2007). Mapping autism risk loci using genetic linkage and chromosomal rearrangements. *Nature Genetics, 39,* 319–328.

Szkrybalo, J., & Ruble, D. N. (1999). God made me a girl: Sex category constancy judgments and explanations revisited. *Developmental Psychology, 35,* 392–403.

Tackett, J. L., Krueger, R. F., Iacono, W. G., & McGue, M. (2005). Symptom-based subfactors of DSM-defined conduct disorder: Evidence for etiologic distinctions. *Journal of Abnormal Psychology, 114,* 483–487.

Tamburro, R. F., Gordon, P. L., D'Apolito, J. P., & Howard, S. C. (2004). Unsafe and violent behavior in commercials aired during televised major sporting events. *Pediatrics, 114,* 694–698.

Tamis-LeMonda, C. S., Bornstein, M. H., & Baumwell, L. (2001). Maternal responsiveness and children's achievement of language milestones. *Child Development, 72*(3), 748–767.

Tamis-LeMonda, C. S., Shannon, J. D., Cabrera, N. J., & Lamb, M. E. (2004). Fathers and mothers at play with their 2- and 3-year-olds: Contributions to language and cognitive development. *Child Development, 75,* 1806–1820.

Tanda, G., Pontieri, F. E., & DiChiara, G. (1997). Cannabinoid and heroin activation of mesolimbic dopamine transmission by a common N1 opiod receptor mechanism. *Science, 276,* 2048–2050.

Tao, K.-T. (1998). An overview of only child family mental health in China. *Psychiatry and Clinical Neurosciences, 52*(Suppl.), S206–S211.

Tarabulsy, G. M., Provost, M. A., Deslandes, J., St-Laurent, D., Moss, E., Lemelin, E., et al. (2003). Individual differences in infant still-face response at 6 months. *Infant Behavior and Development, 26,* 421–438.

Tarkan, L. (2005, November 22). Screening for abnormal embryos offers couples hope after heartbreak. *New York Times.* Retrieved November 22, 2005, from http://www.nytimes.com/2005/11/22/health/22gene.html

Taveras, E. M., Capra, A. M., Braveman, P. A., Jensvold, N. G., Escobar, G. J., & Lieu, T. A. (2003). Clinician support and psychosocial risk factors associated with breastfeeding discontinuation. *Pediatrics, 112,* 108–115.

Taylor, M. G. (1996). The development of children's beliefs about social and biological aspects of gender differences. *Child Development, 67,* 1555–1571.

Taylor, M. (1997). The role of creative control and culture in children's fantasy/reality judgments. *Child Development, 68,* 1015–1017.

Taylor, M., & Carlson, S. M. (1997). The relation between individual differences in fantasy and theory of mind. *Child Development, 68,* 436–455.

Taylor, M., Carlson, S. M., Maring, B. L., Gerow, L., & Charley, C. M. (2004). The characteristics and correlates of fantasy in school-age children: Imaginary companions, impersonation, and social understanding. *Developmental Psychology, 40,* 1173–1187.

Taylor, M., Cartwright, B. S., & Carlson, S. M. (1993). A developmental investigation of children's imaginary companions. *Developmental Psychology, 28,* 276–285.

Taylor, R. D., & Roberts, D. (1995). Kinship support in maternal and adolescent well-being in economically disadvantaged African-American families. *Child Development, 66,* 1585–1597.

Taylor, S., Way, B., Welch, W., Hilmert, C., Lehman, B., & Eisenberger, N. (2006). Early family environment, current adversity, the serotonin transporter promoter polymorphism, and depressive symptomatology. *Biological Psychiatry, 60*(7), 671–676.

Teachman, J. D., Tedrow, L. M., & Crowder, K. D. (2000). The changing demography of America's families. *Journal of Marriage and Family, 62,* 1234–1246.

Teller, D. Y., & Bornstein, M. H. (1987). Infant color vision and color perception. In P. Salapatek & L. B. Cohen (Eds.), *Handbook of infant perception: Vol. 1. From sensation to perception* (pp. 185–236). Orlando, FL: Academic Press.

Temple, J. A., Reynolds, A. J., & Miedel, W. T. (2000). Can early intervention prevent high school dropout? Evidence from the Chicago Child-Parent Centers. *Urban Education, 35*(1), 31–57.

Tennyson, A. (1850). "In Memoriam A. H. H., Canto 54."

Teplin, L. A., McClelland, G. M., Abram, K. M., & Mileusnic, D. (2005). Early violent death among delinquent youth: A prospective study. *Pediatrics, 115,* 1586–1593.

Terman, L. M., & Oden, M. H. (1959). *Genetic studies of genius: Vol. 5. The gifted group at mid-life.* Stanford, CA: Stanford University Press.

Termine, N. T., & Izard, C. E. (1988). Infants' responses to their mothers' expressions of joy and sadness. *Developmental Psychology, 24,* 223–229.

Tester, D. J., Carturan, E., Dura, M., Reiken, S., Wronska, A., Marks, A. R., et al. (2006, May). *Molecular and functional characterization of novel RyR2-encoded cardiac ryanodine receptor/calcium release channel mutations in sudden infant death syndrome.* Presentation at Heart Rhythm 2006, the 27th Annual Scientific Sessions of the Heart Rhythm Society, Boston.

Test-tube baby: It's a girl. (1978, August 7). *Time,* p. 68.

Teti, D. M., & Ablard, K. E. (1989). Security of attachment and infant-sibling relationships: A laboratory study. *Child Development, 60,* 1519–1528.

Teti, D. M., Gelfand, D. M., Messinger, D. S., & Isabella, R. (1995). Maternal depression and the quality of early attachment: An examination of infants, preschoolers, and their mothers. *Developmental Psychology, 31,* 364–376.

Teti, D. M., Sakin, J. W., Kucera, E., Corns, K. M., & Eiden, R. D. (1996). And baby makes four: Predictors of attachment security among preschoolage firstborns during the transition to siblinghood. *Child Development, 67,* 579–596.

Thal, D., Tobias, S., & Morrison, D. (1991). Language and gesture in late talkers: A one-year follow-up. *Journal of Speech and Hearing Research, 34,* 604–612.

Thapar, A., Fowler, T., Rice, F., Scourfield, J., van den Bree, M., Thomas, H., et al. (2003). Maternal smoking during pregnancy and attention deficit hyperactivity disorder symptoms in offspring. *American Journal of Psychiatry, 160,* 1985–1989.

Thapar, A., Langley, K., Fowler, T., Rice, F., Turic, D., Whittinger, N., et al. (2005). Catechol O-methyltransferase gene variant and birth weight predict early-onset antisocial behavior in children with attention-deficit/hyperactivity disorder. *Archives of General Psychiatry, 62,* 1275–1278.

Thelen, E. (1994). Three-month-old infants can learn task-specific patterns of interlimb coordination. *Psychological Science, 5,* 280–285.

Thelen, E. (1995). Motor development: A new synthesis. *American Psychologist, 50*(2), 79–95.

Thelen, E., & Fisher, D. M. (1982). Newborn stepping: An explanation for a "disappearing" reflex. *Developmental Psychology, 18,* 760–775.

Thelen, E., & Fisher, D. M. (1983). The organization of spontaneous leg movements in newborn infants. *Journal of Motor Behavior, 15,* 353–377.

Theodore, A. D., Chang, J. J., Runyan, D. K., Hunter, W. M., Bangdiwala, S. I., & Agans, R. (2005). Epidemiological features of the physical and sexual maltreatment of children in the Carolinas. *Pediatrics, 115,* 331–337.

Thoma, S. J., & Rest, J. R. (1999). The relationship between moral decision making and patterns of consolidation and transition in moral judgment development. *Developmental Psychology, 35,* 323–334.

Thomas, A., & Chess, S. (1977). *Temperament and development.* New York: Brunner/Mazel.

Thomas, A., & Chess, S. (1984). Genesis and evolution of behavioral disorders: From infancy to early adult life. *American Journal of Orthopsychiatry, 141*(1), 1–9.

Thomas, A., Chess, S., & Birch, H. G. (1968). *Temperament and behavior disorders in children.* New York: New York University Press.

Thomas, C. R., Holzer, C. E., & Wall, J. (2002). The Island Youth Programs: Community interventions for reducing youth violence and delinquency. In L. T. Flaherty, (Ed.), *Adolescent psychiatry: Developmental and clinical studies: Vol. 26. Annals of the American Society for Adolescent Psychiatry* (pp. 125–143). Hillsdale, NJ: Analytic Press.

Thomas, R. M. (1996). *Comparing theories of child development* (4th ed.). Pacific Grove, CA: Brooks-Cole.

Thomas, W. P., & Collier, V. P. (1997). *School effectiveness for language minority students.* Washington, DC: National Clearinghouse for Bilingual Education.

Thomas, W. P., & Collier, V. P. (1998). Two languages are better than one. *Educational Leadership, 55*(4), 23–28.

Thompson, L. A., Goodman, D. C., Chang, C.-H., & Stukel, T. A. (2005). Regional variation in rates of low birth weight. *Pediatrics, 116,* 1114–1121.

Thompson, P. M., Cannon, T. D., Narr, K. L., van Erp, T., Poutanen, V., Huttunen, M., et al. (2001). Genetic influences on brain structure. *Nature Neuroscience, 4,* 1253–1258.

Thompson, P. M., Giedd, J. N., Woods, R. P., MacDonald, D., Evans, A. C., & Toga, A. W. (2000). Growth patterns in the developing brain detected by using continuum mechanical tensor maps. *Nature, 404,* 190–193.

Thompson, R. A. (1990). Vulnerability in research: A developmental perspective on research risk. *Child Development, 61,* 1–16.

Thompson, R. A. (1991). Emotional regulation and emotional development. *Educational Psychology Review, 3,* 269–307.

Thompson, R. A. (1998). Early sociopersonality development. In W. Damon (Series Ed.) & N. Eisenberg (Vol. Ed.), *Handbook of child psychology: Vol. 3. Social, emotional, and personality development* (4th ed., pp. 25–104). New York: Wiley.

Thompson, S. L. (2001). The social skills of previously institutionalized children adopted from Romania. *Dissertation Abstracts International: Section B. The Sciences and Engineering, 61*(7-B), 3906.

Thomson, E., Mosley, J., Hanson, T. L., & McLanahan, S. S. (2001). Remarriage, cohabitation, and changes in mothering behavior. *Journal of Marriage and Family, 63,* 370–380.

Thorne, A., & Michaelieu, Q. (1996). Situating adolescent gender and self-esteem with personal memories. *Child Development, 67,* 1374–1390.

Tiedemann, D. (1897). *Beobachtunge über die entwickelung der seelenfähigkeiten bei kindern (Record of an infant's life).* Altenburg, Germany: Oscar Bonde. (Original work published 1787)

Tilghman, S. M. (1999). The sins of the fathers and mothers: Genomic imprinting in mammalian development. *Cell, 96,* 185–193.

Tincoff, R., & Jusczyk, P. W. (1999). Some beginnings of word comprehension in 6-month-olds. *Psychological Science, 10,* 172–177.

Tisdale, S. (1988). The mother. *Hippocrates, 2*(3), 64–72.

Toga, A. W., Thompson, P. M., & Sowell, E. R. (2006). Mapping brain maturation. *Trends in Neurosciences, 29*(3), 148–159.

Tolan, P. H., Gorman-Smith, D., & Henry, D. B. (2003). The developmental ecology of urban males' youth violence. *Developmental Psychology, 39,* 274–291.

Tomashek, K. M., Hsia, J., & Iyasu, S. (2003). Trends in postneonatal mortality attributable to injury, United States, 1988–1998. *Pediatrics, 111,* 1215–1218.

Tomlinson, M., Cooper, P., & Murray, L. (2005). The mother-infant relationship and infant attachment in a South African peri-urban settlement. *Child Development, 76,* 1044–1054.

Torrance, E. P. (1966). *The Torrance Tests of Creative Thinking: Technical norms manual* (Research ed.). Princeton, NJ: Personnel Press.

Torrance, E. P. (1974). *The Torrance Tests of Creative Thinking: Technical norms manual.* Bensonville, IL: Scholastic Testing Service.

Torrance, E. P., & Ball, O. E. (1984). *Torrance Tests of Creative Thinking: Streamlined (revised) manual, Figural A and B.* Bensonville, IL: Scholastic Testing Service.

Totsika, V., & Sylva, K. (2004). The Home Observation for Measurement of the Environment revisited. *Child and Adolescent Mental Health, 9,* 25–35.

Townsend, N. W. (1997). Men, migration, and households in Botswana: An exploration of connections over time and space. *Journal of Southern African Studies, 23,* 405–420.

Trautner, H. M., Ruble, D. N., Cyphers, L., Kirsten, B., Behrendt, R., & Hartmann, P. (2005). Rigidity and flexibility of gender stereotypes in childhood: Developmental or differential? *Infant and Child Development, 14,* 365–381.

Treffers, P. E., Hanselaar, A. G., Helmerhorst, T. J., Koster, M. E., & van Leeuwen, F. E. (2001). [Consequences of diethylstilbestrol during pregnancy; 50 years later still a significant problem.] *Ned Tijdschr Geneeskd, 145,* 675–680.

Trimble, J. E., & Dickson, R. (2005). Ethnic gloss. In C. B. Fisher & R. M. Lerner (Eds.), *Encyclopedia of applied developmental science* (Vol. I, pp. 412–415). Thousand Oaks, CA: Sage.

Troiano, R. P. (2002). Physical inactivity among young people. *New England Journal of Medicine, 347,* 706–707.

Tronick, E. (1972). Stimulus control and the growth of the infant's visual field. *Perception and Psychophysics, 11,* 373–375.

Tronick, E., Als, H., Adamson, L.,Wise, S., & Brazelton, T. B. (1978). The infant's response to entrapment between contradictory messages in face-to-face interaction. *American Academy of Child Psychiatry, 17,* 1–13.

Tronick, E. Z. (1980). On the primacy of social skills. In D. B. Sawin, L. O. Walker, & J. H. Penticuff (Eds.), *The exceptional infant: Psychosocial risk in infant environment transactions.* New York: Brunner/Mazel.

Tronick, E. Z. (1989). Emotions and emotional communication in infants. *American Psychologist, 44*(2), 112–119.

Tronick, E. Z., Morelli, G. A, & Ivey, P. (1992). The Efe forager infant and toddler's pattern of social relationships: Multiple and simultaneous. *Developmental Psychology, 28,* 568–577.

Troseth, G. L., & DeLoache, J. S. (1998). The medium can obscure the message: Young children's understanding of video. *Child Development, 69,* 950–965.

Troseth, G. L., Saylor, M. M., & Archer, A. H. (2006). Young children's use of video as a source of socially relevant information. *Child Development, 77,* 786–799.

Truffaut, F. (1969). *L'enfant sauvage* [*The Wild Child*].

Tryba, A. K., Peña, F., & Ramirez, J. M. (2006). Gasping activity in vitro: A rhythm dependent on 5-HT2A receptors. *Journal of Neuroscience, 26*(10), 2623–2634.

Tsai, J., & Floyd, R. L. (2004). Alcohol consumption among women who are pregnant or who might become pregnant—United States, 2002. *Morbidity and Mortality Weekly Report, 53*(50), 1178–1181.

Tsao, F. M., Liu, H. M., & Kuhl, P. K. (2004). Speech perception in infancy predicts language development in the second year of life: A longitudinal study. *Child Development, 75,* 1067–1084.

Turati, C., Simion, F., Milani, I., & Umilta, C. (2002). Newborns' preference for faces: What is crucial? *Developmental Psychology, 38,* 875–882.

Turkheimer, E., Haley, A., Waldron, J., D'Onofrio, B., & Gottesman, I. I. (2003). Socioeconomic status modifies heritability of IQ in young children. *Psychological Science, 14,* 623–628.

Turner, C. F., Ku, L., Rogers, S. M., Lindberg, L. D., Pleck, J. H., & Sonenstein, F. L. (1998). Adolescent sexual behavior, drug use, and violence: Increased reporting with computer survey technology. *Science, 280,* 867–873.

Turner, P. J., & Gervai, J. (1995). A multidimensional study of gender typing in preschool children and their parents: Personality, attitudes, preferences, behavior, and cultural differences. *Developmental Psychology, 31,* 759–772.

Turrisi, R., Wiersman, K. A., & Hughes, K. K. (2000). Binge-drinking-related consequences in college students: Role of drinking beliefs and mother-teen communication. *Psychology of Addictive Behaviors, 14*(4), 342–345.

Tuulio-Henriksson, A., Haukka, J., Partonen, T., Varilo, T., Paunio, T., Ekelund, J., et al. (2002). Heritability and number of quantitative trait loci of neurocognitive functions in families with schizophrenia. *American Journal of Medical Genetics, 114*(5), 483–490.

Twenge, J. M. (2000). The age of anxiety? Birth cohort change in anxiety and neuroticism, 1952–1993. *Journal of Personality and Social Psychology, 79,* 1007–1021.

Tygiel, J. (1983). *Baseball's great experiment: Jackie Robinson and his legacy.* New York: Oxford University Press.

Tygiel, J. (Ed.). (1997). *The Jackie Robinson reader.* New York: Dutton.

Umberger, F. G., & Van Reenen, J. S. (1995). Thumb sucking management: A review. *International Journal of Orofacial Myology, 21,* 41–47.

UNAIDS. (2006). *Report on the global AIDS epidemic.* Geneva: Author.

UNAIDS/WHO Joint United Nations Programme on HIV/AIDS and World Health Organization (2004). *AIDS epidemic update* (Publication No. UNAIDS/04.45E). Geneva: Author.

UNESCO. (2004). *Education for All Global Monitoring Report 2005—The quality imperative.* Retrieved November 10, 2004, from http://www.unesco.org/education/GMR2005/press

UNICEF. (2002). *Official summary of the State of the World's Children 2002.* Retrieved September 19, 2002, from http://www.unicef.org/pubsgen/sowc02summary/index.html

UNICEF. (2003). *Social monitor 2003.* Florence, Italy: Innocenti Social Monitor, UNICEF Innocenti Research Centre.

United Nations Children's Fund and World Health Organization (WHO). (2004). *Low birthweight: Country, regional and global estimates.* New York: UNICEF.

United Nations High Commissioner for Human Rights. (1989, November 20.). *Convention on the Rights of the Child.* General Assembly Resolution 44/25.

University of Virginia Health System. (2004). *How chromosome abnormalities happen: Meiosis, mitosis, maternal age, environment.* Retrieved September 16, 2004, from http://www.healthsystem.virginia.edu/UVAHealth/pedsgenetics/happen.cfm

U.S. Census Bureau. (1930). *Population in the United States: Population characteristics. January, 1930.* Washington, DC: U.S. Government Printing Office.

U.S. Census Bureau. (2003). *Population in the United States: Population characteristics. June, 2002.* Washington, DC: U.S. Government Printing Office.

U.S. Census Bureau. (2006). Living arrangements of children in 2003. In *The population profile of the United States: Dynamic Version* (*Internet Release*). Retrieved January 1, 2007, from http://www.census.gov/population/www/pop-profile/profiledynamic.html

U.S. Conference of Mayors. (2003). *A status report on hunger and homelessness in*

America's cities: 2003. Washington, DC: Author.

U.S. Department of Agriculture & U.S. Department of Health and Human Services. (2000). *Dietary guidelines for Americans* (5th ed.), USDA Home and Garden Bulletin No. 232. Washington, DC: U.S. Department of Agriculture.

U.S. Department of Health and Human Services (USDHHS). (1996a). *Health, United States, 1995* (DHHS Publication No. PHS 96–1232). Washington, DC: U.S. Government Printing Office.

U.S. Department of Health and Human Services (USDHHS). (1996b). *HHS releases study of relationship between family structure and adolescent substance abuse.* [Press release]. Retrieved from http://www.hhs.gov

U.S. Department of Health and Human Services (USDHHS). (1999a). *Blending perspectives and building common ground: A report to Congress on substance abuse and child protection.* Washington, DC: U.S. Government Printing Office.

U.S. Department of Health and Human Services (USDHHS). (1999b). *Mental health: A report of the Surgeon General.* Rockville, MD: U.S. Department of Health and Human Services, Substance Abuse and Mental Health Services Administration, National Institutes of Health, National Institute of Mental Health.

U.S. Department of Health and Human Services (USDHHS). (2000, December 6). *Statistics on child care help* [HHS press release]. Retrieved December 6, 2000, from http://www.hhs.gov/search/press.html

U.S. Department of Health and Human Services (USDHHS). (2003a). *State funded pre-kindergarten: What the evidence shows.* Retrieved from http://aspe.hhs.gov/hsp/statefunded-k/index.htm

U.S. Department of Health and Human Services (USDHHS). (2003b). *Strengthening Head Start: What the evidence shows.* Retrieved from http://aspe.hhs.gov/hsp/StrengthenHeadStart03/index.htm

U.S. Department of Health and Human Services (USDHHS). (2004). *Child maltreatment 2002.* Retrieved from http://www.acf.hhs.gov/programs/cb/publications/cm02/index.htm

U.S. Department of Health and Human Services Administration on Children, Youth, and Families. (2006). *Child maltreatment 2004.* Washington, DC: U.S. Government Printing Office.

U.S. Department of Health and Human Services Maternal and Child Health Bureau. (2005). *Newborn screening: Toward a uniform screening panel and system—Report for public comment.* Retrieved September 13, 2005, from www.mchb.hrsa.gov/screening

U. S. Preventive Services Task Force. (2006). Screening for speech and language delay in preschool children: Recommendation statement. *Pediatrics, 117,* 497–501.

Vainio, S., Heikkiia, M., Kispert, A., Chin, N., & McMahon, A. P. (1999). Female development in mammals is regulated by Wnt-4 signaling. *Nature, 397,* 405–409.

Valadez-Meltzer, A., Silber, T. J., Meltzer, A. A., & D'Angelo, L. J. (2005). Will I be alive in 2005? Adolescent level of involvement in risk behaviors and belief in near-future death. *Pediatrics, 116,* 24–31.

Valeski, T. N., & Stipek, D. J. (2001). Young children's feelings about school. *Child Development, 72*(4), 1198–1213.

Van, P. (2001). Breaking the silence of African American women: Healing after pregnancy loss. *Health Care Women International, 22,* 229–243.

Van den Boom, D. C. (1989). Neonatal irritability and the development of attachment. In G. A. Kohnstamm, J. E. Bates, & M. K. Rothbart (Eds.), *Temperament in childhood* (pp. 299–318). Chichester, England: Wiley.

Van den Boom, D. C. (1994). The influence of temperament and mothering on attachment and exploration: An experimental manipulation of sensitive responsiveness among lower-class mothers with irritable infants. *Child Development, 65,* 1457–1477.

Van Dyck, J. (1995). *Manufacturing babies and public consent: Debating the new reproductive technologies.* New York: New York University Press.

van Goozen, S. H. M., Fairchild, G., Snoek, H., & Harold, G. T. (2007). The evidence for a neurobiological model of childhood antisocial behavior. *Psychological Bulletin, 133,* 149–182.

van IJzendoorn, M. H. (1995). Adult attachment representations, parental responsiveness, and infant attachment: A meta-analysis on the predictive validity of the Adult Attachment Interview. *Psychological Bulletin, 117*(3), 387–403.

van IJzendoorn, M. H., & Juffer, F. (2005). Adoption is a successful natural intervention enhancing adopted children's IQ and school performance. *Current Directions in Psychological Science, 14,* 326–330.

van IJzendoorn, M. H., Juffer, F., & Poelhuis, C. W. K. (2005). Adoption and cognitive development: A meta-analytic comparison of adopted and nonadopted children's IQ and school performance. *Psychological Bulletin, 131,* 301–316.

van IJzendoorn, M. H., & Kroonenberg, P. M. (1988). Cross-cultural patterns of attachment: A meta-analysis of the Strange Situation. *Child Development, 59,* 147–156.

van IJzendoorn, M. H., & Sagi, A. (1997). Cross-cultural patterns of attachment: Universal and contextual dimensions. In J. Cassidy & P. R. Shaver (Eds.), *Handbook on attachment theory and research.* New York: Guilford.

van IJzendoorn, M. H., & Sagi, A. (1999). Cross-cultural patterns of attachment: Universal and contextual dimensions. In J. Cassidy & P. R. Shaver (Eds.), *Handbook*

of attachment: Theory, research, and clinical applications (pp. 713–734). New York: Guilford.

van IJzendoorn, M. H., Schuengel, C., & Bakermans-Kranenburg, M. J. (1999). Disorganized attachment in early childhood: Meta-analysis of precursors, concomitants, and sequelae. *Development and Psychopathology, 11,* 225–250.

van IJzendoorn, M. H., Vereijken, C.M. J. L., Bakermans-Kranenburg, M. J., & Riksen-Walraven, J. M. (2004). Assessing attachment security with the Attachment Q Sort: Meta-analytic evidence for the validity of the observer AQS. *Child Development, 75,* 1188.

van Noord-Zaadstra, B. M., Looman, C. W., Alsbach, H., Habbema, J. D., te Velde, E. R., & Karbaat, J. (1991). Delayed childbearing: Effect of age on fecundity and outcome of pregnancy. *British Medical Journal, 302,* 1361–1365.

Van Voorhis, B. J. (2007). In vitro fertilization. *New England Journal of Medicine, 356,* 379–386.

Van Voorhis, B. J., Greensmith, J. E., Dokras, A., Sparks, A. E., Simmons, S. T., & Syrop, C. H. (2005). Hyperbaric oxygen and ovarian follicular stimulation for in vitro fertilization: A pilot study. *Fertility and Sterility, 83*(1), 226–228.

Vance, M. L., & Mauras, N. (1999). Growth hormone therapy in adults and children. *New England Journal of Medicine, 341*(16), 1206–1216.

Vandell, D. L. (2000). Parents, peer groups, and other socializing influences. *Developmental Psychology, 36,* 699–710.

Vandell, D. L., & Bailey, M. D. (1992). Conflicts between siblings. In C. U. Shantz & W. W. Hartup (Eds.), *Conflict in child and adolescent development* (pp. 242–269). New York: Cambridge University Press.

Vandell, D. L., & Ramanan, J. (1992). Effects of early and recent maternal employment on children from low income families. *Child Development, 63,* 938–949.

Vargha-Khadem, F., Gadian, D. G., Watkins, K. E., Connelly, A., Van Paesschen, W., & Mishkin, M. (1997). Differential effects of early hippocampal pathology on episodic and semantic memory. *Science, 277,* 376–380.

Vasilyeva, M. & Huttenlocher, J. (2004). Early development of scaling ability. *Developmental Psychology, 40,* 682–690.

Vasilyeva, M., Huttenlocher, J., & Waterfall, H. (2006). Effects of language intervention on syntactic skill levels in preschoolers. *Developmental Psychology, 42,* 164-174.

Vaswani, M., & Kapur, S. (2001). Genetic basis of schizophrenia: Trinucleotide repeats: An update. *Progress in Neuro-Psychopharmacology and Biological Psychiatry, 25*(6), 1187–1201.

Vaughn, B. E., Stevenson-Hinde, J., Waters, E., Kotsaftis, A., Lefever, G. B., Shouldice,

A., et al. (1992). Attachment security and temperament in infancy and early childhood: Some conceptual clarifications. *Developmental Psychology, 28,* 463–473.

Vecchiotti, S. (2003). Kindergarten: An overlooked educational policy priority. *SRCD Social Policy Report, 17*(2), 1–19.

Veenstra, R., Lindenberg, S., Oldehinkel, A. J., De Winter, A. F., Verhulst, F. C., & Ormel, J. (2005). Bullying and victimization in elementary schools: A comparison of bullies, victims, bully/victims, and uninvolved preadolescents. *Developmental Psychology, 41,* 672–682.

Ventura, S. J., Mathews, T. J., & Hamilton, B. E. (2001). Births to teenagers in the United States, 1940–2000. *National Vital Statistics Reports, 49*(10). Hyattsville, MD: National Center for Health Statistics.

Vereecken, C., & Maes, L. (2000). Eating habits, dental care and dieting. In C. Currie, K. Hurrelmann, W. Settertobulte, R. Smith, & J. Todd (Eds.), *Health and health behaviour among young people: A WHO crossnational study (HBSC) international report* (pp. 83–96). WHO Policy Series: Healthy Policy for Children and Adolescents, Series No. 1. Copenhagen, Denmark: World Health Organization Regional Office for Europe.

Verlinsky, Y., Rechitsky, S., Verlinsky, O., Masciangelo, C., Lederer, K., & Kuliev, A. (2002). Preimplantation diagnosis for early-onset Alzheimer disease caused by V717L mutation. *Journal of the American Medical Association, 287,* 1018–1021.

Verma, S., & Larson, R. (2003). Editors' notes. In S. Verma & R. Larson (Eds.), Chromosomal congenital anomalies and residence near hazardous waste landfill sites. *Lancet, 359,* 320–322.

Verschueren, K., Buyck, P., & Marcoen, A. (2001). Self representations and socioemotional competence in young children: A 3-year longitudinal study. *Developmental Psychology, 37,* 126–134.

Verschueren, K., Marcoen, A., & Schoefs, V. (1996). The internal working model of the self, attachment, and competence in five-year-olds. *Child Development, 67,* 2493–2511.

Vgontzas, A. N., & Kales, A. (1999). Sleep and its disorders. *Annual Review of Medicine, 50,* 387–400.

Viner, R. M., & Cole, T. J. (2005). Television viewing in early childhood predicts adult body mass index. *Journal of Pediatrics, 147,* 429–435.

Vink, T., Hinney, A., van Elburg, A. A., van Goozen, S. H. M., Sandkuijl, L. A., Sinke, R. J., et al. (2001). Association between an agouti-related protein gene polymorphism and anorexia nervosa. *Molecular Psychiatry, 6,* 325–328.

Vitaro, F., Tremblay, R. E., Kerr, M., Pagani, L., & Bukowski, W. M. (1997). Disruptiveness, friends' characteristics, and delinquency in early adolescence: A test of two competing models of development. *Child Development, 68,* 676–689.

Vohr, B. R., Wright, L. L., Poole, K., & McDonald, S. A., for the NICHD Neonatal Research Network Follow-up Study. (2005). Neurodevelopmental outcomes of extremely low birth weight infants < 30 weeks' gestation between 1993 and 1998. *Pediatrics, 116,* 635–643.

Vondra, J. I., & Barnett, D. (1999). A typical attachment in infancy and early childhood among children at developmental risk. *Monographs of the Society for Research in Child Development, Serial No. 258, 64*(3).

Vosniadou, S. (1987). Children and metaphors. *Child Development, 58,* 870–885.

Votruba-Drzal, E., Coley, R. L., & Chase-Lansdale, P. L. (2004). Child care and low-income children's development: Direct and moderated effects. *Child Development, 75,* 296–312.

Vrijheld, M., Dolk, H., Armstrong, B., Abramsky, L., Bianchi, F., Fazarinc, I., et al. (2002). Chromosomal congenital anomalies and residence near hazardous waste landfill sites. *Lancet, 359*(9303), 320–322.

Vuchinich, S., Angelelli, J., & Gatherum, A. (1996). Context and development in family problem solving with preadolescent children. *Child Development, 67,* 1276–1288.

Vuori, L., Christiansen, N., Clement, J., Mora, J., Wagner, M., & Herrera, M. (1979). Nutritional supplementation and the outcome of pregnancy: 2. Visual habitation at 15 days. *Journal of Clinical Nutrition, 32,* 463–469.

Vygotsky, L. S. (1962). *Thought and language.* Cambridge, MA: MIT Press. (Original work published 1934)

Vygotsky, L. S. (1978). *Mind in society: The development of higher psychological processes.* Cambridge, MA: Harvard University Press.

Wade, N. (2001, October 4). Researchers say gene is linked to language. *New York Times,* p. Al.

Wagner, C. L., Katikaneni, L. D., Cox, T. H., & Ryan, R. M. (1998). The impact of prenatal drug exposure on the neonate. *Obstetrics and Gynecology Clinics of North America, 25,* 169–194.

Wahlbeck, K., Forsen, T., Osmond, C., Barker, D. J. P., & Erikkson, J. G. (2001). Association of schizophrenia with low maternal body mass index, small size at birth, and thinness during childhood. *Archives of General Psychiatry, 58,* 48–55.

Wainright, J. L., Russell, S. T., & Patterson, C. J. (2004). Psychosocial adjustment, school outcomes, and romantic relationships of adolescents with same-sex parents. *Child Development, 75,* 1886–1898.

Waisbren, S. E., Albers, S., Amato, S., Ampola, M., Brewster, T. G., Demmer, L., et al. (2003). Effect of expanded newborn screening for biochemical disorders on child outcomes and parental stress. *Journal of the American Medical Association, 290,* 2564–2572.

Wakefield, M., Reid, Y., Roberts, L., Mullins, R., & Gillies, P. (1998). Smoking and smoking cessation among men whose partners are pregnant: A qualitative study. *Social Science and Medicine, 47,* 657–664.

Waknine, Y. (2006). Highlights from MMWR: Prevalence of U.S. birth defects and more. *Medscape.* Retrieved January 9, 2006, from http://www.medscape.com/viewarticle/521056

Wakschlag, L. S., Lahey, B. B., Loeber, R., Green, S. M., Gordon, R. A., & Leventhal, B. L. (1997). Maternal smoking during pregnancy and the risk of conduct disorders in boys. *Archives of General Psychiatry, 54,* 670–676.

Wald, N. J. (2004). Folic acid and the prevention of neural-tube defects. *New England Journal of Medicine, 350,* 101–103.

Waldman, I. D. (1996). Aggressive boys' hostile perceptual and response biases: The role of attention and impulsivity. *Child Development, 67,* 1015–1033.

Walk, R. D., & Gibson, E. J. (1961). A comparative and analytical study of visual depth perception. *Psychology Monographs, 75*(15).

Waller, M. W., Hallfors, D. D., Halpern, C. T., Iritani, B., Ford, C. A., & Guo, G. (2006). Gender differences in associations between depressive symptoms and patterns of substance use and risky sexual behavior among a nationally representative sample of U.S. adolescents. *Archives of Women's Mental Health, 9,* 139–150.

Wallerstein, J., & Corbin, S. B. (1999). The child and the vicissitudes of divorce. In R. M. Galatzer-Levy & L. Kraus (Eds.), *The scientific basis of child custody decisions* (pp. 73–95). New York: Wiley.

Wallerstein, J. S., Lewis, J. M., & Blakeslee, S. (2000). *The unexpected legacy of divorce: A 25-year landmark study.* New York: Hyperion.

Walma van der Molen, J. (2004). Violence and suffering in television news: Toward a broader conception of harmful television content for children. *Pediatrics, 113,* 1771–1775.

Wang, D. W., Desai, R. R., Crotti, L., Arnestad, M., Insolia, R., Pedrazzini, M., et al. (2007). Cardiac sodium channel dysfunction in sudden infant death syndrome. *Circulation, 115,* 368–376.

Wang, H., Parry, S., Macones, G., Sammel, M. D., Kuivaniemi, H., Tromp, G., et al. (2006). A functional SNP in the promoter of the SERPINH1 gene increases risk of preterm premature rupture of membranes in African Americans. *Proceedings of the National Academy of Sciences, USA, 103,* 13463–13467.

Wang, H., Xie, H., Guo, Y., Zhang, H., Takahashi, T., Kingsley, P. J., et al. (2006). Fatty acid amide hydrolase deficiency limits early pregnancy events. *The Journal of Clinical Investigation, 116*(8), 2122–2131.

Wang, Q. (2004). The emergence of cultural self-constructs: Autobiographical memory and self-description in European American and Chinese children. *Developmental Psychology, 40*, 3–15.

Wang, Y., & Lobstein, T. (2006). Worldwide trends in childhood overweight and obesity. *International Journal of Obesity, 1*(1), 11–25.

Wardle, J., Robb, K. A., Johnson, F., Griffith, J., Brunner, E., Power, C., et al. (2004). Socioeconomic variation in attitudes to eating and weight in female adolescents. *Health Psychology, 23*, 275–282.

Wasik, B. H., Ramey, C. T., Bryant, D. M., & Sparling, J. J. (1990). A longitudinal study of two early intervention strategies: Project CARE. *Child Development, 61*, 1682–1696.

Watamura, S. E., Donzella, B., Alwin, J., & Gunnar, M. R. (2003). Morning-to-afternoon increases in cortisol concentrations for infants and toddlers at child care: Age differences and behavioral correlates. *Child Development, 74*, 1006–1020.

Waters, E., & Deane, K. E. (1985). Defining and assessing individual differences in attachment relationships: Q-methodology and the organization of behavior in infancy and early childhood. *Monographs of the Society for Research in Child Development, 50*, 41–65.

Waters, E., Wippman, J., & Sroufe, L. A. (1979). Attachment, positive affect, and competence in the peer group: Two studies in construct validation. *Child Development, 50*, 821–829.

Waters, K. A., Gonzalez, A., Jean, C., Morielli, A., & Brouillette, R. T. (1996). Face-straight-down and face-near-straight-down positions in healthy prone-sleeping infants. *Journal of Pediatrics, 128*, 616–625.

Watkins, M., Rasmussen, S. A., Honein, M. A., Botto, L. D., & Moore, C. A. (2003). Maternal obesity and risk for birth defects. *Pediatrics, 111*, 1152–1158.

Watson, A. C., Nixon, C. L., Wilson, A., & Capage, L. (1999). Social interaction skills and theory of mind in young children. *Developmental Psychology, 35*(2), 386–391.

Watson, J. B., & Rayner, R. (1920). Conditioned emotional reactions. *Journal of Experimental Psychology, 3*, 1–14.

Weese-Mayer, D. E., Berry-Kravis, E. M., Maher, B. S., Silvestri, J. M., Curran, M. E., & Marazita, M. L. (2003). Sudden infant death syndrome: Association with a promoter polymorphism of the serotonin transporter gene. *American Journal of Medical Genetics, 117A*, 268–274.

Weese-Mayer, D. E., Berry-Kravis, E. M., Zhou, L., Maher, B. S., Curran, M. E., Silvestri, J. M., et al. (2004). Sudden Infant Death Syndrome: Case-control frequency differences at genes pertinent to autonomic nervous system embryological development. *Pediatric Research, 56*, 391–395.

Wegman, M. E. (1992). Annual summary of vital statistics—1991. *Pediatrics, 90*, 835–845.

Wellman, H. M., & Cross, D. (2001). Theory of mind and conceptual change. *Child Development, 72*, 702–707.

Wellman, H. M., Cross, D., & Watson, J. (2001). Meta-analysis of theory-of-mind development: The truth about false belief. *Child Development, 72*, 655–684.

Wellman, H. M., & Gelman, S. A. (1998). Knowledge acquisition in foundational domains. In W. Damon (Series Ed.), D. Kuhn, & R. S. Siegler (Vol. Eds.), *Handbook of child psychology: Vol. 2. Cognition, perception, and language* (5th ed., pp. 523–573). New York: Wiley.

Wellman, H. M., & Woolley, J. D. (1990). From simple desires to ordinary beliefs: The early development of everyday psychology. *Cognition, 35*, 245–275.

Wells, G. (1985). Preschool literacy-related activities and success in school. In D. R. Olson, N. Torrence, & A. Hilyard (Eds.), *Literacy, language, and learning* (pp. 229–255). New York: Cambridge University Press.

Weinberg, M. K., & Tronick, E. Z. (1996). Infant affective reactions to the resumption of maternal interaction after stillface. *Child Development, 67*, 905–914.

Weinberger, B., Anwar, M., Hegyi, T., Hiatt, M., Koons, A., & Paneth, N. (2000). Antecedents and neonatal consequences of low Apgar scores in preterm newborns. *Archives of Pediatric and Adolescent Medicine, 154*, 294–300.

Weinberger, D. R. (2001, March 10). A brain too young for good judgment. *New York Times*. Retrieved from http://www.nytimes.com/2001/03/10/opinion/10WEIN.html?ex_985250309&ei_1&en_995bc03f7a8c7207

Weinreb, L., Wehler, C., Perloff, J., Scott, R., Hosmer, D., Sagor, L., et al. (2002). Hunger: Its impact on children's health and mental health. *Pediatrics, 110*, 816.

Weinstock, H., Berman, S., & Cates, W., Jr. (2004). Sexually transmitted diseases among American youth: Incidence and prevalence estimates, 2000. *Perspectives on Sexual and Reproductive Health, 36*, 6–10.

Weisner, T. S. (1993). Ethnographic and eco-cultural perspectives on sibling relationships. In Z. Stoneman & P. W. Berman (Eds.), *The effects of mental retardation, visibility, and illness on sibling relationships* (pp. 51–83). Baltimore, MD: Brookes.

Weiss, B., Amler, S., & Amler, R. W. (2004). Pesticides. *Pediatrics, 113*, 1030–1036.

Weiss, B., Dodge, K. A., Bates, J. E., & Pettit, G. S. (1992). Some consequences of early harsh discipline: Child aggression and a maladaptive social information processing style. *Child Development, 63*, 1321–1335.

Weissman, M. M., Warner, V., Wickramaratne, P. J., & Kandel, D. B. (1999). Maternal smoking during pregnancy and psychopathology in offspring followed to adulthood. *Journal of the American Academy of Child and Adolescent Psychiatry, 38*, 892–899.

Weisz, J. R., McCarty, C. A., & Valeri, S. M. (2006). Effects of psychotherapy for depression in children and adolescents: A meta-analysis. *Psychological Bulletin, 132*, 132–149.

Weisz, J. R., Weiss, B., Han, S. S., Granger, D. A., & Morton, T. (1995). Effects of psychotherapy with children and adolescents revisited: A meta-analysis of treatment outcome studies. *Psychological Bulletin, 117*(3), 450–468.

Weitzman, M., Gortmaker, S., & Sobol, A. (1992). Maternal smoking and behavior problems of children. *Pediatrics, 90*, 342–349.

Welch-Ross, M. K. (1997). Mother-child participation in conversation about the past: Relationships to preschoolers' theory of mind. *Developmental Psychology, 33*(4), 618–629.

Welch-Ross, M. K., & Schmidt, C. R. (1996). Gender-schema development and children's story memory: Evidence for a developmental model. *Child Development, 67*, 820–835.

Wender, P. H. (1995). *Attention-deficit hyperactivity disorder in adults.* New York: Oxford University Press.

Wentworth, N., Benson, J. B., & Haith, M. M. (2000). The development of infants' reaches for stationary and moving targets. *Child Development, 71*, 576–601.

Wentzel, K. R. (2002). Are effective teachers like good parents? Teaching styles and student adjustment in early adolescence. *Child Development, 73*, 287–301.

Wenzel, D. (1990). *Ann Bancroft: On top of the world.* Minneapolis, MN: Dillon.

Werker, J. F. (1989). Becoming a native listener. *American Scientist, 77*, 54–59.

Werker, J. F., Pegg, J. E., & McLeod, P. J. (1994). A cross-language investigation of infant preference for infant-directed communication. *Infant Behavior and Development, 17*, 323–333.

Werler, M. M., Louik, C., Shapiro, S., & Mitchell, A. A. (1996). Prepregnant weight in relation to risk of neural tube defects. *Journal of the American Medical Association, 275*, 1089–1092.

Werner, E., Bierman, L., French, F. E., Simonian, K., Conner, A., Smith, R., et al. (1968). Reproductive and environmental casualties: A report on the 10-year follow-up of the children of the Kauai pregnancy study. *Pediatrics, 42*, 112–127.

Werner, E., & Smith, R. S. (2001). *Journeys from childhood to midlife.* Ithaca, NY: Cornell University Press.

Werner, E. E. (1985). Stress and protective factors in children's lives. In A. R. Nichol (Ed.), *Longitudinal studies in child psychology and psychiatry.* New York: Wiley.

Werner, E. E. (1987, July 15). *Vulnerability and resiliency: A longitudinal study of Asian Americans from birth to age 30.* Invited address at the Ninth Biennial Meeting of the International Society for the Study of Behavioral Development, Tokyo, Japan.

Werner, E. E. (1989). Children of the garden island. *Scientific American, 260*(4), 106–111.

Werner, E. E. (1993). Risk and resilience in individuals with learning disabilities: Lessons learned from the Kauai longitudinal study. *Learning Disabilities Research and Practice, 8,* 28–34.

Werner, E. E. (1995). Resilience in development. *Current Directions in Psychological Science, 4*(3), 81–85.

Westen, D. (1998). The scientific legacy of Sigmund Freud: Toward a psychodynamically informed psychological science. *Psychological Bulletin, 124,* 333–371.

Wexler, I. D., Branski, D., & Kerem, E. (2006). War and children. *Journal of the American Medical Association, 296,* 579–581.

Whalen, C. K., Jamner, L. D., Henker, B., Delfino, R. J., & Lozano, J. M. (2002). The ADHD spectrum and everyday life: Experience sampling of adolescent moods, activities, smoking, and drinking. *Child Development, 73,* 209–228.

Whalley, L. J., & Deary, I. J. (2001). Longitudinal cohort study of childhood IQ and survival up to age 76. *British Medical Journal, 322,* 819.

Whalley, L. J., Starr, J. M., Athawes, R., Hunter, D., Pattie, A., & Deary, I. J. (2000). Childhood mental ability and dementia. *Neurology, 55,* 1455–1459.

Whitaker, R. C., Wright, J. A., Pepe, M. S., Seidel, K. D., & Dietz, W. H. (1997). Predicting obesity in young adulthood from childhood and parental obesity. *New England Journal of Medicine, 337,* 869–873.

White, A. (2001). *Alcohol and adolescent brain development.* Retrieved from http://www.duke.edu/~amwhite/alc_adik_pf.html

White, B. L. (1971, October). *Fundamental early environmental influences on the development of competence.* Paper presented at the Third Western Symposium on Learning: Cognitive Learning, Western Washington State College, Bellingham, WA.

White, B. L., Kaban, B., & Attanucci, J. (1979). *The origins of human competence.* Lexington, MA: Heath.

Whitehurst, G. J., Falco, F. L., Lonigan, C. J., Fischel, J. E., DeBaryshe, B. D., Valdez-Menchaca, M. D., et al. (1988). Accelerating language development through picture book reading. *Developmental Psychology, 24,* 552–559.

Whitehurst, G. J., & Lonigan, C. J. (1998). Child development and emergent literacy. *Child Development, 69,* 848–872.

Whitrow, G. J. (1967). *Einstein: The man and his achievement.* New York: Dover.

Whyatt, R. M., Rauh, V., Barr, D. B., Camann, D. E., Andrews, H. F., Garfinkel, R., et al. (2004). Prenatal insecticide exposures and birth weight and length among an urban minority cohort. *Environmental Health Perspectives, 112*(110), 1125–1132.

Wiggins, S., Whyte, P., Higgins, M., Adams, S., Theilmann, J., Bloch, M., et al. (1992). The psychological consequences of predictive testing for Huntington's disease. *New England Journal of Medicine, 327,* 1401–1405.

Wilcox, A. J., Baird, D. D., Weinberg, C. R., Hornsby, P. P., & Herbst, A. L. (1995). Fertility in men exposed prenatally to diethylstilbestrol. *New England Journal of Medicine, 332,* 1411–1416.

Wilcox, A. J., Dunson, D., & Baird, D. D. (2000). The timing of the "fertile window" in the menstrual cycle: Day specific estimates from a prospective study. *British Medical Journal, 321,* 1259–1262.

Wilens, T. E., Faraone, S. V., & Biederman, J. (2004). Attention-Deficit Hyperactivity Disorder in adults. *Journal of the American Medical Association, 292,* 619–623.

Wilgoren, J. (2005, September 25). "Mothering the mother" during childbirth and after. *New York Times.* Retrieved September 27, 2005, from http://www.nytimes.com/2005/09/25/national/25doula.html?

Williams, D. L., Goldstein, G., & Minshew, N. J. (2006). Neuropsychologic functioning in children with autism: Further evidence for disordered complex information-processing. *Child Neuropsychology: A Journal on Normal and Abnormal Development in Childhood and Adolescence, 12*(4–5), 279–298.

Williams, E. R., & Caliendo, M. A. (1984). *Nutrition: Principles, issues, and applications.* New York: McGraw-Hill.

Williams, G. J. (2001). The clinical significance of visual-verbal processing in evaluating children with potential learning related visual problems. *Journal of Optometric Vision Development, 32*(2), 107–110.

Williams, J., Wake, M., Hesketh, K., Maher, E., & Waters, E. (2005). Health-related quality of life of overweight and obese children. *Journal of the American Medical Association, 293,* 70–76.

Willinger, M., Hoffman, H. T., & Hartford, R. B. (1994). Infant sleep position and risk for sudden infant death syndrome: Report of meeting held January 13 and 14, 1994. *Pediatrics, 93,* 814–819.

Wilson, E. O. (1975). *Sociobiology: The new synthesis.* Cambridge, MA: Belknap Press of Harvard University Press.

Wilson, G. T., Grillo, C. M., & Vitousek, K. M. (2007). Psychological treatment of eating disorders. *American Psychologist, 62,* 199–216.

Wilson, K., & Ryan, V. (2001). Helping parents by working with their children in individual child therapy. *Child and Family Social Work* (special issue), *6,* 209–217.

Wilson-Costello, D., Friedman, H., Minich, N., Siner, B., Taylor, G., Schluchter, M., et al. (2007). Improved neurodevelopmental outcomes for extremely low birth weight infants in 2000–2002. *Pediatrics, 119,* 37–45.

Winner, E. (1997). Exceptionally high intelligence and schooling. *American Psychologist, 52*(10), 1070–1081.

Winner, E. (2000). The origins and ends of giftedness. *American Psychologist, 55,* 159–169.

Wisner, K. L., Chambers, C., & Sit, D. K. Y. (2006). Postpartum depression: A major public health problem. *Journal of the American Medical Association, 296,* 2616–2618.

Wolchik, S. A., Sandler, I. N., Millsap, R. E., Plummer, B. A., Greene, S. M., Anderson, E. R., et al. (2002). Six year follow-up of a randomized, controlled trial of preventive interventions for children of divorce. *Journal of the American Medical Association, 288,* 1874–1881.

Wolff, P. H. (1963). Observations on the early development of smiling. In B. M. Foss (Ed.), *Determinants of infant behavior* (vol. 2). London: Methuen.

Wolff, P. H. (1966). The causes, controls, and organizations of behavior in the newborn. *Psychological Issues, 5*(1, Whole No. 17), 1–105.

Wolff, P. H. (1969). The natural history of crying and other vocalizations in early infancy. In B. M. Foss (Ed.), *Determinants of infant behavior* (Vol. 4). London: Methuen.

Wolraich, M. L., Wibbelsman, C. J., Brown, T. E., Evans, S. W., Gotlieb, E. M., Knight, J. R., et al. (2005). Attention-deficit/hyperactivity disorder among adolescents: A review of the diagnosis, treatment, and clinical implications. *Pediatrics, 115,* 1734–1746.

Women in History. (2004). *Marian Anderson biography.* Lakewood, OH: Lakewood Public Library. Retrieved November 18, 2004, from http://www.lkwdpl.org/wihohio/ande-mar.htm

Wong, A. H. C., Gottesman, I. I., & Petronia, A. (2005). Phenotypic differences in genetically identical organisms: The epigenetic perspective. *Human Molecular Genetics, 14, Review Issue 1,* doi:10.1093/hmg/ddi116.

Wong, C. A., Scavone, B. M., Peaceman, A. M., McCarthy, R. J., Sullivan, J. T., Diaz, N. T., et al. (2005). The risk of cesarean delivery with neuraxial analgesia given early versus late in labor. *New England Journal of Medicine, 352,* 655–665.

Wong, C. K., Murray, M. L., Camilleri-Novak, D., & Stephens, P. (2004). Increased prescribing trends of paediatric psychtropic medications. *Archives of the Diseases of Children, 89,* 1131–1132.

Wood, D. (1980). Teaching the young child: Some relationships between social interaction, language, and thought. In D. Olson (Ed.), *The social foundations of language and thought* (pp. 280–296). New York: Norton.

Wood, D., Bruner, J., & Ross, G. (1976). The role of tutoring in problem solving. *Journal of Child Psychiatry and Psychology, 17,* 89–100.

Wood, R. M., & Gustafson, G. E. (2001). Infant crying and adults' anticipated caregiving responses: Acoustic and contextual influences. *Child Development, 72,* 1287–1300.

Wood, W., & Eagly, A. (2002). A cross-cultural analysis of the behavior of women and men: Implications for the origins of sex differences. *Psychological Bulletin, 128,* 699–727.

Woodruff, T. J., Axelrad, D. A., Kyle, A. D., Nweke, O., Miller, G. G., & Hurley, B. J. (2004). Trends in environmentally related childhood illnesses. *Pediatrics, 113,* 1133–1140.

Woodward, A. L., Markman, E. M., & Fitzsimmons, C. M. (1994). Rapid word learning in 13- and 18-month olds. *Development Psychology, 30,* 553–566.

Woodward, S. A., McManis, M. H., Kagan, J., Deldin, P., Snidman, N., Lewis, M., et al. (2001). Infant temperament and the brainstem auditory evoked response in later childhood. *Developmental Psychology, 37,* 533–538.

Woolley, J. D. (1997). Thinking about fantasy: Are children fundamentally different thinkers and believers from adults? *Child Development, 68*(6), 991–1011.

Woolley, J. D., & Boerger, E. A. (2002). Development of beliefs about the origins and controllability of dreams. *Developmental Psychology, 38*(1), 24–41.

Woolley, J. D., Phelps, K. E., Davis, D. L., & Mandell, D. J. (1999). Where theories of mind meet magic: The development of children's beliefs about wishing. *Child Development, 70,* 571–587.

World Bank. (2006). *Repositioning nutrition as central to development.* Washington, DC: Author.

World Health Organization. (2003). The world health report—shaping the future. Retrieved February 14, 2004, from http://www.who. int/wrh/2003/chapter1en/index2.html

Wright, J. C., Huston, A. C., Murphy, K. C., St. Peters, M., Pinon, M., Scantlin, R., et al. (2001). The relations of early television viewing to school readiness and vocabulary of children from low-income families: The Early Window Project. *Child Development, 72*(5), 1347–1366.

Wright, V. C., Chang, J., Jeng, G., & Macaluso, M. (2006). Assisted reproduction technology surveillance—United States, 2003. *Morbidity and Mortality Weekly Report* (Surveillance Summaries), *55*(SS04), 1–22.

Wright, V. C., Schieve, L. A., Reynolds, M. A., & Jeng, G. (2003). Assisted Reproductive Technology Surveillance—United States, 2000. Division of Reproductive Health, National Center for Chronic Disease Prevention and Health Promotion. Retrieved from http://www.cdc.gov/reprod

Wrigley, J., & Dreby, J. (2005). Fatalities and the organization of child care in the United States; 1985–2003. *American Sociological Review, 70*(5), 729–757.

Wu, T., Mendola, P., & Buck, G. M. (2002). Ethnic differences in the presence of secondary sex characteristics and menarche among U.S. girls: The Third National Health and Nutrition Survey, 1988–1994. *Pediatrics, 11,* 752–757.

Wulczyn, F. (2004). Family reunification. In David and Lucile Packard Foundation, Children, families, and foster care. *The Future of Children, 14*(1). Retrieved from http://www.futureofchildren.org

Wynn, K. (1990). Children's understanding of counting. *Cognition, 36,* 155–193.

Wynn, K. (1992). Evidence against empiricist accounts of the origins of numerical knowledge. *Mind and Language, 7,* 315–332.

Wyrobek, A. J., Eskenazi, B., Young, S., Arnheim, N., Tiemann-Boege, I., Jabs, E. W., et al. (2006). Advancing age has differential effects on DNA damage, chromatin integrity, gene mutations, and aneuploidies in sperm. *Proceedings of the National Academy of Sciences of the United States of America, 103*(25), 9601–9606.

Xu, B., Wratten, N., Charych, E. I., Buyske, S., Firestein, B. L., & Brzustowicz, L. M. (2005). Increased expression in dorsolateral prefrontal cortex of CAPON in schizophrenia and bipolar disorder. *PLoS Medicine, 2*(10), 999–1007.

Yager, J., & Andersen, A. E. (2005). Anorexia nervosa. *New England Journal of Medicine, 353,* 1481–1488.

Yamada, H. (2004). Japanese mothers' views of young children's areas of personal discretion. *Child Development, 75,* 164–179.

Yamazaki, J. N., & Schull, W. J. (1990). Perinatal loss and neurological abnormalities among children of the atomic bomb. *Journal of the American Medical Association, 264,* 605–609.

Yang, B., Ollendick, T. H., Dong, Q., Xia, Y., & Lin, L. (1995). Only children and children with siblings in the People's Republic of China: Levels of fear, anxiety, and depression. *Child Development, 66,* 1301–1311.

Yingling, C. D. (2001). Neural mechanisms of unconscious cognitive processing. *Clinical Neurophysiology, 112*(1), 157–158.

Yip, T., Seaton, E. K., & Sellers, R. M. (2006). African American racial identity across the lifespan: Identity status, identity content, and depressive symptoms. *Child Development, 77,* 1504–1517.

Yokota, F., & Thompson, K. M. (2000). Violence in G-rated animated films. *Journal of the American Medical Association, 283,* 2716–2720.

Yoshikawa, H. (1994). Prevention as cumulative protection: Effects of early family support and education on chronic delinquency and its risks. *Psychological Bulletin, 115*(1), 28–54.

Young, K. A., Holcomb, L. A., Bonkale, W. L., Hicks, P. B., Yazdani, U., & German, D. C. (2007). 5HTTLPR polymorphism and enlargement of the pulvinar: Unlocking the backdoor to the limbic system. *Biological Psychiatry, 61,* 813–818.

Youngblade, L. M., & Belsky, J. (1992). Parent-child antecedents of 5-year-olds' close friendships: A longitudinal analysis. *Developmental Psychology, 28,* 700–713.

Youngblade, L. M., Theokas, C., Schulenberg, J., Curry, L., Huang, I.-C., & Novak, M. (2007). Risk and promotive factors in families, schools, and communities: A contextual model of positive youth development in adolescence. *Pediatrics, 119,* 47–53.

Youth violence: A report of the Surgeon General. (2001, January). Retrieved from http://www.surgeongeneral.gov/library/youthviolence/default.htm

Yu, S. M., Huang, Z. J., & Singh, G. K. (2004). Health status and health services utilization among U.S. Chinese, Asian Indian, Filipino, and other Asian/Pacific Islander children. *Pediatrics, 113*(1), 101–107.

Yuan, W., Holland, S. K., Cecil, K. M., Dietrich, K. N., Wessel, S. D., Altaye, M., et al. (2006). The impact of early childhood lead exposure on brain organization: A functional magnetic resonance imaging study of language function. *Pediatrics, 118,* 971–977.

Yunger, J. L., Carver, P. R., & Perry, D. G. (2004). Does gender identity influence children's psychological well-being? *Developmental Psychology, 40,* 572–582.

Yurgelon-Todd, D. (2002). Inside the Teen Brain. Retrieved from http://www.pbs.org/wgbh/pages/frontline/shows/teenbrain/interviews/todd.html

Zahn-Waxler, C., Friedman, R. J., Cole, P. M., Mizuta, I., & Hiruma, N. (1996). Japanese and U.S. preschool children's responses to conflict and distress. *Child Development, 67,* 2462–2477.

Zahn-Waxler, C., Radke-Yarrow, M., Wagner, E., & Chapman, M. (1992). Development of concern for others. *Developmental Psychology, 28,* 126–136.

Zametkin, A. J. (1995). Attention-deficit disorder: Born to be hyperactive. *Journal of the American Medical Association, 273*(23), 1871–1874.

Zametkin, A. J., & Ernst, M. (1999). Problems in the management of attention deficit-hyperactivity disorder. *New England Journal of Medicine, 340,* 40–46.

Zeanah, C. H., Smyke, A. T., Koga, S. F., & Carlson, E. (2005). Attachment in institutionalized and community children in Romania. *Child Development, 76,* 1015–1028.

Zeedyk, M. S., Wallace, L., & Spry, L. (2002). Stop, look, listen, and think? What young children really do when crossing the road. *Accident Analysis and Prevention, 34*(1), 43–50.

Zelazo, P. D., & Müller, U. (2002). Executive function in typical and atypical development. In U. Goswami (Ed.), *Handbook of childhood cognitive development* (pp. 445–469). Oxford, UK: Blackwell.

Zelazo, P. D., Müller, U., Frye, D., & Marcovitch, S. (2003). The development of executive function in early childhood. *Monographs of the Society for Research in Child Development, 68* (3, Serial No. 274).

Zelazo, P. R., Kearsley, R. B., & Stack, D. M. (1995). Mental representations for visual sequences: Increased speed of central processing from 22 to 32 months. *Intelligence, 20,* 41–63.

Zeskind, P. S., & Stephens, L. E. (2004). Maternal selective serotonin reuptake inhibitor use during pregnancy and newborn neurobehavior. *Pediatrics, 11,* 368–375.

Zhao, Y. (2002, May 29). Cultural divide over parental discipline. *New York Times.* Retrieved from http://www.nytimes.com/2002/05/29/nyregion/29DISC.html?ex

Zhensun, Z., & Low, A. (1991). *A young painter: The life and paintings of Wang Yani—China's extraordinary young artist.* New York: Scholastic.

Zhu, B.-P., Rolfs, R. T., Nangle, B. E., & Horan, J. M. (1999). Effect of the interval between pregnancies on perinatal outcomes. *New England Journal of Medicine, 340,* 589–594.

Zigler, E. (1998). School should begin at age 3 years for American children. *Journal of Developmental and Behavioral Pediatrics, 19,* 37–38.

Zigler, E., & Styfco, S. J. (1993). Using research and theory to justify and inform Head Start expansion. *Social Policy Report of the Society for Research in Child Development, 7*(2).

Zigler, E., & Styfco, S. J. (1994). Head Start: Criticisms in a constructive context. *American Psychologist, 49*(2), 127–132.

Zigler, E., & Styfco, S. J. (2001). Extended childhood intervention prepares children for school and beyond. *Journal of the American Medical Association, 285,* 2378–2380.

Zigler, E., Taussig, C., & Black, K. (1992). Early childhood intervention: A promising preventative for juvenile delinquency. *American Psychologist, 47,* 997–1006.

Zigler, E. F. (1987). Formal schooling for four-year-olds? *North American Psychologist, 42*(3), 254–260.

Zimmerman, B. J., Bandura, A., & Martinez-Pons, M. (1992). Self motivation for academic attainment: The role of self-efficacy beliefs and personal goal setting. *American Educational Research Journal, 29,* 663–676.

Zimmerman, F. J., & Christakis, D. A. (2005). Children's television viewing and cognitive outcomes: A longitudinal analysis of national data. *Archives of Pediatrics and Adolescent Medicine, 159*(7), 619–625.

Zito, J. M., Safer, D. J., dosReis, S., Gardner, J. F., Magder, L., Soeken, K., et al. (2003). Psychotropic practice patterns for youth: A 10-year perspective. *Archives of Pediatrics and Adolescent Medicine, 57*(1), 17–25.

Zubenko, G. S., Maher, B., Hughes, H. B., III, Zubenko, W. N., Stiffler, J. S., Kaplan, B. B., et al. (2003). Genome-wide linkage survey for genetic loci that influence the development of depressive disorders in families with recurrent, early-onset, major depression. *American Journal of Medical Genetics: Part B. Neuropsychiatric Genetics, 123*(1), 1–18.

Zuckerman, B. S., & Beardslee, W. R. (1987). Maternal depression: A concern for pediatricians. *Pediatrics, 79,* 110–117.

Zuvekas, S. H., Vitiello, B., & Norquist, G. S. (2006). Recent trends in stimulant medication use among U. S. children. *American Journal of Psychiatry, 163,* 574–585.

Credits

Text and Line Art

Chapter 2

Fig. 2-2: From *A Child's World,* 8th ed., by Diane E. Papalia and Sally Wendkos Olds, Fig. 1-3, p. 29. Copyright © 1999 by The McGraw-Hill Companies, Inc. Reprinted by permission of The McGraw-Hill Companies, Inc.

Chapter 3

Fig. 3-3: From *Human Development,* 10th ed., by Diane E. Papalia, Sally Wendkos Olds, and Ruth Duskin Feldman, Fig. 3-2, p. 66. Copyright © 2007 by The McGraw-Hill Companies, Inc. Reprinted by permission of The McGraw-Hill Companies, Inc.; **Fig. 3-4:** From *Human Development,* 10th ed., by Diane E. Papalia, Sally Wendkos Olds, and Ruth Duskin Feldman, p. 67. Copyright © 2007 by The McGraw-Hill Companies, Inc. Reprinted by permission of The McGraw-Hill Companies, Inc.; **Fig. 3-6:** From *Human Development,* 10th ed., by Diane E. Papalia, Sally Wendkos Olds, and Ruth Duskin Feldman, p. 72. Copyright © 2007 by The McGraw-Hill Companies, Inc. Reprinted by permission of The McGraw-Hill Companies, Inc.; **Fig. 3-9:** From "Neurobiology of intelligence: Science and ethics," by Jeremy R. Gray and Paul M. Thompson in *Nature Reviews/Neuroscience,* 5, June 2004, Box 2, p. 477. Copyright © 2004 Nature Publishing Group. Reprinted with permission.

Chapter 4

Fig. 4-2: From *Human Development,* 10th ed., by Diane E. Papalia, Sally Wendkos Olds, and Ruth Duskin Feldman, p. 88. Copyright © 2007 by The McGraw-Hill Companies, Inc. Reprinted by permission of The McGraw-Hill Companies, Inc.; **Fig. 4-3:** From "Preventing birth defects even before pregnancy," by J. E. Brody in *The New York Times,* June 28, 1995. Copyright © 1995 by The New York Times Co. Reprinted with permission; **Fig. 4-5:** From "Advanced maternal age—how old is too old?" by L. J. Heffner in *New England Journal of Medicine,* 351(19), pp. 1927–1929. November 4, 2004. Copyright © 2004 Massachusetts Medical Society. All rights reserved.

Chapter 5

Fig. 5-1: Adapted from "The 'stress' of being born," by H. Lagercrantz and T. A. Slotkin in *Scientific American,* 254(4), April 1986, pp. 100–107. Reprinted by permission of the illustrator, Patricia Wynne; **Table 5-2:** From *Developmental Physiology and Aging* by P. S. Timiras. Copyright © 1972. Reprinted by permission of the author; **Table 5-3:** Adapted from "A proposal for a new method of evaluation of the newborn infant," by Virginia Apgar in *Current Research in Anesthesia &* *Analgesia,* 32, pp. 260–267, July-August 1953. Reprinted by permission of Lippincott, Williams and Wilkins. All Rights Reserved; **Table 5-4:** Adapted with permission from "The neurological examination of the full-term newborn infant," by H. F. R. Prechtl and D. J. Beintema in *Clinics in Developmental Medicine,* no. 12, 1964.

Chapter 6

Table 6-1: Adapted from *Lifelong Motor Development,* 2nd ed., by C. P. Gabbard. Copyright © 1996. Used by permission of the author; **Table 6-2:** Adapted from *The Denver Developmental Screening Test: Reference Manual* by Frankenburg et al. Copyright © 1992. Reprinted with permission; **Fig. 6-3:** From *Brain Facts: A Primer on the Brain and Nervous System,* p. 13. Copyright © 2005, 2006 The Society for Neuroscience. Reprinted with permission; **Fig. 6-4:** From *Brain Facts: A Primer on the Brain and Nervous System,* p. 10. Copyright © 2005, 2006 The Society for Neuroscience. Reprinted with permission; **Fig. 6-5:** From *Human Development,* 10th ed., by Diane E. Papalia, Sally Wendkos Olds, and Ruth Duskin Feldman, Fig.4-6, p. 134. Copyright © 2007 by The McGraw-Hill Companies, Inc. Reprinted by permission of The McGraw-Hill Companies, Inc.; **Fig. 6-7:** From "Fertile Minds," by J. M. Nash in *Time,* February 3, 1997, pp. 49–56. Copyright © 1997 by Time, Inc. Reprinted by permission.

Chapter 7

Fig. 7-2: From "Current theory and research on infant learning and memory: Application to early interventions," by Carolyn Rovee-Collier and Kimberly Boller in *Infants and Young Children,* 7(3), pp. 1–12, January 1995. Reprinted by permission of Lippincott, Williams and Wilkins. All Rights Reserved; **Table 7-1:** From "The Home Observation for Measurement of the Environment Revisited," by Vasiliki Totsika and Kathy Sylva in *Child and Adolescent Mental Health,* 9(1), pp. 25–35, February 2004, Table 1. Reprinted by permission of Blackwell Publishing; **Table 7-4:** From *Human Development,* 10th ed., by Diane E. Papalia, Sally Wendkos Olds, and Ruth Duskin Feldman, Table 5-3, p. 162. Copyright © 2007 by The McGraw-Hill Companies, Inc. Reprinted by permission of The McGraw-Hill Companies, Inc.; **Box 7-2:** From "Zero to six: Electronic media in the lives of infants, toddlers, and preschoolers," by V. J. Rideout, E. A. Vandewater, and E. A. Wartella, #3378, The Henry J. Kaiser Family Foundation, October, 2003. This information was reprinted with permission from the Henry J. Kaiser Family Foundation. The Kaiser Family Foundation, based in Menlo Park, California, is a nonprofit, private operating foundation focusing on the major health care issues facing the nation and is not associated with Kaiser Permanente or Kaiser Industries; **Fig. 7-4:** From "Object permanence in young infants: Further evidence," by R. Baillargeon and J. DeVos in *Child Development,* 62, 1991, pp. 1227–1246. Copyright © 1991 by the Society for Research in Child Development, Inc. Reprinted with permission; **Fig. 7-5:** From "How do infants learn about the physical world?" by R. Baillargeon in *Current Directions in Psychological Science,* 3(5), pp. 133–139, October 1994, Fig. 5, p. 138. Reprinted by permission of Blackwell Publishing.

Chapter 8

Ch. 8, opening quote: From "Life Prayer." Words and music by John Hartford. Copyright © 1968 (renewed 1996) by Ensign Music Corporation International. Reprinted with permission; **Table 8-1:** Adapted from "Socioemotional development," by L. A. Sroufe in *Handbook of Infant Development,* edited by J. Osofsky. Copyright © 1979 by John Wiley & Sons, Inc. Reprinted with permission of John Wiley & Sons, Inc.; **Fig. 8-1:** Adapted from "The self in self-conscious emotions," by M. Lewis in S. G. Snodgrass and R. L. Thompson (eds.), "The self across psychology: Self-recognition, self-awareness, and the self-concept," *Annals of the New York Academy of Sciences,* 818, Fig. 1, p. 120. Copyright © 1997. Reprinted by permission of Blackwell Publishing; **Table 8-2:** Adapted from "Genesis and evolution of behavioral disorders: From infancy to early adult life," by A. Thomas and S. Chess in *American Journal of Psychiatry,* 141(1), pp. 1–9. Copyright © 1984 by the American Psychological Association; **Table 8-3:** Based on "Early sociopersonality development," by R. A. Thompson in *Handbook of Child Psychology, Volume 3,* edited by N. Eisenberg, pp. 37–39. Copyright © 1998 by John Wiley & Sons, Inc. Reprinted by permission of John Wiley & Sons, Inc.

Chapter 9

Fig. 9-1: Reprinted with the permission of Simon & Schuster Adult Publishing Group from *Solve Your Child's Sleep Problems* by R. Ferber. Copyright © 1985 by Richard Ferber, M.D.; **Table 9-2:** From *A Textbook of Motor Development* by C. B. Corbin. Copyright © 1973 by The McGraw-Hill Companies, Inc. Reprinted by permission of The McGraw-Hill Companies, Inc.; **Fig. 9-2:** From *Analyzing Children's Art* by R. Kellogg. Copyright © 1969, 1970 by Rhoda

Kellogg. Published by The McGraw-Hill Companies; **Fig. 9-3:** Bar chart from Ch. 1, "Global Health: Today's Challenges," Fig. 1.4 in *The World Health Report—Shaping the Future*, 2003. Published by the World Health Organization; **Fig. 9-4:** From "WHO estimates of the causes of death in children," by J. Bryce, C. Boschi-Pinto, K. Shibuya, and the WHO Child Health Epidemiology Reference Group in *The Lancet,* 365 (9465), 2005, pp. 1147–1152. This is reprinted with permission from Elsevier; **Fig. 9-5:** From *The State of America's Children,* 2004, p. 19. Reprinted with permission of The Children's Defense Fund, Washington, DC.

Chapter 10

Table 10-3: From "Number sense growth in kindergarten: A longitudinal investigation of children at risk for mathematics difficulties," by Nancy C. Jordan, David Kaplan, Leslie Nabors Olah, and Maria N. Locuniak in *Child Development,* 77(1), January-February 2006, Table 1, p. 104. Reprinted by permission of Blackwell Publishing; **Table 10-5:** Adapted from "Development of private speech among low income Appalachian children," by L. Berk and R. Garvin in *Developmental Psychology,* 202(2), pp. 271–284. Copyright © 1984 by the American Psychological Association.

Chapter 11

Ch. 11, opening quote: Excerpt from *The People, Yes* by Carl Sandburg. Copyright © 1936 by Harcourt, Brace & Company and renewed 1964 by Carl Sandburg. Reprinted by permission of the publisher; **Table 11-3:** Adapted from "Childhood Fears" by R. J. Morris and T. R. Kratochwill in *Treating Children's Fears and Phobias: A Behavioral Approach,* p. 2. Published by Allyn and Bacon. Copyright © 1983 by Pearson Education. And from "Fearfulness: Developmental Consistency," by J. Stevenson-Hinde and A. Shouldice in *The Five to Seven Year Shift: The Age of Reason and Responsibility,* edited by A. J. Sameroff and M. M. Haith (pp. 237–252). Copyright © 1996. Reprinted by permission of The University of Chicago Press.

Chapter 12

Ch. 12, opening quote: From *You Can't Get There From Here* by Ogden Nash. Copyright © 1953, 1954, 1955, 1956, 1957 by Ogden Nash. Copyright © 1953, 1954, 1956 by The Curtis Publishing Company; **Fig. 12-1:** From "Dynamic mapping of human cortical development during childhood through early adulthood," by N. Gogtay, J. N. Giedd, L. Lusk, K. M. Hayashi, D. Greenstein, A. C. Vaituzis, T. F. Hugent, D. H. Herman, L. S. Clasen, A. W. Toga, J. L. Rapoport,

and P. M. Thompson in *Proceedings of the National Academy of Sciences,* 101(21), May 25, 2004, pp. 8174–8179. Copyright © 2004 National Academy of Sciences, U.S.A. Reprinted with permission.

Chapter 13

Table 13-3: Based on *Frames of Mind: The Theory of Multiple Intelligences* by Howard Gardner. New York: Basic Books, 1993. Also based on "Are there additional intelligences?" by Howard Gardner in J. Kane (Ed.), *Education, Information, and Transformation: Essays on Learning and Thinking.* Englewood Cliffs, NJ: Prentice-Hall, 1998. Used by permission of the author.

Chapter 14

Table 14-1: Based on *The Growth of Interpersonal Understanding: Developmental and Clinical Analysis* by R. L. Selman, 1980. Reprinted with the permission of Elsevier. And based on "Children's ideas about friendship: A new theory," by R. L. Selman and A. P. Selman in *Psychology Today,* April 1979, pp. 71–80. Copyright © 1979 by Sessex Publishers, Inc. Reprinted with the permission of *Psychology Today* magazine; **Box 14-2:** From *Human Development,* 10th ed., by Diane E. Papalia, Sally Wendkos Olds, and Ruth Duskin Feldman, pp. 386–387. Copyright © 2007 by The McGraw-Hill Companies, Inc. Reprinted by permission of The McGraw-Hill Companies, Inc.; **Table 14-3:** From "The development of competence in favorable and unfavorable environments: Lessons from research on successful children," by A. S. Masten and J. D. Coatsworth in *American Psychologist,* 53, pp. 205–220. Copyright © 1998 by the American Psychological Association.

Chapter 16

Fig. 16-1: Adapted from *Cognitive Development,* 1st ed., by Melinda Y. Small. Copyright © 1990. Reprinted with permission of Wadsworth, a division of Thomson Learning, www.thomsonrights.com. Fax: 800-730-2215; **Table 16-1:** Adapted from "Stage and Sequence: The cognitive-developmental approach to socialization," by L. Kohlberg, 1969 in *Handbook of Socialization Theory and Research,* edited by David A. Goslin and T. W. Lickona from *Moral Development and Behavior.* Reprinted by permission of the authors.

Chapter 17

Ch. 17, opening quote: From *A Sky Full of Poems* by Eve Merriam. Copyright © 1964, 1970, 1973, 1986 by Eve Merriam. All rights

reserved. Used by permission of Marian Reiner; **Table 17-1:** Adapted from "Developmental and validation of ego identity status," by J. E. Marcia in *Journal of Personality and Social Psychology,* 3(5), pp. 551–558. Copyright © 1966 by the American Psychological Association; **Table 17-2:** From "Ego identity: An overview" in *Discussion of Ego Identity,* edited by J. Kroger, 1993. Reprinted by permission of the author; **Table 17-3:** From "Stages of ethnic identity development in minority group adolescents," by J. S. Phinney in *Journal of Early Adolescence,* 9, pp. 34–39. Copyright © 1989 by Sage Publications. Reprinted by permission of Sage Publications, Inc.; **Table 17-4:** Adapted with permission from *National Survey of Adolescents and Young Adults: Sexual Health Knowledge, Attitudes and Experiences,* (#3218), Table 8, p. 12, and Table 33, p. 39. The Henry J. Kaiser Family Foundation, May 2003. This information was reprinted with permission from the Henry J. Kaiser Family Foundation. The Kaiser Family Foundation, based in Menlo Park, California, is a nonprofit, private operating foundation focusing on the major health care issues facing the nation and is not associated with Kaiser Permanente or Kaiser Industries; **Figs. 17-1 and 17-2:** From "Behind fall in pregnancy, a new teenage culture of restraint," by Nina Bernstein in *The New York Times,* March 17, 2004, p. 36. Copyright © 2004 by The New York Times Co. Reprinted with permission; **Table 17-6:** From "Parental psychological control: Revisiting a neglected construct," by B. K. Barber in *Child Development,* 67(6), pp. 3296–3319, December 1996. Reprinted by permission of Blackwell Publishing; **Table 17-7:** From "Adolescents' and parents' changing conceptions of parental authority," by J. Smetana, H. Crean, and N. Campione-Barr in *Changing boundaries of parental authority during adolescence: New directions for child and adolescent development, no. 108,* edited by J. Smetana (pp. 31-46, Table 3.1). Reprinted by permission of John Wiley & Sons, Inc.; **Box 17-2:** From p. 463 in *Human Development,* 10th ed., by Diane E. Papalia, Sally Wendkos Olds, and Ruth Duskin Feldman. Copyright © 2007 by The McGraw-Hill Companies, Inc. Reprinted by permission of The McGraw-Hill Companies, Inc.; **Table 17-8:** From "Deviant peer influences in intervention and public policy for youth," by Kenneth A. Dodge, Thomas J. Dishion, and Jennifer E. Lansford in *Social Policy Report,* XX(1), 2006, Table 3, p. 8. Reprinted by permission of Blackwell Publishing.

Photo Credits

Part Openers

p. 2: (top) © Rob Melnychuk/Digital Vision/Getty Images; **(bottom)** © Jon

Feingersh; **p. 56: (top)** © Antonio Mo/Getty Images; **(center)** © Jose Luis Pelaez Inc./Blend Images/Getty Images; **(bottom)** © Bob

Daemmrich/Stock Boston; **p. 140: (top)** © Michael Newman/PhotoEdit; **(center)** © Laura Dwight/Corbis Images; **(bottom)**

© Brand X Pictures/PunchStock; **p. 246:** (top) © Ariel Skelley/Corbis Images; (center) © Bob Daemmrich/PhotoEdit; (bottom) © CLEO Photo/Index Stock Imagery; **p. 328:** (top) © Michael Newman/PhotoEdit; (center) © Comstock Images/Alamy; (bottom) © Digital Vision/Punchstock; **p. 414:** (top) © Michael J. Doolittle/The Image Works; (center) © David Young-Wolff/PhotoEdit; (bottom) © Arthur Tilley/Getty Images

Chapter 1
Opener: © Rob Melnychuk/Digital Vision/Getty Images; **p. 5:** © Contemporary portrait of Victor of Aveyron from DE L'EDUCATION D'UN HOMME. Reproduced by permission of The British Library; **p. 10:** © Musées Royaux d'Art et d'Histoire–Brussels; **p. 14:** © Syracuse Newspapers/The Image Works; **p. 17:** Library of Congress, Prints & Photographs Division, FSA/OWI Collection, [LC-USF34-T01-009095-C]

Chapter 2
Opener: © Jon Feingersh; **p. 23:** © Bettmann/Corbis Images; **p. 27:** © National Library of Medicine; **p. 29:** © Bettmann/Corbis Images; **p. 32:** © Joe McNally; **p. 33:** © Yves De Braine/Black Star; **p. 34:** A.R. Luria/Dr. Michael Cole, Laboratory of Human Cognition, University of California, San Diego; **p. 42:** © Howard J. Radzyner/Phototake; **p. 47:** © James Wilson/Woodfin Camp

Chapter 3
Opener: © Antonio Mo/Getty Images; **p. 59:** © Lester Sloan/Woodfin Camp; **p. 65:** © Nancy Richmond/The Image Works; **p. 70:** © David Young-Wolff/PhotoEdit; **p. 75:** © Ellen Senisi/The Image Works; **p. 79:** © Thomas K. Wanstall/The Image Works; **p. 80:** © Peter DeJong/AP Images

Chapter 4
Opener: © Jose Luis Pelaez Inc./Blend Images/Getty Images; **pp. 92 & 93:** (1 mo., 7 wks., 7 mo., 8 mo.) © Petit Format/Nestle/Science Source/Photo Researchers; (3 mo., 6 mo.) © Lennart Nilsson/Albert Bonniers Forlag AB, A CHILD IS BORN, Dell Publishing Company; (4 mo.) © Ralph Hutchings/Visuals Unlimited; (5 mo.) © James Stevenson/Photo Researchers; (9 mo.) © Tom Galliher/Corbis; **p. 98:** PhotoDisc/Getty Images; **p. 101:** © Blend Images/Corbis Images; **p. 102:** © David Young-Wolff/PhotoEdit

Chapter 5
Opener: © Bob Daemmrich/Stock Boston; **p. 113:** © Bettmann/Corbis Images; **p. 121:** © Erol Gurian/Corbis Images; **p. 127:** © Angela Hampton/Alamy; **p. 131:** © John Cole/Photo Researchers; **p. 133:** © Mike Teruya/Free Spirit Photography; **p. 135:** Harlow Primate Laboratory, University of Wisconsin; **p. 136:** © PhotoDisc/Getty Images

Chapter 6
Opener: © Michael Newman/PhotoEdit; **p. 143:** © Library of Congress, Prints & Photographs Division [LC-USZ62-112517]; **p. 147:** © Richard Lord/The Image Works; **p. 156:** (top left) © Mimi Forsyth; (top center) © Lew Merrim/Photo Researchers; (top right) © Laura Dwight; (bottom left) © Elizabeth Crews; (bottom center) Astier/Photo Researchers; (bottom right) © Elizabeth Crews; **p. 157:** (both) Courtesy, Children's Hospital of Michigan; **p. 158:** © Creatas/PictureQuest; **p. 161:** © Kevin Delgado; **p. 163:** © Innervisions; **p. 168:** © Mark Thomas/SPL/Photo Researchers

Chapter 7
Opener: © Laura Dwight/Corbis Images; **p. 177:** Neg. No. 326799 Courtesy Department Library Services/American Museum of Natural History; **p. 181:** Courtesy, Carolyn Rovee-Collier; **p. 189:** (top) © Enrico Ferorelli; (bottom) © Laura Dwight; **p. 191:** © Brand X Pictures/Getty Images; **p. 192:** DeLoache, J. S., Uttal, D. H., & Rosengren, K. S. (2004). Scale errors offer evidence for a perception-action dissociation early in life. *Science, 304,* 1047–1029. Photo by Jackson Smith; **p. 194:** © James Kilkelly; **p. 195:** © Niamh Baldock/Alamy; **p. 204:** © PhotoDisc/Getty Images; **p. 209:** © Michael Newman/PhotoEdit

Chapter 8
Opener: © Brand X Pictures/PunchStock; **p. 215:** © Ken Heyman/Woodfin Camp; **p. 218:** (left) © Bob Daemmrich/Stock Boston; (right) © Amy Etra/PhotoEdit; **p. 222:** © Ruth Duskin Feldman; **p. 227:** © Jonathan Finlay; **p. 228:** © Michael Newman/PhotoEdit; **p. 233:** © Robert Brenner/PhotoEdit; **p. 238:** © Ellen Senisi; **p. 240:** © Ellen Senisi/The Image Works

Chapter 9
Opener: © Ariel Skelley/Corbis Images; **p. 249:** © Cynthia Johnson/Getty Images; **p. 251:** © Michael Newman/PhotoEdit; **p. 253:** © David Young-Wolff/PhotoEdit; **p. 258:** © Laura Dwight/PhotoEdit; **pp. 263 & 264:** © Tony Freeman/PhotoEdit

Chapter 10
Opener: © Bob Daemmrich/PhotoEdit; **p. 267:** © Bettmann/Corbis Images; **p. 271:** © Erika Stone; **p. 275:** © Sheila Sheridan; **p. 282:** © Erika Stone/Photo Researchers; **p. 284:** © PhotoDisc/Getty Images; **p. 289:** © Paul Conklin/PhotoEdit

Chapter 11
Opener: © CLEO Photo/Index Stock Imagery; **p. 295:** © AP Images; **p. 299:** © Laura Dwight/Corbis; **p. 306:** © Erika Stone/Photo Researchers; **p. 312:** (left) © Ellen Senisi/The Image Works; (right) © Ellen Senisi; **p. 314:** © Myrleen Ferguson Cate/PhotoEdit; **p. 319:** © Margaret Miller/Photo Researchers; **p. 320:** (both) © Albert Bandura; **p. 325:** © Nita Winter

Chapter 12
Opener: © Michael Newman/PhotoEdit; **p. 331:** © AP Images; **p. 334:** © Mary Kate Denny/PhotoEdit; **p. 338:** © David Young-Wolff/PhotoEdit; **p. 340:** © Little Blue Wolf Productions/Corbis; **p. 345:** © Bob Daemmrich/Stock Boston; **p. 346:** © Martin Rogers/Stock Boston

Chapter 13
Opener: © Comstock Images/Alamy; **p. 349:** © Rene Burri/Magnum Photos; **p. 354:** © Bob Daemmrich/Stock Boston; **p. 357:** © David Lassman/The Image Works; **p. 361:** © PhotoDisc/Getty Images; **p. 364:** © Ellen Senisi; **p. 368:** © Michael J. Doolittle/The Image Works; **p. 376:** © Allan Tannenbaum/The Image Works; **p. 377:** © Michael Newman/PhotoEdit; **p. 378:** © Ken Kerbs

Chapter 14
Opener: © Digital Vision/Punchstock; **p. 383:** © Bettmann/Corbis Images; **p. 386:** © Michael Justice/The Image Works; **p. 387:** © Laura Dwight/PhotoEdit; **pp. 388 & 391:** © PhotoDisc/Getty Images; **p. 394:** © Amy Etra/PhotoEdit; **p. 397:** © Momatiuk/Eastcott/Woodfin Camp & Associates; **p. 400:** © Dallas & John Heaton/Stock Boston; **p. 404:** © David Young-Wolff/PhotoEdit; **p. 407:** © Bill Aron/PhotoEdit

Chapter 15
Opener: © Michael J. Doolittle/The Image Works; **p. 417:** © Culver Pictures; **p. 420:** © AP Images; **p. 424:** © Elena Rooraid/PhotoEdit; **p. 432:** © Barrett Stinson/The Grand Island Independent/AP Images; **p. 435:** © PhotoDisc/Getty Images; **p. 438:** © Roy Morsch/Corbis Images

Chapter 16
Opener: © David Young-Wolff/PhotoEdit; **p. 443:** © Reuters/Corbis Images; **p. 448:** Laura Dwight; **p. 454:** © Laura Dwight; **p. 459:** © Erika Stone; **p. 463:** © Dennis MacDonald/PhotoEdit

Chapter 17
Opener: © Arthur Tilley/Getty Images; **p. 467:** © AP Images; **p. 470:** © Michael Pole/Corbis Images; **p. 473:** © Bob Daemmrich/Image Works; **p. 475:** © Paula Lerner/Index Stock Imagery; **p. 487:** © Bob Daemmrich/Image Works; **p. 492:** © Laura Rauch/AP Images.

Name Index

Britto, P. R., 389, 390
Broadfield, D. C., 207
Broadhurst, D. D., 171
Brock, J. W., 107
Brockert, J. F., 107, 482
Broderick, C. J., 405
Brodersen, L., 228
Brody D. J., 343
Brody, G. H., 239, 368, 390, 398, 426, 435, 473, 487, 493
Brody, J. E., 96
Brody, L. R., 159
Brody, N., 84, 282, 289, 301, 359, 360, 361
Broffitt, B., 254
Broidy, L. M., 402, 491
Broman, J. E., 256
Bronfenbrenner, U., 28t, 36, 37, 367, 387
Bronner, E., 371
Bronstein, P., 238, 368, 390
Brook, J. S., 439, 491
Brookmeyer, K. A., 491, 492
Brooks, J., 233
Brooks, M. G., 263
Brooks, R., 195
Brooks-Gunn, J., 107, 133, 134, 185, 239, 240, 283, 289, 290, 291, 360, 368, 389, 390, 425, 426, 483
Broude, G. J., 10, 115, 126, 145, 169, 255
Brouillette, R. T., 167
Brousseau, E., 99
Brouwers, P., 103
Browder, J. P., 108
Brown, A. C., 397
Brown, A. L., 447
Brown, A. S., 85, 435
Brown, B. B., 459, 488, 489, 492
Brown, E., 276
Brown, J., 71, 278, 439
Brown, J. D., 478
Brown, J. L., 100, 403, 492
Brown, J. R., 300
Brown, J. S., 16
Brown, John, 59
Brown, L., 59, 60, 64, 71, 85–86
Brown, L. J., 254, 334
Brown, L. M., 472
Brown, Lesley, 59, 62, 71
Brown, M. B., 165
Brown, N. M., 13
Brown, P., 106
Brown, S. L., 286, 393
Brown, S. S., 129
Brown, T. E., 375, 376
Brown, Z. A., 103
Browne, A., 173
Brownell, C. A., 239
Browning, E. B., 143
Bruckner, H., 478
Bruer, J. T., 18
Bruner, A. B., 430
Bruner, J., 35
Brunner, E., 431
Brunson, K. L., 173
Bruschi, C. J., 218, 300, 386
Brust, J. C. M., 103
Bruton, J. R., 433
Bryan, V. E., 226
Bryant, B. K., 386
Bryant, D. M., 184, 185, 241, 282
Bryantwaugh, R., 432
Bryce, J., 147, 165, 254, 259, 260
Bryk, A., 208
Bryson, K. R., 396
Bryson, Y., 344
Brzustowicz, L. M., 85
Buchanan, C. M., 422
Buchanan, P., 190
Büchel, C., 343
Bucholz, K. K., 435
Buck, G. M., 422
Buckholz, K. K., 436
Buckner, J. C., 263
Budnitz, D. S., 261
Buehler, C., 490, 492

Buell, J., 370
Buhrmester, D., 401, 487, 488, 489
Buitelaar, J., 106
Buitendijk, S. E., 128, 132
Buka, S. L., 133
Bukowski, R., 108
Bukowski, W., 310, 311, 324, 325
Bukowski, W. M., 398, 399, 405, 492
Bulik, C. M., 431, 432
Bulkley, K., 372
Bunikowski, R., 103
Burch, M. M., 237
Burchinal, M. R., 183, 185, 241, 242, 282
Bureau of Labor Statistics, 240, 388
Burgess, S. R., 287
Burgoyne, P. S., 319
Burhans, K. K., 299
Buriel, R., 317, 387, 388, 391
Burke, W., 125
Burleson, B. R., 399
Burns, B. J., 172
Burns, T. L., 254
Burraston, B., 487, 492
Burrows, E., 132
Burston, A., 395
Burt, A., 261
Burton, P. B., 103
Burton, R. V., 161
Burts, D. C., 324
Burwinkle, T. M., 340
Bush, D. M., 426
Bushnell, E. W., 18, 159, 162
Busnel, M. C., 98, 203
Bussey, K., 305, 306, 307
Buyck, P., 298
Buyske, S., 85
Bybee, D., 473
Bynner, J., 366, 369
Byrd, R. S., 344
Byrne, M., 85, 108
Byrnes, J., 447, 449, 457, 458, 462
Byrnes, J. P., 43, 272, 365
Bystron, I., 153

Cabrera, N. J., 136, 208, 390, 391
Cabrol, S., 422
Cadrin, C., 109
Caelli, K., 97
Caggiano, D. M., 428
Cain, K. M., 299, 402
Caldji, C., 136
Caldwell, B. M., 182, 184
Calfas, K. J., 431
Calhoun, T., 13
Caliendo, M. A., 252
Calkins, S. D., 229
Call, J., 220
Callicott, J. H., 85
Camann, D. E., 107
Camann, W. R., 119
Camarata, S., 355, 367
Camargo, C. A., 431
Cameron, A. D., 119
Camilleri-Novak, D., 408
Camoin, T. I. L., 422
Campbell, A., 237, 302
Campbell, F. A., 184, 185, 282
Campbell, R. N., 363
Campbell, Y., 172
Campione, J. C., 447
Campione-Barr, N., 485, 486
Campos, J., 61, 227
Campos, J. J., 161, 231, 232, 299, 386
Canadian Paediatrics Society, 256
Canadian Shaken Baby Study Group, 171
Candy, J., 302
Canfield, R. L., 264
Canick, J. A., 108
Cannon, T. D., 85, 359
Cantor, J., 321, 322
Cao, A., 76
Capage, L., 278
Capaldi, D. M., 476
Caplan, M., 239
Cappa, S. F., 375

Cappell, K., 375
Capra, A. M., 148
Caprara, G. V., 367, 368, 462
Capute, A. J., 202
Carey, S., 198
Carlo, G., 319, 386, 412, 456
Carlson, E. A., 225, 226, 229
Carlson, J. J., 237
Carlson, M. J., 486
Carlson, S. M., 275, 276, 277
Carmichael, M., 260
Carnethon, M. R., 429
Carpenter, M., 220
Carper, R., 356
Carra, J. S., 261
Carraher, D. W., 354
Carraher, T. N., 354
Carrel, L., 68
Carriger, M. S., 194, 195, 197
Carrol, B., 243
Carroll, M. D., 253, 333, 339, 430
Carskadon, M. A., 430
Carson, S. A., 66
Cartar, L., 132
Carter, J., 102
Carter, R. C., 102
Carter-Pokras, O., 262, 345
Carturan, E., 167
Cartwright, B. S., 277
Caruncho, H., 85
Carvalhal, J. B., 103
Carver, L. J., 189, 200, 278
Carver, P. R., 240, 241, 306, 389, 398
CASA. See Center on Addiction and Substance Abuse at Columbia University
Casaer, P., 150
Casals, Pablo, 361
Casanova, M. F., 375
Casas, J. F., 319, 402
Case, R., 34, 297, 357, 447
Casella, J. F., 430
Casey, B. M., 124
Casey, P. H., 133, 134
Cashon, C. H., 197, 198
Casper, L. M., 396
Caspi, A., 14, 172, 173, 223, 283, 313, 405, 407, 412, 425, 426
Cassatt, Mary, 361
Cassidy, J., 229
Cassidy, K. W., 277, 278
Cassuto, D., 422
Castellanos, F. X., 334
Castillo, E. M., 375
Castle, J., 158
Castro, M. A., 118, 119
Catalano, R. F., 435, 481, 493
Cates, W., Jr., 478, 480
Cattanach, B. M., 74
Cauce, A. M., 13, 15, 16, 19, 44, 198
Caughey, A. B., 74
Caulfield, L. E., 97
Cavazanna-Calvo, M., 77
CBS News, 339
CDC. See Centers for Disease Control and Prevention
Ceausescu, Nicolae, 157
Ceci, S. J., 84, 282, 289, 301, 359, 360, 361, 374
Celis, W., 172
Cen, G., 399, 400
Center for Autism Research, 152
Center for Education Reform, 372
Center for Effective Discipline, 314, 315
Center for Weight and Health, 253, 339, 340, 341
Center on Addiction and Substance Abuse at Columbia University (CASA), 436
Centers for Disease Control and Prevention (CDC), 62, 66, 71, 75, 105, 110, 152, 166, 169, 264, 421, 429, 477, 478, 489
Cernkovich, S. A., 483
Cervera, S., 432

Cervia, J., 344
Chaika, H., 159
Chalmers, B., 148
Chamberlain, L. B., 148
Chambers, C., 231
Chambers, C. D., 101
Chambers, R. A., 428, 433, 435
Chan, G., 436
Chan, K. A., 101
Chan, O. Y., 108
Chan, R. W., 394
Chanana, N., 289
Chandler, D. W., 303
Chandler, M., 275
Chandler, P., 204
Chandra, A., 474, 476, 477
Chaney, G., 152
Chang, C., 354
Chang, C.-H., 129
Chang, J., 62, 64
Chang, J. J., 170
Chang, L., 314, 316, 320, 405
Chang, S., 254
Chang, V. W., 430
Chao, R., 360
Chao, R. K., 318, 360
Chao, W., 492, 493
Chapieski, M. L., 234
Chapman, C., 372, 403, 429, 457, 458, 460, 461
Chapman, D. P., 173
Chapman, M., 318, 352
Charatan, D. L., 433
Charlesworth, A., 437
Charley, C. M., 277
Charych, E. I., 85
Chase, C., 103
Chase, M., 105
Chase, V. M., 259
Chase-Lansdale, P. L., 240, 243
Chassin, L., 483, 484
Chatzidaki, E. E., 422
Chawla, S., 84
Cheadle, J., 392
Chehab, F. F., 422
Chen, A., 147, 373
Chen, C., 262, 459
Chen, E., 262
Chen, J., 344
Chen, L., 103, 438
Chen, S., 227
Chen, W., 84, 340
Chen, X., 399, 400
Chen, Y., 173
Chen, Y.-F., 398, 473
Cheng, S., 390, 395
Cherkassky, V. L., 152
Cherlin, A. J., 240
Chernick, A. B., 303
Cherny, S. S., 84
Cheruku, S. R., 99
Chervin, R. D., 256
Chesney, J., 405, 408, 437
Chess, S., 84, 135, 221, 222
Cheung, L. W. Y., 129
Chew, S. K., 108
Chia, S. E., 108
Chiang, E., 253
Children's Defense Fund, 14, 262, 263, 480, 481
Childs, C. P., 44
Chin, N., 68
China-U. S. Collaborative Project for Neural Tube Defect Prevention, 100
Chiodo, L. M., 102
Chiriboga, C. A., 103
Chiron, C., 19
Chistovich, I. A., 209
Chistovich, L. A., 209
Chiu, L., 302
Chodirker, B. N., 109
Choi, J., 70
Chomitz, V. R., 129
Chomsky, C. S., 284, 364

Scholten, C. M., 116
Schöner, G., 190
Schonert-Reichl, K. A., 419, 482
School-Associated Violent Deaths Study Group, 405
Schopflocher, D. P., 345
Schore, A. N., 220
Schork, N. J., 474
Schouten, A., 386
Schreiber, G. B., 431
Schuengel, C., 225
Schulenberg, J. E., 421, 434, 435, 495
Schull, W. J., 107
Schulting, A. B., 291
Schulz, L. E., 271
Schulze, P. A., 236
Schumacher, R., 131
Schumann, C. M., 152
Schumann, J., 19
Schust, D. J., 95
Schwab-Stone, M., 491, 492
Schwartz, D., 320, 405
Schwarzmueller, A., 280
Schweinhart, L. J., 481, 493
Schwimmer, J. B., 340
Scott, C., 165, 345
Scott, E. S., 345, 427, 493
Scott, G., 345
Scott, P., 352
Scott, R., 263
Scourfield, J., 103, 376
Scragg, R., 103
Scullin, M. H., 374
Seage, G. R., 344
Seaton, E. K., 473
Sebanc, A. M., 277
Secher, N. J., 102
Sedlak, A. J., 171
Seeley, J. R., 407, 426
Seepersad, S., 483
Segesten, K., 97
Seidel, K. D., 253
Seidman, E., 473
Seifer, R., 103, 222, 227, 430
Seiner, S. H., 231
Seitz, V., 493
Seligman, M. E. P., 457
Sellers, R. M., 473
Selman, A. P., 401
Selman, R. L., 401
Seltzer, J. A., 208, 393
Seltzer, M., 208
Selwitz, R. H., 334
Seminara, S. B., 422
Sen, A., 288, 366, 457, 458
Sen, M. G., 237
Senghas, A., 207
Senman, L., 278
Serbin, L. A., 237, 312, 398
Sergio, L., 207
Seron, K., 84
Serres, L., 200
Service, V., 204
Sethi, A., 235
Setien, F., 65, 83
Setterstein, R. A., Jr., 495
Sevkovskaya, Z., 148
Sexton, A., 89
Shackleton, Ernest, 332
Shaddy, J., 99, 195
Shagoury, J. K., 422
Shah, R., 102, 103
Shah, T., 102
Shakespeare, W., 378
Shamah, T., 100, 148
Shanahan, M., 495
Shanahan, M. J., 463
Shankaran, S., 102, 103
Shankweiler, D. P., 375
Shannon, D., 137
Shannon, F. T., 256
Shannon, J. D., 136, 208, 391
Shannon, M., 261
Shapiro, B. K., 202
Shapiro, S., 99, 148

Sharma, A. R., 395, 396
Shatz, M., 286
Shaw, D., 237, 301
Shaw, G. M., 99
Shaw, H., 431
Shaw, N., 253
Shaw, P., 359
Shayer, M., 354
Shaywitz, S., 375
Shea, K. M., 108
Shea, S., 253, 336
Sheblanova, E., 456
Shen, L., 94
Shepard, S. A., 319, 386, 412
Shetty, S., 319
Shevell, T., 66
Shi, L. M., 108
Shi, T., 302
Shibuya, K., 165, 254, 259, 260
Shields. A. E., 344
Shields, B. J., 161
Shields, Brooke, 231
Shields, M. K., 15
Shine, B., 253
Shinn, M., 263
Shiono, P. H., 108, 129
Shirley, L., 237, 302
Shoda, Y., 235
Shoji, J., 404
Sholl, W., 366
Shonkoff, J., 241
Shonkoff, J. P., 345
Shore, C., 202, 203, 205
Shore, E. L., 456
Short, E., 103
Shouldice, A., 227, 321
Shrestha, S., 300
Shrout, P. E., 161, 163
Shu, X. O., 108
Shulman, S., 229, 392, 396, 399
Shumpert, M. N., 106
Shurkin, J. N., 378
Shwe, H. I., 205
Siadaty, M. S., 168
Sibai, B., 129
Sick, W. T., 375
Sidora, K. J., 173
Siegal, M., 276
Siegel, A. C., 161
Siegler, R. S., 199, 272, 278, 288, 354, 357, 365, 366
Sieving, R. E., 475, 476
Sigman, M., 197
Sigman, M. D., 194, 195, 282
Sigmundson, H. K., 303
Signorello, L. B., 103
Silber, T. J., 449
Silva, P. A., 223, 376, 425, 426
Silver, E. J., 345
Silver, R. M., 119
Silverman, J. M., 108, 152
Silverman, W. K., 409
Silvestri, J. M., 167
Silvestri, L., 256
Simion, F., 194
Simmer, K., 147
Simmons, R. G., 426
Simmons, S. T., 66
Simon, G. E., 408
Simon, T. R., 405
Simon, Théodore, 8, 8f, 182
Simonian, K., 134
Simonoff, E., 287
Simons, R. F., 227
Simons, R. L., 17, 314, 398, 426, 473, 492, 493
Simons-Morton, B., 404, 405
Simonton, D. K., 379
Simos, P. G., 375
Simpson, J. E., 108
Simpson, J. L., 103
Simpson, K., 168, 303, 491
Siner, B., 131
Singer, D. G., 196, 277, 311
Singer, H. S., 302

Singer, J. D., 208
Singer, J. L., 196, 277, 311
Singer, L. T., 103
Singer, M. S., 95
Singh, G. K., 116, 262, 345
Singh, K. K., 344
Singh, S., 475, 481
Singhal, A., 147
Sinke, R. J., 432
Sipos, A., 85
Siqueland, E., 159
Sirnick, A., 171
Sismons-Morton, B. G., 169
Sit, D. K. Y., 231
Siu, B. L., 167
Skadberg, B. T., 167
Skaletsky, H., 77
Skinner, B. F., 8, 28t, 31, 32, 32, 206
Skinner, D., 307
Skinner, M. L., 185
Skoe, E. E., 456
Skolnick, A. A., 432
Skovron, M. L., 106
Slade, A., 229
Slade, L., 278
Slater, C., 253
Slaughter, V., 233
Slay, M., 106
Sleeper, L. A., 167
Slobin, D., 205, 206
Slomkowski, C., 278, 437, 487
Slotkin, T. A., 117, 120
Slutske, W. S., 425, 435
Sly, P. D., 103
Sly, R. M., 343
Slyper, A. H., 422, 425
Smailes, E. M., 491
Small, M. Y., 285, 446
Smedje, J., 256
Smedley, A., 16
Smedley, B. D., 16
Smetana, J. G., 485, 486
Smilansky, S., 310, 311, 326
Smith, A. M., 103
Smith, B. A., 158
Smith, B. J., 344
Smith, B. L., 128, 165, 167, 168, 259, 345
Smith, C. J., 152
Smith, D. F., 102
Smith, E. P., 473
Smith, G. A., 161
Smith, G. C., 207
Smith, G. C. S., 119
Smith, G. D., 147
Smith, J., 313, 314
Smith, J. A., 436
Smith, K. A., 433
Smith, K. E., 283, 370, 390
Smith, L. B., 163, 190
Smith, L. M., 102, 103
Smith, M., 103
Smith, M. C., 324
Smith, P. J. S., 105
Smith, P. K., 308, 309, 310, 311, 312, 337, 338, 404, 405
Smith, R., 117, 134
Smith, R. S., 134
Smith, S. D., 375
Smith, T. E., 238, 301
Smith, T. S., 136, 238, 391
Smith, V. K., 262
Smith-Khuri, E., 492
Smoot, D. L., 399
Smotherman, W. P., 98
Smyke, A. T., 226
Snarey, J. R., 456
Snell, J. L., 405
Snidman, N., 223, 224
Snoek, H., 406, 490
Snow, C. E., 208, 287
Snow, M. E., 238
Snowling, M. J., 287
Snyder, J., 324, 487, 492
Snyder, L., 205
Snyder, T. D., 376, 379, 409, 429, 457

Sobel, D. M., 271
Sobol, A., 103, 437
Sobol, A. M., 431
Sobolewski, J. M., 392, 487
Society for Assisted Reproductive Technology, 66
Society for Neuroscience, 149, 150, 153, 157
Society for Research in Child Development, 51
Soeken, K., 408
Soenens, B., 485
Sokol, R. J., 101, 102
Sokol, R. Z., 107
Solomon, J., 225
Solowij, N., 435
Sommer, M., 343
Sondergaard, C., 102
Sonek, J., 109
Sonenstein, F. L., 41
Sonko, B. J., 100
Sood, B., 102
Sophian, C., 279, 354
Sørensen, H. T., 480
Sorensen, T., 83
Sorof, J. M., 342
Sotres-Alvarez, D., 100, 148
South, S. J., 476
Soutollo, D., 231
Sowell, E. R., 150, 157, 335, 376
Spady, D. W., 345
Sparks, A. E., 119
Sparling, J. J., 184
Spelke, E., 199
Spelke, E. S., 271, 301, 458
Spellman, B. A., 197, 198
Spence, M. J., 98
Spencer, H., 164, 309
Spencer, J. P., 190
Sperling, M. A., 131
Spicer, P., 473
Spickelmier, J., 455
Spieker, S., 231
Spieker, S. J., 243
Spiker, D., 133
Spinath, F. M., 84, 287
Spinrad, T. L., 311, 386, 412
Spira, E. G., 366
Spirito, A., 336
Spitz, R. A., 228
Spohr, H. L., 102
Spong, C. Y., 119
Sprague, B. M., 167
Spry, L., 259
Squire, L. R., 200
Srinivasan, S. R., 84, 340
Srivastav, P., 238
Sroufe, L. A., 217, 219, 220, 228, 229, 399
St. Clair, D., 85
St. Peters, M., 288
Stack, D. M., 194
Staff, J., 463, 464
Stafford, F. P., 337, 338, 340, 387, 483
Stahl, S. A., 365
Stallings, V. A., 148
Stallone, L., 375
Stallone, Sylvester, 375
Standley, J. M., 131
Stanhope, L., 323
Stanhope, R., 333
Stanley, Julian, 379
Stanley, S. E., 70
Stanley-Hagan, M., 394
Stapleton, S., 343
Starnes, R., 320
Starr, J. M., 359
State, M. W., 167
Staub, E., 490, 491
Staubach, Roger, 323
Stauder, J. E. A., 354
Stavy, R., 272
Stedron, J., 75, 76
Stegge, H., 386
Stein, A. D., 253, 336
Stein, M. A., 336

Wilson, S. P., 236
Wilson-Costello, D., 131
Winfrey, Oprah, 14
Winner, E., 276, 377, 378, 379
Winsor, E. J. T., 109
Wippman, J., 229
Wisborg, K., 102
Wise, L. A., 101
Wise, S., 230
Wisenbaker, J., 106
Wisner, K. L., 231
Wit, J.-M., 131
Witkow, M., 462
Wohlfahrt, J., 107
Wolchik, S. A., 392
Wolff, Kaspar Friedrich, 61
Wolff, P. H., 126, 218, 219
Wolke, D., 132
Wolraich, M. L., 375, 376
Women in History, 383
Wondimu, E. A., 254, 345
Wondoloski, R. L., 181
Wong, A., 275
Wong, A, C., 70
Wong, A. H. C., 83, 120
Wong, C. A., 120
Wong, C. K., 408
Wong, I. C. K., 408
Wong, L.-Y. C., 100
Wong, M. Y.-Y., 314
Wong, W. W., 333
Wood, A., 279, 354
Wood, A. M., 167
Wood, D., 35
Wood, F. B., 375
Wood, R. M., 218
Wood, W., 303, 304, 308
Woodcock, R., 355, 367
Woodruff, T. J., 107, 264, 374, 375, 376
Woods, R. P., 335
Woods, Tiger, 16
Woodward, A. L., 205

Woodward, S. A., 224
Woodward-Lopez, G., 253
Woolley, J. D., 275, 277
Working Group on Sleepiness in
    Adolescents/Young Adults,
    429, 430
World Bank., 148
World Health Organization (WHO),
    129, 130, 169, 260, 344, 346,
    428, 429
Worsley, K., 334
Worthman, C., 340
Woudhuysen, J. S., 267
Wozniak, P., 324
Wratten, N., 85
Wright, E. C., 131
Wright, J., 288
Wright, J. A., 253
Wright, J. C., 288, 403
Wright, L. L., 102, 103, 131
Wright, R. O., 99
Wright, V. C., 62, 64, 65, 66
Wrigley, J., 171
Writing Committee for the International
    Intersex Consensus Conference
    Participants, 303
Wronska, A., 167
Wu, F., 227
Wu, H.-X., 237, 301, 319
Wu, T., 422
Wulczyn, F., 173
Wulf, D., 475
Wyatt, R. J., 85
Wynn, K., 199, 272
Wyrobek, A. J., 108

Xia, Y., 324
Xie, H., 103, 130
Xie, X., 98
Xing, Z. W., 323
Xu, B., 85
Xu, F., 230

Xu, J., 319
Xu, M., 85
Xu, Y., 320

Yaeger, J., 285
Yager, J., 432, 433
Yakub I., 85
Yamada, E., 231
Yamada, H., 318
Yamamoto, Kajiro, 349
Yamazaki, J. N., 107
Yanagihara, T. K., 173
Yanez, E., 363
Yang, B., 324, 409
Yazdani, U., 407
Ye, B., 167
Ye, H. H., 98
Yingling, C. D., 35
Yip, T., 473, 483
Yokota, F., 403
Yoshikawa, H., 493
Young, A., 204
Young, J. K., 102
Young, K. A., 407
Young, S., 108
Youngblade, L. M., 229, 278, 421
Youngstrom, E., 412
Youngstrom, E. A., 132
Youth violence: A report of the Surgeon
    General, 491, 492
Ytteroy, E. A., 395
Yu, J., 133
Yu, S. M., 262, 345
Yu, Y., 85
Yunger, J. L., 306, 398
Yurgelon-Todd, D., 428
Yvon, E., 77

Zabinski, M. F., 431
Zahn-Waxler, C., 26, 231, 318,
    319, 321
Zain, A. F., 311

Zajac, R., 366
Zametkin, A. J., 375, 376
Zavaleta, N., 97
Zeanah, C. H., 222, 226
Zee, P. C., 429, 430
Zeedyk, M. S., 259
Zeffiro, T. A., 375
Zelazo, P. D., 152, 279, 355, 375
Zelazo, P. R., 159, 194, 195
Zerwas, S., 239
Zeskind, P. S., 101
Zhang, F., 85
Zhang, H., 103, 130
Zhang, T., 167
Zhang, W., 375
Zhang, X., 261
Zhao, Y., 318
Zheng, W., 108
Zhensun, Z., 249, 250
Zhou, H., 107
Zhou, L., 167
Zhu, B.-P., 129
Ziegler, T. E., 173
Zigler, E. F., 288, 289, 439, 493
Zijdenbos, A., 334
Zimmerman, B. J., 367, 457
Zimmerman, F. J., 195
Zimmerman, R. R., 136
Zimmern, R. L., 77
Ziol-Guest, K. M., 487
Zito, J. M., 408
Zoccolillo, M., 237, 301, 319
Zola, I. K., 346
Zoran, N., 396
Zubernis, L. S., 277, 278
Zuckerman, B., 103
Zuckerman, B. S., 231
Zuker, K. J., 303
Zupan, J., 165
Zuvekas, S. H., 376
Zwaigenbaum, L., 152
Zybert, P., 253, 336

Subject Index

Note: Page numbers in *italics* indicate photos and in **bold** indicate key terms; page numbers followed by *t* indicate tables and by *f* indicate illustrations.

A, not-B error, 190, **190**
AAI. *See* Adult Attachment Interview
ABC. *See* Abecedarian Project
Abecedarian (ABC) Project, 184, 185
abuse. *See also* emotional maltreatment; neglect; physical abuse
  adolescence drug, 433–437
  child, 172, 313–314
  in infancy and toddlerhood, 170–173
  parent and family, 171–172
  physical, 170, **170,** 172
  sexual, 170, **170,** 172, 173
  substance, 172, **433,** 433–437
academic motivation, 460
academically-directed preschool, 288
acceleration, 379, **379**
"accelerators," 463–464
accidental injury, 259–261, 345
accommodation, 34, **34**
acculturation, 15
Accutane, 101
ACE. *See* angiotensin-converting enzyme
Ache, Paraguay, motor development in, 164
acne, 423
acquired immune deficiency syndrome (AIDS), 105, **105.** *See also* HIV/AIDS
active correlations, 82
active engagement, 461
acute medical conditions, 342, **342**
adaptation, 34, **34**
adaptive behavior, 182
addiction, 433
ADHD. *See* attention-deficit/hyperactivity disorder
adolescence, 8, 11*t,* 414–415, **419.** *See also* adolescence, cognitive development in; adolescence, physical development and health; adolescence, psychosocial development; *specific topics*
  alcohol use, 435–436
  death in, 438–439
  decision making capacity deficiencies of, 427
  depression in, 437
  dialect of, 450
  drug use, 433–437
  eating disorders, 430–431
  friendships in, 488–489
  globalization of, 420
  identity-statuses during, 470–472
  immaturity in, 447–449
  information processing in, 449–451
  nutrition, 430–431
  protective factors, 439
  resilience in, 410*t*
  risks and opportunities during, 419, 421
  sequence of physiological changes in, 423*t*
  siblings and, 487
  sleep needs in, 429–430
  smoking, 435–436
  as social construction, 419
  unformed character in, 427
  vulnerability to peer influence in, 427
Adolescence (Hall, G. S.), 8
adolescence, cognitive development in, 434–464
  educational and vocational issues, 457–464
  language, 449
  maturation, 445–451
  moral development, 451–457
adolescence, physical development and health, 417–440
  brain, 426–428
  exercise, 428–429, 429*f*
  health problems, 428
  health-related behaviors, 428
  puberty, 421–426
  transition in, 419–421

adolescence, psychosocial development, 467–497
  adulthood emerging, 495
  antisocial behavior, 490–494
  family relationships, 482–490
  identity search, 469–473
  juvenile delinquency, 490–494
  peer relationships, 482–490
  sexuality, 474–482
adolescent growth spurt, **423,** 423–424
adolescent rebellion, 482, **482**
adoption
  families, 395–396
  intelligence and, 84
  studies, 78
adrenarche, 421, **421**
Adult Attachment Interview (AAI), 229
adulthood, 495
affective sharing, 230
affordance, 162, **162**
Africa. *See also* central Africa; South Africa
  adolescence in, 420
  attachment of babies in, 225
  early childhood death in, 260
  fathering in, 238
  immunization of, 169
  motor development in, 164
  pictorial competence in, 192
  rough-and-tumble play in, 338
  siblings in, 396
  undernutrition in, 254
African Americans, 15
  academic achievement of, 459
  adolescent obesity, 430
  asthma of, 343
  condom use of high school, 477*f*
  ethnic identity of, 473
  genetic disorders of, 73*t*
  as high school drop outs, 460
  identity status of adolescent, 473
  infant mortality rates among, 165, 166, 166*f,* 166*t*
  IQ, 360
  Kwanzaa celebration of, *14*
  low-birth-weight babies of, 129
  menstruation of, girls, 425
  muscle and bone mass of, 333
  obesity of, 167, 339
  one-parent families of, 392
  poverty of, in U.S., 389, 390
  prejudice felt by, 398
  prenatal care of, 110*f*
  preschool study of, 288–289
  reaching adulthood, 495
  sibling relationships, 487
  sickle-cell anemia in, 71
  suicide of girls, 438
  time usage of teens, 483
  twins of, 65
  virginity loss in, 475
Afrikaner, genetic disorders of, 73*t*
age, 106–107
  father's, 108
agency, 232
agency adoptions, 395
aggression. *See also* bullying; violence
  as behavioral concerns in early childhood, 319–321
  direct, 319, **319**
  female, 319, 402
  gender differences, 319–320
  hostile, **402,** 402–403
  influences on, 320
  instrumental, 319, **319, 401,** 401–403
  male, 319
  media violence associated with, 403–404
  in middle childhood, 401–405
  mothers influence on, 321
  overt, 319, **319**

  parenting influencing, 320
  preschool, 320–321
  proactive, 402
  psychological, 315, **315**
  relational, 319, **319**
  social, 319, **319**
  types of, 402–403
AID. *See* artificial insemination by a donor
AIDS. *See* acquired immune deficiency syndrome
air pollution, danger from exposure to, 263–264
Aka, of central Africa, 136
Alaska Natives, obesity of, 167
alcohol, 101–102, 107
  adolescents using, 435–436
  peer influence on, 436–437
  use by age, 436*f*
alleles, 69, **69**
alpha antitrypsin deficiency, 72*t*
alpha thalassemia, 72*t*
altruism, 318, **318**
ambivalent attachment, 225, **225**
American Indians, 15, 16
  prenatal care of, 110*f,* 167
amniocentesis, 109*t*
amniotic sac, 95
anal stage, 28, 30*t*
analgesic, 119
androgens, 303
anencephaly, 72*t,* 100
angiotensin-converting enzyme (ACE), 101
angry cry, 218
animalcules, 61
animalculists, 61
animism, 270*t,* 271, **271**
anorexia nervosa, 431, **432,** 432–433
anoxia, 123, **123**
anthropology, 23–24
antisocial behavior. *See also* juvenile delinquency
  in adolescence, 490–494
  positive alternatives for, 493
  tendency toward, 398
anxiety. *See also* stress
  separation, 228, **228**
  social, 406
  stranger, 228, **228**
anxiety disorders, 406–407, 408
  generalized, 406, **406**
  separation, 406, **406**
Apgar scale, **124,** 124–125, 124*t*
appearance
  of emotions, 219–220
  of newborns, 120
  reality distinguished from, 270*t,* 276
  reality v., 276
apprenticeships, 462
AQS. *See* Attachment Q-set
Arabian peninsula, early childhood death in, 260
areolae, 422
argumentativeness, 448
Armenian, genetic disorders of, 73*t*
Around the World boxes
  childbirth in Himalayas, 121
  cross-cultural research purposes, 44
  globalization of adolescence, 420
  health care and cultural attitudes, 346
  playing peekaboo, 191
  popularity cross culturally, 400
  sleep customs, 169
  struggles with toddlers, 235
  teenage pregnancy prevention, 481
  toddler struggles, 235
ART. *See* assisted reproductive technology
art therapy, 408, **408**
artificial insemination, 64
artificial insemination by a donor (AID), 64
artistic development, 249–250
  in early childhood, 258–259

child development, **7**. *See also specific stages*
  activity during, 25–26
  adolescence, 11*t*
  basic concepts of, 9–12
  contexts of, 13–16
  culture, race/ethnicity, 15–16
  differences in, 25–27, 26*f*
  divorce influencing, 391–392
  early approaches, 7
  early childhood, 11*t*
  emerging consensus, 20
  faith and, 455
  family influences, 13
  five periods of, 11*t*
  historical context of, 16
  infancy, 11*t*
  influences on, 12–18
  life span studies, 9
  middle childhood, 11*t*
  new frontiers in, 9
  normative and nonnormative influences on, 16, 17
  passivity during, 25–26
  prenatal period, 11*t*
  psychology developmental, 7–9
  research methods, 39–51
  study of, 1–21
  theoretical issues, 25–27
  theoretical perspectives, 27–38
  timing of influences, 18
  toddlerhood, 11*t*
  with working parents, 240–243
child welfare, to discourage deviant behavior, 494
childbearing, 480–482
childbirth, 113–138
  bonding and, 135
  complications of, 128–134, 128*f*
  culture and, 115–116
  electronic fetal monitoring, 118, **118**
  in Himalayas, 121
  process of, 118–120
  risk reduction in, 116
  settings for, 116
  stages of, 117, 117*f*
child-directed speech (CDS), 209, **209**
childhood depression, 407, **407**
childhood intervention programs, 493
child-initiated preschool, 288
China, 136
  adolescence in, 420
  attachment of babies in, 225
  attachment research in, 227
  child abuse rare in, 172
  early childhood death in, 260
  memory of children in, 281
  obesity in, 339
  parenting in, 317–318
  popularity in, 399
  stress and fear study, 409
Chinese Americans, infant mortality rates among, 166
Chippewa Indians, 10
chlamydia, 478, 479*t*
chlorpyrifos, 107
chorionic villus sampling (CVS), 109*t*
chromosomal abnormalities, 75–76. *See also* genetic
      abnormalities
chromosomes, 66, **66**
chronic medical conditions, 342, **342**
chronosystem, 37, **37**, 37*f*
circular reactions, 185, **185**
class inclusion, 352, **352**
"Classical Baby," 196
classical conditioning, 31, **31**, 180, **180**
  three steps of, 180*f*
classification, 270*t*. *See also* categorization
cliques, 470, 488, 489
  -coded language, 450
cocaine, 103
code mixing, 209, **209**
code switching, 209, **209**
cognition, 80
cognitive advances, 351–354
  categorization, 351*t*, 352
  cause and effect, 351*t*, 352
  conservation, 353
  deductive reasoning, 352–353

  in early childhood, 270*t*
  inductive reasoning, 352–353
  number and mathematics, 353–354
  spatial thinking, 351*t*, 352
cognitive approaches, to gender development
  gender-schema theory, 306, **306**
  Kohlberg's theory, 305
cognitive behavioral therapy
  for anxiety disorders, 408
  for bulimia, 433
cognitive complexity, of play, 309
cognitive development, 9–10, **10**. *See also* cognitive
      development, in adolescence; cognitive
      development, in early childhood; cognitive
      development, in infancy and toddlerhood
  adoption influencing, 395
  in prenatal period, 11*f*
cognitive development, in adolescence, 443–464
  educational and vocational issues, 457–464
  language, 449
  maturation, 445–451
  moral development, 451–457
cognitive development, in early childhood, 267–293
  education, 288–291
  information-processing approach, 278–281
  intelligence, 281–283
  language development, 283–288
  memory, 278–281
  Piagetian approach, 269–278, 270*t*
  preoperational child, 269–278, 270*t*
  psychometric approach, 281–282
cognitive development, in infancy and toddlerhood,
      177–212
  behaviorist approach, 179–187
  brain structure, 200
  information-processing approach, 193–200
  language development, 201–210
  Piagetian approach (sensorimotor stage), 185–193,
      186*t*, 188*t*
  psychometric approach, 182–185
  social-contextual approach, 201
cognitive development, in middle childhood, 349–381
  children in school, 366–373
  concrete operational child (Piaget), 351–355
  information-processing approach, 355–357
  language and literacy, 363–366
  psychometric approach, 358–363
cognitive learning theories, 33–36
  cognitive-stage theory, 33–34
  information-processing approach, 35, **35**
  non-Piagetian, 35
  sociocultural, 34–35
cognitive maturation, 445–451
cognitive neuroscience approach, 43, **43**, 179, **180**
cognitive perspective, 28*t*, 33, **33**
cognitive stage theory, **33**, 33–34
cognitive stages, 30*t*
cognitive-state theory, Piaget, 28*t*
cohabiting family, 393–394
cohort, 18, **18**
collaborative research, 51
collective efficacy, 493
Colombia, attachment research in, 227
Columbine High School, Colorado, 491–492
Coming of Age in Samoa (Mead), 23
commitment, 470, **470**
committed compliance, 236, **236**
communication
  pragmatics and, 364–365
  private speech, 285
community programs, to discourage deviant
      behavior, 494
community service, 456
competence
  fostering, 184*t*
  self-esteem and, 385
complications, of childbirth, 128–134
  low birth weight, 128–132
  postmaturity, 132, **132**
  stillbirth, **132**, 132–133
  supportive environment for, 133–134
componential element, 362, **362**
computer and Internet, 372, 372*f*
conception, 61–62
conceptual knowledge, 450, **450**

conceptual understanding, 199
concordant, 79, **79**
concrete operational child, Piagetian approach, 30*t*,
      351–355
  categorization, 352
  cognitive advances, 351–354
  conservation, 353
  moral reasoning, 354–355
  neurological development and schooling, 354
  numbers and mathematics, 353–354
  reasoning, 352–353
  space and causality, 352
concrete operations, **351**
conduct disorder (CD), 406, **406**
confidentiality, 53
conflict, 239
  parent/adolescent relationship, 484
congenital adrenal hyperplasia (CAH), 303
congenital malformations. *See* birth defects
connectedness, 473
conscience, 236, **236**
conservation, **273**, 273–274, 351*t*, 353
  kinds of, 274*t*
constructive math, 371
constructive play, 310, **310**
contextual element, 362, **362**
contextual perspective, 28*t*, **36**, 36–37
continuity theory, 26, 26*f*
contraception, 477, 477*f*
control group, 46, **46**
controversial children, 399
conventional morality, 452, **452**, 452*t*, 453*t*
convergent thinking, 378, **378**
conversational style, 280
cooing, 203
Cooley's anemia, 72*t*
cooperative parenting, 392
coordination, 250
  of secondary schemes, 186, 186*t*, *189*
co-parenting, 391–392
cordocentesis, 109*t*
core knowledge, 199
coregulation, **387**, 387, 388
corporal punishment, 172, 313, **313**, 314–315
corpus callosum, 335
correlation studies, 43*t*, 45, **45**, 45*f*
correlations, 43*t*, 45, 45*f*, 82
  passive genotype-environment, 183
corticotropin-releasing hormone (CRH), 117
"cosmic" stage, of Kohlberg, 453
counting, 272, 272*t*
creativity, of gifted children, 378–379
CRH. *See* corticotropin-releasing hormone
crib death, 167. *See also* sudden infant death
      syndrome (SIDS)
crisis, 29, 470, **470**
critical period, 18, **18**
criticalness, 448
cross-modal transfer, 195, **195**
cross-sectional study, 49, **49**, 49*f*, 50*t*
crowds, 488, 489
crying, 203, 218, *218*
  comforting baby when, 127
Cubans, prenatal care of, 110*f*
cultural and cross-cultural influences, research
      purposes, 44
cultural bias, 360, **360**
cultural socialization, 473, **473**
culture, **15**, 15–16
  aggression influenced by, 320–321
  childbirth and, 115–116
  dialect and, 450
  gender development influenced by, 307–308
  health care influenced by, 346
  identity and categorization influenced by, 271–272
  IQ influenced by, 360–361
  maltreatment association with, 172
  memory influenced by, 281
  middle childhood and family influenced by, 387
  motor development influenced by, 164
  play influenced by, 312
  reasoning of adolescents influenced by, 447
  shyness/boldness influenced by, 223
  time usage, 483
culture-fair, 361, **361**

language—*Cont.*
   evolution of, 201–202
   milestones in infancy and toddlerhood, 202*t*
   symbols for, 269
   theory of mind development and, 277–278
language acquisition device (LAD), **206,** 206–207
language and literacy
   reading, 365–366
   vocabulary, grammar and syntax, 363–364
language development, 201–210, 202*t*
   acquisition theories in, 206–207
   delayed, 286–287
   early childhood, 283–288
   early speech characteristics, 206
   early vocalization, 203–205
   first sentences, 205
   first words, 204–205
   gestures, 204
   grammar and syntax, 284–285
   influences on, 207–209
   literacy preparation, 210, 287–288
   perceiving sounds and structure, 203–204
   pragmatics and social speech, 285–286
   sequence of early, 202
   vocabulary, 283–284
lanugo, 122
latency stage, 28, 30*t*
laterilization, 150, **150**
Latin America
   adolescence in, 420
   early childhood death in, 260
   extended family households in, 396
   illness in, 346
   undernutrition in, 254
Latinos
   academic achievement of, 459
   ethnic identity of, 473
   reaching adulthood, 495
   sibling relationships, 487
   virginity loss in, 475–476
laughing, 219
lawn mowing, 261*t*
LDs. *See* learning disabilities
lead poisoning, 263–264
learning
   behaviorism theory, 31–32
   from imitation, 239
   mechanics of, 179–187
   perspective, 28*t*, **30,** 30–33
   problems, 373–376
   social cognitive theory, 32–33
learning disabilities (LDs), 374, **374**
legal custody, 392
leptin, 422
lesbians
   parents, 394–395
   virginity loss, 476
leukemia, 107
lies, 275–276
"Life Prayer" (Hartford), 215
life span studies, 9
linguistic speech, 204, **204**
literacy, **210**
   cognitive development and, 363–366
   preparation, 210, 287–288
"Little Albert" study, 51, 311
Littleton, Colorado, 491–492
living arrangements, 389*f*
locomotion, 161–162, 163
locomotor play, 309
locomotor reflexes, 155
longitudinal study, 49, **49,** 49*f*, 50*t*
long-term memory, 278, 279, **279**
love, withdrawal of, 315, **315**
low-birth-weight babies, 128–132, **129.** *See also*
   preterm (premature) infants
   IHDP and, 133
   percentages of, 128–129, 128*f*
   treatment and outcomes for, 131–132
   by United Nations regions, 130*t*
low-income homes
   grandparents as caregivers in, 396, 487
   preschool study of, 288–289
   working parents influences, 243
L-selectin, 95

macrosystem, 36, **36,** 37*f*
magical thinking, 276–277, 455
magnetic resonance imaging (MRI), 42, 42*f*
malaria, 260, 260*f*
males. *See also* fathers/fathering; homosexuality
   acne, 423
   adolescent obesity, 430
   adoption and, 395
   aggression in, 319, 402
   androgens, 303
   bond with babies, 135
   as bullies, 404
   care-related moral reasoning of, 456
   competitiveness of, 304
   condom use in high school, 477*f*
   divorce adjustment of, 394
   in early childhood, 301
   early childhood obesity, 253
   education achievements of, 458
   exercise in high school, 429*f*
   females different from, 237–238
   fertility/infertility, 61–64, 63*t*
   friendships among, 401
   genetic disorders by, 73*t*
   gonadarche, 421, **421**
   growth in infancy and toddlerhood, 145
   growth spurt in, 423–424
   identity formation in adolescence, 472
   infant, 98
   literacy development of, 288
   low-income family influences, 240
   maturing early/late, 426
   motor development in middle childhood, 337–340, 337*t*
   muscle and bone mass in middle childhood, 333
   nutrition needs of adolescent, 430
   parent/adolescent relationship for, 485
   peer groups influencing, 398
   play of, 312
   popularity among, 399
   pressure to lose virginity, 476–477
   prosocial behavior of, 456
   rough-and-tumble play in, 338
   in school, 367
   school discipline differences for, 459
   sex characteristics, 422
   siblings, 322–323
   socialization and gender development in, 307
   sperm production, 424–425
   spermarche, 424, **424**
   stillborn, 132
   as victims, 405
   virginity loss in, 475
   volunteerism associated with, 456
   younger siblings influence on, 239
   youth violence among, 491–492
Mali, virginity loss in, 475
malnutrition, 100, 254
   of infants and toddlers, 148
maltreatment
   community characteristics and, 172
   contributing factors, 170–172
   deaths from, 170, 170*f*
   ecological view of, 170–172
   facts and figures, 170
   helping families in trouble, 172–173
   in infancy and toddlerhood, 170–173
   long-term effects of, 173
   parent and family abuse, 171–172
   suicide associated with, 438
marijuana, 103, 107
   adolescents using, 435–436
   use by age, 436*f*
marriage, 410
maternal blood tests, 109*t*
maternal factors, in prenatal development, 99–108
   age, 106–107
   alcohol intake, 101–102
   caffeine, 103
   drug intake, 101–103
   environmental factors, 107
   harmful substance ingestion, 101–104
   HIV/AIDS, 105
   illness, 105–106
   malnutrition, 100
   marijuana, cocaine, and methamphetamine, 103

nicotine, 102–103
nutrition, 99–100
   physical activity, 100
   strenuous work, 100
   stress, 106
   weight, 99–100
math
   family influencing success in, 458
   self-esteem associated with skill in, 385
math wars, 371
maturation, **12,** 12–13, 163
   cognitive, 445–451
   effects of late or early, 426
measles, early childhood death caused by, 260, 260*f*
measles-mumps-rubella (MMR) vaccines, 169
mechanistic model, 25, **25**
meconium, 123
media
   sexual activity of teens influenced by, 478
   substance abuse in, 437
   violence, 403–404
   weight and body image in, 431
media-induced aggressiveness, 404
Medicaid, 262
medical conditions, in middle childhood, 342
medical drugs, 101
medical genetics, 77
Mediterranean, early childhood death in, 260
melatonin, 430
memory, 180–181, 200, 450. *See also* memory
   development
   adolescence and changes in, 449–450
   aids, **356,** 357, 358*t*
   of children, 281
   culture influencing, 281
   declarative, 200
   early, 279–280
   in early childhood, 278–281
   episodic, 279, **279**
   explicit, 200, **200**
   generic, 279, **279**
   implicit, 200, **200**
   infant, 180–181
   long-term, 278, 279, **279**
   retention, 280–281
   sensory, 278, **278**
   span, 356
   strategies, 358*t*
   techniques, 356–357
   visual recognition, 194, **194,** 195
   working, 200, **200,** 278, **278**
memory development
   basic processes and capacities, 278–279
   in early childhood, 278–281
   forming and maintaining memories, 279–280
   recognition and recall, 278
menarche, 424, **424,** 425
menopause, 147
mental combinations, 186*t*
mental disorders, heredity and, 85
mental health
   common emotional disturbances, 405–407
   to discourage deviant behavior, 494
   in middle childhood, 405–412
mental retardation, 374, **374**
mental states, 275
mesoderm, 95
mesosystem, 36, **36,** 37*f*
metacognition, 365, **365**
metamemory, 356, **356**
methamphetamine, 103
Mexican Americans
   adolescent obesity, 430
   early childhood obesity of, 253
   muscle and bone mass of, 333
   obesity of, 339
   prenatal care of, 110*f*
   time usage of teens, 483
Mexico
   rough-and-tumble play in, 338
   toddlers in, 235
microsystem, 36, **36,** 37*f*
middle childhood, 11*t*
   adoption in, 395
   drug abuse starting in, 435–436

overweight—*Cont.*
    in infancy and toddlerhood, 148
    leptin, 422
    in middle childhood, 336, 338–342
    prevention and treatment for middle childhood,
        341–342
    prevention for preschoolers, 253
    as serious concern, 340
    strategy to overcome epidemic of, 341*t*
OxyContin, 434

pacifiers, 168
pain
    cry, 218
    in infancy and toddlerhood, 158
Pakistan, early childhood death in, 260
parallel constructive play, 310
parent/adolescent relationship
    authority, 486*t*
    conflict, 484
    economic stress, 486–487
    individuation, 484
    monitoring, 485
    working mother, 486–487
parental self-reports, 40
parent/child relationship
    power shared in, 387–388
    siblings influencing, 397
parentese, 209
Parents Anonymous, 172
parents/parenting/parenthood, 61–62. *See also*
    authoritarian parenting; authoritative parenting;
        parent/adolescent relationship; parent/child
        relationship; working parents
    abusive and neglectful, 171–172
    academic achievement values of, 462
    adolescent rebellion dealt with by, 483
    of adolescents, 439
    aggression influenced by, 320
    alternative ways to, 64, 66–67
    antisocial behavior shaped by, 490
    attachment of, 229
    attitude toward child's weight, 431
    authority of, 484–485
    Baumrind's model, 316–317
    co-, 391–392
    competence influenced by, 385
    coregulation and discipline, 387–388
    cultural differences in, 317–318
    discipline forms, 313–316
    divorce of, 391–392
    early childhood influenced by, 313–318
    education achievements influenced by, 459
    education and schooling and, 368
    executive skill development influenced by, 356
    gay or lesbian, 394–395
    gender differences shaped by, 237–238
    moral development influenced by, 455
    newborns and, 135–137
    obesity addressed by, 341*t*
    peer relationships influenced by, 324
    play encouraged by, 309
    poverty and, 389–390, 390*f*
    prosocial behavior influenced by, 386, 456
    quality of, 242
    romantic relationships of teens influenced by, 490
    sexually activity of teens influenced by, 478
    social interaction and language development, 208–209
    student aspirations influenced by, 462
    styles, 316–318, 484–485
    vocational choice influenced by, 462
    working, 240–243
    working, influences, 388–389
Parten's categories of play, 311*t*
participant observation, 44, **44**
Partners for Learning, 184, 185
parturition, 117, **117**
passive correlations, 82
passive genotype-environment correlation, 183
passive vocabulary, 205
paternal age, 85
paternal factors, in prenatal development, 107–108
Paula (Allende), 295
pedunal block, 119
peekaboo, 191

peers/peer groups, 27, 397–405, 427
    acceptance, schooling and, 369
    in adolescence, 488
    adolescent relationships, 482–490
    antisocial, 492
    education achievements influenced by, 459
    gender development influenced by, 307
    gender differences in, 398
    juvenile delinquency influences, 490–493
    moral development influenced by, 455, 456
    popularity, 398–399
    romantic relationships and, 489–490
    sex-segregated, 402
    sexual activity influenced by, 476
    status groups, 399
    time usage of adolescents, 483
penile removal, 303
penis envy, 28
perceived popularity, 398, 399
perception, 199, 232
    motor development and, 162
performance measures, 42–43
periods of development, 10, 11*t*, 12
peripheral nervous system, 149*f*
permissive parenting, 316, **316**
    education achievements influenced by, 459
personal fable, **448**, 448–449
personality, 80
    anorexia related to, 432
    heredity, environment and, 84–85
pesticides, 107
    danger from exposure to, 263–264
PET scans, 157, *157*
phallic stage, 28, 30*t*
phenotypes, 71, **71**
phenylketonuria (PKU), 72*t*, 79, 125
Philippines
    rough-and-tumble play in, 338
    virginity loss in, 475
phonemes, 203, 287
phonemic awareness, 287
phonetic, or code-emphasis, approach, 365, **365**
physical abuse, 170, **170,** 172
physical activity. *See* exercise
physical development and health, 9–10, **10,** 11*f*. *See
    also* health and safety
physical development and health, in adolescence,
    417–440
    brain, 426–428
    exercise, 428–429, 429*f*
    health problems, 428
    health-related behaviors, 428
    puberty, 421–426
physical development and health, in early childhood,
    249–265
    mortality rates comparisons, 260*f*
    motor development, 257–259
    physiological development, 251–255
    safety, 259–264
    sleep patterns and problems, 255–257
physical development and health, in infancy and
    toddlerhood, 140–141, 143–174
    abuse, 170–173
    brain and reflex behavior in, 149–158
    breastfeeding, 146–148
    growth, 145–148, 145*f*, 146*f*
    health, 164–169
    immunization, 168–169
    maltreatment, 170–173
    motor development, 159–164
    neglect, 170–173
    nourishment, 146–148
    nutrition, 145–148
    nutritional concerns, 148
    reflexes in, 154–156
    sensory capacity, 158–159
    sudden infant death syndrome (SIDS), 167–168, 168*t*
physical development and health, in middle childhood,
    331–347
    brain development, 334–335
    health and safety, 338–346
    height and weight, 333
    motor development and physical play, 337–340
    nutrition and sleep, 335–337
    tooth development and dental care, 334

physical traits, heredity and environment and, 83–84
physiological development, 251–255
    bodily growth and change, 251–252
    malnutrition, 254
    nutrition, 252–254
    oral health, 254
physiological traits, 83–84
Piagetian approach, **179**
    cognitive development in early childhood,
        269–278, 270*t*
    cognitive development in infancy and toddlerhood,
        185–193, 186*t*, 188*t*
    cognitive development in middle childhood, 351–355
    cognitive-state theory, 28*t*
    concrete operational child, 351–355
    early childhood cognitive development, 269–278, 270*t*
    formal operations stage, 30*t*, **445**, 445–447
    habituation contrasted with, 194
    imitation, 188–189
    information-processing, 197–200, 357
    preoperational stage, 30*t*, **269**, 269–278
    sensorimotor stage, 185–193, 186*t*, 188*t*
pictorial competence, 189–192, 259
PKU. *See* phenylketonuria
placenta, 95
plasticity, 18, **18,** 157, **157**
play
    cognitive levels of, 309–310
    culture influencing, 312
    in early childhood, 308–313
    evolutionary basis of, 309
    gender influences in, 312
    Parten's categories of, 311*t*
    peekaboo, 191
    physical, in middle childhood, 337–340
    pretend, 269, **269,** 310
    social dimension of, 310–311, 311*t*
    therapy, 408, **408**
playgrounds, 261, 261*t*
playmates and friends
    characteristics and effects of, 324
    choosing, 324
    parents influencing, 325
pleasure principle, 27
pneumonia, early childhood death caused by, 260, 260*f*
polycystic kidney disease, 72*t*
polygenic inheritance, 70, **70**
polymorphic genes, 67
pons, 207
popularity, 398–399
    cross-cultural view of, 400
positive reinforcement, 32
postconventional morality, 452, **452,** 453*t*, 454
postmature, 132, **132**
postpartum depression, influencing early
    development, 231
postural reflexes, 154
poverty
    early childhood death influenced by, 260
    health influenced, 344–345
    influence of, 13–14, 14*t*
    parenting and, 389–390
    transitory, 390
power assertion, 315, **315**
pragmatics, **285**, 285–286, **364**, 364–365
preconception care, 110
preconventional morality, **451**, 451–452, 452*t*
prefrontal cortex, 200, 278
pregnancy, 89–111, 489
    signs and symptoms of, 91*t*
    teenage, 480–482
preimplantation genetic diagnosis, 109*t*
prejudice, 398, **398**
prekindergarten, 290
prelinguistic period, 208
prelinguistic speech, 202, **202**
premature infants. *See* preterm (premature) infants
prenatal development, 92*t*–93*t*
    assessment techniques, 109*t*
    care disparities, 108–110
    embryonic stage, **95**, 95–96
    environmental influences, 99–108
    fetal stage, 96–98
    germinal stage, 94–95
    maternal factors, 99–108

waking smiles, 219
Wales, late-talker studies in, 287
walking
    reflex, 156*t*, 163
    in sleep, 256
war
    causing psychological harm, 409–410
    talking about, 411
Wechsler Intelligence Scale for Children (WISC-III),
    358, **358**
Wechsler Preschool and Primary Scale of Intelligence,
    Revised (WPPSI-III), 282, **282**
weight
    infant mortality rate associated with, 165,
        166*f*, 166*t*
    in middle childhood, 333
wet dream, 424
Whites
    adolescent obesity, 430
    asthma of, 343
    condom use of high school, 477*f*
    genetic disorders of, 73*t*
    as high school drop outs, 460

IQ, 360
    low birth weight babies of, 129
    menstruation of, girls, 425
    muscle and bone mass of, 333
    one-parent families of, 393
whole math, 371
whole-language approach, 365, **365**
The Wild Child (film), 5
Wilderness Inquiry, 332
will, 233
wire-raised monkeys, 135
WISC-II. *See* Wechsler Intelligence Scale
    for Children
witch's milk, 123
With a Daughter's Eye (Bateson), *215*
withdrawal of love, 315, **315**
Wnt-4, 68
word meanings, 206
working memory, 200, **200**, 278, **278**
    span, 356
working parents, disadvantaged children impacted
    by, 243
workplace, adolescents in, 462–464

world boxes. *See* Around the World boxes; Everyday
    World boxes; Research World boxes; Social
    World boxes
WPPSI-III. *See* Wechsler Preschool and Primary Scale
    of Intelligence, Revised
writing, 366

X-rays, 107, 108

You Can't Get There from Here (Nash), 331
youth employment, 462–464
Youth Self-Report, 485*t*
youth violence, 491–492
    myths about, 491–492
Yup'ok Eskimo children, 362

ZIFT. *See* zygote intrafallopian transfer
Zoloft, 231
zone of proximal development (ZPD), 35, **35,** 283, **283**
ZPD. *See* zone of proximal development
zygote, 62, **62,** 94
    composition of, 68*f*
zygote intrafallopian transfer (ZIFT), 66

Developmental Landmarks: A Holistic View

Age	Physical Developments	Neurological Developments	Cognitive Developments	Language Developments	Emotional Developments	Social Developments	Self/Gender/ Identity Developments	Moral Developments
4 years	Child dresses self with help. Child can copy a circle and draw designs, cut with scissors, and write recognizable letters.	Myelination of pathways related to hearing is complete.	Child can classify by two criteria. Child shows intuitive understanding of fractional quantities.	Child uses longer sentences, more complex grammar. Private speech increases.	Little explicit awareness of pride or shame.	Sibling conflicts over property are common. Pretend play has sociodramatic themes.	Self-definition is concrete, focused on external traits and skills. Thinking about the self is all-or-none; real self is thought to be the same as ideal self.	Guilt and concern about wrongdoing peaks. Moral reasoning is rigid. "Problem behavior" declines among girls.
5–6 years	Child can descend stairway unaided, alternating feet. Child can hop, jump, and change directions. Child dresses self without help. Child can draw a person and copy figures (pictorial stage). Primary teeth begin to fall out, replaced by permanent teeth.	Brain is almost adult size, but not fully developed. Cortical regions connected with language are maturing.	Theory of mind matures: child can distinguish between appearance or fantasy and reality. Memory span extends to two digits. Development of metamemory enables use of memory strategies. Automatization, encoding, generalization, and strategy construction begin to become more efficient. Child can count in head.	Speech is almost adultlike. Spoken vocabulary is about 2,600 words. Child understands about 20,000 words. Child appreciates pragmatic aspects of language. Child begins to decode written words. Child can retell plot of a movie, book, or TV show.	Negativism declines. Child recognizes pride and shame in others, but not in self.	Patterns of bullying and victimization may be established.	Sense of competence is developing. Self-concept links various aspects of the self, mostly in positive terms. Gender constancy is achieved.	Moral reasoning is becoming less inflexible.
7–8 years	Balance and control of body improve. Speed and throwing ability improve.		Stage of concrete operations begins. Child shows better understanding of cause and effect, seriation, transitive inference, class inclusion, inductive reasoning, and conservation. Processing of more than one task at a time becomes easier. Children play formal games with rules. Child can solve complex story problems using addition.	Pragmatic skills improve.	Child is aware of own pride or shame.	Rough-and-tumble play is common in boys, as a way to jockey for dominance.	Self-concept is more balanced and realistic. Sense of self-worth becomes explicit.	Moral reasoning is increasingly flexible. Child believes punishment should take intent into account. Empathic and prosocial behavior increase. Aggression, especially hostile type, declines.